CODE OF FEDERAL REGULATIONS

Title 13
Business Credit and Assistance

Revised as of January 1, 2019

Containing a codification of documents of general applicability and future effect

As of January 1, 2019

Published by the Office of the Federal Register
National Archives and Records Administration
as a Special Edition of the Federal Register

Table of Contents

Cite this Code: CFR

To cite the regulations in this volume use title, part and section number. Thus, 13 CFR 101.100 *refers to title 13, part 101, section 100.*

Explanation

The Code of Federal Regulations is a codification of the general and permanent rules published in the Federal Register by the Executive departments and agencies of the Federal Government. The Code is divided into 50 titles which represent broad areas subject to Federal regulation. Each title is divided into chapters which usually bear the name of the issuing agency. Each chapter is further subdivided into parts covering specific regulatory areas.

Each volume of the Code is revised at least once each calendar year and issued on a quarterly basis approximately as follows:

Title 1 through Title 16..........as of January 1
Title 17 through Title 27..........as of April 1
Title 28 through Title 41..........as of July 1
Title 42 through Title 50..........as of October 1

The appropriate revision date is printed on the cover of each volume.

LEGAL STATUS

The contents of the Federal Register are required to be judicially noticed (44 U.S.C. 1507). The Code of Federal Regulations is prima facie evidence of the text of the original documents (44 U.S.C. 1510).

HOW TO USE THE CODE OF FEDERAL REGULATIONS

The Code of Federal Regulations is kept up to date by the individual issues of the Federal Register. These two publications must be used together to determine the latest version of any given rule.

To determine whether a Code volume has been amended since its revision date (in this case, January 1, 2019), consult the "List of CFR Sections Affected (LSA)," which is issued monthly, and the "Cumulative List of Parts Affected," which appears in the Reader Aids section of the daily Federal Register. These two lists will identify the Federal Register page number of the latest amendment of any given rule.

EFFECTIVE AND EXPIRATION DATES

Each volume of the Code contains amendments published in the Federal Register since the last revision of that volume of the Code. Source citations for the regulations are referred to by volume number and page number of the Federal Register and date of publication. Publication dates and effective dates are usually not the same and care must be exercised by the user in determining the actual effective date. In instances where the effective date is beyond the cut-off date for the Code a note has been inserted to reflect the future effective date. In those instances where a regulation published in the Federal Register states a date certain for expiration, an appropriate note will be inserted following the text.

OMB CONTROL NUMBERS

The Paperwork Reduction Act of 1980 (Pub. L. 96–511) requires Federal agencies to display an OMB control number with their information collection request.

Many agencies have begun publishing numerous OMB control numbers as amendments to existing regulations in the CFR. These OMB numbers are placed as close as possible to the applicable recordkeeping or reporting requirements.

PAST PROVISIONS OF THE CODE

Provisions of the Code that are no longer in force and effect as of the revision date stated on the cover of each volume are not carried. Code users may find the text of provisions in effect on any given date in the past by using the appropriate List of CFR Sections Affected (LSA). For the convenience of the reader, a "List of CFR Sections Affected" is published at the end of each CFR volume. For changes to the Code prior to the LSA listings at the end of the volume, consult previous annual editions of the LSA. For changes to the Code prior to 2001, consult the List of CFR Sections Affected compilations, published for 1949-1963, 1964-1972, 1973-1985, and 1986-2000.

"[RESERVED]" TERMINOLOGY

The term "[Reserved]" is used as a place holder within the Code of Federal Regulations. An agency may add regulatory information at a "[Reserved]" location at any time. Occasionally "[Reserved]" is used editorially to indicate that a portion of the CFR was left vacant and not accidentally dropped due to a printing or computer error.

INCORPORATION BY REFERENCE

What is incorporation by reference? Incorporation by reference was established by statute and allows Federal agencies to meet the requirement to publish regulations in the Federal Register by referring to materials already published elsewhere. For an incorporation to be valid, the Director of the Federal Register must approve it. The legal effect of incorporation by reference is that the material is treated as if it were published in full in the Federal Register (5 U.S.C. 552(a)). This material, like any other properly issued regulation, has the force of law.

What is a proper incorporation by reference? The Director of the Federal Register will approve an incorporation by reference only when the requirements of 1 CFR part 51 are met. Some of the elements on which approval is based are:

(a) The incorporation will substantially reduce the volume of material published in the Federal Register.

(b) The matter incorporated is in fact available to the extent necessary to afford fairness and uniformity in the administrative process.

(c) The incorporating document is drafted and submitted for publication in accordance with 1 CFR part 51.

What if the material incorporated by reference cannot be found? If you have any problem locating or obtaining a copy of material listed as an approved incorporation by reference, please contact the agency that issued the regulation containing that incorporation. If, after contacting the agency, you find the material is not available, please notify the Director of the Federal Register, National Archives and Records Administration, 8601 Adelphi Road, College Park, MD 20740-6001, or call 202-741-6010.

CFR INDEXES AND TABULAR GUIDES

A subject index to the Code of Federal Regulations is contained in a separate volume, revised annually as of January 1, entitled CFR INDEX AND FINDING AIDS. This volume contains the Parallel Table of Authorities and Rules. A list of CFR titles, chapters, subchapters, and parts and an alphabetical list of agencies publishing in the CFR are also included in this volume.

An index to the text of "Title 3—The President" is carried within that volume.

The Federal Register Index is issued monthly in cumulative form. This index is based on a consolidation of the "Contents" entries in the daily Federal Register.

A List of CFR Sections Affected (LSA) is published monthly, keyed to the revision dates of the 50 CFR titles.

REPUBLICATION OF MATERIAL

There are no restrictions on the republication of material appearing in the Code of Federal Regulations.

INQUIRIES

For a legal interpretation or explanation of any regulation in this volume, contact the issuing agency. The issuing agency's name appears at the top of odd-numbered pages.

For inquiries concerning CFR reference assistance, call 202–741–6000 or write to the Director, Office of the Federal Register, National Archives and Records Administration, 8601 Adelphi Road, College Park, MD 20740-6001 or e-mail *fedreg.info@nara.gov.*

SALES

The Government Publishing Office (GPO) processes all sales and distribution of the CFR. For payment by credit card, call toll-free, 866-512-1800, or DC area, 202-512-1800, M-F 8 a.m. to 4 p.m. e.s.t. or fax your order to 202-512-2104, 24 hours a day. For payment by check, write to: US Government Publishing Office – New Orders, P.O. Box 979050, St. Louis, MO 63197-9000.

ELECTRONIC SERVICES

The full text of the Code of Federal Regulations, the LSA (List of CFR Sections Affected), The United States Government Manual, the Federal Register, Public Laws, Public Papers of the Presidents of the United States, Compilation of Presidential Documents and the Privacy Act Compilation are available in electronic format via *www.govinfo.gov.* For more information, contact the GPO Customer Contact Center, U.S. Government Publishing Office. Phone 202-512-1800, or 866-512-1800 (toll-free). E-mail, *ContactCenter@gpo.gov.*

The Office of the Federal Register also offers a free service on the National Archives and Records Administration's (NARA) World Wide Web site for public law numbers, Federal Register finding aids, and related information. Connect to NARA's web site at *www.archives.gov/federal-register.*

The e-CFR is a regularly updated, unofficial editorial compilation of CFR material and Federal Register amendments, produced by the Office of the Federal Register and the Government Publishing Office. It is available at *www.ecfr.gov.*

OLIVER A. POTTS,
Director,
Office of the Federal Register
January 1, 2019.

THIS TITLE

Title 13—BUSINESS CREDIT AND ASSISTANCE is composed of one volume. This volume contains chapter I—Small Business Administration, chapter III—Economic Development Administration, Department of Commerce, chapter IV—Emergency Steel Guarantee Loan Board, and chapter V—Emergency Oil and Gas Guaranteed Loan Board. The contents of this volume represent all current regulations codified under this title of the CFR as of January 1, 2019.

For this volume, Susannah C. Hurley was Chief Editor. The Code of Federal Regulations publication program is under the direction of John Hyrum Martinez, assisted by Stephen J. Frattini.

Title 13—Business Credit and Assistance

ABBREVIATIONS USED IN THIS CHAPTER:

SBA = *Small Business Administration*. SBID = *The Small Business Investment Division of SBA*. RFC = *Reconstruction Finance Corporation*.

CHAPTER I—SMALL BUSINESS ADMINISTRATION

EDITORIAL NOTE: The Small Business Administration has asked the Director of the Federal Register to inform users of this chapter that parts 143, 145, and 146 are common rule regulations that cannot be amended by the Small Business Administration unilaterally.

PARTS 1–100 [RESERVED]

PART 101—ADMINISTRATION

AUTHORITY: 5 U.S.C. 552 and App. 3, secs. 2, 4(a), 6(a), and 9(a)(1)(T); 15 U.S.C. 633, 634, 687; 31 U.S.C. 6506; 44 U.S.C. 3512; 42 U.S.C. 6307(d); 15 U.S.C. 657h; E.O. 12372 (July 14, 1982), 47 FR 30959, 3 CFR, 1982 Comp., p. 197, as amended by E.O. 12416 (April 8, 1983), 48 FR 15887, 3 CFR, 1983 Comp., p. 186.

SOURCE: 61 FR 2394, Jan. 26, 1996, unless otherwise noted.

Subpart A—Overview

§ 101.100 What is the purpose of SBA?

The U.S. Small Business Administration (SBA) aids, counsels, assists, and protects the interests of small business concerns, and advocates on their behalf within the Government. It also helps victims of disasters. It provides financial assistance, contractual assistance, and business development assistance. For a more detailed description of the functions of SBA see The United States Government Manual, a special publication of the FEDERAL REGISTER, which is available from Superintendent of Documents, P.O. Box 371954, Pittsburgh, PA 15250–7954.

§ 101.101 Who manages SBA?

(a) An Administrator, appointed by the President with the advice and consent of the Senate, manages SBA. The Administrator—

(1) Is responsible to the President and Congress for exercising direction, authority, and control over SBA.

(2) Determines and approves all policies covering SBA's programs to aid, counsel, assist, and protect the interests of the nation's small businesses.

(3) Employs or appoints employees necessary to implement the Small Business Act, as amended, the Small Business Investment Act, as amended, and other laws and directives.

(4) Delegates certain activities, by issuing regulations or otherwise, to Headquarters and field positions.

(b) A Deputy Administrator, appointed by the President with the advice and consent of the Senate, serves as Acting Administrator during the absence or disability of the Administrator or in the event of a vacancy in the Office of the Administrator.

§ 101.102 Where is SBA's Headquarters located?

The Headquarters of SBA is at 409 3rd Street, SW., Washington, DC 20416.

§ 101.103 Where are SBA's field offices located?

A list of SBA's field offices with addresses, phone numbers and jurisdictions served is periodically published in the FEDERAL REGISTER. You can also obtain the address and phone number of an SBA office to serve you by calling 1-800-8-ASK-SBA or 1-800-827-5722.

§ 101.104 What are the functions of SBA's field offices?

(a) *Regional offices.* Regional offices are managed by a Regional Administrator who is responsible to the Administrator and to the Associate Administrator for Field Operations. They are located in major cities and have geographical boundaries which cover multi-state areas. Regional offices exercise limited authority over field activities within their region.

(b) *District offices.* District offices are managed by a District Director and are located in cities within a region. District offices are responsible to Headquarters, the Associate Administrator for Field Operations, and to a regional office. Within their delegated authority, district offices have authority for—

(1) Conducting all program delivery activities within the district boundaries;

(2) Supervising all branch offices located within the district boundaries; and

(3) Providing subordinate branch offices with the technical capability necessary to execute assigned programs.

(c) *Branch offices.* Branch offices are managed by a Branch Manager and are located in cities within a district. Branch offices are responsible to the district office within whose boundaries it is located. Branch offices execute one or more elements of the business or disaster loan programs and have limited authority for program execution.

(d) *Disaster assistance offices.* The Office of Disaster Assistance maintains five permanent field offices which are named according to the particular functions they perform in the disaster loan making process. The office names are: Disaster Assistance Customer Service Center, Disaster Assistance Processing and Disbursement Center, Disaster Assistance Field Operations Center East, Disaster Assistance Field Operations Center West, and the Disaster Assistance Personnel and Administrative Services Center. Each office is managed by a Center Director who reports to the Deputy Associate Administrator for Disaster Assistance. The offices provide loan services to victims of declared disasters, or support the efforts of the other offices to do so. Temporary disaster offices may be established in areas where disasters have occurred.

(e) *Responsibilities.* Each field office has responsibilities within a defined geographical area as periodically set forth in the FEDERAL REGISTER.

[61 FR 2394, Jan. 26, 1996, as amended at 71 FR 63676, Oct. 31, 2006]

§ 101.105 Who may use SBA's official seal and for what purpose?

(a) *General.* This section describes the official seal of the SBA and prescribes rules for its use.

(b) *Official Seal.* The official seal of the SBA is illustrated below.

(c) *Authorized Use.* The official seal and reproductions of the seal may only be used as follows:

(1) Certify and authenticate originals and copies of any books, records, papers or other documents on file within SBA or extracts taken from them or to provide certification for the purposes authorized in 28 U.S.C. 1733;

(2) SBA award certificates and medals;

(3) SBA awards for career service;

(4) Security credentials and employee identification cards;

(5) Business cards for SBA employees;

(6) Official SBA signs;

(7) Plaques; the design of the SBA seal may be incorporated in plaques for display in Agency auditoriums, presentation rooms, lobbies, offices and on buildings occupied by SBA;

(8) The SBA flag;

(9) Officially authorized reports or publications of the SBA; or

(10) For such other purposes as determined necessary by the Administrator.

(d) *Unauthorized use.* The official seal shall not be used, except as authorized by the Administrator, in connection with:

(1) Contractor operated facilities;

(2) Souvenir or novelty items;

(3) Toys or commercial gifts or premiums;

(4) Letterhead design, except on official SBA stationery;

(5) Clothing or equipment; or

(6) Any article which may disparage the seal or reflect unfavorably upon SBA.

(e) SBA's seal will not be used in any manner which implies SBA endorsement of commercial products or services or of the user's policies or activities.

(f) *Reproduction of Official Seal.* Requests for permission to reproduce the SBA seal in circumstances other than those listed in paragraph (c) of this section must be made in writing to the Administrator. The decision whether to grant permission will be made in writing on a case-by-case basis, in consultation with the General Counsel, with consideration of any relevant factors which may include the benefit or cost to the Agency of granting the request; the unintended appearance of endorsement or authentication by SBA; the potential for misuse; the reputability of the use; the extent of control by SBA over the use; and the extent of control by SBA over distribution of any products or publications bearing the SBA seal.

(g) *Penalties for Unauthorized Use.* Fraudulent or wrongful use of SBA's seal can lead to criminal penalties under 18 U.S.C. 506 or 18 U.S.C. 1017.

[72 FR 1963, Jan. 11, 2008]

§ 101.106 Does Federal law apply to SBA programs and activities?

(a) SBA makes loans and provides other services that are authorized and executed under Federal programs to achieve national purposes.

(b) The following are construed and enforced in accordance with Federal law—

(1) Instruments evidencing loans;

(2) Security interests in real or personal property payable to or held by SBA or the Administrator such as promissory notes, bonds, guarantee agreements, mortgages, and deeds of trust;

(3) Other evidences of debt or security;

(4) Contracts or agreements to which SBA is a party, unless expressly provided otherwise.

(c) To the extent feasible, SBA uses local or state procedures, especially for recordation and notification purposes, in implementing and facilitating SBA's loan programs. This use of local or state procedures is not a waiver by SBA of any Federal immunity from any local or state control, penalty, tax, or liability.

(d) No person, corporation, or organization that applies for and receives any benefit or assistance from SBA, or that offers any assurance or security upon which SBA relies for the granting of such benefit or assistance, is entitled to claim or assert any local or state law to defeat the obligation incurred in obtaining or assuring such Federal benefit or assistance.

§ 101.107 What SBA forms are approved for public use?

(a) SBA uses forms approved by the Office of Management and Budget (OMB) under the Paperwork Reduction Act of 1995 (44 U.S.C. 3501 *et seq.*), as amended. You may obtain approved forms for use by the public when applying for or obtaining SBA assistance, or when providing services for SBA, from any field office (see § 101.103). You may also use forms which you have prepared yourself, or have obtained from another source, if those forms are identical in every respect to the forms approved by OMB for the same purpose.

(b) Any member of the public who has reason to believe any SBA office or agent is in violation of the Public Protection Clause of the Paperwork Reduction Act (44 U.S.C. 3512 and see 5 CFR 1320.6) should notify SBA. Direct such comments to the Director, Office of Business Operations at 409 3rd Street, SW., Washington, DC 20416.

[61 FR 2394, Jan. 26, 1996, as amended at 72 FR 50038, Aug. 30, 2007]

§ 101.108 Has SBA waived any of the public participation exemptions of the Administrative Procedure Act?

Yes. Despite these exemptions, SBA will follow the public participation requirements of the Administrative Procedure Act, 5 U.S.C. 553, in rulemakings relating to public property, loans, grants, benefits, or contracts.

§ 101.109 Do SBA regulations include the section headings?

Yes. All SBA regulations must be interpreted as including the section headings.

Subpart B—Employment of Private Counsel

§ 101.200 When does SBA hire private counsel?

(a) *Business loans.* SBA may hire private counsel to represent it in regard to business loans when the volume of activity in an area is not sufficient to require a full-time SBA employee, or the area is too remote for economical use of a full-time SBA employee.

(b) *Disaster loans.* SBA may hire private counsel in regard to disaster loans when the disaster presents an emergency and a volume of activity that cannot be promptly and economically serviced by available SBA employees.

§ 101.201 What are the minimum terms of private counsel's employment?

(a) Private counsel must perform all requested work in compliance with SBA's regulations, policies, and instructions, and take such action as is legally required under the Small Business Act, the Small Business Investment Act, and other laws applicable to SBA.

(b) Private counsel must adhere to the highest standards of professional conduct and maintain confidentiality appropriate to the attorney-client relationship.

(c) Private counsel acts under the supervision of the SBA General Counsel (and designees).

(d) Private counsel usually is compensated at an hourly rate as approved by SBA. Contingency fee agreements may be used if approved by the General Counsel.

(e) Either party may terminate the employment upon written notice.

Subpart C—Inspector General

§ 101.300 What is the Inspector General's authority to conduct audits, investigations, and inspections?

The Inspector General Act of 1978, as amended (5 U.S.C. App. 3) authorizes SBA's Inspector General to provide policy direction for, and to conduct, supervise, and coordinate such audits, investigations, and inspections relating to the programs and operations of SBA as appears necessary or desirable.

§ 101.301 Who should receive information or allegations of waste, fraud, and abuse?

The Office of Inspector General should receive all information or allegations of waste, fraud, or abuse regarding SBA programs and operations.

§ 101.302 What is the scope of the Inspector General's authority?

To obtain the necessary information and evidence, the Inspector General (and designees) have the right to:

(a) Have access to all records, reports, audits, reviews, documents, papers, recommendations, and other materials available to SBA and relating to SBA's programs and operations;

(b) Require by subpoena the production of all information, documents, reports, answers, records, accounts, papers, and other data and documentary evidence;

(c) Administer oaths and affirmations or take affidavits; and

(d) Request information or assistance from any Federal, state, or local government agency or unit.

§ 101.303 How are Inspector General subpoenas served?

(a) Service of subpoenas may be effected by any of the following means—

(1) If by mail, a copy of the subpoena must be addressed to the person, partnership, corporation, or unincorporated association to be served at a residence or usual dwelling place, or a principal office or place of business, and mailed first class by registered or certified mail (postage prepaid, return receipt requested), or by a commercial or U.S. Postal Service overnight or express delivery service.

(2) If by personal delivery, a copy of the subpoena must be delivered to the person to be served, or to a member of the partnership to be served, or to an executive officer or a director of the corporation or unincorporated association to be served, or to a person authorized by appointment or by law to receive process for the person or entity named in the subpoena.

(3) If by delivery to an address, a copy of the subpoena must be left at the principal office or place of business of the person, partnership, corporation, or unincorporated association to be served, or at the residence or usual dwelling place of the person, member of the partnership, or officer or director of the corporation or unincorporated association to be served, with someone of suitable age and discretion.

(b) Proof of service—

(1) When service is by registered, certified, overnight, or express mail, it is complete upon delivery of the document by the Postal Service or commercial service.

(2) The return Postal Service receipt for a document that was registered or certified and mailed, the signed receipt for a document delivered by an overnight or express delivery service, or the Return of Service completed by the individual serving the subpoena by personal delivery shall be proof of service.

Subpart D—Intergovernmental Partnership

§ 101.400 What is the purpose of this subpart?

(a) This subpart implements section 401 of the Intergovernmental Cooperation Act (31 U.S.C. 6506 *et seq.*) which promotes intergovernmental partnership and strengthens Federalism by relying on state processes and state, area-wide, regional, and local coordination for the review of proposed Federal financial assistance and direct Federal development.

(b) While guiding SBA's management, this subpart does not create any right or benefit enforceable at law.

§ 101.401 What programs and activities of SBA are subject to this subpart?

SBA publishes in the FEDERAL REGISTER a list of programs and activities subject to this subpart.

§ 101.402 What procedures apply to the selection of SBA programs and activities?

(a) A state may—

(1) Select any program or activity published in the FEDERAL REGISTER under § 101.401 for intergovernmental review (providing it consults with local elected officials before doing so) and then notify the Administrator of the programs and activities selected; and

(2) Notify the Administrator of changes in its selections at any time. For each change, the state submits to the Administrator an assurance that it consulted with local elected officials regarding the change.

(b) SBA may establish deadlines by which states must inform the Administrator of changes in their program selections.

(c) After receiving notice of a state's selections, the Administrator uses a state's process as soon as feasible depending on individual programs and activities.

(d) "State" means any of the 50 States, the District of Columbia, the Commonwealth of Puerto Rico, the Commonwealth of the Northern Mariana Islands, Guam, American Samoa, the U.S. Virgin Islands, or the Trust Territory of the Pacific Islands.

§ 101.403 What are the notice and comment procedures?

(a) The Administrator provides notice to directly affected state, area-wide, regional, and local entities in a state of proposed SBA financial assistance or direct SBA development if—

(1) The state has not adopted a process under Executive Order 12372 (3 CFR, 1982 Comp., p. 197), as amended by Executive Order 12416 (3 CFR, 1983 Comp., p. 186); or

(2) The assistance or development involves a program or activity not selected for the state process.

(b) Notice may be made by publication in the FEDERAL REGISTER or other means as SBA deems appropriate.

(c) Except in unusual circumstances the Administrator gives state processes or directly affected state, area-wide, regional, and local officials and entities at least 60 days to comment on proposed SBA financial assistance or direct SBA development.

(d) In cases where SBA delegates the review, coordination, and communication authority under this subpart, this section also applies.

§ 101.404 How does the Administrator receive comments?

(a) The Administrator follows the procedures of § 101.405 if—

(1) A state office or official is designated to act as a single point of contact between a state process and all Federal agencies; and

(2) That office or official transmits a state process recommendation for a program selected under § 101.402(a).

(b)(1) The single point of contact is not obligated to transmit comments from state, area-wide, regional, or local officials and entities where there is no state process recommendation.

(2) If a state process recommendation is transmitted by a single point of contact, all comments from state, area-wide, regional, and local officials and entities that differ from it must also be transmitted.

(c) If a state has not established a process, or is unable to submit a state process recommendation, state, area-wide, regional, and local officials and entities may submit comments to SBA.

(d) If a program or activity is not selected for a state process, state, area-wide, regional, and local officials and entities may submit comments to SBA. In addition, if a state process recommendation for a non-selected program or activity is transmitted to SBA by the single point of contact, the Administrator follows the procedures of § 101.405.

(e) The Administrator considers comments which do not constitute a state process recommendation submitted under this subpart and for which the Administrator is not required to apply the procedures of § 101.405 when such comments are provided by a single point of contact directly to SBA by a commenting party.

§ 101.405 How does the Administrator respond to comments?

(a) If a state process provides a recommendation to SBA through its single point of contact, the Administrator:

(1) Accepts the recommendation; or

(2) Reaches a mutually agreeable solution with the state process; or

(3) Provides the single point of contact with a written explanation of the decision in a form the Administrator deems appropriate. The Administrator may also supplement the written explanation by telephone or other means.

(b) In any explanation under paragraph (a)(3) of this section, the Administrator informs the single point of contact that—

(1) SBA will not implement its decision for at least 10 days after the single point of contact receives the explanation; or

(2) Because of unusual circumstances the waiting period of at least 10 days is not feasible.

(c) For purposes of computing the waiting period under paragraph (b)(1) of this section, a single point of contact is presumed to have received written notification 5 days after the date of mailing.

§ 101.406 What are the Administrator's responsibilities in interstate situations?

The Administrator is responsible for—

(a) Identifying proposed SBA financial assistance and direct SBA development that have an impact on interstate areas;

(b) Notifying appropriate officials and entities in states which have adopted a process and selected an SBA program or activity;

(c) Making efforts to identify and notify the affected state, area-wide, regional, and local officials and entities in states that have not adopted a process or selected an SBA program or activity;

(d) Using the procedures of § 101.405 if a recommendation of a designated area-wide agency is transmitted by a single point of contact in cases in which the review, coordination, and communication with SBA has been delegated; and

(e) Using the procedures of § 101.405 if a state process provides a state recommendation to SBA through a single point of contact.

§ 101.407 May the Administrator waive these regulations?

The Administrator may waive any provision of §§ 101.400 through and including 101.406 in an emergency.

Subpart E—Small Business Energy Efficiency

§ 101.500 Small Business Energy Efficiency Program.

(a) The Administration has developed and coordinated a Government-wide program, which is located at *http://www.sba.gov/energy*, building on the Energy Star for Small Business Program, to assist small business concerns in becoming more energy efficient, understanding the cost savings from improved energy efficiency, and identifying financing options for energy efficiency upgrades.

(b) The Program has been developed and coordinated in consultation with the Secretary of the Department of Energy and the Administrator of the Environmental Protection Agency, and in cooperation with entities the Administrator has considered appropriate, for example, such as industry trade associations, industry members, and energy efficiency organizations. SBA's Office of Policy and Strategic Planning will be responsible for overseeing the program but will coordinate with the Department of Energy and EPA.

(c) The Administration is distributing and making available online, the information and materials developed under the program to small business concerns, including smaller design, engineering, and construction firms, and other Federal programs for energy efficiency, such as the Energy Star for Small Business Program.

(d) The Administration will develop a strategy to educate, encourage, and assist small business concerns in adopting energy efficient building fixtures and equipment.

[73 FR 61666, Oct. 17, 2008]

PART 102—RECORD DISCLOSURE AND PRIVACY

Subpart A—Disclosure of Information

Subpart B—Protection of Privacy and Access to Individual Records Under the Privacy Act of 1974

AUTHORITY: 5 U.S.C. 301, 552, 552a; 31 U.S.C. 3717, 9701; 44 U.S.C. 3501.

SOURCE: 61 FR 2673, Jan. 29, 1996, unless otherwise noted.

Subpart A—Disclosure of Information

SOURCE: 82 FR 46371, Oct. 5, 2017, unless otherwise noted.

§ 102.1 General provisions.

(a) This subpart contains the rules that SBA follows in processing requests for records under the Freedom of Information Act ("FOIA"), 5 U.S.C. 552. The rules in this subpart should be read in conjunction with the text of the FOIA and the Uniform Freedom of Information Fee Schedule and Guidelines published by the Office of Management and Budget ("OMB Guidelines"). Requests made by individuals for records about themselves under the Privacy Act of 1974, 5 U.S.C. 552a, are processed under subpart B of this part as well as under this subpart.

(b) As referenced in this subpart, "component" means each separate bureau, office, division, district office, regional office, area office, service center, loan processing center or central office duty location within the SBA that is responsible for processing FOIA requests. See appendix A to this subpart for a list of information generally exempt from disclosure. For contact information for each office visit *https://www.sba.gov/foia* and for a detailed description of the function of each office to help ascertain the types of records maintained by each component, please visit *https://www.sba.gov/about-sba*. The rules described in this regulation that apply to SBA also apply to its components.

(c) The SBA has a decentralized system for processing requests, with each component handling requests for its records.

(d) The term record means:

(1) Any information that would be an agency record subject to the requirements of this section when maintained by SBA in any format, including written or electronic format; and

(2) Any information described under paragraph (d)(1) of this section that is maintained for SBA by an entity under Government contract, for purposes of records management.

§ 102.2 Proactive disclosure of records.

Records that are required by the FOIA to be made available for public inspection in an electronic format may be accessed through the SBA's Web site at *https://www.sba.gov/foia*. Each component of SBA is responsible for determining which of its records are required to be made publicly available, as well as for identifying additional records of interest to the public that are appropriate for public disclosure, and for posting and indexing such records. Each component shall ensure that its Web site of posted records and indices is reviewed and updated on an ongoing basis. Each component has a FOIA Public Liaison who can assist individuals in locating records particular to a component. A list of the SBA's FOIA Public Liaisons is available at *https://www.sba.gov/foia*.

§ 102.3 Requirements pertaining to the submission of requests.

(a) *General information.* (1) The SBA has a decentralized system for responding to FOIA requests, with each component handling requests for its records. All components have the capability to receive requests electronically either through email or a web portal. To make a request for records, a requester should write directly to the Freedom of Information/Privacy Acts (FOI/PA) Office by mail to 409 3rd St SW., Washington, DC 20416 or submit a fax to 202–205–7059 or email to *foia@sba.gov*. Requesters may also submit their request through the FOIA online portal at *https://foiaonline.regulations.gov/foia/action/public/home.* Additional information for submitting a request to SBA is listed at *https://www.sba.gov/foia.* However, a request will receive the quickest possible response if it is addressed to the component that maintains the records sought.

(2) A requester who is making a request for records about himself or herself must comply with the verification of identity provision set forth in subpart B of this part. The Certification of Identity form, available at *http://www.justice.gov/oip/forms/cert_ind.pdf,* may be used by individuals who are making requests for records pertaining to themselves.

(3) Where a request for records pertains to another individual, a requester may receive greater access by submitting either a notarized authorization signed by that individual or a declaration made in compliance with the requirements set forth in 28 U.S.C. 1746 by that individual authorizing disclosure of the records to the requester, or by submitting proof that the individual is deceased (e.g., a copy of a death certificate or an obituary). As an exercise of administrative discretion, each component can require a requester to supply additional information if necessary in order to verify that a particular individual has consented to disclosure.

(b) *Description of records sought.* Requesters must describe the records sought in sufficient detail to enable agency personnel to locate them with a reasonable amount of effort. To the extent possible, requesters should include specific information that may help the component in identifying the requested records, such as the date, title or name, author, recipient, subject matter of the record, case number, file designation, reference number, the timeframe for which the records are sought, the office that created the records, or any other information that will assist the component in locating documents responsive to the request. Before submitting their requests, requesters may contact the component's FOIA Contact or FOIA Public Liaison to discuss the records they are seeking and to receive assistance in describing the records. If, after receiving a request, a component determines that the request does not adequately describe the records sought, the component will inform the requester what additional information is needed or why the request is otherwise insufficient. The component will also notify the requester that it will not be able to comply with their request unless the additional information it has requested is received from them in writing within 20 working days after the component has requested it. If this type of notification is received, a requester may wish to discuss it with the FOIA Public Liaison. If the component does not receive a written response containing the additional information within 20 working days after it has been requested, the SBA will presume that the requester is no longer interested in the records and will close the file on the request. Requesters who are attempting to reformulate or modify such a request may discuss their request with the component's designated FOIA Contact or its FOIA Public Liaison, or a representative of the FOI/PA Office, each of whom is available to assist the requester in reasonably describing the records sought. If a request does not reasonably describe the records sought, the SBA's response to the request may be delayed.

(c) *Form or format.* Requests may specify the preferred form or format (including electronic formats) for the records sought. The SBA will accommodate the request if the record is readily reproducible in that form or format.

(d) *Contact information.* Requesters must provide contact information, such as their phone number, email address, and mailing address, to assist the SBA in communicating with the requester and providing the released records.

§ 102.4 Responsibility for responding to requests.

(a) *In general.* Except in the instances described in paragraphs (c) and (d) of this section, the component that first receives a request for a record and maintains that record is the component responsible for responding to the request. In determining which records are responsive to a request, a component ordinarily will include only records in its possession as of the date that it begins its search. If any other date is used, the component shall inform the requester of that date. A record that is excluded from the requirements of the FOIA pursuant to 5 U.S.C. 552(c) is not considered responsive to a request.

(b) *Authority to grant or deny requests.* The head of a component, or designee, is authorized to grant or to deny any requests for records that are maintained by that component.

(c) *Re-routing of misdirected requests.* Where a component determines that a request was misdirected within the SBA, the receiving component shall route the request to the proper component(s).

(d) *Consultation, referral, and coordination.* When reviewing records located by a component in response to a request, the component shall determine whether another component of SBA or another agency of the Federal Government is better able to determine whether the record is exempt from disclosure under the FOIA. As to any such record, the component shall proceed in one of the following ways:

(1) *Consultation.* When records originated with the component processing the request, but contain within them information of interest to another component, agency, or other Federal Government office, the component processing the request should typically consult with that other component or agency prior to making a release determination.

(2) *Referral.* (i) When the component processing the request believes that a different component, agency, or other Federal Government office is best able to determine whether to disclose the record, the component typically should refer the responsibility for responding to the request regarding that record, as long as the referral is to a component or agency that is subject to the FOIA. Ordinarily, the component or agency that originated the record will be presumed to be best able to make the disclosure determination. However, if the component processing the request and the originating component or agency jointly agrees that the former is in the best position to respond regarding the record, then the record may be handled as a consultation.

(ii) Whenever a component refers any part of the responsibility for responding to a request to another component or agency, it shall document the referral, maintain a copy of the record that it refers, and notify the requester of the referral and inform the requester of the name(s) of the component or agency to which the record was referred, including that component's or agency's FOIA Contact information.

(3) *Coordination.* The standard referral procedure is not appropriate where disclosure of the identity of the component or agency to which the referral would be made could harm an interest protected by an applicable exemption, such as the exemptions that protect personal privacy or national security interests. For example, if a non-law enforcement component responding to a request for records on a living third party locates within its files records originating with a law enforcement agency, and if the existence of that law enforcement interest in the third party was not publicly known, then to disclose that law enforcement interest could cause an unwarranted invasion of the personal privacy of the third party. Similarly, if a component locates within its files material originating with an Intelligence Community agency and the involvement of that agency in the matter is classified and not publicly acknowledged, then to disclose or give attribution to the involvement of that Intelligence Community agency could cause national security harms. In such instances, in order to avoid harm to an interest protected by an applicable exemption, the component that received the request should coordinate with the originating component or agency to seek its views on the disclosure of the record. The release determination for the record that is the subject of the coordination should then be conveyed to the requester by the component that originally received the request.

(e) *Classified information.* On receipt of any request involving classified information, the component shall determine whether the information is currently and properly classified and take appropriate action to ensure compliance. Whenever a request involves a record containing information that has been classified or may be appropriate for classification by another component or agency under any applicable executive order concerning the classification of records, the receiving component shall refer the responsibility for responding to the request regarding that information to the component or agency that classified the information, or that should consider the information for classification. Whenever a component's record contains information that has been derivatively classified (for example, when it contains information classified by another component or agency), the component shall refer the responsibility for responding to that portion of the request to the component or agency that classified the underlying information.

(f) *Agreements regarding consultations and referrals.* Components of SBA may establish agreements with other components of SBA or other Federal agencies to eliminate the need for consultations or referrals with respect to particular types of records.

(g) *Timing of responses to consultations and referrals.* All consultations and referrals received by the SBA will be handled according to the date that the FOIA request initially was received by the first component or agency.

§ 102.5 Timing of responses to requests.

(a) *In general.* Components ordinarily will respond to requests according to their order of receipt. In instances involving misdirected requests that are re-routed pursuant to § 102.4(c), the response time will commence on the date that the request is received by the proper component's office that is designated to receive requests, but in any event not later than 10 working days after the request is first received by any component's office that is designated by these regulations to receive requests.

(b) *Multitrack processing.* All components will designate a specific track for requests that are granted expedited processing, in accordance with the standards set forth in paragraph (e) of this section. A component may also designate additional processing tracks that distinguish between simple and more complex requests based on the estimated amount of work or time needed to process the request. Among the factors that may be considered are the number of records requested, the number of pages involved in processing the request and the need for consultations or referrals. Components shall advise requesters of the track into which their request falls and, when appropriate, should offer the requester an opportunity to narrow or modify the request so that it can be placed in a different processing track.

(c) *Unusual circumstances.* Whenever the statutory time limit for processing a request cannot be met because of "unusual circumstances," as defined in the FOIA, and the component extends the time limit on that basis, the component shall, before expiration of the 20-working day period to respond, notify the requester in writing of the unusual circumstances involved and of the date by which the component estimates processing of the request will be completed. Where the extension exceeds 10 working days, the component shall, as prescribed by the FOIA, provide the requester with an opportunity to modify the request or to arrange an alternative time period for processing the original or modified request. The component shall make available its designated FOIA Contact or its FOIA Public Liaison for this purpose. The component must also alert requesters to the availability of the Office of Government Information Services (OGIS) to provide dispute resolution services.

(d) *Aggregating requests.* For the purposes of determining unusual circumstances under the FOIA, components may aggregate requests in cases where it reasonably appears that multiple requests, submitted either by a requester or by a group of requesters acting in concert, constitute a single request that would otherwise involve unusual circumstances. Components shall not aggregate multiple requests that involve unrelated matters.

(e) *Expedited processing.* (1) Requests and appeals shall be processed on an expedited basis whenever it is determined that they involve:

(i) Circumstances in which the lack of expedited processing could reasonably be expected to pose an imminent threat to the life or physical safety of an individual;

(ii) An urgency to inform the public about an actual or alleged Federal Government activity, if made by a person who is primarily engaged in disseminating information.

(iii) The loss of substantial due process rights; or

(iv) A matter of widespread and exceptional media interest in which there exist possible questions about the government's integrity that affect public confidence.

(2) A request for expedited processing may be made at any time. Requests based on paragraphs (e)(1)(i) through (iii) of this section must be submitted to the component that maintains the records requested. When making a request for expedited processing of an administrative appeal, the request should be submitted to the FOI/PA Office. Requests for expedited processing that are based on paragraph (e)(1)(iv) of this section must be submitted to the component processing the request. A component that receives a misdirected request for expedited processing under the standard set forth in paragraph (e)(1)(iv) of this section shall forward it immediately to the FOI/PA Office for its determination. The time period for making the determination on the request for expedited processing under paragraph (e)(1)(iv) of this section shall commence on the date that the FOI/PA Office receives the request, provided that it is routed within 10 working days.

(3) A requester who seeks expedited processing must submit a notarized statement, such as an affidavit or declaration, certified to be true and correct, explaining in detail the basis for making the request for expedited processing. For example, under paragraph (e)(1)(ii) of this section, a requester who is not a full-time member of the news media must establish that the requester is a person whose primary professional activity or occupation is information dissemination, though it need not be the requester's sole occupation. Such a requester also must establish a particular urgency to inform the public about the government activity involved in the request—one that extends beyond the public's right to know about government activity generally. The existence of numerous articles published on a given subject can be helpful in establishing the requirement that there be an "urgency to inform" the public on the topic. As a matter of administrative discretion, the SBA may waive the formal certification requirement.

(4) A component shall notify the requester within 10 working days of the receipt of a request for expedited processing of its decision whether to grant or deny expedited processing. If expedited processing is granted, the request must be given priority, placed in the processing track for expedited requests, and must be processed as soon as practicable. If a request for expedited processing is denied, any appeal of that decision shall be acted on expeditiously.

§ 102.6 Responses to requests.

(a) *In general.* Components should, to the extent practicable, communicate with requesters having access to the Internet using electronic means, such as email or web portal.

(b) *Acknowledgments of requests.* A component shall acknowledge the request in writing and assign it an individualized tracking number. Components shall include in the acknowledgment a brief description of the records sought to allow requesters to more easily keep track of their requests.

(c) *Estimated dates of completion and interim responses.* Upon request, components shall provide an estimated date by which they expect to provide a response to the requester. If a request involves a voluminous amount of material, or searches in multiple locations, the SBA or component may provide interim responses, releasing the records on a rolling basis.

(d) *Grants of requests.* Once a component determines it will grant a request in full or in part, it will notify the requester in writing. The component shall inform the requester of any fees charged under § 102.8 and shall disclose the requested records to the requester promptly upon payment of any applicable fees. The component must inform the requester of the availability of its FOIA Public Liaison to offer assistance.

(e) *Adverse determinations of requests.* A component making an adverse determination denying a request in any respect shall notify the requester of that determination in writing. Adverse determinations, or denials of requests, include denials involving fees or fee waiver matters, denials of requests for expedited processing, and decisions where:

(1) The requested record is exempt, in whole or in part;

(2) The request does not reasonably describe the records sought;

(3) The information requested is not a record subject to the FOIA;

(4) The requested record does not exist, cannot be located, or has been destroyed; or

(5) The requested record is not readily reproducible in the form or format sought by the requester.

(f) *Content of denial.* The denial must be signed by the head of the component or designee and must include:

(1) The name and title or position of the person responsible for the denial;

(2) A brief statement of the reasons for the denial, including any FOIA exemption applied by the component in denying the request;

(3) An estimate of the volume of any records or information withheld, such as the number of pages or some other reasonable form of estimation, although such an estimate is not required if the volume is otherwise indicated by deletions marked on records that are disclosed in part or if providing an estimate would harm an interest protected by an applicable exemption;

(4) A statement that the denial may be appealed under § 102.9, and a description of the appeal requirements; and

(5) A statement notifying the requester of the assistance available from the component's FOIA Public Liaison or designee, and the dispute resolution services offered by OGIS.

(g) *Markings on released documents.* Records disclosed in part must be marked clearly to show the amount of information deleted and the exemption under which the deletion was made unless doing so would harm an interest protected by an applicable exemption.

§ 102.7 Confidential commercial information.

(a) *Definitions.* For purposes of this section:

Confidential commercial information means commercial or financial information obtained by the SBA from a submitter that may be protected from disclosure under Exemption 4 of the FOIA, 5 U.S.C. 552(b)(4).

Submitter means any person or entity, including a corporation, State, or foreign government, but not including another Federal Government entity, that provides information, either directly or indirectly to the Federal Government.

(b) *Designation of confidential commercial information.* A submitter of confidential commercial information must use good faith efforts to designate by appropriate markings, either at the time of submission or within a reasonable time thereafter, any portion of its submission that it considers to be protected from disclosure under Exemption 4. These designations shall expire 10 years after the date of the submission unless the submitter requests and provides justification for a longer designation period.

(c) *When notice to submitters is required.* (1) A component shall promptly provide written notice to a submitter of confidential commercial information whenever records containing such information are requested under the FOIA if, after reviewing the request, the responsive records, and any appeal by the requester, the component determines that it may be required to disclose the records, provided:

(i) The requested information has been designated in good faith by the submitter as information considered protected from disclosure under Exemption 4; or

(ii) The component has a reason to believe that the requested information may be protected from disclosure under Exemption 4, but has not yet determined whether the information is protected from disclosure under that exemption or any other applicable exemption.

(2) The notice shall either describe the commercial information requested or include a copy of the requested

records or portions of records containing the information. In cases involving a voluminous number of submitters, notice may be made by posting or publishing the notice in a place or manner reasonably likely to accomplish it.

(d) *Exceptions to submitter notice requirements.* The notice requirements of this section shall not apply if:

(1) The component determines that the information is exempt under the FOIA;

(2) The information has been lawfully published or has been officially made available to the public;

(3) Disclosure of the information is required by a statute other than the FOIA or by a regulation issued in accordance with the requirements of Executive Order 12600 of June 23, 1987; or

(4) The designation made by the submitter under paragraph (b) of this section appears obviously frivolous, except that, in such a case, the component shall give the submitter written notice of any final decision to disclose the information and must provide that notice within a reasonable number of days prior to a specified disclosure date.

(e) *Opportunity to object to disclosure.* (1) A component shall specify a reasonable time period within which the submitter must respond to the notice referenced above. If the submitter has any objections to disclosure, it should provide the component a detailed written statement that specifies all grounds for withholding the particular information under any exemption of the FOIA. In order to rely on Exemption 4 as the basis for nondisclosure, the submitter must explain why the information constitutes a trade secret or commercial or financial information that is privileged or confidential.

(2) A submitter who fails to respond within the time period specified in the notice shall be considered to have no objection to disclosure of the information. Information received by the component after the date of any disclosure decision shall not be considered by the component. Any information provided by a submitter under this subpart may itself be subject to disclosure under the FOIA.

(f) *Analysis of objections.* A component shall consider a submitter's objections and specific grounds for nondisclosure in deciding whether to disclose the requested information.

(g) *Notice of intent to disclose.* Whenever a component decides to disclose information over the objection of a submitter, the component shall provide the submitter written notice, which shall include:

(1) A statement of the reasons why each of the submitter's disclosure objections was not sustained;

(2) A description of the information to be disclosed; and

(3) A specified disclosure date, which shall be a reasonable time subsequent to the notice.

§ 102.8 Fees.

(a) *In general.* Components shall charge for processing requests under the FOIA in accordance with the provisions of this section and with the OMB Guidelines. In order to resolve any fee issues that arise under this section, a component may contact a requester for additional information. Components shall ensure that searches, review, and duplication are conducted in the most efficient and the least expensive manner. A component ordinarily will collect all applicable fees before sending copies of records to a requester. Requesters must pay fees by check or money order made payable to the Small Business Administration, addressed to the component assessing the fee.

(b) *Categories of requesters.* Different fees are assessed depending on the requester category. Requesters may seek a fee waiver. Requests for fee waivers will be considered in accordance with the requirements in paragraph (l) of this section. For purposes of assessing fees, the FOIA establishes four categories of requesters:

(1) Commercial use requesters;

(2) Non-commercial scientific/educational institutions requesters;

(3) News media requesters, and;

(4) All other requesters.

(c) *Definitions.* For purposes of this section:

(1) *Commercial use request* is a request that asks for information for a use or a purpose that furthers a commercial,

trade, or profit interest, which can include furthering those interests through litigation. A component's decision to place a requester in the commercial use category will be made on a case-by-case basis based on the requester's intended use of the information.

(2) *Direct costs* are those expenses that the SBA incurs in searching for and duplicating (and, in the case of commercial use requests, reviewing) records in order to respond to a FOIA request. For example, direct costs include the salary of the employee performing the work (*i.e.*, the basic rate of pay for the employee, plus 16 percent of that rate to cover benefits) and the cost of operating computers and other electronic equipment, such as photocopiers and scanners. Direct costs do not include overhead expenses such as the costs of space, and of heating or lighting a facility. This will be in addition to search, review, and duplication fees, and shall be paid by requesters categorized as commercial and other.

(3) *Duplication* is reproducing a copy of a record, or of the information contained in it, necessary to respond to a FOIA request. Copies can take the form of paper, audiovisual materials, or electronic records, among others.

(4) *Educational institution* is any school that operates a program of scholarly research. A requester in this fee category must show that the request is made in connection with his or her role at the educational institution. Components may seek verification from the requester that the request is in furtherance of scholarly research and will advise requesters of their placement in this category.

Example 1 to paragraph (c)(4). A request from a professor of geology at a university for records relating to soil erosion, written on letterhead of the Department of Geology, would be presumed to be from an educational institution.

Example 2 to paragraph (c)(4). A request from the same professor of geology seeking drug information from the Food and Drug Administration in furtherance of a murder mystery he is writing would not be presumed to be an institutional request, regardless of whether it was written on institutional stationery.

Example 3 to paragraph (c)(4). A student, who makes a request in furtherance of their coursework or other school-sponsored activities and provides a copy of a course syllabus or other reasonable documentation to indicate the research purpose for the request, would qualify as part of this fee category.

(5) *Noncommercial scientific institution* is an institution that is not operated on a "commercial" basis, as defined in paragraph (c)(1) of this section and that is operated solely for the purpose of conducting scientific research, the results of which are not intended to promote any particular product or industry. A requester in this category must show that the request is authorized by and is made under the auspices of a qualifying institution and that the records are sought to further scientific research and are not for a commercial use.

(6) *Representative of the news media* is any person or entity that gathers information of potential interest to a segment of the public, uses its editorial skills to turn the raw materials into a distinct work, and distributes that work to an audience. The term "news" means information that is about current events or that would be of current interest to the public. Examples of news media entities include television or radio stations that broadcast "news" to the public at large and publishers of periodicals that disseminate "news" and make their products available through a variety of means to the general public, including news organizations that disseminate solely on the Internet. A request for records supporting the news-dissemination function of the requester will not be considered to be for a commercial use. "Freelance" journalists who demonstrate a solid basis for expecting publication through a news media entity will be considered as a representative of the news media. A publishing contract would provide the clearest evidence that publication is expected; however, a requester's past publication record will be considered in making a determination.

(7) *Review* is the examination of a record located in response to a request in order to determine whether any portion of it is exempt from disclosure. Review time includes processing any record for disclosure, such as doing all that is necessary to prepare the record for disclosure, including the process of

redacting the record and marking the appropriate exemptions. Review costs are properly charged even if a record ultimately is not disclosed. Review time also includes time spent both obtaining and considering any formal objection to disclosure made by a confidential commercial information submitter under § 102.7, but it does not include time spent resolving general legal or policy issues regarding the application of exemptions.

(8) *Search* is the process of looking for and retrieving records or information responsive to a request. Search time includes page-by-page or line-by-line identification of information within records and the reasonable efforts expended to locate and retrieve information from electronic records.

(d) *Charging fees.* In responding to FOIA requests, components will charge the following fees unless a waiver or reduction of fees has been granted under paragraph (l) of this section. Because the fee amounts provided below already account for the direct costs associated with a given fee type, components will not add any additional costs to charges calculated under this section.

(1) *Search.* (i) Requests made by educational institutions, noncommercial scientific institutions, or representatives of the news media are not subject to search fees. Search fees shall be charged for all other requesters, subject to the restrictions of paragraph (e) of this section. Components may properly charge for time spent searching even if they do not locate any responsive records or if they determine that the records are entirely exempt from disclosure.

(ii) For each hour spent by personnel searching for requested records, including electronic searches that do not require new programming, the fees will be charged as follows: Professional (GS 9–14)—$46; and managerial (GS 15 and above)—$83.

(iii) Requesters shall be charged the direct costs associated with conducting any search that requires the creation of a new computer program to locate the requested records. Requesters shall be notified of the costs associated with creating such a program and must agree to pay the associated costs before the costs may be incurred.

(iv) For requests that require the retrieval of records stored by SBA at a Federal Records Center operated by the National Archives and Records Administration (NARA), additional costs shall be charged in accordance with the Transactional Billing Rate Schedule established by NARA.

(2) *Duplication.* Duplication fees will be assessed to all requesters, subject to the restrictions of paragraph (e) of this section. A component shall honor a requester's preference for receiving a record in a particular form or format where it can be readily reproduced in the form or format requested. Where photocopies are supplied, SBA will provide one copy per request at the cost of $.10 per page. For copies of records produced on tapes, disks, or other media, SBA will charge the direct costs of producing the copy, including operator time. Where paper documents must be scanned in order to comply with a requester's preference to receive the records in an electronic format, the requester must also pay the direct costs associated with scanning those materials. For other forms of duplication, components shall charge the direct costs.

(3) *Review.* (i) Review fees will be assessed to requesters who make commercial use requests. Review fees will be assessed in connection with the initial review of the record, *i.e.*, the review conducted by a component to determine whether an exemption applies to a particular record or portion of a record. No charge will be made for review at the administrative appeal stage of exemptions applied at the initial review stage. However, if a particular exemption is deemed to no longer apply, any costs associated with SBA's re-review of the records in order to consider the use of other exemptions may be assessed as review fees. Review fees will be charged at the same rates as those charged for a search under paragraph (d)(1)(ii) of this section.

(ii) The following table summarizes the fees for each type of requester.

TABLE 1 TO § 102.8—SUMMARY OF FEES

Requester category	Search	Review	Duplication fees	Direct costs
Commercial Use	Yes	Yes	Yes	Yes.
Educational/Noncommercial Scientific Institutions.	No	No	Yes (first 100 pages, or equivalent volume free).	No.
News Media	No	No	Yes (first 100 pages, or equivalent volume free).	No.
All Others	Yes (first 2 hours free)	No	Yes (first 100 pages, or equivalent volume free).	Yes.

(e) *Restrictions on charging fees.* (1) When a component determines that a requester is an educational institution, non-commercial scientific institution, or representative of the news media, and the records are not sought for commercial use, it will not charge search fees.

(i) If a component fails to comply with the time limits in which to respond to a request, it may not charge search fees, or, in the instances of requests from requesters described in paragraph (c)(1) of this section, may not charge duplication fees, except as described in paragraphs (d)(1)(ii) through (iv) of this section.

(ii) If a component has determined that unusual circumstances as defined by the FOIA apply and SBA provided timely written notice to the requester in accordance with the FOIA, a failure to comply with the time limit shall be excused for an additional 10 working days.

(iii) If a component has determined that unusual circumstances, as defined by the FOIA, apply and more than 5,000 pages are necessary to respond to the request, the component may charge search fees, or, in the case of requesters described in paragraph (c)(1) of this section, may charge duplication fees, if the following steps are taken. The component shall provide a timely written notice of unusual circumstances to the requester in accordance with the FOIA and SBA must have discussed with the requester via written mail, email, or telephone (or made not less than three good-faith attempts to do so) how the requester could effectively limit the scope of the request in accordance with 5 U.S.C. 552(a)(6)(B)(ii). If this exception is satisfied, the component may charge all applicable fees incurred in the processing of the request.

(iv) If a court has determined that exceptional circumstances exist, as defined by the FOIA, a failure to comply with the time limits shall be excused for the length of time provided by the court order.

(2) No search or review fees will be charged for a quarter-hour period unless more than half of that period is required for search or review.

(3) Except for requesters seeking records for a commercial use, components shall provide without charge:

(i) The first 100 pages of duplication (or the cost equivalent for other media); and

(ii) The first two hours of search.

(4) No fee will be charged when the total fee, after deducting the 100 free pages (or its cost equivalent) and the first two hours of search, is equal to or less than $46.00.

(f) *Notice of anticipated fees in excess of $46.00.* (1) When a component determines or estimates that the fees to be assessed in accordance with this section will exceed $46.00, the component shall notify the requester of the actual or estimated amount of the fees, including a breakdown of the fees for search, review, or duplication, unless the requester has indicated a willingness to pay fees as high as those anticipated. If only a portion of the fee can be estimated readily, the component shall advise the requester accordingly. If the request is not for noncommercial use, the notice will specify that the requester is entitled to the statutory entitlements of 100 pages of duplication at no charge and, if the requester is charged search fees, two hours of search time at no charge, and will advise the requester whether those entitlements have been provided.

(2) In cases in which a requester has been notified that the actual or estimated fees are in excess of $46.00, the

request shall not be considered received and further work will not be completed until the requester commits in writing to pay the actual or estimated total fee, or designates some amount of fees the requester is willing to pay, or in the case of a noncommercial use requester who has not yet been provided with the requester's statutory entitlements, designates that the requester seeks only that which can be provided by the statutory entitlements. The requester must provide the commitment or designation in writing, and must, when applicable, designate an exact dollar amount the requester is willing to pay. Components are not required to accept payments in installments.

(3) If the requester has indicated a willingness to pay some designated amount of fees, but the component estimates that the total fee will exceed that amount, the component will toll the processing of the request when it notifies the requester of the estimated fees in excess of the amount the requester has indicated a willingness to pay. The component shall inquire whether the requester wishes to revise the amount of fees the requester is willing to pay or modify the request. Once the requester responds, the time to respond will resume from where it was at the date of the notification.

(4) Components shall make available their FOIA Public Liaison or other designee to assist any requester in reformulating a request to meet the requester's needs at a lower cost.

(g) *Charges for other services.* Although not required to provide special services, if a component chooses to do so as a matter of administrative discretion, the direct costs of providing the service will be charged. Examples of such services include certifying that records are true copies, providing multiple copies of the same document, or sending records by means other than first class mail.

(h) *Charging interest.* Components may charge interest on any unpaid bill starting on the 31st day following the date of billing the requester. Interest charges will be assessed at the rate provided in 31 U.S.C. 3717 and will accrue from the billing date until payment is received by the component. Components shall follow the provisions of the Debt Collection Act of 1982 (Pub. L. 97–365, 96 Stat. 1749), as amended, and its administrative procedures, including the use of consumer reporting agencies, collection agencies, and offset.

(i) *Aggregating requests.* When a component reasonably believes that a requester or a group of requesters acting in concert is attempting to divide a single request into a series of requests for the purpose of avoiding fees, the component may aggregate those requests and charge accordingly. Components may presume that multiple requests of this type made within a 30-day period have been made in order to avoid fees. For requests separated by a longer period, components shall aggregate them only where there is a reasonable basis for determining that aggregation is warranted in view of all the circumstances involved. Multiple requests involving unrelated matters cannot be aggregated.

(j) *Advance payments.* (1) For requests other than those described in paragraphs (j)(2) or (j)(3) of this section, components cannot require the requester to make an advance payment before work is commenced or continued on a request. Payment owed for work already completed (*i.e.*, payment before copies are sent to a requester) is not an advance payment.

(2) When a component determines or estimates that a total fee to be charged under this section will exceed $250.00, it may require that the requester make an advance payment up to the amount of the entire anticipated fee before beginning to process the request. Components may elect to process the request prior to collecting fees when it receives a satisfactory assurance of full payment from a requester with a history of prompt payment.

(3) Where a requester has previously failed to pay a properly charged FOIA fee to any component or SBA within 30 working days of the billing date, a component may require that the requester pay the full amount due, plus any applicable interest on that prior request, and the component may require that the requester make an advance payment of the full amount of any anticipated fee before SBA begins

to process a new request or continues to process a pending request or any pending appeal. When a component has a reasonable basis to believe that a requester has misrepresented the requester's identity in order to avoid paying outstanding fees, it may require that the requester provide proof of identity.

(4) In cases in which advanced payment is required, the request will not be considered received and further work will not be completed until the required payment is received. If the requester does not pay the advance payment within 30 working days after the date of the fee determination, the request will be closed.

(k) *Other statutes specifically providing for fees.* The fee schedule of this section does not apply to fees charged under any statute that specifically requires SBA to set and collect fees for particular types of records. In instances where records responsive to a request are subject to a statutorily-based fee schedule program, the requester will be informed of the contact information for that program.

(l) *Requirements for waiver or reduction of fees.* (1) Requesters may seek a waiver of fees by submitting written correspondence demonstrating how disclosure of the requested information is in the public interest because it is likely to contribute significantly to public understanding of the operations or activities of the government and is not primarily in the commercial interest of the requester. Records responsive to a request shall be furnished without charge or at a reduced rate below the rate established under paragraph (d) of this section, where a component determines, based on all available information, that the requester has demonstrated that:

(i) Disclosure of the requested information is in the public interest because it is likely to contribute significantly to public understanding of the operations or activities of the government, and

(ii) Disclosure of the information is not primarily in the commercial interest of the requester.

(2) Components shall furnish records responsive to a request without charge or at a reduced rate when it determines, based on all available information, that the factors described in paragraphs (l)(2)(i) through (iii) of this section are satisfied:

(i) Disclosure of the requested information would shed light on the operations or activities of the government. The subject of the request must concern identifiable operations or activities of the Federal Government with a connection that is direct and clear, not remote or attenuated.

(ii) Disclosure of the requested information is likely to contribute significantly to public understanding of those operations or activities. This factor is satisfied when the following criteria are met:

(A) Disclosure of the requested records must be meaningfully informative about government operations or activities. The disclosure of information that already is in the public domain, in either the same or a substantially identical form, would not be meaningfully informative if nothing new would be added to the public's understanding.

(B) The disclosure must contribute to the understanding of a reasonably broad audience of persons interested in the subject, as opposed to the individual understanding of the requester. A requester's expertise in the subject area as well as the requester's ability and intention to effectively convey information to the public must be considered. Components shall presume that a representative of the news media will satisfy this consideration.

(iii) The disclosure must not be primarily in the commercial interest of the requester. To determine whether disclosure of the requested information is primarily in the commercial interest of the requester, the following criteria will be considered:

(A) Identify whether the requester has any commercial interest that would be furthered by the requested disclosure. A commercial interest includes any commercial, trade, or profit interest. Requesters must be given an opportunity to provide explanatory information regarding this consideration.

(B) If there is an identified commercial interest, a determination will be made whether the primary interest is furthered by the request. A waiver or reduction of fees is justified when the requirements of paragraphs (l)(2)(i) and (ii) of this section are satisfied and any commercial interest is not the primary interest furthered by the request. Ordinarily there will be a presumption, that when a news media requester has satisfied factors (l)(2)(i) and (ii) of this section, the request is not primarily in the commercial interest of the requester. Disclosure to data brokers or others who merely compile and market government information for direct economic return will not be presumed to primarily serve the public interest.

(3) Where only some of the records to be released satisfy the requirements for a waiver of fees, a waiver must be granted for those records.

(4) Requests for a waiver or reduction of fees should be made when the request is first submitted and should address the criteria referenced above. A requester may submit a fee waiver request at a later time so long as the underlying record request is pending or on administrative appeal. When a requester who has committed to pay fees subsequently asks for a waiver of those fees and that waiver is denied, the requester must pay any costs incurred up to the date the fee waiver request was received.

§ 102.9 Administrative appeals.

(a) *Requirements for making an appeal.* A requester may appeal any adverse determinations to the FOI/PA Office. The contact information is contained in § 102.3(a)(1). Examples of adverse determinations are provided in § 102.6(e). The requester must make the appeal in writing and to be considered timely it must be postmarked, or in the case of electronic submissions, transmitted, within 90 working days after the date of the response. The appeal should clearly identify the component's determination that is being appealed and the assigned request number. To facilitate handling, the requester should mark both the appeal letter and envelope, or subject line of the electronic transmission, "Freedom of Information Act Appeal."

(b) *Adjudication of appeals.* (1) The Chief, FOI/PA or designee will act on behalf of the SBA on all appeals under this section.

(2) An appeal ordinarily will not be adjudicated if the request becomes a matter of FOIA litigation.

(3) On receipt of any appeal involving classified information, the FOI/PA Office shall take appropriate action to ensure compliance with Executive Orders 13467 and 13526.

(c) *Decisions on appeals.* A decision on an appeal will be made in writing. A decision that upholds a component's determination will contain a statement that identifies the reasons for the affirmance, including any FOIA exemptions applied. The decision will provide the requester with notification of the statutory right to file a lawsuit and will inform the requester of the mediation services offered by OGIS as a non-exclusive alternative to litigation. If a component's decision is remanded or modified on appeal, the requester will be notified of that determination in writing. The component will thereafter, further process the request in accordance with that appeal determination and respond directly to the requester.

(d) Time limit for issuing appeal decision. The statutory time limit for responding to appeals is generally 20 working days after receipt. However, the Appeals Officer may extend the time limit for responding to an appeal provided the circumstances set forth in 5 U.S.C. 552(a)(6)(B)(i) are met.

(e) *Engaging in dispute resolution services provided by OGIS.* Mediation is a voluntary process. If a component agrees to participate in the mediation services provided by OGIS, it will actively engage as a partner to the process in an attempt to resolve the dispute.

(f) *When an appeal is required.* Before seeking review by a court of a component's adverse determination, a requester generally must first submit a timely administrative appeal.

§ 102.10 Preservation of records.

Each component shall preserve all correspondence pertaining to the requests that it receives under this subpart, as well as copies of all requested records, until disposition or destruction is authorized pursuant to title 44 of the United States Code or the General Records Schedule 14 of the National Archives and Records Administration. Records shall not be disposed of or destroyed while they are the subject of a pending request, appeal, or lawsuit under the FOIA.

§ 102.11 Subpoenas.

(a) The person to whom the subpoena is directed must consult with SBA counsel in the relevant SBA office, who will seek approval for compliance from the Associate General Counsel for Litigation. Except where the subpoena requires the testimony of an employee of the Inspector General's office, or records within the possession of the Inspector General, the Associate General Counsel may delegate the authorization for appropriate production of documents or testimony to local SBA counsel.

(b) If SBA counsel approves compliance with the subpoena, SBA will comply.

(c) If SBA counsel disapproves compliance with the subpoena, SBA will not comply, and will base such noncompliance on an appropriate legal basis such as privilege or a statute.

(d) SBA counsel must provide a copy of any subpoena relating to a criminal matter to SBA's Inspector General prior to its return date.

APPENDIX A TO SUBPART A OF PART 102—RECORDS MAINTAINED BY SBA

I. INFORMATION GENERALLY EXEMPT FROM DISCLOSURE

a. Non-statistical information on pending, declined, withdrawn, or canceled applications.

b. Non-statistical information on defaults, delinquencies, losses etc.

c. Loan status, other than charged-off or paid-in-full.

d. Home disaster loan status and interest rate.

e. Financial statements, credit reports, business plans, plant lay-outs, marketing strategy, advertising plans, fiscal projections, pricing information, payroll information, private sector experience and contracts, IRS forms, purchase information, banking information, corporate structure, research plans and client list of applicant/recipient.

f. Portions of: Certificate of Competency records, Requests for Size Determinations, 8(a) Business Development Plans, loan applications, SBIC applications, loan officer's reports.

g. Internal documents not incorporated into final Agency action, pending internal recommendations on applications for assistance, SBA/attorney-client communications, pending litigation documents and investigatory documents. Discretionary disclosure policy must be utilized.

h. Personal history and financial statements, tax forms, resumes, all non-government career experience, communications regarding applicant's character, home addresses and telephone numbers, social security numbers, birth dates and medical records. Portions of Inspector General (IG) reports, audit reports, program investigation records and any other records which, if released, would interfere with the Government's law enforcement proceedings and/or would reveal the identity of a confidential source and documents relating to pending litigation and investigations. Requests for IG documents must be referred to the Office of the Inspector General, Counsel Division.

i. Financial information on portfolio companies.

j. Information originating from other agencies should be referred to those agencies for disclosure determinations.

II. INFORMATION GENERALLY DISCLOSED

a. Names and business addresses of recipients of approved loans, SBIC licenses, Certificates of Competency, lease guarantees, surety bond guarantees and requests for counseling.

b. Names of officers, directors, stockholders or partners of recipient firms.

c. Kinds and amounts of loans, loan terms, interest rates (except on home disaster loans), maturity dates, general purpose, etc.

d. Statistical data on assistance, loans, defaults, contracts, counseling, etc.

e. Decisions, rulings and records showing final Agency actions in specific factual situations if identifying details exempt from disclosure are first deleted.

f. Awarded contracts: names, amounts, dates, contracting agencies.

g. Identity of participating banks.

h. List of 8(a) participants, date of entry, FPPT dates and NAICS codes.

i. OHA opinions and decisions.

j. Names of SBA employees, grades, titles, and duty stations.

Subpart B—Protection of Privacy and Access to Individual Records Under the Privacy Act of 1974

SOURCE: 72 FR 17369, Apr. 9, 2007, unless otherwise noted.

§ 102.20 General provisions.

(a) *Purpose and scope.* This subpart implements the provisions of the Privacy Act of 1974, 5 U.S.C. 552a. These regulations apply to all records which are contained in systems of records maintained by the U.S. Small Business Administration (SBA) and that are retrieved by an individual's name or personal identifier. These regulations set forth the procedures by which individuals may request access to records about themselves, request amendment or correction of those records, and request an accounting of disclosures of those records by the SBA. These regulations also set forth the requirements applicable to SBA employees maintaining, collecting, using or disseminating records pertaining to individuals. This subpart applies to SBA and all of its offices and is mandatory for use by all SBA employees.

(b) *Definitions.* As used in this subpart:

(1) *Agency* means the U.S. Small Business Administration (SBA) and includes all of its offices wherever located;

(2) *Employee* means any employee of the SBA, regardless of grade, status, category or place of employment;

(3) *Individual* means a citizen of the United States or an alien lawfully admitted for permanent residence. This term shall not encompass entrepreneurial enterprises (e.g. sole proprietors, partnerships, corporations, or other forms of business entities);

(4) *Maintain* includes maintain, collect, use, or disseminate;

(5) *Record* means any item, collection, or grouping of information about an individual that is maintained by the SBA, including, but not limited to education, financial transactions, medical history, and criminal or employment history and that contains the individual's name, or an identifying number, symbol, or other identifying particular assigned to the individual such as a finger or voice print or photograph;

(6) *System of records* means a group of any records under the control of SBA from which information is retrieved by the name of the individual or by an identifying number, symbol, or other identifying particular assigned to the individual;

(7) *Statistical record* means a record in a system of records maintained for statistical research or reporting purposes only and not used in whole or in part in making any determination about an identifiable individual;

(8) *Routine use* means, with respect to the disclosure of a record, the use of such record for a purpose which is compatible with the purpose for which it was collected;

(9) *Request for access* to a record means a request made under Privacy Act subsection (d)(1) allowing an individual to gain access to his or her record or to any information pertaining to him or her which is contained in a system of records;

(10) *Request for amendment or correction* of a record means a request made under Privacy Act subsection (d)(2), permitting an individual to request amendment or correction of a record that he or she believes is not accurate, relevant, timely, or complete;

(11) *Request for an accounting* means a request made under Privacy Act subsection (c)(3) allowing an individual to request an accounting of any disclosure to any SBA officers and employees who have a need for the record in the performance of their duties;

(12) *Requester* is an individual who makes a request for access, a request for amendment or correction, or a request for an accounting under the Privacy Act; and

(13) *Authority to request records for a law enforcement purpose* means that the head of an Agency or a United States Attorney, or either's designee, is authorized to make written requests under subsection (b)(7) of the Privacy Act for records maintained by other agencies that are necessary to carry out an authorized law enforcement activity.

§ 102.21 Agency employees responsible for the Privacy Act of 1974.

(a) *Program/Support Office Head* is the SBA employee in each field office and major program and support area responsible for implementing and overseeing this regulation in that office.

(b) *Privacy Act Systems Manager* (PASM) is the designated SBA employee in each office responsible for the development and management of any

Privacy Act systems of records in that office.

(c) *Senior Agency Official for Privacy* is SBA's Chief Information Officer (CIO) who has overall responsibility and accountability for ensuring the SBA's implementation of information privacy protections, including the SBA's full compliance with Federal laws, regulations, and policies relating to information privacy such as the Privacy Act and the E-Government Act of 2002.

(d) *Chief, Freedom of Information/Privacy Acts (FOI/PA) Office* oversees and implements the record access, amendment, and correction provisions of the Privacy Act.

§ 102.22 Requirements relating to systems of records.

(a) *In general.* Each SBA office shall, in accordance with the Privacy Act:

(1) Maintain in its records only such information about an individual as is relevant and necessary to accomplish a purpose of the Agency required to be accomplished by a statute or by Executive Order of the President;

(2) Collect information to the greatest extent practicable directly from the subject individual when the information may affect an individual's rights, benefits, and privileges under Federal programs;

(b) *Requests for information from individuals.* If a form is being used to collect information from individuals, either the form used to collect the information, or a separate form that can be retained by the individual, must state the following:

(1) The authority (whether granted by statute, or by Executive Order of the President) which authorizes the solicitation of the information and whether disclosure of such information is mandatory or voluntary;

(2) The principal purpose or purposes for which the information is intended to be used;

(3) The routine uses which may be made of the information; and

(4) The effects on such individual, if any, of not providing all or any part of the requested information.

(c) *Report on new systems.* Each SBA office shall provide adequate advance notice to Congress and OMB through the FOI/PA Office of any proposal to establish or alter any system of records in order to permit an evaluation of the probable or potential effect of such proposal on the privacy and other personal or property rights of individuals or the disclosure of information relating to such individuals.

(d) *Accurate and secure maintenance of records.* Each SBA office shall:

(1) Maintain all records which are used in making any determination about any individual with such accuracy, relevance, timeliness, and completeness as is reasonably necessary to assure fairness to the individual in the determination;

(2) Prior to disseminating any record from a system of records about an individual to any requestor, including an agency, make reasonable efforts to assure that such records are accurate, complete, timely, and relevant for SBA purposes; and

(3) Establish appropriate administrative, technical, and physical safeguards to insure the security and confidentiality of records and to protect against any anticipated threats or hazards to their security or integrity which could result in substantial harm, embarrassment, inconvenience, or unfairness to any individual on whom information is maintained.

(i) PASMs, with the approval of the head of their offices, shall establish administrative and physical controls, consistent with SBA regulations, to insure the protection of records systems from unauthorized access or disclosure and from physical damage or destruction. The controls instituted shall be proportional to the degree of sensitivity of the records but at a minimum must ensure that records other than those available to the general public under the FOIA, are protected from public view, that the area in which the records are stored is supervised during all business hours and physically secured during non-business hours to prevent unauthorized personnel from obtaining access to the records.

(ii) PASMs, with the approval of the head of their offices, shall adopt access restrictions to insure that only those individuals within the agency who have a need to have access to the records for the performance of their duties have access to them. Procedures shall also be adopted to prevent accidental access to, or dissemination of, records.

(e) *Prohibition against maintenance of records concerning First Amendment rights.* No SBA office shall maintain a record describing how any individual exercises rights guaranteed by the First Amendment (e.g. speech), unless the maintenance of such record is:

(1) Expressly authorized by statute, or

(2) Expressly authorized by the individual about whom the record is maintained, or

(3) Pertinent to and within the scope of an authorized law enforcement activity.

§ 102.23 Publication in the Federal Register—Notices of systems of records.

(a) *Notices of systems of records to be published in the* FEDERAL REGISTER. (1) The SBA shall publish in the FEDERAL REGISTER upon establishment or revision a notice of the existence and character of any new or revised systems of records. Unless otherwise instructed, each notice shall include:

(i) The name and location of the system;

(ii) The categories of individuals on who records are maintained in the system;

(iii) The categories of records maintained in the system;

(iv) Each routine use of the records contained in the system, including the categories of users and the purpose of such use;

(v) The policies and practices of the office regarding storage, retrievability, access controls, retention, and disposal of the records;

(vi) The title and business address of the SBA official who is responsible for the system of records;

(vii) A statement that SBA procedures allow an individual, at his or her request, to determine whether a system of records contains a record pertaining to him or her, to review such records and to contest or amend such records, located in sections 102.25 through 102.29 of these regulations.

(viii) A statement that such requests may be directed to the SBA's FOI/PA Office, 409 3rd St., SW., Washington, DC 20416 or faxed to 202–205–7059; and

(ix) The categories of sources of records in the system.

(2) Minor changes to systems of records shall be published annually.

(b) *Notice of new or modified routine uses to be published in the* FEDERAL REGISTER. At least 30 days prior to disclosing records pursuant to a new use or modification of a routine use, as published under paragraph (a)(1)(iv) of this section, each SBA office shall publish in the FEDERAL REGISTER notice of such new or modified use of the information in the system and provide an opportunity for any individual or persons to submit written comments.

§ 102.24 Requests for access to records.

(a) *How made and addressed.* An individual, or his or her legal guardian, may make a request for access to an SBA record about himself or herself by appearing in person or by writing directly to the SBA office that maintains the record or to the FOI/PA Office by mail to 409 3rd St., SW., Washington, DC 20416 or fax to 202–205–7059. A request received by the FOI/PA Office will be forwarded to the appropriate SBA Office where the records are located.

(b) *Description of records sought.* A request for access to records must describe the records sought in sufficient detail to enable SBA personnel to locate the system of records containing them with a reasonable amount of effort. A request should also state the date of the record or time period in which the record was compiled, and the name or identifying number of each system of records in which the requester believes the record is kept. The SBA publishes notices in the FEDERAL REGISTER that describe its systems of records. A description of the SBA's systems of records also may be found at *http://www.sba.gov/foia/systemrecords.doc.*

(c) *Verification of identity.* Any individual who submits a request for access to records must verify his or her identity. No specific form is required; however, the requester must state his or her full name, current address, and date and place of birth. The request must be signed and the requester's signature must either be notarized or submitted under 28 U.S.C. 1746. This law permits statements to be made under penalty of perjury as a substitute for notarization, the language states:

(1) If executed outside the United States: "I declare (or certify, verify, or state) under penalty of perjury under the laws of the United States of America that the foregoing is true and correct. Executed on (date). Signature"; or

(2) If executed within the Untied States, its territories, possessions or commonwealths: "I declare (or certify, verify, or state) under penalty of perjury that the foregoing is true and correct. Executed on (date). Signature".

(d) *Verification of guardianship.* When making a request as a legal agent or the parent or guardian of a minor or as the guardian of someone determined by a court to be incompetent, for access to records about that individual, the requester must establish:

(1) The identity of the individual who is the subject of the record, by stating the name, current address, date and place of birth, and, at the requester's option, the social security number of the individual;

(2) The requester's own identity, as required in paragraph (c) of this section;

(3) That the requester is the legal agent or parent or guardian of that individual, which may be proven by providing a copy of the individual's birth certificate showing his parentage or by providing a court order establishing guardianship; and

(4) That the requester is acting on behalf of that individual in making the request.

§ 102.25 Responsibility for responding to requests for access to records.

(a) *In general.* Except as stated in paragraphs (c), (d), and (e) of this section and in § 102.24(a), the office that first receives a request for access to a record, and has possession of that record, is the office responsible for responding to the request. That office shall acknowledge receipt of the request not later than 10 days (excluding Saturdays, Sundays, and legal public holidays) after the date of receipt of the request in writing. In determining which records are responsive to a request, an office ordinarily shall include only those records in its possession as of the date the office begins its search for them. If any other date is used, the office shall inform the requester of that date.

(b) *Authority to grant or deny requests.* The Program/Support Office Head, or designee, is authorized to grant or deny any request for access to a record of that office.

(c) *Consultations and referrals.* When an office receives a request for access to a record in its possession, it shall determine whether another office, or another agency of the Federal Government, is better able to determine whether the record is exempt from access under the Privacy Act. If the receiving office determines that it is best able to process the record in response to the request, then it shall do so. If the receiving office determines that it is not best able to process the record, then it shall either:

(1) Respond to the request regarding that record, after consulting with the office or agency best able to determine whether the record is exempt from access and with any other office or agency that has a substantial interest in it; or

(2) Refer the responsibility for responding to the request to the office best able to determine whether the record is exempt from access or to another agency that originated the record (but only if that agency is subject to the Privacy Act). Ordinarily the office or agency that originated a record will be presumed to be best able to determine whether it is exempt from access.

(d) *Law enforcement information.* Whenever a request is made for access to a record containing information that relates to an investigation of a possible violation of law and that was originated by SBA's Office of the Inspector General (OIG) or another agency, the receiving office shall refer the responsibility for responding to the request regarding that information to either SBA's OIG or the other agency "depending on where the investigation originated."

(e) *Classified information.* Whenever a request is made for access to a record containing information that has been classified by or may be appropriate for classification by another office or agency under Executive Order 12958 or any other executive order concerning the classification of records, the receiving office shall refer the responsibility for responding to the request regarding that information to the office or agency that classified the information, should consider the information for classification, or has the primary interest in it, as appropriate. Whenever a record contains information that has been derivatively classified by an office because it contains information classified by another office or agency, the office shall refer the responsibility for responding to the request regarding that information to the office or agency that classified the underlying information. Information determined to no longer require classification shall not be withheld from a requester on the basis of Exemption (k)(1) of the Privacy Act.

(f) *Notice of referral.* Whenever an office refers all or any part of the responsibility for responding to a request to another office or agency, it shall notify the requester of the referral and inform the requester of the name of each office or agency to which the request has been referred and of the part of the request that has been referred.

(g) *Responses to consultations and referrals.* All consultations and referrals shall be processed according to the date the access request was initially received by the first office or agency, not any later date.

(h) *Agreements regarding consultations and referrals.* Offices may make agreements with other offices or agencies to eliminate the need for consultations or referrals for particular types of records.

§ 102.26 Responses to requests for access to records.

(a) *Acknowledgements of requests.* On receipt of a request, an office shall send an acknowledgement letter to the requester.

(b) *Grants of requests for access.* Once an office makes a determination to grant a request for access in whole or in part, it shall notify the requester in writing. The Program/Support Office Head or designee shall inform the requester in the notice of any fee charged under § 102.31 and shall disclose records to the requester promptly on payment of any applicable fee. If a request is made in person, the office may disclose records to the requester directly, in a manner not unreasonably disruptive of its operations, on payment of any applicable fee and with a written record made of the grant of the request. If a requester is accompanied by another person, he or she shall be required to authorize in writing any discussion of the records in the presence of the other person.

(c) *Adverse determinations of requests for access.* A Program/Support Office Head or designee making an adverse determination denying a request for access in any respect shall notify the requester of that determination in writing. Adverse determinations, or denials of requests, consist of: a determination to withhold any requested record in whole or in part; a determination that a requested record does not exist or cannot be located; a determination that the requested information is not a record subject to the Privacy Act; a determination on any disputed fee matter; and a denial of a request for expedited treatment. The notification letter shall be signed by the Program/Support Office Head or designee, and shall include:

(1) The name and title or position of the person responsible for the denial;

(2) A brief statement of the reason(s) for the denial, including any FOIA or Privacy Act exemption(s) applied in denying the request; and

(3) A statement that the denial may be appealed under § 102.27(a) and a description of the requirements of § 102.27(a).

§ 102.27 Appeals from denials of requests for access to records.

(a) *Appeals.* If the requester is dissatisfied with an office's response to his or her request for access to records, the requester may make a written appeal of the adverse determination denying the request in any respect to the SBA's FOI/PA Office, 409 3rd St., SW., Washington, DC 20416. The appeal must be received by the FOI/PA Office within 60 days of the date of the letter denying the request. The requester's appeal letter should include as much information as possible, including the identity of the office whose adverse determination is being appealed. Unless otherwise directed, the Chief, FOI/PA will decide all appeals under this subpart.

(b) *Responses to appeals.* The decision on a requester's appeal will be made in writing not later than 30 days (excluding Saturdays, Sundays, and legal public holidays) after the date of receipt of such appeal. A decision affirming an adverse determination in whole or in part will include a brief statement of the reason(s) for the affirmation, including any Privacy Act exemption applied, and will inform the requester of the Privacy Act provisions for court review of the decision. If the adverse determination is reversed or modified on appeal in whole or in part, the requester will be notified in a written decision and his request will be reprocessed in accordance with that appeal decision.

(c) *Judicial review.* In order to seek judicial review by a court of any adverse determination or denial of a request, a requester must first appeal it to the FOI/PA Office under this section.

§ 102.28 Requests for amendment or correction of records.

(a) *How made and addressed.* Unless the record is not subject to amendment or correction as stated in paragraph (f) of this section, an individual may make a request for amendment or correction of an SBA record about himself or herself by writing directly to the office that maintains the record, following the procedures in § 102.24. The request should identify each particular record in question, state the amendment or correction sought, and state why the record is not accurate, relevant, timely, or complete. The requester may submit any documentation that he or she thinks would be helpful. If the requester believes that the same record is in more than one system of records, that should be stated and the request should be sent to each office that maintains a system of records containing the record.

(b) *Office responses.* Within ten (10) days (excluding Saturdays, Sundays, and legal public holidays) of receiving a request for amendment or correction of records, an office shall send the requester a written acknowledgment of receipt, and the office shall notify the requester within 30 days (excluding Saturdays, Sundays, and legal public holidays) of receipt of the request whether it is granted or denied. If the Program/Support Office Head or designee grants the request in whole or in part, the amendment or correction must be made, and the requester advised of his or her right to obtain a copy of the corrected or amended record. If the office denies a request in whole or in part, it shall send the requester a letter signed by the Program/ Support Office Head or designee that shall state:

(1) The reason(s) for the denial; and

(2) The procedure for appeal of the denial under paragraph (c) of this section, including the name and business address of the official who will act on your appeal.

(c) *Appeals.* An individual may appeal a denial of a request for amendment or correction to the FOI/PA Office in the same manner as a denial of a request for access to records (see § 102.27), and the same procedures shall be followed. If the appeal is denied, the requester shall be advised of his or her right to file a Statement of Disagreement as described in paragraph (d) of this section and of his or her right under the Privacy Act for court review of the decision.

(d) *Statement of Disagreement.* If an appeal under this section is denied in whole or in part, the requester has the right to file a Statement of Disagreement that states the reason(s) for disagreeing with the SBA's denial of his or her request for amendment or correction. A Statement of Disagreement must be concise, must clearly identify each part of any record that is disputed, and should be no longer than one typed page for each fact disputed. An individual's Statement of Disagreement must be sent to the office that maintains the record involved, which shall place it in the system of records in which the disputed record is maintained and shall mark the disputed record to indicate that a Statement of Disagreement has been filed and where in the system of records it may be found.

(e) *Notification of amendment/correction or disagreement.* Within 30 days (excluding Saturdays, Sundays, and legal public holidays) of the amendment or correction of a record, the office that maintains the record shall notify all persons, organizations, or agencies to which it previously disclosed the record, if an accounting of that disclosure was made, that the record has been amended or corrected. If an individual has filed a Statement of Disagreement, the office shall append a copy of it to the disputed record whenever the record is disclosed and may also append a concise statement of its reason(s) for denying the request to amend or correct the record.

(f) *Records not subject to amendment or correction.* The following records are not subject to amendment or correction:

(1) Transcripts of testimony given under oath or written statements made under oath;

(2) Transcripts of grand jury proceedings, judicial proceedings, or quasi-judicial proceedings, which are the official record of those proceedings;

(3) Pre-sentence records that originated with the courts; and

(4) Records in systems of records that have been exempted from amendment and correction under Privacy Act, 5 U.S.C. 552a (j) or (*k*) by notice published in the FEDERAL REGISTER.

§ 102.29 Requests for an accounting of record disclosures.

(a) *How made and addressed.* Except where accountings of disclosures are not required to be kept (as stated in paragraph (b) of this section), an individual may make a request for an accounting of any disclosure that has been made by the SBA to another person, organization, or agency of any record in a system of records about him or her. This accounting contains the date, nature, and purpose of each disclosure, as well as the name and address of the person, organization, or agency to which the disclosure was made. The request for an accounting should identify each particular record in question and should be made by writing directly to the SBA office that maintains the record, following the procedures in § 102.24.

(b) *Where accountings are not required.* Offices are not required to provide accountings where they relate to:

(1) Disclosures for which accountings are not required to be kept; disclosures that are made to employees within the SBA and disclosures that are made under the FOIA;

(2) Disclosures made to law enforcement agencies for authorized law enforcement activities in response to written requests from those law enforcement agencies specifying the civil or criminal law enforcement activities for which the disclosures are sought; or

(3) Disclosures made from law enforcement systems of records that have been exempted from accounting requirements under Privacy Act, 5 U.S.C. 552a(j) or (k) by notice published in the FEDERAL REGISTER.

(c) *Appeals.* An individual may appeal a denial of a request for an accounting to the FOI/PA Office in the same manner as a denial of a request for access to records (see § 102.27), and the same procedures will be followed.

§ 102.30 Preservation of records.

Each office will preserve all correspondence pertaining to the requests that it receives under this subpart, as well as copies of all requested records, until disposition or destruction is authorized by title 44 of the United States Code or the National Archives and Records Administration's General Records Schedule 14. Records will not be disposed of while they are the subject of a pending request, appeal, or lawsuit under the Privacy Act.

§ 102.31 Fees.

SBA offices shall charge fees for duplication of records under the Privacy Act in the same way in which they charge duplication fees under § 102.6(b)(3). No search or review fee may be charged for any record unless the record has been exempted from access under Exemptions (j)(2) or (k)(2) of the Privacy Act. SBA will waive fees under $25.00.

§ 102.32 Notice of court-ordered and emergency disclosures.

(a) *Court-ordered disclosures.* When a record pertaining to an individual is required to be disclosed by order of a court of competent jurisdiction, the office that maintains the record shall make reasonable efforts to provide notice of this to the individual. Notice shall be given within a reasonable time after the office's receipt of the order, except that in a case in which the order is not a matter of public record, the notice shall be given only after the order becomes public. This notice shall be mailed to the individual's last known address and shall contain a copy of the order and a description of the information disclosed. Notice shall not be given if disclosure is made from a criminal law enforcement system of records that has been exempted from the notice requirement.

(b) *Emergency disclosures.* Upon disclosing a record pertaining to an individual made under compelling circumstances affecting health or safety, the office shall notify that individual of the disclosure. This notice shall be mailed to the individual's last known address and shall state the nature of the information disclosed; the person, organization, or agency to which it was disclosed; the date of disclosure; and the compelling circumstances justifying the disclosure.

§ 102.33 Security of systems of records.

(a) Each Program/Support Office Head or designee shall establish administrative and physical controls to prevent unauthorized access to its systems of records, to prevent unauthorized disclosure of records, and to prevent physical damage to or destruction of records. The stringency of these controls shall correspond to the sensitivity of the records that the controls protect. At a minimum, each office's administrative and physical controls shall ensure that:

(1) Records are protected from public view;

(2) The area in which records are kept is supervised during business hours to prevent unauthorized persons from having access to them;

(3) Records are inaccessible to unauthorized persons outside of business hours; and

(4) Records are not disclosed to unauthorized persons or under unauthorized circumstances in either oral or written form.

(b) Each Program/Support Office Head or designee shall establish procedures that restrict access to records to only those individuals within the SBA who must have access to those records in order to perform their duties and that prevent inadvertent disclosure of records.

(c) The OCIO shall provide SBA offices with guidance and assistance for privacy and security of electronic systems and compliance with pertinent laws and requirements.

§ 102.34 Contracts for the operation of record systems.

When SBA contracts for the operation or maintenance of a system of records or a portion of a system of records by a contractor, the record system or the portion of the record affected, are considered to be maintained by the SBA, and subject to this subpart. The SBA is responsible for applying the requirements of this subpart to the contractor. The contractor and its employees are to be considered employees of the SBA for purposes of the sanction provisions of the Privacy Act during performance of the contract.

§ 102.35 Use and collection of Social Security Numbers.

Each Program/Support Office Head or designee shall ensure that collection and use of SSN is performed only when the functionality of the system is dependant on use of the SSN as an identifier. Employees authorized to collect information must be aware:

(a) That individuals may not be denied any right, benefit, or privilege as a result of refusing to provide their social security numbers, unless:

(1) The collection is authorized either by a statute; or

(2) The social security numbers are required under statute or regulation adopted prior to 1975 to verify the identity of an individual; and

(b) That individuals requested to provide their social security numbers must be informed of:

(1) Whether providing social security numbers is mandatory or voluntary;

(2) Any statutory or regulatory authority that authorizes the collection of social security numbers; and

(3) The uses that will be made of the numbers.

§ 102.36 Privacy Act standards of conduct.

Each Program/Support Office Head or designee shall inform its employees of the provisions of the Privacy Act, including its civil liability and criminal penalty provisions. Unless otherwise permitted by law, an employee of the SBA shall:

(a) Collect from individuals only the information that is relevant and necessary to discharge the responsibilities of the SBA;

(b) Collect information about an individual directly from that individual whenever practicable;

(c) Inform each individual from whom information is collected of:

(1) The legal authority to collect the information and whether providing it is mandatory or voluntary;

(2) The principal purpose for which the SBA intends to use the information;

(3) The routine uses the SBA may make of the information; and

(4) The effects on the individual, if any, of not providing the information;

(d) Ensure that the office maintains no system of records without public notice and that it notifies appropriate SBA officials of the existence or development of any system of records that is not the subject of a current or planned public notice;

(e) Maintain all records that are used by the SBA in making any determination about an individual with such accuracy, relevance, timeliness, and completeness as is reasonably necessary to ensure fairness to the individual in the determination;

(f) Except as to disclosures made to an agency or made under the FOIA, make reasonable efforts, prior to disseminating any record about an individual, to ensure that the record is accurate, relevant, timely, and complete;

(g) Maintain no record describing how an individual exercises his or her First Amendment rights, unless it is expressly authorized by statute or by the individual about whom the record is maintained, or is pertinent to and within the scope of an authorized law enforcement activity;

(h) When required by the Privacy Act, maintain an accounting in the specified form of all disclosures of records by the SBA to persons, organizations, or agencies;

(i) Maintain and use records with care to prevent the unauthorized or inadvertent disclosure of a record to anyone; and

(j) Notify the appropriate SBA official of any record that contains information that the Privacy Act does not permit the SBA to maintain.

§ 102.37 Training requirements.

All employees should attend privacy training within one year of employment with SBA. All employees with Privacy Act responsibilities must attend Privacy Act training, whenever needed, that is offered by the SBA.

§ 102.38 Other rights and services.

Nothing in this subpart shall be construed to entitle any person, as a right, to any service or to the disclosure of any record to which such person is not entitled under the Privacy Act.

§ 102.39 SBA's exempt Privacy Act systems of records.

(a) Systems of records subject to investigatory material exemption under 5 U.S.C. 552a(k)(2), or 5 U.S.C. 552a(k)(5) or both:

(1) Office of Inspector General Records Other Than Investigation Records—SBA 4, contains records pertaining to audits, evaluations, and other non-audit services performed by the OIG;

(2) Equal Employment Opportunity Complaint Cases—SBA 13, contains complaint files, Equal Employment Opportunity counselor's reports, investigation materials, notes, reports, and recommendations;

(3) Investigative Files—SBA 16, contains records gathered by the OIG in the investigation of allegations that are within the jurisdiction of the OIG;

(4) Investigations Division Management Information System—SBA 17, contains records gathered or created during preparation for, conduct of, and follow-up on investigations conducted by the OIG, the Federal Bureau of Investigation (FBI), and other Federal,

State, local, or foreign regulatory or law enforcement agency;

(5) Litigation and Claims Files—SBA 19, contains records relating to recipients classified as "in litigation" and all individuals involved in claims by or against the Agency;

(6) Personnel Security Files—SBA 24, contains records on active and inactive personnel security files, employee or former employee's name, background information, personnel actions, OPM, and/or authorized contracting firm background investigations;

(7) Security and Investigations Files—SBA 27, contains records gathered or created during preparation for, conduct of, and follow-up on investigations conducted by OIG, the FBI, and other Federal, State, local, or foreign regulatory or law enforcement agencies as well as other material submitted to or gathered by OIG in furtherance of its investigative function; and

(8) Standards of Conduct Files—SBA 29, contains records on confidential employment and financial statements of employees Grade 13 and above.

(b) These systems of records are exempt from the following provisions of the Privacy Act and all regulations in this part promulgated under these provisions:

(1) 552a(c)(3) (Accounting of Certain Disclosures);

(2) 552a(d) (Access to Records);

(3) 552a(e)(1), 4G, H, and I (Agency Requirements); and

(4) 552a(f) (Agency Rules).

(c) The systems of records described in paragraph (a) of this section are exempt from the provisions of the Privacy Act described in paragraph (b) of this section in order to:

(1) Prevent the subject of investigations from frustrating the investigatory process;

(2) Protect investigatory material compiled for law enforcement purposes;

(3) Fulfill commitments made to protect the confidentiality of sources and to maintain access to necessary sources of information; or

(4) Prevent interference with law enforcement proceedings.

(d) In addition to the foregoing exemptions in paragraphs (a) through (c) of this section, the systems of records described in paragraph (a) of this section numbered SBA 4, 16, 17, 24, and 27 are exempt from the Privacy Act except for subsections (b), (c)(1) and (2), (e)(4)(A) through F, (e)(6), (7), (9), (10) and (11) and (i) to the extent that they contain:

(1) Information compiled to identify individual criminal offenders and alleged offenders and consisting only of identifying data and notations of arrests, confinement, release, and parole and probation status;

(2) Information, including reports of informants and investigators, associated with an identifiable individual compiled to investigate criminal activity; or

(3) Reports compiled at any stage of the process of enforcement of the criminal laws from arrest or indictment through release from supervision associated with an identifiable individual.

(e) The systems of records described in paragraph (d) of this section are exempt from the Privacy Act to the extent described in that paragraph because they are records maintained by the Investigations Division of the OIG, which is a component of SBA which performs as its principal function activities pertaining to the enforcement of criminal laws within the meaning of 5 U.S.C. 552a(j)(2). They are exempt in order to:

(1) Prevent the subjects of OIG investigations from using the Privacy Act to frustrate the investigative process;

(2) Protect the identity of Federal employees who furnish a complaint or information to the OIG, consistent with section 7(b) of the Inspector General Act of 1978, 5 U.S.C. app. 3;

(3) Protect the confidentiality of other sources of information;

(4) Avoid endangering confidential sources and law enforcement personnel;

(5) Prevent interference with law enforcement proceedings;

(6) Assure access to sources of confidential information, including that contained in Federal, State, and local criminal law enforcement information systems;

(7) Prevent the disclosure of investigative techniques; or

(8) Prevent the disclosure of classified information.

§ 102.40 Computer matching.

The OCIO will enforce the computer matching provisions of the Privacy Act. The FOI/PA Office will review and concur on all computer matching agreements prior to their activation and/or renewal.

(a) *Matching agreements.* SBA will comply with the Computer Matching and Privacy Protection Act of 1988 (5 U.S.C. 552a(o), 552a notes) . The Privacy Protection Act establishes procedures Federal agencies must use if they want to match their computer lists. SBA shall not disclose any record which is contained in a system of records to a recipient agency or non-Federal agency for use in a computer matching program except pursuant to a written agreement between SBA and the recipient agency or non-Federal agency specifying:

(1) The purpose and legal authority for conducting the program;

(2) The justification for the purpose and the anticipated results, including a specific estimate of any savings;

(3) A description of the records that will be matched, including each data element that will be used, the approximate number of records that will be matched, and the projected starting and completion dates of the matching program;

(4) Procedures for providing individualized notice at the time of application, and periodically thereafter as directed by the Data Integrity Board, that any information provided by any of the above may be subject to verification through matching programs to:

(i) Applicants for and recipients of financial assistance or payments under Federal benefit programs, and

(ii) Applicants for and holders of positions as Federal personnel.

(5) Procedures for verifying information produced in such matching program as required by paragraph (c) of this section.

(6) Procedures for the retention and timely destruction of identifiable records created by a recipient agency or non-Federal agency in such matching program;

(7) Procedures for ensuring the administrative, technical, and physical security of the records matched and the results of such programs;

(8) Prohibitions on duplication and redisclosure of records provided by SBA within or outside the recipient agency or non-Federal agency, except where required by law or essential to the conduct of the matching program;

(9) Procedures governing the use by a recipient agency or non-Federal agency of records provided in a matching program by SBA, including procedures governing return of the records to SBA or destruction of records used in such programs;

(10) Information on assessments that have been made on the accuracy of the records that will be used in such matching programs; and

(11) That the Comptroller General may have access to all records of a recipient agency or non-Federal agency that the Comptroller General deems necessary in order to monitor or verify compliance with the agreement.

(b) *Agreement specifications.* A copy of each agreement entered into pursuant to paragraph (a) of this section shall be transmitted to OMB, the Committee on Governmental Affairs of the Senate and the Committee on Governmental Operations of the House of Representatives and be available upon request to the public.

(1) No such agreement shall be effective until 30 days after the date on which a copy is transmitted.

(2) Such an agreement shall remain in effect only for such period, not to exceed 18 months, as the Data Integrity Board determines is appropriate in light of the purposes, and length of time necessary for the conduct, of the matching program.

(3) Within three (3) months prior to the expiration of such an agreement, the Data Integrity Board may without additional review, renew the matching agreement for a current, ongoing matching program for not more than one additional year if:

(i) Such program will be conducted without any change; and

(ii) Each party to the agreement certifies to the Board in writing that the program has been conducted in compliance with the agreement.

(c) *Verification.* In order to protect any individual whose records are used in matching programs, SBA and any recipient agency or non-Federal agency may not suspend, terminate, reduce, or make a final denial of any financial assistance or payment under the Federal benefit program to such individual, or take other adverse action against such individual as a result of information produced by such matching programs until such information has been independently verified.

(1) Independent verification requires independent investigation and confirmation of any information used as a basis for an adverse action against an individual including, where applicable:

(i) The amount of the asset or income involved,

(ii) Whether such individual actually has or had access to such asset or income or such individual's own use, and

(iii) The period or periods when the individual actually had such asset or income.

(2) SBA and any recipient agency or non-Federal agency may not suspend, terminate, reduce, or make a final denial of any financial assistance or payment under a Federal benefit program, or take other adverse action as a result of information produced by a matching program,

(i) Unless such individual has received notice from such agency containing a statement of its findings and information of the opportunity to contest such findings, and

(ii) Until the subsequent expiration of any notice period provided by the program's governing statute or regulations, or 30 days. Such opportunity to contest may be satisfied by notice, hearing, and appeal rights governing such Federal benefit program. The exercise of any such rights shall not affect rights available under the Privacy Act.

(3) SBA may take any appropriate action otherwise prohibited by the above if SBA determines that the public health or safety may be adversely affected or significantly threatened during the notice period required by paragraph (c)(2)(ii) of this section.

(d) *Sanctions.* Notwithstanding any other provision of law, SBA may not disclose any record which is contained in a system of records to a recipient agency or non-Federal agency for a matching program if SBA has reason to believe that the requirements of paragraph (c) of this section, or any matching agreement entered into pursuant to paragraph (b) of this section or both, are not being met by such recipient agency.

(1) SBA shall not renew a matching agreement unless,

(i) The recipient agency or non-Federal agency has certified that it has complied with the provisions of that agreement; and

(ii) SBA has no reason to believe that the certification is inaccurate.

(e) Review annually each ongoing matching program in which the Agency has participated during the year, either as a source or as a matching agency in order to assure that the requirements of the Privacy Act, OMB guidance, and any Agency regulations and standard operating procedures, operating instructions, or guidelines have been met.

(f) *Data Integrity Board.* SBA shall establish a Data Integrity Board (Board) to oversee and coordinate the implementation of the matching program. The Board shall consist of the senior officials designated by the Administrator, to include the Inspector General (who shall not serve as chairman), and the Senior Agency Official for Privacy. The Board shall:

(1) Review, approve and maintain all written agreements for receipt or disclosure of Agency records for matching programs to ensure compliance with paragraph (a) of this section and with all relevant statutes, regulations, and guidance;

(2) Review all matching programs in which SBA has participated during the year, determine compliance with applicable laws, regulations, guidelines, and Agency agreements, and assess the costs and benefits of such programs;

(3) Review all recurring matching programs in which SBA has participated during the year, for continued justification for such disclosures;

(4) At the instruction of OMB, compile a report to be submitted to the Administrator and OMB, and made available to the public on request, describing the matching activities of SBA, including,

(i) Matching programs in which SBA has participated;

(ii) Matching agreements proposed that were disapproved by the Board;

(iii) Any changes in membership or structure of the Board in the preceding year;

(iv) The reasons for any waiver of the requirement described below for completion and submission of a cost-benefit analysis prior to the approval of a matching program;

(v) Any violations of matching agreements that have been alleged or identified and any corrective action taken; and

(vi) Any other information required by OMB to be included in such report;

(5) Serve as clearinghouse for receiving and providing information on the accuracy, completeness, and reliability of records used in matching programs;

(6) Provide interpretation and guidance to SBA offices and personnel on the requirements for matching programs;

(7) Review Agency recordkeeping and disposal policies and practices for matching programs to assure compliance with the Privacy Act; and

(8) May review and report on any SBA matching activities that are not matching programs.

(g) *Cost-benefit analysis.* Except as provided in paragraphs (e)(2) and (3) of this section, the Data Integrity Board shall not approve any written agreement for a matching program unless SBA has completed and submitted to such Board a cost-benefit analysis of the proposed program and such analysis demonstrates that the program is likely to be cost effective. The Board may waive these requirements if it determines, in writing, and in accordance with OMB guidelines, that a cost-benefit analysis is not required. Such an analysis also shall not be required prior to the initial approval of a written agreement for a matching program that is specifically required by statute.

(h) *Disapproval of matching agreements.* If a matching agreement is disapproved by the Data Integrity Board, any party to such agreement may appeal to OMB. Timely notice of the filing of such an appeal shall be provided by OMB to the Committee on Governmental Affairs of the Senate and the Committee on Government Operations of the House of Representatives.

(1) OMB may approve a matching agreement despite the disapproval of the Data Integrity Board if OMB determines that:

(i) The matching program will be consistent with all applicable legal, regulatory, and policy requirements;

(ii) There is adequate evidence that the matching agreement will be cost-effective; and

(iii) The matching program is in the public interest.

(2) The decision of OMB to approve a matching agreement shall not take effect until 30 days after it is reported to the committees described in paragraph (h) of this section.

(3) If the Data Integrity Board and the OMB disapprove a matching program proposed by the Inspector General, the Inspector General may report the disapproval to the Administrator and to the Congress.

§ 102.41 Other provisions.

(a) *Personnel records.* All SBA personnel records and files, as prescribed by OPM, shall be maintained in such a way that the privacy of all individuals concerned is protected in accordance with regulations of OPM (5 CFR parts 293 and 297).

(b) *Mailing lists.* The SBA will not sell or rent an individual's name or address. This provision shall not be construed to require the withholding of names or addresses otherwise permitted to be made public.

(c) *Changes in systems.* The SBA shall provide adequate advance notice to Congress and OMB of any proposal to establish or alter any system of records in order to permit an evaluation of the probable or potential effect of such proposal on the privacy and other personal or property rights of individuals or the disclosure of information relating to such individuals, and its effect on the preservation of the constitutional principles of federalism and separation of powers.

(d) *Medical records.* Medical records shall be disclosed to the individual to whom they pertain. SBA may, however, transmit such information to a medical doctor named by the requesting individual. In regard to medical records in personnel files, see also 5 CFR 297.205.

PART 103—STANDARDS FOR CONDUCTING BUSINESS WITH SBA

Sec.

AUTHORITY: Secs. 5, 13, 72 Stat. 385, 394 (15 U.S.C. 634, 642).

SOURCE: 61 FR 2681, Jan. 29, 1996, unless otherwise noted.

§ 103.1 Key definitions.

(a) *Agent* means an authorized representative, including an attorney, accountant, consultant, packager, lender service provider, or any other person representing an applicant or participant by conducting business with SBA.

(b) The term *conduct business with SBA* means:

(1) Preparing or submitting on behalf of an applicant an application for financial assistance of any kind, assistance from the Investment Division of SBA, or assistance in procurement and technical matters;

(2) Preparing or processing on behalf of a lender or a participant in any of SBA's programs an application for federal financial assistance;

(3) Participating with or communicating in any way with officers or employees of SBA on an applicant's, participant's, or lender's behalf;

(4) Acting as a lender service provider; and

(5) Such other activity as SBA reasonably shall determine.

(c) *Applicant* means any person, firm, concern, corporation, partnership, cooperative or other business enterprise applying for any type of assistance from SBA.

(d) *Lender Service Provider* means an Agent who carries out lender functions in originating, disbursing, servicing, or liquidating a specific SBA business loan or loan portfolio for compensation from the lender. SBA determines whether or not one is a "Lender Service Provider" on a loan-by-loan basis.

(e) *Packager* means an Agent who is employed and compensated by an Applicant or lender to prepare the Applicant's application for financial assistance from SBA. SBA determines whether or not one is a "Packager" on a loan-by-loan basis.

(f) *Referral Agent* means a person or entity who identifies and refers an Applicant to a lender or a lender to an Applicant. The Referral Agent may be employed and compensated by either an Applicant or a lender.

(g) *Participant* means a person or entity that is participating in any of the financial, investment, or business development programs authorized by the Small Business Act or Small Business Investment Act of 1958.

§ 103.2 Who may conduct business with SBA?

(a) If you are an Applicant, a Participant, a partner of an Applicant or Participant partnership, or serve as an officer of an Applicant, Participant corporation, or limited liability company, you may conduct business with SBA without a representative.

(b) If you are an Agent, you may conduct business with SBA on behalf of an Applicant, Participant or lender, unless representation is otherwise prohibited by law or the regulations in this part or any other part in this chapter. For example, persons debarred under the SBA or Government-wide debarment regulations may not conduct business with SBA. SBA may request that any Agent supply written evidence of his or her authority to act on behalf of an Applicant, Participant, or lender as a condition of revealing any information about the Applicant's, Participant's, or lender's current or prior dealings with SBA.

§ 103.3 May SBA suspend or revoke an Agent's privilege?

The Administrator of SBA or designee may, for good cause, suspend or revoke the privilege of any Agent to conduct business with SBA. Part 134 of this chapter states the procedures for appealing the decision to suspend or revoke the privilege. The suspension or revocation remains in effect during the pendency of any administrative proceedings under part 134 of this chapter.

§ 103.4 What is "good cause" for suspension or revocation?

Any unlawful or unethical activity is good cause for suspension or revocation of the privilege to conduct business. This includes:

(a) Attempting to influence any employee of SBA or a lender, by gifts, bribes or other unlawful or unethical activity, with respect to any matter involving SBA assistance.

(b) Soliciting for the provision of services to an Applicant by another entity when there is an undisclosed business relationship between the two parties.

(c) Violating ethical guidelines which govern the profession or business of the Agent or which are published at any time by SBA.

(d) Implying or stating that the work to be performed for an Applicant will include use of political or other special influence with SBA. Examples include indicating that the entity is affiliated with or paid, endorsed or employed by SBA, advertising using the words *Small Business Administration* or *SBA* in a manner that implies SBA's endorsement or sponsorship, use of SBA's seal or symbol, and giving a "guaranty" to an Applicant that the application will be approved.

(e) Charging or proposing to charge any fee that does not bear a necessary and reasonable relationship to the services actually rendered or expenses actually incurred in connection with a matter before SBA or which is materially inconsistent with the provisions of an applicable compensation agreement or Lender Service Provider agreement. A fee based solely on a percentage of a loan or guarantee amount can be reasonable, depending on the circumstances of a case and the services actually rendered.

(f) Engaging in any conduct indicating a lack of business integrity or business honesty, including debarment, criminal conviction, or civil judgment within the last seven years for fraud, embezzlement, theft, forgery, bribery, falsification or destruction of records, false statements, conspiracy, receiving stolen property, false claims, or obstruction of justice.

(g) Acting as both a Lender Service Provider or Referral Agent and a Packager for an Applicant on the same SBA business loan and receiving compensation for such activity from both the Applicant and lender. A limited exception to this "two master" prohibition exists when an Agent acts as a Packager and is compensated by the Applicant for packaging services; also acts as a Referral Agent and is compensated by the lender for those activities; discloses the referral activities to the Applicant; and discloses the packaging activities to the lender.

(h) Violating materially the terms of any compensation agreement or Lender Service Provider agreement provided for in § 103.5.

(i) Violating or assisting in the violation of any SBA regulations, policies, or procedures of which the Applicant has been made aware.

§ 103.5 How does SBA regulate an Agent's fees and provision of service?

(a) Any Applicant, Agent, or Packager must execute and provide to SBA a compensation agreement, and any Lender Service Provider must execute and provide to SBA a Lender Service Provider agreement. Each agreement governs the compensation charged for services rendered or to be rendered to the Applicant or lender in any matter involving SBA assistance. SBA provides the form of compensation agreement and a suggested form of Lender Service Provider agreement to be used by Agents.

(b) Compensation agreements must provide that in cases where SBA deems the compensation unreasonable, the Agent or Packager must: reduce the charge to an amount SBA deems reasonable, refund any sum in excess of the amount SBA deems reasonable to the Applicant, and refrain from charging or collecting, directly or indirectly, from the Applicant an amount in excess of the amount SBA deems reasonable.

(c) Each Lender Service Provider must enter into a written agreement with each lender for whom it acts in that capacity. SBA will review all such agreements. Such agreements need not contain each and every provision found in the SBA's suggested form of agreement. However, each agreement must indicate that both parties agree not to engage in any sharing of secondary market premiums, that the services to be provided are accurately described, and that the agreement is otherwise consistent with SBA requirements. Subject to the prohibition on splitting premiums, lenders have reasonable discretion in setting compensation for Lender Service Providers. However, such compensation may not be directly charged to an Applicant or borrower.

PART 105—STANDARDS OF CONDUCT AND EMPLOYEE RESTRICTIONS AND RESPONSIBILITIES

AUTHORITY: 5 U.S.C. 7301; 15 U.S.C. 634, 637(a)(18) and (a)(19), 642, and 645(a).

SOURCE: 61 FR 2399, Jan. 26, 1996, unless otherwise noted.

STANDARDS OF CONDUCT

§ 105.101 Cross-reference to employee ethical conduct standards and financial disclosure regulations.

In addition to this part, Small Business Administration (SBA) employees should refer to the Standards of Ethical Conduct for Employees of the Executive Branch at 5 CFR part 2635 and the regulations at 5 CFR part 2634 entitled, Executive Branch Financial Disclosure, Qualified Trusts and Certificates of Divestiture.

[69 FR 63922, Nov. 3, 2004]

RESTRICTIONS AND RESPONSIBILITIES RELATED TO SBA EMPLOYEES AND FORMER EMPLOYEES

§ 105.201 Definitions.

(a) *Employee* means an officer or employee of the SBA regardless of grade, status or place of employment, including employees on leave with pay or on leave without pay other than those on extended military leave. Unless stated otherwise. Employee shall include those within the category of Special Government Employee.

(b) *Special Government Employee* means an officer or employee of SBA, who is retained, appointed or employed to perform temporary duties on a full-time or intermittent basis, with or without compensation, for not to exceed 130 days during any period of 365 consecutive days.

(c) *Person* means an individual, a corporation, a company, an association, a firm, a partnership, a society, a joint stock company, or any other organization or institution.

(d) *Household member* means spouse and minor children of an employee, all blood relations of the employee and any spouse who resides in the same place of abode with the employee.

(e) *SBA Assistance* means financial, contractual, grant, managerial or other aid, including size determinations, section 8(a) participation, licensing, certification, and other eligibility determinations made by SBA. The term also includes an express decision to compromise or defer possible litigation or other adverse action.

§ 105.202 Employment of former employee by person previously the recipient of SBA Assistance.

(a) No former employee, who occupied a position involving discretion over, or who exercised discretion with respect to, the granting or administration of SBA Assistance may occupy a position as employee, partner, agent, attorney or other representative of a concern which has received this SBA Assistance for a period of two years following the date of granting or administering such SBA Assistance if—

(1) The date of granting or administering such SBA Assistance was within the period of the employee's term of employment; or

(2) The date of granting or administering such SBA Assistance was within one year following the termination of such employment.

(b) Failure of a recipient of SBA Assistance to comply with these provisions may result, in the discretion of SBA, in the requirement for immediate repayment of SBA financial Assistance, the immediate termination of other SBA Assistance involved or other appropriate action.

§ 105.203 SBA Assistance to person employing former SBA employee.

(a) SBA will not provide SBA Assistance to any person who has, as an employee, owner, partner, attorney, agent, owner of stock, officer, director, creditor or debtor, any individual who, within one year prior to the request for such SBA Assistance was an SBA employee, without the prior approval of the SBA Standards of Conduct Counselor. The Standards of Conduct Counselor will refer matters of a controversial nature to the Standards of Conduct Committee for final decision; otherwise, his or her decision is final.

(b) In reviewing requests for approval, the Standards of Conduct Counselor will consider:

(1) The relationship of the former employee with the applicant concern;

(2) The nature of the SBA Assistance requested;

(3) The position held by the former employee with SBA and its relationship to the SBA Assistance requested; and

(4) Whether an apparent conflict of interest might exist if the SBA Assistance were granted.

§ 105.204 Assistance to SBA employees or members of their household.

Without the prior written approval of the Standards of Conduct Committee, no SBA Assistance, other than Disaster loans under subparagraphs (1) and (2) of section 7(b) of the Small Business Act, shall be furnished to a person when the sole proprietor, partner, officer, director or significant stockholder of the person is an SBA employee or a household member.

§ 105.205 Duty to report irregularities.

Every employee shall immediately report to the SBA Inspector General any acts of malfeasance or misfeasance or other irregularities, either actual or suspected, arising in connection with the performance by SBA of any of its official functions.

§ 105.206 Applicable rules and directions.

Every employee shall follow all agency rules, regulations, operating procedures, instructions and other proper directions in the performance of his official functions.

§ 105.207 Politically motivated activities with respect to the Minority Small Business Program.

(a) Any employee who has authority to take, direct others to take, recommend, or approve any action with respect to any program or activity conducted pursuant to section 8(a) or section 7(j) of the Small Business Act, shall not, with respect to any such action, exercise or threaten to exercise such authority on the basis of the political activity or affiliation of any party. Employees shall expeditiously report to the SBA Inspector General any such action for which such employee's participation has been solicited or directed.

(b) Any employee who willfully and knowingly violates this section shall be subject to disciplinary action, which may consist of separation from service, reduction in grade, suspension, or reprimand.

(c) This section shall not apply to any action taken as a penalty or other enforcement of a violation of any law, rule, or regulation prohibiting or restricting political activity.

(d) The prohibitions in and remedial measures provided for under this section with regard to such prohibitions, shall be in addition to, and not in lieu of, any other prohibitions, measures or liabilities that may arise under any other provision of law.

§ 105.208 Penalties.

Any employee guilty of violating any of the provisions in this part may be disciplined, including removal or suspension from SBA employment.

RESTRICTIONS ON SBA ASSISTANCE TO OTHER INDIVIDUALS

§ 105.301 Assistance to officers or employees of other Government organizations.

(a) SBA must receive a written statement of no objection by the pertinent Department or military service before it gives any SBA Assistance, other than Disaster loans under subparagraphs (1) and (2) of section 7(b) of the Small Business Act, to a person when its sole proprietor, partner, officer, director or stockholder with a 10 percent or more interest, or a household member, is an employee of another Government Department or Agency having a grade of at least GS–13 or its equivalent.

(b) The Standards of Conduct Committee must approve an SBA contract with an entity if a sole proprietor, general partner, officer, director, or stockholder with a 10 or more percent interest (or a household member of such individuals) is an employee of a Government Department or Agency. See also 48 CFR part 35, subpart 3.6.

(c) The Standards of Conduct Committee must approve SBA Assistance, other than disaster loans under subparagraphs (1) and (2) of section 7(b) of the Small Business Act, to a person if its sole proprietor, general partner, officer, director or stockholder with a 10 percent or more interest (or a household member of such individual) is a member of Congress or an appointed official or employee of the legislative or judicial branch of the Government.

§ 105.302 Assistance to employees or members of quasi-Government organizations.

(a) The Standards of Conduct Committee must approve SBA Assistance, other than Disaster loans under subparagraphs (1) and (2) of section 7(b) of the Small Business Act, to a person if its sole proprietor, general partner, officer, director or stockholder with a 10 percent or more interest (or a household member) is a member or employee of a Small Business Advisory Council or is a SCORE volunteer.

(b) In reviewing requests for approval, factors the Standards of Conduct Committee may consider include whether the granting of the SBA Assistance might result in or create the appearance of giving preferential treatment, the loss of complete independence or impartiality, or adversely affect the confidence of the public in the integrity of the Government.

ADMINISTRATIVE PROVISIONS

§ 105.401 Standards of Conduct Committee.

(a) The Standards of Conduct Committee will:

(1) Advise and give direction to SBA management officials concerning the administration of this part and any other rules, regulations or directives dealing with conflicts of interest and ethical standards of SBA employees; and

(2) Make decisions on specific requests when its approval is required.

(b) The Standards of Conduct Committee will consist of:

(1) The General Counsel or, in his or her absence, the Deputy General Counsel or, in his or her absence, the Acting General Counsel who shall act as Chairman of the Committee;

(2) The Associate Administrator, Office of Management and Administration, or in his or her absence, the Director, Office of Business Operations; and

(3) The Chief Human Capital Officer, or in his or her absence, the Deputy Chief Human Capital Officer.

[61 FR 2399, Jan. 26, 1996, as amended at 72 FR 50038, Aug. 30, 2007]

§ 105.402 Standards of Conduct Counselors.

(a) The SBA Standards of Conduct Counselor is the Designated Agency Ethics Official, as appointed by the Administrator. Assistant Standards of Conduct Counselors may be designated by the Standards of Conduct Counselor.

(b) The Standards of Conduct Counselors and Assistants:

(1) Provide general advice, assistance and guidance to employees concerning this part and the regulations referred to in § 105.101;

(2) Monitor the Standards of Conduct Program within their assigned areas and provide required reports thereon; and

(3) Review Confidential Financial Disclosure reports as required under 5 CFR part 2634, subpart I, and provide an annual report on compliance with filing requirements to the SBA Standards of Conduct Counselor as of February 1 of each year.

(c) Each employee will be periodically informed of the name, address and telephone number of the Assistant Standards of Conduct Counselor to contact for advice and assistance.

(d) Employee requests for advice or rulings should be directed to the appropriate Standards of Conduct Counselor for appropriate action.

[61 FR 2399, Jan. 26, 1996, as amended at 62 FR 48477, Sept. 16, 1997; 69 FR 63922, Nov. 3, 2004]

§ 105.403 Designated Agency Ethics Officials.

The Designated Agency Ethics Official and Alternates administer the program for Financial Disclosure Statements under 5 CFR 2634.201, receive and evaluate these statements, and provide advice and counsel regarding matters relating to the Ethics in Government Act of 1978 and its implementing regulations. The duties and responsibilities of the Designated Agency Ethics Official and Alternates are set forth in more detail in 5 CFR 2638.203, which is promulgated and amended by the Office of Government Ethics.

[62 FR 2399, Jan. 26, 1996, as amended at 62 FR 48477, Sept. 16, 1997]

PART 106—COSPONSORSHIPS, FEE AND NON-FEE BASED SBA-SPONSORED ACTIVITIES AND GIFTS

Subpart A—Scope and Definitions

Subpart B—Cosponsored Activities

Subpart C—Fee Based SBA-Sponsored Activities

Subpart D—Non-Fee Based SBA-Sponsored Activities

Subpart E—Gifts

AUTHORITY: 15 U.S.C. 633 (g) and (h); 15 U.S.C. 637(b)(1)(A); 15 U.S.C. 637(b)(G).

SOURCE: 70 FR 70704, Nov. 23, 2005, unless otherwise noted.

Subpart A—Scope and Definitions

§106.100 Scope.

The regulations in this part apply to SBA-provided assistance for the benefit of small business through Fee Based SBA-Sponsored Activities or through Cosponsored Activities with Eligible Entities authorized under section 4(h) of the Small Business Act, and to SBA assistance provided directly to small business concerns through Non-Fee Based SBA-Sponsored Activities authorized under section 8(b)(1)(A) of the Small Business Act. The regulations in this part also apply to SBA's solicitation and acceptance of Gifts under certain sections (sections 4(g), 8(b)(1)(G), 5(b)(9) and 7(k)(2)) of the Small Business Act (15 U.S.C. 631 *et seq.*), including Gifts of cash, property, services and subsistence. Under section 4(g) of the Small Business Act, Gifts may be solicited and accepted for marketing and outreach purposes including the cost of promotional items and wearing apparel.

§106.101 Definitions.

The following definitions apply to this part. Defined terms are capitalized wherever they appear.

(a) *Cosponsor* means an entity or individual designated in §106.201 that has signed a written Cosponsorship Agreement with SBA and who actively and substantially participates in planning and conducting an agreed upon Cosponsored Activity.

(b) *Cosponsored Activity* means an activity, event, project or initiative, designed to provide assistance for the benefit of small business as authorized by section 4(h) of the Small Business Act, which has been set forth in an approved written Cosponsorship Agreement. The Cosponsored Activity must be planned and conducted by SBA and one or more Cosponsors. Assistance for purposes of Cosponsored Activity does not include grant or any other form of financial assistance. A Participant Fee may be charged by SBA or another Cosponsor at any Cosponsored Activity.

(c) *Cosponsorship Agreement* means an approved written document (as outlined in §§106.203 and 106.204 which has been duly executed by SBA and one or more Cosponsors. The Cosponsorship Agreement shall contain the parties' respective rights, duties and responsibilities regarding implementation of the Cosponsored Activity.

(d) *Donor* means an individual or entity that provides a Gift, bequest or devise (in cash or in-kind) to SBA.

(e) An *Eligible Entity* is a potential Cosponsor. An Eligible Entity must be a for-profit or not-for-profit entity, or a Federal, State or local government official or entity.

(f) *Fee Based SBA-Sponsored Activity Record* (Fee Based Record) means a written document, as outlined in §106.302, describing a Fee Based SBA-Sponsored Activity and approved in writing pursuant to §106.303.

(g) *Fee Based SBA-Sponsored Activity* means an activity, event, project or initiative designed to provide assistance for the benefit of small business, as authorized by section 4(h) of the Small Business Act, at which SBA may charge a Participant Fee. Assistance for purposes of Fee Based SBA-Sponsored Activity does not include grant or any other form of financial assistance. A Fee Based SBA-Sponsored Activity must be planned, conducted, controlled and sponsored solely by SBA.

(h) *Gift* (including a bequest or a device) is the voluntary transfer to SBA of something of value without the Donor receiving legal consideration.

(i) *Non-Fee Based SBA-Sponsored Activity Record* (Non-Fee Based Record) means a written document describing a Non-Fee Based SBA-Sponsored Activity which has been approved pursuant to §106.403.

(j) *Non-Fee Based SBA-Sponsored Activity* means an activity, event, project or initiative designed to provide assistance directly to small business concerns as authorized by section 8(b)(1)(A) of the Small Business Act. Assistance for purposes of a Non-Fee Based SBA-Sponsored Activity does not include grant or any other form of financial assistance. A Non-Fee Based SBA-Sponsored Activity must be planned, conducted, controlled and sponsored solely by SBA. No fees including Participant Fees may be charged for a Non-Fee Based SBA-Sponsored Activity.

(k) *Participant Fee* means a minimal fee assessed against a person or entity that participates in a Cosponsored Activity or Fee Based SBA-Sponsored Activity and is used to cover the direct costs of such activity.

(l) *Responsible Program Official* is an SBA senior management official from the originating office who is accountable for the solicitation and/or acceptance of a Gift to the SBA; a Cosponsored Activity; a Fee Based SBA-Sponsored Activity; or a Non-Fee Based SBA-Sponsored Activity. If the originating office is a district or branch office, the Responsible Program Official is the district director or their deputy. In headquarters, the Responsible Program Official is the management board member or their deputy with responsibility for the relevant program area.

Subpart B—Cosponsored Activities

§ 106.200 Cosponsored Activity.

The Administrator (or designee), after consultation with the General Counsel (or designee), may provide assistance for the benefit of small business through Cosponsored Activities pursuant to section 4(h) of the Small Business Act.

§ 106.201 Who may be a Cosponsor?

(a) Except as specified in paragraph (b) of this section, SBA may enter into a Cosponsorship Agreement with an Eligible Entity as defined in § 106.101(e).

(b) SBA may not enter into a Cosponsorship Agreement with an Eligible Entity if the Administrator (or designee), after consultation with the General Counsel (or designee), determines that such agreement would create a conflict of interest.

§ 106.202 What are the minimum requirements applicable to Cosponsored Activities?

While SBA may subject a Cosponsored Activity to additional requirements through internal policy, procedure and the Cosponsorship Agreement, the following requirements apply to all Cosponsored Activities:

(a) Cosponsored Activities must be set forth in a written Cosponsorship Agreement signed by the Administrator (or designee) and each Cosponsor;

(b) Appropriate recognition must be given to SBA and each Cosponsor but shall not constitute or imply an endorsement by SBA of any Cosponsor or any Cosponsor's products or services;

(c) Any printed or electronically generated material used to publicize or conduct the Cosponsored Activity, including any material which has been developed, prepared or acquired by a Cosponsor, must be approved in advance by the Responsible Program Official and must include a prominent disclaimer stating that the Cosponsored Activity does not constitute or imply an endorsement by SBA of any Cosponsor or the Cosponsor's products or services;

(d) No Cosponsor shall make a profit on any Cosponsored Activity. SBA grantees who earn program income on Cosponsored Activities must use that program income for the Cosponsored Activity;

(e) Participant Fee(s) charged for a Cosponsored Activity may not exceed the minimal amount needed to cover the anticipated direct costs of the Cosponsored Activity and must be liquidated prior to other sources of funding for the Cosponsored Activity. If SBA charges a Participant Fee, the collection of the Participant Fees is subject to internal SBA policies and procedures as well as applicable U.S. Treasury rules and guidelines;

(f) SBA may not provide a Cosponsor with lists of names and addresses of small business concerns compiled by SBA which are otherwise protected by law or policy from disclosure; and

(g) Written approval must be obtained as outlined in § 106.204.

§ 106.203 What provisions must be set forth in a Cosponsorship Agreement?

While SBA may require additional provisions in the Cosponsorship Agreement through internal policy and procedure, the following provisions must be in all Cosponsorship Agreements:

(a) A written statement agreed to by each Cosponsor that they will abide by all of the provisions of the Cosponsorship Agreement, the requirements of this subpart as well the applicable definitions in § 106.100;

(b) A narrative description of the Cosponsored Activity;

(c) A listing of SBA's and each Cosponsor's rights, duties and responsibilities with regard to the Cosponsored Activity;

(d) A proposed budget demonstrating:

(1) The type and source of financial contribution(s) (including but not limited to cash, in-kind, Gifts, and Participant Fees) that the SBA and each Cosponsor will make to the Cosponsored Activity; and

(2) A reasonable estimation of all anticipated expenses;

(e) A written statement that each Cosponsor agrees that they will not make a profit on the Cosponsored Activity; and

(f) A written statement that Participant Fees, if charged, will not exceed the minimal amount needed to cover the anticipated direct costs of the Cosponsored Activity as outlined in the budget and will be liquidated prior to other sources of funding for the Cosponsored Activity.

§ 106.204 Who has the authority to approve and sign a Cosponsorship Agreement?

The Administrator, or upon his/her written delegation, the Deputy Administrator, an associate or assistant administrator, after consultation with the General Counsel (or designee), has the authority to approve each Cosponsored Activity and sign each Cosponsorship Agreement. This authority cannot be re-delegated.

Subpart C—Fee Based SBA-Sponsored Activities

§ 106.300 Fee Based SBA-Sponsored Activity.

The Administrator (or designee), after consultation with the General Counsel (or designee), may provide assistance for the benefit of small business through Fee-Based SBA-Sponsored Activities pursuant to section 4(h) of the Small Business Act.

§ 106.301 What are the minimum requirements applicable to Fee Based SBA-Sponsored Activities?

While SBA may subject a Fee Based SBA-Sponsored Activity to additional requirements through internal policy and procedure, the following requirements apply to all Fee Based SBA-Sponsored Activities:

(a) A Fee Based Record must be prepared by the Responsible Program Official in advance of the activity;

(b) Any Participant Fees charged will not exceed the minimal amount needed to cover the anticipated direct costs of the activity;

(c) Gifts of cash accepted and the collection of Participant Fees for Fee Based SBA-Sponsored Activities are subject to the applicable requirements in this part, internal SBA policies and procedures as well as applicable U.S. Treasury rules and guidelines; and

(d) Written approval must be obtained as outlined in § 106.303.

§ 106.302 What provisions must be set forth in a Fee Based Record?

A Fee Based Record must contain the following:

(a) A narrative description of the Fee Based SBA-Sponsored Activity;

(b) A certification by the Responsible Program Official that he or she will abide by the requirements contained in this part, as well as all other applicable statutes, regulations, policies and procedures for Fee Based SBA-Sponsored Activities;

(c) A proposed budget demonstrating:

(1) All sources of funding, including annual appropriations, Participant Fees and Gifts, to be used in support of the Fee Based SBA-Sponsored Activity;

(2) A reasonable estimation of all anticipated expenses, which indicates that no profit is anticipated from the Fee Based SBA-Sponsored Activity; and

(3) A provision stating that Participant Fees, if charged, will not exceed the minimal amount needed to cover the anticipated direct costs of the Fee Based SBA-Sponsored Activity as outlined in the budget;

(d) With regard to any donations made in support of the Fee Based SBA-Sponsored Activity, the Fee Based Record will reflect the following:

(1) Each Donor may receive appropriate recognition for its Gift; and

(2) Any printed or electronically generated material recognizing a Donor will include a prominent disclaimer stating that the acceptance of the Gift does not constitute or imply an endorsement by SBA of the Donor or the Donor's products or services.

§ 106.303 Who has authority to approve and sign a Fee Based Record?

The Administrator, or upon his/her written delegation, the Deputy Administrator, an associate or assistant administrator, after consultation with the General Counsel (or designee), has the authority to approve and sign each Fee Based Record. This authority may not be re-delegated.

Subpart D—Non-Fee Based SBA-Sponsored Activities

§ 106.400 Non-Fee Based SBA-Sponsored Activity.

The Administrator (or designee) may provide assistance directly to small business concerns through Non-Fee Based SBA-Sponsored Activities under section 8(b)(1)(A) of the Small Business Act.

§ 106.401 What are the minimum requirements applicable to a Non-Fee Based SBA-Sponsored Activities?

While SBA may subject Non-Fee Based SBA-Sponsored Activities to additional requirements through internal policy and procedure, the following requirements apply to all Non-Fee Based SBA-Sponsored Activity:

(a) A Non-Fee Based Record must be prepared and approved by the Responsible Program Official in advance of the activity;

(b) Gifts of cash accepted for Non-Fee Based SBA-Sponsored Activities are subject to § 106.500, internal SBA policies and procedures as well as applicable U.S. Treasury rules and guidelines; and

(c) Written approval must be obtained as outlined in § 106.403.

§ 106.402 What provisions must be set forth in a Non-Fee Based Record?

A Non-Fee Based Record must contain the following:

(a) A narrative description of the Non-Fee Based SBA-Sponsored Activity;

(b) A certification by the Responsible Program Official that he or she will abide by the requirements contained in this part, as well as all other applicable statutes, regulations, policies and procedures for Non-Fee Based SBA-Sponsored Activities;

(c) If applicable, a list of Donors supporting the activity; and

(d) With regard to any donations made in support of a Non-Fee Based SBA-Sponsored Activity, the Non-Fee Based Record will reflect the following:

(1) Each Donor may receive appropriate recognition for its Gift; and

(2) Any printed or electronically generated material recognizing a Donor will include a prominent disclaimer stating that the acceptance of the Gift does not constitute or imply an endorsement by SBA of the Donor, or the Donor's products or services.

§ 106.403 Who has authority to approve and sign a Non-Fee Based Record?

The appropriate Responsible Program Official, after consultation with the designated legal counsel, has authority to approve and sign each Non-Fee Based Record.

Subpart E—Gifts

§ 106.500 What is SBA's Gift authority?

This section covers SBA's Gift acceptance authority under sections 4(g), 8(b)(1)(G), 5(b)(9) and 7(k)(2) of the Small Business Act.

§ 106.501 What minimum requirements are applicable to SBA's solicitation and/or acceptance of Gifts?

While SBA may subject the solicitation and/or acceptance of Gifts to additional requirements through internal policy and procedure, the following requirements must apply to all Gift solicitations and/or acceptances under the authority of the Small Business Act sections cited in § 106.500:

(a) SBA is required to use the Gift (whether cash or in-kind) in a manner consistent with the original purpose of the Gift;

(b) There must be written documentation of each Gift solicitation and/or acceptance signed by an authorized SBA official;

(c) Any Gift solicited and/or accepted must undergo a determination, prior to solicitation of the Gift or prior to acceptance of the Gift if unsolicited, of whether a conflict of interest exists between the Donor and SBA; and

(d) All cash Gifts donated to SBA under the authority cited in § 106.500 must be deposited in an SBA trust account at the U.S. Department of the Treasury.

§ 106.502 Who has authority to perform a Gift conflict of interest determination?

(a) For Gifts solicited and/or accepted under sections 4(g), 8(b)(1)(G), and 7(k)(2) of the Small Business Act, the General Counsel, or designee, must make the final conflict of interest determination. No Gift shall be solicited and/or accepted under these sections of the Small Business Act if such solicitation and/or acceptance would, in the determination of the General Counsel (or designee), create a conflict of interest.

(b) For Gifts of services and facilities solicited and/or accepted under section 5(b)(9), the conflict of interest determination may be made by designated disaster legal counsel.

§ 106.503 Are there types of Gifts which SBA may not solicit and/or accept?

Yes. SBA shall not solicit and/or accept Gifts of or for (or use cash Gifts to purchase or engage in) the following:

(a) Alcohol products;

(b) Tobacco products;

(c) Pornographic or sexually explicit objects or services;

(d) Gambling (including raffles and lotteries);

(e) Parties primarily for the benefit of Government employees; and

(f) Any other product or service prohibited by law or policy.

PART 107—SMALL BUSINESS INVESTMENT COMPANIES

Subpart A—Introduction to Part 107

Subpart B—Definition of Terms Used in Part 107

Subpart C—Qualifying for an SBIC License

ORGANIZING AN SBIC

CAPITALIZING AN SBIC

APPLYING FOR AN SBIC LICENSE

Subpart D—Changes in Ownership, Control, or Structure of Licensee; Transfer of License

CHANGES IN CONTROL OR OWNERSHIP OF LICENSEE

AUTHORITY: 15 U.S.C. 681, 683, 687(c), 687b, 687d, 687g, 687m.

SOURCE: 61 FR 3189, Jan. 31, 1996, unless otherwise noted.

Subpart A—Introduction to Part 107

§ 107.20 Legal basis and applicability of this part 107.

(a) The regulations in this part implement Title III of the Small Business Investment Act of 1958, as amended. All Licensees must comply with all applicable regulations, accounting guidelines and valuation guidelines for Licensees.

(b) Provisions of this part which are not mandated by the Act shall not supersede existing State law. A party claiming that a conflict exists shall submit an opinion of independent counsel, citing authorities, for SBA's resolution of the issues involved.

§ 107.30 Amendments to Act and regulations.

A Licensee shall be subject to all existing and future provisions of the Act and parts 107 and 112 of title 13 of the Code of Federal Regulations.

§ 107.40 How to read this part 107.

(a) *Center Headings.* All references in this part to SBA forms, and instructions for their preparation, are to the current issue of such forms. Center headings are descriptive and are used for convenience only. They have no regulatory effect.

(b) *Capitalizing defined terms.* Terms defined in § 107.50 are capitalized in this part 107.

(c) The pronoun "you" as used in this part 107 means a Licensee or license applicant, as appropriate, unless otherwise noted.

Subpart B—Definition of Terms Used in Part 107

§ 107.50 Definition of terms.

Accumulated Prioritized Payments has the meaning set forth in § 107.1520.

Act means the Small Business Investment Act of 1958, as amended.

Adjustments has the meaning set forth in § 107.1520.

Affiliate or *Affiliates* has the meaning set forth in § 121.103 of this chapter.

Articles mean articles of incorporation or charter for a Corporate Licensee and the partnership agreement or certificate for a Partnership Licensee.

Assistance or *Assisted* means Financing of or management services rendered to a Small Business by a Licensee pursuant to the Act and these regulations.

Associate of a Licensee means any of the following:

(1)(i) An officer, director, employee or agent of a Corporate Licensee;

(ii) A Control Person, employee or agent of a Partnership Licensee;

(iii) An Investment Adviser/Manager of any Licensee, including any Person who contracts with a Control Person of a Partnership Licensee to be the Investment Adviser/Manager of such Licensee; or

(iv) Any Person regularly serving a Licensee on retainer in the capacity of attorney at law.

(2) Any Person who owns or controls, or who has entered into an agreement to own or control, directly or indirectly, at least 10 percent of any class of stock of a Corporate Licensee or a limited partner's interest of at least 10 percent of the partnership capital of a Partnership Licensee. However, a limited partner in a Partnership Licensee is not considered an Associate if such Person is an entity Institutional Investor whose investment in the Partnership, including commitments, represents no more than 33 percent of the partnership capital of the Licensee and no more than five percent of such Person's net worth.

(3) Any officer, director, partner (other than a limited partner), manager, agent, or employee of any Associate described in paragraph (1) or (2) of this definition.

(4) Any Person that directly or indirectly Controls, or is Controlled by, or is under Common Control with, a Licensee.

(5) Any Person that directly or indirectly Controls, or is Controlled by, or is under Common Control with, any Person described in paragraphs (1) and (2) of this definition.

(6) Any Close Relative of any Person described in paragraphs (1),(2), (4), and (5) of this definition.

(7) Any Secondary Relative of any Person described in paragraphs (1), (2), (4), and (5) of this definition.

(8) Any concern in which—

(i) Any person described in paragraphs (1) through (6) of this definition is an officer; general partner, or managing member; or

(ii) Any such Person(s) singly or collectively Control or own, directly or indirectly, an equity interest of at least 10 percent (excluding interests that such Person(s) own indirectly through ownership interests in the Licensee).

(9) Any concern in which any Person(s) described in paragraph (7) of this definition singly or collectively own (including beneficial ownership) a majority equity interest, or otherwise have Control. As used in this paragraph (9), "collectively" means together with any Person(s) described in paragraphs (1) though (7) of this definition.

(10) For the purposes of this definition, if any Associate relationship described in paragraphs (1) through (7) of this definition exists at any time within six months before or after the date that a Licensee provides Financing, then that Associate relationship is considered to exist on the date of the Financing.

(11) If any Licensee has any ownership interest in another Licensee, the two Licensees are Associates of each other.

Capital Impairment has the meaning set forth in § 107.1830(c).

Central Registration Agent or *CRA* means one or more agents appointed by SBA for the purpose of issuing TCs and performing the functions enumerated in § 107.1620 and performing similar functions for Debentures and Participating Securities funded outside the pooling process.

Charge means an annual fee on Leverage issued on or after October 1, 1996 (except for Leverage issued pursuant to a commitment made by SBA before October 1, 1996), which is payable to SBA by Licensees, subject to the terms and conditions set forth in § 107.1130(d).

Close Relative of an individual means:

(1) A current or former spouse;

(2) A father, mother, guardian, brother, sister, son, daughter; or

(3) A father-in-law, mother-in-law, brother-in-law, sister-in-law, son-in-law, or daughter-in-law.

Combined Capital means the sum of Regulatory Capital and outstanding Leverage.

Commitment means a written agreement between a Licensee and an eligible Small Business that obligates the Licensee to provide Financing (except a guarantee) to that Small Business in a fixed or determinable sum, by a fixed or determinable future date. In this context the term "agreement" means that there has been agreement on the principal economic terms of the Financing. The agreement may include reasonable conditions precedent to the Licensee's obligation to fund the commitment, but these conditions must be outside the Licensee's control.

Common Control means a condition where two or more Persons, either through ownership, management, contract, or otherwise, are under the Control of one group or Person. Two or more Licensees are presumed to be under Common Control if they are Affiliates of each other by reason of common ownership or common officers, directors, or general partners; or if they are managed or their investments are significantly directed either by a common independent investment advisor or managerial contractor, or by two or more such advisors or contractors that are Affiliates of each other. This presumption may be rebutted by evidence satisfactory to SBA.

Control means the possession, direct or indirect, of the power to direct or cause the direction of the management and policies of a Licensee or other concern, whether through the ownership of voting securities, by contract, or otherwise.

Control Person means any Person that controls a Licensee, either directly or through an intervening entity. A Control Person includes:

(1) A general partner of a Partnership Licensee;

(2) Any Person serving as the general partner, officer, director, or manager (in the case of a limited liability company) of any entity that controls a Licensee, either directly or through an intervening entity;

(3) Any Person that—

(i) Controls or owns, directly or through an intervening entity, at least 10 percent of a Partnership Licensee or any entity described in paragraphs (1) or (2) of this definition; and

(ii) Participates in the investment decisions of the general partner of such Partnership Licensee;

(4) Any Person that controls or owns, directly or through an intervening entity, at least 50 percent of a Partnership Licensee or any entity described in paragraphs (1) or (2) of this definition.

Corporate Licensee. See definition of Licensee in this section.

Cost of Money has the meaning set forth in § 107.855.

Debenture Rate means the interest rate, as published from time to time in the FEDERAL REGISTER by SBA, for ten year debentures issued by Licensees and funded through public sales of certificates bearing SBA's guarantee. User or guarantee fees, if any, paid by a Licensee are not considered in determining the Debenture Rate.

Debentures means debt obligations issued by Licensees pursuant to section 303(a) of the Act and held or guaranteed by SBA.

Debt Securities has the meaning set forth in § 107.815.

Disadvantaged Business means a Small Business that is at least 50 percent owned, and controlled and managed, on a day to day basis, by a person or persons whose participation in the free enterprise system is hampered because of social or economic disadvantages.

Distributable Securities means equity securities that are determined by SBA (with the advice of a third party expert in the marketing of securities) to meet each of the following requirements:

(1) The securities (which may include securities that are salable pursuant to the provisions of Rule 144 (17 CFR 230.144) under the Securities Act of 1933, as amended) are salable immediately without restriction under Federal and state securities laws;

(2) The securities are of a class:

(i) Which is listed and registered on a national securities exchange, or

(ii) For which quotation information is disseminated in the National Association of Securities Dealers Automated Quotation System and as to which transaction reports and last sale data are disseminated pursuant to Rule 11Aa3–1 (17 CFR 240.11Aa3–1) under the Securities Exchange Act of 1934, as amended; and

(3) The quantity of such securities to be distributed to SBA can be sold over a reasonable period of time without having an adverse impact upon the price of the security.

Distribution means any transfer of cash or non-cash assets to SBA, its agent or Trustee, or to partners in a Partnership Licensee, or to shareholders in a Corporate Licensee. Capitalization of Retained Earnings Available for Distribution constitutes a Distribution to the Licensee's non-SBA partners or shareholders.

Early Stage SBIC means a Section 301(c) Partnership Licensee, licensed pursuant to § 107.310 of this part, in which at least 50 percent of all Loans and Investments (in dollars) must be made to Small Businesses that are "early stage" companies at the time of the Licensee's initial Financing (see also § 107.1810(f)(11)). For the purposes of this definition, an "early stage" company is one that has never achieved positive cash flow from operations in any fiscal year.

Earmarked Assets has the meaning set forth in § 107.1510(b). (See also § 107.1590.)

Earmarked Profit (Loss) has the meaning set forth in § 107.1510.

Earned Prioritized Payments has the meaning set forth in § 107.1520.

Energy Saving Activities means any of the following:

(1) Manufacturing or research and development of products, integral product components, integral material, or related software that meet one or more of the following:

(i) Improves residential energy efficiency as demonstrated by meeting Department of Energy or Environmental Protection Agency criteria for use of the Energy Star trademark label;

(ii) Improves commercial energy efficiency as demonstrated by being in the upper 25% of efficiency for all similar products as designated by the Department of Energy's Federal Energy Management Program;

(iii) Improves automobile efficiency or reduces consumption of non-renewable fuels through the use of advanced batteries, power electronics, or electric motors; advanced combustion engine technology; alternative fuels; or advanced materials technologies, such as lightweighting;

(iv) Improves industrial energy efficiency through combined heat and power (CHP) prime mover or power generation technologies, heat recovery units, absorption chillers, desiccant dehumidifiers, packaged CHP systems, more efficient process heating equipment, more efficient steam generation equipment, heat recovery steam generators, or more efficient use of water recapture, purification and reuse for industrial application;

(v) Advances commercialization of technologies developed by recipients of awards from the Department of Energy under the Advanced Research Projects Agency—Energy, Small Business Innovation Research, or Small Business Technology Transfer programs;

(vi) Reduces the consumption of non-renewable energy by providing renewable energy sources, as demonstrated by meeting the standards, applicable to the year in which the investment is made, for receiving a Renewable Electricity Production Tax Credit as defined in Internal Revenue Code Section 45 or an Energy Credit as defined in Internal Revenue Code Section 48;

(vii) Reduces the consumption of non-renewable energy for electric power generation as described in Internal Revenue Code Section 48(c)(1)(A) by providing highly efficient energy conversion systems that can use renewable or non-renewable fuel through fuel cells; or

(viii) Improves electricity delivery efficiency by supporting one or more of the smart grid functions as identified in 42 U.S.C. 17386(d), by means of a product, service, or functionality that serves one or more of the following smart grid operational domains: Equipment manufacturing, customer systems, advanced metering infrastructure, electric distribution systems, electric transmission systems, storage systems, and cyber security.

(2) Installation and/or inspection services associated with the deployment of energy saving products as identified by meeting one or more of the following standards:

(i) Deploys products that qualify, in the year in which the investment is made, for installation-related Federal Tax Credits for Residential Consumer Energy Efficiency;

(ii) Deploys products related to commercial energy efficiency as demonstrated by deploying commercial equipment that is in the upper 25% of efficiency for all similar products as designated by the Department of Energy's Federal Energy Management Program;

(iii) Deploys combined heat and power products, goods, or services;

(iv) Deploys products that qualify, in the year in which the investment is made, for receiving a Renewable Electricity Production Tax Credit as defined in Internal Revenue Code Section 45 or an Energy Credit as defined in Internal Revenue Code Section 48; or

(v) Deploys a product, service, or functionality that improves electricity delivery efficiency by supporting one or more of the smart grid functions as identified in 42 U.S.C. 17386(d), and that serves one or more of the following smart grid operational domains: Equipment manufacturing, customer systems, advanced metering infrastructure, electric distribution systems, electric transmission systems, or grid cyber security.

(3) Auditing or consulting services performed with the objective of identifying potential improvements of the type described in paragraph (1) or (2) of this definition.

(4) Other manufacturing, service, or research and development activities that use less energy to provide the same level of energy service or reduce the consumption of non-renewable energy by providing renewable energy sources, as determined by SBA. A Licensee must obtain such determination in writing prior to providing Financing to a Small Business. SBA will consider factors including but not limited to:

(i) Results of energy efficiency testing performed in accordance with recognized professional standards, preferably by a qualified third-party professional, such as a certified energy assessor, energy auditor, or energy engineer;

(ii) Patents or grants awarded to or licenses held by the Small Business related to Energy Saving Activities listed in subsection (1) or (2) above;

(iii) For research and development of products or services that are anticipated to reduce the consumption of non-renewable energy, written evidence from an independent, certified third-party professional of the feasibility, commercial potential, and projected energy savings of such products or services; and

(iv) Eligibility of the product or service for a Federal tax credit cited in this definition that is not available in the year in which the investment is made, but was available in a previous year.

Energy Saving Qualified Investment means a Financing which:

(1) Is made by a Licensee licensed after September 30, 2008;

(2) Is in the form of a Loan, Debt Security, or Equity Security, each as defined in this section;

(3) Is made to a Small Business that is primarily engaged in Energy Saving Activities. A Licensee must obtain a determination from SBA prior to the provision of Financing as to whether a Small Business is primarily engaged in Energy Saving Activities. SBA will consider the distribution of revenues, employees and expenditures, intellectual property rights held, and Energy Saving Activities described in a business plan presented to investors as part of a formal solicitation in making its determination. However, a Small Business is presumed to be primarily engaged in Energy Saving Activities, and no pre-Financing determination by SBA is required, if:

(i) The Small Business derived at least 50% of its revenues during its most recently completed fiscal year from Energy Saving Activities; or

(ii) The Small Business will utilize 100% of the Financing proceeds received from a Licensee to engage in Energy Saving Activities.

Equity Capital Investments means investments in a Small Business in the form of common or preferred stock, limited partnership interests, options, warrants, or similar equity instruments, including subordinated debt with equity features if such debt provides only for interest payments contingent upon and limited to the extent of earnings. Equity Capital Investments must not require amortization. Equity Capital Investments may be guaranteed; however, neither Equity Capital Investments nor such guarantee may be collateralized or otherwise secured. Investments classified as Debt Securities (see §§ 107.800 and 107.815) are not precluded from qualifying as Equity Capital Investments.

Equity Securities has the meaning set forth in § 107.800.

Financing or *Financed* means outstanding financial assistance provided to a Small Business by a Licensee, whether through:

(1) Loans;

(2) Debt Securities;

(3) Equity Securities;

(4) Guarantees; or

(5) Purchases of securities of a Small Business through or from an underwriter (see § 107.825).

Guaranty Agreement means the contract entered into by SBA which is a guarantee backed by the full faith and credit of the United States Government as to timely payment of principal and interest on Debentures or the Redemption Price of and Prioritized Payments on Participating Securities and SBA's rights in connection with such guarantee.

Includible Non-Cash Gains means those non-cash gains (as reported on SBA Form 468) that are realized in the form of Publicly Traded and Marketable securities or investment grade debt instruments. For purposes of this definition, investment grade debt instruments means those instruments that are rated "BBB" or "Baa", or better, by Standard & Poor's Corporation or Moody's Investors Service, respectively. Non-rated debt may be considered to be investment grade if Licensee obtains a written opinion from an investment banking firm acceptable to SBA stating that the non-rated debt instrument is equivalent in risk to the issuer's investment grade debt.

Inflation Adjustment is the methodology used to increase SBIC administrative fees using the Consumer Price Index for Urban Consumers (CPI–U), calculated by the U.S. Bureau of Labor and Statistics (BLS), using the U.S. city average for all items, not seasonally adjusted, with the base period of 1982 – 84 = 100. To calculate the Inflation Adjustment, each year, SBA will divide the CPI–U from the most recent June by the CPI–U from June of the preceding year. If the result is greater than 1, SBA will increase the relevant fees as follows:

(1) Multiply the result by the current fee; and

(2) Round to the nearest $100.

Institutional Investor means:

(1) *Entities.* Any of the following entities if the entity has a net worth (exclusive of unfunded commitments from investors) of at least $1 million, or such higher amount as is specified in paragraph (1) of this definition. (See also § 107.230(b)(4) for limitations on the amount of an Institutional Investor's commitment that may be included in Private Capital.)

(i) A State or National bank, trust company, savings bank, or savings and loan association.

(ii) An insurance company.

(iii) A 1940 Act Investment Company or Business Development Company (each as defined in the Investment Company Act of 1940, as amended (15 U.S.C. 8a–1 *et seq.*).

(iv) A holding company of any entity described in paragraph (1)(i), (ii) or (iii) of this definition.

(v) An employee benefit or pension plan established for the benefit of employees of the Federal government, any State or political subdivision of a State, or any agency or instrumentality of such government unit.

(vi) An employee benefit or pension plan (as defined in the Employee Retirement Income Security Act of 1974, as amended (Pub. L. 93–406, 88 Stat. 829), excluding plans established under section 401(k) of the Internal Revenue Code of 1986 (26 U.S.C. 401(k)), as amended).

(vii) A trust, foundation or endowment exempt from Federal income taxation under the Internal Revenue Code of 1986, as amended.

(viii) A corporation, partnership or other entity with a net worth (exclusive of unfunded commitments from investors) of more than $10 million.

(ix) A State, a political subdivision of a State, or an agency or instrumentality of a State or its political subdivision.

(x) An entity whose primary purpose is to manage and invest non-Federal funds on behalf of at least three Institutional Investors described in paragraphs (1)(i) through (1)(ix) of this definition, each of whom must have at least a 10 percent ownership interest in the entity.

(xi) Any other entity that SBA determines to be an Institutional Investor.

(2) *Individuals.* (i) Any of the following individuals if he/she is also a permanent resident of the United States:

(A) An individual who is an Accredited Investor (as defined in the Securities Act of 1933, as amended (15 U.S.C. 77a–77aa)) and whose commitment to the Licensee is backed by a letter of credit from a State or National bank acceptable to SBA.

(B) An individual whose personal net worth is at least $2 million and at least ten times the amount of his or her commitment to the Licensee. The individual's personal net worth must not include the value of any equity in his or her most valuable residence.

(C) An individual whose personal net worth (determined in accordance with paragraph (2)(i)(B) of this definition) is at least $10 million.

(ii) Any individual who is not a permanent resident of the United States but who otherwise satisfies paragraph (2)(i) of this definition *provided* such individual has irrevocably appointed an agent within the United States for the service of process.

Investment Adviser/Manager means any Person who furnishes advice or assistance with respect to operations of a Licensee under a written contract executed in accordance with the provisions of § 107.510.

Lending Institution means a concern that is operating under regulations of a state or Federal licensing, supervising, or examining body, or whose shares are publicly traded and listed on a recognized stock exchange or NASDAQ and which has assets in excess of $500 million; and which, in either case, holds itself out to the public as engaged in the making of commercial and industrial loans and whose lending operations are not for the purpose of financing its own or an Associate's sales or business operations.

Leverage means financial assistance provided to a Licensee by SBA, either through the purchase or guaranty of a Licensee's Debentures or Participating Securities, or the purchase of a Licensee's Preferred Securities, and any other SBA financial assistance evidenced by a security of the Licensee.

Leverageable Capital means Regulatory Capital, excluding unfunded commitments.

Licensee means either a corporation (Corporate Licensee), or a limited partnership organized pursuant to § 107.160 (Partnership Licensee), to which a license has been granted pursuant to the Act. For certain purposes, the Entity General Partner of a Partnership Licensee is treated as if it were a Licensee (see § 107.160(b)(2)).

LMI Enterprise means:

(1) A Small Business that has at least 50% of its employees or tangible assets located in LMI Zone(s) or in which at least 35% of the full-time employees have primary residences in LMI Zone(s), in either case determined as of the time of application for SBIC financing; or

(2) A Small Business that does not meet the requirements of paragraph (1) of this definition as of the time of application for SBIC financing but that certifies at such time that it intends to meet the requirements within 180 days after the closing of the SBIC financing. A Small Business qualifying under this paragraph (2) will no longer be an LMI Enterprise as of the 180th day after the closing of the SBIC financing unless, on or before such date, at least 50% of its employees or tangible assets are located in LMI Zones or at least 35% of its full-time employees have primary residences in LMI Zones.

LMI Investment means a financing of an LMI Enterprise, made after September 30, 1999, in the form of equity securities or debt securities that are junior to all existing or future secured borrowings of the business. The debt securities may be guaranteed and may be secured by the assets of the LMI Enterprise, but the guarantee may not be collateralized or otherwise secured.

LMI Zone means any area located within a HUBZone (as defined in 13 CFR 126.103), an Urban Empowerment Zone or Urban Enterprise Community (as designated by the Secretary of the Department of Housing and Urban Development), a Rural Empowerment Zone or Rural Enterprise Community (as designated by the Secretary of the Department of Agriculture), an area of Low Income or Moderate Income (as recognized by the Federal Financial Institutions Examination Council), or a county with Persistent Poverty (as classified by the Economic Research Service of the Department of Agriculture).

Loan has the meaning set forth in § 107.810.

Loans and Investments means Portfolio Securities, Assets Acquired in Liquidation of Portfolio Securities, Operating Concerns Acquired, and Notes and Other Securities Received, as set forth in the Statement of Financial Position of SBA Form 468.

Management Expenses has the meaning set forth in § 107.520.

1940 Act Company means a Licensee which is registered under the Investment Company Act of 1940.

1980 Act Company means a Licensee which is registered under the Small Business Investment Incentive Act of 1980.

Original Issue Price means the price paid by the purchaser for securities at the time of issuance.

Participating Securities means preferred stock, preferred limited partnership interests, or similar instruments issued by Licensees, including debentures having interest payable only to the extent of earnings, all of which are subject to the terms set forth in §§ 107.1500 through 107.1590 and section 303(g) of the Act.

Partnership Licensee. See definition of Licensee in this section.

Payment Date means:

(1) For a Participating Securities issuer, each February 1, May 1, August 1, and November 1 during the term of a Participating Security, or

(2) For an Early Stage SBIC, each March 1, June 1, September 1, and December 1 during the term of a Debenture.

Person means a natural person or legal entity.

Pool means an aggregation of SBA guaranteed Debentures or SBA guaranteed Participating Securities approved by SBA.

Portfolio means the securities representing a Licensee's total outstanding Financing of Small Businesses. It does not include idle funds or assets acquired in liquidation of Portfolio securities.

Portfolio Concern means a Small Business Assisted by a Licensee.

Preferred Securities means nonvoting preferred stock or nonvoting limited partnership interests issued to SBA prior to October 1, 1996, by a Section 301(d) Licensee. Such securities were issued at par value in the case of preferred stock, or at face value in the case of preferred limited partnership interests.

Prioritized Payments has the meaning set forth in § 107.1520.

Private Capital has the meaning set forth in § 107.230.

Profit Participation has the meaning set forth in § 107.1500(c)(3).

Publicly Traded and Marketable means securities that are salable without restriction or that are salable within 12 months pursuant to Rule 144 (17 CFR 230.144) of the Securities Act of 1933, as amended, by the holder thereof (or in the case of an In-kind Distribution by the distributee thereof), and are of a class which is traded on a regulated stock exchange, or is listed in the Automated Quotation System of the National Association of Securities Dealers (NASDAQ), or has, at a minimum, at least two market makers as defined in the relevant sections of the Securities Exchange Act of 1934, as amended (15 U.S.C. 77b *et seq.*), and in all cases the quantity of which can be sold over a reasonable period of time without having an adverse impact upon the price of the stock.

Qualified Non-private Funds has the meaning set forth in § 107.230.

Redemption Price means the amount required to be paid by the issuer, or successor to the issuer, of Preferred or

Participating Securities to repurchase such securities from the holder. The Redemption Price shall be the Original Issue Price less any prepayments or prior redemptions.

Regulatory Capital means:

(1) *General.* Regulatory Capital means Private Capital, excluding non-cash assets contributed to a Licensee or a license applicant, and non-cash assets purchased by a license applicant, unless such assets have been converted to cash or have been approved by SBA for inclusion in Regulatory Capital. For purposes of this definition, sales of contributed non-cash assets with recourse or borrowing against such assets shall not constitute a conversion to cash.

(2) *Exclusion of questionable commitments.* An investor's commitment to a Licensee is excluded from Regulatory Capital if SBA determines that the collectibility of the commitment is questionable.

Retained Earnings Available for Distribution means Undistributed Net Realized Earnings less any Unrealized Depreciation on Loans and Investments (as reported on SBA Form 468), and represents the amount that a Licensee may distribute to investors (including SBA) as a profit Distribution, or transfer to Private Capital.

SBA means the Small Business Administration, 409 Third Street, SW., Washington, DC 20416.

Secondary Relative of an individual means:

(1) A grandparent, grandchild, or any other ancestor or lineal descendent who is not a Close Relative;

(2) An uncle, aunt, nephew, niece, or first cousin; or

(3) A spouse of any person described in paragraph (1) or (2) of this definition.

Section 301(c) Licensee has the meaning set forth in §107.100.

Section 301(d) Licensee means a company licensed prior to October 1, 1996 under section 301(d) of the Act as in effect on the date of licensing, that may provide Assistance only to Disadvantaged Businesses. A Section 301(d) Licensee may be organized as a for-profit corporation, as a non-profit corporation, or as a limited partnership.

Short-term Financing means Financing with a term of less than one year in accordance with the regulations.

Small Business means a small business concern as defined in section 103(5) of the Act (including its Affiliates), which for purposes of size eligibility, meets the applicable criteria set forth in part 121 of this chapter.

Smaller Enterprise has the meaning set forth in §107.710.

Start-up Financing means an Equity Capital Investment in a Small Business that—

(1) Has not had sales exceeding $3,000,000 or positive cash flow from operations in any of its last three full fiscal years; and

(2) Was not formed to acquire any existing business, unless the acquired business satisfies paragraphs (1) and (2) of this definition.

Temporary Debt has the meaning set forth in §107.570.

Trust means the legal entity created for the purpose of holding guaranteed Debentures or Participating Securities and the guaranty agreement related thereto, receiving, holding and making any related payments, and accounting for such payments.

Trust Certificate Rate means a fixed rate determined by the Secretary of the Treasury at the time Participating Securities or Debentures are pooled, taking into consideration the current average market yield on outstanding marketable obligations of the United States with maturities comparable to the maturities of the Trust Certificates being guaranteed by SBA, adjusted to the nearest one-eighth of one percent.

Trust Certificates (TCs) means certificates issued by SBA, its agent or Trustee and representing ownership of all or a fractional part of a Trust or Pool of Debentures or Participating Securities.

Trustee means the trustee or trustees of a Trust.

Undistributed Net Realized Earnings means Undistributed Realized Earnings less Non-cash Gains/Income, each as reported on SBA Form 468.

Unrealized Appreciation means the amount by which a Licensee's valuation of each of its Loans and Investments, as determined by its Board of

Directors or General Partner(s) in accordance with Licensee's valuation policies, exceeds the cost basis thereof.

Unrealized Depreciation means the amount by which a Licensee's valuation of each of its Loans and Investments, as determined by its Board of Directors or General Partner(s) in accordance with Licensee's valuation policies, is below the cost basis thereof.

Unrealized Gain (Loss) on Securities Held means the sum of the Unrealized Appreciation and Unrealized Depreciation on all of a Licensee's Loans and Investments, less estimated future income tax expense or estimated realizable future income tax benefit, as appropriate.

Venture Capital Financing has the meaning set forth in § 107.1160.

Wind-up Plan has the meaning set forth in § 107.590.

[61 FR 3189, Jan. 31, 1996; 61 FR 41496, Aug. 9, 1996, as amended at 62 FR 11759, Mar. 13, 1997; 63 FR 5865, Feb. 5, 1998; 64 FR 52645, Sept. 30, 1999; 64 FR 70995, Dec. 20, 1999; 69 FR 8098, Feb. 23, 2004; 77 FR 23378, Apr. 19, 2012; 77 FR 25051, Apr. 27, 2012; 79 FR 62823, Oct. 21, 2014; 82 FR 39340, Aug. 18, 2017; 82 FR 52184, Nov. 13, 2017]

Subpart C—Qualifying for an SBIC License

ORGANIZING AN SBIC

§ 107.100 Organizing a Section 301(c) Licensee.

Section 301(c) Licensee means a company licensed under section 301(c) of the Act. It may be organized as a for-profit corporation or as a limited partnership created in accordance with the special rules of § 107.160.

§ 107.115 1940 Act and 1980 Act Companies.

A 1940 Act or 1980 Act Company is eligible to apply for an SBIC license, and an existing Licensee is eligible to apply for SBA's approval to convert to a 1940 Act or 1980 Act Company. In either case, the 1940 Act or 1980 Act Company may elect to be taxed as a regulated investment company under section 851 of the Internal Revenue Code of 1986, as amended (26 U.S.C. 851). However, a Licensee making such election may make Distributions only as permitted under the applicable sections of this part (see the definition of Retained Earnings Available for Distribution, § 107.585, and §§ 107.1540 through 107.1580).

§ 107.120 Special rules for a Section 301(d) Licensee owned by another Licensee.

With SBA's prior written approval, a Section 301(d) Licensee may operate as the subsidiary of one or more Licensees (participant Licensees), subject to the following:

(a) Each participant Licensee must own at least 20 percent of the voting securities of the Section 301(d) Licensee.

(b) A participant Licensee must treat its entire capital contribution to the subsidiary as a reduction of its Leverageable Capital. The participant Licensee's remaining Leverageable Capital must be sufficient to support its outstanding Leverage.

(c) A participant Licensee may not transfer its Leverage to a subsidiary Section 301(d) Licensee.

[63 FR 5865, Feb. 5, 1998]

§ 107.130 Requirement for qualified management.

When applying for a license, and while you have a license, you must show, to the satisfaction of SBA, that your current or proposed management team is qualified and has the knowledge, experience and capability necessary for investing in the types of businesses contemplated by the Act, the regulations in this part 107, and your business plan. You must designate at least one individual as the official responsible for contact with SBA.

[61 FR 3189, Jan. 31, 1996, as amended at 77 FR 25051, Apr. 27, 2012]

§ 107.140 SBA approval of initial Management Expenses.

If you plan to obtain Leverage, you must have your Management Expenses approved by SBA at the time of licensing. (See § 107.520 for the definition of Management Expenses.)

§ 107.150 Management-ownership diversity requirement.

(a) *Diversity requirement.* You must satisfy the requirements in paragraphs (b), (c) and (d) of this section:

(1) In order to obtain an SBIC license (unless you do not plan to obtain Leverage),

(2) If at the time you were licensed you did not plan to obtain Leverage, but you now wish to be eligible for Leverage, or

(3) If SBA so requires as a condition of approval of your transfer of Control under § 107.440.

(b) *Percentage ownership requirement.* (1) Except as provided in paragraph (b)(2) of this section, no Person or group of Persons who are Affiliates of one another may own or control, directly or indirectly, more than 70 percent of your Regulatory Capital or your Leverageable Capital.

(2) *Exception.* An investor that is a traditional investment company, as determined by SBA, may own and control more than 70 percent of your Regulatory Capital and your Leverageable Capital. For purposes of this section, a traditional investment company must be a professionally managed firm organized exclusively to pool capital from more than one source for the purpose of investing in businesses that are expected to generate substantial returns to the firm's investors. In determining whether a firm is a traditional investment company for purposes of this section, SBA will also consider:

(i) Whether the managers of the firm are unrelated to and unaffiliated with the investors in the firm;

(ii) Whether the managers of the firm are authorized and motivated to make investments that, in their independent judgment, are likely to produce significant returns to all investors in the firm;

(iii) Whether the firm benefits from the use of the SBIC only through the financial performance of the SBIC; and

(iv) Other related factors.

(c) *Non-affiliation requirement*—(1) *General rule.* At least 30 percent of your Regulatory Capital and Leverageable Capital must be owned and controlled by three Persons unaffiliated with your management and unaffiliated with each other, and whose investments are significant in dollar and percentage terms as determined by SBA. Such Persons must not be your Associates (except for their status as your shareholders, limited partners, or members) and must not Control, be Controlled by, or be under Common Control with any of your Associates. A single "acceptable" Institutional Investor may be substituted for two or three of the three Persons who are otherwise required under this paragraph. The following Institutional Investors are "acceptable" for this purpose:

(i) Entities whose overall activities are regulated and periodically examined by state, Federal or other governmental authorities satisfactory to SBA;

(ii) Entities listed on the New York Stock Exchange;

(iii) Entities that are publicly-traded and that meet both the minimum numerical listing standards and the corporate governance listing standards of the New York Stock Exchange;

(iv) Public or private employee pension funds;

(v) Trusts, foundations, or endowments, but only if exempt from Federal income taxation; and

(vi) Other Institutional Investors satisfactory to SBA.

(2) *Look-through for traditional investment company investors.* SBA, in its sole discretion, may consider the requirement in paragraph (c)(1) of this section to be satisfied if at least 30 percent of your Regulatory Capital and Leverageable Capital is owned and controlled indirectly, through a traditional investment company, by Persons unaffiliated with your management.

(d) *Voting requirement.* (1) Except as provided in paragraph (d)(2) of this section, the investors required for you to satisfy diversity may not delegate their voting rights to any Person who is your Associate, or who Controls, is Controlled by, or is under Common Control with any of your Associates, without prior SBA approval.

(2) *Exception.* Paragraph (d)(1) of this section does not apply to investors in publicly-traded Licensees, to proxies given to vote in accordance with specific instructions for single specified meetings, or to any delegation of voting rights to a Person who is neither a diversity investor in the Licensee nor affiliated with management of the Licensee.

(e) *Requirement to maintain diversity.* If you were required to have management-ownership diversity at any time, you must maintain such diversity while you have outstanding Leverage or Earmarked Assets. To maintain management-ownership diversity, you may continue to satisfy the diversity requirement as in effect at the time it was first applicable to you or you may satisfy the management-ownership diversity requirement as currently in effect. If, at any time, you no longer have the required management-ownership diversity, you must:

(1) Notify SBA within 10 days; and

(2) Re-establish diversity within six months. For the consequences of failure to re-establish diversity, see §§ 107.1810(g) and 107.1820(f).

[65 FR 71055, Nov. 29, 2000]

§ 107.160 Special rules for Licensees formed as limited partnerships.

A limited partnership organized under State law solely for the purpose of performing the functions and conducting the activities contemplated under the Act may apply for a license under section 301(c) or section 301 (d) of the Act (''Partnership Licensee'').

(a) *Number of Licensee's General Partners.* If you are a Partnership Licensee, you must have as your general partner(s) at least two individuals, or at least one corporation, partnership, or limited liability company (LLC), or any combination of individuals, corporations, partnerships, or LLCs.

(b) *Entity General Partner of Licensee.* A general partner which is a corporation, limited liability company or partnership (an ''Entity General Partner'') shall be organized under state law solely for the purpose of serving as the general partner of one or more Licensees.

(1) SBA must approve any person who will serve as an officer, director, manager, or general partner of the Entity General Partner. This provision must be stated in an Entity General Partner's Certificate of Incorporation, member agreement, Limited Partnership Agreement or other similar governing instrument which must, in each case, accompany the license application.

(2) An Entity General Partner is subject to the same examination and reporting requirements as a Licensee under section 310(b) of the Act. The restrictions and obligations imposed upon a Licensee by §§ 107.1800 through 107.1820, and 107.30, 107.410 through 107.450, 107.470, 107.475, 107.500, 107.510, 107.585, 107.600, 107.680, 107.690 through 107.692, 107.865, and 107.1910 apply also to an Entity General Partner of a Licensee.

(3) The general partner(s) of your Entity General Partner(s) will be considered your general partner.

(4) If your Entity General Partner is a limited partnership, its limited partners may be considered your Control Person(s) if they meet the definition for Control Person in § 107.50.

(5) If your Entity General Partner is a limited partnership, it is subject to paragraph (a) of this section.

(c) *Other requirements for Partnership Licensees.* If you are a Partnership Licensee:

(1) You must have a minimum duration of ten years or two years following the maturity of your last-maturing Leverage security, whichever is longer. After 10 years, if all Leverage has been repaid or redeemed and all amounts due SBA, its agent, or Trustee have been paid, the Partnership Licensee may be terminated by a vote of your partners. (For purposes of this provision SBA is not considered a partner.);

(2) None of your general partner(s) may be removed or replaced by your limited partners without prior written approval of SBA;

(3) Any transferee of, or successor in interest to, your general partner shall have only the rights and liabilities of a limited partner pending SBA's written approval of such transfer or succession; and

(4) You must incorporate all the provisions in this paragraph (c) in your Limited Partnership Agreement.

(d) *Obligations of a Control Person.* All Control Persons are bound by the disciplinary provisions of sections 313 and 314 of the Act and by the conflict-of-interest rules under section 312 of the Act. The term Licensee, as used in §§ 107.30, 107.460, and 107.680 includes all of the Licensee's Control Persons. The term Licensee as used in § 107.670 includes only the Licensee's general partner(s). The conditions specified in

§§ 107.1800 through 107.1820 and § 107.1910 apply to all general partners.

(e) *Liability of general partner for partnership debts to SBA.* Subject to section 314 of the Act, your general partner is not liable solely by reason of its status as a general partner for repayment of any Leverage or debts you owe to SBA unless SBA, in the exercise of reasonable investment prudence, and with regard to your financial soundness, determines otherwise prior to the purchase or guaranty of your Leverage.

(f) *Reorganization of Licensee.* A corporate Licensee wishing to reorganize as a Partnership Licensee, or a Partnership Licensee wishing to reorganize as a Corporate Licensee, may apply to SBA for approval under § 107.470.

(g) *Special Leverage requirement.* Before your first issuance of Leverage, you must furnish SBA with evidence that you qualify as a partnership for tax purposes, either by a ruling from the Internal Revenue Service, or by an opinion of counsel.

CAPITALIZING AN SBIC

§ 107.200 Adequate capital for Licensees.

You must meet the requirements of this § 107.200 to qualify for a license, to continue as a Licensee, and to receive Leverage.

(a) You must have enough Regulatory Capital to provide reasonable assurance that:

(1) You will operate soundly and profitably over the long term; and

(2) You will be able to operate actively in accordance with your Articles and within the context of your business plan, as approved by SBA.

(b) In SBA's sole discretion, you must be economically viable, taking into consideration actual and anticipated income and losses on your Loans and Investments, and the experience and qualifications of your owners and managers.

§ 107.210 Minimum capital requirements for Licensees.

(a) *Companies licensed on or after October 1, 1996.* A company licensed on or after October 1, 1996, must have Leverageable Capital of at least $2,500,000 and must meet the applicable minimum Regulatory Capital requirement in this paragraph (a), unless lower Leverageable Capital and Regulatory Capital amounts are approved by SBA as part of a Wind-Up Plan in accordance with § 107.590(c):

(1) *Licensees other than Participating Securities issuers and Early Stage SBICs.* Except for Participating Securities issuers and Early Stage SBICs, a Licensee must have Regulatory Capital of at least $5,000,000. As an exception to this general rule, SBA in its sole discretion and based on a showing of special circumstances and good cause may license an applicant with Regulatory Capital of at least $3,000,000, but only if the applicant:

(i) Has satisfied all licensing standards and requirements except the minimum capital requirement, as determined solely by SBA;

(ii) Has a viable business plan reasonably projecting profitable operations; and

(iii) Has a reasonable timetable for achieving Regulatory Capital of at least $5,000,000.

(2) *Participating Securities issuers.* A Licensee that wishes to be eligible to apply for Participating Securities must have Regulatory Capital of at least $10,000,000, unless it demonstrates to SBA's satisfaction that it can be financially viable over the long term with a lower amount. Under no circumstances can the Licensee have Regulatory Capital of less than $5,000,000.

(3) *Early Stage SBICs.* An Early Stage SBIC must have Regulatory Capital of at least $20 million.

(b) *Companies licensed before October 1, 1996.* A company licensed before October 1, 1996 must meet the minimum capital requirements applicable to such company, as required by the regulations in effect on September 30, 1996. See § 107.1120(c)(2) for Leverage eligibility requirements.

[63 FR 5866, Feb. 5, 1998, as amended at 77 FR 25051, Apr. 27, 2012; 82 FR 39340, Aug. 18, 2017]

§ 107.230 Permitted sources of Private Capital for Licensees.

Private Capital means the contributed capital of a Licensee, plus unfunded binding commitments by Institutional Investors (including commitments evidenced by a promissory note) to contribute capital to a Licensee.

(a) *Contributed capital.* For purposes of this section, contributed capital means the paid-in capital and paid-in surplus of a Corporate Licensee, or the partners' contributed capital of a Partnership Licensee, in either case subject to the limitations in paragraph (b) of this section.

(b) *Exclusions from Private Capital.* Private Capital does not include:

(1) Funds borrowed by a Licensee from any source.

(2) Funds obtained through the issuance of Leverage.

(3) Funds obtained directly or indirectly from any Federal, State, or local government agency or instrumentality, except for:

(i) Funds invested by a public pension fund;

(ii) Funds obtained from the business revenues (excluding any governmental appropriation) of any federally chartered or government-sponsored corporation established before October 1, 1987, to the extent that such revenues are reflected in the retained earnings of the corporation; and

(iii) "Qualified Non-private Funds" as defined in paragraph (d) of this section.

(4) Any portion of a commitment from an Institutional Investor with a net worth of less than $10 million that exceeds 10 percent of such Institutional Investor's net worth and is not backed by a letter of credit from a State or National bank acceptable to SBA.

(c) *Non-cash capital contributions.* Capital contributions in a form other than cash are subject to the limitations in § 107.240.

(d) *Qualified Non-private Funds.* Private Capital includes "Qualified Non-private Funds" as defined in this paragraph (d); however, investors of Qualified Non-private Funds must not control, directly or indirectly, a Licensee's management, or its board of directors or general partner(s). Qualified Non-private Funds are:

(1) Funds directly or indirectly invested in any Licensee on or before August 16, 1982 by any Federal agency except SBA, under a statute explicitly mandating the inclusion of such funds in "Private Capital";

(2) Funds directly or indirectly invested in any Licensee by any Federal agency under a statute that is enacted after September 4, 1992, explicitly mandating the inclusion of such funds in "Private Capital";

(3) Funds invested in any Licensee or license applicant by one or more State or local government entities (including any guarantee extended by such entities) in an aggregate amount that does not exceed 33 percent of Regulatory Capital; and

(4) Funds invested in or committed in writing to any Section 301(d) Licensee prior to October 1, 1996, from the following sources:

(i) A State financing agency, or similar agency or instrumentality, if the funds invested are derived from such agency's net income and not from appropriated State or local funds; and

(ii) Grants made by a state or local government agency or instrumentality into a nonprofit corporation or institution exercising discretionary authority with respect to such funds, if SBA determines that such funds have taken on a private character and the nonprofit corporation or institution is not a mere conduit.

(e) You may not accept any capital contribution made with funds borrowed by a Person seeking to own an equity interest (whether direct or indirect, beneficial or of record) of at least 10 percent of your Private Capital. This exclusion does not apply if:

(1) Such Person's net worth is at least twice the amount borrowed; or

(2) SBA gives its prior written approval of the capital contribution.

[61 FR 3189, Jan. 31, 1996, as amended at 63 FR 5866, Feb. 5, 1998; 64 FR 70995, Dec. 20, 1999]

§ 107.240 Limitations on including non-cash capital contributions in Private Capital.

Non-cash capital contributions to a Licensee or license applicant are included in Private Capital only if they fall into one of the following categories:

(a) Direct obligations of, or obligations guaranteed as to principal and interest by, the United States.

(b) Services rendered or to be rendered to you, priced at no more than their fair market value.

(c) Tangible assets used in your operations, priced at no more than their fair market value.

(d) Shares in a Disadvantaged Business received by a subsidiary Section 301(d) Licensee from its parent Licensee, valued at the lower of cost or fair value.

(e) Other non-cash assets approved by SBA.

§ 107.250 Exclusion of stock options issued by Licensee from Management Expenses.

Stock options issued by any Licensee, including a 1940 or 1980 Act Company, are not considered compensation and therefore do not count as part of a Licensee's Management Expenses.

APPLYING FOR AN SBIC LICENSE

§ 107.300 License application form and fee.

SBA evaluates license applicants in two review phases (initial review and final licensing), as follows:

(a) *Initial review.* Except as provided in this paragraph, SBIC applicants must submit a MAQ and the Initial Licensing Fee. MAQ means the Management Assessment Questionnaire in the form approved by SBA and available on SBA's Web site at *www.sba.gov/sbic*. Initial Licensing Fee means a non-refundable fee of $10,000. An applicant under Common Control with one or more Licensees must submit a written request to SBA, and the Initial Licensing Fee, to be considered for a license and is exempt from the requirement in this paragraph to submit a MAQ unless otherwise determined by SBA in SBA's discretion.

(b) *Final licensing.* (1) An applicant may proceed to the final licensing phase only if notified in writing by SBA that it may do so. Following receipt of such notice, in order to proceed to the final licensing phase, the applicant must submit a complete license application, in the form approved by SBA and available on SBA's Web site at *www.sba.gov/sbic*, within the timeframe identified by SBA; and the Final Licensing Fee. The Final Licensing Fee means a non-refundable fee (determined as of the date SBA accepts the application) adjusted annually as follows:

Time period	Final licensing fee
December 13, 2017 to September 30, 2018	$20,000
October 1, 2018 to September 30, 2019	25,000
October 1, 2019 to September 30, 2020	30,000
October 1, 2020 to September 30, 2021	35,000

(2) Beginning on October 1, 2021, SBA will annually adjust both the Initial Licensing Fee and Final Licensing Fee using the Inflation Adjustment and will publish a Notice prior to such adjustment in the FEDERAL REGISTER identifying the amount of the fee.

[82 FR 52184, Nov. 13, 2017]

§ 107.305 Evaluation of license applicants.

SBA will evaluate a license applicant based on the submitted application materials, any interviews with the applicant's management team, and the results of background investigations, public record searches, and other due diligence conducted by SBA and other Federal agencies. SBA's evaluation will consider factors including the following:

(a) Management qualifications, including demonstrated investment skills and experience as a principal investor; business reputation; adherence to legal and ethical standards; record of active involvement in making and monitoring investments and assisting portfolio companies; successful history of working as a team; and experience in developing appropriate processes for evaluating investments and implementing best practices for investment firms.

(b) Performance of managers' prior investments, including investment returns measured both in percentage terms and in comparison to appropriate industry benchmarks; the extent to which investments have been realized as a result of sales, repayments, or other exit mechanisms; and the contribution of prior investments to the growth of portfolio company revenues and number of employees.

(c) Applicant's proposed investment strategy, including clarity of objectives; strength of management's rationale for pursuing the selected strategy; compliance with this part 107 and applicable provisions of part 121 of this chapter; fit with management's skills and experience; and the availability of sufficient resources to carry out the proposed strategy.

(d) Applicant's proposed organizational structure and fund economics, including compliance with this part 107; soundness of financial projections and underlying assumptions; a compensation plan that provides managers with appropriate economic incentives; a reasonable basis for allocations of profits and fees to Persons not involved in management; and governance procedures that provide appropriate checks and balances.

[77 FR 25052, Apr. 27, 2012]

§ 107.310 When and how to apply for licensing as an Early Stage SBIC.

From time to time, SBA will publish a Notice in the FEDERAL REGISTER, inviting the submission of applications for licensing as an Early Stage SBIC. SBA will not consider an application from an Early Stage SBIC applicant that is under Common Control with another Early Stage SBIC applicant or an existing Early Stage SBIC (unless it has no outstanding Leverage or Leverage commitments and will not seek additional Leverage in the future). Applicants must comply with both the regulations in this part 107 and any requirements specified in the Notice, including submission deadlines. The Notice will specify procedures for a particular application period.

[77 FR 25052, Apr. 27, 2012]

§ 107.320 Evaluation of Early Stage SBICs.

SBA will evaluate an Early Stage SBIC license applicant based on the same factors applicable to other license applicants, as set forth in § 107.305, with particular emphasis on managers' skills and experience in evaluating and investing in early stage companies. In addition, SBA reserves the right to maintain diversification among Early Stage SBICs with respect to:

(a) The year in which they commence operations, and

(b) Their geographic location.

[77 FR 25052, Apr. 27, 2012]

Subpart D—Changes in Ownership, Control, or Structure of Licensee; Transfer of License

CHANGES IN CONTROL OR OWNERSHIP OF LICENSEE

§ 107.400 Changes in ownership of 10 percent or more of Licensee but no change of Control.

(a) *Prior approval requirements.* You must obtain SBA's prior written approval for any proposed transfer or issuance of ownership interests that results in the ownership (beneficial or of record) by any Person, or group of Persons acting in concert, of at least 10 percent of any class of your stock or partnership capital.

(b) *Fee.* A processing fee of $200 must accompany each such request for approval of a change of ownership.

§ 107.410 Changes in Control of Licensee (through change in ownership or otherwise).

(a) *Prior approval requirements.* You must obtain SBA's prior written approval for any proposed transaction or event that results in Control by any Person(s) not previously approved by SBA.

(b) *Fee.* A processing fee equal to the combined Licensing Fee (Initial Licensing Fee plus the Final Licensing Fee then in effect) defined in § 107.300 must accompany any application for approval of one or more transactions or events that will result in a transfer of Control.

[61 FR 3189, Jan. 31, 1996, as amended at 82 FR 52185, Nov. 13, 2017]

§ 107.420 Prohibition on exercise of ownership or Control rights in Licensee before SBA approval.

Without prior written SBA approval, no change of ownership or Control may take effect and no officer, director, employee or other Person acting on your behalf shall:

(a) Register on your books any transfer of ownership interest to the proposed new owner(s);

(b) Permit the proposed new owner(s) to exercise voting rights with respect to such ownership interest (including directly or indirectly procuring or voting any proxy, consent or authorization as to such voting rights at any shareholders' or partnership meeting);

(c) Permit the proposed new owner(s) to participate in any manner in the conduct of your affairs (including exercising control over your books, records, funds or other assets; participating directly or indirectly in any disposition thereof; or serving as an officer, director, partner, employee or agent); or

(d) Allow ownership or Control to pass to another Person.

§ 107.430 Notification to SBA of transactions that may change ownership or Control.

You must promptly notify SBA as soon as you have knowledge of transactions or events that may result in a transfer of Control or ownership of at least 10 percent of your capital. If there is any doubt as to whether a particular transaction or event will result in such a change, report the facts to SBA.

§ 107.440 Standards governing prior SBA approval for a proposed transfer of Control.

SBA approval is contingent upon full disclosure of the real parties in interest, the source of funds for the new owners' interest, and other data requested by SBA. As a condition of approving a proposed transfer of control, SBA may:

(a) Require an increase in your Regulatory Capital;

(b) Require the new owners or the transferee's Control Person(s) to assume, in writing, personal liability for your Leverage, effective only in the event of their direct or indirect participation in any transfer of Control not approved by SBA; or

(c) Require compliance with any other conditions set by SBA, including compliance with the requirements for minimum capital and management-ownership diversity as in effect at such time for new license applicants.

[61 FR 3189, Jan. 31, 1996]

§ 107.450 Notification to SBA of pledge of Licensee's shares.

(a) You must notify SBA in writing, within 30 calendar days, of the terms of any transaction in which:

(1) Any Person, or group of Persons acting in concert, pledges shares of your stock (or equivalent ownership interests) as collateral for indebtedness; and

(2) The shares pledged are at least 10 percent of your Regulatory Capital.

(b) If the transaction creates a change of ownership or Control, you must comply with § 107.400 or § 107.410, as appropriate.

RESTRICTIONS ON COMMON CONTROL OR OWNERSHIP OF TWO OR MORE LICENSEES

§ 107.460 Restrictions on Common Control or ownership of two (or more) Licensees.

(a) *General rule.* Without SBA's prior written approval, you must not have an officer, director, manager, Control Person, or owner (with a direct or indirect ownership interest of at least 10 percent) who is also:

(1) An officer, director, manager, Control Person, or owner (with a direct or indirect ownership interest of at least 10 percent) of another Licensee; or

(2) An officer or director of any Person that directly or indirectly controls, or is controlled by, or is under Common Control with, another Licensee.

(b) *Exceptions to general rule.* This § 107.460 does not apply to:

(1) Common officers, directors, managers, or owners of a Section 301(c) Licensee and its Section 301(d) subsidiary; or

(2) Common officers, directors, managers, Control Persons, or owners of two (or more) Licensees which have no Leverage.

CHANGE IN STRUCTURE OF LICENSEE

§ 107.470 SBA approval of merger, consolidation, or reorganization of Licensee.

(a) *Prior approval requirements.* You may not merge, consolidate, change form of organization (corporation or partnership) or reorganize without SBA's prior written approval. Any such merger or consolidation will be subject to § 107.440.

(b) *Fee.* A processing fee of $5,000 must accompany any application for approval of a change in your form of organization (from corporation to partnership or partnership to corporation).

TRANSFER OF LICENSE

§ 107.475 Transfer of license.

You may not transfer your license in any manner without SBA's prior written approval.

Subpart E—Managing the Operations of a Licensee

GENERAL REQUIREMENTS

§ 107.500 Lawful operations under the Act.

You must engage only in the activities contemplated by the Act and in no other activities.

§ 107.501 Identification as a Licensee.

You must display your SBIC license in a prominent location. You must also have a listed telephone number. Before collecting an application fee or extending Financing to a Small Business, you must obtain a written statement from the concern acknowledging its awareness that you are "a Federal licensee under the Small Business Investment Act of 1958, as amended."

§ 107.502 Representations to the public.

You may not represent or imply to anyone that the SBA, the U.S. Government or any of its agencies or officers has approved any ownership interests you have issued or obligations you have incurred. Be certain to include a statement to this effect in any solicitation to investors. Example: You may not represent or imply that "SBA stands behind the Licensee" or that "Your capital is safe because SBA's experts review proposed investments to make sure they are safe for the Licensee."

§ 107.503 Licensee's adoption of an approved valuation policy.

(a) *Valuation guidelines.* You must prepare, document and report the valuations of your Loans and Investments in accordance with the Valuation Guidelines for SBICs issued by SBA. These guidelines may be obtained from SBA's SBIC Web site at *www.sba.gov/sbic.*

(b) *SBA approval of valuation policy.* You must have a written valuation policy approved by SBA for use in determining the value of your Loans and Investments. You must either:

(1) Adopt without change the model valuation policy set forth in section III of the Valuation Guidelines for SBICs; or

(2) Obtain SBA's prior written approval of an alternative valuation policy.

(c) *Responsibility for valuations.* Your board of directors or general partner(s) will be solely responsible for adopting your valuation policy and for using it to prepare valuations of your Loans and Investments for submission to SBA. If SBA reasonably believes that your valuations, individually or in the aggregate, are materially misstated, it reserves the right to require you to engage, at your expense, an independent third party, acceptable to SBA, to substantiate the valuations.

(d) *Frequency of valuations.* (1) If you have outstanding Leverage or Earmarked Assets, you must value your Loans and Investments at the end of the second quarter of your fiscal year, and at the end of your fiscal year.

(2) Otherwise, you must value your Loans and Investments only at your fiscal year end.

(3) On a case-by-case basis, SBA may require you to perform valuations more frequently.

(4) You must report material adverse changes in valuations at least quarterly, within thirty days following the close of the quarter.

(e) *Review of valuations by independent public accountant.* (1) For valuations performed as of the end of your fiscal year, your independent public accountant must review your valuation procedures and the implementation of such procedures, including adequacy of documentation.

(2) The independent public accountant's report on your audited annual financial statements (SBA Form 468) must include a statement that your valuations were prepared in accordance with your approved valuation policy established in accordance with section 310(d)(2) of the Act.

[61 FR 3189, Jan. 31, 1996, as amended at 63 FR 5866, Feb. 5, 1998; 82 FR 39340, Aug. 18, 2017]

§ 107.504 Equipment and office requirements.

(a) *Computer capability.* You must have a personal computer with a modem, and be able to use this equipment to prepare reports (using SBA-provided software) and transmit them to SBA. In addition, by March 31, 2000, you must have access to the Internet and the capability to send and receive electronic mail via the Internet.

(b) *Facsimile capability.* You must be able to receive facsimile messages 24 hours per day at your primary office.

(c) *Accessible office.* You must maintain an office that is convenient to the public and is open for business during normal working hours.

[64 FR 70995, Dec. 20, 1999]

§ 107.506 Safeguarding Licensee's assets/Internal controls.

You must adopt a plan to safeguard your assets and monitor the reliability of your financial data, personnel, Portfolio, funds and equipment. You must provide your bank and custodian with a certified copy of your resolution or other formal document describing your control procedures.

§ 107.507 Violations based on false filings and nonperformance of agreements with SBA.

The following shall constitute a violation of this part:

(a) *Nonperformance.* Nonperformance of any of the requirements of any Debenture, Participating Security or Preferred Security, or of any written agreement with SBA.

(b) *False statement.* In any document submitted to SBA:

(1) Any false statement knowingly made; or

(2) Any misrepresentation of a material fact; or

(3) Any failure to state a material fact. A material fact is any fact which is necessary to make a statement not misleading in light of the circumstances under which the statement was made.

§ 107.509 Employment of SBA officials.

Without SBA's prior written approval, for a period of two years after the date of your most recent issuance of Leverage (or the receipt of any SBA Assistance as defined in part 105 of this chapter), you are not permitted to employ, offer employment to, or retain for professional services, any person who:

(a) Served as an officer, attorney, agent, or employee of SBA on or within one year before such date; and

(b) As such, occupied a position or engaged in activities which, in SBA's determination, involved discretion with respect to the granting of Assistance under the Act.

MANAGEMENT AND COMPENSATION

§ 107.510 SBA approval of Licensee's Investment Adviser/Manager.

You may employ an Investment Adviser/Manager who will be subject to the supervision of your board of directors or general partner. If you have Leverage or plan to seek Leverage, you must obtain SBA's prior written approval of the management contract. SBA's approval of an Investment Adviser/Manager for one Licensee does not indicate approval of that manager for any other Licensee.

(a) *Management contract.* The contract must:

(1) Specify the services the Investment Adviser/Manager will render to you and to the Small Businesses in your Portfolio; and

(2) Indicate the basis for computing Management Expenses.

(b) *Material change to approved management contract.* If there is a material change, both you and SBA must approve such change in advance. If you are uncertain if the change is material, submit the proposed revision to SBA.

§ 107.520 Management Expenses of a Licensee.

SBA must approve any increases in your Management Expenses if you have outstanding Leverage or Earmarked Assets.

(a) *Definition of Management Expenses.* Management Expenses include:

(1) Salaries;

(2) Office expenses;

(3) Travel;

(4) Business development;

(5) Office and equipment rental;

(6) Bookkeeping; and

(7) Expenses related to developing, investigating and monitoring investments.

(b) Management Expenses do not include services provided by specialized outside consultants, outside lawyers and independent public accountants, if they perform services not generally performed by a venture capital company.

(c) If your Management Expenses have not already been approved by SBA, you must submit such expenses for approval with your SBA Form 468 for your first fiscal year ending after January 31, 1996.

CASH MANAGEMENT BY A LICENSEE

§ 107.530 Restrictions on investments of idle funds by leveraged Licensees.

(a) *Applicability of this section.* This § 107.530 applies if you have outstanding Leverage or if you have applied for Leverage.

(b) *Permitted investments of idle funds.* Funds not invested in Small Businesses must be maintained in:

(1) Direct obligations of, or obligations guaranteed as to principal and interest by, the United States, which mature within 15 months from the date of the investment; or

(2) Repurchase agreements with federally insured institutions, with a maturity of seven days or less. The securities underlying the repurchase agreements must be direct obligations of, or obligations guaranteed as to principal and interest by, the United States. The securities must be maintained in a custodial account at a federally insured institution; or

(3) Mutual funds, securities, or other instruments that exclusively consist of, or represent pooled assets of, investments described in paragraphs (b)(1) or (b)(2) of this section; or

(4) Certificates of deposit with a maturity of one year or less, issued by a federally insured institution; or

(5) A deposit account in a federally insured institution, subject to a withdrawal restriction of one year or less; or

(6) A checking account in a federally insured institution; or

(7) A reasonable petty cash fund.

(c) *Deposit of funds in excess of the insured amount.* (1) You are permitted to deposit funds in a federally insured institution in excess of the institution's insured amount, but only if the institution is "well capitalized" in accordance with the definition set forth in regulations of the Federal Deposit Insurance Corporation, as amended (12 CFR 325.103).

(2) Exception: You may make a temporary deposit (not to exceed 30 days) in excess of the insured amount, in a transfer account established to facilitate the receipt and disbursement of funds or to hold funds necessary to honor Commitments issued.

(d) *Deposit of funds in Associate institution.* A deposit in, or a repurchase agreement with, a federally insured institution that is your Associate is not considered a Financing of such Associate under § 107.730, provided the terms of such deposit or repurchase agreement are no less favorable than those available to the general public.

[61 FR 3189, Jan. 31, 1996, as amended at 77 FR 20294, Apr. 4, 2012]

BORROWING BY LICENSEES FROM NON-SBA SOURCES

§ 107.550 Prior approval of secured third-party debt of leveraged Licensees.

(a) *Definition.* In this § 107.550, "secured third-party debt" means any non-SBA debt secured by any of your assets, including secured guarantees and other contingent obligations that you voluntarily assume, secured lines of credit, and secured Temporary Debt of a Licensee with outstanding Participating Securities.

(b) *General rule.* If you have outstanding Leverage, you must get SBA's written approval before you incur any secured third-party debt or refinance any debt with secured third-party debt, including any renewal of a secured line of credit, increase in the maximum amount available under a secured line of credit, or expansion of the scope of a security interest or lien. For purposes of this paragraph (b), "expansion of the scope of a security interest or lien" does not include the substitution of one asset or group of assets for another, provided the asset values (as reported on your most recent annual Form 468) are comparable.

(c) *Additional rule for secured lines of credit in existence on April 8, 1994.* If you have outstanding Leverage and you have a secured line of credit that was created on or before April 8, 1994, you must receive SBA's written approval of the line before you increase the amounts outstanding thereunder.

(d) *Conditions for SBA approval.* As a condition of granting its approval under this §107.550, SBA may impose such restrictions or limitations as it deems appropriate, taking into account your historical performance, current financial position, proposed terms of the secured debt and amount of aggregate debt you will have outstanding (including Leverage). SBA will not favorably consider any requests for approval which include a blanket lien on all your assets, or a security interest in your investor commitments in excess of 125 percent of the proposed borrowing.

(e) *Thirty day approval.* Unless SBA notifies you otherwise within 30 days after it receives your request, you may consider your request automatically approved if:

(1) You are in regulatory compliance;

(2) The security interest in your assets is limited to either those assets being acquired with the borrowed funds or an asset coverage ratio of no more than 2:1;

(3) Your Leverage does not exceed 150 percent of your Leverageable Capital; and

(4) Your request is for approval of a secured line of credit that would not cause your total outstanding borrowings (not including Leverage) to exceed 50 percent of your Leverageable Capital.

§ 107.560 Subordination of SBA's creditor position.

(a) *Debentures purchased or guaranteed on or before July 1, 1991.* Under the terms of any Debenture purchased or guaranteed by SBA on or before July 1, 1991, SBA's unsecured claims against you, as a Debenture-holder or as subrogee, are subordinated in favor of all your other creditors, except to the extent that such claims may be subject to equitable subordination in SBA's favor.

(b) *Debentures purchased or guaranteed after July 1, 1991, including refinancings of Debentures previously purchased or guaranteed.* (1) Under the terms of any Debenture purchased or guaranteed by SBA after July 1, 1991, SBA's unsecured claims against you, as a Debenture-holder or as subrogee, are subordinated only in favor of non-Associate lenders; and, to the extent that your indebtedness to such lenders exceeds the lesser of $10,000,000 or 200 percent of your Regulatory Capital (determined as of the date your Debentures were purchased or guaranteed), SBA's unsecured claims enjoy parity with those of other unsecured creditors, except with respect to indebtedness created on or before July 1, 1991.

(2) In order to induce others to lend you money after your Debenture has been purchased or guaranteed, SBA may agree in writing on a case-by-case basis to subordinate its unsecured claims, on such terms as it may determine, in favor of one or more of your Associates, or in favor of other lenders in excess of the amounts mentioned in paragraph (b)(1) of this section.

(3) SBA reserves the authority to refuse to subordinate its claims if it determines, at the time you request your Debenture be purchased or guaranteed, that the exercise of reasonable investment prudence and your financial condition warrant such refusal.

§ 107.565 Restrictions on third-party debt of Early Stage SBICs.

If you are an Early Stage SBIC and you have outstanding Leverage or a Leverage commitment, you must get SBA's prior written approval to have, incur, or refinance any third-party debt other than accounts payable from routine business operations.

[77 FR 25052, Apr. 27, 2012]

§ 107.570 Restrictions on third-party debt of issuers of Participating Securities.

(a) *General.* Temporary Debt is the only debt (other than Leverage) that you are permitted to incur if you have applied to issue Participating Securities or if you have outstanding Participating Securities. For additional rules governing secured Temporary Debt, see § 107.550.

(b) *Definition of Temporary Debt.* Temporary Debt means your short-term borrowings if:

(1) Such borrowings are for the purpose of maintaining your operating liquidity or providing funds for a particular Financing of a Small Business;

(2) The funds are borrowed from a regulated financial institution or a regulated credit company (or, if approved by SBA on a case-by-case basis, from non-regulated lenders including shareholders or partners);

(3) Your total outstanding borrowings (not including Leverage) do not exceed 50 percent of your Leverageable Capital; and

(4) All such borrowings are fully paid off for at least 30 consecutive days during your fiscal year so that you have no outstanding third-party debt for 30 days.

VOLUNTARY DECREASE IN LICENSEE'S REGULATORY CAPITAL

§ 107.585 Voluntary decrease in Licensee's Regulatory Capital.

You must obtain SBA's prior written approval to reduce your Regulatory Capital by more than two percent in any fiscal year, unless otherwise permitted under §§ 107.1560 and 107.1570, *provided however,* that if you are an Early Stage SBIC, you must obtain SBA's prior written approval for any reduction of your Regulatory Capital, including any reduction pursuant to a Distribution under § 107.1180 of this part. At all times, you must retain sufficient Regulatory Capital to meet the minimum capital requirements in the Act and § 107.210, and sufficient Leverageable Capital to avoid having excess Leverage in violation of section 303 of the Act and §§ 107.1150 through 107.1170.

[61 FR 3189, Jan. 31, 1996, as amended at 77 FR 25052, Apr. 27, 2012]

REQUIREMENT TO CONDUCT ACTIVE INVESTMENT OPERATIONS

§ 107.590 Licensee's requirement to maintain active operations.

(a) *Activity test.* You must conduct active operations, as determined under this § 107.590, as a condition of your license. You will be considered active if:

(1) During the eighteen months preceding your most recent fiscal year end, you made Financings totaling at least 20 percent of your Regulatory Capital; or

(2) Your idle funds did not exceed 20 percent of your total assets (at cost) at your most recent fiscal year end.

(b) *Permitted exceptions to activity requirements.* You are considered active if your failure to meet the requirements in paragraph (a) of this section is the result of one or more of the following factors:

(1) Your excess idle funds are the result of the receipt, within the previous nine months, of realized gains, repayments, additional capital contributions, or Leverage.

(2) It is necessary for you to maintain excess idle funds to conduct your operations because:

(i) Your unfunded commitments from investors are no more than 20 percent of your Regulatory Capital; and

(ii) You cannot receive additional Leverage, solely because SBA has insufficient funds available.

(3) You have not made sufficient Financings because of a lack of available funds, evidenced by Loans and Investments (at cost) equal to at least 90 percent of your Combined Capital as of your most recent fiscal year end.

(4) You have not made sufficient Financings solely because SBA has restricted your ability to make investments.

(c) *Applicability of activity requirements.* The activity requirements in paragraph (a) of this section do not apply if you have filed a "Wind-up Plan" approved by SBA. "Wind-up Plan" means a plan that you prepare when you decide that you will no longer make any Financings other than follow-on investments, and that you update annually when you file your SBA Form 468. The plan must contain your best estimates of the following:

(1) The remaining number of years you expect to operate.

(2) For each of your Loans and Investments, the expected liquidation date and anticipated proceeds.

(3) The timing of your repayment of obligations to SBA.

(4) The timing and amount of any planned reductions in your Management Expenses.

(d) *Phase-in of activity requirements*—(1) *General rule.* You must meet the activity requirements in this § 107.590 as of the end of your first full fiscal year beginning after January 31, 1996. Until then, you will be considered active if you meet the activity requirements in effect on January 30, 1996.

(2) *Rule for new Licensees.* If you received your license after January 31, 1996, or if you received your license less than eighteen months before the fiscal year end determined under paragraph (d)(1) of this section, you must meet the activity requirements in this § 107.590 as of the end of your second full fiscal year beginning after the date you received your license.

Subpart F—Recordkeeping, Reporting, and Examination Requirements for Licensees

RECORDKEEPING REQUIREMENTS FOR LICENSEES

§ 107.600 General requirement for Licensee to maintain and preserve records.

(a) *Maintaining your accounting records.* You must establish and maintain your accounting records using SBA's standard chart of accounts for Licensees, unless SBA approves otherwise.

(b) *Location of records.* You must keep the following records at your principal place of business or, in the case of paragraph (b)(3) of this section, at the branch office that is primarily responsible for the transaction:

(1) All your accounting and other financial records;

(2) All minutes of meetings of directors, stockholders, executive committees, partners, or other officials; and

(3) All documents and supporting materials related to your business transactions, except for any items held by a custodian under a written agreement between you and a Portfolio Concern or non-SBA lender, or any securities held in a safe deposit box, or by a licensed securities broker in an amount not exceeding the broker's per-account insurance coverage.

(c) *Preservation of records.* You must retain all the records that are the basis for your financial reports. Such records must be preserved for the periods specified in this paragraph (c), and must remain accessible for the first two years of the preservation period.

(1) You must preserve for at least 15 years or, in the case of a Partnership Licensee, at least two years beyond the date of liquidation:

(i) All your accounting ledgers and journals, and any other records of assets, asset valuations, liabilities, equity, income, and expenses.

(ii) Your Articles, bylaws, minute books, and license application.

(iii) All documents evidencing ownership of the Licensee including ownership ledgers, and ownership transfer registers.

(2) You must preserve for at least six years all supporting documentation (such as vouchers, bank statements, or canceled checks) for the records listed in paragraph (b)(1) of this section.

(3) After final disposition of any item in your Portfolio, you must preserve for at least six years:

(i) Financing applications and Financing instruments.

(ii) All loan, participation, and escrow agreements.

(iii) Size status declarations (SBA Form 480) and Financing Eligibility Statements (SBA Form 1941).

(iv) Any capital stock certificates and warrants of the Portfolio Concern that you did not surrender or exercise.

(v) All other documents and supporting material relating to the Portfolio Concern, including correspondence.

(4) You may substitute a computer-scanned or generated copy for the original of any record covered by this paragraph (c).

[61 FR 3189, Jan. 31, 1996, as amended at 79 FR 62823, Oct. 21, 2014]

§ 107.610 Required certifications for Loans and Investments.

For each of your Loans and Investments, you must have the documents listed in this section. Except for information and documentation prepared under paragraphs (f)(2) and (3) of this section, you must keep these documents in your files and make them available to SBA upon request.

(a) SBA Form 480, the Size Status Declaration, executed both by you and by the concern you are financing. By executing this document, both parties certify that the concern is a Small Business. For securities purchased from an underwriter in a public offering, you may substitute a prospectus showing that the concern is a Small Business.

(b) SBA Form 652, a certification by the concern you are financing that it will not illegally discriminate (see part 112 of this chapter).

(c) SBA Form 1941 (for Section 301(d) Licensees only), executed both by you and by the concern you are financing. By executing this document, both parties certify that the concern is a Disadvantaged Business.

(d) A certification by the concern you are financing of the intended use of the proceeds. For securities purchased from an underwriter in a public offering, you may substitute a prospectus indicating the intended use of proceeds.

(e) For each LMI Investment:

(1) A certification by the concern, dated as of the date of application for SBIC financing, as to the basis for its qualification as an LMI Enterprise,

(2) If the concern qualifies as an LMI Enterprise as defined in paragraph (2) of the definition of LMI Enterprise in § 107.50, an additional certification dated no later than the date 180 days after the closing of the LMI Investment, as to the location of the concern's employees or tangible assets or the principal residences of its full-time employees as of the date of such certification, and

(3) Certification(s) by the SBIC, made contemporaneously with the certification(s) of the concern, that the concern qualifies as an LMI Enterprise as of the date(s) of the concern's certification(s) and the basis for such qualification.

(f) For each Energy Saving Qualified Investment:

(1) If a pre-Financing determination of eligibility by SBA is not required under the definition of Energy Saving Activities or Energy Saving Qualified Investment:

(i) A certification by you, dated as of the closing date of the Financing, as to the basis for the qualification of the Financing as an Energy Saving Qualified Investment;

(ii) Supporting documentation of the Energy Saving Activities engaged in by the concern;

(iii) Supporting documentation of either the percentage of its revenues derived from Energy Saving Activities during the concern's most recently completed fiscal year, which must be at least 50 percent, or the concern's intended use of the Financing proceeds, all of which must be used for Energy Saving Activities; and

(iv) A certification by the concern, dated as of the closing date of the Financing, that any information it provided to you in connection with this paragraph (f)(1) is true and correct to the best of its knowledge.

(2) If, prior to providing Financing, you must obtain a determination from SBA that the activities in which a concern is engaged are Energy Saving Activities, submit to SBA in writing a description of the product or service being provided or developed, including all available documentation of the energy savings produced or anticipated, addressing the factors considered under paragraph (4) of the definition of "Energy Saving Activities" in § 107.50 and certified by the concern to be true and correct to the best of its knowledge.

(3) If, prior to providing Financing, you must obtain a determination from SBA that the concern is "primarily engaged" in Energy Saving Activities, submit to SBA in writing all available information concerning the factors considered under paragraph (3) of the definition of "Energy Saving Qualified

Investment" in § 107.50, certified by the concern to be true and correct to the best of its knowledge.

(4) For each Financing closed after you obtain a determination from SBA under paragraph (f)(2) or (3) of this section, a certification by you, dated as of the closing date of the Financing, that to the best of your knowledge, you have no reason to believe that the materials submitted are incorrect.

(5) For each Financing closed based on supporting documentation of the concern's intended use of proceeds for Energy Saving Activities under paragraph (f)(1)(iii) of this section:

(i) Documentation by the concern, dated no later than six months after the closing of the Financing, of the proceeds used to date for Energy Saving Activities, with further updates provided at six month intervals until 100 percent of the Financing proceeds have been accounted for; and

(ii) Documentation that you have reviewed the information submitted by the concern under paragraph (f)(5)(i) of this section and have reasonably determined that 100 percent of the Financing proceeds were used for Energy Saving Activities.

(g) For each passive business financed under § 107.720(b)(3), a certification by you, dated as of the closing date of the Financing, as to the basis for the qualification of the Financing under § 107.720(b)(3) and identifying one or more limited partners for which a direct Financing would cause those investors:

(1) To incur "unrelated business taxable income" under section 511 of the Internal Revenue Code (26 U.S.C. 511); or

(2) To incur "effectively connected income" to foreign investors under sections 871 and 882 of the Internal Revenue Code (26 U.S.C. 871 and 882).

[61 FR 3189, Jan. 31, 1996, as amended at 64 FR 52646, Sept. 30, 1999; 77 FR 23379, Apr. 19, 2012; 82 FR 39340, Aug. 18, 2017]

§ 107.620 Requirements to obtain information from Portfolio Concerns.

All the information required by this section is subject to the requirements of § 107.600 and must be in English.

(a) *Information for initial Financing decision.* Before extending any Financing, you must require the applicant to submit such financial statements, plans of operation (including intended use of financing proceeds), cash flow analyses and projections as are necessary to support your investment decision. The information submitted must be consistent with the size and type of the business and the amount of the proposed Financing.

(b) *Updated financial information.* (1) The terms of each Financing must require the Portfolio Concern to provide, at least annually, sufficient financial information to enable you to perform the following required procedures:

(i) Evaluate the financial condition of the Portfolio Concern for the purpose of valuing your investment;

(ii) Determine the continued eligibility of the Portfolio Concern; and

(iii) Verify the use of Financing proceeds.

(2) The information submitted to you must be certified by the president, chief executive officer, treasurer, chief financial officer, general partner, or proprietor of the Portfolio Concern.

(3) For financial and valuation purposes, you may accept a complete copy of the Federal income tax return filed by the Portfolio Concern (or its proprietor) in lieu of financial statements, but only if appropriate for the size and type of the business involved.

(4) The requirements in this paragraph (b) do not apply when you acquire securities from an underwriter in a public offering (see § 107.825). In that case, you must keep copies of all reports furnished by the Portfolio Concern to the holders of its securities.

(c) *Information required for examination purposes.* You must obtain any information requested by SBA's examiners for the purpose of verifying the certifications made by a Portfolio Concern under § 107.610. In this regard, your Financing documents must contain provisions requiring the Portfolio Concern to give you and/or SBA's examiners access to its books and records for such purpose.

REPORTING REQUIREMENTS FOR LICENSEES

§ 107.630 Requirement for Licensees to file financial statements with SBA (Form 468).

(a) *Annual filing of Form 468.* For each fiscal year, you must submit to SBA financial statements and supplementary information prepared on SBA Form 468. You must file Form 468 on or before the last day of the third month following the end of your fiscal year, except for the information required under paragraph (e) of this section, which must be filed on or before the last day of the fifth month following the end of your fiscal year.

(1) *Audit of Form 468.* The annual Form 468 must be audited by an independent public accountant acceptable to SBA.

(2) *Insurance requirement for public accountant.* Unless SBA approves otherwise, your independent public accountant must carry at least $1,000,000 of Errors and Omissions insurance, or be self-insured and have a net worth of at least $1,000,000.

(b) *Interim filings of Form 468.* When requested by SBA, you must file interim reports on Form 468. SBA may require you to file the entire form or only certain statements and schedules. You must file such reports on or before the last day of the month following the end of the reporting period. If you have an outstanding Leverage commitment from SBA, see the filing requirements in § 107.1220.

(c) *Standards for preparation of Form 468.* You must prepare SBA Form 468 in accordance with SBA's Accounting Standards and Financial Reporting Requirements for Small Business Investment Companies.

(d) *Reporting of economic impact information on Form 468.* Your annual filing of SBA Form 468 must include an assessment of the economic impact of each Financing, specifying the full-time equivalent jobs created or retained, and the impact of the Financing on the revenues and profits of the business and on taxes paid by the business and its employees.

[61 FR 3189, Jan. 31, 1996, as amended at 82 FR 39340, Aug. 18, 2017]

§ 107.640 Requirement to file Portfolio Financing Reports (SBA Form 1031).

For each Financing of a Small Business (excluding guarantees), you must submit a Portfolio Financing Report on SBA Form 1031 within 30 days of the closing date.

§ 107.650 Requirement to report portfolio valuations to SBA.

You must determine the value of your Loans and Investments in accordance with § 107.503. You must report such valuations to SBA within 90 days of the end of the fiscal year in the case of annual valuations, and within 30 days following the close of other reporting periods. You must report material adverse changes in valuations at least quarterly, within thirty days following the close of the quarter.

§ 107.660 Other items required to be filed by Licensee with SBA.

(a) *Reports to owners.* You must give SBA a copy of any report you furnish to your investors, including any prospectus, letter, or other publication concerning your financial operations or those of any Portfolio Concern.

(b) *Documents filed with SEC.* You must give SBA a copy of any report, application or document you file with the Securities and Exchange Commission.

(c) *Litigation reports.* When you become a party to litigation or other proceedings, you must give SBA a report within 30 days that describes the proceedings and identifies the other parties involved and your relationship to them.

(1) The proceedings covered by this paragraph (c) include any action by you, or by your security holder(s) in a personal or derivative capacity, against an officer, director, Investment Adviser or other Associate of yours for alleged breach of official duty.

(2) SBA may require you to submit copies of the pleadings and other documents SBA may specify.

(3) Where proceedings have been terminated by settlement or final judgment, you must promptly advise SBA of the terms.

(4) This paragraph (c) does not apply to collection actions or proceedings to enforce your ordinary creditors' rights.

(d) *Notification of criminal charges.* If any officer, director, or general partner of the Licensee, or any other person who was required by SBA to complete a personal history statement in connection with your license, is charged with or convicted of any criminal offense other than a misdemeanor involving a minor motor vehicle violation, you must report the incident to SBA within 5 calendar days. Such report must fully describe the facts which pertain to the incident.

(e) *Other reports.* You must file any other reports that SBA may require by written directive.

[61 FR 3189, Jan. 31, 1996, as amended at 63 FR 5866, Feb. 5, 1998]

§ 107.665 Civil penalties.

Except as provided in § 107.670, a Licensee that violates any regulation or written directive issued by SBA, requiring the filing of any regular or special report pursuant to this part, shall be fined a civil penalty of not more than $259 for each day the Licensee fails to file such report. The civil penalties provided for in this section shall accrue to the United States and may be recovered in a civil action brought by the SBA.

[81 FR 31491, May 19, 2016, as amended at 82 FR 9969, Feb. 9, 2017; 83 FR 7363, Feb. 21, 2018]

§ 107.670 Application for exemption from civil penalty for late filing of reports.

(a) If it is impracticable to submit any required report within the time allowed, you may apply for an extension. The request for an extension must:

(1) Be filed before the reporting deadline;

(2) Certify to an extraordinary occurrence, not within your control, that makes timely filing of the report impracticable; and

(3) Be accompanied by written evidence of such occurrence, where appropriate.

(b) Upon receipt of your request, SBA may exempt you from the civil penalty stated in § 107.665, in such manner and under such conditions as SBA determines.

[61 FR 3189, Jan. 31, 1996, as amended at 81 FR 31491, May 19, 2016]

§ 107.680 Reporting changes in Licensee not subject to prior SBA approval.

(a) *Changes to be reported for post approval.* (1) This section applies to any changes in your Articles, ownership, capitalization, management, operating area, or investment policies that do not require SBA's prior approval. You must report such changes to SBA within 30 days for post approval. A processing fee of $200 must accompany each request for post approval of new officers, directors, or Control Persons.

(2) *Exception for non-leveraged Licensees.* If you do not have outstanding Leverage or Earmarked Assets, you are not required to obtain post approval of new directors or new officers other than your chief operating officer; however, you must notify SBA of the new directors or officers within 30 days.

(b) *Approval by SBA.* You may consider any change submitted under this section § 107.680 to be approved unless SBA notifies you to the contrary within 90 days after receiving it. SBA's approval is contingent upon your full disclosure of all relevant facts and is subject to any conditions SBA may prescribe.

EXAMINATIONS OF LICENSEES BY SBA FOR REGULATORY COMPLIANCE

§ 107.690 Examinations.

SBA will examine all Licensees for the purpose of evaluating regulatory compliance.

§ 107.691 Responsibilities of Licensee during examination.

You must make all books, records and other pertinent documents and materials available for the examination, including any information required by the examiner under § 107.620(c). In addition, the agreement between you and the independent public accountant performing your audit must provide that any information in the accountant's working papers be made available to SBA upon request.

§ 107.692 Examination fees.

(a) *General.* SBA will assess fees for examinations in accordance with this § 107.692. Unless SBA determines otherwise on a case by case basis, SBA will not assess fees for special examinations to obtain specific information.

(b) *Base Fee.* (1) The Base Fee will be assessed based on your total assets (at cost) as of the date of your latest certified financial statement, including if requested by SBA in connection with the examination, a more recently submitted interim statement. For purposes of this section, Base Fee means the Minimum Base Fee plus 0.024% of assets at cost, rounded to the nearest $100, not to exceed the Maximum Base Fee. The Minimum and Maximum Base Fees are adjusted annually as follows:

Time period (Based on the examination start date)	Minimum base fee	Maximum base fee for non-leveraged SBICs	Maximum base fee for leveraged SBICs
December 13, 2017 to September 30, 2018	$6,000	$22,500	$26,000
October 1, 2018 to September 30, 2019	7,000	25,000	32,000
October 1, 2019 to September 30, 2020	8,000	27,500	38,000
October 1, 2020 to September 30, 2021	9,000	30,000	44,000

(2) In the table in paragraph (b)(1) of this section, a Non-leveraged SBIC means any SBIC that, as of the date of the examination, has no outstanding Leverage or Leverage commitment, has no Earmarked Assets, and certifies to SBA that it will not seek Leverage in the future. Beginning on October 1, 2021, SBA will annually adjust the Minimum Base Fee and Maximum Base Fees using the Inflation Adjustment and will publish a Notice prior to such adjustment in the FEDERAL REGISTER identifying the amount of the fees.

(c) *Adjustments to Base Fee.* In order to determine the amount of your examination fee, your Base Fee, as determined in paragraph (b) of this section, will be increased based on the following criteria:

(1) If you were not fully responsive to the letter of notification of examination (that is, you did not provide all requested documents and information within the time period stipulated in the notification letter in a complete and accurate manner, or you did not prepare or did not have available all information requested by the examiner for on-site review) after a written warning by the SBA, you will pay an additional charge equal to 15% of your Base Fee;

(2) If you maintain your records/files in multiple locations (as permitted under § 107.600(b)), you will pay an additional charge equal to 10% of your Base Fee; and

(3) For any regulatory violation that remains unresolved 90 days from the date SBA notified you that you must take corrective action (as established by the date of the notification letter) or such later date as SBA sets forth in the notice, you will pay an additional charge equal to 5% of the Base Fee for every 30 days or portion thereof that the violation remains unresolved after the cure period, unless SBA resolves the finding in your favor.

(d) *Fee additions table.* The following table summarizes the additions noted in paragraph (c) of this section:

Examination fee additions	Amount of addition – % of base fee
Non-responsive	15%.
Records/Files at multiple locations.	10%.
Unresolved Findings.	5% of Base Fee for every 30 days or portion thereof beyond the 90 day cure period or such later date as SBA sets forth in the notice for each unresolved finding.

(e) *Delay fee.* If, in the judgment of SBA, the time required to complete your examination is delayed due to your lack of cooperation or the condition of your records, SBA may assess an additional fee of $700 per day. Beginning on October 1, 2021, SBA will annually adjust this fee using the Inflation Adjustment and will publish a Notice prior to such adjustment in the FEDERAL REGISTER identifying the amount of the fee.

[62 FR 23338, Apr. 30, 1997, as amended at 77 FR 25052, Apr. 27, 2012; 82 FR 52185, Nov. 13, 2017]

Subpart G—Financing of Small Businesses by Licensees

DETERMINING THE ELIGIBILITY OF A SMALL BUSINESS FOR SBIC FINANCING

§ 107.700 Compliance with size standards in part 121 of this chapter as a condition of Assistance.

You are permitted to provide financial assistance and management services only to a Small Business. To determine whether an applicant is a Small Business, you may use either the financial size standards in § 121.301(c)(2) of this chapter or the industry standard covering the industry in which the applicant is primarily engaged, as set forth in § 121.301(c)(1) of this chapter.

[61 FR 3189, Jan. 31, 1996, as amended at 74 FR 33915, July 14, 2009]

§ 107.710 Requirement to finance smaller enterprises.

Your Portfolio must include Financings to Smaller Enterprises.

(a) *Definition of Smaller Enterprise.* A Smaller Enterprise means any small business concern that:

(1) Both together with its Affiliates, and by itself, meets the size standard of § 121.201 of this chapter at the time of Financing for the industry in which it is then primarily engaged; or

(2) Together with its affiliates has a net worth of not more than $6 million and average net income after Federal income taxes (excluding any carry-over losses) for the preceding two years no greater than $2 million. If the applicant is not required by law to pay Federal income taxes at the enterprise level, but is required to pass income through to its shareholders, partners, beneficiaries, or other equitable owners, the applicant's "net income after Federal income taxes" will be its net income reduced by an amount computed as follows:

(i) If the applicant is not required by law to pay State (and local, if any) income taxes at the enterprise level, multiply its net income by the marginal State income tax rate (or by the combined State and local income tax rates, as applicable) that would have applied if it were a taxable corporation.

(ii) Multiply the applicant's net income, less any deduction for State and local income taxes calculated under paragraph (a)(2)(i) of this section, by the marginal Federal income tax rate that would have applied if the applicant were a taxable corporation.

(iii) Add the results obtained in paragraphs (a)(2)(i) and (a)(2)(ii) of this section.

(b) *Smaller Enterprise Financings.* At the close or each of your fiscal years, and at the time of any application to draw Leverage, you must satisfy the Smaller Enterprise financing requirement in this paragraph (b) that applies to you.

(1) If you were licensed after February 17, 2009, at least 25 percent (in dollars) of your Financings must have been invested in Smaller Enterprises.

(2) If you were licensed on or before February 17, 2009, and you have received no SBA Leverage commitment issued after February 17, 2009, at least 20 percent (in dollars) of your Financings, excluding Financings made in whole or in part with Leverage in excess of $90 million, must have been invested in Smaller Enterprises. In addition, 100 percent of all Financings made in whole or in part with Leverage in excess of $90 million (including aggregate Leverage over $90 million issued by two or more Licensees under Common Control) must have been invested in Smaller Enterprises.

(3) If you were licensed on or before February 17, 2009, and you have received an SBA Leverage commitment after February 17, 2009:

(i) For all Financings made after the date of the first Leverage commitment issued after February 17, 2009, at least 25 percent (in dollars) of your Financings must have been invested in Smaller Enterprises, and

(ii) For all Financings made before February 17, 2009, at least 20 percent (in dollars) of your Financings, excluding Financings made in whole or in part with Leverage in excess of $90 million, must have been invested in Smaller

Enterprises. In addition, 100 percent of all Financings made in whole or in part with Leverage in excess of $90 million (including aggregate Leverage over $90 million issued by two or more Licensees under Common Control) must have been invested in Smaller Enterprises.

(c) *Special requirement for certain leveraged Licensees.* (1) This paragraph (c) applies if you were licensed on or before September 30, 1996, and you issued Leverage after that date, and you have Regulatory Capital of:

(i) Less than $10,000,000 if such Leverage included Participating Securities; or

(ii) Less than $5,000,000 if such Leverage was Debentures only.

(2) At the close of each of your fiscal years, at least 50 percent of the total dollar amount of the Financings you extended after September 30, 1996 must have been invested in Smaller Enterprises.

(d) Financing a change of ownership which results in the creation of a Smaller Enterprises. The Financing of a change of ownership under §107.750 which results in the creation of a Smaller Enterprise qualifies as a Smaller Enterprise Financing.

(e) *Non-compliance with this section.* If you have not reached the required percentage of Smaller Enterprise Financings at the end of any fiscal year, then you must be in compliance by the end of the following fiscal year. However, you will not be eligible for additional Leverage until you reach the required percentage (*see* §107.1120(c) and (g)).

[62 FR 11760, Mar. 13, 1997, as amended at 63 FR 5866, Feb. 5, 1998; 64 FR 70995, Dec. 20, 1999; 66 FR 30647, June 7, 2001; 74 FR 33915, July 14, 2009]

§ 107.720 Small Businesses that may be ineligible for financing.

(a) *Relenders or reinvestors.* You are not permitted to finance any business that is a relender or reinvestor.

(1) *Definition.* Relenders or reinvestors are businesses whose primary business activity involves, directly or indirectly, providing funds to others, purchasing debt obligations, factoring, or long-term leasing of equipment with no provision for maintenance or repair.

(2) *Exception.* You may provide Venture Capital Financing to Disadvantaged Businesses that are relenders or reinvestors (except banks or savings and loans not insured by agencies of the federal government, and agricultural credit companies). Without SBA's prior written approval, total Financings under this paragraph (a)(2) that are outstanding as of the close of your fiscal year must not exceed your Regulatory Capital.

(b) *Passive Businesses.* You are not permitted to finance a passive business.

(1) *Definition.* A business is passive if:

(i) It is not engaged in a regular and continuous business operation (for purposes of this paragraph (b), the mere receipt of payments such as dividends, rents, lease payments, or royalties is not considered a regular and continuous business operation); or

(ii) Its employees are not carrying on the majority of day to day operations, and the company does not provide effective control and supervision, on a day to day basis, over persons employed under contract; or

(iii) It passes through substantially all of the proceeds of the Financing to another entity.

(2) *Exception for pass-through of proceeds to subsidiary.* You may provide Financing directly to a passive business, including a passive business that you have formed, if it is a Small Business and it passes substantially all the proceeds through to (or uses substantially all the proceeds to acquire) one or more subsidiary companies, each of which is an eligible Small Business that is not passive. For the purpose of this paragraph (b)(2), "subsidiary company" means a company in which the financed passive business either:

(i) Directly owns, or will own as a result of the Financing, at least 50 percent of the outstanding voting securities; or

(ii) Indirectly owns, or will own as a result of the Financing, at least 50 percent of the outstanding voting securities (by directly owning the outstanding voting securities of another passive Small Business that is the direct owner of the outstanding voting securities of the subsidiary company).

(3) *Exception for certain Partnership Licensees.* If you are a Partnership Licensee, you may form one or more blocker entities in accordance with this paragraph (b)(3). For the purposes of this paragraph, a "blocker entity" means a corporation or a limited liability company that elects to be taxed as a corporation for Federal income tax purposes. The sole purpose of a blocker entity must be to provide Financing to one or more eligible, unincorporated Small Businesses. You may form such blocker entities only if a direct Financing to such Small Businesses would cause any of your investors to incur "unrelated business taxable income" under section 511 of the Internal Revenue Code (26 U.S.C. 511) or to incur "effectively connected income" to foreign investors under sections 871 and 882 of the Internal Revenue Code (26 U.S.C. 871 and 882). Your ownership and investment of funds in such blocker entities will not constitute a violation of §107.730(a). For each passive business financed under this section 107.720(b)(3), you must provide a certification to SBA as required under §107.610(g). A blocker entity formed under this paragraph may provide Financing:

(i) Directly to one or more eligible non-passive Small Businesses; or

(ii) Directly to a passive Small Business that passes substantially all the proceeds directly to (or uses substantially all the proceeds to acquire) one or more eligible non-passive Small Businesses in which the passive Small Business directly owns, or will own as a result of the Financing, at least 50% of the outstanding voting securities.

(4) *Additional conditions for permitted passive business financings.* Financings permitted under paragraphs (b)(2) or (3) of this section must meet all of the following conditions:

(i) For the purposes of this paragraph (b), "substantially all" means at least 99 percent of the Financing proceeds after deduction of actual application fees, closing fees, and expense reimbursements, which may not exceed those permitted by §107.860.

(ii) If you and/or your Associate charge fees permitted by §107.860 and/or §107.900, the total amount of such fees charged to all passive and non-passive businesses that are part of the same Financing may not exceed the fees that would have been permitted if the Financing had been provided directly to a non-passive Small Business. Any such fees received by your Associate must be paid to you in cash within 30 days of the receipt of such fees.

(iii) For the purposes of this part 107, each passive and non-passive business included in the Financing is a Portfolio Concern. The terms of the financing must provide SBA with access to Portfolio Concern information in compliance with this part 107, including without limitation §§107.600 and 107.620.

(c) *Real Estate Businesses.* (1) You are not permitted to finance any business classified under North American Industry Classification System (NAICS) codes 531110 (lessors of residential buildings and dwellings), 531120 (lessors of nonresidential buildings except miniwarehouses), 531190 (lessors of other real estate property), 237210 (land subdivision), or 236117 (new housing for-sale builders). You are not permitted to finance any business classified under NAICS codes 236118 (residential remodelers), 236210 (industrial building construction), or 236220 (commercial and institutional building construction), if such business is primarily engaged in construction or renovation of properties on its own account rather than as a hired contractor. You are permitted to finance a business classified under NAICS codes 531210 (offices of real estate agents and brokers), 531311 (residential property managers), 531312 (nonresidential property managers), 531320 (offices of real estate appraisers), or 531390 (other activities related to real estate), only if such business derives at least 80 percent of its revenue from non-Affiliate sources.

(2) You are not permitted to finance a Small Business, regardless of NAICS classification, if the Financing is to be used to acquire or refinance real property, unless the Small Business:

(i) Is acquiring an existing property and will use at least 51 percent of the usable square footage for an eligible business purpose; or

(ii) Is building or renovating a building and will use at least 67 percent of the usable square footage for an eligible business purpose; or

(iii) Occupies the subject property and uses at least 67 percent of the usable square footage for an eligible business purpose.

(d) *Project Financing.* You are not permitted to finance a business if:

(1) The assets of the business are to be reduced or consumed, generally without replacement, as the life of the business progresses, and the nature of the business requires that a stream of cash payments be made to the business's financing sources, on a basis associated with the continuing sale of assets. Examples include real estate development projects and oil and gas wells; or

(2) The primary purpose of the Financing is to fund production of a single item or defined limited number of items, generally over a defined production period, and such production will constitute the majority of the activities of the Small Business. Examples include motion pictures and electric generating plants.

(e) *Farm land purchases.* You are not permitted to finance the acquisition of farm land. Farm land means land which is or is intended to be used for agricultural or forestry purposes, such as the production of food, fiber, or wood, or is so taxed or zoned.

(f) *Public interest.* You are not permitted to finance any business if the proceeds are to be used for purposes contrary to the public interest, including but not limited to activities which are in violation of law, or inconsistent with free competitive enterprise.

(g) *Foreign investment*—(1) *General rule.* You are not permitted to finance a business if:

(i) The funds will be used substantially for a foreign operation; or

(ii) At the time of the Financing or within one year thereafter, more than 49 percent of the employees or tangible assets of the Small Business are located outside the United States (unless you can show, to SBA's satisfaction, that the Financing was used for a specific domestic purpose).

(2) *Exception.* This paragraph (g) does not prohibit a Financing used to acquire foreign materials and equipment or foreign property rights for use or sale in the United States.

(h) *Associated supplier.* You are not permitted to finance a business that purchases, or will purchase, goods or services from a supplier who is your Associate, except under the following conditions:

(1) The amount of goods and services purchased (or to be purchased) from your Associate with the proceeds of the Financing, or with funds released as a result of the Financing, is less than 50 percent of the total amount of the Financing (75 percent for a Section 301(d) Licensee);

(2) The price of such goods and services is no higher than that charged other customers of your Associate; and

(3) The Small Business purchases no capital goods from your Associate.

(i) *Financing Licensees.* You are not permitted to provide funds, directly or indirectly, that the Small Business will use:

(1) To purchase stock in or provide capital to a Licensee; or

(2) To repay an indebtedness incurred for the purpose of investing in a Licensee.

[61 FR 3189, Jan. 31, 1996, as amended at 63 FR 5867, Feb. 5, 1998; 64 FR 70995, Dec. 20, 1999; 79 FR 62823, Oct. 21, 2014; 82 FR 39340, Aug. 18, 2017]

§ 107.730 Financings which constitute conflicts of interest.

(a) *General rule.* You must not self-deal to the prejudice of a Small Business, the Licensee, its shareholders or partners, or SBA. Unless you obtain a prior written exemption from SBA for special instances in which a Financing may further the purposes of the Act despite presenting a conflict of interest, you must not directly or indirectly:

(1) Provide Financing to any of your Associates, except for a Financing to an Associate that meets all of the following conditions:

(i) The Small Business that receives the Financing is your Associate, pursuant to paragraph (8)(ii) of the Associate definition in § 107.50, only because an investment fund that is your Associate holds a 10% or greater equity interest in the Small Business.

(ii) You and the Associate investment fund previously invested in the Small Business at the same time and on the same terms and conditions.

(iii) You and the Associate investment fund are providing follow-on financing to the Small Business at the same time, on the same terms and conditions, and in the same proportionate dollar amounts as your respective investments in the previous round(s) of financing (for example, if you invested $2 million and your Associate invested $1 million in the previous round, your respective follow-on investments would be in the same 2:1 ratio).

(2) Provide Financing to an Associate of another Licensee if one of your Associates has received or will receive any direct or indirect Financing or a Commitment from that Licensee or a third Licensee (including Financing or Commitments received under any understanding, agreement, or cross dealing, reciprocal or circular arrangement).

(3) Borrow money from:

(i) A Small Business Financed by you;

(ii) An officer, director, or owner of at least a 10 percent equity interest in such business; or

(iii) A Close Relative of any such officer, director, or equity owner.

(4) Provide Financing to a Small Business to discharge an obligation to your Associate or free other funds to pay such obligation. This paragraph (a)(4) does not apply if the obligation is to an Associate Lending Institution and is a line of credit or other obligation incurred in the normal course of business.

(5) Provide Financing to a Small Business for the purpose of purchasing property from your Associate, except as permitted under § 107.720(h).

(b) *Rules applicable to Associates.* Without SBA' s prior written approval, your Associates must not, directly or indirectly:

(1) Borrow money from any Person described in paragraph (a)(3) of this section.

(2) Receive from a Small Business any compensation in connection with Assistance you provide (except as permitted under §§ 107.825(c) and 107.900), or anything of value for procuring, attempting to procure, or influencing your action with respect to such Assistance.

(c) *Applicability of other laws.* You are also bound by any restrictions in Federal or State laws governing conflicts of interest and fiduciary obligations.

(d) *Financings with Associates*—(1) *Financings with Associates requiring prior approval.* Without SBA's prior written approval, you may not Finance any business in which your Associate has either a voting equity interest, or total equity interests (including potential interests), of at least five percent.

(2) *Other Financings with Associates.* If you and an Associate provide Financing to the same Small Business, either at the same time or at different times, you must be able to demonstrate to SBA's satisfaction that the terms and conditions are (or were) fair and equitable to you, taking into account any differences in the timing of each party's financing transactions.

(3) *Exceptions to paragraphs (d)(1) and (d)(2) of this section.* A Financing that falls into one of the following categories is exempt from the prior approval requirement in paragraph (d)(1) of this section or is presumed to be fair and equitable to you for the purposes of paragraph (d)(2) of this section, as appropriate:

(i) Your Associate is a Lending Institution that is providing financing under a credit facility in order to meet the operational needs of the Small Business, and the terms of such financing are usual and customary.

(ii) Your Associate invests in the Small Business on the same terms and conditions and at the same time as you.

(iii) Both you and your Associate are leveraged Licensees, and both have outstanding Participating Securities or neither has outstanding Participating Securities.

(iv) You have no outstanding Leverage and do not intend to issue Leverage in the future, and your Associate either is not a Licensee or has no outstanding Leverage and does not intend to issue Leverage in the future.

(e) *Use of Associates to manage Portfolio Concerns.* To protect your investment, you may designate an Associate to serve as an officer, director, or other participant in the management of a Small Business. You must identify any such Associate in your records available for SBA's review under § 107.600.

Without SBA's prior written approval, the Associate must not:

(1) Have any other direct or indirect financial interest in the Portfolio Concern that exceeds, or has the potential to exceed, 5 percent of the Portfolio Concern's equity.

(2) Have served for more than 30 days as an officer, director or other participant in the management of the Portfolio Concern before you provided Financing.

(3) Receive any income or anything of value from the Portfolio Concern unless it is for your benefit, with the exception of director's fees, expenses, and distributions based upon the Associate's ownership interest in the Concern.

(f) *1940 and 1980 Act Companies: SEC exemptions.* If you are a 1940 or 1980 Act Company and you receive an exemption from the Securities and Exchange Commission for a transaction described in this § 107.730, you need not obtain SBA's approval of the transaction. However, you must promptly notify SBA of the transaction and satisfy the public notice requirements in paragraph (g) of this section.

(g) *Public notice.* Before granting an exemption under this § 107.730, SBA will publish notice of the transaction in the FEDERAL REGISTER.

[61 FR 3189, Jan. 31, 1996, as amended at 63 FR 5867, Feb. 5, 1998; 64 FR 70996, Dec. 20, 1999; 77 FR 20294, Apr. 4, 2012]

§ 107.740 Portfolio diversification ("overline" limitation).

(a) *General rule.* This § 107.740 applies if you have outstanding Leverage or intend to issue Leverage in the future. Unless SBA approved your license application based upon a plan to issue less than two tiers of Leverage, you may provide Financing or a Commitment to a Small Business if the resulting amount of your aggregate Financings and Commitments to such Small Business and its Affiliates does not exceed 30 percent of the sum of:

(1) Your Regulatory Capital as of the date of the Financing or Commitment; plus

(2) Any Distribution(s) you made under § 107.1570(b), during the five years preceding the date of the Financing or Commitment, which reduced your Regulatory Capital; plus

(3) Any Distribution(s) you made under § 107.585, during the five years preceding the date of the Financing or Commitment, which reduced your Regulatory Capital by no more than two percent or which SBA approves for inclusion in the sum determined in this paragraph (a).

(b) *Lower overline limit.* If SBA approved your license application based upon a plan to issue less than two tiers of Leverage, the applicable percentage of the amount computed in paragraphs (a)(1) though (a)(3) of this section will be:

(1) 20 percent if the plan contemplates one tier of Leverage.

(2) 25 percent if the plan contemplates 1.5 tiers of Leverage.

(c) Outstanding Financings. For the purposes of paragraphs (a) and (b) of this section, you must measure each outstanding Financing at its original cost (including any amount of the Financing that was previously written off).

[74 FR 33915, July 14, 2009]

§ 107.750 Conditions for financing a change of ownership of a Small Business.

You may finance a change of ownership of a Small Business only under the conditions set forth in this section.

(a) The Financing must:

(1) Promote the sound development or preserve the existence of the Small Business;

(2) Help create a Small Business as a result of a corporate divestiture; or

(3) Facilitate ownership in a Disadvantaged Business.

(b) The Resulting Concern (as defined in paragraph (c) of this section) must:

(1) Be a Small Business under § 107.700;

(2) Have 500 or fewer full-time equivalent employees; or meet one of the appropriate debt/equity ratio tests:

(i) If you have outstanding Leverage, the Resulting Concern's ratio of debt to equity must be no more than 5 to 1; or

(ii) If you have no outstanding Leverage, the Resulting Concern's ratio of debt to equity must be no more than 8 to 1.

(c) *Definitions.* (1) The "Resulting Concern" is determined by viewing the business as though the change of ownership had already occurred, giving effect to all contemplated financing, mergers, and acquisitions.

(2) For purposes of this section, "debt" means long-term debt, including contingent liabilities, but excluding accounts payable, operating leases, letters of credit, subordinated notes payable to the seller, any other liabilities approved for exclusion by SBA and short-term working capital loans (so long as the loans carry a zero balance for 30 consecutive days during the concern's fiscal year).

(3) For purposes of this section, "equity" means common and preferred stock (corporation), contributed capital (partnership), or membership interests (limited liability company).

§ 107.760 How a change in size or activity of a Portfolio Concern affects the Licensee and the Portfolio Concern.

(a) *Effect on Licensee of a change in size of a Portfolio Concern.* If a Portfolio Concern no longer qualifies as a Small Business you may keep your investment in the concern and:

(1) Subject to the overline limitations of § 107.740, you may provide additional Financing to the concern up to the time it makes a public offering of its securities.

(2) Even after the concern makes a public offering, you may exercise any stock options, warrants, or other rights to purchase Equity Securities which you acquired before the public offering, or fund Commitments you made before the public offering.

(b) *Effect of a change in business activity occurring within one year of Licensee's initial Financing*—(1) *Retention of Investment.* Unless you receive SBA's written approval, you may not keep your investment in a Portfolio Concern, small or otherwise, which becomes ineligible by reason of a change in its business activity within one year of your initial investment.

(2) *Request for SBA's approval to retain investment.* If you request that SBA approve the retention of your investment, your request must include sufficient evidence to demonstrate that the change in business activity was caused by an unforeseen change in circumstances and was not contemplated at the time the Financing was made.

(3) *Additional Financing.* If SBA approves your request to retain an investment under paragraph (b)(2) of this section, you may provide additional Financing to the Portfolio Concern to the extent necessary to protect against the loss of the amount of your original investment, subject to the overline limitations of § 107.740.

(c) *Effect of a change in business activity occurring more than one year after the initial Financing.* If a Portfolio Concern becomes ineligible because of a change in business activity more than one year after your initial Financing you may:

(1) Retain your investment; and

(2) Provide additional Financing to the Portfolio Concern to the extent necessary to protect against the loss of the amount of your original investment, subject to the overline limitations of § 107.740.

STRUCTURING LICENSEE'S FINANCING OF ELIGIBLE SMALL BUSINESSES: TYPES OF FINANCING

§ 107.800 Financings in the form of Equity Securities.

(a) You may purchase the Equity Securities of a Small Business. You may not, inadvertently or otherwise:

(1) Become a general partner in any unincorporated business; or

(2) Become jointly or severally liable for any obligations of an unincorporated business.

(b) *Definition.* Equity Securities means stock of any class in a corporation, stock options, warrants, limited partnership interests in a limited partnership, membership interests in a limited liability company, or joint venture interests. If the Financing agreement contains debt-type acceleration provisions or includes redemption provisions, other than those permitted under § 107.850, the security will be considered a Debt Security for purposes of § 107.855 and § 107.1150(c)(1).

[61 FR 3189, Jan. 31, 1996, as amended at 74 FR 33915, July 14, 2009]

§ 107.810 Financings in the form of Loans.

You may make Loans to Small Businesses. A Loan means a transaction evidenced by a debt instrument with no provision for you to acquire Equity Securities.

§ 107.815 Financings in the form of Debt Securities.

You may purchase Debt Securities from Small Businesses.

(a) *Definitions.* Debt Securities are instruments evidencing a loan with an option or any other right to acquire Equity Securities in a Small Business or its Affiliates, or a loan which by its terms is convertible into an equity position, or a loan with a right to receive royalties that are excluded from the Cost of Money pursuant to § 107.855(g)(12). Consideration must be paid for all options that you acquire.

(b) *Restriction on options obtained by Licensee's management and employees.* If you have outstanding Leverage or plan to obtain Leverage, your employees, officers, directors or general partners, or the general partners of the management company that is providing services to you or to your general partner, may obtain options in a Financed Small Business only if:

(1) They participate in the Financing on a pari passu basis with you; or

(2) SBA gives its prior written approval; or

(3) The options received are compensation for service as a member of the board of directors of the Small Business, and such compensation does not exceed that paid to other outside directors. In the absence of such directors, fees must be reasonable when compared with amounts paid to outside directors of similar companies.

[61 FR 3189, Jan. 31, 1996, as amended at 65 FR 69432, Nov. 17, 2000]

§ 107.820 Financings in the form of guarantees.

At the request of a Small Business or where necessary to protect your existing investment, you may guarantee the monetary obligation of a Small Business to any non-Associate creditor.

(a) You may not issue a guaranty if:

(1) You would become subject to State regulation as an insurance, guaranty or surety business;

(2) The amount of the guaranty plus any direct Financings to the Small Business exceed the overline limitations of § 107.740, except that a pledge of the Equity Securities of the issuer or a subordination of your lien or creditor position does not count toward your overline; or

(3) The total financing cost to the Small Business exceeds the cost of money limits of § 107.855.

(b) *Pledge of Licensee's assets as guaranty.* For purposes of this section, a guaranty with recourse only to specific asset(s) you have pledged is equal to the fair market value of such asset(s) or the amount of the debt guaranteed, whichever is less.

§ 107.825 Purchasing securities from an underwriter or other third party.

(a) *Securities purchased through or from an underwriter.* You may purchase the securities of a Small Business through or from an underwriter if:

(1) You purchase such securities within 90 days of the date the public offering is first made;

(2) Your purchase price is no more than the original public offering price; and

(3) The amount paid by you for the securities (less ordinary and reasonable underwriting charges and commissions) has been, or will be, paid to the Small Business, and the underwriter certifies in writing that this requirement has been met.

(b) *Recordkeeping requirements.* If you have outstanding Leverage or plan to obtain Leverage, you must keep records available for SBA's inspection which show the relevant details of the transaction, including, but not limited to, date, price, commissions, and the underwriter's certifications required under paragraph (c) of this section.

(c) *Underwriter's requirements.* If you have outstanding Leverage or plan to obtain Leverage, the underwriter must certify whether it is your Associate. You may pay reasonable and customary commissions and expenses to an Associate underwriter for the portion of an offering that you purchase, provided it is no more than 25 percent of the total offering. If you buy more than 25 percent of the offering, the amount you pay to the Associate underwriter must not exceed the total of the application and closing fees and reimbursable expenses permitted by § 107.860.

(d) *Securities purchased from another Licensee or from SBA.* You may purchase from, or exchange with, another Licensee, Portfolio securities (or any interest therein). Such purchase or exchange may only be made on a non-recourse basis. You may not have more than one-third of your total assets(valued at cost) invested in such securities. If you have previously sold Portfolio Securities (or any interest therein) on a recourse basis, you shall include the amount for which you may be contingently liable in your overline computation.

(e) *Purchases of securities from other non-issuers.* You may purchase securities of a Small Business from a non-issuer not previously described in this § 107.825 if:

(1) Such acquisition is a reasonably necessary part of the overall sound Financing of the Small Business under the Act; or

(2) The securities are acquired to finance a change of ownership under § 107.750.

STRUCTURING LICENSEE'S FINANCING OF AN ELIGIBLE SMALL BUSINESS: TERMS AND CONDITIONS OF FINANCING

§ 107.830 Minimum duration/term of financing.

(a) *General rule.* The duration/term of all your Financings must be for a minimum period of one year.

(b) *Restrictions on mandatory redemption of Equity Securities.* If you have acquired Equity Securities, options or warrants on terms that include redemption by the Small Business, you must not require redemption by the Small Business within the first year of your acquisition except as permitted in § 107.850.

(c) *Special rules for Loans and Debt Securities*—(1) *Term.* The minimum term for Loans and Debt Securities starts with the first disbursement of the Financing.

(2) *Prepayment.* You must permit voluntary prepayment of Loans and Debt Securities by the Small Business. You must obtain SBA's prior written approval of any restrictions on the ability of the Small Business to prepay other than the imposition of a reasonable prepayment penalty under paragraph (c)(3) of this section.

(3) *Prepayment penalties.* You may charge a reasonable prepayment penalty which must be agreed upon at the time of the Financing. If SBA determines that a prepayment penalty is unreasonable, you must refund the entire penalty to the Small Business. A prepayment penalty equal to 5 percent of the outstanding balance during the first year of any Financing, declining by one percentage point per year through the fifth year, is considered reasonable.

[61 FR 3189, Jan. 31, 1996, as amended at 69 FR 8098, Feb. 23, 2004]

§ 107.835 Exceptions to minimum duration/term of Financing.

You may make a Short-term Financing for a term less than one year if the Financing is:

(a) An interim Financing in contemplation of long-term Financing. The contemplated long-term Financing must be in an amount at least equal to the short-term Financing, and must be made by you alone or in participation with other investors; or

(b) For protection of your prior investment(s); or

(c) For the purpose of Financing a change of ownership under § 107.750. The total amount of such Financings may not exceed 20 percent of your Loans and Investments (at cost) at the end of any fiscal year; or

(d) For the purpose of aiding a Small Business in performing a contract awarded under a Federal, State, or local government set-aside program for "minority" or "disadvantaged" contractors.

[61 FR 3189, Jan. 31, 1996, as amended at 64 FR 52646, Sept. 30, 1999; 69 FR 8098, Feb. 23, 2004]

§ 107.840 Maximum term of Financing.

The maximum term of any Loan or Debt Security Financing must be no longer than 20 years.

§ 107.845 Maximum rate of amortization on Loans and Debt Securities.

The principal of any Loan (or the loan portion of any Debt Security) with a term of one year or less cannot be amortized faster than straight line. If the term is greater than one year, the principal cannot be amortized faster than straight line for the first year.

[69 FR 8098, Feb. 23, 2004]

§ 107.850 Restrictions on redemption of Equity Securities.

(a) A Portfolio Concern cannot be required to redeem Equity Securities earlier than one year from the date of the first closing unless:

(1) The concern makes a public offering, or has a change of management or control, or files for protection under the provisions of the Bankruptcy Code, or materially breaches your Financing agreement; or

(2) You make a follow-on investment, in which case the new securities may be redeemed in less than one year, but no earlier than the redemption date associated with your earliest Financing of the concern.

(b) The redemption price must be either:

(1) A fixed amount that is no higher than the price you paid for the securities; or

(2) An amount that cannot be fixed or determined before the time of redemption. In this case, the redemption price must be based on:

(i) A reasonable formula that reflects the performance of the concern (such as one based on earnings or book value); or

(ii) The fair market value of the concern at the time of redemption, as determined by a professional appraisal performed under an agreement acceptable to both parties.

(c) Any method for determining the redemption price must be agreed upon no later than the date of the first (or only) closing of the Financing.

[61 FR 3189, Jan. 31, 1996, as amended at 64 FR 52646, Sept. 30, 1999; 69 FR 8098, Feb. 23, 2004]

§ 107.855 Interest rate ceiling and limitations on fees charged to Small Businesses ("Cost of Money").

"Cost of Money" means the interest and other consideration that you receive from a Small Business. Subject to lower ceilings prescribed by local law, the Cost of Money to the Small Business must not exceed the ceiling determined under this section.

(a) *Financings to which the Cost of Money rules apply.* This section applies to all Loans and Debt Securities. As required by § 107.800(b), you must include as Debt Securities any equity interests with redemption provisions that do not meet the restrictions in § 107.850.

(b) *When to determine the Cost of Money ceiling for a Financing.* You may determine your Cost of Money ceiling for a particular Financing as of the date you issue a Commitment or as of the date of the first closing of the Financing. Once determined, the Cost of Money ceiling remains fixed for the duration of the Financing.

(c) *How to determine the Cost of Money ceiling for a Financing.* At a minimum, you may use a Cost of Money ceiling of 19 percent for a Loan and 14 percent for a Debt Security. To determine whether you may charge more, do the following:

(1) Choose a base rate for your Cost of Money computation. The base rate may be either the Debenture Rate currently in effect plus the applicable Charge determined under § 107.1130(d)(1), or your own "Cost of Capital" as determined under paragraph (d) of this section.

(2) For a Loan, add 11 percentage points to the base rate; for a Debt Security, add 6 percentage points. In either case, round the sum down to the nearest eighth of one percent.

(3) If the result is more than 19 percent (for a Loan) or 14 percent (for a Debt Security), you may use it as your Cost of Money ceiling.

(4) If two or more Licensees participate in the same Financing of a Small Business, the base rate used in this paragraph (c) is the highest of the following:

(i) The current Debenture Rate plus the applicable Charge determined under § 107.1130(d)(1);

(ii) The Cost of Capital of the lead Licensee; or

(iii) The weighted average of the Cost of Capital for all Licensees participating in the Financing.

(d) *How to determine your Cost of Capital.* "Cost of Capital" is an optional computation of the weighted average interest rate you pay on your "qualified borrowings". "Qualified borrowings" means your Debentures together with your borrowings at or below the usual interest rate charged by banks in your locality on the date your loan was made.

(1) For any fiscal year, you may compute your Cost of Capital:

(i) As of the first day of your fiscal year, to remain in effect for the entire year; or

(ii) As of the first day of every fiscal quarter during the fiscal year, to remain in effect for the duration of the quarter.

(2) For each qualified borrowing outstanding at your last fiscal year or fiscal quarter end, multiply the ending principal balance (net of related unamortized fees) by the number of days during the past four fiscal quarters that the borrowing was outstanding, and divide the result by 365.

(3) Add together the amounts computed for all borrowings under paragraph (d)(2) of this section. The result is your weighted average borrowings.

(4) For all qualified borrowings outstanding at your last fiscal year or fiscal quarter end, determine the aggregate interest expense for the past four fiscal quarters, excluding amortization of loan fees. For the purposes of this paragraph (d)(4):

(i) Interest expense on Debentures includes the 1 percent Charge paid by a Licensee under § 107.1130(d)(1); and

(ii) Section 301(d) Licensees with outstanding subsidized Debentures are presumed to have paid interest at the rate stated on the face of such Debentures, without regard to any subsidy paid by SBA.

(5) Divide the interest expense from paragraph (d)(4) of this section by the weighted average borrowings from paragraph (d)(3) of this section, and multiply by 100. The result is your Cost of Capital, which you may use to compute a Cost of Money ceiling under paragraph (c) of this section.

(e) *SBA review of Cost of Capital computation.* You must keep your Cost of Capital computations in a separate file available for SBA's review.

(1) A computation that is kept in such a file and is audited by your independent public accountant is considered correct unless SBA demonstrates otherwise.

(2) If a computation is not kept in such a file or is unaudited, you must prove its accuracy to SBA's satisfaction.

(f) *Charges included in the Cost of Money.* The Cost of Money includes all interest, points, discounts, fees, royalties, profit participation, and any other consideration you receive from a Small Business, except for the specific exclusions in paragraph (g) of this section. For equity interests subject to the Cost of Money rules (see paragraph (a) of this section), you must include:

(1) The portion of the fixed redemption price that exceeds your original cost.

(2) Any amount of a redemption that is paid out of accounts other than the Small Business's capital accounts (capital, paid-in surplus, or retained earnings of a corporation; or partners' capital of a partnership).

(g) *Charges excluded from the Cost of Money.* You may exclude from the Cost of Money:

(1) Discount on the loan portion of a Debt Security, if such discount exists solely as the result of the allocation of value to detachable stock purchase warrants in accordance with generally accepted accounting principles.

(2) Closing fees, application fees, and expense reimbursements, each as permitted under § 107.860.

(3) Reasonable prepayment penalties permitted under § 107.830(d)(3).

(4) Out-of-pocket conveyance and/or recordation fees and taxes.

(5) Reasonable closing costs.

(6) Fees for management services as permitted under § 107.900.

(7) Reasonable and necessary out-of-pocket expenses you incur to monitor the Financing.

(8) Board of director fees not in excess of those paid to other outside directors, if your board representation meets the requirements of § 107.730(e).

(9) A reasonable fee for arranging financing for a Small Business from a source that is neither a Licensee nor an Associate of yours. The Small Business must agree in writing to pay such a fee before you arrange the financing.

(10) The difference between the contractual interest rate of the Financing and a default rate of interest permitted as follows:

(i) If a Small Business is in default, you may charge a default rate of interest as much as 7 percentage points higher than the contractual rate until the default is cured.

(ii) For this purpose, "default" means either failure to pay an amount when due or failure to provide information required under the Financing documents.

(11) Royalty payments based on improvement in the performance of the Small Business after the date of the Financing.

(12) Gains realized on the disposition of Equity Securities issued by the Small Business.

(h) *How to evaluate compliance with the Cost of Money ceiling.* You must determine whether a Financing is within the Cost of Money ceiling based on its discounted cash flows, as follows:

(1) Beginning with the date of the first disbursement ("period zero"), identify your cash inflows and cash outflows for each period of the Financing. The appropriate period to use (such as years, quarters, or months) depends on how you have structured the disbursements and payments.

(2) Discount the cash flows back to the first disbursement date using the Cost of Money ceiling from paragraph (d) of this section as the discount rate.

(3) If the result is zero or less, the Financing is within the Cost of Money ceiling; if it is greater than zero, the Financing exceeds the Cost of Money ceiling.

[61 FR 3189, Jan. 31, 1996, as amended at 63 FR 5867, Feb. 5, 1998; 64 FR 52646, Sept. 30, 1999; 65 FR 69432, Nov. 17, 2000; 77 FR 20294, Apr. 4, 2012]

§ 107.860 Financing fees and expense reimbursements a Licensee may receive from a Small Business.

You may collect Financing fees and receive expense reimbursements from a Small Business only as permitted under this § 107.860.

(a) *Application fee.* You may collect a nonrefundable application fee from a Small Business to review its Financing application. The application fee may be collected at the same time as the closing fee under paragraph (c) or (d) of this section, or earlier. The fee must be:

(1) No more than 1 percent of the amount of Financing requested (or, if two or more Licensees participate in the Financing, their combined application fees are no more than 1 percent of the total Financing requested); and

(2) Agreed to in writing by the Financing applicant.

(b) *SBA review of application fees.* For any fiscal year, if the number of application fees you collect is more than twice the number of Financings closed, SBA in its sole discretion may determine that you are engaged in activities not contemplated by the Act, in violation of § 107.500.

(c) *Closing fee—Loans.* You may charge a closing fee on a Loan if:

(1) The fee is no more than 2 percent of the Financing amount (or, if two or more Licensees participate in the Financing, their combined closing fees are no more than 2 percent of the total Financing amount); and

(2) You charge the fee no earlier than the date of the first disbursement.

(d) *Closing fee—Debt or Equity Financings.* You may charge a Closing Fee on a Debt Security or Equity Security Financing if:

(1) The fee is no more than 4 percent of the Financing amount (or, if two or more Licensees participate in the Financing, their combined closing fees are no more than 4 percent of the total Financing amount); and

(2) You charge the fee no earlier than the date of the first disbursement.

(e) *Limitation on dual fees.* If another Licensee or an Associate of yours collects a transaction fee under § 107.900(e) in connection with your Financing of a Small Business, the sum of the transaction fee and your application and closing fees cannot exceed the maximum application and closing fees permitted under this § 107.860.

(f) *Expense reimbursements.* You may charge a Small Business for the reasonable out-of-pocket expenses, other than Management Expenses, that you incur to process its Financing application. If SBA determines that any of your reimbursed expenses are unreasonable or are Management Expenses, SBA will require you to include such amounts in the Cost of Money or refund them to the Small Business.

(g) *Breakup fee.* If a Small Business accepts your Commitment and then fails to close the Financing because it has accepted funds from another source, you may charge a "breakup fee" equal to the closing fee that you would have been permitted to charge under paragraph (c) or (d) of this section.

[61 FR 3189, Jan. 31, 1996; 61 FR 41496, Aug. 9, 1996]

§ 107.865 Control of a Small Business by a Licensee.

(a) *In general.* You, or you and your Associates (in the latter case, the "Investor Group"), may exercise Control over a Small Business for purposes connected to your investment, through ownership of voting securities, management agreements, voting trusts, majority representation on the board of directors, or otherwise. The period of such Control will be limited to the seventh anniversary of the date on which such Control was initially acquired, or any earlier date specified by the terms of any investment agreement.

(b) *Presumption of control.* Control over a Small Business based on ownership of voting securities will be presumed to exist whenever you or the Investor Group own or control, directly or indirectly:

(1) At least 50 percent of the outstanding voting securities, if there are fewer than 50 shareholders; or

(2) More than 25 percent of the outstanding voting securities, if there are 50 or more shareholders; or

(3) At least 20 percent of the outstanding voting securities, if there are 50 or more shareholders and no other party holds a larger block.

(c) *Rebuttals to presumption of Control.* A presumption of Control under paragraph (b) of this section is rebutted if:

(1) The management of the Small Business owns at least a 25 percent interest in the voting securities of the business; and

(2) The management of the Small Business can elect at least 40 percent of the board members of a corporation, general partners of a limited partnership, or managers of a limited liability company, as appropriate, and the Investor Group can elect no more than 40 percent. The balance of such officials may be elected through mutual agreement by management and the Investor Group.

(d) *Extension of Control.* With SBA's prior written approval you, or the Investor Group, may retain Control for such additional period as may be reasonably necessary to complete divestiture of Control or to ensure the financial stability of the portfolio company.

(e) *Additional Financing for businesses under Licensee's Control.* If you assume Control of a Small Business, you may later provide additional Financing, without an exemption under § 107.730(a)(1).

[61 FR 3189, Jan. 31, 1996, as amended at 63 FR 5867, Feb. 5, 1998; 64 FR 52646, Sept. 30, 1999; 67 FR 64790, Oct. 22, 2002]

§ 107.880 Assets acquired in liquidation of Portfolio securities.

You may acquire assets in full or partial liquidation of a Small Business's obligation to you under the conditions permitted by this § 107.880. The assets may be acquired from the Small Business, a guarantor of its obligation, or another party.

(a) *Timely disposition of assets.* You must dispose of assets acquired in liquidation of a Portfolio security within a reasonable period of time.

(b) *Permitted expenditures to preserve assets.* (1) You may incur reasonably necessary expenditures to maintain and preserve assets acquired.

(2) You may incur reasonably necessary expenditures for improvements to render such assets saleable.

(3) You may make payments of mortgage principal and interest (including amounts in arrears when you acquired the asset), pay taxes when due, and pay for necessary insurance coverage.

(c) *SBA approval of expenditures.* This paragraph (c) applies if you have outstanding Leverage or are applying for Leverage. Any application for SBA approval under this paragraph must specify all expenses estimated to be necessary pending disposal of the assets. Without SBA's prior written approval:

(1) Your total expenditures under paragraphs (b)(1) and (b)(2) of this section plus your total Financing(s) to the Small Business must not exceed your overline limit under §107.740; and

(2) Your total expenditures under paragraph (b) of this section plus your total Financing(s) to the Small Business must not exceed 35 percent of your Regulatory Capital.

LIMITATIONS ON DISPOSITION OF ASSETS

§ 107.885 Disposition of assets to Licensee's Associates or to competitors of Portfolio Concern.

Sale of assets to Associate. Except with SBA's prior written approval, you are not permitted to dispose of assets (including assets acquired in liquidation) to any Associate if you have outstanding Leverage or Earmarked Assets. As a prerequisite to such approval, you must demonstrate that the proposed terms of disposal are at least as favorable to you as the terms obtainable elsewhere.

[61 FR 3189, Jan. 31, 1996, as amended at 67 FR 64791, Oct. 22, 2002]

MANAGEMENT SERVICES AND FEES

§ 107.900 Management fees for services provided to a Small Business by Licensee or its Associate.

This §107.900 applies to management services that you or your Associate provide to a Small Business during the term of a Financing or prior to Financing. It does not apply to management services that you or your Associate provide to a Small Business that you do not finance. Fees permitted under this section are not included in the Cost of Money (see §107.855).

(a) *Permitted management fees.* You or your Associate may provide management services to a Small Business financed by you if:

(1) You or your Associate have entered into a written contract with the Small Business;

(2) The fees charged are for services actually performed;

(3) Services are provided on an hourly fee, project fee, or other reasonable basis; and

(4) You can demonstrate to SBA, upon request, that the rate does not exceed the prevailing rate charged for comparable services by other organizations in the geographic area of the Small Business.

(b) *Fees for service as a board member.* You or your Associate may receive fees in the form of cash, warrants, or other payments, for services provided as members of the board of directors of a Small Businesses Financed by you. The fees must not exceed those paid to other outside board members. In the absence of such board members, fees must be reasonable when compared with amounts paid to outside directors of similar companies.

(c) *SBA approval required.* You must obtain SBA's prior written approval of any management contract that does not satisfy paragraphs (a) or (b) of this section.

(d) *Recordkeeping requirements.* You must keep a record of hours spent and amounts charged to the Small Business, including expenses charged.

(e) *Transaction fees.* (1) You may charge reasonable transaction fees for work you or your Associate perform to prepare a client for a public offering, private offering, or sale of all or part of the business, and for assisting with the transaction. Compensation may be in the form of cash, notes, stock, and/or options.

(2) Your Associate may charge market rate investment banking fees to a Small Business on that portion of a Financing that you do not provide.

Subpart H—Non-leveraged Licensees—Exceptions to Regulations

§ 107.1000 Licensees without Leverage—exceptions to the regulations.

The regulatory exceptions in this section apply to Licensees with no outstanding Leverage or Earmarked Assets.

(a) You are exempt from the following provisions (but you must come into compliance with them to become eligible for Leverage):

(1) The overline limitation in § 107.740.

(2) The restrictions in § 107.530 on investments of idle funds, provided you do not engage in activities not contemplated by the Act.

(3) The restrictions in § 107.550 on third-party debt.

(4) The restrictions in § 107.880 on expenses incurred to maintain or improve assets acquired in liquidation of Portfolio securities.

(5) The recordkeeping requirements and fee limitations in § 107.825 (b) and (c), respectively, for securities purchased through or from an underwriter.

(b) You are exempt from the requirements to obtain SBA's prior approval for:

(1) A decrease in your Regulatory Capital of more than two percent under § 107.585 (but not below the minimum required under the Act or these regulations). You must report the reduction to SBA within 30 days.

(2) Disposition of any asset to your Associate under § 107.885.

(3) A contract to employ an Investment Adviser/Manager under § 107.510. However, you must notify SBA of the Management Expenses to be incurred under such contract, or of any subsequent material changes in such Management Expenses, within 30 days of execution. In order to become eligible for Leverage, you must have the contract approved by SBA.

(4) Your initial Management Expenses under § 107.140 and increases in your Management Expenses under § 107.520. However, you must have your Management Expenses approved by SBA in order to become eligible for Leverage.

(5) Options obtained from a Small Business by your management or employees under § 107.815(b).

(c) You are exempt from the requirement in § 107.680 to obtain SBA's post approval of new directors and new officers, other than your chief operating officer. However, you must notify SBA of the new directors or officers within 30 days, and you must have all directors and officers approved by SBA in order to become eligible for Leverage.

Subpart I—SBA Financial Assistance for Licensees (Leverage)

General Information About Obtaining Leverage

§ 107.1100 Types of Leverage and application procedures.

(a) *Types of Leverageable available.* You may apply for Leverage from SBA in one or both of the following forms:

(1) The purchase or guarantee of your Debentures.

(2) The purchase or guarantee of your Participating Securities.

(b) *Applying for Leverage.* The Leverage application process has two parts. You must first apply for SBA's conditional commitment to reserve a specific amount of Leverage for your future use. You may then apply to draw down Leverage against the commitment. See §§ 107.1200 through 107.1240.

[63 FR 5868, Feb. 5, 1998, as amended at 64 FR 70996, Dec. 20, 1999; 82 FR 39341, Aug. 18, 2017]

§ 107.1120 General eligibility requirements for Leverage.

To be eligible for Leverage, you must:

(a) Demonstrate a need for Leverage, evidenced by your investment activity and a lack of sufficient funds for investment. For your first issuance of Leverage, if you have invested at least 50 percent of your Leverageable Capital, you are presumed to lack sufficient funds for investment.

(b) Have adequate Private Capital to satisfy the requirements for financial viability under § 107.200.

(c) Meet the minimum capital requirements of § 107.210, subject to the following additional conditions:

(1) If you were licensed after September 30, 1996 under the exception in § 107.210(a)(1), you will not be eligible for Leverage until you have Regulatory Capital of at least $5,000,000.

(2) If you were licensed on or before September 30, 1996, and have Regulatory Capital of less than $5,000,000 (less than $10,000,000 if you wish to issue Participating Securities):

(i) You must certify in writing that at least 50 percent of the aggregate dollar amount of your Financings extended after September 30, 1996 will be provided to Smaller Enterprises (as defined in § 107.710(a)); and

(ii) You must demonstrate to SBA's satisfaction that the approval of Leverage will not create or contribute to an unreasonable risk of default or loss to the United States government, based on such measurements of profitability and financial viability as SBA deems appropriate.

(d) For any Leverage draw that would cause you and any other Licensees under Common Control to have aggregate outstanding Leverage in excess of $150 million, certify that none of the Licensees has a condition of Capital Impairment. *See* also § 107.1150(b).

(e) For any Leverage request pursuant to § 107.1150(d)(2)(i), certify that at least 50 percent (in dollars) of your Financings made on or after the date of such request will be invested in Small Businesses located in low-income geographic areas.

(f) For any Leverage request pursuant to § 107.1150(d)(2)(ii), certify that at least 50 percent (in dollars) of the Financings made by each Licensee under Common Control on or after the date of such request will be invested in Small Businesses located in low-income geographic areas.

(g) Certify in writing that you are in compliance with the requirement to finance Smaller Enterprises in § 107.710(b).

(h) Show, to the satisfaction of SBA, that your management is qualified and has the knowledge, experience, and capability necessary for investing in the types of businesses contemplated by the Act, the regulations in this part and your business plan.

(i) Be in compliance with the regulations in this part.

(j) If required by SBA, have your Control Person(s) assume, in writing, personal responsibility for your Leverage, effective only if such Control Person(s) participate (directly or indirectly) in a transfer of Control not approved by SBA.

(k) If you are an Early Stage SBIC, certify in writing that in accordance with § 107.1810(f)(11), at least 50 percent of the aggregate dollar amount of your Financings will be provided to "early stage" companies as defined under the definition of Early Stage SBIC in § 107.50 of this part.

[61 FR 3189, Jan. 31, 1996, as amended at 63 FR 5868, Feb. 5, 1998; 64 FR 70996, Dec. 20, 1999; 74 FR 33916, July 14, 2009; 77 FR 25053, Apr. 27, 2012; 79 FR 62824, Oct. 21, 2014]

§ 107.1130 Leverage fees and additional charges payable by Licensee.

(a) *Leverage fee.* You must pay a leverage fee to SBA for each issuance of a Debenture or Participating Security. The fee is 3 percent of the face amount of the Leverage issued.

(b) *Payment of leverage fee.* (1) If you issue a Debenture or Participating Security to repay or redeem existing Leverage, you must pay the leverage fee before SBA will guarantee or purchase the new Leverage security.

(2) If you issue a Debenture or Participating Security that is not used to repay or redeem existing Leverage, SBA will deduct the leverage fee from the proceeds remitted to you, unless you prepaid the fee under § 107.1210.

(c) *Refundability.* The leverage fee is not refundable under any circumstances.

(d) *Additional charge for Leverage*—(1) *Debentures.* You must pay to SBA a Charge, not to exceed 1.38 percent per annum, on the outstanding amount of your Debentures issued on or after October 1, 1996, payable under the same terms and conditions as the interest on the Debentures. This Charge does not apply to Debentures issued pursuant to a Leverage commitment obtained from SBA on or before September 30, 1996.

(2) *Participating Securities.* You must pay to SBA a Charge, not to exceed 1.46 percent per annum, on the outstanding amount of your Participating Securities issued on or after October 1, 1996, payable under the same terms and conditions as the Prioritized Payments on the Participating Securities. This Charge does not apply to Participating Securities issued pursuant to a Leverage commitment obtained from SBA on or before September 30, 1996.

(e) *Other Leverage fees.* SBA may establish a fee structure for services performed by the CRA. SBA will not collect any fee for its guarantee of TCs.

[61 FR 3189, Jan. 31, 1996, as amended at 63 FR 5868, Feb. 5, 1998; 77 FR 25053, Apr. 27, 2012]

§ 107.1140 Licensee's acceptance of SBA remedies under §§ 107.1800 through 107.1820.

If you issue Leverage after April 25, 1994, you automatically agree to the terms and conditions in §§ 107.1800 through 107.1820 as they exist at the time of issuance. The effect of these terms and conditions is the same as if they were fully incorporated in the terms of your Leverage.

MAXIMUM AMOUNT OF LEVERAGE FOR WHICH A LICENSEE IS ELIGIBLE

§ 107.1150 Maximum amount of Leverage for a Section 301(c) Licensee.

A Section 301(c) Licensee, other than an Early Stage SBIC, may have maximum outstanding Leverage as set forth in paragraphs (a), (b), (d), and (e) of this section. An Early Stage SBIC may have maximum outstanding Leverage as set forth in paragraph (c) of this section. In general, SBA will approve Leverage commitment requests in excess of 200 percent of Regulatory Capital and draw requests in excess of 200 percent of Leverageable Capital only after a Licensee has demonstrated consistent, sustainable profitability based on a conservative investment strategy that limits downside risk. Any such Leverage request must be supported by an up-to-date business plan that reflects continuation of the Licensee's successful investment strategy and demonstrates the Licensee's ability to pay all SBA obligations in accordance with their terms.

(a) *Individual Licensee.* Subject to SBA's credit policies, if you are a Section 301(c) Licensee, the maximum amount of Leverage you may have outstanding at any time is the lesser of:

(1) 300 percent of your Leverageable Capital, or

(2) $150 million.

(b) *Multiple Licensees under Common Control.* Subject to SBA's credit policies, two or more Licenses under Common Control may have maximum aggregate outstanding Leverage of $350 million. However, for any Leverage draw(s) by one or more such Licensees that would cause the aggregate outstanding Leverage to exceed $150 million, each of the Licensees under Common Control must certify that it does not have a condition of Capital Impairment. *See* also § 107.1120(d).

(c) *Early Stage SBICs.* Subject to SBA's credit policies, if you are an Early Stage SBIC:

(1) The total amount of any and all Leverage commitments you receive from SBA shall not exceed 100 percent of your highest Regulatory Capital or $50 million, whichever is less;

(2) On a cumulative basis, the total amount of Leverage you have issued shall not exceed the total amount of capital paid in by your investors; and

(3) The maximum amount of Leverage you may have outstanding at any time is the lesser of:

(i) 100 percent of your Leverageable Capital, or

(ii) $50 million.

(d) *Additional Leverage based on investment in low-income geographic areas.* Subject to SBA's credit policies, you may have outstanding Leverage in excess of the amounts permitted by paragraphs (a) and (b) of this section in accordance with this paragraph (d). If you were licensed before October 1, 2009, you may seek additional Leverage under paragraph (d)(1) only. If you were licensed on or after October 1, 2009, you may seek additional Leverage under paragraph (d)(1) or (2), but not both. In this paragraph (d), "low income geographic areas" are as defined in § 108.50 of this chapter. Any investment that you use as a basis to seek additional leverage under this paragraph (d) cannot also be used to seek additional leverage under paragraph (e) of this section.

(1) *Investment in Smaller Enterprises located in low-income geographic areas.* To determine whether you may request a draw that would cause you to have outstanding Leverage in excess of the amount determined under paragraph (a) of this section:

(i) Determine the cost basis, as reported on your most recent filing of SBA Form 468, of any investments in the Equity Securities of a Smaller Enterprise located in a low-income geographic area.

(ii) Calculate the amount that equals 50 percent of your Leverageable Capital.

(iii) Subtract from your outstanding Leverage the lesser of paragraph (d)(1)(i) or (ii).

(iv) If the amount calculated in paragraph (d)(1)(iii) is less than the maximum leverage determined under paragraph (a) of this section, the difference between the two amounts equals your additional Leverage availability.

(2) *Investment in Small Businesses located in low-income geographic areas.* This paragraph (d)(2) applies only to Licensees licensed on or after October 1, 2009. You may substitute a maximum Leverage amount of $175,000,000 for the $150,000,000 set forth in paragraph (a)(2) of this section, and a maximum Leverage amount of $250,000,000 for the $225,000,000 set forth in paragraph (b) of this section, if you satisfy the following conditions:

(i) At least 50 percent (in dollars) of your Financings preceding the date of such request must have been invested in Small Businesses located in low-income geographic areas. In addition, you must certify that at least 50 percent (in dollars) of your Financings on or after the date of such request will be invested in Small Businesses located in low-income geographic areas.

(ii) If you are requesting a draw that would cause you and any other Licensees under Common Control to have aggregate outstanding Leverage in excess of $225,000,000, at least 50 percent (in dollars) of the Financings made by each Licensee under Common Control preceding the date of such request must have been invested in Small Businesses located in low-income geographic areas. In addition, each such Licensee must certify that at least 50 percent (in dollars) of its Financings on or after the date of such request will be invested in Small Businesses located in low-income geographic areas.

(e) *Additional Leverage based on Energy Saving Qualified Investments in Smaller Enterprises.* (1) Subject to SBA's credit policies, if you were licensed on or after October 1, 2008, you may have outstanding Leverage in excess of the amounts permitted by paragraphs (a) and (b) of this section in accordance with this paragraph (e). Any investment that you use as a basis to seek additional Leverage under this paragraph (e) cannot also be used to seek additional Leverage under paragraph (d) of this section.

(2) To determine whether you may request a draw that would cause you to have outstanding Leverage in excess of the amount determined under paragraph (a) of this section:

(i) Determine the cost basis, as reported on your most recent filing of SBA Form 468, of any Energy Saving Qualified Investments in a Smaller Enterprise that individually do not exceed 20% of your Regulatory Capital.

(ii) Calculate the amount that equals 33% of your Leverageable Capital.

(iii) Subtract from your outstanding Leverage the lesser of paragraph (e)(2)(i) or (ii).

(iv) If the amount calculated in paragraph (e)(2)(iii) is less than the maximum Leverage determined under paragraph (a) of this section, the difference between the two amounts equals your additional Leverage availability.

[74 FR 33916, July 14, 2009, as amended at 77 FR 23380, Apr. 19, 2012; 77 FR 25053, Apr. 27, 2012; 79 FR 62824, Oct. 21, 2014; 82 FR 39341, Aug. 18, 2017]

§ 107.1160 Maximum amount of Leverage for a Section 301(d) Licensee.

This section applies to Leverage issued by a Section 301(d) Licensee on or before September 30, 1996. Effective October 1, 1996, a Section 301(d) Licensee may apply to issue new Leverage, or refinance existing Leverage, only on the same terms permitted under § 107.1150.

(a) *Maximum amount of subsidized Leverage.* (1) "Subsidized Leverage" means Debentures with a reduced interest rate and Preferred Securities. If you are a Section 301(d) Licensee:

(i) The maximum amount of subsidized Leverage you may have outstanding at any time is the lesser of 400 percent of your Leverageable Capital, or $35,000,000. The same limit applies to a group of Section 301(d) Licensees under Common Control.

(ii) The maximum amount of Preferred Securities you may have outstanding at any time is 200 percent of your Leverageable Capital.

(2) Certain types and amounts of subsidized Leverage have special eligibility requirements (see paragraphs (c) and (d) of this section).

(b) *Maximum amount of total Leverage.* Use § 107.1150 to determine your maximum amount of Leverage as if you were a Section 301(c) Licensee. If the result is more than your maximum subsidized Leverage, then this is your maximum total (subsidized plus non-subsidized) Leverage. Otherwise, your maximum total Leverage is the same as your maximum subsidized Leverage. For Participating Securities, see § 107.1170.

(c) *Special eligibility requirements for fourth tier of Leverage.* A "fourth tier of Leverage" is any amount of outstanding Leverage in excess of 300 percent of your Leverageable Capital.

(1) To qualify for a fourth tier of Leverage, you must have invested (or have Commitments to invest) at least 30 percent of your "Total Funds Available for Investment" in "Venture Capital Financings" (see the definitions in paragraphs (e) and (f) of this section).

(2) While you have a fourth tier of Leverage, you must maintain Venture Capital Financings (at cost) that equal at least 30 percent of your Total Funds Available for Investment.

(d) *Special eligibility requirements for second tier of Preferred Securities.* A "second tier of Preferred Securities" is any amount of outstanding Preferred Securities in excess of 100 percent of your Leverageable Capital.

(1) To qualify for a second tier of Preferred Securities:

(i) If your license was issued after October 13, 1971, you must have at least $500,000 of Leverageable Capital.

(ii) You must have invested (or have Commitments to invest) at least the same dollar amount in Venture Capital Financings.

(2) While you have a second tier of Preferred Securities, you must maintain at least the same dollar amount of Venture Capital Financings (at cost).

(e) *Definition of "Total Funds Available for Investment".* Total Funds Available for Investment means the result obtained from the following formula:

$$T = .90 \times (CA + LI)$$

Where:

T = Total funds available for investment
CA = Total current assets
LI = Total Loans and Investment at cost (as reported on SBA Form 468), net of current maturities

(f) *Definition of "Venture Capital Financing".* Venture Capital Financing means an investment represented by common or preferred stock, a limited partnership interest, or a similar ownership interest; or by an unsecured debt instrument that is subordinated by its terms to all other borrowings of the issuer.

(1) A debt secured by any agreement with a third party is not a Venture Capital Financing, whether or not you have a security interest in any asset of the third party or have recourse against the third party.

(2) A Financing that originally qualified as a Venture Capital Financing will continue to qualify (at its original cost), even if you later must report it on SBA Form 468 under either Assets Acquired in Liquidation of Portfolio Securities or Operating Concerns Acquired.

[61 FR 3189, Jan. 31, 1996, as amended at 63 FR 5868, Feb. 5, 1998; 74 FR 33916, July 14, 2009]

§ 107.1170 Maximum amount of Participating Securities for any Licensee.

The maximum amount of Participating Securities you may have outstanding at any time is 200 percent of your Leverageable Capital. If you are a Section 301(d) Licensee, the maximum combined amount of Participating Securities and Preferred Securities you may have outstanding at any time is 200 percent of your Leverageable Capital.

SPECIAL RULES FOR LEVERAGE ISSUED BY AN EARLY STAGE SBIC

§ 107.1180 Required distributions to SBA by Early Stage SBICs.

(a) *Distribution requirement.* If you are an Early Stage SBIC with outstanding Leverage, you may make Distributions to your investors and to SBA only as permitted under this section. See also § 107.585. For the purposes of this section, "Distributions" do not include required payments to SBA of interest and Charges and payments of Leverage principal at maturity, all of which shall be paid in accordance with the terms of the Leverage. You may make a Distribution on any Payment Date. Unless SBA permits otherwise, you must notify SBA in writing of any planned distribution under this section, including computations of the amounts distributable to SBA and your investors, at least 10 business days before the distribution date.

(b) *How SBA will apply Distributions.* Any amounts you distribute to SBA, or its designated agent or Trustee, under this section will be applied to repayment of principal of outstanding Debentures in order of issue. You may prepay any Debenture in whole, but not in part, on any Payment Date without penalty.

(c) *Condition for making a Distribution.* You may make a Distribution under this section only if you have paid all interest and Charges on your outstanding Debentures that are due and payable, or will pay such interest and Charges simultaneously with your Distribution.

(d) *SBA's share of Distribution.* For each proposed Distribution, determine SBA's share of the Distribution as follows:

(1) Determine the highest ratio of outstanding Leverage to Leverageable Capital that you have ever attained (your "Highest Leverage Ratio"). For the purpose of determining your Highest Leverage Ratio, any deferred interest Debentures issued at a discount must be included in the computation at their face value.

(2) Determine SBA's percentage share of cumulative Distributions:

(i) If your Capital Impairment Percentage under § 107.1840 is less than 50 percent as of the Distribution date or your Highest Leverage Ratio equals 0.5 or less, except as provided in paragraph (d)(2)(iii) of this section, SBA's percentage share of cumulative Distributions equals:

[Highest Leverage Ratio/(Highest Leverage Ratio + 1)] × 100

For example, if your Highest Leverage Ratio equals 1, then SBA's share of any distribution you make will be 50 percent.

(ii) If your Capital Impairment Percentage under § 107.1840 is 50 percent or greater as of the Distribution date and your Highest Leverage Ratio is greater than 0.5, SBA's percentage share of cumulative Distributions equals 100 percent.

(iii) If you have a condition of Capital Impairment under § 107.1830 and your Highest Leverage Ratio equals 0.5 or less as of the Distribution date, SBA's percentage share of cumulative Distributions equals 100 percent.

(3) Multiply the sum of all your prior Distributions and your current proposed Distribution (including Distributions to SBA, your limited partners and your General Partner) by SBA's percentage share of cumulative Distributions as determined in paragraph (d)(2) of this section.

(4) From the result in paragraph (d)(3) of this section, subtract the sum of all your prior Distributions to SBA under this § 107.1180.

(5) The amount of your Distribution to SBA will be the least of:

(i) The result in paragraph (d)(4) of this section;

(ii) Your current proposed Distribution; or

(iii) Your outstanding Leverage.

(e) *Additional Leverage prepayment.* On any Payment Date, subject to the terms of your Leverage, you may make a payment to SBA to be applied to repayment of the principal of one or more outstanding Debentures in order of issue, without making any Distribution to your investors.

[77 FR 25053, Apr. 27, 2012]

§ 107.1181 Interest reserve requirements for Early Stage SBICs.

(a) *Reserve requirement.* If you are an Early Stage SBIC with outstanding Leverage, for each Debenture which requires periodic interest payments to SBA during the first five years of its term, you must maintain a reserve sufficient to pay the interest and Charges on such Debenture for the first 21 Payment Dates following the date of issuance. This reserve may consist of any combination of the following:

(1) Binding unfunded commitments from your Institutional Investors that cannot be called for any purpose other than the payment of interest and Charges to SBA, or the payment of any amounts due to SBA; and

(2) Cash maintained in a separate bank account or separate investment account permitted under § 107.530 of this part and separately identified in your financial statements as "restricted cash" available only for the purpose of paying interest and Charges to SBA, or for the payment of any amounts due to SBA.

(b) The required reserve associated with an individual Debenture shall be reduced on each Payment Date upon payment of the required interest and Charges. If you prepay a Debenture prior to the 21st Payment Date following its date of issuance, the reserve requirement associated with that Debenture shall be correspondingly eliminated.

(c) Your limited partnership agreement must incorporate the reserve requirement in paragraph (a) of this section.

[77 FR 25053, Apr. 27, 2012]

§ 107.1182 Valuation requirements for Early Stage SBICs based on Capital Impairment Percentage.

(a) If you are an Early Stage SBIC, you must compute your Capital Impairment Percentage and determine whether you have a condition of Capital Impairment in accordance with §§ 107.1830 and 107.1840 of this part.

(b) You must promptly notify SBA in writing if your Capital Impairment Percentage is at least 50 percent, even if your maximum permitted Capital Impairment Percentage is higher.

(c) Upon receipt of your notification under paragraph (b) of this section, or upon making its own determination that your Capital Impairment Percentage is at least 50 percent, SBA has the right to require you to engage, at your expense, an independent third party, acceptable to SBA, to prepare valuations of some or all of your Loans and Investments, as designated by SBA.

[77 FR 25053, Apr. 27, 2012]

CONDITIONAL COMMITMENTS BY SBA TO RESERVE LEVERAGE FOR A LICENSEE

§ 107.1200 SBA's Leverage commitment to a Licensee—application procedure, amount, and term.

(a) *General.* Under the provisions in §§ 107.1200 through 107.1240, you may apply for SBA's conditional commitment to reserve a specific amount and type of Leverage for your future use. You may then apply to draw down Leverage against the commitment.

(b) *Applying for a Leverage commitment.* SBA will notify you when it is accepting requests for Leverage commitments. Upon receipt of your request, SBA will send you a complete application package.

(c) *Limitations on the amount of a Leverage commitment.* The amount of a Leverage commitment must be a multiple of $5,000.

(d) *Term of Leverage commitment.* SBA's Leverage commitment will automatically lapse on the expiration date stated in the commitment letter issued to you by SBA.

[61 FR 3189, Jan. 31, 1996, as amended at 63 FR 5868, Feb. 5, 1998]

§ 107.1210 Payment of leverage fee upon receipt of commitment.

(a) *Partial prepayment of leverage fee.* As a condition of SBA's Leverage commitment, and before you draw any Leverage under such commitment, you must pay to SBA a non-refundable fee equal to 1 percent of the face amount of the Debentures or Participating Securities reserved under the commitment. This amount represents a partial prepayment of the 3 percent leverage fee established under § 107.1130(a).

(b) *Automatic cancellation of commitment.* Unless you pay the fee required under paragraph (a) of this section by 5:00 P.M. Eastern Time on the 30th calendar day following the issuance of SBA's Leverage commitment, the commitment will be automatically canceled.

[63 FR 5868, Feb. 5, 1998]

§ 107.1220 Requirement for Licensee to file quarterly financial statements.

As long as any part of SBA's Leverage commitment is outstanding, you must give SBA a Financial Statement on SBA Form 468 (Short Form) as of the close of each quarter of your fiscal year (other than the fourth quarter, which is covered by your annual filing of Form 468 under § 107.630(a)). You must file this form within 30 days after the close of the quarter. You will not be eligible for a draw if you are not in compliance with this § 107.1220.

[64 FR 70996, Dec. 20, 1999]

§ 107.1230 Draw-downs by Licensee under SBA's Leverage commitment.

(a) *Licensee's authorization of SBA to purchase or guarantee securities.* By submitting a request for a draw against SBA's Leverage commitment, you authorize SBA, or any agent or trustee SBA designates, to guarantee your Debenture or Participating Security and to sell it with SBA's guarantee.

(b) *Limitations on amount of draw.* The amount of a draw must be a multiple of $5,000. SBA, in its discretion, may determine a minimum dollar amount for draws against SBA's Leverage commitments. Any such minimum amounts will be published in Notices in the FEDERAL REGISTER from time to time.

(c) *Effect of regulatory violations on Licensee's eligibility for draws*—(1) *General rule.* You are eligible to make a draw against SBA's Leverage commitment only if you are in compliance with all applicable provisions of the Act and SBA regulations (i.e., no unresolved statutory or regulatory violations).

(2) *Exception to general rule.* If you are not in compliance, you may still be eligible for draws if:

(i) SBA determines that your outstanding violations are of non-substantive provisions of the Act or regulations and that you have not repeatedly violated any non-substantive provisions; or

(ii) You have agreed with SBA on a course of action to resolve your violations and such agreement does not prevent you from issuing Leverage.

(d) *Procedures for funding draws.* You may request a draw at any time during the term of the commitment. With each request, submit the following documentation:

(1) A statement certifying that there has been no material adverse change in your financial condition since your last filing of SBA Form 468 (see also § 107.1220 for SBA Form 468 filing requirements).

(2) If your request is submitted more than 30 days following the end of your fiscal year, but before you have submitted your annual filing of SBA Form 468 (Long Form) in accordance with § 107.630(a), a preliminary unaudited annual financial statement on SBA Form 468 (Short Form).

(3) A statement certifying that to the best of your knowledge and belief, you are in compliance with all provisions of the Act and SBA regulations (i.e., no unresolved regulatory or statutory violations), or a statement listing any specific violations you are aware of. Either statement must be executed by one of the following:

(i) An officer of the Licensee;

(ii) An officer of a corporate general partner of the Licensee; or

(iii) An individual who is authorized to act as or for a general partner of the Licensee.

(4) A statement that the proceeds are needed to fund one or more particular Small Businesses or to provide liquidity for your operations. If required by SBA, the statement must include the name and address of each Small Business, and the amount and anticipated closing date of each proposed Financing.

(e) *Reporting requirements after drawing funds.* (1) Within 30 calendar days after the actual closing date of each Financing funded with the proceeds of your draw, you must file an SBA Form 1031 confirming the closing of the transaction.

(2) If SBA required you to provide information concerning a specific planned Financing under paragraph (d)(3) of this section, and such Financing has not closed within 60 calendar days after the anticipated closing date, you must give SBA a written explanation of the failure to close.

(3) If you do not comply with this paragraph (e), you will not be eligible for additional draws. SBA may also determine that you are not in compliance with the terms of your Leverage under §§ 107.1810 or 107.1820.

[61 FR 3189, Jan. 31, 1996, as amended at 63 FR 5868, Feb. 5, 1998; 64 FR 70996, Dec. 20, 1999]

§ 107.1240 Funding of Licensee's draw request through sale to short-term investor.

(a) *Licensee's authorization of SBA to arrange sale of securities to short-term investor.* By submitting a request for a draw of Debenture or Participating Security Leverage, you authorize SBA, or any agent or trustee SBA designates, to enter into any agreements (and to bind you to such agreements) necessary to accomplish:

(1) The sale of your Debenture or Participating Security to a short-term investor at a rate that may be different from the Trust Certificate Rate which will be established at the time of the pooling of your security;

(2) The purchase of your security from the short-term investor, either by you or on your behalf; and

(3) The pooling of your security with other securities with the same maturity date.

(b) *Sale of Debentures to a short-term investor.* If SBA sells your Debenture to a short-term investor:

(1) The sale price will be the face amount.

(2) At the next scheduled date for the sale of Debenture Trust Certificates, whether or not the sale actually occurs, you must pay interest to the short-term investor for the short-term period. If the actual sale of Trust Certificates takes place after the scheduled date, you must pay the short-term investor interest from the scheduled sale date to the actual sale date. This additional interest is due on the actual sale date.

(3) Failure to pay the interest constitutes noncompliance with the terms of your Leverage (see § 107.1810).

(c) *Sale of Participating Securities to a short-term investor.* If SBA sells your Participating Security to a short-term investor, the sale price will be the face amount.

(d) *Licensee's right to repurchase its Debentures before pooling.* You may repurchase your Debentures from the short-term investor before they are pooled. To do so, you must:

(1) Give SBA written notice at least 10 days before the cut-off date for the pool in which your Debenture is to be included; and

(2) Pay the face amount of the Debenture, plus interest, to the short-term investor.

[61 FR 3189, Jan. 31, 1996, as amended at 63 FR 5868, Feb. 5, 1998]

PREFERRED SECURITIES LEVERAGE—SECTION 301(d) LICENSEES

§ 107.1400 Dividends or partnership distributions on 4 percent Preferred Securities.

If you issued Preferred Securities to SBA on or after November 21, 1989, you must pay SBA a dividend or partnership distribution of 4 percent per year, from the date you issued Preferred Securities to the date you repay them, both inclusive. The dividend or partnership distribution is:

(a) Computed on the par value of the outstanding stock or the face value of the outstanding limited partnership interest.

(b) Cumulative. This means that if you do not pay the entire dividend or partnership distribution for a given fiscal year, the unpaid balance accumulates as a distribution in arrears. You do not have to pay interest on distributions in arrears.

(c) Preferred. This means that you must pay SBA in full (including distributions in arrears) before setting aside or paying any amount to any other equity holder.

(d) Payable at the discretion of your Board of Directors or General Partner(s), except that all distributions in arrears must be paid in full when you redeem the Preferred Securities.

[61 FR 3189, Jan. 31, 1996, as amended at 63 FR 5869, Feb. 5, 1998]

§ 107.1410 Requirement to redeem 4 percent Preferred Securities.

You must redeem 4 percent Preferred Securities not later than 15 years from the date of issuance. At the redemption date, you must pay to SBA:

(a) The par value (of preferred stock) or face value (of a preferred limited partnership interest); plus

(b) Any unpaid dividends or partnership distributions accrued to the redemption date.

§ 107.1420 Articles requirements for 4 percent Preferred Securities.

If you have outstanding 4 percent Preferred Securities, your Articles must contain all the provisions in §§ 107.1400 and 107.1410.

[63 FR 5869, Feb. 5, 1998]

§ 107.1430 Redeeming 4 percent Preferred Securities with proceeds of non-subsidized Debentures.

If SBA approves, a Section 301(d) Licensee may use the proceeds of a Debenture to redeem Preferred Securities at their mandatory redemption date, including any accrued unpaid dividends or partnership distributions.

[61 FR 3189, Jan. 31, 1996, as amended at 63 FR 5869, Feb. 5, 1998]

§ 107.1440 Three percent preferred stock issued before November 21, 1989.

Before November 21, 1989, Preferred Securities were available only in the form of preferred stock and had a preferred and cumulative dividend of 3 percent. If you have such preferred stock outstanding, you must follow § 107.1400 (except for § 107.1400(d)), substituting "3 percent" for "4 percent" throughout.) Dividends on 3 percent preferred stock are payable at the discretion of your Board of Directors or General Partner(s), except that all dividends in arrears must be paid in full before any non-SBA investor receives any distribution. Upon your liquidation, SBA is entitled to payment of all dividends in arrears even if you have no Retained Earnings Available for Distribution at such time.

§ 107.1450 Optional redemption of Preferred Securities.

(a) *Redemption at par or face value.* A Section 301(d) Licensee may redeem Preferred Securities at any time, provided you give SBA at least 30 days written notice. You may redeem all or only part of your Preferred Securities, but the par value or face value of the securities being redeemed must be at least $50,000. At the redemption date, you must pay to SBA:

(1) The par value (of preferred stock) or face value (of a preferred limited partnership interest); plus

(2) Any unpaid dividends or partnership distributions accrued to the redemption date.

(b) *Repurchase of 3 percent preferred stock for less than par value.* If you issued 3 percent preferred stock to SBA, you may ask SBA to sell it back to you at a price less than its par value. The terms and conditions of any such transaction will be as set forth in the Notice published in the FEDERAL REGISTER on April 1, 1994 (Copies of this notice are available from SBA, 409 3rd Street, SW., Washington, DC, 20416). SBA has sole discretion to:

(1) Approve or disapprove the sale.

(2) Determine the sale price after considering any factors SBA considers appropriate.

(3) Determine the form of payment SBA will accept. SBA is not authorized to accept the proceeds of a subsidized Debenture as payment.

PARTICIPATING SECURITIES LEVERAGE

§ 107.1500 General description of Participating Securities.

(a) *Types of Participating Securities.* Participating Securities are redeemable, preferred, equity-type securities. SBA may purchase or guarantee Participating Securities issued by Licensees in the form of limited partnership interests, preferred stock, or debentures with interest payable only to the extent of earnings. The structure, terms and conditions of Participating Securities are set forth in detail in §§ 107.1500 through 107.1590.

(b) *Special eligibility requirements for Participating Securities.* In addition to the general eligibility requirements for Leverage under § 107.1120, Participating Securities issuers must also comply with special rules on:

(1) Minimum capital (see § 107.210).

(2) Liquidity (see § 107.1505).

(3) Non-SBA borrowing (see § 107.570).

(4) Equity investing, as set forth in this paragraph (b)(4). If you issue Participating Securities, you must invest an amount equal to the Original Issue Price of such securities solely in Equity Capital Investments, as defined in § 107.50.

(c) *Special features of Participating Securities—Prioritized Payments, Adjustments, and Profit Participation.* When you issue Participating Securities, you agree to make the following payments:

(1) *Prioritized Payments.* Depending upon the type of Participating Security you issue, Prioritized Payments may be preferred partnership distributions, preferred dividends, or interest. Your obligation to pay Prioritized Payments is contingent upon your profits as determined under § 107.1520.

(2) *Adjustments to Prioritized Payments.* If you have unpaid Prioritized Payments, you must compute Adjustments, which are additional contingent obligations determined under § 107.1520. The conditions for paying Adjustments are the same as for Prioritized Payments.

(3) *SBA Profit Participation.* Profit Participation is an amount payable to SBA under § 107.1530 in consideration for SBA's guarantee of your Participating Securities.

(d) *Distributions by Licensees issuing Participating Securities.* Sections 107.1540 through 107.1580 govern both required and optional Distributions by Participating Securities issuers. Distributions include both profit distributions and returns of capital, paid either to SBA or to your non-SBA investors.

(e) *Mandatory redemption of Participating Securities.* You must redeem Participating Securities at the redemption date, which is the same as the maturity date of the Trust Certificates for the Trust containing such securities. The redemption date can never be later than 15 years after the issue date. You must pay the Redemption Price plus any unpaid Earned Prioritized Payments and any earned Adjustments and earned Charges (see § 107.1520).

(f) *Priority of Participating Securities in liquidation of Licensee.* In the event of your liquidation, the following are senior in priority, for all purposes, to all other equity interests you have issued at any time:

(1) The Redemption Price of Participating Securities;

(2) Any Earned Prioritized Payments and any earned Adjustments and earned Charges (see § 107.1520); and

(3) Any Profit Participation allocated to SBA under § 107.1530.

[61 FR 3189, Jan. 31, 1996, as amended at 63 FR 5869, Feb. 5, 1998]

§ 107.1505 Liquidity requirements for Licensees issuing Participating Securities.

If you have outstanding Participating Securities, you must maintain sufficient liquidity to avoid a condition of Liquidity Impairment. Such a condition will constitute noncompliance with the terms of your Leverage under § 107.1820(e).

(a) *Definition of Liquidity Impairment.* A condition of Liquidity Impairment exists when your Liquidity Ratio, as determined in paragraph (b) of this section, is less than 1.20. You are responsible for calculating whether you have a condition of Liquidity Impairment:

(1) As of the close of your fiscal year;

(2) At the time you apply for Leverage, unless SBA permits otherwise; and

(3) At such time as you contemplate making any Distribution.

(b) *Computation of Liquidity Ratio.* Your Liquidity Ratio equals your Total Current Funds Available (A) divided by your Total Current Funds Required (B), as determined in the following table:

CALCULATION OF LIQUIDITY RATIO

Financial account	Amount reported on SBA form 468	Weight	Weighted amount
(1) Cash and invested idle funds		× 1.00	
(2) Commitments from investors		× 1.00	
(3) Current maturities		× 0.50	
(4) Other current assets		× 1.00	
(5) Publicly Traded and Marketable Securities		× 1.00	
(6) Anticipated operating revenue for next 12 months.	[1]	× 1.00	
(7) Total Current Funds Available			A
(8) Current liabilities		× 1.00	
(9) Commitments to Small Businesses		× 0.75	
(10) Anticipated operating expense for next 12 months.	[1]	× 1.00	

CALCULATION OF LIQUIDITY RATIO—Continued

Financial account	Amount reported on SBA form 468	Weight	Weighted amount
(11) Anticipated interest expense for next 12 months.	[1]	× 1.00	
(12) Contingent liabilities (guarantees)		× 0.25	
(13) Total Current Funds Required			B

[1] As determined by Licensee's management under its business plan.

[61 FR 3189, Jan. 31, 1996, as amended at 63 FR 5869, Feb. 5, 1998]

§ 107.1510 How a Licensee computes Earmarked Profit (Loss).

Computing your Earmarked Profit (Loss) is the first step in determining your obligations to pay Prioritized Payments, Adjustments and Charges under § 107.1520 and Profit Participation under § 107.1530.

(a) *Requirement to compute your Earmarked Profit (Loss).* While you have Participating Securities outstanding or have Earmarked Assets (as defined in paragraph (b) of this section), you must compute your Earmarked Profit (Loss) for:

(1) Each full fiscal year.

(2) Any interim period (consisting of one or more fiscal quarters) for which you want to make a Distribution.

(b) *How to determine your Earmarked Assets.* "Earmarked Assets" means all the Loans and Investments that you have when you issue Participating Securities or that you acquire while you have Participating Securities outstanding, and any non-cash assets that you receive in exchange for such Loans and Investments.

(1) An Earmarked Asset remains earmarked until you dispose of it, even if you no longer have any outstanding Participating Securities.

(2) Investments you make after redeeming all your Participating Securities are not Earmarked Assets. However, if you issue new Participating Securities, all of your Loans and Investments again become Earmarked Assets.

(3) If you were licensed before March 31, 1993, you may be permitted to exclude Loans and Investments held at that date from Earmarked Assets under § 107.1590.

(c) *How to compute your Earmarked Asset Ratio.* You must determine your Earmarked Asset Ratio each time you compute Earmarked Profit (Loss). If all your Loans and Investments are Earmarked Assets, your Earmarked Asset Ratio equals 100 percent. Otherwise, compute your Earmarked Asset Ratio using the following formula:

$$EAR = (EA \div LI) \times 100$$

where:

EAR = Earmarked Asset Ratio.
EA = Average Earmarked Assets (at cost) for the fiscal year or interim period.
LI = Average Loans and Investments (at cost) for the fiscal year or interim period.

(d) *How to compute your Earmarked Profit (Loss) if Earmarked Asset Ratio is 100 percent.* (1) (i) If your Earmarked Asset Ratio from paragraph (b) of this section is 100 percent, use the following formula to compute your Earmarked Profit (Loss):

$$EP = NI + IK + EME$$

where:

EP = Earmarked Profit (Loss)
NI = Net Income (Loss), as reported on SBA Form 468 except as otherwise provided in this paragraph (d)(1)
IK = Unrealized Appreciation (Depreciation) on Earmarked Assets that you are distributing as an In-Kind Distribution under § 107.1580
EME = Excess Management Expenses

(ii) For the purpose of determining Net Income (Loss), leverage fees paid to SBA and partnership syndication costs that you incur must be capitalized and amortized on a straight-line basis over not less than five years.

(2) "Excess Management Expenses" are those that exceed the following limit:

(i) For a full fiscal year, the limit is the lower of:

(A) 2.5 percent of your weighted average Combined Capital for the year, plus

$125,000 if Combined Capital is below $20,000,000; or

(B) Your Management Expenses approved by SBA.

(ii) For less than a full fiscal year, you must prorate the annual amounts in paragraph (d)(2)(i) of this section to determine the limit.

(e) *How to compute your Earmarked Profit (Loss) if Earmarked Asset Ratio is less than 100 percent.* If your Earmarked Asset Ratio is less than 100 percent, compute your Earmarked Profit (Loss) as follows:

(1) Do the Earmarked Profit (Loss) computation in paragraph (d) of this section.

(2) Subtract your net realized gain (loss) (as reported on SBA Form 468) on Loans and Investments that are not Earmarked Assets.

(3) Separate the result from paragraph (e)(2) of this section into:

(i) Net realized gain (loss) (as reported on SBA Form 468) on Earmarked Assets ("EGL"); and

(ii) The remainder ("R").

(4) Your Earmarked Profit (Loss) equals:

EGL + (R × Earmarked Asset Ratio)

(f) *How to compute your cumulative Earmarked Profit (Loss).* Sum your Earmarked Profit (Loss) for all fiscal years and for any interim period following the end of your last fiscal year. The total is your cumulative Earmarked Profit (Loss), which you must use in the Prioritized Payment computations under § 107.1520.

[61 FR 3189, Jan. 31, 1996, as amended at 63 FR 5870, Feb. 5, 1998]

§ 107.1520 How a Licensee computes and allocates Prioritized Payments to SBA.

This section tells you how to compute Prioritized Payments, Adjustments and Charges on Participating Securities and determine the amounts you must pay. To distribute these amounts, see § 107.1540.

(a) *How to compute Prioritized Payments and Adjustments*—(1) *Prioritized Payments.* For a full fiscal year, the Prioritized Payment on an outstanding Participating Security equals the Redemption Price times the related Trust Certificate Rate. For an interim period, you must prorate the annual Prioritized Payment. If your Participating Security was sold to a short-term investor in accordance with § 107.1240, the Prioritized Payment for the short-term period equals the Redemption Price times the short-term rate.

(2) *Adjustments.* Compute Adjustments using paragraph (f) of this section.

(3) *Charges.* Compute Charges in accordance with § 107.1130(d)(2).

(b) *Licensee's obligation to pay Prioritized Payments, Adjustments and Charges.* You are obligated to pay Prioritized Payments, Adjustments and Charges only if you have profit as determined in paragraph (d) of this section.

(1) Prioritized Payments that you must pay (or have already paid) because you have sufficient profit are "Earned Prioritized Payments".

(2) Prioritized Payments that have not become payable because you lack sufficient profit are "Accumulated Prioritized Payments". Treat all Prioritized Payments as "Accumulated" until they become "Earned" under this section.

(3) Adjustments (computed under paragraph (f) of this section) and Charges (computed under § 107.1130(d)(2)) are "earned" according to the same criteria applied to Prioritized Payments.

(c) *How to keep track of Prioritized Payments.* You must establish three accounts to record your Accumulated and Earned Prioritized Payments:

(1) *Accumulation Account.* The Accumulation Account is a memorandum account. Its balance represents your Accumulated Prioritized Payments, unearned Adjustments and unearned Charges.

(2) *Distribution Account.* The Distribution Account is a liability account. Its balance represents your unpaid Earned Prioritized Payments, earned Adjustments and earned Charges.

(3) *Earned Payments Account.* The Earned Payments Account is a memorandum account. Each time you add to the Distribution Account balance, add the same amount to the Earned Payments Account. Its balance represents your total (paid and unpaid) Earned

Prioritized Payments, earned Adjustments and earned Charges.

(d) *How to determine your profit for Prioritized Payment purposes.* As of the end of each fiscal year and any interim period for which you want to make a Distribution:

(1) Bring the Accumulation Account up to date by adding to it all Prioritized Payments and Charges through the end of the appropriate fiscal period.

(2) Determine whether you have profit for the purposes of this section by doing the following computation:

(i) Cumulative Earmarked Profit (Loss) under § 107.1510(f); minus

(ii) The Earned Payments Account balance; minus

(iii) All Distributions previously made under §§ 107.1550, 107.1560 and 107.1570(a); minus

(iv) Any Profit Participation previously allocated to SBA under § 107.1530, but not yet distributed.

(3) The amount computed in paragraph (d)(2) of this section, if greater than zero, is your profit. If the amount is zero or less, you have no profit.

(4) If you have a profit, continue with paragraph (e) of this section. Otherwise, continue with paragraph (f) of this section.

(e) *Allocating Prioritized Payments to the Distribution Account.* (1) If you have a profit under paragraph (d) of this section, determine the lesser of:

(i) Your profit; or

(ii) The balance in your Accumulation Account.

(2) Subtract the result in paragraph (e)(1) of this section from the Accumulation Account and add it to the Distribution Account and the Earned Payments Account.

(f) *How to compute Adjustments.* You must compute Adjustments as of the end of each fiscal year if you have a balance greater than zero in either your Accumulation Account or your Distribution Account, after giving effect to any Distribution that will be made no later than the second Payment Date following the fiscal year end.

(1) Determine the combined average Accumulation Account and Distribution Account balances for the fiscal year, assuming that Prioritized Payments accumulate on a daily basis without compounding.

(2) Multiply the average balance computed in paragraph (f)(1) of this section by the average of the Trust Certificate Rates for all the Participating Securities poolings during the fiscal year.

(3) Add the amounts computed in this paragraph (f) to your Accumulation Account.

(g) *Licensee's obligation to pay Prioritized Payments after redeeming Participating Securities.* This paragraph (g) applies if you have redeemed all your Participating Securities, but you still hold Earmarked Assets and still have a balance in your Accumulation Account.

(1) You must continue to perform all the procedures in this section as of the end of each fiscal quarter and prior to making any Distribution. You must distribute any Earned Prioritized Payments, earned Adjustments and earned Charges in accordance with § 107.1540.

(2) After you dispose of all your Earmarked Assets and make any required Distributions in accordance with § 107.1540, your obligation to pay any remaining Accumulated Prioritized Payments, unearned Adjustments and unearned Charges will be extinguished.

[63 FR 5870, Feb. 5, 1998]

§ 107.1530 How a Licensee computes SBA's Profit Participation.

This section tells you how to compute SBA's Profit Participation. Profit Participation is included in the Distributions you make to SBA under §§ 107.1550 and 107.1560.

(a) *How to compute Profit Participation.* Profit Participation equals your "Base" times your "Profit Participation Rate" (if the Base is zero or less, you do not owe SBA Profit Participation). Compute the Base using paragraph (c) of this section and the Profit Participation Rate using paragraphs (d) through (g) of this section. You must compute your Earmarked Profit (Loss) under § 107.1510 and your Prioritized Payments and Adjustments under § 107.1520 before you can compute Profit Participation.

(b) *How to keep track of Profit Participation.* You must establish a Profit Participation Account to record your computations under this section and payments under §§ 107.1550 and 107.1560. Its balance represents your unpaid Profit Participation.

(c) *How to compute the Base.* As of the end of each fiscal year and any year-to-date interim period for which you want to make a Distribution, compute your Base using the following formula:

$$B = EP - PPA - UL$$

where:

B = Base.

EP = Earmarked Profit (Loss) for the period from § 107.1510.

PPA = Prioritized Payments for the period from § 107.1520(a)(1), Adjustments (if applicable) from § 107.1520(f), and Charges (if applicable) from § 107.1130(d)(2).

UL = "Unused Loss" from prior periods as determined in this paragraph (c).

(1) If the Base computed as of the end of your previous fiscal year (your "Previous Base") was less than zero, your Unused Loss equals your Previous Base.

(2) If your Previous Base was zero or greater, your Unused Loss equals zero, with the following exception: If you made an interim Distribution of Profit Participation during your previous fiscal year, and your Previous Base was lower than the interim Base on which your Distribution was computed, then your Unused Loss equals the difference between the interim Base and the Previous Base. For example, assume you are computing your Base as of December 31, 1997, your fiscal year end. Your Previous Base, computed as of December 31, 1996, was $3,000,000. During 1996, you made an interim Distribution which was computed on a Base of $3,500,000 as of June 30, 1996. The $500,000 difference between the 1996 interim and year-end Bases would be carried forward as Unused Loss in the computation of your Base as of December 31, 1997.

(3) If you had no Participating Securities outstanding as of the end of your last fiscal year, you may request SBA's approval to treat your Undistributed Net Realized Loss, as reported on SBA Form 468 for that year, as Unused Loss. If you did not file SBA Form 468 because you were not yet licensed as of the end of your last fiscal year, you may request SBA's approval to treat pre-licensing losses as Unused Loss.

(d) *How to compute the Profit Participation Rate.* You must determine your Profit Participation Rate each time you compute a Base that is greater than zero. Compute the Rate by following the steps in paragraphs (e) through (g) of this section.

(e) *Compute the "PLC ratio"*—(1) *General rule.* The "PLC ratio" is the highest ratio of outstanding Participating Securities to Leverageable Capital that you have ever attained.

(2) *Exception.* You may reduce the ratio computed under paragraph (e)(1) of this section if you have increased your Leverageable Capital above its highest previous level. The increase must have taken place at least 120 days before the date as of which your Base is computed. In addition, the increase must have been expressly provided for in a plan of operations submitted to and approved by SBA in writing, or must be the result of the takedown of commitments or the conversion of non-cash assets that were included in your Private Capital. If these conditions are satisfied, compute your reduced PLC ratio as follows:

(i) Divide the highest dollar amount of Participating Securities you have ever had outstanding by your increased Leverageable Capital.

(ii) If the result in paragraph (e)(2)(i) of this section is lower than your PLC ratio currently in effect, such result will become your new PLC ratio.

(f) *Compute the Profit Participation Rate (before indexing).* Compute the Profit Participation Rate (before indexing) using the table in this paragraph (f). Then go to paragraph (g) of this section to determine whether to index the Profit Participation Rate.

If your PLC ratio is:	Then your Profit Participation Rate is:
1 or less	9% × PLC Ratio.
More than 1	9% + [3% × (PLC ratio-1)].

(g) *Indexing the Profit Participation Rate.* The Profit Participation Rate is indexed, up or down, to the yield-to-maturity on Treasury bonds with a remaining term of ten (10) years (the "Treasury Rate"). You must perform the indexing procedures in this paragraph (g) unless the Treasury Rate was exactly 8 percent on every date that you issued Participating Securities.

(1) *Licensees that have issued Participating Securities on only one occasion.* Determine the Treasury Rate for the date you issued your Participating Security. Adjust the Profit Participation Rate from paragraph (f) of this section by the percentage difference between the Treasury Rate and 8 percent. For example, assume that you issued Participating Securities when the Treasury Rate was 10 percent. The percentage difference between 10 percent and 8 percent is 25 percent. If you had a PLC ratio of 1, the Profit Participation Rate before indexing would be 9 percent. You would increase this rate by 25 percent, giving you a Profit Participation Rate of 11.25 percent.

(2) *Licensees that have issued Participating Securities on more than one occasion.* Determine the Treasury Rate for each of the dates you issued Participating Securities.

(i) Compute an average of all such Treasury Rates, weighted to reflect the dollar amount of each issuance (ignoring any redemptions) and the number of days from the date of each issuance to the date as of which you are computing the Profit Participation Rate.

Example to paragraph (g)(2)(i) of this section. If you issued $10 million of Participating Securities on the 60th day of Fiscal Year 1 when the Treasury Rate was 8 percent, and another $15 million on the 100th day of Fiscal Year 3 when the Treasury Rate was 10 percent, then the weighted average Treasury Rate computed as of the end of Fiscal Year 3 would be 8.55 percent. [Days elapsed since first issuance of Participating Securities = 1,035; days elapsed since second issuance of Participating Securities = 265; weighted amount of first issuance = $10,000,000 × 1,035/1,035 = $10,000,000; weighted amount of second issuance = $15,000,000 × 265/1035 = $3,840,579; weighted average amount of Participating Securities issued = $10,000,000 + $3,840,579 = $13,840,579; weighted average Treasury Rate= {(.08 × $10,000,000) + (.10 × $3,840,579)} / $13,840,579 = 8.55%]

(ii) Adjust the Profit Participation Rate from paragraph (f) of this section by the percentage difference between the weighted average Treasury Rate and 8 percent. In the example given in paragraph (g)(2)(i) of this section, if the PLC ratio were equal to 2, the Profit Participation Rate for the fiscal year would be 12.83 percent. [{((.0855 − .08) ÷ .08) + 1} × .12 × 100 = 12.83%]

(h) *Computing SBA's Profit Participation.* If the Base from paragraph (c) of this section is greater than zero, you must compute SBA's Profit Participation as follows:

(1) Multiply the Base from paragraph (c) of this section by the Profit Participation Rate from paragraph (g) of this section.

(2) If your last Profit Participation computation was for an interim period during the same fiscal year and used a higher Profit Participation Rate than the Rate you just used in paragraph (h)(1) of this section, you must adjust the amount computed in paragraph (h)(1) of this section as follows:

(i) Determine the difference between the Profit Participation Rate you just used in paragraph (h)(1) of this section and the Rate used in your previous computation;

(ii) Multiply the difference by the Base from your last Profit Participation computation; and

(iii) Add the result to the amount you computed in paragraph (h)(1) of this section.

(3) Reduce the Profit Participation computed in paragraphs (h)(1) and (h)(2) of this section by any amounts of Profit Participation that you distributed or reserved for distribution to SBA, or its designated agent or Trustee, for any previous interim period(s) during the fiscal year. The result is SBA's Profit Participation (unless it is less than zero, in which case SBA's Profit Participation is zero).

(i) *Allocation of Profit Participation.* Before any Distribution and in any case within 120 days following the end of your fiscal year, you must add the amount of Profit Participation computed under this § 107.1530 to the Profit Participation Account. You must reserve funds equal to this amount for distribution to SBA, or its designated agent or Trustee; you may not reinvest these funds or use them for any other purpose.

[61 FR 3189, Jan. 31, 1996; 61 FR 41496, Aug. 9, 1996, as amended at 63 FR 5871, Feb. 5, 1998]

§ 107.1540 Distributions by Licensee—Prioritized Payments and Adjustments.

After you compute Prioritized Payments and Adjustments under § 107.1520, you must distribute them in accordance with this § 107.1540. You must notify SBA of any planned distribution under this section 10 business days before the distribution date, unless SBA permits otherwise.

(a) *Requirement to distribute Prioritized Payments and Adjustments.* This paragraph (a) applies only if you satisfy the liquidity requirement in § 107.1505. All Distributions under this paragraph (a) go to SBA or its designated agent or trustee.

(1) You must distribute the balance in your Distribution Account from § 107.1520 annually on the first or second Payment Date following your fiscal year end, and on any date when you are making any other Distribution.

(2) You may distribute all or part of the balance in your Distribution Account on any Payment Date regardless of whether you are making any other Distribution on that date.

(b) *Additional requirement for Licensees with undistributed Prioritized Payments.* This paragraph (b) applies if you do not distribute the full amount in your Distribution Account by the second Payment Date following the end of your fiscal year. At the end of each fiscal quarter, until you reduce the balance in your Distribution Account to zero, you must:

(1) Do all the steps in § 107.1520; and

(2) Distribute the balance in your Distribution Account on the next Payment Date following the end of your fiscal quarter, provided you satisfy the liquidity requirement in § 107.1505.

[61 FR 3189, Jan. 31, 1996, as amended at 63 FR 5871, Feb. 5, 1998]

§ 107.1550 Distributions by Licensee—permitted "tax Distributions" to private investors and SBA.

If you have outstanding Participating Securities or Earmarked Assets, and you are a limited partnership, "S Corporation," or equivalent pass-through entity for tax purposes, you may make "tax Distributions" to your investors in accordance with this § 107.1550, whether or not they have an actual tax liability. SBA receives a share of any tax Distribution you make. This section tells you when you may make a "tax Distribution" and how to compute it. You must notify SBA of any planned distribution under this section 10 business days before the distribution date, unless SBA permits otherwise.

(a) *Conditions for making a tax Distribution.* You may make a tax Distribution only if:

(1) You have paid all your Prioritized Payments, Adjustments, and Charges, so that the balance in both your Distribution Account and your Accumulation Account is zero (see § 107.1520).

(2) You satisfy the liquidity requirement in § 107.1505.

(3) The tax Distribution does not exceed your Retained Earnings Available for Distribution.

(4) The tax Distribution does not exceed the Maximum Tax Liability from paragraph (b) of this section.

(b) *How to compute the Maximum Tax Liability.* (1) You may compute your Maximum Tax Liability for a full fiscal year or for any calendar quarter. Use the following formula:

$$M = (TOI \times HRO) + (TCG \times HRC)$$

where:

M = Maximum Tax Liability

TOI = Net ordinary income allocated to your partners or other owners for Federal income tax purposes for the fiscal year or calendar quarter for which the Distribution is being made, excluding Prioritized Payments allocated to SBA.

HRO = The highest combined marginal Federal and State income tax rate for corporations or individuals on ordinary income, determined in accordance with paragraphs (b)(2) through (b)(4) of this section.

TCG = Net capital gains allocated to your partners or other owners for Federal income tax purposes for the fiscal year or calendar quarter for which the Distribution is being made, excluding Prioritized Payments allocated to SBA.

HRC = The highest combined marginal Federal and State income tax rate for corporations or individuals on capital gains, determined in accordance with paragraphs (b)(2) through (b)(4) of this section.

(2) You may compute the highest combined marginal Federal and State income tax rate on ordinary income and capital gains using either individual or corporate rates. However, you must apply the same type of rate, either individual or corporate, to both ordinary income and capital gains.

(3) In determining the combined Federal and State income tax rate, you must assume that State income taxes are deductible from Federal income taxes. For example, if the Federal tax rate was 35 percent and the State tax rate was 5 percent, the combined tax rate would be [35% × (1−.05)] + 5% = 38.25%.

(4) For purposes of this paragraph (b), the "State income tax" is that of the State where your principal place of business is located, and does not include any local income taxes.

(c) *SBA's share of the tax Distribution.* (1) SBA's percentage share of the tax Distribution is equal to the Profit Participation Rate computed under § 107.1530.

(2) SBA may direct you to pay its share of the tax Distribution to its designated agent or Trustee.

(3) SBA will apply its share of the tax Distribution in the order set forth in § 107.1560(g).

(d) *Paying a tax Distribution.* You may make an annual tax Distribution on the first or second Payment Date following the end of your fiscal year. You may make a quarterly tax Distribution on the first Payment Date following the end of the calendar quarter for which the Distribution is being made. See also § 107.1575(a).

(e) *Excess tax Distributions.* (1) As of the end of your fiscal year, you must determine whether you made any excess tax Distributions for the year in accordance with paragraph (e)(2) of this section. Any tax Distributions that you make for a subsequent period must be reduced by the excess amount distributed.

(2) Determine your excess tax Distributions by adding together all your quarterly tax Distributions for the year (ignoring any required reductions for excess tax Distributions made in prior years), and subtracting the maximum tax Distribution that you would have been permitted to make based upon a single computation performed for the entire fiscal year. The result, if greater than zero, is your excess tax Distribution for the year.

[61 FR 3189, Jan. 31, 1996, as amended at 63 FR 5871, Feb. 5, 1998; 64 FR 70996, Dec. 20, 1999]

§ 107.1560 Distributions by Licensee—required Distributions to private investors and SBA.

You must make Distributions under this § 107.1560 if you have outstanding Participating Securities or Earmarked Assets and you satisfy the conditions in paragraph (a) of this section. Distributions under this section are determined as of the end of each fiscal year. You must notify SBA of any planned distribution under this section 10 business days before the distribution date, unless SBA permits otherwise.

(a) *Conditions for making Distributions.* Distributions under this section are subject to the following conditions:

(1) You must have paid all Prioritized Payments, Adjustments and Charges, so that the balance in both your Distribution Account and your Accumulation Account is zero (see §§ 107.1520 and 107.1540).

(2) You must have made any permitted tax Distribution that you choose to make under § 107.1550.

(3) You must satisfy the liquidity requirement in § 107.1505.

(4) The amount you distribute under this section must not exceed your remaining Retained Earnings Available for Distribution.

(b) *Total amount you must distribute.* Unless SBA permits otherwise, the total amount you must distribute equals the result (if greater than zero) of the following computation:

(1) Your Retained Earnings Available for Distribution as of the end of your fiscal year, after giving effect to any Distribution under §§ 107.1540 and 107.1550; minus

(2) All previous Distributions under this section and § 107.1570(a) that were applied as redemptions or repayments of Leverage; plus

(3) All previous Distributions under § 107.1570(b) that reduced your Retained Earnings Available for Distribution.

(c) *When you must make Distributions.* You must make the required Distributions on either the first or second Payment Date following the end of your fiscal year.

(d) *Effect of Distributions on Retained Earnings Available for Distribution.* Distributions under this § 107.1560 have the following effect on your Retained Earnings Available for Distribution:

(1) All Distributions to private investors reduce Retained Earnings Available for Distribution.

(2) Distributions to SBA, or its designated agent or Trustee, reduce Retained Earnings Available for Distribution if they are applied as payments of Profit Participation or distributions on Preferred Securities (see paragraph (g) of this section).

(3) Distributions to SBA, or its designated agent or Trustee, do not reduce Retained Earnings Available for Distribution if they are applied as a repayment or redemption of Leverage (see paragraph (g) of this section).

(e) *SBA's share of the total Distribution.* Use the following table to determine the percentage share of the total Distribution (from paragraph (b) of this section) that goes to SBA (or its designated agent or Trustee):

SBA'S PERCENTAGE SHARE OF TOTAL DISTRIBUTION

If your ratio of Leverage to Leverageable Capital as of the fiscal period end is:	Then SBA's percentage share of the Distribution is:
Over 200%	[Leverage / (Leverage + Leverageable Capital)] × 100.
Over 100% but not over 200%.	50%.
100% or less	Profit Participation Rate from § 107.1530.

(f) *Exceptions to the Distribution requirement.* (1) With SBA's prior written approval, you may withhold from distribution reasonable reserves necessary to protect your investments or relative position in Loans and Investments and to meet contingent liabilities.

(i) If you submit a written request for SBA approval, you may consider it approved unless SBA notifies you otherwise within 30 days from receipt.

(ii) Reserves that you withhold from distribution may not be used to make investments in additional portfolio companies.

(iii) Withholding of reserves under this paragraph (f)(1) is not a "payment failure" in violation of § 107.1820(e)(6).

(2) SBA may restrict Distributions under this § 107.1560 if SBA determines that the value of your assets is materially overstated. SBA must give you notice of such a determination in advance of your proposed Distribution.

(g) *How SBA will apply your Distributions.* Your Distributions to SBA (or its designated agent or Trustee) under this § 107.1560 will be applied in the following order:

(1) First, to Profit Participation;

(2) Second, to the extent there remain any Retained Earnings Available for Distribution, to distributions on Preferred Securities;

(3) Third, as a redemption of Participating Securities in order of issue;

(4) Fourth, as a redemption of Preferred Securities; and

(5) Fifth, as the repayment of principal of any outstanding Debentures, with such repayment to be made into escrow on terms and conditions SBA determines.

[61 FR 3189, Jan. 31, 1996, as amended at 63 FR 5872, Feb. 5, 1998]

§ 107.1570 Distributions by Licensee—optional Distribution to private investors and SBA.

If you have outstanding Participating Securities or Earmarked Assets, you may make two types of optional Distributions under this § 107.1570: quarterly Distributions determined the same way as the required annual Distributions in § 107.1560, and Distributions allocated between SBA and your private investors in proportion to the capital contributions of each. You must notify SBA of any planned distribution under this section 10 business days before the distribution date, unless SBA permits otherwise.

(a) *Quarterly Distributions subject to conditions in § 107.1560.* (1) You may make Distributions under this paragraph (a) as of the end of any fiscal quarter, giving SBA (or its designated agent or Trustee) a percentage share determined under § 107.1560(e).

(2) Such Distributions are subject to all the provisions in § 107.1560 (a)(1), (a)(3), (a)(4), (d), (f)(2), and (g).

(3) You may make such Distributions only on the next Payment Date following the end of your fiscal quarter.

(4) The total amount of such Distributions may not exceed the result of the following computation:

(i) Your Retained Earnings Available for Distribution as of the end of your fiscal quarter; minus

(ii) All previous Distributions under this paragraph (a) or § 107.1560 that were applied as redemptions or repayments of Leverage; plus

(iii) All previous Distributions under paragraph (b) of this section that reduced your Retained Earnings Available for Distribution.

(b) *Other optional Distributions.* On any Payment Date, you may make additional Distributions to your private investors and to SBA (or its designated agent or Trustee) under this paragraph (b).

(1) *Conditions for making a Distribution.* You may make a Distribution under this paragraph (b) only if:

(i) You have distributed all Earned Prioritized Payments, earned Adjustments, and earned Charges, so that the balance in your Distribution Account is zero (see § 107.1520).

(ii) You have distributed all Profit Participation computed under § 107.1530 which you are required to distribute under § 107.1560 or permitted to distribute under paragraph (a) of this section, as appropriate, and you have made all required Distributions under § 107.1560.

(iii) You satisfy the liquidity requirement in § 107.1505 or obtain SBA's prior written approval of the Distribution.

(iv) You do not have a condition of Capital Impairment.

(v) The Distribution does not reduce your Regulatory Capital (excluding commitments from Institutional Investors) below the minimum required under § 107.210, unless SBA approves the reduction as part of a plan of liquidation.

(vi) The Distribution does not cause you to have excess Leverage contrary to section 303 of the Act.

(2) *SBA's share of Distribution.* (i) If your Capital Impairment Percentage under § 107.1840 is zero, SBA's percentage share of any Distribution under this paragraph (b) equals:

[Leverage /(Leverage + Leverageable Capital)] × 100

In this formula, use Leverage and Leverageable Capital as of the date of the Distribution, after giving effect to any Distribution under § 107.1560 and paragraph (a) of this section.

(ii) If your Capital Impairment Percentage under § 107.1840 is greater than zero, you must modify the formula in paragraph (b)(2)(i) of this section by replacing Leverageable Capital with:

Leverageable Capital × (100% − CIP)

where "CIP" is your Capital Impairment Percentage or 100 percent, whichever is less.

(3) *How SBA will apply Distributions.* Any amounts you distribute to SBA, or its designated agent or Trustee, under this paragraph (b) will be applied as a repayment or redemption of Leverage in the order set forth in § 107.1560(g)(3) through (g)(5).

(4) *Effect of Distributions on Retained Earnings Available for Distribution.* Any amounts you distribute to non-SBA investors under this paragraph (b) must reduce your Retained Earnings Available for Distribution to zero before reducing your Private Capital.

(5) *Permitted exception to § 107.585.* You may make any Distribution permitted by this paragraph (b), even if the result is a reduction in your Regulatory Capital that would otherwise be prohibited under § 107.585.

[61 FR 3189, Jan. 31, 1996, as amended at 63 FR 5872, Feb. 5, 1998]

§ 107.1575 Distributions on other than Payment Dates.

(a) *Permitted Distributions on other than Payment Dates.* Notwithstanding any provisions to the contrary in §§ 107.1540 through 107.1570, you may make Distributions on dates other than Payment Dates as follows:

(1) Required annual Distributions under § 107.1540(a)(1), annual Distributions under § 107.1550, and any Distributions under § 107.1560 must be made no later than the second Payment Date following the end of your fiscal year.

(2) Required Distributions under § 107.1540(b) must be made no later than the first Payment Date following the end of the applicable fiscal quarter;

(3) Optional Distributions under § 107.1540(a)(2) and § 107.1570 may be made on any date.

(4) Quarterly Distributions under § 107.1550 must be made no earlier than the last day of the calendar quarter for which the Distribution is being made and no later than the first Payment

Date following the end of such calendar quarter.

(b) *Conditions for making Distribution.* All Distributions under this section are subject to the following conditions:

(1) You must obtain SBA's written approval before the distribution date;

(2) The ending date of the period for which you compute your Earmarked Profits, Prioritized Payments, Adjustments, Charges, Profit Participation, Retained Earnings Available for Distribution, liquidity ratio, Capital Impairment, and any other applicable computations required under §§ 107.1500 through 107.1570, must be:

(i) The distribution date, or

(ii) If your Distribution includes annual Distributions under §§ 107.1540(a)(1), 107.1550 and/or 107.1560, your most recent fiscal year end;

(3) If your Distribution includes an amount which SBA will apply as a redemption of Participating Securities, the effective date of such redemption, for all purposes including future computations of Prioritized Payments, will be the next Payment Date following the distribution date.

[63 FR 5872, Feb. 5, 1998, as amended at 64 FR 70997, Dec. 20, 1999]

§ 107.1580 Special rules for In-Kind Distributions by Licensees.

(a) *In-Kind Distributions while Licensee has outstanding Participating Securities.* A Distribution under §§ 107.1540, 107.1560 or 107.1570 may consist of securities (an "In-Kind Distribution"). Such a Distribution must satisfy the conditions in this paragraph (a).

(1) You may distribute only Distributable Securities.

(2) You must distribute each security pro-rata to all investors and to SBA or its designated agent or Trustee, based on the amounts that each party would receive if the Distribution were in cash.

(3) You must impute a gain (loss) on each security being distributed as if it were being sold, using the value of the security as of the declaration date of the Distribution (if you are a Corporate Licensee) or the distribution date (if you are a Partnership Licensee).

(4) You must deposit SBA's share of securities being distributed with a disposition agent designated by SBA. As an alternative, if you agree, SBA may direct you to dispose of its shares. In this case, you must promptly remit the proceeds to SBA.

(b) *In-Kind Distributions after Licensee has redeemed all Participating Securities.* This paragraph (b) applies from the time you redeem all your Participating Securities until you dispose of all your Earmarked Assets.

(1) You may make an In-Kind Distribution of an Earmarked Asset only if you pay SBA the lower of:

(i) An amount equal to the Unrealized Appreciation on the asset; or

(ii) The full amount of your Accumulated Prioritized Payments and unpaid Adjustments.

(2) You must obtain SBA's prior written approval of any In-Kind Distribution of Earmarked Assets that are not Distributable Securities, specifically including approval of the valuation of the assets.

[61 FR 3189, Jan. 31, 1996, as amended at 63 FR 5872, Feb. 5, 1998; 64 FR 70997, Dec. 20, 1999]

§ 107.1585 Exchange of Debentures for Participating Securities.

You may, in SBA's discretion, retire a Debenture through the issuance of Participating Securities. To do so, you must:

(a) Obtain SBA's approval to issue Participating Securities;

(b) Pay all unpaid accrued interest on the Debenture, plus any applicable prepayment penalties, fees, and other charges;

(c) Have outstanding Equity Capital Investments (at cost) equal to the amount of the Debenture being refinanced; and

(d) Classify all your existing Loans and Investments as Earmarked Assets.

[63 FR 5869, Feb. 5, 1998]

§ 107.1590 Special rules for companies licensed on or before March 31, 1993.

This section applies to companies licensed on or before March 31, 1993 that apply to issue Participating Securities.

(a) *Election to exclude pre-existing portfolio.* You may choose to exclude all (but not a portion) of your Loans and Investments as of March 31, 1993, from classification as Earmarked Assets if:

(1) The proceeds of your first issuance of Participating Securities are not used to refinance outstanding Debentures (see § 107.1585(a)). SBA will consider payment or prepayment of any outstanding Debenture to be a refinancing unless you demonstrate to SBA's satisfaction that you can pay the Debenture principal without relying on the proceeds of the Participating Securities.

(2) SBA, in its sole discretion, approves the exclusion.

(b) *Treatment of pre-existing portfolio if not excluded.* If you do not choose to exclude your Loans and Investments as of March 31, 1993, they will be Earmarked Assets for all purposes.

(c) *Requirements for Licensee's first issuance of Participating Securities.* When you apply for your first issuance of Participating Securities, you must comply with the following:

(1) For each of your Loans and Investments, you must submit:

(i) The most recent annual report (or fiscal year-end financial statements) and the most recent interim financial statements of the Small Business; and

(ii) Your valuation reports on the Small Business, prepared as of the end of each of your last three fiscal years. If you have applied for Participating Securities on the basis of interim financial statements, you must also submit a valuation report as of your interim financial statement date.

(2) If you have negative Undistributed Net Realized Earnings and/or a net Unrealized Loss on Securities Held, SBA may require you to undergo a quasi-reorganization in accordance with generally accepted accounting principles.

(3) If your financial statements accompanying the Participating Securities application are for an interim period, you must have your SBA-approved independent public accountant perform a limited-scope audit of the statements. For purposes of this paragraph (d)(3), "limited scope audit" means auditing procedures sufficient to enable the independent public accountant to express an opinion on the Statement of Financial Position and the accompanying Schedule of Loans and Investments.

[61 FR 3189, Jan. 31, 1996, as amended at 63 FR 5873, Feb. 5, 1998]

FUNDING LEVERAGE BY USE OF SBA-GUARANTEED TRUST CERTIFICATES ("TCS")

§ 107.1600 SBA authority to issue and guarantee Trust Certificates.

(a) *Authorization.* Sections 319(a) and (b) of the Act authorize SBA or its CRA to issue TCs, and SBA to guarantee the timely payment of the principal and interest thereon. Any guarantee by SBA of such TC is limited to the principal and interest due on the Debentures or the Redemption Price of and Prioritized Payments on Participating Securities in any Trust or Pool backing such TC. The full faith and credit of the United States is pledged to the payment of all amounts due under the guarantee of any TC.

(b) *Periodic exercise of authority.* SBA will issue guarantees of Debentures and Participating Securities under section 303 and of TCs under section 319 of the Act at six month intervals, or at shorter intervals, taking into account the amount and number of such guarantees or TCs.

(c) *SBA authority to arrange public or private fundings of Leverage.* SBA in its discretion may arrange for public or private financing under its guarantee authority. Such financing arranged by SBA may be accomplished by the sale of individual Debentures or Participating Securities, aggregations of Debentures or Participating Securities, or Pools or Trusts of Debentures or Participating Securities.

(d) *Pass-through provisions.* TCs shall provide for a pass-through to their holders of all amounts of principal and interest paid on the Debentures, or the Redemption Price of and Prioritized Payments on the Participating Securities, in the Pool or Trust against which they are issued.

(e) *Formation of a Pool or Trust holding Leverage Securities.* SBA shall approve the formation of each Pool or Trust. SBA may, in its discretion, establish the size of the Pools and their composition, the interest rate on the TCs issued against Trusts or Pools, fees, discounts, premiums and other charges made in connection with the Pools, Trusts, and TCs, and any other characteristics of a Pool or Trust it deems appropriate.

[61 FR 3189, Jan. 31, 1996, as amended at 63 FR 5873, Feb. 5, 1998]

§ 107.1610 Effect of prepayment or early redemption of Leverage on a Trust Certificate.

(a) The rights, if any, of a Licensee to prepay any Debenture or make early redemption of any Participating Security are established by the terms of such securities, and no such right is created or denied by the regulations in this part.

(b) SBA's rights to purchase or prepay any Debenture without premium are established by the terms of the Guaranty Agreement relating to the Debenture. SBA's rights to redeem, at any time, any Participating Security without premium are established by the terms of the Guaranty Agreement relating to the Participating Security.

(c) Any prepayment of a Debenture or early redemption of a Participating Security pursuant to the terms of the Guaranty Agreement relating to such securities, shall reduce the SBA guarantee of timely payment of principal and interest on a TC in proportion to the amount of principal or Redemption Price that such prepaid Debenture or redeemed Participating Security represents in the Trust or Pool backing such TC.

(d) SBA shall be discharged from its guarantee obligation to the holder or holders of any TC, or any successor or transferee of such holder, to the extent of any such prepayment, whether or not such successor or transferee shall have notice of any such prepayment.

(e) Interest on prepaid Debentures and Prioritized Payments on Participating Securities shall accrue only through the date of such voluntary prepayment or SBA payment, as the case may be.

(f) In the event that all Debentures or Participating Securities constituting a Trust or Pool are prepaid, the TCs backed by such Trust or Pool shall be redeemed by payment of the unpaid principal and interest on the TCs; *Provided, however*, that in the case of the prepayment of a Debenture pursuant to the provisions of the Guaranty Agreement relating to the Debenture, the CRA shall pass through pro rata to the holders of the TCs any such prepayments including any prepayment penalty paid by the obligor Licensee pursuant to the terms of the Debenture.

§ 107.1620 Functions of agents, including Central Registration Agent, Selling Agent and Fiscal Agent.

(a) *Agents.* SBA will appoint or cause to be appointed agent(s) to perform functions necessary to market and service Debentures, Participating Securities, or TCs pursuant to this part.

(1) *Selling Agent.* As a condition of guaranteeing a Debenture or Participating Security, SBA shall cause each Licensee to appoint a Selling Agent to perform functions which include, but are not limited to:

(i) Selecting qualified entities to become pool or Trust assemblers ("Poolers").

(ii) Receiving guaranteed Debentures and Participating Securities as well as negotiating the terms and conditions of periodic offerings of Debentures and/or TCs with Poolers on behalf of Licensees.

(iii) Directing and coordinating periodic sales of Debentures and Participating Securities and/or TCs.

(iv) Arranging for the production of the Offering Circular, certificates, and such other documents as may be required from time to time.

(2) *Fiscal Agent.* SBA shall appoint a Fiscal Agent to:

(i) Establish performance criteria for Poolers.

(ii) Monitor and evaluate the financial markets to determine those factors that will minimize or reduce the cost of funding Debentures or Participating Securities.

(iii) Monitor the performance of the Selling Agent, Poolers, CRA, and the Trustee.

(iv) Perform such other functions as SBA, from time to time, may prescribe.

(3) *Central Registration Agent.* Pursuant to a contract entered into with SBA, the CRA, as SBA's agent, will do the following with respect to the Pools or Trust Certificates for the Debentures or Participating Securities:

(i) Form an SBA-approved Pool or Trust;

(ii) Issue the TCs in the form prescribed by SBA;

(iii) Transfer the TCs upon the sale of original issue TCs in any secondary market transaction;

(iv) Receive payments from Licensees;

(v) Make periodic payments as scheduled or required by the terms of the TCs, and pay all amounts required to be paid upon prepayment of Debentures or redemption of Participating Securities;

(vi) Hold, safeguard, and release all Debentures and Participating Securities constituting Trusts or Pools upon instructions from SBA;

(vii) Remain custodian of such other documentation as SBA shall direct by written instructions;

(viii) Provide for the registration of all pooled Debentures and Participating Securities, all Pools and Trusts, and all TCs;

(ix) Perform such other functions as SBA may deem necessary to implement the provisions of this section.

(b) *Functions.* The function of locating purchasers, and negotiating and closing the sale of Debentures, Participating Securities and TCs, may be performed either by SBA or an agent appointed by SBA. Nothing in the regulations in this part shall be interpreted to prevent the CRA from acting as SBA's agent for this purpose.

§ 107.1630 SBA regulation of Brokers and Dealers and disclosure to purchasers of Leverage or Trust Certificates.

(a) *Disclosure to purchasers.* Prior to any sale of a Debenture, Participating Security, or TC, SBA shall require the seller, or the broker or dealer as agent for the seller, to disclose to the purchaser, in a form prescribed or approved by SBA, specified information on the terms, conditions, and yield of such instrument.

(b) *Brokers and Dealers.* Each broker, dealer, and Pool or Trust assembler approved by SBA pursuant to these regulations shall either be regulated by a Federal financial regulatory agency, or be a member of the National Association of Securities Dealers (NASD), and shall be in good standing in respect to compliance with the financial, ethical, and reporting requirements of such body. They also shall be in good standing with SBA as determined by the SBA Associate Administrator for Investment (see paragraph (d) of this section) and shall provide a fidelity bond or insurance in such amount as SBA may require.

(c) *Suspension and/or termination of Broker or Dealer.* SBA shall exclude from the sale and all other dealings in Debentures, Participating Securities or TCs any broker or dealer:

(1) If such broker's or dealer's authority to engage in the securities business has been revoked or suspended by a supervisory agency. When such authority has been suspended, such broker or dealer will be suspended by SBA for the duration of such suspension by the supervisory agency.

(2) If such broker or dealer has been indicted or otherwise formally charged with a misdemeanor or felony bearing on its fitness, such broker or dealer may be suspended while the charge is pending. Upon conviction, participation may be terminated.

(3) If such broker or dealer has suffered an adverse final civil judgment, holding that such broker or dealer has committed a breach of trust or violation of law or regulation protecting the integrity of business transactions or relationships, participation in the market for Debentures, Participating Securities or TCs may be terminated.

(4) If such broker or dealer has failed to make full disclosure of the information required by SBA in paragraph (a) of this section, such broker's or dealer's participation in the market for Debentures, Participating Securities or TCs may be terminated.

(d) *Termination/suspension proceedings.* A broker's or dealer's participation in the market for Debentures, Participating Securities or TCs will be conducted in accordance with part 134 of this chapter. SBA may, for any of the reasons stated in paragraphs (b)(1) through (b)(4) of this section, suspend the privilege of any broker or dealer to participate in this market. SBA shall give written notice at least ten (10) business days prior to the effective date of such suspension. Such notice shall inform the broker or dealer of the opportunity for a hearing pursuant to part 134 of this chapter.

§ 107.1640 SBA access to records of the CRA, Brokers, Dealers and Pool or Trust assemblers.

The CRA and any broker, dealer and Pool or Trust assembler operating under the regulations in this part shall make all books, records and related materials associated with Debentures, Participating Securities and TCs available to SBA for review and copying purposes. Such access shall be at such party's primary place of business during normal business hours.

MISCELLANEOUS

§ 107.1700 Transfer by SBA of its interest in Licensee's Leverage security.

Upon such conditions and for such consideration as it deems reasonable, SBA may sell, assign, transfer, or otherwise dispose of any Preferred Security, Debenture, Participating Security, or other security held by or on behalf of SBA in connection with Leverage. Upon notice by SBA, Licensee will make all payments of principal, dividends, interest, Prioritized Payments, and redemptions as shall be directed by SBA. Licensee will be liable for all damage or loss which SBA may sustain by reason of such disposal, up to the amount of Licensee's liability under such security, plus court costs and reasonable attorney's fees incurred by SBA.

§ 107.1710 SBA authority to collect or compromise its claims.

SBA may, upon such conditions and for such consideration as it deems reasonable, collect or compromise all claims relating to Preferred or Participating Securities or obligations held or guaranteed by SBA, and all legal or equitable rights accruing to SBA.

§ 107.1720 Characteristics of SBA's guarantee.

If SBA agrees to guarantee a Licensee's Debentures or Participating Securities, such guarantee will be unconditional, irrespective of the validity, regularity or enforceability of the Debentures or Participating Securities or any other circumstances which might constitute a legal or equitable discharge or defense of a guarantor. Pursuant to its guarantee, SBA will make timely payments of principal and interest on the Debentures or the Redemption Price of and Prioritized Payments on the Participating Securities.

[63 FR 5873, Feb. 5, 1998]

Subpart J—Licensee's Noncompliance With Terms of Leverage

§ 107.1800 Licensee's agreement to terms and conditions in §§ 107.1810 and 107.1820.

Any Licensee that violates the terms and conditions of its Leverage is subject to SBA remedies. The terms, conditions and remedies in § 107.1810 apply to outstanding Debentures issued after April 25, 1994. The terms, conditions and remedies in § 107.1820 apply to outstanding Preferred Securities and Participating Securities issued after April 25, 1994, or if you have Earmarked Assets in your portfolio.

§ 107.1810 Events of default and SBA's remedies for Licensee's noncompliance with terms of Debentures.

(a) *Applicability of this section.* This § 107.1810 applies to Debentures issued after April 25, 1994. By issuing such Debentures, you automatically agree to the terms, conditions and remedies in this section, as in effect at the time of issuance and as if fully set forth in the Debentures. Debentures issued before April 25, 1994 continue to be governed by the remedies in effect at the time of their issuance.

(b) *Automatic events of default.* The occurrence of one or more of the events in this paragraph (b) causes the remedies in paragraph (c) of this section to take effect immediately.

(1) *Insolvency.* You become equitably or legally insolvent.

(2) *Voluntary assignment.* You make a voluntary assignment for the benefit of creditors without SBA's prior written approval.

(3) *Bankruptcy.* You file a petition to begin any bankruptcy or reorganization proceeding, receivership, dissolution or other similar creditors' rights proceeding, or such action is initiated against you and is not dismissed within 60 days.

(c) *SBA remedies for automatic events of default.* Upon the occurrence of one or more of the events in paragraph (b) of this section:

(1) Without notice, presentation or demand, the entire indebtedness evidenced by your Debentures, including accrued interest, and any other amounts owed SBA with respect to your Debentures, is immediately due and payable; and

(2) You automatically consent to the appointment of SBA or its designee as your receiver under section 311(c) of the Act.

(d) *Events of default with notice.* For any occurrence (as determined by SBA) of one or more of the events in this paragraph (d), SBA may avail itself of one or more of the remedies in paragraph (e) of this section.

(1) *Fraud.* You commit a fraudulent act which causes detriment to SBA's position as a creditor or guarantor.

(2) *Fraudulent transfers.* You make any transfer or incur any obligation that is fraudulent under the terms of 11 U.S.C. 548.

(3) *Willful conflicts of interest.* You willfully violate § 107.730.

(4) *Willful non-compliance.* You willfully violate one or more of the substantive provisions of the Act, specifically including but not limited to the provisions summarized in section 310(c) of the Act, or any substantive regulation promulgated under the Act.

(5) *Repeated Events of Default.* At any time after being notified by SBA of the occurrence of an event of default under paragraph (f) of this section, you engage in similar behavior which results in another occurrence of the same event of default.

(6) *Transfer of Control.* You violate § 107.475 and/or willfully violate § 107.410, and as a result of such violation you undergo a transfer of Control.

(7) *Non-cooperation under § 107.1810(h).* You fail to take appropriate steps, satisfactory to SBA, to accomplish any action SBA may have required under paragraph (h) of this section.

(8) *Non-notification of Events of Default.* You fail to notify SBA as soon as you know or reasonably should have known that any event of default exists under this section.

(9) *Non-notification of defaults to others.* You fail to notify SBA in writing within ten days from the date of a declaration of an event of default or nonperformance under any note, debenture or indebtedness of yours, issued to or held by anyone other than SBA.

(e) *SBA remedies for events of default with notice.* Upon written notice to you of the occurrence (as determined by SBA) of one or more of the events in paragraph (d) of this section:

(1) SBA may declare the entire indebtedness evidenced by your Debentures, including accrued interest, and/or any other amounts owed SBA with respect to your Debentures, immediately due and payable; and

(2) SBA may avail itself of any remedy available under the Act, specifically including institution of proceedings for the appointment of SBA or its designee as your receiver under section 311(c) of the Act.

(f) *Events of default with opportunity to cure.* For any occurrence (as determined by SBA) of one or more of the events in this paragraph (f), SBA may avail itself of one or more of the remedies in paragraph (g) of this section.

(1) *Excessive Management Expenses.* Without the prior written consent of SBA, you incur Management Expenses in excess of those permitted under § 107.520.

(2) *Improper Distributions.* You make any Distribution to your shareholders or partners, except with the prior written consent of SBA, other than:

(i) Distributions permitted under § 107.585;

(ii) Payments from Retained Earnings Available for Distribution based on either the shareholders' pro-rata interests or the provisions for profit distributions in your partnership agreement, as appropriate;

(iii) Distributions by Participating Securities issuers as permitted under §§ 107.1540 through 107.1580; and

(iv) Distributions by Early Stage SBICs as permitted under § 107.1180.

(3) *Failure to make payment.* Unless otherwise approved by SBA, you fail to make timely payment of any amount due under any security or obligation of yours that is issued to, held or guaranteed by SBA.

(4) *Failure to maintain Regulatory Capital.* You fail to maintain the minimum Regulatory Capital required under these regulations or, without the prior written consent of SBA, you reduce your Regulatory Capital, except as permitted by §§ 107.585 and 107.1560 through 107.1580.

(5) *Capital Impairment.* You have a condition of Capital Impairment as determined under § 107.1830.

(6) *Cross-default.* An obligation of yours that is greater than $100,000 becomes due or payable (with or without notice) before its stated maturity date, for any reason including your failure to pay any amount when due. This provision does not apply if you pay the amount due within any applicable grace period or contest the payment of the obligation in good faith by appropriate proceedings.

(7) *Nonperformance.* You violate or fail to perform one or more of the terms and conditions of any security or obligation of yours that is issued to, held or guaranteed by SBA, or of any agreement with or conditions imposed by SBA in its administration of the Act and the regulations promulgated under the Act.

(8) *Noncompliance.* Except as otherwise provided in paragraph (d)(5) of this section, SBA determines that you have violated one or more of the substantive provisions of the Act, specifically including but not limited to the provisions summarized in section 310(c) of the Act, or any substantive regulation promulgated under the Act.

(9) *Failure to maintain investment ratio.* You fail to maintain the investment ratio for Leverage in excess of 300 percent of Leverageable Capital (see § 107.1160(c)), if applicable to you, as of the end of each fiscal year. In determining whether you have maintained the ratio, SBA will disregard any prepayment, sale, or disposition of Venture Capital Financing, any increase in Leverageable Capital, and any receipt of additional Leverage, within 120 days prior to the end of your fiscal year.

(10) *Failure to maintain diversity.* You fail to maintain diversity between management and ownership as required by § 107.150, if applicable to you.

(11) *Failure by an Early Stage SBIC to meet investment requirements.* You are an Early Stage SBIC and, beginning on the first fiscal quarter end when your cumulative total Financings (in dollars) are at least equal to your Regulatory Capital, you have not made at least 50 percent of such Financings to Small Businesses that at the time of your initial Financing were "early stage" companies, as defined under the definition of Early Stage SBIC in § 107.50 of this part.

(12) *Failure by an Early Stage SBIC to maintain required interest reserve.* You are an Early Stage SBIC and you fail to maintain a sufficient reserve to pay interest and Charges on your Debentures as required under § 107.1181 of this part.

(g) *SBA remedies for events of default with opportunity to cure.* (1) Upon written notice to you of the occurrence (as determined by SBA) of one or more of the events of default in paragraph (f) of this section, and subject to the conditions in paragraph (g)(2) of this section:

(i) SBA may declare the entire indebtedness evidenced by your Debentures, including accrued interest, and/or any other amounts owed SBA with respect to your Debentures, immediately due and payable; and

(ii) SBA may avail itself of any remedy available under the Act, specifically including institution of proceedings for the appointment of SBA or its designee as your receiver under section 311(c) of the Act.

(2) SBA may invoke the remedies in paragraph (g)(1) of this section only if:

(i) It has given you at least 15 days to cure the default(s); and

(ii) You fail to cure the default(s) to SBA's satisfaction within the allotted time.

(h) *Repeated non-substantive violations.* If you repeatedly fail to comply with one or more of the non-substantive provisions of the Act or any non-substantive regulation promulgated under the Act, SBA, after written notification to you and until you cure such condition to SBA's satisfaction, may deny you additional Leverage and/or require you to take such actions as SBA may determine to be appropriate under the circumstances.

(i) *Consent to removal of officers, directors, or general partners and/or appointment of receiver.* The Articles of any Licensee issuing Debentures after April 25, 1994 must include the following provisions as a condition to the purchase or guarantee by SBA of such Leverage. Upon the occurrence of any of the events specified in paragraphs (d)(1) through (d)(6) or (f)(1) through (f)(3) of this section as determined by SBA, SBA shall have the right, and your consent to SBA's exercise of such right:

(1) With respect to a Corporate Licensee, upon written notice, to require you to replace, with individuals approved by SBA, one or more of your officers and/or such number of directors of your board of directors as is sufficient to constitute a majority of such board; or

(2) With respect to a Partnership Licensee, upon written notice, to require you to remove the person(s) responsible for such occurrence and/or to remove the general partner of Licensee, which general partner shall then be replaced in accordance with Licensee's Articles by a new general partner approved by SBA; and/or

(3) With respect to either a Corporate or Partnership Licensee, to obtain the appointment of SBA or its designee as your receiver under section 311(c) of the Act for the purpose of continuing your operations. The appointment of a receiver to liquidate a Licensee is not within such consent, but is governed instead by the relevant provisions of the Act.

(j) *Additional SBA remedies applicable to Debentures issued by Early Stage SBICs.* If you are an Early Stage SBIC, upon SBA's payment pursuant to its guarantee of any of your Debentures, SBA shall have the following additional rights and you consent to SBA's exercise of any or all of such rights:

(1) To prohibit you from making any additional investments except for investments under legally binding commitments you entered into before such payment by SBA and, subject to SBA's prior written approval, investments that are necessary to protect your investments;

(2) Until all Leverage is repaid and amounts related thereto are paid in full, to prohibit Distributions by you to any party other than SBA, its agent or Trustee;

(3) To require all your commitments from investors to be funded at the earliest time(s) permitted in accordance with your Articles;

(4) To review and re-determine your approved Management Expenses; and

(5) To the appointment of SBA or its designee as your receiver under section 311(c) of the Act for the purpose of continuing your operations.

[61 FR 3189, Jan. 31, 1996, as amended at 74 FR 33916, July 14, 2009; 77 FR 25054, Apr. 27, 2012]

§ 107.1820 Conditions affecting issuers of Preferred Securities and/or Participating Securities.

(a) *Applicability of this section.* This section applies if you have Preferred Securities issued after April 25, 1994, or if you issue Participating Securities or have Earmarked Assets in your portfolio. Your Articles must include the provisions of this § 107.1820 as a condition to SBA's purchase of Preferred Securities or guarantee of Participating Securities and for as long as you own Earmarked Assets. Preferred Securities issued before April 25, 1994 continue to be governed by the remedies in effect at the time of their issuance.

(b) *Removal Conditions.* Upon the occurrence (as determined by SBA) of any of the following conditions ("Removal Conditions"), SBA may avail itself of one or more of the remedies in paragraph (d) of this section:

(1) *Insolvency or extreme Capital Impairment.* You become equitably or legally insolvent, or have a Capital Impairment Percentage of 100 percent or more ("extreme Capital Impairment") and have not cured such Capital Impairment within the time limits set by SBA in writing. In this regard:

(i) You are not considered to have a condition of extreme Capital Impairment during the first eight years following your first issuance of Participating Securities.

(ii) This paragraph (b)(1) does not give you an additional opportunity to cure if you have already had an opportunity to cure your Capital Impairment under paragraph (e)(3) of this section.

(2) *Voluntary assignment.* You make a voluntary assignment for the benefit of creditors.

(3) *Bankruptcy.* You begin any bankruptcy or reorganization proceeding, receivership, dissolution or other similar creditors' rights proceeding, or such action is initiated against you and is not dismissed within 60 days.

(4) *Transfer of Control.* You violate § 107.475 and/or willfully violate § 107.410, and such violation results in a transfer of Control.

(5) *Fraud.* You commit a fraudulent act which causes serious detriment to SBA's position as a guarantor or investor.

(6) *Fraudulent transfers.* You make any transfer or incur any obligation that is fraudulent under the terms of 11 U.S.C. 548.

(c) *Contingent Removal Conditions.* Upon the occurrence (as determined by SBA) of any of the following conditions ("Contingent Removal Conditions"), SBA may avail itself of one or more of the remedies in paragraph (d) of this section, but only if you fail to remove the person(s) SBA identifies as responsible for such occurrence and/or cure such occurrence to SBA's satisfaction within a time period determined by SBA (but not less than 15 days):

(1) *Willful conflicts of interest.* You willfully violate § 107.730.

(2) *Willful or repeated noncompliance.* You willfully or repeatedly violate one or more of the substantive provisions of the Act, specifically including but not limited to the provisions summarized in section 310(c) of the Act, or any substantive regulation promulgated under the Act.

(3) *Failure to comply with restrictions under paragraph (f) of this section.* You fail to comply with the restrictions imposed by SBA under paragraph (f) of this section.

(d) *SBA remedies for Removal Conditions and Contingent Removal Conditions.* Upon the occurrence (as determined by SBA) of any Removal Condition, or any Contingent Removal Condition accompanied by your failure to act as set forth in paragraph (c) of this section, SBA has the following rights, and you consent to SBA's exercise of any or all of such rights:

(1) With respect to a Corporate Licensee, upon written notice, to require you to replace, with individuals approved by SBA, one or more of your officers and/or such number of directors as is sufficient to constitute a majority of your board of directors; or

(2) With respect to a Partnership Licensee, upon written notice, to require you to remove the person(s) responsible for such occurrence and/or to remove your general partner, who shall then be replaced in accordance with your Articles by a new general partner approved by SBA; and/or

(3) With respect to either a Corporate or Partnership Licensee, to the appointment of SBA or its designee as your receiver under section 311(c) of the Act for the purpose of continuing your operations. The appointment of a receiver to liquidate a Licensee is not within such consent, but is governed instead by the relevant provisions of the Act.

(e) *Restricted Operations Conditions.* Upon the occurrence (as determined by SBA) of any of the following conditions ("Restricted Operations Conditions"), SBA may avail itself of any of the remedies in paragraph (f) of this section.

(1) *Removal Conditions or Contingent Removal Conditions.* Any condition occurs which is listed in paragraphs (b) or (c) of this section.

(2) *Failure to maintain Regulatory Capital.* You fail to maintain the minimum Regulatory Capital required by this part.

(3) *Capital or Liquidity Impairment.* You have a condition of Capital Impairment as determined under § 107.1830 or, if applicable, a condition of Liquidity Impairment as determined under § 107.1505, and you fail to cure the impairment within time limits set by SBA in writing.

(4) *Improper Distributions.* You make any Distribution to your shareholders or partners other than those permitted by §§ 107.585 and 107.1560 through 107.1580.

(5) *Excessive Management Expenses.* Without the prior written consent of SBA, you incur Management Expenses in excess of those permitted under § 107.520.

(6) *Failure to make payment.* You fail to pay any amounts due under Preferred Securities or required by §§ 107.1500 through 107.1590, unless otherwise permitted by SBA.

(7) *Noncompliance.* Except as otherwise provided for in paragraphs (c)(1) and (c)(2) of this section, SBA determines that you have failed to comply with one or more of the substantive provisions of the Act, specifically including but not limited to the provisions summarized in section 310(c) of the Act, or any substantive regulation promulgated under the Act.

(8) *Failure to maintain diversity.* You fail to maintain diversity between management and ownership as required by § 107.150, if applicable to you.

(9) *Failure to meet investment requirements.* You fail to make the amount of Equity Capital Investments required for Participating Securities (§ 107.1500(b)(4)), if applicable to you; or you fail to maintain as of the end of each fiscal year the investment ratios or amounts required for Leverage in excess of 300 percent of Leverageable Capital (§ 107.1160(c)) or Preferred Securities in excess of 100 percent of Leverageable Capital (§ 107.1160(d)), if applicable to you. In determining whether you have met the maintenance requirements in § 107.1160(c) or (d), SBA will disregard any prepayment, sale, or disposition of Venture Capital Financings, any increase in Leverageable Capital, and any receipt of additional Leverage, within 120 days prior to the end of your fiscal year.

(10) *Nonperformance.* You violate or fail to perform one or more of the terms and conditions of any Participating Security or Preferred Security or of any agreement with or condition imposed by SBA in its administration of the Act and the regulations promulgated thereunder.

(11) *Noncooperation under paragraph (g) of this section.* You fail to take appropriate steps, satisfactory to SBA, to accomplish such action as SBA may have required under paragraph (g) of this section.

(f) *SBA remedies for Restricted Operations Conditions.* Upon the occurrence of any Restricted Operations Condition, and until such condition(s) are cured to SBA's satisfaction within a time period determined by SBA (but not less than 15 days), upon written notice SBA shall have the following rights, and you consent to SBA's exercise of any or all of such rights:

(1) To prohibit you from making any additional investments except for investments under legally binding commitments you entered into before such notice and, subject to SBA's prior written approval, investments that are necessary to protect your investments;

(2) Until all Leverage is redeemed and amounts due are paid, to prohibit Distributions by you to any party other than SBA, its agent or Trustee;

(3) To require all your commitments from investors to be funded at the earliest time(s) permitted in accordance with your Articles; and

(4) To review and re-determine your approved Management Expenses.

(g) *Repeated non-substantive violations.* If you repeatedly fail to comply with one or more of the non-substantive provisions of the Act or any non-substantive regulation promulgated thereunder, SBA, after written notification to you and until such condition is cured to SBA's satisfaction, will deny you additional Leverage and/or require you to take such actions as SBA may determine to be appropriate under the circumstances.

[61 FR 3189, Jan. 31, 1996, as amended at 63 FR 5873, Feb. 5, 1998]

COMPUTATION OF LICENSEE'S CAPITAL IMPAIRMENT

§ 107.1830 Licensee's Capital Impairment—definition and general requirements.

(a) *Applicability of this section.* This section applies to Leverage issued on or after April 25, 1994. For Leverage issued before April 25, 1994, you must comply with paragraphs (e) and (f) of this section and the Capital Impairment regulations in this part in effect when you issued your Leverage. For all Leverage issued, you must also comply with any contractual provisions to which you have agreed.

(b) *Significance of Capital Impairment condition.* If you have a condition of Capital Impairment, you are not in compliance with the terms of your Leverage. As a result, SBA has the right to impose the applicable remedies for noncompliance in §§ 107.1810(g) and 107.1820(f).

(c) *Definition of Capital Impairment condition.* You have a condition of Capital Impairment if your Capital Impairment Percentage, as computed in § 107.1840, exceeds:

(1) For Section 301(d) Licensees, 75 percent.

(2) For Section 301(c) Licensees, the appropriate percentage from the following table:

MAXIMUM PERMITTED CAPITAL IMPAIRMENT PERCENTAGES FOR SECTION 301(c) LICENSEES

If the percentage of equity capital investments (at cost) in your portfolio is:	And your ratio of outstanding leverage to leverageable capital is:	Then your maximum permitted capital impairment percentage is:
67%	100% or less	70
	Over 100% but not over 200%	60
	Over 200%	50
At least 40% but under 67%	100% or less	55
	Over 100% but not over 200%	50
	Over 200%	40
Under 40%	100% or less	45
	Over 100% but not over 200%	40
	Over 200%	35

(d) *Phase-in of maximum permitted Capital Impairment Percentages for Section 301(c) Licensees.* If you are a Section 301(c) Licensee, regardless of your maximum permitted Capital Impairment Percentage under paragraph (c) of this section, you will not have a condition of Capital Impairment if:

(1) Your Capital Impairment Percentage does not exceed 50 percent; and

(2) You have not reached your first fiscal year end occurring after April 25, 1995.

(e) *Quarterly computation requirement and procedure.* You must determine whether you have a condition of Capital Impairment as of the end of each fiscal quarter. You must notify SBA promptly if you are capitally impaired.

(f) *SBA's right to determine Licensee's Capital Impairment condition.* SBA may make its own determination of your Capital Impairment condition at any time.

[61 FR 3189, Jan. 31, 1996, as amended at 63 FR 5873, Feb. 5, 1998]

§ 107.1840 Computation of Licensee's Capital Impairment Percentage.

(a) *General.* This section contains the procedures you must use to determine your Capital Impairment Percentage if you have outstanding Leverage issued after April 25, 1994. You must compare your Capital Impairment Percentage to the maximum permitted under § 107.1830(c) to determine whether you have a condition of Capital Impairment.

(b) *Preliminary impairment test.* If you satisfy the preliminary impairment test, your Capital Impairment Percentage is zero and you do not have to perform any more procedures in this § 107.1840. Otherwise, you must continue with paragraph (c) of this section. You satisfy the test if the following amounts are both zero or greater:

(1) The sum of Undistributed Net Realized Earnings, as reported on SBA Form 468, and Includible Non-Cash Gains.

(2) Unrealized Gain (Loss) on Securities Held.

(c) *How to compute your Capital Impairment Percentage.* (1) If you have an Unrealized Gain on Securities Held, compute your Adjusted Unrealized Gain using paragraph (d) of this section. If you have an Unrealized Loss on Securities Held, continue with paragraph (c)(2) of this Section.

(2) Add together your Undistributed Net Realized Earnings, your Includible Non-cash Gains, and either your Unrealized Loss on Securities Held or your Adjusted Unrealized Gain.

(3) If the sum in paragraph (c)(2) of this section is zero or greater, your Capital Impairment Percentage is zero.

(4) If the sum in paragraph (c)(2) of this section is less than zero, drop the negative sign, divide by your Regulatory Capital (excluding Treasury

Stock), and multiply by 100. The result is your Capital Impairment Percentage.

(d) *How to compute your Adjusted Unrealized Gain.* (1) Subtract Unrealized Depreciation from Unrealized Appreciation. This is your "Net Appreciation".

(2) Determine your Unrealized Appreciation on Publicly Traded and Marketable securities. This is your "Class 1 Appreciation".

(3) Determine your Unrealized Appreciation on securities that are not Publicly Traded and Marketable and meet the following criteria, which must be substantiated to the satisfaction of SBA (this is your "Class 2 Appreciation"):

(i) The Small Business that issued the security received a significant subsequent equity financing by an investor whose objectives were not primarily strategic and at a price that conclusively supports the Unrealized Appreciation;

(ii) Such financing represents a substantial investment in the form of an arm's length transaction by a sophisticated new investor in the issuer's securities; and

(iii) Except as provided for Early Stage SBICs in § 107.1845, such financing occurred within 24 months of the date of the Capital Impairment computation, or the Small Business's pretax cash flow from operations for its most recent fiscal year was at least 10 percent of the Small Business's average contributed capital for such fiscal year.

(4) Except as provided for Early Stage SBICs in § 107.1845, perform the appropriate computation from the following table:

ADJUSTED UNREALIZED GAIN BEFORE ESTIMATED TAX EFFECTS

If:	And:	Then adjusted unrealized gain before taxes is:
Class 1 Appreciation ≤Net Appreciation	Class 1 Appreciation + Class 2 Appreciation ≤Net Appreciation.	(80% × Class 1 Appreciation) + (50% × Class 2 Appreciation).
Class 1 Appreciation ≤Net Appreciation	Class 1 Appreciation + Class 2 Appreciation >Net Appreciation.	(80% × Class 1 Appreciation) + [(50% × (Net Appreciation − Class 1 Appreciation)].
Class 1 Appreciation >Net Appreciation	....	80% × Net Appreciation.

(5) Reduce the gain computed in paragraph (d)(4) of this section by your estimate of related future income tax expense. Subject to any adjustment required by paragraph (d)(6) of this section, the result is your Adjusted Unrealized Gain for use in paragraph (c)(2) of this section.

(6) If any securities that are the source of either Class 1 or Class 2 Appreciation are pledged or encumbered in any way, you must reduce the Adjusted Unrealized Gain computed in paragraph (d)(5) of this section by the amount of the related borrowing or other obligation, up to the amount of the Unrealized Appreciation on the securities.

[61 FR 3189, Jan. 31, 1996, as amended at 77 FR 25054, Apr. 27, 2012]

§ 107.1845 Determination of Capital Impairment Percentage for Early Stage SBICs.

This section applies to Early Stage SBICs only. Except as modified by this section, all provisions of § 107.1840 apply to an Early Stage SBIC.

(a) To determine your Class 2 Appreciation under § 107.1840(d)(3), use the following provisions instead of § 107.1840(d)(3)(iii):

(1) Such financing occurred within 24 months of the date of the Capital Impairment computation. At the end of the 24 month period following the financing, you may request SBA's written approval to retain the use of the original Class 2 Appreciation on the investment for up to 24 additional months.

(2) In considering your request, SBA may obtain its own valuation of the investment, require you to obtain a valuation performed by an independent third party acceptable to SBA, and may consider any other information that it deems relevant. To the extent that the valuation and any other relevant information conclusively support the original Class 2 appreciation, SBA may approve an extension to use all or

part of the original Class 2 Appreciation for up to an additional 24 months (the "extension period").

(3) At the end of any extension period, you may submit a new request to retain the use of the original Class 2 Appreciation, repeating the steps in paragraphs (a)(1) and (2) of this section.

(4) SBA may reconsider its approval to retain the use of the original Class 2 Appreciation at any time based on information that may affect the value of an investment.

(b) Any time you submit a request for SBA approval to retain the use of the original Class 2 Appreciation under paragraph (a) of this section, you may also request SBA's written approval to modify your computation of Adjusted Unrealized Gain under §107.1840(d)(4) as provided in paragraph (c) of this section.

(c) If SBA determines that the appreciation on an investment, based on its current fair value, is at least two times the original Class 2 Appreciation on the investment, SBA may allow you, based on relevant information, to compute your Adjusted Unrealized Gain for the duration of the extension period as follows:

(1) Compute Adjusted Unrealized Gain in accordance with §107.1840(d)(4).

(2) If your result in paragraph (c)(1) of this section was computed using the first line of the table in §107.1840(d)(4):

(i) Calculate 50 percent of the original Class 2 Appreciation on the individual investment that is the subject of this paragraph (c), and

(ii) Add it to the result from paragraph (c)(1) of this section to determine your Adjusted Unrealized Gain.

(3) If your result in paragraph (c)(1) of this section was computed using the second line of the table in §107.1840(d)(4):

(i) Calculate 50 percent of the original Class 2 Appreciation on the individual investment that is the subject of this paragraph (c).

(ii) Subtract your Class 1 Appreciation from your Net Appreciation, and multiply the result by 50 percent.

(iii) Add the lesser of (c)(3)(i) and (ii) of this section to the result from paragraph (c)(1) of this section to determine your Adjusted Unrealized Gain.

[77 FR 25054, Apr. 27, 2012]

§107.1850 Exceptions to Capital Impairment provisions for Licensees with outstanding Participating Securities.

The provisions in this §107.1850 apply only if at least two-thirds of your outstanding Leverage consists of Participating Securities, and at least two-thirds of your Loans and Investments (at cost) consist of Equity Capital Investments.

(a) *Forbearance period for Participating Securities issuers.* During the first forty-eight (48) months following your first issuance of Participating Securities, you will not have a condition of Capital Impairment if your Capital Impairment Percentage is below 85 percent.

(b) *Extended forbearance period for early stage investors.* If at least two-thirds of your Loans and Investments (at cost) are in Start-Up Financings, the forbearance period in paragraph (a) of this section is extended to 60 months.

(c) *Forbearance based on actions by Licensee.* The provisions of this paragraph (c) apply only during the fifth and sixth years following your first issuance of Participating Securities. If your Capital Impairment Percentage, as determined either by you or by SBA, exceeds the maximum permitted under §107.1830(c) but is below 85 percent, you will not have a condition of Capital Impairment if you do either of the following within thirty (30) days of such determination:

(1) Increase your Regulatory Capital by a cash contribution placed in an escrow account or other account satisfactory to SBA, for its benefit. The contribution must equal, during the fifth year, 15 percent of your outstanding Leverage or, during the sixth year, 30 percent.

(2) Provide a guarantee, satisfactory to SBA and for its benefit, for the amount of the cash contribution required in paragraph (c)(1) of this section. SBA will credit any escrowed funds or guarantee received in the fifth year toward the requirements for the sixth year.

(d) *Conditions for forbearance under paragraph (c) of this section.* (1) You cannot count any funds placed in an escrow or other account under paragraph

(c) of this section as Leverageable Capital.

(2) Any fee and/or any claim to repayment by the party making the capital contribution or by the guarantor must be deferred and subordinate to all outstanding Leverage plus any unpaid Earned Prioritized Payments and earned Adjustments.

(3) If there is an acceleration or mandatory redemption under § 107.1810 or § 107.1820, any funds in the escrow account and/or any guarantee received under paragraph (c) of this section will be applied toward repaying any amounts due SBA.

(4) If you reduce your Capital Impairment Percentage to zero, SBA will release and return any escrowed funds and/or any guarantee received under paragraph (c) of this section.

Subpart K—Ending Operations as a Licensee

§ 107.1900 Surrender of license.

You may not surrender your license without SBA's prior written approval. Your request for approval must be accompanied by an offer of immediate repayment of all of your outstanding Leverage (including any prepayment penalties thereon), or by a plan satisfactory to SBA for the orderly liquidation of the Licensee.

Subpart L—Miscellaneous

§ 107.1910 Non-waiver of SBA's rights or terms of Leverage security.

SBA's failure to exercise or delay in exercising any right or remedy under the Act or the regulations in this part does not constitute a waiver of such right or remedy. SBA's failure to require you to perform any term or provision of your Leverage does not affect SBA's right to enforce such term or provision. Similarly, SBA's waiver of, or failure to enforce, any term or provision of your Leverage or of any event or condition set forth in § 107.1810 or § 107.1820 does not constitute a waiver of any succeeding breach of such term or provision or condition.

§ 107.1920 Licensee's application for exemption from a regulation in this part 107.

You may file an application in writing with SBA to have a proposed action exempted from any procedural or substantive requirement, restriction, or prohibition to which it is subject under this part, unless the provision is mandated by the Act. SBA may grant an exemption for such applicant, conditionally or unconditionally, provided the exemption would not be contrary to the purposes of the Act. Your application must be accompanied by supporting evidence which demonstrates to SBA's satisfaction that:

(a) The proposed action is fair and equitable; and

(b) The exemption requested is reasonably calculated to advance the best interests of the SBIC program in a manner consonant with the policy objectives of the Act and the regulations in this part.

§ 107.1930 Effect of changes in this part 107 on transactions previously consummated.

The legality of a transaction covered by the regulations in this part is governed by the regulations in this part in effect at the time the transaction was consummated, regardless of later changes. Nothing in this part bars SBA enforcement action with respect to any transaction consummated in violation of provisions applicable at the time, but no longer in effect.

PART 108—NEW MARKETS VENTURE CAPITAL ("NMVC") PROGRAM

Subpart A—Introduction to Part 108

Sec.

Subpart B—Definition of Terms Used in This Part 108

Subpart C—Qualifications for the NMVC Program

ORGANIZING A NMVC COMPANY

108.100 Business form.
108.110 Qualified management.
108.120 Economic development primary mission.
108.130 Identified Low Income Geographic Areas.
108.140 SBA approval of initial Management Expenses.
108.150 Management and ownership diversity requirement.
108.160 Special rules for NMVC Companies formed as limited partnerships.

CAPITALIZING A NMVC COMPANY

108.200 Adequate capital for NMVC Companies.
108.210 Minimum capital requirements for NMVC Companies.
108.230 Private Capital for NMVC Companies.

Subpart D—Application and Approval Process for NMVC Company Designation

108.300 When and how to apply for designation as a NMVC Company.
108.310 Contents of application.
108.320 Contents of comprehensive business plan.
108.330 Grant issuance fee.

Subpart E—Evaluation and Selection of NMVC Companies

108.340 Evaluation and selection—general.
108.350 Eligibility and completeness.
108.360 Evaluation criteria.
108.370 Conditional approval.
108.380 Final approval as a NMVC Company.

Subpart F—Changes in Ownership, Structure, or Control

CHANGES IN CONTROL OR OWNERSHIP OF NMVC COMPANY

108.400 Changes in ownership of 10 percent or more of NMVC Company but no change of Control.
108.410 Changes in Control of NMVC Company (through change in ownership or otherwise).
108.420 Prohibition on exercise of ownership or Control rights in NMVC Company before SBA approval.
108.430 Notification to SBA of transactions that may change ownership or Control.
108.440 Standards governing prior SBA approval for a proposed transfer of Control.
108.450 Notification to SBA of pledge of NMVC Company's shares.

RESTRICTIONS ON COMMON CONTROL OR OWNERSHIP OF TWO OR MORE NMVC COMPANIES

108.460 Restrictions on Common Control or ownership of two (or more) NMVC Companies.

CHANGE IN STRUCTURE OF NMVC COMPANY

108.470 SBA approval of merger, consolidation, or reorganization of NMVC Company.

Subpart G—Managing the Operations of a NMVC Company

GENERAL REQUIREMENTS

108.500 Lawful operations under the Act.
108.502 Representations to the public.
108.503 NMVC Company's adoption of an approved valuation policy.
108.504 Equipment and office requirements.
108.506 Safeguarding the NMVC Company's assets/Internal controls.
108.507 Violations based on false filings and nonperformance of agreements with SBA.
108.509 Employment of SBA officials.

MANAGEMENT AND COMPENSATION

108.510 SBA approval of NMVC Company's Investment Adviser/Manager.
108.520 Management Expenses of a NMVC Company.

CASH MANAGEMENT BY A NMVC COMPANY

108.530 Restrictions on investments of idle funds by NMVC Companies.

BORROWING BY NMVC COMPANIES FROM NON-SBA SOURCES

108.550 Prior approval of secured third-party debt of NMVC companies.

VOLUNTARY DECREASE IN REGULATORY CAPITAL

108.585 Voluntary decrease in NMVC Company's Regulatory Capital.

Subpart H—Recordkeeping, Reporting, and Examination Requirements for NMVC Companies

RECORDKEEPING REQUIREMENTS FOR NMVC COMPANIES

108.600 General requirement for NMVC Company to maintain and preserve records.
108.610 Required certifications for Loans and Investments.
108.620 Requirements to obtain information from Portfolio Concerns.

REPORTING REQUIREMENTS FOR NMVC COMPANIES

108.630 Requirement for NMVC companies to file financial statements and supplementary information with SBA (SBA Form 468).
108.640 Requirement to file portfolio financing reports (SBA Form 1031).
108.650 Requirement to report portfolio valuations to SBA.
108.660 Other items required to be filed by NMVC Company with SBA.
108.680 Reporting changes in NMVC Company not subject to prior SBA approval.

EXAMINATIONS OF NMVC COMPANIES BY SBA FOR REGULATORY COMPLIANCE

108.690 Examinations.
108.691 Responsibilities of NMVC Company during examination.
108.692 Examination fees.

Subpart I—Financing of Small Businesses by NMVC Companies

DETERMINING THE ELIGIBILITY OF A SMALL BUSINESS FOR NMVC FINANCING

108.700 Compliance with size standards in part 121 of this chapter as a condition of Assistance.
108.710 Requirement to finance Low-Income Enterprises.
108.720 Small Businesses that may be ineligible for financing.
108.730 Financings which constitute conflicts of interest.
108.740 Portfolio diversification ("overline" limitation).
108.760 How a change in size or activity of a Portfolio Concern affects the NMVC Company and the Portfolio Concern.

STRUCTURING NMVC COMPANY'S FINANCING OF ELIGIBLE SMALL BUSINESSES

108.800 Financings in the form of equity interests.
108.820 Financings in the form of guarantees.
108.825 Purchasing securities from an underwriter or other third party.

LIMITATIONS ON DISPOSITION OF ASSETS

108.885 Disposition of assets to NMVC Company's Associates.

MANAGEMENT SERVICES AND FEES

108.900 Fees for management services provided to a Small Business by a NMVC Company or its Associate.

Subpart J—SBA Financial Assistance for NMVC Companies (Leverage)

GENERAL INFORMATION ABOUT OBTAINING LEVERAGE

108.1100 Type of Leverage and application procedures.
108.1120 General eligibility requirement for Leverage.
108.1130 Leverage fees payable by NMVC Company.
108.1140 NMVC Company's acceptance of SBA remedies under § 108.1810.

MAXIMUM AMOUNT OF LEVERAGE FOR WHICH A NMVC COMPANY IS ELIGIBLE

108.1150 Maximum amount of Leverage for a NMVC Company.

CONDITIONAL COMMITMENTS BY SBA TO RESERVE LEVERAGE FOR A NMVC COMPANY

108.1200 SBA's Leverage commitment to a NMVC Company's application procedure, amount, and term.
108.1220 Requirement for NMVC Company to file financial statements at the time of request for a draw.
108.1230 Draw-downs by NMVC Company under SBA's Leverage commitment.
108.1240 Funding of NMVC Company's draw request through sale to third-party.

FUNDING LEVERAGE BY USE OF SBA GUARANTEED TRUST CERTIFICATES ("TCS")

108.1600 SBA authority to issue and guarantee Trust Certificates.
108.1610 Effect of prepayment or early redemption of Leverage on a Trust Certificate.
108.1620 Functions of agents, including Central Registration Agent, Selling Agent and Fiscal Agent.
108.1630 SBA regulation of Brokers and Dealers and disclosure to purchasers of Leverage or Trust Certificates.
108.1640 SBA access to records of the CRA, Brokers, Dealers and Pool or Trust assemblers.

MISCELLANEOUS

108.1700 Transfer by SBA of its interest in a NMVC Company's Leverage security.
108.1710 SBA authority to collect or compromise its claims.
108.1720 Characteristics of SBA's guarantee.

Subpart K—NMVC Company's Noncompliance With Terms of Leverage

108.1810 Events of default and SBA's remedies for NMVC Company's noncompliance with terms of Debentures.

AUTHORITY: 15 U.S.C. 689–689q.

SOURCE: 66 FR 28609, May 23, 2001, unless otherwise noted.

Subpart A—Introduction to Part 108

§ 108.10 Description of the New Markets Venture Capital Program.

The New Markets Venture Capital ("NMVC") Program is a developmental venture capital program for the purpose of promoting economic development and the creation of wealth and job opportunities in low-income geographic areas and among individuals living in such areas. SBA selects and then enters into participation agreements with selected newly formed venture capital companies, and provides leverage in the form of debenture guarantees to such companies to allow them to make equity capital investments in smaller enterprises located in low-income geographic areas. SBA also awards grants to such companies and to Specialized Small Business Investment Companies so that they can provide operational assistance to such smaller enterprises in connection with such investments.

§ 108.20 Legal basis and applicability of this part 108.

The regulations in this part implement Part B of Title III of the Small Business Investment Act of 1958, as amended (15 U.S.C. 661 *et seq.*). All NMVC Companies must comply with all applicable SBA regulations, accounting guidelines and valuation guidelines for NMVC Companies, available from SBA.

§ 108.30 Amendments to Act and regulations.

A NMVC Company is subject to all provisions of the Act and parts 108 and 112 of title 13 of the Code of Federal Regulations.

§ 108.40 How to read this part 108.

(a) *Center headings.* All references in this part to SBA forms, and instructions for their preparation, are to the current issue of such forms (available from Investment Division, SBA). Center headings are descriptive and are used for convenience only. They have no regulatory effect.

(b) *Capitalizing defined terms.* Terms defined in § 108.50 have initial capitalization in this part 108.

(c) "*You.*" The pronoun "you" as used in this part 108 means a NMVC Company unless otherwise noted.

Subpart B—Definition of Terms Used in This Part 108

§ 108.50 Definition of terms.

The following definitions apply to this part 108:

Act means the Small Business Investment Act of 1958, as amended (15 U.S.C. 661 *et seq.*).

Affiliate or *Affiliates* has the meaning set forth in § 121.103 of this chapter.

Applicant means any entity submitting an application to SBA for designation as a NMVC Company under this part.

Articles mean articles of incorporation or charter for a Corporate NMVC Company, the partnership agreement or certificate for a Partnership NMVC Company, and the operating agreement or other organizational documents for a LLC NMVC Company.

Assistance or *Assisted* means Financing of or management services rendered to a Small Business by or through a NMVC Company pursuant to the Act and this part.

Associate of a NMVC Company means any of the following:

(1)(i) An officer, director, employee or agent of a Corporate NMVC Company;

(ii) A Control Person, employee or agent of a Partnership NMVC Company;

(iii) A managing member of a LLC NMVC Company;

(iv) An Investment Adviser/Manager of any NMVC Company, including any Person who contracts with a Control Person of a Partnership NMVC Company to be the Investment Adviser/Manager of such NMVC Company; or

(v) Any Person regularly serving a NMVC Company on retainer in the capacity of attorney at law.

(2) Any Person who owns or controls, or who has entered into an agreement to own or control, directly or indirectly, at least 10 percent of any class of stock of a Corporate NMVC Company or 10 percent of the membership interests of an LLC NMVC Company, or a limited partner's interest of at least 10 percent of the partnership capital of a Partnership NMVC Company. However, neither a limited partner in a Partnership NMVC Company nor a non-managing member in an LLC NMVC Company is considered an Associate if such Person is an entity Institutional Investor whose investment in the Partnership, including commitments, represents no more than 33 percent of the capital of the NMVC Company and no more than five percent of such Person's net worth.

(3) Any officer, director, partner (other than a limited partner), manager, agent, or employee of any Associate described in paragraph (1) or (2) of this definition.

(4) Any Person that directly or indirectly Controls, or is Controlled by, or is under Common Control with, a NMVC Company.

(5) Any Person that directly or indirectly Controls, or is Controlled by, or is under Common Control with, any Person described in paragraphs (1) and (2) of this definition.

(6) Any Close Relative of any Person described in paragraphs (1), (2), (4), and (5) of this definition.

(7) Any Secondary Relative of any Person described in paragraphs (1), (2), (4), and (5) of this definition.

(8) Any concern in which—

(i) Any person described in paragraphs (1) through (6) of this definition is an officer; general partner, or managing member; or

(ii) Any such Person(s) singly or collectively Control or own, directly or indirectly, an equity interest of at least 10 percent (excluding interests that such Person(s) own indirectly through ownership interests in the NMVC Company).

(9) Any concern in which any Person(s) described in paragraph (7) of this definition singly or collectively own (including beneficial ownership) a majority equity interest, or otherwise have Control. As used in this paragraph (9), "collectively" means together with any Person(s) described in paragraphs (1) though (7) of this definition.

(10) For the purposes of this definition, if any Associate relationship described in paragraphs (1) through (7) of this definition exists at any time within six months before or after the date that a NMVC Company provides Financing, then that Associate relationship is considered to exist on the date of the Financing.

(11) If any NMVC Company has any ownership interest in another NMVC Company, the two NMVC companies are Associates of each other.

Capital Impairment has the meaning set forth in § 108.1830(b).

Central Registration Agent or *CRA* means one or more agents appointed by SBA for the purpose of issuing TCs and performing the functions enumerated in § 108.1620 and performing similar functions for Debentures funded outside the pooling process.

Close Relative of an individual means:

(1) A current or former spouse;

(2) A father, mother, guardian, brother, sister, son, daughter; or

(3) A father-in-law, mother-in-law, brother-in-law, sister-in-law, son-in-law, or daughter-in-law.

Commitment means a written agreement between a NMVC Company and an eligible Small Business that obligates the NMVC Company to provide Financing (except a guarantee) to that Small Business in a fixed or determinable sum, by a fixed or determinable future date. In this context the term "agreement" means that there has been agreement on the principal economic terms of the Financing. The agreement may include reasonable conditions precedent to the NMVC Company's obligation to fund the commitment, but these conditions must be outside the NMVC Company's control.

Common Control means a condition where two or more Persons, either through ownership, management, contract, or otherwise, are under the Control of one group or Person. Two or more NMVC companies are presumed to be under Common Control if they are Affiliates of each other by reason of common ownership or common officers, directors, or general partners; or if they are managed or their investments are significantly directed either by a common independent investment advisor or managerial contractor, or by two or more such advisors or contractors that are Affiliates of each other. This presumption may be rebutted by evidence satisfactory to SBA.

Community Development Finance means debt and equity-type investments in low-income communities.

Conditionally Approved NMVC Company means a company that—

(1) Has applied for participation as a NMVC Company, and

(2) SBA has conditionally approved to participate in the NMVC program for a specified period of time not to exceed two years, subject to the company fulfilling the requirements to be a NMVC Company within that specified period of time.

Control means the possession, direct or indirect, of the power to direct or cause the direction of the management and policies of a NMVC Company or other concern, whether through the ownership of voting securities, by contract, or otherwise.

Control Person means any Person that controls a NMVC Company, either directly or through an intervening entity. A Control Person includes:

(1) A general partner of a Partnership NMVC Company;

(2) Any Person serving as the general partner, officer, director, or manager (in the case of a limited liability company) of any entity that controls a NMVC Company, either directly or through an intervening entity;

(3) Any Person that—

(i) Controls or owns, directly or through an intervening entity, at least 10 percent of a Partnership NMVC Company or any entity described in paragraphs (1) or (2) of this definition; and

(ii) Participates in the investment decisions of the general partner of such Partnership NMVC Company;

(4) Any Person that controls or owns, directly or through an intervening entity, at least 50 percent of a Partnership NMVC Company or any entity described in paragraphs (1) or (2) of this definition.

Corporate NMVC Company. See definition of NMVC Company in this section.

Debentures means debt obligations issued by NMVC companies pursuant to section 355 of the Act and held or guaranteed by SBA.

Debt Securities are instruments evidencing a loan with an option or any other right to acquire Equity Securities in a Small Business or its Affiliates, or a loan which by its terms is convertible into an equity position. Consideration must be paid for all options that you acquire.

Developmental Venture Capital means capital in the form of Equity Capital Investments in Smaller Enterprises made with a primary objective of fostering economic development in Low-Income Geographic Areas.

Distribution means any transfer of cash or non-cash assets to SBA, its agent or Trustee, or to partners in a Partnership NMVC Company, or to shareholders in a Corporate NMVC Company, or to members in an LLC NMVC Company. Capitalization of Retained Earnings Available for Distribution constitutes a Distribution to the NMVC Company's non-SBA partners, shareholders, or members.

Equity Capital Investments means investments in the form of common or preferred stock, limited partnership interests, options, warrants, or similar equity instruments, including subordinated debt with equity features if such debt provides only for interest payments contingent upon and limited to the extent of earnings. Equity Capital Investments must not require amortization. Equity Capital Investments may be guaranteed by one or more third parties; however, neither Equity Capital Investments nor such guarantee may be collateralized or otherwise secured. Investments classified as Debt Securities are not precluded from qualifying as Equity Capital Investments. Equity Capital Investments may provide for royalty payments only if the royalty payments are based on the earnings of the concern.

Equity Securities means stock of any class in a corporation, stock options, warrants, limited partnership interests in a limited partnership, membership interests in a limited liability company, or joint venture interests.

Financing or *Financed* means outstanding financial assistance provided to a Small Business by a NMVC Company, whether through:

(1) Loans;

(2) Debt Securities;

(3) Equity Securities;

(4) Guarantees; or

(5) Purchases of securities of a Small Business through or from an underwriter (see § 108.825).

Guaranty Agreement means the contract entered into by SBA which is a guarantee backed by the full faith and credit of the United States Government as to timely payment of principal and interest on Debentures and SBA's rights in connection with such guarantee.

Includible Non-Cash Gains means those non-cash gains (as reported on SBA Form 468) that are realized in the form of Publicly Traded and Marketable securities or investment grade debt instruments. For purposes of this definition, investment grade debt instruments means those instruments that are rated "BBB" or "Baa", or better, by Standard & Poor's Corporation or Moody's Investors Service, respectively. Non-rated debt may be considered to be investment grade if a NMVC Company obtains a written opinion from an investment banking firm acceptable to SBA stating that the non-rated debt instrument is equivalent in risk to the issuer's investment grade debt.

Institutional Investor means:

(1) *Entities.* Any of the following entities if the entity has a net worth (exclusive of unfunded commitments from investors) of at least $1 million, or such higher amount as is specified in this paragraph (1). (See also § 108.230(c)(4) for limitations on the amount of an Institutional Investor's commitment that may be included in Private Capital.)

(i) A State or National bank, trust company, savings bank, or savings and loan association.

(ii) An insurance company.

(iii) A 1940 Act Investment Company or Business Development Company (each as defined in the Investment Company Act of 1940, as amended (15 U.S.C. 8a–1 *et seq.*).

(iv) A holding company of any entity described in paragraph (1)(i), (ii) or (iii) of this definition.

(v) An employee benefit or pension plan established for the benefit of employees of the Federal government, any State or political subdivision of a State, or any agency or instrumentality of such government unit.

(vi) An employee benefit or pension plan (as defined in the Employee Retirement Income Security Act of 1974, as amended (Public Law 93–406, 88 Stat. 829), excluding plans established under section 401(k) of the Internal Revenue Code of 1986 (26 U.S.C. 401(k)), as amended).

(vii) A trust, foundation or endowment exempt from Federal income taxation under the Internal Revenue Code of 1986, as amended.

(viii) A corporation, partnership or other entity with a net worth (exclusive of unfunded commitments from investors) of more than $10 million.

(ix) A State, a political subdivision of a State, or an agency or instrumentality of a State or its political subdivision.

(x) An entity whose primary purpose is to manage and invest non-Federal funds on behalf of at least three Institutional Investors described in paragraphs (1)(i) through (1)(ix) of this definition, each of whom must have at least a 10 percent ownership interest in the entity.

(xi) Any other entity that SBA determines to be an Institutional Investor.

(2) *Individuals.* (i) Any of the following individuals if he/she is also a permanent resident of the United States:

(A) An individual who is an Accredited Investor (as defined in the Securities Act of 1933, as amended (15 U.S.C. 77a-77aa)) and whose commitment to the NMVC Company is backed by a letter of credit from a State or National bank acceptable to SBA.

(B) An individual whose personal net worth is at least $2 million and at least ten times the amount of his or her commitment to the NMVC Company. The individual's personal net worth must not include the value of any equity in his or her most valuable residence.

(C) An individual whose personal net worth, not including the value of any equity in his or her most valuable residence, is at least $10 million.

(ii) Any individual who is not a permanent resident of the United States but who otherwise satisfies paragraph (2)(i) of this definition provided such individual has irrevocably appointed an agent within the United States for the service of process.

Investment Adviser/Manager means any Person who furnishes advice or assistance with respect to operations of a NMVC Company under a written contract executed in accordance with the provisions of § 108.510.

Lending Institution means a concern that is operating under regulations of a state or Federal licensing, supervising, or examining body, or whose shares are publicly traded and listed on a recognized stock exchange or NASDAQ and which has assets in excess of $500 million; and which, in either case, holds itself out to the public as engaged in the making of commercial and industrial loans and whose lending operations are not for the purpose of financing its own or an Associate's sales or business operations.

Leverage means financial assistance provided to a NMVC Company by SBA through the guaranty of a NMVC Company's Debentures, and any other SBA financial assistance evidenced by a security of the NMVC Company.

Leverageable Capital means Regulatory Capital, excluding unfunded commitments.

LLC NMVC Company. See definition of NMVC Company in this section.

Loan means a transaction evidenced by a debt instrument with no provision for you to acquire Equity Securities.

Loans and Investments means Portfolio securities, assets acquired in liquidation of Portfolio securities, operating concerns acquired, and notes and other securities received, as set forth in the Statement of Financial Position of SBA Form 468.

Low-Income Enterprise means a Smaller Enterprise that, as of the time of the initial Financing, has its Principal Office located in a Low-Income Geographic Area.

Low-Income Geographic Area ("LI Area") means—

(1) Any population census tract (or in the case of an area that is not tracted for population census tracts, the equivalent county division, as defined by the Bureau of the Census of the United States Department of Commerce for purposes of defining poverty areas), if—

(i) The poverty rate for that census tract is not less than 20 percent;

(ii) In the case of a tract—

(A) That is located within a metropolitan area, 50 percent or more of the households in that census tract have an income equal to less than 60 percent of the area median gross income; or

(B) That is not located within a metropolitan area, the median household income for such tract does not exceed 80 percent of the statewide median household income; or

(C) As determined by the Administrator in accordance with § 108.1940 of this part, a substantial population of Low-Income Individuals reside, an inadequate access to investment capital exists, or other indications of economic distress exist in that census tract; or

(2) Any area located within—

(i) A Historically Underutilized Business Zone ("HUBZone") as defined in section 3(p) of the Small Business Act and 13 CFR 126.103;

(ii) An Urban Empowerment Zone or Urban Enterprise Community (as designated by the Secretary of the United States Department of Housing and Urban Development); or

(iii) A Rural Empowerment Zone or Rural Enterprise Community (as designated by the Secretary of the United States Department of Agriculture).

Low-Income Individual means an individual whose income (adjusted for family size) does not exceed—

(1) For metropolitan areas, 80 percent of the area median income; and

(2) For nonmetropolitan areas, the greater of—

(i) 80 percent of the area median income, or

(ii) 80 percent of the statewide nonmetropolitan area median income.

Low-Income Investment means an Equity Capital Investment in a Low-Income Enterprise.

Management Expenses has the meaning set forth in § 108.520.

NAICS Manual means the latest issue of the North American Industrial Classification System Manual, prepared by the Office of Management and Budget, and available from the U.S. Government Printing Office, Superintendent of Documents, P.O. Box 371954, Pittsburgh, Pa., 15250–7954.

New Markets Tax Credit program means the tax credit created by the Consolidated Appropriations Act of 2001, Public Law 106–554 (114 Stat. 2762A), enacted December 21, 2000, to be implemented by the Internal Revenue Service, United States Department of Treasury.

New Markets Venture Capital Company or *NMVC Company* means a corporation (Corporate NMVC Company), a limited partnership organized as required by § 108.160 (Partnership NMVC Company), or a limited liability company (LLC NMVC Company) that—

(1) Has been granted final approval by SBA under § 108.380, and

(2) Has entered into a Participation Agreement with SBA. For certain purposes, the Entity General Partner of a Partnership NMVC Company is treated as if it were a NMVC Company (see § 108.160(a)).

1940 Act Company means a NMVC Company which is registered under the Investment Company Act of 1940 (15 U.S.C. 80a-1 *et seq.*).

1980 Act Company means a NMVC Company which is registered under the Small Business Investment Incentive Act of 1980 (Public Law 96–447, 94 Stat. 2275).

Operational Assistance means management, marketing, and other technical assistance that assists a Small Business with its business development.

Original Issue Price means the price paid by the purchaser for securities at the time of issuance.

Participation Agreement means an agreement between SBA and a company to which SBA has granted final approval under § 108.380, that—

(1) Details the company's operating plan and investment criteria; and

(2) Requires the company to make investments in Smaller Enterprises at least 80 percent of which Smaller Enterprises are located in LI Areas.

Partnership NMVC Company. See definition of NMVC Company in this section.

Person means a natural person or legal entity.

Pool means an aggregation of SBA guaranteed Debentures approved by SBA.

Portfolio means the securities representing a NMVC Company's total outstanding Financing of Smaller Enterprises. It does not include idle funds or assets acquired in liquidation of Portfolio securities.

Portfolio Concern means a Small Business Assisted by a NMVC Company.

Principal Office means the location where the greatest number of the concern's employees at any one location perform their work. However, for those concerns whose "primary industry" (see 13 CFR 121.107) is service or construction (see 13 CFR 121.201), the determination of principal office excludes the concern's employees who perform the majority of their work at job-site locations to fulfill specific contract obligations.

Private Capital has the meaning set forth in § 108.230.

Publicly Traded and Marketable means securities that are salable without restriction or that are salable within 12 months pursuant to Rule 144 (17 CFR 230.144) of the Securities Act of 1933, as amended, by the holder thereof, and are of a class which is traded on a regulated stock exchange, or is listed in the Automated Quotation System of the National Association of Securities Dealers (NASDAQ), or has, at a minimum, at least two market makers as defined in the relevant sections of the Securities Exchange Act of 1934, as amended (15 U.S.C. 77b *et seq.*), and in all cases the quantity of which can be sold over a reasonable period of time without having an adverse impact upon the price of the stock.

Regulatory Capital means Private Capital, excluding any portion of Private Capital that is designated as matching resources in accordance with § 108.2030(b)(3).

Relevant Venture Capital Finance means Equity Capital Investments in small businesses in low-income communities or benefiting low-income communities.

Retained Earnings Available for Distribution means Undistributed Net Realized Earnings less any Unrealized Depreciation on Loans and Investments (as reported on SBA Form 468), and represents the amount that a NMVC Company may distribute to investors (including SBA) as a profit Distribution, or transfer to Private Capital.

SBA means the Small Business Administration, 409 Third Street, SW., Washington, DC 20416.

Secondary Relative of an individual means:

(1) A grandparent, grandchild, or any other ancestor or lineal descendent who is not a Close Relative;

(2) An uncle, aunt, nephew, niece, or first cousin; or

(3) A spouse of any person described in paragraph (1) or (2) of this definition.

Small Business means a small business concern as defined in section 103(5) of the Act (including its Affiliates), and which meets the criteria applicable to the Small Business Investment Company program as set forth in part 121 of this chapter.

Small Business Investment Company (SBIC) means a Licensee, as that term is defined in § 107.50 of this chapter.

Smaller Enterprise means any Small Business that:

(1) Together with its Affiliates has a net worth of not more than $6.0 million and average net income after Federal income taxes (excluding any carry-over losses) for the preceding two years no greater than $2.0 million; or

(2) Both together with its Affiliates, and by itself, meets the size standard of § 121.201 of this chapter at the time of Financing for the industry in which it is then primarily engaged.

Specialized Small Business Investment Companies (SSBICs) means any Small Business Investment Company that—

(1) Invests solely in small business concerns that contribute to a well-balanced national economy by facilitating ownership in such concerns by persons whose participation in the free enterprise system is hampered because of social or economic disadvantages; and

(2) Was licensed under section 301(d) of the Small Business Investment Act, as in effect before September 30, 1996.

Trust means the legal entity created for the purpose of holding guaranteed Debentures and the guaranty agreement related thereto, receiving, holding and making any related payments, and accounting for such payments.

Trust Certificate Rate means a fixed rate determined at the time Debentures are pooled.

Trust Certificates (TCs) means certificates issued by SBA, its agent or Trustee and representing ownership of all or a fractional part of a Trust or Pool of Debentures.

Trustee means the trustee or trustees of a Trust.

Undistributed Net Realized Earnings means Undistributed Realized Earnings less Non-cash Gains/Income, each as reported on SBA Form 468.

Unrealized Appreciation means the amount by which a NMVC Company's valuation of each of its Loans and Investments, as determined by its Board of Directors or General Partner(s) in accordance with NMVC Company's valuation policies, exceeds the cost basis thereof.

Unrealized Depreciation means the amount by which a NMVC Company's valuation of each of its Loans and Investments, as determined by its Board of Directors or General Partner(s) in accordance with NMVC Company's valuation policies, is below the cost basis thereof.

Unrealized Gain (Loss) on Securities Held means the sum of the Unrealized Appreciation and Unrealized Depreciation on all of a NMVC Company's Loans and Investments, less estimated future income tax expense or estimated realizable future income tax benefit, as appropriate.

[66 FR 28609, May 23, 2001, as amended at 67 FR 68502, Nov. 12, 2002]

Subpart C—Qualifications for the NMVC Program

ORGANIZING A NMVC COMPANY

§ 108.100 Business form.

A NMVC Company must be a newly formed for-profit entity or, subject to § 108.150, a newly formed for-profit subsidiary of an existing entity. It must be organized under State law solely for the purpose of performing the functions and conducting the activities contemplated under the Act. It may be organized as a corporation ("Corporate NMVC Company"), a limited partnership ("Partnership NMVC Company"), or a limited liability company ("LLC NMVC Company").

§ 108.110 Qualified management.

An Applicant must show, to the satisfaction of SBA, that its current or proposed management team is qualified and has the knowledge, experience, and capability in Community Development Finance or Relevant Venture Capital Finance, necessary for investing in the types of businesses contemplated by the Act, the regulations in this part and its business plan. In determining whether an Applicant's current or proposed management team has sufficient qualifications, SBA will consider information provided by the Applicant and third parties concerning the background, capability, education, training and reputation of its general partners, managers, officers, key personnel, and investment committee and governing board members. The Applicant must designate at least one individual as the official responsible for contact with SBA.

§ 108.120 Economic development primary mission.

The primary mission of a NMVC Company must be economic development of one or more LI Areas.

§ 108.130 Identified Low Income Geographic Areas.

A NMVC Company must identify the specific LI Areas in which it intends to make Developmental Venture Capital investments and provide Operational Assistance under the NMVC program.

§ 108.140 SBA approval of initial Management Expenses.

A NMVC Company must have its Management Expenses approved by SBA at the time of designation as a NMVC Company. (See § 108.520 for the definition of Management Expenses.)

§ 108.150 Management and ownership diversity requirement.

(a) *Diversity requirement.* You must have diversity between management and ownership in order to be a NMVC Company. To establish diversity, you must meet the requirements in paragraphs (b) and (c) of this section.

(b) *Percentage ownership requirement.* No Person or group of Persons who are Affiliates of one another may own or control, directly or indirectly, more than 70 percent of your Regulatory Capital or your Leverageable Capital.

(c) *Non-affiliation requirement.* At least 30 percent of your Regulatory Capital and Leverageable Capital must be owned and controlled by three Persons unaffiliated with your management and unaffiliated with each other, whose investments are significant in dollar and percentage terms as determined by SBA. Such Persons must not be your Associates (except for their status as your shareholders, limited partners or members) and must not Control, be Controlled by, or be under Common Control with any of your Associates. A single "acceptable" Institutional Investor may be substituted for two or three of the three investors who are otherwise required. The following Institutional Investors are "acceptable" for this purpose:

(1) Entities whose overall activities are regulated and periodically examined by state, Federal or other governmental authorities satisfactory to SBA;

(2) Entities listed on the New York Stock Exchange;

(3) Entities that are publicly-traded and that meet both the minimum numerical listing standards and the corporate governance listing standards of the New York Stock Exchange:

(4) Public or private employee pension funds;

(5) Trusts, foundations, or endowments, but only if exempt from Federal income taxation; and

(6) Other Institutional Investors satisfactory to SBA.

(d) *Voting requirement.* The investors required for you to satisfy diversity may not delegate their voting rights to any Person who is your Associate, or who Controls, is Controlled by, or is under Common Control with any of your Associates, without prior SBA approval.

(e) *Requirement to maintain diversity.* You must maintain management-ownership diversity while you are a NMVC Company. If, at any time, you no longer have the required management-ownership diversity, you must:

(1) Notify SBA within 10 days; and

(2) Re-establish diversity within six months.

[66 FR 28609, May 23, 2001; 66 FR 32894, June 19, 2001]

§ 108.160 Special rules for NMVC Companies formed as limited partnerships.

(a) *Entity General Partner.* (1) A general partner which is a corporation, limited liability company or partnership (an "Entity General Partner") shall be organized under state law solely for the purpose of serving as the general partner of one or more NMVC companies.

(2) SBA must approve any person who will serve as an officer, director, manager, or general partner of the Entity General Partner. This provision must be stated in an Entity General Partner's Certificate of Incorporation, operating agreement, limited partnership agreement or other similar governing instrument.

(3) An Entity General Partner is subject to the same examination and reporting requirements as a NMVC Company under sections 361 and 362 of the Act. The restrictions and obligations imposed upon a NMVC Company by §§ 108.1810, 108.30, 108.410 through 108.450, 108.470, 108.500, 108.510, 108.585, 108.600, 108.680, 108.690 through 108.692, and 108.1910 apply also to an Entity General Partner of a NMVC Company.

(4) The general partner(s) of your Entity General Partner(s) will be considered your general partner.

(5) If your Entity General Partner is a limited partnership, its limited partners may be considered your Control Person(s) if they meet the definition for Control Person in § 108.50.

(b) *Other requirements for Partnership NMVC Companies.* If you are a Partnership NMVC Company:

(1) You must have a minimum duration of 10 years or two years following the maturity of your last-maturing Leverage security, whichever is longer. After 10 years, if all Leverage has been repaid or redeemed and all amounts due SBA, its agent, or Trustee have been paid, the Partnership NMVC Company may be terminated by a vote of your partners;

(2) None of your general partner(s) may be removed or replaced by your limited partners without prior written approval of SBA;

(3) Any transferee of, or successor in interest to, your general partner shall have only the rights and liabilities of a limited partner pending SBA's written approval of such transfer or succession; and

(4) You must incorporate all the provisions in this paragraph (b) in your limited partnership agreement.

(c) *Obligations of a Control Person.* All Control Persons are bound by the disciplinary provisions of sections 365 and

366 of the Act and by the conflict-of-interest rules under § 108.730. The term NMVC Company, as used in §§ 108.30, 108.460, and 108.680, includes all of the NMVC Company's Control Persons. The conditions specified in § 108.1810 and § 108.1910 apply to all general partners.

(d) *Liability of general partner for partnership debts to SBA.* Subject to section 365 of the Act, your general partner is not liable solely by reason of its status as a general partner for repayment of any Leverage or debts you owe to SBA unless SBA, in the exercise of reasonable investment prudence, and with regard to your financial soundness, determines otherwise prior to the purchase or guaranty of your Leverage.

(e) *Special Leverage requirement.* Before your first issuance of Leverage, you must furnish SBA with evidence that you qualify as a partnership for tax purposes, either by a ruling from the Internal Revenue Service or by an opinion of counsel.

CAPITALIZING A NMVC COMPANY

§ 108.200 Adequate capital for NMVC Companies.

You must meet the requirements of §§ 108.200–108.230 in order to qualify for designation as a NMVC Company and to receive Leverage.

§ 108.210 Minimum capital requirements for NMVC Companies.

You must have Regulatory Capital of at least $5,000,000 and Leverageable Capital of at least $500,000 to become a NMVC Company.

§ 108.230 Private Capital for NMVC Companies.

(a) *General.* Private Capital means the contributed capital of a NMVC Company, plus unfunded binding commitments by Institutional Investors (including commitments evidenced by a promissory note) to contribute capital to a NMVC Company.

(b) *Contributed capital.* For purposes of this section, contributed capital means the paid-in capital and paid-in surplus of a Corporate NMVC Company, the members' paid-in capital of a LLC NMVC Company, or the partners' paid-in capital of a Partnership NMVC Company, in each case subject to the limitations in paragraph (c) of this section.

(c) *Exclusions from Private Capital.* Private Capital does not include:

(1) Funds borrowed by a NMVC Company from any source.

(2) Funds obtained through the issuance of Leverage.

(3) Funds obtained directly from any Federal agency or department.

(4) Any portion of a commitment from an Institutional Investor with a net worth of less than $10 million that exceeds 10 percent of such Institutional Investor's net worth.

(5) A commitment from an investor if SBA determines that the collectability of the commitment is questionable.

(d) *Limitations on including non-cash capital contributions in Private Capital.* Private Capital does not include capital contributions in a form other than cash, except as provided in this paragraph (d). Subject to SBA's prior approval, Private Capital may include payments made on behalf of an Applicant or Conditionally Approved NMVC Company before the Applicant or Conditionally Approved NMVC Company becomes a NMVC Company for organizational expenses and Management Expenses incurred by the Applicant or the Conditionally Approved NMVC Company prior to its becoming a NMVC Company.

(e) *Contributions with borrowed funds.* You may not accept any capital contribution made with funds borrowed by a Person seeking to own an equity interest (whether direct or indirect, beneficial or of record) of at least 10 percent of your Private Capital. This exclusion does not apply if:

(1) Such Person's net worth is at least twice the amount borrowed; or

(2) SBA gives its prior written approval of the capital contribution.

[66 FR 28609, May 23, 2001, as amended at 67 FR 68502, Nov. 12, 2002]

Subpart D—Application and Approval Process for NMVC Company Designation

§ 108.300 When and how to apply for designation as a NMVC Company.

(a) *Notice of Funds Availability ("NOFA").* SBA will publish a NOFA in the FEDERAL REGISTER, advising potential applicants of the availability of funds for the NMVC program. An entity may then submit an application for designation as a NMVC Company. When submitting its application, an Applicant must comply with both these regulations and any requirements specified in the NOFA, including submission deadlines. The NOFA may specify limitations, special rules, procedures, and restrictions for a particular funding round.

(b) *Application form.* An Applicant must apply for designation as a NMVC Company using the application packet provided by SBA. Upon receipt of an application, SBA may request clarifying or technical information on the materials submitted as part of the application.

§ 108.310 Contents of application.

Each Applicant must submit a complete application, including the following:

(a) *Amounts.* The Applicant must indicate—

(1) The specific amount of Regulatory Capital it proposes to raise (which amount must be at least $5,000,000); and

(2) The specific amount of binding commitments for contributions in cash or in-kind it proposes to raise, and/or an annuity it proposes to purchase, in accordance with the requirements of § 108.2030, as its matching resources for its Operational Assistance grant award (the aggregate of which must be not less than $1,500,000 or 30 percent of the Regulatory Capital it proposes to raise under paragraph (a)(1) of this section, whichever is greater).

(b) *Comprehensive business plan.* The Applicant must submit a comprehensive business plan covering at least a five-year period, addressing the specific items described in § 108.320, and which demonstrates that the Applicant has the capacity to operate successfully as a NMVC Company.

(c) *New Markets Tax Credit program.* Applicant must address if and to what extent it intends to conform its activities to the New Markets Tax Credit laws. If Applicant plans to seek a New Markets Tax Credit, Applicant also must state the amount of tax credit allocation it intends to seek.

[66 FR 28609, May 23, 2001, as amended at 67 FR 68502, Nov. 12, 2002]

§ 108.320 Contents of comprehensive business plan.

(a) *Executive summary.* The executive summary must include a description of—

(1) The Applicant;

(2) Its strategy for how it proposes to make successful Developmental Venture Capital investments in identified LI Areas;

(3) The markets in the LI Areas it proposes to serve; and

(4) How it intends to work with community organizations in and be accountable to the residents of identified LI Areas in order to facilitate its Developmental Venture Capital investments.

(b) *Capacity, skills, and experience of the management team.* An Applicant must provide information generally as to the background, capability, education, reputation and training of its general partners, managers, officers, key personnel, investment committee and governing board members. The Applicant also must provide information specifically on these individuals' qualifications and reputation in the areas of Community Development Finance and/or Relevant Venture Capital Finance, including the impact of these individuals' activities in these areas.

(c) *Market analysis.* An Applicant must provide an analysis of the LI Areas in which it intends to focus its Developmental Venture Capital investments and Operational Assistance to Smaller Enterprises, demonstrating that the Applicant understands the market and the unmet capital needs in such areas and how its activities will meet these unmet capital needs through Developmental Venture Capital investments and will have a positive economic impact on those areas. The analysis must include a description of the extent of the economic distress in the identified LI Areas. An Applicant also must analyze the extent of the demand in such areas for Developmental Venture Capital investments and any factors or trends that may affect the Applicant's ability to make effective Developmental Venture Capital investments.

(d) *Operational capacity and investment strategies.* An Applicant must submit information concerning its policies and procedures for underwriting and approving its Developmental Venture Capital investments, monitoring its portfolio, and maintaining internal controls and operations.

(e) *Regulatory Capital.* An Applicant must include a detailed description of how it plans to raise its Regulatory Capital. An Applicant must discuss its potential sources of Regulatory Capital, the estimated timing on raising such funds, and the extent of the expressions of interest to commit such funds to the Applicant.

(f) *Plan for providing Operational Assistance.* An Applicant must describe how it plans to use its grant funds to provide Operational Assistance to Smaller Enterprises in which it will make Developmental Venture Capital investments. Its plan must address the types of Operational Assistance it proposes to provide, and how it plans to provide the Operational Assistance through the use of licensed professionals, when necessary, either from its own staff or from outside entities.

(g) *Matching resources for Operational Assistance grant.* An Applicant must include a detailed description of how it plans to obtain binding commitments for cash or in-kind contributions, and/or to purchase an annuity, to match the funds requested from SBA for the Applicant's Operational Assistance grant. If it proposes to obtain commitments for cash and in-kind contributions, it also must estimate the ratio of cash to in-kind contributions (in no event may in-kind contributions exceed 50 percent of the total contributions). Applicant must discuss its potential sources of matching resources, the estimated timing on raising such funds, and the extent of the expressions of interest to commit such funds to the Applicant. Potential sources of matching resources must satisfy the requirements in § 108.2030(b)(1).

(h) *Projected amount of investment in LI Areas.* An Applicant must describe the amount of its total Regulatory Capital and Leverage that it proposes to invest in Smaller Enterprises located in LI Areas, as compared to the amount that it proposes to invest in Small Businesses located outside of LI Areas.

(i) *Projected impact.* An Applicant must describe the criteria and economic measurements to be used to evaluate whether and to what extent it has met the objectives of the NMVC program. It must include:

(1) A description of the extent to which it will concentrate its Developmental Venture Capital investments and Operational Assistance activities in identified LI Areas;

(2) An estimate of the social, economic, and community development benefits to be created within identified LI Areas over the next five years or more as a result of its activities;

(3) A description of the criteria to be used to measure the benefits created as a result of its activities;

(4) A discussion about the amount of such benefits created that it will consider to constitute successfully meeting the objectives of the NMVC program.

(j) *Affiliates and business relationships.* Applicant must submit information regarding the management and financial strength of any parent or holding entity, affiliated firm or entity, or any other firm or entity essential to the success of the Applicant's business plan.

[66 FR 28609, May 23, 2001, as amended at 67 FR 68503, Nov. 12, 2002]

§ 108.330 Grant issuance fee.

An Applicant must pay to SBA a grant issuance fee of $5,000. An Applicant must submit this fee in advance, at the time of application submission. If SBA does not select an Applicant as a Conditionally Approved NMVC Company or designate an Applicant as a NMVC Company, SBA will refund this fee to the Applicant.

Subpart E—Evaluation and Selection of NMVC Companies

§ 108.340 Evaluation and selection—general.

SBA will evaluate and select an Applicant to participate in the NMVC program solely at SBA's discretion, based on SBA's review of the Applicant's application materials, interviews or site visits with the Applicant (if any), and background investigations conducted by SBA and other Federal agencies. SBA's evaluation and selection process is intended to—

(a) Ensure that Applicants are evaluated on a competitive basis and in a fair and consistent manner;

(b) Take into consideration the unique proposals presented by Applicants;

(c) Ensure that each Applicant that SBA designates as a NMVC Company can fulfill successfully the goals of its comprehensive business plan; and

(d) Ensure that SBA selects Applicants in such a way as to promote Developmental Venture Capital investments nationwide and in both urban and rural areas.

§ 108.350 Eligibility and completeness.

SBA will not consider any application that is not complete or that is submitted by an Applicant that does not meet the eligibility criteria described in subpart C of this part. SBA, at its sole discretion, may request from an Applicant additional information concerning eligibility criteria or easily completed portions of the application in order to allow SBA to consider that Applicant's application.

§ 108.360 Evaluation criteria.

SBA will evaluate and select an Applicant for participation in the NMVC program by considering the following criteria—

(a) The quality of the Applicant's comprehensive business plan in terms of meeting the objectives of the NMVC program;

(b) The likelihood that the Applicant will fulfill the goals described in its comprehensive business plan;

(c) The capability of the Applicant's management team;

(d) The strength and likelihood for success of the Applicant's operations and investment strategies;

(e) The need for Developmental Venture Capital investments in the LI Areas in which the Applicant intends to invest;

(f) The extent to which the Applicant will concentrate its activities on serving the LI Areas in which it intends to invest, including the ratio of resources that it proposes to invest in such areas as compared to other areas;

(g) The Applicant's demonstrated understanding of the markets in the LI Areas in which it intends to focus its activities;

(h) The likelihood that and the time frame within which the Applicant will be able to—

(1) Raise the Regulatory Capital it proposes to raise for its investments, and

(2) Obtain the binding commitments for contributions in cash or in-kind and/or an annuity it proposes to obtain as its matching resources for its Operational Assistance grant award;

(i) The strength of the Applicant's proposal to provide Operational Assistance to Smaller Enterprises in which it plans to invest;

(j) The extent to which the activities proposed by the Applicant will promote economic development and the creation of wealth and job opportunities in the LI Areas in which it intends to invest and among individuals living in LI Areas; and

(k) The strength of the Applicant's application compared to applications submitted by other Applicants and by SSBICs intending to invest in the same or proximate LI Areas.

[66 FR 28609, May 23, 2001, as amended at 67 FR 68503, Nov. 12, 2002]

§ 108.370 Conditional approval.

From among the Applicants submitting eligible and complete applications, SBA will select a number of Applicants and will conditionally approve such selected Applicants to participate in the NMVC program. SBA will give each such Conditionally Approved NMVC Company a specific period of time, not to exceed two years, to satisfy the requirements to become a NMVC Company.

§ 108.380 Final approval as a NMVC Company.

(a) *General rule.* With respect to each Conditionally Approved NMVC Company, SBA will either:

(1) Grant final approval to participate in the NMVC program and designate such company as a NMVC Company, if such Conditionally Approved NMVC Company:

(i) Within the specific period of time SBA gave to it when SBA conditionally approved it for participation in the NMVC program, has raised:

(A) The amount of Regulatory Capital set forth in its application, pursuant to § 108.310(a)(1); and

(B) The amount of matching resources for its Operational Assistance grant award set forth in its application, pursuant to § 108.310(a)(2); and

(ii) Enters into a Participation Agreement with SBA; or

(2) Revoke SBA's conditional approval of the company, at which time it is no longer a Conditionally Approved NMVC Company and must not participate in the NMVC program or represent itself as a Conditionally Approved NMVC Company.

(b) *Exception to requirement to raise matching resources*—(1) *General.* At its discretion and based upon a showing of good cause, SBA may consider a Conditionally Approved NMVC Company to have satisfied the requirement in paragraph (a)(1)(i)(B) of this section to raise matching resources in the amount of at least 30 percent of its Regulatory Capital if the Conditionally Approved NMVC Company—

(i) Already has raised at least 20 percent of the total amount of required matching resources; and

(ii) Has a viable plan that reasonably projects its capacity to raise the remainder of the required amount of matching resources.

(2) *Request for exception.* Before the expiration of the time period given to it by SBA to meet the requirements to become a NMVC Company, a Conditionally Approved NMVC Company may submit to SBA a request that SBA grant the exception described in paragraph (b)(1) of this section. Such Conditionally Approved NMVC must present to SBA evidence of good cause for such request, as well as evidence supporting the elements of the exception described in paragraph (b)(1) of this section.

(3) *No applicability to Regulatory Capital.* The exception described in this section applies only to matching resources for the Operational Assistance grant award. Under no circumstances will SBA designate a Conditionally Approved NMVC Company as a NMVC Company if such Conditionally Approved NMVC Company does not raise the required amount of Regulatory Capital within the time period SBA gave it to do so.

[66 FR 28609, May 23, 2001, as amended at 67 FR 68503, Nov. 12, 2002]

Subpart F—Changes in Ownership, Structure, or Control

CHANGES IN CONTROL OR OWNERSHIP OF NMVC COMPANY

§ 108.400 Changes in ownership of 10 percent or more of NMVC Company but no change of Control.

You must obtain SBA's prior written approval for any proposed transfer or issuance of ownership interests that results in the ownership (beneficial or of record) by any Person, or group of Persons acting in concert, of at least 10 percent of any class of your stock, partnership capital or membership interests.

§ 108.410 Changes in Control of NMVC Company (through change in ownership or otherwise).

You must obtain SBA's prior written approval for any proposed transaction or event that results in Control by any Person(s) not previously approved by SBA.

§ 108.420 Prohibition on exercise of ownership or Control rights in NMVC Company before SBA approval.

Without prior written SBA approval, no change of ownership or Control may take effect and no officer, director, employee or other Person acting on your behalf shall:

(a) Register on your books any transfer of ownership interest to the proposed new owner(s);

(b) Permit the proposed new owner(s) to exercise voting rights with respect to such ownership interest (including directly or indirectly procuring or voting any proxy, consent or authorization as to such voting rights at any meeting of shareholders, partners or members);

(c) Permit the proposed new owner(s) to participate in any manner in the conduct of your affairs (including exercising control over your books, records, funds or other assets; participating directly or indirectly in any disposition thereof; or serving as an officer, director, partner, manager, employee or agent); or

(d) Allow ownership or Control to pass to another Person.

§ 108.430 Notification to SBA of transactions that may change ownership or Control.

You must promptly notify SBA as soon as you have knowledge of transactions or events that may result in a transfer of Control or ownership of at least 10 percent of your capital. If there is any doubt as to whether a particular transaction or event will result in such a change, report the facts to SBA.

§ 108.440 Standards governing prior SBA approval for a proposed transfer of Control.

SBA approval is contingent upon full disclosure of the real parties in interest, the source of funds for the new owners' interest, and other data requested by SBA. As a condition of approving a proposed transfer of control, SBA may:

(a) Require an increase in your Regulatory Capital;

(b) Require the new owners or the transferee's Control Person(s) to assume, in writing, personal liability for your Leverage, effective only in the event of their direct or indirect participation in any transfer of Control not approved by SBA; or

(c) Require compliance with any other conditions set by SBA, including compliance with the requirements for minimum capital and management-ownership diversity as in effect at such time for new NMVC Companies.

§ 108.450 Notification to SBA of pledge of NMVC Company's shares.

(a) You must notify SBA in writing, within 30 calendar days, of the terms of any transaction in which:

(1) Any Person, or group of Persons acting in concert, pledges shares of your stock (or equivalent ownership interests) as collateral for indebtedness; and

(2) The shares pledged are at least 10 percent of your Regulatory Capital.

(b) If the transaction creates a change of ownership or Control, you must comply with § 108.400 or § 108.410, as appropriate.

RESTRICTIONS ON COMMON CONTROL OR OWNERSHIP OF TWO OR MORE NMVC COMPANIES

§ 108.460 Restrictions on Common Control or ownership of two (or more) NMVC Companies.

Without SBA's prior written approval, you must not have an officer, director, manager, Control Person, or owner (with a direct or indirect ownership interest of at least 10 percent) who is also:

(a) An officer, director, manager, Control Person, or owner (with a direct or indirect ownership interest of at least 10 percent) of another NMVC Company; or

(b) An officer or director of any Person that directly or indirectly controls, or is controlled by, or is under Common Control with, another NMVC Company.

CHANGE IN STRUCTURE OF NMVC COMPANY

§ 108.470 SBA approval of merger, consolidation, or reorganization of NMVC Company.

You may not merge, consolidate, change form of organization (corporation or partnership) or reorganize without SBA's prior written approval. Any such merger or consolidation will be subject to § 108.440.

Subpart G—Managing the Operations of a NMVC Company

GENERAL REQUIREMENTS

§ 108.500 Lawful operations under the Act.

You must engage only in the activities contemplated by the Act and in no other activities.

§ 108.502 Representations to the public.

You may not represent or imply to anyone that the SBA, the U.S. Government or any of its agencies or officers has approved any ownership interests you have issued or obligations you have incurred. Be certain to include a statement to this effect in any solicitation to investors. Example: You may not represent or imply that "SBA stands behind the NMVC Company" or that "Your capital is safe because SBA's experts review proposed investments to make sure they are safe for the NMVC Company."

§ 108.503 NMVC Company's adoption of an approved valuation policy.

(a) *Valuation guidelines.* You must prepare, document and report the valuations of your Loans and Investments in accordance with the Valuation Guidelines for SBICs issued by SBA. These guidelines may be obtained from SBA's Investment Division.

(b) *SBA approval of valuation policy.* You must have a written valuation policy approved by SBA for use in determining the value of your Loans and Investments. You must either:

(1) Adopt without change the model valuation policy set forth in section III of the Valuation Guidelines for SBICs; or

(2) Obtain SBA's prior written approval of an alternative valuation policy.

(c) *Responsibility for valuations.* Your board of directors, managing members, or general partner(s) will be solely responsible for adopting your valuation policy and for using it to prepare valuations of your Loans and Investments for submission to SBA. If SBA reasonably believes that your valuations, individually or in the aggregate, are materially misstated, it reserves the right to require you to engage, at your expense, an independent third party acceptable to SBA to substantiate the valuations.

(d) *Frequency of valuations.* (1) You must value your Loans and Investments at the end of the second quarter of your fiscal year, and at the end of your fiscal year.

(2) On a case-by-case basis, SBA may require you to perform valuations more frequently.

(3) You must report material adverse changes in valuations at least quarterly, within thirty days following the close of the quarter.

(e) *Review of valuations by independent public accountant.* (1) For valuations performed as of the end of your fiscal year, your independent public accountant must review your valuation procedures and the implementation of such procedures, including adequacy of documentation.

(2) The independent public accountant's report on your audited annual financial statements (SBA Form 468) must include a statement that your valuations were prepared in accordance with your approved valuation policy.

§ 108.504 Equipment and office requirements.

(a) *Computer capability.* You must have a personal computer with a modem, and be able to use this equipment to prepare reports (using SBA provided software) and transmit them to SBA. In addition, you must have access to the Internet and the capability to send and receive electronic mail via the Internet.

(b) *Facsimile capability.* You must be able to receive facsimile messages 24 hours per day at your primary office.

(c) *Accessible office.* You must maintain an office that is convenient to the public and is open for business during normal working hours.

§ 108.506 Safeguarding the NMVC Company's assets/Internal controls.

You must adopt a plan to safeguard your assets and monitor the reliability of your financial data, personnel, Portfolio, funds and equipment. You must provide your bank and custodian with a certified copy of your resolution or other formal document describing your control procedures.

§ 108.507 Violations based on false filings and nonperformance of agreements with SBA.

The following shall constitute a violation of this part:

(a) *Nonperformance.* Nonperformance of any of the requirements of any Debenture or of any written agreement with SBA.

(b) *False statement.* In any document submitted to SBA:

(1) Any false statement knowingly made; or

(2) Any misrepresentation of a material fact; or

(3) Any failure to state a material fact. A material fact is any fact that is necessary to make a statement not misleading in light of the circumstances under which the statement was made.

§ 108.509 Employment of SBA officials.

Without SBA's prior written approval, for a period of two years after the date of your most recent issuance of Leverage (or the receipt of any SBA Assistance as defined in part 105 of this chapter), you are not permitted to employ, offer employment to, or retain for professional services, any person who:

(a) Served as an officer, attorney, agent, or employee of SBA on or within one year before such date; and

(b) As such, occupied a position or engaged in activities which, in SBA's determination, involved discretion with respect to the granting of SBA Assistance.

MANAGEMENT AND COMPENSATION

§ 108.510 SBA approval of NMVC Company's Investment Adviser/Manager.

You may employ an Investment Adviser/Manager who will be subject to the supervision of your board of directors, managing members, or general partner. If you have Leverage or plan to seek Leverage, you must obtain SBA's prior written approval of the management contract. SBA's approval of an Investment Adviser/Manager for one NMVC Company does not indicate approval of that manager for any other NMVC Company.

(a) *Management contract.* The contract must:

(1) Specify the services the Investment Adviser/Manager will render to you and to the Small Businesses in your Portfolio; and

(2) Indicate the basis for computing Management Expenses.

(b) *Material change to approved management contract.* If there is a material change, both you and SBA must approve such change in advance. If you are uncertain if the change is material, submit the proposed revision to SBA.

§ 108.520 Management Expenses of a NMVC Company.

SBA must approve your initial Management Expenses and any increases in your Management Expenses.

(a) *Definition of Management Expenses.* Management Expenses include:

(1) Salaries;

(2) Office expenses;

(3) Travel;

(4) Business development;

(5) Office and equipment rental;

(6) Bookkeeping; and

(7) Expenses related to developing, investigating and monitoring investments.

(b) Management Expenses do not include services provided by specialized outside consultants, outside lawyers and independent public accountants, if they perform services not generally performed by a venture capital company.

CASH MANAGEMENT BY A NMVC COMPANY

§ 108.530 Restrictions on investments of idle funds by NMVC Companies.

(a) *Permitted investments of idle funds.* Funds not invested in Small Businesses must be maintained in:

(1) Direct obligations of, or obligations guaranteed as to principal and interest by, the United States, which mature within 15 months from the date of the investment; or

(2) Repurchase agreements with federally insured institutions, with a maturity of seven days or less. The securities underlying the repurchase agreements must be direct obligations of, or obligations guaranteed as to principal and interest by, the United States. The

securities must be maintained in a custodial account at a federally insured institution; or

(3) Certificates of deposit with a maturity of one year or less, issued by a federally insured institution; or

(4) A deposit account in a federally insured institution, subject to a withdrawal restriction of one year or less; or

(5) A checking account in a federally insured institution; or

(6) A reasonable petty cash fund.

(b) *Deposit of funds in excess of the insured amount.* (1) You are permitted to deposit funds in a federally insured institution in excess of the institution's insured amount, but only if the institution is "well capitalized" in accordance with the definition set forth in regulations of the Federal Deposit Insurance Corporation, as amended (12 CFR 325.103).

(2) Exception: You may make a temporary deposit (not to exceed 30 days) in excess of the insured amount, in a transfer account established to facilitate the receipt and disbursement of funds or to hold funds necessary to honor Commitments issued.

(c) *Deposit of funds in Associate institution.* A deposit in, or a repurchase agreement with, a federally insured institution that is your Associate is not considered a Financing of such Associate under § 108.730, provided the terms of such deposit or repurchase agreement are no less favorable than those available to the general public.

BORROWING BY NMVC COMPANIES FROM NON-SBA SOURCES

§ 108.550 Prior approval of secured third-party debt of NMVC companies.

(a) *Definition.* In this section, "secured third-party debt" means any non-SBA debt secured by any of your assets, including secured guarantees and other contingent obligations that you voluntarily assume and secured lines of credit.

(b) *General rule.* You must get SBA's written approval before you incur any secured third-party debt or refinance any debt with secured third-party debt, including any renewal of a secured line of credit, increase in the maximum amount available under a secured line of credit, or expansion of the scope of a security interest or lien. For purposes of this paragraph (b), "expansion of the scope of a security interest or lien" does not include the substitution of one asset or group of assets for another, provided the asset values (as reported on your most recent annual Form 468) are comparable.

(c) *Conditions for SBA approval.* As a condition of granting its approval under this section, SBA may impose such restrictions or limitations as it deems appropriate, taking into account your historical performance, current financial position, proposed terms of the secured debt and amount of aggregate debt you will have outstanding (including Leverage). SBA will not favorably consider any requests for approval which include a blanket lien on all your assets, or a security interest in your investor commitments in excess of 125 percent of the proposed borrowing.

(d) *Thirty-day approval.* Unless SBA notifies you otherwise within 30 days after it receives your request, you may consider your request automatically approved if:

(1) You are in regulatory compliance;

(2) The security interest in your assets is limited to either those assets being acquired with the borrowed funds or an asset coverage ratio of no more than 2:1;

(3) Your request is for approval of a secured line of credit that would not cause your total outstanding borrowings (not including Leverage) to exceed 50 percent of your Leverageable Capital.

VOLUNTARY DECREASE IN REGULATORY CAPITAL

§ 108.585 Voluntary decrease in NMVC Company's Regulatory Capital.

You must obtain SBA's prior written approval to reduce your Regulatory Capital by more than two percent in any fiscal year. At all times, you must retain sufficient Regulatory Capital to meet the minimum capital requirements in the Act and § 108.210, and sufficient Leverageable Capital to avoid having excess Leverage in violation of section 355(d) of the Act.

Subpart H—Recordkeeping, Reporting, and Examination Requirements for NMVC Companies

RECORDKEEPING REQUIREMENTS FOR NMVC COMPANIES

§ 108.600 General requirement for NMVC Company to maintain and preserve records.

(a) *Maintaining your accounting records.* You must establish and maintain your accounting records using SBA's standard chart of accounts for SBICs, unless SBA approves otherwise. You may obtain this chart of accounts from SBA.

(b) *Location of records.* You must keep the following records at your principal place of business or, in the case of paragraph (b)(3) of this section, at the branch office that is primarily responsible for the transaction:

(1) All your accounting and other financial records;

(2) All minutes of meetings of directors, stockholders, executive committees, partners, or other officials; and

(3) All documents and supporting materials related to your business transactions, except for any items held by a custodian under a written agreement between you and a Portfolio Concern or non-SBA lender, or any securities held in a safe deposit box, or by a licensed securities broker in an amount not exceeding the broker's per-account insurance coverage.

(c) *Preservation of records.* You must retain all the records that are the basis for your financial reports. Such records must be preserved for the periods specified in this paragraph (c), and must remain accessible for the first two years of the preservation period.

(1) You must preserve for at least 15 years or, in the case of a Partnership NMVC Company or LLC NMVC Company, at least two years beyond the date of liquidation:

(i) All your accounting ledgers and journals, and any other records of assets, asset valuations, liabilities, equity, income, and expenses.

(ii) Your Articles, bylaws, minute books, and NMVC Company application.

(iii) All documents evidencing ownership of the NMVC Company including ownership ledgers, and ownership transfer registers.

(2) You must preserve for at least six years all supporting documentation (such as vouchers, bank statements, or canceled checks) for the records listed in paragraph (b)(1) of this section.

(3) After final disposition of any item in your Portfolio, you must preserve for at least six years:

(i) Financing applications and Financing instruments.

(ii) All loan, participation, and escrow agreements.

(iii) Size status declarations (SBA Form 480).

(iv) Any capital stock certificates and warrants of the Portfolio Concern that you did not surrender or exercise.

(v) All other documents and supporting material relating to the Portfolio Concern, including correspondence.

(4) You may substitute a microfilm or computer-scanned or generated copy for the original of any record covered by this paragraph (c).

(d) *Additional requirement.* You must comply with the recordkeeping and record retention requirements set forth in Circular A–110 of the Office of Management and Budget. (OMB circulars are available from the addresses in 5 CFR 1310.3.)

§ 108.610 Required certifications for Loans and Investments.

For each of your Loans and Investments, you must have the documents listed in this section. You must keep these documents in your files and make them available to SBA upon request.

(a) SBA Form 480, the Size Status Declaration, executed both by you and by the concern you are financing. By executing this document, both parties certify that the concern is a Small Business. For securities purchased from an underwriter in a public offering, you may substitute a prospectus showing that the concern is a Small Business.

(b) SBA Form 652, a certification by the concern you are financing that it will not illegally discriminate (see part 112 of this chapter).

(c) A certification by the concern you are financing of the intended use of the proceeds. For securities purchased from an underwriter in a public offering, you may substitute a prospectus indicating the intended use of proceeds.

(d) For each Low-Income Investment, a certification by the concern you are financing as to the basis for its qualification as a Low-Income Enterprise.

§ 108.620 Requirements to obtain information from Portfolio Concerns.

All the information required by this section is subject to the requirements of § 108.600 and must be in English.

(a) *Information for initial Financing decision.* Before extending any Financing, you must require the applicant to submit such financial statements, plans of operation (including intended use of financing proceeds), cash flow analyses, projections, and such community economic development information about the company, as are necessary to support your investment decision. The information submitted must be consistent with the size and type of the business and the amount of the proposed Financing.

(b) *Updated financial and community economic development information.* (1) The terms of each Financing must require the Portfolio Concern to provide, at least annually, sufficient financial and community economic development information to enable you to perform the following required procedures:

(i) Evaluate the financial condition of the Portfolio Concern for the purpose of valuing your investment;

(ii) Determine the continued eligibility of the Portfolio Concern;

(iii) Verify the use of Financing proceeds; and

(iv) Evaluate the community economic development impact of the Financing.

(2) The president, chief executive officer, treasurer, chief financial officer, general partner, or proprietor of the Portfolio Concern must certify the information submitted to you.

(3) For financial and valuation purposes, you may accept a complete copy of the Federal income tax return filed by the Portfolio Concern (or its proprietor) in lieu of financial statements, but only if appropriate for the size and type of the business involved.

(4) The requirements in this paragraph (b) do not apply when you acquire securities from an underwriter in a public offering (see § 108.825). In that case, you must keep copies of all reports furnished by the Portfolio Concern to the holders of its securities.

(c) *Information required for examination purposes.* You must obtain any information requested by SBA's examiners for the purpose of verifying the certifications made by a Portfolio Concern under § 108.610. In this regard, your Financing documents must contain provisions requiring the Portfolio Concern to give you and/or SBA's examiners access to its books and records for such purpose.

REPORTING REQUIREMENTS FOR NMVC COMPANIES

§ 108.630 Requirement for NMVC companies to file financial statements and supplementary information with SBA (SBA Form 468).

(a) *Annual filing of Form 468.* For each fiscal year, you must submit to SBA financial statements and supplementary information prepared on SBA Form 468. You must file Form 468 on or before the last day of the third month following the end of your fiscal year, except for the information required under paragraphs (e) and (f) of this section, which must be filed on or before the last day of the fifth month following the end of your fiscal year.

(1) *Audit of Form 468.* An independent public accountant acceptable to SBA must audit the annual Form 468.

(2) *Insurance requirement for public accountant.* Unless SBA approves otherwise, your independent public accountant must carry at least $1,000,000 of Errors and Omissions insurance, or be self-insured and have a net worth of at least $1,000,000.

(b) *Interim filings of Form 468.* When requested by SBA, you must file interim reports on Form 468. SBA may require you to file the entire form or only certain statements and schedules. You must file such reports on or before the last day of the month following the end of the reporting period. When you submit a request for a draw under an SBA Leverage commitment, you must also comply with any applicable filing requirements set forth in § 108.1220.

(c) *Standards for preparation of Form 468.* You must prepare SBA Form 468 in accordance with SBA's Accounting Standards and Financial Reporting Requirements for Small Business Investment Companies, which you may obtain from SBA.

(d) *Where to file Form 468.* Submit all filings of Form 468 to the Office of New Markets Venture Capital in the Investment Division of SBA.

(e) *Reporting of social, economic, or community development impact information on Form 468.* Your annual filing of SBA Form 468 must include an assessment of the social, economic, or community development impact of each Financing. This assessment must specify the fulltime equivalent jobs created, the impact of the Financing on the revenues and profits of the business and on taxes paid by the business and its employees, and a listing of the number and percentage of employees who reside in LI Areas.

(f) *Reporting of community development information.* For each Financing of a Low-Income Enterprise, your Form 468 must include an assessment of such Financing with respect to:

(1) The social, economic or community development benefits achieved as a result of the Financing;

(2) How and to what extent such benefits fulfilled the goals of your comprehensive business plan and Participation Agreement;

(3) Whether you consider the Financing or the results of the Financing to have fulfilled the objectives of the NMVC program; and

(4) Whether, and if so, how you achieved accountability to the residents of the LI Area in connection with that Financing.

§ 108.640 Requirement to file portfolio financing reports (SBA Form 1031).

For each Financing you make (excluding guarantees), you must submit a Portfolio Financing Report on SBA Form 1031 within 30 days of the closing date.

§ 108.650 Requirement to report portfolio valuations to SBA.

You must determine the value of your Loans and Investments in accordance with § 108.503. You must report such valuations to SBA within 90 days of the end of the fiscal year in the case of annual valuations, and within 30 days following the close of other reporting periods. You must report material adverse changes in valuations at least quarterly, within thirty days following the close of the quarter.

§ 108.660 Other items required to be filed by NMVC Company with SBA.

(a) *Reports to owners.* You must give SBA a copy of any report you furnish to your investors, including any prospectus, letter, or other publication concerning your financial operations or those of any Portfolio Concern.

(b) *Documents filed with SEC.* You must give SBA a copy of any report, application or document you file with the Securities and Exchange Commission.

(c) *Litigation reports.* When you become a party to litigation or other proceedings, you must give SBA a report within 30 days that describes the proceedings and identifies the other parties involved and your relationship to them.

(1) The proceedings covered by this paragraph (c) include any action by you, or by your security holder(s) in a personal or derivative capacity, against an officer, director, Investment Adviser or other Associate of yours for alleged breach of official duty.

(2) SBA may require you to submit copies of the pleadings and other documents SBA may specify.

(3) Where proceedings have been terminated by settlement or final judgment, you must promptly advise SBA of the terms.

(4) This paragraph (c) does not apply to collection actions or proceedings to enforce your ordinary creditors' rights.

(d) *Notification of criminal charges.* If any officer, director, or general partner of the NMVC Company, or any other person who was required by SBA to complete a personal history statement, is charged with or convicted of any criminal offense other than a misdemeanor involving a minor motor vehicle violation, you must report the incident to SBA within 5 calendar days. Such report must fully describe the facts that pertain to the incident.

(e) *Reports concerning Operational Assistance grant funds.* You must comply with all reporting requirements set forth in Circular A–110 of the Office of Management and Budget and any grant award document executed between you and SBA.

(f) *Other reports.* You must file any other reports SBA may require in writing.

§ 108.680 Reporting changes in NMVC Company not subject to prior SBA approval.

(a) *Changes to be reported for post-approval.* This section applies to any changes in your Articles, ownership, capitalization, management, operating area, or investment policies that do not require SBA's prior approval. You must report such changes to SBA within 30 days for post approval.

(b) *Approval by SBA.* You may consider any change submitted under this section to be approved unless SBA notifies you to the contrary within 90 days after receiving it. SBA's approval is contingent upon your full disclosure of all relevant facts and is subject to any conditions SBA may prescribe.

EXAMINATIONS OF NMVC COMPANIES BY SBA FOR REGULATORY COMPLIANCE

§ 108.690 Examinations.

All NMVC companies must submit to annual examinations by or at the direction of SBA for the purpose of evaluating regulatory compliance.

§ 108.691 Responsibilities of NMVC Company during examination.

You must make all books, records and other pertinent documents and materials available for the examination, including any information required by the examiner under § 108.620(c). In addition, the agreement between you and the independent public accountant performing your audit must provide that any information in the accountant's working papers be made available to SBA upon request.

§ 108.692 Examination fees.

(a) *General.* SBA will assess fees for examinations in accordance with this section. Unless SBA determines otherwise on a case by case basis, SBA will not assess fees for special examinations to obtain specific information.

(b) *Base fee.* A base fee of $3,500 will be assessed, subject to adjustment in accordance with paragraph (c) of this section.

(c) *Adjustments to base fee.* The base fee will be decreased based on the following criteria:

(1) If you have no outstanding regulatory violations at the time of the commencement of the examination and SBA did not identify any violations as a result of the most recent prior examination, you will receive a 15% discount on your base fee; and

(2) If you were fully responsive to the letter of notification of examination (that is, you provided all requested documents and information within the time period stipulated in the notification letter in a complete and accurate manner, and you prepared and had available all information requested by the examiner for on-site review), you will receive a 10% discount on your base fee.

(d) *Delay fee.* If, in the judgment of SBA, the time required to complete your examination is delayed due to your lack of cooperation or the condition of your records, SBA may assess an additional fee of up to $500 per day.

Subpart I—Financing of Small Businesses by NMVC Companies

DETERMINING THE ELIGIBILITY OF A SMALL BUSINESS FOR NMVC FINANCING

§ 108.700 Compliance with size standards in part 121 of this chapter as a condition of Assistance.

You are permitted to provide financial assistance and management services only to a Small Business. To determine whether an applicant meets the size standards for a Small Business, you may use either the financial size standards in § 121.301(c)(1) of this chapter or the industry standard covering the industry in which the applicant is primarily engaged, as set forth in § 121.301(c)(2) of this chapter.

§ 108.710 Requirement to finance Low-Income Enterprises.

(a) *Low-Income Enterprise Financings.* At the close of each of your fiscal years—

(1) At least 80 percent of your Portfolio Concerns must be Low-Income Enterprises in which you have an Equity Capital Investment; and

(2) For all Financings you have extended, you must have invested at least 80 percent (in total dollars) in Equity Capital Investments in Low-Income Enterprises.

(b) *Non-compliance with this section.* If you have not reached the percentages required in paragraph (a) of this section at the end of any fiscal year, then you must be in compliance by the end of the following fiscal year. However, you will not be eligible for additional Leverage until such time as you reach the required percentages (see § 108.1120).

§ 108.720 Small Businesses that may be ineligible for financing.

(a) *Relenders or reinvestors.* You are not permitted to finance any business that is a relender or reinvestor. Relenders or reinvestors are businesses whose primary business activity involves, directly or indirectly, providing funds to others, purchasing debt obligations, factoring, or long-term leasing of equipment with no provision for maintenance or repair.

(b) *Passive Businesses.* You are not permitted to finance a passive business.

(1) *Definition.* A business is passive if:

(i) It is not engaged in a regular and continuous business operation (for purposes of this paragraph (b), the mere receipt of payments such as dividends, rents, lease payments, or royalties is not considered a regular and continuous business operation); or

(ii) Its employees are not carrying on the majority of day to day operations, and the company does not provide effective control and supervision, on a day to day basis, over persons employed under contract; or

(iii) It passes through substantially all of the proceeds of the Financing to another entity.

(2) *Exception for pass-through of proceeds to subsidiary.* With the prior written approval of SBA, you may finance a passive business if it is a Small Business and it passes substantially all the proceeds through to one or more subsidiary companies, each of which is an eligible Small Business that is not passive. For the purpose of this paragraph (b) (2), "subsidiary company" means a company in which at least 50 percent of the outstanding voting securities are owned by the Financed passive business.

(3) *Exception for certain Partnership NMVC companies.* With the prior written approval of SBA, if you are a Partnership NMVC Company, you may form one or more wholly owned corporations in accordance with this paragraph (b) (3). The sole purpose of such corporation(s) must be to provide Financing to one or more eligible, unincorporated Small Businesses. You may form such corporation(s) only if a direct Financing to such Small Businesses would cause any of your investors to incur unrelated business taxable income under section 511 of the Internal Revenue Code of 1986, as amended (26 U.S.C. 511). Your investment of funds in such corporation(s) will not constitute a violation of § 108.730(a).

(c) *Real Estate Businesses.* (1) You are not permitted to finance:

(i) Any business classified under subsector 5311 (Lessors of Real Estate) of the NAICS Manual; or

(ii) Any business listed under subsector 5312 (Offices of Real Estate Agents and Brokers) unless at least 80 percent of the revenue is derived from non-Affiliate sources.

(2) You are not permitted to finance a business, regardless of NAICS classification, if the Financing is to be used to acquire or refinance real property, unless the Small Business:

(i) Is acquiring an existing property and will use at least 51 percent of the usable square footage for an eligible business purpose; or

(ii) Is building or renovating a building and will use at least 67 percent of the usable square footage for an eligible business purpose; or

(iii) Occupies the subject property and uses at least 67 percent of the usable square footage for an eligible business purpose.

(d) *Project Financing.* You are not permitted to finance a business if:

(1) The assets of the business are to be reduced or consumed, generally without replacement, as the life of the business progresses, and the nature of the business requires that a stream of cash payments be made to the business's financing sources, on a basis associated with the continuing sale of assets. Examples include real estate development projects and oil and gas wells; or

(2) The primary purpose of the Financing is to fund production of a single item or defined limited number of items, generally over a defined production period, and such production will constitute the majority of the activities of the Small Business. Examples include motion pictures and electric generating plants.

(e) *Farm land purchases.* You are not permitted to finance the acquisition of farmland. Farmland means land, which is or is intended to be used for agricultural or forestry purposes, such as the production of food, fiber, or wood, or is so taxed or zoned.

(f) *Public interest.* You are not permitted to finance any business if the proceeds are to be used for purposes contrary to the public interest, including but not limited to activities which are in violation of law, or inconsistent with free competitive enterprise.

(g) *Foreign investment*—(1) *General rule.* You are not permitted to finance a business if:

(i) The funds will be used substantially for a foreign operation; or

(ii) At the time of the Financing or within one year thereafter, more than 49 percent of the employees or tangible assets of the Small Business are located outside the United States (unless you can show, to SBA's satisfaction, that the Financing was used for a specific domestic purpose).

(2) *Exception.* This paragraph (g) does not prohibit a Financing used to acquire foreign materials and equipment or foreign property rights for use or sale in the United States.

(h) *Financing NMVC companies or SBICs.* You are not permitted to provide funds, directly or indirectly, that the Small Business will use:

(1) To purchase stock in or provide capital to a NMVC Company or SBIC; or

(2) To repay an indebtedness incurred for the purpose of investing in a NMVC Company or SBIC.

§ 108.730 Financings which constitute conflicts of interest.

(a) *General rule.* You must not self-deal to the prejudice of a Small Business, the NMVC Company, its shareholders or partners, or SBA. Unless you obtain a prior written exemption from SBA for special instances in which a Financing may further the purposes of the Act despite presenting a conflict of interest, you must not directly or indirectly:

(1) Provide Financing to any of your Associates, except for a Small Business that satisfies all of the following conditions:

(i) Your Associate relationship with the Small Business is described by paragraph (8) or (9) of the definition of Associate in § 108.50;

(ii) No Person triggering the Associate relationship identified in paragraph (a)(1)(i) of this section is a Close Relative or Secondary Relative of any Person described in paragraph (1), (2), (4), or (5) of the definition of Associate in § 108.50; and

(iii) No single Associate of yours has either a voting interest or an economic interest in the Small Business exceeding 20 percent, and no two or more of your Associates have either a voting interest or an economic interest exceeding 33 percent. Economic interests shall be computed on a fully diluted basis, and both voting and economic interests shall exclude any interest owned through the NMVC Company.

(2) Provide Financing to an Associate of another NMVC Company if one of your Associates has received or will receive any direct or indirect Financing or a Commitment from that NMVC Company or a third NMVC Company (including Financing or Commitments received under any understanding, agreement, or cross dealing, reciprocal or circular arrangement).

(3) Borrow money from:

(i) A Small Business Financed by you;

(ii) An officer, director, or owner of at least a 10 percent equity interest in such business; or

(iii) A Close Relative of any such officer, director, or equity owner.

(4) Provide Financing to a Small Business to discharge an obligation to your Associate or free other funds to pay such obligation. This paragraph (a)(4) does not apply if the obligation is to an Associate Lending Institution and is a line of credit or other obligation incurred in the normal course of business.

(b) *Rules applicable to Associates.* Without SBA' s prior written approval, your Associates must not, directly or indirectly:

(1) Borrow money from any Person described in paragraph (a)(3) of this section.

(2) Receive from a Small Business any compensation in connection with Assistance you provide (except as permitted under §108.825(c)), or anything of value for procuring, attempting to procure, or influencing your action with respect to such Assistance.

(c) *Applicability of other laws.* You are also bound by any restrictions in Federal or State laws governing conflicts of interest and fiduciary obligations.

(d) *Financings with Associates*—(1) *Financings with Associates requiring prior approval.* Without SBA's prior written approval, you may not Finance any business in which your Associate has either a voting equity interest or total equity interests (including potential interests) of at least five percent, except as otherwise permitted under paragraph (a)(1) of this section.

(2) *Other Financings with Associates.* If you and an Associate provide Financing to the same Small Business, either at the same time or at different times, you must be able to demonstrate to SBA's satisfaction that the terms and conditions are (or were) fair and equitable to you, taking into account any differences in the timing of each party's financing transactions.

(3) *Exceptions to paragraphs (d)(1) and (d)(2) of this section.* A Financing that falls into one of the following categories is exempt from the prior approval requirement in paragraph (d)(1) of this section or is presumed to be fair and equitable to you for the purposes of paragraph (d)(2) of this section, as appropriate:

(i) Your Associate is a Lending Institution that is providing financing under a credit facility in order to meet the operational needs of the Small Business, and the terms of such financing are usual and customary.

(ii) Your Associate invests in the Small Business on the same terms and conditions and at the same time as you.

(iii) Both you and your Associate are NMVC companies.

(e) *Use of Associates to manage Portfolio Concerns.* To protect your investment, you may designate an Associate to serve as an officer, director, or other participant in the management of a Small Business. You must identify any such Associate in your records available for SBA's review under §108.600. Without SBA's prior written approval, the Associate must not:

(1) Have any other direct or indirect financial interest in the Portfolio Concern that exceeds, or has the potential to exceed, the percentages of the Portfolio Concern's equity set forth in paragraph (a)(1) of this section.

(2) Receive any income or anything of value from the Portfolio Concern unless it is for your benefit, with the exception of director's fees, expenses, and distributions based upon the Associate's ownership interest in the Concern.

(f) *1940 and 1980 Act Companies: SEC exemptions.* If you are a 1940 or 1980 Act Company and you receive an exemption from the Securities and Exchange Commission for a transaction described in this section, you need not obtain SBA's approval of the transaction. However, you must promptly notify SBA of the transaction.

(g) *Restriction on options obtained by NMVC Company's management and employees.* Your employees, officers, directors, managing members or general partners, or the general partners of the management company that is providing services to you or to your general partner, may obtain options in a Financed Small Business only if:

(1) They participate in the Financing on a *pari passu* basis with you; or

(2) SBA gives its prior written approval; or

(3) The options received are compensation for service as a member of

the board of directors of the Small Business, and such compensation does not exceed that paid to other outside directors. In the absence of such directors, fees must be reasonable when compared with amounts paid to outside directors of similar companies.

§ 108.740 Portfolio diversification ("overline" limitation).

(a) Without SBA's prior written approval, you may provide Financing or a Commitment to a Small Business only if the resulting amount of your aggregate outstanding Financings and Commitments to such Small Business and its Affiliates does not exceed 10 percent of the sum of:

(1) Your Regulatory Capital as of the date of the Financing or Commitment; plus

(2) The total amount of leverage projected in your participation agreement with SBA; plus

(3) Any permitted Distribution(s) you made during the five years preceding the date of the Financing or Commitment which reduced your Regulatory Capital.

(b) For the purposes of paragraph (a) of this section, you must measure each outstanding Financing at its current cost plus any amount of the Financing that was previously written off.

[66 FR 28609, May 23, 2001, as amended at 76 FR 63545, Oct. 12, 2011]

§ 108.760 How a change in size or activity of a Portfolio Concern affects the NMVC Company and the Portfolio Concern.

(a) *Effect on NMVC Company of a change in size of a Portfolio Concern.* If a Portfolio Concern no longer qualifies as a Small Business you may keep your investment in the concern and:

(1) Subject to the overline limitations of § 108.740, you may provide additional Financing to the concern up to the time it makes a public offering of its securities.

(2) Even after the concern makes a public offering, you may exercise any stock options, warrants, or other rights to purchase Equity Securities which you acquired before the public offering, or fund Commitments you made before the public offering.

(b) *Effect of a change in business activity occurring within one year of NMVC Company's initial Financing*—(1) *Retention of Investment.* Unless you receive SBA's written approval, you may not keep your investment in a Portfolio Concern, small or otherwise, which becomes ineligible by reason of a change in its business activity within one year of your initial investment.

(2) *Request for SBA 's approval to retain investment.* If you request that SBA approve the retention of your investment, your request must include sufficient evidence to demonstrate that the change in business activity was caused by an unforeseen change in circumstances and was not contemplated at the time the Financing was made.

(3) *Additional Financing.* If SBA approves your request to retain an investment under paragraph (b)(2) of this section, you may provide additional Financing to the Portfolio Concern to the extent necessary to protect against the loss of the amount of your original investment, subject to the overline limitations of § 108.740.

(c) *Effect of a change in business activity occurring more than one year after the initial Financing.* If a Portfolio Concern becomes ineligible because of a change in business activity more than one year after your initial Financing you may:

(1) Retain your investment; and

(2) Provide additional Financing to the Portfolio Concern to the extent necessary to protect against the loss of the amount of your original investment, subject to the overline limitations of § 108.740.

STRUCTURING NMVC COMPANY'S FINANCING OF ELIGIBLE SMALL BUSINESSES

§ 108.800 Financings in the form of equity interests.

You may not, inadvertently or otherwise:

(a) Become a general partner in any unincorporated business; or

(b) Become jointly or severally liable for any obligations of an unincorporated business.

§ 108.820 Financings in the form of guarantees.

(a) *General rule.* At the request of a Small Business or where necessary to protect your existing investment, you may guarantee the monetary obligation of a Small Business to any non-Associate creditor.

(b) *Exception.* You may not issue a guaranty if:

(1) You would become subject to State regulation as an insurance, guaranty or surety business; or

(2) The amount of the guaranty plus any direct Financings to the Small Business exceed the overline limitations of § 108.740, except that a pledge of the Equity Securities of the issuer or a subordination of your lien or creditor position does not count toward your overline.

(c) *Pledge of NMVC Company's assets as guaranty.* For purposes of this section, a guaranty with recourse only to specific asset(s) you have pledged is equal to the fair market value of such asset(s) or the amount of the debt guaranteed, whichever is less.

§ 108.825 Purchasing securities from an underwriter or other third party.

(a) *Securities purchased through or from an underwriter.* You may purchase the securities of a Small Business through or from an underwriter if:

(1) You purchase such securities within 90 days of the date the public offering is first made;

(2) Your purchase price is no more than the original public offering price; and

(3) The amount paid by you for the securities (less ordinary and reasonable underwriting charges and commissions) has been, or will be, paid to the Small Business, and the underwriter certifies in writing that this requirement has been met.

(b) *Recordkeeping requirements.* You must keep records available for SBA's inspection which show the relevant details of the transaction, including, but not limited to, date, price, commissions, and the underwriter's certifications required under paragraphs (a)(3) and (c) of this section.

(c) *Underwriter's requirements.* The underwriter must certify whether it is your Associate. You may pay reasonable and customary commissions and expenses to an Associate underwriter for the portion of an offering that you purchase.

(d) *Securities purchased from another NMVC Company or from SBA.* You may purchase from, or exchange with, another NMVC Company, Portfolio securities (or any interest therein). Such purchase or exchange may only be made on a non-recourse basis. You may not have more than one-third of your total assets (valued at cost) invested in such securities. If you have previously sold Portfolio securities (or any interest therein) on a recourse basis, you shall include the amount for which you may be contingently liable in your overline computation.

(e) *Purchases of securities from other non-issuers.* You may purchase securities of a Small Business from a non-issuer not previously described in this section if such acquisition is a reasonably necessary part of the overall sound Financing of the Small Business.

LIMITATIONS ON DISPOSITION OF ASSETS

§ 108.885 Disposition of assets to NMVC Company's Associates.

Except with SBA's prior written approval, you are not permitted to dispose of assets (including assets acquired in liquidation) to any Associate. As a prerequisite to such approval, you must demonstrate that the proposed terms of disposal are at least as favorable to you as the terms obtainable elsewhere.

MANAGEMENT SERVICES AND FEES

§ 108.900 Fees for management services provided to a Small Business by a NMVC Company or its Associate.

(a) *General.* This section applies to management services that you or your Associate provide to a Small Business during the term of a Financing or prior to a Financing. It does not apply to management services that your Associate provides to a Small Business that you do not finance. It also does not apply to Operational Assistance that you or your Associate provide to a Smaller Enterprise that you have Financed or in which you expect to make a Financing, for which neither you nor your Associate may charge the Smaller Enterprise.

(b) *SBA approval.* You must obtain SBA's prior written approval of any management services fees and other fees described in this section that you or your Associate charge.

(c) *Permitted management services fees.* You or your Associate may provide management services to a Small Business financed by you if:

(1) You or your Associate have entered into a written contract with the Small Business;

(2) The fees charged are for services actually performed;

(3) Services are provided on an hourly fee, project fee, or other reasonable basis;

(4) You can demonstrate to SBA, upon request, that the rate does not exceed the prevailing rate charged for comparable services by other organizations in the geographic area of the Small Business; and

(5) At least 50 percent of any management services fees paid to your Associate by a Small Business for management services provided by the Associate is allocated back to you for your benefit.

(d) *Fees for service as a board member.* You or your Associate may charge a Small Business Financed by you for services provided as members of the Small Business' board of directors. The fees must not exceed those paid to other outside board members. In the absence of such board members, fees must be reasonable when compared with amounts paid to outside directors of similar companies. Fees may be in the form of cash, warrants, or other payments. At least 50 percent of any such fees paid to your Associate by a Small Business for service by the Associate as a board member must be allocated back to you for your benefit.

(e) *Transaction fees.* (1) You or your Associate may charge reasonable transaction fees for work performed such as preparing a Small Business for a public offering, private offering, or sale of all or part of the business, and for assisting with the transaction. Fees may be in the form of cash, notes, stock, and/or options. At least 50 percent of any such fees paid to your Associate by a Small Business for transactions work done by the Associate must be allocated back to you for your benefit.

(2) Your Associate may charge market rate investment banking fees to a Small Business on that portion of a Financing that you do not provide.

(f) *Recordkeeping requirements.* You must keep a record of hours spent and amounts charged to the Small Business, including expenses charged.

[67 FR 68503, Nov. 12, 2002]

Subpart J—SBA Financial Assistance for NMVC Companies (Leverage)

GENERAL INFORMATION ABOUT OBTAINING LEVERAGE

§ 108.1100 Type of Leverage and application procedures.

(a) *Type of Leverage available.* You may apply for Leverage from SBA in the form of a guarantee of your Debentures.

(b) *Applying for Leverage.* The Leverage application process has two parts. You must first apply for SBA's conditional commitment to reserve a specific amount of Leverage for your future use. You may then apply to draw down Leverage against the commitment. See §§ 108.1200 through 108.1240.

(c) *Where to send your application.* Send all Leverage applications to SBA, Investment Division Office of New Markets Venture Capital, 409 Third Street, SW., Washington, DC 20416.

§ 108.1120 General eligibility requirement for Leverage.

To be eligible for Leverage, you must be in compliance with the Act, the regulations in this part, and your Participation Agreement.

§ 108.1130 Leverage fees payable by NMVC Company.

There is no fee for the issuance of Debentures by a NMVC Company.

§ 108.1140 NMVC Company's acceptance of SBA remedies under § 108.1810.

If you issue Leverage, you automatically agree to the terms and conditions in § 108.1810 as it exists at the time of issuance. The effect of these terms and conditions is the same as if they were fully incorporated in the terms of your Leverage.

MAXIMUM AMOUNT OF LEVERAGE FOR WHICH A NMVC COMPANY IS ELIGIBLE

§ 108.1150 Maximum amount of Leverage for a NMVC Company.

The face amount of a NMVC Company's outstanding Debentures may not exceed 150 percent of its Leverageable Capital.

CONDITIONAL COMMITMENTS BY SBA TO RESERVE LEVERAGE FOR A NMVC COMPANY

§ 108.1200 SBA's Leverage commitment to a NMVC Company—application procedure, amount, and term.

(a) *General.* Under the provisions in §§ 108.1200 through 108.1240, you may apply for SBA's conditional commitment to reserve a specific amount and type of Leverage for your future use. You may then apply to draw down Leverage against the commitment.

(b) *Applying for a Leverage commitment.* SBA will notify you when it is accepting requests for Leverage commitments. Upon receipt of your request, SBA will send you a complete application package.

(c) *Limitations on the amount of a Leverage commitment.* The amount of a Leverage commitment must be a multiple of $5,000. SBA, in its discretion, may determine a minimum dollar amount for Leverage commitments. Any such minimum amounts will be published in Notices in the FEDERAL REGISTER from time to time.

(d) *Term of Leverage commitment.* SBA's Leverage commitment will automatically lapse on the expiration date stated in the commitment letter issued to you by SBA.

§ 108.1220 Requirement for NMVC Company to file financial statements at the time of request for a draw.

(a) If you submit a request for a draw against SBA's Leverage commitment more than 90 days since your submission of an annual Form 468 or a Form 468 (Short Form), you must:

(1) Give SBA a financial statement on Form 468 (Short Form); and

(2) File a statement of no material adverse change in your financial condition since your last filing of Form 468.

(b) You will not be eligible for a draw if you are not in compliance with this section.

§ 108.1230 Draw-downs by NMVC Company under SBA's Leverage commitment.

(a) *NMVC Company's authorization of SBA to guarantee securities.* By submitting a request for a draw against SBA's Leverage commitment, you authorize SBA, or any agent or trustee SBA designates, to guarantee your Debenture and to sell it with SBA's guarantee.

(b) *Limitations on amount of draw.* The amount of a draw must be a multiple of $5,000. SBA, in its discretion, may determine a minimum dollar amount for draws against SBA's Leverage commitments. Any such minimum amounts will be published in Notices in the FEDERAL REGISTER from time to time.

(c) *Effect of regulatory violations on NMVC Company's eligibility for draws*—(1) *General rule.* You are eligible to make a draw against SBA's Leverage commitment only if you are in compliance with all applicable provisions of the Act and SBA regulations (i.e., no unresolved statutory or regulatory violations) and your Participation Agreement.

(2) *Exception to general rule.* If you are not in compliance, you may still be eligible for draws if:

(i) SBA determines that your outstanding violations are of non-substantive provisions of the Act or regulations or your Participation Agreement and that you have not repeatedly violated any non-substantive provisions; or

(ii) You have agreed with SBA on a course of action to resolve your violations and such agreement does not prevent you from issuing Leverage.

(d) *Procedures for funding draws.* You may request a draw at any time during the term of the commitment. With each request, submit the following documentation:

(1) A statement certifying that there has been no material adverse change in your financial condition since your last

filing of SBA Form 468 (see also § 108.1220 for SBA Form 468 filing requirements).

(2) If your request is submitted more than 30 days following the end of your fiscal year, but before you have submitted your annual filing of SBA Form 468 (Long Form) in accordance with § 108.630(a), a preliminary unaudited annual financial statement on SBA Form 468 (Short Form).

(3) A statement certifying that to the best of your knowledge and belief, you are in compliance with all provisions of the Act and SBA regulations (i.e., no unresolved regulatory or statutory violations) and your Participation Agreement, or a statement listing any specific violations you are aware of. Either statement must be executed by one of the following:

(i) An officer of the NMVC Company;

(ii) An officer of a corporate general partner of the NMVC Company;

(iii) An individual who is authorized to act as or for a general partner of the NMVC Company; or

(iv) An individual who is authorized to act as or for a member-manager of the NMVC Company.

(4) A statement that the proceeds are needed to fund one or more particular Small Businesses or to provide liquidity for your operations. If required by SBA, the statement must include the name and address of each Small Business, and the amount and anticipated closing date of each proposed Financing.

(e) *Reporting requirements after drawing funds.* (1) Within 30 calendar days after the actual closing date of each Financing funded with the proceeds of your draw, you must file an SBA Form 1031 confirming the closing of the transaction.

(2) If SBA required you to provide information concerning a specific planned Financing under paragraph (d)(4) of this section, and such Financing has not closed within 60 calendar days after the anticipated closing date, you must give SBA a written explanation of the failure to close.

(3) If you do not comply with this paragraph (e), you will not be eligible for additional draws. SBA may also determine that you are not in compliance with the terms of your Leverage under § 108.1810.

§ 108.1240 Funding of NMVC Company's draw request through sale to third-party.

(a) *NMVC Company's authorization of SBA to arrange sale of securities to third-party.* By submitting a request for a draw of Debenture Leverage, you authorize SBA, or any agent or trustee SBA designates, to enter into any agreements (and to bind you to such agreements) necessary to accomplish:

(1) The sale of your Debenture to a third-party at a rate approved by SBA; and

(2) The purchase of your security from the third-party and the pooling of your security with other securities with the same maturity date.

(b) *Sale of Debentures to a third-party.* If SBA arranges for the sale of your Debenture to a third-party, the sale price may be an amount discounted from the face amount of the Debenture.

Funding Leverage by Use of SBA Guaranteed Trust Certificates ("TCs")

§ 108.1600 SBA authority to issue and guarantee Trust Certificates.

(a) *Authorization.* Section 356 of the Act authorizes SBA to issue TCs and to guarantee the timely payment of the principal and interest thereon. Any guarantee by SBA of such TC is limited to the principal and interest due on the Debentures in any Trust or Pool backing such TC. The full faith and credit of the United States is pledged to the payment of all amounts due under the guarantee of any TC.

(b) *SBA authority to arrange public or private fundings of Leverage.* SBA in its discretion may arrange for public or private financing under its guarantee authority. Such financing arranged by SBA may be accomplished by the sale of individual Debentures, aggregations of Debentures, or Pools or Trusts of Debentures.

(c) *Pass-through provisions.* TCs shall provide for a pass-through to their holders of all amounts of principal and interest paid on the Debentures in the Pool or Trust against which they are issued.

(d) *Formation of a Pool or Trust holding Leverage Securities.* SBA shall approve the formation of each Pool or Trust. SBA may, in its discretion, establish the size of the Pools and their composition, the interest rate on the TCs issued against Trusts or Pools, fees, discounts, premiums and other charges made in connection with the Pools, Trusts, and TCs, and any other characteristics of a Pool or Trust it deems appropriate.

§ 108.1610 Effect of prepayment or early redemption of Leverage on a Trust Certificate.

(a) The rights, if any, of a NMVC Company to prepay any Debenture is established by the terms of such security, and no such right is created or denied by the regulations in this part.

(b) SBA's rights to purchase or prepay any Debenture without premium are established by the terms of the Guaranty Agreement relating to the Debenture.

(c) Any prepayment of a Debenture pursuant to the terms of the Guaranty Agreement relating to such security shall reduce the SBA guarantee of timely payment of principal and interest on a TC in proportion to the amount of principal that such prepaid Debenture represents in the Trust or Pool backing such TC.

(d) SBA shall be discharged from its guarantee obligation to the holder or holders of any TC, or any successor or transferee of such holder, to the extent of any such prepayment. whether or not such successor or transferee shall have notice of any such prepayment.

(e) Interest on prepaid Debentures shall accrue only through the date of prepayment.

(f) In the event that all Debentures constituting a Trust or Pool are prepaid, the TCs backed by such Trust or Pool shall be redeemed by payment of the unpaid principal and interest on the TCs; provided, however, that in the case of the prepayment of a Debenture pursuant to the provisions of the Guaranty Agreement relating to the Debenture, the CRA shall pass through pro rata to the holders of the TCs any such prepayments including any prepayment penalty paid by the obligor NMVC Company pursuant to the terms of the Debenture.

§ 108.1620 Functions of agents, including Central Registration Agent, Selling Agent and Fiscal Agent.

(a) *Agents.* SBA may appoint or cause to be appointed agent(s) to perform functions necessary to market and service Debentures or TCs pursuant to this part.

(1) *Selling Agent.* As a condition of guaranteeing a Debenture, SBA may cause each NMVC Company to appoint a Selling Agent to perform functions that include, but are not limited to:

(i) Selecting qualified entities to become pool or Trust assemblers ("Poolers").

(ii) Receiving guaranteed Debentures as well as negotiating the terms and conditions of sales or periodic offerings of Debentures and/or TCs on behalf of NMVC companies.

(iii) Directing and coordinating periodic sales of Debentures and/or TCs.

(iv) Arranging for the production of Offering Circulars, certificates, and such other documents as may be required from time to time.

(2) *Fiscal Agent.* SBA shall appoint a Fiscal Agent to:

(i) Establish performance criteria for Poolers.

(ii) Monitor and evaluate the financial markets to determine those factors that will minimize or reduce the cost of funding Debentures.

(iii) Monitor the performance of the Selling Agent, Poolers, CRA, and the Trustee.

(iv) Perform such other functions as SBA, from time to time, may prescribe.

(3) *Central Registration Agent.* Pursuant to a contract entered into with SBA, the CRA, as SBA's agent, will do the following with respect to the Pools or Trust Certificates for the Debentures:

(i) Form an SBA-approved Pool or Trust;

(ii) Issue the TCs in the form prescribed by SBA;

(iii) Transfer the TCs upon the sale of original issue TCs in any secondary market transaction;

(iv) Receive payments from NMVC companies;

(v) Make periodic payments as scheduled or required by the terms of the TCs, and pay all amounts required to be paid upon prepayment of Debentures;

(vi) Hold, safeguard, and release all Debentures constituting Trusts or Pools upon instructions from SBA;

(vii) Remain custodian of such other documentation as SBA shall direct by written instructions;

(viii) Provide for the registration of all pooled Debentures, all Pools and Trusts, and all TCs;

(ix) Perform such other functions as SBA may deem necessary to implement the provisions of this section.

(b) *Functions.* Either SBA or an agent appointed by SBA may perform the function of locating purchasers, and negotiating and closing the sale of Debentures and TCs. Nothing in the regulations in this part shall be interpreted to prevent the CRA from acting as SBA's agent for this purpose.

§ 108.1630 SBA regulation of Brokers and Dealers and disclosure to purchasers of Leverage or Trust Certificates.

(a) *Brokers and Dealers.* Each broker, dealer, and Pool or Trust assembler approved by SBA pursuant to these regulations shall either be regulated by a Federal financial regulatory agency, or be a member of the National Association of Securities Dealers (NASD), and shall be in good standing in respect to compliance with the financial, ethical, and reporting requirements of such body. They also shall be in good standing with SBA as determined by the SBA Associate Administrator for Investment (see paragraph (c) of this section) and shall provide a fidelity bond or insurance in such amount as SBA may require.

(b) *Suspension and/or termination of Broker or Dealer.* SBA shall exclude from the sale and all other dealings in Debentures or TCs any broker or dealer:

(1) If such broker's or dealer's authority to engage in the securities business has been revoked or suspended by a supervisory agency. When such authority has been suspended, SBA will suspend such broker or dealer for the duration of such suspension by the supervisory agency.

(2) If such broker or dealer has been indicted or otherwise formally charged with a misdemeanor or felony bearing on its fitness, such broker or dealer may be suspended while the charge is pending. Upon conviction, participation may be terminated.

(3) If such broker or dealer has suffered an adverse final civil judgment holding that such broker or dealer has committed a breach of trust or violation of law or regulation protecting the integrity of business transactions or relationships, participation in the market for Debentures or TCs may be terminated.

(c) *Termination/suspension proceedings.* A broker's or dealer's participation in the market for Debentures or TCs will be conducted in accordance with part 134 of this chapter. SBA may, for any of the reasons stated in paragraphs (b)(1) through (b)(3) of this section, suspend the privilege of any broker or dealer to participate in this market. SBA shall give written notice at least ten (10) business days prior to the effective date of such suspension. Such notice shall inform the broker or dealer of the opportunity for a hearing pursuant to part 134 of this chapter.

§ 108.1640 SBA access to records of the CRA, Brokers, Dealers and Pool or Trust assemblers.

The CRA and any broker, dealer and Pool or Trust assembler operating under the regulations in this part shall make all books, records and related materials associated with Debentures and TCs available to SBA for review and copying purposes. Such access shall be at such party's primary place of business during normal business hours.

MISCELLANEOUS

§ 108.1700 Transfer by SBA of its interest in a NMVC Company's Leverage security.

Upon such conditions and for such consideration as it deems reasonable, SBA may sell, assign, transfer, or otherwise dispose of any Debenture held by or on behalf of SBA. Upon notice by SBA, a NMVC Company will make all payments of principal and interest as shall be directed by SBA. A NMVC Company will be liable for all damage or loss which SBA may sustain by reason of such disposal, up to the amount of the NMVC Company's liability under such security, plus court costs and reasonable attorney's fees incurred by SBA.

§ 108.1710 SBA authority to collect or compromise its claims.

SBA may, upon such conditions and for such consideration as it deems reasonable, collect or compromise all claims relating to obligations held or guaranteed by SBA, and all legal or equitable rights accruing to SBA.

§ 108.1720 Characteristics of SBA's guarantee.

If SBA agrees to guarantee a NMVC Company's Debentures, such guarantee will be unconditional, irrespective of the validity, regularity or enforceability of the Debentures or any other circumstances that might constitute a legal or equitable discharge or defense of a guarantor. Pursuant to its guarantee, SBA will make timely payments of principal and interest on the Debentures.

Subpart K—NMVC Company's Noncompliance With Terms of Leverage

§ 108.1810 Events of default and SBA's remedies for NMVC Company's noncompliance with terms of Debentures.

(a) *Applicability of this section.* By issuing Debentures, you automatically agree to the terms, conditions and remedies in this section, as in effect at the time of issuance and as if fully set forth in the Debentures.

(b) *Automatic events of default.* The occurrence of one or more of the events in this paragraph (b) causes the remedies in paragraph (c) of this section to take effect immediately.

(1) *Insolvency.* You become equitably or legally insolvent.

(2) *Voluntary assignment.* You make a voluntary assignment for the benefit of creditors without SBA's prior written approval.

(3) *Bankruptcy.* You file a petition to begin any bankruptcy or reorganization proceeding, receivership, dissolution or other similar creditors' rights proceeding, or such action is initiated against you and is not dismissed within 60 days.

(c) *SBA remedies for automatic events of default.* Upon the occurrence of one or more of the events in paragraph (b) of this section:

(1) Without notice, presentation or demand, the entire indebtedness evidenced by your Debentures, including accrued interest, and any other amounts owed SBA with respect to your Debentures, is immediately due and payable; and

(2) You automatically consent to the appointment of SBA or its designee as your receiver under section 363(c) of the Act.

(d) *Events of default with notice.* For any occurrence (as determined by SBA) of one or more of the events in this paragraph (d), SBA may avail itself of one or more of the remedies in paragraph (e) of this section.

(1) *Fraud.* You commit a fraudulent act that causes detriment to SBA's position as a creditor or guarantor.

(2) *Fraudulent transfers.* You make any transfer or incur any obligation that is fraudulent under the terms of 11 U.S.C. 548.

(3) *Willful conflicts of interest.* You willfully violate § 108.730.

(4) *Willful non-compliance.* You willfully violate one or more of the substantive provisions of the Act or any substantive regulation promulgated under the Act or any substantive provision of your Participation Agreement.

(5) *Repeated Events of Default.* At any time after being notified by SBA of the occurrence of an event of default under paragraph (f) of this section, you engage in similar behavior that results in another occurrence of the same event of default.

(6) *Transfer of Control.* You willfully violate § 108.410, and as a result of such violation you undergo a transfer of Control.

(7) *Non-cooperation under paragraph (h) of this section.* You fail to take appropriate steps, satisfactory to SBA, to accomplish any action SBA may have required under paragraph (h) of this section.

(8) *Non-notification of Events of Default.* You fail to notify SBA as soon as you know or reasonably should have known that any event of default exists under this section.

(9) *Non-notification of defaults to others.* You fail to notify SBA in writing within ten days from the date of a declaration of an event of default or nonperformance under any note, debenture or indebtedness of yours, issued to or held by anyone other than SBA.

(e) *SBA remedies for events of default with notice.* Upon written notice to you of the occurrence (as determined by SBA) of one or more of the events in paragraph (d) of this section:

(1) SBA may declare the entire indebtedness evidenced by your Debentures, including accrued interest, and/or any other amounts owed SBA with respect to your Debentures, immediately due and payable; and

(2) SBA may avail itself of any remedy available under the Act, specifically including institution of proceedings for the appointment of SBA or its designee as your receiver under section 363 (c) of the Act.

(f) *Events of default with opportunity to cure.* For any occurrence (as determined by SBA) of one or more of the events in this paragraph (f), SBA may avail itself of one or more of the remedies in paragraph (g) of this section.

(1) *Excessive Management Expenses.* Without the prior written consent of SBA, you incur Management Expenses in excess of those permitted under §§108.510 and 108.520.

(2) *Improper Distributions.* You make any Distribution to your shareholders or partners, except with the prior written consent of SBA, other than:

(i) Distributions permitted under §108.585; and

(ii) Payments from Retained Earnings Available for Distribution based on either the shareholders' or members' pro-rata interests or the provisions for profit distributions in your partnership agreement, as appropriate.

(3) *Failure to make payment.* Unless otherwise approved by SBA, you fail to make timely payment of any amount due under any security or obligation of yours that is issued to, held or guaranteed by SBA.

(4) *Failure to maintain Regulatory Capital.* You fail to maintain the minimum Regulatory Capital required under these regulations or, without the prior written consent of SBA, you reduce your Regulatory Capital except as permitted by §108.585.

(5) *Capital Impairment.* You have a condition of Capital Impairment as determined under §108.1830.

(6) *Cross-default.* An obligation of yours that is greater than $100,000 becomes due or payable (with or without notice) before its stated maturity date, for any reason including your failure to pay any amount when due. This provision does not apply if you pay the amount due within any applicable grace period or contest the payment of the obligation in good faith by appropriate proceedings.

(7) *Nonperformance.* You violate or fail to perform one or more of the terms and conditions of any security or obligation of yours that is issued to, held or guaranteed by SBA, or of any agreement (including your Participation Agreement) with or conditions imposed by SBA in its administration of the Act and the regulations promulgated under the Act.

(8) *Noncompliance.* Except as otherwise provided in paragraph (d) (5) of this section, SBA determines that you have violated one or more of the substantive provisions of the Act or any substantive regulation promulgated under the Act.

(9) *Failure to maintain diversity.* You fail to maintain diversity between management and ownership as required by §108.150.

(g) *SBA remedies for events of default with opportunity to cure.* (1) Upon written notice to you of the occurrence (as determined by SBA) of one or more of the events of default in paragraph (f) of this section, and subject to the conditions in paragraph (g)(2) of this section:

(i) SBA may declare the entire indebtedness evidenced by your Debentures, including accrued interest, and/or any other amounts owed SBA with respect to your Debentures, immediately due and payable; and

(ii) SBA may avail itself of any remedy available under the Act, specifically including institution of proceedings for the appointment of SBA or its designee as your receiver under section 363(c) of the Act.

(2) SBA may invoke the remedies in paragraph (g)(1) of this section only if:

(i) It has given you at least 15 days to cure the default(s); and

(ii) You fail to cure the default(s) to SBA's satisfaction within the allotted time.

(h) *Repeated non-substantive violations.* If you repeatedly fail to comply with one or more of the non-substantive provisions of the Act or any non-substantive regulation promulgated under the Act, SBA, after written notification to you and until you cure such condition to SBA's satisfaction, may deny you additional Leverage and/or require you to take such actions as SBA may determine to be appropriate under the circumstances.

(i) *Consent to removal of officers, directors, or general partners and/or appointment of receiver.* The Articles of each NMVC Company must include the following provisions as a condition to the purchase or guarantee by SBA of Leverage. Upon the occurrence of any of the events specified in paragraphs (d)(1) through (d)(6) or (f)(1) through (f)(3) of this section as determined by SBA, SBA shall have the right, and you consent to SBA's exercise of such right:

(1) With respect to a Corporate NMVC Company, upon written notice, to require you to replace, with individuals approved by SBA, one or more of your officers and/or such number of directors of your board of directors as is sufficient to constitute a majority of such board; or

(2) With respect to a Partnership NMVC Company or an LLC NMVC Company, upon written notice, to require you to remove the person(s) responsible for such occurrence and/or to remove the general partner or manager of the NMVC Company, which general partner or manager shall then be replaced in accordance with NMVC Company's Articles by a new general partner or manager approved by SBA; and/or

(3) With respect to a Corporate or Partnership or LLC NMVC Company, to obtain the appointment of SBA or its designee as your receiver under section 363(c) of the Act for the purpose of continuing your operations. The appointment of a receiver to liquidate a NMVC Company is not within such consent, but is governed instead by the relevant provisions of the Act.

COMPUTATION OF NMVC COMPANY'S CAPITAL IMPAIRMENT

§ 108.1830 NMVC Company's Capital Impairment definition and general requirements.

(a) *Significance of Capital Impairment condition.* If you have a condition of Capital Impairment, you are not in compliance with the terms of your Leverage. As a result, SBA has the right to impose the applicable remedies for noncompliance in § 108.1810(g).

(b) *Definition of Capital Impairment condition.* You have a condition of Capital Impairment if your Capital Impairment Percentage, as computed in § 108.1840, exceeds 70 percent.

(c) *Quarterly computation requirement and procedure.* You must determine whether you have a condition of Capital Impairment as of the end of each fiscal quarter. You must notify SBA promptly if you are capitally impaired.

(d) *SBA's right to determine NMVC Company's Capital Impairment condition.* SBA may make its own determination of your Capital Impairment condition at any time.

§ 108.1840 Computation of NMVC Company's Capital Impairment Percentage.

(a) *General.* This section contains the procedures you must use to determine your Capital Impairment Percentage. You must compare your Capital Impairment Percentage to the maximum permitted under § 108.1830(b) to determine whether you have a condition of Capital Impairment.

(b) *Preliminary impairment test.* If you satisfy the preliminary impairment test, your Capital Impairment Percentage is zero and you do not have to perform any more procedures in this section. Otherwise, you must continue with paragraph (c) of this section. You satisfy the test if the following amounts are both zero or greater:

(1) The sum of Undistributed Net Realized Earnings, as reported on SBA Form 468, and Includible Non-Cash Gains.

(2) Unrealized Gain (Loss) on Securities Held.

(c) *How to compute your Capital Impairment Percentage.* (1) If you have an Unrealized Gain on Securities Held, compute your Adjusted Unrealized Gain using paragraph (d) of this section. If you have an Unrealized Loss on Securities Held, continue with paragraph (c)(2) of this section.

(2) Add together your Undistributed Net Realized Earnings, your Includible Non-cash Gains, and either your Unrealized Loss on Securities Held or your Adjusted Unrealized Gain.

(3) If the sum in paragraph (c)(2) of this section is zero or greater, your Capital Impairment Percentage is zero.

(4) If the sum in paragraph (c)(2) of this section is less than zero, drop the negative sign, divide by your Regulatory Capital (excluding Treasury Stock), and multiply by 100. The result is your Capital Impairment Percentage.

(d) *How to compute your Adjusted Unrealized Gain.* (1) Subtract Unrealized Depreciation from Unrealized Appreciation. This is your "Net Appreciation".

(2) Determine your Unrealized Appreciation on Publicly Traded and Marketable securities. This is your "Class I Appreciation".

(3) Determine your Unrealized Appreciation on securities that are not Publicly Traded and Marketable and meet the following criteria, which must be substantiated to the satisfaction of SBA (this is your "Class 2 Appreciation"):

(i) The Small Business that issued the security received a significant subsequent equity financing by an investor whose objectives were not primarily strategic and at a price that conclusively supports the Unrealized Appreciation;

(ii) Such financing represents a substantial investment in the form of an arm's length transaction by a sophisticated new investor in the issuer's securities; and

(iii) Such financing occurred within 24 months of the date of the Capital Impairment computation, or the Small Business' pre-tax cash flow from operations for its most recent fiscal year was at least 10 percent of the Small Business' average contributed capital for such fiscal year.

(4) Perform the appropriate computation from the table in §107.1840(d)(4) of this chapter.

(5) Reduce the gain computed in paragraph (d) (4) of this section by your estimate of related future income tax expense. Subject to any adjustment required by paragraph (d)(6) of this section, the result is your Adjusted Unrealized Gain for use in paragraph (c)(2) of this section.

(6) If any securities that are the source of either Class 1 or Class 2 Appreciation are pledged or encumbered in any way, you must reduce the Adjusted Unrealized Gain computed in paragraph (d)(5) of this section by the amount of the related borrowing or other obligation, up to the amount of the Unrealized Appreciation on the securities.

Subpart L—Ending Operations as a NMVC Company

§ 108.1900 Termination of participation as a NMVC Company.

You may not terminate your participation as a NMVC Company without SBA's prior written approval. Your request for approval must be accompanied by an offer of immediate repayment of all of your outstanding Leverage (including any prepayment penalties thereon), or by a plan satisfactory to SBA for the orderly liquidation of the NMVC Company.

Subpart M—Miscellaneous

§ 108.1910 Non-waiver of SBA's rights or terms of Leverage security.

SBA's failure to exercise or delay in exercising any right or remedy under the Act or the regulations in this part does not constitute a waiver of such right or remedy. SBA's failure to require you to perform any term or provision of your Leverage does not affect SBA's right to enforce such term or provision. Similarly, SBA's waiver of, or failure to enforce, any term or provision of your Leverage or of any event or condition set forth in § 108.1810 does not constitute a waiver of any succeeding breach of such term or provision or condition.

§ 108.1920 NMVC Company's application for exemption from a regulation in this part 108.

(a) *General.* You may file an application in writing with SBA to have a proposed action exempted from any procedural or substantive requirement, restriction, or prohibition to which it is subject under this part, unless the provision is mandated by the Act. SBA may grant an exemption for such applicant, conditionally or unconditionally, provided the exemption would not be contrary to the purposes of the Act.

(b) *Contents of application.* Your application must be accompanied by supporting evidence that demonstrates to SBA's satisfaction that:

(1) The proposed action is fair and equitable; and

(2) The exemption requested is reasonably calculated to advance the best interests of the NMVC program in a manner consistent with the policy objectives of the Act and the regulations in this part.

§ 108.1930 Effect of changes in this part 108 on transactions previously consummated.

The legality of a transaction covered by the regulations in this part is governed by the regulations in this part in effect at the time the transaction was consummated, regardless of later changes. Nothing in this part bars SBA enforcement action with respect to any transaction consummated in violation of provisions applicable at the time, but no longer in effect.

§ 108.1940 Procedures for designation of additional Low-Income Geographic Areas

(a) *General.* On its own initiative or upon written request by a Person which addresses the relevant factor(s) set forth in paragraph (b) of this section, SBA may consider whether to designate additional census tracts (or equivalent county divisions) as LI Areas.

(b) *Criteria.* SBA will consider one or more of the following factors in determining whether to designate a particular census tract (or equivalent county division) as an additional LI Area:

(1) A substantial number of Low-Income Individuals reside in that census tract (or equivalent county division).

(2) As adequately supported by studies or other analyses or reliable data, that census tract (or equivalent county division) has a pattern of unmet needs for investment capital.

(3) As adequately supported by studies or other analyses or reliable data, that census tract (or equivalent county division) has indications of economic distress.

(c) *Procedure for designation.* (1) If SBA decides to consider the designation of an additional LI Area, SBA will publish in the FEDERAL REGISTER a notice that it is considering such designation. SBA will advise the public that it will consider any comments supporting or opposing the designation, submitted within a specified time period.

(2) In making a final decision on whether to designate a particular census tract (or equivalent county division) as an additional LI Area, SBA will consider evidence submitted by any requester, SBA's own research, any public comments submitted, and any other information deemed relevant by SBA.

(3) If SBA designates a particular census tract (or equivalent county division) as an additional LI Area, SBA will publish a notice in the FEDERAL REGISTER and, if appropriate, will amend this part to include the additional LI Area.

Subpart N—Requirements and Procedures for Operational Assistance Grants to NMVC Companies and SSBICs

§ 108.2000 Operational Assistance Grants to NMVC Companies and SSBICs.

(a) *NMVC Companies.* Regulations governing Operational Assistance grants to NMVC Companies may be found in subparts D and E of this part 108, and in §§ 108.2010 through 108.2040.

(b) *SSBICs.* Regulations governing Operational Assistance grants to SSBICs may be found in §§ 108.2001 through 108.2040.

[67 FR 68503, Nov. 12, 2002]

§ 108.2001 When and how SSBICs may apply for Operational Assistance grants.

(a) *Notice of Funds Availability ("NOFA").* SBA will publish a NOFA in the FEDERAL REGISTER, advising SSBICs of the availability of funds for Operational Assistance grants to SSBICs. This NOFA will be the same NOFA described in § 108.300(a), or will be published simultaneously with that NOFA. An SSBIC may submit an application for an Operational Assistance grant only during the time period specified for such purpose in the NOFA.

(b) *Application form.* An SSBIC must apply for an Operational Assistance grant using the application packet provided by SBA. Upon receipt of an application, SBA may request clarifying or technical information on the materials submitted as part of the application.

[67 FR 68503, Nov. 12, 2002]

§ 108.2002 Eligibility of SSBICs to apply for Operational Assistance grants.

An SSBIC is eligible to apply for an Operational Assistance grant if:

(a) It intends to increase its Regulatory Capital, as in effect on December 21, 2000, and to make Low-Income Investments in the amount of such increase;

(b) It intends to raise binding commitments for contributions in cash or in-kind, and/or to purchase an annuity, in an amount not less than 30 percent of the intended increase in its Regulatory Capital described in paragraph (a) of this section; and

(c) It has a plan describing how it intends to use the requested grant funds to provide Operational Assistance to Smaller Enterprises in which it has made or expects to make Low-Income Investments after December 21, 2000.

[67 FR 68503, Nov. 12, 2002]

§ 108.2003 Grant issuance fee for SSBICs.

An SSBIC must pay to SBA a grant issuance fee of $5,000. An SSBIC must submit this fee in advance, at the time of application submission. If SBA does not award a grant to the SSBIC, SBA will refund this fee to the SSBIC.

[67 FR 68503, Nov. 12, 2002]

§ 108.2004 Contents of application submitted by SSBICs.

Each application submitted by an SSBIC for an Operational Assistance grant must contain the information specified in the application packet provided by SBA, including the following information:

(a) *Amounts.* An SSBIC must specify the amount of Regulatory Capital it intends to raise after December 21, 2000, and the amount of Operational Assistance grant funds it seeks from SBA, which must be at least 30 percent of its intended increase in its Regulatory Capital since December 21, 2000.

(b) *Plan.* An SSBIC must submit a plan addressing the specific items described in § 108.2005.

[67 FR 68503, Nov. 12, 2002]

§ 108.2005 Contents of plan submitted by SSBICs.

(a) *Plan for providing Operational Assistance.* The SSBIC must describe how it plans to use its grant funds to provide Operational Assistance to Smaller Enterprises in which it will make Low-Income Investments. Its plan must address the types of Operational Assistance it proposes to provide, and how it plans to provide the Operational Assistance through the use of licensed professionals, when necessary, either from its own staff or from outside entities.

(b) *Matching resources for Operational Assistance grant.* The SSBIC must include a detailed description of how it plans to obtain binding commitments for contributions in cash or in-kind, and/or to purchase an annuity, to match the funds requested from SBA for the SSBIC's Operational Assistance grant. If it proposes to obtain commitments for cash and in-kind contributions, it also must estimate the ratio of cash to in-kind contributions (in no event may in-kind contributions exceed 50 percent of the total contributions). The SSBIC must discuss its potential sources of matching resources, the estimated timing on raising such match, and the extent of the expressions of interest to commit such match to the SSBIC.

(c) *Identification of LI Areas.* The SSBIC must identify the specific LI

Areas in which it intends to make Low-Income Investments and provide Operational Assistance under the NMVC program.

(d) *Projected allocation of investments among identified LI Areas.* The SSBIC must describe the amount of Low-Income Investments it intends to make in each of the identified LI Areas.

(e) *Track record of management team in obtaining public policy results through investments.* The SSBIC must provide information concerning the past track record of the SSBIC in making investments that have had a demonstrable impact on the socially or economically disadvantaged businesses targeted by the SSBIC program (for example, new businesses created, jobs created, or wealth created). Such information might include case studies or examples of the SSBIC's successful Financings.

(f) *Market analysis.* The SSBIC must provide an analysis of the LI Areas in which it intends to makes its Low-Income Investments and provide its Operational Assistance to Smaller Enterprises, demonstrating that the SSBIC understands the market and the unmet capital needs in such areas and how its activities will meet these unmet capital needs through Low-Income Investments and have a positive economic impact on those areas. The analysis must include a description of the extent of the economic distress in the identified LI Areas. The SSBIC also must analyze the extent of the demand in such areas for Low-Income Investments and any factors or trends that may affect the SSBIC's ability to make effective Low-Income Investments.

(g) *Regulatory Capital.* The SSBIC must include a detailed description of how it plans to raise its Regulatory Capital. The SSBIC must discuss its potential sources of Regulatory Capital, the estimated timing on raising such funds, and the extent of the expressions of interest to commit such funds to the SSBIC.

(h) *Projected impact.* The SSBIC must describe the criteria and economic measurements to be used to evaluate whether and to what extent it has met the objectives of the NMVC program. It must include:

(1) An estimate of the social, economic, and community development benefits to be created within identified LI Areas over the next five years or more as a result of its activities;

(2) A description of the criteria to be used to measure the benefits created as a result of its activities; and

(3) A discussion about the amount of such benefits created that it will consider to constitute successfully meeting the objectives of the NMVC program.

[67 FR 68503, Nov. 12, 2002]

§ 108.2006 Evaluation and selection of SSBICs.

SBA will evaluate and select an SSBIC for an Operational Assistance grant award under the NMVC program solely at SBA's discretion, based on SBA's review of the SSBIC's application materials, interviews or site visits with the SSBIC (if any), and information in SBA's records relating to the SSBIC's regulatory compliance status and track record as an SSBIC. SBA's evaluation and selection process is intended to ensure that SSBIC requests are evaluated on a competitive basis and in a fair and consistent manner. SBA will evaluate and select SSBICs for an Operational Assistance grant award by considering the following criteria:

(a) The strength of the SSBIC's application, including the strength of its proposal to provide Operational Assistance to Smaller Enterprises in which it intends to invest;

(b) The SSBIC's regulatory compliance status and past track record in being able to accomplish program goals through its investment activity;

(c) The likelihood that and the time frame within which the SSBIC will be able to raise the Regulatory Capital it intends to raise and obtain the matching resources described in § 108.2005(b) and (g);

(d) The need for Low-Income Investments in the LI Areas in which the SSBIC intends to invest;

(e) The SSBIC's demonstrated understanding of the markets in the LI Areas in which it intends to invest;

(f) The extent to which the activities proposed by the SSBIC will promote economic development and the creation of wealth and job opportunities in the LI Areas in which it intends to invest and among individuals living in LI Areas;

(g) The likelihood that the SSBIC will fulfill the goals described in its application and meet the objectives of the NMVC program; and

(h) The strength of the SSBIC's application compared to applications submitted by other SSBICs and by Applicants intending to invest in the same or proximate LI Areas.

[67 FR 68503, Nov. 12, 2002]

§ 108.2007 Grant award to SSBICs.

An SSBIC selected for an Operational Assistance grant award will receive a grant award only if, by a date established by SBA, it increases its Regulatory Capital in the specific amount set forth in its application, pursuant to § 108.2004(a), and raises matching resources for the grant in the amount required by § 108.2030(d)(2).

[67 FR 68503, Nov. 12, 2002]

§ 108.2010 Restrictions on use of Operational Assistance grant funds.

(a) *Restrictions applicable only to SSBICs.* An SSBIC that receives an Operational Assistance grant must use both grant funds awarded by SBA and its matching resources only to provide Operational Assistance in connection with a Low-Income Investment made by the SSBIC with Regulatory Capital raised after December 21, 2000.

(b) *Restrictions applicable only to NMVC Companies.* A NMVC Company must use at least 80 percent of both grant funds awarded by SBA and its matching resources to provide Operational Assistance to Smaller Enterprises whose Principal Office at the time the Operational Assistance commences is located in an LI Area.

(c) *Restrictions applicable to NMVC Companies and SSBICs.* A NMVC Company or a SSBIC that receives an Operational Assistance grant must not use either grant funds awarded by SBA or its matching resources for "general and administrative expense," as defined in the Federal Acquisition Regulations, "Definitions of Words and Terms," 48 CFR 2.101.

[66 FR 28609, May 23, 2001; 66 FR 32894, June 19, 2001, as amended at 67 FR 68505, Nov. 12, 2002]

§ 108.2020 Amount of Operational Assistance grant.

(a) *Amount of grant to NMVC Company.* NMVC Companies are eligible for an Operational Assistance grant award equal to the amount of matching resources raised by the NMVC Company in accordance with §§ 108.380(a)(1)(i)(B) and 108.2030.

(b) *Amount of grant to SSBIC.* SSBICs are eligible for an Operational Assistance grant award equal to the amount of matching resources raised by the SSBIC in accordance with §§ 108.2007 and 108.2030.

(c) *Pro rata reductions.* In the event that the total amount of funds available to SBA for purposes of making Operational Assistance grant awards to NMVC Companies and SSBICs is not sufficient to award grants in the amounts described in paragraphs (a) and (b) of this section, SBA will make pro rata reductions in the amounts otherwise awarded to each such NMVC Company and SSBIC.

[66 FR 28609, May 23, 2001, as amended at 67 FR 68505, Nov. 12, 2002]

§ 108.2030 Matching requirements.

(a) *General.* All Operational Assistance grant funds SBA awards to an NMVC Company or a SSBIC must be matched on a dollar for dollar basis with funds or other resources raised by the NMVC Company or SSBIC.

(b) *Allowable sources.* (1) Any source other than SBA is an allowable source of matching resources for an Operational Assistance grant award.

(2) Neither a NMVC Company nor a SSBIC may use funds or other resources that it has used to satisfy a legal requirement for obtaining funds under any other Federal program, to satisfy the matching resources requirements described in this part.

(3) A portion of Private Capital may be designated as matching resources if the designated funds are used to purchase an annuity pursuant to paragraph (c)(2)(iv) of this section or are otherwise segregated in a manner acceptable to SBA.

(c) *Type and form of matching resources.* (1) Matching resources may come from cash contributions or in-kind contributions. In-kind contributions cannot exceed 50 percent of the total amount of match raised by the NMVC Company or SSBIC.

(2) Matching resources may be in the form of:

(i) Cash;

(ii) In-kind contributions;

(iii) Binding commitments for cash or in-kind contributions that may be payable over a multiyear period acceptable to SBA (but not to exceed the term of the Operational Assistance grant from SBA and in no event more than 10 years); and/or

(iv) An annuity, purchased with funds other than Regulatory Capital, from an insurance company acceptable to SBA and that may be payable over a multiyear period acceptable to SBA (but not to exceed the term of the Operational Assistance grant from SBA and in no event more than 10 years).

(d) *Amount of matching resources*—(1) *NMVC Companies.* The amount of matching resources required of an NMVC Company is set forth in § 108.380(a)(1)(i)(B).

(2) *SSBICs.* The amount of matching resources required of an SSBIC is equal to the amount of Operational Assistance grant funds requested by the SSBIC, as set forth in its application pursuant to § 108.2004(a).

[66 FR 28609, May 23, 2001, as amended at 67 FR 68505, Nov. 12, 2002]

§ 108.2040 Reporting and recordkeeping requirements.

(a) *NMVC Companies.* Policies governing reporting, record retention, and recordkeeping requirements applicable to NMVC Companies may be found in subpart H of this part. NMVC Companies also must comply with all reporting, record retention, and recordkeeping requirements set forth in Circular A–110 of the Office of Management and Budget (for availability, see 5 CFR 1310.3) and any grant award document executed between SBA and the NMVC Company.

(b) *SSBICs.* An SSBIC receiving an Operational Assistance grant award must comply with all reporting, record retention and recordkeeping requirements set forth in Circular A–110 of the Office of Management and Budget and any grant award document executed between SBA and the SSBIC, as well as the reporting requirements in § 108.630(f) and the filing requirement in § 108.640.

[66 FR 28609, May 23, 2001, as amended at 67 FR 68505, Nov. 12, 2002]

PART 109—INTERMEDIARY LENDING PILOT PROGRAM

Subpart A—Introduction

Subpart B—ILP Intermediary Application and Selection Process

Subpart C—ILP Program Requirements

Subpart D—Requirements for ILP Intermediary Loans to Small Businesses

Subpart E—Oversight

AUTHORITY: 15 U.S.C. 634(b)(6), (b)(7), and 636(l).

SOURCE: 76 FR 18015, Apr. 1, 2011, unless otherwise noted.

Subpart A—Introduction

§ 109.10 Description of the Intermediary Lending Pilot program.

The Small Business Intermediary Lending Pilot program (ILP program) provides direct loans to ILP Intermediaries to make loans of up to $200,000 to startup, newly established, or growing small businesses. ILP Intermediaries continue to relend a portion of the payments received on small business loans made under the program until they have fully repaid their loans to SBA.

§ 109.20 Definitions.

Affiliate is defined in § 121.301(f) of this chapter.

Associate. (1) An Associate of an ILP Intermediary is:

(i) An officer, director, key employee, or holder of 20 percent or more of the value of the ILP Intermediary or its debt instruments, or an agent involved in the loan process;

(ii) Any entity in which one or more individuals referred to in paragraph (1)(i) of this definition or a Close Relative of any such individual owns or controls at least 20 percent;

(2) An Associate of an Eligible Small Business Concern is:

(i) An officer director, owner of more than 20 percent of the equity, or key employee of the Eligible Small Business Concern;

(ii) Any entity in which one or more individuals referred to in paragraphs (2)(i) of this definition owns or controls at least 20 percent; and

(iii) Any individual or entity in control of or controlled by the small business (except a Small Business Investment Company (SBIC) licensed by SBA).

(3) For the purposes of this definition, the time during which an Associate relationship exists commences six months before the following dates and continues as long as the ILP Note or the loan to the Eligible Small Business Concern is outstanding:

(i) For an ILP Intermediary, the date of the ILP Note;

(ii) For an Eligible Small Business Concern, the date of the loan application to the ILP Intermediary.

Close Relative is a spouse; a parent; a child or sibling, or the spouse of any such person.

Eligible Small Business Concern is a small business that meets the requirements of § 109.400.

ILP Intermediary means a private, nonprofit entity that has applied for and been selected by SBA to receive an ILP Loan through the competitive application process described in this Part.

ILP Loan means a direct loan made by SBA to an ILP Intermediary under this program.

ILP Note means the instrument that represents the obligation of the ILP Intermediary to repay the ILP Loan to SBA.

ILP Program Activities Report means the quarterly report that identifies the use and management of ILP program funds.

ILP Program Requirements are requirements imposed upon an ILP Intermediary by statute, SBA regulations, any agreement executed between SBA and the ILP Intermediary, SBA SOPs, SBA procedural guidance, official SBA notices and forms applicable to the ILP program, any NOFA applicable to the ILP program, and the ILP Note and Loan Authorization, as such requirements are issued and revised by SBA from time to time.

ILP Relending Fund means a federally insured depository account established by the ILP Intermediary at a well-capitalized financial institution which includes, at a minimum, the ILP Loan proceeds and the principal portion of repayments from Eligible Small Business Concerns.

Intermediary Lending Program Electronic Reporting System (ILPERS) means the web-based, electronic reporting system used by the ILP Intermediary to report each loan made to Eligible Small Business Concerns, to provide aging information on each loan, and to update the outstanding principal balance of each loan until all loans are either paid in full or charged off.

Native American Tribal Government means the governing body of any Native American tribe, band, nation, or other organized group or community, including any Alaska Native village or regional or village corporation as defined in or established pursuant to the Alaska Native Claims Settlement Act (43 U.S.C.A. § 1601 *et seq.*), which is recognized as eligible for the special programs and services provided by the United States to Native Americans because of their status as Native Americans.

Portfolio Identification Report means the electronic report that collects identifying information on loans made to Eligible Small Business Concerns, including demographic information, use of proceeds, payment terms, and jobs created and retained.

Portfolio Status Report means the quarterly electronic report that summarizes the payment status and outstanding principal balances of an ILP Intermediary's loans to Eligible Small Business Concerns.

[76 FR 18015, Apr. 1, 2011, as amended at 81 FR 41428, June 27, 2016]

Subpart B—ILP Intermediary Application and Selection Process

§ 109.100 ILP Intermediary eligibility and continuing participation requirements.

(a) *Organization type:* An ILP Intermediary must be a private, nonprofit entity other than an intermediary participating in the SBA Microloan program as described in subpart G of Part 120. Eligible entities include:

(1) Private, nonprofit community development corporations;

(2) Consortiums of private, nonprofit organizations or nonprofit community development corporations; and

(3) Agencies of or nonprofit entities established by Native American tribal governments.

(b) *Prior experience:* An ILP Intermediary must have at least one year of successful experience making and servicing loans to startup, newly established, or growing small businesses.

(c) *Management and operations.* (1) An ILP Intermediary must have paid staff with loan making and servicing experience acceptable to SBA.

(2) An ILP Intermediary must have a continuing ability to evaluate, process, close, disburse, service and liquidate small business loans including, but not limited to:

(i) Holding sufficient permanent capital (as determined by SBA) to support lending activities under this program; and

(ii) Maintaining satisfactory SBA performance, as determined by SBA in its discretion.

(3) An ILP Intermediary must meet and maintain the ethical requirements of 13 CFR 120.140.

(4) An ILP Intermediary (and any Affiliates) that participates in other SBA programs must be in compliance with those program requirements.

(5) An ILP Intermediary must be in good standing with its Federal and/or State regulator, as applicable.

(6) An ILP Intermediary must have the ability to comply with the ILP Program Requirements, including reporting requirements, as such requirements are revised from time to time, and maintain compliance with ILP Program Requirements for as long as the ILP Intermediary participates in the ILP program.

§ 109.200 Application to become an ILP Intermediary.

(a) *Notice of Funds Availability (NOFA).* SBA will periodically publish a NOFA in the FEDERAL REGISTER, advising potential applicants of the availability of funds for the ILP program. Any eligible entity may then submit an application to become an ILP Intermediary. When submitting its application, an applicant must comply with both these regulations and any requirements specified in the NOFA, including submission deadlines. The NOFA may specify limitations, special rules, procedures, and restrictions for a particular funding round.

(b) *Contents of application.* The application to become an ILP Intermediary must include:

(1) Documentation that the applicant meets the eligibility and continuing

participation requirements for the ILP program set forth in § 109.100;

(2) A completed ILP Intermediary application form provided by SBA;

(3) A description of:

(i) The type of small businesses to be assisted;

(ii) The size and range of loans to be made;

(iii) The interest rate and terms of the loans to be made;

(iv) The geographic area to be served and the economic, poverty, and unemployment characteristics of the area;

(v) The status of small businesses in the area to be served and an analysis of the availability of credit; and

(4) Any additional forms and documentation required by SBA.

§ 109.210 Evaluation and selection of ILP Intermediaries.

(a) *General.* SBA will evaluate and select applicants to participate in the ILP program in accordance with this section and the NOFA. SBA reserves the right, in its discretion, to loan less than all available funds.

(b) *Number of ILP Intermediaries.* SBA will make loans to not more than 20 of the selected ILP Intermediaries in each of the fiscal years for which funding is available.

(c) *Eligibility and completeness.* SBA will not consider any application that is not complete or that is submitted by an applicant that does not meet the eligibility and participation criteria established by SBA. SBA, at its sole discretion, may request from an applicant additional information, including information concerning participation criteria or the application, in order to allow SBA to consider that applicant's application. Failure to provide such additional information may be considered grounds to reject the application.

(d) *Evaluation criteria.* Eligible and complete applications will be evaluated and scored based on the criteria established by SBA, as set forth in the NOFA. In general, eligible applications with the highest scores will be granted ILP Intermediary status, up to the maximum number allowed by statute. SBA reserves the right to select ILP Intermediaries in such a way as to ensure geographic diversity of areas served by ILP Intermediaries.

§ 109.220 Loan limits—loans to ILP Intermediaries.

No ILP Intermediary (including Affiliates) may receive more than $1,000,000 in ILP Loans.

Subpart C—ILP Program Requirements

§ 109.300 General.

An ILP Intermediary must maintain compliance with all ILP Program Requirements until the ILP Intermediary has repaid its ILP Loan to SBA. With respect to its activities in the ILP program, the ILP Intermediary is subject to the requirements of §§ 120.140 (What ethical requirements apply to participants?), 120.197 (Notifying SBA's Office of Inspector General of suspected fraud), 120.412 (Other services Lenders may provide Borrowers), and 120.413 (Advertisement of relationship with SBA) of this chapter, in addition to the regulations specifically set forth in this Part. The ILP Intermediary and any contractor(s) it may have are independent contractors that are responsible for their own actions with respect to small business loans made under this program. SBA has no responsibility or liability for any claim by an Eligible Small Business Concern or other party for any injury as a result of any wrongful action taken by the ILP Intermediary or an employee, agent or contractor of an ILP Intermediary.

§ 109.310 Terms of loans to ILP Intermediaries.

(a) *Disbursement.* An ILP Intermediary must be in compliance with ILP Program Requirements in order to draw down its ILP Loan funds. SBA may place restrictions on disbursement, including the amount disbursed to an ILP Intermediary at one time or conditions on subsequent disbursements.

(b) *Term.* An ILP Loan must be repaid within 20 years from the date of the ILP Note.

(c) *Interest rate.* The interest rate for an ILP Loan to an ILP Intermediary is fixed at one percent per annum.

(d) *Repayment.* Payments of principal and interest must be made on a quarterly basis, except SBA will defer the first payment on an ILP Loan for two years from the date of the first disbursement. Interest will accrue on all disbursed funds during the deferment period. Accrued interest will be added to the outstanding principal balance at the end of the deferment period and amortized over the remaining life of the loan. An ILP Intermediary may prepay an ILP Loan at any time without penalty.

(e) *Collateral.* SBA does not require the ILP Intermediary to provide any collateral for an ILP Loan.

(f) *Fees.* SBA does not charge an ILP Intermediary any fees for an ILP Loan.

§ 109.320 ILP Loan purposes.

(a) ILP Loan funds must only be used to provide direct loans to Eligible Small Business Concerns for working capital, real estate, or the acquisition of materials, supplies, furniture, fixtures, or equipment.

(b) ILP Loan funds must not be used for any other purpose, including maintenance of loan loss reserves or payment of administrative costs or expenses of the ILP Intermediary.

§ 109.330 ILP Relending Fund.

(a) *General.* The ILP Intermediary must establish and maintain an ILP Relending Fund for as long as it has an outstanding balance owed to SBA under this program. The ILP Relending Fund must be in an account separate and distinct from the ILP Intermediary's other assets and financial activities.

(b) *Contents of the ILP Relending Fund.* All ILP Loan proceeds disbursed from SBA to the ILP Intermediary must be deposited into the ILP Relending Fund. All payments received by the ILP Intermediary on loans made to Eligible Small Business Concerns must also be deposited into the ILP Relending Fund. The ILP Intermediary must not commingle funds from any other public programs (including other SBA programs) in this account.

(c) *Interest earned.* The ILP Intermediary is not required to retain the interest portion of payments received on loans made to Eligible Small Business Concerns in the ILP Relending Fund or to retain the interest earned on the ILP Relending Fund in the ILP Relending Fund.

(d) *Allowable uses of the ILP Relending Fund.* The ILP Intermediary must use the ILP Relending Fund to disburse loans made to Eligible Small Business Concerns under this program and to make payments to SBA on its ILP Loan; it may not use the ILP Relending Fund for any other purposes.

§ 109.340 Lending requirements.

(a) *Initial lending requirement.* The ILP Intermediary must commit 100% of its ILP Loan funds to Eligible Small Business Concerns within two years of the date of the ILP Note. The Associate Administrator for Capital Access (AA/CA) or designee may approve extensions to the initial lending requirement on a case-by-case basis.

(b) *Ongoing relending requirement.* After meeting the initial lending requirement, the ILP Intermediary must relend the funds in the ILP Relending Fund so that the total principal balance of loans outstanding to Eligible Small Business Concerns does not fall below 75% of the outstanding principal balance of the ILP Loan at any time while the ILP Loan is outstanding. Exceptions to this requirement will be considered by the AA/CA or designee on a case by case basis based on the particular facts and circumstances of the ILP Intermediary.

§ 109.350 Maintenance of loan loss reserve.

The ILP Intermediary must maintain a reasonable loan loss reserve appropriate for the quality of the ILP Intermediary's portfolio in a federally insured depository account established by the ILP Intermediary at a well-capitalized financial institution. The loan loss reserve must be in an account separate and distinct from the ILP Intermediary's other assets and financial activities. This reserve must be maintained at not less than 5% of the principal balance of all outstanding loans to Eligible Small Business Concerns made from the ILP Relending Fund. The AA/CA or designee may require the ILP Intermediary to maintain a larger loss reserve if the AA/CA determines that the ILP

Intermediary's loss reserve level is potentially inadequate to protect SBA from loss. ILP Relending Fund proceeds must not be used to establish or maintain the loan loss reserve.

§ 109.360 Recordkeeping and reporting requirements.

(a) *Maintenance of records.* The ILP Intermediary must maintain at its principal business office accurate and current financial records, including books of accounts, and all documents and supporting materials relating to the ILP Intermediary's activities in the ILP program, including files on loans made to Eligible Small Business Concerns. Records may be preserved electronically if the original is available for retrieval within 15 calendar days.

(b) *ILP Intermediary reporting.* The ILP Intermediary must submit the following to SBA:

(1) *Portfolio Identification Reports.* All loans made by the ILP Intermediary to an Eligible Small Business Concern under this program must be entered into the Intermediary Lending Program Electronic Reporting System (ILPERS) within seven calendar days of closing the loan.

(2) *Quarterly reports.* By the 30th calendar day following the end of each calendar quarter, each ILP Intermediary must submit a Portfolio Status Report via ILPERS to update the payment status and outstanding principal balances of its loans to Eligible Small Business Concerns. Additionally, each ILP Intermediary must submit an ILP Program Activities Report with accompanying bank statements to demonstrate the use and management of ILP program funds.

(3) *Audited financial statements.* Within four months after the close of the ILP Intermediary's fiscal year, the ILP Intermediary must submit to SBA audited financial statements as prepared by an independent certified public accountant, except that ILP Intermediaries subject to OMB Circular A–133 must submit audits prepared in accordance with that circular. The AA/CA or designee may provide extensions to the filing deadline.

(4) *Reports of changes.* An ILP Intermediary must submit to SBA a summary of any changes in the ILP Intermediary's organization or financing (within 30 calendar days of the change), such as:

(i) Any change in its name, address or telephone number;

(ii) Any change in its charter, bylaws, or its officers or directors (to be accompanied by a statement of personal history on the form approved by SBA);

(iii) Any material change in capitalization or financial condition; and

(iv) Any change affecting the ILP Intermediary's eligibility to continue to participate in the ILP program.

(5) *Other reports.* Each ILP Intermediary must submit such other reports as SBA may require from time to time.

Subpart D—Requirements for ILP Intermediary Loans to Small Businesses

§ 109.400 Eligible Small Business Concerns.

(a) To be eligible to receive loans from an ILP Intermediary under this program, a small business must:

(1) Be organized for profit;

(2) Be located in the U.S.;

(3) Be small under the size requirements applicable to 7(a) business loans (including Affiliates);

(4) Be a startup, newly established, or growing small business;

(5) Together with Affiliates and principal owners, not have credit elsewhere; and

(6) Be creditworthy and demonstrate reasonable assurance of repayment of the loan.

(b) The following types of businesses are not eligible to receive a loan from an ILP Intermediary under this program:

(1) Nonprofit businesses (for-profit subsidiaries are eligible);

(2) Financial businesses primarily engaged in the business of lending;

(3) Passive businesses owned by developers and landlords that do not actively use or occupy the assets acquired or improved with the loan proceeds;

(4) Life insurance companies;

(5) Businesses located in a foreign country;

(6) Pyramid sale distribution plans;

(7) Businesses deriving more than one-third of gross annual revenue from legal gambling activities;

(8) Businesses engaged in any illegal activity;

(9) Private clubs and businesses which limit the number of memberships for reasons other than capacity;

(10) Government-owned entities (except for businesses owned or controlled by a Native American tribe);

(11) Businesses principally engaged in teaching, instructing, counseling or indoctrinating religion or religious beliefs, whether in a religious or secular setting;

(12) [Reserved]

(13) Loan packagers earning more than one third of their gross annual revenue from packaging SBA loans;

(14) Businesses in which the ILP Intermediary or any of its Associates owns an equity interest;

(15) Businesses with an Associate who is incarcerated, on probation, on parole, or has been indicted for a felony or a crime of moral turpitude;

(16) Businesses which:

(i) Present live performances of a prurient sexual nature; or

(ii) Derive directly or indirectly more than de minimis gross revenue through the sale of products or services, or the presentation of any depictions or displays, of a prurient sexual nature;

(17) Businesses that have previously defaulted on a Federal loan or Federally assisted financing, resulting in the Federal government or any of its agencies or Departments sustaining a loss in any of its programs, and businesses owned or controlled by an applicant or any of its Associates which previously owned, operated, or controlled a business which defaulted on a Federal loan (or guaranteed a loan which was defaulted) and caused the Federal government or any of its agencies or Departments to sustain a loss in any of its programs. For purposes of this section, a compromise agreement shall also be considered a loss unless the agreement provides otherwise;

(18) Businesses primarily engaged in political or lobbying activities; and

(19) Speculative businesses (such as oil wildcatting);

(20) Businesses located in a Coastal Barrier Resource Area (as defined in the Coastal Barriers Resource Act);

(21) Businesses owned or controlled by an applicant or any of its Associates who are more than 60 days delinquent in child support under the terms of any administrative order, court order, or repayment agreement;

(22) Businesses in which any Associate is an undocumented (illegal) alien; or

(23) Businesses owned or controlled by an applicant or any of its Associates who are presently debarred, suspended, proposed for debarment, declared ineligible, or voluntarily excluded from participation by any Federal department or agency.

[76 FR 18015, Apr. 1, 2011, as amended at 82 FR 39501, Aug. 21, 2017]

§ 109.410 Loan limits—loans to Eligible Small Business Concerns.

No small business (including Affiliates) may have more than $200,000 outstanding under this program at one time. The provisions of § 120.151 do not apply to loans under this program.

§ 109.420 Terms of loans from ILP Intermediaries to Eligible Small Business Concerns.

(a) *General.* The terms of a loan made by the ILP Intermediary to an Eligible Small Business Concern must be agreed to by the ILP Intermediary and the Eligible Small Business Concern. The loan terms must be within the limits established by SBA in these regulations.

(b) *Maximum loan size.* The maximum amount of a loan by the ILP Intermediary to an Eligible Small Business Concern under this program is $200,000.

(c) *Maturity.* The term of a loan by the ILP Intermediary to an Eligible Small Business Concern under this program must be the shortest appropriate term. The maximum loan term is 10 years or less, unless the loan finances or refinances real estate or equipment with a useful life exceeding ten years, in which case the maximum loan term is 25 years.

(d) *Interest rate.* The maximum interest rate the ILP Intermediary may charge for loans less than or equal to $50,000 is 8.75 percent. The maximum interest rate the ILP Intermediary may charge for loans greater than $50,000 is 7%. SBA may adjust the maximum interest rates from time to time; SBA will publish any such change by Notice in the FEDERAL REGISTER. Changes to the maximum interest rate do not apply to loans made to Eligible Small Business Concerns prior to publication of the change in the FEDERAL REGISTER.

(e) *Fees.* The ILP Intermediary must not impose any fees or direct costs on an Eligible Small Business Concern, except for the following allowed fees or direct costs:

(1) Necessary out-of-pocket expenses, such as filing or recording fees;

(2) The reasonable direct costs of any liquidation;

(3) A late payment fee not to exceed 5 percent of the scheduled loan payment; and

(4) Reasonable application and origination fees, subject to a maximum total fee cap of 1 percent of the amount of the loan to the Eligible Small Business Concern. SBA may adjust the maximum total fee cap from time to time; SBA will publish any such change by Notice in the FEDERAL REGISTER.

§ 109.430 Loan purposes.

(a) An Eligible Small Business Concern may only use the proceeds of a loan under this program for the following purposes:

(1) Working capital;

(2) Real estate (except for real estate acquired and held primarily for sale, lease, or investment); and

(3) The acquisition of materials, supplies, furniture, fixtures, or equipment.

(b) Revolving lines of credit are permitted. However, if, at any time, SBA determines that the ILP Intermediary's operation of revolving lines of credit is causing excessive risk of loss for the intermediary or the Government, the AA/CA or designee may terminate the ILP Intermediary's authority to use the ILP Relending Fund proceeds for revolving lines of credit. Such termination will be by written notice and will prevent the ILP Intermediary from approving any new lines of credit or extending any existing revolving lines of credit beyond the effective date of termination contained in the notice.

§ 109.440 Requirements imposed under other laws and orders.

Loans made by the ILP Intermediary under this program must comply with all applicable laws, including §§ 120.170 (Flood insurance), 120.172 (Flood-plain and wetlands management), 120.173 (Lead-based paint), 120.173 (Earthquake hazards), and the civil rights laws (see parts 112, 113, 117, and 136 of this chapter) prohibiting discrimination on the grounds of race, color, national origin, religion, sex, marital status, disability or age.

§ 109.450 SBA review of ILP Intermediary loans to Eligible Small Business Concerns.

(a) *Review restrictions.* SBA does not review loans made by an ILP Intermediary under this program before approval of the loan by the ILP Intermediary. The ILP Intermediary is responsible for all loan decisions regarding eligibility (including size).

(b) *Subsequent review.* SBA will periodically review loans made by an ILP Intermediary after approval of the loan by the ILP Intermediary as part of the on-site and off-site reviews described in § 109.510. If SBA discovers that an ILP Intermediary has made a loan under this program to an ineligible business or for an ineligible purpose, SBA will require the ILP Intermediary to refinance the ineligible loan with non-ILP program funds and to deposit into its ILP Relending Fund an amount equal to the outstanding principal balance on the ineligible loan.

§ 109.460 Prohibition on sales of ILP Intermediary Loans to Eligible Small Business Concerns.

An ILP Intermediary may not sell all or any portion of a loan made to an Eligible Small Business Concern without prior written consent from the AA/CA or designee.

Subpart E—Oversight

§ 109.500 SBA access to ILP Intermediary files.

The ILP Intermediary must allow SBA's authorized representatives, including other officers of any other Federal agency and representatives authorized by the SBA Inspector General, during normal business hours, timely access to its facility and files to review, inspect, and copy all records and documents, including electronic and hard copy, relating to the operations of the ILP Intermediary, the ILP Loan, and the loans made from the ILP Relending Fund and other records and documents as requested for oversight of the ILP Intermediary.

§ 109.510 Reviews.

(a) *General.* SBA may conduct reviews and monitoring of ILP Intermediaries, including ILP Intermediaries' self-assessments. SBA may also perform reviews of ILP Intermediaries as needed, as determined by SBA in its discretion.

(b) *Corrective actions.* SBA may require an ILP Intermediary to take corrective actions to address findings from reviews. Failure to take required corrective actions may constitute an event of default, as described in § 109.520(c).

(c) *Confidentiality of reports.* Review reports and other SBA prepared review related documents are subject to the confidentiality requirements of § 120.1060.

[82 FR 39501, Aug. 21, 2017]

§ 109.520 Events of default and revocation of authority to participate in the ILP program.

(a) *Automatic events of default.* Upon the occurrence of one or more of the events in this paragraph (a), the ILP Loan balance, including accrued interest, is immediately due and payable to SBA without notice and the ILP Intermediary's authority to participate in the ILP program is revoked.

(1) *Insolvency.* The ILP Intermediary becomes equitably or legally insolvent.

(2) *Voluntary assignment.* The ILP Intermediary makes a voluntary assignment for the benefit of creditors without SBA's prior written approval.

(3) *Bankruptcy.* The ILP Intermediary files a petition to begin any bankruptcy or reorganization proceeding, receivership, dissolution or other similar creditors' rights proceeding, or such action is initiated against the ILP Intermediary and is not dismissed within 60 calendar days.

(b) *Events of default with notice and possible opportunity to cure.* Except as provided in paragraph (c) of this section, upon receipt of written notice to the ILP Intermediary of the occurrence (as determined by SBA) of one or more of the events in this paragraph (b), the ILP loan balance, including accrued interest, is immediately due and payable to SBA and the ILP Intermediary's authority to participate in the ILP program is revoked.

(1) *Fraud.* The ILP Intermediary commits a fraudulent act.

(2) *Violation of SBA's ethical requirements.* The ILP Intermediary violates 13 CFR § 120.140.

(3) *Non-notification of events of default.* The ILP Intermediary fails to notify SBA in writing as soon as it knows or reasonably should have known that any event of default exists under this section.

(4) *Non-notification of defaults to others.* The ILP Intermediary fails to notify SBA in writing within ten calendar days from the date of a declaration of an event of default or nonperformance under any note, debenture or indebtedness, issued to or held by anyone other than SBA.

(5) *Failure to make timely payment.* Unless otherwise approved by the AA/CA or designee in writing, the ILP Intermediary fails to make timely payment to SBA on its ILP Loan.

(6) *Failure to take adequate corrective actions.* The ILP Intermediary fails to take adequate corrective actions, to SBA's satisfaction, as required by SBA under § 109.510 within the timeframe requested by SBA.

(7) *Violation of ILP Program Requirements.* The ILP Intermediary violates one or more ILP Program Requirement.

(8) *Actions that increase risk.* The ILP Intermediary takes other action which increases the risk of loss to SBA.

(c) *Opportunity to Cure.* SBA may, in its discretion, provide the ILP Intermediary with an opportunity to cure an event of default identified in paragraph (b) of this section. If SBA provides the ILP Intermediary with such a cure opportunity, SBA will issue written notice discussing the relevant facts, and directing the ILP Intermediary to cure the default and provide SBA with documentation to show that the default has been cured within a specified period of time (generally 15 days). SBA will then provide the ILP Intermediary with a final notification advising whether the default has been satisfactorily cured. In the event SBA determines the default has not been cured, the ILP Loan balance, including accrued interest, is immediately due and payable to SBA and the ILP Intermediary's authority to participate in the ILP program is revoked upon the ILP Intermediary's receipt of this final notification.

(d) *Appeals.* Notification of default without opportunity to cure under paragraph (b) of this section and final notification of uncured default under paragraph (c) of this section are final agency decisions. An ILP Intermediary may appeal a final agency decision only in the appropriate federal district court.

§ 109.530 Debarment and Suspension.

In accordance with 2 CFR Parts 180 and 2700, SBA may take any necessary action to debar or suspend an ILP Intermediary or any officer, director, general partner, manager, employee, agent or other participant in the affairs of an ILP Intermediary's SBA operations.

PART 112—NONDISCRIMINATION IN FEDERALLY ASSISTED PROGRAMS OF SBA—EFFECTUATION OF TITLE VI OF THE CIVIL RIGHTS ACT OF 1964

Sec.

AUTHORITY: Sec. 602, 78 Stat. 252 (42 U.S.C. 2000d–1).

SOURCE: 30 FR 298, Jan. 9, 1965, unless otherwise noted.

§ 112.1 Purpose.

The purpose of this part is to effectuate the provisions of Title VI of the Civil Rights Act of 1964 (hereinafter referred to as the *Act*) to the end that no person in the United States shall, on the ground of race, color, or national origin, be excluded from participation in, be denied the benefits of, or be otherwise subjected to discrimination under any financial assistance activities of the Small Business Administration to which the Act applies.

§ 112.2 Application of this part.

(a) This part applies to all recipients of Federal financial assistance administered by the Small Business Administration. (See appendix A)

(b) The term *Federal financial assistance* includes: (1) Grants and loans of Federal funds; (2) the grant or donation of Federal property and interests in property; (3) the detail of Federal personnel; (4) the sale and lease of, and the permission to use (on other than a casual or transient basis), Federal property or any interest in such property without consideration, or at a nominal consideration, or at a consideration which is reduced for the purpose of assisting the recipient, or in recognition of the public interest to be served by such sale or lease to the recipient; and (5) any Federal agreement, arrangement, or other contract which has as one of its purposes the provision of assistance.

(c) This part does not apply to financial assistance extended by way of insurance or guarantee.

(d) The terms *applicant* and *recipient* mean, respectively, one who applies for and one who receives any of the financial assistance under any of the statutes referred to in paragraph (a) of this section. The term *recipient* also shall be deemed to include *subrecipients* of SBA financial assistance, i.e., concerns which secondarily receive financial assistance from the primary recipients of such financial assistance.

(e) The terms *program or activity* and *program* mean all of the operations of any entity described in paragraphs (e)(1) through (4) of this section, any part of which is extended Federal financial assistance:

(1)(i) A department, agency, special purpose district, or other instrumentality of a State or of a local government; or

(ii) The entity of such State or local government that distributes such assistance and each such department or agency (and each other State or local government entity) to which the assistance is extended, in the case of assistance to a State or local government;

(2)(i) A college, university, or other postsecondary institution, or a public system of higher education; or

(ii) A local educational agency (as defined in 20 U.S.C. 7801), system of vocational education, or other school system;

(3)(i) An entire corporation, partnership, or other private organization, or an entire sole proprietorship—

(A) If assistance is extended to such corporation, partnership, private organization, or sole proprietorship as a whole; or

(B) Which is principally engaged in the business of providing education, health care, housing, social services, or parks and recreation; or

(ii) The entire plant or other comparable, geographically separate facility to which Federal financial assistance is extended, in the case of any other corporation, partnership, private organization, or sole proprietorship; or

(4) Any other entity which is established by two or more of the entities described in paragraph (e)(1),(2), or (3) of this section.

[30 FR 298, Jan. 9, 1965, as amended at 38 FR 17934, July 5, 1973; 50 FR 1441 Jan. 11, 1985; 68 FR 51348, 51349, Aug. 26, 2003]

§ 112.3 Discrimination prohibited.

(a) *General.* To the extent that this part applies, no person in the United States shall, on the ground of race, color or national origin be excluded from participation in, be denied the benefits of, or be otherwise subjected to discrimination by any business or other activity.

(b) *Specific discriminatory actions prohibited.* (1) To the extent that this part applies, a business or other activity may not, directly or through contractual or other arrangements, on ground of race, color or national origin:

(i) Deny an individual any services, financial aid or other benefit provided by the business or other activity;

(ii) Provide any service, financial aid or other benefit to an individual which is different or is provided in a different manner, from that provided to others by the business or other activity;

(iii) Subject an individual to segregation or separate treatment in any manner related to his receipt of any service, financial aid or other benefit from the business or other activity;

(iv) Restrict an individual in any way in the enjoyment of any advantage or privilege enjoyed by others receiving any service, financial aid or other benefit from the business or other activity;

(v) Treat an individual differently from others in determining whether he satisfies any admission, enrollment, quota, eligibility, membership or other requirement or condition which individuals must meet in order to be provided any service, financial aid or other benefit provided by the business or other activity.

(2) The enumeration of specific forms of prohibited discrimination in this paragraph does not limit the generality of the prohibition in paragraph (a) of this section.

(3) This regulation does not prohibit the consideration of race, color, or national origin if the purpose and effect are to remove or overcome the consequences of practices or impediments which have restricted the availability of, or participation in, a program or activity receiving Federal financial assistance, on the grounds of race, color, or national origin. Where previous discriminatory practice or usage tends, on

the grounds of race, color, or national origin, to exclude individuals from participation in, to deny them the benefits of, or to subject them to discrimination under any program or activity to which this regulation applies, the applicant or recipient has an obligation to take reasonable action to remove or overcome the consequences of the prior discriminatory practice or usage, and to accomplish the purposes of the Act.

[30 FR 298, Jan. 9, 1965, as amended at 38 FR 17934, July 5, 1973; 68 FR 51349, Aug. 26, 2003]

§ 112.4 Discrimination in employment.

Small business concerns and development companies which apply for or receive any financial assistance of the kind described in § 112.2(a) (1) and (2), including concerns which are identifiable beneficiaries of loans made under § 112.2(a)(2), may not discriminate on the grounds of race, color, or national origin in their employment practices. Such assistance is deemed to have as a primary objective the providing of employment. Where a primary objective of the Federal financial assistance is not to provide employment, but discrimination on the grounds of race, color, or national origin in the employment practices of the recipient or other persons subject to the regulation tends, on the grounds of race, color, or national origin, to exclude individuals from participation in, to deny them the benefits of, or to subject them to discrimination under any program to which this regulation applies, the provisions of § 112.7(a) shall apply to the employment practices of the recipient or other persons subject to the regulation, to the extent necessary to assure equality of opportunity and nondiscriminatory treatment.

[38 FR 17934, July 5, 1973]

§ 112.5 Discrimination in providing financial assistance.

Development companies and small business investment companies which apply for or receive any of the financial assistance described in § 112.2(a) may not discriminate, on the ground of race, color or national origin, in providing financial assistance to small business concerns.

§ 112.6 Discrimination in accommodations or services.

Small business concerns which apply for or receive any financial assistance of the kind described in § 112.2(a)(1), concerns which are identifiable beneficiaries of loans made under § 112.2(a)(2), and physicians, hospitals, schools, libraries, and other individuals or organizations which apply for or receive financial assistance of the kind described in § 112.2(a)(5), may not discriminate in the treatment accommodations or services they provide to their patients, students, visitors, guests, members, passengers, or patrons in the conduct of such businesses or other enterprises, whether or not operated for profit.

[31 FR 2374, Feb. 4, 1966]

§ 112.7 Illustrative applications.

(a) *Employment.* The discrimination prohibited by § 112.4 includes but is not limited to any action (taken directly or through contractual or other arrangements) which subjects an individual to discrimination on the ground of race, color or national origin in any employment practice, including recruitment or recruitment advertising, employment, layoff or termination, upgrading, demotion, or transfer, rates of pay or other forms of compensation, and use of facilities.

(b) *Financial assistance.* The discrimination prohibited by § 112.5 includes but is not limited to the failure or refusal, because of the race, color, or national origin of a person, to extend a loan or equity financing to him or to any business concern of which he is an owner or employee; or, in the case of financing which has actually been extended, the failure or refusal, because of the race, color, or national origin of the borrower or of an owner or employee of the borrower, to accord the borrower fair treatment and the customary courtesies regarding such matters as default, grace periods and the like.

(c) *Accommodations or services.* The discrimination prohibited by § 112.6 includes but is not limited to the failure or refusal, because of the race, color, or national origin of a person, to accept him on a nonsegregated basis as a patient, student, visitor, guest, member, customer, passenger or patron.

(d) *Affirmative action.* (1) In some situations even though past discriminatory practices have been abandoned, the consequences of such practices continue to impede the full availability of equal opportunity. If the efforts required of the applicant or recipient under § 112.3(b)(3) to provide information as to the availability of equal opportunity, and the rights of individuals under this regulation, have failed to overcome these consequences, it will become necessary for such applicant or recipient to take additional steps to make equal opportunity fully available to racial and nationality groups previously subjected to discrimination.

(2) Even though an applicant or recipient has never used discriminatory policies, the opportunities in the business it operates may not in fact be equally available to some racial or nationality groups. In such circumstances a recipient may properly give special consideration to race, color, or national origin to make opportunity more widely available to such groups.

[30 FR 298, Jan. 9, 1965, as amended at 38 FR 17934, July 5, 1973]

§ 112.8 Assurances required.

An application for any of the financial assistance described in § 112.2(a) shall, as a condition to its approval and the extension of such assistance, contain or be accompanied by an assurance that the recipient will comply with this part. Such an assurance shall contain provisions authorizing the acceleration of the maturity of the recipient's financial obligation to the SBA in the event of a failure to comply, and provisions which give the United States a right to seek judicial enforcement of the terms of the assurance. SBA shall specify the form of the foregoing assurance, and the extent to which like assurances will be required of contractors and subcontractors, transferees, successors in interest, and other participants.

[30 FR 298, Jan. 9, 1965, as amended at 68 FR 51349, Aug. 26, 2003]

§ 112.9 Compliance information.

(a) *Cooperation and assistance.* SBA shall to the fullest extent practicable seek the cooperation of applicants and recipients in obtaining compliance with this part and shall provide assistance and guidance to applicants and recipients to help them comply voluntarily with this part.

(b) *Compliance reports.* Each applicant or recipient shall keep such records and submit to SBA timely, complete and accurate compliance reports at such times, and in such form and containing such information, as SBA may determine to be necessary to enable SBA to ascertain whether the applicant or recipient has complied or is complying with this part. In the case of a small business concern which receives financial assistance from a development company or from a small business investment company, such concern shall submit to the company such information as may be necessary to enable the company to meet its reporting requirements under this part.

(c) *Access to sources of information.* Each applicant or recipient shall permit access by SBA during normal business hours to such of its books, records, accounts, and other sources of information, and its facilities as may be pertinent to ascertain compliance with this part. Where any information required of an applicant or recipient is in the exclusive possession of any other agency, institution or person and this agency, institution or person shall fail or refuse to furnish this information, the applicant or recipient shall so certify in its report and shall set forth what efforts it has made to obtain this information.

(d) *Information to the public.* Each recipient shall make available to persons entitled under the Act and under this part to protection against discrimination by the recipient such information as SBA may find necessary to apprise them of their rights to such protection.

[30 FR 298, Jan. 9, 1965, as amended at 38 FR 17934, July 5, 1973]

§ 112.10 Conduct of investigations.

(a) *Periodic compliance reviews.* SBA shall from time to time review the practices of recipients to determine whether they are complying with this part.

(b) *Complaints.* Any person who believes himself or any specific class of individuals to be subjected to discrimination prohibited by this part may, by himself or by a representative, file with SBA a written complaint. A complaint must be filed not later than 180 days from the date of the alleged discrimination, unless the time for filing is extended by SBA.

(c) *Investigations.* SBA will make a prompt investigation whenever a compliance review, report, complaint, or any other information indicates a possible failure to comply with this part. The investigation should include, where appropriate, a review of the pertinent practices and policies of the applicant or recipient, the circumstances under which the possible noncompliance with this part occurred, and other factors relevant to a determination as to whether the applicant or recipient has failed to comply with this part.

(d) *Resolution of matters.* (1) If an investigation pursuant to paragraph (c) of this section indicates a failure to comply with this part, SBA will so inform the applicant or recipient and the matter will be resolved by informal means whenever possible. If it has been determined that the matter cannot be resolved by informal means, action will be taken as provided for in §112.11.

(2) If an investigation does not warrant action pursuant to paragraph (d)(1) of this section, SBA will so inform the applicant or recipient and the complainant, if any, in writing.

(e) *Intimidatory or retaliatory acts prohibited.* No applicant or recipient or other person shall intimidate, threaten, coerce, or discriminate against any individual for the purpose of interfering with any right or privilege secured by section 601 of the Act or by this part or because he has made a complaint, testified, assisted, or participated in any manner in an investigation, proceeding, or hearing under this part. The identity of complainants shall be kept confidential except to the extent necessary to carry out the purposes of this part, including the conduct of any investigation, hearing, or judicial proceeding arising thereunder.

[30 FR 298, Jan. 9, 1965, as amended at 38 FR 17934, July 5, 1973]

§112.11 Procedure for effecting compliance.

(a) *General.* (1) If there appears to be a failure or threatened failure to comply with this part and if the noncompliance or threatened noncompliance cannot be corrected by informal means, compliance with this part may be effected by suspending, terminating, or refusing any financial assistance approved but not yet disbursed to an applicant or, in the case of a loan which has been partially disbursed, by refusing to make further disbursements. In addition, compliance may be effected by any other means authorized by law.

(2) Such other means may include but are not limited to (i) legal action by SBA to enforce its right, embodied in the assurances described in §112.8, to accelerate the maturity of the recipient's obligation; (ii) a reference to the Department of Justice with a recommendation that appropriate proceedings be brought to enforce any rights of the United States under any law of the United States, including other titles of the Act; and (iii) any applicable proceedings under State or local law.

(b) *Noncompliance with §112.8.* If an applicant fails or refuses to furnish an assurance required under §112.8 or otherwise fails or refuses to comply with a requirement imposed by or pursuant to that section Federal financial assistance may be refused in accordance with the procedures of paragraph (c) of this section. SBA shall not be required to provide assistance in such a case during the pendency of the administrative proceedings under such paragraph except that SBA shall continue assistance during the pendency of such proceedings where such assistance is due and payable pursuant to an application therefor approved prior to the effective date of this part. Such proceedings shall be conducted in accordance with the provisions of part 134 of this chapter by an Administrative Law Judge of the Office of Hearings and Appeals, who shall issue an initial decision in the case. The Administrator shall be the reviewing official for purposes of § 134.228. The applicant's failure to file a timely motion in accordance with §§ 134.222 and 134.211, requesting that the matter be scheduled for an oral hearing, shall constitute waiver of the right to an oral hearing but shall not prevent the submission of written information and argument for the record in accordance with the provisions of part 134.

(c) *Conditions precedent.* No order suspending, terminating, or refusing financial assistance shall become effective until (1) SBA has advised the applicant or recipient of his failure to comply and has determined that compliance cannot be secured by voluntary means; (2) there has been an express finding on the record after an opportunity for an oral hearing, of a failure by the applicant or recipient to comply with a requirement imposed by or pursuant to this part; (3) the initial decision has become final pursuant to § 134.227(b); and (4) the expiration of 30 days after SBA has filed with the committee of the House and the committee of the Senate having legislative jurisdiction of the form of financial assistance involved, a full written report of the circumstances and the grounds for such action.

(d) *Other means authorized by law.* No action to effect compliance by any other means authorized by law shall be taken until (1) SBA has determined that compliance cannot be secured by voluntary means; (2) the action has been approved by the Administrator or his designee; (3) the applicant or recipient or other person has been notified of its failure to comply and of the action to be taken to effect compliance; and (4) the expiration of at least 10 days from the mailing of such notice to the applicant or recipient or other person. During this period of at least 10 days from the mailing of such notice to the applicant or recipient or other person. During this period of at least 10 days additional efforts shall be made to persuade the applicant or recipient or other person to comply with this part and to take such corrective action as may be appropriate.

[30 FR 298, Jan. 9, 1965, as amended at 38 FR 17934, July 5, 1973; 49 FR 33629, Aug. 24, 1984; 61 FR 2691, Jan. 29, 1996]

§ 112.12 Effect on other regulations; forms and instructions.

(a) *Effect on other regulations.* All regulations, orders or like directions heretofore issued by SBA which impose requirements designed to prohibit any discrimination against individuals on the grounds of race, color, or national origin and which authorize the suspension or termination of or refusal to grant to or to continue financial assistance to any applicant for or recipient of such assistance for failure to comply with such requirements, are hereby superseded to the extent that such discrimination is prohibited by this part, except that nothing in this part shall be deemed to relieve any person of any obligation assumed or imposed under any such superseded regulation, order, instruction, or like direction prior to the effective date of this part. Nothing in this part, however, shall be deemed to supersede any of the following (including future amendments thereof):

(1) Executive Order 11246 and regulations issued thereunder, or (2) any other orders, regulations or instructions, insofar as such order, regulations, or instructions prohibit discrimination on the grounds of race, color, or national origin in any program or situation to which this part is inapplicable or prohibit discrimination on any other ground.

(b) *Forms and instructions.* SBA shall issue and promptly make available to interested persons forms and detailed instructions and procedures for effectuating this part.

(c) *Supervision and coordination.* The Administrator may from time to time assign to officials of SBA or to officials of other agencies of the Government with the consent of such agencies, responsibilities in connection with the effectuation of the purpose of Title VI of the Act and this part (other than responsibility for final decision as provided in § 112.13), including the achievement of effective coordination and maximum uniformity within SBA and within the Executive Branch of the Government in the application of Title VI and this part to similar programs and in similar situations. Any action taken, determination made, or requirement imposed by an official of another Department or agency acting pursuant to an assignment of responsibility under this subsection shall have the same effect as though such action had been taken by the Administrator of SBA.

[30 FR 298, Jan. 9, 1965, as amended at 38 FR 17935, July 5, 1973. Redesignated at 49 FR 33629, Aug. 24, 1984]

APPENDIX A TO PART 112

Name of Federal financial assistance	Authority
Federal Financial Assistance Involving Grants of Funds	
Regular business loans	Small Business Act, sec. 7(a) and 7(a)(11).
Handicapped assistance loans.	Small Business Act, sec. 7(a)(10)
Small business energy loans	Small Business Act, sec. 7(a)(12).
Small general contractors	Small Business Act, sec. 7(a)(9).
Vietnam-era and Disabled Veterans Loan Program.	Pub. L. 97–72.
Debtor State development company loans (501) and their small business concerns.	Small Business Investment Act, title V, and Small Business Act, sec. 7(a)(13).
Debtor small business investment companies and their small business concerns.	Small Business Investment Act, title III.
Disaster Loans	
Physical	Small Business Act, sec. 7(b)(1).
Economic injury (EIDL)	Small Business Act, sec. 7(b)(2).
Federal action—economic injury.	Small Business Act, sec. 7(b)(3).
Currency fluctuation—economic injury.	Small Business Act, sec. 7(b)(4).
Other Federal Financial Assistance	
Women's business enterprise	Executive Order 12138.
Small business innovation and research.	Small Business Act, sec. 9.
Procurement automated source system.	Small Business Act, sec. 8 and Pub. L. 96–302.
Business Development Program.	Small Business Act, sec. 8(a) and Pub. L. 95–507, as amended by Pub. L. 96–481.
Small Business Institute Program.	Small Business Act, sec. 8(b)(1) and Pub. L. 85–536.
Certificate of competency	Small Business Act, sec. 8(b)(7) and Pub. L 95–89.
Subcontracting Assistance Program.	Small Business Act, sec. 8(d) and Pub. L. 95–507.
Technology Assistance Program.	Small Business Act, sec. 9.
Small business development centers.	Small Business Act, sec. 21 and Pub. L. 96–302.
International Trade Program	Small Business Act, sec. 22 and Pub. L. 96–481.
Service Corps of Retired Executives and Active Corps of Executives.	Small Business Act, secs. 101 and 8(b)(1) and Pub. L. 95–510.
Veterans affairs programs	Pub. L. 93–237.
Private sector initiatives	Small Business Act, sec. 8(b)(1).

NOTE: All types of Federal financial assistance listed above are also covered by part 113 of title 13 of the Code of Federal Regulations.

[50 FR 1441, Jan. 11, 1985, as amended at 68 FR 51348, 51349, Aug. 26, 2003]

PART 113—NONDISCRIMINATION IN FINANCIAL ASSISTANCE PROGRAMS OF SBA—EFFECTUATION OF POLICIES OF FEDERAL GOVERNMENT AND SBA ADMINISTRATOR

Subpart A—General Provisions

Subpart B—Nondiscrimination on the Basis of Sex in Education Programs or Activities Receiving Federal Financial Assistance

INTRODUCTION

COVERAGE

AUTHORITY: 15 U.S.C. 633, 634, 687, 1691; 20 U.S.C. 1681, 1682, 1683, 1685, 1686, 1687, 1688; 29 U.S.C. 794; Sec. 5, Pub. L. 85–536, 72 Stat. 385, as amended; Sec. 308, Pub. L. 85–699, 72 Stat. 694, as amended.

SOURCE: 44 FR 20068, Apr. 4, 1979, unless otherwise noted.

Subpart A—General Provisions

§ 113.1 Purpose.

(a) Part 112 of this chapter, issued pursuant to Title VI of the Civil Rights Act of 1964, prohibits discrimination on the basis of race, color, or national origin by some recipients of financial assistance from SBA. The purpose of this part is to reflect to the fullest extent possible the nondiscrimination policies of the Federal Government as expressed in the several statutes, Executive Orders, and messages of the President dealing with civil rights and equality of opportunity, and in the previous determination of the Administrator of the Small Business Administration that discrimination based on race, color, religion, sex, marital status, handicap or national origin shall be prohibited, to the extent that it is not prohibited by part 112 of this chapter, to all recipients of financial assistance from SBA.

(b) In accordance with Pub. L. 94–239, 15 U.S.C. 1691, cited as the Equal Credit Act Amendments of 1976, it is unlawful for any recipient creditor to discriminate against any applicant, with respect to any aspect of a credit transaction because of race, color, religion, national origin, sex, marital status, age: (*Provided*, the applicant has the capacity to contract), because all or part of the applicant's income derives from any public assistance program, or because the applicant has in good faith exercised any right under the Consumer Credit Protection Act.

(c) It is the intention of the Administrator that the prohibitions in this part supplement those in part 112 of this chapter, that the two parts be read in pari materia, and that the procedures established herein be harmonized to the maximum extent feasible with those established in part 112 of this chapter.

§ 113.2 Definitions.

As used in this part:

(a) The term *Federal financial assistance* includes (1) grants and loans of Federal funds, (2) the grant or donation of Federal property and interests in property, (3) the detail of Federal personnel, (4) the sale and lease of, and the permission to use (on other than a casual or transient basis), Federal property or any interest in such property without consideration, or at a nominal consideration, or at a consideration which is reduced for the purpose of assisting the recipient, or in recognition of the public interest to be served by such sale or lease to the recipient, and (5) any Federal agreement, arrangement, or other contract which has as one of its purposes the provision of assistance.

(b) The terms *applicant* and *recipient* mean, respectively, one who applies for and one who receives any of the financial assistance under any of the statutes referred to in paragraph (a) of this section. The term *recipient* also shall be deemed to include *subrecipients* of SBA financial assistance, i.e., concerns which secondarily receive financial assistance from the primary recipients of such financial assistance. For the purposes of this part, a paragraph (b) lender (13 CFR 120.4(b)) shall be deemed a recipient of financial assistance.

(c) The term *religion* includes all aspects of religious observance and practice, as well as belief.

(d) The term *qualified handicapped person* means (1) with respect to employment, a handicapped person who, with reasonable accommodation, can perform the essential functions of the job in question and (2) with respect to services, a handicapped person who meets the essential eligibility requirements for the receipt of such services.

(e) The term *handicapped person*, as defined by the guideline set forth by the Department of Health, Education, and Welfare in §85.31 of title 45 of the CFR (43 FR 2137, dated January 13, 1978), means any person who has a physical or mental impairment that substantially limits one or more major life activities, has a record of such an impairment, or is regarded as having such an impairment.

(f) As used in paragraph (e) of this section, the phrase:

(1) *Physical or mental impairment* means (i) any physiological disorder or condition, cosmetic disfigurement, or anatomical loss affecting one or more of the following body systems: Neurological; musculoskeletal; special sense organs; respiratory, including speech organs; cardiovascular; reproductive; digestive; genitourinary; hemic and lymphatic; skin; and endocrine; or (ii) any mental or psychological disorder, such as mental retardation, organic brain syndrome, emotional or mental illness, and specific learning disabilities. The term *physical or mental impairment* includes, but is not limited to, such diseases and conditions as orthopedic, visual, speech, and hearing impairments, cerebral palsy, epilepsy, muscular dystrophy, multiple sclerosis, cancer, heart disease, diabetes, mental retardation, emotional illness, drug addiction and alcoholism.

(2) *Major life activities* means functions such as caring for one's self, performing manual tasks, walking, seeing, hearing, speaking, breathing, learning, and working.

(3) *Has a record of such an impairment* means has a history of, or has been misclassified as having, a mental or physical impairment that substantially limits one or more major life activities.

(4) *Is regarded as having an impairment* means (i) has a physical or mental impairment that does not substantially limit major life activities but is treated by a recipient as constituting such a limitation; (ii) has a physical or mental impairment that substantially limits major life activities only as a result of the attitudes of others toward such impairment; or (iii) has none of the impairments defined in paragraph (f)(1) of this section but is treated by a recipient as having such an impairment.

(g) The term *reasonable accommodation* as used in these Regulations may include: (1) making facilities used by employees readily accessible to and usable by handicapped persons; and (2) job restructuring, part-time or modified work schedules, acquisition or modification of equipment or devices, the provision of readers or interpreters, and other similar actions.

(h) The term *facility* means all or any portion of buildings, structures, equipment, roads, walks, parking lots, or other real or personal property.

[44 FR 20068, Apr. 4, 1979, as amended at 48 FR 14891, Apr. 6, 1983]

§ 113.3 Discrimination prohibited.

To the extent not covered or prohibited by part 112 of this chapter, recipients of financial assistance may not:

(a) Discriminate with regard to goods, services, or accommodations offered or provided by the aided business or other enterprise, whether or not operated for profit, because of race, color, religion, sex, handicap, or national origin of a person, or fail or refuse to accept a person on a nonsegregated basis as a patient, student, visitor, guest, customer, passenger, or patron.

(b) With regard to employment practices within the aided business or other enterprise, whether or not operated for profit; fail or refuse, because of race, color, religion, sex or national origin of a person, to seek or retain the person's services, or to provide the person with opportunities for advancement or promotion, or accord an employee the rank and rate of compensation, including fringe benefits, merited by the employee's services and abilities.

(c) With regard to employment practices within the aided business or other enterprise, whether or not operated for profit; discriminate against a qualified handicapped person; or because of handicap, fail or refuse to seek or retain the person's services or to provide the person with opportunities for advancement or promotion, or accord an employee the rank and rate of compensation, including fringe benefits, merited by the employee's services and abilities. All employment decisions shall be made in a manner which ensures that discrimination on the basis of handicap does not occur. Such decisions may not limit, segregate, or classify job applicants or employees in any way that adversely affects the opportunities or status of qualified handicapped individuals.

(d) Participate in a contractual or other relationship that has the effect of subjecting job applicants or employees to discrimination prohibited by this part. The relationships referred to in this paragraph include those with employment and referral agencies, labor unions, organizations providing or administering fringe benefits to employees of the recipient, and organizations providing training and apprenticeship programs. Activities covered by this part are as follows:

(1) Recruitment, advertising, and the processing of applications for employment;

(2) Hiring, upgrading, promotion, award of tenure, demotion, transfer, layoff, termination, right of return from layoff, and rehiring;

(3) Rates of pay or any other form of compensation and changes in compensation;

(4) Job assignments, job classifications, organizational structures, position descriptions, lines of progression, and seniority lists;

(5) Leaves of absence, sick leave, or any other leave;

(6) Fringe benefits available by virtue of employment, whether or not administered by the recipient;

(7) Selection and financial support for training, including apprenticeship, professional meetings, conferences, and other related activities, and selection for leaves of absence to pursue training;

(8) Employer sponsored activities, including social or recreational programs; and

(9) Any other term, condition, or privilege of employment.

(e) Use employment tests or criteria that discriminate on the basis of race, color, religion, sex, marital status, handicap, or national origin. Employment tests which are used for all other job applicants shall be adapted in an appropriate mode for use by persons who have handicaps that impair sensory, manual, or speaking skills.

(f) Conduct a preemployment medical examination, unless required of all job applicants, and subsequent to a conditional offer of employment. The results of all such medical examinations shall be kept confidential.

(g) Make a preemployment inquiry as to whether a job applicant is a handicapped person or as to the nature or severity of a handicap: EXCEPT when a recipient is taking remedial action to overcome the effects of conditions which resulted in past discrimination, or when a recipient is taking affirmative action pursuant to section 503 of the Rehabilitation Act of 1973, as amended.

(1) Such preemployment inquiry may only be made after the job applicant has been informed that such disclosure is for the purposes set forth in paragraph (g) of this section; that the disclosure is voluntary and will be kept confidential; and that refusal of the job applicant to provide such information will not subject the applicant to any adverse action.

(2) Information elicited from qualified handicapped job applicants concerning their medical history or condition shall be kept confidential EXCEPT that:

(i) Supervisors and managers may be informed about restrictions on or accommodations to be made for the qualified handicapped individual;

(ii) First aid and safety personnel may be informed, where appropriate, of the need for possible emergency treatment; and

(iii) Compliance officials shall be given relevant information, if requested.

(h) Discriminate on the basis of race, color, religion, handicap or national origin in the use of toilets or any facilities for rest or comfort. Discriminate on the basis of race, color, religion, sex, handicap or national origin in the use of cafeterias, recreational programs or other programs sponsored by the applicant or recipient.

(i) With regard to all recipients offering credit, such as Small Business Investment Companies and Community Development Companies, discriminate against debtors on the basis of race, color, religion, sex, marital status, handicap, or national origin.

(j) With regard to the granting of credit by all recipient creditors, discriminate against any credit applicant, with respect to any aspect of a credit transaction because of race, color, religion, national origin, sex, marital status, handicap, age (provided the applicant has the capacity to contract), because all or part of the applicant's income derives from any public assistance program, or because the applicant has in good faith exercised any right under the Consumer Credit Protection Act.

§ 113.3-1 Consideration of race, color, religion, sex, marital status, handicap, or national origin.

(a) This regulation does not prohibit the consideration of race, color, religion, sex, marital status, handicap, or national origin if the purpose and effect are to remove or overcome the consequences of practices or impediments which have restricted the availability of, or participation in, the program or activity receiving Federal financial assistance, on the grounds of race, color, religion, sex, marital status, handicap, or national origin. Where previous discriminatory practices or usage tends, on the grounds of race, color, religion, sex, marital status, handicap, or national origin, to exclude individuals from participation in, to deny them the benefits of, or to subject them to discrimination under any program or activity to which this regulation applies, the applicant or recipient has an obligation to take reasonable action to remove or overcome the consequences of the prior discriminatory practice or usage, and to accomplish the purposes of this regulation. All programs and activities shall be administered in the most integrated setting possible.

(b) Nothing in this part shall prohibit the restriction of certain jobs to members of one sex if a bona fide occupational qualification can be demonstrated by the applicant or recipient. Custom or tradition is not a bona fide occupational qualification.

(c) Recipients shall take steps to ensure that communications with job applicants and employees who have vision and/or hearing disabilities are available in appropriate modes.

(d) Recipients shall make reasonable accommodation to the known physical or mental limitations of an otherwise qualified handicapped job applicant or employee UNLESS the recipient can demonstrate that the accommodation would impose an undue hardship on the operation of the business. Factors to be considered in determining whether an accommodation would impose an undue hardship on the operation of a recipient's business include:

(1) The overall size of the recipient's business with respect to number of employees, number and type of facilities,

size of budget, and the financial condition of the business;

(2) The type of the recipient's operation, including the composition and structure of the recipient's workforce; and

(3) The nature and cost of the accommodation needed.

(e) Such accommodation may include making facilities used by employees readily accessible to and usable by handicapped persons, job restructuring, part-time or modified work schedules, acquisition or modification of equipment or devices, the provision of readers or interpreters, and other similar actions.

(f) The final decision, when making a review or investigation of a complaint, as to whether an accommodation would impose an undue hardship on the operation of a recipient business will be made by the compliance officials of the Small Business Administration.

(g) Recipients shall administer programs and activities in the most integrated setting appropriate to the needs of qualified handicapped persons, and shall not participate in a contractual relationship that has the effect of subjecting qualified handicapped job applicants or employees to discrimination prohibited by this part. The relationships referred to in this paragraph include those with referral agencies, labor unions, organizations providing or administering fringe benefits to employees of the recipient, and organizations providing training and apprenticeship programs.

(h) Nothing in this part shall apply to a religious corporation, association, educational institution or society with respect to the membership or the employment of individuals of a particular religion to perform work connected with the carrying on by such corporation, association, educational institution or society of its religious activities.

§ 113.3–2 Accommodations to religious observance and practice.

A recipient of financial assistance must accommodate to the religious observances and practices of an employee or prospective employee unless the recipient demonstrates that it is unable to reasonably accommodate to an employee's or prospective employee's religious observance or practice without undue hardship on the conduct of the employer's business. As part of this obligation, recipient must make reasonable accommodations to the religious observances and practices of an employee or prospective employee who regularly observes Friday evening and Saturday, or some other day of the week, as Sabbath and/or who observes certain religious holidays during the year and who is conscientiously opposed to performing work or engaging in similar activity on such days, when such accommodations can be made without undue hardship on the conduct of the employer's business. In determining the extent of a recipient's obligations under this section, at least the following factors should be considered: (a) Business necessity, (b) financial costs and expenses, and (c) resulting personnel problems.

§ 113.3–3 Structural accommodations for handicapped clients.

(a) *Existing facilities.* Recipients in preexisting structures shall make their goods or services accessible to and usable by handicapped clients. Where structural changes are necessary to make the recipient's goods or services accessible, such changes shall be made as soon as practicable, but in no event later than three years after the effective date of this Regulation. A plan setting forth the steps necessary to complete such structural changes shall be developed and submitted to SBA. If practical, interested persons, including handicapped persons or organizations representing handicapped persons, will be consulted.

(b) *Design, construction, and alteration.* New facilities shall be designed and constructed to be readily accessible to and usable by persons with handicaps. Alterations to existing facilities that affect usability shall, to the maximum extent feasible, be designed and constructed to be readily accessible to and usable by handicapped persons.

(c) *Conformance with Uniform Federal Accessibility Standards.* (1) Effective as of January 18, 1991, design, construction, or alteration of buildings in conformance with sections 3-8 of the Uniform Federal Accessibility Standards

(UFAS) (appendix A to 41 CFR subpart 101–19.6) shall be deemed to comply with the requirements of this section with respect to those buildings. Departures from particular technical and scoping requirements of UFAS by the use of other methods are permitted where substantially equivalent or greater access to and usability of the building is provided.

(2) For purposes of this section, section 4.1.6(1)(g) of UFAS shall be interpreted to exempt from the requirements of UFAS only mechanical rooms and other spaces that, because of their intended use, will not require accessibility to the public or beneficiaries or result in the employment or residence therein of persons with physical handicaps.

(3) This section does not require recipients to make building alterations that have little likelihood of being accomplished without removing or altering a load-bearing structural member.

[44 FR 20068, Apr. 4, 1979, as amended at 45 FR 81734, Dec. 12, 1980; 55 FR 52138, 52140, Dec. 19, 1990]

§ 113.4 Assurances required.

An application for financial assistance shall, as a condition to its approval and the extension of such assistance, contain or be accompanied by an assurance that the recipient will comply with this part. Such an assurance shall contain provisions authorizing the acceleration of the maturity of the recipient's financial obligations to SBA in the event of a failure to comply, and provisions which give the United States a right to seek judicial enforcement of the terms of the assurance. SBA shall specify the form of the foregoing assurance for each program, and the extent to which like assurances will be required of contractors and subcontractors, transferees, successors in interest, and other participants in the program.

§ 113.5 Compliance information.

(a) *Cooperation and assistance:* SBA shall to the fullest extent practicable seek the cooperation of applicants and recipients in obtaining compliance with this part and shall provide assistance and guidance to applicants and recipients to help them comply voluntarily with this part. Recipients are expected to continually evaluate their compliance status, with the assistance of interested persons, including handicapped persons or organizations representing handicapped persons.

(b) *Compliance reports:* Each applicant or recipient shall keep such records and submit to SBA timely, complete and accurate compliance reports at such times, and in such form and containing such information, as SBA may determine to be necessary to enable SBA to ascertain whether the applicant or recipient has complied or is complying with this part. In the case of a small business concern which receives financial assistance from a development company or from a small business investment company, such concern shall submit to the company such information as may be necessary to enable the company to meet its reporting requirements under this part.

(c) *Access to sources of information:* Each applicant or recipient shall permit access by SBA during normal business hours to such of its books, records, accounts and other sources of information, and its facilities as may be pertinent to ascertain compliance with this part. Where any information required of an applicant or recipient is in the exclusive possession of any other agency, institution or person; and such agency, institution or person shall fail or refuse to furnish this information, the applicant or recipient shall so certify in its report and shall set forth what efforts it has made to obtain this information.

(d) *Information to the Public.* Each recipient shall make available to persons entitled under this part to protection against discrimination by the recipient such information as SBA may find necessary to apprise them of their rights to such protection.

(1) In some situations even though past discriminatory practices have been abandoned, the consequences of such practices continue to impede the full availability of equal opportunity. If the efforts required of the applicant or recipient under § 113.5(b) to provide information as to the availability of equal opportunity, and the rights of individuals under this regulation, have failed to overcome these consequences,

it will become necessary for such applicant or recipient to take additional steps to make equal opportunity fully available to racial, qualified handicapped, nationality groups and persons who because of their sex were previously subjected to discrimination.

(2) Even though an applicant or recipient has never used discriminatory policies, the opportunities in the business it operates may not in fact be equally available to some racial, qualified handicapped, or nationality groups. In such circumstances a recipient may properly give special consideration to race, color, religion, sex, marital status, qualified handicap or national origin to make the opportunities more widely available to such groups.

§ 113.6 Conduct of investigations.

(a) *Periodic compliance reviews.* SBA shall from time to time review the practices of recipients to determine whether they are complying with this part.

(b) *Complaints.* Any person who believes that he, she or any class of individuals has been subjected to discrimination prohibited by this part may, personally or through a representative, file with SBA a written complaint. A complaint must be filed not later than 180 days from the date of the alleged discrimination, unless the time for filing is extended by SBA.

(c) *Investigations.* SBA will make a prompt investigation whenever a compliance review, report, complaint, or any other information indicates a possible failure to comply with this part. The investigation should include, where appropriate, a review of the pertinent practices and policies of the applicant or recipient, the circumstances under which the possible noncompliance with this part occurred, and other factors relevant to a determination as to whether the applicant or recipient has failed to comply with this part.

(d) *Resolution of matters.* (1) If an investigation pursuant to paragraph (c) of this section indicates a failure to comply with this part, SBA will so inform the applicant or recipient and the matter will be resolved by informal means whenever possible. If it has been determined that the matter cannot be resolved by informal means, action will be taken as provided for in § 113.7.

(2) If an investigation does not warrant action pursuant to paragraph (d)(1) of this section, SBA will so inform the applicant or recipient and the complainant, if any, in writing.

(e) *Intimidatory or retaliatory acts prohibited.* No applicant or recipient or other person shall intimidate, threaten, coerce, or discriminate against any individual for the purpose of interfering with any right or privilege secured by this part or because he has made a complaint, testified, assisted, or participated in any manner in an investigation, proceeding, or hearing under this part. The identity of complainants shall be kept confidential except to the extent necessary to carry out the purposes of this part, including the conduct of any investigation, hearing, or judicial proceeding arising thereunder.

§ 113.7 Procedure for effecting compliance.

(a) *General.* (1) If there appears to be a failure or threatened failure to comply with this part and if the noncompliance or threatened noncompliance cannot be corrected by informal means, compliance with this part may be effected by suspending, terminating, or refusing any financial assistance approved but not yet disbursed to an applicant. In the case of loans partially or fully disbursed, compliance with this part may be effected by calling, canceling, terminating, accelerating repayment, or suspending in whole or in part the financial assistance provided. In addition compliance may be effected by any other means authorized by law.

(2) Such other means may include but are not limited to (i) legal action by SBA to enforce its rights, embodied in the assurances described in § 113.4; (ii) a reference to the Department of Justice with a recommendation that appropriate proceedings be brought to enforce any rights of the United States under any law of the United States; and (iii) any applicable proceedings under State or local law.

(b) *Noncompliance with § 113.4.* If an applicant fails or refuses to furnish an assurance required under § 113.4 or otherwise fails or refuses to comply with a requirement imposed by or pursuant to that section, Federal financial assistance may be refused in accordance with the procedures of paragraph (c) of this section. SBA shall not be required to provide assistance in such a case during the pendency of the administrative proceedings under such paragraph except that SBA shall continue assistance during the pendency of such proceedings where such assistance is due and payable pursuant to an application therefor approved prior to the effective date of this part. Such proceedings shall be conducted in accordance with the provisions of part 134 of this chapter by an Administrative Law Judge of the Office of Hearings and Appeals, who shall issue an initial decision in the case. The Admininstrator shall be the reviewing official for purposes of § 134.228. The applicant's failure to file a timely motion in accordance with §§ 134.222 and 134.211, requesting that the matter be scheduled for an oral hearing, shall constitute waiver of the right to an oral hearing but shall not prevent the submission of written information and argument for the record in accordance with the provisions of part 134.

(c) *Condition precedent.* Under this part 113, no order suspending, terminating, refusing, calling, canceling, or accelerating repayment of financial assistance in whole or in part shall become effective until (1) SBA has advised the applicant or recipient of his failure to comply and has determined that compliance cannot be secured by voluntary means; (2) there has been an express finding on the record after an opportunity for an oral hearing, of a failure by the applicant or recipient to comply with a requirement imposed by or pursuant to this part; and (3) the initial decision has become final pursuant to § 134.227(b).

(d) Other means authorized by law. No action to effect compliance by any other means authorized by law shall be taken until:

(1) SBA has determined that compliance cannot be secured by voluntary means.

(2) The action has been approved by the Administrator or the Administrator's designee.

(3) The applicant or recipient or other person has been notified of its failure to comply and of the action to be taken to effect compliance.

(4) The expiration of at least 10 days from the mailing of such notice to the applicant or recipient or other person. During this period of at least 10 days, additional efforts shall be made to persuade the applicant or recipient or other person to comply with this part and to take such corrective action as may be appropriate.

[44 FR 20068, Apr. 4, 1979, as amended at 49 FR 33629, Aug. 24, 1984; 61 FR 2691, Jan. 29, 1996]

§ 113.8 Effect on other regulations, forms and instructions.

(a) *Effect on other regulations.* All regulations, orders of like directions heretofore issued by SBA which impose requirements designed to prohibit any discrimination against individuals on the grounds of race, color, religion, sex, handicap, marital status, age, or national origin and which authorize the suspension or termination of a refusal to grant to or to continue financial assistance to any applicant for or recipient of such assistance for failure to comply with such requirements, are hereby superseded to the extent that such discrimination is prohibited by this part, except that nothing in this part shall be deemed to relieve any person of any obligation assumed or imposed under any such superseded regulation, order, instruction or like direction prior to the effective date of this part.

(b) *Forms and instructions.* SBA shall issue and promptly make available to interested persons forms and detailed instructions and procedures for effectuating this part.

(c) *Supervision and coordination.* The Administrator may from time-to-time assign to officials of SBA or to officials of other agencies of the Government, with the consent of such agencies, responsibilities in connection with the effectuation of the purposes of this part (other than responsibility of first decisions as provided in §113.9) including the achievement of effective coordination and maximum uniformity within SBA and within the executive branch of the Government in the application of this part and of comparable regulations issued by other agencies of the Government to similar situations. Any action taken, determination made, or requirement imposed by an official of another department or agency acting pursuant to an assignment of responsibility under this subsection shall have the same effect as though such action had been taken by the Administrator of SBA.

[44 FR 20068, Apr. 4, 1979. Redesignated at 49 FR 33629, Aug. 24, 1984]

APPENDIX A TO SUBPART A OF PART 113

Name of program	Authority
Financial Programs	
Regular business loans	Small Business Act, sec. 7(a).
Handicapped assistance loans.	Small Business Act, sec. 7(a)(10).
Small business energy loans	Small Business Act, sec. 7(a)(12).
Small general contractors loans.	Small Business Act, sec. 7(a)(9).
Export revolving line of credit	Small Business Act, sec. 7(a)(14).
Vietnam-era and Disabled Veterans Loan Program.	Pub. L. 97–72.
Debtor State development company loans (501) and their small business concerns.	Small Business Investment Act, Title V and Small Business Act, sec. 7(a)(13).
Debtor State and local development company loans (502) and their small business concerns.	Small Business Investment Act, Title V and Small Business Act, sec. 7(a)(13).
Debtor certified development companies (503) and their small business concerns.	Small Business Investment Act, Title V and Small Business Act, sec. 7(a)(13).
Debtor small business investment companies and their small business concerns.	Small Business Investment Act, Title III.
Pollution Control	Small Business Investment Act, Title IV, Part A.
Surety bond guarantees	Small Business Investment Act, Title IV, Part B.
Lease guarantees (not funded) disaster loans.	Small Business Investment Act, Title IV.
Physical	Small Business Act, sec. 7(b)(1).
Economic injury (EIDL)	Small Business Act, sec. 7(b)(2).
Federal action—economic injury.	Small Business Act, sec. 7(b)(3).
Currency fluctuation—economic injury.	Small Business Act, sec 7(b)(4).
Nonfinancial Programs	
Women's business enterprise	Executive Order 12138.
Small business innovation and research.	Small Business Act, sec. 9.
Procurement automated source system..	Small Business Act, sec. 8 and Pub. L. 96–302.
Business Development Program.	Small Business Act, sec. 8(a) and Pub. L. 95–507, as amended by Pub. L. 96–481.
Small Business Institute	Small Business Act, sec. 8(b)(1).
Certificate of competency	Small Business Act, sec. 8(b)(7) and Pub. L. 95–89.
Subcontracting Assistance Program.	Small Business Act, sec. 8(d) and Pub. L. 95–507.
Technology Assistance Program.	Small Business Act, sec. 9.
Small business development centers.	Small Business Act, sec. 21 and Pub. L. 96–302.
International Trade Program	Small Business Act, sec. 22 and Pub. L. 96–481.
Service Corps of Retired Executives and Active Corps of Executives.	Small Business Act, secs. 101 and 8(b)(1) and Pub. L. 95–510.
Veterans Affairs Programs	Pub. L. 93–237.
Private sector initiatives	Small Business Act, sec. 8(b)(1).

[50 FR 1442, Jan. 11, 1985]

Subpart B—Nondiscrimination on the Basis of Sex in Education Programs or Activities Receiving Federal Financial Assistance

AUTHORITY: 20 U.S.C. 1681, 1682, 1683, 1685, 1686, 1687, 1688.

SOURCE: 65 FR 52865, 52876, Aug. 30, 2000, unless otherwise noted.

INTRODUCTION

§113.100 Purpose and effective date.

The purpose of these Title IX regulations is to effectuate Title IX of the Education Amendments of 1972, as amended (except sections 904 and 906 of those Amendments) (20 U.S.C. 1681, 1682, 1683, 1685, 1686, 1687, 1688), which is designed to eliminate (with certain exceptions) discrimination on the basis of sex in any education program or activity receiving Federal financial assistance, whether or not such program or activity is offered or sponsored by an educational institution as defined in these Title IX regulations. The effective date of these Title IX regulations shall be September 29, 2000.

§113.105 Definitions.

As used in these Title IX regulations, the term:

Administratively separate unit means a school, department, or college of an educational institution (other than a local educational agency) admission to which is independent of admission to any other component of such institution.

Admission means selection for part-time, full-time, special, associate, transfer, exchange, or any other enrollment, membership, or matriculation in or at an education program or activity operated by a recipient.

Applicant means one who submits an application, request, or plan required to be approved by an official of the Federal agency that awards Federal financial assistance, or by a recipient, as a condition to becoming a recipient.

Designated agency official means Assistant Administrator for Equal Employment and Civil Rights Compliance.

Educational institution means a local educational agency (LEA) as defined by 20 U.S.C. 8801(18), a preschool, a private elementary or secondary school, or an applicant or recipient that is an institution of graduate higher education, an institution of undergraduate higher education, an institution of professional education, or an institution of vocational education, as defined in this section.

Federal financial assistance means any of the following, when authorized or extended under a law administered by the Federal agency that awards such assistance:

(1) A grant or loan of Federal financial assistance, including funds made available for:

(i) The acquisition, construction, renovation, restoration, or repair of a building or facility or any portion thereof; and

(ii) Scholarships, loans, grants, wages, or other funds extended to any entity for payment to or on behalf of students admitted to that entity, or extended directly to such students for payment to that entity.

(2) A grant of Federal real or personal property or any interest therein, including surplus property, and the proceeds of the sale or transfer of such property, if the Federal share of the fair market value of the property is not, upon such sale or transfer, properly accounted for to the Federal Government.

(3) Provision of the services of Federal personnel.

(4) Sale or lease of Federal property or any interest therein at nominal consideration, or at consideration reduced for the purpose of assisting the recipient or in recognition of public interest to be served thereby, or permission to use Federal property or any interest therein without consideration.

(5) Any other contract, agreement, or arrangement that has as one of its purposes the provision of assistance to any education program or activity, except a contract of insurance or guaranty.

Institution of graduate higher education means an institution that:

(1) Offers academic study beyond the bachelor of arts or bachelor of science degree, whether or not leading to a certificate of any higher degree in the liberal arts and sciences;

(2) Awards any degree in a professional field beyond the first professional degree (regardless of whether the first professional degree in such field is awarded by an institution of undergraduate higher education or professional education); or

(3) Awards no degree and offers no further academic study, but operates ordinarily for the purpose of facilitating research by persons who have received the highest graduate degree in any field of study.

Institution of professional education means an institution (except any institution of undergraduate higher education) that offers a program of academic study that leads to a first professional degree in a field for which there is a national specialized accrediting agency recognized by the Secretary of Education.

Institution of undergraduate higher education means:

(1) An institution offering at least two but less than four years of college-level study beyond the high school level, leading to a diploma or an associate degree, or wholly or principally creditable toward a baccalaureate degree; or

(2) An institution offering academic study leading to a baccalaureate degree; or

(3) An agency or body that certifies credentials or offers degrees, but that may or may not offer academic study.

Institution of vocational education means a school or institution (except an institution of professional or graduate or undergraduate higher education) that has as its primary purpose preparation of students to pursue a technical, skilled, or semiskilled occupation or trade, or to pursue study in a technical field, whether or not the school or institution offers certificates, diplomas, or degrees and whether or not it offers full-time study.

Recipient means any State or political subdivision thereof, or any instrumentality of a State or political subdivision thereof, any public or private agency, institution, or organization, or other entity, or any person, to whom Federal financial assistance is extended directly or through another recipient and that operates an education program or activity that receives such assistance, including any subunit, successor, assignee, or transferee thereof.

Student means a person who has gained admission.

Title IX means Title IX of the Education Amendments of 1972, Public Law 92–318, 86 Stat. 235, 373 (codified as amended at 20 U.S.C. 1681–1688) (except sections 904 and 906 thereof), as amended by section 3 of Public Law 93–568, 88 Stat. 1855, by section 412 of the Education Amendments of 1976, Public Law 94–482, 90 Stat. 2234, and by Section 3 of Public Law 100–259, 102 Stat. 28, 28–29 (20 U.S.C. 1681, 1682, 1683, 1685, 1686, 1687, 1688).

Title IX regulations means the provisions set forth at §§ 113.100 through 113.605.

Transition plan means a plan subject to the approval of the Secretary of Education pursuant to section 901(a)(2) of the Education Amendments of 1972, 20 U.S.C. 1681(a)(2), under which an educational institution operates in making the transition from being an educational institution that admits only students of one sex to being one that admits students of both sexes without discrimination.

§ 113.110 Remedial and affirmative action and self-evaluation.

(a) *Remedial action.* If the designated agency official finds that a recipient has discriminated against persons on the basis of sex in an education program or activity, such recipient shall take such remedial action as the designated agency official deems necessary to overcome the effects of such discrimination.

(b) *Affirmative action.* In the absence of a finding of discrimination on the basis of sex in an education program or activity, a recipient may take affirmative action consistent with law to overcome the effects of conditions that resulted in limited participation therein by persons of a particular sex. Nothing in these Title IX regulations shall be interpreted to alter any affirmative action obligations that a recipient may have under Executive Order 11246, 3 CFR, 1964–1965 Comp., p. 339; as amended by Executive Order 11375, 3 CFR, 1966–1970 Comp., p. 684; as amended by Executive Order 11478, 3 CFR, 1966–1970 Comp., p. 803; as amended by Executive Order 12086, 3 CFR, 1978 Comp., p. 230; as amended by Executive Order 12107, 3 CFR, 1978 Comp., p. 264.

(c) *Self-evaluation.* Each recipient education institution shall, within one year of September 29, 2000:

(1) Evaluate, in terms of the requirements of these Title IX regulations, its current policies and practices and the effects thereof concerning admission of students, treatment of students, and employment of both academic and non-academic personnel working in connection with the recipient's education program or activity;

(2) Modify any of these policies and practices that do not or may not meet the requirements of these Title IX regulations; and

(3) Take appropriate remedial steps to eliminate the effects of any discrimination that resulted or may have resulted from adherence to these policies and practices.

(d) *Availability of self-evaluation and related materials.* Recipients shall maintain on file for at least three years following completion of the evaluation required under paragraph (c) of this section, and shall provide to the designated agency official upon request, a description of any modifications made pursuant to paragraph (c)(2) of this section and of any remedial steps taken pursuant to paragraph (c)(3) of this section.

§113.115 Assurance required.

(a) *General.* Either at the application stage or the award stage, Federal agencies must ensure that applications for Federal financial assistance or awards of Federal financial assistance contain, be accompanied by, or be covered by a specifically identified assurance from the applicant or recipient, satisfactory to the designated agency official, that each education program or activity operated by the applicant or recipient and to which these Title IX regulations apply will be operated in compliance with these Title IX regulations. An assurance of compliance with these Title IX regulations shall not be satisfactory to the designated agency official if the applicant or recipient to whom such assurance applies fails to commit itself to take whatever remedial action is necessary in accordance with §113.110(a) to eliminate existing discrimination on the basis of sex or to eliminate the effects of past discrimination whether occurring prior to or subsequent to the submission to the designated agency official of such assurance.

(b) *Duration of obligation.* (1) In the case of Federal financial assistance extended to provide real property or structures thereon, such assurance shall obligate the recipient or, in the case of a subsequent transfer, the transferee, for the period during which the real property or structures are used to provide an education program or activity.

(2) In the case of Federal financial assistance extended to provide personal property, such assurance shall obligate the recipient for the period during which it retains ownership or possession of the property.

(3) In all other cases such assurance shall obligate the recipient for the period during which Federal financial assistance is extended.

(c) *Form.* (1) The assurances required by paragraph (a) of this section, which may be included as part of a document that addresses other assurances or obligations, shall include that the applicant or recipient will comply with all applicable Federal statutes relating to nondiscrimination. These include but are not limited to: Title IX of the Education Amendments of 1972, as amended (20 U.S.C. 1681–1683, 1685–1688).

(2) The designated agency official will specify the extent to which such assurances will be required of the applicant's or recipient's subgrantees, contractors, subcontractors, transferees, or successors in interest.

§113.120 Transfers of property.

If a recipient sells or otherwise transfers property financed in whole or in part with Federal financial assistance to a transferee that operates any education program or activity, and the Federal share of the fair market value of the property is not upon such sale or transfer properly accounted for to the Federal Government, both the transferor and the transferee shall be deemed to be recipients, subject to the provisions of §§113.205 through 113.235(a).

§113.125 Effect of other requirements.

(a) *Effect of other Federal provisions.* The obligations imposed by these Title IX regulations are independent of, and do not alter, obligations not to discriminate on the basis of sex imposed by Executive Order 11246, 3 CFR, 1964–1965 Comp., p. 339; as amended by Executive Order 11375, 3 CFR, 1966–1970 Comp., p. 684; as amended by Executive Order 11478, 3 CFR, 1966–1970 Comp., p. 803; as amended by Executive Order 12087, 3 CFR, 1978 Comp., p. 230; as amended by Executive Order 12107, 3 CFR, 1978 Comp., p. 264; sections 704 and 855 of the Public Health Service Act (42 U.S.C. 295m, 298b-2); Title VII of the Civil Rights Act of 1964 (42 U.S.C. 2000e *et seq.*); the Equal Pay Act of 1963 (29 U.S.C. 206); and any other Act of Congress or Federal regulation.

(b) *Effect of State or local law or other requirements.* The obligation to comply with these Title IX regulations is not obviated or alleviated by any State or local law or other requirement that would render any applicant or student ineligible, or limit the eligibility of any applicant or student, on the basis of sex, to practice any occupation or profession.

(c) *Effect of rules or regulations of private organizations.* The obligation to comply with these Title IX regulations is not obviated or alleviated by any rule or regulation of any organization, club, athletic or other league, or association that would render any applicant or student ineligible to participate or limit the eligibility or participation of any applicant or student, on the basis of sex, in any education program or activity operated by a recipient and that receives Federal financial assistance.

§ 113.130 Effect of employment opportunities.

The obligation to comply with these Title IX regulations is not obviated or alleviated because employment opportunities in any occupation or profession are or may be more limited for members of one sex than for members of the other sex.

§ 113.135 Designation of responsible employee and adoption of grievance procedures.

(a) *Designation of responsible employee.* Each recipient shall designate at least one employee to coordinate its efforts to comply with and carry out its responsibilities under these Title IX regulations, including any investigation of any complaint communicated to such recipient alleging its noncompliance with these Title IX regulations or alleging any actions that would be prohibited by these Title IX regulations. The recipient shall notify all its students and employees of the name, office address, and telephone number of the employee or employees appointed pursuant to this paragraph.

(b) *Complaint procedure of recipient.* A recipient shall adopt and publish grievance procedures providing for prompt and equitable resolution of student and employee complaints alleging any action that would be prohibited by these Title IX regulations.

§ 113.140 Dissemination of policy.

(a) *Notification of policy.* (1) Each recipient shall implement specific and continuing steps to notify applicants for admission and employment, students and parents of elementary and secondary school students, employees, sources of referral of applicants for admission and employment, and all unions or professional organizations holding collective bargaining or professional agreements with the recipient, that it does not discriminate on the basis of sex in the educational programs or activities that it operates, and that it is required by Title IX and these Title IX regulations not to discriminate in such a manner. Such notification shall contain such information, and be made in such manner, as the designated agency official finds necessary to apprise such persons of the protections against discrimination assured them by Title IX and these Title IX regulations, but shall state at least that the requirement not to discriminate in education programs or activities extends to employment therein, and to admission thereto unless §§ 113.300 through 113.310 do not apply to the recipient, and that inquiries concerning the application of Title IX and these Title IX regulations to such recipient may be referred to the employee designated pursuant to § 113.135, or to the designated agency official.

(2) Each recipient shall make the initial notification required by paragraph (a)(1) of this section within 90 days of September 29, 2000 or of the date these Title IX regulations first apply to such recipient, whichever comes later, which notification shall include publication in:

(i) Newspapers and magazines operated by such recipient or by student, alumnae, or alumni groups for or in connection with such recipient; and

(ii) Memoranda or other written communications distributed to every student and employee of such recipient.

(b) *Publications.* (1) Each recipient shall prominently include a statement of the policy described in paragraph (a) of this section in each announcement, bulletin, catalog, or application form that it makes available to any person of a type, described in paragraph (a) of this section, or which is otherwise used in connection with the recruitment of students or employees.

(2) A recipient shall not use or distribute a publication of the type described in paragraph (b)(1) of this section that suggests, by text or illustration, that such recipient treats applicants, students, or employees differently on the basis of sex except as such treatment is permitted by these Title IX regulations.

(c) *Distribution.* Each recipient shall distribute without discrimination on the basis of sex each publication described in paragraph (b)(1) of this section, and shall apprise each of its admission and employment recruitment representatives of the policy of nondiscrimination described in paragraph (a) of this section, and shall require such representatives to adhere to such policy.

COVERAGE

§ 113.200 Application.

Except as provided in §§ 113.205 through 113.235(a), these Title IX regulations apply to every recipient and to each education program or activity operated by such recipient that receives Federal financial assistance.

§ 113.205 Educational institutions and other entities controlled by religious organizations.

(a) *Exemption.* These Title IX regulations do not apply to any operation of an educational institution or other entity that is controlled by a religious organization to the extent that application of these Title IX regulations would not be consistent with the religious tenets of such organization.

(b) *Exemption claims.* An educational institution or other entity that wishes to claim the exemption set forth in paragraph (a) of this section shall do so by submitting in writing to the designated agency official a statement by the highest-ranking official of the institution, identifying the provisions of these Title IX regulations that conflict with a specific tenet of the religious organization.

§ 113.210 Military and merchant marine educational institutions.

These Title IX regulations do not apply to an educational institution whose primary purpose is the training of individuals for a military service of the United States or for the merchant marine.

§ 113.215 Membership practices of certain organizations.

(a) *Social fraternities and sororities.* These Title IX regulations do not apply to the membership practices of social fraternities and sororities that are exempt from taxation under section 501(a) of the Internal Revenue Code of 1954, 26 U.S.C. 501(a), the active membership of which consists primarily of students in attendance at institutions of higher education.

(b) *YMCA, YWCA, Girl Scouts, Boy Scouts, and Camp Fire Girls.* These Title IX regulations do not apply to the membership practices of the Young Men's Christian Association (YMCA), the Young Women's Christian Association (YWCA), the Girl Scouts, the Boy Scouts, and Camp Fire Girls.

(c) *Voluntary youth service organizations.* These Title IX regulations do not apply to the membership practices of a voluntary youth service organization that is exempt from taxation under section 501(a) of the Internal Revenue Code of 1954, 26 U.S.C. 501(a), and the membership of which has been traditionally limited to members of one sex and principally to persons of less than nineteen years of age.

§ 113.220 Admissions.

(a) Admissions to educational institutions prior to June 24, 1973, are not covered by these Title IX regulations.

(b) *Administratively separate units.* For the purposes only of this section, §§ 113.225 and 113.230, and §§ 113.300 through 113.310, each administratively separate unit shall be deemed to be an educational institution.

(c) *Application of §§ 113.300 through 113.310.* Except as provided in paragraphs (d) and (e) of this section, §§ 113.300 through 113.310 apply to each recipient. A recipient to which §§ 113.300 through 113.310 apply shall not discriminate on the basis of sex in admission or recruitment in violation of §§ 113.300 through 113.310.

(d) *Educational institutions.* Except as provided in paragraph (e) of this section as to recipients that are educational institutions, §§ 113.300 through

113.310 apply only to institutions of vocational education, professional education, graduate higher education, and public institutions of undergraduate higher education.

(e) *Public institutions of undergraduate higher education.* §§ 113.300 through 113.310 do not apply to any public institution of undergraduate higher education that traditionally and continually from its establishment has had a policy of admitting students of only one sex.

§ 113.225 Educational institutions eligible to submit transition plans.

(a) *Application.* This section applies to each educational institution to which §§ 113.300 through 113.310 apply that:

(1) Admitted students of only one sex as regular students as of June 23, 1972; or

(2) Admitted students of only one sex as regular students as of June 23, 1965, but thereafter admitted, as regular students, students of the sex not admitted prior to June 23, 1965.

(b) *Provision for transition plans.* An educational institution to which this section applies shall not discriminate on the basis of sex in admission or recruitment in violation of §§ 113.300 through 113.310.

§ 113.230 Transition plans.

(a) *Submission of plans.* An institution to which § 113.225 applies and that is composed of more than one administratively separate unit may submit either a single transition plan applicable to all such units, or a separate transition plan applicable to each such unit.

(b) *Content of plans.* In order to be approved by the Secretary of Education, a transition plan shall:

(1) State the name, address, and Federal Interagency Committee on Education Code of the educational institution submitting such plan, the administratively separate units to which the plan is applicable, and the name, address, and telephone number of the person to whom questions concerning the plan may be addressed. The person who submits the plan shall be the chief administrator or president of the institution, or another individual legally authorized to bind the institution to all actions set forth in the plan.

(2) State whether the educational institution or administratively separate unit admits students of both sexes as regular students and, if so, when it began to do so.

(3) Identify and describe with respect to the educational institution or administratively separate unit any obstacles to admitting students without discrimination on the basis of sex.

(4) Describe in detail the steps necessary to eliminate as soon as practicable each obstacle so identified and indicate the schedule for taking these steps and the individual directly responsible for their implementation.

(5) Include estimates of the number of students, by sex, expected to apply for, be admitted to, and enter each class during the period covered by the plan.

(c) *Nondiscrimination.* No policy or practice of a recipient to which § 113.225 applies shall result in treatment of applicants to or students of such recipient in violation of §§ 113.300 through 113.310 unless such treatment is necessitated by an obstacle identified in paragraph (b)(3) of this section and a schedule for eliminating that obstacle has been provided as required by paragraph (b)(4) of this section.

(d) *Effects of past exclusion.* To overcome the effects of past exclusion of students on the basis of sex, each educational institution to which § 113.225 applies shall include in its transition plan, and shall implement, specific steps designed to encourage individuals of the previously excluded sex to apply for admission to such institution. Such steps shall include instituting recruitment programs that emphasize the institution's commitment to enrolling students of the sex previously excluded.

§ 113.235 Statutory amendments.

(a) This section, which applies to all provisions of these Title IX regulations, addresses statutory amendments to Title IX.

(b) These Title IX regulations shall not apply to or preclude:

(1) Any program or activity of the American Legion undertaken in connection with the organization or operation of any Boys State conference, Boys Nation conference, Girls State conference, or Girls Nation conference;

(2) Any program or activity of a secondary school or educational institution specifically for:

(i) The promotion of any Boys State conference, Boys Nation conference, Girls State conference, or Girls Nation conference; or

(ii) The selection of students to attend any such conference;

(3) Father-son or mother-daughter activities at an educational institution or in an education program or activity, but if such activities are provided for students of one sex, opportunities for reasonably comparable activities shall be provided to students of the other sex;

(4) Any scholarship or other financial assistance awarded by an institution of higher education to an individual because such individual has received such award in a single-sex pageant based upon a combination of factors related to the individual's personal appearance, poise, and talent. The pageant, however, must comply with other nondiscrimination provisions of Federal law.

(c) *Program or activity* or *program* means:

(1) All of the operations of any entity described in paragraphs (c)(1)(i) through (iv) of this section, any part of which is extended Federal financial assistance:

(i)(A) A department, agency, special purpose district, or other instrumentality of a State or of a local government; or

(B) The entity of such State or local government that distributes such assistance and each such department or agency (and each other State or local government entity) to which the assistance is extended, in the case of assistance to a State or local government;

(ii)(A) A college, university, or other postsecondary institution, or a public system of higher education; or

(B) A local educational agency (as defined in section 8801 of title 20), system of vocational education, or other school system;

(iii)(A) An entire corporation, partnership, or other private organization, or an entire sole proprietorship—

(*1*) If assistance is extended to such corporation, partnership, private organization, or sole proprietorship as a whole; or

(*2*) Which is principally engaged in the business of providing education, health care, housing, social services, or parks and recreation; or

(B) The entire plant or other comparable, geographically separate facility to which Federal financial assistance is extended, in the case of any other corporation, partnership, private organization, or sole proprietorship; or

(iv) Any other entity that is established by two or more of the entities described in paragraphs (c)(1)(i), (ii), or (iii) of this section.

(2)(i) *Program or activity* does not include any operation of an entity that is controlled by a religious organization if the application of 20 U.S.C. 1681 to such operation would not be consistent with the religious tenets of such organization.

(ii) For example, all of the operations of a college, university, or other postsecondary institution, including but not limited to traditional educational operations, faculty and student housing, campus shuttle bus service, campus restaurants, the bookstore, and other commercial activities are part of a "program or activity" subject to these Title IX regulations if the college, university, or other institution receives Federal financial assistance.

(d)(1) Nothing in these Title IX regulations shall be construed to require or prohibit any person, or public or private entity, to provide or pay for any benefit or service, including the use of facilities, related to an abortion. Medical procedures, benefits, services, and the use of facilities, necessary to save the life of a pregnant woman or to address complications related to an abortion are not subject to this section.

(2) Nothing in this section shall be construed to permit a penalty to be imposed on any person or individual because such person or individual is seeking or has received any benefit or service related to a legal abortion. Accordingly, subject to paragraph (d)(1) of this section, no person shall be excluded from participation in, be denied the benefits of, or be subjected to discrimination under any academic, extracurricular, research, occupational training, employment, or other educational program or activity operated by a recipient that receives Federal financial assistance because such individual has sought or received, or is seeking, a legal abortion, or any benefit or service related to a legal abortion.

DISCRIMINATION ON THE BASIS OF SEX IN ADMISSION AND RECRUITMENT PROHIBITED

§ 113.300 Admission.

(a) *General.* No person shall, on the basis of sex, be denied admission, or be subjected to discrimination in admission, by any recipient to which §§ 113.300 through §§ 113.310 apply, except as provided in §§ 113.225 and §§ 113.230.

(b) *Specific prohibitions.* (1) In determining whether a person satisfies any policy or criterion for admission, or in making any offer of admission, a recipient to which §§ 113.300 through 113.310 apply shall not:

(i) Give preference to one person over another on the basis of sex, by ranking applicants separately on such basis, or otherwise;

(ii) Apply numerical limitations upon the number or proportion of persons of either sex who may be admitted; or

(iii) Otherwise treat one individual differently from another on the basis of sex.

(2) A recipient shall not administer or operate any test or other criterion for admission that has a disproportionately adverse effect on persons on the basis of sex unless the use of such test or criterion is shown to predict validly success in the education program or activity in question and alternative tests or criteria that do not have such a disproportionately adverse effect are shown to be unavailable.

(c) *Prohibitions relating to marital or parental status.* In determining whether a person satisfies any policy or criterion for admission, or in making any offer of admission, a recipient to which §§ 113.300 through 113.310 apply:

(1) Shall not apply any rule concerning the actual or potential parental, family, or marital status of a student or applicant that treats persons differently on the basis of sex;

(2) Shall not discriminate against or exclude any person on the basis of pregnancy, childbirth, termination of pregnancy, or recovery therefrom, or establish or follow any rule or practice that so discriminates or excludes;

(3) Subject to § 113.235(d), shall treat disabilities related to pregnancy, childbirth, termination of pregnancy, or recovery therefrom in the same manner and under the same policies as any other temporary disability or physical condition; and

(4) Shall not make pre-admission inquiry as to the marital status of an applicant for admission, including whether such applicant is "Miss" or "Mrs." A recipient may make pre-admission inquiry as to the sex of an applicant for admission, but only if such inquiry is made equally of such applicants of both sexes and if the results of such inquiry are not used in connection with discrimination prohibited by these Title IX regulations.

§ 113.305 Preference in admission.

A recipient to which §§ 113.300 through 113.310 apply shall not give preference to applicants for admission, on the basis of attendance at any educational institution or other school or entity that admits as students only or predominantly members of one sex, if the giving of such preference has the effect of discriminating on the basis of sex in violation of §§ 113.300 through 113.310.

§ 113.310 Recruitment.

(a) *Nondiscriminatory recruitment.* A recipient to which §§ 113.300 through 113.310 apply shall not discriminate on the basis of sex in the recruitment and admission of students. A recipient may be required to undertake additional recruitment efforts for one sex as remedial action pursuant to § 113.110(a), and may choose to undertake such efforts as affirmative action pursuant to § 113.110(b).

(b) *Recruitment at certain institutions.* A recipient to which §§ 113.300 through 113.310 apply shall not recruit primarily or exclusively at educational institutions, schools, or entities that admit as students only or predominantly members of one sex, if such actions have the effect of discriminating on the basis of sex in violation of §§ 113.300 through 113.310.

DISCRIMINATION ON THE BASIS OF SEX IN EDUCATION PROGRAMS OR ACTIVITIES PROHIBITED

§ 113.400 Education programs or activities.

(a) *General.* Except as provided elsewhere in these Title IX regulations, no person shall, on the basis of sex, be excluded from participation in, be denied the benefits of, or be subjected to discrimination under any academic, extracurricular, research, occupational training, or other education program or activity operated by a recipient that receives Federal financial assistance. Sections 113.400 through 113.455 do not apply to actions of a recipient in connection with admission of its students to an education program or activity of a recipient to which §§ 113.300 through 113.310 do not apply, or an entity, not a recipient, to which §§ 113.300 through 113.310 would not apply if the entity were a recipient.

(b) *Specific prohibitions.* Except as provided in §§ 113.400 through 113.455, in providing any aid, benefit, or service to a student, a recipient shall not, on the basis of sex:

(1) Treat one person differently from another in determining whether such person satisfies any requirement or condition for the provision of such aid, benefit, or service;

(2) Provide different aid, benefits, or services or provide aid, benefits, or services in a different manner;

(3) Deny any person any such aid, benefit, or service;

(4) Subject any person to separate or different rules of behavior, sanctions, or other treatment;

(5) Apply any rule concerning the domicile or residence of a student or applicant, including eligibility for in-state fees and tuition;

(6) Aid or perpetuate discrimination against any person by providing significant assistance to any agency, organization, or person that discriminates on the basis of sex in providing any aid, benefit, or service to students or employees;

(7) Otherwise limit any person in the enjoyment of any right, privilege, advantage, or opportunity.

(c) *Assistance administered by a recipient educational institution to study at a foreign institution.* A recipient educational institution may administer or assist in the administration of scholarships, fellowships, or other awards established by foreign or domestic wills, trusts, or similar legal instruments, or by acts of foreign governments and restricted to members of one sex, that are designed to provide opportunities to study abroad, and that are awarded to students who are already matriculating at or who are graduates of the recipient institution; *Provided,* that a recipient educational institution that administers or assists in the administration of such scholarships, fellowships, or other awards that are restricted to members of one sex provides, or otherwise makes available, reasonable opportunities for similar studies for members of the other sex. Such opportunities may be derived from either domestic or foreign sources.

(d) *Aids, benefits or services not provided by recipient.* (1) This paragraph (d) applies to any recipient that requires participation by any applicant, student, or employee in any education program or activity not operated wholly by such recipient, or that facilitates, permits, or considers such participation as part of or equivalent to an education program or activity operated by such recipient, including participation in educational consortia and cooperative employment and student-teaching assignments.

(2) Such recipient:

(i) Shall develop and implement a procedure designed to assure itself that the operator or sponsor of such other education program or activity takes no action affecting any applicant, student, or employee of such recipient that these Title IX regulations would prohibit such recipient from taking; and

(ii) Shall not facilitate, require, permit, or consider such participation if such action occurs.

§ 113.405 Housing.

(a) *Generally.* A recipient shall not, on the basis of sex, apply different rules or regulations, impose different fees or requirements, or offer different services or benefits related to housing, except as provided in this section (including housing provided only to married students).

(b) *Housing provided by recipient.* (1) A recipient may provide separate housing on the basis of sex.

(2) Housing provided by a recipient to students of one sex, when compared to that provided to students of the other sex, shall be as a whole:

(i) Proportionate in quantity to the number of students of that sex applying for such housing; and

(ii) Comparable in quality and cost to the student.

(c) *Other housing.* (1) A recipient shall not, on the basis of sex, administer different policies or practices concerning occupancy by its students of housing other than that provided by such recipient.

(2)(i) A recipient which, through solicitation, listing, approval of housing, or otherwise, assists any agency, organization, or person in making housing available to any of its students, shall take such reasonable action as may be necessary to assure itself that such housing as is provided to students of one sex, when compared to that provided to students of the other sex, is as a whole:

(A) Proportionate in quantity; and

(B) Comparable in quality and cost to the student.

(ii) A recipient may render such assistance to any agency, organization, or person that provides all or part of such housing to students of only one sex.

§ 113.410 Comparable facilities.

A recipient may provide separate toilet, locker room, and shower facilities on the basis of sex, but such facilities provided for students of one sex shall be comparable to such facilities provided for students of the other sex.

§ 113.415 Access to course offerings.

(a) A recipient shall not provide any course or otherwise carry out any of its education program or activity separately on the basis of sex, or require or refuse participation therein by any of its students on such basis, including health, physical education, industrial, business, vocational, technical, home economics, music, and adult education courses.

(b)(1) With respect to classes and activities in physical education at the elementary school level, the recipient shall comply fully with this section as expeditiously as possible but in no event later than one year from September 29, 2000. With respect to physical education classes and activities at the secondary and post-secondary levels, the recipient shall comply fully with this section as expeditiously as possible but in no event later than three years from September 29, 2000.

(2) This section does not prohibit grouping of students in physical education classes and activities by ability as assessed by objective standards of individual performance developed and applied without regard to sex.

(3) This section does not prohibit separation of students by sex within physical education classes or activities during participation in wrestling, boxing, rugby, ice hockey, football, basketball, and other sports the purpose or major activity of which involves bodily contact.

(4) Where use of a single standard of measuring skill or progress in a physical education class has an adverse effect on members of one sex, the recipient shall use appropriate standards that do not have such effect.

(5) Portions of classes in elementary and secondary schools, or portions of education programs or activities, that deal exclusively with human sexuality may be conducted in separate sessions for boys and girls.

(6) Recipients may make requirements based on vocal range or quality that may result in a chorus or choruses of one or predominantly one sex.

§ 113.420 Access to schools operated by LEAs.

A recipient that is a local educational agency shall not, on the basis of sex, exclude any person from admission to:

(a) Any institution of vocational education operated by such recipient; or

(b) Any other school or educational unit operated by such recipient, unless such recipient otherwise makes available to such person, pursuant to the same policies and criteria of admission, courses, services, and facilities comparable to each course, service, and facility offered in or through such schools.

§ 113.425 Counseling and use of appraisal and counseling materials.

(a) *Counseling.* A recipient shall not discriminate against any person on the basis of sex in the counseling or guidance of students or applicants for admission.

(b) *Use of appraisal and counseling materials.* A recipient that uses testing or other materials for appraising or counseling students shall not use different materials for students on the basis of their sex or use materials that permit or require different treatment of students on such basis unless such different materials cover the same occupations and interest areas and the use of such different materials is shown to be essential to eliminate sex bias. Recipients shall develop and use internal procedures for ensuring that such materials do not discriminate on the basis of sex. Where the use of a counseling test or other instrument results in a substantially disproportionate number of members of one sex in any particular course of study or classification, the recipient shall take such action as is necessary to assure itself that such disproportion is not the result of discrimination in the instrument or its application.

(c) *Disproportion in classes.* Where a recipient finds that a particular class contains a substantially disproportionate number of individuals of one sex, the recipient shall take such action as is necessary to assure itself that such disproportion is not the result of discrimination on the basis of sex in counseling or appraisal materials or by counselors.

§ 113.430 Financial assistance.

(a) *General.* Except as provided in paragraphs (b) and (c) of this section, in providing financial assistance to any of its students, a recipient shall not:

(1) On the basis of sex, provide different amounts or types of such assistance, limit eligibility for such assistance that is of any particular type or source, apply different criteria, or otherwise discriminate;

(2) Through solicitation, listing, approval, provision of facilities, or other services, assist any foundation, trust, agency, organization, or person that provides assistance to any of such recipient's students in a manner that discriminates on the basis of sex; or

(3) Apply any rule or assist in application of any rule concerning eligibility for such assistance that treats persons of one sex differently from persons of the other sex with regard to marital or parental status.

(b) *Financial aid established by certain legal instruments.* (1) A recipient may administer or assist in the administration of scholarships, fellowships, or other forms of financial assistance established pursuant to domestic or foreign wills, trusts, bequests, or similar legal instruments or by acts of a foreign government that require that awards be made to members of a particular sex specified therein; *Provided,* that the overall effect of the award of such sex-restricted scholarships, fellowships, and other forms of financial assistance does not discriminate on the basis of sex.

(2) To ensure nondiscriminatory awards of assistance as required in paragraph (b)(1) of this section, recipients shall develop and use procedures under which:

(i) Students are selected for award of financial assistance on the basis of nondiscriminatory criteria and not on the basis of availability of funds restricted to members of a particular sex;

(ii) An appropriate sex-restricted scholarship, fellowship, or other form of financial assistance is allocated to each student selected under paragraph (b)(2)(i) of this section; and

(iii) No student is denied the award for which he or she was selected under paragraph (b)(2)(i) of this section because of the absence of a scholarship, fellowship, or other form of financial assistance designated for a member of that student's sex.

(c) *Athletic scholarships.* (1) To the extent that a recipient awards athletic scholarships or grants-in-aid, it must provide reasonable opportunities for such awards for members of each sex in proportion to the number of students of each sex participating in interscholastic or intercollegiate athletics.

(2) A recipient may provide separate athletic scholarships or grants-in-aid for members of each sex as part of separate athletic teams for members of each sex to the extent consistent with this paragraph (c) and § 113.450.

§ 113.435 Employment assistance to students.

(a) *Assistance by recipient in making available outside employment.* A recipient that assists any agency, organization, or person in making employment available to any of its students:

(1) Shall assure itself that such employment is made available without discrimination on the basis of sex; and

(2) Shall not render such services to any agency, organization, or person that discriminates on the basis of sex in its employment practices.

(b) *Employment of students by recipients.* A recipient that employs any of its students shall not do so in a manner that violates §§ 113.500 through 113.550.

§ 113.440 Health and insurance benefits and services.

Subject to § 113.235(d), in providing a medical, hospital, accident, or life insurance benefit, service, policy, or plan to any of its students, a recipient shall not discriminate on the basis of sex, or provide such benefit, service, policy, or plan in a manner that would violate §§ 113.500 through 113.550 if it were provided to employees of the recipient. This section shall not prohibit a recipient from providing any benefit or service that may be used by a different proportion of students of one sex than of the other, including family planning services. However, any recipient that provides full coverage health service shall provide gynecological care.

§ 113.445 Marital or parental status.

(a) *Status generally.* A recipient shall not apply any rule concerning a student's actual or potential parental, family, or marital status that treats students differently on the basis of sex.

(b) *Pregnancy and related conditions.* (1) A recipient shall not discriminate against any student, or exclude any student from its education program or activity, including any class or extracurricular activity, on the basis of such student's pregnancy, childbirth, false pregnancy, termination of pregnancy, or recovery therefrom, unless the student requests voluntarily to participate in a separate portion of the program or activity of the recipient.

(2) A recipient may require such a student to obtain the certification of a physician that the student is physically and emotionally able to continue participation as long as such a certification is required of all students for other physical or emotional conditions requiring the attention of a physician.

(3) A recipient that operates a portion of its education program or activity separately for pregnant students, admittance to which is completely voluntary on the part of the student as provided in paragraph (b)(1) of this section, shall ensure that the separate portion is comparable to that offered to non-pregnant students.

(4) Subject to § 113.235(d), a recipient shall treat pregnancy, childbirth, false pregnancy, termination of pregnancy and recovery therefrom in the same manner and under the same policies as any other temporary disability with respect to any medical or hospital benefit, service, plan, or policy that such recipient administers, operates, offers, or participates in with respect to students admitted to the recipient's educational program or activity.

(5) In the case of a recipient that does not maintain a leave policy for its students, or in the case of a student who does not otherwise qualify for leave under such a policy, a recipient shall treat pregnancy, childbirth, false pregnancy, termination of pregnancy, and recovery therefrom as a justification

for a leave of absence for as long a period of time as is deemed medically necessary by the student's physician, at the conclusion of which the student shall be reinstated to the status that she held when the leave began.

§ 113.450 Athletics.

(a) *General.* No person shall, on the basis of sex, be excluded from participation in, be denied the benefits of, be treated differently from another person, or otherwise be discriminated against in any interscholastic, intercollegiate, club, or intramural athletics offered by a recipient, and no recipient shall provide any such athletics separately on such basis.

(b) *Separate teams.* Notwithstanding the requirements of paragraph (a) of this section, a recipient may operate or sponsor separate teams for members of each sex where selection for such teams is based upon competitive skill or the activity involved is a contact sport. However, where a recipient operates or sponsors a team in a particular sport for members of one sex but operates or sponsors no such team for members of the other sex, and athletic opportunities for members of that sex have previously been limited, members of the excluded sex must be allowed to try out for the team offered unless the sport involved is a contact sport. For the purposes of these Title IX regulations, contact sports include boxing, wrestling, rugby, ice hockey, football, basketball, and other sports the purpose or major activity of which involves bodily contact.

(c) *Equal opportunity.* (1) A recipient that operates or sponsors interscholastic, intercollegiate, club, or intramural athletics shall provide equal athletic opportunity for members of both sexes. In determining whether equal opportunities are available, the designated agency official will consider, among other factors:

(i) Whether the selection of sports and levels of competition effectively accommodate the interests and abilities of members of both sexes;

(ii) The provision of equipment and supplies;

(iii) Scheduling of games and practice time;

(iv) Travel and per diem allowance;

(v) Opportunity to receive coaching and academic tutoring;

(vi) Assignment and compensation of coaches and tutors;

(vii) Provision of locker rooms, practice, and competitive facilities;

(viii) Provision of medical and training facilities and services;

(ix) Provision of housing and dining facilities and services;

(x) Publicity.

(2) For purposes of paragraph (c)(1) of this section, unequal aggregate expenditures for members of each sex or unequal expenditures for male and female teams if a recipient operates or sponsors separate teams will not constitute noncompliance with this section, but the designated agency official may consider the failure to provide necessary funds for teams for one sex in assessing equality of opportunity for members of each sex.

(d) *Adjustment period.* A recipient that operates or sponsors interscholastic, intercollegiate, club, or intramural athletics at the elementary school level shall comply fully with this section as expeditiously as possible but in no event later than one year from September 29, 2000. A recipient that operates or sponsors interscholastic, intercollegiate, club, or intramural athletics at the secondary or postsecondary school level shall comply fully with this section as expeditiously as possible but in no event later than three years from September 29, 2000.

§ 113.455 Textbooks and curricular material.

Nothing in these Title IX regulations shall be interpreted as requiring or prohibiting or abridging in any way the use of particular textbooks or curricular materials.

DISCRIMINATION ON THE BASIS OF SEX IN EMPLOYMENT IN EDUCATION PROGRAMS OR ACTIVITIES PROHIBITED

§ 113.500 Employment.

(a) *General.* (1) No person shall, on the basis of sex, be excluded from participation in, be denied the benefits of, or be subjected to discrimination in employment, or recruitment, consideration, or selection therefor, whether full-time or part-time, under any education program or activity operated by a recipient that receives Federal financial assistance.

(2) A recipient shall make all employment decisions in any education program or activity operated by such recipient in a nondiscriminatory manner and shall not limit, segregate, or classify applicants or employees in any way that could adversely affect any applicant's or employee's employment opportunities or status because of sex.

(3) A recipient shall not enter into any contractual or other relationship which directly or indirectly has the effect of subjecting employees or students to discrimination prohibited by §§ 113.500 through 113.550, including relationships with employment and referral agencies, with labor unions, and with organizations providing or administering fringe benefits to employees of the recipient.

(4) A recipient shall not grant preferences to applicants for employment on the basis of attendance at any educational institution or entity that admits as students only or predominantly members of one sex, if the giving of such preferences has the effect of discriminating on the basis of sex in violation of these Title IX regulations.

(b) *Application.* The provisions of §§ 113.500 through 113.550 apply to:

(1) Recruitment, advertising, and the process of application for employment;

(2) Hiring, upgrading, promotion, consideration for and award of tenure, demotion, transfer, layoff, termination, application of nepotism policies, right of return from layoff, and rehiring;

(3) Rates of pay or any other form of compensation, and changes in compensation;

(4) Job assignments, classifications, and structure, including position descriptions, lines of progression, and seniority lists;

(5) The terms of any collective bargaining agreement;

(6) Granting and return from leaves of absence, leave for pregnancy, childbirth, false pregnancy, termination of pregnancy, leave for persons of either sex to care for children or dependents, or any other leave;

(7) Fringe benefits available by virtue of employment, whether or not administered by the recipient;

(8) Selection and financial support for training, including apprenticeship, professional meetings, conferences, and other related activities, selection for tuition assistance, selection for sabbaticals and leaves of absence to pursue training;

(9) Employer-sponsored activities, including social or recreational programs; and

(10) Any other term, condition, or privilege of employment.

§ 113.505 Employment criteria.

A recipient shall not administer or operate any test or other criterion for any employment opportunity that has a disproportionately adverse effect on persons on the basis of sex unless:

(a) Use of such test or other criterion is shown to predict validly successful performance in the position in question; and

(b) Alternative tests or criteria for such purpose, which do not have such disproportionately adverse effect, are shown to be unavailable.

§ 113.510 Recruitment.

(a) *Nondiscriminatory recruitment and hiring.* A recipient shall not discriminate on the basis of sex in the recruitment and hiring of employees. Where a recipient has been found to be presently discriminating on the basis of sex in the recruitment or hiring of employees, or has been found to have so discriminated in the past, the recipient shall recruit members of the sex so discriminated against so as to overcome the effects of such past or present discrimination.

(b) *Recruitment patterns.* A recipient shall not recruit primarily or exclusively at entities that furnish as applicants only or predominantly members of one sex if such actions have the effect of discriminating on the basis of sex in violation of §§ 113.500 through 113.550.

§ 113.515 Compensation.

A recipient shall not make or enforce any policy or practice that, on the basis of sex:

(a) Makes distinctions in rates of pay or other compensation;

(b) Results in the payment of wages to employees of one sex at a rate less than that paid to employees of the opposite sex for equal work on jobs the performance of which requires equal skill, effort, and responsibility, and that are performed under similar working conditions.

§ 113.520 Job classification and structure.

A recipient shall not:

(a) Classify a job as being for males or for females;

(b) Maintain or establish separate lines of progression, seniority lists, career ladders, or tenure systems based on sex; or

(c) Maintain or establish separate lines of progression, seniority systems, career ladders, or tenure systems for similar jobs, position descriptions, or job requirements that classify persons on the basis of sex, unless sex is a bona fide occupational qualification for the positions in question as set forth in § 113.550.

§ 113.525 Fringe benefits.

(a) *"Fringe benefits" defined.* For purposes of these Title IX regulations, *fringe benefits* means: Any medical, hospital, accident, life insurance, or retirement benefit, service, policy or plan, any profit-sharing or bonus plan, leave, and any other benefit or service of employment not subject to the provision of § 113.515.

(b) *Prohibitions.* A recipient shall not:

(1) Discriminate on the basis of sex with regard to making fringe benefits available to employees or make fringe benefits available to spouses, families, or dependents of employees differently upon the basis of the employee's sex;

(2) Administer, operate, offer, or participate in a fringe benefit plan that does not provide for equal periodic benefits for members of each sex and for equal contributions to the plan by such recipient for members of each sex; or

(3) Administer, operate, offer, or participate in a pension or retirement plan that establishes different optional or compulsory retirement ages based on sex or that otherwise discriminates in benefits on the basis of sex.

§ 113.530 Marital or parental status.

(a) *General.* A recipient shall not apply any policy or take any employment action:

(1) Concerning the potential marital, parental, or family status of an employee or applicant for employment that treats persons differently on the basis of sex; or

(2) Which is based upon whether an employee or applicant for employment is the head of household or principal wage earner in such employee's or applicant's family unit.

(b) *Pregnancy.* A recipient shall not discriminate against or exclude from employment any employee or applicant for employment on the basis of pregnancy, childbirth, false pregnancy, termination of pregnancy, or recovery therefrom.

(c) *Pregnancy as a temporary disability.* Subject to § 113.235(d), a recipient shall treat pregnancy, childbirth, false pregnancy, termination of pregnancy, recovery therefrom, and any temporary disability resulting therefrom as any other temporary disability for all job-related purposes, including commencement, duration, and extensions of leave, payment of disability income, accrual of seniority and any other benefit or service, and reinstatement, and under any fringe benefit offered to employees by virtue of employment.

(d) *Pregnancy leave.* In the case of a recipient that does not maintain a leave policy for its employees, or in the case of an employee with insufficient leave or accrued employment time to qualify for leave under such a policy, a recipient shall treat pregnancy, childbirth, false pregnancy, termination of pregnancy, and recovery therefrom as a justification for a leave of absence without pay for a reasonable period of time, at the conclusion of which the employee shall be reinstated to the status that she held when the leave began or to a comparable position, without decrease in rate of compensation or loss of promotional opportunities, or any other right or privilege of employment.

§ 113.535 Effect of state or local law or other requirements.

(a) *Prohibitory requirements.* The obligation to comply with §§ 113.500

through 113.550 is not obviated or alleviated by the existence of any State or local law or other requirement that imposes prohibitions or limits upon employment of members of one sex that are not imposed upon members of the other sex.

(b) *Benefits.* A recipient that provides any compensation, service, or benefit to members of one sex pursuant to a State or local law or other requirement shall provide the same compensation, service, or benefit to members of the other sex.

§ 113.540 Advertising.

A recipient shall not in any advertising related to employment indicate preference, limitation, specification, or discrimination based on sex unless sex is a bona fide occupational qualification for the particular job in question.

§ 113.545 Pre-employment inquiries.

(a) *Marital status.* A recipient shall not make pre-employment inquiry as to the marital status of an applicant for employment, including whether such applicant is "Miss" or "Mrs."

(b) *Sex.* A recipient may make pre-employment inquiry as to the sex of an applicant for employment, but only if such inquiry is made equally of such applicants of both sexes and if the results of such inquiry are not used in connection with discrimination prohibited by these Title IX regulations.

§ 113.550 Sex as a bona fide occupational qualification.

A recipient may take action otherwise prohibited by §§ 113.500 through 113.550 provided it is shown that sex is a bona fide occupational qualification for that action, such that consideration of sex with regard to such action is essential to successful operation of the employment function concerned. A recipient shall not take action pursuant to this section that is based upon alleged comparative employment characteristics or stereotyped characterizations of one or the other sex, or upon preference based on sex of the recipient, employees, students, or other persons, but nothing contained in this section shall prevent a recipient from considering an employee's sex in relation to employment in a locker room or toilet facility used only by members of one sex.

PROCEDURES

§ 113.600 Notice of covered programs.

Within 60 days of September 29, 2000, each Federal agency that awards Federal financial assistance shall publish in the FEDERAL REGISTER a notice of the programs covered by these Title IX regulations. Each such Federal agency shall periodically republish the notice of covered programs to reflect changes in covered programs. Copies of this notice also shall be made available upon request to the Federal agency's office that enforces Title IX.

§ 113.605 Enforcement procedures.

The investigative, compliance, and enforcement procedural provisions of Title VI of the Civil Rights Act of 1964 (42 U.S.C. 2000d) ("Title VI") are hereby adopted and applied to these Title IX regulations. These procedures may be found at 13 CFR part 112.

[65 FR 52876, Aug. 30, 2000]

PART 114—ADMINISTRATIVE CLAIMS UNDER THE FEDERAL TORT CLAIMS ACT AND REPRESENTATION AND INDEMNIFICATION OF SBA EMPLOYEES

Subpart A—Administrative Tort Claims

Sec.

Subpart B—Representation and Indemnification of SBA Employees

114.111 Does the attorney-client privilege apply when SBA employees are represented by the Government?

AUTHORITY: 15 U.S.C. 634 (b)(1), (b)(6); 28 U.S.C. 2672; 28 CFR 14.11.

SOURCE: 61 FR 2401, Jan. 26, 1996, unless otherwise noted.

Subpart A—Administrative Tort Claims

§ 114.100 Definitions.

As used throughout this part 114, *date of accrual* means the date you know or reasonably should have known of your injury. The date of accrual will depend on the facts of each case. *Site* means the geographic location where the incident giving rise to your claim occurred.

§ 114.101 What do these regulations cover?

This part applies only to monetary claims you assert under the Federal Tort Claims Act, 28 U.S.C. 2671 *et seq.*, for injury to or loss of property, personal injury, or death arising from the negligent or wrongful act or omission of any SBA employee acting within the scope of his or her employment.

§ 114.102 When, where and how do I present a claim?

(a) *When.* You must present your claim within 2 years of the date of accrual.

(b) *Where.* You may present your claim at the SBA District Office nearest to the site of the action giving rise to the claim and within the same state as the site. If your claim is based on the acts or omissions of an employee of SBA's Disaster Assistance Program, you may present your claim either to the appropriate SBA District Office or to the Disaster Assistance Office nearest to the site of the action giving rise to the claim.

(c) *How.* You must use an official form which can be obtained from the SBA office where you file the claim or give other written notice of your claim, stating the specific amount of your alleged damages and providing enough information to enable SBA to investigate your claim. You may present your claim in person or by mail, but your claim will not be considered presented until SBA receives the written information.

[64 FR 40283, July 26, 1999]

§ 114.103 Who may file a claim?

(a) If a claim is based on factors listed in the first column, then it may be presented by persons listed in the second column.

Claim factors	Claim presenters
Injury to or loss of property	The owner of the property, his or her duly authorized agent, or legal representative.
Personal injury	The injured person, his or her duly authorized agent, or legal representative.
Death	The executor, administrator, or legal representative of the decedent's estate, or any other person entitled to assert the claim under applicable state law.
Loss wholly compensated by an insurer with rights as a subrogee.	The parties individually, as their interests appear, or jointly.

(b) An agent or legal representative may present your claim in your name, but must sign the claim, state his or her title or legal capacity, and include documentation of authority to present the claim on your behalf.

§ 114.104 What evidence and information may SBA require relating to my claim?

(a) For a claim based on injury to or loss of property:

(1) Proof you own the property.

(2) A specific statement of the damage you claim with respect to each item of property.

(3) Itemized receipts for payment for necessary repairs or itemized written estimates of the cost of such repairs.

(4) A statement listing date of purchase, purchase price and salvage value, where repair is not economical.

(5) Full information about potential insurance coverage and any insurance claims or payments relating to your claim.

(6) Any other information that may be relevant to the government's alleged liability or the damages you claim.

(b) For a claim based on personal injury, including pain and suffering:

(1) A written report from your health care provider stating the nature and extent of your injury and treatment,

the degree of your temporary or permanent disability, your prognosis, period of hospitalization, and any diminished earning capacity.

(2) A written report following a physical, dental or mental examination of you by a physician employed by SBA or another Federal Agency. If you want a copy of this report, you must request it in writing, furnish SBA with the written report of your health care provider, if SBA requests it, and make or agree to make available to SBA any other medical reports relevant to your claim.

(3) Itemized bills for medical, dental and hospital expenses you have incurred, or itemized receipts of payment for these expenses.

(4) Your health care provider's written statement of the expected expenses related to any necessary future treatment.

(5) A statement from your employer showing actual time lost from employment, whether you are a full or part-time employee, and the wages or salary you actually lost.

(6) Documentary evidence showing the amount of earnings you actually lost if you are self-employed.

(7) Information about the existence of insurance coverage and any insurance claims or payments relating to the claim in question.

(8) Any other information that may be relevant to the government's alleged liability or the damages you claim.

(c) For a claim based on death:

(1) An authenticated death certificate or other competent evidence showing cause of death, date of death, and age of the decedent.

(2) Evidence of decedent's employment or occupation at the time of death, including monthly or yearly salary or earnings, and the duration of such employment or occupation.

(3) Full names, addresses, birth dates, kinship, and marital status of the decedent's survivors, including identification of those survivors who were dependent upon the decedent for support at the time of his or her death.

(4) Evidence of the support provided by the decedent to each dependent survivor at the time of his or her death.

(5) A summary of the decedent's general physical and mental condition before death.

(6) Itemized bills or receipts for payments for medical and burial expenses.

(7) For pain and suffering damage claims, a physician's detailed statement specifying the injuries suffered, the duration of pain and suffering, any drugs administered for pain, and the decedent's physical condition in the interval between injury and death.

(8) Any other information that may be relevant to the government's alleged liability or the damages claimed.

§ 114.105 Who investigates and considers my claim?

(a) SBA may investigate, or ask another Federal agency to investigate, your claim. SBA also may request any Federal agency to conduct a physical examination of you and provide a report to SBA. SBA will reimburse the Federal agency for the costs of that examination when authorized or required by statute or regulation.

(b) In those cases in which SBA investigates your claim, and which arise out of the acts or omissions of employees other than employees of the Disaster Assistance Program, the SBA District Counsel in the office with jurisdiction over the site where the action giving rise to the claim occurred will investigate and make recommendations or determination with respect to your claim. In those cases in which SBA investigates your claim, and which arise out of acts or omissions of Disaster Assistance Program employees, the SBA Disaster Area Counsel in the office with jurisdiction over the site where the action giving rise to the claim occurred will investigate and make recommendations or a determination with respect to your claim. The District Counsel, or Disaster Area Counsel, where appropriate, may negotiate with you, and is authorized to use alternative dispute resolution mechanisms, which are non-binding on SBA, when they may promote the prompt, fair and efficient resolution of your claim.

(c) If your claim is for $5,000 or less, the District Counsel or Disaster Area Counsel who investigates your claim may deny the claim, or may recommend approval, compromise, or settlement of the claim to the Associate General Counsel for Litigation, who will in such a case take final action.

[61 FR 2401, Jan. 26, 1996, as amended at 64 FR 40283, July 26, 1999]

§114.106 What if my claim exceeds $5,000?

The District Counsel or Disaster Area Counsel, as appropriate, must review and investigate your claim and forward it with a report and recommendation to the Associate General Counsel for Litigation, who may approve or deny an award, compromise, or settlement of claims in excess of $5,000, but not exceeding $25,000.

[64 FR 40283, July 26, 1999]

§114.107 What if my claim exceeds $25,000 or has other special features?

(a) The U.S. Attorney General or designee must approve in writing any award, compromise, or settlement of a claim in excess of $25,000. For this purpose, a principal claim and any derivative or subrogated claim are considered a single claim.

(b) SBA must consult with the Department of Justice before adjusting, determining, compromising, or settling a claim whenever the General Counsel or designee determines:

(1) The claim involves a new precedent or a new point of law; or

(2) The claim involves or may involve a question of policy; or

(3) The United States is or may be entitled to indemnity or contribution from a third party and SBA is unable to adjust the third party claim; or

(4) Approval of a claim, as a practical matter, will or may control the disposition of a related claim in which the amount to be paid may exceed $25,000.

(c) SBA must consult with the Department of Justice before adjusting, determining, compromising, or settling a claim whenever SBA learns that the United States, or any of its employees, agents, or cost-plus contractors, is involved in litigation based on a claim arising out of the same incident or transaction.

(d) SBA, acting through its General Counsel or designee, must make any referrals to the Department of Justice for approval or consultation by transmitting them in writing to the Assistant Attorney General, Civil Division.

(1) The referral must contain a short and concise statement of the facts and the reason for the request or referral, copies of the relevant portions of the claim file, and SBA's views and recommendations.

(2) SBA may make this referral at any time after a claim is presented.

§114.108 What if my claim is approved?

SBA will notify you in writing if it approves your claim. The District Counsel or Disaster Area Counsel investigating your claim will forward to you, your agent or legal representative the forms necessary to indicate satisfaction of your claim and your acceptance of the payment. Acceptance by you, your agent or your legal representative of any award, compromise or settlement releases all your claims against the United States under the Federal Tort Claims Act. This means that it binds you, your agent or your legal representative, and any other person on whose behalf or for whose benefit the claim was presented. It also constitutes a complete release of your claim against the United States and its employees. If you are represented by counsel, SBA will designate you and your counsel as joint payees and will deliver the check to counsel. Payment is contingent upon the waiver of your claim and is subject to the availability of appropriated funds.

[64 FR 40283, July 26, 1999]

§114.109 What if my claim is denied?

SBA will notify you or your agent or legal representative in writing by certified or registered mail if it denies your claim. You have a right to file suit in an appropriate U.S. District Court not later than six months after the date the notification was mailed.

Subpart B—Representation and Indemnification of SBA Employees

§ 114.110 What is SBA's policy with respect to indemnifying and providing legal representation to SBA employees?

(a) If an SBA employee engages in conduct, within the scope of his or her employment, which gives rise to a claim, and the SBA Administrator or designee determines that any of the following actions relating to the claim are in SBA's interest, SBA may:

(1) Indemnify the employee after a verdict, judgment, or other monetary award is rendered personally against the employee in any civil suit in state or federal court or any arbitration proceeding;

(2) Settle or compromise the claim; and/or

(3) Pay for, or request that the Department of Justice provide, legal representation to the employee once personally named in such a suit.

(b) If you are an SBA employee, you may ask SBA to settle or compromise your claim, provide you with legal representation, or provide you with indemnification for a verdict, judgment or award entered against you in a suit. To do so, you must submit a timely, written request to the General Counsel, with appropriate documentation, including copies of any pleadings, verdict, judgment, award, or settlement proposal. The General Counsel will decide all requests for representation or settlement, and will forward to the Administrator, with the accompanying documentation and a recommendation, any requests for indemnification.

(c) Any payments by SBA under this section will be contingent upon the availability of appropriated funds.

§ 114.111 Does the attorney-client privilege apply when SBA employees are represented by the Government?

When attorneys employed by SBA participate in any process in which SBA seeks to determine whether SBA should request the Department of Justice to provide representation to an SBA employee sued, subpoenaed, or charged in his or her individual capacity, or whether attorneys employed by SBA should provide representational assistance for such an employee, those attorneys undertake a full and traditional attorney-client relationship with the employee with respect to the attorney-client privilege. If representation is authorized, SBA attorneys who assist in the representation of an SBA employee also undertake a full and traditional attorney-client relationship with the employee with respect to the attorney-client privilege. Unless authorized by the employee, the attorney must not disclose to anyone other than attorneys also responsible for the employee's representation information communicated to the attorney by the client-employee during the course of the attorney-client relationship. The attorney-client privilege will continue with respect to that information whether or not representation is provided, and even if the employee's representation is denied or discontinued.

PART 115—SURETY BOND GUARANTEE

Subpart C—Preferred Surety Bond (PSB) Guarantees

AUTHORITY: 5 U.S.C. app 3; 15 U.S.C. 687b, 687c, 694a, 694b note; and Pub. L. 110–246, Sec. 12079, 122 Stat. 1651.

SOURCE: 61 FR 3271, Jan. 31, 1996, unless otherwise noted.

EDITORIAL NOTE: Nomenclature changes to part 115 appear at 72 FR 50038, Aug. 30, 2007.

§ 115.1 Overview of regulations.

The regulations in this part cover the SBA's Surety Bond Guarantee Programs under Part B of Title IV of the Small Business Investment Act of 1958, as amended. Subpart A of this part contains regulations common to both the program requiring prior SBA approval of each bond guarantee (the Prior Approval Program) and the program not requiring prior approval (the PSB Program). Subpart B of this part contains the regulations applicable only to the Prior Approval Program. Subpart C of this part contains the regulations applicable only to the PSB Program.

§ 115.2 Savings clause.

Transactions affected by this part 115 are governed by the regulations in effect at the time they occur.

Subpart A—Provisions for All Surety Bond Guarantees

§ 115.10 Definitions.

Affiliate is defined in § 121.301(f) of this chapter.

Ancillary Bond means a bond incidental and essential to the performance of a Contract for which there is a guaranteed Final Bond.

Applicable Statutory Limit means the maximum amount, set forth below, of any Contract or Order for which SBA is authorized to guarantee, or commit to guarantee, a Bid Bond, Payment Bond, Performance Bond, or Ancillary Bond:

(1) $6.5 million (as adjusted for inflation in accordance with 41 U.S.C. 1908);

(2) $10 million if a contracting officer of a Federal agency certifies, in accordance with section 115.12(e)(3), that such guarantee is necessary; or

(3) if SBA is guaranteeing the bond in connection with a procurement related to a major disaster pursuant to section 12079 of Pub. L. 110–246, see section 115.12(e)(4).

Bid Bond means a bond conditioned upon the bidder on a Contract entering into the Contract, and furnishing the required Payment and Performance Bonds. The term does not include a forfeiture bond unless it is issued for a jurisdiction where statute or settled decisional law requires forfeiture bonds for public works.

Contract means a written obligation of the Principal, including an Order, requiring the furnishing of services, supplies, labor, materials, machinery, equipment, or construction. A Contract must not prohibit a Surety from performing the Contract upon default of the Principal. A contract does not include a permit, subdivision contract, lease, land contract, evidence of debt, financial guarantee (e.g., a contract requiring any payment by the Principal to the Obligee, except for contracts in connection with bid and performance bonds for the sale of timber and/or other forest products, such as biomass, that require the Principal to pay the Obligee), warranty of performance or efficiency, warranty of fidelity, or release of lien (other than for claims under a guaranteed bond). It includes a maintenance agreement of 2 years or less which covers defective workmanship or materials only. With SBA's written approval, it can also include a longer maintenance agreement covering defective workmanship or materials, or a maintenance agreement covering something other than defective workmanship or materials. To qualify for such approval, the agreement must be ancillary to the Contract for which SBA is guaranteeing a bond, must be required to be performed by the same Principal, and must be customarily required in the relevant trade or industry.

D/SG means SBA's Director, Office of Surety Guarantees.

Execution means signing by a representative or agent of the Surety with the authority and power to bind the Surety.

Final Bond means a Performance Bond and/or a Payment Bond.

Head of Agency means in the case of a cabinet department, the Secretary; and in the case of an independent commission, board, or agency, the Chair or Administrator; or any person to whom the Secretary, Chair, or Administrator has directly delegated the authority to request SBA to guarantee bonds on Contracts or Orders in excess of $5,000,000.

Imminent Breach means a threat to the successful completion of a bonded Contract which, unless remedied by the Surety, makes a default under the bond appear to be inevitable.

Investment Act means the Small Business Investment Act of 1958 (15 U.S.C. 661 *et seq.*), as amended.

Loss has the meaning set forth in § 115.16.

Obligee means:

(1)(i) In the case of a Bid Bond, the Person requesting bids for the performance of a Contract; or

(ii) In the case of a Final Bond, the Person who has contracted with a Principal for the completion of the Contract and to whom the primary obligation of the Surety runs in the event of a breach by the Principal.

(2) In either case, no Person (other than a Federal department or agency) may be named co-Obligee or Obligee on a bond or on a rider to the bond unless that Person is bound by the Contract to the Principal (or to the Surety, if the Surety has arranged completion of the Contract) to the same extent as the original Obligee. In no event may the addition of one or more co-Obligees increase the aggregate liability of the Surety under the bond.

Order means a task order for services or delivery order for supplies issued under an indefinite delivery Contract (definite quantity, indefinite quantity, or requirements).

OSG means SBA's Office of Surety Guarantees.

Payment Bond means a bond which is conditioned upon the payment by the Principal of money to persons who have a right of action against such bond, including those who have furnished labor, materials, equipment and supplies for use in the performance of the Contract. A Payment Bond can not require the Surety to pay an amount which exceeds the claimant's actual loss or damage.

Performance Bond means a bond conditioned upon the completion by the Principal of a Contract in accordance with its terms.

Person means a natural person or a legal entity.

Premium means the amount charged by a Surety to issue bonds. The Premium is determined by applying an approved rate (see §§ 115.32(a) and 115.60(a)(2)) to the bond or contract amount. The Premium does not include surcharges for extra services, whether or not considered part of the "premium" under local law.

Principal means, in the case of a Bid Bond, the Person bidding for the award of a Contract. In the case of Final Bonds and Ancillary Bonds, Principal means the Person primarily liable to complete the Contract, or to make Contract-related payments to other persons, and is the Person whose performance or payment is bonded by the Surety. A Principal may be a prime contractor or a subcontractor.

Prior Approval Agreement means the Surety Bond Guarantee Agreement (SBA Form 990) or Quick Bond Guarantee Application and Agreement (SBA Form 990A) entered into between a Prior Approval Surety and SBA under which SBA agrees to guarantee a specific bond.

Prior Approval Surety means a Surety which must obtain SBA's prior approval on each guarantee and which has entered into one or more Prior Approval Agreements with SBA.

PSB Agreement means the Preferred Surety Bond Guarantee Agreement entered into between a PSB Surety and SBA.

PSB Surety means a Surety that has been admitted to the Preferred Surety Bond (PSB) Program.

Service-Disabled Veteran means a veteran with a disability that is service-connected, as defined in Section 101(16) of Title 38, United States Code.

Small Business Owned and Controlled by Service-Disabled Veterans means:

(1) A Small Concern of which not less than 51 percent is owned by one or more Service-Disabled Veterans; or a publicly-owned Small concern of which not less than 51 percent of the stock is owned by one or more Service-Disabled Veterans; and

(2) The management and daily business operations of which are controlled by one or more Service-Disabled Veterans, or in the case of a Service-Disabled Veteran with permanent and severe disability, the spouse or permanent caregiver of such Veteran.

Small Business Owned and Controlled by Veterans means:

(1) A Small Concern of which not less than 51 percent is owned by one or more Veterans; or a publicly-owned Small Concern of which not less than 51 percent of the stock is owned by one or more Veterans; and

(2) The management and daily business operations of which are controlled by one or more Veterans.

Surety means a company which:

(1)(i) Under the terms of a Bid Bond, agrees to pay a sum of money to the Obligee if the Principal breaches the conditions of the bond;

(ii) Under the terms of a Performance Bond, agrees to pay a sum of money or to incur the cost of fulfilling the terms of a Contract if the Principal breaches the conditions of the Contract; and

(iii) Under the terms of a Payment or an Ancillary Bond, agrees to make payment to all who have a right of action against such bond, including those who have furnished labor, materials, equipment and supplies in the performance of the Contract.

(2) The term Surety includes an agent, independent agent, underwriter, or any other company or individual empowered to act on behalf of the Surety.

Veteran has the meaning given the term in Section 101(2) of Title 38, United States Code.

[61 FR 3271, Jan. 31, 1996, as amended at 61 FR 7985, Mar. 1, 1996; 72 FR 34599, June 25, 2007; 72 FR 50038, Aug. 30, 2007; 74 FR 36109, July 22, 2009; 76 FR 2572, Jan. 14, 2011; 76 FR 9963, Feb. 23, 2011; 77 FR 41665, July 16, 2012; 79 FR 2086, Jan. 13, 2014; 81 FR 41428, June 27, 2016]

§ 115.11 Applying to participate in the Surety Bond Guarantee Program.

Sureties interested in participating as Prior Approval Sureties or PSB Sureties should apply in writing to the D/SG at 409 3rd Street, SW., Washington, DC 20416. OSG will determine the eligibility of the applicant considering its standards and procedures for underwriting, administration, claims and recovery. Each applicant must be a corporation listed by the U.S. Treasury as eligible to issue bonds in connection with Federal procurement contracts. At a minimum, each applicant must have salaried staff that is employed directly (not an agent or other individual or entity under contract with the applicant) to oversee its underwriting function and perform all claims and recovery functions other than specialized services the costs of which may be reimbursable under 13 CFR 115.16(e)(1). Final settlement authority for claims and recovery must be vested only in the applicant's salaried claims staff. The applicant must continue to comply with SBA's standards and procedures for underwriting, administration, claims, recovery, and staffing requirements while participating in SBA's Surety Bond Guarantee Programs.

[61 FR 3271, Jan. 31, 1996, as amended at 81 FR 23565, Apr. 22, 2016]

§ 115.12 General program policies and provisions.

(a) *Description of Surety Bond Guarantee Programs.* SBA guarantees Sureties participating in the Surety Bond Guarantee Programs against a portion of their Losses incurred and paid as a result of a Principal's breach of the terms of a Bid Bond, Final Bond or Ancillary Bond, on any eligible Contract. In the Prior Approval Program, the

Surety must obtain SBA's approval before a guaranteed bond can be issued. In the PSB Program, selected Sureties may issue, monitor, and service SBA guaranteed bonds without further SBA approval.

(b) *Eligibility of bonds.* Bid Bonds and Final Bonds are eligible for an SBA guarantee if they are executed in connection with an eligible Contract, as defined in § 115.10, Definitions. Commercial and Fidelity bonds are not eligible for SBA guarantees. Ancillary Bonds may also be eligible for SBA's guarantee. A performance bond must not prohibit a Surety from performing the Contract upon default of the Principal.

(c) *Expiration of Bid Bond Guarantee.* A Bid Bond guarantee expires 120 days after Execution of the Bid Bond, unless the Surety notifies SBA in writing before the 120th day that a later expiration date is required. The notification must include the new expiration date.

(d) *Guarantee agreement.* The terms and conditions of SBA's bond guarantee agreements, including the guarantee percentage, may vary from Surety to Surety, depending on past experience with SBA. If the guarantee percentage is not fixed by the Investment Act, it is determined by OSG after considering, among other things, the rating or ranking assigned to the Surety by recognized authority, and the Surety's Loss rate, average Contract amount, average bond penalty per guaranteed bond, and ratio of Bid Bonds to Final Bonds, all in comparison with other Sureties participating in the same SBA Surety Bond Guarantee Program (Prior Approval or PSB) to a comparable degree. Any guarantee agreement under this part is made exclusively for the benefit of SBA and the Surety, and does not confer any rights (such as a right of action against SBA) or benefits on any other party.

(e) *Amount of Contract*—(1) *Determination of Amount of Contract.* For a fixed price Contract, the amount of the Contract is the price excluding any options. For a requirements Contract, the amount of the Contract is the price of the total estimated quantity to be ordered under the Contract. For an indefinite quantity Contract, the amount of the Contract is the price of the specified minimum quantity to be ordered under the Contract and, for each Order issued under such Contract, the price of each such Order. The amount of the Contract or Order to be bonded must not exceed the Applicable Statutory Limit as of the date:

(i) SBA approves a Prior Approval Surety's request for a Bid Bond guarantee;

(ii) A Preferred Surety Executes a Bid Bond; or

(iii) The date Final Bonds (and any Ancillary Bonds) unrelated to an SBA-guaranteed Bid Bond are Executed by a Preferred Surety or by a Prior Approval Surety following SBA's approval of its request for a guarantee of Final Bonds.

(2) *Aggregation of Contract and Order amounts.* (i) The amounts of two or more formally separate Contracts for a single construction project are aggregated to determine the Contract amount unless the Contracts are to be performed in phases and the prior bond is released before the beginning of each succeeding phase. A bond may be considered released even if the warranty period it is covering has not yet expired. For purposes of this paragraph, a "single construction project" means one represented by two or more Contracts of one Principal or its Affiliates with one Obligee or its Affiliates for performance at the same location, regardless of job title or nature of the work to be performed.

(ii) The amounts of two or more Contracts or Orders for supplies and services awarded to the same Principal or its Affiliates are aggregated to determine the Contract or Order amount if SBA determines, after discussion with the contracting official responsible for the award of the contract, that award of a single Contract or Order could reasonably have satisfied the supply or service requirement at the time of issuance.

(3) *Federal Contracts or Orders in excess of $6,500,000 (as adjusted for inflation in accordance with section 1908 of title 41, United States Code).* SBA is authorized to guarantee bonds on Federal Contracts or Orders greater than $6,500,000 (as adjusted for inflation in accordance with 41 U.S.C. 1908), but not exceeding $10,000,000, upon a signed certification

of a Federal contracting officer. The contracting officer's certification must include a statement that the small business is experiencing difficulty obtaining a bond and that an SBA bond guarantee would be in the best interests of the Government. The certification must be express mailed to SBA, Office of Surety Guarantees, 409 Third Street, SW., Suite 8600, Washington, DC 20416, or faxed to the Office of Surety Guarantees at 202–481–0390, with a copy provided to the small business, and must include the following additional information:

(i) Name, address and telephone number of the small business;

(ii) Offer or Contract number and brief description of the contract; and

(iii) Estimated Contract value and date of anticipated award determination.

(4) *Alternative authority to guarantee bonds for Contracts and Orders related to a major disaster area.* Subject to the availability of funds appropriated in advance specifically for the purpose of guaranteeing bonds for any Contract or Order related to a major disaster, SBA may, as an alternative to the authority otherwise set forth in this Part, guarantee bonds on any Contract or Order under the following terms and conditions:

(i) The Contract or Order does not exceed $5,000,000 at the time of bond execution, and:

(A) For products or services procured under a Federal Contract or Order, the products will be manufactured or the services will be performed in the major disaster area identified in the Federal Emergency Management Agency (FEMA) Web site at *http://www.fema.gov*, or the products will be manufactured or the services will be performed outside the major disaster area and the products or services will directly assist in the recovery efforts in the major disaster area; or

(B) For products or services procured under any other Contract or Order, the products will be manufactured or the services will be performed in the major disaster area identified in the FEMA Web site at *http://www.fema.gov;*

(ii) At the request of the Head of the Agency involved in reconstruction efforts in response to a major disaster, SBA may guarantee bonds on Federal Contracts or Orders in excess of $5,000,000, but not more than $10,000,000;

(iii) A guarantee may be issued under this paragraph (e)(4) for any Contract or Order for which an offer is submitted or an award is made within 12 months from the date an area is designated a major disaster area in the FEDERAL REGISTER. SBA may, at its discretion, extend this time period for any particular disaster, and will publish a notice of the extension in the FEDERAL REGISTER.

(f) *Transfers or sales by Surety.* Sureties must not sell or otherwise transfer their files or accounts, whether before or after a default by the Principal has occurred, without the prior written approval of SBA. A violation of this provision is grounds for termination from participation in the program. This provision does not apply to the sale of an entire business division, subsidiary or operation of the Surety.

[61 FR 3271, Jan. 31, 1996, as amended at 66 FR 30804, June 8, 2001; 74 FR 36109, July 22, 2009; 76 FR 2572, Jan. 14, 2011; 79 FR 2086, Jan. 13, 2014]

§ 115.13 Eligibility of Principal.

(a) *General eligibility.* In order to be eligible for a bond guaranteed by SBA, the Principal must comply with the following requirements:

(1) *Size.* Together with its Affiliates, it must qualify as a small business under part 121 of this title.

(2) *Character.* It must possess good character and reputation. A Principal meets this standard if each owner of 20% or more of its equity, and each of its officers, directors, or general partners, possesses good character and reputation. A Person's good character and reputation is presumed absent when:

(i) The Person is under indictment for, or has been convicted of a felony, or a final civil judgment has been entered stating that such Person has committed a breach of trust or has violated a law or regulation protecting the integrity of business transactions or business relationships; or

(ii) A regulatory authority has revoked, canceled, or suspended a license of the Person which is necessary to perform the Contract; or

(iii) The Person has obtained a bond guarantee by fraud or material misrepresentation (as described in § 115.19(b)), or has failed to keep the Surety informed of unbonded contracts or of a contract bonded by another Surety, as required by a bonding line commitment under § 115.33.

(3) *Need for bond.* It must certify that a bond is expressly required by the bid solicitation or the original Contract in order to bid on the Contract or to serve as a prime contractor or subcontractor.

(4) *Availability of bond.* It must certify that a bond is not obtainable on reasonable terms and conditions without SBA's guarantee.

(5) *Partial subcontract.* It must certify the percentage of work under the Contract to be subcontracted. SBA will not guarantee bonds for Principals who are primarily brokers. In addition, the Principal must retain full responsibility for the oversight and management of the Contract, including any work performed by any subcontractor, and may not subcontract the full scope of the statement of work.

(6) *Debarment.* It must certify that the Principal is not presently debarred, suspended, proposed for debarment, declared ineligible, or voluntarily excluded from transactions with any Federal department or agency, under governmentwide debarment and suspension rules.

(7) *No loss of eligibility.* Neither the Principal nor any of its Affiliates is ineligible for an SBA-guaranteed bond under § 115.14.

(b) *Conflict of interest.* A Principal is not eligible for an SBA-guaranteed bond issued by a particular Surety if that Surety, or an Affiliate of that Surety, or a close relative or member of the household of that Surety or Affiliate owns, directly or indirectly, 10% or more of the Principal. This prohibition also applies to ownership interests in any of the Principal's Affiliates.

[61 FR 3271, Jan. 31, 1996, as amended at 79 FR 2087, Jan. 13, 2014; 81 FR 23565, Apr. 22, 2016]

§ 115.14 Loss of Principal's eligibility for future assistance and reinstatement of Principal.

(a) *Ineligibility.* A Principal and its Affiliates lose eligibility for further SBA bond guarantees if any of the following occurs under an SBA-guaranteed bond issued on behalf of the Principal:

(1) Legal action under the guaranteed bond has been initiated.

(2) The Obligee has declared the Principal to be in default under the Contract.

(3) The Surety has established a claim reserve for the bond of at least $1000.

(4) The Principal, or any of its Affiliates, has defaulted on an SBA-guaranteed bond resulting in a Loss that has not been fully reimbursed to SBA, or SBA has not been fully reimbursed for any Imminent Breach payments.

(5) The guarantee fee has not been paid by the Principal.

(6) The Principal committed fraud or material misrepresentation in obtaining the guaranteed bond.

(b) *Reinstatement of Principal's eligibility.* At any time after a Principal becomes ineligible for further bond guarantees under paragraph (a) of this section:

(1) A Prior Approval Surety may recommend that such Principal's eligibility be reinstated, and OSG may agree to reinstate the Principal if:

(i) The Surety has settled its claim with the Principal, or any of its Affiliates, for an amount that results in no Loss to SBA or in no amount owed for Imminent Breach payments, or OSG finds good cause for reinstating the Principal notwithstanding the Loss to SBA or amount owed for Imminent Breach payments; or

(ii) OSG and the Surety determine that further bond guarantees are appropriate after the Principal was deemed ineligible for further SBA bond guarantees under paragraph (a)(1), (2), (3), (5) or (6) of this section.

(2) A PSB Surety may:

(i) Recommend that such Principal's eligibility be reinstated, and OSG may agree to reinstate the Principal, if the Surety has settled its claim with the Principal, or any of its Affiliates, for an amount that results in no Loss to SBA or in no amount owed for Imminent Breach payments, or OSG finds good cause for reinstating the Principal notwithstanding the Loss to SBA or amount owed for Imminent Breach payments; or

(ii) Reinstate a Principal's eligibility upon the Surety's determination that further bond guarantees are appropriate after the Principal was deemed ineligible for further SBA bond guarantees under paragraph (a)(1), (2), (3), (5) or (6) of this section.

(c) *Underwriting after reinstatement.* A guarantee application submitted after reinstatement of the Principal's eligibility is subject to a very stringent underwriting review.

[61 FR 3271, Jan. 31, 1996, as amended at 81 FR 23565, Apr. 22, 2016]

§ 115.15 Underwriting and servicing standards.

(a) *Underwriting.* (1) Sureties must evaluate the credit, capacity, and character of a Principal using standards generally accepted by the surety industry and in accordance with SBA's Standard Operating Procedures on underwriting and the Surety's principles and practices on unguaranteed bonds. The Principal must satisfy the eligibility requirements set forth in § 115.13. The Surety must reasonably expect that the Principal will successfully perform the Contract to be bonded.

(2) The terms and conditions of the bond and the Contract must be reasonable in light of the risks involved and the extent of the Surety's participation. The bond must satisfy the eligibility requirements set forth in § 115.12(b). The Surety must be satisfied as to the reasonableness of cost and the feasibility of successful completion of the Contract.

(b) *Servicing.* The Surety must ensure that the Principal remains viable and eligible for SBA's Surety Bond Guarantee Program, must monitor the Principal's progress on bonded Contracts guaranteed by SBA, and must request job status reports from Obligees of Final Bonds guaranteed by SBA. Documentation of the job status requests must be maintained by the Surety.

§ 115.16 Determination of Surety's Loss.

Loss is determined as follows:

(a) *Loss under a Bid Bond* is the lesser of the penal sum or the amount which is the difference between the bonded bid and the next higher responsive bid. In either case, the Loss is reduced by any amounts the Surety recovers by reason of the Principal's defenses against the Obligee's demand for performance by the Principal and any sums the Surety recovers from indemnitors and other salvage.

(b) *Loss under a Payment Bond* is, at the Surety's option, the sum necessary to pay all just and timely claims against the Principal for the value of labor, materials, equipment and supplies furnished for use in the performance of the bonded Contract and other covered debts, or the penal sum of the Payment Bond. In either case, the Loss includes interest (if any), but Loss is reduced by any amounts recovered (through offset or otherwise) by reason of the Principal's claims against laborers, materialmen, subcontractors, suppliers, or other rightful claimants, and by any amounts recovered from indemnitors and other salvage.

(c) *Loss under a Performance Bond* is, at the Surety's option, the sum necessary to meet the cost of fulfilling the terms of a bonded Contract or the penal sum of the bond. In either case, the Loss includes interest (if any), but Loss is reduced by any amounts recovered (through offset or otherwise) by reason of the Principal's defenses or causes of action against the Obligee, and by any amounts recovered from indemnitors and other salvage.

(d) *Loss under an Ancillary Bond* is the amount covered by such bond which is attributable to the Contract for which guaranteed Final Bonds were Executed.

(e) *Loss includes* the following expenses if they are itemized, documented and attributable solely to the Loss under the guaranteed bond:

(1) Amounts actually paid by the Surety for specialized services that are provided under contract by an outside consultant, which is not an Affiliate of the Surety, provided that such services are beyond the capability of the Surety's salaried claims staff, and amounts actually paid by the Surety for travel expenses of the Surety's claims staff. The cost of the consultant's services and the travel expenses of the Surety's claims staff must be reasonable and

necessary and must specifically concern the investigation, adjustment, negotiation, compromise, settlement of, or resistance to a claim for Loss resulting from the breach of the terms of the bonded Contract. The cost allocation method must be reasonable and must comply with generally accepted accounting principles; and

(2) Amounts actually paid by the Surety for court costs and reasonable attorney's fees incurred to mitigate any Loss under paragraphs (a) through (e)(1) of this section including suits to obtain sums due from Obligees, indemnitors, Principals and others.

(f) *Loss does not include* the following expenses:

(1) Any unallocated expenses, all direct and indirect costs incurred by the Surety's salaried claims staff (except for reasonable and necessary travel expenses of such staff), or any clear mark-up on expenses or any overhead of the Surety, its attorney, or any other consultant hired by the Surety or the attorney;

(2) Expenses paid for any suits, cross-claims, or counterclaims filed against the United States of America or any of its agencies, officers, or employees unless the Surety has received, prior to filing such suit or claim, written concurrence from SBA that the suit may be filed;

(3) Attorney's fees and court costs incurred by the Surety in a suit by or against SBA or its Administrator;

(4) Fees, costs, or other payments, including tort damages, arising from a successful tort suit or claim by a Principal or any other Person against the Surety; and

(5) Any costs that arise from the Principal's failure to secure and maintain insurance coverage required by the Contract or Order, or any costs that result from any claims or judgments that exceed the amount of any insurance coverage required by the Contract or Order, as well as any costs that arise as a result of any agreement by the Principal in the Contract or Order to indemnify the Obligee or any other Persons.

[61 FR 3271, Jan. 31, 1996, as amended at 76 FR 2572, Jan. 14, 2011; 81 FR 23566, Apr. 22, 2016]

§ 115.17 Minimization of Surety's Loss.

(a) *Indemnity agreements and collateral*—(1) *Requirements*. The Surety must take all reasonable action to minimize risk of Loss including, but not limited to, obtaining from each Principal a written indemnity agreement which covers actual Losses under the Contract and Imminent Breach payments under § 115.34(a) or § 115.69. The indemnity agreement must be secured by such collateral as the Surety or SBA finds appropriate. Indemnity agreements from other Persons, secured or unsecured, may also be required by the Surety or SBA.

(2) *Prohibitions*. No indemnity agreement may be obtained from the Surety, its agent or any other representative of the Surety. The Surety must not separately collateralize the portion of its bond which is not guaranteed by SBA.

(b) *Salvage and recovery*—(1) *General*. The Surety must pursue all possible sources of salvage and recovery. Salvage and recovery includes all payments made in settlement of the Surety's claim, even though the Surety has incurred other losses as a result of that Principal which are not reimbursable by SBA.

(2) *SBA's share*. SBA is entitled to its guaranteed percentage of all salvage and recovery from a defaulted Principal, its guarantors and indemnitors, and any other party, received by the Surety in connection with the guaranteed bond or any other bond issued by the Surety on behalf of the Principal unless such recovery is unquestionably identifiable as related solely to the non-guaranteed bond. The Surety must reimburse or credit SBA (in the same proportion as SBA's share of Loss) within 45 days of receipt of any recovery by the Surety.

(3) *Multiple Sureties*. In any dispute between two or more Sureties concerning recovery under SBA guaranteed bonds, the dispute must first be brought to the attention of OSG for an attempt at mediation and settlement.

[61 FR 3271, Jan. 31, 1996, as amended at 79 FR 2087, Jan. 13, 2014]

§ 115.18 Refusal to issue further guarantees; suspension and termination of PSB status.

(a) *Improper surety bond guarantee practices*—(1) *Imprudent practices.* SBA may refuse to issue further guarantees to a Prior Approval Surety or may suspend the preferred status of a PSB Surety, by written notice stating all reasons for such decision and the effective date. Reasons for such a decision include, but are not limited to, a determination that the Surety (in its underwriting, its efforts to minimize Loss, its claims or recovery practices, or its documentation related to SBA guaranteed bonds) has failed to adhere to prudent standards or practices, including any standards or practices required by SBA, as compared to those of other Sureties participating in the same SBA Surety Bond Guarantee Program to a comparable degree.

(2) *Regulatory violations, fraud.* Acts of wrongdoing such as fraud, material misrepresentation, breach of the Prior Approval or PSB Agreement, the Surety's failure to continue to comply with the requirements set forth in § 115.11, or regulatory violations (as defined in § 115.19(d) and (h)) also constitute sufficient grounds for refusal to issue further guarantees, or in the case of a PSB Surety, termination of preferred status.

(3) *Audit; records.* The failure of a Surety to consent to SBA's audit or to maintain and produce records constitutes grounds for SBA to refuse to issue further guarantees for a Prior Approval Surety, to suspend a PSB Surety from participation, and to refuse to honor claims submitted by a Prior Approval or PSB Surety until the Surety consents to the audit.

(4) *Excessive Losses.* If a Surety experiences excessive Losses on SBA guaranteed bonds relative to those of other Sureties participating in the same SBA Surety Bond Guarantee Program to a comparable degree, SBA may also require the renegotiation of the guarantee percentage and/or SBA's charge to the Surety for bonds executed thereafter.

(b) *Lack of business integrity.* A Surety's participation in the Surety Bond Guarantee Programs may be denied, suspended, or terminated upon the occurrence of any event in paragraphs (b) (1) through (5) of this section involving any of the following Persons: The Surety or any of its officers, directors, partners, or other individuals holding at least 20% of the Surety's voting securities, and any agents, underwriters, or any individual empowered to act on behalf of any of the preceding Persons.

(1) If a State or other authority has revoked, canceled, or suspended the license required of such Person to engage in the surety business, the right of such Person to participate in the SBA Surety Bond Guarantee Program may be denied, terminated, or suspended, as applicable, in that jurisdiction or in other jurisdictions. Ineligibility or suspension from the Surety Bond Guarantee Programs is for at least the duration of the license suspension.

(2) If such Person has been indicted or otherwise formally charged with a misdemeanor or felony bearing on such Person's fitness to participate in the Surety Bond Guarantee Programs, the participation of such Person may be suspended pending disposition of the charge. Upon conviction, participation may be denied or terminated.

(3) If a final civil judgment is entered holding that such Person has committed a breach of trust or violation of a law or regulation protecting the integrity of business transactions or relationships, participation may be denied or terminated.

(4) If such Person has made a material misrepresentation or willfully false statement in the presentation of oral or written information to SBA in connection with an application for a surety bond guarantee or the presentation of a claim, or committed a material breach of the Prior Approval or PSB Agreement or a material violation of the regulations (all as described in § 115.19), participation may be denied or terminated.

(5) If such Person is debarred, suspended, voluntarily excluded from, or declared ineligible for participation in Federal programs, participation may be denied or terminated.

(c) *Notification requirement.* The Prior Approval or PSB Surety must promptly notify SBA of the occurrence of any event in paragraphs (b) (1) through (5) of this section, or if any of the Persons described in paragraph (b) of this section does not, or ceases to, qualify as a Surety. SBA may require submission of a Statement of Personal History (SBA Form 912) from any of these Persons.

(d) *SBA proceedings.* Decisions to suspend, terminate, deny participation in, or deny reinstatement in the Surety Bond Guarantee program are made by the D/SG. A Surety may file a petition for review of suspensions and terminations with the SBA Office of Hearings and Appeals (OHA) under part 134 of this chapter. SBA's Administrator may, pending a decision pursuant to part 134 of this chapter, suspend the participation of any Surety for any of the causes listed in paragraphs (b) (1) through (5) of this section.

(e) *Effect on guarantee.* A guarantee issued by SBA before a suspension or termination under this section remains in effect, subject to SBA's right to deny liability under the guarantee.

[61 FR 3271, Jan. 31, 1996, as amended at 81 FR 23566, Apr. 22, 2016]

§ 115.19 Denial of liability.

In addition to equitable and legal defenses and remedies under contract law, the Act, and the regulations in this Part, SBA is relieved of liability in whole or in part within its discretion if any of the circumstances in paragraphs (a) through (h) of this section exist, except that SBA shall not deny liability on Prior Approval bonds based solely upon material information that was provided to SBA as part of the Surety's guarantee application.

(a) *Excess Contract or bond amount.* The total Contract or Order amount at the time of Execution of the bond exceeds the Applicable Statutory Limit (see § 115.10) or the bond amount at any time exceeds the total Contract or Order amount.

(b) *Misrepresentation or fraud.* The Surety obtained the Prior Approval or PSB Agreement, or applied for reimbursement for losses, by fraud or material misrepresentation. Material misrepresentation includes (but is not limited to) both the making of an untrue statement of material fact and the omission of a statement of material fact necessary to make a statement not misleading in light of the circumstances in which it was made. Material misrepresentation also includes the adoption by the Surety of a material misstatement made by others which the Surety knew or under generally accepted underwriting standards should have known to be false or misleading. The Surety's failure to disclose its ownership (or the ownership by any owner of at least 20% of the Surety's equity) of an interest in a Principal or an Obligee is considered the omission of a statement of material fact.

(c) *Material breach.* The Surety has committed a material breach of one or more terms or conditions of its Prior Approval or PSB Agreement. A material breach is considered to have occurred if:

(1) Such breach (or such breaches in the aggregate) causes an increase in the Contract amount or in the bond amount of at least 25% or $500,000 of the original contract or bond amount, whichever is less; or

(2) One of the conditions under Part B of Title IV of the Investment Act is not met.

(d) *Substantial regulatory violation.* The Surety has committed a "substantial violation" of SBA regulations. For purposes of this paragraph, a "substantial violation" is a violation which causes an increase in the bond amount of at least 25% or $500,000 of the original contract or bond amount, whichever is less in the aggregate, or is contrary to the purposes of the Surety Bond Guarantee Programs.

(e) *Alteration.* Without obtaining prior written approval from SBA (which may be conditioned upon payment of additional fees), the Surety agrees to or acquiesces in any material alteration in the terms, conditions, or provisions of the bond, including but not limited to the following acts:

(1) Naming as an Obligee or co-Obligee any Person that does not qualify as an Obligee under § 115.10; or

(2) In the case of a Prior Approval Surety, acquiescing in any alteration to the bond which would increase the bond amount by at least 25% or $500,000 of the original contract or bond amount, whichever is less.

(f) *Timeliness.* (1) Either:

(i) The bond was Executed prior to the date of SBA's guarantee; or

(ii) The bond was Executed (or approved, if the Surety is legally bound by such approval) after the work under the Contract had begun, unless SBA executes a "Surety Bond Guarantee Agreement Addendum" (SBA Form 991) after receiving all of the following from the Surety:

(A) Satisfactory evidence, including a certified copy of the Contract (or a sworn affidavit from the Principal), showing that the bond requirement was contained in the original Contract, or other documentation satisfactory to SBA, showing why a bond was not previously obtained and is now being required;

(B) Certification by the Principal that all taxes and labor costs are current, and listing all suppliers and subcontractors, indicating that they are all paid to date, and attaching a waiver of lien from each; or an explanation satisfactory to SBA why such documentation cannot be produced; and

(C) Certification by the Obligee that all payments due under the Contract to date have been made and that the job has been satisfactorily completed to date.

(2)(i) For purposes of paragraph (f)(1)(ii) of this section, work under a Contract is considered to have begun when a Principal takes any action at the job site which would have exposed its Surety to liability under applicable law had a bond been Executed (or approved, if the Surety is legally bound by such approval) at the time.

(ii) For purposes of this paragraph (f), the Surety must maintain a contemporaneous record of the Execution and approval of each bond.

(g) *Delinquent fees.* The Surety has not remitted to SBA the Principal's payment for the full amount of the guarantee fee within the time period required under § 115.30(d) for Prior Approval Sureties or § 115.66 for PSB Sureties, or has not made timely payment of the Surety's fee within the time period required by § 115.32(c). SBA may reinstate the guarantee upon showing that the contract is not in default and that a valid reason exists why a timely remittance or payment was not made.

(h) *Other regulatory violations.* The occurrence of any of the following:

(1) The Principal on the bonded Contract is not a small business;

(2) The bond was not required under the bid solicitation or the original Contract;

(3) The bond was not eligible for guarantee by SBA because the bonded contract was not a Contract as defined in § 115.10;

(4) The loss occurred under a bond that was not guaranteed by SBA;

(5) The loss incurred by the Surety was not a Loss as determined under § 115.16; or

(6) The Surety's loss under a Performance Bond did not result from the Principal's breach or Imminent Breach of the Contract.

[61 FR 3271, Jan. 31, 1996, as amended at 66 FR 30804, June 8, 2001; 72 FR 34599, July 25, 2007; 74 FR 36110, July 22, 2009; 79 FR 2087, Jan. 13, 2014; 82 FR 39501, Aug. 21, 2017]

§ 115.20 Insolvency of Surety.

(a) *Successor in interest.* If a Surety becomes insolvent, all rights or benefits conferred on the Surety under a valid and binding Prior Approval or PSB Agreement will accrue only to the trustee or receiver of the Surety. SBA will not be liable to the trustee or receiver of the insolvent Surety except for the guaranteed portion of any Loss incurred and actually paid by such Surety or its trustee or receiver under the guaranteed bonds.

(b) *Filing requirement.* The trustee or receiver must submit to SBA quarterly status reports accounting for all funds received and all settlements being considered.

§ 115.21 Audits and investigations.

(a) *Audits*—(1) *Scope of audit.* SBA may audit in the office of a Prior Approval or PSB Surety, the Surety's attorneys or consultants, or the Principal or its subcontractors, all documents, files, books, records, tapes, disks and other material relevant to SBA's guarantee, commitments to guarantee a surety bond, or agreements to indemnify the Prior Approval or PSB Surety. See § 115.18(a)(3) for consequences of failure to comply with this section.

(2) *Frequency of PSB audits*. Each PSB Surety is subject to an audit at least once every 3 years by examiners selected and approved by SBA.

(b) *Records*. The Surety must maintain the records listed in this paragraph (b) for the term of each bond, plus any additional time required to settle any claims of the Surety for reimbursement from SBA and to attempt salvage or other recovery, plus an additional 3 years. If there are any unresolved audit findings in relation to a particular bond, the Surety must maintain the related records until the findings are resolved. The records to be maintained include the following:

(1) A copy of the bond;

(2) A copy of the bonded Contract;

(3) All documentation submitted by the Principal in applying for the bond;

(4) All information gathered by the Surety in reviewing the Principal's application;

(5) All documentation of any of the events set forth in § 115.35(a) or § 115.65(c)(2);

(6) All records of any transaction for which the Surety makes payment under or in connection with the bond, including but not limited to claims, bills (including lawyers' and consultants' bills), judgments, settlement agreements and court or arbitration decisions, consultants' reports, Contracts and receipts;

(7) All documentation relating to efforts to mitigate Losses, including documentation required by § 115.34(a) or § 115.69 concerning Imminent Breach;

(8) All records of any accounts into which fees and funds obtained in mitigation of Losses were paid and from which payments were made under the bond, and any other trust accounts, and any reconciliations of such accounts;

(9) Job status reports received from Obligees and documentation of each unanswered request for a job status report; and

(10) All documentation relating to any collateral held by or available to the Surety.

(c) *Purpose of audit*. SBA's audit will determine, but not be limited to:

(1) The adequacy and sufficiency of the Surety's underwriting and credit analysis, its documentation of claims and claims settlement procedures and activities, and its recovery procedures and practices;

(2) The Surety's minimization of Loss, including the exercise of bond options upon Contract default; and

(3) The Surety's loss ratio in comparison with other Sureties participating in the same SBA Surety Bond Guarantee Program to a comparable degree.

(d) *Investigations*. SBA may conduct investigations to inquire into the possible violation by any Person of the Small Business Act or the Investment Act, or of any rule or regulation under those Acts, or of any order issued under those Acts, or of any Federal law relating to programs and operations of SBA.

[61 FR 3271, Jan. 31, 1996, as amended at 72 FR 34599, June 25, 2007]

§ 115.22 Quarterly Contract Completion Report.

The Surety must submit a Quarterly Contract Completion Report within 45 days after the close of each fiscal year quarter ending December 31, March 31, June 30, and September 30, that identifies each contract successfully completed during the quarter. The report shall include:

(a) The SBA Surety Bond Guarantee Number,

(b) Name of the Principal,

(c) The original Contract Dollar Amount,

(d) The revised Contract Dollar Amount (if applicable),

(e) The date of Contract completion, and

(f) A summary specifying the fee amounts paid to SBA by the Surety and Principal, the fee amounts due to SBA as a result of any increases in the Contract amount, and the fee amounts to be refunded to the Principal or rebated to the Surety as a result of any decreases in the Contract amount.

[82 FR 39501, Aug. 21, 2017]

Subpart B—Guarantees Subject to Prior Approval

§ 115.30 Submission of Surety's guarantee application.

(a) *Legal effect of application*. By submitting an application to SBA for a bond guarantee, the Prior Approval Surety certifies that the Principal meets the eligibility requirements set forth in § 115.13 and that the underwriting standards set forth in § 115.15 have been met.

(b) *SBA's determination.* SBA's approval or decline of a guarantee application is made in writing by an authorized SBA officer. The officer may provide telephone notice before the Prior Approval Surety receives SBA's guarantee approval form if the officer has already signed the form. In the event of a conflict between the telephone notice and the written form, the written form controls.

(c) *Reconsideration-appeal of SBA determination.* A Prior Approval Surety may request reconsideration of a decline from the SBA officer who made the decision. If the decision on reconsideration is negative, the Surety may appeal to an individual designated by the D/SG. If the decision is again adverse, the Surety may appeal to the D/SG, who will make the final decision.

(d) *Prior Approval Agreement.* To apply for a bond guarantee, a Prior Approval Surety must submit one of the following forms:

(1) *Surety Bond Guarantee Agreement (SBA Form 990).* A Prior Approval Surety may complete and submit a Surety Bond Guarantee Agreement (SBA Form 990) to SBA for each Bid Bond or Final Bond, and this Form must be approved by SBA prior to the Surety's Execution of the bond, except in the case of a surety bonding line approved by SBA under § 115.33(d). The guarantee fees owed in connection with Final Bonds must be paid in accordance with § 115.32.

(2) *Quick Bond Guarantee Application and Agreement (SBA Form 990A)*—(i) *General procedures.* Except as provided in paragraph (d)(2)(ii) of this section, a Prior Approval Surety may complete and submit the Quick Bond Guarantee Application and Agreement (SBA Form 990A) to SBA for each Bid Bond or Final Bond, and this Form must be approved by SBA prior to the Surety's Execution of the bond. SBA Form 990A is a streamlined application form that may be used only for contract amounts that do not exceed $400,000 at the time of application. The guarantee fees owed in connection with Final Bonds must be paid in accordance with § 115.32.

(ii) *Exclusions.* SBA Form 990A may not be used under the following circumstances:

(A) The Principal has previously defaulted on any contract or has had any claims or complaints filed against it with any court or administrative agency;

(B) Work on the Contract commenced before a bond is Executed;

(C) The time for completion of the Contract exceeds 12 months;

(D) The Contract includes a provision for liquidated damages that exceed $1,000 per day;

(E) The Contract involves asbestos abatement, hazardous waste removal, demolition, or timber sales; or

(F) The bond would be issued under a surety bonding line approved under § 115.33.

[61 FR 3271, Jan. 31, 1996, as amended at 77 FR 41665, July 16, 2012; 79 FR 2087, Jan. 13, 2014; 82 FR 39501, Aug. 21, 2017]

§ 115.31 Guarantee percentage.

(a) *Ninety percent.* SBA reimburses a Prior Approval Surety for 90% of the Loss incurred and paid if:

(1) The total amount of the Contract at the time of Execution of the bond is $100,000 or less; or

(2) The bond was issued on behalf of a small business owned and controlled by socially and economically disadvantaged individuals, on behalf of a qualified HUBZone small business concern, or on behalf of a small business owned and controlled by veterans or a small business owned and controlled by Service-disabled veterans.

(b) *Eighty percent.* SBA reimburses a Prior Approval Surety in an amount not to exceed 80% of the Loss incurred and paid on bonds for Contracts in excess of $100,000 which are executed on behalf of non-disadvantaged concerns.

(c) *Contract increase to over $100,000.* If the Contract amount increases to more than $100,000 after Execution of the bond, the guarantee percentage decreases by one percentage point for each $5,000 of increase or part thereof, but it does not decrease below 80%. This provision applies only to guarantees which qualify under paragraph (a)(1) of this section.

(d) *Contract or Order increases exceed Applicable Statutory Limit.* If the Contract or Order amount is increased above the Applicable Statutory Limit after Execution of the bond, SBA's share of the Loss is limited to that percentage of the increased Contract or Order amount that the Applicable Statutory Limit represents multiplied by the guarantee percentage approved by SBA. For example, if a contract amount increases to $6,800,000, SBA's share of the loss under an 80% guarantee is limited to 76.5% [6,500,000/6,800,000 = 95.6% x 80% = 76.5%].

(e) *Contract or Order decrease to $100,000 or less.* If the Contract or Order amount decreases to $100,000, or less, after Execution of the bond, SBA's guarantee percentage increases to 90% if the Surety provides SBA with evidence supporting the decrease and any other information or documents requested.

[61 FR 3271, Jan. 31, 1996, as amended at 64 FR 18324, Apr. 14, 1999; 66 FR 30804, June 8, 2001; 72 FR 34599, June 25, 2007; 74 FR 36110, July 22, 2009; 79 FR 2087, Jan. 13, 2014]

§ 115.32 Fees and Premiums.

(a) *Surety's Premium.* A Prior Approval Surety must not charge a Principal an amount greater than that authorized by the appropriate insurance department. The Surety must not require the Principal to purchase casualty or other insurance or any other services from the Surety or any Affiliate or agent of the Surety. The Surety must not charge non-Premium fees to a Principal unless the Surety performs other services for the Principal, the additional fee is permitted by State law, and the Principal agrees to the fee.

(b) *SBA charge to Principal.* SBA does not charge Principals application or Bid Bond guarantee fees. If SBA guarantees a Final Bond, the Principal must pay a guarantee fee equal to a certain percentage of the Contract amount. The percentage is determined by SBA and is published in Notices in the FEDERAL REGISTER from time to time. The Principal's fee is rounded to the nearest dollar, and is to be remitted to SBA with the form submitted under either § 115.30(d)(1) or (2). See paragraph (d) of this section for additional requirements when the Contract amount changes.

(c) *SBA charge to Surety.* SBA does not charge Sureties application or Bid Bond guarantee fees. Subject to § 115.18(a)(4), the Surety must pay SBA a guarantee fee on each guaranteed bond (other than a Bid Bond) within 60 calendar days after SBA's approval of the Prior Approval Agreement. The fee is a certain percentage of the bond premium determined by SBA and published in Notices in the FEDERAL REGISTER from time to time. The fee is rounded to the nearest dollar. SBA does not receive any portion of a Surety's non-premium charges. See paragraph (d) of this section for additional requirements when the Contract or bond amount changes.

(d) *Contract or bond increases/decreases*—(1) *Notification and approval.* The Prior Approval Surety must notify SBA of any increases or decreases in the Contract or bond amount that aggregate 25% or $500,000 of the original contract or bond amount, whichever is less, as soon as the Surety acquires knowledge of the change. Whenever the original bond amount increases as a result of a single change order of at least 25% or $500,000 of the original contract or bond amount, whichever is less, the prior written approval of such increase by SBA is required on a supplemental Prior Approval Agreement and is conditioned upon payment by the Surety of the increase in the Principal's guarantee fee as set forth in paragraph (d)(2) of this section. In notifying SBA of any increase or decrease in the Contract or bond amount, the Surety must use the same form (SBA Form 990 or SBA Form 990A) that it used in applying for the original bond guarantee.

(2) *Increases; fees.* The payment for the increase in the Principal's guarantee fee, which is computed on the increase in the Contract amount, is due upon notification of the increase in the Contract or bond amount under this paragraph (d). If the increase in the Principal's fee is less than $40, no payment is due until the total amount of increases in the Principal's fee equals or exceeds $40. The Surety's payment of the increase in the Surety's guarantee fee, computed on the increase in the bond Premium, must be submitted

to SBA within 60 calendar days of SBA's approval of the Prior Approval Agreement, unless the amount of such increased guarantee fee is less than $40. When the total amount of increase in the guarantee fee equals or exceeds $40, the Surety must remit the fee within 60 calendar days.

(3) *Decreases; refunds.* Whenever SBA is notified of a decrease in the Contract or bond amount, SBA will refund to the Principal a proportionate amount of the Principal's guarantee fee and rebate to the Surety a proportionate amount of SBA's Premium share in the ordinary course of business. If the amount to be refunded or rebated is less than $40, such refund or rebate will not be made until the amounts to be refunded or rebated, respectively, aggregate at least $40. Upon receipt of the refund, the Surety must promptly pay a proportionate amount of its Premium to the Principal.

[61 FR 3271, Jan. 31, 1996, as amended at 72 FR 34599, June 25, 2007; 77 FR 41665, July 16, 2012; 79 FR 2087, Jan. 13, 2014; 82 FR 39502, Aug. 21, 2017]

§ 115.33 Surety bonding line.

A surety bonding line is a written commitment by SBA to a Prior Approval Surety which provides for the Surety's Execution of multiple bonds for a specified small business strictly within pre-approved terms, conditions and limitations. In applying for a bonding line, the Surety must provide SBA with information on the applicant as requested. In addition to the other limitations and provisions set forth in this part 115, the following conditions apply to each surety bonding line:

(a) *Underwriting.* A bonding line may be issued by SBA for a Principal only if the underwriting evaluation is satisfactory. The Prior Approval Surety must require the Principal to keep it informed of all its contracts, whether bonded by the same or another surety or unbonded, during the term of the bonding line.

(b) *Bonding line conditions.* The bonding line contains limitations on the following:

(1) The term of the bonding line, not to exceed 1 year subject to renewal in writing;

(2) The total dollar amount of the Principal's bonded and unbonded work on hand at any time, including outstanding bids, during the term of the bonding line;

(3) The number of such bonded and unbonded contracts outstanding at any time during the term of the bonding line;

(4) The maximum dollar amount of any single guaranteed bonded Contract;

(5) The timing of Execution of bonds under the bonding line—bonds must be dated and Executed before the work on the underlying Contract has begun, or the Surety must submit to SBA the documentation required under § 115.19(f)(1)(ii); and

(6) Any other limitation related to type, specialty of work, geographical area, or credit.

(c) *Excess bonding.* If, after a bonding line is issued, the Principal desires a bond and the Surety desires a guarantee exceeding a limitation of the bonding line, the Surety must submit an application to SBA under regular procedures.

(d) *Submission of forms to SBA*—(1) *Bid Bonds.* Within 15 business days after the Execution of any Bid Bonds under a bonding line, the Surety must submit a "Surety Bond Guarantee Underwriting Review" (SBA Form 994B) to SBA for approval. If the Surety fails to submit the form within this time period, SBA's guarantee of the bond will be void from its inception unless SBA determines otherwise upon a showing that a valid reason exists why the timely submission was not made.

(2) *Final Bonds.* Within 15 business days after the Execution of any Final Bonds under a bonding line, the Surety must submit a Surety Bond Guarantee Underwriting Review (SBA Form 994B) and a Surety Bond Guarantee Agreement (SBA Form 990) to SBA for approval. If the surety fails to submit these forms within the time period or the guarantee fees are not paid in accordance with § 115.32, SBA's guarantee of the bond will be void from its inception unless SBA determines otherwise upon a showing that the Contract is not in default and a valid reason exists why the timely submission was not made.

(3) *Additional information.* The Surety must submit any other data SBA requests.

(e) *Cancellation of bonding line*—(1) *Optional cancellation.* Either SBA or the Surety may cancel a bonding line at any time, with or without cause, upon written notice to the other party. Upon the receipt of any adverse information concerning the Principal, the Surety must promptly notify SBA, and SBA may cancel the bonding line.

(2) *Mandatory cancellation.* Upon the occurrence of a default by the Principal, whether under a contract bonded by the same or another surety or an unbonded contract, the Surety must immediately cancel the bonding line.

(3) *Effect of cancellation.* Cancellation of a bonding line by SBA is effective upon receipt of written notice by the Surety. Bonds issued before the effective date of cancellation remain guaranteed by SBA. Upon cancellation by SBA or the Surety, the Surety must promptly notify the Principal in writing.

[61 FR 3271, Jan. 31, 1996, as amended at 77 FR 41665, July 16, 2012]

§ 115.34 Minimization of Surety's Loss.

(a) *Imminent Breach*—(1) *Prior approval requirement.* SBA will reimburse its guaranteed share of payments made by a Surety to avoid or attempt to avoid an Imminent Breach of the terms of a Contract covered by an SBA guaranteed bond only if the payments were made with the prior approval of OSG. OSG's prior approval will be given only if the Surety demonstrates to SBA's satisfaction that a breach is imminent and that there is no other recourse to prevent such breach.

(2) *Amount of reimbursement.* The aggregate of the payments by SBA to avoid Imminent Breach cannot exceed 10% of the Contract amount, unless the Administrator finds that a greater payment (not to exceed the guaranteed share of the bond penalty) is necessary and reasonable. In no event will SBA make any duplicate payment pursuant to this or any other provision of this part 115.

(3) *Recordkeeping requirement.* The Surety must keep records of payments made to avoid Imminent Breach.

(b) *Salvage and recovery.* A Prior Approval Surety must pursue all possible sources of salvage and recovery until SBA concurs with the Surety's recommendation for a discontinuance or for a settlement. The Surety must certify that continued pursuit of salvage and recovery would be neither economically feasible nor a viable strategy in maximizing recovery. See also § 115.17(b).

§ 115.35 Claims for reimbursement of Losses.

(a) *Notification requirements*—(1) *Events requiring notification.* A Prior Approval Surety must notify OSG of the occurrence of any of the following:

(i) Legal action under the bond has been initiated.

(ii) The Obligee has declared the Principal to be in default under the Contract.

(iii) The Surety has established a claim reserve for the bond.

(iv) The Surety has received any adverse information concerning the Principal's financial condition or possible inability to complete the project or to pay laborers or suppliers.

(2) *Timing of notification.* Notification must be made in writing at the earlier of the time the Surety applies for a guarantee on behalf of an affected Principal, or within 30 days of the date the Surety acquires knowledge, or should have acquired knowledge, of any of the listed events.

(b) *Surety action.* The Surety must take all necessary steps to mitigate Losses resulting from any of the events in paragraph (a) of this section, including the disposal at fair market value of any collateral held by or available to the Surety. Unless SBA notifies the Surety otherwise, the Surety must take charge of all claims or suits arising from a defaulted bond, and compromise, settle and defend such suits. The Surety must handle and process all claims under the bond and all settlements and recoveries as it does on non-guaranteed bonds.

(c) *Claim reimbursement requests.* (1) Claims for reimbursement for Losses which the Surety has paid must be submitted (together with a copy of the bond, the bonded Contract, and any indemnity agreements) with the initial claim to OSG on a "Default Report, Claim for Reimbursement and Report of Recoveries" (SBA Form 994H), within 90 days from the time of each disbursement. Claims submitted after 90 days must be accompanied by substantiation satisfactory to SBA. The date of the claim for reimbursement is the date of receipt of the claim by SBA, or such later date as additional information requested by SBA is received.

(2) The Surety must also submit evidence of the disposal of all collateral at fair market value.

(3) SBA may request additional information prior to reimbursing the Surety for its Loss.

(4) Subject to the offset provisions of part 140, SBA pays its share of the Loss incurred and paid by the Surety within 45 days of receipt of the requisite information.

(5) Claims for reimbursement and any additional information submitted are subject to review and audit by SBA, including but not limited to the Surety's compliance with SBA's regulations and forms.

(d) *Status updates.* The Surety must submit semiannual status reports on each claim 6 months after the initial default notice, and then every 6 months. The Surety must notify SBA immediately of any substantial changes in the status of the claim or the amounts of Loss reserves.

(e) *Reservation of SBA rights.* The payment by SBA of a Surety's claim does not waive or invalidate any of the terms of the Prior Approval Agreement, the regulations set forth in this part 115, or any defense SBA may have against the Surety. Within 30 days of receipt of notification that a claim or any portion of a claim should not have been paid by SBA, the Surety must repay the specified amounts to SBA.

[61 FR 3271, Jan. 31, 1996, as amended at 79 FR 2087, Jan. 13, 2014]

§115.36 Indemnity settlements.

(a) An indemnity settlement occurs when a defaulted Principal and its Surety agree upon an amount, less than the actual loss under the bond, which will satisfy the Principal's indebtedness to the Surety. Sureties must not agree to any indemnity settlement proposal or enter into any such agreement without SBA's concurrence.

(b) Any settlement proposal submitted for SBA's consideration must include current financial information, including financial statements, tax returns, and credit reports, together with the Surety's written recommendations. It should also indicate whether the Principal is interested in further bonding.

(c) The Surety must pay SBA its *pro rata* share of the settlement amount within 45 days of receipt. Prior to closing the file on a Principal, the Surety must certify that SBA has received its *pro rata* share of all indemnity recovery.

[61 FR 3271, Jan. 31, 1996, as amended at 79 FR 2087, Jan. 13, 2014; 81 FR 23566, Apr. 22, 2016]

Subpart C—Preferred Surety Bond (PSB) Guarantees

§115.60 Selection and admission of PSB Sureties.

(a) *Selection of PSB Sureties.* SBA's selection of PSB Sureties will be guided by, but not limited to, these factors:

(1) An underwriting limitation of at least $6,500,000 on the U.S. Treasury Department list of acceptable sureties;

(2) An agreement that the Surety will neither charge a bond premium in excess of that authorized by the appropriate State insurance department, nor impose any non-premium fee unless such fee is permitted by applicable State law and approved by SBA.

(3) Premium income from contract bonds guaranteed by any government agency (Federal, State or local) of no more than one- quarter of the total contract bond premium income of the Surety;

(4) The vesting of underwriting authority for SBA guaranteed bonds only in employees of the Surety;

(5) The rating or ranking designations assigned to the Surety by recognized authority.

(b) *Admission of PSB Sureties.* A Surety admitted to the PSB program must execute a PSB Agreement before approving SBA guaranteed bonds. No SBA guarantee attaches to bonds approved before the D/SG or designee has countersigned the Agreement. For a period of nine months following admission to the PSB program, the Surety must obtain SBA's prior written approval before executing a bond greater than $2 million so that SBA may evaluate the Surety's performance in its underwriting and claims and recovery functions. At the end of this nine month period, SBA may in its discretion extend this period to allow SBA to further evaluate the Surety's performance.

[61 FR 3271, Jan. 31, 1996, as amended at 66 FR 30804, June 8, 2001; 72 FR 34600, June 25, 2007; 81 FR 23566, Apr. 22, 2016; 82 FR 39502, Aug. 21, 2017]

§ 115.61 [Reserved]

§ 115.62 Prohibition on participation in Prior Approval program.

A PSB Surety is not eligible to submit applications under subpart B of this part. This prohibition does not extend to an Affiliate, as defined in 13 CFR § 121.103, of a PSB Surety that is not itself a PSB Surety provided that the relationship between the PSB Surety and the Affiliate has been fully disclosed to SBA and that such Affiliate has been approved by SBA to participate as a Prior Approval Surety pursuant to § 115.11.

[72 FR 34600, June 25, 2007]

§ 115.63 Allotment of guarantee authority.

(a) *General.* SBA allots to each PSB Surety a periodic maximum guarantee authority. No SBA guarantee attaches to bonds approved by a PSB Surety if the bonds exceed the allotted authority for the period in which the bonds are approved. No reliance on future authority is permitted. An allotment can be increased only by prior written permission of SBA.

(b) *Execution of Bid Bonds.* When the PSB Surety Executes a Bid Bond, SBA debits the Surety's allotment for an amount equal to the guarantee percentage of the estimated penal sum of the Final Bond SBA would guarantee if the Contract were awarded. If the Contract is then awarded for an amount other than the bid amount, or if the bid is withdrawn or the Bid Bond guarantee has expired (see § 115.12(c)), SBA debits or credits the Surety's allotment accordingly.

(c) *Execution of Final Bonds.* If the PSB Surety Executes a guaranteed Final Bond, but not the related Bid Bond, SBA debits the Surety's allotment for an amount equal to the guarantee percentage of the penal sum of the Final Bond. SBA will debit the allotment for increases, and credit the allotment for decreases, in the bond amount.

(d) *Release and non-issuance of Final Bonds.* The release of Final Bonds upon completion of the Contract does not restore the corresponding allotment. If, however, a PSB Surety approves a Final Bond but never issues the bond, SBA will credit the Surety's allotment for an amount equal to the guarantee percentage of the penal sum of the bond. In that event, the Surety must notify SBA as soon as possible, but in no event later than 5 business days after the non-issuance has been determined. Until the Surety has so notified SBA, it cannot rely on such credit.

§ 115.64 Timeliness requirement.

There must be no Execution or approval of a bond by a PSB Surety after commencement of work under a Contract unless the Surety obtains written approval from the D/SG. To apply for such approval, the Surety must submit a completed "Surety Bond Guarantee Agreement Addendum" (SBA Form 991), together with the evidence and certifications described in § 115.19(f)(1)(ii).

§ 115.65 General PSB procedures.

(a) *Retention of information.* A PSB Surety must comply with all applicable SBA regulations and obtain from its applicants all the information and certifications required by SBA. The PSB Surety must document compliance with SBA regulations and retain such certifications in its files, including a contemporaneous record of the date of approval and Execution of each bond. See also § 115.19(f). The certifications and other information must be made available for inspection by SBA or its agents and must be available for submission to SBA in connection with the Surety's claims for reimbursement.

The PSB Surety must retain the certifications and other information for the term of the bond, plus such additional time as may be required to settle any claims of the Surety for reimbursement from SBA and to attempt salvage or other recovery, plus an additional 3 years. If there are any unresolved audit findings in relation to a particular bond, the Surety must maintain the related certifications and other information until the findings are resolved.

(b) *Usual staff and procedures.* The approval, Execution and administration by a PSB Surety of SBA guaranteed bonds must be handled in the same manner and with the same staff as the Surety's activity outside the PSB program. The Surety must request job status reports from Obligees in accordance with its own procedures.

(c) *Notification to SBA*—(1) *Approvals.* A PSB Surety must notify SBA by electronic transmission or monthly bordereau, as agreed between the Surety and SBA, of all approved Bid and Final Bonds, and of the Surety's approval of increases and decreases in the Contract or bond amount. The notice must contain the information specified from time to time in agreements between the Surety and SBA. SBA may deny liability with respect to Final Bonds for which SBA has not received timely notice.

(2) *Other events requiring notification.* The PSB Surety must notify SBA within 30 calendar days of the name and address of any Principal against whom legal action on the bond has been instituted; whenever an Obligee has declared a default; whenever the Surety has established or added to a claim reserve; of the recovery of any amounts on the guaranteed bond; and of any decision by the Surety to bond any such Principal again.

§ 115.66 Fees.

The PSB Surety must pay SBA a certain percentage of the Premium it charges on Final Bonds. The PSB Surety must also remit to SBA the Principal's payment for its guarantee fee, equal to a certain percentage of the Contract amount. The fee percentages are determined by SBA and are published in Notices in the FEDERAL REGISTER from time to time. Each fee is rounded to the nearest dollar. The Surety must remit SBA's Premium share and the Principal's guarantee fee with the bordereau listing the related Final Bond, as required in the PSB Agreement.

§ 115.67 Changes in Contract or bond amount.

(a) *Increases.* The PSB Surety must process Contract or bond amount increases within its allotment in the same manner as initial guaranteed bond issuances (see § 115.65(c)(1)). The Surety must present checks for additional fees due from the Principal and the Surety on any increases aggregating 25% of the original Contract or bond amount or $500,000, whichever is less, and attach such payments to the respective monthly bordereau. If the additional Principal's fee or Surety's fee is less than $40, such fee is not due until all unpaid increases in such fee aggregate at least $40.

(b) *Decreases.* If the Contract or bond amount is decreased, SBA will refund to the Principal a proportionate amount of the guarantee fee, and adjust SBA's Premium share accordingly in the ordinary course of business. No refund or adjustment will be made until the amounts to be refunded or rebated, respectively, aggregate at least $40.

[61 FR 3271, Jan. 31, 1996, as amended at 79 FR 2087, Jan. 13, 2014; 82 FR 39502, Aug. 21, 2017]

§ 115.68 Guarantee percentage.

SBA reimburses a PSB Surety in the same percentages and under the same terms as set forth in § 115.31.

[82 FR 39502, Aug. 21, 2017]

§ 115.69 Imminent Breach.

(a) *No prior approval requirement.* SBA will reimburse a PSB Surety for the guaranteed portion of payments the Surety makes to avoid or attempt to avoid an Imminent Breach of the terms of a Contract covered by an SBA guaranteed bond. The aggregate of the payments by SBA under this section cannot exceed 10% of the Contract amount, unless the Administrator finds that a greater payment (not to exceed the guaranteed portion of the bond penalty) is necessary and reasonable. The PSB Surety does not need to obtain prior SBA approval to make Imminent Breach payments, except that the PSB Surety may request SBA to approve payments that exceed 10% of the Contract amount prior to the Surety making the payment. In no event will SBA make any duplicate payment under any provision of these regulations in this part.

(b) *Recordkeeping requirement.* The PSB Surety must keep records of payments made to avoid Imminent Breach.

[79 FR 2087, Jan. 13, 2014]

§ 115.70 Claims for reimbursement of Losses.

(a) *How claims are submitted.* A PSB Surety must submit claims for reimbursement on a form approved by SBA no later than 90 days from the date the Surety paid the amount. Loss is determined as of the date of receipt by SBA of the claim for reimbursement, or as of such later date as additional information requested by SBA is received. Subject to the offset provisions of part 140, SBA pays its share of Loss within 45 days of receipt of the requisite information. Claims for reimbursement and any additional information submitted are subject to review and audit by SBA.

(b) *Surety responsibilities.* The PSB Surety must take all necessary steps to mitigate Losses when legal action against a bond has been instituted, when the Obligee has declared a default, and when the Surety has established a claim reserve. The Surety may dispose of collateral at fair market value only. Unless SBA notifies the Surety otherwise, the Surety must take charge of all claims or suits arising from a defaulted bond, and compromise, settle or defend the suits. The Surety must handle and process all claims under the bond and all settlements and recoveries in the same manner as it does on non-guaranteed bonds.

(c) *Reservation of SBA's rights.* The payment by SBA of a PSB Surety's claim does not waive or invalidate any of the terms of the PSB Agreement, the regulations in this part 115, or any defense SBA may have against the Surety. Within 30 days of receipt of notification that a claim or any portion of a claim should not have been paid by SBA, the Surety must repay the specified amounts to SBA.

[61 FR 3271, Jan. 31, 1996, as amended at 79 FR 2087, Jan. 13, 2014]

§ 115.71 Denial of liability.

In addition to the grounds set forth in § 115.19, SBA may deny liability to a PSB Surety if:

(a) The PSB Surety's guaranteed bond was in an amount which, together with all other guaranteed bonds, exceeded the allotment for the period during which the bond was approved, and no prior SBA approval had been obtained;

(b) The PSB Surety's loss was incurred under a bond which was not listed on the bordereau for the period when it was approved; or

(c) The loss incurred by the PSB Surety is not attributable to the particular Contract for which an SBA guaranteed bond was approved.

PART 117—NONDISCRIMINATION IN FEDERALLY ASSISTED PROGRAMS OR ACTIVITIES OF SBA—EFFECTUATION OF THE AGE DISCRIMINATION ACT OF 1975, AS AMENDED

Sec.

AUTHORITY: Age Discrimination Act of 1975, 42 U.S.C. 6101 *et seq.*

SOURCE: 50 FR 41648, Oct. 11, 1985, unless otherwise noted.

EDITORIAL NOTE: Nomenclature changes to part 117 appear at 68 FR 51349, Aug. 26, 2003.

§ 117.1 Purpose.

The purpose of this part is to effectuate the provisions of The Age Discrimination Act of 1975, as amended (hereinafter referred to as the *Act*), to the end that no person in the United States shall, on the basis of age, be excluded from participation in, be denied the benefits of, or be subjected to discrimination under programs or activities receiving financial assistance or any financial activities of the Small Business Administration to which this Act applies. The Act also permits recipients of Federal funds to continue to use certain age distinctions and other factors other than age which meet the requirements of the Act and these regulations in the conduct of programs or activities and the provision of services to the public.

§ 117.2 Application of this part.

(a) This part applies to all recipients of Federal financial assistance administered by the Small Business Administration, whether or not the specific type of Federal financial assistance administered is listed in appendix A.

(b) For the purposes of this part, the prohibition against age discrimination applies to natural persons of all ages.

(c) This part does not apply to the employment practices of any recipients.

[50 FR 41648, Oct. 11, 1985, as amended at 68 FR 51349, Aug. 26, 2003]

§ 117.3 Definitions.

As used in this part:

(a) The term *act* means the Age Discrimination Act of 1975, as amended (Title III of Pub. L. 94–135).

(b) The term *action* means any act, activity, policy, rule, standard, or method of administration; or the use of any policy, rule, standard, or method of administration.

(c) The term *age* means how old a person is, or the number of years from the date of a person's birth.

(d) The term *age distinction* means any action using age or an age-related term.

(e) The term *age-related* means a word or words which necessarily imply a particular age or range of ages (for example, *children, adult, older persons*, but not *student*).

(f) The term *agency* means a Federal department or agency that is empowered to extend financial assistance.

(g) The term *applicant* means one who applies for Federal financial assistance.

(h) The term *Federal financial assistance* includes: (1) Grants and loans of Federal funds; (2) the grant or donation of Federal property and interests in property; (3) the detail of Federal personnel; (4) the sale and lease of, and the permission to use (on other than a casual or transient basis), Federal property or any interest in such property without consideration, or at a nominal consideration, or at a consideration which is reduced for the purpose of assisting the recipient, or in recognition of the public interest to be served by such sale or lease to the recipient; and (5) any Federal agreement, arrangement, or other contract which has as one of its purposes the provision of assistance.

(i) The term *normal operation* means the operation of a business or activity without significant changes that would impair its ability to meet its objectives.

(j) The term *program or activity* means all of the operations of any entity described in paragraphs (j)(1) through (4) of this section, any part of which is extended Federal financial assistance:

(1)(i) A department, agency, special purpose district, or other instrumentality of a State or of a local government; or

(ii) The entity of such State or local government that distributes such assistance and each such department or agency (and each other State or local government entity) to which the assistance is extended, in the case of assistance to a State or local government;

(2)(i) A college, university, or other postsecondary institution, or a public system of higher education; or

(ii) A local educational agency (as defined in 20 U.S.C. 7801), system of vocational education, or other school system;

(3)(i) An entire corporation, partnership, or other private organization, or an entire sole proprietorship—

(A) If assistance is extended to such corporation, partnership, private organization, or sole proprietorship as a whole; or

(B) Which is principally engaged in the business of providing education, health care, housing, social services, or parks and recreation; or

(ii) The entire plant or other comparable, geographically separate facility to which Federal financial assistance is extended, in the case of any other corporation, partnership, private organization, or sole proprietorship; or

(4) Any other entity which is established by two or more of the entities described in paragraph (j)(1), (2), or (3) of this section.

(k) The term *recipient* means one who receives any Federal financial assistance administered by the Small Business Administration. (See Appendix A.) The term *recipient* also shall be deemed to include *subrecipients* of SBA financial assistance.

(l) The term *SBA* means the Small Business Administration.

(m) The term *subrecipient* means any business concern that receives Federal financial assistance from the primary recipient of such financial assistance. A subrecipient is generally regarded as a recipient of Federal financial assistance and has all the duties of a recipient in these regulations.

(n) The term *statutory objective* means the purposes of the legislation as stated in an act, statute or ordinance or can be shown in the legislative history of any Federal statute, State statute, or local statute or ordinance adopted by an elected, general purpose legislative body.

[50 FR 41648, Oct. 11, 1985, as amended at 68 FR 51349, Aug. 26, 2003]

§ 117.4 Discrimination prohibited and exceptions.

(a) *General.* To the extent that this part applies, no person in the United States shall, on the basis of age, be excluded from participation in, be denied the benefits of, or be subjected to discrimination under any business or activity receiving Federal financial assistance.

(b) *Specific discriminatory actions prohibited.* To the extent that this part applies, a recipient business or other activity may not, directly or through contractual arrangements, on the ground of age:

(1) Deny an individual any services, financial aid or other benefit provided by the business or other activity, except where sanctioned by one of the exceptions stated in § 117.4 (d), (e) or (f) of this section.

(2) Provide any service, financial aid or other benefit, except as sanctioned by one of the exceptions stated below, in such a way as to deny or limit persons in their efforts to participate in federally-assisted programs or activities;

(3) Treat an individual differently from others, except as sanctioned by an exception stated below, in determining whether the person satisfied any admission, enrollment, eligibility, membership, or other requirement or condition which individuals must meet in order to be provided any service, financial aid or other benefit provided by the business or activity.

(c) The specific forms of prohibited discrimination in paragraph (b) of this section does not limit the generality of the prohibition in paragraph (a) of this section.

(d) *Exception 1.* A recipient is permitted to take an action otherwise prohibited by paragraphs (a) and (b) of this section, if the action reasonably takes into account age as a factor necessary to the normal operation or the achievement of any statutory objective of a business or activity. An action reasonably takes into account age as a factor necessary to the normal operation or the achievement of any statutory objective of a business or activity, if:

(1) Age is used as a measure or approximation of one or more other characteristics; and

(2) The other characteristic(s) must be measured or approximated in order for the normal operation of the business or activity to continue, or to achieve any statutory objective of the business or activity; and

(3) The other characteristic(s) can be reasonably measured or approximated by the use of age; and

(4) The other characteristic(s) are impractical to measure directly on an individual basis.

NOTE: All of the above factors must be met in order to exclude a business activity from the provisions of this part.

(e) *Exception 2.* A recipient is permitted to take an action otherwise prohibited by paragraphs (a) and (b) of this section which is based on a factor other than age, even though that action may have a disproportionate effect on persons of different ages. An action may be based on a factor other than age if the factor bears a direct and substantial relationship to the normal operation of the business or activity or to the achievement of a statutory objective.

(f) *Exception 3.* A recipient is permitted to take an action otherwise prohibited by paragraphs (a) and (b) of this section if an age distinction is contained in that part of a Federal, State or local statute or ordinance adopted by an elected general purpose legislative body which provides any benefits or assistance to, establishes criteria for participation in, or describes intended beneficiaries or target groups in age-related terms.

(g) The burden of proving that an age distinction or other action falls within the exceptions outlined in paragraphs (d), (e), and (f) of this section on the recipient of Federal financial assistance.

§ 117.5 Illustrative applications.

(a) *Discrimination in providing financial assistance.* Development companies and small business investment companies, which apply for or receive any financial assistance may not discriminate on the ground of age in providing financial assistance to small business concerns. Such discrimination prohibited by § 117.4 includes but is not limited to the failure or refusal, because of the age of the applicant, or the age of the applicant's principal owner or operating official to extend a loan or equity financing to any business concern; or, in the case of financing which has actually been extended, the failure or refusal because of the age of the recipient, or the age of recipient's principal owner or operating official to accord the recipient fair treatment and the customary courtesies regarding such matters as default, grace periods and the like.

(b) *Discrimination in accommodations or services.* Small Business Concerns and others who or which apply for or receive any financial assistance administered by the Small Business Administration, such as but not limited to physicians, dentists, hospitals, schools, libraries, and other individuals or organizations may not discriminate in the treatment, accommodations or services they provide to their patients, students, members, passengers, or members of the public, except when the normal operation or statutory objective of the business or activity of the intended beneficiary is designated in age-related terms, whether or not operated for profit. Action by such business or activity to be excluded from compliance with this regulation must fall within the exceptions enumerated in § 117.4 (d), (e), and (f) of this part.

(c) The discrimination prohibited by § 117.5(b) includes, but is not limited to the failure or refusal, because of age, to accept a patient, student, member, customer, client, or passenger, except when the imposition of this prohibition would interfere with the normal operation of the business, e.g., pediatricians, nursery schools, geriatric clinics.

§ 117.6 Remedial and affirmative action by recipients.

(a) Where a recipient is found to have discriminated on the basis of age, the recipient shall take any remedial action which the Agency may require to overcome the effects of the discrimination. If another recipient exercises control over the recipient that has discriminated, both recipients may be required to take remedial action.

(b) Even in the absence of a finding of discrimination, a recipient may take affirmative action to overcome the effects of conditions that resulted in limited participation in the recipient's program or activity on the basis of age.

(c) If a recipient operating a program or activity which serves the elderly or children in addition to persons of other ages, provides special benefits to the elderly or to children, the provision of those benefits shall be presumed to be voluntary affirmative action provided that it does not have the effect of excluding otherwise eligible persons from participation in the program or activity.

§ 117.7 Assurances required.

An application for financial assistance administered by the Small Business Administration shall, as a condition of its approval and the extension of such assistance, contain or be accompanied by an assurance that the recipient will comply with this part. SBA shall specify the form of the foregoing assurance, and the extent to which like assurances will be required of contractors and subcontractors, transferees, successors, and other participants.

§ 117.8 Responsibilities of SBA recipients.

(a) Each SBA recipient has the primary responsibility to ensure that its programs or activities are in compliance with the Act and these regulations, and shall take steps to eliminate violations of the Act. A recipient also has responsibility to maintain records, provide information, and to afford SBA access to its records to the extent SBA finds necessary to determine whether the recipient is in compliance with the Act and these regulations. (OMB No. 3245 0076)

(b) Where a recipient passes on Federal financial assistance from SBA to subrecipients, the recipient shall provide the subrecipients written notice of their obligations under the Act and these regulations.

(c) Each recipient shall make necessary information about the Act and these regulations available to the beneficiaries of its programs or activities in order to inform them about the protections against discrimination provided by the Act and these regulations.

(d) Whenever an assessment indicates a violation of the Act and the SBA regulations, the recipient shall take corrective action.

§ 117.9 Compliance information.

(a) *Cooperation and assistance.* SBA shall, to the fullest extent practicable, seek the cooperation of recipients in obtaining compliance with this part and shall provide assistance and guidance to recipients to help them comply voluntarily with this part.

(b) *Record Keeping.* Each recipient shall keep records in such form, and containing such information which SBA determines may be necessary to ascertain whether the recipient has complied or is complying with this part (OMB No. 3245 0076). In the case of a small business concern which receives financial assistance from a development company or from a small business investment company, the small business concern shall also keep such records and information as may be necessary to enable SBA to determine if the small business concern is complying with this part.

(c) Each recipient shall provide to SBA, upon request, information and reports which SBA determines are necessary to ascertain whether the recipient is complying with the Act and these regulations.

(d) *Access to sources of information.* Each recipient shall permit reasonable access by SBA during normal business hours to such of its books, records, accounts, and other sources of information, and its facilities as may be pertinent to ascertain compliance with this part. Where any information required of an applicant or recipient is in the exclusive possession of any other agency, institution or person and that agency, institution or person shall fail or refuse to furnish the information, the recipient shall so certify and shall set forth what efforts it has made to obtain the required information. The recipient will be held responsible for submitting the information. Failure to submit information or permit access to sources of information required by SBA will subject the recipient to enforcement procedure as provided in § 117.15 of this part.

(Information collection requirements in paragraph (c) were approved by the Office of Management and Budget under control number 3245–0076)

§ 117.10 Review procedures.

(a) SBA shall from time to time review the practices of recipients to determine whether they are complying with this part. As part of a compliance review or complaint investigation, SBA may require a recipient employing 15 or more full-time employees to complete a written self-evaluation, in a manner specified by the Agency, of any age distinction imposed in its program or activity receiving Federal financial assistance.

(b) If a compliance review or pre-award review indicates a violation of the Act or these regulations, SBA will attempt to achieve voluntary compliance with the Act. If voluntary compliance with the recipient cannot be achieved, such recipient will be subject to the enforcement procedure contained in § 117.15 of these regulations. A refusal to permit an on-site compliance review during normal working hours may constitute noncompliance with this part.

§ 117.11 Complaint procedures.

(a) Any person who believes that he/she or any specific class of individuals is being or has been subjected to discrimination by SBA, a recipient, or an applicant for assistance, prohibited by this part may, by himself/herself or by a representative, file with SBA a written complaint. The complainant has the right to have a representative at all stages of the complaint procedure.

(b) A complaint must be filed not later than 180 days from the date of the alleged discrimination, unless the time filing is extended by SBA. The Adminstrator, the Assistant Administrator, Office of Equal Employment Opportunity & Civil Rights Compliance, are the only officials who may waive the 180-day time limit for filing complaints under this part. SBA will consider the date a complaint is filed to be the date upon which the complaint is sufficient to be processed.

(c) Each complaint will be reviewed to ensure that it falls within the coverage of the Act and contains all information necessary for further processing.

(d) SBA will attempt to facilitate the filing of complaints wherever possible, including taking the following actions:

(1) Accepting as a sufficient complaint, any written statement which identifies the parties involved and the date the complainant first had knowledge of the alleged violation, describes generally the action or practice complained of, and is signed by the complainant.

(2) Freely permitting a complainant to add information to the complaint to meet the requirements of a sufficient complaint.

(3) Notifying the complainant and the recipient of their rights and obligations under the complaint procedure, including the right to have a representative at all stages of the complaint procedure.

(4) Notifying the complainant and the recipient (or their representatives) of their right to contact the Assistant Administrator, Office of Equal Employment Opportunity & Civil Rights Compliance, for information and assistance regarding the complaint resolution process.

(e) SBA will return to the complainant any complaint filed under the jurisdiction of this regulation, but found to be outside the jurisdiction of this regulation, and will state the reason(s) why it is outside the jurisdiction of this regulation.

[50 FR 41648, Oct. 11, 1985, as amended at 72 FR 50038, Aug. 30, 2007]

§ 117.12 Mediation.

(a) SBA shall, after ensuring that the complaint falls within the coverage of this Act and all information necessary for further processing is contained therein, unless the age distinction complained of is clearly within an exception, promptly refer the complaint to the Federal Mediation and Conciliation Service (FMCS).

(b) SBA shall, to the extent possible, require the participation of the recipient and the complainant in the mediation process in an effort to reach a mutually satisfactory settlement of the complaint or make an informed judgment that an agreement is not possible. Both parties need not meet with the mediator at the same time.

(c) If the complainant and the recipient reach a mutually satisfactory resolution of the complaint during the mediation period, the mediator shall prepare a written statement of the agreement and have the complainant and recipient sign it.

(d) A copy of the written mediation agreement will be referred to SBA, and no further action will be taken unless it appears that either the complainant or the recipient (or other alleged discriminator subject to this part) fails to comply with the agreement.

(e) If at the end of 60 days after the receipt of a complaint by SBA, or at any time prior thereto, an agreement is reached or the mediator determines an agreement cannot be reached through mediation, the agreement or complaint will be returned to SBA.

(f) This 60-day period may be extended by the mediator, with the concurrence of SBA for not more than 30 days if the mediator determines that an agreement will likely be reached during the extended period.

(g) The mediator shall protect the confidentiality of all information obtained in the course of the mediation process. No mediator shall testify in any adjudicative proceeding, produce any document, or otherwise disclose any information obtained during the course of the mediation process without prior approval of the head of the agency appointing the mediator.

§ 117.13 Investigation and resolution of matters.

(a) SBA will make a prompt investigation whenever a compliance review indicates a possible failure to comply with this part by the recipient and additional information is needed by SBA to assure compliance with this part, or when an unresolved complaint has been returned by the FMCS, or when it appears that the complainant or the recipient is failing to comply with a mediation agreement. The investigation shall include a review of the pertinent practices and policies of the recipient, the circumstances under which the possible noncompliance with this part occurred, and other factors relevant to a determination as to whether the recipient is complying, is not complying, or has failed to comply with this part.

(b) *Resolution of matters.* If an investigation indicates a failure to comply with this part, SBA will so inform the complainant, if applicable, and the recipient that the matter will be resolved by informal means that are mutually agreeable to the parties, whenever possible.

(1) If, during the course of an investigation, the matter is resolved by informal means, SBA will put any agreement in writing and have it signed by the parties and an authorized official of SBA.

(2) If investigation indicates a violation of the Act or these regulations, SBA will attempt to achieve voluntary compliance. If SBA cannot achieve voluntary compliance, it will begin enforcement as described in § 117.15.

(3) If an investigation does not warrant action, SBA will so inform the complainant, if applicable, and the recipient in writing.

§ 117.14 Intimidating or retaliatory acts prohibited.

No complainant, recipient or other person shall intimidate, threaten, coerce, or discriminate against any individual for the purpose of interfering with any right or privilege secured by this part or because an individual or group has made a complaint, testified, assisted, or participated in any manner in an investigation, review, enforcement process, or hearing under this part. The identity of complainants shall be kept confidential except to the extent necessary to carry out the purposes of this part, including the conduct of any investigation, hearing, mediation, or judicial proceeding.

§ 117.15 Procedure for effecting compliance.

(a) *General.* (1) If there appears to be a failure or threatened failure to comply with this part by an applicant or recipient and if the noncompliance or threatened noncompliance cannot be resolved by informal means, compliance with this part may be effected by suspending, terminating, or refusing any financial assistance approved but not yet disbursed to an applicant. In the case of loans partially or fully disbursed, compliance with this part may be effected by calling, canceling, terminating, accelerating repayment, or suspending in whole or in part the Federal financial assistance provided. The determination of the recipient's violation may be made only after a recipient has had an opportunity for a hearing on the record before an administrative law judge.

(2) In addition, compliance may be effected by any other means authorized by law. Such other means may include, but are not limited to:

(i) Action by SBA to accelerate the maturity of the recipient's obligation;

(ii) Referral to the Department of Justice with a recommendation that appropriate proceedings be brought to enforce any rights of the United States under any law of the United States or obligations of the recipient created by the Act or this part; and

(iii) Use of any requirement of or referral to any Federal, State or local government agency that will have the effect of correcting a violation of the Act or these regulations.

(3) If there appears to be a failure or threatened failure to comply with this part by an SBA office or official, the Assistant Administrator, Office of Equal Employment Opportunity & Civil Rights Compliance, will recommend appropriate corrective action to the Administrator. Any resulting adverse action against an SBA employee shall follow Office of Personnel Management and SBA procedures for such action.

(b) *Noncompliance with §§ 117.7 and 117.9.* If an applicant fails or refuses to furnish an assurance required under § 117.7, or fails to provide information or allow SBA access to information under § 117.9 or otherwise fails or refuses to comply with a requirement imposed by or pursuant to those sections, Federal financial assistance may be deferred for a period not to exceed 60 days after the applicant has received a notice for an opportunity for hearing under § 117.16, or unless a hearing has begun within that time, or the time for beginning the hearing has been extended by mutual consent of the recipient and the Agency, for purposes of determining what constitutes mutual consent, the Agency shall be deemed to have consented to any extension requested by the recipient and granted by the administrative law judge (hearing officer), whether or not the Agency initially approved the extension. A deferral may not continue for more than 30 days after the close of the hearing, unless the hearing results in a finding against the applicant or recipient.

(c) SBA will not take action toward accelerating repayment, suspending, terminating, or refusing financial assistance until:

(1) SBA has advised the applicant or recipient of the failure to comply and has determined that compliance cannot be secured by voluntary means;

(2) There has been an express finding on the record, after an opportunity for hearing, of a failure by the applicant or recipient to comply with a requirement imposed by or pursuant to this part;

(3) The action has been approved by the Administrator of SBA pursuant to § 117.17; and

(4) The expiration of 30 days after SBA has filed with the committee of the House and the committee of the Senate having legislative jurisdiction over the form of financial assistance involved, a full written report of the circumstances and the grounds for such action.

(d) Other means authorized by law. No action to effect compliance by any other means authorized by law shall be taken until:

(1) SBA has determined that compliance cannot be secured by voluntary means;

(2) The action has been approved by the Administrator or designee;

(3) The expiration of 30 days after SBA has filed with the committee of the House and the committee of the Senate having legislative jurisdiction over the form of financial assistance involved, a full written report of the circumstances and the grounds for such action;

(4) The applicant or recipient has been notified of the failure to comply, and of the action to be taken to effect compliance; and

(5) The expiration of at least 10 days from the mailing of such notice to the applicant or recipient or other person. During this period of at least 10 days from the mailing of such notice to the applicant or recipient or other person, additional efforts shall be made to persuade the applicant or recipient to comply with this part and to take such

corrective action as may be appropriate.

[50 FR 41648, Oct. 11, 1985, as amended at 72 FR 50038, Aug. 30, 2007]

§ 117.16 Hearings.

(a) *Opportunity for hearing.* Whenever an opportunity for a hearing is required by § 117.15, reasonable notice shall be given by registered or certified mail, return receipt requested, to the affected applicant or recipient. This notice shall advise the applicant or recipient of the action proposed to be taken, the specific provision under which the proposed action against it is to be taken, and the matters of fact or law asserted as the basis for this action, and either.

(1) Fix a date not less than 20 days after the date of such notice within which the applicant or recipient may request the Office of Hearings and Appeals (OHA) that the matter be scheduled for hearing; or

(2) Advise the applicant or recipient that the matter in question has been set down for hearing at a stated place and time. The time and place so fixed shall be reasonable and shall be subject to change for cause. The complainant shall be advised of the time and place of the hearing. An applicant or recipient may waive a hearing and submit written information and argument for the record. The failure of an applicant or recipient to appear at a hearing for which a date has been set shall be deemed to be a waiver of the right to a hearing and as consent to the making of a decision on the basis of such information as is available.

(b) *Time and place of hearing.* Hearings shall be held at OHA in Washington, DC, at a time fixed by OHA unless that office determines that the convenience of the complainant, applicant, recipient or SBA requires that another place be selected. Hearings shall be held before an administrative law judge designated in accordance with the Administrative Procedure Act.

(c) *Right to counsel.* In all proceedings under this section, the applicant or recipient and SBA shall have the right to be represented by counsel.

(d) *Procedures, evidence, and record.* (1) The hearings, decisions, and any administrative review shall be conducted in conformity with the Administrative Procedure Act and 13 CFR part 134. Such rules of procedure should be consistent with this section, relate to the conduct of the hearing, provide for giving of notices to those referred to in paragraph (a) of this section, taking of testimony, exhibits, arguments, and briefs, request for findings and other related matters. SBA, the complainant, if any, and the applicant or recipient shall be entitled to introduce all relevant evidence on the issues as stated in the notice for hearing, or as determined by the administrative law judge conducting the hearing at the outset of or during the hearing.

(2) Technical rules of evidence may be waived by the administrative law judge conducting a hearing pursuant to this part, but rules or principles designed to assure production of the most credible evidence available, and subject testimony to test by cross-examination shall be applied where reasonably necessary. The administrative law judge may exclude irrelevant, immaterial, or unduly repetitious evidence. All documents and other evidence offered or taken for the record shall be open to examination by the parties and opportunity shall be given to refute facts and arguments advanced on either side of the issues. A transcript shall be made of the oral evidence except to the extent the substance thereof is stipulated for the record. All decisions shall be based upon the hearing record and written findings shall be made.

(e) *Consolidated or joint hearings.* In cases in which the same or related facts are asserted to constitute noncompliance or threatened noncompliance with this part, with respect to two or more forms of financial assistance to which this part applies, or noncompliance with this part and the regulations of one or more other Federal agencies issued under the Act, the Administrator may, by agreement with such other agencies, provide for the conduct of consolidated or joint hearings, and for the application to such hearings of rules and procedures not inconsistent with this part. Final decisions in such cases, insofar as this part is concerned, shall be made in accordance with § 117.17.

§117.17 Decisions and notices.

(a) *Decision by an administrative law judge.* If the hearing is held by an administrative law judge, such administrative law judge shall either make an initial decision, if so authorized, or certify the entire record, including recommended findings and proposed decision, to the Administrator for a final decision and a copy of such initial decision or certification shall be mailed to the applicant or recipient and the complainant. Where the initial decision is made by the administrative law judge, the applicant or recipient may, within 30 days of the mailing of such notice of initial decision, file with the Administrator exceptions to the initial decision, with the reasons therefor. In the absence of exceptions, the Administrator may, by motion within 45 days after the initial decision, serve on the applicant or recipient a notice that he/she will review the decision. Upon the filing of such exceptions or of such notice of review, the Administrator shall review the initial decision and issue his/her decision thereon, including the reasons therefor. The decision of the Administrator shall be mailed promptly to the applicant or recipient, and the complainant, if any. In the absence of either exceptions or a notice of review, the initial decision shall constitute the final decision of the Administrator.

(b) *Decisions on record or review by the Administrator.* Whenever a record is certified to the Administrator for decision or the Administrator reviews the decision of an administrative law judge pursuant to paragraph (a) of this section, or whenever the Secretary of the Department of Health and Human Services or the Department of Justice conducts the hearing, the applicant or recipient shall be given reasonable opportunity to file briefs or other written statements of its contentions and a copy of the final decision of the Administrator shall be given in writing to the applicant or recipient and the complainant, if any.

(c) *Decisions on record where a hearing is waived.* Whenever a hearing is waived pursuant to §117.16, a decision shall be made by the Administrator on the record and a copy of such decision shall be given in writing to the applicant or recipient, and to the complainant, if any.

(d) *Rulings required.* Each decision of an administrative law judge or the Administrator shall set forth the ruling on each finding, conclusion, or exception presented, and shall identify the requirement or requirements imposed by or pursuant to this part with which it is found that the applicant or recipient has failed to comply.

(e) *Decision by the Administrator.* The Administrator shall make any final decision which provides for the suspension or termination of, or the refusal to grant or continue Federal financial assistance, acceleration repayment or the imposition of any other sanction available under the regulations or taken under other means authorized by law.

(f) *Content of orders.* The final decision may provide for accelerating of repayment, suspension or termination of, or refusal to approve, disburse, or continue Federal financial assistance, in whole or in part, to which this regulation applies, and may contain such terms, conditions, and other provisions as are consistent with and will effectuate the purposes of the Act and this part, including provisions designed to assure that no Federal financial assistance to which this regulation applies will, thereafter, be extended to the applicant or recipient determined by such decision to have failed to comply with this part, unless and until it corrects its noncompliance and satisfies the Administrator that it will fully comply with this part.

(g) *Post termination proceedings.* (1) An applicant or recipient adversely affected by an order issued under paragraph (e) of this section shall be restored to full eligibility to receive Federal financial assistance only if it satisfies the terms and conditions of that order for such eligibility and it brings itself into compliance with this regulation and provides reasonable assurance that it will fully comply with this regulation.

(2) Any applicant or recipient adversely affected by an order entered

pursuant to paragraph (f) of this section may at any time request the Administrator to restore fully its eligibility to receive Federal financial assistance. Any such request shall be supported by information showing that the applicant or recipient has met the requirements of paragraph (g)(1) of this section. If the Administrator determines that those requirements have been satisfied, he/she shall restore such eligibility.

(3) If the Administrator denies any such request, the applicant or recipient may submit a request for a hearing in writing, specifying why it believes the denial to have been in error. It shall there upon be given an expeditious hearing, with a decision on the record, in accordance with rules and procedures issued by the Administrator. The applicant or recipient shall be restored to such eligibility if it proves at such hearing that it satisfied the requirements of paragraph (g)(1) of this section. While proceedings under this paragraph are pending, the sanctions imposed by the order issued under paragraph (f) of this section shall remain in effect.

§ 117.18 Judicial review.

(a) The complainant may file a civil action following the exhaustion of administrative remedies under the Act. Administrative remedies are exhausted if:

(1) 180 days have elapsed since the complainant filed the complaint and the Agency has made no finding with regard to the complaint; or

(2) The Agency has issued a finding in favor of the recipient.

(b) If the Agency fails to make a finding within 180 days or issues a finding in favor of the recipient, the Agency shall:

(1) Advise the complainant of this fact;

(2) Advise the complainant of the right to file a civil action for injunctive relief; and

(3) Inform the complainant:

(i) That the complainant may bring a civil action only in a United States district court for the district in which the recipient is found or transacts business;

(ii) That a complainant prevailing in a civil action has the right to be awarded the costs of the action, including reasonable attorney's fees, but that the complainant must demand these costs in the complaint;

(iii) That before commencing the action the complainant shall give 30 days notice by registered mail to the Secretary of the Department of Health and Human Services, the Attorney General of the United States and the recipient;

(iv) That the notice must state: The alleged violation of the Act; the relief requested; the court in which the complainant is bringing the action; and whether or not attorney's fees are demanded in the event the complainant prevails; and

(v) That the complainant may not bring an action if the same alleged violation of the Act by the same recipient is the subject of a pending action in any court of the United States.

§ 117.19 Effect on other regulations.

(a) All regulations, orders or like directions heretofore issued by SBA which impose requirements designed to prohibit any discrimination against individuals on the grounds of age and which authorize the suspension or termination of or refusal to grant or to continue financial assistance to any applicant for or recipient of such assistance for failure to comply with such requirements, are hereby superseded to the extent that such discrimination is prohibited by this part, except that nothing in this part shall be deemed to relieve any person of any obligation assumed or imposed under any such superseded regulation, order, instruction, or like direction prior to the effective date of this part. Nothing in this part, however, shall be deemed to supersede any of the following (including future amendments thereof):

(1) Executive Order 11246, as amended, and regulations issued thereunder;

(2) Title VI of the Civil Rights Act of 1964, as amended;

(3) The Equal Credit Opportunity Act, as amended and Regulation B of the Board of Governors of the Federal Reserve System, (12 CFR part 202);

(4) Section 504 of the Rehabilitation Act of 1973, as amended;

(5) Title VIII of the Civil Rights Act of 1968;

(6) Title IX of the Educational Amendments of 1972;

(7) Section 633(b) of the Small Business Act;

(8) Part 113 of title 13 of the Code of Federal Regulations (13 CFR part 113); or

(9) Any other statute, order, regulation or instruction, insofar as such order, regulations, or instruction prohibits discrimination on the grounds of age in any program or activity or situation to which this part is inapplicable on any other ground.

§ 117.20 Supervision and coordination.

The Administrator may from time to time assign to officials of SBA or to officials of other agencies of the Government with the consent of such agencies, responsibilities in connection with the effectuation of the purpose of the Act and this part (other than responsibility for final decision as provided in § 117.17), including the achievement of effective coordination and maximum uniformity within SBA and within the Executive Branch of the Government in the application of the Act and this part to similar programs or activities and in similar situations. Responsibility for administering and enforcing this part is assigned by the Administrator, to the Office of Civil Rights Compliance, Office of Equal Employment Opportunity and Compliance of the Small Business Administration.

APPENDIX A TO PART 11[1]

Type of Federal financial assistance	Authority
Business Loans	Small Business Act, section 7(a).
Debtor State Development companies (501) and their small business concerns.	Small Business Investment Act, Title V.
Debtor State Development companies (502) and their small business concerns.	Small Business Investment Act, Title V.
Debtor certified development companies (503) and their small business concerns.	Small Business Investment Act, Title V.
Debtor small business investment companies and their small business concerns.	Small Business Investment Act, Title III.
Pollution Control	Small Business Investment Act, Title IV, Part A.
Disaster Loans:	
Physical, including riot	Small Business Act, section 7(b)(1).
Economic Injury (EIDL)	Small Business Act, section 7(b)(2).
Federal Action Loan Program.	Small Business Act, section 7(b)(3).
Small Business Institute	Small Business Act, section 8(b)(1).
Small Business Development Centers.	Small Business Act, section 21.
International Trade Program.	Small Business Act, section 22.
Technical and Management Assistance.	Small Business Act, section 7(j).

[1] None of the programs administered have any age distinctions except as statutorily required.

PART 119—PROGRAM FOR INVESTMENT IN MICROENTREPRENEURS ("PRIME" OR "THE ACT")

Sec.

AUTHORITY: 15 U.S.C. 634(b)(6) and Pub. L. 106–102.

SOURCE: 66 FR 29013, May 29, 2001, unless otherwise noted.

§ 119.1 What is the Program for Investment in Microentrepreneurs ("PRIME" or "the Act")?

PRIME authorizes SBA to make grants to "qualified organizations" to fund training and technical assistance for disadvantaged entrepreneurs, build these organizations' own capacity to give training and technical assistance, fund research and development of "best practices" in microenterprise development and technical assistance programs for disadvantaged microentrepreneurs, and to fund other undertakings the Administrator or designee deems consistent with these purposes.

§ 119.2 Definitions.

For the purposes of this part, the following definitions apply:

Capacity Building Grant means a grant made under the Act identified under § 119.4(b).

Capacity building services means services provided to an organization or program that is currently, or is developing as, a microenterprise development organization or program, for the purpose of enhancing its ability to provide training and technical assistance to disadvantaged microentrepreneurs.

Collaborative means two or more nonprofit entities that agree to act jointly as a qualified organization under this part.

Developer means a person interested in starting or acquiring a microenterprise.

Disadvantaged entrepreneur, or *disadvantaged microentrepreneur*, means the owner, majority owner, or developer, of a microenterprise who is also—

(1) A low-income person;

(2) A very low-income person; or

(3) An entrepreneur who lacks adequate access to capital or other resources essential for business success, or is economically disadvantaged, as defined in this part.

Discretionary Grant means a grant made under the Act identified under § 119.4(d).

Economically disadvantaged entrepreneur, or *economically disadvantaged* microentrepreneur, means an owner, majority owner, or developer of a microenterprise whose ability to compete in the free enterprise system has been impaired due to diminished capital and credit opportunities as compared to others in the industry such that his or her ownership of a small business would help to qualify the small business for assistance under section 7(j) or section 8(a) programs of the Small Business Act.

Grantee means a recipient of a grant under the Act.

Group has the same meaning as "collaborative" as defined in this section.

Indian tribe means any Indian tribe, band, pueblo, nation, or other organized group or community, including any Alaska Native village or regional or village corporation, as defined in or established pursuant to the Alaska Native Claims Settlement Act, which is recognized as eligible for the special programs and services the United States provides to Indians because of their status as Indians.

Indian tribe jurisdiction means Indian country, as defined in 18 U.S.C. 1151, and any other lands, title to which is either held by the United States in trust for the benefit of any Indian tribe or individual or held by any tribe or individual subject to a restriction by the United States against alienation, and any land held by Alaska Native groups, regional corporations, and village corporations, as defined in or established under the Alaska Native Claims Settlement Act, public domain Indian allotments, and former Indian reservations in the State of Oklahoma.

Intermediary means a private, nonprofit entity serving or seeking to serve microenterprise development organizations or programs identified under § 119.3.

Large microenterprise development organization or program means a microenterprise development organization or program with 10 or more full time employees or equivalents, including its executive director, as of the date it files its application with SBA for a PRIME grant.

Local community means an identifiable area and population constituting a political subdivision of a state.

Low-income person means a person having an income, adjusted for family size, of not more than—

(1) For metropolitan areas, 80 percent of the median income; and

(2) For non-metropolitan areas, the greater of—

(i) 80 percent of the area median income; or

(ii) 80 percent of the statewide non-metropolitan area median income.

Microenterprise means a sole proprietorship, partnership or corporation that—

(1) Has fewer than 5 employees, including the owner; and

(2) Generally lacks access to conventional loans, equity, or other banking services.

Microenterprise development organization or program means a nonprofit entity, or a program administered by such an entity, including community development corporations or other nonprofit development organizations and social service organizations, that provides services to disadvantaged microentrepreneurs.

Qualified organization means an organization eligible for a PRIME grant identified under § 119.3.

Research and Development Grant means a grant made under the Act identified under § 119.4(c).

Severe constraints on available sources of matching funds means the documented inability of a qualified organization applying for a PRIME grant to raise matching funds or in-kind resources from non-Federal sources during the 2 years immediately prior to the date of its application because of a lack of or increased scarcity of monetary or in-kind resources from potential non-Federal sources.

Small microenterprise development organization or program means a microenterprise development organization or program with less than 10 full time employees or equivalents, including its executive director, as of the date it files its application with SBA for a PRIME grant.

Technical Assistance Grant means a grant made under the Act identified under § 119.4(a).

Training and technical assistance means services and support provided to disadvantaged entrepreneurs, such as, but not limited to, assistance intended to enhance business planning, marketing, management, financial management skills, business operations, or assistance for the purpose of increasing access to loans and other financial services.

Very low-income person means having an income adjusted for family size of not more than 150 percent of the poverty line, as defined in section 673(2) of the Community Services Block Grant Act, 42 U.S.C. 9902(2), including any revision required by that section.

§ 119.3 What types of organizations are eligible for PRIME grants?

An organization eligible for a PRIME grant ("qualified organization") is one that is:

(a) A microenterprise development organization or program as defined in § 119.2(q) (or a group or collaborative thereof) that has a demonstrated record of delivering microenterprise services to disadvantaged microentrepreneurs;

(b) An intermediary, as defined in § 119.2(l);

(c) A microenterprise development organization or program as defined in § 119.2(q) that is accountable to a local community, working with a State or local government or Indian tribe; or

(d) An Indian tribe acting on its own, if the Indian tribe can certify that no private organization or program referred to in paragraphs (a), (b) and (c) of this section exists within its jurisdiction.

§ 119.4 What services or activities must PRIME grant funds be used for?

A recipient of a PRIME grant ("grantee") must use PRIME grants to—

(a) Provide training and technical assistance to disadvantaged microentrepreneurs ("Technical Assistance Grant");

(b) Provide training and capacity building services to microenterprise development organizations and programs to assist them to develop microenterprise training and services ("Capacity Building Grant");

(c) Aid in researching and developing the best practices in the field of microenterprise development and technical assistance programs for disadvantaged microentrepreneurs ("Research and Development Grant"); or

(d) Conduct such other activities as the Administrator or designee determines to be consistent with the purposes of the Act ("Discretionary Grant").

§ 119.5 How are PRIME grant awards allocated?

(a) At least 50 percent of the number of grant awards made under this part will be awarded to qualified organizations that benefit very low-income persons, including those residing on Indian reservations. In general, SBA will make grant award decisions to serve diverse populations by including as recipients both large and small microenterprise development organizations, and organizations serving urban, rural, and Indian tribal communities.

(b) SBA will allocate the funding available for awards as follows:

(1) A minimum of 75 percent for Technical Assistance Grants;

(2) A minimum of 15 percent for Capacity Building Grants; and

(3) The remaining 10 percent or less may be allocated by SBA, in its sole discretion to be used for:

(i) Research and Development Grants; or

(ii) Discretionary Grants.

§ 119.6 What are the minimum and maximum amounts for an award?

(a) The minimum grant award for Technical Assistance and Capacity Building Grants will be $50,000 during the first year of the award, subject to the availability of funds.

(b) There is no minimum grant award for Research and Development or Discretionary Grants.

(c) The maximum amount that an individual grant recipient may receive in any fiscal year from a single award or multiple awards, under any of the purposes of the program, may not exceed $250,000 or 10 percent of the total grant funds available for award in that fiscal year, whichever is less.

§ 119.7 How long and in what amounts will grant funding be available to a single grantee?

(a) Generally, the funding period for a PRIME grant will be one year. Subject to availability of funds and continuing authorization, funding may be available on an annual basis allowing for the initial grant plus up to four option years, for a project period of up to five years. Decisions regarding option year awards and the funding levels of these awards will depend upon availability of funding and the grantee's performance as measured against project objectives and milestones. A grantee that enters into a cooperative agreement must submit a separate application to have the support continued for each subsequent year. In all cases, continuation awards require a determination by SBA that continued funding is in the best interest of the Federal government. Neither the approval of any application nor the entering into of any cooperative agreement commits or obligates the Federal Government in any way to make any additional, supplemental, continuation or other award with respect to any grantee.

(b) For Technical Assistance and Capacity Building Grants, after a grantee receives an initial grant, funding for any option year(s) must be no more than 67 percent of the initial grant amount.

(c) For Research and Development and Discretionary Grants, after a grantee receives an initial grant, funding for any option year(s) will be approved at the discretion of the SBA.

(d) In the final year of a project, grantees may apply to extend the expiration date of a grant if additional time beyond the established expiration date is required to assure adequate completion of the original scope of work within the funds already made available. For this purpose, the grantee may make an extension request for a one-time, no-cost extension, not to exceed 12 months, prior to the established expiration date. Written notification of such an extension, with the supporting reasons, must be received by the SBA

Grant Officer at least 60 days prior to the expiration of the award. SBA reserves the right to disapprove the extension if the requirements set forth in OMB Circular A–110, paragraph .25(e)(2) are not met or if the extension is not in the best interests of SBA.

§ 119.8 Are there matching requirements for grantees?

Applicants and grantees must match SBA funding as follows:

(a) Except as provided in paragraph (c) of this section, applicants and grantees must match Federal assistance with funds from sources other than the Federal Government in an amount not less than 50 percent of the grant amount awarded each year. Sources such as fees, grants, gifts, income from loan sources, and in-kind resources of a grant recipient from non-Federal public or private sources may be used to comply with the matching funds requirement;

(b) Grantees receiving funds in option years as described in § 119.7(b) through (c) are subject to the matching requirements of this section.

(c) Applicants or grantees with severe constraints on available sources of matching funds may request that the Administrator or designee reduce or eliminate the matching requirements. Any reductions or eliminations must not exceed 10 percent of the aggregate of all PRIME grant funds made available by SBA in any fiscal year. By requesting a waiver, the applicant is implying that, but for the waiver, the proposed programming will not be possible at the levels requested.

(d) An applicant may request a waiver of the matching fund requirement by submitting a written request with its application for funding. The request must justify, and evidence, the need for a waiver. As evidence, the request must include, but is not limited to:

(1) The cause and extent of the constraints on the historical and projected ability to raise matching funds as demonstrated by financial statements and letters of rejection from previous funders and potential new funding sources;

(2) Evidence of efforts to raise match specific to the subject application, including negative responses, and

(3) Based on those efforts, a list of any matching funds expected for the PRIME grant.

(e) Subject to § 119.12 (a) through (d), applications will be evaluated on merit before being matched with cost proposals. Any organization requesting a waiver of matching funds, therefore, will not be rejected solely on the basis of such a request.

(f) Applications will be ranked, within their respective categories, from the most to least qualified. The best qualified applicants in each category will be selected whether or not a waiver is requested until the availability of waivers is exhausted.

§ 119.9 How will a qualified organization apply for PRIME grant awards?

(a) SBA will issue Program Announcements specifying the terms, conditions, and evaluation criteria for each potential set of awards. Program Announcements will summarize the purpose of the available funds; will advise potential applicants regarding how to obtain an application packet; and will provide summary information regarding deadlines and other requirements. Program Announcements may specify any limitations, special rules, procedures, and restrictions for available funding.

(b) Applicants may submit applications in response to the Program Announcements. Each applicant shall submit an application for a grant in accordance with this part and the applicable Program Announcement.

(c) SBA reserves the right to consider at the same time multiple applications from a single applicant when appropriate.

§ 119.10 Will SBA give preferential consideration to other SBA program participants?

In making grants under this part, SBA will not give preferential consideration to an applicant that is a participant in programs established under section 7(m) of the Small Business Act.

§ 119.11 What information will be requested in an application under the PRIME program?

Each application must contain the information and documentation specified in the applicable Program Announcement including, but not limited to, the following items.

(a) For applications seeking Technical Assistance Grants:

(1) Identifying information and core documentation for the applicant including such items as the applicant's articles of incorporation, by-laws, proof of IRS tax-exempt status, financial statements, and reference contacts.

(2) A description of past and present activities and technical qualifications of the applicant, including workshops, programs and other technical assistance services, with specific descriptions of the extent to which such services have reached low and very low-income individuals, and the success rates of clients.

(3) A list of applicant's community partnerships and collaborations with state and local entities, and a description of how such partnerships and collaborations are serving microentrepreneurs.

(4) A description of the proposed activity for which the applicant will use PRIME grant funds, including training programming plans; a plan for outreach and delivery; applicant's capacity to provide thorough and detailed reports; and a description of the applicant's current data collection and management system, such as computer hardware, software and internet capabilities.

(5) In the event the applicant is a collaborative, a plan for maintaining internal controls, accountability, and program quality control among the participants of the collaborative.

(6) Resumes of the personnel that will be administering and managing the proposed activities under the PRIME grant, showing knowledge in such areas as business development, business structures, financial management, and business training and counseling.

(7) A list of grants received, and/or contracts entered into, that are similar in scope to the subject grant, including name of Federal or other agency providing funding, grant or contract number, and a summary of services provided.

(b) For applicants seeking Capacity Building Grants:

(1) See paragraphs (a)(1), (5), (6) and (7) of this section.

(2) A description of past and present activities and technical qualifications of the applicant, including workshops, programs, operational services, and other technical assistance services, or program development services with specific descriptions of the extent to which such services have improved the operations of client MDOs, assisted client MDOs with operational issues, and assisted client MDOs in reaching low and very low-income individuals.

(3) A description of the proposed activity for which the applicant will use PRIME grant funds, including training programming plans, a plan for outreach and delivery, applicant's capacity to provide thorough and detailed reports; a description of the applicant's current data collection and management system, such as computer hardware, software, and internet capabilities and a description of how these capabilities will or will not be integrated into the training of MDOs.

(c) For applicants seeking Research and Development Grants:

(1) See paragraphs (a)(1), (6), and (7) of this section.

(2) A research proposal indicating the thesis, method(s), scope, duration, and implementation plans (if any).

(3) A description of the expected effect of the research on services to disadvantaged microentrepreneurs.

(d) For applicants seeking Discretionary Grants:

(1) See paragraph (a)(1) of this section.

(2) A description of the proposed activity for which the applicant will use PRIME grant funds, including applicant's capacity to provide thorough and detailed reports, and a description of the applicant's current data collection and management system, such as computer hardware, software and internet capabilities.

§ 119.12 What criteria will SBA use to evaluate applications for funding under the PRIME program?

During the first year for which funding is available for the PRIME program, SBA will give special consideration to organizations located in and serving areas of, or with a history of successful outreach to, low-income and very low-income persons, to enable the PRIME program to assist those with the greatest need first. SBA will evaluate applications for funding in accordance with the specific goals of the Act, and as more fully described in the Program Announcements. Evaluation criteria include, but are not limited to, the following:

(a) Applications for Technical Assistance Grants:

(1) Applicants will compete based on expertise and ability to fulfill the purposes of the Act.

(2) SBA will evaluate organizational structure, financial stability, financial management systems, personnel capacity, and electronic communication capabilities (or potential for same). SBA will also evaluate data collection capabilities, reporting capacities, and ability to account for performance and outcome.

(3) SBA will evaluate the applicant's history of providing technical assistance to low-income and very low-income microentrepreneurs. This factor includes patterns of program growth, client success, outcomes of training, success in establishing new businesses, and success in arranging micro-level financing when the client indicates financing as a goal.

(4) SBA will evaluate the applicant's ability to use community partnerships and collaborations with state and local entities to better serve low-income and very low-income microentrepreneurs.

(b) Applications for Capacity Building Grants:

(1) SBA will evaluate the criteria set forth in paragraph (a)(2) of this section.

(2) SBA will evaluate the applicant's history of providing capacity building services to MDOs, as an indication of the organization's understanding of the goals and purposes of capacity building, its historical effectiveness with the microenterprise development industry, and its ability to provide quality programming to the targeted market. SBA will evaluate patterns of program growth, outcomes of training, types of services provided, delivery systems used, the number and types of clients served, and the successes realized within the client's organizational goals.

(3) SBA will evaluate expected impact on client MDOs; expected impact on services to low-and very-low income microentrepreneurs; and a plan for service and delivery.

(c) Applications for Research and Development Grants:

(1) SBA will evaluate the criteria set forth in paragraph (a)(2) of this section.

(2) SBA will evaluate how the research potentially will enhance microenterprise-oriented technical assistance services to disadvantaged entrepreneurs. Applicants must show the method(s), scope, duration, and implementation plans of the proposed research.

(3) SBA will evaluate applicant's plan of action incorporating original and secondary research. Applicants must show impact on improved access to microenterprise development services for disadvantaged microentrepreneurs, and the expected replicability/transferability of the finished product to the field.

(d) Applications for Discretionary Grants will be evaluated based on the goals and the viability of the project.

§ 119.13 How will an applicant make a subgrant?

(a) An applicant that wants to make subgrants using PRIME grant funds must receive written approval from SBA prior to making subgrants. The applicant must identify the subgrantee(s) and describe in detail what the subgrantee(s) will do to help the grantee implement its proposal. An applicant must submit information to SBA demonstrating that, through the subgrantee(s), the grantee's program will:

(1) Provide expanded services to the community,

(2) Provide a method by which one or more previously unserved communities will gain access to the program, or

(3) Provide other specific benefits to the clients, such as specialized training, expanded schedules of operation, or other benefits.

(b) If an applicant has identified potential subgrantee(s) at the time it submits an application for a PRIME grant, the applicant must include the information requested in paragraph (a) of this section in the application. Otherwise, the applicant or grantee may submit the requested information at such time that approvals for subgrantee(s) are requested.

(c) A grantee may not use more than 7.5 percent of the assistance received under its PRIME grant for administrative expenses in connection with the making of subgrants.

§ 119.14 Are there limitations regarding the use of program income?

Program income, as defined in OMB Circular A–110, may only be used to further PRIME program objectives. As such, fees collected from clients, and other program income as defined, may be used to help fund the matching requirement. All program income, as defined, shall be reported on financial reports submitted to SBA and added to funds committed to the project by SBA and the recipient organization. However, any interest earned in excess of the maximum allowable amount as specified in the OMB circular incorporated into the grant must be returned to the Federal Government by the grantee.

§ 119.15 If a grantee is unable to spend the entire amount allotted for a single fiscal year, can the funds be carried over to the next year?

(a) The grantee may request approval to use unexpended funds in the next budget period. This is permissible if funds are to be used for a non-severable, non-recurring project or activity within the scope of the PRIME program. Non-severable means a project in its entirety that cannot be subdivided. The request for using unexpended funds in the next budget period must include the following:

(1) SF 424, budget pages, and justification;

(2) Explanation of why the funds were not expended during the period in which they were awarded; and

(3) Evidence of match. The match requirement for funds carried over to the next budget period can be met by using any excess of matching funds from the current budget period, new matching funds, or a combination of both.

(b) The request must be made no later than 60 days before the end of the budget/project period or the de-obligation process will begin. Approved requests will require the issuance of a revised Notice of Award. Expenditures for funds carried over to the next budget period must be tracked separately.

§ 119.16 What are the reporting, record keeping, and related requirements for grantees?

A grantee must keep records and meet the other requirements of section 115 of the Riegle Community Development and Regulatory Improvement Act of 1994 (Riegle Act), as if it were a community development financial institution. (See 12 U.S.C. 4714). In addition to meeting requirements of the Riegle Act, a grantee must also maintain data allowing it to measure the impact of services provided by it and any subgrantees, and, if specifically required by the terms of the PRIME grant, measure the success rate of individual clients whom the grantees assist. SBA will detail such requirements in its Program Announcements.

§ 119.17 What types of oversight will SBA provide to grantees?

(a) In addition to reports required under the Riegle Act, SBA will require reports in accordance with applicable OMB circulars. Such reports will include the following information:

(1) For recipients of Technical Assistance and Capacity Building Grants, for the first two years of receiving grant funding, narrative performance reports and financial status reports will be required quarterly within 15 calendar days of the end of each quarter. Thereafter, grantees may request that SBA reduce the frequency of reports from quarterly to semi-annually. The frequency of reporting then will be determined at the discretion of SBA. In addition, details of expenditures will be

required with each request for payment. Grantees will be required to submit audited financial statements on an annual basis, if available, or annual financial statements prepared by a licensed, independent public accountant, within 120 calendar days of the end of the grantee's fiscal year.

(2) For recipients of Research and Development Grants, reports will be required in accordance with agreed upon milestones and as part of the disbursement process.

(3) For recipients of Discretionary Grants, reports will be required as appropriate for the project, or on a schedule as described in paragraph (a)(1) of this section, whichever is more frequent.

(b) In addition, SBA may, from time to time, make site visits to the grantee, and review all applicable books and records.

§ 119.18 What are the restrictions against lobbying?

No assistance made available under the PRIME program may be expended by a grantee or subgrantee to pay any person to influence, or attempt to influence, any agency, elected official, officer, or employee of a Federal, State, or local government in connection with its participation in the program.

§ 119.19 Is fundraising an allowable expense under the PRIME program?

Expenditures of grant funds for fundraising activities are not allowable costs under this program. Applicants must be able to raise matching funds without the assistance of grant funds. Unless the full requirement for matching funds is waived, the applicant must demonstrate that it has adequate fundraising resources to obtain the required non-Federal matching funds to perform the project.

§ 119.20 Should grantees and subgrantees raise conflict of interest matters with SBA?

Each grantee or subgrantee must provide SBA with a copy of its conflicts of interest policies prior to receipt of funding under the program. Such policies must clearly describe the grantee's or subgrantee's protections from conflicts of interest or the appearance thereof in the handling of grant funding and program provision under this program.

PART 120—BUSINESS LOANS

GENERAL DESCRIPTIONS OF SBA'S BUSINESS LOAN PROGRAMS

DEFINITIONS

Subpart A—Policies Applying to All Business Loans

ELIGIBILITY REQUIREMENTS

INELIGIBLE BUSINESSES AND ELIGIBLE PASSIVE COMPANIES

USES OF PROCEEDS

ETHICAL REQUIREMENTS

CREDIT CRITERIA FOR SBA LOANS

REQUIREMENTS IMPOSED UNDER OTHER LAWS AND ORDERS

Subpart D—Lenders

Subpart E—Servicing, Liquidation and Debt Collection Litigation of 7(a) and 504 Loans

AUTHORITY: 15 U.S.C. 634(b) (6), (b) (7), (b) (14), (h), and note, 636(a), (h) and (m), 650, 687(f), 696(3) and (7), and 697(a) and (e); Pub. L. 111–5, 123 Stat. 115, Pub. L. 111–240, 124 Stat. 2504.

SOURCE: 61 FR 3235, Jan. 31, 1996, unless otherwise noted.

EDITORIAL NOTE: Nomenclature changes to part 120 appear at 72 FR 50039, Aug. 30, 2007.

GENERAL DESCRIPTIONS OF SBA'S BUSINESS LOAN PROGRAMS

§ 120.1 Which loan programs does this part cover?

This part regulates SBA's financial assistance to small businesses under its general business loan programs ("7(a) loans") authorized by section 7(a) of the Small Business Act ("the Act"), 15 U.S.C. 636(a), its microloan demonstration loan program ("Microloans") authorized by section 7(m) of the Act, 15 U.S.C. 636(m), and its development company program ("504 loans") authorized by Title V of the Small Business Investment Act, 15 U.S.C. 695 to 697f ("Title V"). These three programs constitute the business loan programs of the SBA.

§ 120.2 Descriptions of the business loan programs.

(a) *7(a) loans.* (1) 7(a) loans provide financing for general business purposes and may be:

(i) A direct loan by SBA;

(ii) An immediate participation loan by a Lender and SBA; or

(iii) A guaranteed loan (deferred participation) by which SBA guarantees a portion of a loan made by a Lender.

(2) A guaranteed loan is initiated by a Lender agreeing to make an SBA guaranteed loan to a small business and applying to SBA for SBA's guarantee under a blanket guarantee agreement (participation agreement) between SBA and the Lender. If SBA agrees to guarantee (authorizes) a portion of the loan, the Lender funds and services the loan. If the small business defaults on the loan, SBA's guarantee requires SBA to purchase its portion of the outstanding balance, upon demand by the Lender and subject to specific conditions. Regulations specific to 7(a) loans are found in subpart B of this part.

(b) *Microloans.* SBA makes loans and loan guarantees to non-profit Intermediaries that make short-term loans up to $50,000 to eligible small businesses for general business purposes, except payment of personal debts. SBA also makes grants to Intermediaries for use in providing management assistance and counseling to small businesses. Regulations specific to these loans are found in subpart G of this part.

(c) *504 loans.* Projects involving 504 loans require long-term fixed-asset financing for small businesses. A Certified Development Company (CDC) provides the final portion of this financing with a 504 loan made from the proceeds of a Debenture issued by the CDC, guaranteed 100 percent by SBA (with the full faith and credit of the United States), and sold to investors. The regulations specific to these loans are found in subpart H of this part.

[61 FR 3235, Jan. 31, 1996, as amended at 76 FR 63545, Oct. 12, 2011]

§ 120.3 Pilot programs.

The Administrator of SBA may from time to time suspend, modify, or waive rules for a limited period of time to test new programs or ideas. The Administrator shall publish a document in the FEDERAL REGISTER explaining the reasons for these actions.

DEFINITIONS

§ 120.10 Definitions.

The following terms have the same meaning wherever they are used in this part. Defined terms are capitalized wherever they appear.

Acceptable Risk Rating is an SBA-assigned Risk Rating, currently defined by SBA as "1", "2" or "3" on a scale of 1 to 5, which represents an acceptable level of risk as determined by SBA, and which may be revised by SBA from time to time as published in the FEDERAL REGISTER through notice and comment.

Associate. (1) An Associate of a Lender or CDC is:

(i) An officer, director, key employee, or holder of 20 percent or more of the value of the Lender's or CDC's stock or debt instruments, or an agent involved in the loan process;

(ii) Any entity in which one or more individuals referred to in paragraphs (1)(i) of this definition or a Close Relative of any such individual owns or controls at least 20 percent.

(2) An Associate of a small business is:

(i) An officer, director, owner of more than 20 percent of the equity, or key employee of the small business;

(ii) Any entity in which one or more individuals referred to in paragraphs (2)(i) of this definition owns or controls at least 20 percent; and

(iii) Any individual or entity in control of or controlled by the small business (except a Small Business Investment Company ("SBIC") licensed by SBA).

(3) For purposes of this definition, the time during which an Associate relationship exists commences six months before the following dates and continues as long as the certification, participation agreement, or loan is outstanding:

(i) For a CDC, the date of certification by SBA;

(ii) For a Lender, the date of application for a loan guarantee on behalf of an applicant; or

(iii) For a small business, the date of the loan application to SBA, the CDC, the Intermediary, or the Lender.

Authorization is SBA's written agreement providing the terms and conditions under which SBA will make or guarantee business loans. It is not a contract to make a loan.

Authorized CDC Liquidator is a CDC in good standing with authority under the Act and SBA regulations to conduct liquidation and certain debt collection litigation in connection with 504 loans, as authorized by § 120.975.

Borrower is the obligor of an SBA business loan.

Certified Development Company ("CDC") is an entity authorized by SBA to deliver 504 financing to small businesses.

Close Relative is a spouse; a parent; or a child or sibling, or the spouse of any such person.

Eligible Passive Company is a small entity or trust which does not engage in regular and continuous business activity, which leases real or personal property to an Operating Company for use in the Operating Company's business, and which complies with the conditions set forth in § 120.111.

Federal Financial Institution Regulator is the federal banking regulator of a 7(a) Lender and may include the Federal Deposit Insurance Corporation, the Federal Reserve Board, the Office of the Comptroller of the Currency, the Office of Thrift Supervision, the National Credit Union Administration, and the Farm Credit Administration.

Intermediary is the entity in the Microloan program that receives SBA financial assistance and makes loans to small businesses in amounts up to $50,000.

Lender or 7(a) Lender is an institution that has executed a participation agreement with SBA under the guaranteed loan program.

Lender Oversight Committee is a committee within SBA, with responsibilities as outlined in Delegations of Authority, as published in the FEDERAL REGISTER.

Less Than Acceptable Risk Rating is an SBA-assigned Risk Rating, currently defined by SBA as "4" or "5" on a scale of 1 to 5, which represents a higher level of risk as determined by SBA, and which may be revised by SBA from time to time as published in the FEDERAL REGISTER through notice and comment.

Loan Instruments are the Authorization, note, instruments of hypothecation, and all other agreements and documents related to a loan.

Loan program requirements are requirements imposed upon Lenders or CDCs by statute, SBA regulations, any agreement the Lender or CDC has executed with SBA, SBA SOPs, official SBA notices and forms applicable to the 7(a) and 504 loan programs, and loan authorizations, as such requirements are issued and revised by SBA from time to time. For CDCs, this term also includes requirements imposed by Debentures, as that term is defined in § 120.802.

Management Official is an officer, director, general partner, manager, employee participating in management, agent or other participant in the management of the affairs of the SBA Supervised Lender's activities under the 7(a) program.

Non-Federally Regulated Lender (NFRL) is a business concern that is authorized by the SBA to make loans under section 7(a) and is subject to regulation by a state but whose lending activities are not regulated by a Federal Financial Institution Regulator.

Operating Company is an eligible small business actively involved in conducting business operations now or about to be located on real property owned by an Eligible Passive Company, or using or about to use in its business operations personal property owned by an Eligible Passive Company.

Other Regulated SBLC is a Small Business Lending Company whose SBA operations receive regular safety and soundness examinations by a state banking regulator or a Federal Financial Institution Regulator, and which meets the requirements set forth in § 120.1511.

Person is any individual, corporation, partnership, association, unit of government, or legal entity, however organized.

Preference is any arrangement giving a Lender or a CDC a preferred position compared to SBA relating to the making, servicing, or liquidation of a business loan with respect to such things as repayment, collateral, guarantees, control, maintenance of a compensating balance, purchase of a Certificate of deposit or acceptance of a separate or companion loan, without SBA's consent.

Rentable Property is the total square footage of all buildings or facilities used for business operations.

Risk Rating is an SBA internal composite rating assigned to individual SBA Lenders, Intermediaries, or NTAPs that reflects the risk associated with the SBA Lender's or Intermediary's portfolio of SBA loans or with the NTAP. Risk Ratings currently range from one to five, with one representing the least risk and five representing the most risk, and may be revised by SBA from time to time as published in the FEDERAL REGISTER through notice and comment.

Rural Area is a political subdivision or unincorporated area in a non-metropolitan county (as defined by the Department of Agriculture), or, if in a metropolitan county, any such subdivision or area with a resident population under 20,000 which is designated by SBA as rural.

SBA Lender is a 7(a) Lender or a CDC. This term includes SBA Supervised Lenders.

SBA Supervised Lender is a 7(a) Lender that is either a Small Business Lending Company or a NFRL.

Service Provider is an entity that contracts with a Lender or CDC to perform management, marketing, legal or other services.

Small Business Lending Company (SBLC) is a nondepository lending institution that is SBA licensed and is authorized by SBA to only make loans pursuant to section 7(a) of the Small Business Act and loans to Intermediaries in SBA's Microloan program. SBA has imposed a moratorium on licensing new SBLCs since January 1982.

SOPs are SBA Standard Operating Procedures, as issued and revised by SBA from time to time. SOPs are publicly available on SBA's Web site at *http://www.sba.gov* in the online library.

[61 FR 3235, Jan. 31, 1996, as amended at 64 FR 2117, Jan. 13, 1999; 68 FR 57980, Oct. 7, 2003; 72 FR 18360, Apr. 12, 2007; 73 FR 75510, Dec. 11, 2008; 76 FR 63545, Oct. 12, 2011]

Subpart A—Policies Applying to All Business Loans

ELIGIBILITY REQUIREMENTS

§ 120.100 What are the basic eligibility requirements for all applicants for SBA business loans?

To be eligible for an SBA business loan, a small business applicant must:

(a) Be an operating business (except for loans to Eligible Passive Companies);

(b) Be organized for profit;

(c) Be located in the United States;

(d) Be small under the size requirements of part 121 of this chapter (including affiliates). See subpart H of this part for the size standards of part 121 of this chapter which apply only to 504 loans; and

(e) Be able to demonstrate a need for the desired credit.

§ 120.101 Credit not available elsewhere.

SBA provides business loan assistance only to applicants for whom the desired credit is not otherwise available on reasonable terms from non-Federal sources. SBA requires the Lender or CDC to certify or otherwise show that the desired credit is unavailable to the applicant on reasonable terms and conditions from non-Federal sources without SBA assistance, taking into consideration the prevailing rates and terms in the community in or near where the applicant conducts business, for similar purposes and periods of time. Submission of an application to SBA by a Lender or CDC constitutes certification by the Lender or CDC that it has examined the availability of credit to the applicant, has based its certification upon that examination, and has substantiation in its file to support the certification.

§ 120.103 Are farm enterprises eligible?

Federal financial assistance to agricultural enterprises is generally made by the United States Department of Agriculture (USDA), but may be made by SBA under the terms of a Memorandum of Understanding between SBA and USDA. Farm-related businesses which are not agricultural enterprises are eligible businesses under SBA's business loan programs.

§ 120.104 Are businesses financed by SBICs eligible?

SBA may make or guarantee loans to a business financed by an SBIC if SBA's collateral position will be superior to that of the SBIC. SBA may also make or guarantee a loan to an otherwise eligible small business which temporarily is owned or controlled by an SBIC under the regulations in part 107 of this chapter. SBA neither guarantees SBIC loans nor makes loans jointly with SBICs.

§ 120.105 Special consideration for veterans.

SBA will give special consideration to a small business owned by a veteran or, if the veteran chooses not to apply, to a business owned or controlled by one of the veteran's dependents. If the veteran is deceased or permanently disabled, SBA will give special consideration to one survivor or dependent. SBA will process the application of a business owned or controlled by a veteran or dependent promptly, resolve close questions in the applicant's favor, and pay particular attention to maximum loan maturity. For SBA loans, a veteran is a person honorably discharged from active military service.

Ineligible Businesses and Eligible Passive Companies

§ 120.110 What businesses are ineligible for SBA business loans?

The following types of businesses are ineligible:

(a) Non-profit businesses (for-profit subsidiaries are eligible);

(b) Financial businesses primarily engaged in the business of lending, such as banks, finance companies, and factors (pawn shops, although engaged in lending, may qualify in some circumstances);

(c) Passive businesses owned by developers and landlords that do not actively use or occupy the assets acquired or improved with the loan proceeds (except Eligible Passive Companies under § 120.111);

(d) Life insurance companies;

(e) Businesses located in a foreign country (businesses in the U.S. owned by aliens may qualify);

(f) Pyramid sale distribution plans;

(g) Businesses deriving more than one-third of gross annual revenue from legal gambling activities;

(h) Businesses engaged in any illegal activity;

(i) Private clubs and businesses which limit the number of memberships for reasons other than capacity;

(j) Government-owned entities (except for businesses owned or controlled by a Native American tribe);

(k) Businesses principally engaged in teaching, instructing, counseling or indoctrinating religion or religious beliefs, whether in a religious or secular setting;

(l) [Reserved]

(m) Loan packagers earning more than one third of their gross annual revenue from packaging SBA loans;

(n) Businesses with an Associate who is incarcerated, on probation, on parole, or has been indicted for a felony or a crime of moral turpitude;

(o) Businesses in which the Lender or CDC, or any of its Associates owns an equity interest;

(p) Businesses which:

(1) Present live performances of a prurient sexual nature; or

(2) Derive directly or indirectly more than *de minimis* gross revenue through the sale of products or services, or the presentation of any depictions or displays, of a prurient sexual nature;

(q) Unless waived by SBA for good cause, businesses that have previously defaulted on a Federal loan or Federally assisted financing, resulting in the Federal government or any of its agencies or Departments sustaining a loss in any of its programs, and businesses owned or controlled by an applicant or any of its Associates which previously owned, operated, or controlled a business which defaulted on a Federal loan (or guaranteed a loan which was defaulted) and caused the Federal government or any of its agencies or Departments to sustain a loss in any of its programs. For purposes of this section, a compromise agreement shall also be considered a loss;

(r) Businesses primarily engaged in political or lobbying activities; and

(s) Speculative businesses (such as oil wildcatting).

[61 FR 3235, Jan. 31, 1996, as amended at 82 FR 39502, Aug. 21, 2017]

§ 120.111 What conditions must an Eligible Passive Company satisfy?

An Eligible Passive Company must use loan proceeds only to acquire or lease, and/or improve or renovate, real or personal property (including eligible refinancing), that it leases to one or more Operating Companies for conducting the Operating Company's business, or to finance a change of ownership between the existing owners of the Eligible Passive Company. When the Operating Company is a co-borrower on the loan, loan proceeds also may be used by the Operating Company for working capital and/or the purchase of other assets, including intangible assets, for the Operating Company's use as provided in paragraph (a)(5) of this section. (References to Operating Company in paragraphs (a) and (b) of this section mean each Operating Company.) In the 504 loan program, if the Eligible Passive Company owns assets in addition to the real estate or other eligible long-term fixed assets, loan proceeds may not be used to finance a change of ownership between existing owners of the Eligible Passive Company unless the additional assets owned by the Eligible Passive Company are directly related to the real estate or other eligible long-term fixed assets, the amount attributable to the additional assets is de minimis, and the additional assets are excluded from the Project financing. Any ownership structure or legal form may qualify as an Eligible Passive Company. Any ownership structure or legal form may qualify as an Eligible Passive Company.

(a) Conditions that apply to all legal forms:

(1) The Operating Company must be an eligible small business, and the proposed use of the proceeds must be an eligible use if the Operating Company were obtaining the financing directly;

(2) The Eligible Passive Company (with the exception of a trust) and the Operating Company each must be small under the appropriate size standards in part 121 of this chapter;

(3) The lease between the Eligible Passive Company and the Operating Company must be in writing and must be subordinate to SBA's mortgage, trust deed lien, or security interest on the property. The Eligible Passive Company (as landlord) must furnish as collateral for the loan an assignment of all rents paid under the lease. The rent or lease payments cannot exceed the amount necessary to make the loan payment to the lender, and an additional amount to cover the Eligible Passive Company's direct expenses of holding the property, such as maintenance, insurance and property taxes;

(4) The lease between the Eligible Passive Company and the Operating Company, including options to renew exercisable solely by the Operating Company, must have a remaining term at least equal to the term of the loan;

(5) The Operating Company must be a guarantor or co-borrower with the Eligible Passive Company. In a 7(a) loan that includes working capital and/or the purchase of other assets, including intangible assets, for the Operating Company's use, the Operating Company must be a co-borrower.

(6) Each holder of an ownership interest constituting at least 20 percent of either the Eligible Passive Company or the Operating Company must guarantee the loan. The trustee shall execute the guaranty on behalf of any trust. When deemed necessary for credit or other reasons, SBA or, for a loan processed under an SBA Lender's delegated authority, the SBA Lender may require other appropriate individuals or entities to provide full or limited guarantees of the loan without regard to the percentage of their ownership interests, if any.

(b) *Additional conditions that apply to trusts.* The eligibility status of the trustor will determine trust eligibility. All donors to the trust will be deemed to have trustor status for eligibility purposes. A trust qualifying as an Eligible Passive Company may engage in other activities as authorized by its trust agreement. The trustee must warrant and certify that the trust will not be revoked or substantially amended for the term of the loan without the consent of SBA. The trustor must guarantee the loan. For purposes of this section, the trustee shall certify to SBA that:

(1) The trustee has authority to act;

(2) The trust has the authority to borrow funds, pledge trust assets, and lease the property to the Operating Company;

(3) The trustee has provided accurate, pertinent language from the trust agreement confirming the above; and

(4) The trustee has provided and will continue to provide SBA with a true and complete list of all trustors and donors.

[61 FR 3235, Jan. 31, 1996; 61 FR 7986, Mar. 1, 1996, as amended at 64 FR 2117, Jan. 13, 1999; 77 FR 19533, Apr. 2, 2012; 82 FR 39502, Aug. 21, 2017]

Uses of Proceeds

§ 120.120 What are eligible uses of proceeds?

A small business must use an SBA business loan for sound business purposes. The uses of proceeds are prescribed in each loan's Authorization.

(a) A Borrower may use loan proceeds from any SBA loan to:

(1) Acquire land (by purchase or lease);

(2) Improve a site (e.g., grading, streets, parking lots, landscaping), including up to 5 percent for community improvements such as curbs and sidewalks;

(3) Purchase one or more existing buildings;

(4) Convert, expand or renovate one or more existing buildings;

(5) Construct one or more new buildings; and/or

(6) Acquire (by purchase or lease) and install fixed assets (for a 504 loan, these assets must have a useful life of at least 10 years and be at a fixed location, although short-term financing for equipment, furniture, and furnishings may be permitted where essential to and a minor portion of the 504 Project).

(b) A Borrower may also use 7(a) and microloan proceeds for:

(1) Inventory;

(2) Supplies;

(3) Raw materials; and

(4) Working capital (if the Operating Company is a co-borrower with the Eligible Passive Company, part of the loan proceeds may be applied for working capital and/or the purchase of other assets, including intangible assets, for use by the Operating Company).

(c) A Borrower may use 7(a) loan proceeds for refinancing certain outstanding debts.

[61 FR 3235, Jan. 31, 1996, as amended at 77 FR 19533, Apr. 2, 2012]

§ 120.130 Restrictions on uses of proceeds.

SBA will not authorize nor may a Borrower use loan proceeds for the following purposes (including the replacement of funds used for any such purpose):

(a) Payments, distributions or loans to Associates of the applicant (except for ordinary compensation for services rendered);

(b) Refinancing a debt owed to a Small Business Investment Company ("SBIC") or a New Markets Venture Capital Company ("NMVCC");

(c) Floor plan financing or other revolving line of credit, except under § 120.340 or § 120.390;

(d) Investments in real or personal property acquired and held primarily for sale, lease, or investment (except for a loan to an Eligible Passive Company or to a small contractor under § 120.310);

(e) The applicant may not use any of the proceeds to pay past-due Federal, state, or local payroll taxes, sales taxes, or other similar taxes that are required to be collected by the applicant and held in trust on behalf of a Federal, state, or local government entity.

(f) A purpose which does not benefit the small business; or

(g) Any use restricted by §§ 120.201, 120.202, and 120.884 (specific to 7(a) loans and 504 loans respectively).

[61 FR 3235, Jan. 31, 1996, as amended at 76 FR 9218, Feb. 17, 2011; 76 FR 63545, Oct. 12, 2011; 82 FR 39502, Aug. 21, 2017]

§ 120.131 Leasing part of new construction or existing building to another business.

(a) If the SBA financing (whether 7(a) or 504) is for the construction of a new building, a Borrower may permanently lease up to 20 percent of the Rentable Property to one or more tenants if the Borrower permanently occupies and uses no less than 60 percent of the Rentable Property, and plans to permanently occupy and use within three years some of the remaining space not immediately occupied and not permanently leased and plans to permanently occupy and use within ten years all of the remaining space not permanently leased. If the Borrower is an Eligible Passive Company which leases 100 percent of the new building's space to one or more Operating Companies, the Operating Company, or Operating Companies together, must follow the same rules set forth in this paragraph.

(b) If the SBA financing (whether 7(a) or 504) is for the acquisition, renovation, or reconstruction of an existing building, the Borrower may permanently lease up to 49 percent of the Rentable Property if the Borrower permanently occupies and uses no less than 51 percent of the Rentable Property. If the Borrower is an Eligible Passive Company which leases 100 percent of the space of the existing building to one or more Operating Companies, the Operating Company, or Operating Companies together, must follow the same rules set forth in this paragraph.

[68 FR 51679, Aug. 28, 2003]

ETHICAL REQUIREMENTS

§ 120.140 What ethical requirements apply to participants?

Lenders, Intermediaries, and CDCs (in this section, collectively referred to as "Participants"), must act ethically and exhibit good character. Ethical indiscretion of an Associate of a Participant or a member of a CDC will be attributed to the Participant. A Participant must promptly notify SBA if it obtains information concerning the unethical behavior of an Associate. The following are examples of such unethical behavior. A Participant may not:

(a) Self-deal;

(b) Have a real or apparent conflict of interest with a small business with which it is dealing (including any of its Associates or an Associate's Close Relatives) or SBA;

(c) Own an equity interest in a business that has received or is applying to receive SBA financing (during the term of the loan or within 6 months prior to the loan application);

(d) Be incarcerated, on parole, or on probation;

(e) Knowingly misrepresent or make a false statement to SBA;

(f) Engage in conduct reflecting a lack of business integrity or honesty;

(g) Be a convicted felon, or have an adverse final civil judgment (in a case involving fraud, breach of trust, or other conduct) that would cause the public to question the Participant's business integrity, taking into consideration such factors as the magnitude, repetition, harm caused, and remoteness in time of the activity or activities in question;

(h) Accept funding from any source that restricts, prioritizes, or conditions the types of small businesses that the Participant may assist under an SBA program or that imposes any conditions or requirements upon recipients of SBA assistance inconsistent with SBA's loan programs or regulations;

(i) Fail to disclose to SBA all relationships between the small business and its Associates (including Close Relatives of Associates), the Participant, and/or the lenders financing the Project of which it is aware or should be aware;

(j) Fail to disclose to SBA whether the loan will:

(1) Reduce the exposure of a Participant or an Associate of a Participant in a position to sustain a loss;

(2) Directly or indirectly finance the purchase of real estate, personal property or services (including insurance) from the Participant or an Associate of the Participant;

(3) Repay or refinance a debt due a Participant or an Associate of a Participant; or

(4) Require the small business, or an Associate (including Close Relatives of Associates), to invest in the Participant (except for institutions which require an investment from all members

as a condition of membership, such as a Production Credit Association);

(k) Issue a real estate forward commitment to a builder or developer; or

(l) Engage in any activity which taints its objective judgment in evaluating the loan.

[61 FR 3235, Jan. 31, 1996, as amended at 68 FR 57980, Oct. 7, 2003]

CREDIT CRITERIA FOR SBA LOANS

§ 120.150 What are SBA's lending criteria?

The applicant (including an Operating Company) must be creditworthy. Loans must be so sound as to reasonably assure repayment. SBA will consider:

(a) Character, reputation, and credit history of the applicant (and the Operating Company, if applicable), its Associates, and guarantors;

(b) Experience and depth of management;

(c) Strength of the business;

(d) Past earnings, projected cash flow, and future prospects;

(e) Ability to repay the loan with earnings from the business;

(f) Sufficient invested equity to operate on a sound financial basis;

(g) Potential for long-term success;

(h) Nature and value of collateral (although inadequate collateral will not be the sole reason for denial of a loan request); and

(i) The effect any affiliates (as defined in part 121 of this chapter) may have on the ultimate repayment ability of the applicant.

§ 120.151 What is the statutory limit for total loans to a Borrower?

The aggregate amount of the SBA portions of all loans to a single Borrower, including the Borrower's affiliates as defined in § 121.301(f) of this chapter, must not exceed a guaranty amount of $3,750,000, except as otherwise authorized by statute for a specific program. The maximum loan amount for any one 7(a) loan is $5,000,000. The amount of any loan received by an Eligible Passive Company applies to the loan limit of both the Eligible Passive Company and the Operating Company.

[61 FR 3235, Jan. 31, 1996, as amended at 68 FR 51680, Aug. 28, 2003; 76 FR 63546, Oct. 12, 2011; 81 FR 41428, June 27, 2016]

§ 120.160 Loan conditions.

The following requirements are normally required by SBA for all business loans:

(a) *Personal guarantees.* Holders of at least a 20 percent ownership interest generally must guarantee the loan. When deemed necessary for credit or other reasons, SBA or, for a loan processed under an SBA Lender's delegated authority, the SBA Lender, may require other appropriate individuals or entities to provide full or limited guarantees of the loan without regard to the percentage of their ownership interests, if any.

(b) *Appraisals.* SBA may require professional appraisals of the applicant's and principals' assets, a survey, or a feasibility study.

(c) *Hazard Insurance.* SBA requires hazard insurance on all collateral.

[61 FR 3235, Jan. 31, 1996, as amended at 82 FR 39502, Aug. 21, 2017]

REQUIREMENTS IMPOSED UNDER OTHER LAWS AND ORDERS

§ 120.170 Flood insurance.

Under the Flood Disaster Protection Act of 1973 (Sec. 205(b) of Pub. L. 93–234; 87 Stat. 983 (42 U.S.C. 4000 *et seq.*)), a loan recipient must obtain flood insurance if any building (including mobile homes), machinery, or equipment acquired, installed, improved, constructed, or renovated with the proceeds of SBA financial assistance is located in a special flood hazard area. The requirement applies also to any inventory (business loan program), fixtures or furnishings contained or to be contained in the building. Mobile homes on a foundation are buildings. SBA, Lenders, CDCs, and Intermediaries must notify Borrowers that flood insurance must be maintained.

§ 120.171 Compliance with child support obligations.

Any holder of 50% or more of the ownership interest in the recipient of an SBA loan must certify that he or she is not more than 60 days delinquent on any obligation to pay child support arising under:

(a) An administrative order;

(b) A court order;

(c) A repayment agreement between the holder and a custodial parent; or

(d) A repayment agreement between the holder and a State agency providing child support enforcement services.

§ 120.172 Flood-plain and wetlands management.

(a) All loans must conform to requirements of Executive Orders 11988, "Flood Plain Management" (3 CFR, 1977 Comp., p. 117) and 11990, "Protection of Wetlands" (3 CFR, 1977 Comp., p. 121). Lenders, Intermediaries, CDCs, and SBA must comply with requirements applicable to them. Applicants must show:

(1) Whether the location for which financial assistance is proposed is in a floodplain or wetland;

(2) If it is in a floodplain, that the assistance is in compliance with local land use plans; and

(3) That any necessary construction or use permits will be issued.

(b) Generally, there is an 8-step decision making process with respect to:

(1) Construction or acquisition of anything, other than a building;

(2) Repair and restoration equal to more than 50% of the market value of a building; or

(3) Replacement of destroyed structures.

(c) SBA may determine for the following types of actions, on a case-by-case basis, that the full 8-step process is not warranted and that only the first step (determining if a proposed action is in the base floodplain) need be completed:

(1) Actions located outside the base floodplain;

(2) Repairs, other than to buildings, that are less than 50% of the market value;

(3) Replacement of building contents, materials, and equipment;

(4) Hazard mitigation measures;

(5) Working capital loans; or

(6) SBA loan assistance of $1,500,000 or less.

§ 120.173 Lead-based paint.

If loan proceeds are for the construction or rehabilitation of a residential structure, lead-based paint may not be used on any interior surface, or on any exterior surface that is readily accessible to children under the age of seven years.

§ 120.174 Earthquake hazards.

When loan proceeds are used to construct a new building or an addition to an existing building, the construction must conform with the "National Earthquake Hazards Reduction Program ("NEHRP") Recommended Provisions for the Development of Seismic Regulations for New Buildings" (which can be obtained from the Federal Emergency Management Agency, Publications Office, Washington, DC) or a code identified by SBA as being substantially equivalent.

§ 120.175 Coastal barrier islands.

SBA and Intermediaries may not make or guarantee any loan within the Coastal Barrier Resource System.

§ 120.176 Compliance with other laws.

All SBA loans are subject to all applicable laws, including (without limitation) the civil rights laws (*see* parts 112, 113, 117 and 136 of this chapter), prohibiting discrimination on the grounds of race, color, national origin, religion, sex, marital status, disability or age. SBA requests agreements or evidence to support or document compliance with these laws, including reports required by applicable statutes or the regulations in this chapter.

APPLICABILITY AND ENFORCEABILITY OF LOAN PROGRAM REQUIREMENTS

§ 120.180 Lender and CDC compliance with Loan Program Requirements.

Lenders must comply and maintain familiarity with Loan Program Requirements for the 7(a) program, as such requirements are revised from time to time. CDCs must comply and maintain familiarity with Loan Program Requirements for the 504 program, as such requirements are revised from time to time. Loan Program Requirements in effect at the time that a

Lender or CDC takes an action in connection with a particular loan govern that specific action. For example, although loan closing requirements in effect when a Lender or CDC closes a loan will govern the closing actions, a Lender or CDC's liquidation actions on the same loan are subject to the liquidation requirements in effect at the time that a liquidation action is taken.

[72 FR 18360, Apr. 12, 2007]

§ 120.181 Status of Lenders and CDCs.

Lenders, CDCs and their contractors are independent contractors that are responsible for their own actions with respect to a 7(a) or 504 loan. SBA has no responsibility or liability for any claim by a borrower, guarantor or other party alleging injury as a result of any allegedly wrongful action taken by a Lender, CDC or an employee, agent, or contractor of a Lender or CDC.

[72 FR 18360, Apr. 12, 2007]

LOAN APPLICATIONS

§ 120.190 Where does an applicant apply for a loan?

An applicant for a business loan should apply to:

(a) A Lender for a guaranteed or immediate participation loan;

(b) A CDC for a 504 loan;

(c) An Intermediary for a Microloan; or

(d) SBA for a direct loan.

§ 120.191 The contents of a business loan application.

For most business loans, SBA requires that an application for a business loan contain, among other things, a description of the history and nature of the business, the amount and purpose of the loan, the collateral offered for the loan, current financial statements, historical financial statements (or tax returns if appropriate) for the past three years, IRS tax verification, and a business plan, when applicable. Personal histories and financial statements will be required from principals of the applicant (and the Operating Company, if applicable).

§ 120.192 Approval or denial.

Applicants receive notice of approval or denial by the Lender, CDC, Intermediary, or SBA, as appropriate. Notice of denial will include the reasons. If a loan is approved, an Authorization will be issued.

§ 120.193 Reconsideration after denial.

An applicant or recipient of a business loan may request reconsideration of a denied loan or loan modification request within 6 months of denial. Applicants denied due to a size determination can appeal that determination under part 121 of this chapter. All others must be submitted to the office that denied the original request. To prevail, the applicant must demonstrate that it has overcome all legitimate reasons for denial. Six months after denial, a new application is required. If the reconsideration is denied, a second and final reconsideration may be considered by the Director, Office of Financial Assistance (D/FA), whose decision is final.

COMPUTERIZED SBA FORMS

§ 120.194 [Reserved]

REPORTING

§ 120.195 Disclosure of fees.

An Applicant for a business loan must identify to SBA the name of each Agent as defined in part 103 of this chapter that helped the applicant obtain the loan, describing the services performed, and disclosing the amount of each fee paid or to be paid by the applicant to the Agent in conjunction with the performance of those services.

§ 120.197 Notifying SBA's Office of Inspector General of suspected fraud.

Lenders, CDCs, Borrowers, and others must notify the SBA Office of Inspector General of any information which indicates that fraud may have occurred in connection with a 7(a) or 504 loan. Send the notification to the Assistant Inspector General for Investigations, Office of Inspector General, U.S. Small Business Administration, 409 3rd Street, SW., Washington, DC 20416.

[72 FR 18360, Apr. 12, 2007]

Subpart B—Policies Specific to 7(a) Loans

BONDING REQUIREMENTS

§ 120.200 What bonding requirements exist during construction?

On 7(a) loans which finance construction, the Borrower must supply a 100 percent payment and performance bond and builder's risk insurance, unless waived by SBA.

LIMITATIONS ON USE OF PROCEEDS

§ 120.201 Refinancing unsecured or undersecured loans.

A Borrower may not use 7(a) loan proceeds to pay any creditor in a position to sustain a loss causing a shift to SBA of all or part of a potential loss from an existing debt.

§ 120.202 Restrictions on loans for changes in ownership.

A Borrower may not use 7(a) loan proceeds to purchase a portion of a business or a portion of another owner's interest. One or more current owners may use loan proceeds to purchase the entire interest of another current owner, or a Borrower can purchase ownership of an entire business.

MATURITIES; INTEREST RATES; LOAN AND GUARANTEE AMOUNTS

§ 120.210 What percentage of a loan may SBA guarantee?

SBA's guarantee percentage must not exceed the applicable percentage established in section 7(a) of the Act. The maximum allowable guarantee percentage on a loan will be determined by the loan amount. Loans of $150,000 or less may receive a maximum guaranty of 85 percent. Loans more than $150,000 may receive a maximum guaranty of 75 percent, except as otherwise authorized by law.

[61 FR 3235, Jan. 31, 1996, as amended at 68 FR 51680, Aug. 28, 2003; 76 FR 63546, Oct. 12, 2011]

§ 120.211 What limits are there on the amounts of direct loans?

(a) The statutory limit for direct loans made under the authority of section 7(a)(1)-(19) of the Small Business Act is $350,000. SBA has established an administrative limit of $150,000 for direct loans. The D/FA may authorize acceptance of an application up to the statutory limit.

(b) The statutory limit for direct loans made under the authority of section 7(a)(20) is $750,000. SBA has established an administrative limit of $150,000. The Associate Administrator for Business Development may authorize the acceptance of an application that exceeds the administrative limit.

(c) The statutory limit on SBA's portion of an immediate participation loan is $350,000. The administrative limit is the lesser of 75 percent of the loan or $150,000. The D/FA may authorize exceptions to the administrative limit up to $350,000.

[61 FR 3235, Jan. 31, 1996, as amended at 74 FR 45753, Sept. 4, 2009]

§ 120.212 What limits are there on loan maturities?

The term of a loan shall be:

(a) The shortest appropriate term, depending upon the Borrower's ability to repay;

(b) Ten years or less, unless it finances or refinances real estate or equipment with a useful life exceeding ten years; and

(c) A maximum of 25 years, including extensions. (A portion of a loan used to acquire or improve real property may have a term of 25 years plus an additional period needed to complete the construction or improvements.)

§ 120.213 What fixed interest rates may a Lender charge?

(a) *Fixed Rates for Guaranteed Loans.* A loan may have a reasonable fixed interest rate. SBA periodically publishes the maximum allowable rate in the FEDERAL REGISTER.

(b) *Direct loans.* A statutory formula based on the cost of money to the Federal government determines the interest rate on direct loans. SBA publishes the rate periodically in the FEDERAL REGISTER.

§ 120.214 What conditions apply for variable interest rates?

A Lender may use a variable rate of interest, upon SBA's approval. SBA's maximum allowable rates apply only to the initial rate on the date SBA received the loan application. SBA shall approve the use of a variable interest rate under the following conditions:

(a) *Frequency.* The first change may occur on the first calendar day of the month following initial disbursement, using the base rate (see paragraph (c) of this section) in effect on the first business day of the month. After that, changes may occur no more often than monthly.

(b) *Range of fluctuation.* The amount of fluctuation shall be equal to the movement in the base rate. The difference between the initial rate and the ceiling rate may be no greater than the difference between the initial rate and the floor rate.

(c) *Base rate.* The base rate will be one of the following: (i) The prime rate; (ii) the thirty-day (1-month) London Interbank Offered Rate (LIBOR) plus 3 percentage points, or (iii) the Optional Peg Rate. The prime or LIBOR rate will be that which is in effect on the first business day of the month, as printed in a national financial newspaper published each business day. SBA publishes the Optional Peg Rate quarterly in the FEDERAL REGISTER.

(d) *Maturities under 7 years.* For loans with maturities under seven years, the maximum interest rate shall not exceed two and one-quarter (2 1/4) percentage points over the base rate.

(e) *Maturities of 7 years or more.* For loans with maturities of seven or more years, the maximum interest rate shall not exceed two and three-quarters (2 3/4) percentage points over the base rate.

(f) *Amortization.* Initial amortization of principal and interest may be recomputed and reassessed as interest rates fluctuate, as directed by SBA. With prior approval of SBA, the Lender may use certain other amortization methods, except that SBA does not allow balloon payments.

[61 FR 3235, Jan. 31, 1996, as amended at 73 FR 67101, Nov. 13, 2008]

§ 120.215 What interest rates apply to smaller loans?

For a loan over $25,000 but not exceeding $50,000, the interest rate may be one percent more than the maximum interest rate described above. For a loan of $25,000 or less, the maximum interest rate described above may be increased by two percentage points.

[61 FR 3235, Jan. 31, 1996; 61 FR 7986, Mar. 1, 1996]

FEES FOR GUARANTEED LOANS

§ 120.220 Fees that Lender pays SBA.

A Lender must pay a guaranty fee to SBA for each loan it makes. If the guarantee fee is not paid, SBA may terminate the guarantee. Acceptance of the guaranty fee by SBA does not waive any right of SBA arising from a Lender's negligence, misconduct or violation of any provision of these regulations, the guaranty agreement, or the loan authorization.

(a) *Amount of guaranty fee*—(1) *In general.* Except to the extent paragraph (a)(2) of this section applies, for a loan with a maturity of twelve (12) months or less, the guarantee fee which the Lender must pay to SBA is one-quarter (¼) of one percent of the guaranteed portion of the loan. For a loan with a maturity of more than twelve (12) months, the guarantee fee is payable as follows:

(i) Not more than 2 percent of the guaranteed portion of a loan if the total amount of the loan is not more than $150,000;

(ii) Not more than 3 percent of the guaranteed portion of a loan if the total amount of the loan is more than $150,000 but not more than $700,000;

(iii) Except as provided in paragraph (a)(1)(iv) of this section, not more than 3.5 percent of the guaranteed portion of a loan if the total amount of the loan is more than $700,000; and

(iv) An additional 0.25 percent of the guaranteed portion of a loan if the total amount of the loan is more than $1,000,000.

(2) *For loans approved October 1, 2002, through September 30, 2004.* For a loan with a maturity of twelve (12) months or less, the guarantee fee which the Lender must pay to SBA is one-quarter (¼) of one percent of the guaranteed portion of the loan. For a loan with a maturity of more than twelve (12) months, the guarantee fee is:

(i) 1 percent of the guaranteed portion of the loan if the total loan amount is not more than $150,000,

(ii) 2.5 percent of the guaranteed portion of a loan if the total loan amount is more than $150,000, but not more than $700,000, and

(iii) 3.5 percent of the guaranteed portion if the total loan amount is more than $700,000.

(3) *For loans approved under section 7(a)(31) of the Small Business Act (SBA Express loans) to veterans and/or the spouse of a veteran.* In fiscal years when the 7(a) program is at zero subsidy, SBA will not collect a guarantee fee in connection with a loan made under section 7(a)(31) of the Small Business Act to a business owned and controlled by a veteran or the spouse of a veteran.

(b) *When the guaranty fee is payable.* For a loan with a maturity of twelve (12) months or less, the Lender must pay the guaranty fee to SBA electronically within 10 business days after receiving SBA loan approval. The Lender may only charge the Borrower for the fee after the Lender pays the guaranty fee. For a loan with a maturity in excess of twelve (12) months, the Lender must pay the guaranty fee to SBA electronically within 90 days after SBA gives its loan approval. The Lender may charge the Borrower the fee after the Lender has made the first disbursement of the loan. The Borrower may use the loan proceeds to pay the guaranty fee. However, the first disbursement must not be made solely or primarily to pay the guaranty fee.

(c) *Refund of guaranty fee.* For a loan with a maturity of more than twelve (12) months, SBA will refund the guaranty fee if the Lender has not made any disbursement and the lender requests in writing the refund and cancellation of the SBA guaranty.

(d) *Lender's retention of portion of guaranty fee.* With respect to a loan with a maturity of more than twelve (12) months, where the total loan amount is no more than $150,000 Lender may retain not more than 25 percent of the guaranty fee.

(e) If the guarantee fee is not paid, SBA may terminate the guarantee. The Borrower may use working capital loan proceeds to reimburse the Lender for the guarantee fee. Acceptance of the guarantee fee by SBA shall not waive any right of SBA arising from the Lender's misconduct or violation of any provision of this part, the guarantee agreement, the Authorization, or other loan documents.

(f) *Lender's annual service fee payable to SBA*—(1) *In general.* Except to the extent paragraph (f)(2) of this section applies, the lender shall pay SBA an annual service fee in an amount not to exceed 0.55 percent of the outstanding balance of the guaranteed portion of each loan. The service fee cannot be charged to the Borrower. SBA may institute a late fee charge for delinquent payments of the annual service fee to cover administrative costs associated with collecting delinquent fees.

(2) *For loans approved from October 1, 2002, through September 30, 2004.* The lender shall pay SBA an annual service fee equal to 0.25 percent of the outstanding balance of the guaranteed portion of each loan. The service fee cannot be charged to the Borrower. SBA may institute a late fee charge for delinquent payments of the annual service fee to cover administrative costs associated with collecting delinquent fees.

[61 FR 3235, Jan. 31, 1996; 61 FR 11471, Mar. 20, 1996, as amended at 68 FR 51680, Aug. 28, 2003; 68 FR 56554, Oct. 1, 2003; 76 FR 63546, Oct. 12, 2011; 82 FR 39502, Aug. 21, 2017]

§ 120.221 Fees and expenses which the Lender may collect from a loan applicant or Borrower.

Unless otherwise allowed by SBA Loan Program Requirements, the Lender may charge and collect from the applicant or Borrower only the following fees and expenses:

(a) *Service and packaging fees.* The Lender may charge an applicant reasonable fees (customary for similar Lenders in the geographic area where the loan is being made) for packaging and other services. The Lender must advise the applicant in writing that the applicant is not required to obtain or pay for unwanted services. The applicant is responsible for deciding whether fees are reasonable. SBA may review these fees at any time. Lender must refund any such fee considered unreasonable by SBA.

(b) *Extraordinary servicing.* Subject to prior written SBA approval, if all or part of a loan will have extraordinary servicing needs, the Lender may charge the applicant a service fee not to exceed 2 percent per year on the outstanding balance of the part requiring special servicing.

(c) *Out-of-pocket expenses.* The Lender may collect from the applicant necessary out-of-pocket expenses such as filing or recording fees.

(d) *Late payment fee.* The Lender may charge the Borrower a late payment fee not to exceed 5 percent of the regular loan payment.

(e) *Legal services.* Lender may charge the Borrower for legal services rendered on an hourly basis.

[61 FR 3235, Jan. 31, 1996, as amended at 82 FR 39503, Aug. 21, 2017]

§ 120.222 Prohibition on sharing premiums for secondary market sales.

The Lender or its Associates may not share in any premium received from the sale of an SBA guaranteed loan in the secondary market with a Service Provider, packager, or other loan-referral source.

[82 FR 39503, Aug. 21, 2017]

§ 120.223 Subsidy recoupment fee payable to SBA by Borrower.

(a) The subsidy recoupment fee is payable to SBA when:

(1) Loan has a maturity of 15 years or more.

(2) Borrower makes a voluntary prepayment (or several prepayments in the aggregate) during any one of the first three successive 12 month periods following the first disbursement of the loan. Prepayment is defined as a payment of principal in excess of the amount due according to the amortization schedule.

(3) The prepayment (or several prepayments in the aggregate) is more than 25 percent of the highest outstanding principal balance of the loan in any one of the first three successive 12 month periods following the first disbursement.

(b) When all the conditions above exist, the following subsidy recoupment fees apply:

(1) If the prepayment is made during the first 12 month period after first disbursement, the charge is 5 percent of the total amount of all prepayments made during such period;

(2) If the prepayment is made during the second 12 month period after first disbursement, the charge is 3 percent of the total amount of all prepayments made during that period; and

(3) If the prepayment is made during the third 12 month period after first disbursement, the charge is 1 percent of the total amount of all prepayments made during that period.

[68 FR 51680, Aug. 28, 2003]

Subpart C—Special Purpose Loans

§ 120.300 Statutory authority.

Congress has authorized several special purpose programs in various subsections of section 7(a) of the Act. Generally, 7(a) loan policies, eligibility requirements and credit criteria enumerated in subpart B of this part apply to these programs. The sections of this subpart prescribe the special conditions applying to each special purpose program. As with other business loans, special purpose loans are available only to the extent funded by annual appropriations.

DISABLED ASSISTANCE LOAN PROGRAM (DAL)

§ 120.310 What assistance is available for the disabled?

Section 7(a)(10) of the Act authorizes SBA to guarantee or make direct loans to the disabled. SBA distinguishes two kinds of assistance:

(a) *DAL–1.* DAL–1 Financial Assistance is available to non-profit public or private organizations for disabled individuals that employ such individuals; or

(b) *DAL–2.* DAL–2 Financial Assistance is available to:

(1) Small businesses wholly owned by disabled individuals; and

(2) Disabled individuals to establish, acquire, or operate a small business.

§ 120.311 Definitions.

(a) *Organization for the disabled* means one which:

(1) Is organized under federal or state law to operate in the interest of disabled individuals;

(2) Is non-profit;

(3) Employs disabled individuals for seventy-five percent of the time needed

to produce commodities or services for sale; and

(4) Complies with occupational and safety standards prescribed by the Department of Labor.

(b) *Disabled individual* means a person who has a permanent physical, mental or emotional impairment, defect, ailment, disease or disability which limits the type of employment for which the person would otherwise be qualified.

§ 120.312 DAL–1 use of proceeds and other program conditions.

(a) DAL–1 applicants must submit appropriate documents to establish program eligibility.

(b) Generally, applicants may use loan proceeds for any 7(a) loan purposes. Loan proceeds may not be used:

(1) To purchase or construct facilities if construction grants and mortgage assistance are available from another Federal source; or

(2) For supportive services (expenses incurred by a DAL–1 organization to subsidize wages of low producers, health and rehabilitation services, management, training, education, and housing of disabled workers).

(c) SBA does not consider a DAL–1 organization to have a conflict of interest if one or more of its Associates is an Associate of the Lender.

§ 120.313 DAL–2 use of proceeds and other program conditions.

(a) The DAL–2 loan proceeds may be used for any 7(a) loan purposes.

(b) An applicant may use DAL–2 loan proceeds to acquire an eligible small business without complying with the change of ownership conditions in § 120.202.

(c) A DAL–2 applicant must submit evidence from a physician, psychiatrist, or other qualified professional as to the permanent nature of the disability and the limitation it places on the applicant.

§ 120.314 Resolving doubts about creditworthiness.

For the purpose of the DAL Program, SBA shall resolve doubts concerning the creditworthiness of an applicant in favor of the applicant. However, the applicant must present satisfactory evidence of repayment ability. Personal guarantees of Associates are not required for purposes of DAL–1 financial assistance.

§ 120.315 Interest rate and loan limit.

The interest rate on direct DAL loans is three percent. There is an administrative limit of $150,000 on a direct DAL loan.

BUSINESSES OWNED BY LOW INCOME INDIVIDUALS

§ 120.320 Policy.

Section 7(a)(11) of the Act authorizes SBA to guarantee or make direct loans to establish, preserve or strengthen small business concerns:

(a) Located in an area having high unemployment according to the Department of Labor;

(b) Located in an area in which a high percentage of individuals have a low income inadequate to satisfy basic family needs; and

(c) More than 50 percent owned by low income individuals.

ENERGY CONSERVATION

§ 120.330 Who is eligible for an energy conservation loan?

SBA may make or guarantee loans to assist a small business to design, engineer, manufacture, distribute, market, install, or service energy devices or techniques designed to conserve the Nation's energy resources.

§ 120.331 What devices or techniques are eligible for a loan?

Eligible energy conservation devices or techniques include:

(a) Solar thermal equipment;

(b) Photovoltaic cells and related equipment;

(c) A product or service which increases the energy efficiency of existing equipment, methods of operation or systems which use fossil fuels, and which is on the Energy Conservation Measures list of the Secretary of Energy;

(d) Equipment producing energy from wood, biological waste, grain or other biomass energy sources;

(e) Equipment for cogeneration of energy, district heating or production of energy from industrial waste;

(f) Hydroelectric power equipment;

(g) Wind energy conversion equipment; and

(h) Engineering, architectural, consulting, or other professional services necessary or appropriate for any of the devices or techniques in paragraphs (a) through (g) of this section.

§ 120.332 What are the eligible uses of proceeds?

(a) *Acquire property.* The Borrower may use the loan proceeds to acquire land necessary for imminent plant construction, buildings, machinery, equipment, furniture, fixtures, facilities, supplies, and material needed to accomplish any of the eligible program purposes in § 120.330.

(b) *Research and development.* Up to 30% of loan proceeds may be used for research and development:

(1) Of an existing product or service; or

(2) A new product or service.

(c) *Working capital.* The Borrower may use proceeds for working capital for entering or expanding in the energy conservation market.

§ 120.333 Are there any special credit criteria?

In addition to regular credit evaluation criteria, SBA shall weigh the greater risk associated with energy projects. SBA shall consider such factors as quality of the product or service, technical qualifications of the applicant's management, sales projections, and financial status.

EXPORT WORKING CAPITAL PROGRAM (EWCP)

§ 120.340 What is the Export Working Capital Program?

Under the EWCP, SBA guarantees short-term working capital loans made by participating lenders to exporters (section 7(a)(14) of the Act). Loan maturities may be for up to three years with annual renewals. Proceeds can be used only to finance export transactions. Loans can be for single or multiple export transactions. An export transaction is the production and payment associated with a sale of goods or services to a foreign buyer. The maximum loan amount for any one EWCP loan is $5,000,000. EWCP loans shall receive a guaranty of 90 percent, not to exceed $4,500,000.

[61 FR 3235, Jan. 31, 1996, as amended at 76 FR 63546, Oct. 12, 2011]

§ 120.341 Who is eligible?

In addition to the eligibility criteria applicable to all 7(a) loans, an applicant must be in business for one full year at the time of application, but not necessarily in the exporting business. SBA may waive this requirement if the applicant has sufficient export trade experience or other managerial experience.

§ 120.342 What are eligible uses of proceeds?

Loan proceeds may be used:

(a) To acquire inventory;

(b) To pay the manufacturing costs of goods for export;

(c) To purchase goods or services for export;

(d) To support standby letters of credit;

(e) For pre-shipment working capital; and

(f) For post-shipment foreign accounts receivable financing.

§ 120.343 Collateral.

A Borrower must give SBA a first security interest sufficient to cover 100 percent of the EWCP loan amount (such as insured accounts receivable or letters of credit). Collateral must be located in the United States, its territories or possessions.

§ 120.344 Unique requirements of the EWCP.

(a) An applicant must submit cash flow projections to support the need for the loan and the ability to repay. After the loan is made, the loan recipient must submit continual progress reports.

(b) SBA does not limit the amount of extraordinary servicing fees, as referenced in § 120.221(b), under the EWCP.

(c) SBA does not prescribe the interest rates for the EWCP, but will monitor these rates for reasonableness.

INTERNATIONAL TRADE LOANS

§ 120.345 Policy.

Section 7(a)(16) of the Act authorizes SBA to guarantee loans to small businesses that are:

(a) Engaged or preparing to engage in international trade; or

(b) Adversely affected by import competition.

§ 120.346 Eligibility.

(a) An applicant must establish that:

(1) The loan proceeds will significantly expand an existing export market or develop new export markets; or

(2) The applicant business is adversely affected by import competition; and

(3) The loan will improve the applicant's competitive position.

(b) The applicant must have a business plan reasonably supporting its projected export sales.

[61 FR 3235, Jan. 31, 1996, as amended at 76 FR 63546, Oct. 12, 2011]

§ 120.347 Use of proceeds.

The Borrower may use loan proceeds to acquire, construct, renovate, modernize, improve, or expand facilities and equipment to be used in the United States to produce goods or services involved in international trade, and to develop and penetrate foreign markets. The Borrower may also use proceeds in the refinancing of existing indebtedness that is not structured with reasonable terms and conditions, including any debt that qualifies for refinancing under 7(a) Loan Program Requirements, and to provide working capital.

[61 FR 3235, Jan. 31, 1996, as amended at 76 FR 63546, Oct. 12, 2011]

§ 120.348 Amount of guarantee.

The maximum loan amount for any one International Trade (IT) loan is $5,000,000. IT loans may receive a maximum guaranty of 90 percent or $4,500,000, except that the maximum guaranty amount for any working capital component of an IT loan is limited to $4,000,000. To the extent that the Borrower has a separate EWCP loan or any other 7(a) loan for working capital, the guaranty amount for the other loan is counted against the $4,000,000 guaranty limit for the IT loan.

[76 FR 63546, Oct. 12, 2011]

§ 120.349 Collateral.

Each IT loan must be secured either by a first lien position or first mortgage on the property or equipment financed by the IT loan or on other assets of the Borrower, except that an IT loan may be secured by a second lien position on the property or equipment financed by the IT loan or on other assets of the Borrower, if the SBA determines the second lien position provides adequate assurance of the payment of the IT loan.

[76 FR 63546, Oct. 12, 2011]

QUALIFIED EMPLOYEE TRUSTS (ESOP)

§ 120.350 Policy.

Section 7(a)(15) of the Act authorizes SBA to guarantee a loan to a qualified employee trust ("ESOP") to:

(a) Help finance the growth of its employer's small business; or

(b) Purchase ownership or voting control of the employer.

§ 120.351 Definitions.

All terms specific to ESOPs have the same definition for purposes of this section as in the Internal Revenue Service (IRS) Code (title 26 of the United States Code) or regulations (26 CFR chapter I).

§ 120.352 Use of proceeds.

Loan proceeds may be used for two purposes.

(a) *Qualified employer securities.* A qualified employee trust may relend loan proceeds to the employer by purchasing qualified employer securities. The small business concern may use these funds for any general 7(a) purpose.

(b) *Control of employer.* A qualified employee trust may use loan proceeds to purchase a controlling interest (51 percent) in the employer. Ownership and control must vest in the trust by the time the loan is repaid.

§ 120.353 Eligibility.

SBA may assist a qualified employee trust (or equivalent trust) that meets the requirements and conditions for an ESOP prescribed in all applicable IRS, Treasury and Department of Labor (DOL) regulations. In addition, the following conditions apply:

(a) The small business must provide the funds needed by the trust to repay the loan; and

(b) The small business must provide adequate collateral.

§ 120.354 Creditworthiness.

In determining repayment ability, SBA shall not consider the personal assets of the employee-owners of the trust. SBA shall consider the earnings history and projected future earnings of the employer small business. SBA may consider the business and management experience of the employee-owners.

VETERANS LOAN PROGRAM

§ 120.360 Which veterans are eligible?

SBA may guarantee or make direct loans to a small business 51 percent owned by one or more of the following eligible veterans:

(a) Vietnam-era veterans who served for a period of more than 180 days between August 5, 1964, and May 7, 1975, and were discharged other than dishonorably;

(b) Disabled veterans of any era with a minimum compensable disability of 30 percent; or

(c) A veteran of any era who was discharged for disability.

§ 120.361 Other conditions of eligibility.

(a) Management and daily operations of the business must be directed by one or more of the veteran owners whose veteran status was used to qualify for the loan.

(b) This direct loan program is available only if private sector financing and guaranteed loans are not available.

(c) A veteran may qualify only once for this program on a direct loan basis.

POLLUTION CONTROL PROGRAM

§ 120.370 Policy.

Section 7(a)(12) of the Act authorizes SBA to guarantee loans up to $1,000,000 to an eligible small business to plan, design or install a pollution control facility. An applicant must meet the eligibility requirements for 7(a) loans.

LOANS TO PARTICIPANTS IN THE 8(a) PROGRAM

§ 120.375 Policy.

Section 7(a)(20) of the Act authorizes SBA to provide direct (unilaterally or together with Lenders) or guaranteed loans to firms participating in the 8(a) Program.

§ 120.376 Special requirements.

The following special conditions apply (otherwise, 7(a) loan eligibility criteria apply):

(a) The Associate Administrator for Business Development may waive the direct loan administrative ceiling of $150,000, and raise it to $750,000.

(b) The SBA portion of a guaranteed loan must not exceed $750,000.

(c) The interest rate on a guaranteed loan shall be the same as on 7(a) guaranteed business loans. The interest rate on a direct loan shall be one percent less than on a regular direct loan.

(d) For a direct loan or SBA's portion of an immediate participation loan, SBA shall subordinate its security interest on all collateral to other debt of the applicant.

[61 FR 3235, Jan. 31, 1996, as amended at 74 FR 45753, Sept. 4, 2009]

§ 120.377 Use of proceeds.

The loan proceeds shall not be used for debt refinancing. Only a manufacturing concern may use loan proceeds for working capital.

DEFENSE ECONOMIC TRANSITION ASSISTANCE

§ 120.380 Program.

Section 7(a)(21) of the Act authorizes SBA to guarantee loans to help eligible small businesses transition from defense to civilian markets, or eligible individuals adversely impacted by base closures or defense cutbacks to acquire or open and operate a small business.

§ 120.381 Eligibility.

(a) *Eligible small businesses.* A small business is eligible if it has been detrimentally impacted by the closure (or substantial reduction) of a Department of Defense installation, or the termination (or substantial reduction) of a Department of Defense Program on which the small business was a prime contractor, subcontractor, or supplier at any tier.

(b) *Eligible individual.* An eligible individual, for purposes of this program, includes the following persons involuntarily separated from their position or voluntarily terminated under a program offering inducements to encourage early retirement:

(1) A member of the Armed Forces of the United States (honorably discharged);

(2) A civilian employee of the Department of Defense; or

(3) An employee of a prime contractor, sub-contractor, or supplier at any tier of a Department of Defense program.

(c) *Defense loan and technical assistance (DELTA).* The DELTA program provides financial and technical assistance to defense dependent small businesses which have been adversely affected by defense reductions. The goal of the program is to assist these businesses to diversify into the commercial market while remaining part of the defense industrial base. Complete information on eligibility and other rules is available from each SBA district office.

§ 120.382 Repayment ability.

SBA shall resolve reasonable doubts concerning the small business' proposed business plan for transition to non-defense-related markets in favor of the loan applicant in determining the sound value of the proposed loan.

§ 120.383 Restrictions on loan processing.

Since greater risk may be associated with a loan to an applicant under this program, a Certified Lender or Preferred Lender shall not make a defense economic assistance loan under the PLP or CLP programs.

CapLines Program

§ 120.390 Revolving credit.

(a) CapLines finances eligible small businesses' short-term, revolving and non-revolving working-capital needs. SBA regulations governing the 7(a) loan program govern business loans made under this program. The maximum guaranteed amount and the maximum loan amount are the same under CapLines as other 7(a) loans, as stated in § 120.151.

(b) CapLines proceeds can be used to finance the cyclical, recurring, or other identifiable short-term operating capital needs of small businesses. Proceeds can be used to create current assets or used to provide financing against the current assets that already exist.

[61 FR 3235, Jan. 31, 1996, as amended at 76 FR 63546, Oct. 12, 2011]

Builders Loan Program

§ 120.391 What is the Builders Loan Program?

Under section 7(a)(9) of the Act, SBA may make or guarantee loans to finance small general contractors to construct or rehabilitate residential or commercial property for resale. This program provides an exception under specified conditions to the general rule against financing investment property. "Construct" and "rehabilitate" mean only work done on-site to the structure, utility connections and landscaping.

§ 120.392 Who may apply?

A construction contractor or homebuilder with a past history of profitable construction or rehabilitation projects of comparable type and size may apply. An applicant may subcontract the work. Subcontracts in excess of $25,000 may require 100 percent payment and performance bonds.

§ 120.393 Are there special application requirements?

(a) An applicant must submit documentation from:

(1) A mortgage lender indicating that permanent mortgage money is available to qualified purchasers to buy such properties;

(2) A real estate broker indicating that a market exists for the proposed building and that it will be compatible with its neighborhood; and

(3) An architect, appraiser or engineer agreeing to make inspections and

certifications to support interim disbursements.

(b) The Borrower may substitute a letter from a qualified Lender for one or more of the letters.

§ 120.394 What are the eligible uses of proceeds?

A Borrower must use the loan proceeds solely to acquire, construct or substantially rehabilitate an individual residential or commercial building for sale. "Substantial" means rehabilitation expenses of more than one-third of the purchase price or fair market value at the time of the application. A Borrower may use up to 33 percent of the proceeds to acquire land, and up to 5 percent for community improvements such as curbs and sidewalks.

[61 FR 3235, Jan. 31, 1996, as amended at 82 FR 39503, Aug. 21, 2017]

§ 120.395 What is SBA's collateral position?

SBA will require a lien on the building which must be in no less than a second position.

§ 120.396 What is the term of the loan?

The loan must not exceed sixty (60) months plus the estimated time to complete construction or rehabilitation.

§ 120.397 Are there any special restrictions?

The borrower must not use loan proceeds to purchase vacant land for possible future construction or to operate or hold rental property for future rehabilitation. SBA may allow rental of the property only if the rental will improve the ability to sell the property. The sale must be a legitimate change of ownership.

America's Recovery Capital (Business Stabilization) Loan Program—ARC Loan Program

§ 120.398 America's Recovery Capital (ARC) Loan Program.

(a) *Purpose.* The purpose of the ARC Loan Program is to enable SBA to guarantee certain loans to viable small businesses that are experiencing immediate financial hardship. Loans made under this loan program are referred to as ARC Loans and are subject to the requirements set forth in this Part for 7(a) loans except as noted in this section.

(b) *Definitions.* (1) (i) *Eligible Borrower* is a small business concern as defined in Section 3 of the Small Business Act and § 120.100. Eligible Borrower does not include:

(A) Ineligible small businesses as listed in § 120.110; and

(B) Small business concerns with the following primary industry North American Industry Classification System (NAICS) codes:

(*1*) 713210 (Casinos (Except Casino Hotels));

(*2*) 721120 (Casino Hotels);

(*3*) 713290 (Other Gambling Industries);

(*4*) 713910 (Golf Courses and Country Clubs); and

(*5*) 712130 (Zoos and Botanical Gardens).

(ii) Applications submitted by small business concerns with a primary industry NAICS code of 713940 (Fitness and Recreational Sports Centers) will be identified and reviewed by SBA to determine eligibility in accordance with the statutory restriction on assistance to swimming pools.

(2) *Going Concern* is a small business concern actively engaging in business with the expectation of indefinite continuance.

(3) *Qualifying Small Business Loan* is a loan previously made to an Eligible Borrower for any of the purposes set forth in § 120.120 and not for any of the purposes set forth in § 120.130 or 120.160(d). Qualifying Small Business Loans may include credit card obligations, capital leases for major equipment and vehicles, notes payable to vendors or suppliers, loans in the first lien position made by commercial lenders in connection with the Development Company Loan Program (504), home equity loans used to finance business operations, other loans to small businesses made without an SBA guaranty, and loans made by or with an SBA guaranty on or after February 17, 2009. Loans made or guaranteed by SBA before February 17, 2009 are not Qualifying Small Business Loans for the purposes of the ARC Loan Program. A

Qualifying Small Business Loan may not be used as the basis for more than one ARC Loan but ARC Loans may be used to pay multiple Qualifying Small Business Loans.

(4) *Viable small business* is a small business that is a Going Concern but which is having difficulty making periodic payments of principal and interest on Qualifying Small Business Loan(s) and/or meeting operating expenses of the business although it can reasonably demonstrate its projected continued operation for a reasonable period beyond the six month period of payment assistance with an ARC Loan.

(c) *Period of program.* The ARC Loan Program is authorized through September 30, 2010, or until appropriated funds are exhausted, whichever is sooner.

(d) *Use of proceeds.* Loans made under the ARC Loan Program are for the sole purpose of making periodic payments of principal and interest (including default interest), in full or in part, for up to six (6) months, on one or more existing Qualifying Small Business Loans. ARC Loan proceeds cannot be used to make payments on loans made or guaranteed by SBA prior to February 17, 2009.

(e) *Loan terms.* (1) *Guaranty percentage.* ARC Loans are 100% guaranteed by SBA.

(2) *Maximum loan size.* An ARC Loan may not exceed $35,000.

(3) *Interest rate.* The interest rate for ARC Loans will be published by SBA in the FEDERAL REGISTER.

(4) *Loan maturity.* An ARC Loan may be made with a maturity of up to six and one-half years.

(5) *Disbursement period.* The disbursement period for an ARC Loan is up to six consecutive months.

(6) *Loan payments.*

(i) *Borrower's payments.* The borrower will be responsible for all principal payments.

(ii) *Payment of interest by SBA.* SBA will make periodic interest payments to the lender on ARC Loans. Interest will accrue only until the date 120 days after the earliest uncured payment default on the ARC Loan. However, the amount paid by SBA on a defaulted ARC Loan, when it honors its guarantee, will be adjusted to reconcile for any overpayments or underpayments of interest previously paid to the Lender. Interim adjustments to interest paid by SBA to lenders may be made during the term of the ARC Loan and interest payments due the Lender will be adjusted to accommodate the interim interest adjustments.

(iii) *Deferral period.* No principal repayment is required during the disbursement period or for 12 months following the final loan disbursement.

(iv) *Repayment period.* The borrower will be required to pay the loan principal over five years beginning in the 13th month following the final loan disbursement. The ARC Loan balance will be fully amortized over the five year repayment period. Balloon payments may not be required by lenders. The borrower may prepay all or a portion of the principal during the life of the loan without penalty.

(f) *Number of ARC Loans per small business.* No small business may obtain more than one ARC Loan, but the proceeds of the ARC loan may be used to pay more than one Qualifying Small Business Loan.

(g) *Personal guarantees.* Holders of at least a 20 percent ownership interest in the borrower generally must guarantee the ARC Loan.

(h) *Collateral.* SBA requires each lender to follow the collateral policies and procedures that it has established and implemented for similarly-sized non-SBA guaranteed commercial loans. The lender's collateral policies must be commercially reasonable and prudent. Lenders will certify that the collateral policies applied to the ARC Loan meet this standard. Lenders may charge borrowers the direct cost of securing and liquidating collateral for ARC Loans. SBA will reimburse Lenders for the direct cost of liquidating collateral that are not reimbursed by the borrower in the event of default. Reimbursement of the direct costs of liquidation by SBA to the Lender is limited to the amount of the recovery received on the ARC Loan.

(i) *Credit criteria.* To be approved for an ARC Loan, the applicant must be a creditworthy small business with a reasonable expectation of repayment, taking into consideration the following:

(1) Character, reputation, and credit history of the applicant (and the Operating Company, if applicable) and its Associates;

(2) Experience and depth of management;

(3) Strength of the business;

(4) Past earnings, current earnings, and projected cash flow; and

(5) Ability to repay the loan with earnings from the business.

(j) *Statement of hardship.* In addition to the certifications required for 7(a) loans generally, ARC Loan recipients must submit a statement certifying that they are experiencing immediate financial hardship and provide documentation to support the certification.

(k) *Loan application.* The provisions of § 120.191 do not apply for ARC Loans. A lender making an ARC Loan will provide an application with information on the small business that includes the nature and history of the business, current and historical financial statements (or tax returns), and other information that SBA may require.

(l) *Preferences and refinancing.* A lender may make an ARC Loan to an Eligible Borrower that intends to use the proceeds of the ARC Loan to make periodic payments of principal and interest on a Qualifying Small Business Loan that is owned or serviced by that same lender. The provisions of §§ 120.10, 120.536(a)(2) and 120.925 with regard to Preference for repayments without prior SBA approval do not apply to ARC Loans. The provisions of § 120.201 restricting refinancing also do not apply to ARC Loans.

(m) *Loan fees.* Neither the lender nor SBA shall impose any fees or direct costs on a borrower of an ARC Loan, except that lenders may charge borrowers for the direct costs of securing and liquidating collateral for the ARC Loan. Fees include, but are not limited to, points, bonus points, prepayment penalties, brokerage fees, fees for processing, origination, or application, and out of pocket expenses (other than the direct costs of securing and liquidating collateral). SBA will not impose any fees on a lender making an ARC Loan.

(n) *Lender reporting.* Lenders shall report on its ARC Loans in accordance with requirements established by SBA from time to time for 7a loans and loans made under the American Recovery and Reinvestment Act of 2009.

(o) *Loan servicing.* Each originating lender shall service all of its ARC Loans in accordance with the existing practices and procedures that the Lender uses for its non-SBA guaranteed commercial loans. In all circumstances, such practices and procedures must be commercially reasonable and consistent with prudent lending standards and in accordance with SBA Loan Program Requirements as defined in § 120.10. SBA's prior written consent is required for servicing actions that may have significant exposure implications for SBA. SBA may require written notice of other servicing actions it considers necessary for portfolio management purposes.

(p) *Liquidations.* Each Lender shall be responsible for liquidating any defaulted ARC Loan originated by the Lender. ARC Loans will be liquidated in accordance with the existing practices and procedures that the Lender uses for its non-SBA guaranteed commercial loans. In all circumstances, such practices and procedures must be commercially reasonable and consistent with prudent lending standards and in accordance with SBA Loan Program Requirements as defined in Section 120.10. Loans with de minimis value may, at the Lender's request and with SBA's approval, be liquidated by SBA or its agent(s). Significant liquidation actions taken on ARC Loans must be documented. The reimbursement of liquidation related fees by SBA to the Lender is limited to the amount of the recovery on the ARC Loan.

(q) *Purchase requests.* Any purchase request to SBA to honor its guaranty on a defaulted ARC Loan shall be made by the originating lender. Lenders may request SBA to purchase an ARC Loan when there has been an uncured payment default exceeding 60 days or when the borrower has declared bankruptcy. SBA requires Lenders to submit loans for purchase no later than 120 days after the earliest uncured payment default on the ARC Loan. Additionally, SBA may honor its guarantee and require a Lender to submit an ARC Loan for purchase at any time. Except as noted above, the Lender is required to complete all recovery actions on the ARC Loan after purchase.

(r) *Prohibition on secondary market sales and loan participations.* A lender may not sell an ARC loan into the secondary market nor may a lender participate a portion of an ARC loan with another lender.

(s) *Loan volume.* SBA reserves the right to allocate loan volume under the ARC Loan Program among Lenders (as defined in § 120.10).

(t) *Delegated authority.* SBA may allow lenders to use their delegated authority to process ARC Loans.

(u) *Personal resources test.* The personal resources test provisions of § 120.102 do not apply to ARC Loans.

(v) *Statutory loan limit.* The provisions of § 120.151 do not apply to ARC Loans.

[74 FR 27247, June 9, 2009]

Subpart D—Lenders

§ 120.400 Loan Guarantee Agreements.

SBA may enter into a Loan Guarantee Agreement with a Lender to make deferred participation (guaranteed) loans. Such an agreement does not obligate SBA to participate in any specific proposed loan that a Lender may submit. The existence of a Loan Guarantee Agreement does not limit SBA's rights to deny a specific loan or establish general policies. *See also* § 120.440(c) concerning Supplemental Guarantee Agreements.

[61 FR 3235, Jan. 31, 1996, as amended at 82 FR 39503, Aug. 21, 2017]

PARTICIPATION CRITERIA

§ 120.410 Requirements for all participating Lenders.

A Lender must:

(a) Have a continuing ability to evaluate, process, close, disburse, service, liquidate and litigate small business loans including, but not limited to:

(1) Holding sufficient permanent capital to support SBA lending activities (for SBA Lenders with a Federal Financial Institution Regulator, meeting capital requirements for an adequately capitalized financial institution is considered sufficient permanent capital to support SBA lending activities; for SBLCs, meeting its SBA minimum capital requirement; and for NFRLs, meeting its state minimum capital requirement); and

(2) Maintaining satisfactory SBA performance, as determined by SBA in its discretion. The 7(a) Lender's Risk Rating, among other factors, will be considered in determining satisfactory SBA performance. Other factors may include, but are not limited to, review/examination assessments, historical performance measures (like default rate, purchase rate and loss rate), loan volume to the extent that it impacts performance measures, and other performance related measurements and information (such as contribution toward SBA mission);

(b) Be open to the public for the making of such loans (not be a financing subsidiary, engaged primarily in financing the operations of an affiliate);

(c) Have continuing good character and reputation, and otherwise meet and maintain the ethical requirements of § 120.140

(d) Be supervised and examined by either:

(1) A Federal Financial Institution Regulator,

(2) A state banking regulator satisfactory to SBA, or

(3) SBA;

(e) Be in good standing with SBA, as defined in § 120.420(f) (and determined by SBA in its discretion), and, as applicable, with its state regulator and be considered Satisfactory by its Federal Financial Institution Regulator (as determined by SBA and based on, for example, information in published orders/agreements and call reports); and

(f) Operate in a safe and sound condition using commercially reasonable lending policies, procedures, and standards employed by prudent Lenders.

[61 FR 3235, Jan. 31, 1996, as amended at 62 FR 302, Jan. 3, 1997; 73 FR 75510, Dec. 11, 2008; 82 FR 39503, Aug. 21, 2017]

§ 120.411 Preferences.

An agreement to participate under the Act may not establish any Preferences in favor of the Lender.

§ 120.412 Other services Lenders may provide Borrowers.

Subject to § 120.140 Lenders, their Associates or the designees of either may provide services to and contract for goods with a Borrower only after full disbursement of the loan to the small business or to an account not controlled by the Lender, its Associate, or the designee. A Lender, an Associate, or a designee providing such services must do so under a written contract with the small business, based on time and hourly charges, and must maintain time and billing records for examination by SBA. Fees cannot exceed those charged by established professional consultants providing similar services. *See also* § 120.195.

§ 120.413 Advertisement of relationship with SBA.

A Lender may refer in its advertising to its participation with SBA. The advertising may not:

(a) State or imply that the Lender, or any of its Borrowers, has or will receive preferential treatment from SBA;

(b) Be false or misleading; or

(c) Make use of SBA's seal.

PARTICIPATING LENDER FINANCINGS

SOURCE: Sections 120.420 through 120.428 appear at 64 FR 6507, Feb. 10, 1999, unless otherwise noted.

§ 120.420 Definitions.

(a) *7(a) Loans*—All references to 7(a) loans under this subpart include loans made under section 7(a) of the Small Business Act (15 U.S.C. 631 *et seq.*) and loans made under section 502 of the Small Business Investment Act (15 U.S.C. 661 *et seq.*), both of which may be securitized under this subpart.

(b) *Bank Regulatory Agencies*—The bank regulatory agencies are the Federal Deposit Insurance Corporation, the Federal Reserve Board, the Office of the Comptroller of the Currency, and the Office of Thrift Supervision.

(c) *Benchmark Number*—The maximum number of percentage points that a securitizer's Currency Rate can decrease without triggering the PLP suspension provision set forth in § 120.425. SBA will publish the Benchmark Number in the FEDERAL REGISTER.

(d) *Currency Rate*—A securitizer's "Currency Rate" is the dollar balance of its 7(a) guaranteed loans that are less than 30 days past due divided by the dollar balance of its portfolio of 7(a) guaranteed loans outstanding, as calculated quarterly by SBA, excluding loans approved in SBA's current fiscal year.

(e) *Currency Rate Percentage*—The relationship between the securitizer's Currency Rate and the SBA 7(a) loan portfolio Currency Rate as calculated by dividing the securitizer's Currency Rate by the SBA 7(a) loan portfolio Currency Rate.

(f) *Good Standing*—In general, a Lender is in "good standing" with SBA if it:

(1) Is in compliance with all applicable:

(i) Laws and regulations;

(ii) Policies; and

(iii) Procedures;

(2) Is in good financial condition as determined by SBA;

(3) Is not under investigation or indictment for, or has not been convicted of, or had a judgment entered against it for felony or fraud, or charges relating to a breach of trust or violation of a law or regulation protecting the integrity of business transactions or relationships, unless the Lender Oversight Committee has determined that good standing exists despite the existence of such factors.

(4) Does not have any officer or employee who has been under investigation or indictment for, or has been convicted of or had a judgment entered against him for, a felony or fraud, or charges relating to a breach of trust or violation of a law or regulation protecting the integrity of business transactions or relationships, unless the Lender Oversight Committee has determined that good standing exists despite the existence of such person.

(g) *Initial Currency Rate*—The Initial Currency Rate (ICR) is the securitizer's benchmark Currency Rate. SBA will calculate the securitizer's ICR as of the end of the calendar quarter immediately prior to the first securitization completed after April 12, 1999. This calculation will include all 7(a) loans which are outstanding and were approved in any fiscal year prior to SBA's current fiscal year. Each quarter, SBA will compare each securitizer's Currency Rate to its ICR.

(h) *Initial Currency Rate Percentage*—The Initial Currency Rate Percentage (ICRP) measures the relationship between a securitizer's Initial Currency Rate and the SBA 7(a) loan portfolio Currency Rate at the time of the first securitization after April 12, 1999. The ICRP is calculated by dividing the securitizer's Currency Rate by the SBA 7(a) loan portfolio Currency Rate. SBA will calculate the securitizer's ICRP as of the end of the calendar quarter immediately prior to the first securitization completed after April 12, 1999.

(i) *Loss Rate*—A securitizer's "loss rate," as calculated by SBA, is the aggregate principal amount of the securitizer's 7(a) loans determined uncollectible by SBA for the most recent 10-year period, excluding SBA's current fiscal year activity, divided by the aggregate original principal amount of 7(a) loans disbursed by the securitizer during that period.

(j) *Nondepository Institution*—A "nondepository institution" is a Small Business Lending Company ("SBLC") regulated by SBA or a Business and Industrial Development Company ("BIDCO") or other nondepository institution participating in SBA's 7(a) program.

(k) *Securitization*—A "securitization" is the pooling and sale of the unguaranteed portion of SBA guaranteed loans to a trust, special purpose vehicle, or other mechanism, and the issuance of securities backed by those loans to investors in either a private placement or public offering.

[64 FR 6507, Feb. 10, 1999, as amended at 73 FR 75511, Dec. 11, 2008]

§ 120.421 Which Lenders may securitize?

All SBA participating Lenders may securitize subject to SBA's approval.

§ 120.422 Are all securitizations subject to this subpart?

All securitizations are subject to this subpart. Until additional regulations are promulgated, SBA will consider securitizations involving multiple Lenders on a case by case basis, using the conditions in § 120.425 as a starting point. SBA will consider securitizations by affiliates as single Lender securitizations for purposes of this subpart.

§ 120.423 Which 7(a) loans may a Lender securitize?

A Lender may only securitize 7(a) loans that will be fully disbursed within 90 days of the securitization's closing date. If the amount of a fully disbursed loan increases after a securitization settles, the Lender must retain the increased amount.

§ 120.424 What are the basic conditions a Lender must meet to securitize?

To securitize, a Lender must:

(a) Be in good standing with SBA as defined in § 120.420(f) of this chapter and determined by SBA in its discretion;

(b) Have satisfactory SBA performance, as determined by SBA in its discretion. The Lender's Risk Rating, among other factors, will be considered in determining satisfactory SBA performance. Other factors may include, but are not limited to, review/examination assessments, historical performance measures (like default rate, purchase rate and loss rate), loan volume to the extent that it impacts performance measures, and other performance related measurements and information (such as contribution toward SBA mission);

(c) Use a securitization structure which is satisfactory to SBA;

(d) Use documents acceptable to SBA, including SBA's model multiparty agreement, as amended from time to time;

(e) Obtain SBA's written consent, which it may withhold in its sole discretion, prior to executing a commitment to securitize; and

(f) Cause the original notes to be stored at the FTA, as defined in § 120.600, and other loan documents to be stored with a party approved by SBA.

[64 FR 6507, Feb. 10, 1999, as amended at 73 FR 75511, Dec. 11, 2008; 82 FR 39503, Aug. 21, 2017]

§ 120.425 What are the minimum elements that SBA will require before consenting to a securitization?

A securitizer must comply with the following three conditions:

(a) Capital Requirement—All securitizers must be considered to be "well capitalized" by their regulator. SBA will consider a depository institution to be in compliance with this section if it meets the definition of "well capitalized" used by its bank regulator. SBA's capital requirement does not change the requirements that banks already meet. For nondepository institutions, SBA, as the regulator, will consider a non-depository institution to be "well capitalized" if it maintains a minimum unencumbered paid in capital and paid in surplus equal to at least 10 percent of its assets, excluding the guaranteed portion of 7(a) loans. The capital charge applies to the remaining balance outstanding on the unguaranteed portion of the securitizer's 7(a) loans in its portfolio and in any securitization pools. Each nondepository institution must submit annual audited financial statements demonstrating that it has met SBA's capital requirement.

(b) Subordinated Tranche—A securitizer or its wholly owned subsidiary must retain a tranche of the securities issued in the securitization (subordinated tranche) equal to the greater of two times the securitizer's Loss Rate or 2 percent of the principal balance outstanding at the time of securitization of the unguaranteed portion of the loans in the securitization. This tranche must be subordinate to all other securities issued in the securitization including other subordinated tranches. The securitizer or its wholly owned subsidiary may not sell, pledge, transfer, assign, sell participations in, or otherwise convey the subordinated tranche during the first 6 years after the closing date of the securitization. The securities evidencing the subordinated tranche must bear a legend stating that the securities may not be sold until 6 years after the issue date. SBA's Securitization Committee may modify the formula for determining the tranche size for a securitizer creating a securitization from a pool of loans located in a region affected by a severe economic downturn if the Securitization Committee concludes that enforcing this section might exacerbate the adverse economic conditions in the region. SBA will work with the securitizer to verify the accuracy of the data used to make the Loss Rate calculation.

(c) PLP Privilege Suspension.

(1) *Suspension:* If a securitizer's Currency Rate declines, SBA may suspend the securitizer's PLP unilateral loan approval privileges (PLP approval privileges) if the decline from the securitizer's ICR is more than the Benchmark Number as published in the FEDERAL REGISTER from time to time and the securitizer's Currency Rate Percentage is less than its ICRP. The securitizer will first be placed on probation for one quarter. If, at the end of the probationary quarter the securitizer has not met either of the following conditions in paragraph (c)(1)(i) or (c)(1)(ii) of this section, SBA will suspend the securitizer's PLP approval privileges and will not approve additional securitization requests from that securitizer. SBA will provide written notice at least 10 days prior to the effective date of suspension. The suspension will last a minimum of 3 months. During the suspension period, the securitizer must use Certified Lender or Regular Procedures to process 7(a) loan applications. The prohibition will end if, at the end of the probationary quarter: (i) the securitizer has improved its Currency Rate to above its ICR less the Benchmark Number; or (ii) its Currency Rate Percentage is either the same or greater than its ICRP.

(2) *Reinstatement:* The suspension will remain in effect until the securitizer meets either the condition in paragraph (c)(1)(i) or (c)(1)(ii) of this section. If the securitizer meets either condition by the end of the 3-month period, notifies SBA with acceptable documentation, and SBA agrees, SBA will reinstate the securitizer. If the securitizer cannot meet either condition, the suspension will remain in effect. The securitizer may then petition the Lender Oversight Committee (Committee) for reinstatement. The Committee will review the reinstatement petition and determine if the securitizer's PLP approval privilege

and securitization status should be reinstated. The Committee may consider the economic conditions in the securitizer's market area, the securitizer's efforts to improve its Currency Rate, and the quality of the securitizer's 7(a) loan packages and servicing. The Committee will consider only one petition by a securitizer per quarter.

(3) *The Benchmark Number*. SBA will monitor the Benchmark Number. If economic conditions or policy considerations warrant, SBA may modify the Benchmark Number to protect the safety and soundness of the 7(a) program.

(4) *Data*. SBA will calculate Currency Rate and Currency Rate Percentages quarterly from financial information that securitizers provide. SBA will work with a securitizer to verify the accuracy of the data used to make the Currency Rate calculation.

[64 FR 6508, Feb. 10, 1999, as amended at 65 FR 49481, Aug. 14, 2000; 73 FR 75511, Dec. 11, 2008]

§ 120.426 What action will SBA take if a securitizer transfers the subordinated tranche prior to the termination of the holding period?

If a securitizer transfers the subordinated tranche prior to the termination of the holding period, SBA will suspend immediately the securitizer's ability to make new 7(a) loans. The securitizer will have 30 calendar days to submit an explanation to Lender Oversight Committee ("Committee"). The Committee will have 30 calendar days to review the explanation and determine whether to lift the suspension. If an explanation is not received within 30 calendar days or the explanation is not satisfactory to the Committee, SBA may transfer the servicing of the applicable securitized loans, including the securitizers' servicing fee on the guaranteed and unguaranteed portions and the premium protection fee on the guaranteed portion, to another SBA participating Lender.

[64 FR 6507, Feb. 10, 1999, as amended at 73 FR 75511, Dec. 11, 2008]

§ 120.427 Will SBA approve a securitization application from a capital impaired Securitizer?

If a securitizer does not maintain the level of capital required by this subpart, SBA will not approve a securitization application from that securitizer.

§ 120.428 What happens to a securitizer's other PLP responsibilities if SBA suspends its PLP approval privilege?

The securitizer must continue to service and liquidate loans according to its PLP Supplemental Agreement.

OTHER CONVEYANCES

SOURCE: Sections 120.430 through 120.435 appear at 64 FR 6509, 6510, Feb. 10, 1999, unless otherwise noted.

§ 120.430 What conveyances are covered by §§ 120.430 through 120.435?

Sections 120.430 through 120.435 cover all other transactions in which a Lender sells, sells a participating interest in, or pledges an SBA guaranteed loan other than for the purpose of securitizing and other than conveyances covered under Subpart F, Secondary Market, of this part.

§ 120.431 Which Lenders may sell, sell participations in, or pledge 7(a) loans?

All Lenders may sell, sell participations in, or pledge 7(a) loans in accordance with this subpart.

§ 120.432 Under what circumstances does this subpart permit sales of, or sales of participating interests in, 7(a) loans?

(a) A Lender may sell all of its interest in a 7(a) loan to another Lender operating under a current Loan Guarantee Agreement (SBA Form 750) ("participating Lender"), with SBA's prior written consent, which SBA may withhold in its sole discretion. A Lender may not sell any of its interest in a 7(a) loan to a nonparticipating Lender. The purchasing Lender must take possession of the promissory note and other loan documents, and service the sold 7(a) loan. The purchasing Lender purchases the loan subject to SBA's existing rights including its right to deny liability on its guarantee as provided in § 120.524. After purchase, the purchased loan will be subject to the purchasing Lender's Loan Guarantee Agreement.

(b) A Lender may sell, or sell a participating interest in, a part of a 7(a) loan to another participating Lender. If the Lender retains ownership of a part of the unguaranteed portion of the loan equal to at least 10 percent of the outstanding principal balance of the loan, the Lender must give SBA prior written notice of the transaction, and the Lender must continue to hold the note and service the loan. If a Lender retains ownership of a part of the unguaranteed portion of the loan equal to less than 10 percent of the outstanding principal balance of the loan, the Lender must obtain SBA's prior written consent to the transaction, which consent SBA may withhold in its sole discretion. The Lender must continue to hold the note and other loan documents, and service the loan unless SBA otherwise agrees in its sole discretion.

(c) For purposes of determining the percentage of ownership a Lender has retained, SBA will not consider a Lender to be the owner of the part of a loan in which it has sold a participating interest.

§ 120.433 What are SBA's other requirements for sales and sales of participating interests?

SBA requires the following:

(a) The Lender must be in good standing with SBA as defined in § 120.420(f) and determined by SBA in its discretion;

(b) The Lender has satisfactory SBA performance, as determined by SBA in its discretion. The Lender's Risk Rating, among other factors, will be considered in determining satisfactory SBA performance. Other factors may include, but are not limited to, review/examination assessments, historical performance measures (like default rate, purchase rate and loss rate), loan volume to the extent that it impacts performance measures, and other performance related measurements and information (such as contribution toward SBA mission); and

(c) In transactions requiring SBA's consent, all documentation must be satisfactory to SBA, including, if SBA determines it to be necessary, a multiparty agreement.

[64 FR 6507, Feb. 10, 1999, as amended at 73 FR 75511, Dec. 11, 2008; 82 FR 39503, Aug. 21, 2017]

§ 120.434 What are SBA's requirements for loan pledges?

(a) Except as set forth in § 120.435, SBA must give its prior written consent to all pledges of any portion of a 7(a) loan, which consent SBA may withhold in its sole discretion;

(b) The Lender must be in good standing with SBA as defined in § 120.420(f) and determined by SBA in its discretion;

(c) The Lender has satisfactory SBA performance, as determined by SBA in its discretion. The Lender's Risk Rating, among other factors, will be considered in determining satisfactory SBA performance. Other factors may include, but are not limited to, review/examination assessments, historical performance measures (like default rate, purchase rate and loss rate), loan volume to the extent that it impacts performance measures, and other performance related measurements and information (such as contribution toward SBA mission);

(d) All loan documents must be satisfactory to SBA and must include a multi-party agreement among SBA, Lender, the pledgee, FTA and such other parties as SBA determines are necessary;

(e) The Lender must use the proceeds of the loan secured by the 7(a) loans only for financing 7(a) loans and for costs and expenses directly connected with the borrowing for which the loans are pledged;

(f) The Lender must remain the servicer of the loans and retain possession of all loan documents other than the original promissory notes;

(g) The Lender must deposit the original promissory notes at the FTA; and

(h) The Lender must retain an economic interest in and the ultimate risk of loss on the unguaranteed portion of the loans.

[64 FR 6507, Feb. 10, 1999, as amended at 73 FR 75511, Dec. 11, 2008; 82 FR 39503, Aug. 21, 2017]

§ 120.435 Which loan pledges do not require notice to or consent by SBA?

Notwithstanding the provisions of § 120.434(e), 7(a) loans may be pledged for the following purposes without notice to or consent by SBA:

(a) Treasury tax and loan accounts;

(b) The deposit of public funds;

(c) Uninvested trust funds;

(d) Discount borrowings at a Federal Reserve Bank; or

(e) Advances by a Federal Home Loan Bank.

[64 FR 6507, Feb. 10, 1999, as amended at 73 FR 75511, Dec. 11, 2008]

DELEGATED AUTHORITY CRITERIA

§ 120.440 How does a 7(a) Lender obtain delegated authority?

(a) In making its decision to grant or renew a delegated authority, SBA considers whether the Lender, as determined by SBA in its discretion:

(1) Has the continuing ability to evaluate, process, close, disburse, service, liquidate and litigate SBA loans. This includes the ability to develop and analyze complete loan packages. SBA may consider the experience and capability of Lender's management and staff.

(2) Has satisfactory SBA performance (as defined in § 120.410(a)(2));

(3) Is in compliance with SBA Loan Program Requirements (*e.g.*, Form 1502 reporting, timely payment of all fees to SBA);

(4) Has completed to SBA's satisfaction all required corrective actions;

(5) Whether Lender is subject to any enforcement action, order or agreement with a regulator or the presence of other regulatory concerns as determined by SBA; and

(6) Whether Lender exhibits other risk factors (*e.g.*, has rapid growth; low SBA activity; SBA loan volume; Lender, an officer or director is under investigation or indictment).

(b) Delegated authority decisions are made by the appropriate SBA official in accordance with Delegations of Authority, and are final.

(c) If delegated authority is approved or renewed, Lender must execute a Supplemental Guarantee Agreement, which will specify a term not to exceed two years. SBA may grant shortened renewals based on risk or any of the other delegated authority criteria. Lenders with less than 3 years of SBA lending experience will be limited to a term of 1 year or less.

[82 FR 39503, Aug. 21, 2017]

§ 120.441 [Reserved]

PREFERRED LENDERS PROGRAM (PLP)

§ 120.450 What is the Preferred Lenders Program?

Under the Preferred Lenders Program (PLP), designated Lenders process, close, service, and liquidate SBA guaranteed loans with reduced requirements for documentation to and prior approval by SBA.

§ 120.451 [Reserved]

§ 120.452 What are the requirements of PLP loan processing?

(a) Subparts A and B of this part govern the making of PLP loans, except for the following:

(1) Certain types of businesses, loans, and loan programs are not eligible for PLP, as detailed in published SBA policy and procedures.

(2) A Lender may not make a PLP business loan which reduces its existing credit exposure for any Borrower, except in cases where an interim loan(s) has been made for other than real estate construction purposes to the Borrower which was approved by the Lender within 90 days of receipt of the issuance fo a subsequent PLP loan number.

(3) SBA will not guarantee more than the specified statutory percentage of any PLP loan.

(b) A PLP Lender notifies SBA of its approval of a PLP loan by submitting to SBA's loan processing center appropriate documentation signed by two of the PLP's authorized representatives. SBA will attach the SBA guarantee and notify the PLP Lender of the SBA loan number (if it does not identify a problem with eligibility, and funds are available).

(c) The PLP Lender is responsible for all PLP loan decisions regarding eligibility (including size) and creditworthiness. The PLP Lender is also responsible for confirming that all PLP loan closing decisions are correct, and that it has complied with all requirements of law and SBA regulations.

§ 120.453 Responsibilities of PLP Lenders for servicing and liquidating 7(a) loans.

Servicing and Liquidation responsibilities for PLP Lenders are set forth in subpart E of this part.

[72 FR 18360, Apr. 12, 2007]

SBA SUPERVISED LENDERS

§ 120.460 What are SBA's additional requirements for SBA Supervised Lenders?

(a) In general. In addition to complying with SBA's requirements for SBA Lenders, an SBA Supervised Lender must meet the additional requirements set forth in this regulation and the SBA Supervised Lender regulations that follow.

(b) Operations and internal controls. Each SBA Supervised Lender's board of directors (or management, if the SBA Supervised Lender is a division of another company and does not have its own board of directors) must adopt an internal control policy which provides adequate direction to the institution in establishing effective control over and accountability for operations, programs, and resources. The internal control policy must, at a minimum:

(1) Direct management to assign responsibility for the internal control function (covering financial, credit, credit review, collateral, and administrative matters) to an officer or officers of the SBA Supervised Lender;

(2) Adopt and set forth procedures for maintenance and periodic review of the internal control function; and

(3) Direct the operation of a program to review and assess the SBA Supervised Lender's assets. The asset review program policies must specify the following:

(i) Loan, loan-related asset, and appraisal review standards, including standards for scope of selection for review (of any such loan, loan-related asset or appraisal) and standards for work papers and supporting documentation;

(ii) Asset quality classification standards consistent with the standardized classification systems used by the Federal Financial Institution Regulators;

(iii) Specific internal control requirements for the SBA Supervised Lender's major asset categories (cash and investment securities), lending, and the issuance of debt;

(iv) Specific internal control requirements for the SBA Supervised Lender's oversight of Lender Service Providers; and

(v) Standards for training to implement the asset review program.

[73 FR 75512, Dec. 11, 2008]

§ 120.461 What are SBA's additional requirements for SBA Supervised Lenders concerning records?

(a) *Report filing.* All SBA Supervised Lender-specific reports (including all SBLC-only reports) must be filed with the appropriate Office of Capital Access official in accordance with Delegations of Authority.

(b) *Maintenance of records.* An SBA Supervised Lender must maintain at its principal business office accurate and current financial records, including books of accounts, minutes of stockholder, directors, and executive committee meetings, and all documents and supporting materials relating to the SBA Supervised Lender's transactions. However, securities held by a custodian pursuant to a written agreement are exempt from this requirement.

(c) *Permanent preservation of records.* An SBA Supervised Lender must permanently preserve in a manner permitting immediate (one business day) retrieval the following documentation for the financial statements and other reports required by § 120.464 (and the accompanying certified public accountant's opinion):

(1) All general and subsidiary ledgers (or other records) reflecting asset, liability, capital stock and additional paid-in capital, income, and expense accounts;

(2) All general and special journals (or other records forming the basis for entries in such ledgers); and

(3) The corporate charter, bylaws, application for determination of eligibility to participate with SBA, and all minutes books, capital stock certificates or stubs, stock ledgers, and stock transfer registers.

(d) *Other preservation of records.* An SBA Supervised Lender must preserve for at least 6 years following final disposition of each individual SBA loan:

(1) All applications for financing;

(2) Lending, participation, and escrow agreements;

(3) Financing instruments; and

(4) All other documents and supporting material relating to such loans, including correspondence.

(e) *Electronic preservation.* Records and other documents referred to in this section may be preserved electronically if the original is available for retrieval within 15 working days.

[73 FR 75512, Dec. 11, 2008]

§ 120.462 What are SBA's additional requirements on capital maintenance for SBA Supervised Lenders?

(a) *Capital adequacy.* The board of directors (or management, if the SBA Supervised Lender is a division of another company and does not have its own board of directors) of each SBA Supervised Lender must determine capital adequacy goals; that is, the total amount of capital needed to assure the SBA Supervised Lender's continued financial viability and provide for any necessary growth. The minimum standards set in § 120.471 for SBLCs and those established by state regulators for NFRLs are not to be adopted as the ideal capital level for a given SBA Supervised Lender. Rather, the minimum standards are to serve as minimum levels of capital that each SBA Supervised Lender must maintain to protect against the credit risk and other general risks inherent in its operation.

(b) *Capital plan.* (1) The board of directors of each SBA Supervised Lender must establish, adopt, and maintain a formal written capital plan. The plan must include any interim capital targets that are necessary to achieve the SBA Supervised Lender's capital adequacy goals as well as the minimum capital standards. The plan must address any projected dividend goals, equity retirements, or any other anticipated action that may decrease the SBA Supervised Lender's capital. The plan must set forth the circumstances in which capital retirements (e.g., dividends, distributions of capital or purchase of treasury stock) can occur. In addition to factors described above that must be considered in meeting the minimum standards, the board of directors must also address the following factors in developing the SBA Supervised Lender's capital adequacy plan:

(i) Management capability;

(ii) Quality of operating policies, procedures, and internal controls;

(iii) Quality and quantity of earnings;

(iv) Asset quality and the adequacy of the allowance for loan losses within the loan portfolio;

(v) Sufficiency of liquidity; and

(vi) Any other risk-oriented activities or conditions that warrant additional capital (e.g., portfolio growth rate).

(2) An SBA Supervised Lender must keep its capital plan current, updating it at least annually or more often as operating conditions may warrant.

(c) *Certification of compliance.* Within 45 days of the end of each fiscal quarter, each SBA Supervised Lender must furnish the SBA with a calculation of capital and certification of compliance with its minimum capital requirement as set forth in §§ 120.471, 120.472, or 120.474, as applicable, for SBLCs and as established by state regulators for NFRLs. The SBA Supervised Lender's chief financial officer must certify the calculation to be correct. The quarterly calculation and certification of compliance may be included in the SBA Supervised Lender's Quarterly Condition Report.

(d) *Capital impairment.* An SBA Supervised Lender must meet its minimum regulatory capital requirement and avoid capital impairment. Capital impairment exists if an SBA Supervised Lender fails to meet its minimum regulatory capital requirement under §§ 120.471, 120.472, and 120.474 for SBLCs or as established by state regulators for NFRLs. An SBA Supervised Lender must provide the appropriate Office of Capital Access official in accordance with Delegations of Authority written notice of any failure to meet its minimum capital requirement within 30 calendar days of the month-end in which the impairment occurred. Unless otherwise waived by the appropriate Office of Capital Access official in accordance with Delegations of Authority in writing, an SBA Supervised Lender may not present any loans to SBA for guaranty until the impairment is cured. SBA may waive the presentment prohibition for good cause as determined by SBA in its discretion. In the case of differences in calculating capital or capital requirements between the SBA Supervised Lender and SBA, SBA's calculations will prevail until differences between the two calculations are resolved.

(e) *Capital restoration plan*— (1) *Filing requirement*. An SBA Supervised Lender must file a written capital restoration plan with SBA within 45 days of the date that the SBA Supervised Lender provides notice to SBA under paragraph (d) of this section or receives notice from SBA (whichever is earlier) that the SBA Supervised Lender has not met its minimum capital requirement, unless SBA notifies the SBA Supervised Lender in writing that the plan is to be filed within a different time period.

(2) *Plan content*. An SBA Supervised Lender must detail the steps it will take to meet its minimum capital requirement; the time within which each step will be taken; the timeframe for accomplishing the entire capital restoration; and the person or department at the SBA Supervised Lender charged with carrying out the capital restoration plan.

(3) *SBA response*. SBA will provide written notice of whether the capital restoration plan is approved or not or whether SBA will seek additional information. If the capital restoration plan is not approved by SBA, the SBA Supervised Lender will submit a revised capital restoration plan within the timeframe specified by SBA.

(4) *Amendment of capital restoration plan*. An SBA Supervised Lender that has submitted an approved capital restoration plan may, after prior written notice to and approval by SBA, amend the plan to reflect a change in circumstance. Until such time as a proposed amendment has been approved, the SBA Supervised Lender must implement the capital restoration plan as approved prior to the proposed amendment.

(5) *Failure*. If an SBA Supervised Lender fails to submit a capital restoration plan that is acceptable to SBA within its discretion within the required timeframe, or fails to implement, in any material respect as determined by SBA in its discretion, its SBA approved capital restoration plan within the plan timeframe, SBA may undertake enforcement actions under § 120.1500.

[73 FR 75512, Dec. 11, 2008]

§ 120.463 Regulatory accounting—What are SBA's regulatory accounting requirements for SBA Supervised Lenders?

(a) *Books and records*. The books and records of an SBA Supervised Lender must be kept on an accrual basis in accordance with Generally Accepted Accounting Principles (GAAP) as promulgated by the Financial Accounting Standards Board (FASB), supplemented by Regulatory Accounting Principles (RAP) as identified by SBA in Policy, Procedural or Information Notices, from time to time.

(b) *Annual audit*. Each SBA Supervised Lender must have its financial statements audited annually by a certified public accountant experienced in auditing financial institutions. The audit must be performed in accordance with generally accepted auditing standards as adopted by the Auditing Standards Board of the American Institute of Certified Public Accountants (AICPA) for non-public companies and by the Public Company Accounting Oversight Board (PCAOB) for public companies. Annually, the auditor must issue an audit report with an opinion as to the fairness of the SBA Supervised Lender's financial statements and their compliance with GAAP.

(c) *Auditor qualifications*. The audit shall be conducted by an independent certified public accountant who:

(1) Is registered or licensed to practice as a certified public accountant,

and is in good standing, under the laws of the state or other political subdivision of the United States in which the SBA Supervised Lender's principal office is located;

(2) Agrees in the engagement letter with the SBA Supervised Lender to provide the SBA with access to and copies of any work papers, policies, and procedures relating to the services performed;

(3)(i) Is in compliance with the AICPA Code of Professional Conduct; and

(ii) Meets the independence requirements and interpretations of the Securities and Exchange Commission and its staff;

(4) Has received a peer review or is enrolled in a peer review program, that meets AICPA guidelines; and

(5) Is otherwise acceptable to SBA.

(d) *Change of auditor.* If an SBA Supervised Lender discharges or changes its auditor, it must notify SBA in writing within ten days of the occurrence. Such notification must provide:

(1) The name, address, and telephone number of the discharged auditor; and

(2) If the discharge/change involved a dispute over the financial statements, a reasonably detailed statement of all the reasons for the discharge or change. This statement must set out the issue in dispute, the position of the auditor, the position of the SBA Supervised Lender, and the effect of each position on the balance sheet and income statement of the SBA Supervised Lender.

(e) *Specific accounting requirements.* (1) Each SBA Supervised Lender must maintain an allowance for losses on loans and other assets that is sufficient to absorb all probable and estimated losses that may reasonably be expected based on the SBA Supervised Lender's historical performance and reasonably-anticipated events. Each SBA Supervised Lender must maintain documentation of its loan loss allowance calculations and analysis in sufficient detail to permit the SBA to understand the assumptions used and the application of those assumptions to the assets of the SBA Supervised Lender.

(2) The unguaranteed portions of loans determined to be uncollectible must be charged-off promptly. If the portion determined to be uncollectible by the SBA Supervised Lender is different from the amount determined by its auditors or the SBA, the SBA Supervised Lender must charge-off such amount as the SBA may direct.

(3) Each SBA Supervised Lender must classify loans as:

(i) "Nonaccrual," if any portion of the principal or interest is determined to be uncollectible and

(ii) "Formally restructured," if the loan meets the "troubled debt restructuring" definition set forth in FASB Statement of Financial Accounting Standards No. 15, Accounting by Debtors and Creditors for Troubled Debt Restructurings.

(4) When one loan to a borrower is classified as nonaccrual or formally restructured, all loans to that borrower must be so classified unless the SBA Supervised Lender can document that the loans have independent sources of repayment.

(f) *Valuing loan servicing rights and residual interests.* Each SBA Supervised Lender must account for loan sales transactions and the valuation of loan servicing rights in accordance with GAAP. At the end of each quarter, the SBA Supervised Lender must review for reasonableness the existing environmental assumptions used in the valuation. Particular attention must be given to interest rate and repayment rate assumptions. Assumptions considered no longer reasonable must be modified and modifications must be reflected in the valuation and must be documented and supported by a market analysis. Work papers reflecting the analysis of assumptions and any resulting adjustment in the valuation must be maintained for SBA review in accordance with § 120.461. SBA may require an SBA Supervised Lender to use industry averages for the valuation of servicing rights.

[73 FR 75513, Dec. 11, 2008]

§ 120.464 Reports to SBA.

(a) An SBA Supervised Lender must submit the following to SBA:

(1) *Annual Report.* Within three months after the close of each fiscal year, each SBA Supervised Lender must submit to SBA two copies of an

annual report including audited financial statements as prepared by a certified public accountant in accordance with § 120.463. Specifically, the annual report must, at a minimum, include the following:

(i) Audited balance sheet;

(ii) Audited statement of income and expense;

(iii) Audited reconciliation of capital accounts;

(iv) Audited source and application of funds;

(v) Such footnotes as are necessary to an understanding of the report;

(vi) Auditor's letter to management on internal control weaknesses; and

(vii) The auditor's report.

(2) *Quarterly Condition Reports.* By the 45th calendar day following the end of each calendar quarter, each SBA Supervised Lender must submit a Quarterly Condition Report in a form and content as the SBA may prescribe from time to time. At a minimum, the Quarterly Condition Report must include the SBA Supervised Lender's quarterly financial statements, which may be internally prepared. The SBA Supervised Lender must apply uniform definitions to categories of nonperforming loans and include recovery amounts on liquidated loans. SBA may, on a case-by-case basis, depending on an SBA Supervised Lender's size and the quality of its assets, adjust the requirements for content and frequency of filing Quarterly Condition Reports.

(3) *Legal and Administrative Proceeding Report.* Each SBA Supervised Lender must report any legal or administrative proceeding by or against the SBA Supervised Lender, or against any officer, director or employee of the SBA Supervised Lender for an alleged breach of official duty, within ten business days after initiating or learning of the proceeding, and also must notify the SBA of the terms of any settlement or final judgment. The SBA Supervised Lender must include such information in any reporting required under other provisions of SBA regulations.

(4) *Stockholder Reports.* Each SBA Supervised Lender must submit to SBA a copy of any report furnished to its stockholders in any manner, within 30 calendar days after submission to stockholders, including any prospectus, letter, or other document, concerning the financial operations or condition of the SBA Supervised Lender.

(5) *Reports of Changes.* Each SBA Supervised Lender must submit to SBA a summary of any changes in the SBA Supervised Lender's organization or financing (within 30 calendar days of the change), such as:

(i) Any change in its name, address or telephone number;

(ii) Any change in its charter, bylaws, or its officers or directors (to be accompanied by a statement of personal history on the form approved by SBA);

(iii) Any change in capitalization, including such types of change as are identified in this part 120;

(iv) Any changes affecting an SBA Supervised Lender's eligibility to continue to participate as an SBA Supervised Lender; and

(v) Notice of any pledge of stock (within 30 calendar days of the transaction) if 10 percent or more of the stock is pledged by any person (or group of persons acting in concert) as collateral for indebtedness.

(6) *Report of Changes in Financial Condition.* In addition to other reports required under this part 120, each SBA Supervised Lender must submit a report to SBA on any material change in financial condition. The SBA Supervised Lender must submit such report promptly, but no later than ten days after its management becomes aware of such change (except as provided for in § 120.462(d)). Failure to promptly notify SBA concerning a material change in financial condition may lead to enforcement action.

(7) *Other Reports.* Each SBA Supervised Lender must submit such other reports as SBA from time to time may in writing require.

(b) *Preparing financial reports for filing.* Each SBA Supervised Lender must prepare financial reports:

(1) In accordance with all applicable laws, regulations, procedures, standards, and such instructions and specifications and in such form and media format as may be prescribed by SBA from time to time;

(2) On an accrual basis, in accordance with GAAP principles and such other accounting requirements, standards,

and procedures as may be prescribed by the SBA from time to time;

(3) That contain all applicable footnotes in accordance with GAAP principals, one of which includes a brief analysis of how the SBA Supervised Lender complies with SBA's capital regulations, as applicable; and

(4) In such manner as to facilitate the reconciliation of these reports with the books and records of the SBA Supervised Lender.

(c) *Responsibility for assuring the accuracy of filed financial reports.* Each financial report filed with SBA must be certified as having been prepared in accordance with all applicable regulations, SOPs, notices, and instructions and to be a true, accurate, and complete representation of the financial condition and financial performance of the SBA Supervised Lender to which it applies. The reports must be certified by the officer of the reporting SBA Supervised Lender named for that purpose by action of the institution's board of directors. If the institution's board of directors has not acted to name an officer to certify the correctness of its reports of financial condition and financial performance, then the reports must be certified by the president or chief executive officer of the reporting SBA Supervised Lender.

(d) *Waiver.* The appropriate Office of Capital Access official in accordance with Delegations of Authority may in his/her discretion waive any § 120.464 reporting requirement for SBA Supervised Lenders for good cause (including, but not limited to, where an SBA Supervised Lender has a relatively small SBA loan portfolio), as determined by SBA. SBA Supervised Lenders must request the waiver in writing and include all supporting reasons and documentation. The waiver decision of the appropriate Office of Capital Access official in accordance with Delegations of Authority is final.

[73 FR 75514, Dec. 11, 2008]

§ 120.465 Civil penalty for late submission of required reports.

(a) *Obligation to submit required reports by applicable due dates.* SBA Supervised Lenders must submit complete reports by the due dates described in the regulations or as directed in writing by SBA. SBA considers any report that an SBA Supervised Lender sends to SBA by the applicable due date but that is submitted only in part, to have not been submitted by the applicable due date. SBA also considers any report that is postmarked by the due date to be submitted by the due date.

(b) *Amount of civil penalty.* For each day past the due date for such report, the SBA Supervised Lender must pay to SBA a civil penalty of not more than $6,460 per day per report. Such civil penalty continues to accrue until and including the date upon which SBA Supervised Lender submits the complete report. In determining the amount of the civil penalty to be assessed, SBA may consider the financial resources and good faith of the SBA Supervised Lender, the gravity of the violation, the history of previous violations and any such other matters as justice may require.

(c) *Notification of amount of civil penalty.* SBA will notify the SBA Supervised Lender in writing of the amount of civil penalties imposed either upon receiving the required complete report or at such other time as SBA determines. The SBA Supervised Lender must pay this amount to SBA within 30 days of the date of SBA's written demand.

(d) *Identification during examination.* SBA may also impose on an SBA Supervised Lender a civil penalty as described in this section if SBA discovers, during an examination pursuant to subpart I of this Part 120 or otherwise, that the SBA Supervised Lender did not submit a required report by the due date.

(e) *Extensions of submission due dates.* (1) An SBA Supervised Lender may request in writing to SBA that SBA extend its report due date. The request must reference the report and its due date, state the reasonable cause for extension, and assert how much additional time is needed in order to submit a complete report. SBA will advise SBA Supervised Lender in writing as to whether it approved or denied the extension request. If SBA determines that there is reasonable cause to grant an extension and it is not due to willful neglect, SBA will establish a new due date. Such determination as to willful neglect and reasonable cause is in SBA's discretion. SBA will consider the following factors in determining willful neglect:

(i) Whether the SBA Supervised Lender failed to file required reports for more than two reporting periods and

(ii) If SBA provided the SBA Supervised Lender notice of the failure to file and the SBA Supervised Lender failed to respond or failed to provide a reasonable explanation for the filing failure in its response.

(2) If SBA disapproves the extension, the due date remains the same. The civil penalty accrues regardless of whether the SBA Supervised Lender files an extension request. If SBA approves the extension, SBA will waive the civil penalty that has accrued so far for that particular report. However, a new civil penalty will accrue if the SBA Supervised Lender does not submit a complete report by the new due date established by SBA.

(f) *Requests for reduction or exemption.* (1) An SBA Supervised Lender may request a reduction or exemption from the civil penalty in writing to SBA. The request must reference the required report, its due date and the amount sought for reduction, and state in detail the reasons for the reduction. SBA will consider the following factors:

(i) Whether there is reasonable cause for failure to file timely and it was not due to willful neglect;

(ii) Whether the SBA Supervised Lender has demonstrated to SBA's satisfaction that it has modified its internal procedures to comply with reporting requirements in the future; and

(iii) Whether the SBA Supervised Lender has demonstrated to SBA's satisfaction, based on financial information fully disclosed together with its request, that it would have difficulty paying the civil penalty assessed.

(2) SBA must also determine that a reduction or exemption is not inconsistent with the public interest or the protection of SBA.

(3) SBA may in writing approve the exemption, reduce the civil penalty, or deny the exemption.

(4) If SBA grants the reduction request or denies the reduction or exemption, the SBA Supervised Lender must pay the amount owed within 30 days of the letter date. Civil penalties will accrue while the request is pending.

(g) *Reconsideration of decisions.* An SBA Supervised Lender may request in writing to the Associate Administrator for Capital Access (AA/CA) to reconsider its request for extension, reduction, or exemption. The reconsideration request must be received by SBA within 30 days of the date of the letter denying the SBA Supervised Lender's original request. SBA will not consider untimely requests. The SBA Supervised Lender must include any additional information or documentation to support its reconsideration request. SBA will issue a written decision on the reconsideration request. The decision is a final agency decision. If on reconsideration, a civil penalty remains due, the SBA Supervised Lender must pay to SBA the civil penalty within 30 days of the written decision or as otherwise directed. Civil penalties will continue to accrue while the reconsideration request is pending.

(h) *Other enforcement actions.* SBA may seek additional remedies for failure to timely file reports as authorized by law.

(i) *Exception for affiliate of SBLC.* Civil penalties under this section do not apply to any affiliate of an SBLC that procures at least 10% of its annual purchasing requirements from small manufacturers.

[73 FR 75515, Dec. 11, 2008, as amended at 81 FR 31491, May 19, 2016; 82 FR 9969, Feb. 9, 2017; 83 FR 7363, Feb. 21, 2018]

SMALL BUSINESS LENDING COMPANIES (SBLC)

§ 120.470 What are SBA's additional requirements for SBLCs?

In addition to complying with SBA's requirements for SBA Lenders and SBA Supervised Lenders, an SBLC must meet the requirements contained in this regulation and the SBLC regulations that follow.

(a) *Lending.* An SBLC may only make:

(1) Loans under section 7(a) (except section 7(a)(13) of the Act in participation with SBA); and/or

(2) SBA guaranteed loans to Intermediaries (see subpart G of this part). Such loans are subject to the same conditions as guaranteed loans made to Intermediaries by 7(a) Lenders.

(b) *Business structure.* An SBLC must be a corporation (profit or non-profit) or a limited liability company or limited partnership.

(c) *Written agreement.* An SBLC must sign a written agreement with SBA.

(d) *Dual control.* An SBLC must maintain dual control over disbursement of funds and withdrawal of securities.

(1) An SBLC may disburse funds only by checks or wire transfers authorized by signatures of two or more officers covered by the SBLC's fidelity bond, except that checks in an amount of $1,000 or less may be signed by one bonded officer, provided that such action is permitted under the SBLC's fidelity bond.

(2) There must be two or more bonded officers, or one bonded officer and a bonded employee to open safe deposit boxes or withdraw securities from safekeeping. The SBLC must furnish to each depository bank, custodian, or entity providing safe deposit boxes a certified copy of the resolution implementing control procedures.

(e) *Fidelity insurance.* An SBLC must maintain a Brokers Blanket Bond, Standard Form 14, or Finance Companies Blanket Bond, Standard Form 15, or such other form of coverage as SBA may approve, in a minimum amount of $2,000,000 executed by a surety holding a certificate of authority from the Secretary of the Treasury pursuant to 31 U.S.C. 9304–9308.

(f) *Common control.* (1) An SBLC must not control, be controlled by, or be under common control with another SBLC.

(2) In the case of a purchase of an SBLC by an organization that already owns an SBLC, the purchasing entity will have six months to submit a plan to SBA for the divestiture of one of the SBLCs. All divestiture plans must be approved by SBA and SBA may withhold approval in its discretion. Divestiture of the SBLC must occur within one year of purchase date.

(3) Without prior written SBA approval, an Associate of one SBLC must not be an Associate of another SBLC or of any entity which directly or indirectly controls, or is under common control with, another SBLC.

(4) For purposes of paragraph (f) of this section, common control means a condition where two or more SBLCs, either through ownership, management, contract, or otherwise, are under the Control of one group or Person (as defined in § 120.10 of this chapter). Two or more SBLCs are presumed to be under common control if they are Affiliates of each other by reason of common ownership or common officers, directors, or general partners.

(5) "Affiliate" has the meaning set forth in § 121.103 of this chapter.

(6) "Control" means the possession, direct or indirect, of the power to direct or cause the direction of the management and policies of an SBLC or other concern, whether through the ownership of voting securities, by contract, or otherwise. The common control presumption may be rebutted by evidence satisfactory to SBA.

(g) *Management.* An SBLC must employ full time professional management.

(h) *Borrowed funds.* In general, an SBLC may not be capitalized with borrowed funds. Shareholders owning 10 percent or more of any class of its stock must not use personally-borrowed funds to purchase the stock unless the net worth of the shareholder is at least twice the amount borrowed or unless the shareholder receives SBA's prior written approval for a lower ratio.

[73 FR 75515, Dec. 11, 2008]

§ 120.471 What are the minimum capital requirements for SBLCs?

(a) *Minimum capital requirements.* Each SBLC must maintain, at a minimum, unencumbered paid-in capital and paid-in surplus of at least $1,000,000, or ten percent of the aggregate of its share of all outstanding loans, whichever is more.

(b) *Composition of capital.* For purposes of complying with paragraph (a) of this section, capital consists only of one or more of the following:

(1) Common stock;

(2) Preferred stock that is noncumulative as to dividends and does not have a maturity date;

(3) Additional paid-in capital representing amounts paid for stock in excess of the par value;

(4) Retained earnings of the business; and/or

(5) For limited liability companies and limited partnerships, capital contributions must not be subject to repayment at any specific time, must not be subject to withdrawal and must have no cumulative priority return.

(c) *Voluntary capital reduction.* Without prior written SBA approval, an SBLC must not voluntarily reduce its capital, or repurchase and hold more than 2 percent of any class or combination of classes of its stock.

(d) *Issuance of securities.* Without prior written SBA approval, an SBLC must not issue any securities (including stock options and debt securities) except stock dividends.

[73 FR 75516, Dec. 11, 2008]

§ 120.472 Higher individual minimum capital requirement.

The Associate Administrator for Capital Access (AA/CA) may require, under § 120.473(d), an SBLC to maintain a higher level of capital, if the AA/CA determines, in his/her discretion, that the SBLC's level of capital is potentially inadequate to protect the SBA from loss due to the financial failure of the SBLC. The factors to be considered in the determination will vary in each case and may include, for example:

(a) Specific conditions or circumstances pertaining to the SBLC;

(b) Exigency of those circumstances or potential problems;

(c) Overall condition, management strength, and future prospects of the SBLC and, if applicable, its parent or affiliates;

(d) The SBLC's liquidity and existing capital level, and the performance of its SBA loan portfolio;

(e) The management views of the SBLC's directors and senior management; and

(f) Other risk-related factors, as determined by SBA.

[73 FR 75516, Dec. 11, 2008]

§ 120.473 Procedures for determining individual minimum capital requirement.

(a) *Notice.* When SBA determines that an individual minimum capital requirement above that set forth in this subpart or other legal authority is necessary or appropriate for a particular SBLC, SBA will notify the SBLC in writing of the proposed individual minimum capital requirement, the date by which it should be reached and will provide an explanation of why the requirement proposed is considered necessary or appropriate.

(b) *SBLC response.* The SBLC may respond to the notice. The response should include any matters which the SBLC would have SBA consider in deciding whether individual minimum capital requirements should be established for the SBLC, what those capital requirements should be, and, if applicable, when they should be achieved. The response must be in writing and delivered to the AA/CA within 30 days after the date on which the SBLC received the notice. SBA may shorten the time for response when, in the opinion of SBA, the condition of the SBLC so warrants, provided that the SBLC is informed promptly of the new time period, or the SBLC consents to the shortening of its response time. In its discretion, SBA may extend the time period for good cause.

(c) *Failure to respond.* An SBLC that does not respond within 30 days or such other time period as may be specified by SBA will have waived any objections to the proposed minimum capital requirement and the deadline for its achievement. Failure to respond will also constitute consent to the individual minimum capital requirement.

(d) *Decision.* After the close of the SBLC's response period, the AA/CA will decide, based on a review of SBA reasons for proposing the individual minimum capital requirement, the SBLC's response, and other information concerning the SBLC, whether the individual minimum capital requirement should be established for the SBLC and, if so, the requirement and the date it will become effective. The SBLC will be notified of the decision in writing. The notice will include an explanation of the decision; except for a decision not to establish an individual minimum capital requirement for the SBLC.

(e) *Submission of plan.* The decision may require the SBLC to develop and submit to SBA, within a time period specified, an acceptable plan to reach the individual minimum capital requirement by the date required.

(f) *Change in circumstances.* If, after SBA's decision in paragraph (d) of this section, there is a change in the circumstances affecting the SBLC's capital adequacy or its ability to reach the required individual minimum capital requirement by the specified date, either the SBLC or the AA/CA may propose to the other a change in the individual minimum capital requirement for the SBLC, the date when the individual minimum must be achieved, and/or the SBLC's plan (if applicable). The AA/CA may decline to consider proposals that are not based on a significant change in circumstances or are repetitive or frivolous. Pending a decision by the AA/CA on reconsideration, SBA's original decision and any plan required under that decision will continue in full force and effect.

[73 FR 75516, Dec. 11, 2008]

§ 120.474 Relation to other actions.

In lieu of, or in addition to, the procedures in this subpart, the individual minimum capital requirement for an SBLC may be established or revised through a written agreement or cease and desist proceedings under subpart I of this part.

[73 FR 75517, Dec. 11, 2008]

§ 120.475 Change of ownership or control.

(a) Any change of ownership or control without prior written approval of SBA is prohibited. An SBLC must request approval of any such change from the appropriate Office of Capital Access official in accordance with Delegations of Authority.Pending the approval, the SBLC may not register the proposed new owners on its transfer books nor permit them to participate in any manner in the conduct of the SBLC's affairs. Change of ownership or control includes:

(1) Any transfer of 10 percent or more of any class of the SBLC's stock, and any agreement providing for such transfer;

(2) Any transfer that could result in the beneficial ownership by any person or group of persons acting in concert of 10 percent or more of any class of its stock, and any agreement providing for such transfer;

(3) Any merger, consolidation, or reorganization; or

(4) Any other transaction or agreement that transfers control of the SBLC.

(b) If transfer of ownership or control is subject to the approval of any State or Federal chartering, licensing, or other regulatory authority, copies of any documents filed with such authority must, at the same time, be transmitted to the appropriate Office of Capital Access official in accordance with Delegations of Authority.

[61 FR 3235, Jan. 31, 1996. Redesignated and amended at 73 FR 75516, Dec. 11, 2008]

§ 120.476 Prohibited financing.

An SBLC may not make a loan to a small business that has received financing (or a commitment for financing) from an SBIC that is an Associate of the SBLC.

[61 FR 3235, Jan. 31, 1996. Redesignated at 73 FR 75516, Dec. 11, 2008]

§ 120.490 Audits.

Every SBLC is subject to periodic audits by SBA's Office of Inspector General, Auditing Division, and the cost of such audits will be assessed against the SBLC, except for the first audit. Fees are structured based on the SBLC's assets as of the date of the latest audited financial statement submitted to SBA before the audit. The fee schedule is set forth in SBA's Standard Operating Procedures manual.

[61 FR 3235, Jan. 31, 1996. Redesignated at 73 FR 75516, Dec. 11, 2008]

Subpart E—Servicing, Liquidation and Debt Collection Litigation of 7(a) and 504 Loans

SBA'S PURCHASE OF A GUARANTEED PORTION

§ 120.520 Purchase of 7(a) loan guarantees.

(a) *When SBA will purchase*—(1) *For loans approved on or after May 14, 2007.* A Lender may demand in writing that SBA honor its guarantee if the Borrower is in default on any installment for more than 60 calendar days (or less if SBA agrees) and the default has not been cured, provided all business personal property securing the defaulted SBA loan has been liquidated. A Lender may also submit a request for purchase of a defaulted 7(a) loan when a Borrower files for federal bankruptcy once a period of at least 60 days has elapsed since the last full installment payment. If a Borrower cures a default before a Lender requests purchase by SBA, the Lender's right to request purchase on that default lapses. SBA considers liquidation of business personal property collateral to be completed when a Lender has exhausted all prudent and commercially reasonable efforts to collect upon these assets. In addition, SBA, in its sole discretion, may purchase the guaranteed portion of a loan at any time whether in default or not, with or without the request from a Lender.

(2) *For loans approved before May 14, 2007.* The regulations applicable to the time that a Lender may make demand for purchase that were in effect immediately prior to this date will govern such loans.

(b) *Documentation for purchase.* SBA will not purchase its guaranteed portion of a loan from a Lender unless the Lender has submitted to SBA documentation that SBA deems sufficient to allow SBA to determine whether purchase of the guarantee is warranted under § 120.524.

(c) *Purchase of loans sold in Secondary Market.* When the Lender has sold the guaranteed portion of a loan in the Secondary Market, under subpart F of this part, Lenders must perform all necessary servicing and liquidation actions for such loan even after SBA has purchased the guaranteed portion of such loan from a Registered Holder (as that term is defined in § 120.600(i)). In the event that SBA purchases its guaranteed portion of such a loan from the Registered Holder, Lenders must provide SBA with a loan status report within 15 business days of such purchase. This report should include but not be limited to, a status report on the borrower and current condition of the collateral, plans for any type of loan workout or loan restructuring, existing liquidation activities including the sale of loan collateral, or the status of ongoing foreclosure proceedings. The report should accompany requested documentation that SBA deems sufficient to be able to review the Lender's administration of the loan under § 120.524. A Lender's failure to provide sufficient documentation may constitute a material failure to comply with SBA requirements under § 120.524(a)(1), and may lead to initiation of an action for recovery from the Lender of all or some of the moneys SBA paid to a Registered Holder on a guarantee. SBA will also evaluate the Lender's continued participation in the Secondary Market and may restrict further sale of guaranteed portions into the Secondary Market until SBA determines that the Lender has provided sufficient documentation for purchases.

(d) *No waiver of SBA's rights.* Purchase by SBA of the guaranteed portion of a loan, or of a portion of SBA's guarantee of a loan, either through a negotiated agreement with a Lender or otherwise, does not waive any of SBA's rights to recover from the responsible Lender any money paid on the guarantee based upon the occurrence of any of the events set forth in § 120.524(a) in connection with that loan.

[72 FR 18360, Apr. 12, 2007]

§ 120.521 What interest rate applies after SBA purchases its guaranteed portion?

When SBA purchases the guaranteed portion of a fixed interest rate loan, the rate of interest remains as stated in the note. On loans with a fluctuating interest rate, the interest rate that the Borrower owes will be at the rate in effect at the time of the earliest uncured payment default, or the rate in effect at the time of purchase (where no default has occurred).

§ 120.522 Payment of accrued interest to the Lender or Registered Holder when SBA purchases the guaranteed portion.

(a) *Rate of interest.* If SBA purchases the guaranteed portion from a Lender or from a Registered Holder (if sold in the Secondary Market), it will pay accrued interest at:

(1) The rate in the note if it is a fixed rate loan; or

(2) The rate in effect on the date of the earliest uncured payment default, or of SBA's purchase (if there has been no default).

(b) *Payment to Lender*—(1) *For loans approved on or after May 14, 2007.* SBA will pay up to a maximum of 120 days interest to a Lender at the time of guarantee purchase.

(2) *For loans approved before May 14, 2007.* The regulations applicable to the amount of interest that SBA will pay to a Lender upon loan default that were in effect immediately prior to this date will govern such loans.

(c) *Payment to Registered Holder.* SBA will pay a Registered Holder all accrued interest up to the date of payment.

[61 FR 3235, Jan. 31, 1996, as amended at 72 FR 18361, Apr. 12, 2007]

§ 120.523 What is the "earliest uncured payment default"?

The earliest uncured payment default is the date of the earliest failure by a Borrower to pay a regular installment of principal and/or interest when due. Payments made by the Borrower before a Lender makes its request to SBA to purchase are applied to the earliest uncured payment default. If the installment is paid in full, the earliest uncured payment default date will advance to the next unpaid installment date. If a Borrower makes any payment after the Lender makes its request to SBA to purchase, the earliest uncured payment default date does not change because the Lender has already exercised its right to request purchase.

§ 120.524 When is SBA released from liability on its guarantee?

(a) SBA is released from liability on a loan guarantee (in whole or in part, within SBA's exclusive discretion), if any of the events below occur:

(1) The Lender has failed to comply materially with any Loan Program Requirement for 7(a) loans.

(2) The Lender has failed to make, close, service, or liquidate a loan in a prudent manner;

(3) The Lender's improper action or inaction has placed SBA at risk;

(4) The Lender has failed to disclose a material fact to SBA regarding a guaranteed loan in a timely manner;

(5) The Lender has misrepresented a material fact to SBA regarding a guaranteed loan;

(6) SBA has received a written request from the Lender to terminate the guarantee;

(7) The Lender has not paid the guarantee fee within the period required under SBA rules and regulations;

(8) The Lender has failed to request that SBA purchase a guarantee within 180 days after maturity of the loan. However, if the Lender is conducting liquidation or debt collection litigation in connection with a loan that has matured, SBA will be released from its guarantee only if the Lender fails to request that SBA purchase the guarantee within 180 days after the completion of the liquidation or debt collection litigation;

(9) The Lender has failed to use required SBA forms or exact electronic copies; or

(10) The Borrower has paid the loan in full.

(b) If SBA determines, at any time, that any of the events set forth in paragraph (a) of this section occurred in connection with that loan, SBA is entitled to recover any moneys paid on the guarantee plus interest from the Lender. In the exercise of its rights, SBA may utilize all legal means available, including offset and judicial remedies.

(c) If the Lender's loan documentation or other information indicates that one or more of the events in paragraph (a) of this section occurred, SBA may undertake such investigation as it deems necessary to determine whether to honor or deny the guarantee, and may withhold a decision on whether to honor the guarantee until the completion of such investigation.

(d) Any information provided to SBA by a Lender or other party will not prejudice, or be construed as effecting any waiver of, SBA's right to deny liability for a guarantee if one or more of the events listed in paragraph (a) of this section occur.

(e) Unless SBA provides written notice to the contrary, the Lender remains responsible for all loan servicing ad liquidation actions until SBA honors its guarantee in full.

[61 FR 3235, Jan. 31, 1996, as amended at 72 FR 18361, Apr. 12, 2007; 82 FR 39503, Aug. 21, 2017]

§ 120.530 Deferment of payment.

SBA may agree to defer payments on a business loan for a stated period of time, and use such other methods as it considers necessary and appropriate to help in the successful operation of the Borrower. This policy applies to all business loan programs, including 504 loans.

§ 120.531 Extension of maturity.

SBA may agree to extend the maturity of a loan for up to 10 years beyond its original maturity if the extension will aid in the orderly repayment of the loan.

§ 120.532 What is a loan Moratorium?

SBA may assume a Borrower's obligation to repay principal and interest on a loan by agreeing to make the payments to the Lender on behalf of the Borrower under terms and conditions set by SBA. This relief is called a "Moratorium." Complete information concerning this program may be obtained from local SBA offices.

§ 120.535 Standards for Lender and CDC loan servicing, loan liquidation and debt collection litigation.

(a) *Service using prudent lending standards.* Lenders and CDCs must service 7(a) and 504 loans in their portfolio no less diligently than their non-SBA portfolio, and in a commercially reasonable manner, consistent with prudent lending standards, and in accordance with Loan Program Requirements. Those Lenders and CDCs that do not maintain a non-SBA loan portfolio must adhere to the same prudent lending standards for loan servicing followed by commercial lenders on loans without a government guarantee.

(b) *Liquidate using prudent lending standards.* Lenders and Authorized CDC Liquidators must liquidate and conduct debt collection litigation for 7(a) and 504 loans in their portfolio no less diligently than for their non-SBA portfolio, and in a prompt, cost-effective and commercially reasonable manner, consistent with prudent lending standards, and in accordance with Loan Program Requirements and with any SBA approval of either a liquidation or litigation plan or any amendment of such a plan. Lenders and CDCs that do not maintain a non-SBA loan portfolio must adhere to the same prudent lending standards followed by commercial lenders that liquidate loans without a government guarantee. They are also to operate in accordance with Loan Program Requirements and with any SBA approval of either a liquidation or litigation plan or any amendment of such a plan.

(c) *Absence of actual or apparent conflict of interest.* A CDC must not take any action in the liquidation or debt collection litigation of a 504 loan that would result in an actual or apparent conflict of interest between the CDC (or any employee of the CDC) and any Third Party Lender, associate of a Third Party Lender, or any person participating in a liquidation, foreclosure or loss mitigation action.

(d) *SBA rights to take over servicing or liquidation.* SBA may, in its sole discretion, undertake the servicing, liquidation and/or litigation of any 7(a) or 504 loan. If SBA elects to service, liquidate and/or litigate a loan, it will notify the relevant Lender or CDC in writing, and, upon receiving such notice, the Lender or CDC must assign the Loan Instruments to SBA and provide any needed assistance to allow SBA to service, liquidate and/or litigate the loan. SBA will notify the Borrower of the change in servicing. SBA may use contractors to perform these actions.

[72 FR 18361, Apr. 12, 2007]

§ 120.536 Servicing and liquidation actions that require the prior written consent of SBA.

(a) *Actions by Lenders and CDCs.* Except as otherwise provided in a Supplemental Guarantee Agreement with a Lender or an Agreement with a CDC, SBA must give its prior written consent before a Lender or CDC takes any of the following actions:

(1) Increases the principal amount of a loan above that authorized by SBA at loan origination.

(2) Confers a Preference on the Lender or CDC or engages in an activity that creates a conflict of interest.

(3) Compromises the principal balance of a loan.

(4) Takes title to any property in the name of SBA.

(5) Takes title to environmentally contaminated property, or takes over operation and control of a business that handles hazardous substances or hazardous wastes.

(6) Transfers, sells or pledges more than 90% of a loan.

(7) Takes any action for which prior written consent is required by a Loan Program Requirement.

(b) *Actions by CDCs only (other than PCLP CDCs).* SBA must give its prior written consent before a CDC, other than a PCLP CDC, takes any of the following actions with respect to a 504 loan:

(1) Alters substantially the terms or conditions of any Loan Instrument.

(2) Releases collateral having a cumulative market value in excess of 10 percent of the Debenture amount or $10,000, whichever is less.

(3) Accelerates the maturity of the note.

(4) Compromises or releases any claim against any Borrower or obligor, or against any guarantor, standby creditor, or any other person that is contingently liable for moneys owed on the loan.

(5) Purchases or pays off any indebtedness secured by the property that serves as collateral for a defaulted 504 loan, such as payment of the debt(s) owed to a lien holder or lien holders with priority over the lien securing the loan.

(6) Accepts a workout plan to restructure the material terms and conditions of a loan that is in default or liquidation.

(7) Takes any action for which prior written consent is required by a Loan Program Requirement.

(c) *Documentation requirements.* For all servicing/liquidation actions not requiring SBA's prior written consent, Lenders and CDCs must document the justifications for their decisions and retain these and supporting documents in their file for future SBA review to determine if the actions taken by the Lender or CDC were prudent, commercially reasonable, and complied with all Loan Program Requirements.

[72 FR 18361, Apr. 12, 2007]

§ 120.540 Liquidation and litigation plans.

(a) *SBA oversight.* SBA may monitor or review liquidation through the review of liquidation plans which all Authorized CDC Liquidators and certain Lenders must submit to SBA for approval prior to undertaking liquidation, and through liquidation wrap-up reports which Lenders must submit to SBA at the completion of liquidation. SBA will monitor debt collection litigation, such as judicial foreclosures, bankruptcy proceedings and other state and federal insolvency proceedings, through the review of litigation plans, as set forth in this section.

(b) *Liquidation plan.* An Authorized CDC Liquidator and a Lender for a loan made under its authority as a CLP Lender must, prior to undertaking any liquidation, submit a written proposed liquidation plan to SBA and receive SBA's written approval of that plan.

(c) *Litigation plan.* An Authorized CDC Liquidator and a Lender must obtain SBA's prior approval of a litigation plan before proceeding with any Non-Routine Litigation, as defined in paragraph (c)(1) of this section. SBA's prior approval is not required for Routine Litigation, as defined in paragraph (c)(2) of this section.

(1) Non-Routine Litigation includes:

(i) All litigation where factual or legal issues are in dispute and require resolution through adjudication;

(ii) Any litigation where legal fees are estimated to exceed $10,000;

(iii) Any litigation involving a loan where a Lender or Authorized CDC Liquidator has an actual or potential conflict of interest with SBA; and

(iv) Any litigation involving a 7(a) or 504 loan where the Lender or CDC has made a separate loan to the same borrower which is not a 7(a) or 504 loan.

(2) Routine Litigation means uncontested litigation, such as non-adversarial matters in bankruptcy and undisputed foreclosure actions, having estimated legal fees not exceeding $10,000.

(d) *Decision by SBA to take over litigation.* If a Lender or Authorized CDC Liquidator is conducting, or proposes to conduct, debt collection litigation on a 7(a) loan or 504 loan, SBA may take over the litigation if SBA determines that the outcome of the litigation could adversely affect SBA's administration of the loan program or that the Government is entitled to legal remedies that are not available to the Lender or Authorized CDC Liquidator. Examples of cases that could adversely affect SBA's administration of a loan program include, but are not limited to, situations where SBA determines that:

(1) The litigation involves important governmental policy or program issues.

(2) The case is potentially of great precedential value or there is a risk of adverse precedent to the Government.

(3) The Lender or Authorized CDC Liquidator has an actual or potential conflict of interest with SBA.

(4) The legal fees of the Lender or Authorized CDC Liquidator's outside counsel are unnecessary, unreasonable or not customary in the locality.

(e) *Amendments to a liquidation or litigation plan.* Lenders and Authorized CDC Liquidators must submit an amended liquidation or litigation plan to address any material changes arising during the course of the liquidation or litigation that were not addressed in the original plan or an amended plan. Lenders and Authorized CDC Liquidators must obtain SBA's written approval of the amended plan prior to taking any further liquidation or litigation action. Examples of such material changes that would require the approval of an amended plan include, but are not limited to:

(1) Changes arising during the course of Routine Litigation that transform the litigation into Non-Routine Litigation, such as when the debtor contests a foreclosure or when the actual legal fees incurred exceed $10,000.

(2) If SBA has approved a litigation plan where anticipated legal fees exceed $10,000, or has approved an amended plan, and thereafter the anticipated or actual legal fees increase by more than 15 percent.

(3) If SBA has approved a liquidation plan, or an amended plan, and thereafter the anticipated or actual costs of conducting the liquidation increase by more than 15 percent.

(f) *Limited waiver of need for a written liquidation or litigation plan.* SBA may, in its discretion, and upon request by a Lender or Authorized CDC Liquidator, waive the requirements of paragraphs (b), (c) or (e) of this section, if one of the following extraordinary circumstances warrant such a waiver: the need for expeditious action to avoid the potential risk of loss on the loan or dissipation of collateral exists; an immediate response is required to litigation by a borrower, guarantor or third party; or another urgent reason arises. The Lender or Authorized CDC Liquidator must obtain SBA's written consent to such waiver before undertaking the Emergency action, if at all practicable. SBA's waiver will apply only to the specific action(s) which the Lender or Authorized CDC Liquidator has identified to SBA as being necessary to address the Emergency. The Lender or Authorized CDC Liquidator must, as soon after the Emergency as is practicable, submit a written liquidation or litigation plan to SBA or, if appropriate, a written amended plan, and may not take further liquidation or litigation action without written approval of such plan or amendment by SBA.

(g) *Appeals.* A Lender for loans made under its authority as a CLP Lender or an Authorized CDC Liquidator that disagrees with an SBA office's decision pertaining to an original or amended liquidation plan, other than such portions of the plan that address litigation matters, may submit a written appeal to the D/FA within 30 days of the decision. The D/FA or designee will make the final Agency decision in consultation with the Associate General Counsel for Litigation. A Lender or Authorized CDC Liquidator that disagrees with an SBA office's decision pertaining to an original or amended litigation plan, or the portion of a liquidation plan addressing litigation matters, may submit a written appeal to the Associate General Counsel for Litigation within 30 days of the decision. The Associate General Counsel for Litigation will make the final Agency decision in consultation with the D/FA.

[72 FR 18362, Apr. 12, 2007, as amended at 74 FR 45753, Sept. 4, 2009]

§ 120.541 Time for approval by SBA.

(a) Except as set forth in paragraph (c) of this section, in responding to a request for approval under §§ 120.540(b), 120.540(c), 120.536(b)(5) or 120.536(b)(6), SBA will approve or deny the request within 15 business days of the date when SBA receives the request. If SBA is unable to approve or deny the request within this 15-day period, SBA will provide a written notice of no decision to the Lender or Authorized CDC Liquidator, stating the reason for SBA's inability to act; an estimate of the additional time required to act on the plan or request; and, if SBA deems appropriate, requesting additional information.

(b) Except as set forth in paragraph (c) of this section, unless SBA gives its written consent to a proposed liquidation or litigation plan, or a proposed amendment of a plan, or any of the actions set forth in § 120.536(b)(5) or § 120.536(b)(6), SBA will not be deemed to have approved the proposed action.

(c) If a Lender seeks to perform liquidation on a loan made under its authority as a CLP Lender by submitting a liquidation plan to SBA for approval, SBA will approve or deny such plan within ten business days. If SBA fails to approve or deny the plan within ten business days, SBA will be deemed to have approved such plan.

[72 FR 18362, Apr. 12, 2007]

§ 120.542 Payment by SBA of legal fees and other expenses.

(a) *Legal fees SBA will not pay.* (1) SBA will not pay legal fees or other costs that a Lender or Authorized CDC Liquidator incurs:

(i) In asserting a claim, cross claim, counterclaim, or third-party claim against SBA or in defense of an action brought by SBA, unless payment of such fees or costs is otherwise required by federal law.

(ii) In connection with actions of a Lender or Authorized CDC Liquidator's outside counsel for performing non-legal liquidation services, unless authorized by SBA prior to the action.

(iii) In taking actions which solely benefit a Lender or Authorized CDC Liquidator and which do not benefit SBA, as determined by SBA.

(2) SBA will not pay legal fees or other costs a Lender or CDC incurs in the defense of, or pay for any settlement or adverse judgment resulting from, a suit, counterclaim or other claim by a borrower, guarantor, or other party that seeks damages based upon a claim that the Lender or CDC breached any duty or engaged in any wrongful actions, unless SBA expressly directed the Lender or CDC to undertake the allegedly wrongful action that is the subject of the suit, counterclaim or other claim.

(b) *Legal fees SBA may decline to pay.* In addition to any right or authority SBA may have under law or contract, SBA may, in its discretion, decline to pay a Lender or Authorized CDC Liquidator for all, or a portion, of legal fees and/or other costs incurred in connection with the liquidation and/or litigation of a 7(a) loan or 504 loan under any of the following circumstances:

(1) SBA determines that the Lender or Authorized CDC Liquidator failed to perform liquidation or litigation promptly and in accordance with commercially reasonable standards, in a prudent manner, or in accordance with any Loan Program Requirement or SBA approvals of either a liquidation or litigation plan or any amendment of such a plan.

(2) A Lender or Authorized CDC Liquidator fails to obtain prior written approval from SBA for any liquidation or litigation plan, or for any amended liquidation or litigation plan, or for any action set forth in § 120.536, when such approval is required by these regulations or a Loan Program Requirement.

(3) If SBA has not specifically approved fees or costs identified in an original or amended liquidation or litigation plan under § 120.540, and SBA determines that such fees or costs are not reasonable, customary or necessary in the locality in question. In such cases, SBA will pay only such fees as it deems are necessary, customary and reasonable in the locality in question.

(c) *Fees for liquidation actions performed by Authorized CDC Liquidators.* Subject to paragraph (d) of this section, SBA will compensate Authorized CDC Liquidators for their liquidation actions on 504 loans, whether such actions are performed by the CDC or the CDC's contractor retained in accordance with § 120.975(a)(2) or (b)(2)(ii). The compensation fee will be a percentage (to be published in the FEDERAL REGISTER from time to time, but not to exceed 10%) of the net recovery proceeds realized from the sale of collateral or other liquidation actions on an individual loan, up to a fee of $25,000 for such loan, and a lower percentage (also to be published in the FEDERAL REGISTER from time to time, but not to exceed 5%) of the realized net recovery proceeds above such amounts. The compensation fee limits set forth in this paragraph (c) do not include reasonable, customary and necessary administrative costs related to liquidation activities on such loan that are incurred in accordance with the liquidation plan, or amendments thereto, approved by SBA pursuant to § 120.540(b). The Authorized CDC Liquidator may compensate its contractor up to the amount it receives from SBA. All requests for compensation fees must be received by SBA within nine months from the date of SBA's purchase of the defaulted debenture. Fee requests not received within such timeframe will be automatically rejected.

(d) *Appeals—liquidation costs.* A Lender or Authorized CDC Liquidator that disagrees with a decision by an SBA office to decline to reimburse all, or a portion, of the fees and/or costs incurred in conducting liquidation may appeal this decision in writing to the D/FA within 30 days of the decision. The decision of the D/FA or designee will be made in consultation with the Associate General Counsel for Litigation, and will be the final Agency decision.

(e) *Appeals—litigation costs.* A Lender or Authorized CDC Liquidator that disagrees with a decision by SBA to decline to reimburse all, or a portion, of the legal fees and/or costs incurred in conducting debt collection litigation may appeal this decision in writing to the Associate General Counsel for Litigation within 30 days of the decision. The decision of the Associate General Counsel for Litigation will be made in consultation with the D/FA, and will be the final Agency decision.

[72 FR 18362, Apr. 12, 2007, as amended at 74 FR 45753, Sept. 4, 2009]

§ 120.545 What are SBA's policies concerning the liquidation of collateral and the sale of business loans and physical disaster assistance loans, physical disaster business loans and economic injury disaster loans?

(a) *Liquidation policy.* SBA or the Lender may liquidate collateral securing a loan if the loan is in default or there is no reasonable prospect that the loan can be repaid within a reasonable period.

(b) *Sale and conversion of loans.* Without the consent of the Borrower, SBA may:

(1) Sell a direct loan;

(2) Convert a guaranteed or immediate participation loan to a direct loan; or

(3) Convert an immediate participation loan to a guaranteed loan or a loan owned solely by the Lender.

(4) Sell direct and purchased 7(a) and 501, 502, 503 and 504 loans and physical disaster home loans, physical disaster business loans and economic injury disaster loans in asset sales. SBA will offer these loans for sale to qualified bidders by means of competitive procedures at publicly advertised sales. Bidder qualifications will be set for each sale in accordance with the terms and conditions of each sale.

(c) *Disposal of collateral and assets acquired through foreclosure or conveyance.* SBA or the Lender may sell real and personal property (including contracts and claims) pledged to secure a loan that is in default in accordance with the provisions of the related security instrument (*see* § 120.550 for Homestead Protection for Farmers).

(1) *Competitive bids or negotiated sales.* Generally, SBA will offer loan collateral and acquired assets for public sale through competitive bids at auctions or sealed bid sales. The Lender may use negotiated sales if consistent with its usual practice for similar non-SBA assets.

(2) *Lease of acquired property.* Normally, neither SBA nor a Lender will rent or lease acquired property or grant options to purchase. SBA and the Lender will consider proposals for a lease if it appears a property cannot be sold advantageously and the lease may be terminated on reasonable notice upon receipt of a favorable purchase offer.

(d) *Recoveries and security interests shared.* SBA and the Lender will share pro rata (in accordance with their respective interests in a loan) all loan payments or recoveries, including proceeds from asset sales, all reasonable expenses (including advances for the care, preservation, and maintenance of collateral securing the loan and the payment of senior lienholders), and any security interest or guarantee (excluding SBA's guarantee) which the Lender or SBA may hold or receive in connection with a loan.

(e) *Guarantors.* Guarantors of financial assistance have no rights of contribution against SBA on an SBA guaranteed or direct loan. SBA is not deemed to be a co-guarantor with any other guarantors.

[61 FR 3235, Jan. 31, 1996, as amended at 64 FR 44110, Aug. 13, 1999; 65 FR 17133, Mar. 31, 2000; 68 FR 51680, Aug. 28, 2003. Redesignated and amended at 72 FR 18362, Apr. 12, 2007]

§ 120.546 Loan asset sales.

(a) *General.* Loan asset sales are governed by § 120.545(b)(4) and by this section.

(b) *7(a) loans*—(1) *For loans approved on or after May 14, 2007.* The Lender will be deemed to have consented to SBA's sale of the loan (guaranteed and unguaranteed portions) in an asset sale conducted or overseen by SBA upon the occurrence any of the following:

(i) SBA's purchase of the guaranteed portion of the loan from the Registered Holder for a loan where the guaranteed portion has been sold in the Secondary Market pursuant to subpart F of this part and after default, the Lender has not exercised its option to purchase such guaranteed portion; or

(ii) SBA's purchase of the guaranteed portion from the Lender, provided however, that if SBA purchased the guaranteed portion pursuant to § 120.520(a)(1) prior to the Lender's completion of liquidation for the loan, then SBA will not sell such loan in an asset sale until nine months from the date of SBA's purchase; or

(iii) SBA receives written consent from the Lender.

(2) For loans identified in paragraph (b)(1)(i) of this section, the Lender may request that SBA withhold the loan from an asset sale if the Lender submits a written request to SBA within 15 business days of SBA's purchase of the guaranteed portion of the loan from the Registered Holder and if such request addresses the issues described in this subparagraph. The Lender's written request must advise SBA of the status of the loan, the Lender's plans for workout and/or liquidation, including and pending sale of loan collateral or foreclosure proceedings arranged prior to SBA's purchase that already are underway, and the Lender's estimated schedule for restructuring the loan or liquidating the collateral. SBA will consider the Lender's request and, based on the circumstances, SBA in its sole discretion may elect to defer including the loan in an asset sale in order to provide the Lender additional time to complete the planned restructuring and/or liquidation actions.

(3) *For loans approved before May 14, 2007.* SBA must obtain written consent from the Lender for the sale of such loans in an asset sale.

(4) After SBA has purchased the guaranteed portion of a loan from the Registered Holder or from the Lender, the Lender must continue to perform all necessary servicing and liquidation actions for the loan up to the point the loan is transferred to the purchaser in an asset sale. The Lender also must cooperate and take all necessary actions to effectuate both the asset sale and the transfer of the loan to the purchaser in the asset sale.

(c) *504 loans*—(1) *PCLP Loans.* After SBA's purchase of a Debenture, SBA may at its sole discretion sell a defaulted PCLP Loan in an asset sale conducted or overseen by SBA, after providing to the PCLP CDC that made the loan advance notice of not less than 90 days before the date upon which SBA first makes its records concerning such loan available to prospective purchasers for examination.

(2) *All other 504 loans.* After SBA's purchase of a Debenture, SBA may at its sole discretion sell a defaulted 504 loan in an asset sale conducted or overseen by SBA.

[72 FR 18364, Apr. 12, 2007]

HOMESTEAD PROTECTION FOR FARMERS

§ 120.550 What is homestead protection for farmers?

SBA may lease to a farmer-Borrower the farm residence occupied by the Borrower and a reasonable amount of adjoining property (no more than 10 acres and seven farm buildings), if they were acquired by SBA as a result of a defaulted farm loan made or guaranteed by SBA (*see* the Consolidated Farm and Rural Development Act, 7 U.S.C. 1921, for qualifying loan purposes).

§ 120.551 Who is eligible for homestead protection?

SBA must notify the Borrower in possession of the availability of these homestead protection rights within 30 days after SBA acquires the property. A farmer-Borrower must:

(a) Apply for the homestead occupancy to the SBA field office which serviced the loan within 90 days after SBA acquires the property;

(b) Provide evidence that the farm produces farm income reasonable for the area and economic conditions;

(c) Show that at least 60 percent of the Borrower and spouse's gross annual income came from farm or ranch operations in at least any two out of the last six calendar years;

(d) Have resided on the property during the previous six years; and

(e) Be personally liable for the debt.

§ 120.552 Lease.

If approved, the applicant must personally occupy the residence during the term of the lease and pay a reasonable rent to SBA. The lease will be for a period of at least 3 years, but no more than 5 years. A lease of less than 5 years may be renewed, but not beyond 5 years from the original lease date. During or at the end of the lease period, the lessee has a right of first refusal to reacquire the homestead property under terms and conditions no less favorable than those offered to any other purchaser.

§ 120.553 Appeal.

If the application is denied, the Borrower may appeal the decision to the D/FA. Until the conclusion of any appeal, the Borrower may retain possession of the homestead property.

§ 120.554 Conflict of laws.

In the event of a conflict between the homestead provisions at §§ 120.550 through 120.553 of this part, and any state law relating to the right of a Borrower to designate for separate sale or to redeem part or all of the real property securing a loan foreclosed by the Lender, state law shall prevail.

Subpart F—Secondary Market

FISCAL AND TRANSFER AGENT (FTA)

§ 120.600 Definitions.

(a) *Certificate* is the document the FTA issues representing either a beneficial fractional undivided interest in a Pool (Pool Certificate), or a fractional undivided interest in some or all of the guaranteed portion of an individual 7(a) guaranteed loan (Individual Certificate).

(b) *Current* means that no repayment from a Borrower to a Lender is over 29 days late measured from the due date of the payment on the records of the FTA's central registry (Pools) or the entity servicing the loan (individual guaranteed portion).

(c) *Dollar-Weighted Average Net Rate* of a Pool is calculated by multiplying the interest rate of each loan in the Pool by the ratio of that loan's current outstanding guaranteed principal to the current outstanding guaranteed principal of all loans in the Pool, and adding the sum of the resulting products. The Dollar-Weighted Average Net Rate of a Pool will fluctuate over the life of the Pool as loan defaults, prepayments and normal loan repayments occur.

(d) *FTA* is the SBA's fiscal and transfer agent.

(e) *Note Rate* is the interest rate on the Borrower's note.

(f) *Net Rate* is the interest rate on an individual guaranteed portion of a loan in a Pool.

(g) *Pool* is an aggregation of SBA guaranteed portions of loans made by Lenders.

(h) *Pool Assembler* is a financial institution that:

(1) Organizes and packages a Pool by acquiring the SBA guaranteed portions of loans from Lenders;

(2) Resells fractional interests in the Pool to Registered Holders; and

(3) Directs the FTA to issue Certificates.

(i) *Pool Rate* is the interest rate on a Pool Certificate.

(j) *Registered Holder* is the Certificate owner listed in FTA's records.

(k) *SBA's Secondary Market Program Guide* is an issuance from SBA which describes the characteristics of Secondary Market transactions.

(l) *Weighted Average Coupon (WAC) Pool* is a Pool where the interest rate payable to the investor is equal to the Dollar-Weighted Average Net Rate of the Pool.

[61 FR 3235, Jan. 31, 1996, as amended at 73 FR 67102, Nov. 13, 2008; 76 FR 63546, Oct. 12, 2011]

§ 120.601 SBA Secondary Market.

The SBA secondary market ("Secondary Market") consists of the sale of Certificates, representing either a fractional undivided interest in some or all of the guaranteed portion of an individual 7(a) guaranteed loan or a fractional undivided interest in a Pool consisting of the SBA guaranteed portions of a number of 7(a) guaranteed loans. Transactions involving interests in Pools or the sale of individual guaranteed portions of loans are governed by the contracts entered into by the parties, SBA's Secondary Market Program Guide, and this subpart. See sections 5(f), (g), and (h) of the Small Business Act (15 U.S.C. 634(f), (g), and (h)).

[76 FR 63546, Oct. 12, 2011]

CERTIFICATES

§ 120.610 Form and terms of Certificates.

(a) *General form and content.* Each Certificate must be registered with the FTA. SBA must approve the terms of the Certificate.

(b) *Face amount of Pool Certificate.* The face amount of a Pool Certificate cannot be less than a minimum amount as specified in the Program Guide, and the dollar amount of Certificates must be in increments which SBA will specify in the Program Guide (except for one Certificate in each Pool). SBA may change these requirements based upon an analysis of market conditions and program experience, and will publish any such change in the FEDERAL REGISTER.

(c) *Basis of payment for Pool Certificates.* Principal installments and interest payments are based on the unpaid principal balance of the portion of the Pool represented by a Pool Certificate. All prepayments on loans in the Pool must be passed through to the appropriate Registered Holders with the regularly scheduled payments to such Holders.

(d) *Basis of payment for Individual Certificates.* Principal installments and interest payments are based on the unpaid principal balance of the SBA guaranteed portion of the loan supporting an Individual Certificate. The Certificate must provide for a pass through to the Registered Holder of payments which the FTA receives from a Lender or any entity servicing the loan, less applicable fees.

(e) *Interest rate on Pool Certificate.* The interest rate on a Pool Certificate will be either the lowest Net Rate of any individual guaranteed portion of a loan in the Pool or the Dollar-Weighted Average Net Rate of the Pool.

[61 FR 3235, Jan. 31, 1996, as amended at 73 FR 67102, Nov. 13, 2008]

§ 120.611 Pools backing Pool Certificates.

(a) *Pool characteristics.* As set forth in the Program Guide, each Pool must have:

(1) A minimum number of guaranteed portions of loans;

(2) A minimum aggregate principal balance of the guaranteed portions;

(3) A maximum percentage of the Pool which an individual guaranteed portion may constitute;

(4) A maximum allowable difference between the highest and lowest note interest rates;

(5) A maximum allowable difference between the remaining terms to maturity of the loans in the Pool;

(6) A minimum weighted average maturity at Pool formation; and

(7) A maximum allowable difference between the highest and lowest Net Rate on the guaranteed portions that are placed in a WAC Pool.

(b) *Adjustment of Pool characteristics.* SBA may adjust the Pool characteristics periodically based upon program experience and market conditions.

(c) *Increments of guaranteed portion.* If the amount of the guaranteed portion of an individual 7(a) guaranteed loan is more than $500,000, a Pool Assembler may elect to divide the guaranteed portion into increments of $500,000 and one increment of any remaining amount less than $500,000, in order to permit the maximum amount of any guaranteed portion in a Pool to be not more than $500,000. Only one increment from a loan to a specific borrower may be included in a Pool.

[61 FR 3235, Jan. 31, 1996, as amended at 73 FR 67102, Nov. 13, 2008; 76 FR 63546, Oct. 12, 2011]

§ 120.612 Loans eligible to back Certificates.

(a) Pool Certificates are backed by the SBA guaranteed portions of loans comprising the Pool. An Individual Certificate is backed by the SBA guaranteed portion of a single loan. Any such loan must:

(1) Be current as of the date the Pool is formed or the individual guaranteed portion of a loan is initially sold in the Secondary Market;

(2) Be guaranteed under the Act; and

(3) Meet such other standards as SBA may determine to be necessary for the successful operation of the Secondary Market program.

(b) The loans that back a Pool must meet the SBA requirements in effect at the time the Pool is formed.

§ 120.613 Secondary Participation Guarantee Agreement.

When a Lender wants to sell the guaranteed portion of a loan, it enters into a Secondary Participation Guarantee Agreement ("SPGA") with SBA and the prospective purchaser. The terms of sale between the Lender and the purchaser cannot require the Lender or SBA to repurchase the guaranteed portion of the loan except in accordance with the terms of the SPGA. Before execution of the SPGA, the Lender must:

(a) Submit to FTA a copy of the proposed SPGA, the note, and such other documents as SBA may require;

(b) Except for export working capital loans, disburse to the Borrower the full amount of the loan; and

(c) Pay SBA all guarantee fees relevant to the loan in full.

[61 FR 3235, Jan. 31, 1996, as amended at 68 FR 51680, Aug. 28, 2003]

THE SBA GUARANTEE OF A CERTIFICATE

§ 120.620 SBA guarantee of a Pool Certificate.

(a) *Extent of Guarantee.* SBA guarantees to a Registered Holder the timely payment of principal and interest installments and any prepayment or other recovery of principal to which the Registered Holder is entitled. If the Borrower of a loan in a Pool backing the Certificates does not make a required installment payment, SBA, through the FTA, will make advances to maintain the schedule of interest and principal payments to the Registered Holders.

(b) *SBA guarantee backed by full faith and credit.* SBA's guarantee of the Pool Certificate is backed by the full faith and credit of the United States.

§ 120.621 SBA guarantee of an Individual Certificate.

(a) *Extent of SBA guarantee.* With respect to Individual Certificates, SBA guarantees to purchase from the Registered Holder the guaranteed portion of the loan for an amount equal to the unpaid principal and accrued interest due as of the date of SBA's purchase, less deductions for applicable fees. Unlike the SBA guarantee with respect to pooled loans, SBA does not guarantee timely payment on Individual Certificates.

(b) *What triggers the SBA guarantee.* SBA's guarantee to the Registered Holder may be called upon when:

(1) The Borrower remains in uncured default for 60 days on payments of principal or interest due on the note;

(2) The Lender fails to send to the FTA on a timely basis payments it received from the Borrower; or

(3) The FTA fails to send to the Registered Holder on a timely basis any payments it has received from the Lender.

(c) *Full faith and credit.* SBA's guarantee to the Registered Holder is backed by the full faith and credit of the United States.

POOL ASSEMBLERS

§ 120.630 Qualifications to be a Pool Assembler.

(a) *Application to become Pool Assembler.* The application to become a Pool Assembler is available from the D/FA. In order to qualify as a Pool Assembler, an entity must send the application to the D/FA, with an application fee, and certify that it:

(1) Is regulated by the appropriate agency as defined in section 3(a)(34)(G) of the Securities Exchange Act of 1934 (15 U.S.C. 78c(a)(34)(G));

(2) Meets all financial and other applicable requirements of its regulatory authority and the Government Securities Act of 1986, as amended (Pub. L. 99–571, 100 Stat. 3208);

(3) Has the financial capability to assemble acceptable and eligible guaranteed loan portions in sufficient quantity to support the issuance of Pool Certificates; and

(4) Is in good standing with SBA (as the D/FA determines in his or her discretion), and is Satisfactory with the Office of the Comptroller of the Currency ("OCC") if it is a national bank, the Federal Deposit Insurance Corporation if it is a bank not regulated by the OCC, or the Financial Industry Regulatory Authority ("FINRA") if it is a member as determined by SBA.

(5) For any pool assembler that is an SBA Lender, that the SBA Lender has satisfactory SBA performance, as determined by SBA in its discretion. The Lender's Risk Rating, among other factors, will be considered in determining satisfactory SBA performance. Other factors may include, but are not limited to, review/examination assessments, historical performance measures (like default rate, purchase rate and loss rate), loan volume to the extent that it impacts performance measures, and other performance related measurements and information (such as contribution toward SBA mission).

(b) *Approval by SBA.* An entity may not submit Pool applications to the FTA until SBA has approved the application to become a Pool Assembler.

(c) *Conduct of business by Pool Assembler.* An entity continues to qualify as a Pool Assembler so long as it:

(1) Meets the eligibility standards in paragraph (a) of this section;

(2) Conducts its business in accordance with SBA regulations and accepted securities or banking industry practices, ethics, and standards; and

(3) Maintains its books and records in accordance with generally accepted accounting principles or in accordance with the guidelines of the regulatory body governing its activities.

[61 FR 3235, Jan. 31, 1996, as amended at 73 FR 75517, Dec. 11, 2008; 82 FR 39503, Aug. 21, 2017]

§ 120.631 Suspension or termination of Pool Assembler.

(a) *Suspension or termination.* The D/FA may suspend a Pool Assembler from operating in the Secondary Market for up to 18 months or terminate its status as a Pool Assembler, if the Pool Assembler (and/or its Associates):

(1) Does not comply with any of the requirements in § 120.630 (a) and (c);

(2) Has been indicted or otherwise formally charged with, or convicted of, a misdemeanor or felony;

(3) Has received an adverse civil judgment that it has committed a breach of

trust or a violation of a law or regulation protecting the integrity of business transactions or relationships;

(4) Has not formed a Pool for at least three years; or

(5) Is under investigation by its regulating authority for activities which may affect its fitness to participate in the Secondary Market.

(b) *Suspension procedures.* The D/FA shall notify a Pool Assembler by certified mail, return receipt requested, of the decision to suspend and the reasons therefore at least 10 business days prior to the effective date of the suspension. The Pool Assembler may appeal the suspension made under this section pursuant to the procedures set forth in part 134 of this chapter. The action of the D/FA shall remain in effect pending resolution of the appeal.

(c) *Notice of termination.* In order to terminate a Pool Assembler, the D/FA must issue an order to show cause why the SBA should not terminate the Pool Assembler's participation in the Secondary Market. The Pool Assembler may appeal the termination made under this section pursuant to procedures set forth in part 134 of this chapter. The action of the D/FA shall remain in effect pending resolution of the appeal.

MISCELLANEOUS PROVISIONS

§ 120.640 Administration of the Pool and Individual Certificates.

(a) *FTA responsibility.* The FTA has the responsibility to administer each Pool or Individual Certificate. It shall maintain a registry of Registered Holders and other information as SBA requires.

(b) *Self-liquidating.* Each Pool or individual guaranteed portion of a loan in the Secondary Market is self-liquidating because of Borrower payments or prepayments, redemption by SBA, and/or payments by SBA or the Lender after default by the Borrower. Substitution of the guaranteed portions of existing loans for defaulted loans is not permitted.

(c) *SBA's right to subrogation.* If SBA pays a claim under a guarantee with respect to a Certificate issued under this subpart, it must be subrogated fully to the rights satisfied by such payment.

(d) *SBA ownership rights not limited.* No Federal, State or local law can preclude or limit the exercise by SBA of its ownership rights in the portions of loans constituting the Pool against which the Certificates are issued.

§ 120.641 Disclosure to purchasers.

(a) *Information to purchaser.* Prior to any sale, the Pool Assembler, Registered Holder of an Individual Certificate, or any subsequent seller must disclose to the purchaser, verbally or in writing, information on the terms, conditions, and yield as described in the SBA Secondary Market Program Guide.

(b) *Information on transfer document.* The seller must provide the same information described in paragraph (a) of this section in writing on the transfer document when the seller submits it to the FTA. After the sale of an Individual Certificate, the FTA will provide the disclosure information in writing to the purchaser.

(c) *Information in prospectus.* If the Registered Holder is a trust, investment Pool, mutual fund or other security, it must disclose the information in paragraph (a) of this section to investors through a prospectus and other promotional material if an Individual Certificate or Pool Certificate is placed into or used as the backing for the investment vehicle.

§ 120.642 Requirements before the FTA issues Pool Certificates.

Before the FTA issues any Pool Certificate, the Pool Assembler must deliver to it the following documents:

(a) A properly completed Pool application form;

(b) Either:

(1) Individual Certificates evidencing the guaranteed portions comprising the Pool; or

(2) An executed SPGA and related documentation for the loans whose guaranteed portions are to be part of the Pool; and

(c) Any other documentation which SBA may require.

§ 120.643 Requirements before the FTA issues Individual Certificates.

(a) *FTA issuance of initial Certificate.* Before the FTA can issue the Individual Certificate for a guaranteed portion of a loan, the original seller must provide the following documents to the FTA:

(1) An executed SPGA;

(2) A copy of the note representing the guaranteed loan; and

(3) Any other documentation which SBA may require.

(b) Review of documentation. SBA may review or require the FTA to review any documentation before the FTA issues a Certificate.

§ 120.644 Transfers of Certificates.

(a) *General rule.* Certificates are transferable. Transfers in the Secondary Market must comply with Article 8 of the Uniform Commercial Code of the State of New York. The seller must use the detached form of assignment (SBA Form 1088), unless the seller and purchaser choose to use another form which the SBA approves. The FTA may refuse to issue a Certificate until it is satisfied that the documents of transfer are complete.

(b) *Transfer on FTA records.* In order for the transfer of a Certificate to be effective the FTA must reflect it on its records.

(c) *Contents of letter of transmittal accompanying the transfer of Certificates.* (1) A letter of transmittal must accompany each Certificate which a Registered Holder submits to the FTA for transfer. The Registered Holder must supply the following information in the letter:

(i) Pool number, if applicable;

(ii) Certificate number;

(iii) Name of purchaser of Certificate;

(iv) Address and tax identification number of the purchaser;

(v) Name and telephone number of the person handling or facilitating the transfer;

(vi) Instructions for the delivery of the new Certificate.

(2) The Registered Holder must also send the fee which the FTA charges for this service. The FTA will supply fee information to the Registered Holder.

(d) *Lender cannot purchase guaranteed portion of loan it made.* The Lender (or its Associate) that made a 7(a) guaranteed loan cannot purchase the guaranteed portion of that loan in the Secondary Market. If a Lender does purchase the guaranteed portion of one of its own loans, it shall not have the unconditional guarantee of SBA.

§ 120.645 Redemption of Certificates.

(a) *Redemption of Individual Certificate.* The prepayment of the underlying loan or a default on such loan will trigger the redemption of the Certificate by FTA/SBA in accordance with the procedures prescribed in the SPGA.

(b) *Redemption of Pool Certificate.* The FTA and SBA may redeem a Pool Certificate because of prepayment or default of all loans in a Pool.

§ 120.650 Registration duties of FTA in Secondary Market.

The FTA registers all Certificates. This means it issues, transfers title to, and redeems them. All financial transactions relating to a guaranteed portion of a loan flow through the FTA. In fulfilling its obligation to keep the central registry current, the FTA may, with SBA's approval, obtain any necessary information from the parties involved in the Secondary Market.

§ 120.651 Claim to FTA by Registered Holder to replace Certificate.

(a) To replace a Certificate because of loss, theft, destruction, mutilation, or defacement, the Registered Holder must:

(1) Give the FTA information about the Certificate and the facts relating to the claim;

(2) File an indemnity bond acceptable to SBA and the FTA with a surety to protect the interests of SBA and the FTA;

(3) Pay the FTA its fee to replace a Certificate; and

(4) Use an affidavit of loss (form available from the FTA) to report:

(i) The name and address of the Registered Holder (and the name and capacity of any representative actually filing the claim);

(ii) The Certificate by Pool number, if applicable;

(iii) The Certificate number;

(iv) The original principal amount;

(v) The name in which the Certificate was registered;

(vi) Any assignment, endorsement or other writing on the Certificate; and

(vii) A statement of the circumstances of the theft or loss.

(b) When the FTA receives notice of the theft or loss, it will stop any transfer of the Certificate. The Registered Holder must send to the FTA all available portions of a mutilated or defaced Certificate. When the Registered Holder completes these steps, the FTA will replace the Certificate.

§ 120.652 FTA fees.

The FTA may charge reasonable servicing fees, transfer fees, and other fees as the SBA and FTA may negotiate under contract.

SUSPENSION OR REVOCATION OF PARTICIPANT IN SECONDARY MARKET

§ 120.660 Suspension or revocation.

(a) *Temporary suspension or revocation of Lender, broker, dealer, or Registered Holder for violation of Secondary Market rules and regulations or other risks to SBA.* The D/FA together with the Director, Office of Credit Risk Management (D/OCRM) may suspend for a period of no more than 120 calendar days or revoke for a period of no more than two (2) years, the privilege of a Lender, broker, dealer, or Registered Holder to sell, purchase, broker, or deal in loans or Certificates for:

(1) Committing a serious violation, in SBA's discretion, of:

(i) The regulations governing the Secondary Market; or

(ii) Any provisions in the contracts entered into by the parties, including SBA Forms 1086, 1088 and 1454;

(2) Knowingly submitting false or fraudulent information to the SBA or FTA; or

(3) A Lender's receipt, from its primary Federal or state regulator (including SBA), of a cease and desist order, a consent agreement affecting capital or commercial lending issues, a supervisory action citing unsafe or unsound banking practices, or any other supervisory action a primary regulator establishes hereafter that addresses unsafe or unsound lending practices; or a going concern opinion issued by the Lender's auditor. A Lender subject to a public action or going concern opinion must notify the D/FA and the D/OCRM within five (5) business days (or as soon as practicable thereafter) of the public issuance of any such action or the issuance of a going concern opinion. The Lender notice shall include copies of all relevant documents for SBA review.

(b) *Additional rules for suspension or revocation of broker or dealer.* In addition to acting under paragraph (a) of this section, the D/FA may suspend or revoke the privilege of any broker or dealer to sell or otherwise deal in Certificates in the Secondary Market if:

(1) Its supervisory agency has revoked or suspended the broker or dealer from engaging in the securities business, or is investigating the firm or broker for a practice which SBA considers, in its sole discretion, to be relevant to the broker's or dealer's fitness to participate in the Secondary Market;

(2) The broker or dealer has been indicted or otherwise formally charged with a misdemeanor or felony which bears on its fitness to participate in the Secondary Market; or

(3) A civil judgment is entered holding that the broker or dealer has committed a breach of trust or a violation of any law or regulation protecting the integrity of business transactions or relationships.

(c) *Notice to suspend or revoke.* The D/FA and the D/OCRM shall notify the affected party in writing, providing the reasons therefore, at least 10 business days prior to the effective date of the suspension or revocation. The affected party may appeal the suspension or revocation made under this section pursuant to the procedures set forth in part 134 of this chapter. The action taken by the D/FA and the D/OCRM will remain in effect pending resolution of the appeal.

(d) *Early termination of suspension or revocation.* SBA may, by written notice, terminate a Secondary Market suspension or revocation under this section, if the D/FA and the D/OCRM, in their sole discretion, determine that such termination is warranted for good cause.

[61 FR 3235, Jan. 31, 1996, as amended at 82 FR 39503, Aug. 21, 2017]

Subpart G—Microloan Program

§ 120.700 What is the Microloan Program?

The Microloan Program assists women, low income individuals, minority entrepreneurs, and other small businesses which need small amounts of financial assistance. Under this program, SBA makes direct and guaranteed loans to Intermediaries (as defined below) who use the proceeds to make loans to eligible borrowers. SBA may also make grants under the program to Intermediaries and other qualified nonprofit entities to be used for marketing, management, and technical assistance to the program's target population.

[61 FR 3235, Jan. 31, 1996, as amended at 66 FR 47073, Sept. 11, 2001]

§ 120.701 Definitions.

(a) *Deposit account* is a demand, time, savings, passbook, or similar account maintained with an insured depository institution (not including an account evidenced by a Certificate of Deposit).

(b) *Grant* is a Federal award of money, or property in lieu of money (including cooperative agreements) to an eligible grantee that must account for its use. The term does not include the provision of technical assistance, revenue sharing, loans, loan guarantees, interest subsidies, insurance, direct appropriations, or any fellowship or other lump sum award.

(c) *Insured depository institution* means any Federally insured bank, savings association, or credit union.

(d) *Intermediary* is an entity participating in the Microloan Program which makes and services Microloans to eligible small businesses and which provides marketing, management, and technical assistance to its borrowers. It may be:

(1) A private, nonprofit community development corporation or other entity;

(2) A consortium of private, nonprofit community development corporations or other entities;

(3) A quasi-governmental economic development entity, other than a state, county, municipal government or any agency thereof; or

(4) An agency of or a nonprofit entity established by a Native American Tribal Government.

(e) *Microloan* is a short-term, fixed interest rate loan of not more than $50,000 made by an Intermediary to an eligible small business.

(f) *Non-Federal sources* are sources of funds other than the Federal Government and may include indirect costs or in-kind contributions paid for under non-Federal programs. Community Block Development Grants are considered non-Federal sources.

(g) *Non-lending technical assistance provider* (NTAP) is an entity which receives grant funds from SBA to provide technical assistance to Microloan borrowers.

(h) *Specialized Intermediary* is an Intermediary which maintains a portfolio of Microloans averaging $10,000 or less.

[61 FR 3235, Jan. 31, 1996, as amended at 66 FR 47073, Sept. 11, 2001; 66 FR 47878, Sept. 14, 2001; 76 FR 63546, Oct. 12, 2011; 80 FR 34046, June 15, 2015]

§ 120.702 Are there limitations on who can be an Intermediary or on where an Intermediary may operate?

(a) *Prior experience requirement.* To be eligible to be an Intermediary, an organization must:

(1) Have made and serviced short-term fixed rate loans of not more than $50,000 to newly established or growing small businesses for at least one year: and

(2) Have at least one year of experience providing technical assistance to its borrowers.

(b) *Limitation to one state.* An Intermediary may not operate in more than one state unless the appropriate Office of Capital Access official in accordance with Delegations of Authority determines that it would be in the best interests of the small business community for it to operate across state lines.

[61 FR 3235, Jan. 31, 1996, as amended at 66 FR 47878, Sept. 14, 2001; 73 FR 75517, Dec. 11, 2008; 76 FR 63546, Oct. 12, 2011]

§ 120.703 How does an organization apply to become an Intermediary?

(a) *Application Process.* Organizations interested in becoming Intermediaries should contact SBA for information on the application process.

(b) *Documentation in support of application.* The application must include a detailed narrative statement describing:

(1) The types of businesses assisted in the past and those the applicant intends to assist with Microloans;

(2) The average size of the loans made in the past and the average size of intended Microloans;

(3) The extent to which the applicant will make Microloans to small businesses in rural areas;

(4) The geographic area in which the applicant intends to operate, including a description of the economic and demographic conditions existing in the intended area of operations;

(5) The availability and cost of obtaining credit for small businesses in the area;

(6) The applicant's experience and qualifications in providing marketing, management, and technical assistance to small businesses; and

(7) Any plan to use other technical assistance resources (such as counselors from the Service Corps of Retired Executives) to help Microloan borrowers.

§ 120.704 How are applications evaluated?

(a) *Evaluation criteria.* In selecting Intermediaries, SBA will attempt to insure that Microloans are available to small businesses in all industries and particularly to small businesses located in urban and rural areas.

(b) *Preference for organizations which make very small loans.* In selecting Intermediaries, SBA will give priority to applicants which maintain a portfolio of loans averaging $10,000 or less.

(c) *Consideration of quasi-governmental organizations.* Generally, SBA will consider applications by quasi-governmental organizations only when it determines that program services for a particular geographic area would be best provided by such organization.

[61 FR 3235, Jan. 31, 1996, as amended at 66 FR 47878, Sept. 14, 2001]

§ 120.705 What is a Specialized Intermediary?

At the end of an Intermediary's first year of participation in the program, SBA will determine whether it qualifies as a Specialized Intermediary. An Intermediary qualifies as a Specialized Intermediary if it maintains a portfolio of Microloans averaging $10,000 or less. Specialized Intermediaries qualify for more favorable interest rates on SBA loans. If, after the first year, an Intermediary qualifies as a Specialized Intermediary, the special interest rate is applied retroactively to SBA loans made to the Intermediary. After the first year SBA will determine an Intermediary's qualifications as a Specialized Intermediary annually, based on its lending practices during the term of its participation in the program. Specialized Intermediaries also qualify for a greater amount of technical assistance grant funding.

[61 FR 3235, Jan. 31, 1996, as amended at 66 FR 47878, Sept. 14, 2001]

§ 120.706 What are the terms and conditions of an SBA loan to an Intermediary?

(a) *Loan Amount.* An Intermediary may not borrow more than $750,000 in the first year of participation in the program. In later years, the Intermediary's obligation to SBA may not exceed an aggregate of $5 million, subject to statutory limitations on the total amount of funds available per state.

(b) *Repayment terms.* During the first year of the loan, an Intermediary is not required to make any payments, but interest accrues from the date that SBA disburses the loan proceeds to the Intermediary. After that, SBA will determine the periodic payments. The loan must be repaid within 10 years.

(c) *Interest rate.* The interest rate is equal to the rate applicable to five-year obligations of the United States Treasury, adjusted to the nearest one-eighth percent, less 1.25 percent. However, the interest rate for Specialized Intermediaries is equal to the rate applicable to five-year obligations of the United States Treasury, adjusted to the nearest one-eighth percent, less two percent.

(d) *Collateral.* As security for repayment of the SBA loan, an Intermediary must pledge to SBA a first lien position in the MRF (described below), LLRF (described below), and all notes receivable from Microloans.

(e) *Default.* If for any reason an Intermediary is unable to make payment to SBA when due, SBA may accelerate maturity of the loan and demand payment in full. In this event, or if an Intermediary violates this part or the terms of its loan agreement, it must surrender possession of all collateral described in paragraph (d) of this section to SBA. The Intermediary is not obligated to pay SBA any loss or deficiency which may remain after liquidation of the collateral unless the loss was caused by fraud, negligence, violation of any of the ethical requirements of § 120.140, or violation of any other provision of this part.

(f) *Fees.* SBA does not charge Intermediaries any fees for loans under this Program. An Intermediary may, however, pay minimal closing costs to third parties, such as filing and recording fees.

[61 FR 3235, Jan. 31, 1996, as amended at 66 FR 47073, Sept. 11, 2001; 76 FR 63546, Oct. 12, 2011]

§ 120.707 What conditions apply to loans by Intermediaries to Microloan borrowers?

(a) Except as otherwise provided in this paragraph, an Intermediary may only make Microloans to small businesses eligible to receive financial assistance under this part. A borrower may also use Microloan proceeds to establish a nonprofit child care business. An Intermediary may also make Microloans to businesses with an Associate who is currently on probation or parole; provided, however, that the Associate is not on probation or parole for an offense involving fraud or dishonesty or, in the case of a child care business, is not on probation or parole for an offense against children. Proceeds from Microloans may be used only for working capital and acquisition of materials, supplies, furniture, fixtures, and equipment. SBA does not review Microloans for creditworthiness.

(b) *Amount and maturity.* Generally, Intermediaries should not make a Microloan of more than $10,000 to any borrower. An Intermediary may not make a Microloan of more than $20,000 unless the borrower demonstrates that it is unable to obtain credit elsewhere at comparable interest rates and that it has good prospects for success. An Intermediary may not make a Microloan of more than $50,000, and no borrower may owe an Intermediary more than $50,000 at any one time. Each Microloan must be repaid within six years.

(c) *Interest rate.* The maximum interest rate that can be charged a Microloan borrower is:

(1) On loans of more than $10,000, the interest rate charged on the SBA loan to the Intermediary, plus 7.75 percentage points; and

(2) On loans of $10,000 or less, the interest rate charged on the SBA loan to the Intermediary, plus 8.5 percentage points.

[61 FR 3235, Jan. 31, 1996, as amended at 66 FR 47073, Sept. 11, 2001; 66 FR 47878, Sept. 14, 2001; 76 FR 63547, Oct. 12, 2011; 80 FR 34046, June 15, 2015]

§ 120.708 What is the Intermediary's financial contribution?

The Intermediary must contribute from non-Federal sources an amount equal to 15 percent of any loan that it receives from SBA. The contribution may not be borrowed. For purposes of this program, Community Development Block Grants are considered non-Federal sources.

§ 120.709 What is the Microloan Revolving Fund?

The Microloan Revolving Fund ("MRF") is a Deposit Account into which an Intermediary must deposit the proceeds from SBA loans, its contributions from non-Federal sources, and payments from its Microloan borrowers. An Intermediary may only withdraw from this account the money needed to establish the Loan Loss Reserve Fund (§ 120.710), proceeds for each Microloan it makes, and any payments to be made to SBA.

[61 FR 3235, Jan. 31, 1996, as amended at 80 FR 34046, June 15, 2015]

§ 120.710 What is the Loan Loss Reserve Fund?

(a) *General.* The Loan Loss Reserve Fund ("LLRF") is a Deposit Account which an Intermediary must establish to pay any shortage in the MRF caused by delinquencies or losses on Microloans.

(b) *Level of Loan Loss Reserve Fund.* Until it is in the Microloan program for at least five years, an Intermediary must maintain a balance on deposit in its LLRF equal to 15 percent of the outstanding balance of the notes receivable owed to it by its Microloan borrowers ("Portfolio").

(c) *SBA review of Loan Loss Reserve Fund.* After an Intermediary has been in the Microloan program for five years, it may request SBA's appropriate Office of Capital Access official in accordance with Delegations of Authority to reduce the percentage of its Portfolio which it must maintain in its LLRF to an amount equal to the actual average loan loss rate during the preceding five-year period. Upon receipt of such request, he/she will review the Intermediary's annual loss rate for the most recent five-year period preceding the request.

(d) *Reduction of Loan Loss Reserve Fund.* The appropriate Office of Capital Access official in accordance with Delegations of Authority has the authority to reduce the percentage of an Intermediary's Portfolio that it must maintain in its LLRF to an amount equal to the actual average loan loss rate during the preceding five-year period. The appropriate Office of Capital Access official in accordance with Delegations of Authority cannot reduce the LLRF to less than ten percent of the Portfolio.

(e) *What must an intermediary demonstrate to get a reduction in Loan Loss Reserve Fund?* To receive a reduction in its LLRF, an Intermediary must:

(1) Have satisfactory SBA performance, as determined by SBA in its discretion. The Intermediary's Risk Rating, among other factors, will be considered in determining satisfactory SBA performance. Other factors may include, but are not limited to, review/examination assessments, historical performance measures (like default rate, purchase rate and loss rate), loan volume to the extent that it impacts performance measures, and other performance related measurements and information (such as contribution toward SBA mission); and

(2) No other factors exist that may impair the Intermediary's ability to repay all obligations which it owes to the SBA under the Microloan program.

[61 FR 3235, Jan. 31, 1996, as amended at 65 FR 17439, Apr. 3, 2000; 73 FR 75517, Dec. 11, 2008; 80 FR 34046, June 15, 2015; 82 FR 39504, Aug. 21, 2017]

§ 120.711 What rules govern Intermediaries?

Intermediaries must operate in accordance with applicable statutes, regulations, policy notices, SBA's Standard Operating Procedures (SOPs), and the information in the application.

§ 120.712 How does an Intermediary get a grant to assist Microloan borrowers?

(a) *General.* An Intermediary is eligible to receive grant funding from SBA of not more than 25 percent of the outstanding balance of all SBA loans to the Intermediary. The Intermediary must contribute, solely from non-Federal sources, an amount equal to 25 percent of the grant. Contributions may be made in cash or in kind.

(b) *Limitations on grant funds.* An Intermediary may not borrow its contribution. It may only use grant funds to provide Microloan borrowers with marketing, management, and technical assistance, except that:

(1) Up to 25 percent of the grant funds may be used to provide information and technical assistance to prospective Microloan borrowers; and

(2) Grant monies may be used to attend training required by SBA.

(c) *Intermediaries eligible to receive additional grant monies.* An Intermediary may receive an additional SBA grant equal to five percent of the outstanding balance of all loans received from SBA (with no obligation to contribute additional matching funds) if the Intermediary is a Specialized Intermediary.

(d) *Third party contracts for technical assistance.* An Intermediary may use no more than 25 percent of the grant funds it receives from SBA for contracts with third parties for the latter to provide technical assistance to Microloan borrowers.

[61 FR 3235, Jan. 31, 1996, as amended at 66 FR 47073, Sept. 11, 2001; 76 FR 63547, Oct. 12, 2011; 80 FR 34047, June 15, 2015]

§ 120.713 Does SBA provide technical assistance to Intermediaries?

SBA may procure technical assistance for an Intermediary to improve its knowledge, skill, and understanding of microlending by awarding a grant to a more experienced Intermediary. SBA may also obtain such assistance for prospective Intermediaries in areas of the country that are either not served or underserved by an existing Intermediary.

§ 120.714 How are grants made to non-lending technical assistance providers (NTAP)?

SBA selects non-lending technical assistance providers (NTAP) to receive grant funds for technical assistance to Microloan borrowers.

(a) *Grant procedure for non-Intermediaries.* Any nonprofit entity that is not an Intermediary may apply to SBA for a grant to provide marketing, management and technical assistance to low-income individuals for the purpose of assisting them in obtaining private sector financing in amounts of $50,000 or less. To qualify, it must submit information regarding its ability to provide this assistance. If approved, the grant agreement will establish the terms and conditions for the grant.

(b) *Number and amount of grants.* In each year of the Microloan Program, SBA may make no more than 55 grants to non-Intermediaries for terms of up to five years. A grant may not exceed $200,000.

(c) *Contribution by nonprofit entity.* The nonprofit entity must contribute an amount equal to 20 percent of the grant. The contribution from the nonprofit entity must come solely from non-Federal sources, and may include direct costs or in-kind contributions paid for under non-Federal programs.

[61 FR 3235, Jan. 31, 1996, as amended at 66 FR 47073, Sept. 11, 2001; 66 FR 47878, Sept. 14, 2001; 76 FR 63547, Oct. 12, 2011]

§ 120.715 Does SBA guarantee any loans an Intermediary obtains from another source?

(a) SBA may guarantee not less than 90 percent of loans made by for-profit or nonprofit entities (or an alliance of such entities) to no more than 10 Intermediaries in urban areas and 10 Intermediaries in Rural Areas (as defined in § 120.10).

(b) Any loan guaranteed by SBA under this section will have a term of 10 years. If an Intermediary receives such a loan, it will not need to repay any principal or interest during the first year, although the interest will accrue. During the second through fifth years, the Intermediary will pay interest only. During the sixth through tenth years, it will pay interest and fully amortize the principal.

(c) The interest rate on any loan under this section shall be calculated as described in § 120.706.

[61 FR 3235, Jan. 31, 1996, as amended at 66 FR 47073, Sept. 11, 2001]

§ 120.716 What is the minimum number of loans an Intermediary must make each Federal fiscal year?

(a) *Minimum loan requirement.* Intermediaries must close and fund the required number of microloans per year (October 1–September 30) as follows, except that an Intermediary entering the program will not be required to meet the minimum in that year:

(1) For fiscal year 2015, four microloans,

(2) For fiscal year 2016, six microloans,

(3) For fiscal year 2017, eight microloans, and

(4) For fiscal years 2018 and thereafter, ten microloans per year.

(b) Intermediaries that do not meet the minimum loan requirement are not eligible to receive new grant funding unless they submit a corrective action plan acceptable to SBA, in its discretion. Intermediaries that have submitted acceptable corrective action plans may receive a reduced grant at SBA's discretion.

[80 FR 34047, June 15, 2015]

Subpart H—Development Company Loan Program (504)

§ 120.800 The purpose of the 504 program.

As authorized by Congress, SBA has established this program to foster economic development, create or preserve job opportunities, and stimulate growth, expansion, and modernization of small businesses.

§ 120.801 How a 504 Project is financed.

(a) One or more small businesses may apply for 504 financing through a CDC serving the area where the 504 Project is located. SBA issues an Authorization if it agrees to guarantee part of the funding for a Project.

(b) Usually, a Project requires interim financing from an interim lender (often the same lender that later provides a portion of the permanent financing).

(c) Generally, permanent financing of the Project consists of:

(1) A contribution by the small business in an amount of at least 10 percent of the Project costs;

(2) A loan made with the proceeds of a CDC Debenture for up to 40 percent of the Project costs and certain administrative costs, collateralized by a second lien on the Project Property; and

(3) A *Third Party Loan* comprising the balance of the financing, collateralized by a first lien on the Project property (see § 120.920).

(d) The Debenture is guaranteed 100 percent by SBA (with the full faith and credit of the United States), and sold to Underwriters who form Debenture Pools. Investors purchase interests in Debenture Pools and receive Certificates representing ownership of all or part of a Debenture Pool. SBA and CDCs use various agents to facilitate the sale and service of the Certificates and the orderly flow of funds among the parties.

[61 FR 3235, Jan. 31, 1996, as amended at 64 FR 2118, Jan. 13, 1999]

§ 120.802 Definitions.

The following terms have the same meaning wherever they are used in this subpart. Defined terms are capitalized wherever they appear.

Area of Operations is the geographic area where SBA has approved a CDC's request to provide 504 program services to small businesses on a permanent basis. The minimum Area of Operations is the State in which the CDC is incorporated.

Central Servicing Agent (CSA) is an entity that receives and disburses funds among the various parties involved in 504 financing under a master servicing agent agreement with SBA.

Certificate is a document issued by SBA or its agent representing ownership of all or part of a Debenture Pool.

Debenture is an obligation issued by a CDC and guaranteed 100 percent by SBA, the proceeds of which are used to fund a 504 loan.

Debenture Pool is an aggregation of Debentures.

Designated Attorney is the CDC closing attorney that SBA has approved to close loans under an expedited closing process for a Priority CDC.

Investor is an owner of a beneficial interest in a Debenture Pool.

Job Opportunity is a full time (or equivalent) permanent job created within two years of receipt of 504 funds, or retained in the community because of a 504 loan.

Lead SBA Office is the SBA District Office designated by SBA as the primary liaison between SBA and a CDC and with responsibility for managing SBA's relationship with that CDC.

Local Economic Area is an area, as determined by SBA, that is in a State other than the State in which an existing CDC (or an applicant applying to become a CDC) is incorporated, is contiguous to the CDC's existing Area of Operations (or the applicant's proposed Area of Operations) of its State of incorporation, and is a part of a local trade area that is contiguous to the CDC's Area of Operations (or applicant's proposed Area of Operations) of its State of incorporation. Examples of a local trade area would be a city that is bisected by a State line or a metropolitan statistical area that is bisected by a State line.

Multi-State CDC is a CDC that is incorporated in one State and is authorized by SBA to operate as a CDC in a

State contiguous to its State of incorporation beyond any contiguous Local Economic Areas.

Net Debenture Proceeds are the portion of Debenture proceeds that finance eligible Project costs (excluding administrative costs).

Priority CDC is a CDC certified to participate on a permanent basis in the 504 program (see § 120.812) that SBA has approved to participate in an expedited 504 loan and Debenture closing process.

Project is the purchase or lease, and/or improvement or renovation of long-term fixed assets by a small business, with 504 financing, for use in its business operations.

Project Property is one or more long-term fixed assets, such as land, buildings, machinery, and equipment, acquired or improved by a small business, with 504 financing, for use in its business operations.

Third Party Loan is a loan from a commercial or private lender, investor, or Federal (non-SBA), State or local government source that is part of the Project financing.

Underwriter is an entity approved by SBA to form Debenture Pools and arrange for the sale of Certificates.

[61 FR 3235, Jan. 31, 1996, as amended at 64 FR 2118, Jan. 13, 1999; 65 FR 42632, July 11, 2000; 68 FR 57980, Oct. 7, 2003]

CERTIFICATION PROCEDURES TO BECOME A CDC

§ 120.810 Applications for certification as a CDC.

(a) An applicant for certification as a CDC must apply to the SBA District Office serving the jurisdiction in which the applicant has or proposes to locate its headquarters (see § 101.103 of this chapter).

(b) The applicant must apply for an Area of Operations. The applicant's proposed Area of Operations must include the entire State in which the applicant is incorporated, and may include Local Economic Areas. An applicant may not apply to cover an area as a Multi-State CDC.

(c) The applicant must demonstrate that it satisfies the CDC certification and operational requirements in §§ 120.820, and 120.822 through 120.824. The applicant also must include an operating budget, approved by the applicant's Board of Directors, which demonstrates the required financial ability (as described in § 120.825), and a plan to meet CDC operational requirements (without specializing in a particular industry) in §§ 120.821, and 120.826 through 120.830.

(d) The District Office will forward the application and its recommendation to the D/FA, who will make the final decision. SBA will notify the CDC in writing of its decision, and, if the petition is declined, the reasons for the decision.

[68 FR 57980, Oct. 7, 2003]

§ 120.812 Probationary period for newly certified CDCs.

(a) Newly certified CDCs will be on probation for a period of two years from the date of certification, at the end of which the CDC must petition the Lead SBA Office for:

(1) Permanent CDC status; or

(2) A single, one-year extension of probation.

(b) SBA will consider the failure to file a petition before the end of the probationary period as a withdrawal from the 504 program. If the CDC elects withdrawal, SBA will direct the CDC to transfer all funded and/or approved loans to another CDC, SBA, or another servicer approved by SBA.

(c) The Lead SBA Office will send the petition and its recommendation to the D/FA, who will make the final decision. SBA will determine permanent CDC status or an extension of probation, in part, based upon the CDC's compliance with the certification and operational requirements in §§ 120.820 through 120.830. To be considered for permanent CDC status or an extension of probation, the CDC must have satisfactory SBA performance, as determined by SBA in its discretion. The CDC's Risk Rating, among other factors, will be considered in determining satisfactory SBA performance. Other factors may include, but are not limited to, review/examination assessments, historical performance measures, loan volume to the extent that it impacts performance measures, and other performance related measurements and information (such as contribution toward SBA mission).

(d) SBA will notify the CDC in writing of its decision, and, if the petition is declined, the reasons for the decision.

[68 FR 57980, Oct. 7, 2003, as amended at 73 FR 75517, Dec. 11, 2008; 82 FR 39504, Aug. 21, 2017]

REQUIREMENTS FOR CDC CERTIFICATION AND OPERATION

§ 120.816 CDC non-profit status and good standing.

A CDC must be a non-profit corporation, except that for-profit CDCs certified by SBA prior to January 1, 1987 may retain their certifications. An SBIC may not become a CDC. A CDC must be in good standing based upon the following criteria:

(a) In good standing in the State in which the CDC is incorporated and any other State in which the CDC conducts business.

(b) In compliance with all laws, including taxation requirements, in the State in which the CDC is incorporated and any other State in which the CDC conducts business.

(c) Must have satisfactory SBA performance, as determined by SBA in its discretion. The CDC's Risk Rating, among other factors, will be considered in determining satisfactory SBA performance. Other factors may include, but are not limited to, review/examination assessments, historical performance measures, loan volume to the extent that it impacts performance measures, and other performance related measurements and information (such as contribution toward SBA mission).

[68 FR 57980, Oct. 7, 2003, as amended at 73 FR 75518, Dec. 11, 2008. Redesignated at 79 FR 15649, Mar. 21, 2014; 82 FR 39504, Aug. 21, 2017]

§ 120.818 Applicability to existing for-profit CDCs.

Unless expressly provided otherwise in the regulations, any Loan Program Requirement that applies to non-profit CDCs also applies to for-profit CDCs.

[79 FR 15649, Mar. 21, 2014]

§ 120.820 CDC Affiliation.

(a) A CDC must be independent and must not be affiliated (as determined in accordance with § 121.103 of this chapter) with any Person (as defined in § 120.10) except as permitted under this section.

(b) A CDC may be affiliated with an entity (other than a 7(a) Lender or another CDC) whose function is economic development in the same Area of Operations and that is either a non-profit entity or a State or local government or political subdivision (e.g., council of governments).

(c) A CDC must not be affiliated (as determined in accordance with § 121.103) with or invest, directly or indirectly, in a 7(a) Lender. A CDC that was affiliated with a 7(a) Lender as of November 6, 2003 may continue such affiliation.

(d) A CDC must not be affiliated (as determined in accordance with § 121.103 of this chapter) with another CDC. In addition, a CDC must not directly or indirectly invest in or finance another CDC, except with the prior written approval of D/FA or designee and D/OCRM or designee if they determine in their discretion that such approval is in the best interests of the 504 Loan Program.

(e) A CDC may remain affiliated with a for-profit entity (other than a 7(a) Lender) if such affiliation existed prior to March 21, 2014. A CDC may also be affiliated with a for-profit entity (other than a 7(a) Lender) whose function is economic development in the same Area of Operations with the prior written approval of the D/FA or designee if he or she determines in his or her discretion that such approval is in the best interests of the 504 Loan Program.

(f) A CDC must not directly or indirectly invest in a Licensee (as defined in § 107.50 of this chapter) licensed by SBA under the SBIC program authorized in Part A of Title III of the Small Business Investment Act, 15 U.S.C. 681 et seq. A CDC that has an SBA-approved investment in a Licensee as of November 6, 2003 may retain such investment.

[79 FR 15649, Mar. 21, 2014]

§ 120.821 CDC Area of Operations.

A CDC must operate only within its designated Area of Operations approved by SBA except as provided in § 120.839.

[68 FR 57980, Oct. 7, 2003]

§ 120.823 CDC Board of Directors.

(a) The CDC, whether for-profit or nonprofit, must have a Board of Directors with at least nine (9) voting directors. A CDC may request the approval of the D/FA or designee to have a Board with fewer directors than 9 for good cause. SBA recommends that the CDC create a Board with no more than 25 voting directors. The Board must be actively involved in encouraging economic development in the Area of Operations. The initial Board may be created by any method permitted by applicable State law. At a minimum, the Board must have directors with background and expertise in internal controls, financial risk management, commercial lending, legal issues relating to commercial lending, and corporate governance. Directors may be either currently employed or retired. A CDC must have at least one voting director that represents the economic, community or workforce development fields, and at least two voting directors that represent the commercial lending field.

(b) At least two voting members of the Board of Directors, other than the CDC manager, must possess commercial lending experience satisfactory to SBA. When the Board votes on SBA loan approval or servicing actions, at least two voting Board members, with such commercial lending experience, other than the CDC manager, must be present and vote.

(c) The Board of Directors must meet at least quarterly and shall be responsible for the actions of the CDC and any committees established by the Board of Directors. In addition, the Board of Directors is subject to the following requirements:

(1) Except for the CDC manager, no person on the CDC's staff may be a voting director of the Board;

(2) A quorum must be present to transact business. The quorum shall be set by the CDC but shall be no less than 50% of the voting members of the Board of Directors;

(3) Attendance at meetings may be through any format permitted by State law;

(4) Directors from the commercial lending fields must comprise less than 50% of the representation on the Board; and

(5) No CDC Board member may serve on the Board of another CDC.

(d) The Board shall have and exercise all corporate powers and authority and be responsible for all corporate actions and business. There must be no actual or appearance of a conflict of interest with respect to any actions of the Board. The Board is responsible for ensuring that the structure and operation of the CDC, as set forth in the Bylaws, comply with SBA's Loan Program Requirements. The responsibilities of the Board include, but are not limited, to the following:

(1) Approving the mission and the policies for the CDC;

(2) Hiring, firing, supervising and annually evaluating the CDC manager;

(3) Setting the salary for the CDC manager and reviewing all salaries;

(4) Establishing committees, at its discretion, including the following:

(i) *Executive Committee.* To the extent authorized in the Bylaws, the Board of Directors may establish an Executive Committee. The Executive Committee may exercise the authority of the Board; however, the delegation of its authority does not relieve the Board of its responsibility imposed by law or Loan Program Requirements. No further delegation or redelegation of this authority is permitted. If the Board establishes an Executive Committee and delegates any of its authority to the Executive Committee as set forth in the Bylaws of the CDC, the Executive Committee must:

(A) Be chosen by and from the Board of Directors from the Board; and

(B) Meet the same organizational and representational requirements as the Board of Directors, except that the Executive Committee must have a minimum of five voting members who must be present to conduct business.

(ii) *Loan Committee.* The Board of Directors may establish a Loan Committee. The Loan Committee may exercise the authority of the Board only as set forth below; however, the delegation of its authority does not relieve the Board of its responsibility imposed by law or Loan Program Requirements. If the Board of Directors chooses to establish a Loan Committee, no CDC staff or manager may serve on the

Loan Committee. The Loan Committee must:

(A) Be chosen by the Board of Directors, and consist of individuals with a background in either financial risk management, commercial lending, or legal issues relating to commercial lending who are not associated with another CDC;

(B) Have a Quorum of at least five (5) Loan Committee members authorized to vote;

(C) Have at least two (2) Loan Committee members with commercial lending experience satisfactory to SBA;

(D) Have no actual or appearance of a conflict of interest, including for example, a Loan Committee member participating in deliberations on a loan for which the Third Party Lender is the member's employer or the member is otherwise associated with the Third Party Lender; and

(E) Consist of Loan Committee members who live or work in the Area of Operations of the State where the 504 project they are voting on is located unless the project falls under one of the exceptions listed in § 120.839.

(5) Ensuring that the CDC's expenses are reasonable and customary;

(6) Hiring directly an independent auditor to provide the financial statements in accordance with Loan Program Requirements;

(7) Monitoring the CDC's portfolio performance on a regular basis;

(8) Reviewing a semiannual report on portfolio performance from the CDC manager, which would include, but not be limited to, asset quality and industry concentration;

(9) Ensuring that the CDC establishes and maintains adequate reserves for operations;

(10) Ensuring that the CDC invests in economic development in each of the States in its Area of Operations in which it has a portfolio, and approving each investment. If the investment is included in the CDC's budget, the Board's approval of the budget may be deemed approval of the investment. If the investment is not included in the budget, the Board must separately approve the investment;

(11) Establishing a policy in the Bylaws of the CDC prohibiting an actual conflict of interest or the appearance of same, and enforcing such policy (see § 120.140 and § 120.851);

(12) Retaining accountability for all of the actions of the CDC;

(13) Establishing written internal control policies, in accordance with § 120.826;

(14) Establishing commercially reasonable loan approval policies, procedures, and standards. The Bylaws must include any delegations of authority to the Loan Committee and Executive Committee, if either Committee has been established. In addition, the CDC must establish and set forth in detail in a policy manual its credit approval process. All 504 loan applications must have credit approval prior to submission to the Agency. The Loan Committee, if established, may be delegated the authority to provide credit approval for loans up to $2,000,000 but, for loans of $1,000,000 to $2,000,000, the Loan Committee's action must be ratified by the Board or Executive Committee prior to Debenture closing. Only the Board or Executive Committee, if authorized by the Board, may provide credit approval for loans greater than $2,000,000.

(15) All members of the Board of Directors must annually certify in writing that they have read and understand this section, and copies of the certification must be included in the Annual Report to SBA.

(e) The Board of Directors shall maintain Directors' and Officers' Liability and Errors and Omissions insurance in amounts established by SBA that are based on the size of the CDC's portfolio and other relevant factors.

[79 FR 15649, Mar. 21, 2014, as amended at 82 FR 39504, Aug. 21, 2017]

§ 120.824 Professional management and staff.

A CDC must have full-time professional management, including an Executive Director (or the equivalent) managing daily operations. It must also have a full-time professional staff qualified by training and experience to market the 504 Program, package and process loan applications, close loans, service, and, if authorized by SBA, liquidate the loan portfolio, and sustain a sufficient level of service and activity in the Area of Operations. CDCs may obtain, under written contract, management, marketing, packaging, processing, closing, servicing or liquidation services provided by qualified individuals and entities under the following circumstances:

(a) The CDC must have at least one salaried professional employee that is employed directly (not a contractor or an Associate of a contractor) full-time to manage the CDC. The CDC manager must be hired by the CDC's board of directors and subject to termination only by the board. A CDC may petition SBA to waive the requirement of the manager being employed directly if:

(1) Another non-profit entity that has the economic development of the CDC's Area of Operations as one of its principal activities will contribute the management of the CDC, and the management contributed by the other entity also may work on and operate that entity's economic development programs, but must be available to small businesses interested in the 504 program and to 504 loan borrowers during regular business hours; or

(2) The CDC petitioning SBA for such waiver is rural; has insufficient loan volume to justify having management employed directly by the CDC; and has contracted with another CDC located in the same general area to provide the management.

(b) SBA must pre-approve contracts the CDC makes for managing, marketing, packaging, processing, closing, servicing, or liquidation functions. (CDCs may contract for legal and accounting services without SBA approval, except for legal services in connection with loan liquidation or litigation.)

(c) Contracts must clearly identify terms and conditions satisfactory to SBA that permit the CDC to terminate the contract prior to its expiration date on a reasonable basis.

(d) The CDC must provide copies of these contracts to SBA for review annually.

(e) If a CDC's Board believes that it is in the best interest of the CDC to contract for a management, marketing, packaging, processing, closing, servicing or liquidation function, the CDC's Board must explain its reasoning to SBA. The CDC's Board must demonstrate to SBA that:

(1) The compensation under the contract is only from the CDC, reasonable and customary for similar services in the Area of Operations, and is only for actual services performed;

(2) The full term of the contract (including options) is reasonable; and

(3) The contract does not evidence any actual or apparent conflict of interest or self-dealing on the part of any of the CDC's officers, management, and staff, including members of the Board and any Loan Committee.

(f) No contractor (under this section) or Associate of a contractor may be a voting or non-voting member of the CDC's Board.

[65 FR 42632, July 11, 2000, as amended at 68 FR 57981, Oct. 7, 2003]

§ 120.825 Financial ability to operate.

A CDC must be able to sustain its operations continuously, with reliable sources of funds (such as income from services rendered and contributions from government or other sponsors). Any funds generated from 503 and 504 loan activity by a CDC remaining after payment of staff and overhead expenses must be retained by the CDC as a reserve for future operations or for investment in other local economic development activity in its Area of Operations. If a CDC is operating as a Multi-State CDC, it must maintain a separate accounting for each State of all 504 fee income and expenses and provide, upon SBA's request, evidence that the funds resulting from its Multi-State CDC operations are being invested in economic development activities in each State in which they were generated.

[65 FR 42633, July 11, 2000]

§ 120.826 Basic requirements for operating a CDC.

A CDC must operate in accordance with the following requirements:

(a) *In general.* CDCs must meet all 504 Loan Program Requirements. In its Area of Operations, a CDC must market the 504 program, package and process 504 loan applications, close and service 504 loans, and if authorized by SBA, liquidate and litigate 504 loans. It must supply to SBA current and accurate information about all certification and operational requirements, and maintain the records and submit all reports required by SBA.

(b) *Operations and internal controls.* Each CDC's board of directors must adopt an internal control policy which provides adequate direction to the institution for effective control over and accountability for operations, programs, and resources. The board adopted internal control policy must, at a minimum:

(1) Direct management to assign the responsibility for the internal control function (covering financial, credit, credit review, collateral, and administrative matters) to an officer or officers of the CDC;

(2) Adopt and set forth procedures for maintenance and periodic review of the internal control function;

(3) Direct the operation of a program to review and assess the CDC's 504-related loans. For the 504 review program, the internal control policies must specify the following:

(i) Loan, loan-related collateral, and appraisal review standards, including standards for scope of selection (for review of any such loan, loan-related collateral or appraisal) and standards for work papers and supporting documentation;

(ii) Loan quality classification standards consistent with the standardized classification systems used by the Federal Financial Institution Regulators;

(iii) Specific control requirements for the CDC's oversight of Lender Service Providers; and

(iv) Standards for training to implement the loan review program; and

(4) Address other control requirements as may be established by SBA.

(c) *Annual Audited/Reviewed Financial Statements.* Each CDC with a 504 loan portfolio balance of $20 million or more (as calculated by SBA) must have its financial statements audited annually by a certified public accountant that is independent and experienced in auditing financial institutions. The audit must be performed in accordance with generally accepted auditing standards as adopted by the Auditing Standards Board of the American Institute of Certified Public Accountants (AICPA). The auditor must be independent, as defined by the AICPA, of the CDC. Annually, the auditor must issue an opinion as to the fairness of the CDC's financial statements and their compliance with GAAP. For CDCs with a 504 portfolio balance of less than $20 million (as calculated by SBA), the CDC's annual financial statements submitted to SBA must be reviewed by an independent CPA in accordance with GAAP.

(d) *Auditor qualifications.* The audit or review must be conducted by an independent certified public accountant who:

(1) Is registered or licensed to practice as a public accountant, and is in good standing, under the laws of the state or other political subdivision of the United States in which the CDC's principal office is located;

(2) Agrees in the engagement letter with the CDC to provide the SBA with access to and copies of any work papers, policies, and procedures relating to the services performed;

(3)(i) Is in compliance with the AICPA Code of Professional Conduct; and

(ii) Meets the independence requirements and interpretations of the Securities and Exchange Commission and its staff;

(4) Has received a peer review or is enrolled in a peer review program that meets AICPA guidelines; and

(5) Is otherwise acceptable to SBA.

[73 FR 75518, Dec. 11, 2008]

§ 120.827 Other services a CDC may provide to small businesses.

A CDC may provide a small business with assistance unrelated to the 504 loan program as long as the CDC does not make such assistance a condition of the CDC accepting from that small business an application for a 504 loan. An example of other services a CDC may provide is assisting a small business in applying for a 7(a) loan (as described in § 120.2). A CDC is subject to part 103 of this chapter when providing such assistance.

[68 FR 57981, Oct. 7, 2003]

§ 120.828 Minimum level of 504 loan activity and restrictions on portfolio concentrations.

(a) A CDC is required to receive SBA approval of at least four 504 loan approvals during two consecutive fiscal years.

(b) A CDC's 504 loan portfolio must be diversified by business sector.

[68 FR 57981, Oct. 7, 2003]

§ 120.829 Job Opportunity average a CDC must maintain.

(a) A CDC's portfolio must maintain a minimum average of one Job Opportunity per an amount of 504 loan funding that will be specified by SBA from time to time in a FEDERAL REGISTER notice. Such Job Opportunity average remains in effect until changed by subsequent FEDERAL REGISTER publication. A CDC is permitted two years from its certification date to meet this average.

(b) A CDC must indicate in its annual report the Job Opportunities actually or estimated to be provided by each Project.

(c) If a CDC does not maintain the required average, it may retain its certification if it justifies to SBA's satisfaction its failure to do so in its annual report and shows how it intends to attain the required average.

[61 FR 3235, Jan. 31, 1996, as amended at 68 FR 57981, Oct. 7, 2003]

§ 120.830 Reports a CDC must submit.

A CDC must submit the following reports to SBA:

(a) An Annual Report within one hundred-eighty days after the end of the CDC's fiscal year (to include Federal tax returns for that year). A CDC that is certified by SBA within 6 months of the CDC's fiscal year-end is not required to submit an Annual Report for that year. The Annual Report must include, but is not limited to, the following:

(1) Audited or Reviewed Financial Statements as required in § 120.826(c) and (d) for the CDC and any affiliates or subsidiaries of the CDC.

(i) Audited financial statements must, at a minimum, include the following:

(A) Audited balance sheet;

(B) Audited statement of income (or receipts) and expenses;

(C) Audited statement of source and application of funds;

(D) Such footnotes as are necessary to an understanding of the financial statements;

(E) Auditor's letter to management on internal control weaknesses; and

(F) The auditor's report; and

(ii) Reviewed financial statements must, at a minimum, include the following:

(A) Balance sheet;

(B) Statement of income (or receipts) and expenses;

(C) Statement of source and application of funds;

(D) Such footnotes as are necessary to an understanding of the financial statements;

(E) The accountant's review report; and

(2) Report on compensation: CDCs are required to provide detailed information on total compensation (including salary, bonuses and expenses) paid within the CDC's most recent tax year for current and former officers and directors, and for current and former employees and independent contractors with total compensation of more than $100,000 during that period.

(3) Certification of members of the Board of Directors. Written annual certification by each Board member that he or she has read and understands the requirements set forth in § 120.823.

(4) Report on investment in economic development. Written report on investments in economic development in each State in which the CDC has an outstanding 504 loan.

(b) For each new associate and staff, a Statement of Personal History (for use by non-bank lenders and CDCs) and other information required by SBA;

(c) Reports of involvement in any legal proceeding;

(d) Changes in organizational status;

(e) Changes in any condition that affects its eligibility to continue to participate in the 504 program; and

(f) Quarterly service reports on each loan in its portfolio which is 60 days or more past due (and interim reports upon request by SBA).

(g) Other reports as required by SBA.

[61 FR 3235, Jan. 31, 1996, as amended at 68 FR 57981, Oct. 7, 2003; 73 FR 75518, Dec. 11, 2008; 79 FR 15650, Mar. 21, 2014]

EXTENDING A CDC'S AREA OF OPERATIONS

§ 120.835 Application to expand an Area of Operations.

(a) *General.* A CDC that has been certified to participate in the 504 program may apply to expand its Area of Operations if it meets all requirements to be an Accredited Lender Program (ALP) CDC, as set forth in § 120.840(c), and demonstrates that it can competently fulfill its 504 program responsibilities in the proposed area.

(b) *Local Economic Area Expansion.* A CDC seeking to expand its Area of Operations into a Local Economic Area must apply in writing to the Lead SBA Office.

(c) A CDC seeking to become a Multi-State CDC must apply to the SBA District Office that services the area within each State where the CDC intends to locate its principal office for that State. A CDC may apply to be a Multi-State CDC only if the State the CDC seeks to expand into is contiguous to the State of the CDC's incorporation and the CDC establishes a loan committee in that State meeting the requirements of § 120.823.

[68 FR 57981, Oct. 7, 2003, as amended at 79 FR 15650, Mar. 21, 2014]

§ 120.837 SBA decision on application for a new CDC or for an existing CDC to expand Area of Operations.

The processing District Office must solicit the comments of any other District Office in which the CDC operates or proposes to operate. The processing District Office must determine that the CDC is in compliance with SBA's regulations, policies, and performance benchmarks, including pre-approval and annual review by SBA of any management or staff contracts, and the timely submission of all annual reports. In making its recommendation on the application, the District Office may consider any information presented to it regarding the requesting CDC, the existing CDC, or CDCs that may be affected by the application, and the proposed Area of Operations.

(a) The SBA District office will submit the application, recommendation, and supporting materials within 60 days of the receipt of a complete application from the CDC to the D/FA, who will make the final decision. The D/FA may consider any information submitted or available related to the applicant and the application.

(b) SBA will notify the CDC of its decision in writing, and if the application is denied, the reasons for its decision.

(c) If a CDC is approved to operate as a Multi-State CDC, the CDC's ALP, PCLP, or Priority CDC authority will carry over into every additional State in which it is approved to operate as a Multi-State CDC.

[65 FR 42633, July 11, 2000, as amended at 68 FR 57981, Oct. 7, 2003]

§ 120.839 Case-by-case application to make a 504 loan outside of a CDC's Area of Operations.

A CDC may apply to make a 504 loan for a Project outside its Area of Operations by submitting a request to the 504 loan processing center. The applicant CDC must demonstrate that it can adequately fulfill its 504 program responsibilities for the 504 loan, including proper servicing. In addition, the CDC must have satisfactory SBA performance, as determined by SBA in its discretion. The CDC's Risk Rating, among other factors, will be considered in determining satisfactory SBA performance. Other factors may include, but are not limited to, review/examination assessments, historical performance measures, loan volume to the extent that it impacts performance measures, and other performance related measurements and information (such as contribution toward SBA mission). The 504 loan processing center may approve the application if:

(a) The applicant CDC has previously assisted the business to obtain a 504 loan; or

(b) The existing CDC or CDCs serving the area agree to permit the applicant CDC to make the 504 loan; or

(c) There is no CDC within the Area of Operations.

[68 FR 57982, Oct. 7, 2003, as amended at 73 FR 75518, Dec. 11, 2008; 82 FR 39504, Aug. 21, 2017]

ACCREDITED LENDERS PROGRAM (ALP)

§ 120.840 Accredited Lenders Program (ALP).

(a) *General.* Under the ALP program, SBA designates qualified CDCs as ALP CDCs, gives them increased authority to process, close, and service 504 loans, and provides expedited processing of loan approval and servicing actions.

(b) *Application.* A CDC must apply for ALP status to the Lead SBA Office. The Lead SBA Office will send its recommendation and the application to the D/FA for final decision.

(c) *Eligibility.* In order for a CDC to be eligible to receive ALP status, its application must show that it meets the criteria set forth in § 120.841.

(d) *Additional application requirements.* The CDC's application must include the following:

(1) Certified copy of the CDC's Board of Directors' resolution authorizing the application for ALP status.

(2) Summary of the experience of each of the CDC's loan processing, closing, and servicing staff members with significant authority.

(3) Name, address, and summary of experience of Designated Attorney.

(4) Documentation of any SBA required insurance.

(5) Any other documentation required by SBA.

(e) *Term of ALP designation.* SBA generally will designate a CDC as an ALP CDC for a two-year period. SBA may renew the designation for additional two-year periods if the CDC continues to meet the ALP program eligibility requirements.

(f) *SBA approval or decline decision.* SBA will notify the CDC in writing of an approval or decline of either an ALP application or of an ALP renewal. If the SBA approves the CDC's application, the ALP CDC may exercise its ALP authority in its entire Area of Operations. If an application or renewal is declined, SBA will notify the CDC of the reasons for the decision.

[68 FR 57982, Oct. 7, 2003]

§ 120.841 Qualifications for the ALP.

An applicant for ALP status must show that it substantially meets the following criteria:

(a) *CDC staff experience.* The CDC's staff must have well-trained, qualified loan officers who are knowledgeable concerning SBA's lending policies and procedures for the 504 program. The CDC must have at least one loan officer with three years of 504 loan processing experience and at least one loan officer with three years of 504 servicing experience or two years experience plus satisfactory completion of SBA-approved processing and servicing training. The same loan officer may meet these qualifications. In addition, the CDC's staff must have demonstrated satisfactorily to SBA the ability to process and service 504 loans.

(b) *Number of 504 loans approved and size of portfolio.* SBA must have approved at least 20 504 loan applications by the CDC in the most recent three years, and the CDC must have a portfolio of at least 30 active 504 loans. (An "active" 504 loan is a loan that was approved and closed by the CDC and has a status of either current, delinquent, or in liquidation.)

(c) *CDC reviews.* CDC reviews conducted by SBA must be current (within the last 24 months, if applicable) for applicants for ALP status. The CDC must have received a review assessment of either "Acceptable" or "Acceptable With Corrective Actions Required." In addition, the CDC must have satisfactory SBA performance, as determined by SBA in its discretion. The CDC's Risk Rating, among other factors, will be considered in determining satisfactory SBA performance. Other factors may include, but are not limited to, review/examination assessments, historical performance measures, loan volume to the extent that it impacts performance measures, and other performance related measurements and information (such as contribution toward SBA mission);

(d) *Record of compliance with 504 program requirements.* The CDC must have a record of conforming to SBA's policies and procedures and of satisfactorily underwriting, closing and servicing 504 loans. SBA will consider all relevant material information, which will include but is not limited to whether the CDC meets all SBA's CDC portfolio benchmarks, when determining the CDC's record of compliance, including:

(1) Submission of satisfactory 504 loan analyses and applications, and all required, and properly completed, loan documents.

(2) Careful and thorough analysis and screening of all 504 loan applications for conformance with SBA credit and eligibility standards;

(3) Proper completion of required 504 loan closing documents and compliance with SBA 504 loan closing policies and procedures.

(4) Compliance with SBA loan servicing policies and procedures.

(5) Compliance with the certification and operational requirements as set forth in §§ 120.820 through 120.830.

(6) Submission of timely, complete and acceptable annual reports.

(7) Compliance with CDC ethical requirements (see § 120.851).

(e) *Priority CDC*. The CDC must be a Priority CDC with a Designated Attorney and SBA required insurance.

(f) *Record of Cooperation*. The CDC must have a record of effective communication and a cooperative relationship with all SBA offices including district offices and SBA's loan processing and servicing centers.

[68 FR 57982, Oct. 7, 2003, as amended at 72 FR 18364, Apr. 12, 2007; 73 FR 75519, Dec. 11, 2008; 82 FR 39504, Aug. 21, 2017]

PREMIER CERTIFIED LENDERS PROGRAM

§ 120.845 Premier Certified Lenders Program (PCLP).

(a) *General*. Under the PCLP, SBA designates qualified CDCs as PCLP CDCs and delegates to them increased authority to process, close, service, and liquidate 504 loans. SBA also may give PCLP CDCs increased authority to litigate 504 loans.

(b) *Application*. A CDC must apply for PCLP status to the Lead SBA Office. The Lead SBA Office will send its written recommendation and the application to SBA's PCLP Loan Processing Center. The PCLP Loan Processing Center will review these materials and forward them to the appropriate Office of Capital Access official in accordance with Delegations of Authority for final determination.

(c) *Eligibility*. In order for a CDC to be eligible to receive PCLP status, its application must show that it meets the following criteria:

(1) The CDC must be an ALP CDC in substantial compliance with Loan Program Requirements or meet the criteria to be an ALP CDC set forth in § 120.841(a) through (h).

(2) The CDC can adequately comply with SBA liquidation and litigation requirements.

(d) *Additional application requirements*. The application must include the following:

(1) Certified copy of the CDC's Board of Directors' resolution authorizing the application for PCLP status.

(2) Summary of the experience of each of the CDC's loan processing, closing, servicing and liquidation staff members with significant authority.

(3) Name, address and summary of experience of Designated Attorney.

(4) Documentation of any SBA required insurance.

(5) Any other documentation required by SBA.

(e) *Term of designation*. If approved, SBA generally will confer PCLP status for a period of two years. However, if SBA deems it appropriate, it may confer PCLP status for a period of less than two years.

(f) *Area of Operations for PCLP CDCs*. If the SBA approves the CDC's application, the PCLP CDC may exercise its PCLP authority in its entire Area of Operations.

(g) *SBA approval or decline decision*. SBA will notify the CDC in writing of an approval or decline of a PCLP application. If an application is declined, SBA will notify the CDC of the reasons for the decision.

[68 FR 57982, Oct. 7, 2003, as amended at 72 FR 18364, Apr. 12, 2007; 73 FR 75519, Dec. 11, 2008]

§ 120.846 Requirements for maintaining and renewing PCLP status.

(a) To maintain its status as a PCLP CDC, a CDC must continue to:

(1) Meet the PCLP eligibility requirements in § 120.845.

(2) Timely conform with all requirements and deadlines set forth in SBA's regulations and policy and procedural

guidance concerning properly establishing, funding and reporting a PCLP Loan Loss Reserve Fund (LLRF).

(3) Substantially comply with all Loan Program Requirements.

(4) Remain an active CDC.

(5) In accordance with statutory requirements set forth in section 508(i) of Title V, 15 U.S.C. 697e(i), establish a goal of processing at least 50 percent of its 504 loans using PCLP procedures.

(b) SBA will notify the PCLP CDC in writing of a renewal or non-renewal of PCLP status. If PCLP status is not renewed, SBA will notify the CDC of the reasons for the decision.

[68 FR 57983, Oct. 7, 2003, as amended at 72 FR 18364, Apr. 12, 2007]

§ 120.847 Requirements for the Loan Loss Reserve Fund (LLRF).

(a) *General.* PCLP CDCs must establish and maintain a LLRF (or multiple accounts which together constitute one LLRF) which complies with paragraphs (b) through (g) of this section. A PCLP CDC must use the LLRF or other funds to reimburse the SBA for 10 percent of any loss sustained by SBA as a result of a default in the payment of principal or interest on a Debenture it issued under the PCLP ("PCLP Debenture"). A CDC that is participating in the PCLP as of January 1, 2004, and a CDC that has participated in the PCLP in the past but which does not have PCLP status as of that date, must establish a LLRF within 30 days of that date to cover potential losses for all 504 loans made in connection with PCLP Debentures that remain outstanding as of that date. A CDC that receives PCLP status after that date must establish and maintain a LLRF prior to closing any 504 loans processed under its PCLP status. The LLRF is the accumulation of deposits that a PCLP CDC must establish and maintain for each PCLP Debenture that it issues. PCLP CDCs must coordinate with their Lead SBA Office to ensure that the LLRF is properly established, that all necessary documentation is executed and delivered by all parties in a timely fashion, and that all required deposits are made.

(b) *PCLP CDC Exposure and LLRF deposit requirements.* A PCLP CDC's "Exposure" is defined as its reimbursement obligation to SBA with respect to default in the payment of any PCLP Debenture. The amount of a PCLP CDC's Exposure is 10 percent of any loss (including attorney's fees; litigation costs; and care of collateral, appraisal and other liquidation costs and expenses) sustained by SBA as a result of a default in the payment of principal or interest on a PCLP Debenture. For each PCLP Debenture a PCLP CDC issues, it must establish and maintain an LLRF equal to one percent of the original principal amount (the face amount) of the PCLP Debenture. The amount the PCLP CDC must maintain in the LLRF for each PCLP Debenture remains the same even as the principal balance of the PCLP Debenture is paid down over time.

(c) *Establishing a LLRF.* The LLRF must be a deposit account (or accounts) with a federally insured depository institution selected by the PCLP CDC. A "deposit account" is a demand, time, savings, or passbook account, including a certificate of deposit (CD) which is either uncertificated or, if certificated, non-transferable. A "deposit account" is not an investment account and must not contain securities or other investment properties. A deposit account may contain only cash and CDs credited to that account. A PCLP CDC may pool its deposits for multiple PCLP Debentures in a single account in one institution. The LLRF must be segregated from the PCLP CDC's other operating accounts. The PCLP CDC is responsible for all fees, costs and expenses incurred in connection with establishing, managing and maintaining the LLRF, including fees associated with transferring funds or early withdrawal of CDs, and related income tax expenses.

(d) *Creating and perfecting a security interest in a LLRF.* A PCLP CDC must give SBA a first priority, perfected security interest in the LLRF to secure the PCLP CDC's obligation to reimburse SBA for the PCLP CDC's Exposure under all of its outstanding PCLP Debentures. (If a PCLP CDC's LLRF is comprised of multiple deposit accounts, it must give SBA this security interest with respect to each such account.) The PCLP CDC must grant to SBA the security interest in the LLRF pursuant to a security agreement between the PCLP CDC and SBA, and a control agreement between the PCLP CDC, SBA, and the applicable depository institution. The control agreement must include provisions requiring the depository institution to follow SBA instructions regarding withdrawal from the account without a requirement for obtaining further consent from the PCLP CDC, and must restrict the PCLP CDC's ability to make withdrawals from the account without SBA consent. When establishing the LLRF, a PCLP CDC must coordinate with its Lead SBA Office to execute and deliver the required documentation. The PCLP CDC must provide to the Lead SBA Office a fully executed original of the security and control agreements. All documents must be satisfactory to SBA in both form and substance.

(e) *Schedule for contributions to a LLRF.* The PCLP CDC must contribute to the LLRF the required deposits for each PCLP Debenture in accordance with the following schedule:

(1) At least 50 percent of the required deposits to the LLRF on or about the date that it issues the PCLP Debenture.

(2) At least an additional 25 percent of the required deposits to the LLRF no later than one year after it issues the PCLP Debenture.

(3) Any remainder of the required deposits to the LLRF no later than two years after it issues the PCLP Debenture.

(f) *LLRF reporting requirements.* Each PCLP CDC must periodically report to SBA the amount in the LLRF in a form that will readily facilitate reconciliation of the amount maintained in the LLRF with the amount required to meet a PCLP CDC's Exposure for its entire portfolio of PCLP Debentures.

(g) *Withdrawal of excess funds.* Interest and other funds in the LLRF that exceed the required minimums as set forth in paragraph (b) of this section, within the time frames set forth in paragraph (e) of this section, accrue to the benefit of the PCLP CDC. PCLP CDCs are authorized to withdraw excess funds, including interest, from the LLRF if such funds exceed the required minimums set forth in paragraph (b) of this section. The PCLP CDC must forward requests for withdrawals to the Lead SBA Office, which will verify the existence and amount of excess funds and notify the financial institution to transfer the excess funds to the PCLP CDC.

(h) *Determining SBA loss.* When a PCLP CDC has concluded the liquidation of a defaulted 504 loan made with the proceeds of a PCLP Debenture and has submitted a liquidation wrap-up report to SBA, or when SBA otherwise determines that the PCLP CDC has exhausted all reasonable collection efforts with respect to that 504 loan, SBA will determine the amount of the loss to SBA. SBA will notify the PCLP CDC of the amount of its reimbursement obligation to SBA (if any) and will explain how SBA calculated the loss.

(1) If the PCLP CDC agrees with SBA's calculations of the loss, it must reimburse SBA for ten percent of the amount of that loss no later than 30 days after SBA's notification to the PCLP CDC of the CDC's reimbursement obligation.

(2) If the PCLP CDC disputes SBA's calculations, it must reimburse SBA for ten percent of any loss amount that is not in dispute no later than 30 days after SBA's notification to the PCLP CDC of the CDC's reimbursement obligation. No later than 30 days after SBA's notification, the PCLP CDC may submit to the D/FA or his or her delegate a written appeal of any disagreement regarding the calculation of SBA's loss. The PCLP CDC must include with that appeal an explanation of its reasons for the disagreement. Upon the D/FA's final decision as to the disputed amount of the loss, the PCLP CDC must promptly reimburse SBA for ten percent of that amount.

(i) *Reimbursing SBA for loss.* A PCLP CDC may use funds in the LLRF or other funds to reimburse SBA for the PCLP CDC's Exposure on a defaulted PCLP Debenture. If a PCLP CDC does not satisfy the entire reimbursement obligation within 30 days after SBA's notification to the PCLP CDC's of its reimbursement obligation, SBA may cause funds in the LLRF to be transferred to SBA in order to cover the PCLP CDC's Exposure, unless the PCLP CDC has filed an appeal under paragraph (h)(2) of this section. If the

PCLP CDC has filed such an appeal, SBA may cause such a transfer of funds to SBA 30 days after the D/FA's or his or her delegate's decision. If the LLRF does not contain sufficient funds to reimburse SBA for any unpaid Exposure with respect to any PCLP Debenture, the PCLP CDC must pay SBA the difference within 30 days after demand for payment by SBA.

(j) *Insufficient funding of LLRF.* A PCLP CDC must diligently monitor the LLRF to ensure that it contains sufficient funds to cover its Exposure for its entire portfolio of PCLP Debentures. If, at any time, the LLRF does not contain sufficient funds, the PCLP CDC must, within 30 days of the earlier of the date it becomes aware of this deficiency or the date it receives notification from SBA of this deficiency, make additional contributions to the LLRF to make up this difference.

[68 FR 57983, Oct. 7, 2003]

§ 120.848 Requirements for 504 loan processing, closing, servicing, liquidating, and litigating by PCLP CDCs.

(a) *General.* In processing closing, servicing, liquidating and litigating 504 loans under the PCLP ("PCLP Loans"), the PCLP CDC must comply with Loan Program Requirements and conduct such activities in accordance with prudent and commercially reasonable lending standards.

(b) *Documentation of decision making.* For each PCLP Loan, the PCLP CDC must document in its files the basis for its decisions with respect to loan processing, closing, servicing, liquidating, and litigating.

(c) *Processing requirements.* SBA expects PCLP CDCs to handle most 504 loan processing situations, although SBA may require that the PCLP CDC process 504 loans involving complex or problematic eligibility issues through the SBA using standard 504 loan processing procedures. The PCLP CDC is responsible for properly determining borrower creditworthiness and establishing the terms and conditions under which the PCLP Loan will be made. The PCLP CDC also is responsible for properly undertaking such other processing actions as SBA may delegate to the PCLP CDC.

(d) *Submission of loan documents.* A PCLP CDC must notify SBA of its approval of a 504 loan by submitting to SBA's PCLP Loan Processing Center all documentation required by SBA, including SBA's PCLP eligibility checklist, signed by an authorized representative of the PCLP CDC. The PCLP Loan Processing Center will review these documents to determine whether the PCLP CDC has identified any problems with the PCLP Loan approval, and whether SBA funds are available for the PCLP Loan. If appropriate, the PCLP Processing Center will notify the PCLP CDC of the loan number assigned to the loan.

(e) *Loan and Debenture closing.* After receiving notification from SBA PCLP Loan Processing Center, the PCLP CDC is responsible for properly undertaking all actions necessary to close the PCLP Loan and Debenture in accordance with the expedited loan closing procedures applicable to a Priority CDC and with § 120.960.

(f) *Servicing, liquidation and litigation responsibilities.* The PCLP CDC generally must service, liquidate and litigate its entire portfolio of PCLP Loans, although SBA may in certain circumstances elect to handle such duties with respect to a particular PCLP Loan or Loans. Additional servicing and liquidation requirements are set forth in subpart E of this part.

(g) *Making a 504 loan previously considered by another CDC.* A PCLP CDC also may utilize its PCLP status to process a 504 loan application from an applicant whose application was declined or rejected by another CDC operating in that same Area of Operations, if the applicant is located within that area and as long as SBA has not previously declined that applicant's 504 loan application. This may include the processing of a 504 loan application from an applicant that has withdrawn its application from another CDC.

[68 FR 57984, Oct. 7, 2003, as amended at 72 FR 18364, Apr. 12, 2007]

ASSOCIATE DEVELOPMENT COMPANIES (ADCs)

§ 120.850 Expiration of Associate Development Company designation.

The designation of Associate Development Company (ADC) will cease to exist on January 1, 2004. After that date, former ADCs may continue to contract with CDCs as Lender Service Providers (see part 103 of this chapter) or to perform other services.

[68 FR 57984, Oct. 7, 2003]

OTHER CDC REQUIREMENTS

§ 120.851 CDC ethical requirements.

CDCs and their Associates must act ethically and exhibit good character. They must meet all of the ethical requirements of § 120.140. In addition, they are subject to the following:

(a) Any benefit flowing to a CDC's Associate or his or her employer from activities as an Associate must be merely incidental (this requirement does not prevent an Associate or an Associate's employer from providing interim financing as described in § 120.890 or Third Party Loans as described in § 120.920, as long as such activity does not violate § 120.140); and

(b) A CDC's Associate may not be an officer, director, or manager of more than one CDC.

[68 FR 57984, Oct. 7, 2003]

§ 120.852 [Reserved]

§ 120.853 Inspector General audits of CDCs.

The SBA Office of Inspector General may also conduct, supervise or coordinate audits pursuant to the Inspector General Act. The CDC must cooperate and make its staff, records, and facilities available.

[68 FR 57985, Oct. 7, 2003, as amended at 73 FR 75519, Dec. 11, 2008]

§ 120.857 Voluntary transfer and surrender of CDC certification.

A CDC may not transfer its certification or withdraw from the 504 program without SBA's consent. The CDC must provide a plan to SBA to transfer its portfolio. The portfolio may only be transferred with SBA's written consent. If a CDC desires to withdraw from the 504 program, it must forfeit its portfolio to SBA. SBA may conduct an audit of the transferring or withdrawing CDC.

[61 FR 3235, Jan. 31, 1996. Redesignated at 68 FR 57987, Oct. 7, 2003]

PROJECT ECONOMIC DEVELOPMENT GOALS

§ 120.860 Required objectives.

A Project must achieve at least one of the economic development objectives set forth in § 120.861 or § 120.862.

§ 120.861 Job creation or retention.

A Project must create or retain one Job Opportunity per an amount of 504 loan funding that will be specified by SBA from time to time in a FEDERAL REGISTER notice. Such Job Opportunity average remains in effect until changed by subsequent FEDERAL REGISTER publication.

[68 FR 57987, Oct. 7, 2003]

§ 120.862 Other economic development objectives.

A Project that achieves any of the following community development or public policy goals is eligible if the CDC's overall portfolio of 504 loans, including the subject loan, meets or exceeds the CDC's required Job Opportunity average. Loan applications must indicate how the Project will meet the specified economic development objective.

(a) Community Development goals:

(1) Improving, diversifying or stabilizing the economy of the locality;

(2) Stimulating other business development;

(3) Bringing new income into the community;

(4) Assisting manufacturing firms (North American Industry Classification System (NAICS), Sectors 31 " 33); or

(5) Assisting businesses in Labor Surplus Areas as defined by the Department of Labor.

(b) Public Policy goals:

(1) Revitalizing a business district of a community with a written revitalization or redevelopment plan;

(2) Expansion of exports;

(3) Expansion of small businesses owned and controlled by women as defined in section 29(a)(3) of the Act, 15 U.S.C. 656(a)(3);

(4) Expansion of small businesses owned and controlled by veterans (especially service-disabled veterans) as defined in section 3(q) of the Act, 15 U.S.C. 632(q);

(5) Expansion of minority enterprise development (see §124.103(b) of this chapter for minority groups who qualify for this description);

(6) Aiding rural development;

(7) Increasing productivity and competitiveness (retooling, robotics, modernization, competition with imports);

(8) Modernizing or upgrading facilities to meet health, safety, and environmental requirements;

(9) Assisting businesses in or moving to areas affected by Federal budget reductions, including base closings, either because of the loss of Federal contracts or the reduction in revenues in the area due to a decreased Federal presence; or

(10) Reduction of rates of unemployment in labor surplus areas, as such areas are determined by the Secretary of Labor.

[61 FR 3235, Jan. 31, 1996, as amended at 64 FR 2118, Jan. 13, 1999; 68 FR 57987, Oct. 7, 2003; 76 FR 63547, Oct. 12, 2011]

LEASING POLICIES SPECIFIC TO 504 LOANS

§ 120.870 Leasing Project Property.

(a) A Borrower may use the proceeds of a 504 loan to acquire, construct, or modify buildings and improvements, and/or to purchase and install machinery and equipment located on land leased to the Borrower by an unrelated lessor if:

(1) The remaining term of the lease, including options to renew, exercisable only by the lessee, equals or exceeds the term of the Debenture;

(2) The Borrower assigns its interest in the lease to the CDC with right of reassignment to SBA; and

(3) The 504 loan is secured by a recorded lien against the leasehold estate and other collateral as necessary.

(b) If the Project is for new construction, the Borrower may lease long term up to 20 percent of the Rentable Property in the Project to one or more tenants if the Borrower immediately occupies at least 60 percent of the Rentable Property, plans to occupy within three years some of the remaining space not immediately occupied and not leased long term, and plans to occupy all of the remaining space not leased long term within ten years.

[61 FR 3235, Jan. 31, 1996, as amended at 64 FR 2118, Jan. 13, 1999; 68 FR 57987, Oct. 7, 2003]

§ 120.871 Leasing part of Project Property to another business.

(a) The costs of interior finishing of space to be leased out to another business are not eligible Project costs.

(b) Third-party loan proceeds used to renovate the leased space do not count towards the 504 first mortgage requirement or the Borrower's contribution.

LOAN-MAKING POLICIES SPECIFIC TO 504 LOANS

§ 120.880 Basic eligibility requirements.

In addition to the eligibility requirements specified in subpart A, to be an eligible Borrower for a 504 loan, a small business must:

(a) Use the Project Property (except that an Eligible Passive Company may lease to an Operating Company); and

(b) Together with its Affiliates, meet one of the size standards set forth in §121.301(b) of this chapter.

[61 FR 3235, Jan. 31, 1996, as amended at 68 FR 57987, Oct. 7, 2003]

§ 120.881 Ineligible Projects for 504 loans.

In addition to the ineligible businesses and uses of proceeds specified in subpart A of this part, the following Projects are ineligible for 504 financing:

(a) Relocation of any of the operations of a small business which will cause a net reduction of one-third or more in the workforce of a relocating small business or a substantial increase in unemployment in any area of the country, unless the CDC can justify the loan because:

(1) The relocation is for key economic reasons and crucial to the continued existence, economic wellbeing,

and/or competitiveness of the applicant; and

(2) The economic development benefits to the applicant and the receiving community outweigh the negative impact on the community from which the applicant is moving; and

(b) Projects in foreign countries (loans financing real or personal property located outside the United States or its possessions).

§ 120.882 Eligible Project costs for 504 loans.

Eligible Project costs which may be paid with the proceeds of 504 loans are:

(a) Costs directly attributable to the Project including expenditures incurred by the Borrower (with its own funds or from a loan) to acquire land used in the Project, or for any other expense directly attributable to the Project, prior to applying to SBA for the 504 loan;

(b) In Projects involving construction, a contingency reserve for cost overruns not to exceed 10 percent of construction cost;

(c) Professional fees directly attributable and essential to the Project, such as title insurance, opinion of title, architectural and engineering costs, appraisals, environmental studies, and legal fees related to zoning, permits, or platting; and

(d) Repayment of interim financing including points, fees and interest.

(e) If the project involves expansion of a small business concern, any amount of existing indebtedness that does not exceed 50 percent of the project cost of the expansion may be refinanced and added to the expansion cost if:

(1) Substantially all (85% or more) of the proceeds of the indebtedness were used to acquire land, including a building situated thereon, to construct a building thereon, or to purchase equipment. The assets acquired must be eligible for financing under the 504 loan program. If the acquisition, construction or purchase of the asset was originally financed through a commercial loan that would have satisfied the "substantially all" requirement and that was subsequently refinanced one or more times, with the current commercial loan being the most recent refinancing, the current commercial loan will be deemed to satisfy this paragraph (e)(1).

(2) The existing indebtedness is collateralized by fixed assets. The 504 eligible fixed assets collateralizing any debt to be refinanced or relating to the portion of debt being refinanced in the case of a partial refinance must also collateralize the 504 Loan unless SBA approves a waiver due to extraordinary circumstances. PCLP CDCs may not use their delegated authority to approve a loan requiring this waiver;

(3) The existing indebtedness was incurred for the benefit of the small business concern for which any new Project costs are incurred. Existing 7(a) and 504 loans may be refinanced under this section in accordance with SBA policies or procedures;

(4) The financing will be used only for refinancing existing indebtedness or costs relating to the project financed;

(5) The financing will provide a substantial benefit to the borrower when prepayment penalties, financing fees, and other financing costs are accounted for. For purposes of this paragraph, "substantial benefit" means that the portion of the new installment amount attributable to the debt being refinanced must be at least 10 percent less than the existing installment amount(s). Prepayment penalties, financing fees, and other financing costs must also be added to the amount being refinanced in calculating the percentage reduction in the new installment payment. Exceptions to the 10% reduction requirement may be approved by the D/FA or designee for good cause. PCLP CDCs may not use their delegated authority to approve a loan requiring this exception;

(6) The borrower has been current on all payments due on the existing debt for not less than 1 year preceding the date of refinancing. For purposes of this section, "date of refinancing" refers to the date the 504 loan is approved by SBA. Any unremedied delinquency after approval must be reported to SBA as an adverse change;

(7) The financing under section 504 will provide better terms or rate of interest than the existing indebtedness on the date of refinancing. For purposes of this paragraph, "better terms

or rate of interest" may include longer maturity (but always commensurate with the assets' useful life), a lower interest rate committed on the Third Party Lender Loan or projected on the 504 loan, improved collateral conditions, or less restrictive loan covenants.

(8) The authority to approve the refinancing of same institution debt must be approved by SBA and is not delegated to the PCLP CDCs. For the purposes of this paragraph, "same institution debt" means any debt of the CDC or the Third Party Lender financing the new project, or of affiliates of either.

(f) For the purposes of paragraph (e), the phrase "project involves expansion of a small business concern" includes any project that involves the acquisition, construction or improvement of land, building or equipment for use by the small business concern.

(g) SBA may approve a Refinancing Project of a qualified debt subject to the following conditions and requirements:

(1) The Refinancing Project does not involve the expansion of a small business;

(2) The applicant for the refinancing available under this paragraph (g) has been in operation for all of the 2 year period ending on the date of application;

(3) The cost to the Federal Government of making guarantees under this subsection (g) and under section 503 of the Small Business Investment Act of 1958 (15 U.S.C. 697) during the fiscal year in which the guarantee is made is zero;

(4) In addition to the annual guarantee fee assessed under § 120.971(d)(2), Borrower must pay SBA a supplemental annual guarantee fee to cover the additional cost attributable to the refinancing in an amount established by SBA each fiscal year.

(5) The funding for the Refinancing Project must come from three sources based on the current fair market value of the fixed assets serving as collateral for the Refinancing Project, including a Third Party Loan that is at least as much as the 504 loan, not less than 10% from the Borrower (excluding administrative costs), and not more than 40% from the 504 loan. If the Refinancing Project involves a limited or single purpose building or structure, the Borrower must contribute not less than 15% (excluding administrative costs), unless SBA determines, in its discretion, and publishes a notice in the FEDERAL REGISTER, that due to an economic recession, as determined by the National Bureau of Economic Research or its equivalent, Borrowers may contribute not less than 10% for Refinancing Projects involving a limited or single purpose property during the recession. The lower required contribution by the Borrower will be in effect until the first day of the calendar quarter following the end of the economic recession as determined by the National Bureau of Economic Research or its equivalent. SBA will publish a notice in the FEDERAL REGISTER announcing the date on which the requirement of the lower Borrower contribution ended. In addition to a cash contribution, the Borrower's contribution may be satisfied as set forth in § 120.910 or by the equity in any other fixed assets that are acceptable to SBA as collateral for the Refinancing Project, provided that there is an independent appraisal of the fair market value of the asset;

(6)(i) The portion of the Refinancing Project provided by the 504 loan and the Third Party Loan may be no more than 90% of the fair market value of the fixed assets that will serve as collateral, except that if the Borrower's application includes a request to finance the Eligible Business Expenses described in paragraph (g)(6)(ii) of this section, the portion of the Refinancing Project provided by the 504 loan and the Third Party Loan may be no more than 85% of the fair market value of the fixed assets that will serve as collateral and the Borrower may receive no more than 20% of the fair market value of the Eligible Fixed Asset(s) securing the Qualified Debt for Eligible Business Expenses;

(ii) The Borrower's application may include a request to finance eligible business expenses as part of the Refinancing Project if the amount of cash funds that will be provided for the Refinancing Project exceeds the amount to be paid to the lender of the Qualified

Debt. The Borrower's application must include a specific description of the business expenses for which the financing is requested and an itemization of the amount of each expense. For the purposes of this paragraph (g), "Eligible Business Expenses" are limited to the operating expenses of the business that were incurred but not paid prior to the date of application or that will become due for payment within 18 months after the date of application. These expenses may include salaries, rent, utilities, inventory, and other expenses of the business that are not capital expenditures. Debt is not included as an Eligible Business Expense, except debt that was incurred with a credit card or a business line of credit may be included if the credit card or business line of credit is issued in the name of the small business and the Applicant certifies that the debt being refinanced was incurred exclusively for business related purposes. Loan proceeds must not be used to refinance any personal expenses. Both the CDC and the Borrower must certify in the application that the funds will be used to cover Eligible Business Expenses. Borrower must, upon request, substantiate the use of the funds provided for business expenses through, for example, bank statements, invoices marked "paid," cleared checks, or any other documents that demonstrate that a business obligation was satisfied with the funds provided.

(7) If the qualified debt is not fully satisfied by the funding provided by the Refinancing Project, the lender of the qualified debt must take one of the following actions, or some combination thereof, to address the deficiency:

(i) Forgiveness of all or part of the deficiency;

(ii) Acceptance of payment by the Borrower, or

(iii) Acceptance of a Note executed by the Borrower for the balance, or any portion of the balance. Such Note must be subordinate to the 504 loan if the Note and the 504 loan are secured by any of the same collateral. The Note is subject to any other restrictions that SBA may establish to protect its creditor position, including standby requirements;

(8) The Third Party Lender must have a first lien position, and the 504 loan must have a second lien position, on all Eligible Fixed Assets securing the Refinancing Project. Any other lien must be junior in priority to these lien positions. For other fixed assets serving as collateral for the Refinancing Project, the lien positions of the Third Party Lender and the 504 loan may be junior to any existing liens acceptable to SBA;

(9) Eligible Project costs which may be paid with the proceeds of the 504 loan are the amount used to refinance the qualified debt and other costs under § 120.882(c) and (d) and eligible administrative costs under § 120.883;

(10) A CDC must limit the amount of its loans under this paragraph (g) so that, during any Federal fiscal year, the amount of the new loans approved under this paragraph (g) does not exceed 50% of the total dollar amount of the CDC's 504 loans approved (including the loans approved under this paragraph (g)) during the previous fiscal year. This limitation may be waived upon application by the CDC and upon a determination by SBA that the 504 loan is needed for good cause.

(11) The authority to approve the refinancing under this paragraph (g) is not delegated to PCLP CDCs;

(12) The 504 loans approved under this paragraph (g) must be disbursed within 9 months after loan approval. The Director, Office of Financial Assistance, or his or her designee, may approve a request for extension of the disbursement period for an additional 6 months for good cause.

(13) The Third Party Loan may not be sold on the secondary market as a part of a pool guaranteed under subpart J of this part, or any successor to this program, when the debt being refinanced is same institution debt;

(14) The Third Party Lender must certify that it would not refinance the qualified debt except for the assistance provided under this paragraph (g);

(15) *Definitions.* For the purposes of this paragraph (g), the terms below are defined as follows:

Date of application refers to the date the 504 loan application is received by SBA.

Eligible Fixed Assets are one or more long-term fixed assets, such as land, buildings, machinery, and equipment, acquired, constructed or improved by a small business for use in its business operations.

Fair market value refers to the current appraised value of an asset that is established by an independent appraiser in accordance with the standards established by SBA in its SOPs.

Qualified debt is a commercial loan:

(i) That was incurred not less than 2 years before the date of the application for the refinancing available under this paragraph (g). A commercial loan that was refinanced within the two years prior to the date of application (the most recent loan) may be deemed incurred not less than 2 years before the date of the application provided that the effect of the most recent loan was to extend the maturity date without advancing any additional proceeds (except to cover closing costs) and the collateral for the most recent loan includes, at a minimum, the same Eligible Fixed Asset(s) that served as collateral for the former loan that was refinanced. The loan documents and lien instruments for the most recent loan, as well as the loan documents and lien instruments for the loan that was replaced by the most recent loan, must be submitted to SBA as part of the application.

(ii) That is not subject to a guarantee by a Federal agency or department;

(iii) Substantially all (85% or more) of which was for an Eligible Fixed Asset. If the Eligible Fixed Asset was originally financed through a commercial loan that would have satisfied the "substantially all" standard (the "original loan") and that was subsequently refinanced one or more times, with the current commercial loan being the most recent refinancing, the current commercial loan will be deemed to satisfy this paragraph (iii). If the original loan was for the construction of a new building, or the acquisition, renovation, or reconstruction of an existing building, and such loan would not have satisfied the leasing policies set forth in 13 CFR 120.131 and 13 CFR 120.870(b), the current commercial loan will be deemed to satisfy these policies, provided that Borrower demonstrates compliance with 13 CFR 120.131(b) for existing buildings as of the date of application.

(iv) That was for the benefit of the small business concern;

(v) That is collateralized by Eligible Fixed Assets;

(vi) That is not a Third Party Loan that is part of an existing 504 Project; and

(vii) For which the applicant for the refinancing available under this paragraph (g) has been current on all payments due for not less than one year preceding the date of application. For the purposes of this paragraph (vii), "current on all payments due" means that no payment was more than 30 days past due from either the original payment terms or modified payment terms (whether through a modification to an existing Note or through a refinancing that results in a new Note). The modification (or refinancing) must have been agreed to in writing by the Borrower and the lender of the existing debt no less than one year preceding the date of application, except that a modified (or refinanced) loan may be allowed if the purpose of the modification (or refinancing) was to extend the maturity date of the loan, including any balloon payment, and if, during the one year period prior to the date of application (*i.e.*, in the months prior to and after the modification or refinancing), the Borrower was current on all payments due, there have been no deferments of any payments, and no additional proceeds were advanced through the modification or refinancing (except to cover closing costs). Any delinquency in payment on the loan to be refinanced after approval and before debenture funding must be reported to SBA as an adverse change.

Refinancing Project means the fair market value of the Eligible Fixed Asset(s) securing the qualified debt and any other fixed assets acceptable to SBA, except that if the Refinancing Project includes the financing of Eligible Business Expenses, SBA will not accept as collateral any fixed assets other than the Eligible Fixed Asset(s) securing the Qualified Debt.

Same institution debt means any debt of the Third Party Lender that is providing funds for the refinancing, or of its affiliates.

[61 FR 3235, Jan. 31, 1996, as amended at 68 FR 57987, Oct. 7, 2003; 74 FR 29591, June 23, 2009; 76 FR 9218, Feb. 17, 2011; 76 FR 63155, Oct. 12, 2011; 79 FR 15650, Mar. 21, 2014; 81 FR 33125, May 25, 2016; 83 FR 19920, May 7, 2018]

§ 120.883 Eligible administrative costs for 504 loans.

The following administrative costs are not part of Project costs, but may be paid with the proceeds of the 504 loan and the Debenture (see § 120.971):

(a) SBA guarantee fee;

(b) Funding fee (to cover the cost of a public issuance of securities and the Trustee);

(c) CDC processing fee;

(d) Borrower's out-of-pocket costs associated with 504 loan and Debenture closing other than legal fees (for example, certifications and the copying costs associated with them, overnight delivery, postage, and messenger services) but not to include fees and costs described in § 120.882;

(e) CDC Closing Fee (see § 120.971(a)(2)) up to a maximum of $2,500; and

(f) Underwriters' fee.

[64 FR 2118, Jan. 13, 1999, as amended at 68 FR 57987, Oct. 7, 2003]

§ 120.884 Ineligible costs for 504 loans.

Costs not directly attributable and necessary for the Project may not be paid with proceeds of the 504 loan. These include, but are not limited to, the following:

(a) Debt refinancing (other than interim financing), except as provided in § 120.882(e) and (g).

(b) A CDC may not use 504 loan proceeds to pay any creditor in a position to sustain a loss causing a shift to SBA of all or part of a potential loss from an existing debt.

(c) Third-Party Loan fees (commitment, broker, finders, origination, processing fees of permanent financing).

(d) Ancillary business expenses, such as:

(1) Working capital;

(2) Counseling or management services fees;

(3) Incorporation/organization costs;

(4) Franchise fees; and

(5) Advertising.

(e) Fixed-asset Project components, such as:

(1) Short-term equipment, furniture, and furnishings (unless essential to and a minor portion of the Project);

(2) Automobiles, trucks, and airplanes; and

(3) Construction equipment (except for heavy duty construction equipment integral to the business' operations with a remaining useful life of a minimum of 10 years).

[61 FR 3235, Jan. 31, 1996, as amended at 64 FR 2118, Jan. 13, 1999; 74 FR 29591, June 23, 2009; 76 FR 9219, Feb. 17, 2011; 82 FR 39504, Aug. 21, 2017]

Interim Financing

§ 120.890 Source of interim financing.

A Project may use interim financing for all Project costs except the Borrower's contribution. Any source (including a CDC) may supply interim financing provided:

(a) The financing is not derived from any SBA program, directly or indirectly;

(b) The terms and conditions of the financing are acceptable to SBA;

(c) The source is not the Borrower or an Associate of the Borrower; and

(d) The source has the experience and qualifications to monitor properly all Project construction and progress payments. (If the source lacks such experience or qualifications, SBA may require the interim loan to be managed by a third party such as a bank or professional construction manager.)

§ 120.891 Certifications of disbursement and completion.

Before the Debenture is issued, the interim lender must certify the amount disbursed. The CDC must certify that the Project was completed in accordance with the final plans and specifications (except as provided in § 120.961).

§ 120.892 Certifications of no adverse change.

Following completion of the Project, the following certifications must be made before the 504 loan closing:

(a) The interim lender must certify to the CDC that it has no knowledge of any unremedied substantial adverse change in the condition of the small business since the application to the interim lender;

(b) The Borrower (or Operating Company) must certify to the CDC that there has been no unremedied substantial adverse change in its financial condition or its ability to repay the 504 loan since the date of application, and must furnish interim financial statements, current within 120 days of closing; and

(c) The CDC must issue an opinion to the best of its knowledge that there has been no unremedied substantial adverse change in the Borrower's (or Operating Company's) ability to repay the 504 loan since its submission of the loan application to SBA.

[61 FR 3235, Jan. 31, 1996, as amended at 68 FR 57987, Oct. 7, 2003]

PERMANENT FINANCING

§ 120.900 Sources of permanent financing.

Permanent financing for each Project must come from three sources: the Borrower's contribution, Third-Party Loans, and the 504 loan. Typically, the Borrower contributes 10 percent of the permanent financing, Third-Party Loans 50 percent and the 504 loan 40 percent.

THE BORROWER'S CONTRIBUTION

§ 120.910 Borrower contributions.

(a) The Borrower must contribute to the Project cash (or property acceptable to SBA obtained with the cash) or land (that is part of the Project Property), in an amount equal to the following percentage of the Project cost, excluding administrative costs:

(1) At least 15 percent, if the Borrower (or Operating Company if the Borrower is an Eligible Passive Company) has operated for two years or less;

(2) At least 15 percent, if the Project involves the acquisition, construction, conversion, or expansion of a limited or single purpose building or structure;

(3) At least 20 percent, if the Project involves conditions described in paragraphs (a)(1) and (2) of this section; or

(4) At least 10 percent, in all other circumstances.

(b) The source of the contribution may be a CDC or any other source except an SBA business loan program (see § 120.913 for SBIC exception).

[64 FR 2118, Jan. 13, 1999]

§ 120.911 Land contributions.

The Borrower's contribution may be land (including buildings, structures and other site improvements which will be part of the Project Property) previously acquired by the Borrower.

[68 FR 57987, Oct. 7, 2003]

§ 120.912 Borrowed contributions.

The Borrower may borrow its cash contribution from the CDC or a third party. If any of the contribution is borrowed, the interest rate must be reasonable. If the loan is secured by any of the Project assets, the loan must be subordinate to the liens securing the 504 Loan, and the loan may not be repaid at a faster rate than the 504 Loan unless SBA gives prior written approval. A third party lender may not receive voting rights, stock options, or any other actual or potential voting interest in the small business.

§ 120.913 Limitations on any contributions by a Licensee.

Subject to part 107 of this chapter, a Licensee may provide financing for all or part of the Borrower's contribution to the Project. SBA will consider Licensee funds to be derived from federal sources if the Licensee has Leverage (as defined in § 107.50 of this chapter). If the Licensee does not have Leverage, SBA will consider the investment to be from private funds. Licensee financing must be subordinated to the 504 loan and must not be repaid at a faster rate than the Debenture. (Refer to § 120.930(a) for additional limitations.)

[68 FR 57987, Oct. 7, 2003]

THIRD PARTY LOANS

§ 120.920 Required participation by the Third Party Lender.

(a) *Amount of Third Party Loans.* A Project financing must include one or more Third Party Loans totaling at least as much as the 504 loan. However, the Third Party Loans must total at least 50 percent of the total cost of the Project if:

(1) The Borrower (or Operating Company, if the Borrower is an Eligible Passive Company) has operated for two years or less, or

(2) The Project is for the acquisition, construction, conversion or expansion of a limited or single purpose asset.

(b) *Third party loan collateral.* The 504 loan is usually collateralized by a second lien on Project Property. The Third Party Lender may obtain additional collateral or other security for the Third Party Loan ("Additional Collateral") only if in the event of liquidation and unless otherwise approved in writing by SBA:

(1) The Third Party Lender liquidates or otherwise exhausts all reasonable avenues of collection with respect to the Additional Collateral no later than the disposition of the Project Property, and

(2) The Third Party Lender applies any proceeds received as a result of the Additional Collateral to the balance outstanding on the Third Party Loan prior to the application of proceeds from the disposition of the Project Property to the Third Party Loan.

[64 FR 2118, Jan. 13, 1999, as amended at 79 FR 15650, Mar. 21, 2014]

§ 120.921 Terms of Third Party loans.

(a) *Maturity.* A Third Party Loan must have a term of at least 7 years when the 504 loan is for a term of 10 years and 10 years when the 504 loan is for 20 years. If there is more than one Third Party Loan, an overall loan maturity must be calculated, taking into account the maturities and amounts of each loan. If there is a balloon payment, it must be justified in the loan report and clearly identified in the Loan Authorization.

(b) *Interest rates.* Interest rates must be reasonable. SBA must establish and publish in the FEDERAL REGISTER a maximum interest rate for any Third Party Loan from commercial financial institutions. The rate shall remain in effect until changed.

(c) *Other terms.* The Third Party Loan must not have any early call feature or contain any demand provisions unless the loan is in default. By participating, a Third Party Loan lender waives, as to the CDC/SBA financing, any provision in its deed of trust, or mortgage, or other documents prohibiting further encumbrances or subordinate debt. In the event of default, the Third Party Lender must give the CDC and SBA written notice of default within 30 days of the event of default and at least 60 days prior to foreclosure.

(d) *Future advances.* The Third Party Loan must not be open-ended. After completion of the Project, the Third Party Lender may not make future advances under the Third Party Loan except expenditures to collect amounts due the Third Party Loan notes, maintain collateral and protect the Third Party Lender's lien position on the Third Party Loan.

(e) *Subordination.* The Third Party Lender's lien will be subordinate to the CDC/SBA lien regarding any prepayment penalties, late fees, other default charges, and escalated interest after default due under the Third Party Loan.

(f) *Escalation upon default.* A Third-Party Lender may not escalate the rate of interest upon default to a rate greater than the maximum rate set forth in paragraph (b) of this section. Regarding any Project that SBA approved after September 30, 1996, SBA will only pay the interest rate on the note in effect before the date of the Borrower's default.

[61 FR 3235, Jan. 31, 1996, as amended at 64 FR 2118, Jan. 13, 1999]

§ 120.922 Pre-existing debt on the Project Property.

In addition to its share of Project cost, a Third-Party Loan may include consolidation of existing debt on the Project Property. The consolidation must not improve the lien position of the Lender on the pre-existing debt, unless the debt is a previous Third-Party Loan.

§ 120.923 Policies on subordination.

(a) Financing provided by the seller of Project Property must be subordinate to the 504 loan. SBA may waive the subordination requirement if the property is classified as "other real estate owned" by a national bank or other Federally regulated lender and SBA considers the property to be of sufficient value to support the 504 loan.

(b) A Borrower is eligible for a 504 loan even if part of the Project financing is tax-exempt. SBA's lien position must not be subordinate to loans made from the proceeds of the tax-exempt obligation.

(c) The Borrower must not prepay any Project financing subordinate to the 504 loan without SBA's prior written consent.

[61 FR 3235, Jan. 31, 1996, as amended at 68 FR 57988, Oct. 7, 2003]

§ 120.925 [Reserved]

§ 120.926 Referral fee.

The CDC can receive a reasonable referral fee from the Third Party Lender if the CDC secured the Third Party Lender for the Borrower under a written contract between the CDC and the Third Party Lender. Both the CDC and the Third Party Lender are prohibited from charging this fee to the Borrower. If a CDC charges a referral fee, the CDC will be construed as a Referral Agent under part 103 of this chapter.

[68 FR 57988, Oct. 7, 2003]

504 Loans and Debentures

§ 120.930 Amount.

(a) Generally, a 504 loan may not exceed 40 percent of total Project cost plus 100 percent of eligible administrative costs. For good cause shown, SBA may authorize an increase in the percentage of Project costs covered up to 50 percent. No more than 50 percent of eligible Project costs can be from Federal sources, whether received directly or indirectly through an intermediary.

(b) A 504 loan must not be less than $25,000.

(c) Upon completion of the Project, the Debenture amount will be reduced by the amount that the unused contingency reserve exceeds 2 percent of the anticipated Debenture.

[61 FR 3235, Jan. 31, 1996, as amended at 68 FR 57988, Oct. 7, 2003]

§ 120.931 504 Lending limits.

504 loan amounts shall be limited to:

(a) An outstanding balance of $5,000,000 for each Borrower and its affiliates if the loan proceeds will not be directed towards a Project in paragraph (c) of this section,

(b) An outstanding balance of $5,000,000 for each Borrower and its affiliates if one or more of the public policy goals enumerated in § 120.862(b) applies to the Project; and

(c) $5,500,000 for each Project for:

(1) Small Manufacturers (NAICS Codes 31–33) with all production facilities located in the United States;

(2) Reduction of the Borrower's, or if the Borrower is an Eligible Passive Company, the Operating Company's energy consumption by at least 10%; or

(3) Plant, equipment and process upgrades of renewable energy sources such as the small-scale production of energy for individual buildings' or communities' consumption, commonly known as micropower, or renewable fuel producers including biodiesel and ethanol producers.

[76 FR 63547, Oct. 12, 2011]

§ 120.932 Interest rate.

The interest rate of the 504 Loan and the Debenture which funds it is set by the SBA and approved by the Secretary of the Treasury.

§ 120.933 Maturity.

From time to time, SBA will publish in the Federal Register the available maturities for a 504 loan and the Debenture that funds it. Such available maturities remain in effect until changed by subsequent Federal Register publication.

[68 FR 57988, Oct. 7, 2003]

§ 120.934 Collateral.

The CDC usually takes a second lien position on the Project Property to secure the 504 loan. Sometimes additional collateral is required. (In rare circumstances, SBA may permit other collateral substituted for Project Property.) All collateral must be insured against such hazards and risks as SBA may require, with provisions for notice to SBA and the CDC in the event of impending lapse of coverage.

[68 FR 57988, Oct. 7, 2003]

§ 120.935 Deposit from the Borrower that a CDC may require.

At the time of application for a 504 loan, the CDC may require a deposit from the Borrower of $2,500 or 1 percent of the Net Debenture Proceeds, whichever is less. The deposit may be applied to the loan processing fee if the application is accepted, but must be refunded if the application is denied. If the small business withdraws its application, the CDC may deduct from the deposit reasonable costs incurred in packaging and processing the application.

§ 120.937 Assumption.

A 504 loan may be assumed with SBA's prior written approval.

§ 120.938 Default.

(a) Upon occurrence of an event of default specified in the 504 note which requires automatic acceleration, the note becomes due and payable. Upon occurrence of an event of default which does not require automatic acceleration, SBA may forbear acceleration of the note and attempt to resolve the default. If the default is not cured subsequently, the note shall be accelerated. In either case, upon acceleration of the note, the Debenture which funded it is also due immediately, and SBA must honor its guarantee of the Debenture. SBA shall not reimburse the investor for any premium paid.

(b) If a CDC defaults on a Debenture, SBA generally shall limit its recovery to the payments made by the small business to the CDC on the loan made from the Debenture proceeds, and the collateral securing the defaulted loan. However, SBA will look to the CDC for the entire amount of the Debenture in the case of fraud, negligence, or misrepresentation by the CDC.

§ 120.939 Borrower prohibition.

Neither a Borrower nor an Associate of the Borrower may purchase an interest in a Debenture Pool in which the Debenture that funded its 504 loan has been placed.

§ 120.940 Prepayment of the 504 loan or Debenture.

The Borrower may prepay its 504 loan, if it pays the entire principal balance, unpaid interest, any unpaid fees, and any prepayment premium established in the note. If the Borrower prepays, the CDC must prepay the corresponding Debenture with interest and premium. If one of the Debentures in a Debenture Pool is prepaid, the Investors in that Debenture Pool must be paid pro rata, and SBA's guarantee on the entire Debenture Pool must be proportionately reduced. If the entire Debenture Pool is paid off, SBA may call all Certificates backed by the Pool for redemption.

§ 120.941 Certificates.

(a) The face value of a Certificate must be at least $25,000. Certificates are issued in registered form and transferred only by entry on the central registry maintained by the Trustee. SBA guarantees the timely payment of principal and interest on the Certificates.

(b) Before the sale of a Certificate, the seller, or the broker or dealer acting as the seller's agent, must disclose to the purchaser the terms, conditions, yield, and premium and other characteristics not guaranteed by SBA.

DEBENTURE SALES AND SERVICE AGENTS

§ 120.950 SBA and CDC must appoint agents.

SBA and the CDC must appoint the following agents to facilitate the sale and service of the Certificates and disbursement of the proceeds.

§ 120.951 Selling agent.

The CDC, with SBA approval, shall appoint a Selling Agent to select underwriters, negotiate the terms and conditions of Debenture offerings with the underwriters, and direct and coordinate Debenture sales.

§ 120.952 Fiscal agent.

SBA shall appoint a Fiscal Agent to assess the financial markets, minimize the cost of sales, arrange for the production of the Offering Circular, Debenture Certificates, and other required documents, and monitor the performance of the Trustee and the underwriters.

§ 120.953 Trustee.

SBA must appoint a Trustee to:

(a) Issue Certificates;

(b) Transfer the Certificates upon resale in the secondary market;

(c) Maintain physical possession of the Debentures for SBA and the Certificate holders;

(d) Establish and maintain a central registry of:

(1) Debenture Pools, including the CDC obligors and the interest rate payable on the Debentures in each Pool;

(2) Certificates issued or transferred, including the Debenture Pool backing the Certificate, name and address of the purchaser, price paid, the interest rate on the Certificate, and fees or charges assessed by the transferror; and

(3) Brokers and dealers in Certificates, and the commissions, fees or discounts granted to the brokers and dealers;

(e) Receive semi-annual Debenture payments and prepayments;

(f) Make regularly scheduled and prepayment payments to Investors; and

(g) Assure before any resale of a Debenture or Certificate is recorded in the registry that the seller has provided the purchaser a written disclosure statement approved by SBA.

§ 120.954 Central Servicing Agent.

(a) SBA has entered into a Master Servicing Agreement designating a Central Servicing Agent (CSA) to support the orderly flow of funds among Borrowers, CDCs, and SBA. The CDC and Borrower must enter into an individual Servicing Agent Agreement with the CSA for each 504 loan, constituting acceptance by the CDC and the Borrower of the terms of the Master Servicing Agreement.

(b) The CSA has established a master reserve account. All funds related to the 504 loans and Debentures flow through the master reserve account under the provisions of the Master Servicing Agreement. The master reserve account will be funded by a guarantee fee, a funding fee to be published from time to time in the FEDERAL REGISTER, and by principal and interest payments of 504 loans. At SBA's direction, the CSA may use funds in the master reserve account to defray program expenses. In the event a Borrower defaults and its 504 note is accelerated, SBA shall add funds under its guarantee to ensure the full and timely payment of the Debenture which funded the 504 loan. At SBA's direction, the CSA must pay to the CDC servicing each loan the interest accruing in the master reserve account on loan payments made by each Borrower between the date of receipt of each monthly payment and the date of disbursement to investors. The CSA may disburse such interest periodically to CDCs on a pro rata basis. SBA may use interest accruals in the master reserve account earned prior to October 1991 (not previously distributed to the CDCs) for the costs of 504 program administration.

§ 120.955 Agent bonds and records.

(a) Each agent (in §§ 120.951 through 120.954) must provide a fidelity bond or insurance in such amount as necessary to fully protect the interest of the government.

(b) SBA must have access at the agent's place of business to all books, records and other documents relating to Debenture activities.

§ 120.956 Suspension or revocation of brokers and dealers.

The appropriate Office of Capital Access official in accordance with Delegations of Authority may suspend or revoke the privilege of any broker or dealer to participate in the sale or marketing of Debentures and Certificates for actions or conduct bearing negatively on the broker's fitness to participate in the securities market. SBA must give the broker or dealer written notice, stating the reasons, at least 10 business days prior to the effective date of the suspension or revocation. A broker or dealer may appeal the suspension or revocation made under this section pursuant to the procedures set forth in part 134 of this chapter. The action of this official will remain in effect pending resolution of the appeal.

[73 FR 75519, Dec. 11, 2008]

CLOSINGS

§ 120.960 Responsibility for closing.

(a) The CDC is responsible for the 504 loan closing.

(b) The Debenture closing is the joint responsibility of the CDC and SBA.

(c) SBA may, within its sole discretion, decline to close the Debenture; direct the transfer of the 504 loan to another CDC; or cancel its guarantee of the Debenture, prior to sale, if any of the following occur:

(1) The CDC has failed to comply materially with any requirement imposed by statute, regulation, SOP, policy and procedural notice, any agreement the CDC has executed with SBA, or the terms of a Debenture or loan authorization;

(2) The CDC has failed to make or close the 504 loan or prepare the Debenture closing in a prudent or commercially reasonable manner;

(3) The CDC's improper action or inaction places SBA at risk;

(4) The CDC has failed to use required SBA forms or electronic versions of those forms;

(5) The CDC, Third Party Lender or Borrower has failed to timely disclose to SBA a material fact regarding the Project or 504 loan;

(6) The CDC, Third Party Lender or Borrower has misrepresented a material fact to SBA regarding the Project or 504 loan; or

(7) SBA determines that there has been an unremedied material adverse change, such as deterioration in the Borrower's financial condition, since the 504 loan was approved, or that approving the closing of the Debenture will put SBA at unacceptable financial risk.

[68 FR 57988, Oct. 7, 2003]

§ 120.961 Construction escrow accounts.

The CSA, title company, CDC attorney, or bank may hold Debenture proceeds in escrow to complete Project components such as landscaping and parking lots, and acquire machinery and equipment if the component or acquisition is a minor portion of the total Project and has been contracted for completion or delivery at a specified price and specific future date. The escrow agent must disburse funds upon approval by the CDC and the SBA, supported by invoices and payable jointly to the small business and the designated contractor.

SERVICING

§ 120.970 Servicing of 504 loans and Debentures.

(a) In servicing 504 loans, CDCs must comply with Loan Program Requirements and in accordance with prudent and commercially reasonable lending standards.

(b) The CDC is responsible for routine servicing including receipt and review of the Borrower's or Operating Company's financial statements on an annual or more frequent basis and monitoring the status of the Borrower and 504 loan collateral.

(c) The CDC is responsible for assuring that the Borrower makes all required insurance premium payments and has paid all taxes when due.

(d) The CDC is responsible for filing renewals and extensions of security interests on collateral for the 504 loan, as required.

(e) The CDC must timely respond to Borrower requests for loan modifications.

(f) For any 504 loan that is more than three months past due, the CDC must promptly request that SBA purchase the Debenture unless the 504 loan has an SBA-approved deferment or is in compliance with an SBA-approved plan to allow the Borrower to catch up on delinquent loan payments.

(g) The CDC must cooperate with SBA to cure defaults and initiate workouts.

(h) Additional servicing requirements are set forth in subpart E of this part.

[68 FR 57988, Oct. 7, 2003, as amended at 72 FR 18364, Apr. 12, 2007]

FEES

§ 120.971 Allowable fees paid by Borrower.

(a) *CDC fees.* The fees a CDC may charge the Borrower in connection with a 504 loan and Debenture are limited to the following:

(1) *Processing fee.* The CDC may charge up to 1.5 percent of the net Debenture proceeds to process the financing. Two-thirds of this fee will be considered earned and may be collected by the CDC when the Authorization for the Debenture is issued by SBA. The portion of the processing fee paid by the Borrower may be reimbursed from the Debenture proceeds;

(2) *Closing fee.* The CDC may charge a reasonable closing fee sufficient to reimburse it for the expenses of its in-house or outside legal counsel, and other miscellaneous closing costs (CDC Closing Fee). Some closing costs may be funded out of the Debenture proceeds (see § 120.883 for limitations);

(3) *Servicing fee.* The CDC will charge a monthly servicing fee of at least 0.625 percent per annum and no more than 2 percent per annum on the unpaid balance of the loan as determined at five-year anniversary intervals. A servicing fee greater than 1.5 percent in a rural area and 1 percent everywhere else requires SBA's prior written approval, based on evidence of substantial need. The servicing fee may be paid only from loan payments received. The fees may be accrued without interest and collected from the CSA when the payments are made.

(4) *Late fees.* Loan payments received after the 15th of each month may be subject to a late payment fee of 5 percent of the late payment or $100, whichever is greater. These fees will be collected by the CSA on behalf of the CDC; and

(5) *Assumption fee.* Upon SBA's written approval, a CDC may charge an assumption fee not to exceed 1 percent of the outstanding principal balance of the loan being assumed.

(b) *CSA fees.* The CSA may charge an initiation fee on each loan and a monthly servicing fee under the terms of the Master Servicing Agreement.

(c) *Other agent fees.* Agent fees and charges necessary to market and service Debentures and Certificates may be assessed to the Borrower or the investor. The fees must be approved by SBA and published periodically in the FEDERAL REGISTER.

(d) *SBA fees.* (1) SBA charges a 0.5 percent guarantee fee on the Debenture.

(2) For loans approved by SBA after September 30, 1996, SBA charges a fee of not more than 0.9375 percent annually on the unpaid principal balance of the loan as determined at five-year anniversary intervals.

(e) *Miscellaneous fees.* A funding fee not to exceed 0.25 percent of the Debenture may be charged to cover costs incurred by the trustee, fiscal agent, transfer agent.

[61 FR 3235, Jan. 31, 1996, as amended at 64 FR 2119, Jan. 13, 1999; 68 FR 57988, Oct. 7, 2003]

§ 120.972 Third Party Lender participation fee and CDC fee.

(a) *Participation fee.* For loans approved by SBA after September 30, 1996, SBA must collect a one-time fee equal to 50 basis points on the Third Party Lender's participation in a Project when the Third Party Lender occupies a senior credit position to SBA in the Project.

(b) *CDC fee.* For loans approved by SBA after September 30, 1996, SBA must collect an annual fee from the CDC equal to 0.125 percent of the outstanding principal balance of the Debenture. The fee must be paid from the servicing fees collected by the CDC and cannot be paid from any additional fees imposed on the Borrower.

[68 FR 57988, Oct. 7, 2003]

AUTHORITY OF CDCS TO PERFORM LIQUIDATION AND DEBT COLLECTION LITIGATION

§ 120.975 CDC Liquidation of loans and debt collection litigation.

(a) *PCLP CDCs.* If a CDC is designated as a PCLP CDC under § 120.845, the CDC must liquidate and handle debt collection litigation with respect to all PCLP Loans in its portfolio on behalf of SBA as required by § 120.848(f), in accordance with subpart E of this part. With respect to all other 504 loans that a PCLP CDC makes, the PCLP CDC is an Authorized CDC Liquidator and must exercise its delegated authority to liquidate and handle debt-collection litigation in accordance with subpart E of this part for such loans, if the PCLP CDC is notified by SBA that it meets either of the following requirements to be an Authorized CDC Liquidator, as determined by SBA:

(1) The PCLP CDC has one or more employees who have not less than two years of substantive, decision-making experience in administering the liquidation and workout of defaulted or problem loans secured in a manner substantially similar to loans funded with 504 loan program debentures, and who have completed a training program on loan liquidation developed by the Agency in conjunction with qualified CDCs that meet the requirements of this section; or

(2) The PCLP CDC has entered into a contract with a qualified third party for the performance of its liquidation responsibilities and obtains the approval of SBA with respect to the qualifications of the contractor and the terms and conditions of the contract.

(b) *All other CDCs.* A CDC that is not authorized under paragraph (a) of this section may apply to become an Authorized CDC Liquidator with authority to liquidate and handle debt collection litigation with respect to 504 loans on behalf of SBA, in accordance with subpart E of this part, if the CDC meets the following requirements:

(1) The CDC meets either of the following criteria:

(i) The CDC participated in the loan liquidation pilot program established by the Small Business Programs Improvement Act of 1996 prior to October 1, 2006; or

(ii) During the three fiscal years immediately prior to seeking such authority, the CDC made an average of not less than ten 504 loans per year; and

(2) The CDC meets either of the following requirements:

(i) The CDC has one or more employees who have not less than two years of substantive, decision-making experience in administering the liquidation and workout of defaulted or problem loans secured in a manner substantially similar to loans funded with 504 loan program debentures, and who have completed a training program on loan liquidation developed by the Agency in conjunction with qualified CDCs that meet the requirements of this section; or

(ii) The CDC has entered into a contract with a qualified third party for the performance of its liquidation responsibilities and obtains the approval of SBA with respect to the qualifications of the contractor and the terms and conditions of the contract.

(c) *CDC counsel.* To perform debt collection litigation under paragraphs (a) or (b) of this section, a CDC must also have either in-house counsel with adequate experience as approved by SBA or entered into a contract for the performance of debt collection litigation with an experienced attorney or law firm as approved by SBA.

(d) *Application for authority to liquidate and litigate.* To seek authority to perform liquidation and debt collection litigation under paragraphs (b) and (c) of this section, a CDC other than a PCLP CDC must submit a written application to SBA and include documentation demonstrating that the CDC meets the requirements of paragraph (b) and (c) of this section. If a CDC intends to use a contractor to perform liquidation, it must obtain approval from SBA of both the qualifications of the contractor and the terms and conditions in the contract covering the CDC's retention of the contractor. SBA will notify a CDC in writing when the CDC can begin to perform liquidation and/or debt collection litigation under this section.

[72 FR 18365, Apr. 12, 2007]

ENFORCEABILITY OF 501, 502 AND 503 LOANS AND OTHER LAWS

§ 120.990 501, 502 and 503 loans.

SBA has discontinued loan programs for 501, 502, and 503 loans. Outstanding loans remain under these programs, and Borrowers, CDCs, and SBA must comply with the terms and conditions of the corresponding notes and Debentures, and the regulations in this part in effect when the obligations were undertaken or last in effect, if applicable.

§ 120.991 Effect of other laws.

No State or local law may preclude or limit SBA's exercise of its rights with respect to notes, guarantees, Debentures and Debenture Pools, or of its enforcement rights to foreclose on collateral.

Subpart I—Risk-Based Lender Oversight

SOURCE: 72 FR 25194, May 4, 2007, unless otherwise noted.

SUPERVISION

§ 120.1000 Risk-Based Lender Oversight.

(a) *Risk-Based Lender Oversight.* SBA supervises, examines, and regulates, and enforces laws against, SBA Supervised Lenders and the SBA operations of SBA Lenders, Intermediaries, and NTAPs.

(b) *Scope.* Most rules and standards set forth in this subpart apply to SBA Lenders as well as Intermediaries and NTAPs, However, SBA has separate regulations for enforcement grounds and enforcement actions for Intermediaries and NTAPs at §120.1425 and §120.1540.

[73 FR 75519, Dec. 11, 2008]

§ 120.1005 Bureau of PCLP Oversight.

SBA's Bureau of PCLP Oversight within OCRM, monitors the capitalization of PCLP CDC pilot participants' LLRFs and performs other related functions.

[73 FR 75519, Dec. 11, 2008]

§ 120.1010 SBA access to SBA Lender, Intermediary, and NTAP files.

An SBA Lender, Intermediary, and NTAP must allow SBA's authorized representatives, including representatives authorized by the SBA Inspector General, during normal business hours, access to its files to review, inspect, and copy all records and documents, relating to SBA guaranteed loans or as requested for SBA oversight.

[73 FR 75519, Dec. 11, 2008]

§ 120.1015 Risk Rating System.

(a) *Risk Rating.* SBA may assign a Risk Rating to all SBA Lenders, Intermediaries, and NTAPs on a periodic basis. Risk Ratings are based on certain risk-related portfolio performance factors as set forth in notices or SBA's SOPs and as published from time to time.

(b) *Rating categories.* Risk Ratings fall into one of two broad categories: Acceptable Risk Ratings or Less Than Acceptable Risk Ratings.

[73 FR 75519, Dec. 11, 2008]

§ 120.1025 Monitoring.

SBA may conduct monitoring of SBA Lenders, Intermediaries, and NTAPs, including SBA Lenders', Intermediaries' or NTAPs' self-assessments.

[73 FR 75519, Dec. 11, 2008, as amended at 82 FR 39504, Aug. 21, 2017]

§ 120.1050 Reviews and examinations.

(a) *Reviews.* SBA may conduct reviews of the SBA loan operations of SBA Lenders. The review may include, but is not limited to, an evaluation of the following:

(1) Portfolio performance;

(2) SBA operations management;

(3) Credit administration; and

(4) Compliance with Loan Program Requirements.

(b) *Examinations.* SBA may conduct safety and soundness examinations of SBA Supervised Lenders, except SBA will not conduct safety and soundness examinations of Other Regulated SBLCs under §§120.1510 and 1511. The safety and soundness examination may include, but is not limited to, an evaluation of:

(1) Capital adequacy;

(2) Asset quality (including credit administration and allowance for loan losses);

(3) Management quality (including internal controls, loan portfolio management, and asset/liability management);

(4) Earnings;

(5) Liquidity; and

(6) Compliance with Loan Program Requirements.

(c) *Reviews/examinations of Intermediaries and NTAPs.* SBA may perform reviews or examinations of Intermediaries and NTAPs.

(d) *Other reviews or examinations.* SBA may perform other reviews/examinations as needed as determined by SBA in its discretion.

[73 FR 75519, Dec. 11, 2008, as amended at 82 FR 39504, Aug. 21, 2017]

§ 120.1051 Frequency of reviews and examinations.

SBA may conduct reviews and examinations of SBA Lenders, Intermediaries, and NTAPs on a periodic basis. SBA may consider, but is not limited to, the following factors in determining frequency:

(a) Results of monitoring, including an SBA Lender's, Intermediary's or NTAP's Risk Rating;

(b) SBA loan portfolio size;

(c) Previous review or examination findings;

(d) Responsiveness in correcting deficiencies noted in prior reviews or examinations; and

(e) Such other risk-related information as SBA, in its discretion, determines to be appropriate.

[73 FR 75519, Dec. 11, 2008, as amended at 82 FR 39504, Aug. 21, 2017]

§ 120.1055 Review and examination results.

(a) *Written Reports.* SBA will provide an SBA Lender, Intermediary, and NTAP a copy of SBA's written report prepared as a result of the SBA Lender review or examination ("Report"). The Report may contain findings, conclusions, corrective actions and recommendations. Each director (or manager, in the absence of a Board of Directors) of the SBA Lender, Intermediary, and NTAP, in keeping with his or her responsibilities, must become fully informed regarding the contents of the Report.

(b) *Response to review and examination Reports.* SBA Lenders, Intermediaries, and NTAPs must respond to Report findings and corrective actions, if any, in writing to SBA and, if requested, submit proposed corrective actions and/or a capital restoration plan. An SBA Lender, Intermediary, or NTAP must respond within 30 days from the Report date unless SBA notifies the SBA Lender, Intermediary, or NTAP in writing that the response, proposed corrective actions or capital restoration plan is to be filed within a different time period. The SBA Lender, Intermediary, or NTAP response must address each finding and corrective action. In proposing a corrective action or capital restoration plan, the SBA Lender, Intermediary, or NTAP must detail: The steps it will take to correct the finding(s); the time within which each step will be taken; the timeframe for accomplishing the entire corrective action plan; and the person(s) or department at the SBA Lender, Intermediary, or NTAP charged with carrying out the corrective action or capital restoration plan, as applicable.

(c) *SBA response.* SBA will provide written notice of whether the response and, if applicable, any corrective action or capital restoration plan, is approved, or whether SBA will seek additional information or require other action.

(d) *Failure to respond or to submit or implement an acceptable plan.* If an SBA Lender, Intermediary, or NTAP fails to respond in writing to SBA, respond timely to SBA, or provide a response acceptable to SBA within SBA's discretion, or respond to all findings and required corrective actions in a Report, then SBA may take enforcement action under Subpart I. If an SBA Lender, Intermediary, or NTAP that is requested to submit a corrective action plan or capital restoration plan to SBA fails to do so in writing; fails to submit timely such plan to SBA; or fails to submit a plan acceptable to SBA within SBA's discretion, then SBA may take enforcement action under § 120.1500 through § 120.1540. If an SBA Lender, Intermediary, or NTAP fails to implement in any material respect a corrective action or capital restoration plan within the required timeframe, then SBA may undertake enforcement action under § 120.1500 through § 120.1540.

[73 FR 75519, Dec. 11, 2008]

§ 120.1060 Confidentiality of Reports, Risk Ratings and related Confidential Information.

(a) *In general.* Reports and other SBA prepared review or examination related documents are the property of SBA and are loaned to an SBA Lender, Intermediary, or NTAP for its confidential use only. The Reports, Risk Ratings, and related Confidential Information are privileged and confidential as more fully explained in paragraph (b) of this section. The Report, Risk Rating, and Confidential Information must not be relied upon for any purpose other than SBA's Lender oversight and SBA's portfolio management purposes. An SBA Lender, Intermediary, or NTAP must not make any representations concerning the Report (including its findings, conclusions, and recommendations), the Risk Rating, or the Confidential Information. For purposes of this regulation, Report means the review or examination report and related documents. For purposes of this regulation, Confidential Information is defined in the SBA Lender information portal and by notice issued from time to time. Access to the Lender information portal may be obtained by contacting the OCRM.

(b) *Disclosure prohibition.* Each SBA Lender, Intermediary, and NTAP is prohibited from disclosing its Report, Risk Rating, and Confidential Information, in full or in part, in any manner, without SBA's prior written permission. An SBA Lender, Intermediary, and NTAP may use the Report, Risk Rating, and Confidential Information for confidential use within its own immediate corporate organization. SBA Lenders, Intermediaries, and NTAPs must restrict access to their Report, Risk Rating and Confidential Information to their respective parent entities, officers, directors, employees, auditors and consultants, in each case who demonstrate a legitimate need to know such information for the purpose of assisting in improving the SBA Lender's, Intermediary's, or NTAP's SBA program operations in conjunction with SBA's Program and SBA's portfolio management (for purposes of this regulation, each referred to as a "permitted party"), and to those for whom SBA has approved access by prior written consent, and those for whom access is required by applicable law or legal process. If such law or process requires SBA Lender, Intermediary, or NTAP to disclose the Report, Risk Rating, or Confidential Information to any person other than a permitted party, SBA Lender, Intermediary, or NTAP will promptly notify SBA and SBA's Information Provider in writing and in advance of such disclosure so that SBA and the Information Provider have, within their discretion, the opportunity to seek appropriate relief such as an injunction or protective order prior to disclosure. For purposes of this regulation, "consultants" means only those consultants that are under written contract with an SBA Lender, Intermediary or NTAP specifically to assist with addressing its Report Findings and Corrective Actions to SBA's satisfaction. The consultant contract must provide for both the consultant's agreement to abide by the disclosure prohibition in this paragraph and the consultant's agreement not to use the Report, Risk Rating, and Confidential Information for any purpose other than to assist with addressing the Report Findings and Corrective Actions. "Information Provider" means any contractor that provides SBA with the Risk Rating. Each SBA Lender, Intermediary, and NTAP must ensure that each permitted party is aware of and agrees to these regulatory requirements and must ensure that each such permitted party abides by them. Any disclosure of the Report, Risk Rating, or Confidential Information other than as permitted by this regulation may result in appropriate action as authorized by law. An SBA Lender, Intermediary, and NTAP will indemnify and hold harmless SBA from and against any and all claims, demands, suits, actions, and liabilities to any degree based upon or resulting from any unauthorized use or disclosure of the Report, Risk Rating, or Confidential Information. Information Provider contact information is available from the Office of Capital Access.

[73 FR 75519, Dec. 11, 2008, as amended at 82 FR 39504, Aug. 21, 2017]

§ 120.1070 SBA Lender oversight fees.

Lenders are required to pay to SBA fees to cover costs of examinations and reviews and, if assessed by SBA, other Lender oversight activities.

(a) *Fee components:* The fees may cover the following:

(1) *Examinations.* The costs of conducting a safety and soundness examination and related activities of an SBA-Supervised Lender, including any expenses that are incurred in relation to the examination and such activities.

(2) *Reviews.* The costs of conducting a review of a 7(a) Lender or a 7(a) Lender's loans, and related review activities (*e.g.*, corrective action assessments, delegated loan reviews), including any expenses that are incurred in relation to the review and such activities.

(3) *Monitoring.* The costs of conducting monitoring reviews of a 7(a) Lender, including any expenses that are incurred in relation to the monitoring review activities.

(4) *Other lender oversight activities.* The costs of additional expenses that SBA incurs in carrying out other lender oversight activities (for example, the salaries and travel expenses of SBA employees and equipment expenses that are directly related to carrying out lender oversight activities, technical assistance and analytics to support the monitoring and review program, and supervision and enforcement activity costs).

(b) *Allocation.* SBA will assess to 7(a) Lender(s) the costs associated with the review, examination, monitoring, or other lender oversight activity, as determined by SBA in its discretion. In general:

(1) Where the costs that SBA incurs for a review, exam, monitoring or other lender oversight activity are specific to a particular 7(a) Lender, SBA will charge that 7(a) Lender a fee for the actual costs of conducting the review, exam, monitoring or other lender oversight activity; and

(2) Where the costs that SBA incurs for the lender oversight activity are not sufficiently specific to a particular Lender, SBA will assess a fee based on each 7(a) Lender's portion of the total dollar amount of SBA guarantees in SBA's total portfolio or in the relevant portfolio segment being reviewed or examined, to cover the costs of such activity. SBA may waive the assessment of this fee for all 7(a) Lenders owing less than a threshold amount below which SBA determines that it is not cost effective to collect the fee.

(c) *Billing process.* For the examinations or reviews conducted under paragraphs (a)(1) and (2) of this section, SBA will bill each 7(a) Lender for the amount owed following completion of the examination, review or related activity. For monitoring conducted under paragraph (a)(3) of this section and the other lender oversight activity expenses incurred under paragraph (a)(4) of this section, SBA will bill each 7(a) Lender for the amount owed on an annual basis. SBA will state in the bill the date by which payment is due SBA and the approved payment method(s). The payment due date will be no less than 30 calendar days from the bill date.

(d) *Delinquent payment and late-payment charges.* Payments that are not received by the due date specified in the bill shall be considered delinquent. SBA will charge interest, and other applicable charges and penalties, on delinquent payments, as authorized by 31 U.S.C. 3717. SBA may waive or abate the collection of interest, charges and/or penalties if circumstances warrant. In addition, a 7(a) Lender's failure to pay any of the fee components described in this section, or to pay interest, charges and penalties that have been charged, may result in a decision to suspend or revoke a participant's eligibility, limit a participant's delegated authority, or other remedy available under law.

[61 FR 3235, Jan. 31, 1996, as amended at 82 FR 39505, Aug. 21, 2017]

ENFORCEMENT ACTIONS

§ 120.1400 Grounds for enforcement actions—SBA Lenders.

(a) *Agreements.* By making SBA 7(a) guaranteed loans or 504 loans, SBA Lenders automatically agree to the terms, conditions, and remedies in Loan Program Requirements, as promulgated or issued from time to time and as if fully set forth in the SBA Form 750 (Loan Guaranty Agreement), Development Company 504 Debenture, CDC Certification, Servicing Agent Agreement, or other applicable participation, guaranty, or supplemental agreement. SBA Lenders further agree that a violation of Loan Program Requirements constitutes default under their respective agreements with SBA.

(1) *Additional agreements by CDCs.* By obtaining approval for 504 loans after October 20, 2017, a CDC consents to the remedies in § 120.1500(e)(3) and waives in advance any right it may have to contest the validity of the appointment of a receiver. The CDC agrees that its consent to SBA's application to a Federal court of competent jurisdiction for appointment of a receiver of SBA's choosing, an injunction or other equitable relief, and the CDC's consent in advance to the court's granting of SBA's application, may be enforced upon any basis in law or equity recognized by the court.

(2) *Additional agreements by SBA Supervised Lenders (except Other Regulated SBLCs).* By making SBA 7(a) guaranteed loans after October 20, 2017, an SBA Supervised Lender (except an Other Regulated SBLC) consents to the remedies in § 120.1500(c)(3) and waives in advance any right it may have to contest the validity of the appointment of a receiver. The SBA Supervised Lender agrees that its consent to SBA's application to a Federal court of competent jurisdiction for appointment of a receiver of SBA's choosing, an injunction or other equitable relief, and the SBA Supervised Lender's consent in advance to the court's granting of SBA's application, may be enforced upon any basis in law or equity recognized by the court.

(b) *Scope.* SBA may undertake one or more of the enforcement actions listed in § 120.1500 or as otherwise authorized by law, if SBA determines that the grounds applicable to the enforcement action exist. Paragraphs (c) through (e) of this section list the grounds that trigger enforcement actions against each type of SBA Lender. In general, the grounds listed in paragraph (c) apply to all SBA Lenders. However, certain enforcement actions against SBA Supervised Lenders require the existence of certain grounds, as set forth in paragraphs (d) and (e). In addition, paragraph (f) of this section lists two additional grounds for taking enforcement action against CDCs that do not apply to other SBA Lenders.

(c) *Grounds in general.* Except as provided in paragraphs (d) and (e) of this section, the grounds that may trigger an enforcement action against any SBA Lender (regardless of its Risk Rating) include:

(1) Failure to maintain eligibility requirements for specific SBA programs and delegated authorities, including but not limited to: 7(a), PLP, SBAExpress, 504, ALP, PCLP, the alternative loss reserve pilot program and any pilot loan program;

(2) Failure to comply materially with any requirement imposed by Loan Program Requirements;

(3) Making a material false statement or failure to disclose a material fact to SBA. (A material fact is any fact which is necessary to make a statement not misleading in light of the circumstances under which the statement was made.);

(4) Not performing underwriting, closing, disbursing, servicing, liquidation, litigation or other actions in a commercially reasonable and prudent manner for 7(a) or 504 loans, respectively, as applicable. Evidence of such performance or actions may include, but is not limited to, the SBA Lender having a repeated Less Than Acceptable Risk Rating (generally in conjunction with other evidence) or an on-site review/examination assessment which is Less Than Acceptable;

(5) Failure within the time period specified to correct an underwriting, closing, disbursing, servicing, liquidation, litigation, or reporting deficiency, or failure in any material respect to take other corrective action, after receiving notice from SBA of a deficiency and the need to take corrective action;

(6) Engaging in a pattern of uncooperative behavior or taking an action that SBA determines is detrimental to an SBA program, that undermines management or administration of a program, or that is not consistent with standards of good conduct. Prior to issuing a notice of a proposed enforcement action or immediate suspension under § 120.1500 based upon this paragraph, SBA must send prior written notice to the SBA Lender explaining why the SBA Lender's actions were uncooperative, detrimental to the program,

undermined SBA's management of the program, or were not consistent with standards of good conduct. The prior notice must also state that the SBA Lender's actions could give rise to a specified enforcement action, and provide the SBA Lender with a reasonable time to cure the deficiency before any further action is taken;

(7) Repeated failure to correct continuing deficiencies;

(8) Unauthorized disclosure of Reports, Risk Rating, or Confidential Information;

(9) Any other reason that SBA determines may increase SBA's financial risk (for example, repeated Less Than Acceptable Risk Ratings (generally in conjunction with other indicators of increased financial risk) or indictment on felony or fraud charges of an officer, key employee, or loan agent involved with SBA loans for the SBA Lender);

(10) As otherwise authorized by law; and

(11) For immediate suspension of all SBA Lenders from delegated authorities—upon a determination by SBA that one or more of the grounds in paragraph (c) or paragraph (f) of this section, as applicable, exist and that immediate action is needed to prevent significant impairment of the integrity of the 7(a) or 504 loan program.

(12) For immediate suspension of all SBA Lenders except SBA Supervised Lenders from the authority to participate in the SBA loan program, including the authority to make, service, liquidate, or litigate 7(a) or 504 loans—upon a determination by SBA that one or more of the grounds in paragraph (c) or paragraph (f) of this section, as applicable, exist and that immediate action is needed to prevent significant impairment of the integrity of the 7(a) or 504 loan program.

(d) *Grounds required for certain enforcement actions against SBA Supervised Lenders (except Other Regulated SBLCs) or, as applicable, Other Persons.* For purposes of Subpart I, Other Person means a Management Official, attorney, accountant, appraiser, Lender Service Provider or other individual involved in the SBA Supervised Lender's operations. For the below listed SBA Supervised Lender enforcement actions, the grounds that are required to take the enforcement action are:

(1) *For SBA program suspensions and revocations*—

(i) False statements knowingly made in any required written submission to SBA; or

(ii) An omission of a material fact from any written submission required by SBA; or

(iii) A willful or repeated violation of the Small Business Act (the Act) or SBA regulations; or

(iv) A willful or repeated violation of any condition imposed by SBA with respect to any application, request, or agreement with SBA; or

(v) A violation of any cease and desist order of SBA.

(2) *For SBA program immediate suspension*—SBA may suspend an SBA Supervised Lender, effective immediately, if in addition to meeting the grounds set forth in paragraph (d)(1) of this section, the Administrator (or the Deputy Administrator, only if the Administrator is unavailable to take such action) finds extraordinary circumstances and takes such action in order to protect the financial or legal position of the United States.

(3) *For cease and desist orders*—

(i) A violation of the Act or SBA regulations, or

(ii) Where an SBA Supervised Lender or Other Person engages in or is about to engage in any acts or practices that will violate the Act or SBA's regulations.

(4) *For an emergency cease and desist order*—

(i) Where grounds for cease and desist order are met,

(ii) The Administrator (or the Deputy Administrator, only if the Administrator is unavailable to take such action) finds extraordinary circumstances, and

(iii) In order to protect the financial or legal position of the United States.

(5) *For transfer of Loan portfolio*—

(i) Where a court has appointed a receiver; or

(ii) The SBA Supervised Lender is either not in compliance with capital requirements or is insolvent. An SBA Supervised Lender is insolvent within the meaning of this provision when all of its capital, surplus, and undivided profits are absorbed in funding losses and the remaining assets are not sufficient to pay and discharge its contracts, debts, and other obligations as they come due.

(6) *For transfer of servicing activity*—

(i) Where grounds for transfer of Loan portfolio are met; or

(ii) Where the SBA Supervised Lender is otherwise operating in an unsafe and unsound condition.

(7) *For order to remove Management Official*—where, in the opinion of the Administrator or his/her delegatee, the Management Official—

(i) Willfully and knowingly committed a substantial violation of the Act, SBA regulation, a final cease and desist order, or any agreement by the Management Official or the SBA Supervised Lender under the Act or SBA regulations, or

(ii) Willfully and knowingly committed a substantial breach of a fiduciary duty of that person as a Management Official and the violation or breach of fiduciary duty is one involving personal dishonesty on the part of such Management Official, or

(iii) The Management Official is convicted of a felony involving dishonesty or breach of trust and the conviction is no longer subject to further judicial review (excludes writ of habeas corpus).

(8) *For order to suspend or prohibit participation of Management Official* (interim measure pending removal)—where SBA is undertaking enforcement action of removal of a Management Official.

(9) *For order to suspend or prohibit participation of Management Official due to criminal charges*—where the Management Official is charged in any information, indictment or complaint authorized by a United States attorney with a felony involving dishonesty or breach of trust.

(e) *Grounds required for certain enforcement actions against SBLCs and Other Regulated SBLCs*—(1) *Capital directive.* If the AA/CA determines that an SBLC is capitally impaired or is otherwise being operated in an imprudent manner, the AA/CA may, in addition to any other action authorized by law, issue a directive to the SBLC to increase capital consistent with § 120.1500(d)(1).

(2) *Civil action for termination.* If an SBLC violates the Act or SBA regulations, SBA may institute a civil action to terminate SBLC rights, privileges, and the franchise under § 120.1500(d)(2).

(f) *Additional grounds specific to CDCs.* In addition to the grounds set forth in paragraphs (b) and (c) of this section, SBA may take enforcement action against a CDC for:

(1) Failure to receive SBA approval for at least four 504 loans during the last two consecutive fiscal years, or

(2) For PCLP CDCs, failure to establish or maintain a LLRF as required by the PCLP.

[73 FR 75521, Dec. 11, 2008, as amended at 82 FR 39505, Aug. 21, 2017]

§ 120.1425 Grounds for enforcement actions—Intermediaries participating in the Microloan Program and NTAPs.

(a) *Agreement.* By participating in the SBA Microloan or NTAP program, Intermediaries and NTAPs automatically agree to the terms, conditions, and remedies in this Part 120 as if fully set forth in their participation agreement and all other agreements jointly executed by the Intermediary or NTAP and SBA.

(b) *Scope.* SBA may undertake one or more of the enforcement actions listed in § 120.1540, or as otherwise authorized by law, if SBA determines that any of the grounds listed in paragraphs (c) through (e) of this section exist.

(c) *Grounds in general*—For any Intermediary or NTAP, grounds that may trigger enforcement action against the Intermediary or NTAP (regardless of its Risk Rating) include:

(1) Violation of any laws, regulations, or policies of the program; or

(2) Failure to meet any one of the following performance standards:

(i) Coverage of the service territory assigned by SBA, including honoring SBA's determined boundaries of neighboring intermediaries and NTAPs;

(ii) Fulfill reporting requirements;

(iii) Manage program funds and matching funds in a satisfactory and financially sound manner;

(iv) Communicate and file reports within six months after beginning participation in program;

(v) Maintain a currency rate of 85% or more for the Intermediary's SBA Microloan portfolio (that is, loans that are no more than 30 days late in scheduled payments);

(vi) Maintain a default rate in the Intermediary's Microloan portfolio of 15% or less of the cumulative dollars loaned under the program;

(vii) Maintain a staff trained in Microloan program issues and requirements; or

(viii) Any other reason that SBA determines may increase SBA's financial or program risk (for example, repeated Less Than Acceptable Risk Ratings (generally in conjunction with other indicators of increased risk) or indictment on felony or fraud charges of an officer, key employee, or loan agent involved with SBA programs for the Intermediary or NTAP).

(d) *Additional grounds specific to Intermediaries.* In addition to the grounds set forth in paragraph (c) of this section, SBA may take enforcement action against an Intermediary for:

(1) Failure to satisfactorily provide in-house technical assistance to Microloan clients and prospective Microloan clients; or

(2) Failure to close and fund the required number of microloans per year under § 120.716.

(e) *Additional grounds specific to NTAPs.* In addition to grounds set forth in paragraph (c) of this section, SBA may take enforcement action against an NTAP for failure to show that, for every 30 clients for which the NTAP provided technical assistance, at least one client received a loan from the private sector.

[73 FR 75521, Dec. 11, 2008, as amended at 80 FR 34047, June 15, 2015]

§ 120.1500 Types of enforcement actions—SBA Lenders.

Upon a determination that the grounds set forth in § 120.1400 exist, SBA may undertake, in SBA's discretion, one or more of the following enforcement actions for each of the types of SBA Lenders listed. SBA will take such action in accordance with procedures set forth in § 120.1600. If enforcement action is taken under this section and the SBA Lender fails to implement required corrective action in any material respect within the required timeframe in response to the enforcement action, SBA may take further enforcement action, as authorized by law. SBA's decision to take an enforcement action will not, by itself, invalidate a guaranty previously provided by SBA.

(a) *Enforcement actions for all SBA Lenders*—(1) *Imposition of portfolio guaranty dollar limit.* SBA may limit the maximum dollar amount that SBA will guarantee on the SBA Lender's SBA loans or debentures.

(2) *Suspension or revocation of delegated authority.* SBA may suspend or revoke an SBA Lender's delegated authority (including, but not limited to, PLP, SBA Express, or PCLP delegated authorities).

(3) *Suspension or revocation from SBA program.* SBA may suspend or revoke an SBA Lender's authority to participate in the SBA loan program, including the authority to make, service, liquidate, or litigate 7(a) or 504 loans. Section 120.1400(d)(1) sets forth the grounds for SBA program suspension or revocation of an SBA Supervised Lender (except Other Regulated SBLCs). The grounds for SBA program suspension or revocation for all other SBA Lenders are set forth in § 120.1400(c) and, as applicable, paragraph (f) of § 120.1400.

(4) *Immediate suspension.* SBA may suspend, effective immediately, an SBA Lender's delegated authority or authority to participate in the SBA loan program, or the authority to make, service, liquidate, or litigate 7(a) or 504 loans. Section 120.1400(d)(2) sets forth the grounds for SBA program immediate suspension of an SBA Supervised Lender (except Other Regulated SBLCs). The grounds for SBA program immediate suspension for all other SBA Lenders and the grounds for immediate suspension of delegated authority for all SBA Lenders are set forth in § 120.1400(c)(11) and § 120.1400(c)(12).

(5) *Debarment.* In accordance with 2 CFR Parts 180 and 2700, SBA may take any necessary action to debar a Person, as defined in § 120.10, including but not limited to an officer, a director, a

general partner, a manager, an employee, an agent or other participant in the affairs of an SBA Lender's SBA operations.

(6) *Other actions available under law.* SBA may take all other enforcement actions against SBA Lenders available under law.

(b) *Enforcement actions specific to 7(a) Lenders.* In addition to those enforcement actions applicable to all SBA Lenders, SBA may suspend or revoke a 7(a) Lender's authority to sell or purchase loans or certificates in the Secondary Market.

(c) *Enforcement actions specific to SBA Supervised Lenders and Other Persons (except Other Regulated SBLCs).* In addition to those enforcement actions listed in paragraphs (a) and (b) of this section, SBA may take any one or more of the following enforcement actions specific to SBA Supervised Lenders and as applicable, Other Persons:

(1) *Cease and desist order.* SBA may issue a cease and desist order against the SBA Supervised Lender or Other Person. The Cease and Desist order may either require the SBA Supervised Lender or the Other Person to take a specific action, or to refrain from a specific action. The Cease and Desist Order may be issued as effective immediately (or as a proposal for Order). SBA may include in the cease and desist order the suspension of authority to lend.

(2) *Remove Management Official.* SBA may issue an order to remove a Management Official from office. SBA may suspend a Management Official from office or prohibit a Management Official from participating in management of the SBA Supervised Lender or in reviewing, approving, closing, servicing, liquidating or litigating any 7(a) loan, or any other activities of the SBA Supervised Lender while the removal proceeding is pending in order to protect an SBA Supervised Lender or the interests of SBA or the United States.

(3) *Initiate request for appointment of receiver and/or other relief.* The SBA may make application to any Federal court of competent jurisdiction for the court to take exclusive jurisdiction, without notice, of an SBA Supervised Lender, and SBA shall be entitled to the appointment of a receiver of SBA's choosing to hold, administer, operate, and/or liquidate the SBA Supervised Lender; and to such injunctive or other equitable relief as may be appropriate. Without limiting the foregoing and with SBA's written consent, the receiver may take possession of the portfolio of 7(a) loans and sell such loans to a third party, and/or take possession of servicing activities of 7(a) loans and sell such servicing rights to a third party.

(4) *Civil monetary penalties for report filing failure.* SBA may seek civil penalties, in accordance with § 120.465, of not more than $5,000 a day against an SBA Supervised Lender that fails to file any regular or special report by its due date as specified by regulation or SBA written directive.

(d) *Enforcement actions specific to SBLCs.* In addition to those supervisory actions listed in paragraphs (a), (b), and (c) of this section, SBA may take the following enforcement actions specific to SBLCs.

(1) *Capital directive.* The AA/CA may issue a capital directive upon a determination that the grounds in § 120.1400(e)(1) exist. A directive may order the SBLC to:

(i) Achieve its minimum capital requirement applicable to it by a specified date;

(ii) Adhere to a previously submitted capital restoration plan (provided under § 120.462 or § 120.1055) to achieve the applicable capital requirement;

(iii) Submit and adhere to a capital restoration plan acceptable to SBA describing the means and time schedule by which the SBLC will achieve the applicable capital requirement (The SBLC must provide its capital restoration plan within 30 days from the date of the SBA order unless SBA notifies the SBLC that the plan is to be filed within a different time period. SBA may perform an on-site examination (generally within 90 days after the restoration plan is submitted) to verify the implementation of the plan and verify that the SBLC meets minimum capital requirements.);

(iv) Refrain from taking certain actions without obtaining SBA's prior written approval (Such actions may include but are not limited to: paying any dividend; retiring any equity;

maintaining a rate of growth that causes further deterioration in the capital percentage; securitizing any unguaranteed portion of its 7(a) loans; or selling participations in any of its 7(a) loans); or

(v) Undertake a combination of any of these or similar actions.

(2) *Civil action for termination.* SBA may institute a civil action to terminate the rights, privileges, and franchises of an SBLC.

(e) *Enforcement actions specific to CDCs.* In addition to those enforcement actions listed in paragraph (a) of this section, SBA may take any one or more of the following enforcement actions specific to CDCs:

(1) Require the CDC to transfer part or all of its existing 504 loan portfolio and/or part or all of its pending 504 loan applications to SBA, another CDC, or any other entity designated by SBA. Any such transfer may be on a temporary or permanent basis, in SBA's discretion; or

(2) Instruct the Central Servicing Agent to withhold payment of servicing, late and/or other fee(s) to the CDC.

(3) Apply to any Federal court of competent jurisdiction for the court to take exclusive jurisdiction, without notice, of the CDC, and SBA shall be entitled to the appointment of a receiver of SBA's choosing to hold, administer, operate and/or liquidate the CDC; and to such injunctive or other equitable relief as may be appropriate. Without limiting the foregoing and with SBA's consent, the receiver may take possession of the portfolio of 504 loans and/or pending 504 loan applications, including for the purpose of carrying out an enforcement order under paragraph (e)(1) of this section.

[73 FR 75521, Dec. 11, 2008, as amended at 82 FR 39506, Aug. 21, 2017]

§ 120.1510 Other Regulated SBLCs.

Other Regulated SBLCs are exempt from §§ 120.465, 120.1050(b), 120.1400(d), 120.1500(c), and 120.1600(b). This exemption is not intended to preclude SBA from seeking any other remedy authorized by law or equity.

[73 FR 75521, Dec. 11, 2008]

§ 120.1511 Certification and other reporting and notification requirements for Other Regulated SBLCs.

(a) *Certification.* An SBLC seeking Other Regulated SBLC status must certify to SBA in writing that its lending activities are subject to regulation by a Federal Financial Institution Regulator or state banking regulator. This certification must be executed by the chair of the board of directors of the SBLC and submitted to SBA either:

(1) Within 60 calendar days of the effective date of this section or

(2) If the SBLC becomes subject to regulation by a Federal Financial Institution Regulator or state banking regulator after the effective date of this section for any reason (e.g. license transfers), within 60 days of the date that the SBLC becomes directly examined and directly regulated by such regulator.

(b) *Contents of Certification:* This certification must include:

(1) The identity of the Federal Financial Institution Regulator or state banking regulator that regulates the lending activities of the SBLC;

(2) A statement that the Federal Financial Institution Regulator or state banking regulator identified in paragraph (b)(1) of this section regularly conducts safety and soundness examinations on the SBLC itself and not only on the SBLC's parent company or affiliate, if any; and

(3) The date of the most recent safety and soundness examination conducted on the SBLC by the Federal Financial Institution Regulator or state banking regulator. To qualify as an Other Regulated SBLC, the SBLC must have received this examination within the past 3 years of the date of certification.

(c) *Notification of examination.* An Other Regulated SBLC must notify SBA in writing each time a Federal Financial Institution Regulator or state banking regulator conducts a safety and soundness examination, and this notification must be submitted to SBA within 30 calendar days of the SBLC receiving the results of the examination. To retain its status as an Other Regulated SBLC, the Other Regulated SBLC must receive such examination, and provide the written notification to

SBA, at least once every two years following initial certification.

(d) *Report.* An Other Regulated SBLC must report in writing to SBA on its interactions with other Federal Financial Institution Regulators or state banking regulator (e.g., the results of the safety and soundness examinations and any order issued against the Other Regulated SBLC), to the extent allowed by law.

(e) *Notification of change in status.* If, for any reason, an Other Regulated SBLC becomes no longer subject to regulation by a Federal Financial Institution Regulator or state banking regulator, the Other Regulated SBLC must immediately notify SBA in writing, and the exemption provided in § 120.1510 will immediately no longer apply.

(f) *Extension of timeframes.* SBA may in its discretion extend any timeframe imposed on the SBLC under this section if the SBLC can show good cause for any delay in meeting the time requirement. The SBLC may appeal this decision to the AA/CA.

(g) *Failure to satisfy requirements.* In the event that an SBLC fails to satisfy the requirements set forth in paragraphs (a), (b), and (c) of this section, then the exemption provided in § 120.1510 will not apply to the SBLC.

[73 FR 75521, Dec. 11, 2008]

§ 120.1540 Types of enforcement actions—Intermediaries participating in the Microloan Program and NTAPs.

Upon a determination that any ground set out in § 120.1425 exists, the SBA may take in its discretion, one or more of the following enforcement actions against an Intermediary or NTAP:

(a) Suspension or pre-revocation sanctions which may include, but are not limited to:

(1) Accelerated reporting requirements;

(2) Accelerated loan repayment requirements for outstanding program debt to SBA, as applicable;

(3) Imposition of a temporary lending moratorium, as applicable; or

(4) Imposition of a temporary training moratorium.

(b) Revocation of authority to participate in the Microloan program which will include:

(1) Removal from the program;

(2) Liquidation of Intermediary's Microloan Revolving Fund and Loan Loss Reserve Fund accounts by SBA, and application of the liquidated funds to any outstanding balance owed to SBA;

(3) Payment of outstanding debt to SBA by the Intermediary;

(4) Forfeiture or repayment of any unused grant funds by the Intermediary or NTAP;

(5) Debarment of the organization from receipt of federal funds until loan and grant repayments are met; or

(6) Taking such other actions available under law.

[73 FR 75521, Dec. 11, 2008]

§ 120.1600 General procedures for enforcement actions against SBA Lenders, SBA Supervised Lenders, Other Regulated SBLCs, Management Officials, Other Persons, Intermediaries, and NTAPs.

(a) *In general.* Except as otherwise set forth for the enforcement actions listed in paragraphs (a)(6), (b) and (c) of this section, SBA will follow the procedures listed below.

(1) *SBA's notice of enforcement action.* (i) When undertaking an immediate suspension under § 120.1500(a)(4), or prior to undertaking an enforcement action set forth in § 120.1500(a), (b), and (e) and § 120.1540, SBA will issue a written notice to the affected SBA Lender, Intermediary, or NTAP identifying the proposed enforcement action or notifying it of an immediate suspension. The notice will set forth in reasonable detail the underlying facts and reasons for the proposed action or immediate suspension. If the notice is for a proposed or immediate suspension, SBA will also state the scope and term of the proposed or immediate suspension.

(ii) If a proposed enforcement action or immediate suspension is based upon information obtained from a third party other than the SBA Lender, Intermediary, NTAP or SBA, SBA's notice of proposed action or immediate suspension will provide copies of documentation received from such third party, or the name of the third party in case of oral information, unless SBA determines that there are compelling reasons not to provide such information. If compelling reasons exist, SBA will provide a summary of the information it received to the SBA Lender, Intermediary, or NTAP.

(2) *SBA Lender, Intermediary, or NTAP's opportunity to object.* (i) An SBA Lender, Intermediary, or NTAP that desires to contest a proposed enforcement action or an immediate suspension must file, within 30 calendar days of its receipt of the notice or within some other term established by SBA in its notice, a written objection with the appropriate Office of Capital Access official in accordance with Delegations of Authority or other SBA official identified in the notice. Notice will be presumed to have been received within five days of the date of the notice unless the SBA Lender, Intermediary, or NTAP can provide compelling evidence to the contrary.

(ii) The objection must set forth in detail all grounds known to the SBA Lender, Intermediary, or NTAP to contest the proposed action or immediate suspension and all mitigating factors, and must include documentation that the SBA Lender, Intermediary, or NTAP believes is most supportive of its objection. An SBA Lender, Intermediary, or NTAP must exhaust this administrative remedy in order to preserve its objection to a proposed enforcement action or an immediate suspension.

(iii) If an SBA Lender, Intermediary, or NTAP can show legitimate reasons as determined by SBA in SBA's discretion why it does not understand the reasons given by SBA in its notice of the action, the Agency will provide clarification. SBA will provide the requested clarification in writing to the SBA Lender, Intermediary, or NTAP or notify the SBA Lender, Intermediary, or NTAP in writing that SBA has determined that such clarification is not necessary. SBA, in its discretion, will further advise in writing whether the SBA Lender, Intermediary, or NTAP may have additional time to present its objection to the notice. Requests for clarification must be made to the appropriate Office of Capital Access official in accordance with Delegations of Authority in writing and received by SBA within the 30 day timeframe or the timeframe given by the notice for response.

(iv) An SBA Lender, Intermediary, or NTAP may request additional time to respond to SBA's notice if it can show that there are compelling reasons why it is not able to respond within the 30 day timeframe or the response timeframe given by the notice. If such requests are submitted to the Agency, SBA may, in its discretion, provide the SBA Lender, Intermediary, or NTAP with additional time to respond to the notice of proposed action or immediate suspension. Requests for additional time to respond must be made in writing to the appropriate Office of Capital Access official in accordance with Delegations of Authority or other official identified in the notice and received by SBA within the 30 day timeframe or the response timeframe given by the notice.

(v) Prior to the issuance of a final decision by SBA, if an SBA Lender, Intermediary, or NTAP can show that there is newly discovered material evidence which, despite the SBA Lender, Intermediary, or NTAP's exercise of due diligence, could not have been discovered within the timeframe given by SBA to respond to a notice, or that there are compelling reasons beyond the SBA Lender, Intermediary, or NTAP's control as to why it was not able to present a material fact or argument to SBA, and that the SBA Lender, Intermediary, or NTAP has been prejudiced by not being able to present such information, the SBA Lender, Intermediary, or NTAP may submit such information to SBA and request that the Agency consider such information in its final decision.

(3) *SBA's notice of final agency decision where SBA Lender, Intermediary, or NTAP filed objection to the proposed action or immediate suspension.* (i) If the affected SBA Lender, Intermediary, or NTAP files a timely written objection to a proposed enforcement action other than an immediate suspension in accordance with this section, SBA must issue a written notice of final decision to the affected SBA Lender, Intermediary, or NTAP advising whether

SBA is undertaking the proposed enforcement action and setting forth the grounds for the decision. SBA will issue such a notice of decision within 90 days of either receiving the objection or from when additional information is provided under paragraph (a)(2)(v) or (a)(3)(iii) of this section, whichever is later, unless SBA provides notice that it requires additional time.

(ii) If the affected SBA Lender, Intermediary, or NTAP files a timely written objection to a notice of immediate suspension, SBA must issue a written notice of final decision to the affected SBA Lender, Intermediary, or NTAP within 30 days of receiving the objection advising whether SBA is continuing with the immediate suspension, unless SBA provides notice that it requires additional time. If the SBA Lender, Intermediary, or NTAP submits additional information to SBA (under paragraph (a)(2)(v) or (a)(3)(iii) of this section) after submitting its objection but before SBA issues its final decision, SBA must issue its final decision within 30 days of receiving such information, unless SBA provides notice that it requires additional time.

(iii) Prior to issuing a notice of decision, SBA in its discretion can request additional information from the affected SBA Lender, Intermediary, NTAP or other parties and conduct any other investigation it deems appropriate. If SBA determines, in its discretion, to consider an untimely objection, it must issue a notice of final decision pursuant to this paragraph (a)(3).

(4) *SBA's notice of final agency decision where no filed objection or untimely objection not considered.* If SBA chooses not to consider an untimely objection or if the affected SBA Lender, Intermediary, or NTAP fails to file a written objection to a proposed enforcement action or an immediate suspension, and if SBA continues to believe that such proposed enforcement action or immediate suspension is appropriate, SBA must issue a written notice of final decision to the affected SBA Lender, Intermediary, or NTAP that SBA is undertaking one or more of the proposed enforcement actions against the SBA Lender, Intermediary, or NTAP or that an immediate suspension of the SBA Lender, Intermediary, or NTAP will continue. Such a notice of final decision need not state any grounds for the action other than to reference the SBA Lender, Intermediary, or NTAP's failure to file a timely objection, and represents the final agency decision.

(5) *Appeals.* An SBA Lender, Intermediary, or NTAP may appeal the final agency decision only in the appropriate federal district court.

(6) *Receiverships of Certified Development Companies and/or other relief.* If SBA undertakes the appointment of a receiver for a Certified Development Company and/or injunctive or other equitable relief, paragraphs (a)(1) through (5) of this section will not apply and SBA will follow the applicable procedures under Federal law to obtain such remedies and to enforce the Certified Development Company's consent and waiver in advance to those remedies.

(b) *Procedures for certain enforcement actions against SBA Supervised Lenders (except Other Regulated SBLCs) and, where applicable, Management Officials and Other Persons*—(1) *Suspension and revocation actions and cease and desist orders.* If SBA seeks to suspend or revoke loan program authority (including, the authority to make, service, liquidate, or litigate SBA loans), or issue a cease and desist order to an SBA Supervised Lender or, as applicable, Other Person, SBA will follow the procedures below in lieu of those in paragraph (a) of this section.

(i) *Show cause order and hearing.* The Administrator will serve upon the SBA Supervised Lender or Other Person an order to show cause why an order suspending or revoking the authority or why a cease and desist order should not be issued. The show cause order will contain a statement of the matters of fact and law asserted by SBA, as well as the legal authority and jurisdiction under which an administrative hearing will be held, and will set forth the place and time of the administrative hearing. The hearing will be conducted by an administrative law judge in accordance with 5 U.S.C. 554–557, 15 U.S.C. 650, and applicable sections of part 134 of this chapter. The Administrative Law Judge will issue a recommended decision based on the record.

(ii) *Witnesses.* The party calling witnesses will pay the witness the same fees and mileage paid witnesses for their appearance in U.S. courts.

(iii) *Administrator finding and order issuance.* If after the administrative hearing, or the SBA Supervised Lender's or Other Person's waiver of the administrative hearing, the Administrator determines that the order should be issued, the Administrator will issue an order to suspend or revoke authority or a cease and desist order, as applicable. The order will include a statement of findings, the grounds and reasons, and will specify the order's effective date. SBA will serve the order on the SBA Supervised Lender or Other Person. The Administrator may delegate the power to issue a cease and desist order or to suspend or revoke loan program authority only if the Administrator is unavailable and only to the Deputy Administrator.

(iv) *Judicial review.* The order constitutes a final agency action. The SBA Supervised Lender or Other Person will have 20 days from the order issuance date to file an appeal in the appropriate federal district court.

(2) *Immediate suspension or immediate cease and desist order.* If SBA undertakes an immediate suspension of authority to participate in the 7(a) loan program or immediate cease and desist order against an SBA Supervised Lender or, as applicable, Other Person, SBA will within two business days follow the procedures set forth in paragraph (b)(1) of this section.

(3) *Removal of Management Official.* If SBA undertakes the removal of a Management Official of an SBA Supervised Lender, SBA will follow the procedures below in lieu of those in paragraph (a) of this section.

(i) *Notice and hearing.* SBA will serve upon the Management Official and the SBA Supervised Lender written notice of intention to remove that includes a statement of the facts constituting the grounds and the date, time, and place for an administrative hearing. The administrative hearing will be held between 30 and 60 days from the date notice is served, unless an earlier or later date is set at the request of the Management Official for good cause shown or at the request of the Attorney General. The hearing will be conducted in accordance with 5 U.S.C. 554–557, 15 U.S.C. 650 and applicable sections of part 134 of this chapter. Failure of the Management Official to appear at the administrative hearing will constitute consent to the removal order. SBA will serve on the SBA Supervised Lender a copy of each notice that is served on a Management Official.

(ii) *Suspension from office or prohibition in participation, pending removal.* The suspension or prohibition will take effect upon service of intention to remove the Management Official or such subsequent time as the Administrator or his/her delegate deems appropriate and serves notice. It will remain in effect pending the completion of the administrative proceedings to remove and until such time as either SBA dismisses the charges in the removal notice or, if an order to remove or prohibit participation is issued, until the effective date of an order to remove or prohibit. In the case of suspension or prohibition following criminal charges, it may remain in effect until the information, indictment, or complaint is finally disposed of, or until the suspension is terminated by SBA or by order of a district court. A Management Official may appeal to the appropriate federal district court for a stay of the suspension or prohibition pending completion of the administrative hearing not later than 10 days from the suspension or prohibition's effective date.

(iii) *Decision.* SBA may issue the order of removal if the Management Official consents or is convicted of the criminal charges and the judgment is not subject to further judicial review (not including writ of habeas corpus), or if upon a record of a hearing, SBA finds that any of the notice grounds have been established. After the hearing, in the latter case, and within 30 days after SBA has notified the parties that the case has been submitted for final decision, SBA will render a decision (which includes findings of fact upon which the decision is predicated) and issue and serve an order upon each party to the proceeding. The decision will constitute final agency action.

(iv) *Effective date and judicial review.* The removal order will take effect 30 days after date of service upon the SBA

Supervised Lender and the Management Official except in case of consent which will be effective at the time specified in the order or in case of removal for conviction on criminal charges the order will be effective upon removal order service on the SBA Supervised Lender and the Management Official. The order will remain effective and enforceable, except to the extent it is stayed, modified, terminated, or set aside by Administrator or a reviewing court. The adversely affected party will have 20 days from the order issuance date to seek judicial review in the appropriate federal district court.

(4) *Receiverships, transfer of assets and servicing activities.* If SBA undertakes the appointment of a receiver for, or the transfer of assets or servicing rights of an SBA Supervised Lender and/or injunctive or other equitable relief, SBA will follow the applicable procedures under Federal law to obtain such remedies and to enforce the SBA Supervised Lender's consent and waiver in advance to those remedies.

(5) *Civil penalties for report filing failure.* If SBA seeks to impose civil penalties against an SBA Supervised Lender for failure to file a report in accordance with SBA regulations or written directive, SBA will follow the procedures set forth for enforcement actions in § 120.465.

(c) *Additional procedures for certain enforcement actions against SBLCs. Capital directive*—(1) *Notice of intent to issue capital directive.* SBA will notify an SBLC in writing of its intention to issue a directive. The notice will state:

(i) Reasons for issuance of the directive and

(ii) The proposed contents of the directive.

(2) *Response to notice.* (i) An SBLC may respond to the notice by stating why a capital directive should not be issued and/or by proposing alternative contents for the capital directive or seeking other appropriate relief. The response must include any information, mitigating circumstances, documentation, or other relevant evidence that supports its position. The response may include a plan for achieving the minimum capital requirement applicable to the SBLC. The response must be in writing and delivered to the SBA within 30 days after the date on which the SBLC received the notice. In its discretion, SBA may extend the time period for good cause. SBA may shorten the 30-day time period:

(A) When, in the opinion of SBA, the condition of the SBLC so requires, provided that the SBLC will be informed promptly of the new time period;

(B) With the consent of the SBLC; or

(C) When the SBLC already has advised SBA that it cannot or will not achieve its applicable minimum capital requirement.

(ii) Failure to respond within 30 days or such other time period as may be specified by SBA will constitute a waiver of any objections to the proposed capital directive.

(3) *Decision.* After the closing date of the SBLC's response period, or receipt of the SBLC's response, if earlier, SBA may seek additional information or clarification of the response. Thereafter, SBA will determine whether or not to issue a capital directive, and if one is to be issued, whether it should be as originally proposed or in modified form.

(4) *Issuance of a capital directive.* (i) A capital directive will be served by delivery to the SBLC. It will include, or be accompanied by, a statement of reasons for its issuance.

(ii) A capital directive is effective immediately upon its receipt by the SBLC, or upon such later date as may be specified therein, and will remain effective and enforceable until it is stayed, modified, or terminated by SBA.

(5) *Reconsideration based on change in circumstances.* Upon a change in circumstances, an SBLC may request SBA to reconsider the terms of its capital directive or may propose changes in the plan to achieve the SBLC's applicable minimum capital requirement. SBA also may take such action on its own initiative. SBA may decline to consider requests or proposals that are not based on a significant change in circumstances or are repetitive or frivolous. Pending a decision on reconsideration, the capital directive and plan will continue in full force and effect.

(6) *Relation to other administrative actions.* A capital directive may be issued in addition to, or in lieu of, any other

action authorized by law, including cease and desist proceedings. SBA also may, in its discretion, take any action authorized by law, in lieu of a capital directive, in response to an SBLC's failure to achieve or maintain the applicable minimum capital requirement.

(7) *Appeals.* The capital directive constitutes a final agency action. An SBLC may appeal the final agency decision only in the appropriate federal district court.

[73 FR 75521, Dec. 11, 2008, as amended at 82 FR 39506, Aug. 21, 2017]

Subpart J—Establishment of SBA Secondary Market Guarantee Program for First Lien Position 504 Loan Pools

SOURCE: 74 FR 56093, Oct. 30, 2009, unless otherwise noted.

§ 120.1700 Definitions used in subpart J.

504 financing. The loans made to a small business to fund a Project under the SBA's development company loan program authorized by Title V of the Small Business Investment Act of 1958.

Affiliate. A person or entity SBA determines to be an affiliate of a Program Participant pursuant to the application of the principles and guidelines set forth in § 121.103 of this Title.

Central Servicing Agent or CSA. The entity serving as SBA's central servicing agent for the Program.

Certified Development Company or CDC. An entity that meets the definition of a Certified Development Company as defined in § 120.10 of this Part.

Current. That no scheduled payment owed by an Obligor pursuant to a Pool Note is over 29 days past due.

First Lien Position 504 Loan. The financing provided by the First Lien Position 504 lender that is part of the 504 project financing.

First Lien Position 504 Loan Pool Guarantee Agreement. The agreement, in the form approved by SBA, wherein entities agree to participate in the forming of a Pool under the Program, available at *http://www.sba.gov/aboutsba/sbaprograms/elending/index.html/.*

Guide. The First Lien Position 504 Loan Pooling Program Guide published by SBA which provides information applicable to the Program including, among other things, requirements relating to the formation of a Pool, available at *http://www.sba.gov/aboutsba/sbaprograms/elending/index.html/.*

Liquidation Proceeds. Cash, including insurance proceeds, proceeds of any foreclosed-on property disposition, revenues received with respect to the conservation and disposition of a foreclosed-on property or repossessed collateral, including any real property securing the Pool Loan, consisting of a commercial property or residential property and any improvements thereon, and any other amounts received in connection with the liquidation of the Pool Loan, whether through Seller's sale, foreclosure sale, any offset or workout, or otherwise.

Loan Interest. The right to receive the owned portion of the principal balance of the Pool Loan together with interest thereon at a per annum rate in effect from time to time in accordance with the First Lien Position 504 Loan Pool Guarantee Agreement.

Maturity. The maturity of the Loan Interest in the Pool that has the longest remaining term of any Loan Interest in the Pool. The maturity will change from time to time due to prepayment or default on Loan Interests in the Pool.

Ongoing Guarantee Fee. An annual fee collected monthly and based on the percentage of the Pool Loan amount, pursuant to section 503(C)(3)(B)(ii) of the Recovery Act, to result in a cost of the loan guarantee of zero as determined under the Federal Credit Reform Act of 1990, as amended. The funds generated by the fee serve as a reserve to pay for program losses.

Obligor. The obligor(s) under a Pool Note.

Pool. The aggregate of Loan Interests formed into a single pool by the Pool Originator in accordance with the Program. The Pool is comprised of an unguaranteed portion and an SBA-guaranteed portion. The unguaranteed portion of the Pool backs the Pool Originator Receipt, and cannot be sold to Pool Investors. The SBA-guaranteed portion of the Pool backs the Pool Certificates sold to Pool Investors. The

Seller's Loan Interest is not included in the Pool.

Pool Assembler. An entity that meets the qualifications of a Pool Assembler as set forth in section 120.630 of this Part and has been approved as such by SBA.

Pool Certificate. The document representing a beneficial fractional interest in the SBA-guaranteed portion of a Pool.

Pooled. When one or more Loan Interests in a Pool Loan has been put into a Pool.

Pooling. The transfer of one or more Loan Interests in a Pool Loan into a Pool.

Pool Investor. An entity which holds a Pool Certificate in accordance with Program Rules and Regulations.

Pool Loan. A loan that meets the Program eligibility requirements as set forth in § 120.1704 of this subpart J and has been pooled.

Pool Loan Receivables. Pool Loan payments, prepayments, or collections made in connection with the Pool Loan by the Obligor pursuant to Pool Note or any other Pool Loan documents or agreements, or by another person or entity made on behalf of any such Pool Loan obligor, and Liquidation Proceeds.

Pool Note. The document evidencing a Pool Loan.

Pool Originator. An entity approved by SBA to pool Loan Interests under the Program.

Pool Originator Receipt. The document evidencing the Pool Originator's retained ownership in a Pool it has formed under the Program.

Premier Certified Lenders Program. The program defined in § 120.845 of this Part.

Program. The program authorized by section 503 of the American Recovery and Reinvestment Act of 2009.

Program Participant. An entity that executes the First Lien Position 504 Loan Pool Guarantee Agreement as Seller, Pool Originator, or Pool Investor, and any successors or assignees thereof.

Program Participant Associate. (1) An officer, director, key employee, or holder of 20 percent or more of the value of a Program Participant's stock or debt instruments, or (2) Any individual in which one or more individuals referred to in paragraph (1) of this definition, or a spouse, or child, or sibling, or the spouse of any such individual, owns or controls at least 20 percent.

Program Preference. Any arrangement giving the Seller, Pool Originator, or a Program Associate or Affiliate of Seller or Pool Originator, a preference or benefit of proportion greater than its Loan Interest as compared to Pool Originator, Pool Investor, or SBA relating to the making, servicing, or liquidation of the Loan with respect to such things as repayment, collateral, guarantees, control, maintenance of a compensating balance, purchase of a certificate of deposit or acceptance of a separate or companion loan, without SBA's consent. Seller's agreement to grant a Pool Loan's Obligor a deferment in return for receiving more collateral on a different loan owned by Seller is an example of a preference.

Program Rules and Regulations. This subpart J, as may be amended from time to time by SBA (the Program Regulations), the First Lien Position 504 Loan Pool Guarantee Agreement, any other Program agreements signed by a Program Participant, if applicable, the Guide, the Recovery Act, and the provisions of subpart H governing Third Party Loans and Third Party Lenders.

Project. A project as defined by § 120.802 of the Part.

SBA. The United States Small Business Administration, an agency of the United States Government.

Seller. An entity that has sold a Pool Loan to a Pool Originator to be Pooled and any successor entity that has executed the First Lien Position 504 Loan Pool Guaranty Agreement pursuant to § 120.1707.

Seller's Pool Loan. The Pool Loan sold to a Pool Originator pursuant to the First Lien Position 504 Loan Pool Guarantee Agreement.

Seller Receipt. The document that evidences a Seller's Loan Interest.

Servicing Retention Amount. The amount of a Pool Loan interest payment retained by Seller for servicing the Pool Loan that is payable and calculated pursuant to the First Lien Position 504 Loan Pool Guarantee Agreement.

Weighted Average Interest Rate. The dollar-weighted average interest rate of a Pool Certificate calculated by multiplying the interest rate of each Loan Interest in the Pool by the ratio of that Loan Interest's current outstanding principal in the SBA-guaranteed portion of the Pool (that is, the portion of the Pool Loan backing the Pool Certificates) to the current aggregate or outstanding principal of each Loan Interest in the SBA-guaranteed portion of the Pool, and adding the sum of the resulting products. The Pool Certificate interest rate will fluctuate over the life of the Pool as defaults, prepayments and normal repayments applicable to Loan Interests in the Pool occur.

Weighted Average Maturity. The weighted average maturity of a Pool Certificate is a dollar weighted average maturity that is calculated by multiplying the remaining term, in months, of each Loan Interest in a Pool by the ratio of that Loan Interest's current outstanding pooled principal to the current aggregate outstanding pooled principal of all Loan Interests in the Pool, and adding the sum of the resulting products. The weighted average maturity of a Pool Certificate will fluctuate over the life of the Pool as Loan Interest defaults, prepayments and normal Loan Interest repayments occur.

§ 120.1701 Program purpose.

As authorized by the American Recovery and Reinvestment Act of 2009 (Recovery Act), SBA establishes the Program to authorize an entity to apply for SBA's guarantee of Pools comprised of portions of First Lien Position 504 Loans backing Pool Certificates to be sold to Pool Investors. The purpose of the Program is to temporarily provide a federal guarantee for Pools of First Lien Position 504 Loans to facilitate the sale of such loans and increase the liquidity of the lenders holding the loans so that the lenders can use the sale proceeds to fund more such loans. The Program's authorization expires on September 23, 2012 and the Administrator may guarantee not more than $3,000,000,000 of pools under this authority pursuant to section 503(c)(B)(iii) of the Recovery Act, as amended by section 1119 of the Small Business Jobs Act of 2010.

[61 FR 3235, Jan. 31, 1996, as amended at 76 FR 63547, Oct. 12, 2011]

§ 120.1702 Program fee.

Ongoing Guarantee Fee. The Ongoing Guarantee Fee is payable to SBA, and it is calculated and payable monthly from the amounts received in respect of interest on Loan Interests in the SBA-guaranteed portion of a Pool. This amount is set forth in the First Lien Position 504 Loan Pool Guarantee Agreement. This fee is used to pay program losses.

§ 120.1703 Qualifications to be a Pool Originator.

(a) *Application to become Pool Originator*. The application to become a Pool Originator is available from the SBA and can be found on SBA's website. In order to qualify as a Pool Originator, an entity must send the application to the SBA and certify that it is a Pool Assembler or it:

(1) Is regulated by the appropriate agency as defined in section 3(a)(34)(G) of the Securities Exchange Act of 1934 (15 U.S.C. 78c(a)(34)(G));

(2) Meets all financial and other applicable requirements of its regulatory authority and the Government Securities Act of 1986, as amended (Pub. L. 99–571, 100 Stat. 3208);

(3) Has the financial capability to originate acceptable pools consisting of eligible First Lien Position 504 Loans in sufficient quantity to support the issuance of Pool Certificates;

(4) Is in good standing with SBA (as the SBA determines), and is Satisfactory with the Office of the Comptroller of the Currency (OCC) if it is a national bank, the Federal Deposit Insurance Corporation if it is a bank not regulated by the OCC, the Financial Institutions Regulatory Authority if it is a member, the National Credit Union Administration if it is a credit union, as determined by SBA; and

(5) for any Pool Originator that is an SBA Lender, that the SBA Lender has satisfactory SBA performance, as determined by SBA in its sole discretion.

(b) *Approval by SBA*. An entity may not submit applications to form Pools to the CSA until SBA has approved its application to become a Pool Originator.

(c) *Conduct of business by Pool Originator.* An entity continues to qualify as a Pool Originator so long as it:

(1) Meets the eligibility standards in paragraph (a) of this section;

(2) Conducts its business in accordance with SBA regulations and accepted securities or banking industry practices, ethics, and standards;

(3) Maintains its books and records in accordance with generally accepted accounting principles or in accordance with the guidelines of the regulatory body governing its activities; and

(4) Has not been suspended or terminated from the Program by SBA.

[74 FR 56093, Oct. 30, 2009, as amended at 82 FR 39506, Aug. 21, 2017]

§ 120.1704 Pool Loans eligible for Pooling.

(a) *General Pool Loan eligibility requirements.* For a First Lien Position 504 Loan to be eligible for Pooling it must:

(1) Be a loan that is:

(i) A Third Party Loan as defined in § 120.801(c)(3);

(ii) Made by a private sector lender acceptable to SBA in its sole discretion; and

(iii) Secured by a first lien on the Project Property as defined in § 120.801 of this chapter;

(2) Be part of a 504 financing that is comprised of only one Third Party Loan and one CDC 504 loan; the CDC 504 loan must be funded by a Debenture that was been sold on or after February 17, 2009;

(3) Be Current and have been Current for the six-month-period immediately prior to the date the Pool is formed or for the life of the Pool Loan, whichever time period is shorter;

(4) Have been made and closed in a commercially reasonable manner, consistent with prudent lending standards;

(5) Be part of a completed 504 financing, funded by a 504 debenture, which means that the Pool Loan must be fully disbursed and the debenture funding the related loan by a CDC must have been sold on or after February 17, 2009; and

(6) Not be:

(i) To a business deriving more than one-third of its gross annual revenue from legal gambling activities;

(ii) To a casino, gambling establishment, or casino hotel;

(iii) For financing the acquisition, construction or renovation of an aquarium, zoo, golf course, or swimming pool; or

(iv) To a business covered by a six-digit North American Industry Classification System (NAICS) code for casinos—713210 ("Casinos (Except Casino Hotels)"); casino hotels—721120 ("Casino Hotels"); other gambling institutions—713290 ("Other Gambling Industries"); golf courses—713910 ("Golf Courses and Country Clubs"); or aquariums and zoos—712130 ("Zoos and Botanical Gardens").

(b) *SBA review of a Pool Loan prior to pool formation.* SBA has the right to review any Pool Loan before a Loan Interest in it is added to a Pool, and SBA may prohibit the Pool's formation as proposed based on SBA's review in SBA's sole discretion. In the event SBA decides to review Pool Loan documents related to a Loan Interest prior to the requested Pool formation, that Loan Interest may not be added to the Pool until SBA reviews and approves the Pool Loan for such purpose. Copies of Pool Loan documents related to underwriting and origination, and any other Pool Loan-related documents SBA may, in its sole discretion, request to review in writing, must be sent to SBA's Sacramento Pool Loan Processing Center. The Pool Originator must identify and SBA must review Pool Loan documents before a Loan Interest is added to a Pool if:

(1) The Pool Loan is to a business within NAICS code 713940 covering Fitness and Recreational Sports Centers; (If SBA determines that a Pool Loan has had any of its proceeds used for any of the restricted purposes listed above, the Pool Loan will be prohibited from being part of a Pool.)

(2) The Pool Loan was part of a 504 financing involving a 504 loan that was processed under SBA's Premier Certified Lenders Program; or

(3) The Project the Pool Loan financed included the refinancing of existing debt owed to the Seller or Third

Party Lender (not including interim financing associated with the Project).

§ 120.1705 Pool formation requirements.

(a) *Initiation of Pool formation.* Only an entity approved by SBA to be a Pool Originator under the Program that continues to qualify to be a Pool Originator pursuant to this subpart may initiate the formation of a Pool. The Pool Originator creates the Pool subject to Program Rules and Regulations, including the parameters set forth in the Guide, and SBA approval.

(b) *Adjustment of Pool requirements.* SBA may adjust the Pool characteristics periodically based on program experience and market conditions and will publish a revised version of the Guide in the FEDERAL REGISTER to implement such adjustments. Any such adjustments shall not affect Pools formed prior to the adjustment.

(c) *When the Pool Originator is the Seller.* When a Pool Originator proposes to form a Pool involving a Pool Loan it owns, it must execute the First Lien Position 504 Loan Pool Guarantee Agreement as Pool Originator and as Seller and, consequently, will be subject to all applicable Program Rules and Regulations pertaining to both roles.

(d) *When the Pool Originator does not own the Pool Loan.* When a Pool Originator proposes to form a Pool involving a Pool Loan it does not own, it must purchase the Loan Interest it proposes to pool from a Seller that owns the whole Pool Loan and that has the servicing rights. The Pool Originator must purchase the Loan Interest and take it into inventory or settle the purchase of the Loan Interest through the CSA concurrently with the formation of the Pool. The entity selling the Loan Interest to the Pool Originator must execute the First Lien Position 504 Loan Pool Guarantee Agreement as Seller and, consequently, will be subject to all applicable Program Rules and Regulations pertaining to a Seller. The Pool Originator must also execute the First Lien Position 504 Loan Pool Guaranty Agreement.

(e) *What CSA must receive prior to Pool formation.* Before the CSA may carry out its responsibilities relating to the formation of a Pool, it must receive:

(1) From the Pool Originator: A properly completed First Lien Position 504 Loan Pool application form, First Lien Position 504 Loan Guarantee Agreement, and any other documentation which SBA may require, if applicable; and

(2) All cost reimbursement due and payable to the CSA prior to Pool formation owed by the Participants participating in the formation of the Pool.

§ 120.1706 Pool Originator's retained interest in Pool.

The Pool Originator must retain an ownership interest in any Pool it has formed that is equal to at least 5% of the aggregate of the total outstanding principal balance of each Pool Loan with a Loan Interest in the Pool as calculated at the time of Pool formation. Such interest will decline with Loan Interest payments, prepayments, defaults and any other early termination. At Pool formation, the CSA will issue the Pool Originator a Pool Originator Receipt evidencing the Pool Originator's retained interest in the Pool. The Pool Originator may not sell, pledge, participate, or otherwise transfer its Pool Originator Receipt or any interest therein for the life of the Pool.

§ 120.1707 Seller's retained Loan Interest.

The Seller must retain a 15% or greater Loan Interest in each of its loans included in a Pool. At Pool formation, the CSA will issue the Seller a Seller Receipt evidencing the Seller's retained ownership in the Pool Loan. With SBA's written permission, the Seller may sell the Seller Receipt and Servicing Retention Amount in whole, but not in part, to a single entity at one time. The Seller may not sell less than 100% of the Seller Receipt and Servicing Retention Amount, and may not sell a participation interest in any portion of any of its Pooled loans. In addition, in order to complete such sale, Seller must have the purchaser of its rights to the Pool Loan execute an allonge to the Seller's First Lien Position 504 Loan Pool Guarantee Agreement in a form acceptable to SBA, acknowledging and accepting all terms of the Seller's First Lien Position 504 Loan Pool Guarantee Agreement, and deliver the executed original allonge and a copy of the corresponding First Lien Position 504 Loan Pool Guarantee Agreement to the CSA. All Pool Loan payments related to a Seller Receipt and Servicing Retention Amount proposed for sale will be withheld by the CSA pending SBA acknowledgement of receipt of all executed documents required to complete the transfer.

[74 FR 56093, Oct. 30, 2009, as amended at 82 FR 39506, Aug. 21, 2017]

§ 120.1708 Pool Certificates.

(a) *SBA Guarantee of Pool Certificates.* SBA guarantees to a Pool Investor the timely payment of principal and interest installments and any prepayment or other recovery of principal to which the Pool Investor is entitled. If an Obligor misses a scheduled payment pursuant to the terms of the Pool Note underlying a Loan Interest backing a Pool Certificate, SBA, through the CSA, will make advances to maintain the schedule of interest and principal payments to the Pool Investor. If SBA makes such payments, it is subrogated fully to the rights satisfied by such payment.

(b) *SBA guarantee backed by full faith and credit.* SBA's guarantee of the Pool Certificate is backed by the full faith and credit of the United States.

(c) *SBA purchase of a Loan Interest.* SBA will determine whether to purchase a Loan Interest backing a Pool Certificate with an underlying Pool Note that is 60 days or more in arrears. SBA reserves the right to purchase a Loan Interest from a Pool at any time.

(d) *Self-liquidating.* A Pool Certificate represents a fractional beneficial interest in a Pool that is self-liquidating by Pool Loan Receivables and/or SBA Loan Interest payment or redemption.

(e) *Pool Certificate form.* The CSA prepares the Pool Certificate. SBA must approve the form and terms of the Pool Certificate.

(f) *Pool Certificate registration.* A Pool Certificate must be registered with the CSA.

(g) *Face amount of Pool Certificate.* The face amount of a Pool Certificate cannot be less than a minimum amount as specified in the Guide, and the dollar amount of Pool Certificates must be in increments which SBA will specify in the Guide (except for one Pool Certificate for each Pool). SBA may change these requirements based upon an analysis of market conditions and program experience, and will publish any such change in the FEDERAL REGISTER.

(h) *Basis of payment for Pool Certificates.* All payments on a Pool Certificate are due pursuant to terms, conditions, and percentages set forth or referenced therein and are based on the unpaid principal balance of the Pool represented by the Pool Certificate. Any Pool Loan Receivables applicable to a Loan Interest in the SBA-guaranteed portion of a Pool will be passed through to the appropriate Pool Investors with the regularly scheduled payments to such Pool Investors.

(i) *Pool Certificate interest rate.* A Pool Certificate must have a Weighted Average Interest Rate.

(j) *Pool Certificate maturity.* A Pool Certificate must have a Maturity and a Weighted Average Maturity.

(k) *Early Pool Certificate redemption.* SBA, or the CSA on behalf of SBA, may redeem a Pool Certificate prior to its Maturity because of Obligor prepayment and/or SBA purchase of all Loan Interests in the Pool backing the Pool Certificate.

§ 120.1709 Transfers of Pool Certificates.

(a) *Transfer of Pool Certificates.* A Pool Certificate is transferable. A transfer of a Pool Certificate must comply with Article 8 of the Uniform Commercial Code of the State of New York. The seller may use any form of assignment acceptable to SBA and the CSA. The CSA may refuse to issue a Pool Certificate until it is satisfied that the documents of transfer are complete.

(b) *Transfer on CSA records.* In order for the transfer of a Pool Certificate to be effective, the CSA must reflect the transfer on its records.

(c) *Contents of letter of transmittal for Pool Certificate.* A letter of transmittal must accompany each Pool Certificate which a Pool Investor submits to the CSA for transfer. The Pool Investor must supply the following information in the letter:

(1) Pool number;

(2) Pool Certificate number;

(3) Name of purchaser of Pool Certificate;

(4) Address and tax identification number of the purchaser;

(5) Name, e-mail address and telephone number of the person handling or facilitating the transfer; and

(6) Instructions for the delivery of the new Pool Certificate.

(d) *CSA transfer cost recovery.* At the same time a Pool Investor submits a letter of transmittal for a Pool Certificate pursuant to this section, it must send to the CSA sufficient funds to cover its cost for this service. The CSA will supply the transfer information to the Pool Investor.

§ 120.1710 Central servicing of the Program.

(a) *Pool Certificates and Receipts issued at Pool formation.* As part of its role as Central Servicing Agent for the Pool, at Pool formation, CSA issues a Seller Receipt to the Seller, a Pool Originator Receipt to the Pool Originator, and a Pool Certificate to each Pool Investor.

(b) *CSA fiscal transfer responsibilities.* All Pool Loan Receivables on a Pool Loan received by the CSA must be forwarded by it to pay the Servicing Retention Amount, Ongoing Guarantee Fee, Seller Receipt, Pool Originator Receipt, Pool Certificates, any SBA-purchased Loan Interest, and any other payment applicable to the Pooling of such Pooled Loan, in accordance with Program Rules and Regulations.

(c) *Administration of the Pool Certificates.* CSA must administer each Pool Certificate. It shall maintain a registry of Pool Investors and other information as SBA requires. CSA registers all Pool Certificates. This means it issues, transfers title to, and redeems them. It shall maintain a registry of Pool Investors and other information as SBA requires. In fulfilling its obligation to keep the central registry current, the CSA may, with SBA's approval, obtain any necessary information from the parties involved in the Program.

(d) *CSA Monthly Report.* CSA must provide SBA with a list, by Pool, of each Loan Interest with an underlying Pool Note that is 60 days or more in arrears on a monthly basis.

§ 120.1711 Suspension or termination of Program participation privileges.

(a) *Participant suspension or termination.* The SBA may suspend or terminate the privilege of a Participant, and/or any Associate or Affiliate of the Participant, to sell, purchase, broker, or deal in Pool Loans, Loan Interests, or Pool Certificates under the Program if any such Participant or its Associate or Affiliate has:

(1) Failed to comply materially with any requirement imposed by the Program Rules and Regulations or other SBA rules and regulations; or

(2) Made a material false statement or failed to disclose a material fact to SBA.

(b) *Additional rules for suspension or termination of Pool Originator.* In addition to the conditions set forth in paragraph (a) above, SBA may also suspend or terminate the Program participation privileges of a Pool Originator if the Pool Originator (and/or its Associates):

(1) Does not comply with any of the requirements in 120.1703(a) or (c);

(2) Has been revoked or suspended it from engaging in the securities business by its supervisory agency, or is under investigation for a practice which SBA considers, in its sole discretion, to be relevant to its fitness to participate in the Program;

(3) Has been indicted or otherwise formally charged with, or convicted of, a felony, or a misdemeanor which, in SBA's sole discretion, bears on its fitness to participate in the Program;

(4) Has received an adverse civil judgment that it has committed a breach of trust or a violation of a law or regulation protecting the integrity of business transactions or relationships; or

(5) Has been suspended or terminated as a Pool Assembler under 120.631.

(c) *Suspension procedures.* SBA may undertake suspension or enforcement actions under this section using the procedures set forth in § 120.1600(a).

§ 120.1712 Seller responsibilities with respect to Seller's Pool Loan.

Seller shall remain obligated for servicing and liquidating Seller's Pool Loan until the Pool Loan is repaid in full unless SBA provides written approval or notice to the contrary.

§ 120.1713 Seller's Pool Loan origination.

SBA is entitled to recover from the Seller losses incurred by SBA on its guarantee of a Pool if such losses resulted because Seller's Pool Loan was not made and closed in a commercially reasonable manner, consistent with prudent lending standards, and in accordance with any applicable Program Rules and Regulations.

§ 120.1714 Seller's Pool Loan servicing.

Subject to § 120.1718 of this subpart J, the Seller must service Seller's Pool Loan in a commercially reasonable manner, consistent with prudent lending standards, and in accordance with applicable Program Rules and Regulations. The Seller receives the Servicing Retention Amount for servicing the Seller's Pool Loan.

§ 120.1715 Seller's Pool Loan liquidation.

Subject to § 120.1718 of this subpart J, the Seller must liquidate and conduct debt collection litigation for Seller's Pool Loan in a prompt, cost-effective and commercially reasonable manner, consistent with prudent lending standards, in accordance with applicable Program Rules and Regulations, and with SBA approval of a liquidation plan and any litigation plan, and any amendment of either such a plan, if applicable.

§ 120.1716 Required SBA approval of servicing actions.

Seller shall not, without prior written consent of SBA, take the following actions with respect to Seller's Pool Loan:

(a) Make or consent to any substantial alteration in the terms ("substantial" includes, but is not limited to, any changes to the principal amount or interest rate);

(b) Accelerate the maturity;

(c) Sue; or

(d) Waive or release any claim. Guidance on other servicing actions, some of which may need prior SBA approval, is provided in the Guide.

§ 120.1717 Seller's Pool Loan deferments.

Without the prior written consent of SBA, Seller, at the request of Obligor, may grant one deferment of Obligor's scheduled payments for a continuous period not to exceed three months of past or future installments. Seller shall immediately notify CSA of any payment deferment and that notification shall include:

(a) The SBA Pool Loan number;

(b) The Obligor's name;

(c) The terms of such deferment;

(d) The date Obligor is to resume payment; and

(e) Reconfirmation of the basis of interest calculation (e.g. 30/360 or Actual Days/365).

§ 120.1718 SBA's right to assume Seller's responsibilities.

SBA may, in its sole discretion, undertake the servicing, liquidation and/or litigation of Seller's Pool Loan at any time and, in such event, Seller must take any steps necessary to facilitate the assumption by SBA of such responsibilities, which can be transferred by SBA at its discretion to a contractor, agent or other entity, and such steps shall include, among other things, providing or assigning to SBA any documents requested by SBA within 15 calendar days of Seller's receipt of such request. SBA will notify the Obligor of the change in servicing.

§ 120.1719 SBA's right to recover from Seller.

SBA is entitled to recover from Seller any monies paid on SBA's guarantee of a Pool Certificate backed in part by Seller's Pool Loan, plus interest, if SBA in its sole discretion determines that any of the following events has occurred:

(a) Seller's improper action or inaction has put SBA at risk;

(b) Seller has failed to disclose a material fact to SBA regarding a Seller's Pool Loan in a timely manner;

(c) Seller has misrepresented a material fact to SBA regarding Seller's Pool Loan;

(d) Seller has failed to comply materially with § 120.1720 of this subpart;

(e) SBA has received a written request from Seller to terminate the

SBA's guarantee on the Loan Interest in Seller's Pool Loan;

(f) Seller has failed to comply materially with Program Rules and Regulations; or

(g) Seller has failed to make, close, service or liquidate Seller's Pool Loan in a prudent manner.

§ 120.1720 SBA's right to review Pool Loan documents.

In the event that SBA purchases a Loan Interest in Seller's Pool Loan, Seller must provide to SBA copies of the Pool Loan collateral documents, Pool Loan underwriting documents, and any other documents SBA may require in writing within 15 calendar days of a written request from SBA (which SBA will review in connection with its efforts to determine if Seller is obligated to reimburse SBA pursuant to this subpart). A Seller's failure to provide the requested documentation may constitute a material failure to comply with the Program Rules and Regulations and may lead to an action for recovery under § 120.1719. SBA will also evaluate a Seller's continued participation in the Program and may restrict further sales under the Program until SBA determines that the Seller has provided sufficient documentation.

§ 120.1721 SBA's right to investigate.

SBA may undertake such investigation as it deems necessary to determine whether it is entitled to seek recovery from the Seller and Seller agrees to take whatever actions are necessary to facilitate such investigation.

§ 120.1722 SBA's offset rights.

SBA shall have the right to offset any amount owed by Lender to SBA, including, without limitation, an offset against CSA's obligation to pay Lender pursuant to any Section 504 First Mortgage Loan Pool Guarantee Agreement.

§ 120.1723 Pool Loan receivables received by Seller.

Any Pool Loan Receivables received by Seller in connection with obligations under Seller's Pool Loan must be forwarded by Seller to CSA within two business days of receipt of collected funds.

§ 120.1724 Servicing and liquidation expenses.

All ordinary and reasonable expenses of servicing and liquidating Seller's Pool Loan shall be paid by, or be recoverable from, Obligor, and all such ordinary and reasonable expenses incurred by Seller or SBA which are not recoverable from Obligor shall be shared ratably by Seller, SBA, and the Pool Originator pursuant to the applicable percentages set forth in the First Lien Position 504 Loan Pool Guarantee Agreement.

§ 120.1725 No Program Preference by Seller or Pool Originator.

The Seller and the Pool Originator must not establish a Program Preference, which is defined in 13 CFR 120.10.

§ 120.1726 Pool Certificates a Seller cannot purchase.

Neither a Seller, nor any of its Program Associates or Affiliates, may purchase a Pool Certificate that is backed by a Loan Interest in a Pool Loan that the Seller, or any of its Program Associates or Affiliates, originated or owned, and, in the event such purchase occurs, SBA's guarantee shall not be in effect with respect to any such Pool Certificate.

PART 121—SMALL BUSINESS SIZE REGULATIONS

Subpart A—Size Eligibility Provisions and Standards

PROVISIONS OF GENERAL APPLICABILITY

Sec.

121.110 What must a concern do in order to be identified as a small business concern in any Federal procurement databases?

SIZE STANDARDS USED TO DEFINE SMALL BUSINESS CONCERNS

121.201 What size standards has SBA identified by North American Industry Classification System codes?

SIZE ELIGIBILITY REQUIREMENTS FOR SBA FINANCIAL ASSISTANCE

121.301 What size standards and affiliation principles are applicable to financial assistance programs?
121.302 When does SBA determine the size status of an applicant?
121.303 What size procedures are used by SBA before it makes a formal size determination?
121.304 What are the size requirements for refinancing an existing SBA loan?
121.305 What size eligibility requirements exist for obtaining financial assistance relating to particular procurements?

SIZE ELIGIBILITY REQUIREMENTS FOR GOVERNMENT PROCUREMENT

121.401 What procurement programs are subject to size determinations?
121.402 What size standards are applicable to Federal Government Contracting programs?
121.403 Are SBA size determinations and NAICS code designations binding on parties?
121.404 When is the size status of a business concern determined?
121.405 May a business concern self-certify its small business size status?
121.406 How does a small business concern qualify to provide manufactured products or other supply items under a small business set-aside, service-disabled veteran-owned small business, HUBZone, WOSB or EDWOSB, or 8(a) contract?
121.407 What are the size procedures for multiple item procurements?
121.408 What are the size procedures for SBA's Certificate of Competency Program?
121.409 What size standard applies in an unrestricted procurement for Certificate of Competency purposes?
121.410 What are the size standards for SBA's Section 8(d) Subcontracting Program?
121.411 What are the size procedures for SBA's Section 8(d) Subcontracting Program?
121.412 What are the size procedures for partial small business set-asides?
121.413 [Reserved]

SIZE ELIGIBILITY REQUIREMENTS FOR SALES OR LEASE OF GOVERNMENT PROPERTY

121.501 What programs for sales or leases of Government property are subject to size determinations?
121.502 What size standards are applicable to programs for sales or leases of Government property?
121.503 Are SBA size determinations binding on parties?
121.504 When does SBA determine the size status of a business concern?
121.505 What is the effect of a self-certification?
121.506 What definitions are important for sales or leases of Government-owned timber?
121.507 What are the size standards and other requirements for the purchase of Government-owned timber (other than Special Salvage Timber)?
121.508 What are the size standards and other requirements for the purchase of Government-owned Special Salvage Timber?
121.509 What is the size standard for leasing of Government land for coal mining?
121.510 What is the size standard for leasing of Government land for uranium mining?
121.511 What is the size standard for buying Government-owned petroleum?
121.512 What is the size standard for stockpile purchases?

SIZE ELIGIBILITY REQUIREMENTS FOR THE 8(a) BUSINESS DEVELOPMENT PROGRAM

121.601 What is a small business for purposes of admission to SBA's 8(a) Business Development program?
121.602 At what point in time must a 8(a) BD applicant be small?
121.603 How does SBA determine whether a Participant is small for a particular 8(a) BD subcontract?
121.604 Are 8(a) BD Participants considered small for purposes of other SBA assistance?

SIZE AND ELIGIBILITY REQUIREMENTS FOR THE SMALL BUSINESS INNOVATION RESEARCH (SBIR) AND SMALL BUSINESS TECHNOLOGY TRANSFER (STTR) PROGRAMS

121.701 What SBIR and STTR programs are subject to size and eligibility determinations and what definitions are important?
121.702 What size and eligibility standards are applicable to the SBIR and STTR programs?
121.703 Are formal size determinations binding on parties?
121.704 When does SBA determine the size and eligibility status of a business concern?
121.705 Must a business concern self-certify its size and eligibility status?

AUTHORITY: 15 U.S.C. 632, 634(b)(6), 662, and 694a(9).

SOURCE: 61 FR 3286, Jan. 31, 1996, unless otherwise noted.

EDITORIAL NOTE: Nomenclature changes to part 121 appear at 72 FR 50039 and 50040, Aug. 30, 2007.

Subpart A—Size Eligibility Provisions and Standards

PROVISIONS OF GENERAL APPLICABILITY

§ 121.101 What are SBA size standards?

(a) SBA's size standards define whether a business entity is small and, thus, eligible for Government programs and preferences reserved for "small business" concerns. Size standards have been established for types of economic activity, or industry, generally under the North American Industry Classification System (NAICS).

(b) NAICS is described in the North American Industry Classification Manual–United States, which is available from the National Technical Information Service, 5285 Port Royal Road, Springfield, VA 22161; by calling 1(800) 553–6847 or 1(703) 605–6000; or via the Internet at *http://www.ntis.gov/products/naics.aspx*. The manual includes definitions for each industry, tables showing relationships between 1997 NAICS and 1987 SICs, and a comprehensive index. NAICS assigns codes to all economic activity within twenty broad sectors. Section 121.201 provides a full table of small business size standards matched to the U.S. NAICS industry codes. A full table matching a size standard with each NAICS Industry or U.S. Industry code is also published annually by SBA in the FEDERAL REGISTER.

[65 FR 30840, May 15, 2000, as amended at 67 FR 52602, Aug. 13, 2002; 74 FR 46313, Sept. 9, 2009]

§ 121.102 How does SBA establish size standards?

(a) SBA considers economic characteristics comprising the structure of an industry, including degree of competition, average firm size, start-up costs and entry barriers, and distribution of firms by size. It also considers technological changes, competition from other industries, growth trends, historical activity within an industry, unique factors occurring in the industry which may distinguish small firms from other firms, and the objectives of its programs and the impact on those programs of different size standard levels.

(b) As part of its review of a size standard, SBA will investigate if any concern at or below a particular standard would be dominant in the industry. SBA will take into consideration market share of a concern and other appropriate factors which may allow a concern to exercise a major controlling influence on a national basis in which a number of business concerns are engaged. Size standards seek to ensure that a concern that meets a specific size standard is not dominant in its field of operation.

(c) As part of its review of size standards, SBA's Office of Size Standards will examine the impact of inflation on monetary-based size standards (e.g., receipts, net income, assets) at least once every five years and submit a report to the Administrator or designee. If SBA finds that inflation has significantly eroded the value of the monetary-based size standards, it will issue a proposed rule to increase size standards.

(d) Please address any requests to change existing size standards or establish new ones for emerging industries to the Division Chief, Office of Size Standards, Small Business Administration, 409 3rd Street, SW., Washington, DC 20416.

(e) When SBA publishes a final rule in the FEDERAL REGISTER revising, modifying, or establishing a size standard, SBA will include in the final rule, an instruction that interested persons may file a petition for reconsideration of a revised, modified, or established size standard at SBA's Office of Hearings and Appeals (OHA) within 30 calendar days after publication of the final rule in accordance with 15 U.S.C. 632(a)(9) and part 134, subpart I of this chapter. The instruction will provide the mailing address, facsimile number, and email address of OHA.

(f) Within 14 calendar days after a petition for reconsideration of a size standard is filed, unless it appears OHA will dismiss the petition for reconsideration, SBA will publish a document in the FEDERAL REGISTER announcing the size standard or standards that have been challenged, the FEDERAL REGISTER citation of the final rule, the assigned OHA docket number, and the date of the close of record. The document will further state that interested parties may contact OHA to intervene in the dispute pursuant to § 134.906 of this chapter.

(g) Where OHA grants a petition for reconsideration of a size standard that had been revised or modified, OHA will remand the case to SBA's Office of Size Standards for further action in accordance with § 134.916(a) of this chapter.

[61 FR 3286, Jan. 31, 1996, as amended at 67 FR 3045, Jan. 23, 2002; 82 FR 25506, June 2, 2017]

§ 121.103 How does SBA determine affiliation?

(a) *General Principles of Affiliation.* (1) Concerns and entities are affiliates of each other when one controls or has the power to control the other, or a third party or parties controls or has the power to control both. It does not matter whether control is exercised, so long as the power to control exists.

(2) SBA considers factors such as ownership, management, previous relationships with or ties to another concern, and contractual relationships, in determining whether affiliation exists.

(3) Control may be affirmative or negative. Negative control includes, but is not limited to, instances where a minority shareholder has the ability, under the concern's charter, by-laws, or shareholder's agreement, to prevent

a quorum or otherwise block action by the board of directors or shareholders.

(4) Affiliation may be found where an individual, concern, or entity exercises control indirectly through a third party.

(5) In determining whether affiliation exists, SBA will consider the totality of the circumstances, and may find affiliation even though no single factor is sufficient to constitute affiliation.

(6) In determining the concern's size, SBA counts the receipts, employees, or other measure of size of the concern whose size is at issue and all of its domestic and foreign affiliates, regardless of whether the affiliates are organized for profit.

(7) For SBA's Small Business Innovation Research (SBIR) and Small Business Technology Transfer (STTR) programs, the bases for affiliation are set forth in § 121.702.

(8) For applicants in SBA's Business Loan, Disaster Loan, and Surety Bond Guarantee Programs, the size standards and bases for affiliation are set forth in § 121.301.

(b) *Exceptions to affiliation coverage.* (1) Business concerns owned in whole or substantial part by investment companies licensed, or development companies qualifying, under the Small Business Investment Act of 1958, as amended, are not considered affiliates of such investment companies or development companies.

(2)(i) Business concerns owned and controlled by Indian Tribes, Alaska Native Corporations (ANCs) organized pursuant to the Alaska Native Claims Settlement Act (43 U.S.C. 1601 *et seq.*), Native Hawaiian Organizations (NHOs), Community Development Corporations (CDCs) authorized by 42 U.S.C. 9805, or wholly-owned entities of Indian Tribes, ANCs, NHOs, or CDCs are not considered affiliates of such entities.

(ii) Business concerns owned and controlled by Indian Tribes, ANCs, NHOs, CDCs, or wholly-owned entities of Indian Tribes, ANCs, NHOs, or CDCs, are not considered to be affiliated with other concerns owned by these entities because of their common ownership or common management. In addition, affiliation will not be found based upon the performance of common administrative services so long as adequate payment is provided for those services. Affiliation may be found for other reasons.

(A) Common administrative services which are subject to the exception to affiliation include, bookkeeping, payroll, recruiting, other human resource support, cleaning services, and other duties which are otherwise unrelated to contract performance or management and can be reasonably pooled or otherwise performed by a holding company, parent entity, or sister business concern without interfering with the control of the subject firm.

(B) Contract administration services include both services that could be considered "common administrative services" under the exception to affiliation and those that could not.

(*1*) Contract administration services that encompass actual and direct day-to-day oversight and control of the performance of a contract/project are not shared common administrative services, and would include tasks or functions such as negotiating directly with the government agency regarding proposal terms, contract terms, scope and modifications, project scheduling, hiring and firing of employees, and overall responsibility for the day-to-day and overall project and contract completion.

(*2*) Contract administration services that are administrative in nature may constitute administrative services that can be shared, and would fall within the exception to affiliation. These administrative services include tasks such as record retention not related to a specific contract (*e.g.*, employee time and attendance records), maintenance of databases for awarded contracts, monitoring for regulatory compliance, template development, and assisting accounting with invoice preparation as needed.

(C) Business development may include both services that could be considered "common administrative services" under the exception to affiliation and those that could not. Efforts at the holding company or parent level to identify possible procurement opportunities for specific subsidiary companies may properly be considered "common administrative services" under the exception to affiliation. However, at some point the opportunity identified by the holding company's or parent entity's business development efforts becomes concrete enough to assign to a subsidiary and at that point the subsidiary must be involved in the business development efforts for such opportunity. At the proposal or bid preparation stage of business development, the appropriate subsidiary company for the opportunity has been identified and a representative of that company must be involved in preparing an appropriate offer. This does not mean to imply that one or more representatives of a holding company or parent entity cannot also be involved in preparing an offer. They may be involved in assisting with preparing the generic part of an offer, but the specific subsidiary that intends to ultimately perform the contract must control the technical and contract specific portions of preparing an offer. In addition, once award is made, employee assignments and the logistics for contract performance must be controlled by the specific subsidiary company and should not be performed at a holding company or parent entity level.

(3) Business concerns which are part of an SBA approved pool of concerns for a joint program of research and development or for defense production as authorized by the Small Business Act are not affiliates of one another because of the pool.

(4) Business concerns which lease employees from concerns primarily engaged in leasing employees to other businesses or which enter into a co-employer arrangement with a Professional Employer Organization (PEO) are not affiliated with the leasing company or PEO solely on the basis of a leasing agreement.

(5) For financial, management or technical assistance under the Small Business Investment Act of 1958, as amended, (an applicant is not affiliated with the investors listed in paragraphs (b)(5) (i) through (vi) of this section.

(i) Venture capital operating companies, as defined in the U.S. Department of Labor regulations found at 29 CFR 2510.3–101(d);

(ii) Employee benefit or pension plans established and maintained by the Federal government or any state, or their political subdivisions, or any agency or instrumentality thereof, for the benefit of employees;

(iii) Employee benefit or pension plans within the meaning of the Employee Retirement Income Security Act of 1974, as amended (29 U.S.C. 1001, *et seq.*);

(iv) Charitable trusts, foundations, endowments, or similar organizations exempt from Federal income taxation under section 501(c) of the Internal Revenue Code of 1986, as amended (26 U.S.C. 501(c));

(v) Investment companies registered under the Investment Company Act of 1940, as amended (1940 Act) (15 U.S.C. 80a-1, *et seq.*); and

(vi) Investment companies, as defined under the 1940 Act, which are not registered under the 1940 Act because they are beneficially owned by less than 100 persons, if the company's sales literature or organizational documents indicate that its principal purpose is investment in securities rather than the operation of commercial enterprises.

(6) A firm that has an SBA-approved mentor-protégé agreement authorized under § 124.520 or § 125.9 of this chapter is not affiliated with its mentor firm solely because the protégé firm receives assistance from the mentor under the agreement. Similarly, a protégé firm is not affiliated with its mentor solely because the protégé firm receives assistance from the mentor under a federal mentor-protégé program where an exception to affiliation is specifically authorized by statute or by SBA under the procedures set forth in § 121.903. Affiliation may be found in either case for other reasons as set forth in this section.

(7) The member shareholders of a small agricultural cooperative, as defined in the Agricultural Marketing Act (12 U.S.C. 1141j), are not considered affiliated with the cooperative by virtue of their membership in the cooperative.

(8) These exceptions to affiliation and any others set forth in § 121.702 apply for purposes of SBA's SBIR and STTR programs.

(9) In the case of a solicitation for a bundled contract, a small business contractor may enter into a Small Business Teaming Arrangement with one or more small business subcontractors and submit an offer as a small business without regard to affiliation, so long as each team member is small for the size standard assigned to the contract or subcontract. The agency shall evaluate the offer in the same manner as other offers with due consideration of the capabilities of the subcontractors.

(c) *Affiliation based on stock ownership.* (1) A person (including any individual, concern or other entity) that owns, or has the power to control, 50 percent or more of a concern's voting stock, or a block of voting stock which is large compared to other outstanding blocks of voting stock, controls or has the power to control the concern.

(2) If two or more persons (including any individual, concern or other entity) each owns, controls, or has the power to control less than 50 percent of a concern's voting stock, and such minority holdings are equal or approximately equal in size, and the aggregate of these minority holdings is large as compared with any other stock holding, SBA presumes that each such person controls or has the power to control the concern whose size is at issue. This presumption may be rebutted by a showing that such control or power to control does not in fact exist.

(3) If a concern's voting stock is widely held and no single block of stock is large as compared with all other stock holdings, the concern's Board of Directors and CEO or President will be deemed to have the power to control the concern in the absence of evidence to the contrary.

(d) *Affiliation arising under stock options, convertible securities, and agreements to merge.* (1) In determining size, SBA considers stock options, convertible securities, and agreements to merge (including agreements in principle) to have a present effect on the power to control a concern. SBA treats such options, convertible securities, and agreements as though the rights granted have been exercised.

(2) Agreements to open or continue negotiations towards the possibility of a merger or a sale of stock at some later date are not considered "agreements in principle" and are thus not given present effect.

(3) Options, convertible securities, and agreements that are subject to conditions precedent which are incapable of fulfillment, speculative, conjectural, or unenforceable under state or Federal law, or where the probability of the transaction (or exercise of the rights) occurring is shown to be extremely remote, are not given present effect.

(4) An individual, concern or other entity that controls one or more other concerns cannot use options, convertible securities, or agreements to appear to terminate such control before actually doing so. SBA will not give present effect to individuals', concerns' or other entities' ability to divest all or part of their ownership interest in order to avoid a finding of affiliation.

(e) *Affiliation based on common management.* Affiliation arises where one or more officers, directors, managing members, or partners who control the board of directors and/or management of one concern also control the board of directors or management of one or more other concerns.

(f) *Affiliation based on identity of interest.* Affiliation may arise among two or more persons with an identity of interest. Individuals or firms that have identical or substantially identical business or economic interests (such as family members, individuals or firms with common investments, or firms that are economically dependent through contractual or other relationships) may be treated as one party with such interests aggregated. Where SBA determines that such interests should be aggregated, an individual or firm may rebut that determination with evidence showing that the interests deemed to be one are in fact separate.

(1) Firms owned or controlled by married couples, parties to a civil union, parents, children, and siblings are presumed to be affiliated with each other if they conduct business with each other, such as subcontracts or joint ventures or share or provide loans, resources, equipment, locations or employees with one another. This presumption may be overcome by

showing a clear line of fracture between the concerns. Other types of familial relationships are not grounds for affiliation on family relationships.

(2) SBA may presume an identity of interest based upon economic dependence if the concern in question derived 70% or more of its receipts from another concern over the previous three fiscal years.

(i) This presumption may be rebutted by a showing that despite the contractual relations with another concern, the concern at issue is not solely dependent on that other concern, such as where the concern has been in business for a short amount of time and has only been able to secure a limited number of contracts.

(ii) A business concern owned and controlled by an Indian Tribe, ANC, NHO, CDC, or by a wholly-owned entity of an Indian Tribe, ANC, NHO, or CDC, is not considered to be affiliated with another concern owned by that entity based solely on the contractual relations between the two concerns.

Example 1 to paragraph (f). Firm A has been in business for 9 months and has two contracts. Contract 1 is with Firm B and is valued at $900,000 and Contract 2 is with Firm C and is valued at $200,000. Thus, Firm B accounts for over 70% of Firm A's receipts. Absent other connections between A and B, the presumption of affiliation between A and B is rebutted because A is a new firm.

Example 2 to paragraph (f). Firm A has been in business for five years. It has over 200 contracts. Of that 200, 195 are with Firm B, and the value of those contracts is greater than 70% of the revenue over the previous three years. In this case, SBA would most likely find the two firms affiliated unless the firm could provide some other compelling rebuttal to the very strong presumption that it should be considered affiliated with Firm B.

(g) *Affiliation based on the newly organized concern rule.* Affiliation may arise where former officers, directors, principal stockholders, managing members, or key employees of one concern organize a new concern in the same or related industry or field of operation, and serve as the new concern's officers, directors, principal stockholders, managing members, or key employees, and the one concern is furnishing or will furnish the new concern with contracts, financial or technical assistance, indemnification on bid or performance bonds, and/or other facilities, whether for a fee or otherwise. A concern may rebut such an affiliation determination by demonstrating a clear line of fracture between the two concerns. A "key employee" is an employee who, because of his/her position in the concern, has a critical influence in or substantive control over the operations or management of the concern.

(h) *Affiliation based on joint ventures.* A joint venture is an association of individuals and/or concerns with interests in any degree or proportion consorting to engage in and carry out no more than three specific or limited-purpose business ventures for joint profit over a two year period, for which purpose they combine their efforts, property, money, skill, or knowledge, but not on a continuing or permanent basis for conducting business generally. This means that a specific joint venture entity generally may not be awarded more than three contracts over a two year period, starting from the date of the award of the first contract, without the partners to the joint venture being deemed affiliated for all purposes. Once a joint venture receives one contract, SBA will determine compliance with the three awards in two years rule for future awards as of the date of initial offer including price. As such, an individual joint venture may be awarded more than three contracts without SBA finding general affiliation between the joint venture partners where the joint venture had received two or fewer contracts as of the date it submitted one or more additional offers which thereafter result in one or more additional contract awards. The same two (or more) entities may create additional joint ventures, and each new joint venture entity may be awarded up to three contracts in accordance with this section. At some point, however, such a longstanding inter-relationship or contractual dependence between the same joint venture partners will lead to a finding of general affiliation between and among them. For purposes of this provision and in order to facilitate tracking of the number of contract awards made to a joint venture, a joint venture: Must be in writing and must do business under its own name; must be identified as a joint venture in the System for Award Management (SAM); may be in the form of a formal or informal partnership or exist as a separate limited liability company or other separate legal entity; and, if it exists as a formal separate legal entity, may not be populated with individuals intended to perform contracts awarded to the joint venture (*i.e.*, the joint venture may have its own separate employees to perform administrative functions, but may not have its own separate employees to perform contracts awarded to the joint venture). SBA may also determine that the relationship between a prime contractor and its subcontractor is a joint venture, and that affiliation between the two exists, pursuant to paragraph (h)(5) of this section. For purposes of this paragraph (h), contract refers to prime contracts, and any subcontract in which the joint venture is treated as a similarly situated entity as the term is defined in part 125 of this chapter.

Example 1 to paragraph (h) introductory text. Joint Venture AB has received two contracts. On April 2, Joint Venture AB submits an offer for Solicitation 1. On June 6, Joint Venture AB submits an offer for Solicitation 2. On July 13, Joint Venture AB submits an offer for Solicitation 3. In September, Joint Venture AB is found to be the apparent successful offeror for all three solicitations. Even though the award of the three contracts would give Joint Venture AB a total of five contract awards, it could receive those awards without causing general affiliation between its joint venture partners because Joint Venture AB had not yet received three contract awards as of the dates of the offers for each of three solicitations at issue.

Example 2 to paragraph (h) introductory text. Joint Venture XY receives a contract on December 19, year 1. It may receive two additional contracts through December 19, year 3. On August 6, year 2, XY receives a second contract. It receives no other contract awards through December 19, year 3 and has submitted no additional offers prior to December 19, year 3. Because two years have passed since the date of the first contract award, after December 19, year 3, XY cannot receive an additional contract award. The individual parties to XY must form a new joint venture if they want to seek and be awarded additional contracts as a joint venture.

Example 3 to paragraph (h) introductory text. Joint Venture XY receives a contract on December 19, year 1. On May 22, year 2, XY submits an offer for Solicitation 1. On June 10, year 2, XY submits an offer for Solicitation 2. On June 19, year 2, XY receives a second contract responding to Solicitation 1. XY is not awarded a contract responding to Solicitation 2. On December 15, year 3, XY submits an offer for Solicitation 3. In January, XY is found to be the apparent successful offeror for Solicitation 3. XY is eligible for the contract award because compliance with the three awards in two years rule is determined as of the date of the initial offer including price, XY submitted its offer prior to December 19, year 3, and XY had not received three contract awards prior to its offer on December 15.

(1) Parties to a joint venture are affiliates if any one of them seeks SBA financial assistance for use in connection with the joint venture.

(2) Except as provided in paragraph (h)(3) of this section, concerns submitting offers on a particular procurement or property sale as joint venturers are affiliated with each other with regard to the performance of that contract.

(3) *Exception to affiliation for certain joint ventures.* (i) A joint venture of two or more business concerns may submit an offer as a small business for a Federal procurement, subcontract or sale so long as each concern is small under the size standard corresponding to the NAICS code assigned to the contract.

(ii) Two firms approved by SBA to be a mentor and protégé under § 125.9 of this chapter may joint venture as a small business for any Federal government prime contract or subcontract, provided the protégé qualifies as small for the size standard corresponding to the NAICS code assigned to the procurement, and the joint venture meets the requirements of §§ 124.513 (c) and (d), §§ 125.8(b) and (c), §§ 125.18(b)(2) and (3), §§ 126.616(c) and (d), or §§ 127.506(c) and (d) of this chapter, as appropriate.

(iii) Two firms approved by SBA to be a mentor and protégé under § 124.520 of these regulations may joint venture as a small business for any Federal government prime contract or subcontract, provided the protégé qualifies as small for the size standard corresponding to the NAICS code assigned to the procurement and, for purposes of 8(a) sole source requirements, has not reached the dollar limit set forth in § 124.519 of these regulations. If the procurement is to be awarded through the 8(a) BD program, SBA must approve the joint venture pursuant to § 124.513.

If the procurement is to be awarded other than through the 8(a) BD program (*e.g.*, small business set aside, HUBZone set aside), SBA need not approve the joint venture prior to award, but if the size status of the joint venture is protested, the provisions of §§ 124.513(c) and (d) will apply. This means that the joint venture must meet the requirements of §§ 124.513(c) and (d) in order to receive the exception to affiliation authorized by this paragraph. In either case, after contract performance is complete, the 8(a) partner to the joint venture must submit a report to its servicing SBA district office explaining how the applicable performance of work requirements were met for the contract.

(4) A contractor and its ostensible subcontractor are treated as joint venturers, and therefore affiliates, for size determination purposes. An ostensible subcontractor is a subcontractor that is not a similarly situated entity, as that term is defined in § 125.1 of this chapter, and performs primary and vital requirements of a contract, or of an order, or is a subcontractor upon which the prime contractor is unusually reliant. All aspects of the relationship between the prime and subcontractor are considered, including, but not limited to, the terms of the proposal (such as contract management, technical responsibilities, and the percentage of subcontracted work), agreements between the prime and subcontractor (such as bonding assistance or the teaming agreement), and whether the subcontractor is the incumbent contractor and is ineligible to submit a proposal because it exceeds the applicable size standard for that solicitation.

(5) For size purposes, a concern must include in its receipts its proportionate share of joint venture receipts, and in its total number of employees its proportionate share of joint venture employees.

(i) *Affiliation based on franchise and license agreements.* The restraints imposed on a franchisee or licensee by its franchise or license agreement relating to standardized quality, advertising, accounting format and other similar provisions, generally will not be considered in determining whether the franchisor or licensor is affiliated with the franchisee or licensee provided the franchisee or licensee has the right to profit from its efforts and bears the risk of loss commensurate with ownership. Affiliation may arise, however, through other means, such as common ownership, common management or excessive restrictions upon the sale of the franchise interest.

[61 FR 3286, Jan. 31, 1996]

EDITORIAL NOTE: For FEDERAL REGISTER citations affecting § 121.103, see the List of CFR Sections Affected, which appears in the Finding Aids section of the printed volume and at *www.govinfo.gov*.

§ 121.104 How does SBA calculate annual receipts?

(a) *Receipts* means all revenue in whatever form received or accrued from whatever source, including from the sales of products or services, interest, dividends, rents, royalties, fees, or commissions, reduced by returns and allowances. Generally, receipts are considered "total income" (or in the case of a sole proprietorship "gross income") plus "cost of goods sold" as these terms are defined and reported on Internal Revenue Service (IRS) tax return forms (such as Form 1120 for corporations; Form 1120S and Schedule K for S corporations; Form 1120, Form 1065 or Form 1040 for LLCs; Form 1065 and Schedule K for partnerships; Form 1040, Schedule F for farms; Form 1040, Schedule C for other sole proprietorships). Receipts do not include net capital gains or losses; taxes collected for and remitted to a taxing authority if included in gross or total income, such as sales or other taxes collected from customers and excluding taxes levied on the concern or its employees; proceeds from transactions between a concern and its domestic or foreign affiliates; and amounts collected for another by a travel agent, real estate agent, advertising agent, conference management service provider, freight forwarder or customs broker. For size determination purposes, the only exclusions from receipts are those specifically provided for in this paragraph. All other items, such as subcontractor costs, reimbursements for purchases a contractor makes at a customer's request, investment income, and employee-based costs such as payroll taxes, may not be excluded from receipts.

(1) The Federal income tax return and any amendments filed with the IRS on or before the date of self-certification must be used to determine the size status of a concern. SBA will not use tax returns or amendments filed with the IRS after the initiation of a size determination.

(2) When a concern has not filed a Federal income tax return with the IRS for a fiscal year which must be included in the period of measurement, SBA will calculate the concern's annual receipts for that year using any other available information, such as the concern's regular books of account, audited financial statements, or information contained in an affidavit by a person with personal knowledge of the facts.

(b) *Completed fiscal year* means a taxable year including any short year. "Taxable year" and "short year" have the meanings attributed to them by the IRS.

(c) *Period of measurement.* (1) Annual receipts of a concern that has been in business for three or more completed fiscal years means the total receipts of the concern over its most recently completed three fiscal years divided by three.

(2) Annual receipts of a concern which has been in business for less than three complete fiscal years means the total receipts for the period the concern has been in business divided by the number of weeks in business, multiplied by 52.

(3) Where a concern has been in business three or more complete fiscal years but has a short year as one of the years within its period of measurement, annual receipts means the total receipts for the short year and the two full fiscal years divided by the total number of weeks in the short year and the two full fiscal years, multiplied by 52.

(d) *Annual receipts of affiliates.* (1) The average annual receipts size of a business concern with affiliates is calculated by adding the average annual receipts of the business concern with the average annual receipts of each affiliate.

(2) If a concern has acquired an affiliate or been acquired as an affiliate during the applicable period of measurement or before the date on which it self-certified as small, the annual receipts used in determining size status includes the receipts of the acquired or acquiring concern. Furthermore, this aggregation applies for the entire period of measurement, not just the period after the affiliation arose.

(3) If the business concern or an affiliate has been in business for a period of less than three years, the receipts for the fiscal year with less than a 12 month period are annualized in accordance with paragraph (c)(2) of this section. Receipts are determined for the concern and its affiliates in accordance with paragraph (c) of this section even though this may result in using a different period of measurement to calculate an affiliate's annual receipts.

(4) The annual receipts of a former affiliate are not included if affiliation ceased before the date used for determining size. This exclusion of annual receipts of a former affiliate applies during the entire period of measurement, rather than only for the period after which affiliation ceased.

(e) Unless otherwise defined in this section, all terms shall have the meaning attributed to them by the IRS.

[61 FR 3286, Jan. 31, 1996, as amended at 65 FR 48604, Aug. 9, 2000; 69 FR 29203, May 21, 2004; 81 FR 34258, May 31, 2016]

§ 121.105 How does SBA define "business concern or concern"?

(a)(1) Except for small agricultural cooperatives, a business concern eligible for assistance from SBA as a small business is a business entity organized for profit, with a place of business located in the United States, and which operates primarily within the United States or which makes a significant contribution to the U.S. economy through payment of taxes or use of American products, materials or labor.

(2) A small agricultural cooperative is an association (corporate or otherwise) acting pursuant to the provisions of the Agricultural Marketing Act (12 U.S.C.A. 1141j) whose size does not exceed the size standard established by

SBA for other similar agricultural small business concerns. A small agricultural cooperative's member shareholders are not considered to be affiliates of the cooperative by virtue of their membership in the cooperative. However, a business concern or cooperative that does not qualify as small under this part may not be a member of a small agricultural cooperative.

(b) A business concern may be in the legal form of an individual proprietorship, partnership, limited liability company, corporation, joint venture, association, trust or cooperative, except that where the form is a joint venture there can be no more than 49 percent participation by foreign business entities in the joint venture.

(c) A firm will not be treated as a separate business concern if a substantial portion of its assets and/or liabilities are the same as those of a predecessor entity. In such a case, the annual receipts and employees of the predecessor will be taken into account in determining size.

[61 FR 3286, Jan. 31, 1996, as amended at 70 FR 51248, Aug. 30, 2005]

§ 121.106 How does SBA calculate number of employees?

(a) In determining a concern's number of employees, SBA counts all individuals employed on a full-time, part-time, or other basis. This includes employees obtained from a temporary employee agency, professional employee organization or leasing concern. SBA will consider the totality of the circumstances, including criteria used by the IRS for Federal income tax purposes, in determining whether individuals are employees of a concern. Volunteers (*i.e.*, individuals who receive no compensation, including no in-kind compensation, for work performed) are not considered employees.

(b) Where the size standard is number of employees, the method for determining a concern's size includes the following principles:

(1) The average number of employees of the concern is used (including the employees of its domestic and foreign affiliates) based upon numbers of employees for each of the pay periods for the preceding completed 12 calendar months.

(2) Part-time and temporary employees are counted the same as full-time employees.

(3) If a concern has not been in business for 12 months, the average number of employees is used for each of the pay periods during which it has been in business.

(4)(i) The average number of employees of a business concern with affiliates is calculated by adding the average number of employees of the business concern with the average number of employees of each affiliate. If a concern has acquired an affiliate or been acquired as an affiliate during the applicable period of measurement or before the date on which it self-certified as small, the employees counted in determining size status include the employees of the acquired or acquiring concern. Furthermore, this aggregation applies for the entire period of measurement, not just the period after the affiliation arose.

(ii) The employees of a former affiliate are not counted if affiliation ceased before the date used for determining size. This exclusion of employees of a former affiliate applies during the entire period of measurement, rather than only for the period after which affiliation ceased.

[61 FR 3286, Jan. 31, 1996, as amended at 69 FR 29203, May 21, 2004]

§ 121.107 How does SBA determine a concern's "primary industry"?

In determining the primary industry in which a concern or a concern combined with its affiliates is engaged, SBA considers the distribution of receipts, employees and costs of doing business among the different industries in which business operations occurred for the most recently completed fiscal year. SBA may also consider other factors, such as the distribution of patents, contract awards, and assets.

§ 121.108 What are the penalties for misrepresentation of size status?

(a) *Presumption of Loss Based on the Total Amount Expended.* In every contract, subcontract, cooperative agreement, cooperative research and development agreement, or grant which is set aside, reserved, or otherwise classified as intended for award to small business concerns, there shall be a presumption of loss to the United States based on the total amount expended on the contract, subcontract, cooperative agreement, cooperative research and development agreement, or grant whenever it is established that a business concern other than a small business concern willfully sought and received the award by misrepresentation.

(b) *Deemed Certifications*. The following actions shall be deemed affirmative, willful and intentional certifications of small business size and status:

(1) Submission of a bid, proposal, application or offer for a Federal grant, contract, subcontract, cooperative agreement, or cooperative research and development agreement reserved, set aside, or otherwise classified as intended for award to small business concerns.

(2) Submission of a bid, proposal, application or offer for a Federal grant, contract, subcontract, cooperative agreement or cooperative research and development agreement which in any way encourages a Federal agency to classify the bid or proposal, if awarded, as an award to a small business concern.

(3) Registration on any Federal electronic database for the purpose of being considered for award of a Federal grant, contract, subcontract, cooperative agreement, or cooperative research and development agreement, as a small business concern.

(c) *Signature Requirement*. Each offer, proposal, bid, or application for a Federal contract, subcontract, or grant shall contain a certification concerning the small business size and status of a business concern seeking the Federal contract, subcontract or grant. An authorized official must sign the certification on the same page containing the size status claimed by the concern.

(d) *Limitation of Liability*. Paragraphs (a) through (c) of this section may be determined not to apply in the case of unintentional errors, technical malfunctions, and other similar situations that demonstrate that a misrepresentation of size was not affirmative, intentional, willful or actionable under the False Claims Act, 31 U.S.C. §§ 3729, et seq. A prime contractor acting in good faith should not be held liable for misrepresentations made by its subcontractors regarding the subcontractors' size. Relevant factors to consider in making this determination may include the firm's internal management procedures governing size representation or certification, the clarity or ambiguity of the representation or certification requirement, and the efforts made to correct an incorrect or invalid representation or certification in a timely manner. An individual or firm may not be held liable where government personnel have erroneously identified a concern as small without any representation or certification having been made by the concern and where such identification is made without the knowledge of the individual or firm.

(e) *Penalties for Misrepresentation*. (1) *Suspension or debarment*. The SBA suspension and debarment official or the agency suspension and debarment official may suspend or debar a person or concern for misrepresenting a firm's size status pursuant to the procedures set forth in 48 CFR subpart 9.4.

(2) *Civil Penalties*. Persons or concerns are subject to severe penalties under the False Claims Act, 31 U.S.C. 3729–3733, the Program Fraud Civil Remedies Act, 31 U.S.C. 3801–3812 and any other applicable laws or regulations, including 13 CFR part 142.

(3) *Criminal Penalties*. Persons or concerns are subject to severe criminal penalties for knowingly misrepresenting the small business size status of a concern in connection with procurement programs pursuant to section 16(d) of the Small Business Act, 15 U.S.C. 645(d), as amended, 18 U.S.C. 1001, 18 U.S.C. 287, and any other applicable laws. Persons or concerns are subject to criminal penalties for knowingly making false statements or misrepresentations to SBA for the purpose of influencing any actions of SBA pursuant to section 16(a) of the Small Business Act, 15 U.S.C. 645(a), as amended, including failure to correct "continuing representations" that are no longer true.

(4) *Limitation on Liability*. An individual or business concern will not be subject to the penalties imposed under 15 U.S.C. 645(a) where it acted in good

faith reliance on a small business status advisory opinion accepted by SBA under § 121.109.

[78 FR 38816, June 28, 2013, as amended at 80 FR 7536, Feb. 11, 2015; 81 FR 31491, May 19, 2016]

§ 121.109 What is a small business status advisory opinion?

(a) *Defined.* A small business status advisory opinion is a written opinion issued by either a Small Business Development Center (SBDC) operating under part 130 of this chapter or a Procurement Technical Assistance Center (PTAC) operating under 10 U.S.C. chapter 142 which concludes that a firm is entitled to represent itself as a small business concern for purposes of federal government procurement opportunities.

(b) *Submission.* An SBDC or PTAC must submit a copy of each small business status advisory opinion it issues to the following Agency official for review: Associate General Counsel, Office of Procurement Law, U.S. Small Business Administration, 409 Third Street SW., Washington, DC 20416 or by fax to (202) 205–6390 marked Attn: Small Business Status Advisory Opinion. A small business status advisory opinion must:

(1) Provide a written analysis explaining the reasoning underlying the SBDC or PTAC's determination that the covered concern, along with its affiliates, either does or does not exceed the size standard(s). This analysis must be dated and signed by an SBDC or PTAC business counselor or similarly qualified individual.

(2) Include, as an attachment, a completed copy of an SBA Form 355 for the covered concern and its affiliates.

(3) Include, as an attachment, copies of the evidence (such as payroll records, time sheets, federal income tax returns, etc.) provided by the covered concern to the SBDC or PTAC clearly documenting its annual receipts and/or number of employees as those terms are defined by §§ 121.104 and 121.106.

(c) *Review.* Unless a referral is made under paragraph (e) of this section, SBA will decide within 10 business days of receiving a small business status advisory opinion to accept or reject it based on its consistency with part 121. SBA will provide written notification of that decision to the SBDC or PTAC that issued the small business status advisory opinion as well as to the covered concern.

(d) *Reliance.* A concern that receives a small business status advisory opinion holding that it does not exceed the applicable size standard(s) may rely upon that determination for purposes of responding to Federal procurement opportunities from the date it is issued unless and until that advisory opinion is rejected by SBA in accordance with paragraph (c) of this section or the concern undergoes a significant change in its ownership, management, or other factors bearing on its status as a small business concern. However, the firm's size may be protested by interested parties in connection with a specific procurement.

(e) *Referral for size determination.* Nothing in this section precludes the Associate General Counsel, Office of Procurement Law from requesting a formal size determination for a concern that is the subject of a small business status advisory opinion pursuant to § 121.1001(b)(9).

(f) *Penalties for misrepresentation*—(1) *Suspension or debarment.* The SBA suspension and debarment official may suspend or debar a person or concern for misrepresenting a concern's size for purposes of obtaining a small business size status advisory opinion pursuant to the procedures set forth in 48 CFR subpart 9.4.

(2) *Civil penalties.* Persons or concerns are subject to severe penalties under the False Claims Act, 31 U.S.C. 3729–3733, and under the Program Fraud Civil Remedies Act, 331 U.S.C. 3801–3812, and any other applicable laws.

(3) *Criminal Penalties.* Persons or concerns are subject to severe criminal penalties for knowingly misrepresenting the small business size status of a concern in connection with procurement programs pursuant to section 16(d) of the Small Business Act, 15 U.S.C. 645(d), as amended, 18 U.S.C. 1001, 18 U.S.C. 287, and any other applicable laws. Persons or concerns are subject to criminal penalties for knowingly making false statements or misrepresentations for the purpose of influencing any actions of SBA pursuant

to section 16(a) of the Small Business Act, 15 U.S.C. 645(a), as amended, including failure to correct "continuing representations" that are no longer true.

[80 FR 7536, Feb. 11, 2015]

§ 121.110 What must a concern do in order to be identified as a small business concern in any Federal procurement databases?

(a) In order to be identified as a small business concern in the System for Award Management (SAM) database (or any successor thereto), a concern must certify its size in connection with specific size standards at least annually.

(b) If a firm identified as a small business concern in SAM fails to certify its size within one year of a size certification, the firm will not be listed as a small business concern in SAM, unless and until the firm recertifies its size.

[78 FR 38817, June 28, 2013. Redesignated at 80 FR 7536, Feb. 11, 2015.]

Size Standards Used To Define Small Business Concerns

§ 121.201 What size standards has SBA identified by North American Industry Classification System codes?

The size standards described in this section apply to all SBA programs unless otherwise specified in this part. The size standards themselves are expressed either in number of employees or annual receipts in millions of dollars, unless otherwise specified. The number of employees or annual receipts indicates the maximum allowed for a concern and its affiliates to be considered small.

Small Business Size Standards by NAICS Industry

NAICS codes	NAICS U.S. industry title	Size standards in millions of dollars	Size standards in number of employees
Sector 11—Agriculture, Forestry, Fishing and Hunting			
Subsector 111—Crop Production			
111110	Soybean Farming	$0.75	
111120	Oilseed (except Soybean) Farming	$0.75	
111130	Dry Pea and Bean Farming	$0.75	
111140	Wheat Farming	$0.75	
111150	Corn Farming	$0.75	
111160	Rice Farming	$0.75	
111191	Oilseed and Grain Combination Farming	$0.75	
111199	All Other Grain Farming	$0.75	
111211	Potato Farming	$0.75	
111219	Other Vegetable (except Potato) and Melon Farming	$0.75	
111310	Orange Groves	$0.75	
111320	Citrus (except Orange) Groves	$0.75	
111331	Apple Orchards	$0.75	
111332	Grape Vineyards	$0.75	
111333	Strawberry Farming	$0.75	
111334	Berry (except Strawberry) Farming	$0.75	
111335	Tree Nut Farming	$0.75	
111336	Fruit and Tree Nut Combination Farming	$0.75	
111339	Other Noncitrus Fruit Farming	$0.75	
111411	Mushroom Production	$0.75	
111419	Other Food Crops Grown Under Cover	$0.75	
111421	Nursery and Tree Production	$0.75	
111422	Floriculture Production	$0.75	
111910	Tobacco Farming	$0.75	
111920	Cotton Farming	$0.75	
111930	Sugarcane Farming	$0.75	
111940	Hay Farming	$0.75	
111991	Sugar Beet Farming	$0.75	
111992	Peanut Farming	$0.75	
111998	All Other Miscellaneous Crop Farming	$0.75	
Subsector 112—Animal Production and Aquaculture			
112111	Beef Cattle Ranching and Farming	$0.75	
112112	Cattle Feedlots	$7.5	
112120	Dairy Cattle and Milk Production	$0.75	

SMALL BUSINESS SIZE STANDARDS BY NAICS INDUSTRY—Continued

NAICS codes	NAICS U.S. industry title	Size standards in millions of dollars	Size standards in number of employees
112210	Hog and Pig Farming	$0.75	
112310	Chicken Egg Production	$15.0	
112320	Broilers and Other Meat Type Chicken Production	$0.75	
112330	Turkey Production	$0.75	
112340	Poultry Hatcheries	$0.75	
112390	Other Poultry Production	$0.75	
112410	Sheep Farming	$0.75	
112420	Goat Farming	$0.75	
112511	Finfish Farming and Fish Hatcheries	$0.75	
112512	Shellfish Farming	$0.75	
112519	Other Aquaculture	$0.75	
112910	Apiculture	$0.75	
112920	Horse and Other Equine Production	$0.75	
112930	Fur-Bearing Animal and Rabbit Production	$0.75	
112990	All Other Animal Production	$0.75	
	Subsector 113—Forestry and Logging		
113110	Timber Tract Operations	$11.0	
113210	Forest Nurseries and Gathering of Forest Products	$11.0	
113310	Logging		500
	Subsector 114—Fishing, Hunting and Trapping		
114111	Finfish Fishing	$20.5	
114112	Shellfish Fishing	$5.5	
114119	Other Marine Fishing	$7.5	
114210	Hunting and Trapping	$5.5	
	Subsector 115—Support Activities for Agriculture and Forestry		
115111	Cotton Ginning	$11.0	
115112	Soil Preparation, Planting, and Cultivating	$7.5	
115113	Crop Harvesting, Primarily by Machine	$7.5	
115114	Postharvest Crop Activities (except Cotton Ginning)	$27.5	
115115	Farm Labor Contractors and Crew Leaders	$15.0	
115116	Farm Management Services	$7.5	
115210	Support Activities for Animal Production	$7.5	
115310	Support Activities for Forestry	$7.5	
Except,	Forest Fire Suppression [17]	$19.0 [17]	
Except,	Fuels Management Services [17]	$19.0 [17]	
	Sector 21—Mining, Quarrying, and Oil and Gas Extraction		
	Subsector 211—Oil and Gas Extraction		
211120	Crude Petroleum Extraction		1,250
211130	Natural Gas Extraction		1,250
	Subsector 212—Mining (except Oil and Gas)		
212111	Bituminous Coal and Lignite Surface Mining		1,250
212112	Bituminous Coal Underground Mining		1,500
212113	Anthracite Mining		250
212210	Iron Ore Mining		750
212221	Gold Ore Mining		1,500
212222	Silver Ore Mining		250
212230	Copper, Nickel, Lead, and Zinc Mining		750
212291	Uranium-Radium-Vanadium Ore Mining		250
212299	All Other Metal Ore Mining		750
212311	Dimension Stone Mining and Quarrying		500
212312	Crushed and Broken Limestone Mining and Quarrying		750
212313	Crushed and Broken Granite Mining and Quarrying		750
212319	Other Crushed and Broken Stone Mining and Quarrying		500
212321	Construction Sand and Gravel Mining		500
212322	Industrial Sand Mining		500
212324	Kaolin and Ball Clay Mining		750
212325	Clay and Ceramic and Refractory Minerals Mining		500
212391	Potash, Soda, and Borate Mineral Mining		750
212392	Phosphate Rock Mining		1,000
212393	Other Chemical and Fertilizer Mineral Mining		500

SMALL BUSINESS SIZE STANDARDS BY NAICS INDUSTRY—Continued

NAICS codes	NAICS U.S. industry title	Size standards in millions of dollars	Size standards in number of employees
212399	All Other Nonmetallic Mineral Mining		500
	Subsector 213—Support Activities for Mining		
213111	Drilling Oil and Gas Wells		1,000
213112	Support Activities for Oil and Gas Operations	$38.5	
213113	Support Activities for Coal Mining	$20.5	
213114	Support Activities for Metal Mining	$20.5	
213115	Support Activities for Nonmetallic Minerals (except Fuels)	$7.5	
	Sector 22—Utilities		
	Subsector 221—Utilities		
221111	Hydroelectric Power Generation		500
221112	Fossil Fuel Electric Power Generation		750
221113	Nuclear Electric Power Generation		750
221114	Solar Electric Power Generation		250
221115	Wind Electric Power Generation		250
221116	Geothermal Electric Power Generation		250
221117	Biomass Electric Power Generation		250
221118	Other Electric Power Generation		250
221121	Electric Bulk Power Transmission and Control		500
221122	Electric Power Distribution		1,000
221210	Natural Gas Distribution		1,000
221310	Water Supply and Irrigation Systems	$27.5	
221320	Sewage Treatment Facilities	$20.5	
221330	Steam and Air-Conditioning Supply	$15.0	
	Sector 23—Construction		
	Subsector 236—Construction of Buildings		
236115	New Single-family Housing Construction (Except For-Sale Builders)	$36.5	
236116	New Multifamily Housing Construction (except For-Sale Builders)	$36.5	
236117	New Housing For-Sale Builders	$36.5	
236118	Residential Remodelers	$36.5	
236210	Industrial Building Construction	$36.5	
236220	Commercial and Institutional Building Construction	$36.5	
	Subsector 237—Heavy and Civil Engineering Construction		
237110	Water and Sewer Line and Related Structures Construction	$36.5	
237120	Oil and Gas Pipeline and Related Structures Construction	$36.5	
237130	Power and Communication Line and Related Structures Construction	$36.5	
237210	Land Subdivision	$27.5	
237310	Highway, Street, and Bridge Construction	$36.5	
237990	Other Heavy and Civil Engineering Construction	$36.5	
Except,	Dredging and Surface Cleanup Activities[2]	$27.5[2]	
	Subsector 238—Specialty Trade Contractors		
238110	Poured Concrete Foundation and Structure Contractors	$15.0	
238120	Structural Steel and Precast Concrete Contractors	$15.0	
238130	Framing Contractors	$15.0	
238140	Masonry Contractors	$15.0	
238150	Glass and Glazing Contractors	$15.0	
238160	Roofing Contractors	$15.0	
238170	Siding Contractors	$15.0	
238190	Other Foundation, Structure, and Building Exterior Contractors	$15.0	
238210	Electrical Contractors and Other Wiring Installation Contractors	$15.0	
238220	Plumbing, Heating, and Air-Conditioning Contractors	$15.0	
238290	Other Building Equipment Contractors	$15.0	
238310	Drywall and Insulation Contractors	$15.0	
238320	Painting and Wall Covering Contractors	$15.0	
238330	Flooring Contractors	$15.0	
238340	Tile and Terrazzo Contractors	$15.0	
238350	Finish Carpentry Contractors	$15.0	
238390	Other Building Finishing Contractors	$15.0	
238910	Site Preparation Contractors	$15.0	
238990	All Other Specialty Trade Contractors	$15.0	

SMALL BUSINESS SIZE STANDARDS BY NAICS INDUSTRY—Continued

NAICS codes	NAICS U.S. industry title	Size standards in millions of dollars	Size standards in number of employees
Except,	Building and Property Specialty Trade Services [13]	$15.0 [13]	
	Sectors 31–33—Manufacturing		
	Subsector 311—Food Manufacturing		
311111	Dog and Cat Food Manufacturing		1,000
311119	Other Animal Food Manufacturing		500
311211	Flour Milling		1,000
311212	Rice Milling		500
311213	Malt Manufacturing		500
311221	Wet Corn Milling		1,250
311224	Soybean and Other Oilseed Processing		1,000
311225	Fats and Oils Refining and Blending		1,000
311230	Breakfast Cereal Manufacturing		1,000
311313	Beet Sugar Manufacturing		750
311314	Cane Sugar Manufacturing		1,000
311340	Nonchocolate Confectionery Manufacturing		1,000
311351	Chocolate and Confectionery Manufacturing from Cacao Beans		1,250
311352	Confectionery Manufacturing from Purchased Chocolate		1,000
311411	Frozen Fruit, Juice, and Vegetable Manufacturing		1,000
311412	Frozen Specialty Food Manufacturing		1,250
311421	Fruit and Vegetable Canning [3]		1,000 [3]
311422	Specialty Canning		1,250
311423	Dried and Dehydrated Food Manufacturing		750
311511	Fluid Milk Manufacturing		1,000
311512	Creamery Butter Manufacturing		750
311513	Cheese Manufacturing		1,250
311514	Dry, Condensed, and Evaporated Dairy Product Manufacturing		750
311520	Ice Cream and Frozen Dessert Manufacturing		1,000
311611	Animal (except Poultry) Slaughtering		1,000
311612	Meat Processed from Carcasses		1,000
311613	Rendering and Meat Byproduct Processing		750
311615	Poultry Processing		1,250
311710	Seafood Product Preparation and Packaging		750
311811	Retail Bakeries		500
311812	Commercial Bakeries		1,000
311813	Frozen Cakes, Pies, and Other Pastries Manufacturing		750
311821	Cookie and Cracker Manufacturing		1,250
311824	Dry Pasta, Dough, and Flour Mixes Manufacturing from Purchased Flour		750
311830	Tortilla Manufacturing		1,250
311911	Roasted Nuts and Peanut Butter Manufacturing		750
311919	Other Snack Food Manufacturing		1,250
311920	Coffee and Tea Manufacturing		750
311930	Flavoring Syrup and Concentrate Manufacturing		1,000
311941	Mayonnaise, Dressing, and Other Prepared Sauce Manufacturing		750
311942	Spice and Extract Manufacturing		500
311991	Perishable Prepared Food Manufacturing		500
311999	All Other Miscellaneous Food Manufacturing		500
	Subsector 312—Beverage and Tobacco Product Manufacturing		
312111	Soft Drink Manufacturing		1,250
312112	Bottled Water Manufacturing		1,000
312113	Ice Manufacturing		750
312120	Breweries		1,250
312130	Wineries		1,000
312140	Distilleries		1,000
312230	Tobacco Manufacturing		1,500
	Subsector 313—Textile Mills		
313110	Fiber, Yarn, and Thread Mills		1,250
313210	Broadwoven Fabric Mills		1,000
313220	Narrow Fabric Mills and Schiffli Machine Embroidery		500
313230	Nonwoven Fabric Mills		750
313240	Knit Fabric Mills		500
313310	Textile and Fabric Finishing Mills		1,000
313320	Fabric Coating Mills		1,000

SMALL BUSINESS SIZE STANDARDS BY NAICS INDUSTRY—Continued

NAICS codes	NAICS U.S. industry title	Size standards in millions of dollars	Size standards in number of employees
	Subsector 314—Textile Product Mills		
314110	Carpet and Rug Mills		1,500
314120	Curtain and Linen Mills		750
314910	Textile Bag and Canvas Mills		500
314994	Rope, Cordage, Twine, Tire Cord, and Tire Fabric Mills		1,000
314999	All Other Miscellaneous Textile Product Mills		500
	Subsector 315—Apparel Manufacturing		
315110	Hosiery and Sock Mills		750
315190	Other Apparel Knitting Mills		750
315210	Cut and Sew Apparel Contractors		750
315220	Men's and Boys' Cut and Sew Apparel Manufacturing		750
315240	Women's, Girls', and Infants' Cut and Sew Apparel Manufacturing		750
315280	Other Cut and Sew Apparel Manufacturing		750
315990	Apparel Accessories and Other Apparel Manufacturing		500
	Subsector 316—Leather and Allied Product Manufacturing		
316110	Leather and Hide Tanning and Finishing		500
316210	Footwear Manufacturing		1,000
316992	Women's Handbag and Purse Manufacturing		750
316998	All Other Leather Good and Allied Product Manufacturing		500
	Subsector 321—Wood Product Manufacturing		
321113	Sawmills		500
321114	Wood Preservation		500
321211	Hardwood Veneer and Plywood Manufacturing		500
321212	Softwood Veneer and Plywood Manufacturing		1,250
321213	Engineered Wood Member (except Truss) Manufacturing		750
321214	Truss Manufacturing		500
321219	Reconstituted Wood Product Manufacturing		750
321911	Wood Window and Door Manufacturing		1,000
321912	Cut Stock, Resawing Lumber, and Planing		500
321918	Other Millwork (including Flooring)		500
321920	Wood Container and Pallet Manufacturing		500
321991	Manufactured Home (Mobile Home) Manufacturing		1,250
321992	Prefabricated Wood Building Manufacturing		500
321999	All Other Miscellaneous Wood Product Manufacturing		500
	Subsector 322—Paper Manufacturing		
322110	Pulp Mills		750
322121	Paper (except Newsprint) Mills		1,250
322122	Newsprint Mills		750
322130	Paperboard Mills		1,250
322211	Corrugated and Solid Fiber Box Manufacturing		1,250
322212	Folding Paperboard Box Manufacturing		750
322219	Other Paperboard Container Manufacturing		1,000
322220	Paper Bag and Coated and Treated Paper Manufacturing		750
322230	Stationery Product Manufacturing		750
322291	Sanitary Paper Product Manufacturing		1,500
322299	All Other Converted Paper Product Manufacturing		500
	Subsector 323—Printing and Related Support Activities		
323111	Commercial Printing (except Screen and Books)		500
323113	Commercial Screen Printing		500
323117	Books Printing		1,250
323120	Support Activities for Printing		500
	Subsector 324—Petroleum and Coal Products Manufacturing		
324110	Petroleum Refineries[4]		1,500[4]
324121	Asphalt Paving Mixture and Block Manufacturing		500
324122	Asphalt Shingle and Coating Materials Manufacturing		750
324191	Petroleum Lubricating Oil and Grease Manufacturing		750
324199	All Other Petroleum and Coal Products Manufacturing		500

SMALL BUSINESS SIZE STANDARDS BY NAICS INDUSTRY—Continued

NAICS codes	NAICS U.S. industry title	Size standards in millions of dollars	Size standards in number of employees
	Subsector 325—Chemical Manufacturing		
325110	Petrochemical Manufacturing		1,000
325120	Industrial Gas Manufacturing		1,000
325130	Synthetic Dye and Pigment Manufacturing		1,000
325180	Other Basic Inorganic Chemical Manufacturing		1,000
325193	Ethyl Alcohol Manufacturing		1,000
325194	Cyclic Crude, Intermediate, and Gum and Wood Chemical Manufacturing		1,250
325199	All Other Basic Organic Chemical Manufacturing		1,250
325211	Plastics Material and Resin Manufacturing		1,250
325212	Synthetic Rubber Manufacturing		1,000
325220	Artificial and Synthetic Fibers and Filaments Manufacturing		1,000
325311	Nitrogenous Fertilizer Manufacturing		1,000
325312	Phosphatic Fertilizer Manufacturing		750
325314	Fertilizer (Mixing Only) Manufacturing		500
325320	Pesticide and Other Agricultural Chemical Manufacturing		1,000
325411	Medicinal and Botanical Manufacturing		1,000
325412	Pharmaceutical Preparation Manufacturing		1,250
325413	In-Vitro Diagnostic Substance Manufacturing		1,250
325414	Biological Product (except Diagnostic) Manufacturing		1,250
325510	Paint and Coating Manufacturing		1,000
325520	Adhesive Manufacturing		500
325611	Soap and Other Detergent Manufacturing		1,000
325612	Polish and Other Sanitation Good Manufacturing		750
325613	Surface Active Agent Manufacturing		750
325620	Toilet Preparation Manufacturing		1,250
325910	Printing Ink Manufacturing		500
325920	Explosives Manufacturing		750
325991	Custom Compounding of Purchased Resins		500
325992	Photographic Film, Paper, Plate, and Chemical Manufacturing		1,500
325998	All Other Miscellaneous Chemical Product and Preparation Manufacturing		500
	Subsector 326—Plastics and Rubber Products Manufacturing		
326111	Plastics Bag and Pouch Manufacturing		750
326112	Plastics Packaging Film and Sheet (including Laminated) Manufacturing		1,000
326113	Unlaminated Plastics Film and Sheet (except Packaging) Manufacturing		750
326121	Unlaminated Plastics Profile Shape Manufacturing		500
326122	Plastics Pipe and Pipe Fitting Manufacturing		750
326130	Laminated Plastics Plate, Sheet (except Packaging), and Shape Manufacturing.		500
326140	Polystyrene Foam Product Manufacturing		1,000
326150	Urethane and Other Foam Product (except Polystyrene) Manufacturing		750
326160	Plastics Bottle Manufacturing		1,250
326191	Plastics Plumbing Fixture Manufacturing		750
326199	All Other Plastics Product Manufacturing		750
326211	Tire Manufacturing (except Retreading) [5]		1,500 [5]
326212	Tire Retreading		500
326220	Rubber and Plastics Hoses and Belting Manufacturing		750
326291	Rubber Product Manufacturing for Mechanical Use		750
326299	All Other Rubber Product Manufacturing		500
	Subsector 327—Nonmetallic Mineral Product Manufacturing		
327110	Pottery, Ceramics, and Plumbing Fixture Manufacturing		1,000
327120	Clay Building Material and Refractories Manufacturing		750
327211	Flat Glass Manufacturing		1,000
327212	Other Pressed and Blown Glass and Glassware Manufacturing		1,250
327213	Glass Container Manufacturing		1,250
327215	Glass Product Manufacturing Made of Purchased Glass		1,000
327310	Cement Manufacturing		1,000
327320	Ready-Mix Concrete Manufacturing		500
327331	Concrete Block and Brick Manufacturing		500
327332	Concrete Pipe Manufacturing		750
327390	Other Concrete Product Manufacturing		500
327410	Lime Manufacturing		750
327420	Gypsum Product Manufacturing		1,500
327910	Abrasive Product Manufacturing		750
327991	Cut Stone and Stone Product Manufacturing		500
327992	Ground or Treated Mineral and Earth Manufacturing		500
327993	Mineral Wool Manufacturing		1,500

SMALL BUSINESS SIZE STANDARDS BY NAICS INDUSTRY—Continued

NAICS codes	NAICS U.S. industry title	Size standards in millions of dollars	Size standards in number of employees
327999	All Other Miscellaneous Nonmetallic Mineral Product Manufacturing		500
	Subsector 331—Primary Metal Manufacturing		
331110	Iron and Steel Mills and Ferroalloy Manufacturing		1,500
331210	Iron and Steel Pipe and Tube Manufacturing from Purchased Steel		1,000
331221	Rolled Steel Shape Manufacturing		1,000
331222	Steel Wire Drawing		1,000
331313	Alumina Refining and Primary Aluminum Production		1,000
331314	Secondary Smelting and Alloying of Aluminum		750
331315	Aluminum Sheet, Plate, and Foil Manufacturing		1,250
331318	Other Aluminum Rolling, Drawing, and Extruding		750
331410	Nonferrous Metal (except Aluminum) Smelting and Refining		1,000
331420	Copper Rolling, Drawing, Extruding, and Alloying		1,000
331491	Nonferrous Metal (except Copper and Aluminum) Rolling, Drawing and Extruding.		750
331492	Secondary Smelting, Refining, and Alloying of Nonferrous Metal (except Copper and Aluminum).		750
331511	Iron Foundries		1,000
331512	Steel Investment Foundries		1,000
331513	Steel Foundries (except Investment)		500
331523	Nonferrous Metal Die-Casting Foundries		500
331524	Aluminum Foundries (except Die-Casting)		500
331529	Other Nonferrous Metal Foundries (except Die-Casting)		500
	Subsector 332—Fabricated Metal Product Manufacturing		
332111	Iron and Steel Forging		750
332112	Nonferrous Forging		750
332114	Custom Roll Forming		500
332117	Powder Metallurgy Part Manufacturing		500
332119	Metal Crown, Closure, and Other Metal Stamping (except Automotive)		500
332215	Metal Kitchen Cookware, Utensil, Cutlery, and Flatware (except Precious) Manufacturing.		750
332216	Saw Blade and Handtool Manufacturing		750
332311	Prefabricated Metal Building and Component Manufacturing		750
332312	Fabricated Structural Metal Manufacturing		500
332313	Plate Work Manufacturing		750
332321	Metal Window and Door Manufacturing		750
332322	Sheet Metal Work Manufacturing		500
332323	Ornamental and Architectural Metal Work Manufacturing		500
332410	Power Boiler and Heat Exchanger Manufacturing		750
332420	Metal Tank (Heavy Gauge) Manufacturing		750
332431	Metal Can Manufacturing		1,500
332439	Other Metal Container Manufacturing		500
332510	Hardware Manufacturing		750
332613	Spring Manufacturing		500
332618	Other Fabricated Wire Product Manufacturing		500
332710	Machine Shops		500
332721	Precision Turned Product Manufacturing		500
332722	Bolt, Nut, Screw, Rivet and Washer Manufacturing		500
332811	Metal Heat Treating		750
332812	Metal Coating, Engraving (except Jewelry and Silverware), and Allied Services to Manufacturers.		500
332813	Electroplating, Plating, Polishing, Anodizing and Coloring		500
332911	Industrial Valve Manufacturing		750
332912	Fluid Power Valve and Hose Fitting Manufacturing		1,000
332913	Plumbing Fixture Fitting and Trim Manufacturing		1,000
332919	Other Metal Valve and Pipe Fitting Manufacturing		750
332991	Ball and Roller Bearing Manufacturing		1,250
332992	Small Arms Ammunition Manufacturing		1,250
332993	Ammunition (except Small Arms) Manufacturing		1,500
332994	Small Arms, Ordnance, and Ordnance Accessories Manufacturing		1,000
332996	Fabricated Pipe and Pipe Fitting Manufacturing		500
332999	All Other Miscellaneous Fabricated Metal Product Manufacturing		750
	Subsector 333—Machinery Manufacturing [6]		
333111	Farm Machinery and Equipment Manufacturing		1,250
333112	Lawn and Garden Tractor and Home Lawn and Garden Equipment Manufacturing.		1,500

SMALL BUSINESS SIZE STANDARDS BY NAICS INDUSTRY—Continued

NAICS codes	NAICS U.S. industry title	Size standards in millions of dollars	Size standards in number of employees
333120	Construction Machinery Manufacturing		1,250
333131	Mining Machinery and Equipment Manufacturing		500
333132	Oil and Gas Field Machinery and Equipment Manufacturing		1,250
333241	Food Product Machinery Manufacturing		500
333242	Semiconductor Machinery Manufacturing		1,500
333243	Sawmill, Woodworking, and Paper Machinery Manufacturing		500
333244	Printing Machinery and Equipment Manufacturing		750
333249	Other Industrial Machinery Manufacturing		500
333314	Optical Instrument and Lens Manufacturing		500
333316	Photographic and Photocopying Equipment Manufacturing		1,000
333318	Other Commercial and Service Industry Machinery Manufacturing		1,000
333413	Industrial and Commercial Fan and Blower and Air Purification Equipment Manufacturing.		500
333414	Heating Equipment (except Warm Air Furnaces) Manufacturing		500
333415	Air-Conditioning and Warm Air Heating Equipment and Commercial and Industrial Refrigeration Equipment Manufacturing.		1,250
333511	Industrial Mold Manufacturing		500
333514	Special Die and Tool, Die Set, Jig and Fixture Manufacturing		500
333515	Cutting Tool and Machine Tool Accessory Manufacturing		500
333517	Machine Tool Manufacturing		500
333519	Rolling Mill and Other Metalworking Machinery Manufacturing		500
333611	Turbine and Turbine Generator Set Units Manufacturing		1,500
333612	Speed Changer, Industrial High-Speed Drive, and Gear Manufacturing		750
333613	Mechanical Power Transmission Equipment Manufacturing		750
333618	Other Engine Equipment Manufacturing		1,500
333912	Air and Gas Compressor Manufacturing		1,000
333914	Measuring, Dispensing, and Other Pumping Equipment Manufacturing		750
333921	Elevator and Moving Stairway Manufacturing		1,000
333922	Conveyor and Conveying Equipment Manufacturing		500
333923	Overhead Traveling Crane, Hoist, and Monorail System Manufacturing		1,250
333924	Industrial Truck, Tractor, Trailer and Stacker Machinery Manufacturing		750
333991	Power-Driven Hand Tool Manufacturing		500
333992	Welding and Soldering Equipment Manufacturing		1,250
333993	Packaging Machinery Manufacturing		500
333994	Industrial Process Furnace and Oven Manufacturing		500
333995	Fluid Power Cylinder and Actuator Manufacturing		750
333996	Fluid Power Pump and Motor Manufacturing		1,250
333997	Scale and Balance Manufacturing		500
333999	All Other Miscellaneous General Purpose Machinery Manufacturing		500
	Subsector 334—Computer and Electronic Product Manufacturing [6]		
334111	Electronic Computer Manufacturing		1,250
334112	Computer Storage Device Manufacturing		1,250
334118	Computer Terminal and Other Computer Peripheral Equipment Manufacturing.		1,000
334210	Telephone Apparatus Manufacturing		1,250
334220	Radio and Television Broadcasting and Wireless Communications Equipment Manufacturing.		1,250
334290	Other Communications Equipment Manufacturing		750
334310	Audio and Video Equipment Manufacturing		750
334412	Bare Printed Circuit Board Manufacturing		750
334413	Semiconductor and Related Device Manufacturing		1,250
334416	Capacitor, Resistor, Coil, Transformer, and Other Inductor Manufacturing		500
334417	Electronic Connector Manufacturing		1,000
334418	Printed Circuit Assembly (Electronic Assembly) Manufacturing		750
334419	Other Electronic Component Manufacturing		750
334510	Electromedical and Electrotherapeutic Apparatus Manufacturing		1,250
334511	Search, Detection, Navigation, Guidance, Aeronautical, and Nautical System and Instrument Manufacturing.		1,250
334512	Automatic Environmental Control Manufacturing for Residential, Commercial and Appliance Use.		500
334513	Instruments and Related Products Manufacturing for Measuring, Displaying, and Controlling Industrial Process Variables.		750
334514	Totalizing Fluid Meter and Counting Device Manufacturing		750
334515	Instrument Manufacturing for Measuring and Testing Electricity and Electrical Signals.		750
334516	Analytical Laboratory Instrument Manufacturing		1,000
334517	Irradiation Apparatus Manufacturing		1,000
334519	Other Measuring and Controlling Device Manufacturing		500

SMALL BUSINESS SIZE STANDARDS BY NAICS INDUSTRY—Continued

NAICS codes	NAICS U.S. industry title	Size standards in millions of dollars	Size standards in number of employees
334613	Blank Magnetic and Optical Recording Media Manufacturing		1,000
334614	Software and Other Prerecorded Compact Disc, Tape, and Record Reproducing.		1,250
	Subsector 335—Electrical Equipment, Appliance and Component Manufacturing [6]		
335110	Electric Lamp Bulb and Part Manufacturing		1,250
335121	Residential Electric Lighting Fixture Manufacturing		750
335122	Commercial, Industrial and Institutional Electric Lighting Fixture Manufacturing.		500
335129	Other Lighting Equipment Manufacturing		500
335210	Small Electrical Appliance Manufacturing		1,500
335220	Major Household Appliance Manufacturing		1,500
335311	Power, Distribution and Specialty Transformer Manufacturing		750
335312	Motor and Generator Manufacturing		1,250
335313	Switchgear and Switchboard Apparatus Manufacturing		1,250
335314	Relay and Industrial Control Manufacturing		750
335911	Storage Battery Manufacturing		1,250
335912	Primary Battery Manufacturing		1,000
335921	Fiber Optic Cable Manufacturing		1,000
335929	Other Communication and Energy Wire Manufacturing		1,000
335931	Current-Carrying Wiring Device Manufacturing		500
335932	Noncurrent-Carrying Wiring Device Manufacturing		1,000
335991	Carbon and Graphite Product Manufacturing		750
335999	All Other Miscellaneous Electrical Equipment and Component Manufacturing.		500
	Subsector 336—Transportation Equipment Manufacturing [6]		
336111	Automobile Manufacturing		1,500
336112	Light Truck and Utility Vehicle Manufacturing		1,500
336120	Heavy Duty Truck Manufacturing		1,500
336211	Motor Vehicle Body Manufacturing		1,000
336212	Truck Trailer Manufacturing		1,000
336213	Motor Home Manufacturing		1,250
336214	Travel Trailer and Camper Manufacturing		1,000
336310	Motor Vehicle Gasoline Engine and Engine Parts Manufacturing		1,000
336320	Motor Vehicle Electrical and Electronic Equipment Manufacturing		1,000
336330	Motor Vehicle Steering and Suspension Components (except Spring) Manufacturing.		1,000
336340	Motor Vehicle Brake System Manufacturing		1,250
336350	Motor Vehicle Transmission and Power Train Parts Manufacturing		1,500
336360	Motor Vehicle Seating and Interior Trim Manufacturing		1,500
336370	Motor Vehicle Metal Stamping		1,000
336390	Other Motor Vehicle Parts Manufacturing		1,000
336411	Aircraft Manufacturing		1,500
336412	Aircraft Engine and Engine Parts Manufacturing		1,500
336413	Other Aircraft Parts and Auxiliary Equipment Manufacturing [7]		1,250 [7]
336414	Guided Missile and Space Vehicle Manufacturing		1,250
336415	Guided Missile and Space Vehicle Propulsion Unit and Propulsion Unit Parts Manufacturing.		1,250
336419	Other Guided Missile and Space Vehicle Parts and Auxiliary Equipment Manufacturing.		1,000
336510	Railroad Rolling Stock Manufacturing		1,500
336611	Ship Building and Repairing		1,250
336612	Boat Building		1,000
336991	Motorcycle, Bicycle, and Parts Manufacturing		1,000
336992	Military Armored Vehicle, Tank, and Tank Component Manufacturing		1,500
336999	All Other Transportation Equipment Manufacturing		1,000
	Subsector 337—Furniture and Related Product Manufacturing		
337110	Wood Kitchen Cabinet and Countertop Manufacturing		750
337121	Upholstered Household Furniture Manufacturing		1,000
337122	Nonupholstered Wood Household Furniture Manufacturing		750
337124	Metal Household Furniture Manufacturing		750
337125	Household Furniture (except Wood and Metal) Manufacturing		750
337127	Institutional Furniture Manufacturing		500
337211	Wood Office Furniture Manufacturing		1,000
337212	Custom Architectural Woodwork and Millwork Manufacturing		500
337214	Office Furniture (except Wood) Manufacturing		1,000

SMALL BUSINESS SIZE STANDARDS BY NAICS INDUSTRY—Continued

NAICS codes	NAICS U.S. industry title	Size standards in millions of dollars	Size standards in number of employees
337215	Showcase, Partition, Shelving, and Locker Manufacturing		500
337910	Mattress Manufacturing		1,000
337920	Blind and Shade Manufacturing		1,000
	Subsector 339—Miscellaneous Manufacturing		
339112	Surgical and Medical Instrument Manufacturing		1,000
339113	Surgical Appliance and Supplies Manufacturing		750
339114	Dental Equipment and Supplies Manufacturing		750
339115	Ophthalmic Goods Manufacturing		1,000
339116	Dental Laboratories		500
339910	Jewelry and Silverware Manufacturing		500
339920	Sporting and Athletic Goods Manufacturing		750
339930	Doll, Toy, and Game Manufacturing		500
339940	Office Supplies (except Paper) Manufacturing		750
339950	Sign Manufacturing		500
339991	Gasket, Packing, and Sealing Device Manufacturing		500
339992	Musical Instrument Manufacturing		1,000
339993	Fastener, Button, Needle, and Pin Manufacturing		750
339994	Broom, Brush and Mop Manufacturing		500
339995	Burial Casket Manufacturing		1,000
339999	All Other Miscellaneous Manufacturing		500
	Sector 42—Wholesale Trade		
	(These NAICS codes shall not be used to classify Government acquisitions for supplies. They also shall not be used by Federal Government contractors when subcontracting for the acquisition for supplies. The applicable manufacturing NAICS code shall be used to classify acquisitions for supplies. A Wholesale Trade or Retail Trade business concern submitting an offer or a quote on a supply acquisition is categorized as a nonmanufacturer and deemed small if it has 500 or fewer employees and meets the requirements of 13 CFR 121.406.)		
	Subsector 423—Merchant Wholesalers, Durable Goods		
423110	Automobile and Other Motor Vehicle Merchant Wholesalers		250
423120	Motor Vehicle Supplies and New Parts Merchant Wholesalers		200
423130	Tire and Tube Merchant Wholesalers		200
423140	Motor Vehicle Parts (Used) Merchant Wholesalers		100
423210	Furniture Merchant Wholesalers		100
423220	Home Furnishing Merchant Wholesalers		100
423310	Lumber, Plywood, Millwork, and Wood Panel Merchant Wholesalers		150
423320	Brick, Stone, and Related Construction Material Merchant Wholesalers		150
423330	Roofing, Siding, and Insulation Material Merchant Wholesalers		200
423390	Other Construction Material Merchant Wholesalers		100
423410	Photographic Equipment and Supplies Merchant Wholesalers		200
423420	Office Equipment Merchant Wholesalers		200
423430	Computer and Computer Peripheral Equipment and Software Merchant Wholesalers.		250
423440	Other Commercial Equipment Merchant Wholesalers		100
423450	Medical, Dental, and Hospital Equipment and Supplies Merchant Wholesalers.		200
423460	Ophthalmic Goods Merchant Wholesalers		150
423490	Other Professional Equipment and Supplies Merchant Wholesalers		150
423510	Metal Service Centers and Other Metal Merchant Wholesalers		200
423520	Coal and Other Mineral and Ore Merchant Wholesalers		100
423610	Electrical Apparatus and Equipment, Wiring Supplies, and Related Equipment Merchant Wholesalers.		200
423620	Household Appliances, Electric Housewares, and Consumer Electronics Merchant Wholesalers.		200
423690	Other Electronic Parts and Equipment Merchant Wholesalers		250
423710	Hardware Merchant Wholesalers		150
423720	Plumbing and Heating Equipment and Supplies (Hydronics) Merchant Wholesalers.		200
423730	Warm Air Heating and Air-Conditioning Equipment and Supplies Merchant Wholesalers.		150
423740	Refrigeration Equipment and Supplies Merchant Wholesalers		100
423810	Construction and Mining (except Oil Well) Machinery and Equipment Merchant Wholesalers.		250
423820	Farm and Garden Machinery and Equipment Merchant Wholesalers		100
423830	Industrial Machinery and Equipment Merchant Wholesalers		100
423840	Industrial Supplies Merchant Wholesalers		100
423850	Service Establishment Equipment and Supplies Merchant Wholesalers		100

SMALL BUSINESS SIZE STANDARDS BY NAICS INDUSTRY—Continued

NAICS codes	NAICS U.S. industry title	Size standards in millions of dollars	Size standards in number of employees
423860	Transportation Equipment and Supplies (except Motor Vehicle) Merchant Wholesalers.		150
423910	Sporting and Recreational Goods and Supplies Merchant Wholesalers		100
423920	Toy and Hobby Goods and Supplies Merchant Wholesalers		150
423930	Recyclable Material Merchant Wholesalers		100
423940	Jewelry, Watch, Precious Stone, and Precious Metal Merchant Wholesalers.		100
423990	Other Miscellaneous Durable Goods Merchant Wholesalers		100
	Subsector 424—Merchant Wholesalers, Nondurable Goods		
424110	Printing and Writing Paper Merchant Wholesalers		200
424120	Stationery and Office Supplies Merchant Wholesalers		150
424130	Industrial and Personal Service Paper Merchant Wholesalers		150
424210	Drugs and Druggists' Sundries Merchant Wholesalers		250
424310	Piece Goods, Notions, and Other Dry Goods Merchant Wholesalers		100
424320	Men's and Boys' Clothing and Furnishings Merchant Wholesalers		150
424330	Women's, Children's, and Infants' Clothing and Accessories Merchant Wholesalers.		100
424340	Footwear Merchant Wholesalers		200
424410	General Line Grocery Merchant Wholesalers		250
424420	Packaged Frozen Food Merchant Wholesalers		200
424430	Dairy Product (except Dried or Canned) Merchant Wholesalers		200
424440	Poultry and Poultry Product Merchant Wholesalers		150
424450	Confectionery Merchant Wholesalers		200
424460	Fish and Seafood Merchant Wholesalers		100
424470	Meat and Meat Product Merchant Wholesalers		150
424480	Fresh Fruit and Vegetable Merchant Wholesalers		100
424490	Other Grocery and Related Products Merchant Wholesalers		250
424510	Grain and Field Bean Merchant Wholesalers		200
424520	Livestock Merchant Wholesalers		100
424590	Other Farm Product Raw Material Merchant Wholesalers		100
424610	Plastics Materials and Basic Forms and Shapes Merchant Wholesalers		150
424690	Other Chemical and Allied Products Merchant Wholesalers		150
424710	Petroleum Bulk Stations and Terminals		200
424720	Petroleum and Petroleum Products Merchant Wholesalers (except Bulk Stations and Terminals).		200
424810	Beer and Ale Merchant Wholesalers		200
424820	Wine and Distilled Alcoholic Beverage Merchant Wholesalers		250
424910	Farm Supplies Merchant Wholesalers		200
424920	Book, Periodical, and Newspaper Merchant Wholesalers		200
424930	Flower, Nursery Stock, and Florists' Supplies Merchant Wholesalers		100
424940	Tobacco and Tobacco Product Merchant Wholesalers		250
424950	Paint, Varnish, and Supplies Merchant Wholesalers		150
424990	Other Miscellaneous Nondurable Goods Merchant Wholesalers		100
	Subsector 425—Wholesale Electronic Markets and Agents and Brokers		
425110	Business to Business Electronic Markets		100
425120	Wholesale Trade Agents and Brokers		100
	Sector 44–45—Retail Trade		
	(These NAICS codes shall not be used to classify Government acquisitions for supplies. They also shall not be used by Federal Government contractors when subcontracting for the acquisition for supplies. The applicable manufacturing NAICS code shall be used to classify acquisitions for supplies. A Wholesale Trade or Retail Trade business concern submitting an offer or a quote on a supply acquisition is categorized as a nonmanufacturer and deemed small if it has 500 or fewer employees and meets the requirements of 13 CFR 121.406.)		
	Subsector 441—Motor Vehicle and Parts Dealers		
441110	New Car Dealers		200
441120	Used Car Dealers	$25.0	
441210	Recreational Vehicle Dealers	$32.5	
441222	Boat Dealers	$32.5	
441228	Motorcycle, ATV, and All Other Motor Vehicle Dealers	$32.5	
441310	Automotive Parts and Accessories Stores	$15.0	
441320	Tire Dealers	$15.0	

SMALL BUSINESS SIZE STANDARDS BY NAICS INDUSTRY—Continued

NAICS codes	NAICS U.S. industry title	Size standards in millions of dollars	Size standards in number of employees
	Subsector 442—Furniture and Home Furnishings Stores		
442110	Furniture Stores	$20.5	
442210	Floor Covering Stores	$7.5	
442291	Window Treatment Stores	$7.5	
442299	All Other Home Furnishings Stores	$20.5	
	Subsector 443—Electronics and Appliance Stores		
443141	Household Appliance Stores	$11.0	
443142	Electronics Stores	$32.5	
	Subsector 444—Building Material and Garden Equipment and Supplies Dealers		
444110	Home Centers	$38.5	
444120	Paint and Wallpaper Stores	$27.5	
444130	Hardware Stores	$7.5	
444190	Other Building Material Dealers	$20.5	
444210	Outdoor Power Equipment Stores	$7.5	
444220	Nursery and Garden Centers	$11.0	
	Subsector 445—Food and Beverage Stores		
445110	Supermarkets and Other Grocery (except Convenience) Stores	$32.5	
445120	Convenience Stores	$29.5	
445210	Meat Markets	$7.5	
445220	Fish and Seafood Markets	$7.5	
445230	Fruit and Vegetable Markets	$7.5	
445291	Baked Goods Stores	$7.5	
445292	Confectionery and Nut Stores	$7.5	
445299	All Other Specialty Food Stores	$7.5	
445310	Beer, Wine and Liquor Stores	$7.5	
	Subsector 446—Health and Personal Care Stores		
446110	Pharmacies and Drug Stores	$27.5	
446120	Cosmetics, Beauty Supplies and Perfume Stores	$27.5	
446130	Optical Goods Stores	$20.5	
446191	Food (Health) Supplement Stores	$15.0	
446199	All Other Health and Personal Care Stores	$7.5	
	Subsector 447—Gasoline Stations		
447110	Gasoline Stations with Convenience Stores	$29.5	
447190	Other Gasoline Stations	$15.0	
	Subsector 448—Clothing and Clothing Accessories Stores		
448110	Men's Clothing Stores	$11.0	
448120	Women's Clothing Stores	$27.5	
448130	Children's and Infants' Clothing Stores	$32.5	
448140	Family Clothing Stores	$38.5	
448150	Clothing Accessories Stores	$15.0	
448190	Other Clothing Stores	$20.5	
448210	Shoe Stores	$27.5	
448310	Jewelry Stores	$15.0	
448320	Luggage and Leather Goods Stores	$27.5	
	Subsector 451—Sporting Good, Hobby, Book and Music Stores		
451110	Sporting Goods Stores	$15.0	
451120	Hobby, Toy and Game Stores	$27.5	
451130	Sewing, Needlework and Piece Goods Stores	$27.5	
451140	Musical Instrument and Supplies Stores	$11.0	
451211	Book Stores	$27.5	
451212	News Dealers and Newsstands	$7.5	
	Subsector 452—General Merchandise Stores		
452210	Department Stores	$32.5	
452311	Warehouse Clubs and Supercenters	$29.5	

SMALL BUSINESS SIZE STANDARDS BY NAICS INDUSTRY—Continued

NAICS codes	NAICS U.S. industry title	Size standards in millions of dollars	Size standards in number of employees
452319	All Other General Merchandise Stores	$32.5	
	Subsector 453—Miscellaneous Store Retailers		
453110	Florists	$7.5	
453210	Office Supplies and Stationery Stores	$32.5	
453220	Gift, Novelty and Souvenir Stores	$7.5	
453310	Used Merchandise Stores	$7.5	
453910	Pet and Pet Supplies Stores	$20.5	
453920	Art Dealers	$7.5	
453930	Manufactured (Mobile) Home Dealers	$15.0	
453991	Tobacco Stores	$7.5	
453998	All Other Miscellaneous Store Retailers (except Tobacco Stores)	$7.5	
	Subsector 454—Nonstore Retailers		
454110	Electronic Shopping and Mail-Order Houses	$38.5	
454210	Vending Machine Operators	$11.0	
454310	Fuel Dealers		100
454390	Other Direct Selling Establishments	$7.5	
	Sectors 48–49—Transportation and Warehousing		
	Subsector 481—Air Transportation		
481111	Scheduled Passenger Air Transportation		1,500
481112	Scheduled Freight Air Transportation		1,500
481211	Nonscheduled Chartered Passenger Air Transportation		1,500
481212	Nonscheduled Chartered Freight Air Transportation		1,500
481219	Other Nonscheduled Air Transportation	$15.0	
	Subsector 482—Rail Transportation		
482111	Line-Haul Railroads		1,500
482112	Short Line Railroads		1,500
	Subsector 483—Water Transportation		
483111	Deep Sea Freight Transportation		500
483112	Deep Sea Passenger Transportation		1,500
483113	Coastal and Great Lakes Freight Transportation		750
483114	Coastal and Great Lakes Passenger Transportation		500
483211	Inland Water Freight Transportation		750
483212	Inland Water Passenger Transportation		500
	Subsector 484—Truck Transportation		
484110	General Freight Trucking, Local	$27.5	
484121	General Freight Trucking, Long-Distance, Truckload	$27.5	
484122	General Freight Trucking, Long-Distance, Less Than Truckload	$27.5	
484210	Used Household and Office Goods Moving	$27.5	
484220	Specialized Freight (except Used Goods) Trucking, Local	$27.5	
484230	Specialized Freight (except Used Goods) Trucking, Long-Distance	$27.5	
	Subsector 485—Transit and Ground Passenger Transportation		
485111	Mixed Mode Transit Systems	$15.0	
485112	Commuter Rail Systems	$15.0	
485113	Bus and Other Motor Vehicle Transit Systems	$15.0	
485119	Other Urban Transit Systems	$15.0	
485210	Interurban and Rural Bus Transportation	$15.0	
485310	Taxi Service	$15.0	
485320	Limousine Service	$15.0	
485410	School and Employee Bus Transportation	$15.0	
485510	Charter Bus Industry	$15.0	
485991	Special Needs Transportation	$15.0	
485999	All Other Transit and Ground Passenger Transportation	$15.0	
	Subsector 486—Pipeline Transportation		
486110	Pipeline Transportation of Crude Oil		1,500

SMALL BUSINESS SIZE STANDARDS BY NAICS INDUSTRY—Continued

NAICS codes	NAICS U.S. industry title	Size standards in millions of dollars	Size standards in number of employees
486210	Pipeline Transportation of Natural Gas	$27.5	
486910	Pipeline Transportation of Refined Petroleum Products		1,500
486990	All Other Pipeline Transportation	$37.50	
	Subsector 487—Scenic and Sightseeing Transportation		
487110	Scenic and Sightseeing Transportation, Land	$7.5	
487210	Scenic and Sightseeing Transportation, Water	$7.5	
487990	Scenic and Sightseeing Transportation, Other	$7.5	
	Subsector 488—Support Activities for Transportation		
488111	Air Traffic Control	$32.5	
488119	Other Airport Operations	$32.5	
488190	Other Support Activities for Air Transportation	$32.5	
488210	Support Activities for Rail Transportation	$15.0	
488310	Port and Harbor Operations	$38.5	
488320	Marine Cargo Handling	$38.5	
488330	Navigational Services to Shipping	$38.5	
488390	Other Support Activities for Water Transportation	$38.5	
488410	Motor Vehicle Towing	$7.5	
488490	Other Support Activities for Road Transportation	$7.5	
488510	Freight Transportation Arrangement [10]	$15.0 [10]	
Except,	Non-Vessel Owning Common Carriers and Household Goods Forwarders	$27.5	
488991	Packing and Crating	$27.5	
488999	All Other Support Activities for Transportation	$7.5	
	Subsector 491—Postal Service		
491110	Postal Service	$7.5	
	Subsector 492—Couriers and Messengers		
492110	Couriers and Express Delivery Services		1,500
492210	Local Messengers and Local Delivery	$27.5	
	Subsector 493—Warehousing and Storage		
493110	General Warehousing and Storage	$27.5	
493120	Refrigerated Warehousing and Storage	$27.5	
493130	Farm Product Warehousing and Storage	$27.5	
493190	Other Warehousing and Storage	$27.5	
	Sector 51—Information		
	Subsector 511—Publishing Industries (except Internet)		
511110	Newspaper Publishers		1,000
511120	Periodical Publishers		1,000
511130	Book Publishers		1,000
511140	Directory and Mailing List Publishers		1,250
511191	Greeting Card Publishers		1,500
511199	All Other Publishers		500
511210	Software Publishers [20]	$38.5	
	Subsector 512—Motion Picture and Sound Recording Industries		
512110	Motion Picture and Video Production	$32.5	
512120	Motion Picture and Video Distribution	$32.0	
512131	Motion Picture Theaters (except Drive-Ins)	$38.5	
512132	Drive-In Motion Picture Theaters	$7.5	
512191	Teleproduction and Other Postproduction Services	$32.0	
512199	Other Motion Picture and Video Industries	$20.5	
512230	Music Publishers		750
512240	Sound Recording Studios	$7.5	
512250	Record Production and Distribution		250
512290	Other Sound Recording Industries	$11.0	
	Subsector 515—Broadcasting (except Internet)		
515111	Radio Networks	$32.5	

SMALL BUSINESS SIZE STANDARDS BY NAICS INDUSTRY—Continued

NAICS codes	NAICS U.S. industry title	Size standards in millions of dollars	Size standards in number of employees
515112	Radio Stations	$38.5	
515120	Television Broadcasting	$38.5	
515210	Cable and Other Subscription Programming	$38.5	
Subsector 517—Telecommunications			
517311	Wired Telecommunications Carriers		1,500
517312	Wireless Telecommunications Carriers (except Satellite)		1,500
517410	Satellite Telecommunications	$32.5	
517911	Telecommunications Resellers		1,500
517919	All Other Telecommunications	$32.5	
Subsector 518—Data Processing, Hosting, and Related Services			
518210	Data Processing, Hosting, and Related Services	$32.5	
Subsector 519—Other Information Services			
519110	News Syndicates	$27.5	
519120	Libraries and Archives	$15.0	
519130	Internet Publishing and Broadcasting and Web Search Portals		1,000
519190	All Other Information Services	$27.5	
Sector 52—Finance and Insurance			
Subsector 522—Credit Intermediation and Related Activities			
522110	Commercial Banking [8]	$550 million in assets [8]	
522120	Savings Institutions [8]	$550 million in assets [8]	
522130	Credit Unions [8]	$550 million in assets [8]	
522190	Other Depository Credit Intermediation [8]	$550 million in assets [8]	
522210	Credit Card Issuing [8]	$550 million in assets [8]	
522220	Sales Financing	$38.5	
522291	Consumer Lending	$38.5	
522292	Real Estate Credit	$38.5	
522293	International Trade Financing	$38.5	
522294	Secondary Market Financing	$38.5	
522298	All Other Nondepository Credit Intermediation	$38.5	
522310	Mortgage and Nonmortgage Loan Brokers	$7.5	
522320	Financial Transactions Processing, Reserve, and Clearinghouse Activities	$38.5	
522390	Other Activities Related to Credit Intermediation	$20.5	
Subsector 523—Securities, Commodity Contracts, and Other Financial Investments and Related Activities			
523110	Investment Banking and Securities Dealing	$38.5	
523120	Securities Brokerage	$38.5	
523130	Commodity Contracts Dealing	$38.5	
523140	Commodity Contracts Brokerage	$38.5	
523210	Securities and Commodity Exchanges	$38.5	
523910	Miscellaneous Intermediation	$38.5	
523920	Portfolio Management	$38.5	
523930	Investment Advice	$38.5	
523991	Trust, Fiduciary and Custody Activities	$38.5	
523999	Miscellaneous Financial Investment Activities	$38.5	
Subsector 524—Insurance Carriers and Related Activities			
524113	Direct Life Insurance Carriers	$38.5	
524114	Direct Health and Medical Insurance Carriers	$38.5	
524126	Direct Property and Casualty Insurance Carriers		1,500
524127	Direct Title Insurance Carriers	$38.5	
524128	Other Direct Insurance (except Life, Health and Medical) Carriers	$38.5	
524130	Reinsurance Carriers	$38.5	
524210	Insurance Agencies and Brokerages	$7.5	
524291	Claims Adjusting	$20.5	
524292	Third Party Administration of Insurance and Pension Funds	$32.5	

SMALL BUSINESS SIZE STANDARDS BY NAICS INDUSTRY—Continued

NAICS codes	NAICS U.S. industry title	Size standards in millions of dollars	Size standards in number of employees
524298	All Other Insurance Related Activities	$15.0	
	Subsector 525—Funds, Trusts and Other Financial Vehicles		
525110	Pension Funds	$32.5	
525120	Health and Welfare Funds	$32.5	
525190	Other Insurance Funds	$32.5	
525910	Open-End Investment Funds	$32.5	
525920	Trusts, Estates, and Agency Accounts	$32.5	
525990	Other Financial Vehicles	$32.5	
	Sector 53—Real Estate and Rental and Leasing		
	Subsector 531—Real Estate		
531110	Lessors of Residential Buildings and Dwellings [9]	$27.5 [9]	
531120	Lessors of Nonresidential Buildings (except Miniwarehouses) [9]	$27.5 [9]	
531130	Lessors of Miniwarehouses and Self Storage Units [9]	$27.5 [9]	
531190	Lessors of Other Real Estate Property [9]	$27.5 [9]	
531210	Offices of Real Estate Agents and Brokers [10]	$7.5 [10]	
531311	Residential Property Managers	$7.5	
531312	Nonresidential Property Managers	$7.5	
531320	Offices of Real Estate Appraisers	$7.5	
531390	Other Activities Related to Real Estate	$7.5	
	Subsector 532—Rental and Leasing Services		
532111	Passenger Car Rental	$38.5	
532112	Passenger Car Leasing	$38.5	
532120	Truck, Utility Trailer, and RV (Recreational Vehicle) Rental and Leasing	$38.5	
532210	Consumer Electronics and Appliances Rental	$38.5	
532281	Formal Wear and Costume Rental	$20.5	
532282	Video Tape and Disc Rental	$27.5	
532283	Home Health Equipment Rental	$32.5	
532284	Recreational Goods Rental	$7.5	
532289	All Other Consumer Goods Rental	$7.5	
532310	General Rental Centers	$7.5	
532411	Commercial Air, Rail, and Water Transportation Equipment Rental and Leasing.	$32.5	
532412	Construction, Mining and Forestry Machinery and Equipment Rental and Leasing.	$32.5	
532420	Office Machinery and Equipment Rental and Leasing	$32.5	
532490	Other Commercial and Industrial Machinery and Equipment Rental and Leasing.	$32.5	
	Subsector 533—Lessors of Nonfinancial Intangible Assets (except Copyrighted Works)		
533110	Lessors of Nonfinancial Intangible Assets (except Copyrighted Works)	$38.5	
	Sector 54—Professional, Scientific and Technical Services		
	Subsector 541—Professional, Scientific and Technical Services		
541110	Offices of Lawyers	$11.0	
541191	Title Abstract and Settlement Offices	$11.0	
541199	All Other Legal Services	$11.0	
541211	Offices of Certified Public Accountants	$20.5	
541213	Tax Preparation Services	$20.5	
541214	Payroll Services	$20.5	
541219	Other Accounting Services	$20.5	
541310	Architectural Services	$7.5	
541320	Landscape Architectural Services	$7.5	
541330	Engineering Services	$15.0	
Except,	Military and Aerospace Equipment and Military Weapons	$38.5	
Except,	Contracts and Subcontracts for Engineering Services Awarded Under the National Energy Policy Act of 1992.	$38.5	
Except,	Marine Engineering and Naval Architecture	$38.5	
541340	Drafting Services	$7.5	
541350	Building Inspection Services	$7.5	
541360	Geophysical Surveying and Mapping Services	$15.0	
541370	Surveying and Mapping (except Geophysical) Services	$15.0	

SMALL BUSINESS SIZE STANDARDS BY NAICS INDUSTRY—Continued

NAICS codes	NAICS U.S. industry title	Size standards in millions of dollars	Size standards in number of employees
541380	Testing Laboratories	$15.0	
541410	Interior Design Services	$7.5	
541420	Industrial Design Services	$7.5	
541430	Graphic Design Services	$7.5	
541490	Other Specialized Design Services	$7.5	
541511	Custom Computer Programming Services	$27.5	
541512	Computer Systems Design Services	$27.5	
541513	Computer Facilities Management Services	$27.5	
541519	Other Computer Related Services	$27.5	
Except,	Information Technology Value Added Resellers [18]		150 [18]
541611	Administrative Management and General Management Consulting Services.	$15.0	
541612	Human Resources Consulting Services	$15.0	
541613	Marketing Consulting Services	$15.0	
541614	Process, Physical Distribution and Logistics Consulting Services	$15.0	
541618	Other Management Consulting Services	$15.0	
541620	Environmental Consulting Services	$15.0	
541690	Other Scientific and Technical Consulting Services	$15.0	
541713	Research and Technology in Nanotechnology [11]		1,000 [11]
541714	Research and Technology in Biotechnology (except Nanobiotechnology) [11]		1,000 [11]
541715	Research and Development in the Physical, Engineering, and Life Sciences (except Nanotechnology and Biotechnology) [11].		1,000 [11]
Except,	Aircraft, Aircraft Engine and Engine Parts [11]		1,500 [11]
Except,	Other Aircraft Parts and Auxiliary Equipment [11]		1,250 [11]
Except,	Guided Missiles and Space Vehicles, Their Propulsion Units and Propulsion Parts [11].		1,250 [11]
541720	Research and Development in the Social Sciences and Humanities	$20.5	
541810	Advertising Agencies [10]	$15.0 [10]	
541820	Public Relations Agencies	$15.0	
541830	Media Buying Agencies	$15.0	
541840	Media Representatives	$15.0	
541850	Outdoor Advertising	$15.0	
541860	Direct Mail Advertising	$15.0	
541870	Advertising Material Distribution Services	$15.0	
541890	Other Services Related to Advertising	$15.0	
541910	Marketing Research and Public Opinion Polling	$15.0	
541921	Photography Studios, Portrait	$7.5	
541922	Commercial Photography	$7.5	
541930	Translation and Interpretation Services	$7.5	
541940	Veterinary Services	$7.5	
541990	All Other Professional, Scientific and Technical Services	$15.0	
	Sector 55—Management of Companies and Enterprises		
	Subsector 551—Management of Companies and Enterprises		
551111	Offices of Bank Holding Companies	$20.5	
551112	Offices of Other Holding Companies	$20.5	
	Sector 56—Administrative and Support, Waste Management and Remediation Services		
	Subsector 561—Administrative and Support Services		
561110	Office Administrative Services	$7.5	
561210	Facilities Support Services [12]	$38.5 [12]	
561311	Employment Placement Agencies	$27.5	
561312	Executive Search Services	$27.5	
561320	Temporary Help Services	$27.5	
561330	Professional Employer Organizations	$27.5	
561410	Document Preparation Services	$15.0	
561421	Telephone Answering Services	$15.0	
561422	Telemarketing Bureaus and Other contact Centers	$15.0	
561431	Private Mail Centers	$15.0	
561439	Other Business Service Centers (including Copy Shops)	$15.0	
561440	Collection Agencies	$15.0	
561450	Credit Bureaus	$15.0	
561491	Repossession Services	$15.0	
561492	Court Reporting and Stenotype Services	$15.0	
561499	All Other Business Support Services	$15.0	
561510	Travel Agencies [10]	$20.5 [10]	
561520	Tour Operators [10]	$20.5 [10]	

SMALL BUSINESS SIZE STANDARDS BY NAICS INDUSTRY—Continued

NAICS codes	NAICS U.S. industry title	Size standards in millions of dollars	Size standards in number of employees
561591	Convention and Visitors Bureaus	$20.5	
561599	All Other Travel Arrangement and Reservation Services	$20.5	
561611	Investigation Services	$20.5	
561612	Security Guards and Patrol Services	$20.5	
561613	Armored Car Services	$20.5	
561621	Security Systems Services (except Locksmiths)	$20.5	
561622	Locksmiths	$20.5	
561710	Exterminating and Pest Control Services	$11.0	
561720	Janitorial Services	$18.0	
561730	Landscaping Services	$7.5	
561740	Carpet and Upholstery Cleaning Services	$5.5	
561790	Other Services to Buildings and Dwellings	$7.5	
561910	Packaging and Labeling Services	$11.0	
561920	Convention and Trade Show Organizers [10]	$11.0 [10]	
561990	All Other Support Services	$11.0	
Subsector 562—Waste Management and Remediation Services			
562111	Solid Waste Collection	$38.5	
562112	Hazardous Waste Collection	$38.5	
562119	Other Waste Collection	$38.5	
562211	Hazardous Waste Treatment and Disposal	$38.5	
562212	Solid Waste Landfill	$38.5	
562213	Solid Waste Combustors and Incinerators	$38.5	
562219	Other Nonhazardous Waste Treatment and Disposal	$38.5	
562910	Remediation Services	$20.5	
Except,	Environmental Remediation Services [14]		750 [14]
562920	Materials Recovery Facilities	$20.5	
562991	Septic Tank and Related Services	$7.5	
562998	All Other Miscellaneous Waste Management Services	$7.5	
Sector 61—Educational Services			
Subsector 611—Educational Services			
611110	Elementary and Secondary Schools	$11.0	
611210	Junior Colleges	$20.5	
611310	Colleges, Universities and Professional Schools	$27.5	
611410	Business and Secretarial Schools	$7.5	
611420	Computer Training	$11.0	
611430	Professional and Management Development Training	$11.0	
611511	Cosmetology and Barber Schools	$7.5	
611512	Flight Training	$27.5	
611513	Apprenticeship Training	$7.5	
611519	Other Technical and Trade Schools	$15.0	
Except,	Job Corps Centers [16]	$38.5 [16]	
611610	Fine Arts Schools	$7.5	
611620	Sports and Recreation Instruction	$7.5	
611630	Language Schools	$11.0	
611691	Exam Preparation and Tutoring	$7.5	
611692	Automobile Driving Schools	$7.5	
611699	All Other Miscellaneous Schools and Instruction	$11.0	
611710	Educational Support Services	$15.0	
Sector 62—Health Care and Social Assistance			
Subsector 621—Ambulatory Health Care Services			
621111	Offices of Physicians (except Mental Health Specialists)	$11.0	
621112	Offices of Physicians, Mental Health Specialists	$11.0	
621210	Offices of Dentists	$7.5	
621310	Offices of Chiropractors	$7.5	
621320	Offices of Optometrists	$7.5	
621330	Offices of Mental Health Practitioners (except Physicians)	$7.5	
621340	Offices of Physical, Occupational and Speech Therapists and Audiologists	$7.5	
621391	Offices of Podiatrists	$7.5	
621399	Offices of All Other Miscellaneous Health Practitioners	$7.5	
621410	Family Planning Centers	$11.0	
621420	Outpatient Mental Health and Substance Abuse Centers	$15.0	
621491	HMO Medical Centers	$32.5	
621492	Kidney Dialysis Centers	$38.5	

SMALL BUSINESS SIZE STANDARDS BY NAICS INDUSTRY—Continued

NAICS codes	NAICS U.S. industry title	Size standards in millions of dollars	Size standards in number of employees
621493	Freestanding Ambulatory Surgical and Emergency Centers	$15.0	
621498	All Other Outpatient Care Centers	$20.5	
621511	Medical Laboratories	$32.5	
621512	Diagnostic Imaging Centers	$15.0	
621610	Home Health Care Services	$15.0	
621910	Ambulance Services	$15.0	
621991	Blood and Organ Banks	$32.5	
621999	All Other Miscellaneous Ambulatory Health Care Services	$15.0	
	Subsector 622—Hospitals		
622110	General Medical and Surgical Hospitals	$38.5	
622210	Psychiatric and Substance Abuse Hospitals	$38.5	
622310	Specialty (except Psychiatric and Substance Abuse) Hospitals	$38.5	
	Subsector 623—Nursing and Residential Care Facilities		
623110	Nursing Care Facilities (Skilled Nursing Facilities)	$27.5	
623210	Residential Intellectual and Developmental Disability Facilities	$15.0	
623220	Residential Mental Health and Substance Abuse Facilities	$15.0	
623311	Continuing Care Retirement Communities	$27.5	
623312	Assisted Living Facilities for the Elderly	$11.0	
623990	Other Residential Care Facilities	$11.0	
	Subsector 624—Social Assistance		
624110	Child and Youth Services	$11.0	
624120	Services for the Elderly and Persons with Disabilities	$11.0	
624190	Other Individual and Family Services	$11.0	
624210	Community Food Services	$11.0	
624221	Temporary Shelters	$11.0	
624229	Other Community Housing Services	$15.0	
624230	Emergency and Other Relief Services	$32.5	
624310	Vocational Rehabilitation Services	$11.0	
624410	Child Day Care Services	$7.5	
	Sector 71—Arts, Entertainment and Recreation		
	Subsector 711—Performing Arts, Spectator Sports and Related Industries		
711110	Theater Companies and Dinner Theaters	$20.5	
711120	Dance Companies	$11.0	
711130	Musical Groups and Artists	$11.0	
711190	Other Performing Arts Companies	$27.5	
711211	Sports Teams and Clubs	$38.5	
711212	Race Tracks	$38.5	
711219	Other Spectator Sports	$11.0	
711310	Promoters of Performing Arts, Sports and Similar Events with Facilities	$32.5	
711320	Promoters of Performing Arts, Sports and Similar Events without Facilities	$15.0	
711410	Agents and Managers for Artists, Athletes, Entertainers and Other Public Figures.	$11.0	
711510	Independent Artists, Writers, and Performers	$7.5	
	Subsector 712—Museums, Historical Sites and Similar Institutions		
712110	Museums	$27.5	
712120	Historical Sites	$7.5	
712130	Zoos and Botanical Gardens	$27.5	
712190	Nature Parks and Other Similar Institutions	$7.5	
	Subsector 713—Amusement, Gambling and Recreation Industries		
713110	Amusement and Theme Parks	$38.5	
713120	Amusement Arcades	$7.5	
713210	Casinos (except Casino Hotels)	$27.5	
713290	Other Gambling Industries	$32.5	
713910	Golf Courses and Country Clubs	$15.0	
713920	Skiing Facilities	$27.5	
713930	Marinas	$7.5	
713940	Fitness and Recreational Sports Centers	$7.5	
713950	Bowling Centers	$7.5	

SMALL BUSINESS SIZE STANDARDS BY NAICS INDUSTRY—Continued

NAICS codes	NAICS U.S. industry title	Size standards in millions of dollars	Size standards in number of employees
713990	All Other Amusement and Recreation Industries	$7.5	
	Sector 72—Accommodation and Food Services		
	Subsector 721—Accommodation		
721110	Hotels (except Casino Hotels) and Motels	$32.5	
721120	Casino Hotels	$32.5	
721191	Bed-and-Breakfast Inns	$7.5	
721199	All Other Traveler Accommodation	$7.5	
721211	RV (Recreational Vehicle) Parks and Campgrounds	$7.5	
721214	Recreational and Vacation Camps (except Campgrounds)	$7.5	
721310	Rooming and Boarding Houses, Dormitories, and Workers' Camps	$7.5	
	Subsector 722—Food Services and Drinking Places		
722310	Food Service Contractors	$38.5	
722320	Caterers	$7.5	
722330	Mobile Food Services	$7.5	
722410	Drinking Places (Alcoholic Beverages)	$7.5	
722511	Full-Service Restaurants	$7.5	
722513	Limited-Service Restaurants	$11.0	
722514	Cafeterias, Grill Buffets, and Buffets	$27.5	
722515	Snack and Nonalcoholic Beverage Bars	$7.5	
	Sector 81—Other Services (Except Public Administration)		
	Subsector 811—Repair and Maintenance		
811111	General Automotive Repair	$7.5	
811112	Automotive Exhaust System Repair	$7.5	
811113	Automotive Transmission Repair	$7.5	
811118	Other Automotive Mechanical and Electrical Repair and Maintenance	$7.5	
811121	Automotive Body, Paint and Interior Repair and Maintenance	$7.5	
811122	Automotive Glass Replacement Shops	$11.0	
811191	Automotive Oil Change and Lubrication Shops	$7.5	
811192	Car Washes	$7.5	
811198	All Other Automotive Repair and Maintenance	$7.5	
811211	Consumer Electronics Repair and Maintenance	$7.5	
811212	Computer and Office Machine Repair and Maintenance	$27.5	
811213	Communication Equipment Repair and Maintenance	$11.0	
811219	Other Electronic and Precision Equipment Repair and Maintenance	$20.5	
811310	Commercial and Industrial Machinery and Equipment (except Automotive and Electronic) Repair and Maintenance.	$7.5	
811411	Home and Garden Equipment Repair and Maintenance	$7.5	
811412	Appliance Repair and Maintenance	$15.0	
811420	Reupholstery and Furniture Repair	$7.5	
811430	Footwear and Leather Goods Repair	$7.5	
811490	Other Personal and Household Goods Repair and Maintenance	$7.5	
	Subsector 812—Personal and Laundry Services		
812111	Barber Shops	$7.5	
812112	Beauty Salons	$7.5	
812113	Nail Salons	$7.5	
812191	Diet and Weight Reducing Centers	$20.5	
812199	Other Personal Care Services	$7.5	
812210	Funeral Homes and Funeral Services	$7.5	
812220	Cemeteries and Crematories	$20.5	
812310	Coin-Operated Laundries and Drycleaners	$7.5	
812320	Drycleaning and Laundry Services (except Coin-Operated)	$5.5	
812331	Linen Supply	$32.5	
812332	Industrial Launderers	$38.5	
812910	Pet Care (except Veterinary) Services	$7.5	
812921	Photofinishing Laboratories (except One-Hour)	$20.5	
812922	One-Hour Photofinishing	$15.0	
812930	Parking Lots and Garages	$38.5	
812990	All Other Personal Services	$7.5	
	Subsector 813—Religious, Grantmaking, Civic, Professional and Similar Organizations		
813110	Religious Organizations	$7.5	

SMALL BUSINESS SIZE STANDARDS BY NAICS INDUSTRY—Continued

NAICS codes	NAICS U.S. industry title	Size standards in millions of dollars	Size standards in number of employees
813211	Grantmaking Foundations	$32.5	
813212	Voluntary Health Organizations	$27.5	
813219	Other Grantmaking and Giving Services	$38.5	
813311	Human Rights Organizations	$27.5	
813312	Environment, Conservation and Wildlife Organizations	$15.0	
813319	Other Social Advocacy Organizations	$7.5	
813410	Civic and Social Organizations	$7.5	
813910	Business Associations	$7.5	
813920	Professional Organizations	$15.0	
813930	Labor Unions and Similar Labor Organizations	$7.5	
813940	Political Organizations	$7.5	
813990	Other Similar Organizations (except Business, Professional, Labor, and Political Organizations).	$7.5	
	Sector 92—Public Administration [19]		
(Small business size standards are not established for this sector. Establishments in the Public Administration sector are Federal, state, and local government agencies which administer and oversee government programs and activities that are not performed by private establishments.)			

Footnotes

1. [Reserved]

2. *NAICS code 237990*—Dredging: To be considered small for purposes of Government procurement, a firm must perform at least 40 percent of the volume dredged with its own equipment or equipment owned by another small dredging concern.

3. *NAICS code 311421*—For purposes of Government procurement for food canning and preserving, the standard of 1,000 employees excludes agricultural labor as defined in 3306(k) of the Internal Revenue Code, 26 U.S.C. 3306(k).

4. *NAICS code 324110*—To qualify as small for purposes of Government procurement, the petroleum refiner, including its affiliates, must be a concern that has either no more than 1,500 employees or no more than 200,000 barrels per calendar day total Operable Atmospheric Crude Oil Distillation capacity. Capacity includes all domestic and foreign affiliates, all owned or leased facilities, and all facilities under a processing agreement or an arrangement such as an exchange agreement or a throughput. To qualify under the capacity size standard, the firm, together with its affiliates, must be primarily engaged in refining crude petroleum into refined petroleum products. A firm's "primary industry" is determined in accordance with 13 CFR 121.107.

5. *NAICS code 326211*—For Government procurement, a firm is small for bidding on a contract for pneumatic tires within Census NAICS Product Classification codes 3262111 and 3262113, provided that:

(a) The value of tires within Census NAICS Product Classification codes 3262111 and 3262113 that it manufactured in the United States during the previous calendar year is more than 50 percent of the value of its total worldwide manufacture,

(b) The value of pneumatic tires within Census NAICS Product Classification codes 3262111 and 3262113 comprising its total worldwide manufacture during the preceding calendar year was less than 5 percent of the value of all such tires manufactured in the United States during that period, and

(c) The value of the principal product that it manufactured, produced, or sold worldwide during the preceding calendar year is less than 10 percent of the total value of such products manufactured or otherwise produced or sold in the United States during that period.

6. *NAICS Subsectors 333, 334, 335* and *336*—For rebuilding machinery or equipment on a factory basis, or equivalent, use the NAICS code for a newly manufactured product. Concerns performing major rebuilding or overhaul activities do not necessarily have to meet the criteria for being a "manufacturer" although the activities may be classified under a manufacturing NAICS code. Ordinary repair services or preservation are not considered rebuilding.

7. *NAICS code 336413*—Contracts for the rebuilding or overhaul of aircraft ground support equipment on a contract basis are classified under NAICS code 336413.

8. *NAICS Codes 522110, 522120, 522130, 522190, and 522210*—A financial institution's assets are determined by averaging the assets reported on its four quarterly financial statements for the preceding year. "Assets" for the purposes of this size standard means the assets defined according to the Federal Financial Institutions Examination Council 041 call report form for NAICS codes 522110, 522120, 522190, and 522210 and the National

Credit Union Administration 5300 call report form for NAICS code 522130.

9. *NAICS codes 531110, 531120, 531130, and 531190*—Leasing of Building Space to the Federal Government by Owners: For Government procurement, a size standard of $38.5 million in gross receipts applies to the owners of building space leased to the Federal Government. The standard does not apply to an agent.

10. *NAICS codes 488510 (part) 531210, 541810, 561510, 561520,* and *561920*—As measured by total revenues, but excluding funds received in trust for an unaffiliated third party, such as bookings or sales subject to commissions. The commissions received are included as revenues.

11. *NAICS code 541713, 541714, and 541715*—

(a) "Research and Development" means laboratory or other physical research and development. It does not include economic, educational, engineering, operations, systems, or other nonphysical research; or computer programming, data processing, commercial and/or medical laboratory testing.

(b) For research and development contracts requiring the delivery of a manufactured product, the appropriate size standard is that of the manufacturing industry.

(c) For purposes of the Small Business Innovation Research (SBIR) and Small Business Transfer Technology (STTR) programs, the term "research" or "research and development" means any activity which is (A) a systematic, intensive study directed toward greater knowledge or understanding of the subject studied; (B) a systematic study directed specifically toward applying new knowledge to meet a recognized need; or (C) a systematic application of knowledge toward the production of useful materials, devices, and systems or methods, including design, development, and improvement of prototypes and new processes to meet specific requirements. See 15 U.S.C. 638(e)(5) and section 3 of the SBIR and STTR policy directives available at *www.sbir.gov*. For size eligibility requirements for the SBIR and STTR programs, see § 121.702 of this part.

(d) "Research and Development" for guided missiles and space vehicles includes evaluations and simulation, and other services requiring thorough knowledge of complete missiles and spacecraft.

12. *NAICS code 561210*—Facilities Support Services:

(a) If one or more activities of Facilities Support Services as defined in paragraph (b) (below in this footnote) can be identified with a specific industry and that industry accounts for 50% or more of the value of an entire procurement, then the proper classification of the procurement is that of the specific industry, not Facilities Support Services.

(b) "Facilities Support Services" requires the performance of three or more separate activities in the areas of services or specialty trade contractors industries. If services are performed, these service activities must each be in a separate NAICS industry. If the procurement requires the use of specialty trade contractors (plumbing, painting, plastering, carpentry, etc.), all such specialty trade contractors activities are considered a single activity and classified as "Building and Property Specialty Trade Services." Since "Building and Property Specialty Trade Services" is only one activity, two additional activities of separate NAICS industries are required for a procurement to be classified as "Facilities Support Services."

13. *NAICS code 238990*—Building and Property Specialty Trade Services: If a procurement requires the use of multiple specialty trade contractors (*i.e.*, plumbing, painting, plastering, carpentry, etc.), and no specialty trade accounts for 50% or more of the value of the procurement, all such specialty trade contractors activities are considered a single activity and classified as Building and Property Specialty Trade Services.

14. *NAICS 562910*—Environmental Remediation Services:

(a) For SBA assistance as a small business concern in the industry of Environmental Remediation Services, other than for Government procurement, a concern must be engaged primarily in furnishing a range of services for the remediation of a contaminated environment to an acceptable condition including, but not limited to, preliminary assessment, site inspection, testing, remedial investigation, feasibility studies, remedial design, containment, remedial action, removal of contaminated materials, storage of contaminated materials and security and site closeouts. If one of such activities accounts for 50 percent or more of a concern's total revenues, employees, or other related factors, the concern's primary industry is that of the particular industry and not the Environmental Remediation Services Industry.

(b) For purposes of classifying a Government procurement as Environmental Remediation Services, the general purpose of the procurement must be to restore or directly support the restoration of a contaminated environment (such as, preliminary assessment, site inspection, testing, remedial investigation, feasibility studies, remedial design, remediation services, containment, removal of contaminated materials, storage of contaminated materials or security and site closeouts), although the general purpose of the procurement need not necessarily include remedial actions. Also, the procurement must be composed of activities in three or more separate industries with separate NAICS codes or, in some instances (*e.g.*, engineering), smaller sub-components of NAICS codes with separate, distinct size standards.

These activities may include, but are not limited to, separate activities in industries such as: Heavy Construction; Specialty Trade Contractors; Engineering Services; Architectural Services; Management Consulting Services; Hazardous and Other Waste Collection; Remediation Services, Testing Laboratories; and Research and Development in the Physical, Engineering and Life Sciences. If any activity in the procurement can be identified with a separate NAICS code, or component of a code with a separate distinct size standard, and that industry accounts for 50 percent or more of the value of the entire procurement, then the proper size standard is the one for that particular industry, and not the Environmental Remediation Service size standard.

15. [Reserved]

16. *NAICS codes 611519*—Job Corps Centers. For classifying a Federal procurement, the purpose of the solicitation must be for the management and operation of a U.S. Department of Labor Job Corps Center. The activities involved include admissions activities, life skills training, educational activities, comprehensive career preparation activities, career development activities, career transition activities, as well as the management and support functions and services needed to operate and maintain the facility. For SBA assistance as a small business concern, other than for Federal Government procurements, a concern must be primarily engaged in providing the services to operate and maintain Federal Job Corps Centers.

17. *NAICS code 115310* (Support Activities for Forestry)—Forest Fire Suppression and Fuels Management Services are two components of Support Activities for Forestry. Forest Fire Suppression includes establishments which provide services to fight forest fires. These firms usually have fire-fighting crews and equipment. Fuels Management Services firms provide services to clear land of hazardous materials that would fuel forest fires. The treatments used by these firms may include prescribed fire, mechanical removal, establishing fuel breaks, thinning, pruning, and piling.

18. *NAICS code 541519*—An Information Technology Value Added Reseller (ITVAR) provides a total solution to information technology acquisitions by providing multi-vendor hardware and software along with significant value added services. Significant value added services consist of, but are not limited to, configuration consulting and design, systems integration, installation of multi-vendor computer equipment, customization of hardware or software, training, product technical support, maintenance, and end user support. For purposes of Government procurement, an information technology procurement classified under this exception and 150-employee size standard must consist of at least 15% and not more than 50% of value added services, as measured by the total contract price. In addition, the offeror must comply with the manufacturing performance requirements, or comply with the non-manufacturer rule by supplying the products of small business concerns, unless SBA has issued a class or contract specific waiver of the non-manufacturer rule. If the contract consists of less than 15% of value added services, then it must be classified under a NAICS manufacturing industry. If the contract consists of more than 50% of value added services, then it must be classified under the NAICS industry that best describes the predominate service of the procurement.

19. *NAICS Sector 92*—Small business size standards are not established for this sector. Establishments in the Public Administration sector are Federal, State, and local government agencies which administer and oversee government programs and activities that are not performed by private establishments. Concerns performing operational services for the administration of a government program are classified under the NAICS private sector industry based on the activities performed. Similarly, procurements for these types of services are classified under the NAICS private sector industry that best describes the activities to be performed. For example, if a government agency issues a procurement for law enforcement services, the requirement would be classified using one of the NAICS industry codes under 56161, Investigation, Guard, and Armored Car Services.

20. *NAICS code 511210*—For purposes of Government procurement, the purchase of software subject to potential waiver of the non-manufacturer rule pursuant to § 121.1203(d) should be classified under this NAICS code.

[65 FR 30840, May 15, 2000]

EDITORIAL NOTES: 1. For FEDERAL REGISTER citations affecting § 121.201, see the List of CFR Sections Affected, which appears in the Finding Aids section of the printed volume and at *www.govinfo.gov*.

2. At 73 FR 12870, Mar. 11, 2008, § 121.201 was amended; however, several amendments could not be incorporated due to inaccurate amendatory instruction.

SIZE ELIGIBILITY REQUIREMENTS FOR SBA FINANCIAL ASSISTANCE

§ 121.301 What size standards and affiliation principles are applicable to financial assistance programs?

(a) For Business Loans (other than for 7(a) Business Loans for the period beginning May 5, 2009 and ending on September 30, 2010) and for Disaster Loans (other than physical disaster loans), an applicant business concern must satisfy two criteria:

(1) The size of the applicant alone (without affiliates) must not exceed the size standard designated for the industry in which the applicant is primarily engaged; and

(2) The size of the applicant combined with its affiliates must not exceed the size standard designated for either the primary industry of the applicant alone or the primary industry of the applicant and its affiliates, which ever is higher. These size standards are set forth in § 121.201.

(b) For Development Company programs and, for the period beginning May 5, 2009 and ending on September 30, 2010, for 7(a) Business Loans, an applicant must meet one of the following standards:

(1) The same standards applicable under paragraph (a) of this section; or

(2) Including its affiliates, tangible net worth not in excess of $8.5 million, and average net income after Federal income taxes (excluding any carry-over losses) for the preceding two completed fiscal years not in excess of $3.0 million. If the applicant is not required by law to pay Federal income taxes at the enterprise level, but is required to pass income through to its shareholders, partners, beneficiaries, or other equitable owners, the applicant's "net income after Federal income taxes" will be its net income reduced by an amount computed as follows:

(i) If the applicant is not required by law to pay State (and local, if any) income taxes at the enterprise level, multiply its net income by the marginal State income tax rate (or by the combined State and local income tax rates, as applicable) that would have applied if it were a taxable corporation.

(ii) Multiply the applicant's net income, less any deduction for State and local income taxes calculated under paragraph (b)(2)(i) of this section, by the marginal Federal income tax rate that would have applied if the applicant were a taxable corporation.

(iii) Sum the results obtained in paragraphs (b)(2)(i) and (b)(2)(ii) of this section.

(c) For the Small Business Investment Company (SBIC) program, an applicant must meet one of the following standards:

(1) The same standards applicable under paragraph (a) of this section; or

(2) Including its affiliates, tangible net worth not in excess of $19.5 million, and average net income after Federal income taxes (excluding any carry-over losses) for the preceding two completed fiscal years not in excess of $6.5 million. If the applicant is not required by law to pay Federal income taxes at the enterprise level, but is required to pass income through to its shareholders, partners, beneficiaries, or other equitable owners, the applicant's "net income after Federal income taxes" will be its net income reduced by an amount computed as follows:

(i) If the applicant is not required by law to pay State (and local, if any) income taxes at the enterprise level, multiply its net income by the marginal State income tax rate (or by the combined State and local income tax rates, as applicable) that would have applied if it were a taxable corporation.

(ii) Multiply the applicant's net income, less any deduction for State and local income taxes calculated under paragraph (c)(2)(i) of this section, by the marginal Federal income tax rate that would have applied if the applicant were a taxable corporation.

(iii) Add the results obtained in paragraphs (c)(2)(i) and (c)(2)(ii) of this section.

(d) For Surety Bond Guarantee assistance—a business concern, combined with its affiliates, must meet the size standard for the primary industry in which such business concern, combined with its affiliates, is engaged.

(e) The applicable size standards for purposes of SBA's financial assistance programs, excluding the Surety Bond Guarantee assistance program, are increased by 25% whenever the applicant agrees to use all of the financial assistance within a labor surplus area. Labor surplus areas are listed monthly in the Department of Labor publication "Area Trends in Employment and Unemployment."

(f) Concerns and entities are affiliates of each other when one controls or has the power to control the other, or a third party or parties controls or has the power to control both. It does not matter whether control is exercised, so long as the power to control exists. Affiliation under any of the circumstances described below is sufficient to establish affiliation for applicants for SBA's Business Loan, Disaster Loan, and Surety Bond Programs. For this rule, the Business Loan Programs consist of the 7(a) Loan Program, the Microloan Program, the Intermediary Lending Pilot Program, and the Development Company Loan Program ("504 Loan Program"). The Disaster Loan Programs consist of Physical Disaster Business Loans, Economic Injury Disaster Loans, Military Reservist Economic Injury Disaster Loans, and Immediate Disaster Assistance Program loans. The following principles apply for the Business Loan, Disaster Loan, and Surety Bond Guarantee Programs:

(1) *Affiliation based on ownership.* For determining affiliation based on equity ownership, a concern is an affiliate of an individual, concern, or entity that owns or has the power to control more than 50 percent of the concern's voting equity. If no individual, concern, or entity is found to control, SBA will deem the Board of Directors or President or Chief Executive Officer (CEO) (or other officers, managing members, or partners who control the management of the concern) to be in control of the concern. SBA will deem a minority shareholder to be in control, if that individual or entity has the ability, under the concern's charter, by-laws, or shareholder's agreement, to prevent a quorum or otherwise block action by the board of directors or shareholders.

(2) *Affiliation arising under stock options, convertible securities, and agreements to merge.* (i) In determining size, SBA considers stock options, convertible securities, and agreements to merge (including agreements in principle) to have a present effect on the power to control a concern. SBA treats such options, convertible securities, and agreements as though the rights granted have been exercised.

(ii) Agreements to open or continue negotiations towards the possibility of a merger or a sale of stock at some later date are not considered "agreements in principle" and are thus not given present effect.

(iii) Options, convertible securities, and agreements that are subject to conditions precedent which are incapable of fulfillment, speculative, conjectural, or unenforceable under state or Federal law, or where the probability of the transaction (or exercise of the rights) occurring is shown to be extremely remote, are not given present effect.

(iv) An individual, concern or other entity that controls one or more other concerns cannot use options, convertible securities, or agreements to appear to terminate such control before actually doing so. SBA will not give present effect to individuals', concerns', or other entities' ability to divest all or part of their ownership interest in order to avoid a finding of affiliation.

(3) *Affiliation based on management.* Affiliation arises where the CEO or President of the applicant concern (or other officers, managing members, or partners who control the management of the concern) also controls the management of one or more other concerns. Affiliation also arises where a single individual, concern, or entity that controls the Board of Directors or management of one concern also controls the Board of Directors or management of one of more other concerns. Affiliation also arises where a single individual, concern or entity controls the management of the applicant concern through a management agreement.

(4) *Affiliation based on identity of interest.* Affiliation arises when there is an identity of interest between close relatives, as defined in 13 CFR 120.10, with identical or substantially, identical business or economic interests (such as where the close relatives operate concerns in the same or similar industry in the same geographic area). Where SBA determines that interests should be aggregated, an individual or firm may rebut that determination with evidence showing that the interests deemed to be one are in fact separate.

(5) *Affiliation based on franchise and license agreements.* The restraints imposed on a franchisee or licensee by its

franchise or license agreement generally will not be considered in determining whether the franchisor or licensor is affiliated with an applicant franchisee or licensee provided the applicant franchisee or licensee has the right to profit from its efforts and bears the risk of loss commensurate with ownership. SBA will only consider the franchise or license agreements of the applicant concern.

(6) *Determining the concern's size.* In determining the concern's size, SBA counts the receipts, employees (§ 121.201), or the alternate size standard (if applicable) of the concern whose size is at issue and all of its domestic and foreign affiliates, regardless of whether the affiliates are organized for profit.

(7) *Exceptions to affiliation.* For exceptions to affiliation, see 13 CFR 121.103(b).

[61 FR 3286, Jan. 31, 1996, as amended at 66 FR 30648, June 7, 2001; 67 FR 3056, Jan. 23, 2002; 69 FR 29204, May 21, 2004; 70 FR 69047, 69052, Nov. 14, 2005; 70 FR 72594, Dec. 6, 2005; 71 FR 62208, Oct. 24, 2006; 73 FR 41254, July 18, 2008; 74 FR 20580, May 5, 2009; 74 FR 36110, July 22, 2009; 75 FR 48550, Aug. 11, 2010; 79 FR 33669, June 12, 2014; 79 FR 71296, Dec. 2, 2014; 81 FR 41428, June 27, 2016]

§ 121.302 When does SBA determine the size status of an applicant?

(a) The size status of an applicant for SBA financial assistance is determined as of the date the application for financial assistance is accepted for processing by SBA, except for applications under the Preferred Lenders Program (PLP), the Disaster Loan program, the SBIC program, and the New Markets Venture Capital (NMCV) program.

(b) For the Preferred Lenders program, size is determined as of the date of approval of the loan by the Preferred Lender.

(c) For disaster loan assistance (other than physical disaster loans), size status is determined as of the date the disaster commenced, as set forth in the Disaster Declaration. For pre-disaster mitigation loans, size status is determined as of the date SBA accepts a complete Pre-Disaster Mitigation Small Business Loan Application for processing. Refer to § 123.408 of this chapter to find out what SBA considers to be a complete Pre-Disaster Mitigation Small Business Loan Application.

(d) For financial assistance from an SBIC licensee or an NMVC company, size is determined as of the date a concern's application is accepted for processing by the SBIC or the NMVC company.

(e) Changes in size after the applicable date when size is determined will not disqualify an applicant for assistance.

[61 FR 3286, Jan. 31, 1996, as amended at 64 FR 48276, Sept. 3, 1999; 67 FR 11880, Mar. 15, 2002; 67 FR 62337, Oct. 7, 2002; 69 FR 29204, May 21, 2004; 70 FR 72594, Dec. 6, 2005; 73 FR 41254, July 18, 2008; 75 FR 48550, Aug. 11, 2010; 79 FR 33669, June 12, 2014]

§ 121.303 What size procedures are used by SBA before it makes a formal size determination?

(a) A concern that submits an application for financial assistance is deemed to have certified that it is small under the applicable size standard. SBA may question the concern's status based on information supplied in the application or from any other source.

(b) A small business investment company, a development company, a surety bond company, or a preferred lender may accept as true the size information provided by an applicant, unless credible evidence to the contrary is apparent.

(c) Size is initially considered by the individual with final financial assistance authority. This is not a formal size determination. A formal determination may be requested prior to a denial of eligibility based on size.

(d) An applicant may request a formal size determination when assistance has been denied for size ineligibility. Except for disaster loan eligibility, a request for a formal size determination must be made to the Government Contracting Area Director serving the area in which the headquarters of the applicant is located, regardless of the location of the parent company or affiliates. For disaster loan assistance, the request for a size determination must be made to the Area Director for the Disaster Area Office which denied the assistance.

(e) There are no time limitations for making a formal size determination for purposes of financial assistance. The official making the formal size determination must provide a copy of the determination to the applicant, to the requesting SBA official, and to other interested SBA program officials.

§ 121.304 What are the size requirements for refinancing an existing SBA loan?

(a) A concern that applies to refinance an existing SBA loan or guarantee will be considered small for the refinancing even though its size has increased since the date of the original financing to exceed its applicable size standard, provided that:

(1) The increase in size is due to natural growth (as distinguished from merger, acquisition or similar management action); and

(2) SBA determines that refinancing is necessary to protect the Government's financial interest.

(b) If a concern's size has increased other than by natural growth, the concern and its affiliates must be small at the time the application for refinancing is accepted for processing by SBA.

§ 121.305 What size eligibility requirements exist for obtaining financial assistance relating to particular procurements?

A concern qualified as small for a particular procurement, including an 8(a) subcontract, is small for financial assistance directly and primarily relating to the performance of the particular procurement.

Size Eligibility Requirements for Government Procurement

§ 121.401 What procurement programs are subject to size determinations?

The rules set forth in §§ 121.401 through 121.413 apply to all Federal procurement programs for which status as a small business is required or advantageous, including the small business set-aside program, SBA's Certificate of Competency program, SBA's 8(a) Business Development program, SBA's HUBZone program, the Women Owned Small Business (WOSB) Federal Contract Program, SBA's Service-Disabled Veteran-Owned Small Business program, the Small Business Subcontracting program, and the Federal Small Disadvantaged Business (SDB) program.

[75 FR 62280, Oct. 7, 2010]

§ 121.402 What size standards are applicable to Federal Government Contracting programs?

(a) A concern must not exceed the size standard for the NAICS code specified in the solicitation. The contracting officer must specify the size standard in effect on the date the solicitation is issued. If SBA amends the size standard and it becomes effective before the date initial offers (including price) are due, the contracting officer may amend the solicitation and use the new size standard.

(b) The procuring agency contracting officer, or authorized representative, designates the proper NAICS code and corresponding size standard in a solicitation, selecting the single NAICS code which best describes the principal purpose of the product or service being acquired. Except for multiple award contracts as set forth in paragraph (c) of this section, every solicitation, including a request for quotations, must contain only one NAICS code and only one corresponding size standard.

(1) Primary consideration is given to the industry descriptions in the U.S. NAICS Manual, the product or service description in the solicitation and any attachments to it, the relative value and importance of the components of the procurement making up the end item being procured, and the function of the goods or services being purchased.

(2) A procurement is usually classified according to the component which accounts for the greatest percentage of contract value. Acquisitions for supplies must be classified under the appropriate manufacturing or supply NAICS code, not under a Wholesale Trade or Retail Trade NAICS code. A concern that submits an offer or quote for a contract, order, or subcontract where the NAICS code assigned to the contract, order, or subcontract is one for supplies, and furnishes a product it did not itself manufacture or produce, is categorized as a nonmanufacturer

and deemed small if it has 500 or fewer employees and meets the requirements of § 121.406(b).

(c) *Multiple Award Contracts* (*see* definition at § 125.1).

(1) For a Multiple Award Contract, the contracting officer must:

(i) Assign the solicitation a single NAICS code and corresponding size standard which best describes the principal purpose of the acquisition as set forth in paragraph (b) of this section, only if the NAICS code will also best describe the principal purpose of each order to be placed under the Multiple Award Contract. If a service NAICS code has been assigned to the Multiple Award Contract, then a service NAICS code must be assigned to the solicitation for the order, including an order for services that also requires some supplies; or

(ii) Divide the solicitation into discrete categories (such as Contract Line Item Numbers (CLINs), Special Item Numbers (SINs), Sectors, Functional Areas (FAs), or the equivalent), and assign each discrete category the single NAICS code and corresponding size standard that best describes the principal purpose of the goods or services to be acquired under that category (CLIN, SIN, Sector, FA or equivalent) as set forth in paragraph (b) of this section. A concern must meet the applicable size standard for each category (CLIN, SIN, Sector, FA or equivalent) for which it seeks an award as a small business concern.

(2)(i) The contracting officer must assign a single NAICS code for each order issued against a Multiple Award Contract. When placing an order under a Multiple Award Contract with multiple NAICS codes, the contracting officer must assign the NAICS code and corresponding size standard that best describes the principle purpose of each order. In cases like the GSA Schedule, where an agency can issue an order against multiple SINs with different NAICS codes, the contracting officer must select the single NAICS code that best represents the acquisition.

(ii) With respect to an order issued against a multiple award contract, an agency will receive small business credit for goaling only if the business concern awarded the order has represented its status as small for the underlying multiple award contract for the same NAICS code as that assigned to the order, provided recertification has not been required or occurred for the contract or order.

(d) The NAICS code assigned to a procurement and its corresponding size standard is final unless timely appealed to SBA's Office of Hearings and Appeals (OHA), or unless SBA assigns an NAICS code or size standard as provided in paragraph (e) of this section.

(e) An unclear, incomplete or missing NAICS code designation or size standard in the solicitation may be clarified, completed or supplied by SBA in connection with a formal size determination or size appeal.

(f) Any offeror or other interested party adversely affected by an NAICS code designation or size standard designation may appeal the designations to OHA under part 134 of this chapter.

[61 FR 3286, Jan. 31, 1996, as amended at 65 FR 30863, May 15, 2000; 69 FR 29205, May 21, 2004; 75 FR 61604, Oct. 6, 2010; 76 FR 5683, Feb. 2, 2011; 76 FR 8252, Feb. 11, 2011; 78 FR 61130, Oct. 2, 2013; 81 FR 34259, May 31, 2016]

§ 121.403 Are SBA size determinations and NAICS code designations binding on parties?

Formal size determinations and NAICS code designations made by authorized SBA officials are binding upon the parties. Opinions otherwise provided by SBA officials to contracting officers or others are advisory in nature, and are not binding or appealable.

[61 FR 3286, Jan. 31, 1996, as amended at 65 FR 30863, May 15, 2000]

§ 121.404 When is the size status of a business concern determined?

(a) SBA determines the size status of a concern, including its affiliates, as of the date the concern submits a written self-certification that it is small to the procuring activity as part of its initial offer (or other formal response to a solicitation), which includes price.

(1) With respect to Multiple Award Contracts and orders issued against a Multiple Award Contract:

(i) SBA determines size at the time of initial offer (or other formal response to a solicitation), which includes price, for a Multiple Award Contract based upon the size standard set forth in the solicitation for the Multiple Award Contract if a single NAICS codes is assigned as set forth in § 121.402(c)(i)(A). If a business is small at the time of offer for the Multiple Award Contract, it is small for each order issued against the contract, unless a contracting officer requests a new size certification in connection with a specific order.

(ii) SBA determines size at the time of initial offer (or other formal response to a solicitation), which includes price, for a Multiple Award Contract based upon the size standard set forth for each discrete category (*e.g.*, CLIN, SIN, Sector, FA or equivalent) for which a business concern submits an offer and represents it is small for the Multiple Award Contract as set forth in § 121.402(c)(i)(B). If the business concern submits an offer for the entire Multiple Award Contract, SBA will determine whether it meets the size standard for each discrete category (CLIN, SIN, Sector, FA or equivalent). If a business is small at the time of offer for a discrete category on the Multiple Award Contract, it is small for each order issued against that category with the same NAICS code and corresponding size standard, unless a contracting officer requests a new size certification in connection with a specific order.

(iii) SBA will determine size at the time of initial offer (or other formal response to a solicitation), which includes price, for an order issued against a Multiple Award Contract if the contracting officer requests a new size certification for the order.

(2) With respect to "Agreements" including Blanket Purchase Agreements (BPAs) (except for BPAs issued against a GSA Schedule Contract), Basic Agreements, Basic Ordering Agreements, or any other Agreement that a contracting officer sets aside or reserves awards to any type of small business, a concern must qualify as small at the time of its initial offer (or other formal response to a solicitation), which includes price, for the Agreement. Because an Agreement is not a contract, the concern must also qualify as small for each order issued pursuant to the Agreement in order to be considered small for the order and for an agency to receive small business goaling credit for the order.

(b) A concern applying to be certified as a Participant in SBA's 8(a) Business Development program (under part 124, subpart A, of this chapter), as a small disadvantaged business (under part 124, subpart B, of this chapter), or as a HUBZone small business (under part 126 of this chapter) must qualify as a small business for its primary industry classification as of the date of its application and, where applicable, the date the SBA program office requests a formal size determination in connection with a concern that otherwise appears eligible for program certification.

(c) The size status of an applicant for a Certificate of Competency (COC) relating to an unrestricted procurement is determined as of the date of the concern's application for the COC.

(d) Size status for purposes of compliance with the nonmanufacturer rule set forth in § 121.406(b)(1) and the ostensible subcontractor rule set forth in § 121.103(h)(4) is determined as of the date of the final proposal revision for negotiated acquisitions and final bid for sealed bidding.

(e) For subcontracting purposes, a concern must qualify as small as of the date that it certifies that it is small for the subcontract. The applicable size standard is that which is set forth in § 121.410 and which is in effect at the time the concern self-certifies that it is small for the subcontract.

(f) For purposes of architect-engineering, design/build or two-step sealed bidding procurements, a concern must qualify as small as of the date that it certifies that it is small as part of its initial bid or proposal (which may or may not include price).

(g) A concern that represents itself as a small business and qualifies as small at the time of its initial offer (or other formal response to a solicitation), which includes price, is considered to be a small business throughout the life of that contract. This means that if a business concern is small at the time of initial offer for a Multiple Award Contract (*see* § 121.1042(c) for designation of NAICS codes on a Multiple Award Contract), then it will be considered small for each order issued against the contract with the same NAICS code and size standard, unless a contracting officer requests a new size certification in connection with a specific order. Where a concern grows to be other than small, the procuring agency may exercise options and still count the award as an award to a small business. However, the following exceptions apply to this paragraph (g):

(1) Within 30 days of an approved contract novation, a contractor must recertify its small business size status to the procuring agency, or inform the procuring agency that it is other than small. If the contractor is other than small, the agency can no longer count the options or orders issued pursuant to the contract, from that point forward, towards its small business goals.

(2)(i) In the case of a merger, sale, or acquisition, where contract novation is not required, the contractor must, within 30 days of the transaction becoming final, recertify its small business size status to the procuring agency, or inform the procuring agency that it is other than small. If the contractor is other than small, the agency can no longer count the options or orders issued pursuant to the contract, from that point forward, towards its small business goals. The agency and the contractor must immediately revise all applicable Federal contract databases to reflect the new size status.

(ii) Recertification is required:

(A) When a concern, or an affiliate of the concern, acquires or is acquired by another concern;

(B) From both the acquired concern and the acquiring concern if each has been awarded a contract as a small business; and

(C) From a joint venture when an acquired concern, acquiring concern, or merged concern is a participant in a joint venture that has been awarded a contract or order as a small business.

(D) If the merger, sale or acquisition occurs after offer but prior to award, the offeror must recertify its size to the contracting officer prior to award.

(3) For the purposes of contracts (including Multiple Award Contracts) with durations of more than five years (including options), a contracting officer must request that a business concern recertify its small business size status no more than 120 days prior to the end of the fifth year of the contract, and no more than 120 days prior to exercising any option thereafter. If the contractor certifies that it is other than small, the agency can no longer count the options or orders issued pursuant to the contract towards its small business prime contracting goals. The agency and the contractor must immediately revise all applicable Federal contract databases to reflect the new size status.

(i) A business concern that certified itself as other than small, either initially or prior to an option being exercised, may recertify itself as small for a subsequent option period if it meets the applicable size standard.

(ii) Re-certification does not change the terms and conditions of the contract. The limitations on subcontracting, non-manufacturer and subcontracting plan requirements in effect at the time of contract award remain in effect throughout the life of the contract. However, a contracting officer may require a subcontracting plan if a prime contractor's size status changes from small to other than small as a result of a size recertification.

(iii) A request for a size re-certification shall include the size standard in effect at the time of re-certification that corresponds to the NAICS code that that was initially assigned to the contract.

(iv) A contracting officer must assign a NAICS code and size standard to each order under a long-term contract. The NAICS code and size standard assigned to an order must correspond to a NAICS code and size standard assigned to the underlying long-term contract and must be assigned in accordance with §§ 121.402(b) and (c). A concern will be considered small for that order only if it certified itself as small under the same or lower size standard.

(v) Where the contracting officer explicitly requires concerns to recertify their size status in response to a solicitation for an order, SBA will determine size as of the date the concern submits its self-representation as part of its response to the solicitation for the order.

(4) The requirements in paragraphs (g)(1), (2), and (3) of this section apply to Multiple Award Contracts. However, if the Multiple Award Contract was set-aside for small businesses, partially set-aside for small businesses, or reserved for small business, then in the case of a contract novation, or merger or acquisition where no novation is required, where the resulting contractor is now other than small, the agency cannot count any new orders issued pursuant to the contract, from that point forward, towards its small business goals. This includes set-asides, partial set-asides, and reserves for 8(a) BD Participants, HUBZone SBCs, SDVO SBCs, and ED/WOSBs.

(5) If during contract performance a subcontractor performs primary and vital requirements of a contract, the contractor and its ostensible subcontractor will be treated as joint venturers. *See* § 121.103(h)(4). If the two firms exceed the applicable size standard in the aggregate, the contractor cannot continue to certify as small for that contract or for any task order under that contract.

(h) A follow-on or renewal contract is a new contracting action. As such, size is determined as of the date the concern submits a written self-certification that it is small to the procuring agency as part of its initial offer including price for the follow-on or renewal contract.

[69 FR 29205, May 21, 2004, as amended at 71 FR 19813, Apr. 18, 2006; 71 FR 66443, Nov. 15, 2006; 76 FR 5683, Feb. 2, 2011; 76 FR 8252, Feb. 11, 2011; 78 FR 42403, July 16, 2013; 78 FR 38817, June 28, 2013; 78 FR 61131, Oct. 2, 2013; 81 FR 34259, May 31, 2016; 81 FR 48578, July 25, 2016; 83 FR 12851, Mar. 26, 2018]

§ 121.405 May a business concern self-certify its small business size status?

(a) A concern must self-certify it is small under the size standard specified in the solicitation, or as clarified, completed or supplied by SBA pursuant to § 121.402(d).

(b) A contracting officer may accept a concern's self-certification as true for the particular procurement involved in the absence of a written protest by other offerors or other credible information which causes the contracting officer or SBA to question the size of the concern.

(c) Procedures for protesting the self-certification of an offeror are set forth in §§ 121.1001 through 121.1009.

§ 121.406 How does a small business concern qualify to provide manufactured products or other supply items under a small business set-aside, service-disabled veteran-owned small business, HUBZone, WOSB or EDWOSB, or 8(a) contract?

(a) *General.* In order to qualify as a small business concern for a small business set-aside, service-disabled veteran-owned small business set-aside or sole source contract, HUBZone set-aside or sole source contract, WOSB or EDWOSB set-aside or sole source contract, 8(a) set-aside or sole source contract, partial set-aside, or set aside of an order against a multiple award contract to provided manufactured products or other supply items, an offeror must either:

(1) Be the manufacturer or producer of the end item being procured (and the end item must be manufactured or produced in the United States); or

(2) Comply with the requirements of paragraph (b), (c) or (d) of this section as a nonmanufacturer, a kit assembler or a supplier under Simplified Acquisition Procedures.

(b) *Nonmanufacturers.* (1) A firm may qualify as a small business concern for a requirement to provide manufactured products or other supply items as a nonmanufacturer if it:

(i) Does not exceed 500 employees;

(ii) Is primarily engaged in the retail or wholesale trade and normally sells the type of item being supplied;

(iii) Takes ownership or possession of the item(s) with its personnel, equipment or facilities in a manner consistent with industry practice; and

(iv) Will supply the end item of a small business manufacturer, processor or producer made in the United States, or obtains a waiver of such requirement pursuant to paragraph (b)(5) of this section.

(2) For size purposes, there can be only one manufacturer of the end item being acquired. The manufacturer is the concern which, with its own facilities, performs the primary activities in

transforming inorganic or organic substances, including the assembly of parts and components, into the end item being acquired. The end item must possess characteristics which, as a result of mechanical, chemical or human action, it did not possess before the original substances, parts or components were assembled or transformed. The end item may be finished and ready for utilization or consumption, or it may be semifinished as a raw material to be used in further manufacturing. Firms which perform only minimal operations upon the item being procured do not qualify as manufacturers of the end item. Firms that add substances, parts, or components to an existing end item to modify its performance will not be considered the end item manufacturer where those identical modifications can be performed by and are available from the manufacturer of the existing end item:

(i) SBA will evaluate the following factors in determining whether a concern is the manufacturer of the end item:

(A) The proportion of total value in the end item added by the efforts of the concern, excluding costs of overhead, testing, quality control, and profit;

(B) The importance of the elements added by the concern to the function of the end item, regardless of their relative value; and

(C) The concern's technical capabilities; plant, facilities and equipment; production or assembly line processes; packaging and boxing operations; labeling of products; and product warranties.

(ii) Firms that provide computer and other information technology equipment primarily consisting of component parts (such as motherboards, video cards, network cards, memory, power supplies, storage devices, and similar items) who install components totaling less than 50% of the value of the end item are generally not considered the manufacturer of the end item.

(3) The nonmanufacturer rule applies only to procurements that have been assigned a manufacturing or supply NAICS code, or the Information Technology Value Added Resellers (ITVAR) exception to NAICS code 541519. The nonmanufacturer rule does not apply to contracts that have been assigned a service (except for the ITVAR exception to NAICS code 541519), construction, or specialty trade construction NAICS code.

(4) The nonmanufacturer rule applies only to the supply component of a requirement classified as a manufacturing, supply, or ITVAR contract. If a requirement is classified as a service contract, but also has a supply component, the nonmanufacturer rule does not apply to the supply component of the requirement. The rental of an item(s) is a service and should be treated as such in the application of the nonmanufacturer rule and the limitation on subcontracting.

Example 1 to paragraph (b)(4). A procuring agency seeks to acquire computer integration and maintenance services. Included within that requirement, the agency also seeks to acquire some computer hardware. If the procuring agency determines that the principal nature of the procurement is services and classifies the procurement as a services procurement, the nonmanufacturer rule does not apply to the computer hardware portion of the requirement. This means that while a contractor must meet the applicable performance of work requirement set forth in §125.6 for the services portion of the contract, the contractor does not have to supply the computer hardware of a small business manufacturer.

Example 2 to paragraph (b)(4). A procuring agency seeks to acquire computer hardware, as well as computer integration and maintenance services. If the procuring agency determines that the principal nature of the procurement is for supplies and classifies the procurement as a supply procurement, the nonmanufacturer rule applies to the computer hardware portion of the requirement. A firm seeking to qualify as a small business nonmanufacturer must supply the computer hardware manufactured by a small business. Because the requirement is classified as a supply contract, the contractor does not have to meet the performance of work requirement set forth in §125.6 for the services portion of the contract.

(5) The Administrator or designee may waive the requirement set forth in paragraph (b)(1)(iv) of this section under the following two circumstances:

(i) The contracting officer has determined that no small business manufacturer or processor reasonably can be expected to offer a product meeting the specifications (including period for performance) required by a particular solicitation and SBA reviews and accepts that determination; or

(ii) SBA determines that no small business manufacturer or processor of the product or class of products is available to participate in the Federal procurement market.

(6) The two waiver possibilities identified in paragraph (b)(5) of this section are called "individual" and "class" waivers respectively, and the procedures for requesting and granting them are contained in § 121.1204.

(7) SBA's waiver of the nonmanufacturer rule means that the firm can supply the product of any size business without regard to the place of manufacture. However, SBA's waiver of the nonmanufacturer rule has no effect on requirements external to the Small Business Act which involve domestic sources of supply, such as the Buy American Act or the Trade Agreements Act.

(c) *Kit assemblers.* (1) Where the manufactured item being acquired is a kit of supplies or other goods provided by an offeror for a special purpose, the offeror cannot exceed 500 employees, and 50 percent of the total value of the components of the kit must be manufactured by business concerns in the United States which are small under the size standards for the NAICS codes of the components being assembled. The offeror need not itself be the manufacturer of any of the items assembled.

(2) Where the Government has specified an item for the kit which is not produced by U.S. small business concerns, such item shall be excluded from the calculation of total value in paragraph (c)(1) of this section.

(d) The performance requirements (limitations on subcontracting) and the nonmanufacturer rule do not apply to small business set-aside acquisitions with an estimated value between the micro-purchase threshold and the simplified acquisition threshold (as both terms are defined in the FAR at 48 CFR 2.101).

(e) *Multiple item acquisitions.* (1) If at least 50% of the estimated contract value is composed of items that are manufactured by small business concerns, then a waiver of the nonmanufacturer rule is not required. There is no requirement that each and every item acquired in a multiple-item procurement be manufactured by a small business.

(2) If more than 50% of the estimated contract value is composed of items manufactured by other than small concerns, then a waiver is required. SBA may grant a contract specific waiver for one or more items in order to ensure that at least 50% of the value of the products to be supplied by the nonmanufacturer comes from domestic small business manufacturers or are subject to a waiver.

(3) If a small business is both a manufacturer of item(s) and a nonmanufacturer of other item(s), the manufacturer size standard should be applied.

(f) These requirements do not apply to small business concern subcontractors.

[61 FR 3286, Jan. 31, 1996; 61 FR 7986, Mar. 1, 1996, as amended at 65 FR 30863, May 15, 2000; 69 FR 29205, May 21, 2004; 76 FR 8252, Feb. 11, 2011; 78 FR 61132, Oct. 2, 2013; 81 FR 4469, Jan. 26, 2016; 81 FR 34259, May 31, 2016; 81 FR 48579, July 25, 2016; 83 FR 12851, Mar. 26, 2018]

§ 121.407 What are the size procedures for multiple item procurements?

If a procurement calls for two or more specific end items or types of services with different size standards and the offeror may submit an offer on any or all end items or types of services, the offeror must meet the size standard for each end item or service item for which it submits an offer. If the procurement calls for more than one specific end item or type of service and an offeror is required to submit an offer on all items, the offeror may qualify as a small business for the procurement if it meets the size standard of the item which accounts for the greatest percentage of the total contract value.

§ 121.408 What are the size procedures for SBA's Certificate of Competency Program?

(a) A firm which applies for a COC must file an "Application for Small Business Size Determination" (SBA Form 355). If the initial review of SBA

Form 355 indicates the applicant, including its affiliates, is small for purposes of the COC program, SBA will process the application for COC. If the review indicates the applicant, including its affiliates is other than small SBA will initiate a formal size determination as set forth in § 121.1001(b)(3)(ii). In such a case, SBA will not further process the COC application until a formal size determination is made.

(b) A concern is ineligible for a COC if a formal SBA size determination finds the concern other than small.

[61 FR 3286, Jan. 31, 1996, as amended at 81 FR 34259, May 31, 2016]

§ 121.409 What size standard applies in an unrestricted procurement for Certificate of Competency purposes?

For the purpose of receiving a Certificate of Competency in an unrestricted procurement, the applicable size standard is that corresponding to the NAICS code set forth in the solicitation. The offeror need not be the manufacturer of any of the items acquired.

[61 FR 3286, Jan. 31, 1996, as amended at 65 FR 30863, May 15, 2000; 81 FR 34259, May 31, 2016]

§ 121.410 What are the size standards for SBA's Section 8(d) Subcontracting Program?

For subcontracting purposes pursuant to sections 8(d) of the Small Business Act, a concern is small for subcontracts which relate to Government procurements if it does not exceed the size standard for the NAICS code that the prime contractor believes best describes the product or service being acquired by the subcontract. However, subcontracts for engineering services awarded under the National Energy Policy Act of 1992 have the same size standard as Military and Aerospace Equipment and Military Weapons under NAICS code 541330.

[61 FR 3286, Jan. 31, 1996, as amended at 65 FR 30863, May 15, 2000; 69 FR 29205, May 21, 2004; 74 FR 46313, Sept. 9, 2009]

§ 121.411 What are the size procedures for SBA's Section 8(d) Subcontracting Program?

(a) Prime contractors may rely on the information contained in the System for Award Management (SAM) (or any successor system or equivalent database maintained or sanctioned by SBA) as an accurate representation of a concern's size and ownership characteristics for purposes of maintaining a small business source list.

(b) Even if a concern is on a small business source list, it must still qualify and self-certify as a small business at the time it submits its offer as a section 8(d) subcontractor. Prime contractors (or subcontractors) may accept paper self-certifications as to size and socioeconomic status or a subcontractor's electronic self-certification as to size or socioeconomic status, if the solicitation for the subcontract contains a clause which provides that the subcontractor verifies by submission of the offer that the size or socioeconomic representations and certifications are accurate and complete. Electronic submission may include any method acceptable to the prime contractor (or subcontractor) including, but not limited to, size representations and certifications made in SAM (or any successor system) and electronic conveyance of subcontractor certifications in prime contractor systems in connection with an offer for a subcontract. Prime contractors or subcontractors may not require the use of SAM (or any successor system) for purposes of representing size or socioeconomic status in connection with a subcontract.

(c) Upon determination of the successful subcontract offeror for a competitive subcontract, but prior to award, the prime contractor must inform each unsuccessful subcontract offeror in writing of the name and location of the apparent successful offeror.

(d) The self-certification of a concern subcontracting or proposing to subcontract under section 8(d) of the Small Business Act may be protested by the contracting officer, the prime contractor, the appropriate SBA official or any other interested party.

(e) *Presumption of Loss Based on the Total Amount Expended.* In every contract, subcontract, cooperative agreement, cooperative research and development agreement, or grant which is set aside, reserved, or otherwise classified as intended for award to small business concerns, there shall be a presumption of loss to the United States based on the total amount expended on the contract, subcontract, cooperative agreement, cooperative research and development agreement, or grant whenever it is established that a business concern other than a small business concern willfully sought and received the award by misrepresentation.

(f) *Deemed Certifications.* The following actions shall be deemed affirmative, willful and intentional certifications of small business size and status:

(1) Submission of a bid, proposal, application or offer for a Federal grant, contract, subcontract, cooperative agreement, or cooperative research and development agreement reserved, set aside, or otherwise classified as intended for award to small business concerns.

(2) Submission of a bid, proposal, application or offer for a Federal grant, contract, subcontract, cooperative agreement or cooperative research and development agreement which in any way encourages a Federal agency to classify the bid or proposal, if awarded, as an award to a small business concern.

(3) Registration on any Federal electronic database for the purpose of being considered for award of a Federal grant, contract, subcontract, cooperative agreement, or cooperative research and development agreement, as a small business concern.

(g) *Signature Requirement.* Each offer, proposal, bid, or application for a Federal contract, subcontract, or grant shall contain a certification concerning the small business size and status of a business concern seeking the Federal contract, subcontract or grant. An authorized official must sign the certification on the same page containing the size status claimed by the concern.

(h) *Limitation of Liability.* Paragraphs (d) through (f) of this section may be determined not to apply in the case of unintentional errors, technical malfunctions, and other similar situations that demonstrate that a misrepresentation of size was not affirmative, intentional, willful or actionable under the False Claims Act, 31 U.S.C. §§ 3729, et seq. A prime contractor acting in good faith should not be held liable for misrepresentations made by its subcontractors regarding the subcontractors' size. Relevant factors to consider in making this determination may include the firm's internal management procedures governing size representation or certification, the clarity or ambiguity of the representation or certification requirement, and the efforts made to correct an incorrect or invalid representation or certification in a timely manner. An individual or firm may not be held liable where government personnel have erroneously identified a concern as small without any representation or certification having been made by the concern and where such identification is made without the knowledge of the individual or firm.

(i) *Penalties for Misrepresentation.* (1) *Suspension or debarment.* The SBA suspension and debarment official or the agency suspension and debarment official may suspend or debar a person or concern for misrepresenting a firm's size status pursuant to the procedures set forth in 48 CFR subpart 9.4.

(2) *Civil Penalties.* Persons or concerns are subject to severe penalties under the False Claims Act, 31 U.S.C. 3729–3733, the Program Fraud Civil Remedies Act, 31 U.S.C. 3801–3812 and any other applicable laws or regulations, including 13 CFR part 142.

(3) *Criminal Penalties.* Persons or concerns are subject to severe criminal penalties for knowingly misrepresenting the small business size status of a concern in connection with procurement programs pursuant to section 16(d) of the Small Business Act, 15 U.S.C. 645(d), as amended, 18 U.S.C. 1001, 18 U.S.C. 287, and any other applicable laws. Persons or concerns are subject to criminal penalties for knowingly making false statements or misrepresentations to SBA for the purpose of influencing any actions of SBA pursuant to section 16(a) of the Small Business Act, 15 U.S.C. 645(a), as

amended, including failure to correct "continuing representations" that are no longer true.

[61 FR 3286, Jan. 31, 1996, as amended at 69 FR 29205, May 21, 2004; 78 FR 42403, July 16, 2013; 78 FR 38817, June 28, 2013; 79 FR 29661, May 23, 2014; 81 FR 31491, May 19, 2016; 81 FR 94250, Dec. 23, 2016]

§ 121.412 What are the size procedures for partial small business set-asides?

A firm is required to meet size standard requirements only for the small business set-aside portion of a procurement, and is not required to qualify as a small business for the unrestricted portion.

§ 121.413 [Reserved]

SIZE ELIGIBILITY REQUIREMENTS FOR SALES OR LEASE OF GOVERNMENT PROPERTY

§ 121.501 What programs for sales or leases of Government property are subject to size determinations?

Sections 121.501 through 121.512 apply to small business size determinations for the purpose of the sale or lease of Government property, including the Timber Sales Program, the Special Salvage Timber Sales Program, and the sale of Government petroleum, coal and uranium.

§ 121.502 What size standards are applicable to programs for sales or leases of Government property?

(a) Unless otherwise specified in this part—

(1) A concern primarily engaged in manufacturing is small for sales or leases of Government property if it does not exceed 500 employees;

(2) A concern not primarily engaged in manufacturing is small for sales or leases of Government property if it has annual receipts not exceeding $7.5 million.

(b) Size status for such sales and leases is determined by the primary industry of the applicant business concern.

[61 FR 3286, Jan. 31, 1996, as amended at 67 FR 3056, Jan. 23, 2002; 70 FR 72594, Dec. 6, 2005; 73 FR 41254, July 18, 2008; 79 FR 33669, June 12, 2014]

§ 121.503 Are SBA size determinations binding on parties?

Formal size determinations based upon a specific Government sale or lease, or made in response to a request from another Government agency under § 121.901, are binding upon the parties. Other SBA opinions provided to contracting officers or others are only advisory, and are not binding or appealable.

§ 121.504 When does SBA determine the size status of a business concern?

SBA determines the size status of a concern (including its affiliates) as of the date the concern submits a written self-certification that it is small to the Government as part of its initial offer including price where there is a specific sale or lease at issue, or as set forth in § 121.903 if made in response to a request of another Government agency.

§ 121.505 What is the effect of a self-certification?

(a) A contracting officer may accept a concern's self-certification as true for the particular sale or lease involved, in the absence of a written protest by other offerors or other credible information which would cause the contracting officer or SBA to question the size of the concern.

(b) Procedures for protesting the self-certification of an offeror are set forth in §§ 121.1001 through 121.1009.

§ 121.506 What definitions are important for sales or leases of Government-owned timber?

(a) *Forest product industry* means logging, wood preserving, and the manufacture of lumber and wood related products such as veneer, plywood, hardboard, particle board, or wood pulp, and of products of which lumber or wood related products are the principal raw materials.

(b) *Logging of timber* means felling and bucking, yarding, and/or loading. It does not mean hauling.

(c) *Manufacture of logs* means, at a minimum, breaking down logs into rough cuts of the finished product.

(d) *Sell* means, in addition to its usual and customary meaning, the exchange of sawlogs for sawlogs on a product-for-product basis with or without monetary adjustment, and an indirect transfer, such as the sale of the assets of a concern after it has been awarded one or more set-aside sales of timber.

(e) *Significant logging of timber* means that a concern uses its own employees to perform at least two of the following: felling and bucking, yarding, and loading.

§ 121.507 What are the size standards and other requirements for the purchase of Government-owned timber (other than Special Salvage Timber)?

(a) To be small for purposes of the sale of Government-owned timber (other than Special Salvage Timber) a concern must:

(1) Be primarily engaged in the logging or forest products industry;

(2) Not exceed 500 employees, taking into account its affiliates; and

(3) If it does not intend at the time of the offer to resell the timber—

(i) Agree that it will manufacture the logs with its own facilities or those of another business which meets the requirements of paragraphs (a)(1) and (a)(2) of this section;

(ii) Agree that if it eventually resells the timber, it will resell no more than 30% of the sawtimber volume to other businesses which do not meet the requirements of paragraphs (a)(1) and (a)(2) of this section; and

(iii) Agree that if it becomes acquired or controlled by a business which does not meet the requirements of paragraphs (a)(1) and (a)(2) of this section, it will require as a condition of the acquisition or change of control that the acquiring or controlling business resell at least 70% of the sawtimber volume to businesses which do meet the requirements of paragraphs (a)(1) and (a)(2) of this section; or

(4) If it intends at the time of offer to resell the timber—

(i) Agree that it will not sell more than 30% of such timber (50% of such timber if the concern is an Alaskan business) to a business which does not meet the requirements of paragraphs (a)(1) and (a)(2) of this section; and

(ii) Agree that if it becomes acquired or controlled by a business which does not meet the requirements of paragraphs (a)(1) and (a)(2) of this section, it will require as a condition of the acquisition or change of control that the acquiring or controlling business resell at least 70% of the sawtimber volume (or at least 50% of the sawtimber volume, if it is an Alaskan business) to businesses which meet the requirements of paragraphs (a)(1) and (a)(2) of this section.

(b) For a period of three years following the date upon which a concern purchases timber under a small business set-aside (other than through the Special Salvage Timber Sale program), it must maintain a record of:

(1) The name, address and size status of every concern to which it sells the timber or sawlogs; and

(2) The species, grades and volumes of sawlogs sold.

(c) For a period of three years following the date upon which a concern purchases timber, it must by contract require all small business repurchasers of the sawlogs or timber it purchased under the small business set-aside to maintain the records described in paragraph (b) of this section.

§ 121.508 What are the size standards and other requirements for the purchase of Government-owned Special Salvage Timber?

(a) In order to purchase Government-owned Special Salvage Timber from the United States Forest Service or the Bureau of Land Management as a small business, a concern must:

(1) Be primarily engaged in the logging or forest product industry;

(2) Have, together with its affiliates, no more than twenty-five employees during any pay period for the last twelve months; and

(3) If it does not intend at the time of offer to resell the timber—

(i) Agree that it will manufacture a significant portion of the logs with its own employees; and

(ii) Agree that it will log the timber only with its own employees or with employees of another business which is eligible for award of a Special Salvage Timber sales contract; or

(4) If it intends at the time of offer to resell the timber, agree that it will perform a significant portion of timber logging with its own employees and that it will subcontract the remainder of the timber logging to a concern which is eligible for award of a Special Salvage Timber sales contract.

§ 121.509 What is the size standard for leasing of Government land for coal mining?

A concern is small for this purpose if it:

(a) Together with its affiliates, does not have more than 250 employees;

(b) Maintains management and control of the actual mining operations of the tract; and

(c) Agrees that if it subleases the Government land, it will be to another small business, and that it will require its sublessors to agree to the same.

§ 121.510 What is the size standard for leasing of Government land for uranium mining?

A concern is small for this purpose if it, together with its affiliates, does not have more than 100 employees.

§ 121.511 What is the size standard for buying Government-owned petroleum?

A concern is small for this purpose if it is primarily engaged in petroleum refining and meets the size standard for a petroleum refining business.

§ 121.512 What is the size standard for stockpile purchases?

A concern is small for this purpose if:

(a) It is primarily engaged in the purchase of materials which are not domestic products; and

(b) Its annual receipts, together with its affiliates, do not exceed $62.5 million.

[61 FR 3286, Jan. 31, 1996, as amended at 67 FR 3056, Jan. 23, 2002; 70 FR 72594, Dec. 6, 2005; 73 FR 41254, July 18, 2008; 79 FR 33669, June 12, 2014]

SIZE ELIGIBILITY REQUIREMENTS FOR THE 8(a) BUSINESS DEVELOPMENT PROGRAM

§ 121.601 What is a small business for purposes of admission to SBA's 8(a) Business Development program?

An applicant must not exceed the size standard corresponding to its primary industry classification in order to qualify for admission to SBA's 8(a) Business Development Program.

[69 FR 29205, May 21, 2004]

§ 121.602 At what point in time must a 8(a) BD applicant be small?

A 8(a) BD applicant must be small for its primary industry at the time SBA certifies it for admission into the program.

[61 FR 3286, Jan. 31, 1996, as amended at 69 FR 29206, May 21, 2004]

§ 121.603 How does SBA determine whether a Participant is small for a particular 8(a) BD subcontract?

(a) *Self certification by Participant.* A 8(a) BD Participant must certify that it qualifies as a small business under the NAICS code assigned to a particular 8(a) BD subcontract as part of its initial offer including price to the procuring agency. The Participant also must submit a copy of its offer, including its self-certification as to size, to the appropriate SBA district office at the same time it submits the offer to the procuring agency. *See* § 121.404 for the time at which size is determined for, and § 121.406 for the applicability of the nonmanufacturer rule to, 8(a) BD procurements.

(b) *Verification of size by SBA.* Within 30 days of its receipt of a Participant's size self-certification for a particular 8(a) BD subcontract, the SBA district office serving the geographic area in which the Participant's principal office is located will review the Participant's self-certification and determine if it is small for purposes of that subcontract. The SBA district office will review the Participant's most recent financial statements and other relevant data and then notify the Participant of its decision.

(c) *Changes in size between date of self-certification and date of award.* (1) Where

SBA verifies that the selected Participant is small for a particular procurement, subsequent changes in size up to the date of award, except those due to merger with or acquisition by another business concern, will not affect the firm's size status for that procurement.

(2) Where a Participant has merged with or been acquired by another business concern between the date of its self-certification and the date of award, the concern must recertify its size status, and SBA must verify the new certification before award can occur.

(d) *Finding Participant to be other than small.* (1) A Participant may request a formal size determination (pursuant to §§ 121.1001 through 121.1009) with the SBA Government Contracting Area Office serving the geographic area in which the principal office of the Participant is located within 5 working days of its receipt of notice from the SBA district office that it is not small for a particular 8(a) BD subcontract.

(2) Where the Participant does not timely request a formal size determination, SBA may accept the procurement in support of another Participant, or may rescind its acceptance of the offer for the 8(a) BD program, as appropriate.

[61 FR 3286, Jan. 31, 1996, as amended at 65 FR 30863, May 15, 2000; 69 FR 29206, May 21, 2004]

§ 121.604 Are 8(a) BD Participants considered small for purposes of other SBA assistance?

A concern which SBA determines to be a small business for the award of a 8(a) BD subcontract will be considered to have met applicable size eligibility requirements of other SBA programs where that assistance directly and primarily relates to the performance of the 8(a) BD subcontract in question.

[61 FR 3286, Jan. 31, 1996, as amended at 69 FR 29206, May 21, 2004]

Size and Eligibility Requirements for the Small Business Innovation Research (SBIR) and Small Business Technology Transfer (STTR) Programs

§ 121.701 What SBIR and STTR programs are subject to size and eligibility determinations and what definitions are important?

(a) These sections apply to SBA's SBIR and STTR programs, 15 U.S.C. 638.

(b) *Definitions*—(1) *Funding agreement officer* means a contracting officer, a grants officer, or a cooperative agreement officer.

(2) *Funding agreement* means any contract, grant or cooperative agreement entered into between any Federal agency and any small business for the purposes of the SBIR or STTR program.

(3) *Hedge fund* has the meaning given that term in section 13(h)(2) of the Bank Holding Company Act of 1956 (12 U.S.C. 1851(h)(2)). The hedge fund must have a place of business located in the United States and be created or organized in the United States, or under the law of the United States or of any State.

(4) *Portfolio company* means any company that is owned in whole or part by a venture capital operating company, hedge fund, or private equity firm.

(5) *Private equity firm* has the meaning given the term "private equity fund" in section 13(h)(2) of the Bank Holding Company Act of 1956 (12 U.S.C. 1851(h)(2)). The private equity firm must have a place of business located in the United States and be created or organized in the United States, or under the law of the United States or of any State.

(6) *Venture capital operating company* means an entity described in § 121.103(b)(5)(i), (v), or (vi). The venture capital operating company must have a place of business located in the United States and be created or organized in the United States, or under the law of the United States or of any State.

[77 FR 76225, Dec. 27, 2012]

§ 121.702 What size and eligibility standards are applicable to the SBIR and STTR programs?

To be eligible for award of funding agreements in SBA's SBIR and STTR programs, a business concern must meet the requirements below at the time of award of an SBIR or STTR Phase I or Phase II funding agreement:

(a) *Ownership and control for the SBIR program.* (1) An SBIR awardee must:

(i) Be a concern which is more than 50% directly owned and controlled by one or more individuals (who are citizens or permanent resident aliens of the United States), other small business concerns (each of which is more than 50% directly owned and controlled by individuals who are citizens or permanent resident aliens of the United States), an Indian tribe, ANC or NHO (or a wholly owned business entity of such tribe, ANC or NHO), or any combination of these;

(ii) Be a concern which is more than 50% owned by multiple venture capital operating companies, hedge funds, private equity firms, or any combination of these (for agencies electing to use the authority in 15 U.S.C. 638(dd)(1)); or

(iii) Be a joint venture in which each entity to the joint venture must meet the requirements set forth in paragraph (a)(1)(i) or (a)(1)(ii) of this section. A joint venture that includes one or more concerns that meet the requirements of paragraph (a)(1)(ii) of this section must comply with §121.705(b) concerning registration and proposal requirements.

(2) No single venture capital operating company, hedge fund, or private equity firm may own more than 50% of the concern unless that single venture capital operating company, hedge fund, or private equity firm qualifies as a small business concern that is more than 50% directly owned and controlled by individuals who are citizens or permanent resident aliens of the United States.

(3) If an Employee Stock Ownership Plan owns all or part of the concern, each stock trustee and plan member is considered an owner.

(4) If a trust owns all or part of the concern, each trustee and trust beneficiary is considered an owner.

(b) *Ownership and control for the STTR program.* (1) An STTR awardee must:

(i) Be a concern which is more than 50% directly owned and controlled by one or more individuals (who are citizens or permanent resident aliens of the United States), other small business concerns (each of which is more than 50% directly owned and controlled by individuals who are citizens or permanent resident aliens of the United States), an Indian tribe, ANC or NHO (or a wholly owned business entity of such tribe, ANC or NHO), or any combination of these; or

(ii) Be a joint venture in which each entity to the joint venture must meet the requirements set forth in paragraph (b)(1)(i) of this section.

(2) If an Employee Stock Ownership Plan owns all or part of the concern, each stock trustee and plan member is considered an owner.

(3) If a trust owns all or part of the concern, each trustee and trust beneficiary is considered an owner.

(c) *Size and affiliation.* An SBIR or STTR awardee, together with its affiliates, must not have more than 500 employees. Concerns and entities are affiliates of each other when one controls or has the power to control the other, or a third party or parties controls or has the power to control both. It does not matter whether control is exercised, so long as the power to control exists. For the purposes of the SBIR and STTR programs, the following bases of affiliation apply:

(1) *Affiliation based on ownership.* For determining affiliation based on equity ownership, a concern is an affiliate of an individual, concern, or entity that owns or has the power to control more than 50 percent of the concern's voting equity. However, SBA may find a concern an affiliate of an individual, concern, or entity that owns or has the power to control 40% or more of the voting equity based upon the totality of circumstances. If no individual, concern, or entity is found to control, SBA will deem the Board of Directors to be in control of the concern.

(2) *Affiliation arising under stock options, convertible securities, and agreements to merge.* In determining size, SBA considers stock options, convertible securities, and agreements to

merge (including agreements in principle) to have a present effect on the power to control a concern. SBA treats such options, convertible securities, and agreements as though the rights granted have been exercised.

(i) Agreements to open or continue negotiations towards the possibility of a merger or a sale of stock at some later date are not considered "agreements in principle" and are thus not given present effect.

(ii) Options, convertible securities, and agreements that are subject to conditions precedent which are incapable of fulfillment, speculative, conjectural, or unenforceable under state or Federal law, or where the probability of the transaction (or exercise of the rights) occurring is shown to be extremely remote, are not given present effect.

(iii) An individual, concern or other entity that controls one or more other concerns cannot use options, convertible securities, or agreements to appear to terminate such control before actually doing so. SBA will not give present effect to individuals', concerns' or other entities' ability to divest all or part of their ownership interest in order to avoid a finding of affiliation.

(3) *Affiliation based on common management.* Affiliation arises where the CEO or President of a concern (or other officers, managing members, or partners who control the management of the concern) also controls the management of one or more other concerns. Affiliation also arises where a single individual, concern, or entity that controls the board of directors of one concern also controls the board of directors or management of one or more other concerns.

(4) *Affiliation based on identity of interest.* Affiliation may arise among two or more persons (including any individual, concern or other entity) with an identity of interest. An individual, concern or entity may rebut a determination of identity of interest with evidence showing that the interests deemed to be one are in fact separate.

(i) SBA may presume an identity of interest between family members with identical or substantially identical business or economic interests (such as where the family members operate concerns in the same or similar industry in the same geographic area).

(ii) SBA may presume an identity of interest based upon economic dependence if the SBIR/STTR awardee relies upon another concern or entity for 70% or more of its receipts.

(iii) An SBIR or STTR awardee is not affiliated with a portfolio company of a venture capital operating company, hedge fund, or private equity firm, solely on the basis of one or more shared investors, though affiliation may be found for other reasons.

(5) *Affiliation based on the newly organized concern rule.* Affiliation may arise where former or current officers, directors, principal stockholders, managing members, general partners, or key employees of one concern organize a new concern in the same or related industry or field of operation, and serve as the new concern's officers, directors, principal stockholders, managing members, general partners, or key employees, and the one concern is furnishing or will furnish the new concern with contracts, financial or technical assistance, indemnification on bid or performance bonds, and/or other facilities, whether for a fee or otherwise. A concern may rebut such an affiliation determination by demonstrating a clear line of fracture between the two concerns. A "key employee" is an employee who, because of his/her position in the concern, has a critical influence in or substantive control over the operations or management of the concern. A concern will be considered "new" for the purpose of this rule if it has been actively operating continuously for less than one year.

(6) *Affiliation based on joint ventures.* Concerns submitting an application as a joint venture are affiliated with each other with regard to the application. SBA will apply the joint venture affiliation exception at § 121.103(h)(3)(iii) for two firms approved to be a mentor and protégé under SBA's 8(a) program.

(7) *Affiliation based on the ostensible subcontractor rule.* A concern and its ostensible subcontractor are treated as joint venturers, and therefore affiliates, for size determination purposes. An ostensible subcontractor is a subcontractor or subgrantee that performs primary and vital requirements of a

funding agreement (*i.e.*, those requirements associated with the principal purpose of the funding agreement), or a subcontractor or subgrantee upon which the concern is unusually reliant. All aspects of the relationship between the concern and subcontractor are considered, including, but not limited to, the terms of the proposal (such as management, technical responsibilities, and the percentage of subcontracted work) and agreements between the concern and subcontractor or subgrantee (such as bonding assistance or the teaming agreement). To determine whether a subcontractor performs primary and vital requirements of a funding agreement, SBA will consider whether the concern's proposal complies with the performance requirements of the SBIR or STTR program.

(8) *Affiliation based on license agreements.* SBA will consider whether there is a license agreement concerning a product or trademark which is critical to operation of the licensee. The license agreement will not cause the licensor to be affiliated with the licensee if the licensee has the right to profit from its efforts and bears the risk of loss. Affiliation may arise, however, through other means, such as common ownership or common management.

(9) *Exception to affiliation for portfolio companies.* If a venture capital operating company, hedge fund, or private equity firm that is determined to be affiliated with an awardee is a minority investor in the awardee, the awardee is not affiliated with a portfolio company of the venture capital operating company, hedge fund, or private equity firm, unless:

(i) The venture capital operating company, hedge fund, or private equity firm owns a majority of the portfolio company; or

(ii) The venture capital operating company, hedge fund, or private equity firms holds a majority of the seats of the board of directors of the portfolio company.

(10) *Totality of the circumstances.* In determining whether affiliation exists, SBA may consider the totality of the circumstances, and may find affiliation even though no single factor is sufficient to constitute affiliation.

(d) *Calculating ownership and control.* SBA will review the small business' equity ownership on a fully diluted basis for purposes of determining ownership, control and affiliation in the SBIR and STTR programs. This means that SBA will consider the total number of shares or equity that would be outstanding if all possible sources of conversion were exercised, including, but not limited to: Outstanding common stock or equity, outstanding preferred stock (on a converted to common basis) or equity, outstanding warrants (on an as exercised and converted to common basis), outstanding options and options reserved for future grants, and any other convertible securities on an as converted to common basis.

[77 FR 76225, Dec. 27, 2012; 78 FR 11745, Feb. 20, 2013, as amended at 81 FR 34259, May 31, 2016; 81 FR 48579, July 25, 2016; 81 FR 71983, Oct. 19, 2016]

§ 121.703 Are formal size determinations binding on parties?

Size determinations by authorized SBA officials are formal actions based upon a specific funding agreement, and are binding upon the parties. Other SBA opinions provided to funding agreement officers or others, are only advisory, and are not binding or appealable.

§ 121.704 When does SBA determine the size and eligibility status of a business concern?

(a) The size and eligibility status of a concern for the purpose of a funding agreement award under the SBIR and STTR programs is determined at the time of award for both Phase I and Phase II SBIR and STTR awards, or on the date of the request for a size determination, if an award is pending.

(b) A concern that qualified as a small business at the time it receives an SBIR or STTR funding agreement is considered a small business throughout the life of that specific funding agreement. Where a concern grows to be other than small, the funding agreement agency may exercise the options on the award that is a contract, grant or cooperative agreement or issue a continuation on a grant or cooperative agreement and still count the award as an award to a small business under the

SBIR or STTR program. However, the following exceptions apply:

(1) In the case of a merger or acquisition, the awardee must, within 30 days of the transaction becoming final (or the approved funding agreement novation if a novation is required), recertify its small business size status to the funding agreement agency or inform the funding agreement agency that it is other than small. If the awardee is other than small, the agency can no longer fund the options or issue a continuation pursuant to the funding agreement, from that point forward, with SBIR or STTR funds. Funding agreement novations for reasons other than a merger or acquisition do not necessarily require re-certification. The funding agreement agency and the awardee must immediately revise all applicable Federal contract and grant databases to reflect the new size status from that point forward.

(2) For the purposes of SBIR and STTR funding agreements with durations of more than five years, a funding agreement officer must request that a business concern re-certify its small business size status no more than 120 days prior to the end of the fifth year of the funding agreement, and no more than 120 days prior to exercising any option or issuing any continuation. If the awardee certifies that it is other than small, the funding agreement agency can no longer fund the options or issue a continuation pursuant to the funding agreement with SBIR or STTR funds. The funding agreement agency and the awardee must immediately revise all applicable Federal contract and grant databases to reflect the new size status from that point forward.

(c) Re-certification does not change the terms and conditions of the funding agreement. The requirements in effect at the time of award remain in effect throughout the life of the funding agreement.

(d) A request for a size re-certification shall include the size standard in effect at the time of re-certification.

[77 FR 76226, Dec. 27, 2012]

§ 121.705 Must a business concern self-certify its size and eligibility status?

(a) A business concern must self-certify that it meets the eligibility requirements set forth in § 121.702 for a Phase I or Phase II SBIR or STTR funding agreement.

(b) A business concern that is more than 50% owned by multiple venture capital operating companies, hedge funds, or private equity firms and a joint venture where one or more parties to the joint venture is more than 50% owned by multiple venture capital operating companies, hedge funds, or private equity firms must be registered with SBA as of the date it submits its initial proposal (or other formal response) to a Phase I or Phase II SBIR announcement or solicitation. The concern must indicate in any SBIR proposal or application that it is registered with SBA as majority-owned by multiple venture capital operating companies, hedge funds, or private equity firms.

(c) A small business concern that did not meet the requirements of paragraph (b) of this section at the time of its SBIR proposal or application must notify the funding agreement officer if, on the date of award, the concern is more than 50% owned by multiple venture capital operating companies, hedge funds, or private equity firms.

(1) The concern is still eligible to receive the award if it becomes majority-owned by multiple venture capital operating companies, hedge funds, or private equity firms after the time it submitted its initial proposal (or other formal response) to a Phase I or Phase II SBIR announcement or solicitation if the agency makes the award on or after the date that is 9 months from the end of the period for submitting applications under the SBIR solicitation.

(2) This small business, known as a covered small business concern, would have to certify that it meets the requirements of the SBIR program set forth in §§ 121.702(a)(1)(ii) or 121.702(a)(1)(iii), and 121.702(a)(2) and 121.702(c) at the time of award of the funding agreement.

(d) A funding agreement officer may accept a concern's self-certification as true for the particular funding agreement involved in the absence of a written protest or other credible information which would cause the funding agreement officer or SBA to question the size or eligibility of the concern.

(e) Procedures for protesting an awardee's self-certification are set forth in §§ 121.1001 through 121.1009. In adjudicating a protest, SBA may address both the size status and eligibility of the SBIR or STTR awardee.

[77 FR 76227, Dec. 27, 2012]

SIZE ELIGIBILITY REQUIREMENTS FOR PAYING REDUCED PATENT FEES

§ 121.801 May patent fees be reduced if a concern is small?

These sections apply to size status for the purpose of paying reduced patent fees authorized by Pub. L. 97–247, 96 Stat. 317. The eligibility requirements for independent inventors and non-profit organizations for the purpose of paying reduced patent fees are set forth in regulations of the Patent and Trademark Office of the Department of Commerce, 37 CFR 1.9, 1.27, 1.28.

§ 121.802 What size standards are applicable to reduced patent fees programs?

A concern eligible for reduced patent fees is one:

(a) Whose number of employees, including affiliates, does not exceed 500 persons; and

(b) Which has not assigned, granted, conveyed, or licensed (and is under no obligation to do so) any rights in the invention to any person who made it and could not be classified as an independent inventor, or to any concern which would not qualify as a non-profit organization or a small business concern under this section.

§ 121.803 Are formal size determinations binding on parties?

Size determinations by authorized SBA officials are formal actions, based upon a specific patent application pursuant to the rules of the Patent and Trademark Office, Department of Commerce, and are binding upon the parties. Other SBA opinions provided to patent applicants or others are only advisory, and are not binding or appealable.

§ 121.804 When does SBA determine the size status of a business concern?

Size status is determined as of the date of the patent applicant's written verification of size.

§ 121.805 May a business concern self-certify its size status?

(a) A concern verifies its size status with its submission of its patent application.

(b) Any attempt to establish small size status improperly (fraudulently, through gross negligence, or otherwise) may result in remedial action by the Patent and Trademark Office.

(c) In the absence of credible information indicating otherwise, the Patent and Trademark Office may accept the verification by the concern as a small business as true.

(d) Questions concerning the size verification are resolved initially by the Patent and Trademark Office. If not verified as small, the applicant may request a formal SBA size determination.

SIZE ELIGIBILITY REQUIREMENTS FOR COMPLIANCE WITH PROGRAMS OF OTHER AGENCIES

§ 121.901 Can other Government agencies obtain SBA size determinations?

Upon request by another Government agency, SBA will provide a size determination, under SBA rules, standards and procedures, for its use in determining compliance with small business requirements of its statutes, regulations or programs.

§ 121.902 What size standards are applicable to programs of other agencies?

SBA size standards. The size standards for compliance with programs of other agencies are those for SBA programs which are most comparable to the programs of such other agencies, unless the agency and SBA agree otherwise.

[67 FR 13716, Mar. 26, 2002]

§ 121.903 How may an agency use size standards for its programs that are different than those established by SBA?

(a) Federal agencies or departments promulgating regulations relating to small businesses usually use SBA size criteria. In limited circumstances, if they decide the SBA size standard is not suitable for their programs, then agency heads may establish a more appropriate small business definition for the exclusive use in such programs, but only when:

(1) The size standard will determine:

(i) The size of a manufacturing concern by its average number of employees based on the preceding twelve calendar months, determined according to § 121.106;

(ii) The size of a services concern by its average annual receipts over a period of at least three years, determined according to § 121.104;

(iii) The size of other concerns on data over a period of at least three years; or,

(iv) Other factors approved by SBA;

(2) The agency has consulted in writing with SBA's Division Chief, office of Size Standards at least fourteen (14) calendar days before publishing the proposed rule which is part of the rulemaking process. The written consultation will include:

(i) What size standard the agency contemplates using;

(ii) To what agency program it will apply;

(iii) How the agency arrived at this particular size standard for this program; and,

(iv) Why SBA's existing size standards do not satisfy the program requirements;

(3) The agency proposes the size standard for public comment pursuant to the Administrative Procedure Act, 5 U.S.C. 553;

(4) The agency provides a copy of the proposed rule, when it publishes it for public comment as part of the rulemaking process, to SBA's Division Chief, Office of Size Standards; and

(5) SBA's Administrator approves the size standard before the agency adopts a final rule or otherwise prescribes the size standard for its use. The agency's request for the SBA Administrator's approval must include:

(i) Copies of all comments on the proposed size standard received in response to the proposed rule;

(ii) A separate written justification for the intended size standard;

(iii) A copy of the intended final rule if available at that time, or a copy of the intended final rule and preamble prior to its publication; and

(iv) Other information SBA may request in connection with the request.

(b) When approving any size standard established pursuant to this section, SBA's Administrator will ensure that the size standard varies from industry to industry to the extent necessary to reflect the differing characteristics of the various industries, and consider other relevant factors.

(c) Where the agency head is developing a size standard for the sole purpose of performing a Regulatory Flexibility Analysis pursuant to section 601(3) of the Regulatory Flexibility Act, the department or agency may, after consultation with the SBA Office of Advocacy, establish a size standard different from SBA's which is more appropriate for such analysis.

[67 FR 13716, Mar. 26, 2002]

§ 121.904 When does SBA determine the size status of a business concern?

For compliance with programs of other agencies, SBA will base its size determination on the size of the concern as of the date set forth in the request of the other agency.

[67 FR 13716, Mar. 26, 2002]

Procedures for Size Protests and Requests for Formal Size Determinations

§ 121.1001 Who may initiate a size protest or request a formal size determination?

(a) *Size Status Protests.* (1) For SBA's Small Business Set-Aside Program, including the Property Sales Program, or any instance in which a procurement or order has been restricted to or reserved for small businesses or a particular group of small businesses (including a partial set-aside), the following entities may file a size protest in connection with a particular procurement, sale or order:

(i) Any offeror that the contracting officer has not eliminated from consideration for any procurement-related reason, such as non-responsiveness, technical unacceptability or outside of the competitive range;

(ii) The contracting officer;

(iii) The SBA Government Contracting Area Director having responsibility for the area in which the headquarters of the protested offeror is located, regardless of the location of a parent company or affiliates, or the Director, Office of Government Contracting; and

(iv) Other interested parties. Other interested parties include large businesses where only one concern submitted an offer for the specific procurement in question. A concern found to be other than small in connection with the procurement is not an interested party unless there is only one remaining offeror after the concern is found to be other than small.

(2) For competitive 8(a) contracts, the following entities may protest:

(i) Any offeror that the contracting officer has not eliminated from consideration for any procurement related reason, such as non-responsiveness, technical unacceptability or outside of the competitive range;

(ii) The contracting officer; or

(iii) The SBA District Director, or designee, in either the district office serving the geographical area in which the procuring activity is located or the district office that services the apparent successful offeror, or the Associate Administrator for Business Development.

(3) For SBA's Subcontracting Program, the following entities may protest:

(i) The prime contractor;

(ii) The contracting officer;

(iii) Other potential subcontractors;

(iv) The responsible SBA Government Contracting Area Director or the Director, Office of Government Contracting; and

(v) Other interested parties.

(4) For SBA's Small Business Innovation Research (SBIR) program and Small Business Technology Transfer (STTR) program, the following entities may protest:

(i) An offeror or applicant for that solicitation;

(ii) The funding agreement officer; and

(iii) The responsible SBA Government Contracting Area Director; the Director, Office of Government Contracting; or the Associate Administrator, Investment Division.

(5) For the Department of Defense's Small Disadvantaged Business (SDB) Program, and any other similar program of another Federal agency, the following entities may file a protest in connection with a particular SDB procurement:

(i) Any offeror for the specific SDB requirement whom the contracting officer has not eliminated for reasons unrelated to size;

(ii) The contracting officer; and

(iii) The responsible SBA Area Director for Government Contracting, the SBA Director, Office of Government Contracting, or the SBA Associate Administrator for Business Development;

(6) For SBA's HUBZone program, the following entities may protest in connection with a particular HUBZone procurement:

(i) Any concern that submits an offer for a specific HUBZone set-aside procurement that the contracting officer has not eliminated for reasons unrelated to size;

(ii) Any concern that submitted an offer in full and open competition and its opportunity for award will be affected by a price evaluation preference given a qualified HUBZone SBC;

(iii) The contracting officer; and

(iv) The SBA Director, Office of HUBZone, or designee.

(7) For any unrestricted Government procurement in which a business concern has represented itself as a small business concern, the following entities may protest in connection with a particular procurement:

(i) Any offeror;

(ii) The contracting officer; and

(iii) The responsible SBA Government Contracting Area Director, the Director, Office of Government Contracting, or the Associate Administrator for Business Development.

(8) For SBA's Service Disabled Veteran-Owned Small Business Concern program, the following entities may protest in connection with a particular service-disabled veteran-owned procurement:

(i) Any concern that submits an offer for a specific service-disabled veteran-owned small business set-aside contract;

(ii) The contracting officer;

(iii) The SBA Government Contracting Area Director; and

(iv) The Director, Office of Government Contracting, or designee.

(9) For SBA's WOSB Federal Contracting Program, the following entities may protest:

(i) Any concern that submits an offer for a specific requirement set aside for WOSBs or WOSBs owned by one or more women who are economically disadvantaged (EDWOSB) pursuant to part 127 of this chapter;

(ii) The contracting officer;

(iii) The SBA Government Contracting Area Director; and

(iv) The Director for Government Contracting, or designee.

(b) *Request for Size Determinations.* (1) For SBA's Financial Assistance Programs, the following entities may request a formal size determination:

(i) The applicant for assistance; and

(ii) The SBA official with authority to take final action on the assistance requested. That official may also request the appropriate Government Contracting Area Office to determine whether affiliation exists between an applicant for financial assistance and one or more other entities for purposes of determining whether the applicant would exceed the loan limit amount imposed by § 120.151 of this chapter.

(iii) The SBA Associate Administrator for Investment or designee may request a formal size determination for any purpose relating to the SBIC program (*see* part 107 of this chapter) or the NMVC program (*see* part 108 of this chapter). A formal size determination includes a request to determine whether or not affiliation exists between two or more entities for any purpose relating to the SBIC program.

(2) For SBA's 8(a) BD program:

(i) Concerning initial or continued 8(a) BD eligibility, the following entities may request a formal size determination:

(A) The 8(a) BD applicant concern or Participant; or

(B) The Director of the Division of Program Certification and Eligibility or the Associate Administrator for Business Development.

(ii) Concerning individual sole source 8(a) contract awards, the following entities may request a formal size determination:

(A) The Participant nominated for award of the particular sole source contract;

(B) The SBA program official with authority to execute the 8(a) contract or, where applicable, the procuring activity contracting officer who has been delegated SBA's 8(a) contract execution functions; or

(C) The SBA District Director in the district office that services the Participant, or the Associate Administrator for Business Development.

(3) For SBA's Certificate of Competency Program, the following entities may request a formal size determination:

(i) The offeror who has applied for a COC; and

(ii) The responsible SBA Government Contracting Area Director or the Director, Office of Government Contracting.

(4) For SBA's sale or lease of government property, the following entities may request a formal size determination:

(i) The responsible SBA Government Contracting Area Director or the Director, Office of Government Contracting; and

(ii) Authorized officials of other Federal agencies administering a property sales program.

(5) For eligibility to pay reduced patent fees, the following entities may request a formal size determination:

(i) The applicant for the reduced patent fees; and

(ii) The Patent and Trademark Office.

(6) For purposes of determining compliance with small business requirements of another Government agency program not otherwise specified in this section, an official with authority to

administer the program involved may request a formal size determination.

(7) In connection with initial or continued eligibility for the Small Disadvantaged Business (SDB) program, the following may request a formal size determination:

(i) The applicant or SDB concern; or

(ii) The Director of the Division of Program Certification and Eligibility or the Associate Administrator for Business Development.

(8) In connection with initial or continued eligibility for the HUBZone program, the following may request a formal size determination:

(i) The applicant or qualified HUBZone business concern; or

(ii) The Director, Office of HUBZone, or designee.

(9) For other purposes related to protecting the integrity of the Federal procurement process, including validating that firms listed in the System for Award Management database are small, the Government Contracting Area Director or the Director, Office of Government Contracting may initiate a formal size determination when sufficient information exists that calls into question a firm's small business status. The current date will be used to determine size, and SBA will initiate the process to remove from the database the small business designation of any firm found to be other than small.

(10) For purposes of the small business mentor-protégé program authorized pursuant to §125.9 of this chapter (based on its status as a small business for its primary or identified secondary NAICS code), the business concern seeking to be a protégé or SBA may request a formal size determination.

(11) For purposes of determining compliance with small business requirements for firms relying upon small business status advisory opinions, the Associate General Counsel, Office of Procurement Law may request a formal size determination. Additionally, any firm that is the subject of a small business status advisory opinion holding that it is other than small may request a formal size determination.

(12) In connection with eligibility for the SDVO SBC and the WOSB/EDWSOB programs, the Director, Office of Government Contracting, may initiate a formal size determination.

(13) The SBA Inspector General may request a formal size determination with respect to any of the programs identified in paragraph (b) of this section.

[61 FR 3286, Jan. 31, 1996, as amended at 63 FR 31907, June 11, 1998; 63 FR 35739, June 30, 1998; 69 FR 25266, May 5, 2004; 69 FR 29206, May 21, 2004; 69 FR 29420, May 24, 2004; 69 FR 44461, July 26, 2004; 73 FR 56947, Oct. 1, 2008; 74 FR 45753, Sept. 4, 2009; 75 FR 62280, Oct. 7, 2010; 76 FR 8253, Feb. 11, 2011; 77 FR 76227, Dec. 27, 2012; 78 FR 61132, Oct. 2, 2013; 80 FR 7536, Feb. 11, 2015; 81 FR 34259, May 31, 2016; 81 FR 48579, July 25, 2016]

§121.1002 Who makes a formal size determination?

The responsible Government Contracting Area Director or designee makes all formal size determinations in response to either a size protest or a request for a formal size determination, with the exception of size determinations for purposes of the Disaster Loan Program, which will be made by the Disaster Area Office Director or designee responsible for the area in which the disaster occurred.

§121.1003 Where should a size protest be filed?

A protest involving a government procurement or sale must be filed with the contracting officer for the procurement or sale, who must forward the protest to the SBA Government Contracting Area Office serving the area in which the headquarters of the protested concern is located, regardless of the location of any parent company or affiliates.

§121.1004 What time limits apply to size protests?

(a) *Protests by entities other than contracting officers or SBA*—(1) *Sealed bids or sales (including protests on partial set-asides and reserves of Multiple Award Contracts and set-asides of orders against Multiple Award Contracts).* A protest must be received by the contracting officer prior to the close of business on the 5th day, exclusive of Saturdays, Sundays, and legal holidays, after bid opening for

(i) The contract; or

(ii) An order issued against a Multiple Award Contract if the contracting officer requested a new size certification in connection with that order.

(2) *Negotiated procurement (including protests on partial set-asides and reserves of Multiple Award Contracts and set-asides of orders against Multiple Award Contracts).* A protest must be received by the contracting officer prior to the close of business on the 5th day, exclusive of Saturdays, Sundays, and legal holidays, after the contracting officer has notified the protestor of the identity of the prospective awardee for

(i) The contract; or

(ii) An order issued against a Multiple Award Contract if the contracting officer requested a new size certification in connection with that order.

(3) *Long-Term Contracts.* For contracts with durations greater than five years (including options), including all existing long-term contracts, Multi-agency contracts, Governmentwide Acquisition Contracts and Multiple Award Contracts:

(i) Protests regarding size certifications made for contracts must be received by the contracting officer prior to the close of business on the 5th day, exclusive of Saturdays, Sundays, and legal holidays, after receipt of notice (including notice received in writing, orally, or via electronic posting) of the identity of the prospective awardee or award.

(ii) Protests regarding size certifications made for an option period must be received by the contracting officer prior to the close of business on the 5th day, exclusive of Saturdays, Sundays, and legal holidays, after receipt of notice (including notice received in writing, orally, or via electronic posting) of the size certification made by the protested concern.

(A) A contracting officer is not required to terminate a contract where a concern is found to be other than small pursuant to a size protest concerning a size certification made for an option period.

(B) [Reserved]

(iii) Protests relating to size certifications made in response to a contracting officer's request for size certifications in connection with an individual order must be received by the contracting officer prior to the close of business on the 5th day, exclusive of Saturdays, Sundays, and legal holidays, after receipt of notice (including notice received in writing, orally, or via electronic posting) of the identity of the prospective awardee or award.

(4) *Electronic notification of award.* Where notification of award is made electronically, such as posting on the Internet under Simplified Acquisition Procedures, a protest must be received by the contracting officer before close of business on the fifth day, exclusive of Saturdays, Sundays, and legal holidays, after the electronic posting.

(5) *No notice of award.* Where there is no requirement for written pre-award notice or notice of award, or where the contracting officer has failed to provide written notification of award, the 5-day protest period will commence upon oral notification by the contracting officer or authorized representative or another means (such as public announcements or other oral communications) of the identity of the apparent successful offeror.

(b) *Protests by contracting officers, funding agreement officers or SBA.* The time limitations in paragraph (a) of this section do not apply to contracting officers, funding agreement officers or SBA, and they may file protests before or after awards, except to the extent set forth in paragraph (e) of this section, including for purposes of the SBIR and STTR programs. Notwithstanding paragraph (e), for purposes of the SBIR and STTR programs the funding agreement officer or SBA may file a protest in anticipation of an award.

(c) *Effect of contract award.* A timely filed protest applies to the procurement in question even though a contracting officer awarded the contract prior to receipt of the protest.

(d) *Untimely protests.* A protest received after the allotted time limits must still be forwarded to SBA. SBA will dismiss untimely protests.

(e) *Premature protests.* A protest filed by any party, including the contracting officer, before bid opening or notification to offerors of the selection of the apparent successful offer will be dismissed as premature.

[61 FR 3286, Jan. 31, 1996, as amended at 69 FR 29206, May 21, 2004; 71 FR 66444, Nov. 15, 2006; 77 FR 76227, Dec. 27, 2012; 78 FR 61132, Oct. 2, 2013]

§ 121.1005 How must a protest be filed with the contracting officer?

A protest must be delivered to the contracting officer by hand, telegram, mail, facsimile, Federal Express or other overnight delivery service, e-mail, or telephone. If a protest is made by telephone, the contracting officer must later receive a confirming letter either within the 5-day period in § 121.1004(a)(1) or postmarked no later than one day after the date of the telephone protest.

[61 FR 3286, Jan. 31, 1996, as amended at 69 FR 29206, May 21, 2004]

§ 121.1006 When will a size protest be referred to an SBA Government Contracting Area Office?

(a) A contracting officer who receives a protest (other than from SBA) must forward the protest promptly to the SBA Government Contracting Area Office serving the area in which the headquarters of the offeror is located.

(b) A contracting officer's referral must contain the following information:

(1) The protest and any accompanying materials;

(2) A copy of the self-certification as to size;

(3) Identification of the applicable size standard;

(4) A copy of the solicitation;

(5) Identification of the date of bid opening or notification provided to unsuccessful offerors;

(6) The date on which the protest was received; and

(7) A complete address and point of contact for the protested concern.

§ 121.1007 Must a protest of size status relate to a particular procurement and be specific?

(a) *Particular procurement.* A protest challenging the size of a concern which does not pertain to a particular procurement or sale will not be acted on by SBA.

(b) *A protest must include specific facts.* A protest must be sufficiently specific to provide reasonable notice as to the grounds upon which the protested concern's size is questioned. Some basis for the belief or allegation stated in the protest must be given. A protest merely alleging that the protested concern is not small or is affiliated with unnamed other concerns does not specify adequate grounds for the protest. No particular form is prescribed for a protest. Where materials supporting the protest are available, they should be submitted with the protest.

(c) *Non-specific protests will be dismissed.* Protests which do not contain sufficient specificity will be dismissed by SBA. The following are examples of allegation specificity:

Example 1: An allegation that concern X is large because it employs more than 500 employees (where 500 employees is the applicable size standard) without setting forth a basis for the allegation is non-specific.

Example 2: An allegation that concern X is large because it exceeds the 500 employee size standard (where 500 employees is the applicable size standard) because a higher employment figure was published in publication Y is sufficiently specific.

Example 3: An allegation that concern X is affiliated with concern Y without setting forth any basis for the allegation is non-specific.

Example 4: An allegation that concern X is affiliated with concern Y because Mr. A is the majority shareholder in both concerns is sufficiently specific.

Example 5: An allegation that concern X has revenues in excess of $5 million (where $5 million is the applicable size standard) without setting forth a basis for the allegation is non-specific.

Example 6: An allegation that concern X exceeds the size standard (where the applicable size standard is $5 million) because it received Government contracts in excess of $5 million last year is sufficiently specific.

[61 FR 3286, Jan. 31, 1996, as amended at 69 FR 29206, May 21, 2004]

§ 121.1008 What occurs after SBA receives a size protest or request for a formal size determination?

(a) When SBA receives a size protest, the SBA Area Director for Government Contracting, or designee, will notify the contracting officer, the protested concern, and the protestor that the protest has been received. If the protest pertains to a requirement involving SBA's HUBZone program, the Area Director will also notify the D/HUB of the protest. If the protest pertains to a requirement set aside for WOSBs or EDWOSBs, the Area Director will also notify SBA's Director for Government Contracting of the protest. If the protest pertains to a requirement involving SBA's SBIR or STTR programs, the Area Director will also notify the Associate Administrator, Investment Division. If the protest involves the size status of an SDB concern (see part 124, subpart B of this chapter) the Area Director will notify SBA's Associate Administrator for Business Development. If the protest pertains to a requirement that has been reserved for competition among eligible 8(a) BD program participants, the Area Director will notify the SBA district office servicing the 8(a) concern whose size status has been protested. SBA will provide a copy of the protest to the protested concern together with SBA Form 355, Application for Small Business Size Determination, by certified mail, return receipt requested, or by any overnight delivery service that provides proof of receipt. SBA will ask the protested concern to complete the form and respond to the allegations in the protest.

(b) When SBA receives a request for a formal size determination in accord with §121.1001(b), SBA will provide a blank copy of SBA Form 355 to the concern whose size is at issue.

(c) The protested concern or concern whose size is at issue must return the completed SBA Form 355 and all other requested information to SBA within 3 working days from the date of receipt of the blank form from SBA. SBA has discretion to grant an extension of time to file the form. The firm must attach to the completed SBA Form 355 its answers to the allegations contained in the protest, where applicable, together with any supporting material.

(d) If a concern whose size status is at issue fails to submit a completed SBA Form 355, responses to the allegations of the protest, or other requested information within the time allowed by SBA, or if it submits incomplete information, SBA may presume that disclosure of the information required by the form or other missing information would demonstrate that the concern is other than a small business. A concern whose size status is at issue must furnish information about its alleged affiliates to SBA, despite any third party claims of privacy or confidentiality, because SBA will not disclose information obtained in the course of a size determination except as permitted by Federal law.

[61 FR 3286, Jan. 31, 1996, as amended at 63 FR 31908, June 11, 1998; 69 FR 29207, May 21, 2004; 73 FR 56948, Oct. 1, 2008; 74 FR 45753, Sept. 4, 2009; 75 FR 62280, Oct. 7, 2010; 77 FR 76227, Dec. 27, 2012]

§ 121.1009 What are the procedures for making the size determination?

(a) *Time frame for making size determination.* (1) After receipt of a protest or a request for a formal size determination, the SBA Area Office will issue a formal size determination within 15 business days, if possible.

(2) The contracting officer may award a contract after receipt of a protest if the contracting officer determines in writing that an award must be made to protect the public interest. Notwithstanding such a determination, the provisions of paragraph (g) of this section apply to the procurement in question.

(3) If SBA does not issue its determination within 15 business days (or request an extension that is granted), the contracting officer may award the contract if he or she determines in writing that there is an immediate need to award the contract and that waiting until SBA makes its determination will be disadvantageous to the Government. Notwithstanding such a determination, the provisions of paragraph (g) of this section apply to the procurement in question.

(b) *Basis for determination.* The size determination will be based primarily on the information supplied by the protestor or the entity requesting the size determination and that provided by the concern whose size status is at issue. The determination, however, may also be based on grounds not raised in the protest or request for size determination. SBA may use other information and may make requests for additional information to the protestor, the concern whose size status is at issue and any alleged affiliates, or other parties.

(c) *Burden of persuasion.* The concern whose size is under consideration has the burden of establishing its small business size.

(d) *Weight of evidence.* SBA will give greater weight to specific, signed, factual evidence than to general, unsupported allegations or opinions. In the case of refusal or failure to furnish requested information within a required time period, SBA may assume that disclosure would be contrary to the interests of the party failing to make disclosure.

(e) *Formal size determination.* The SBA will base its formal size determination upon the record, including reasonable inferences from the record, and will state in writing the basis for its findings and conclusions.

(f) *Notification of determination.* SBA will promptly notify the contracting officer, the protester, and the protested concern. SBA will send the notification by verifiable means, which may include facsimile, electronic mail, or overnight delivery service.

(g) *Results of an SBA Size Determination.* (1) A contracting officer may award a contract to a protested concern after the SBA Area Office has determined either that the protested concern is an eligible small business or has dismissed all protests against it. If OHA subsequently overturns the Area Office's determination or dismissal, the contracting officer may apply the OHA decision to the procurement in question.

(2) A contracting officer shall not award a contract to a protested concern that the Area Office has determined is not an eligible small business for the procurement in question.

(i) If a contracting officer receives such a determination after contract award, and no OHA appeal has been filed, the contracting officer shall terminate the award.

(ii) If a timely OHA appeal is filed after contract award, the contracting officer must consider whether performance can be suspended until an appellate decision is rendered.

(iii) If OHA affirms the size determination finding the protested concern ineligible, the contracting officer shall either terminate the contract or not exercise the next option.

(3) The contracting officer must update the Federal Procurement Data System and other procurement reporting databases to reflect the final agency size decision (the formal size determination if no appeal is filed or the appellate decision).

(4) Once SBA has determined that a concern is other than small for purposes of a particular procurement, the concern cannot later become eligible for the procurement by reducing its size.

(5) A concern determined to be other than small under a particular size standard is ineligible for any procurement or any assistance authorized by the Small Business Act or the Small Business Investment Act of 1958 which requires the same or a lower size standard, unless SBA recertifies the concern to be small pursuant to § 121.1010 or OHA reverses the adverse size determination. After an adverse size determination, a concern cannot self-certify as small under the same or lower size standard unless it is first recertified as small by SBA. If a concern does so, it may be in violation of criminal laws, including section 16(d) of the Small Business Act, 15 U.S.C. 645(d). If the concern has already certified itself as small on a pending procurement or on an application for SBA assistance, the concern must immediately inform the officials responsible for the pending procurement or requested assistance of the adverse size determination.

(h) *Limited reopening of size determinations.* SBA may, in its sole discretion, reopen a formal size determination to correct an error or mistake, provided it is within the appeal period and no appeal has been filed with OHA. Once the agency has issued a final decision (either a formal size determination that is not timely appealed or an appellate decision), SBA cannot re-open the size determination.

[61 FR 3286, Jan. 31, 1996, as amended at 67 FR 47245, July 18, 2002; 69 FR 29207, May 21, 2004; 76 FR 5683, Feb. 2, 2011; 78 FR 38818, June 28, 2013]

§ 121.1010 How does a concern become recertified as a small business?

(a) A concern may request SBA to recertify it as small at any time by filing an application for recertification with the Government Contracting Area Office responsible for the area in which the headquarters of the applicant is located, regardless of the location of parent companies or affiliates. No particular form is prescribed for the application; however, the request for recertification must be accompanied by a current completed SBA Form 355 and any other information sufficient to show a significant change in its ownership, management, or other factors bearing on its status as a small concern.

(b) Recertification will not be required nor will the prohibition against future self-certification apply if the adverse SBA size determination is based solely on a finding of affiliation due to a joint venture (e.g., ostensible subcontracting) limited to a particular Government procurement or property sale, or is based on an ineligible manufacturer where the eligible small business bidder or offeror is a nonmanufacturer on a particular Government procurement.

(c) A denial of an application for recertification is a formal size determination and may be reviewed by OHA at the discretion of that office.

(d) The granting of an application for recertification has future effect only. While it is a formal size determination, notice of recertification is required to be given only to the applicant.

APPEALS OF SIZE DETERMINATIONS AND NAICS CODE DESIGNATIONS

§ 121.1101 Are formal size determinations subject to appeal?

(a) Appeals from formal size determinations may be made to OHA. Unless an appeal is made to OHA, the size determination made by a SBA Government Contracting Area Office or Disaster Area Office is the final decision of the agency. The procedures for appealing a formal size determination to OHA are set forth in part 134 of this chapter. The OHA appeal is an administrative remedy that must be exhausted before judicial review of a formal size determination may be sought in a court.

(b) OHA will review all timely appeals of size determinations.

[69 FR 29207, May 21, 2004, as amended at 76 FR 5683, Feb. 2, 2011]

§ 121.1102 Are NAICS code designations subject to appeal?

A NAICS code designation made by a procuring activity contracting officer may be appealed to OHA. The procedures governing OHA appeals are set forth in part 134 of this chapter. The OHA appeal is an administrative remedy that must be exhausted before judicial review of a NAICS code designation may be sought in a court.

[67 FR 47245, July 18, 2002]

§ 121.1103 What are the procedures for appealing a NAICS code or size standard designation?

(a)(1) Any interested party adversely affected by a NAICS code designation may appeal the designation to OHA. An interested party would include a business concern seeking to change the NAICS code designation in order to be considered a small business for the challenged procurement, regardless of whether the procurement is reserved for small businesses or unrestricted. The only exception is that, for a sole source contract reserved under SBA's 8(a) Business Development program (*see* part 124 of this chapter), only SBA's Associate Administrator for Business Development may appeal the NAICS code designation.

(2) A NAICS code appeal may include an appeal involving the applicable size standard, such as where more than one size standard corresponds to the selected NAICS code, or a question relating to the size standard in effect at the time the solicitation was issued or amended.

(b) The contracting officer's determination of the applicable NAICS code is final unless appealed as follows:

(1) An appeal from a contracting officer's NAICS code or size standard designation must be served and filed within 10 calendar days after the issuance of the solicitation or amendment affecting the NAICS code or size standard. However, SBA may file a NAICS code appeal at any time before offers

are due. OHA will summarily dismiss an untimely NAICS code appeal.

(2)(i) The appeal petition must be in writing and must be sent to the Office of Hearings & Appeals, U.S. Small Business Administration, 409 3rd Street, SW., Suite 5900, Washington, DC 20416.

(ii) There is no required format for a NAICS code appeal, but an appeal must include the following information: the solicitation or contract number; the name, address, and telephone number of the contracting officer; a full and specific statement as to why the NAICS code designation is erroneous, and argument in support thereof; and the name, address and telephone number of the appellant or its attorney.

(3) The appellant must serve the appeal petition upon the contracting officer who assigned the NAICS code to the acquisition and SBA's Office of General Counsel, Associate General Counsel for Procurement Law, 409 3rd Street, SW., Washington, DC 20416.

(c) *Procedure after a NAICS code appeal is filed and served.* (1) Upon receipt of the service copy of a NAICS code appeal, the contracting officer shall:

(i) Stay the solicitation;

(ii) Advise the public, by amendment to the solicitation or other method, of the existence of the NAICS code appeal and the procedures and deadline for interested parties to file and serve arguments concerning the appeal;

(iii) Send a copy of (or an electronic link to) the entire solicitation, including amendments, to OHA;

(iv) File and serve any response to the appeal prior to the close of the record; and

(v) Inform OHA of any amendments, actions or developments concerning the procurement in question.

(2) Upon receipt of a NAICS code appeal, OHA shall:

(i) Notify the appellant, the contracting officer, the SBA and any other known party of the date OHA received the appeal and the date the record will close; and

(ii) Conduct the appeal in accordance with part 134 of this chapter.

(3) Any interested party may file and serve its response to the NAICS code appeal.

[69 FR 29207, May 21, 2004; 74 FR 45753, Sept. 4, 2009, as amended at 76 FR 5683, Feb. 2, 2011; 78 FR 61132, Oct. 2, 2013]

Subpart B—Other Applicable Provisions

WAIVERS OF THE NONMANUFACTURER RULE FOR CLASSES OF PRODUCTS AND INDIVIDUAL CONTRACTS

§ 121.1201 What is the Nonmanufacturer Rule?

The Nonmanufacturer Rule is set forth in § 121.406(b).

§ 121.1202 When will a waiver of the Nonmanufacturer Rule be granted for a class of products?

(a) A waiver for a class of products (class waiver) will be granted when there are no small business manufacturers or processors available to participate in the Federal market for that class of products.

(b) *Federal market* means acquisitions by the Federal Government from offerors located in the United States, or such smaller area as SBA designates if it concludes that the class of products is not supplied on a national basis.

(1) When considering the appropriate market area for a product, SBA presumes that the entire United States is the relevant Federal market, unless it is clearly demonstrated that a class of products cannot be procured on a national basis. This presumption may be particularly difficult to overcome in the case of manufactured products, since such items typically have a market area encompassing the entire United States.

(2) When considering geographic segmentation of a Federal market, SBA will not necessarily use market definitions dependent on airline radius, political, or SBA regional boundaries. Market areas typically follow established transportation routes rather than jurisdictional borders. SBA examines the following factors, among others, in cases where geographic segmentation for a class of products is urged:

(i) Whether perishability affects the area in which the product can practically be sold;

(ii) Whether transportation costs are high as a proportion of the total value of the product so as to limit the economic distribution of the product;

(iii) Whether there are legal barriers to transportation of the item;

(iv) Whether a fixed, well-delineated boundary exists for the purported market area and whether this boundary has been stable over time; and

(v) Whether a small business, not currently selling in the defined market area, could potentially enter the market from another area and supply the market at a reasonable price.

(c) *Available to participate* in the context of the Federal market means that contractors exist that have been awarded or have performed a contract to supply a specific class of products to the Federal Government within 24 months from the date of the request for waiver, either directly or through a dealer, or who have submitted an offer on a solicitation for that class of products within that time frame.

(d) *Class of products* is an individual subdivision within an NAICS Industry Number as established by the Office of Management and Budget in the NAICS Manual.

[61 FR 3286, Jan. 31, 1996, as amended at 65 FR 30863, May 15, 2000]

§ 121.1203 When will a waiver of the Nonmanufacturer Rule be granted for an individual contract?

(a) Where appropriate, SBA will generally grant waivers for an individual contract or order prior to the issuance of a solicitation, or, where a solicitation has been issued, when the contracting officer provides all potential offerors additional time to respond.

(b) SBA may grant a waiver after contract award, where the contracting officer has determined that the modification is within the scope of the contract and the agency followed the regulations prior to issuance of the solicitation and properly and timely requested a waiver for any other items under the contract, where required.

Example to paragraph (b): The Government seeks to buy spare parts to fix Item A. After conducting market research, the government determines that Items B, C, and D that are being procured may be eligible for waivers and requests and receives waivers from SBA for those items prior to issuing the solicitation. After the contract is awarded, the Government determines that it will need additional spare parts to fix Item A. The Government determines that adding the additional parts as a modification to the original contract is within scope. The contracting officer believes that one of the additional parts is also eligible for a waiver from SBA, and requests the waiver at the time of the modification. If all other criteria are met, SBA would grant the waiver, even though the contract has already been awarded.

(c) An individual waiver for an item in a solicitation will be approved when the SBA Director, Office of Government Contracting, reviews and accepts a contracting officer's determination that no small business manufacturer or processor can reasonably be expected to offer a product meeting the specifications of a solicitation, including the period of performance.

(d) *Waivers for the purchase of software.* (1) SBA may grant an individual waiver for the procurement of software provided that the software being sought is an item that is of a type customarily used by the general public or by non-governmental entities for purposes other than governmental purposes, and the item:

(i) Has been sold, leased, or licensed to the general public, or has been offered for sale, lease, or license to the general public;

(ii) Is sold in substantial quantities in the commercial marketplace; and

(iii) Is offered to the Government, without modification, in the same form in which it is sold in the commercial marketplace.

(2) If the value of services provided related to the purchase of a supply item that meets the requirements of paragraph (d)(1) of this section exceeds the value of the item itself, the procurement should be identified as a service procurement, even if the services are provided as part of the same license, lease, or sale terms. If a contracting officer cannot make a determination of the value of services being provided, SBA will assume that the value of the services is greater than the value of items or supplies, and will not grant a waiver.

(3) Subscription services, remote hosting of software, data, or other applications on servers or networks of a party other than the U.S. Government are considered by SBA to be services and not the procurement of a supply item. Therefore SBA will not grant waivers of the nonmanufacturer rule for these types of services.

[81 FR 34260, May 31, 2016]

§ 121.1204 What are the procedures for requesting and granting waivers?

(a) *Waivers for classes of products.* (1) SBA may, at its own initiative, examine a class of products for possible waiver of the Nonmanufacturer Rule.

(2) Any interested person, business, association, or Federal agency may submit a request for a waiver for a particular class of products. Requests should be addressed or hand-carried to the Director, Office of Government Contracting, Small Business Administration, 409 3rd Street SW., Washington, DC 20416.

(3) Requests for a waiver of a class of products need not be in any particular form, but should include a statement of the class of products to be waived, the applicable NAICS code, and detailed information on the efforts made to identify small business manufacturers or processors for the class.

(4) If SBA decides that there are small business manufacturers or processors in the Federal procurement market, it will deny the request for waiver, issue notice of the denial, and provide the names, addresses, and telephone numbers of the sources found. If SBA does not initially confirm the existence of small business manufacturers or processors in the Federal market, it will:

(i) Publish notices in the Commerce Business Daily and the FEDERAL REGISTER seeking information on small business manufacturers or processors, announcing a notice of intent to waive the Nonmanufacturer Rule for that class of products and affording the public a 15-day comment period; and

(ii) If no small business sources are identified, publish a notice in the FEDERAL REGISTER stating that no small business sources were found and that a waiver of the Nonmanufacturer Rule for that class of products has been granted.

(5) An expedited procedure for issuing a class waiver may be used for emergency situations, but only if the contracting officer provides a determination to the Director, Office of Government Contracting that the procurement is proceeding under the authority of FAR § 6.302–2 (48 CFR 6.302–2) for "unusual and compelling urgency," or provides a determination materially the same as one of unusual and compelling urgency. Under the expedited procedure, if a small business manufacturer or processor is not identified by a PASS search, the SBA will grant the waiver for the class of products and then publish a notice in the FEDERAL REGISTER. The notice will state that a waiver has been granted, and solicit public comment for future procurements.

(6) The decision by the Director, Office of Government Contracting to grant or deny a waiver is the final decision by the Agency.

(7) A waiver of the Nonmanufacturer Rule for classes of products has no specific time limitation. SBA will, however, periodically review existing class waivers to the Nonmanufacturer Rule to determine if small business manufacturers or processors have become available to participate in the Federal market for the waived classes of products and the waiver should be terminated.

(i) Upon SBA's receipt of evidence that a small business manufacturer or processor exists in the Federal market for a waived class of products, the waiver will be terminated by the Director, Office of Government Contracting. This evidence may be discovered by SBA during a periodic review of existing waivers or may be brought to SBA's attention by other sources.

(ii) SBA will announce its intent to terminate a waiver for a class of products through the publication of a notice in the FEDERAL REGISTER, asking for comments regarding the proposed termination.

(iii) Unless public comment reveals that no small business manufacturer or processor in fact exists for the class of products in question, SBA will publish a final Notice of Termination in the FEDERAL REGISTER.

(b) *Individual waivers for specific solicitations.* (1) A contracting officer's request for a waiver of the Nonmanufacturer Rule for specific solicitations need not be in any particular form, but must, at a minimum, include:

(i) A definitive statement of the specific item to be waived and justification as to why the specific item is required;

(ii) The proposed solicitation number, NAICS code, dollar amount of the procurement, and a brief statement of the procurement history;

(iii) A determination by the contracting officer that no small business manufacturer or processor reasonably can be expected to offer a product or products meeting the specifications (including period of performance) required by a particular solicitation. Include a narrative describing market research and supporting documentation; and

(iv) For contracts or orders expected to exceed $500,000, a copy of the Statement of Work.

(2) Requests should be addressed to the Director, Office of Government Contracting, Small Business Administration, 409 3rd Street, SW., Washington, DC 20416.

(3) SBA will examine the contracting officer's determination and any other information it deems necessary to make an informed decision on the individual waiver request. If SBA's research verifies that no small business manufacturers or processors exist for the item, the Director, Office of Government Contracting will grant an individual, one-time waiver. If a small business manufacturer or processor is found for the product in question, the Associate Administrator will deny the request. Either decision represents a final decision by SBA.

[61 FR 3286, Jan. 31, 1996, as amended at 65 FR 30863, May 15, 2000; 78 FR 61132, Oct. 2, 2013; 81 FR 34260, May 31, 2016]

§ 121.1205 How is a list of previously granted class waivers obtained?

A list of classes of products for which waivers for the Nonmanufacturer Rule have been granted is maintained in SBA Web site at: *http://www.sba.gov/aboutsba/sbaprograms/gc/programs/gc_waivers_nonmanufacturer.html.* A list of such waivers may also be obtained by contacting the Office of Government Contracting, U.S. Small Business Administration, 409 3rd Street, SW., Washington, DC 20416, or the nearest SBA Government Contracting Area Office.

[69 FR 29208, May 21, 2004, as amended at 74 FR 46313, Sept. 9, 2009]

§ 121.1206 How will potential offerors be notified of applicable waivers?

(a) Contracting officers must provide written notification to potential offerors of any waivers being applied to a specific acquisition, whether it is a class waiver or a contract specific waiver. This notification must be provided at the time a solicitation is issued. If the notification is provided after a solicitation is issued, the contracting officer must provide potential offerors a reasonable amount of additional time to respond to the solicitation.

(b) If a contracting officer does not provide notice, and additional reasonable time for responses when required, then the waiver cannot be applied to the solicitation. This applies to both class waivers and individual waivers.

[81 FR 34260, May 31, 2016]

PART 123—DISASTER LOAN PROGRAM

Subpart A—Overview

Sec.

Subpart B—Home Disaster Loans

Subpart C—Physical Disaster Business Loans

Subpart D—Economic Injury Disaster Loans

Subpart E—Pre-Disaster Mitigation Loans

Subpart F—Military Reservist Economic Injury Disaster Loans

Subpart G—Economic Injury Disaster Loans as a Result of the September 11, 2001 Terrorist Attacks

Subpart H—Immediate Disaster Assistance Program

AUTHORITY: 15 U.S.C. 632, 634(b)(6), 636(b), 636(d), 657n; and Pub. L. 102–395, 106 Stat. 1828, 1864.

SOURCE: 61 FR 3304, Jan. 31, 1996, unless otherwise noted.

Subpart A—Overview

§ 123.1 What do these rules cover?

This part covers the disaster loan programs authorized under the Small Business Act, 15 U.S.C. 636(b), (d), and (f); and 15 U.S.C. 657n. Since SBA cannot predict the occurrence or magnitude of disasters, it reserves the right to change the rules in this part, without advance notice, by publishing interim emergency regulations in the FEDERAL REGISTER.

[61 FR 3304, Jan. 31, 1996, as amended at 75 FR 60597, Oct. 1, 2010]

§ 123.2 What are disaster loans and disaster declarations?

SBA offers low interest, fixed rate loans to disaster victims, enabling them to repair or replace property damaged or destroyed in declared disasters. It also offers such loans to affected small businesses to help them recover from economic injury caused by such disasters. SBA also offers interim guaranteed disaster loans, in participation with financial institutions, to affected small businesses ("IDAP loans"). Disaster declarations are official notices recognizing that specific geographic areas have been damaged by floods and other acts of nature, riots, civil disorders, or industrial accidents such as oil spills. These disasters are sudden events which cause severe physical damage, and do not include slower physical occurrences such as shoreline erosion or gradual land settling. However, *for purposes of economic injury disaster loans only*, they do include droughts and below average water levels in the Great Lakes or on any body of water in the United States that supports commerce by small businesses. Sudden events that cause substantial economic injury may be disasters even if they do not cause physical damage to a victim's property. Past examples include ocean conditions causing significant displacement (major ocean currents) or closure (toxic algae blooms) of customary fishing waters, as well as contamination of food or other products for human consumption from unforeseeable and unintended events beyond the control of the victims.

[61 FR 3304, Jan. 31, 1996, as amended at 71 FR 75409, Dec. 15, 2007; 75 FR 60597, Oct. 1, 2010; 81 FR 67903, Oct. 3, 2016]

§ 123.3 How are disaster declarations made?

(a) There are five ways in which disaster declarations are issued which make SBA disaster loans possible:

(1) The President declares a Major Disaster and authorizes Federal Assistance, including individual assistance (Assistance to Individuals and Households Program).

(2) If the President declares a Major Disaster limited to public assistance only, a private nonprofit facility which provides non-critical services under guidelines of the Federal Emergency Management Agency (FEMA) must first apply to SBA for disaster loan assistance for such non-critical services before it could seek grant assistance from FEMA.

(3) SBA makes a physical disaster declaration, based on the occurrence of at least a minimum amount of physical damage to buildings, machinery, equipment, inventory, homes and other property. Such damage usually must meet the following tests:

(i) In any county or other smaller political subdivision of a State or U.S. possession, at least 25 homes or 25 businesses, or a combination of at least 25 homes, businesses, or other eligible institutions, each sustain uninsured losses of 40 percent or more of the estimated fair replacement value or pre-disaster fair market value of the damaged property, whichever is lower; or

(ii) In any such political subdivision, at least three businesses each sustain uninsured losses of 40 percent or more of the estimated fair replacement value or pre-disaster fair market value of the damaged property, whichever is lower, and, as a direct result of such physical damage, 25 percent or more of the work force in their community would be unemployed for at least 90 days; and

(iii) The Governor of the State in which the disaster occurred submits a written request to SBA for a physical disaster declaration by SBA (OMB Approval No. 3245–0121). This request should be delivered to the Disaster Assistance Field Operations Center serving the jurisdiction within 60 days of the date of the disaster. The addresses, phone numbers, and jurisdictions served by the field operations centers are published in the FEDERAL REGISTER.

(4) SBA makes an economic injury disaster declaration in response to a determination of a natural disaster by the Secretary of Agriculture.

(5) SBA makes an economic injury declaration in reliance on a state certification that at least five small business concerns in a disaster area have suffered substantial economic injury as a result of the disaster and are in need of financial assistance not otherwise available on reasonable terms. The state certification must be signed by the Governor, must specify the county or counties or other political subdivision in which the disaster occurred, and must be delivered (with supporting documentation) to the Disaster Assistance Field Operations Center serving the jurisdiction within 120 days of the disaster occurrence. When a Governor certifies with respect to a drought or to below average water levels, the supporting documentation must include findings which show that conditions during the incident period meet or exceed the U.S. Drought Monitor (USDM) standard of "severe" (Intensity level D–2 to D–4). The USDM may be found at *http://drought.unl.edu/dm/monitor*. With respect to below average water levels, the supplementary information accompanying the certification must include findings which establish long-term average water levels based on recorded historical data, show that current water levels are below long-term average levels, and demonstrate that economic injury has occurred as a direct result of the low water levels. Not later than 30 days after SBA receives a certification by a Governor, it shall respond in writing with its decision and its reasons.

(b) SBA publishes notice of any disaster declaration in the FEDERAL REGISTER. The published notice will identify the kinds of assistance available, the date and nature of the disaster, and the deadline and location for filing loan applications. Additionally, SBA will use the local media to inform potential loan applicants where to obtain loan applications and otherwise to assist victims in applying for disaster loans. SBA will accept applications after the announced deadline only when SBA determines that the late filing resulted from substantial causes beyond the control of the applicant.

[61 FR 3304, Jan. 31, 1996, as amended at 64 FR 13667, Mar. 22, 1999; 67 FR 64518, Oct. 21, 2002; 71 FR 63676, Oct. 31, 2006; 71 FR 75409, Dec. 15, 2006; 73 FR 54675, Sept. 23, 2008; 81 FR 67903, Oct. 3, 2016]

§ 123.4 What is a disaster area and why is it important?

Each disaster declaration defines the geographical areas affected by the disaster. Only those victims located in the declared disaster area are eligible to apply for SBA disaster loans. When the President declares a major disaster, the Federal Emergency Management Agency defines the disaster area. In major disasters, economic injury disaster loans and IDAP loans may be made for victims in contiguous counties or other political subdivisions, provided, however that with respect to major disasters which authorize public assistance only, SBA shall not make economic injury disaster or IDAP loans in counties contiguous to the disaster area. Disaster declarations issued by the Administrator of SBA include contiguous counties for both physical, economic injury and, in some cases, IDAP assistance. Contiguous counties or other political subdivisions are those land areas which abut the land area of the declared disaster area without geographic separation other than by a minor body of water, not to exceed one mile between the land areas of such counties.

[61 FR 3304, Jan. 31, 1996, as amended at 67 FR 64519, Oct. 21, 2002; 75 FR 60597, Oct. 1, 2010]

§ 123.5 What kinds of loans are available?

(a) *Disaster loans authorized under Section 7(b).* SBA offers four kinds of disaster loans as authorized by Section 7(b) of the Small Business Act: Physical disaster home loans, physical disaster business loans, economic injury disaster business loans, and Military Reservist EIDL loans. SBA makes these loans directly or in participation with a financial institution. If a disaster loan authorized under Section 7(b) is made in participation with a financial institution, SBA's share in that loan may not exceed 90 percent.

(b) *IDAP loans.* SBA also offers IDAP loans as authorized by Section 42 of the Small Business Act. SBA makes these interim guaranteed disaster loans to small businesses only in participation with a financial institution. SBA's share in an IDAP loan is equal to 85 percent.

[75 FR 60597, Oct. 1, 2010]

§ 123.6 What does SBA look for when considering a disaster loan applicant?

There must be reasonable assurance that you can repay your loan based on SBA's analysis of your credit or your personal or business cash flow, and you must also have satisfactory character. SBA will not make a loan to you if repayment depends upon the sale of collateral through foreclosure or any other disposition of assets owned by you. SBA is prohibited by statute from making a loan to you if you are engaged in the production or distribution of any product or service that has been determined to be obscene by a court.

[61 FR 3304, Jan. 31, 1996, as amended at 79 FR 22862, Apr. 25, 2014]

§ 123.7 Are there restrictions on how disaster loans can be used?

You must use disaster loans to restore or replace your primary home (including a mobile home used as a primary residence) and your personal or business property as nearly as possible to their condition before the disaster occurred, and within certain limits, to protect damaged or destroyed real property from possible future similar disasters.

§ 123.8 Does SBA charge any fees for obtaining a disaster loan?

SBA does not charge points, closing, or servicing fees on any disaster loan authorized under Section 7(b). You will be responsible for payment of any closing costs owed to third parties on these loans, such as recording fees and title insurance premiums. If your loan is made under Section 7(b) in participation with a financial institution, SBA will charge a guarantee fee to the financial institution, which then may recover the guarantee fee from you. SBA does not charge a guarantee fee for an IDAP loan made under Section 42.

[75 FR 60598, Oct. 1, 2010]

§ 123.9 What happens if I don't use loan proceeds for the intended purpose?

(a) For disaster loans authorized under Section 7(b), when SBA approves each application, it issues a loan authorization which specifies the amount of the loan, repayment terms, any collateral requirements, and the permitted use of loan proceeds. If you wrongfully misapply the proceeds of a disaster loan authorized under Section 7(b), you will be liable to SBA for one and one-half times the proceeds disbursed to you as of the date SBA learns of your wrongful misapplication. Wrongful misapplication means the willful use of any loan proceeds without SBA approval contrary to the loan authorization. If you fail to use loan proceeds for authorized purposes for 60 days or more after receiving a loan disbursement check, such non-use also is considered a wrongful misapplication of the proceeds.

(b) If SBA learns that you may have misapplied your loan proceeds from a disaster loan authorized under Section 7(b), SBA will notify you at your last known address, by certified mail, return receipt requested. You will be given at least 30 days to submit to SBA evidence that you have not misapplied the loan proceeds or that you have corrected any such misapplication. Any failure to respond in time will be considered an admission that you misapplied the proceeds. If SBA finds a wrongful misapplication, it will cancel any undisbursed loan proceeds, call the loan, and begin collection measures to collect your outstanding loan balance and the civil penalty.

(c) If you misapply loan proceeds of any disaster loan under this Part, including an IDAP loan, you may face criminal prosecution or civil or administrative action.

[61 FR 3304, Jan. 31, 1996, as amended at 75 FR 60598, Oct. 1, 2010]

§ 123.10 What happens if I cannot use my insurance proceeds to make repairs?

If you must pay insurance proceeds to the holder of a recorded lien or encumbrance against your damaged property instead of using them to make repairs, you may apply to SBA for the full amount needed to make such repairs. If you voluntarily pay insurance proceeds to a recorded lienholder, your loan eligibility is reduced by the amount of the voluntary payment.

§ 123.11 Does SBA require collateral for any of its disaster loans?

(a) When collateral is not required:

(1) *Economic injury disaster loans.* Generally, SBA will not require that you pledge collateral to secure an economic injury disaster loan of $25,000 or less.

(2) *Physical disaster home and physical disaster business loans.* Generally, SBA will not require that you pledge collateral to secure a physical disaster home or physical disaster business loan of $25,000 or less. This authority expires on November 25, 2018, unless extended by statute.

(3) *IDAP loans.* Collateral requirements for IDAP loans are set forth in Subpart H of this part.

(4) *Military Reservist EIDL.* For the purposes of the Military Reservist EIDL only, as described in section 123.513, SBA will not generally require that you pledge collateral to secure a loan of $50,000 or less.

(b) For loans larger than the amounts outlined in paragraph (a) of this section, you will be required to provide available collateral such as a lien on the damaged or replacement property, a security interest in personal/business property, or both.

(c) Sometimes a borrower, including affiliates as defined in part 121 of this title, will have more than one loan after a single disaster. In deciding whether collateral is required, SBA will add up all physical disaster loans to see if they exceed the applicable unsecured threshold outlined in paragraph (a)(2) of this section and all economic injury disaster loans to see if they exceed $25,000.

(d) SBA will not decline a loan if you lack a particular amount of collateral as long as it is reasonably sure that you can repay your loan. If you refuse to pledge available collateral when requested by SBA, however, SBA may decline or cancel your loan.

[61 FR 3304, Jan. 31, 1996, as amended at 73 FR 54675, Sept. 23, 2008; 75 FR 14332, Mar. 25, 2010; 75 FR 60598, Oct. 1, 2010; 79 FR 22862, Apr. 25, 2014; 81 FR 67903, Oct. 3, 2016]

§ 123.12 Are books and records required?

You must retain complete records of all transactions financed with your SBA loan proceeds, including copies of all contracts and receipts, for a period of 3 years after you receive your final disbursement of loan proceeds. If you have a physical disaster business or economic injury loan, you must also maintain current and accurate books of account, including financial and operating statements, insurance policies, and tax returns. You must retain applicable books and records for 3 years after your loan matures including any extensions, or from the date when your loan is paid in full, whichever occurs first. You must make available to SBA or other authorized government personnel upon request all such books and records for inspection, audit, and reproduction during normal business hours and you must also permit SBA and any participating financial institution to inspect and appraise your assets. (OMB Approval No. 3245–0110.)

§ 123.13 What happens if my loan application is denied?

(a) If SBA denies your loan application, SBA will notify you in writing and set forth the specific reasons for the denial. Any applicant whose request for a loan is declined for reasons other than size (not being a small business) has the right to present information to overcome the reason or reasons for the decline and to request reconsideration in writing.

(b) Any decline due to size can only be appealed as set forth in part 121 of this chapter.

(c) Any request for reconsideration must be received by SBA's Disaster Assistance Processing and Disbursement Center (DAPDC) within six months of the date of the decline notice. After six months, a new loan application is required.

(d) A request for reconsideration must contain all significant new information that you rely on to overcome SBA's denial of your original loan application. Your request for reconsideration of a business loan application must also be accompanied by current business financial statements.

(e) If SBA declines your application a second time, you have the right to appeal in writing to the Director, Disaster Assistance Processing and Disbursement Center. All appeals must be received by the processing center within 30 days of the decline action. Your request must state that you are appealing, and must give specific reasons why the decline action should be reversed.

(f) The decision of the Director, DAPDC, is final unless:

(1) The Director, DAPDC, does not have the authority to approve the requested loan;

(2) The Director, DAPDC, refers the matter to the AA/DA; or

(3) The AA/DA, upon a showing of special circumstances, requests that the Director, DAPDC, forward the matter to him or her for final consideration. Special circumstances may include, but are not limited to, policy considerations or alleged improper acts by SBA personnel or others in processing the application.

(g) This section does not apply to IDAP loans.

[61 FR 3304, Jan. 31, 1996, as amended at 71 FR 63676, Oct. 31, 2006; 75 FR 60598, Oct. 1, 2010; 81 FR 67903, Oct. 3, 2016]

§ 123.14 How does the Federal Debt Collection Procedures Act of 1990 apply?

(a) Under the Federal Debt Collection Procedures Act of 1990 (28 U.S.C. 3201(e)), a debtor who owns property which is subject to an outstanding judgment lien for a debt owed to the United States generally is not eligible to receive a disaster loan. The SBA Associate Administrator for Disaster Assistance, or designee, may waive this restriction as to disaster loans (except IDAP loans) upon a demonstration of good cause. Good cause means a written representation by you under oath which convinces SBA that:

(1) The declared disaster was a major contributing factor to the delinquency

which led to the judgment lien, regardless of when the original debt was incurred; or

(2) The disaster directly prevented you from fulfilling the terms of an agreement with SBA or any other Federal Government entity to satisfy its pre-disaster judgment lien; in this situation, the judgment creditor must certify to SBA that you were complying with the agreement to satisfy the judgment lien when the disaster occurred; or

(3) Other circumstances exist which would justify a waiver.

(b) The waiver determination by the Associate Administrator for Disaster Assistance, or designee, is a final, non-appealable decision. The granting of a waiver does not include loan approval; a waiver recipient must then follow normal loan application procedures.

[61 FR 3304, Jan. 31, 1996, as amended at 75 FR 60598, Oct. 1, 2010]

§ 123.15 What if I change my mind?

If SBA required you to pledge collateral for your loan, you may change your mind and rescind your loan pursuant to the Consumer Credit Protection Act, 15 U.S.C. 1601, and Regulation Z of the Federal Reserve Board, 12 CFR part 226. Your note and any collateral documents signed by you will be canceled upon your return of all loan proceeds and your payment of any interest accrued. This provision does not apply to IDAP loans.

[61 FR 3304, Jan. 31, 1996, as amended at 75 FR 60598, Oct. 1, 2010]

§ 123.16 How are loans administered and serviced?

(a) If you obtained your disaster loan from a participating lender, that lender is responsible for closing and servicing your loan. If you obtained your loan directly from SBA, your loan will be closed and serviced by SBA. The SBA rules on servicing are found in Subpart H of this part and part 120 of this chapter.

(b) If you are unable to pay your SBA loan installments in a timely manner for reasons substantially beyond your control, you may request that SBA suspend your loan payments, extend your maturity, or both.

[61 FR 3304, Jan. 31, 1996, as amended at 75 FR 60598, Oct. 1, 2010]

§ 123.17 Do other Federal requirements apply?

As a condition of disbursement, you must be in compliance with certain requirements relating to flood insurance, lead-based paint, earthquake hazards, coastal barrier islands, and child support obligations, as set forth in §§ 120.170 through 120.175 of this chapter.

§ 123.18 Can I request an increase in the amount of a physical disaster loan?

(a) Generally, SBA will consider your request for an increase in your loan if you can show that the eligible cost of repair or replacement of damages increased because of events occurring after the loan approval that were beyond your control. An eligible cost is one which is related to the disaster for which SBA issued the original loan. For example, if you discover hidden damage within a reasonable time after SBA approved your original disaster loan and before repair, renovation, or reconstruction is complete, you may request an increase. Or, if applicable building code requirements were changed since SBA approved your original loan, you may request an increase in your loan amount.

(b) For all disasters occurring on or after November 25, 2015, you may also request an increase in your loan if you suffered substantial economic damage or substantial risks to health or safety as a result of malfeasance in connection with the repair or replacement of real property or business machinery and equipment for which SBA made a disaster loan. See § 123.105 for limits on home loan amounts and § 123.202 for limits on business loan amounts. Malfeasance may include, but is not limited to, nonperformance of all or any portion of the work for which a contractor was paid, work that does not meet acceptable standards, or use of substandard materials.

[63 FR 15072, Mar. 30, 1998, as amended at 81 FR 67903, Oct. 3, 2016]

§ 123.19 May I request an increase in the amount of an economic injury loan?

SBA will consider your request for an increase in the loan amount if you can show that the increase is essential for your business to continue and is based on events occurring after SBA approved your original loan which were beyond your control. For example, delays may have occurred beyond your control which prevent you from resuming your normal business activity in a reasonable time frame. Your request for an increase in the loan amount must be related to the disaster for which the SBA economic injury disaster loan was originally made.

[63 FR 15072, Mar. 30, 1998]

§ 123.20 How long do I have to request an increase in the amount of a physical disaster loan or an economic injury loan?

(a) You should request a loan increase as soon as possible after you discover the need for the increase, but not later than two years after SBA approved your physical disaster or economic injury loan. After two years, the SBA Associate Administrator for Disaster Assistance (AA/DA) may waive this limitation after finding extraordinary and unforeseeable circumstances.

(b) For physical disaster loan increases requested under § 123.18(b) as a result of malfeasance, the request must be received not later than two years after the date of final disbursement.

[63 FR 15073, Mar. 30, 1998, as amended at 81 FR 67903, Oct. 3, 2016]

§ 123.21 What is a mitigation measure?

A mitigation measure is something done for the purpose of protecting property and occupants against disaster related damage. You may implement mitigation measures after a disaster occurs (post-disaster) to protect against recurring disaster related damage, or before a disaster occurs (pre-disaster) to protect against future disaster related damage. Examples of mitigation measures include building retaining walls, sea walls, grading and contouring land, elevating flood prone structures, relocating utilities, constructing a safe room or similar storm shelter (if such safe room or similar storm shelter is constructed in accordance with applicable standards issued by the Federal Emergency Management Agency), or retrofitting structures to protect against high winds, earthquakes, flood, wildfires, or other physical disasters. Section 123.107 specifically addresses post-disaster mitigation for home disaster loans, and § 123.204 specifically addresses post-disaster mitigation for businesses. Sections 123.400 through 123.412 specifically address pre-disaster mitigation.

[67 FR 62337, Oct. 7, 2002, as amended at 81 FR 67903, Oct. 3, 2016]

Subpart B—Home Disaster Loans

§ 123.100 Am I eligible to apply for a home disaster loan?

(a) You are eligible to apply for a home disaster loan if you:

(1) Own and occupy your primary residence and have suffered a physical loss to your primary residence, personal property, or both; or

(2) Do not own your primary residence, but have suffered a physical loss to your personal property. Family members sharing a residence are eligible if they are not dependents of the owners of the residence.

(b) Losses may be claimed only by the owners of the property at the time of the disaster, and all such losses will be verified by SBA. SBA will consider beneficial ownership as well as legal title (for real or personal property) in determining who suffered the loss.

§ 123.101 When am I not eligible for a home disaster loan?

You are not eligible for a home disaster loan if:

(a) You have been convicted, during the past year, of a felony during and in connection with a riot or civil disorder or other declared disaster;

(b) You acquired voluntarily more than a 50 percent ownership interest in the damaged property after the disaster, and no contract of sale existed at the time of the disaster;

(c) Your damaged property can be repaired or replaced with the proceeds of insurance, gifts or other compensation, including condemnation awards (with one exception), these amounts must either be deducted from the amount of the claimed losses or, if received after SBA has approved and disbursed a loan, must be paid to SBA as principal payments on your loan. You must notify SBA of any such recoveries collected after receiving an SBA disaster loan. The one exception applies to amounts received under the Individuals and Household Program of the Federal Emergency Management Agency solely to meet an emergency need pending processing of an SBA loan. In such an event, you must repay the financial assistance with SBA loan proceeds if it was used for purposes also eligible for an SBA loan;

(d) SBA determines that you assumed the risk (for example, by not maintaining flood insurance as required by an earlier SBA disaster loan when the current loss is also due to flood);

(e) Your damaged property is a secondary home (although if you rented the property out before the disaster and the property would not constitute a "residence" under the provisions of Section 280A of the Internal Revenue Code (26 U.S.C. 280A), you may be eligible for a physical disaster business loan);

(f) Your damaged property is the type of vehicle normally used for recreational purposes, such as motorhomes, aircraft, and boats;

(g) Your damaged property consists of cash or securities;

(h) The replacement value of your damaged personal property is extraordinarily high and not easily verified, such as the value of antiques, artworks, or hobby collections;

(i) You or other principal owners of the damaged property are presently incarcerated, or on probation or parole following conviction for a serious criminal offense;

(j) Your only interest in the damaged property is in the form of a security interest, mortgage, or deed of trust;

(k) The damaged building, including contents, was newly constructed or substantially improved on or after February 9, 1989, and (without a significant business justification) is located seaward of mean high tide or entirely in or over water; or

(l) You voluntarily decide to relocate outside the business area in which the disaster has occurred, and there are no special or unusual circumstances leading to your decision (business area means the municipality which provides general governmental services to your damaged home or, if not located in a municipality, the county or equivalent political entity in which your damaged home is located).

[61 FR 3304, Jan. 31, 1996, as amended at 67 FR 64519, Oct. 21, 2002]

§ 123.102 What circumstances would justify my relocating?

SBA may approve a loan if you intend to relocate outside the business area in which the disaster has occurred if your relocation is caused by such special or unusual circumstances as:

(a) Demonstrable risk that the business area will suffer future disasters;

(b) A change in employment status (such as loss of job, transfer, lack of adequate job opportunities within the business area or scheduled retirement within 18 months after the disaster occurs);

(c) Medical reasons; or

(d) Special family considerations which necessitate a move outside of the business area.

§ 123.103 What happens if I am forced to move from my home?

If you must relocate inside or outside the business area because local authorities will not allow you to repair your damaged property, SBA considers this to be a total loss and a mandatory relocation. In this case, your loan would be an amount that SBA considers sufficient to replace your residence at your new location, plus funds to cover losses of personal property and eligible refinancing.

§ 123.104 What interest rate will I pay on my home disaster loan?

If you can obtain credit elsewhere, your interest rate is set by a statutory formula, but will not exceed 8 percent per annum. If you cannot obtain credit elsewhere, your interest rate is one-half the statutory rate, but will not exceed 4 percent per annum. Credit elsewhere means that, with your cash flow and disposable assets, SBA believes you could obtain financing from non-federal sources on reasonable terms. If you cannot obtain credit elsewhere, you also may be able to borrow from SBA to refinance existing recorded liens against your damaged real property. Under prior legislation, some SBA disaster loans had split interest rates. On any such loan, repayments of principal are applied first to that portion of the loan with the lowest interest rate.

§ 123.105 How much can I borrow with a home disaster loan and what limits apply on use of funds and repayment terms?

(a) There are limits on how much money you can borrow for particular purposes:

(1) $40,000 for repair or replacement of household and personal effects;

(2) $200,000 for repair or replacement of a primary residence (including upgrading in order to meet minimum standards of safety and decency or current building code requirements). Repair or replacement of landscaping and/or recreational facilities cannot exceed $5,000;

(3) $200,000 for eligible refinancing purposes;

(4) 20 percent of the verified loss (not including refinancing or malfeasance), before deduction of compensation from other sources, up to a maximum of $200,000 for post-disaster mitigation (see § 123.107); and

(5) $200,000 for eligible malfeasance, pursuant to § 123.18.

(b) You may not use loan proceeds to repay any debts on personal property, secured or unsecured, unless you incurred those debts as a direct result of the disaster.

(c) SBA determines the loan maturity and repayment terms based on your needs and your ability to pay. Generally, you will pay equal monthly installments of principal and interest, beginning five months from the date of the loan, as shown on the Note securing the loan. SBA will consider other payment terms if you have seasonal or fluctuating income, and SBA may allow installment payments of varying amounts over the first two years of the loan. The maximum maturity for a home disaster loan is 30 years. There is no penalty for prepayment of home disaster loans.

[61 FR 3304, Jan. 31, 1996, as amended at 75 FR 14332, Mar. 25, 2010; 81 FR 67903, Oct. 3, 2016]

§ 123.106 What is eligible refinancing?

(a) If your home (primary residence) is totally destroyed or substantially damaged, and you do not have credit elsewhere, SBA may allow you to borrow money to refinance recorded liens or encumbrances on your home. Your home is totally destroyed or substantially damaged if it has suffered uninsured or otherwise uncompensated damage which, at the time of the disaster, is either:

(1) 40 percent or more of the home's market value or replacement cost at the time of the disaster, including land value, whichever is less; or

(2) 50 percent or more of its market value or replacement cost at the time of the disaster, not including land value, whichever is less.

(b) Your home disaster loan for refinancing existing liens or encumbrances cannot exceed an amount equal to the lesser of $200,000, or the physical damage to your primary residence after reductions for any insurance or other recovery.

§ 123.107 How much can I borrow for post-disaster mitigation for my home?

For mitigation measures implemented after a disaster has occurred, you can request that the approved home disaster loan amount be increased by the lesser of the cost of the mitigation measure, or up to 20 percent of the verified loss (before deducting compensation from other sources), to a maximum of $200,000.

[75 FR 14332, Mar. 25, 2010]

§ 123.108 How do the SBA disaster loan program and the FEMA grant programs interact?

After a Presidential disaster declaration is made, you may be eligible for disaster assistance, including grant assistance, from the Federal Emergency Management Agency's (FEMA) Federal

Assistance to Individuals and Households Program (IHP). After you register with FEMA for disaster assistance, FEMA will consider you for IHP assistance, which includes housing assistance grants to repair or replace your damaged primary residence and temporary housing assistance (including rental assistance) to assist you temporarily with a place to live, and assistance with personal property, medical, dental and funeral expenses. FEMA may also refer you to SBA to apply for loan assistance to help repair or rebuild your home and/or to replace personal property destroyed during the disaster. If SBA is unable to approve your loan application, or if you have damage in excess of the SBA loan amount, SBA may refer you, on a timely basis, to FEMA for IHP grant consideration to assist with your unmet personal property and transportation needs. If you are approved for the SBA disaster loan and you have received grant assistance that duplicates the damage covered by the SBA loan, such grant assistance must be deducted from your loan eligibility as described in section 123.101(c) of the regulations. All grant decisions are made by FEMA. Additionally, if additional disaster assistance is available from state, local or other agencies, SBA may refer you to the appropriate agency for consideration.

[75 FR 7546, Feb. 22, 2010]

Subpart C—Physical Disaster Business Loans

§ 123.200 Am I eligible to apply for a physical disaster business loan?

(a) Almost any business concern or charitable or other non-profit entity whose real or tangible personal property is damaged in a declared disaster area is eligible to apply for a physical disaster business loan. Your business may be a sole proprietorship, partnership, corporation, limited liability company, or other legal entity recognized under State law. Your business' size (average annual receipts or number of employees) is not taken into consideration in determining your eligibility for a physical disaster business loan. If your damaged business occupied rented space at the time of the disaster, and the terms of your business' lease require you to make repairs to your business' building, you may have suffered a physical loss and can apply for a physical business disaster loan to repair the property. In all other cases, the owner of the building is the eligible loan applicant.

(b) Damaged vehicles, of the type normally used for recreational purposes, such as motorhomes, aircraft, and boats, may be repaired or replaced with SBA loan proceeds if you can submit evidence that the damaged vehicles were used in your business at the time of the disaster.

§ 123.201 When am I not eligible to apply for a physical disaster business loan?

(a) You are not eligible for a physical disaster business loan if your business is an agricultural enterprise or if you (or any principal of the business) fit into any of the categories in § 123.101. Agricultural enterprise means a business primarily engaged in the production of food and fiber, ranching and raising of livestock, aquaculture and all other farming and agriculture-related industries.

(b) Sometimes a damaged business entity (whether in the form of a corporation, limited liability company, partnership, or sole proprietorship) is engaged in both agricultural enterprise and a non-agricultural business venture. If the agricultural enterprise part of your business entity has suffered a physical disaster, that enterprise is not eligible for SBA physical disaster assistance. If the non-agricultural business venture of your entity has suffered physical disaster damage, that part of your business operation would be eligible for SBA physical disaster assistance. If both the agricultural enterprise part and the non-agricultural business venture have incurred physical disaster damage, only the non-agricultural business venture of your business entity would be eligible for SBA physical disaster assistance.

(c) If your business is going to relocate voluntarily outside the business area in which the disaster occurred, you are not eligible for a physical disaster business loan. If, however, the relocation is due to uncontrollable or compelling circumstances, SBA will consider the relocation to be involuntary and eligible for a loan. Such circumstances may include, but are not limited to:

(1) The elimination or substantial decrease in the market for your products or services, as a consequence of the disaster;

(2) A change in the demographics of your business area within 18 months prior to the disaster, or as a result of the disaster, which makes it uneconomical to continue operations in your business area;

(3) A substantial change in your cost of doing business, as a result of the disaster, which makes the continuation of your business in the business area not economically viable;

(4) Location of your business in a hazardous area such as a special flood hazard area or an earthquake-prone area;

(5) A change in the public infrastructure in your business area which occurred within 18 months or as a result of the disaster that would result in substantially increased expenses for your business in the business area;

(6) Your implementation of decisions adopted and at least partially implemented within 18 months prior to the disaster to move your business out of the business area; and

(7) Other factors which undermine the economic viability of your business area.

(d) You are not eligible if your business is engaged in any illegal activity.

(e) You are not eligible if you are a government owned entity (except for a business owned or controlled by a Native American tribe).

(f) You are not eligible if your business presents live performances of a prurient sexual nature or derives directly or indirectly more than *de minimis* gross revenue through the sale of products or services, or the presentation of any depictions or displays, of a prurient sexual nature.

[61 FR 3304, Jan. 31, 1996, as amended at 62 FR 35337, July 1, 1997; 63 FR 46644, Sept. 2, 1998]

§ 123.202 How much can my business borrow with a physical disaster business loan?

(a) Disaster business loans, including both physical disaster and economic injury loans to the same borrower, together with its affiliates, cannot exceed the lesser of the uncompensated physical loss and economic injury or $2 million. Physical disaster loans may include amounts to meet current building code requirements. If your business is a major source of employment, SBA may waive the $2 million limitation. A major source of employment is a business concern that has one or more locations in the disaster area, on or after the date of the disaster, which:

(1) Employed 10 percent or more of the entire work force within the commuting area of a geographically identifiable community (no larger than a county), provided that the commuting area does not extend more than 50 miles from such community; or

(2) Employed 5 percent of the work force in an industry within the disaster area and, if the concern is a non-manufacturing concern, employed no less than 50 employees in the disaster area, or if the concern is a manufacturing concern, employed no less than 150 employees in the disaster area; or

(3) Employed no less than 250 employees within the disaster area.

(b) SBA will consider waiving the $2 million loan limit for a major source of employment only if:

(1) Your damaged location or locations are out of business or in imminent danger of going out of business as a result of the disaster, and a loan in excess of $2 million is necessary to reopen or keep open the damaged locations in order to avoid substantial unemployment in the disaster area; and

(2) You have used all reasonably available funds from your business, its affiliates and its principal owners (20% or greater ownership interest) and all available credit elsewhere (as described in § 123.104) to alleviate your physical damage and economic injury.

(c) Physical disaster business borrowers may request refinancing of liens on both damaged real property and machinery and equipment, but for an amount reduced by insurance or other compensation. To do so, your business property must be totally destroyed or substantially damaged, which means:

(1) 40 percent or more of the aggregate value (lesser of market value or replacement cost at the time of the disaster) of the damaged real property (including land) and damaged machinery and equipment; or

(2) 50 percent or more of the aggregate value (lesser of market value or replacement cost at the time of the disaster) of the damaged real property (excluding land) and damaged machinery and equipment.

(d) Loan funds allocated for repair or replacement of landscaping or recreational facilities may not exceed $5,000 unless the landscaping or recreational facilities fulfilled a functional need or contributed to the generation of business.

(e) The SBA Administrator may increase the $2 million loan limit for disaster business physical and economic injury loans under an individual disaster declaration based on appropriate economic indicators for the region(s) in which the disaster occurred. SBA will publish the increased loan amount in the FEDERAL REGISTER.

[61 FR 3304, Jan. 31, 1996, as amended at 63 FR 46644, Sept. 2, 1998; 75 FR 14332, Mar. 25, 2010]

§ 123.203 What interest rate will my business pay on a physical disaster business loan and what are the repayment terms?

(a) SBA will announce interest rates with each disaster declaration. If your business, together with its affiliates and principal owners, has credit elsewhere, your interest rate is set by a statutory formula, but will not exceed 8 percent per annum. If you do not have credit elsewhere, your interest rate will not exceed 4 percent per annum. The maturity of your loan depends upon your repayment ability, but cannot exceed seven years if you have credit elsewhere.

(b) Generally, you must pay equal monthly installments, of principal and interest, beginning five months from the date of the loan as shown on the Note. SBA will consider other payment terms if you have seasonal or fluctuating income, and SBA may allow installment payments of varying amounts over the first two years of the loan. There is no penalty for prepayment for disaster loans.

(c) For certain disaster business physical and economic injury loans, an additional payment, based on a percentage of net earnings, will be required to reduce the balance of the loan. This additional payment will not be required until 5 years after repayment begins.

[61 FR 3304, Jan. 31, 1996, as amended at 75 FR 14333, Mar. 25, 2010; 77 FR 12157, Feb. 29, 2012]

§ 123.204 How much can your business borrow for post-disaster mitigation?

For mitigation measures implemented after a disaster has occurred, you can request an increase in the approved physical disaster business loan by the lesser of the cost of the mitigation measure, or up to 20 percent of the verified loss, before deducting compensation from other sources, to repair or replace your damaged business.

[75 FR 14333, Mar. 25, 2010]

Subpart D—Economic Injury Disaster Loans

§ 123.300 Is my business eligible to apply for an economic injury disaster loan?

(a) If your business is located in a declared disaster area, and suffered substantial economic injury as a direct result of a declared disaster, you are eligible to apply for an economic injury disaster loan.

(1) Substantial economic injury is such that a business concern is unable to meet its obligations as they mature or to pay its ordinary and necessary operating expenses.

(2) Loss of anticipated profits or a drop in sales is not considered substantial economic injury for this purpose.

(b) Economic injury disaster loans are available only if you were a small business (as defined in part 121 of this chapter) or a private non-profit organization when the declared disaster commenced, you and your affiliates and principal owners (20% or more ownership interest) have used all reasonably available funds, and you are unable to obtain credit elsewhere (see § 123.104).

(c) Eligible businesses do not include agricultural enterprises, but do include—

(1) Small nurseries affected by a drought disaster designated by the Secretary of Agriculture (nurseries are commercial establishments deriving 50 percent or more of their annual receipts from the production and sale of ornamental plants and other nursery products, including, but not limited to, bulbs, florist greens, foliage, flowers, flower and vegetable seeds, shrubbery, and sod);

(2) Small agricultural cooperatives;

(3) Producer cooperatives; and

(4) Small aquaculture enterprises.

(d) An eligible private non-profit organization is a non-governmental agency or entity that currently has:

(1) An effective ruling letter from the U.S. Internal Revenue Service, granting tax exemption under sections 510(c), (d), or (e) of the Internal Revenue Code of 1954, or

(2) Satisfactory evidence from the State that the non-revenue producing organization or entity is a non-profit one organized or doing business under State law.

[61 FR 3304, Jan. 31, 1996, as amended at 67 FR 11880, Mar. 15, 2002; 70 FR 72595, Dec. 6, 2005; 73 FR 41254, July 18, 2008; 75 FR 14333, Mar. 25, 2010; 76 FR 63547, Oct. 12, 2011]

§ 123.301 When would my business not be eligible to apply for an economic injury disaster loan?

Your business is not eligible for an economic disaster loan if you (or any principal of the business) fit into any of the categories in §§ 123.101 and 123.201, or if your business is:

(a) Engaged in lending, multi-level sales distribution, speculation, or investment (except for real estate investment with property held for rental when the disaster occurred);

(b) A non-profit or charitable concern, other than a private non-profit organization;

(c) A consumer or marketing cooperative;

(d) Not a small business concern; or

(e) Deriving more than one-third of gross annual revenue from legal gambling activities;

(f) A loan packager which earns more than one-third of its gross annual revenue from packaging SBA loans;

(g) Principally engaged in teaching, instructing, counseling, or indoctrinating religion or religious beliefs, whether in a religious or secular setting; or

(h) Primarily engaged in political or lobbying activities.

[61 FR 3304, Jan. 31, 1996, as amended at 63 FR 46644, Sept. 2, 1998; 75 FR 14333, Mar. 25, 2010]

§ 123.302 What is the interest rate on an economic injury disaster loan?

Your economic injury loan will have an interest rate of 4 percent per annum or less.

§ 123.303 How can my business spend my economic injury disaster loan?

(a) You can only use the loan proceeds for working capital necessary to carry your concern until resumption of normal operations and for expenditures necessary to alleviate the specific economic injury, but not to exceed that which the business could have provided had the injury not occurred.

(b) Loan proceeds may not be used to:

(1) Refinance indebtedness which you incurred prior to the disaster event;

(2) Make payments on loans owned by another federal agency (including SBA) or a Small Business Investment Company licensed under the Small Business Investment Act;

(3) Pay, directly or indirectly, any obligations resulting from a federal, state or local tax penalty as a result of negligence or fraud, or any non-tax criminal fine, civil fine, or penalty for non-compliance with a law, regulation, or order of a federal, state, regional, or local agency or similar matter;

(4) Repair physical damage; or

(5) Pay dividends or other disbursements to owners, partners, officers or stockholders, except for reasonable remuneration directly related to their performance of services for the business.

Subpart E—Pre-Disaster Mitigation Loans

SOURCE: 67 FR 62337, Oct. 7, 2002, unless otherwise noted.

§ 123.400 What is the Pre-Disaster Mitigation Loan Program?

The Pre-Disaster Mitigation Loan Program allows SBA to make low interest, fixed rate loans to small businesses for the purpose of implementing mitigation measures to protect their commercial real property (building) or leasehold improvements or contents from disaster related damage. This program supports the Federal Emergency Management Agency (FEMA's) Pre-Disaster Mitigation Program. This pilot program is authorized for 5 fiscal years (October—September), from 2000 through 2004, and has only been approved for limited funding. Therefore, approved loan requests are funded on a first come, first served basis up to the limit of program funds available (see § 123.411).

§ 123.401 What types of mitigation measures can your business include in an application for a pre-disaster mitigation loan?

To be included in a pre-disaster mitigation loan application, each of your business' mitigation measures must satisfy the following criteria:

(a) The mitigation measure, as described in the application, must serve the purpose of protecting your commercial real property (building) or leasehold improvements or contents from damage that may be caused by future disasters; and

(b) The mitigation measure must conform to the priorities and goals of the State or local government's mitigation plan for the community in which the business subject to the measure is located. To show that this factor is satisfied your business must submit to SBA, as a part of your complete application, a written statement from a State or local emergency management coordinator confirming this fact (see § 123.408). Contact your regional FEMA office for a list of your State's emergency management coordinators or visit the FEMA Web site at *http://www.fema.gov.*

§ 123.402 Can your business include its relocation as a mitigation measure in an application for a pre-disaster mitigation loan?

Yes, you may request a pre-disaster mitigation loan for the relocation of your business if:

(a) Your commercial real property (building) is located in a SFHA (Special Flood Hazard Area); and

(b) Your business relocates outside the SFHA but remains in the same participating pre-disaster mitigation community. Contact your regional FEMA office for a listing of communities participating in the Pre-Disaster Mitigation Program and SFHAs or visit the FEMA Web site at *http://www.fema.gov.*

§ 123.403 When is your business eligible to apply for a pre-disaster mitigation loan?

To be eligible to apply for a pre-disaster mitigation loan your business must meet each of the following criteria:

(a) Your business, which is the subject of the pre-disaster mitigation measure, must be located in a participating pre-disaster mitigation community. Each State, the District of Columbia, Puerto Rico, and the Virgin Islands have at least one participating pre-disaster mitigation community. Contact your regional FEMA office to find out the locations of participating pre-disaster mitigation communities or visit the FEMA Web site at *http://www.fema.gov.*;

(b) If your business is proposing a mitigation measure that protects against a flood hazard, the location of your business which is the subject of the mitigation measure must be located in a Special Flood Hazard Area (SFHA). Contact your FEMA regional office to find out the locations of SFHAs or visit the FEMA Web site at *http://www.fema.gov.*;

(c) As of the date your business submits a complete Pre-Disaster Mitigation Small Business Loan Application to SBA (see § 123.408 for what SBA's considers to be a complete application), your business, along with its affiliates, must be a small business concern as defined in part 121 of this chapter. The definition of small business concern encompasses sole proprietorships, partnerships, corporations, limited liability entities, and other legal entities recognized under State law;

(d) Your business, which is the subject of the mitigation measure, must have operated as a business in its present location for at least one year before submitting its application;

(e) Your business, along with its affiliates and owners, must not have the financial resources to fund the proposed mitigation measures without undue hardship. SBA makes this determination based on the information your business submits as a part of its application; and

(f) If your business is owning and leasing out real property, the mitigation measures must be for protection of a building leased primarily for commercial rather than residential purposes (SBA will determine this based upon a comparative square footage basis).

§ 123.404 When is your business ineligible to apply for a pre-disaster mitigation loan?

Your business is ineligible to apply for a pre-disaster mitigation loan if your business (including its affiliates) satisfies any of the following conditions:

(a) Any of your business' principal owners is presently incarcerated, or on probation or parole following conviction of a serious criminal offense, or has been indicted for a felony or a crime of moral turpitude;

(b) Your business' only interest in the business property is in the form of a security interest, mortgage, or deed of trust;

(c) The building, which is the subject of the mitigation measure, was newly constructed or substantially improved on or after February 9, 1989, and (without significant business justification) is located seaward of mean high tide or entirely in or over water;

(d) Your business is an agricultural enterprise. Agricultural enterprise means a business primarily engaged (see § 121.107 of this chapter) in the production of food and fiber, ranching and raising of livestock, aquaculture and all other farming and agriculture-related industries. Sometimes a business is engaged in both agricultural and non-agricultural business activities. If the primary business activity of your business is not an agricultural enterprise, it may apply for a pre-disaster mitigation loan, but loan proceeds may not be used, directly or indirectly, for the benefit of the agricultural activities;

(e) Your business is engaged in any illegal activity;

(f) Your business is a government owned entity (except for a business owned or controlled by a Native American tribe);

(g) Your business presents live performances of a prurient sexual nature or derives directly or indirectly more than *de minimis* gross revenue through the sale of products or services, or the presentation of any depictions or displays, of a prurient sexual nature;

(h) Your business engages in lending, multi-level sales distribution, speculation, or investment (except for real estate investment with property held for commercial rental);

(i) Your business is a non-profit or charitable concern;

(j) Your business is a consumer or marketing cooperative;

(k) Your business derives more than one-third of its gross annual revenue from legal gambling activities;

(l) Your business is a loan packager that earns more than one-third of its gross annual revenue from packaging SBA loans;

(m) Your business principally engages in teaching, instructing, counseling, or indoctrinating religion or religious beliefs, whether in a religious or secular setting; or

(n) Your business is primarily engaged in political or lobbying activities.

§ 123.405 How much can your business borrow with a pre-disaster mitigation loan?

Your business, together with its affiliates, may borrow up to $50,000 each fiscal year. This loan amount may be used to fund only those projects that were a part of your business' approved loan request. SBA will consider mitigation measures costing more than $50,000 per year if your business can identify, as a part of its Pre-Disaster

Mitigation Small Business Loan Application, sources that will fund the cost above $50,000.

§ 123.406 What is the interest rate on a pre-disaster mitigation loan?

The interest rate on a pre-disaster mitigation loan will be fixed at 4 percent per annum or less. The exact interest rate will be stated in the FEDERAL REGISTER notice announcing each filing period (see § 123.407).

§ 123.407 When does your business apply for a pre-disaster mitigation loan and where does your business get an application?

SBA will publish a notice in the FEDERAL REGISTER announcing the availability of pre-disaster mitigation loans. The notice will designate a 30-day application filing period with a specific opening date and filing deadline, as well as the locations for obtaining and filing loan applications. In addition to the FEDERAL REGISTER, SBA will coordinate with FEMA, and will issue press releases to the local media to inform potential loan applicants where to obtain loan applications. SBA will not accept any applications postmarked after the filing deadline; however, SBA may announce additional application periods each year depending on the availability of program funds.

§ 123.408 How does your business apply for a pre-disaster mitigation loan?

To apply for a pre-disaster mitigation loan your business must submit a complete Pre-Disaster Mitigation Small Business Loan Application (application) within the announced filing period. Complete applications mailed to SBA and postmarked within the announced filing period will be accepted. The complete application serves as your business' loan request. A complete application supplies all of the filing requirements specified on the application form including a written statement from the local or State coordinator confirming:

(a) The business that is the subject of the mitigation measure is located within the participating pre-disaster mitigation community; and

(b) The mitigation measure is in accordance with the specific priorities and goals of the local participating pre-disaster mitigation community in which the business is located. (The local or State coordinator's written statement does not constitute an endorsement or technical approval of the project and is not a guarantee that the project will prevent damage in future disasters).

§ 123.409 Which pre-disaster mitigation loan requests will SBA consider for funding?

(a) SBA will consider a loan request for funding if, after reviewing a complete application, SBA determines that it meets the following selection criteria:

(1) Your business satisfies the requirements of §§ 123.401, 123.402 and 123.403;

(2) None of the conditions specified in § 123.404 apply to your business, its affiliates, or principal owners;

(3) Your business has submitted a reasonable cost estimate for the proposed mitigation measure and has chosen to undertake a mitigation measure that is likely to accomplish the desired mitigation result (SBA's determination of this point is not a guaranty that the project will prevent damage in future disasters);

(4) Your business is creditworthy; and

(5) There is a reasonable assurance of loan repayment in accordance with the terms of a loan agreement.

(b) SBA will notify you in writing if your loan request does not meet the criteria in this section.

§ 123.410 Which loan requests will SBA fund?

SBA will date stamp each application (loan request) as it is received. SBA will fund loan requests which meet the selection criteria specified in § 123.409 on a first come, first served basis using this date stamp, until it has allocated all available program funds. Multiple applications received on the same day will be ranked by a computer based random selection system to determine their funding order. SBA will notify you in writing of its funding decision.

§ 123.411 What if SBA determines that your business loan request meets the selection criteria of § 123.409 but SBA is unable to fund it because SBA has already allocated all program funds?

If SBA determines that your business' loan request meets the selection criteria of § 123.409 but we are unable to fund it because we have already allocated all available program funds, your request will be given priority status, based on the original acceptance date, once more program funds become available. However, if more than 6 months pass since SBA determined to fund your request, SBA may request updated or additional financial information.

§ 123.412 What happens if SBA declines your business' pre-disaster mitigation loan request?

If SBA declines your business' loan request, SBA will notify your business in writing giving specific reasons for decline. If your business disagrees with SBA's decision, it may respond in accordance with § 123.13. If SBA reverses its decision, SBA will use the date it received your business' last request for reconsideration or appeal as the basis for determining the order of funding.

Subpart F—Military Reservist Economic Injury Disaster Loans

SOURCE: 66 FR 38530, July 25, 2001, unless otherwise noted.

§ 123.500 Definitions.

The following terms have the same meaning wherever they are used in this subpart:

(a) *Essential employee* is an individual (whether or not an owner of a small business) whose managerial or technical expertise is critical to the successful day-to-day operations of a small business.

(b) *Military reservist* is a member of a reserve component of the Armed Forces ordered to active duty during a period of military conflict.

(c) *Period of military conflict* means:

(1) A period of war declared by the Congress,

(2) A period of national emergency declared by the Congress or by the President, or

(3) A period of contingency operation, as defined in 10 U.S.C. 101(a).

(d) *Principal owner* is a person or entity which owns 20 percent or more of the small business.

(e) *Substantial economic injury* means an economic harm to the small business such that it cannot:

(1) Meet its obligations as they mature,

(2) Pay its ordinary and necessary operating expenses, or

(3) Market, produce or provide a product or service ordinarily marketed, produced or provided by the business. Loss of anticipated profits or a drop in sales is not considered substantial economic injury for this purpose.

§ 123.501 Under what circumstances is your business eligible to be considered for a Military Reservist Economic Injury Disaster Loan?

Your business is eligible to apply for a Military Reservist EIDL if:

(a) It is a small business as defined in 13 CFR part 121 when the essential employee was called to active duty,

(b) The owner of the business is a military reservist and an essential employee or the business employs a military reservist who is an essential employee,

(c) The essential employee has been called-up to active military duty during a period of military conflict existing on or after March 24, 1999,

(d) The business has suffered or is likely to suffer substantial economic injury as a result of the absence of the essential employee, and

(e) You and your affiliates and principal owners (20% or more ownership interest) have used all reasonably available funds, and you are unable to obtain credit elsewhere (see § 123.104).

[66 FR 38530, July 25, 2001, as amended at 67 FR 64519, Oct. 21, 2002]

§ 123.502 Under what circumstances is your business ineligible to be considered for a Military Reservist Economic Injury Disaster Loan?

Your business is ineligible for a Military Reservist EIDL if it, together with its affiliates, is subject to any of the following conditions:

(a) Any of your business' principal owners has been convicted, during the past year, of a felony during and in connection with a riot or civil disorder;

(b) You have assumed the risk associated with employing the military reservist, as determined by SBA (for example, hiring the "essential employee" after the employee has received call-up orders or been notified that they are imminent);

(c) Any of your business' principal owners is presently incarcerated, or on probation or parole following conviction of a serious criminal offense;

(d) Your business is an agricultural enterprise. Agricultural enterprise means a business primarily engaged in the production of food and fiber, ranching and raising of livestock, aquaculture and all other farming and agriculture-related industries. (See 13 CFR 121.107, "How does SBA determine a concern's primary industry?") Sometimes a business is engaged in both agricultural and non-agricultural business activities. If the primary business activity of the business is not an agricultural enterprise, it may apply for a Military Reservist EIDL, but loan proceeds may not be used, directly or indirectly, for the benefit of the agricultural enterprises;

(e) Your business is engaged in any illegal activity;

(f) Your business is a government owned entity (except for a business owned or controlled by a Native American tribe);

(g) Your business presents live performances of a prurient sexual nature or derives directly or indirectly more than an insignificant gross revenue through the sale of products or services, or through the presentation of any depictions or displays, of a prurient sexual nature;

(h) Your business is engaged in lending, multi-level sales distribution, speculation, or investment (except for real estate investment with property held for commercial rental);

(i) Your business is a non-profit or charitable concern;

(j) Your business is a consumer or marketing cooperative;

(k) Your business is not a small business concern;

(l) Your business derives more than one-third of its gross annual revenue from legal gambling activities;

(m) Your business is a loan packager which earns more than one-third of its gross annual revenue from packaging SBA loans;

(n) Your business' principal activity is teaching, instructing, counseling, or indoctrinating religion or religious beliefs, whether in a religious or secular setting; or

(o) Your business' principal activity is political or lobbying activities.

§ 123.503 When can you apply for a Military Reservist EIDL?

Your small business can apply for a Military Reservist EIDL any time beginning on the date your essential employee receives notice of expected call-up and ending one year after the date the essential employee is discharged or released from active duty. The Associate Administrator for Disaster Assistance (AA/DA) or designee may extend the one year limit by no more then one additional year after finding extraordinary or unforeseeable circumstances.

[73 FR 54675, Sept. 23, 2008]

§ 123.504 How do you apply for a Military Reservist EIDL?

To apply for a Military Reservist EIDL you must complete a SBA Military Reservist EIDL application package (SBA Form 5R and supporting documentation *can be obtained through SBA's Disaster Area Office*) including:

(a) A copy of the essential employee's official call-up orders for active duty showing the date of call-up, and, if known, the date of release from active duty. For an essential employee who expects to be called up and who has not received official call-up orders, the application shall include the notice of the expected call-up including, if known, the expected date of call-up and expected date of release from active duty;

(b) A statement from the business owner that the reservist is essential to the successful day-to-day operations of the business (detailing the employee's duties and responsibilities and explaining why these duties and responsibilities can't be completed in the essential employee's absence);

(c) A certification by the essential employee supporting that he or she concurs with the business owner's statement as described in paragraph (b) of this section;

(d) A written explanation and financial estimate of how the call-up of the essential employee has or will result in economic injury to your business;

(e) The steps your business is taking to alleviate the economic injury; and

(f) The business owners' certification that the essential employee will be offered the same or a similar job upon the employee's return from active duty.

[61 FR 3304, Jan. 31, 1996, as amended at 73 FR 54675, Sept. 23, 2008]

§ 123.505 What if you are both an essential employee and the owner of the small business and you started active duty before applying for a Military Reservist EIDL?

If you are both an essential employee and the owner of the small business and you started active duty before applying for an Military Reservist EIDL, a person who has a power of attorney with the authority to borrow and make other related commitments on your behalf, may complete and submit the EIDL loan application package for you.

§ 123.506 How much can you borrow under the Military Reservist EIDL Program?

You can borrow an amount equal to the substantial economic injury you have suffered or are likely to suffer until normal operations resume as a result of the absence of one or more essential employees called to active duty, up to a maximum of $2 million.

[73 FR 54675, Sept. 23, 2008]

§ 123.507 Under what circumstances will SBA consider waiving the $2 million loan limit?

SBA will consider waiving the $2 million limit if you can certify to the following conditions and SBA approves of such certification based on the information supplied in your application:

(a) Your small business is a major source of employment. A major source of employment is a business concern that, on or after the date of the disaster:

(1) Employs 10 percent or more of the work force within the commuting area of the geographically identifiable community (no larger than a county) in which the business employing the essential employee is located, provided that the commuting area does not extend more than 50 miles from such community; or

(2) Employs 5 percent of the work force in an industry within such commuting area and, if the small business is a non-manufacturing small business, employs no less than 50 employees in the same commuting area, or if the small business is a manufacturing small business, employs no less than 150 employees in the commuting area; or

(3) Employs no less than 250 employees within such commuting area;

(b) Your small business is in imminent danger of going out of business as a result of one or more essential employees being called up to active duty during a period of military conflict, and a loan in excess of $2 million is necessary to reopen or keep open the small business; and

(c) Your small business has used all reasonably available funds from the small business, its affiliates, its principal owners and all available credit elsewhere to alleviate the small business' economic injury. Credit elsewhere means financing from non-Federal sources on reasonable terms given your available cash flow and disposable assets which SBA believes your small business, its affiliates and principal owners could obtain.

[61 FR 3304, Jan. 31, 1996, as amended at 73 FR 54675, Sept. 23, 2008; 75 FR 14333, Mar. 25, 2010]

§ 123.508 How can you use Military Reservist EIDL funds?

Your small business can use Military Reservist EIDL to:

(a) Meet obligations as they mature,

(b) Pay ordinary and necessary operating expenses, or

(c) Enable the business to market, produce or provide products or services ordinarily marketed, produced, or provided by the business, which cannot be done as a result of the essential employee's military call-up.

§ 123.509 What can't you use Military Reservist EIDL funds for?

Your small business can not use Military Reservist EIDL funds for purposes described in § 123.303(b) (See § 123.303, " How can my business spend my economic injury disaster loan?").

§ 123.510 What if you don't use your Military Reservist EIDL funds as authorized?

If your small business does not use Military Reservist EIDL funds as authorized by § 123.508, then § 123.9 applies (See § 123.9, "What happens if I don't use loan proceeds for the intended purpose?").

§ 123.511 How will SBA disburse Military Reservist EIDL funds?

Funds will be disbursed only after the essential employee has been called to active duty, and you have provided a copy of the essential employee's official call-up orders for active duty showing the date of the call-up. SBA will disburse your funds in quarterly installments (unless otherwise specified in your loan authorization agreement) based on a continued need as demonstrated by comparative financial information. On or about 30 days before your scheduled fund disbursement, SBA will request ordinary and usual financial statements (including balance sheets and profit and loss statements). Based on this information, SBA will assess your continued need for disbursements under this program. Upon making such assessment, SBA will notify you of the status of future disbursements.

[73 FR 54675, Sept. 23, 2008]

§ 123.512 What is the interest rate on a Military Reservist EIDL?

The interest rate on a Military Reservist EIDL will be 4 percent per annum or less. SBA will publish the interest rate quarterly in the FEDERAL REGISTER.

§ 123.513 Does SBA require collateral on its Military Reservist EIDL?

SBA will not generally require you to pledge collateral to secure a Military Reservist EIDL of $50,000 or less. For loans larger than $50,000, you will be required to provide available collateral such as a lien on business property, a security interest in personal property, or both. SBA will not decline a loan if you do not have a particular amount of collateral so long as SBA is reasonably sure that you can repay the loan. If you refuse to pledge the available collateral when requested by SBA, however, SBA may decline or cancel your loan.

[73 FR 54675, Sept. 23, 2008]

Subpart G—Economic Injury Disaster Loans as a Result of the September 11, 2001 Terrorist Attacks

SOURCE: 66 FR 53331, Oct. 22, 2001, unless otherwise noted.

§ 123.600 Are economic injury disaster loans under this subpart limited to the geographic areas contiguous to the declared disaster areas?

No. Notwithstanding § 123.4, SBA may make economic injury disaster loans outside the declared disaster areas and the contiguous geographic areas to small business concerns that have suffered substantial economic injury as a direct result of the destruction of the World Trade Center or the damage to the Pentagon on September 11, 2001, or as a direct result of any related federal action taken between September 11, 2001 and October 22, 2001.

§ 123.601 Is my business eligible to apply for an economic injury disaster loan under this subpart?

(a) If your business has suffered substantial economic injury as a direct result of the destruction of the World Trade Center or the damage to the Pentagon on September 11, 2001, or as a direct result of any related federal action taken between September 11, 2001 and October 22, 2001, you are eligible to apply for an economic injury disaster loan under this subpart.

(1) Substantial economic injury is such that a business concern is unable to meet its obligations as they mature or to pay its ordinary and necessary operating expenses.

(2) Loss of anticipated profits or a drop in sales is not considered substantial economic injury for this purpose.

(b) Economic injury disaster loans are available under this subpart only if you were a small business (as defined in part 121 of this chapter) on the date SBA accepts your application for processing (and for applications submitted before March 15, 2002, whether denied or pending, such applications shall be deemed resubmitted on March 15, 2002, you and your affiliates and principal owners (20% or more ownership interest) have used all reasonable available funds, and you are unable to obtain credit elsewhere (see § 123.104).

(c) Eligible businesses do not include agricultural enterprises, but do include small agricultural cooperatives and producer cooperatives.

[66 FR 53331, Oct. 22, 2001, as amended at 67 FR 11880, Mar. 15, 2002]

§ 123.602 When would my business not be eligible to apply for an economic injury disaster loan under this subpart?

Your business is not eligible for an economic injury disaster loan under this subpart if you (or any principal of the business) fit into any of the categories in §§ 123.101 and 123.201, or if your business is:

(a) Engaged in lending, multi-level sales distribution, speculation, or investment (except for real estate investment with property held for rental on September 11, 2001);

(b) A non-profit or charitable concern;

(c) A consumer or marketing cooperative;

(d) Not a small business concern; or

(e) Deriving more than one-third of gross annual revenue from legal gambling activities;

(f) A loan packager which earns more than one-third of its gross annual revenue from packaging SBA loans;

(g) Principally engaged in teaching, instructing, counseling, or indoctrinating religion or religious beliefs, whether in a religious or secular setting; or

(h) Primarily engaged in political or lobbying activities.

§ 123.603 What is the interest rate on an economic injury disaster loan under this subpart?

Your economic injury disaster loan under this subpart will have an interest rate of 4 percent per annum or less.

§ 123.604 How can my business spend my economic injury disaster loan under this subpart?

(a) You can only use the loan proceeds for working capital necessary to carry your concern until resumption of normal operations and for expenditures necessary to alleviate the specific economic injury, but not to exceed that which the business could have provided had the injury not occurred.

(b) Loan proceeds may not be used to:

(1) Refinance indebtedness which you incurred prior to September 11, 2001;

(2) Make payments on loans owned by another federal agency (including SBA) or a Small Business Investment Company licensed under the Small Business Investment Act;

(3) Pay, directly or indirectly, any obligations resulting from a federal, state or local tax penalty as a result of negligence or fraud, or any non-tax criminal fine, civil fine, or penalty for non-compliance with a law, regulation, or order of a federal, state, regional, or local agency or similar matter;

(4) Repair physical damage; or

(5) Pay dividends or other disbursements to owners, partners, officers, or stockholders, except for reasonable remuneration directly related to their performance of services for the business.

§ 123.605 How long do I have to apply for a loan under this subpart?

You have until January 22, 2002 to apply for a loan under this subpart. Your application must be postmarked no later than this date. SBA has the discretion, for good cause, to extend the application deadline by publication of a notice in the FEDERAL REGISTER.

§ 123.606 May I request an increase in the amount of an economic injury disaster loan under this subpart?

Yes. Notwithstanding § 123.20, you may request an increase in the amount of an economic injury disaster loan under this subpart not later than one year after the date SBA approves your initial request.

Subpart H—Immediate Disaster Assistance Program

SOURCE: 75 FR 60598, Oct. 1, 2010, unless otherwise noted.

§ 123.700 What is the Immediate Disaster Assistance Program?

(a) The Immediate Disaster Assistance Program (IDAP) is a guaranteed disaster loan program for small businesses that have suffered physical damage or economic injury due to a Declared Disaster. An IDAP loan is an interim loan in an amount not to exceed $25,000 made by an IDAP Lender to meet the immediate business needs of an IDAP Borrower while approval of long-term financing from a Disaster Loan is pending with SBA.

(b) *Definitions.* As used in this subpart, the terms below are defined as follows:

Contiguous Counties means the counties or other political subdivisions identified in the IDAP-Eligible Disaster Declaration as abutting the Primary Counties.

Credit Elsewhere means that the IDAP Borrower is able to address disaster losses using available personal or business resources or access to nonfederal lending sources at reasonable rates and terms.

Declared Disaster is a disaster event for which an IDAP-Eligible Disaster Declaration has been issued.

Declared Disaster Area means the Primary Counties and the Contiguous Counties identified for a particular Declared Disaster.

Disaster Loan means a disaster loan authorized by Section 7(b) of the Small Business Act.

IDAP Borrower is the obligor of an IDAP loan.

IDAP Lender is a financial institution participating in the IDAP loan program, subject to the requirements of this subpart.

IDAP Loan Program Requirements are requirements imposed upon an IDAP Lender by statute, SBA regulations, any agreement the IDAP Lender has executed with SBA, SBA SOPs, SBA procedural guidance, official SBA notices and forms applicable to the IDAP loan program, and loan authorizations, as such requirements are issued and revised by SBA from time to time.

IDAP-Eligible Disaster Declaration means a Major Disaster Declaration, SBA Administrative Disaster Declaration or SBA EIDL-Only Disaster Declaration in which SBA has indicated that IDAP loans are available.

Initial Period is the IDAP loan repayment period that begins upon the initial disbursement of an IDAP loan and ends upon (i) full repayment of the IDAP loan from the proceeds of the IDAP Borrower's Disaster Loan; (ii) SBA notice to the IDAP Lender of decline of the IDAP Borrower's Disaster Loan Application; or (iii) receipt by the IDAP Lender of partial repayment of the IDAP loan from the proceeds of the Disaster Loan; provided that if the IDAP loan has not been fully disbursed at such time, the Initial Period shall not end until the IDAP loan is fully disbursed.

Major Disaster Declaration means a disaster declaration issued under § 123.3(a)(1) of this part.

Other Recoveries are other compensation for disaster losses and include, but are not limited to: Proceeds of policies of insurance or other indemnifications; grants or other reimbursement (including loans) from government agencies or private organizations; claims for civil liability against other individuals, organizations or governmental entities; gifts; condemnation awards; and salvage (including any sale or re-use) of items of disaster-damaged property. If an IDAP Borrower has voluntarily paid insurance recoveries to a recorded lienholder, the amount paid is considered to be Other Recoveries.

Primary Counties means the counties or other political subdivisions identified in the IDAP-Eligible Disaster Declaration as having been adversely affected by the disaster.

SBA Administrative Disaster Declaration means a disaster declaration issued under § 123.3(a)(3) of this part.

SBA EIDL-Only Disaster Declaration means a disaster declaration issued under § 123.3(a)(5) of this part.

Substantial Economic Injury exists when a business concern is unable to meet its obligations as they mature or to pay its ordinary and necessary operating expenses. Loss of anticipated profits or a drop in sales is not considered substantial economic injury.

Term Period is the repayment period that begins following:

(i) SBA notice to the IDAP Lender of decline of the IDAP Borrower's Disaster Loan application;

(ii) Receipt by the IDAP Lender of partial repayment of the IDAP loan from the proceeds of the Disaster Loan; or

(iii) Final disbursement of the IDAP loan, whichever is later, and ends when the IDAP loan is repaid in full.

§ 123.701 What is the application procedure for an IDAP loan?

A prospective IDAP Borrower must apply to an IDAP Lender for an IDAP loan by the application deadline for prospective IDAP Borrowers established by SBA in the IDAP-Eligible Disaster Declaration. If the IDAP Lender approves the application, it must submit a request for IDAP loan approval to SBA by the application deadline for IDAP Lenders established by SBA in the IDAP-Eligible Disaster Declaration. SBA will issue an approval or a decline of the IDAP Lender's request within 36 hours of receipt by SBA. A prospective IDAP Borrower will receive notice of approval or decline of its loan application from the IDAP Lender. Notice of decline will include the reasons. If an IDAP loan is approved, a loan authorization will be issued.

§ 123.702 What are the eligibility requirements for an IDAP loan?

(a) *Eligible IDAP applicants.* To be eligible for an IDAP loan, an applicant business must meet all of the requirements set forth below. The applicant business must:

(1) Be located within a Declared Disaster Area;

(2) Have eligible disaster losses as follows:

(i) For a Major Disaster Declaration, if located in a Primary County, have sustained damage to real or business personal property in the Declared Disaster or, if located in a Primary or Contiguous County, have sustained Substantial Economic Injury as a direct result of the Declared Disaster; or

(ii) For an SBA Administrative Disaster Declaration, have sustained damage to real or business personal property in the Declared Disaster or sustained Substantial Economic Injury as a direct result of the Declared Disaster; or

(iii) For an SBA EIDL-Only Disaster Declaration, have sustained Substantial Economic Injury as a direct result of the Declared Disaster;

(3) Have been a small business concern under the size requirements applicable to disaster loan assistance under part 121 of this chapter (including affiliates) when the Declared Disaster commenced;

(4) Together with affiliates and principal owners, not have Credit Elsewhere;

(5) Apply to SBA for a Disaster Loan within the applicable deadline and before any disbursement of the IDAP loan; and

(6) Be creditworthy and demonstrate reasonable assurance of repayment of the IDAP loan.

(b) *Ineligible IDAP applicants.* An applicant business is not eligible for an IDAP loan if it is:

(1) A non-profit or charitable concern;

(2) A business that was not a small business concern under the size requirements of part 121 of this chapter (including affiliates) when the Declared Disaster commenced;

(3) A consumer or marketing cooperative;

(4) Deriving more than one-third of gross annual revenue from legal gambling activities or a business whose purpose for being is gambling regardless of its ability to meet the one-third criteria established for otherwise eligible concerns;

(5) A loan packager which earns more than one-third of its gross annual revenue from packaging SBA loans;

(6) Principally engaged in teaching, instructing, counseling, or indoctrinating religion or religious beliefs, whether in a religious or secular setting;

(7) Primarily engaged in political or lobbying activities;

(8) A private club or business that limits the number of memberships for reasons other than capacity;

(9) Presents live performances of a prurient sexual nature or derives directly or indirectly more than *de minimis* gross revenue through the sale of products or services, or the presentation of any depictions or displays, of a prurient sexual nature;

(10) Engaged in the production or distribution of any product or service that has been determined to be obscene by a court;

(11) Engaged in any illegal activity;

(12) A government owned entity (except for a business owned or controlled by a Native American tribe);

(13) A business in which the IDAP Lender or any of its Associates (as defined in §120.10) owns an equity interest;

(14) Primarily engaged in subdividing real property into lots and developing it for resale on its own account;

(15) Engaged in lending, multi-level sales distribution, speculation, or investment (except for real estate investment with property held for rental when the Declared Disaster occurred);

(16) Delinquent on any Federal obligation, including but not limited to any Federal loans, contracts, grants, student loans or taxes, or has a judgment lien for a Federal debt against its property;

(17) Located in a Special Flood Hazard Area (SFHA), as designated by the Federal Emergency Management Agency, and has not maintained required flood insurance on its business property (regardless of the type of disaster);

(18) Located in a SFHA within a non-participating community or a community under sanction;

(19) Located in a building that was newly constructed or substantially improved on or after February 9, 1989, and is currently located seaward of mean high tide or entirely in or over water;

(20) Located in a Coastal Barrier Resource Area (COBRA);

(21) A business that had a substantial change of ownership (more than 50 percent) after the Declared Disaster and no contract of sale existed prior to that time;

(22) A business that was established after the Declared Disaster;

(23) Relocating out of the Declared Disaster Area;

(24) Primarily engaged in the production of food and fiber, ranching and raising of livestock, aquaculture and all other farming and agriculture-related industries (except for a nursery deriving less than 50 percent of annual receipts from the production and sale of ornamental plants and other nursery products, a small agricultural cooperative or a small producer cooperative); or

(25) A sole proprietorship, unincorporated association, partnership or limited liability company in which a Member of Congress (or a household member) has an ownership interest.

(c) *Character requirements.* An applicant business is not eligible for an IDAP loan if any Associate (as defined in §120.10) of the applicant business:

(1) Is presently under indictment, on parole or probation;

(2) Has ever been charged with, arrested for, convicted, placed on pretrial diversion, and/or placed on any form of probation (including adjudication withheld pending probation) for any criminal offense other than a minor motor vehicle violation (including offenses which have been dismissed, discharged, or not prosecuted);

(3) Is at least a 50 percent or more owner of applicant business, and is more than 60 days delinquent on any obligation to pay child support arising under an administrative order, court order, repayment agreement between the holder and a custodial parent, or repayment agreement between the holder and a state agency providing child support enforcement services;

(4) Is an undocumented (illegal) alien; or

(5) Is delinquent on any Federal obligation, including but not limited to any Federal loans, contracts, grants, student loans or taxes.

§ 123.703 What are the terms of an IDAP loan?

(a) *Guaranty percentage.* The SBA guaranteed share of an IDAP loan is 85%.

(b) *Maximum loan size.* (1) If the amount of an IDAP Borrower's disaster losses is $25,000 or less, the principal amount of an IDAP loan must not exceed the amount of disaster losses minus Other Recoveries.

(2) If the amount of an IDAP Borrower's disaster losses is more than $25,000, the principal amount of an IDAP loan must not exceed $25,000 minus Other Recoveries.

(c) *Disbursement.* The disbursement period for an IDAP loan is generally up to 30 days from the date of SBA approval of the IDAP loan. If the IDAP Lender is notified before disbursement of the IDAP loan that the IDAP Borrower has received Other Recoveries, the IDAP Lender must decrease the approved amount of the IDAP loan by the amount of the Other Recoveries. If the IDAP Borrower's Disaster Loan is approved, SBA will contact the IDAP Lender when SBA is ready to disburse the Disaster Loan. Upon receipt of such notification by SBA, the IDAP Lender must cancel any remaining undisbursed amount of the IDAP loan.

(d) *Repayment*—(1) *Initial Period.* During the Initial Period, an IDAP Borrower will pay interest only on the disbursed principal balance of the IDAP loan. If SBA approves the IDAP Borrower's Disaster Loan application, SBA will require that the IDAP loan be repaid first from the proceeds of the Disaster Loan. If the IDAP Borrower receives Other Recoveries during the Initial Period, the IDAP Borrower must, in accordance with § 123.703(h), remit the Other Recoveries to the IDAP Lender, and the IDAP Lender will apply the Other Recoveries to the IDAP loan. If the IDAP Borrower's Disaster Loan application is declined or if the amount of the approved Disaster Loan is insufficient to repay the IDAP loan in full, the remaining balance of the IDAP loan will be repaid during the Term Period as described in paragraph (2). The Initial Period ends upon (i) full repayment of the IDAP loan from the proceeds of the IDAP Borrower's Disaster Loan; (ii) SBA notice to the IDAP Lender of decline of the IDAP Borrower's Disaster Loan Application; or (iii) receipt by the IDAP Lender of partial repayment of the IDAP loan from the proceeds of the Disaster Loan; provided that if the IDAP loan has not been fully disbursed at such time, the Initial Period shall not end until the IDAP loan is fully disbursed. If an IDAP Borrower withdraws an application for a Disaster Loan, fails to close on an approved Disaster Loan or if the approved Disaster Loan is cancelled, the IDAP loan is immediately due and payable by the IDAP Borrower.

(2) *Term Period.* If SBA declines the IDAP Borrower's Disaster Loan application or the approved amount of the Disaster Loan is insufficient to repay the IDAP loan in full, the IDAP Borrower must pay principal and interest on the IDAP loan, with the IDAP loan balance to be fully amortized over a period that is at least 10 years from the date of final disbursement of the IDAP loan, but no more than 25 years from the date of final disbursement. The Term Period begins in the first month following SBA notice to the IDAP Lender of decline of the IDAP Borrower's Disaster Loan application, receipt by the IDAP Lender of partial repayment of the IDAP loan from the proceeds of the Disaster Loan, or final disbursement of the IDAP loan, whichever is later. Balloon payments are not permitted. The IDAP Borrower may prepay all or a portion of the principal during the life of the loan without penalty. If the IDAP Borrower receives Other Recoveries during the Term Period, the IDAP Borrower must, in accordance with § 123.703(h), remit the Other Recoveries to the IDAP Lender, and the IDAP Lender will apply the Other Recoveries to the IDAP loan.

(e) *Interest rate*—(1) *Initial Period.* The maximum interest rate an IDAP Lender may charge an IDAP Borrower during the Initial Period will be published by SBA in the FEDERAL REGISTER from time to time. This rate must be a fixed rate.

(2) *Term Period.* The maximum interest rate an IDAP Lender may charge an IDAP Borrower during the Term Period will be published in the FEDERAL REGISTER from time to time. The IDAP

Lender may charge either a fixed or a variable rate during the Term Period.

(f) *Number of IDAP loans per small business.* No small business (including affiliates) may obtain more than one IDAP loan per Declared Disaster. The provisions of § 120.151 do not apply to IDAP loans.

(g) *Personal guarantees.* Holders of at least a 20 percent ownership interest in the IDAP Borrower must guarantee the IDAP loan.

(h) *Agreement to remit Other Recoveries.* IDAP Borrowers must promptly notify the IDAP Lender of the receipt of Other Recoveries, and must promptly remit the proceeds of Other Recoveries to the IDAP Lender. The IDAP Lender must apply the Other Recoveries to the IDAP loan balance. SBA does not require any additional collateral for IDAP loans.

§ 123.704 Are there restrictions on how IDAP loan funds may be used?

(a) IDAP loan proceeds may only be used for the following purposes:

(1) For a Major Disaster Declaration:

(i) If the IDAP Borrower is located in a Primary County, to restore or replace the IDAP Borrower's real or business personal property to its condition before the Declared Disaster occurred and/or for working capital necessary to carry the IDAP Borrower until resumption of normal operations and for expenditures necessary to alleviate the specific economic injury, but not to exceed that which the IDAP Borrower could have provided had the injury not occurred; or

(ii) If the IDAP Borrower is located in a Contiguous County, for working capital necessary to carry the IDAP Borrower until resumption of normal operations and for expenditures necessary to alleviate the specific economic injury, but not to exceed that which the IDAP Borrower could have provided had the injury not occurred.

(2) For an SBA Administrative Disaster Declaration, if the IDAP Borrower is located in either a Primary County or a Contiguous County, to restore or replace the IDAP Borrower's real or business personal property to its condition before the Declared Disaster occurred and/or for working capital necessary to carry the IDAP Borrower until resumption of normal operations and for expenditures necessary to alleviate the specific economic injury, but not to exceed that which the IDAP Borrower could have provided had the injury not occurred.

(3) For an SBA EIDL-Only Disaster Declaration, if the IDAP Borrower is located in either a Primary County or a Contiguous County, for working capital necessary to carry the IDAP Borrower until resumption of normal operations and for expenditures necessary to alleviate the specific economic injury, but not to exceed that which the IDAP Borrower could have provided had the injury not occurred.

(b) IDAP loan proceeds may not be used to:

(1) Refinance or repay indebtedness incurred prior to the Declared Disaster (other than regularly due installments);

(2) Make payments on loans owned by another federal agency (including SBA) or a Small Business Investment Company licensed under the Small Business Investment Act;

(3) Pay, directly or indirectly, any obligations resulting from a federal, state or local tax penalty as a result of negligence or fraud, or any non-tax criminal fine, civil fine, or penalty for non-compliance with a law, regulation, or order of a federal, state, regional, or local agency or similar matter;

(4) Pay dividends, bonuses or other disbursements to owners, partners, officers or stockholders, except for reasonable remuneration directly related to their performance of services for the business;

(5) Make repairs on a building rented by the IDAP Borrower if the IDAP Borrower's lease does not require the IDAP Borrower to make such repairs;

(6) Make repairs to a condominium unit owned by the IDAP Borrower;

(7) Replace landscaping in excess of $5,000 unless the disaster damaged landscaping fulfilled a functional need or contributed toward the generation of business;

(8) Repair or replace property not located within the Declared Disaster Area at the time of the Declared Disaster;

(9) Repay stockholder/Associate loans, except where the funds were injected on an interim basis as a result of the Declared Disaster and non-repayment would cause undue hardship to the stockholder/Associate;

(10) Expand facilities or acquire fixed assets, except for replacement of disaster-damaged fixed assets;

(11) Pay for contractor malfeasance;

(12) Replace damaged property that consists of cash or securities;

(13) Replace damaged property if the replacement value is extraordinarily high and not easily verified, such as the value of antiques, artworks or hobby collections; or

(14) Repair or replace damaged property where the IDAP Borrower's only interest is in the form of a security interest, mortgage or deed of trust.

§ 123.705 Are there any fees associated with IDAP loans?

(a) *IDAP Lender Fees.* An IDAP Lender must not impose any fees or direct costs on an IDAP Borrower, except for the following allowed fees or direct costs:

(1) The reasonable direct costs of liquidation;

(2) A late payment fee not to exceed 5 percent of the scheduled IDAP loan payment; and

(3) An application fee not to exceed $250. Notwithstanding the provisions of 13 CFR 103.5, no compensation agreement is required for the application fee. If an undisbursed IDAP loan is cancelled pursuant to § 123.703(c), the IDAP Lender may retain the application fee.

(b) *SBA Fees.* SBA will not impose any guarantee fees on an IDAP Lender making an IDAP loan.

(c) *Prohibition on paid loan packagers, referral agents or brokers.* Other than the application fee set forth in (a)(3) of this section, no IDAP Lender or third party may charge an IDAP Borrower a fee to assist in the preparation of an IDAP loan application or application materials. No third party may charge an IDAP Borrower or an IDAP Lender a referral fee or broker's fee in connection with an IDAP loan.

§ 123.706 What are the requirements for IDAP Lenders?

(a) *IDAP Lenders.* An IDAP Lender must be a 7(a) Lender (as defined in § 120.10). Notwithstanding the provisions of § 120.470(a), a Small Business Lending Company (SBLC) that is a 7(a) Lender may make IDAP loans. An IDAP Lender must sign a supplemental Loan Guarantee Agreement for the IDAP loan program. An IDAP Lender must comply and maintain familiarity with the IDAP Loan Program Requirements, as such requirements are revised from time to time. IDAP Loan Program Requirements in effect at the time that an IDAP Lender takes an action in connection with a particular IDAP loan govern that specific action. With respect to their activities in the IDAP loan program, IDAP Lenders are subject to the requirements of §§ 120.140 (What ethical requirements apply to participants?), 120.197 (Notifying SBA's Office of Inspector General of suspected fraud), 120.400 (Loan Guarantee Agreements), 120.410 (Requirements for all participating Lenders), 120.411 (Preferences), 120.412 (Other services Lenders may provide Borrowers), and 120.413 (Advertisement of relationship with SBA) of this chapter. An IDAP Lender and its contractor(s) are independent contractors that are responsible for their own actions with respect to an IDAP loan. SBA has no responsibility or liability for any claim by an IDAP Borrower, guarantor or other party alleging injury as a result of any allegedly wrongful action taken by an IDAP Lender or an employee, agent or contractor of an IDAP Lender.

(b) *Delegated authority.* An IDAP loan must be processed, serviced and liquidated under an IDAP Lender's delegated authority provided by the supplemental Loan Guarantee Agreement for the IDAP loan program. Non-delegated processing is not available for the IDAP loan program. An IDAP Lender is responsible for all IDAP loan decisions regarding eligibility (including size) and creditworthiness. In determining creditworthiness, an IDAP Lender must use the existing practices and procedures that the IDAP Lender uses for its non-SBA guaranteed commercial loans of a similar size. The IDAP

Lender's existing practices and procedures must be appropriate and generally accepted, proven and prudent credit evaluation processes and procedures, which may include credit scoring, and must ensure that there is reasonable assurance of repayment. In disbursing the IDAP loan, the IDAP Lender must use the same disbursement procedures and documentation as it uses for its similarly sized non-SBA guaranteed commercial loans. An IDAP Lender is also responsible for confirming that all IDAP loan processing, closing, servicing and liquidation decisions are correct and that all IDAP Loan Program Requirements have been followed.

(c) *IDAP Lender reporting.* An IDAP Lender must report on its IDAP loans in accordance with requirements established by SBA from time to time.

(d) *Servicing.* Each IDAP Lender must service all of its IDAP loans in accordance with the existing practices and procedures that the IDAP Lender uses for its non-SBA guaranteed commercial loans. In all circumstances, such practices and procedures must be commercially reasonable and consistent with prudent lending standards and in accordance with IDAP Loan Program Requirements. SBA's prior written consent is required for servicing actions that may have significant exposure implications for SBA. SBA may require written notice of other servicing actions it considers necessary for portfolio management purposes.

(e) *Liquidations.* Each IDAP Lender must be responsible for liquidating its defaulted IDAP loans. IDAP loans will be liquidated in accordance with the existing practices and procedures that the IDAP Lender uses for its non-SBA guaranteed commercial loans. In all circumstances, such practices and procedures must be commercially reasonable and consistent with prudent lending standards and in accordance with IDAP Loan Program Requirements. IDAP loans with *de minimis* value may, at the IDAP Lender's request and with SBA's approval, be liquidated by SBA or its agent(s). Significant liquidation actions taken on IDAP loans must be documented. The reimbursement of IDAP Lender liquidation expenses is limited to the amount of the recovery on the IDAP loan.

(f) *Purchase requests.* An IDAP Lender may request SBA to purchase the guaranteed portion of an IDAP loan when there has been an uncured payment default exceeding 60 days or when the IDAP Borrower has declared bankruptcy. IDAP loans are subject to the 7(a) loan program requirements of §§120.520 (Purchase of 7(a) loan guarantees), 120.521 (What interest rate applies after SBA purchases its guaranteed portion?), 120.522 (Payment of accrued interest to the Lender or Registered Holder when SBA purchases the guaranteed portion), 120.523 (What is the "earliest uncured payment default"?), 120.524 (When is SBA released from liability on its guarantee?), 120.542 (Payment by SBA of legal fees and other expenses) and 120.546 (Loan asset sales) of this chapter.

(g) *Prohibition on secondary market sales, securitizations, loan participations and loan sales.* An IDAP Lender may not sell the guaranteed portion of an IDAP loan in the secondary market, securitize the unguaranteed portion of an IDAP loan, participate any portion of an IDAP loan with another lender, or sell all of its interest in an IDAP loan.

(h) *Loan pledges.* An IDAP Lender may pledge an IDAP loan subject to the 7(a) loan program requirements of §§120.434 and 120.435 of this chapter.

(i) *Oversight.* All IDAP Lenders are subject to the supervision and enforcement provisions applicable to 7(a) Lenders in part 120, subpart I of this chapter (§§120.1000 through 120.1600). In addition, an IDAP Lender that is an SBA Supervised Lender (as defined in §120.10) is subject to the requirements of §§120.460 through 120.490, as applicable.

PART 124—8(a) BUSINESS DEVELOPMENT/SMALL DISADVANTAGED BUSINESS STATUS DETERMINATIONS

Subpart A—8(a) Business Development

PROVISIONS OF GENERAL APPLICABILITY

AUTHORITY: 15 U.S.C. 634(b)(6), 636(j), 637(a), 637(d), 644 and Pub. L. 99–661, Pub. L. 100–656, sec.1207, Pub. L. 101–37, Pub. L. 101–574, section 8021, Pub. L. 108–87, and 42 U.S.C. 9815.

SOURCE: 63 FR 35739, June 30, 1998, unless otherwise noted.

EDITORIAL NOTE: Nomenclature changes to part 124 appear at 72 FR 50040, Aug. 30, 2007, and 76 FR 8253, Feb. 11, 2011.

Subpart A—8(a) Business Development

PROVISIONS OF GENERAL APPLICABILITY

§ 124.1 What is the purpose of the 8(a) Business Development program?

Sections 8(a) and 7(j) of the Small Business Act authorize a Minority Small Business and Capital Ownership Development program (designated the 8(a) Business Development or "8(a) BD" program for purposes of the regulations in this part). The purpose of the 8(a) BD program is to assist eligible small disadvantaged business concerns compete in the American economy through business development.

§ 124.2 What length of time may a business participate in the 8(a) BD program?

A Participant receives a program term of nine years from the date of SBA's approval letter certifying the concern's admission to the program. The Participant must maintain its program eligibility during its tenure in the program and must inform SBA of any changes that would adversely affect its program eligibility. The nine year program term may be shortened only by termination, early graduation (including voluntary early graduation) or voluntary withdrawal as provided for in this subpart.

[76 FR 8253, Feb. 11, 2011]

§ 124.3 What definitions are important in the 8(a) BD program?

Alaska Native, as defined by the Alaska Native Claims Settlement Act (43 U.S.C. 1602), means a citizen of the

United States who is a person of one-fourth degree or more Alaskan Indian (including Tsimshian Indians not enrolled in the Metlaktla Indian Community), Eskimo, or Aleut blood, or a combination of those bloodlines. The term includes, in the absence of proof of a minimum blood quantum, any citizen whom a Native village or Native group regards as an Alaska Native if their father or mother is regarded as an Alaska Native.

Alaska Native Corporation or ANC means any Regional Corporation, Village Corporation, Urban Corporation, or Group Corporation organized under the laws of the State of Alaska in accordance with the Alaska Native Claims Settlement Act, as amended (43 U.S.C. 1601, *et seq.*)

Bona fide place of business, for purposes of 8(a) construction procurements, means a location where a Participant regularly maintains an office which employs at least one full-time individual within the appropriate geographical boundary. The term does not include construction trailers or other temporary construction sites.

Community Development Corporation or CDC means a nonprofit organization responsible to residents of the area it serves which has received financial assistance under 42 U.S.C. 9805, *et seq.*

Concern is defined in part 121 of this title.

Days means calendar days unless otherwise specified.

Day-to-day operations of a firm means the marketing, production, sales, and administrative functions of the firm.

Immediate family member means father, mother, husband, wife, son, daughter, brother, sister, grandfather, grandmother, grandson, granddaughter, father-in-law, and mother-in-law.

Indian tribe means any Indian tribe, band, nation, or other organized group or community of Indians, including any ANC, which is recognized as eligible for the special programs and services provided by the United States to Indians because of their status as Indians, or is recognized as such by the State in which the tribe, band, nation, group, or community resides. *See* definition of "tribally-owned concern."

NAICS code means North American Industry Classification System code.

Native Hawaiian means any individual whose ancestors were natives, prior to 1778, of the area which now comprises the State of Hawaii.

Native Hawaiian Organization means any community service organization serving Native Hawaiians in the State of Hawaii which is a not-for-profit organization chartered by the State of Hawaii, is controlled by Native Hawaiians, and whose business activities will principally benefit such Native Hawaiians.

Negative control is defined in part 121 of this title.

Non-disadvantaged individual means any individual who does not claim disadvantaged status, does not qualify as disadvantaged, or upon whose disadvantaged status an applicant or Participant does not rely in qualifying for 8(a) BD program participation.

Participant means a small business concern admitted to participate in the 8(a) BD program.

Primary industry classification means the six digit North American Industry Classification System (NAICS) code designation which best describes the primary business activity of the 8(a) BD applicant or Participant. The NAICS code designations are described in the North American Industry Classification System book published by the U.S. Office of Management and Budget. SBA utilizes §121.107 of this chapter in determining a firm's primary industry classification. A Participant may change its primary industry classification where it can demonstrate to SBA by clear evidence that the majority of its total revenues during a three-year period have evolved from one NAICS code to another.

Principal place of business means the business location where the individuals who manage the concern's day-to-day operations spend most working hours and where top management's business records are kept. If the offices from which management is directed and where the business records are kept are in different locations, SBA will determine the principal place of business for program purposes.

Program year means a 12-month period of an 8(a) BD Participant's program participation. The first program year begins on the date that the concern is certified to participate in the 8(a) BD program and ends one year later. Each subsequent program year begins on the Participant's anniversary of program certification and runs for one 12-month period.

Regularly maintains an office means conducting business activities as an on-going business concern from a fixed location on a daily basis. The best evidence of the regular maintenance of an office is documentation that shows that third parties routinely transact business with a Participant at a location within a particular geographical area. Such evidence includes lease agreements, payroll records, advertisements, bills, correspondence, and evidence that the Participant has complied with all local requirements concerning registering, licensing, or filing with the State or County where the place of business is located. Although a firm would generally be required to have a license to do business in a particular location in order to "regularly maintain an office" there, the firm would not be required to have an additional construction license or other specific type of license in order to regularly maintain an office.

Same or similar line of business means business activities within the same four-digit "Industry Group" of the NAICS Manual as the primary industry classification of the applicant or Participant. The phrase "same business area" is synonymous with this definition.

Self-marketing of a requirement occurs when a Participant identifies a requirement that has not been committed to the 8(a) BD program and, through its marketing efforts, causes the procuring activity to offer that specific requirement to the 8(a) BD program on the Participant's behalf. A firm which identifies and markets a requirement which is subsequently offered to the 8(a) BD program as an open requirement or on behalf of another Participant has not "self-marketed" the requirement within the meaning of this part.

Tribally-owned concern means any concern at least 51 percent owned by an Indian tribe as defined in this section.

Unconditional ownership means ownership that is not subject to conditions precedent, conditions subsequent, executory agreements, voting trusts, restrictions on or assignments of voting rights, or other arrangements causing or potentially causing ownership benefits to go to another (other than after death or incapacity). The pledge or encumbrance of stock or other ownership interest as collateral, including seller-financed transactions, does not affect the unconditional nature of ownership if the terms follow normal commercial practices and the owner retains control absent violations of the terms.

[63 FR 35739, June 30, 1998, as amended at 76 FR 8253, Feb. 11, 2011; 77 FR 28237, May 14, 2012]

§ 124.4 What restrictions apply to fees for applicant and Participant representatives?

(a) The compensation received by any packager, agent or representative of an 8(a) applicant or Participant for assisting the applicant in obtaining 8(a) certification or for assisting the Participant in obtaining 8(a) contracts, or any other assistance to support program participation, must be reasonable in light of the service(s) performed by the packager, agent or representative.

(b) In assisting a Participant obtain one or more 8(a) contracts, a packager, agent or representative cannot receive a fee that is a percentage of the gross contract value.

(c) For good cause, the AA/BD may initiate proceedings to suspend or revoke a packager's, agent's or representative's privilege to assist applicants obtain 8(a) certification, assist Participants obtain 8(a) contracts, or any other assistance to support program participation. Good cause is defined in § 103.4 of these regulations.

(1) The AA/BD may send a show cause letter requesting the agent or representative to demonstrate why the agent or representative should not be suspended or proposed for revocation, or may immediately send a written notice suspending or proposing revocation, depending upon the evidence in the administrative record. The notice

will include a discussion of the relevant facts and the reason(s) why the AA/BD believes that good cause exists.

(2) Unless the AA/BD specifies a different time in the notice, the agent or representative must respond to the notice within 30 days of the date of the notice with any facts or arguments showing why good cause does not exist. The agent or representative may request additional time to respond, which the AA/BD may grant in his or her discretion.

(3) After considering the agent's or representative's response, the AA/BD will issue a final determination, setting forth the reasons for this decision and, if a suspension continues to be effective or a revocation is implemented, the term of the suspension or revocation.

(d) The AA/BD may refer a packager, agent, or other representative to SBA's Suspension and Debarment Official for possible Government-wide suspension or debarment where appropriate, including where it appears that the packager, agent or representative assisted an applicant to or Participant in the 8(a) BD program submit information to SBA that the packager, agent or representative knew was false or materially misleading.

[76 FR 8253, Feb. 11, 2011]

Eligibility Requirements for Participation in the 8(a) Business Development Program

§ 124.101 What are the basic requirements a concern must meet for the 8(a) BD program?

Generally, a concern meets the basic requirements for admission to the 8(a) BD program if it is a small business which is unconditionally owned and controlled by one or more socially and economically disadvantaged individuals who are of good character and citizens of and residing in the United States, and which demonstrates potential for success.

[76 FR 8254, Feb. 11, 2011]

§ 124.102 What size business is eligible to participate in the 8(a) BD program?

(a)(1) An applicant concern must qualify as a small business concern as defined in part 121 of this title. The applicable size standard is the one for its primary industry classification. The rules for calculating the size of a tribally-owned concern, a concern owned by an Alaska Native Corporation, a concern owned by a Native Hawaiian Organization, or a concern owned by a Community Development Corporation are additionally affected by §§ 124.109, 124.110, and 124.111, respectively.

(2) In order to remain eligible to participate in the 8(a) BD program after certification, a firm must generally remain small for its primary industry classification, as adjusted during the program. SBA may graduate a Participant prior to the expiration of its program term where the firm exceeds the size standard corresponding to its primary NAICS code, as adjusted, for three successive program years, unless the firm demonstrates that through its growth and development its primary industry is changing, pursuant to the criteria described in 13 CFR 121.107, to a related secondary NAICS code that is contained in its most recently approved business plan. The firm's business plan must contain specific targets, objectives, and goals for its continued growth and development under its new primary industry.

(b) If 8(a) BD program officials determine that a concern may not qualify as small, they may deny an application for 8(a) BD program admission or may request a formal size determination under part 121 of this title.

(c) A concern whose application is denied due to size by 8(a) BD program officials may request a formal size determination under part 121 of this title. A favorable determination will enable the firm to immediately submit a new 8(a) BD application without waiting one year.

[63 FR 35739, June 30, 1998, as amended at 76 FR 8254, Feb. 11, 2011]

§ 124.103 Who is socially disadvantaged?

(a) *General.* Socially disadvantaged individuals are those who have been subjected to racial or ethnic prejudice or cultural bias within American society because of their identities as members of groups and without regard to their individual qualities. The social disadvantage must stem from circumstances beyond their control.

(b) *Members of designated groups.* (1) There is a rebuttable presumption that the following individuals are socially disadvantaged: Black Americans; Hispanic Americans; Native Americans (Alaska Natives, Native Hawaiians, or enrolled members of a Federally or State recognized Indian Tribe); Asian Pacific Americans (persons with origins from Burma, Thailand, Malaysia, Indonesia, Singapore, Brunei, Japan, China (including Hong Kong), Taiwan, Laos, Cambodia (Kampuchea), Vietnam, Korea, The Philippines, U.S. Trust Territory of the Pacific Islands (Republic of Palau), Republic of the Marshall Islands, Federated States of Micronesia, the Commonwealth of the Northern Mariana Islands, Guam, Samoa, Macao, Fiji, Tonga, Kiribati, Tuvalu, or Nauru); Subcontinent Asian Americans (persons with origins from India, Pakistan, Bangladesh, Sri Lanka, Bhutan, the Maldives Islands or Nepal); and members of other groups designated from time to time by SBA according to procedures set forth at paragraph (d) of this section. Being born in a country does not, by itself, suffice to make the birth country an individual's country of origin for purposes of being included within a designated group.

(2) An individual must demonstrate that he or she has held himself or herself out, and is currently identified by others, as a member of a designated group if SBA requires it.

(3) The presumption of social disadvantage may be overcome with credible evidence to the contrary. Individuals possessing or knowing of such evidence should submit the information in writing to the Associate Administrator for Business Development (AA/BD) for consideration.

(c) *Individuals not members of designated groups.* (1) An individual who is not a member of one of the groups presumed to be socially disadvantaged in paragraph (b)(1) of this section must establish individual social disadvantage by a preponderance of the evidence. Such individual should present corroborating evidence to support his or her claim(s) of social disadvantage where readily available.

(2) Evidence of individual social disadvantage must include the following elements:

(i) At least one objective distinguishing feature that has contributed to social disadvantage, such as race, ethnic origin, gender, physical handicap, long-term residence in an environment isolated from the mainstream of American society, or other similar causes not common to individuals who are not socially disadvantaged;

(ii) The individual's social disadvantage must be rooted in treatment which he or she has experienced in American society, not in other countries;

(iii) The individual's social disadvantage must be chronic and substantial, not fleeting or insignificant; and

(iv) The individual's social disadvantage must have negatively impacted on his or her entry into or advancement in the business world. SBA will consider any relevant evidence in assessing this element, including experiences relating to education, employment and business history (including experiences relating to both the applicant firm and any other previous firm owned and/or controlled by the individual), where applicable.

(A) *Education.* SBA considers such factors as denial of equal access to institutions of higher education, exclusion from social and professional association with students or teachers, denial of educational honors rightfully earned, and social patterns or pressures which discouraged the individual from pursuing a professional or business education.

(B) *Employment.* SBA considers such factors as unequal treatment in hiring, promotions and other aspects of professional advancement, pay and fringe benefits, and other terms and conditions of employment; retaliatory or discriminatory behavior by an employer; and social patterns or pressures which have channeled the individual into nonprofessional or non-business fields.

(C) *Business history.* SBA considers such factors as unequal access to credit or capital, acquisition of credit or capital under commercially unfavorable circumstances, unequal treatment in opportunities for government contracts or other work, unequal treatment by potential customers and business associates, and exclusion from business or professional organizations.

(3) An individual claiming social disadvantage must present facts and evidence that by themselves establish that the individual has suffered social disadvantage that has negatively impacted his or her entry into or advancement in the business world.

(i) Each instance of alleged discriminatory conduct must be accompanied by a negative impact on the individual's entry into or advancement in the business world in order for it to constitute an instance of social disadvantage.

(ii) SBA may disregard a claim of social disadvantage where a legitimate alternative ground for an adverse employment action or other perceived adverse action exists and the individual has not presented evidence that would render his/her claim any more likely than the alternative ground.

Example 1 to paragraph (c)(3)(ii). A woman who is not a member of a designated group attempts to establish her individual social disadvantage based on gender. She certifies that while working for company X, she received less compensation than her male counterpart. Without additional facts, that claim is insufficient to establish an incident of gender bias that could lead to a finding of social disadvantage. Without additional facts, it is no more likely that the individual claiming disadvantage was paid less than her male counterpart because he had superior qualifications or because he had greater responsibilities in his employment position. She must identify her qualifications (education, experience, years of employment, supervisory functions) as being equal or superior to that of her male counterpart in order for SBA to consider that particular incident may be the result of discriminatory conduct.

Example 2 to paragraph (c)(3)(ii). A woman who is not a member of a designated group attempts to establish her individual social disadvantage based on gender. She certifies that while working for company Y, she was not permitted to attend a professional development conference, even though male employees were allowed to attend similar conferences in the past. Without additional facts, that claim is insufficient to establish an incident of gender bias that could lead to a finding of social disadvantage. It is no more likely that she was not permitted to attend the conference based on gender bias than based on non-discriminatory reasons. She must identify that she was in the same professional position and level as the male employees who were permitted to attend similar conferences in the past, and she must identify that funding for training or professional development was available at the time she requested to attend the conference.

(iii) SBA may disregard a claim of social disadvantage where an individual presents evidence of discriminatory conduct, but fails to connect the discriminatory conduct to consequences that negatively impact his or her entry into or advancement in the business world.

Example to paragraph (c)(3)(iii). A woman who is not a member of a designated group attempts to establish her individual social disadvantage based on gender. She provides instances where one or more male business clients utter derogatory statements about her because she is a woman. After each instance, however, she acknowledges that the clients gave her contracts or otherwise continued to do business with her. Despite suffering discriminatory conduct, this individual has not established social disadvantage because the discriminatory conduct did not have an adverse effect on her business.

(4) SBA may request an applicant to provide additional facts to support his or her claim of social disadvantage to substantiate that a negative outcome was based on discriminatory conduct instead of one or more legitimate non-discriminatory reasons.

(5) SBA will discount or disbelieve statements made by an individual seeking to establish his or her individual social disadvantage where such statements are inconsistent with other evidence contained in the record.

(6) In determining whether an individual claiming social disadvantage meets the requirements set forth in this paragraph (c), SBA will determine whether:

(i) Each specific claim establishes an incident of bias or discriminatory conduct;

(ii) Each incident of bias or discriminatory conduct negatively impacted the individual's entry into or advancement in the business world; and

(iii) In the totality, the incidents of bias or discriminatory conduct that negatively impacted the individual's entry into or advancement in the business world establish chronic and substantial social disadvantage.

(d) *Socially disadvantaged group inclusion*—(1) *General.* Representatives of an identifiable group whose members believe that the group has suffered chronic racial or ethnic prejudice or cultural bias may petition SBA to be included as a presumptively socially disadvantaged group under paragraph (b)(1) of this section. Upon presentation of substantial evidence that members of the group have been subjected to racial or ethnic prejudice or cultural bias because of their identity as group members and without regard to their individual qualities, SBA will publish a notice in the FEDERAL REGISTER that it has received and is considering such a request, and that it will consider public comments.

(2) *Standards to be applied.* In determining whether a group has made an adequate showing that it has suffered chronic racial or ethnic prejudice or cultural bias for the purposes of this section, SBA must determine that:

(i) The group has suffered prejudice, bias, or discriminatory practices;

(ii) Those conditions have resulted in economic deprivation for the group of the type which Congress has found exists for the groups named in the Small Business Act; and

(iii) Those conditions have produced impediments in the business world for members of the group over which they have no control and which are not common to small business owners generally.

(3) *Procedure.* The notice published under paragraph (d)(1) of this section will authorize a specified period for the receipt of public comments supporting or opposing the petition for socially disadvantaged group status. If appropriate, SBA may hold hearings. SBA may also conduct its own research relative to the group's petition.

(4) *Decision.* In making a final decision that a group should be considered presumptively disadvantaged, SBA must find that a preponderance of the evidence demonstrates that the group has met the standards set forth in paragraph (d)(2) of this section based on SBA's consideration of the group petition, the comments from the public, and any independent research it performs. SBA will advise the petitioners of its final decision in writing, and publish its conclusion as a notice in the FEDERAL REGISTER. If appropriate, SBA will amend paragraph (b)(1) of this section to include a new group.

[63 FR 35739, June 30, 1998, as amended at 74 FR 45753, Sept. 4, 2009; 76 FR 8254, Feb. 11, 2011; 81 FR 48579, July 25, 2016]

§ 124.104 Who is economically disadvantaged?

(a) *General.* Economically disadvantaged individuals are socially disadvantaged individuals whose ability to compete in the free enterprise system has been impaired due to diminished capital and credit opportunities as compared to others in the same or similar line of business who are not socially disadvantaged.

(b) *Submission of narrative and financial information.* (1) Each individual claiming economic disadvantage must submit personal financial information.

(2) When married, an individual claiming economic disadvantage must submit separate financial information for his or her spouse, unless the individual and the spouse are legally separated. SBA will consider a spouse's financial situation in determining an individual's access to credit and capital where the spouse has a role in the business (*e.g.*, an officer, employee or director) or has lent money to, provided credit support to, or guaranteed a loan of the business. SBA does not take into consideration community property laws when determining economic disadvantage.

(c) *Factors to be considered.* In considering diminished capital and credit opportunities, SBA will examine factors relating to the personal financial condition of any individual claiming disadvantaged status, including income for the past three years (including bonuses and the value of company stock received in lieu of cash), personal net worth, and the fair market value of all assets, whether encumbered or not. An individual who exceeds any one of the thresholds set forth in this paragraph for personal income, net worth or total assets will generally be deemed to have access to credit and capital and not economically disadvantaged.

(1) *Transfers within two years.* (i) Except as set forth in paragraph (c)(1)(ii) of this section, SBA will attribute to

an individual claiming disadvantaged status any assets which that individual has transferred to an immediate family member, or to a trust a beneficiary of which is an immediate family member, for less than fair market value, within two years prior to a concern's application for participation in the 8(a) BD program or within two years of a Participant's annual program review, unless the individual claiming disadvantaged status can demonstrate that the transfer is to or on behalf of an immediate family member for that individual's education, medical expenses, or some other form of essential support.

(ii) SBA will not attribute to an individual claiming disadvantaged status any assets transferred by that individual to an immediate family member that are consistent with the customary recognition of special occasions, such as birthdays, graduations, anniversaries, and retirements.

(iii) In determining an individual's access to capital and credit, SBA may consider any assets that the individual transferred within such two-year period described by paragraph (c)(1)(i) of this section that SBA does not consider in evaluating the individual's assets and net worth (e.g., transfers to charities).

(2) *Net worth.* For initial 8(a) BD eligibility, the net worth of an individual claiming disadvantage must be less than $250,000. For continued 8(a) BD eligibility after admission to the program, net worth must be less than $750,000. In determining such net worth, SBA will exclude the ownership interest in the applicant or Participant and the equity in the primary personal residence (except any portion of such equity which is attributable to excessive withdrawals from the applicant or Participant). Exclusions for net worth purposes are not exclusions for asset valuation or access to capital and credit purposes.

(i) A contingent liability does not reduce an individual's net worth.

(ii) Funds invested in an Individual Retirement Account (IRA) or other official retirement account that are unavailable to an individual until retirement age without a significant penalty will not be considered in determining an individual's net worth. In order to properly assess whether funds invested in a retirement account may be excluded from an individual's net worth, the individual must provide information about the terms and restrictions of the account to SBA and certify that the retirement account is legitimate.

(iii) Income received from an applicant or Participant that is an S corporation, limited liability company (LLC) or partnership will be excluded from an individual's net worth where the applicant or Participant provides documentary evidence demonstrating that the income was reinvested in the firm or used to pay taxes arising in the normal course of operations of the firm. Losses from the S corporation, LLC or partnership, however, are losses to the company only, not losses to the individual, and cannot be used to reduce an individual's net worth.

(iv) The personal net worth of an individual claiming to be an Alaska Native will include assets and income from sources other than an Alaska Native Corporation and exclude any of the following which the individual receives from any Alaska Native Corporation: cash (including cash dividends on stock received from an ANC) to the extent that it does not, in the aggregate, exceed $2,000 per individual per annum; stock (including stock issued or distributed by an ANC as a dividend or distribution on stock); a partnership interest; land or an interest in land (including land or an interest in land received from an ANC as a dividend or distribution on stock); and an interest in a settlement trust.

(3) *Personal income for the past three years.* (i) If an individual's adjusted gross income averaged over the three years preceding submission of the 8(a) application exceeds $250,000, SBA will presume that such individual is not economically disadvantaged. For continued 8(a) BD eligibility, SBA will presume that an individual is not economically disadvantaged if his or her adjusted gross income averaged over the three preceding years exceeds $350,000. The presumption may be rebutted by a showing that this income level was unusual and not likely to occur in the future, that losses commensurate with and directly related to

the earnings were suffered, or by evidence that the income is not indicative of lack of economic disadvantage.

(ii) Income received from an applicant or Participant that is an S corporation, LLC or partnership will be excluded from an individual's income where the applicant or Participant provides documentary evidence demonstrating that the income was reinvested in the firm or used to pay taxes arising in the normal course of operations of the firm. Losses from the S corporation, LLC or partnership, however, are losses to the company only, not losses to the individual, and cannot be used to reduce an individual's personal income.

(4) *Fair market value of all assets.* An individual will generally not be considered economically disadvantaged if the fair market value of all his or her assets (including his or her primary residence and the value of the applicant/Participant firm) exceeds $4 million for an applicant concern and $6 million for continued 8(a) BD eligibility. The only assets excluded from this determination are funds excluded under paragraph (c)(2)(ii) of this section as being invested in a qualified IRA account.

[63 FR 35739, June 30, 1998, as amended at 76 FR 8254, Feb. 11, 2011; 81 FR 48580, July 25, 2016]

§ 124.105 What does it mean to be unconditionally owned by one or more disadvantaged individuals?

An applicant or Participant must be at least 51 percent unconditionally and directly owned by one or more socially and economically disadvantaged individuals who are citizens of the United States, except for concerns owned by Indian tribes, Alaska Native Corporations, Native Hawaiian Organizations, or Community Development Corporations (CDCs). *See* § 124.3 for definition of unconditional ownership; and §§ 124.109, 124.110, and 124.111, respectively, for special ownership requirements for concerns owned by Indian tribes, ANCs, Native Hawaiian Organizations, and CDCs.

(a) *Ownership must be direct.* Ownership by one or more disadvantaged individuals must be direct ownership. An applicant or Participant owned principally by another business entity or by a trust (including employee stock ownership trusts) that is in turn owned and controlled by one or more disadvantaged individuals does not meet this requirement. However, ownership by a trust, such as a living trust, may be treated as the functional equivalent of ownership by a disadvantaged individual where the trust is revocable, and the disadvantaged individual is the grantor, a trustee, and the sole current beneficiary of the trust.

(b) *Ownership of a partnership.* In the case of a concern which is a partnership, at least 51 percent of every class of partnership interest must be unconditionally owned by one or more individuals determined by SBA to be socially and economically disadvantaged. The ownership must be reflected in the concern's partnership agreement.

(c) *Ownership of a limited liability company.* In the case of a concern which is a limited liability company, at least 51 percent of each class of member interest must be unconditionally owned by one or more individuals determined by SBA to be socially and economically disadvantaged.

(d) *Ownership of a corporation.* In the case of a concern which is a corporation, at least 51 percent of each class of voting stock outstanding and 51 percent of the aggregate of all stock outstanding must be unconditionally owned by one or more individuals determined by SBA to be socially and economically disadvantaged.

(e) *Stock options' effect on ownership.* In determining unconditional ownership, SBA will disregard any unexercised stock options or similar agreements held by disadvantaged individuals. However, any unexercised stock options or similar agreements (including rights to convert non-voting stock or debentures into voting stock) held by non-disadvantaged individuals will be treated as exercised, except for any ownership interests which are held by investment companies licensed under the Small Business Investment Act of 1958.

(f) *Dividends and distributions.* One or more disadvantaged individuals must be entitled to receive:

(1) At least 51 percent of the annual distribution of dividends paid on the stock of a corporate applicant concern;

(2) 100 percent of the value of each share of stock owned by them in the event that the stock is sold; and

(3) At least 51 percent of the retained earnings of the concern and 100 percent of the unencumbered value of each share of stock owned in the event of dissolution of the corporation.

(g) *Ownership of another Participant in the same or similar line of business.* (1) An individual may not use his or her disadvantaged status to qualify a concern if that individual has an immediate family member who is using or has used his or her disadvantaged status to qualify another concern for the 8(a) BD program. The AA/BD may waive this prohibition if the two concerns have no connections, either in the form of ownership, control or contractual relationships, and provided the individual seeking to qualify the second concern has management and technical experience in the industry. Where the concern seeking a waiver is in the same or similar line of business as the current or former 8(a) concern, there is a presumption against granting the waiver. The applicant must provide clear and compelling evidence that no connection exists between the two firms.

(2) If the AA/BD grants a waiver under paragraph (g)(1) of this section, SBA will, as part of its annual review, assess whether the firm continues to operate independently of the other current or former 8(a) concern of an immediate family member. SBA may initiate proceedings to terminate a firm for which a waiver was granted from further participation in the 8(a) BD program if it is apparent that there are connections between the two firms that were not disclosed to the AA/BD when the waiver was granted or that came into existence after the waiver was granted. SBA may also initiate termination proceedings if the firm begins to operate in the same or similar line of business as the current or former 8(a) concern of the immediate family member and the firm did not operate in the same or similar line of business at the time the waiver was granted.

(h) *Ownership restrictions for non-disadvantaged individuals and concerns.* (1) A non-disadvantaged individual (in the aggregate with all immediate family members) or a non-Participant concern that is a general partner or stockholder with at least a 10 percent ownership interest in one Participant may not own more than a 10 percent interest in another Participant that is in the developmental stage or more than a 20 percent interest in another Participant in the transitional stage of the program. This restriction does not apply to financial institutions licensed or chartered by Federal, state or local government, including investment companies which are licensed under the Small Business Investment Act of 1958.

(2) A non-Participant concern in the same or similar line of business or a principal of such concern may not own more than a 10 percent interest in a Participant that is in the developmental stage or more than a 20 percent interest in a Participant in the transitional stage of the program, except that a former Participant in the same or similar line of business or a principal of such a former Participant (except those that have been terminated from 8(a) BD program participation pursuant to §§ 124.303 and 124.304) may have an equity ownership interest of up to 20 percent in a current Participant in the developmental stage of the program or up to 30 percent in a transitional stage Participant.

(i) *Change of ownership.* A Participant may change its ownership or business structure so long as one or more disadvantaged individuals own and control it after the change and SBA approves the transaction in writing prior to the change. The decision to approve or deny a Participant's request for a change in ownership or business structure will be made and communicated to the firm by the AA/BD. The decision of the AA/BD is the final decision of the Agency. The AA/BD will issue a decision within 60 days from receipt of a request containing all necessary documentation, or as soon thereafter as possible. If 60 days lapse without a decision from SBA, the Participant cannot presume that it can complete the change without written approval from SBA. A decision to deny a request for change of ownership or business structure may be grounds for program termination where the change is made nevertheless.

(1) Any Participant that was awarded one or more 8(a) contracts may substitute one disadvantaged individual for another disadvantaged individual without requiring the termination of those contracts or a request for waiver under § 124.515, as long as it receives SBA's approval prior to the change.

(2) Where the previous owner held less than a 10 percent interest in the concern, or the transfer results from the death or incapacity due to a serious, long-term illness or injury of a disadvantaged principal, prior approval is not required, but the concern must notify SBA within 60 days.

(3) Continued participation of the Participant with new ownership and the award of any new 8(a) contracts requires SBA's determination that all eligibility requirements are met by the concern and the new owners.

(4) Where a Participant requests a change of ownership or business structure, and proceeds with the change prior to receiving SBA approval (or where a change of ownership results from the death or incapacity of a disadvantaged individual for which a request prior to the change in ownership could not occur), SBA will suspend the Participant from program benefits pending resolution of the request. If the change is approved, the length of the suspension will be restored to the Participant's program term in the case of death or incapacity, or if the firm requested prior approval and waited 60 days for SBA approval.

(5) A change in ownership does not provide the new owner(s) with a new 8(a) BD program term. For example, if a concern has been in the 8(a) BD program for five years when a change in ownership occurs, the new owner will have four years remaining until program graduation.

(j) *Public offering.* A Participant's request for SBA's approval for the issuance of a public offering will be treated as a request for a change of ownership. Such request will cause SBA to examine the concern's continued need for access to the business development resources of the 8(a) BD program.

(k) *Community property laws given effect.* In determining ownership interests when an owner resides in any of the community property states or territories of the United States (Arizona, California, Idaho, Louisiana, Nevada, New Mexico, Puerto Rico, Texas, Washington and Wisconsin), SBA considers applicable state community property laws. If only one spouse claims disadvantaged status, that spouse's ownership interest will be considered unconditionally held only to the extent it is vested by the community property laws. A transfer or relinquishment of interest by the non-disadvantaged spouse may be necessary in some cases to establish eligibility.

[63 FR 35739, June 30, 1998, as amended at 74 FR 45753, Sept. 4, 2009; 76 FR 8255, Feb. 11, 2011; 81 FR 48580, July 25, 2016]

§ 124.106 When do disadvantaged individuals control an applicant or Participant?

Control is not the same as ownership, although both may reside in the same person. SBA regards control as including both the strategic policy setting exercised by boards of directors and the day-to-day management and administration of business operations. An applicant or Participant's management and daily business operations must be conducted by one or more disadvantaged individuals, except for concerns owned by Indian tribes, ANCs, Native Hawaiian Organizations, or Community Development Corporations (CDCs). (*See* §§ 124.109, 124.110, and 124.111, respectively, for the requirements for concerns owned by Indian tribes or ANCs, for concerns owned by Native Hawaiian Organizations, and for CDC-owned concerns.) Management experience need not be related to the same or similar industry as the primary industry classification of the applicant or Participant. Disadvantaged individuals managing the concern must have managerial experience of the extent and complexity needed to run the concern. A disadvantaged individual need not have the technical expertise or possess a required license to be found to control an applicant or Participant if he or she can demonstrate that he or she has ultimate managerial and supervisory control over those who possess the required licenses or technical expertise. However, where a critical license is held by a non-disadvantaged individual having an equity interest in the applicant or Participant firm, the non-disadvantaged individual may be found to control the firm.

(a)(1) An applicant or Participant must be managed on a full-time basis by one or more disadvantaged individuals who possess requisite management capabilities.

(2) A disadvantaged full-time manager must hold the highest officer position (usually President or Chief Executive Officer) in the applicant or Participant and be physically located in the United States.

(3) One or more disadvantaged individuals who manage the applicant or Participant must devote full-time to the business during the normal working hours of firms in the same or similar line of business. Work in a wholly-owned subsidiary of the applicant or participant may be considered to meet the requirement of full-time devotion. This applies only to a subsidiary owned by the 8(a) firm, and not to firms in which the disadvantaged individual has an ownership interest.

(4) Any disadvantaged manager who wishes to engage in outside employment must notify SBA of the nature and anticipated duration of the outside employment and obtain the prior written approval of SBA. SBA will deny a request for outside employment which could conflict with the management of the firm or could hinder it in achieving the objectives of its business development plan.

(5) Except as provided in paragraph (d)(1) of this section, a disadvantaged owner's unexercised right to cause a change in the control or management of the applicant concern does not in itself constitute disadvantaged control and management, regardless of how quickly or easily the right could be exercised.

(b) In the case of a partnership, one or more disadvantaged individuals must serve as general partners, with control over all partnership decisions. A partnership in which no disadvantaged individual is a general partner will be ineligible for participation.

(c) In the case of a limited liability company, one or more disadvantaged individuals must serve as management members, with control over all decisions of the limited liability company.

(d) One or more disadvantaged individuals must control the Board of Directors of a corporate applicant or Participant.

(1) SBA will deem disadvantaged individuals to control the Board of Directors where:

(i) A single disadvantaged individual owns 100% of all voting stock of an applicant or Participant concern;

(ii) A single disadvantaged individual owns at least 51% of all voting stock of an applicant or Participant concern, the individual is on the Board of Directors and no super majority voting requirements exist for shareholders to approve corporation actions. Where super majority voting requirements are provided for in the concern's articles of incorporation, its by-laws, or by state law, the disadvantaged individual must own at least the percent of the voting stock needed to overcome any such super majority voting requirements; or

(iii) More than one disadvantaged shareholder seeks to qualify the concern (i.e., no one individual owns 51%), each such individual is on the Board of Directors, together they own at least 51% of all voting stock of the concern, no super majority voting requirements exist, and the disadvantaged shareholders can demonstrate that they have made enforceable arrangements to permit one of them to vote the stock of all as a block without a shareholder meeting. Where the concern has super majority voting requirements, the disadvantaged shareholders must own at least that percentage of voting stock needed to overcome any such super majority ownership requirements.

(2) Where an applicant or Participant does not meet the requirements set forth in paragraph (d)(1) of this section, the disadvantaged individual(s) upon whom eligibility is based must control the Board of Directors through actual numbers of voting directors or, where permitted by state law, through weighted voting (e.g., in a concern having a two-person Board of Directors where one individual on the Board is disadvantaged and one is not, the disadvantaged vote must be weighted—worth more than one vote—in order for

the concern to be eligible for 8(a) participation). Where a concern seeks to comply with this paragraph:

(i) Provisions for the establishment of a quorum cannot permit non-disadvantaged Directors to control the Board of Directors, directly or indirectly;

(ii) Any Executive Committee of Directors must be controlled by disadvantaged directors unless the Executive Committee can only make recommendations to and cannot independently exercise the authority of the Board of Directors.

(3) An applicant must inform SBA of any super majority voting requirements provided for in its articles of incorporation, its by-laws, by state law, or otherwise. Similarly, after being admitted to the program, a Participant must inform SBA of changes regarding super majority voting requirements.

(4) Non-voting, advisory, or honorary Directors may be appointed without affecting disadvantaged individuals' control of the Board of Directors.

(5) Arrangements regarding the structure and voting rights of the Board of Directors must comply with applicable state law.

(e) Non-disadvantaged individuals may be involved in the management of an applicant or Participant, and may be stockholders, partners, limited liability members, officers, and/or directors of the applicant or Participant. However, no non-disadvantaged individual or immediate family member may:

(1) Exercise actual control or have the power to control the applicant or Participant;

(2) Be a former employer or a principal of a former employer of any disadvantaged owner of the applicant or Participant, unless it is determined by the AA/BD that the relationship between the former employer or principal and the disadvantaged individual or applicant concern does not give the former employer actual control or the potential to control the applicant or Participant and such relationship is in the best interests of the 8(a) BD firm; or

(3) Receive compensation from the applicant or Participant in any form as directors, officers or employees, including dividends, that exceeds the compensation to be received by the highest officer (usually CEO or President). The highest ranking officer may elect to take a lower salary than a non-disadvantaged individual only upon demonstrating that it helps the applicant or Participant. In the case of a Participant, the Participant must also obtain the prior written consent of the AA/BD or designee before changing the compensation paid to the highest ranking officer to be below that paid to a non-disadvantaged individual.

(f) Non-disadvantaged individuals who transfer majority stock ownership or control of the firm to an immediate family member within two years prior to the application and remain involved in the firm as a stockholder, officer, director, or key employee of the firm are presumed to control the firm. The presumption may be rebutted by showing that the transferee has independent management experience necessary to control the operation of the firm.

(g) Non-disadvantaged individuals or entities may be found to control or have the power to control in any of the following circumstances, which are illustrative only and not all inclusive:

(1) In circumstances where an applicant or Participant seeks to establish disadvantaged control of the Board of Directors through paragraph (d)(2) of this section, non-disadvantaged individuals control the Board of Directors of the applicant or Participant, either directly through majority voting membership, or indirectly, where the by-laws allow non-disadvantaged individuals effectively to prevent a quorum or block actions proposed by the disadvantaged individuals.

(2) A non-disadvantaged individual or entity, having an equity interest in the applicant or participant, provides critical financial or bonding support or a critical license to the applicant or Participant which directly or indirectly allows the non-disadvantaged individual significantly to influence business decisions of the Participant.

(3) A non-disadvantaged individual or entity controls the applicant or Participant or an individual disadvantaged owner through loan arrangements. Providing a loan guaranty on commercially reasonable terms does not, by

itself, give a non-disadvantaged individual or entity the power to control a firm.

(4) Business relationships exist with non-disadvantaged individuals or entities which cause such dependence that the applicant or Participant cannot exercise independent business judgment without great economic risk.

(h) Notwithstanding the provisions of this section requiring a disadvantaged owner to control the daily business operations and long-term strategic planning of an 8(a) BD Participant, where a disadvantaged individual upon whom eligibility is based is a reserve component member in the United States military who has been called to active duty, the Participant may elect to designate one or more individuals to control the Participant on behalf of the disadvantaged individual during the active duty call-up period. If such an election is made, the Participant will continue to be treated as an eligible 8(a) Participant and no additional time will be added to its program term. Alternatively, the Participant may elect to suspend its 8(a) BD participation during the active duty call-up period pursuant to §§ 124.305(h)(1)(ii) and 124.305(h)(4).

[63 FR 35739, June 30, 1998, as amended at 74 FR 45753, Sept. 4, 2009; 76 FR 8255, Feb. 11, 2011; 81 FR 48580, July 25, 2016]

§ 124.107 What is potential for success?

The applicant concern must possess reasonable prospects for success in competing in the private sector if admitted to the 8(a) BD program. To do so, it must be in business in its primary industry classification for at least two full years immediately prior to the date of its 8(a) BD application, unless a waiver for this requirement is granted pursuant to paragraph (b) of this section.

(a) Income tax returns for each of the two previous tax years must show operating revenues in the primary industry in which the applicant is seeking 8(a) BD certification.

(b)(1) SBA may waive the two years in business requirement if each of the following five conditions are met:

(i) The individual or individuals upon whom eligibility is based have substantial business management experience;

(ii) The applicant has demonstrated technical experience to carry out its business plan with a substantial likelihood for success if admitted to the 8(a) BD program;

(iii) The applicant has adequate capital to sustain its operations and carry out its business plan as a Participant;

(iv) The applicant has a record of successful performance on contracts from governmental or nongovernmental sources in its primary industry category; and

(v) The applicant has, or can demonstrate its ability to timely obtain, the personnel, facilities, equipment, and any other requirements needed to perform contracts as a Participant.

(2) The concern seeking a waiver under paragraph (b) must provide information on governmental and nongovernmental contracts in progress and completed (including letters of reference) in order to establish successful contract performance, and must demonstrate how it otherwise meets the five conditions for waiver. SBA considers an applicant's performance on both government and private sector contracts in determining whether the firm has an overall successful performance record. If, however, the applicant has performed only government contracts or only private sector contracts, SBA will review its performance on those contracts alone to determine whether the applicant possesses a record of successful performance.

(c) In assessing potential for success, SBA considers the concern's access to credit and capital, including, but not limited to, access to long-term financing, access to working capital financing, equipment trade credit, access to raw materials and supplier trade credit, and bonding capability.

(d) In assessing potential for success, SBA will also consider the technical and managerial experience of the applicant concern's managers, the operating history of the concern, the concern's record of performance on previous Federal and private sector contracts in the primary industry in which the concern is seeking 8(a) BD certification, and its financial capacity. The applicant concern as a whole must demonstrate both technical knowledge in its primary industry category and management experience sufficient to run its day-to-day operations.

(e) The Participant or individuals employed by the Participant must hold all requisite licenses if the concern is engaged in an industry requiring professional licensing (e.g., public accountancy, law, professional engineering).

(f) An applicant will not be denied admission into the 8(a) BD program due solely to a determination that potential 8(a) contract opportunities are unavailable to assist in the development of the concern unless:

(1) The Government has not previously procured and is unlikely to procure the types of products or services offered by the concern; or

(2) The purchase of such products or services by the Federal Government will not be in quantities sufficient to support the developmental needs of the applicant and other Participants providing the same or similar items or services.

§ 124.108 What other eligibility requirements apply for individuals or businesses?

(a) *Good character.* The applicant or Participant and all its principals must have good character.

(1) If during the processing of an application, SBA receives adverse information from the applicant or a credible source regarding possible criminal conduct by the applicant or any of its principals, SBA may suspend further processing of the application and refer it to SBA's Office of Inspector General (OIG) for review. If the SBA suspends the application, but does not hear back from OIG within 45 days, SBA may proceed with application processing. The AA/BD will consider any findings of the OIG when evaluating the application.

(2) Violations of any of SBA's regulations may result in denial of participation in the 8(a) BD program. The AA/BD will consider the nature and severity of the violation in making an eligibility determination.

(3) Debarred or suspended concerns or concerns owned by debarred or suspended persons are ineligible for admission to the 8(a) BD program.

(4) An applicant is ineligible for admission to the 8(a) BD program if the applicant concern or a proprietor, partner, limited liability member, director, officer, or holder of at least 20 percent of its stock, or another person (including key employees) with significant authority over the concern:

(i) Lacks business integrity as demonstrated by information related to an indictment or guilty plea, conviction, civil judgment, or settlement; or

(ii) Is currently incarcerated, or on parole or probation pursuant to a pre-trial diversion or following conviction for a felony or any crime involving business integrity.

(5) If, during the processing of an application, SBA determines that an applicant has knowingly submitted false information, regardless of whether correct information would cause SBA to deny the application, and regardless of whether correct information was given to SBA in accompanying documents, SBA will deny the application. If, after admission to the program, SBA discovers that false information has been knowingly submitted by a firm, SBA will initiate termination proceedings and suspend the firm under §§ 124.304 and 124.305. Whenever SBA determines that the applicant submitted false information, the matter will be referred to SBA's Office of Inspector General for review.

(b) *One-time eligibility.* Once a concern or disadvantaged individual upon whom eligibility was based has participated in the 8(a) BD program, neither the concern nor that individual will be eligible again.

(1) An individual who claims disadvantage and completes the appropriate SBA forms to qualify an applicant has participated in the 8(a) BD program if SBA approves the application.

(2) Use of eligibility will take effect on the date of the concern's approval for admission into the program.

(3) An individual who uses his or her one-time eligibility to qualify a concern for the 8(a) BD program will be

considered a non-disadvantaged individual for ownership or control purposes of another applicant or Participant. The criteria restricting participation by non-disadvantaged individuals will apply to such an individual. *See* §§ 124.105 and 124.106.

(4) When at least 50% of the assets of a concern are the same as those of a former Participant, the concern will not be eligible for entry into the program.

(5) Participants which change their form of business organization and transfer their assets and liabilities to the new organization may do so without affecting the eligibility of the new organization provided the previous business is dissolved and all other eligibility criteria are met. In such a case, the new organization may complete the remaining program term of the previous organization. A request for a change in business form will be treated as a change of ownership under § 124.105(i).

(c) *Wholesalers.* An applicant concern seeking admission to the 8(a) BD program as a wholesaler need not demonstrate that it is capable of meeting the requirements of the nonmanufacturer rule for its primary industry classification.

(d) *Brokers.* Brokers are ineligible to participate in the 8(a) BD program. A broker is a concern that adds no material value to an item being supplied to a procuring activity or which does not take ownership or possession of or handle the item being procured with its own equipment or facilities.

(e) *Federal financial obligations.* Neither a firm nor any of its principals that fails to pay significant financial obligations owed to the Federal Government, including unresolved tax liens and defaults on Federal loans or other Federally assisted financing, is eligible for admission to or participation in the 8(a) BD program.

[63 FR 35739, 35772, June 30, 1998, as amended at 74 FR 45753, Sept. 4, 2009; 76 FR 8255, Feb. 11, 2011; 81 FR 48580, July 25, 2016]

§ 124.109 Do Indian tribes and Alaska Native Corporations have any special rules for applying to the 8(a) BD program?

(a) *Special rules for ANCs.* Small business concerns owned and controlled by ANCs are eligible for participation in the 8(a) program and must meet the eligibility criteria set forth in § 124.112 to the extent the criteria are not inconsistent with this section. ANC-owned concerns are subject to the same conditions that apply to tribally-owned concerns, as described in paragraphs (b) and (c) of this section, except that the following provisions and exceptions apply only to ANC-owned concerns:

(1) Alaska Natives and descendants of Natives must own a majority of both the total equity of the ANC and the total voting powers to elect directors of the ANC through their holdings of settlement common stock. Settlement common stock means stock of an ANC issued pursuant to 43 U.S.C. 1606(g)(1), which is subject to the rights and restrictions listed in 43 U.S.C. 1606(h)(1).

(2) An ANC that meets the requirements set forth in paragraph (a)(1) of this section is deemed economically disadvantaged under 43 U.S.C. 1626(e), and need not establish economic disadvantage as required by paragraph (b)(2) of this section.

(3) Even though an ANC can be either for profit or non-profit, a small business concern owned and controlled by an ANC must be for profit to be eligible for the 8(a) program. The concern will be deemed owned and controlled by the ANC where both the majority of stock or other ownership interest and total voting power are held by the ANC and holders of its settlement common stock.

(4) The Alaska Native Claims Settlement Act provides that a concern which is majority owned by an ANC shall be deemed to be both owned and controlled by Alaska Natives and an economically disadvantaged business. Therefore, an individual responsible for control and management of an ANC-owned applicant or Participant need not establish personal social and economic disadvantage.

(5) Paragraphs (b)(3)(i), (ii) and (iv) of this section are not applicable to an ANC, provided its status as an ANC is

clearly shown in its articles of incorporation.

(6) Paragraph (c)(1) of this section is not applicable to an ANC-owned concern to the extent it requires an express waiver of sovereign immunity or a "sue and be sued" clause.

(b) *Tribal eligibility.* In order to qualify a concern which it owns and controls for participation in the 8(a) BD program, an Indian Tribe must establish its own economic disadvantaged status under paragraph (b)(2) of this section. Once an Indian Tribe establishes that it is economically disadvantaged in connection with the application for one Tribally-owned firm, it need not reestablish such status in order to have other businesses that it owns certified for 8(a) BD program participation, unless specifically requested to do so by the AA/BD. An Indian Tribe may request to meet with SBA prior to submitting an application for 8(a) BD participation for its first applicant firm to better understand what SBA requires for it to establish economic disadvantage. Each Tribally-owned concern seeking to be certified for 8(a) BD participation must comply with the provisions of paragraph (c) of this section.

(1) *Social disadvantage.* An Indian tribe as defined in § 124.3 is considered to be socially disadvantaged.

(2) *Economic disadvantage.* In order to be eligible to participate in the 8(a) BD program, the Indian tribe must demonstrate to SBA that the tribe itself is economically disadvantaged. This must involve the consideration of available data showing the tribe's economic condition, including but not limited to, the following information:

(i) The number of tribal members.

(ii) The present tribal unemployment rate.

(iii) The per capita income of tribal members, excluding judgment awards.

(iv) The percentage of the local Indian population below the poverty level.

(v) The tribe's access to capital.

(vi) The tribal assets as disclosed in a current tribal financial statement. The statement must list all assets including those which are encumbered or held in trust, but the status of those encumbered or in trust must be clearly delineated.

(vii) A list of all wholly or partially owned tribal enterprises or affiliates and the primary industry classification of each. The list must also specify the members of the tribe who manage or control such enterprises by serving as officers or directors.

(3) *Forms and documents required to be submitted.* Except as otherwise provided in this section, the Indian tribe generally must submit the forms and documents required of 8(a) BD applicants as well as the following material:

(i) A copy of all governing documents such as the tribe's constitution or business charter.

(ii) Evidence of its recognition as a tribe eligible for the special programs and services provided by the United States or by its state of residence.

(iii) Copies of its articles of incorporation and bylaws as filed with the organizing or chartering authority, or similar documents needed to establish and govern a non-corporate legal entity.

(iv) Documents or materials needed to show the tribe's economically disadvantaged status as described in paragraph (b)(2) of this section.

(c) *Business eligibility.* In order to be eligible to participate in the 8(a) BD program, a concern which is owned by an eligible Indian tribe (or wholly owned business entities of such tribe) must meet the conditions set forth in paragraphs (c)(1) through (c)(7) of this section.

(1) *Legal business entity organized for profit and susceptible to suit.* The applicant or participating concern must be a separate and distinct legal entity organized or chartered by the tribe, or Federal or state authorities. The concern's articles of incorporation, partnership agreement or limited liability company articles of organization must contain express sovereign immunity waiver language, or a "sue and be sued" clause which designates United States Federal Courts to be among the courts of competent jurisdiction for all matters relating to SBA's programs including, but not limited to, 8(a) BD program participation, loans, and contract performance. Also, the concern must be organized for profit, and the

tribe must possess economic development powers in the tribe's governing documents.

(2) *Size.* (i) A tribally-owned applicant concern must qualify as a small business concern as defined for purposes of Federal Government procurement in part 121 of this title. The particular size standard to be applied is based on the primary industry classification of the applicant concern.

(ii) A tribally-owned Participant must certify to SBA that it is a small business pursuant to the provisions of part 121 of this title for the purpose of performing each individual contract which it is awarded.

(iii) In determining the size of a small business concern owned by a socially and economically disadvantaged Indian tribe (or a wholly owned business entity of such tribe) for either 8(a) BD program entry or contract award, the firm's size shall be determined independently without regard to its affiliation with the tribe, any entity of the tribal government, or any other business enterprise owned by the tribe, unless the Administrator determines that one or more such tribally-owned business concerns have obtained, or are likely to obtain, a substantial unfair competitive advantage within an industry category.

(iv) In determining whether a tribally-owned concern has obtained, or is likely to obtain, a substantial unfair competitive advantage within an industry category, SBA will examine the firm's participation in the relevant six digit NAICS code nationally as compared to the overall small business share of that industry.

(A) SBA will consider the firm's percentage share of the national market and other relevant factors to determine whether the firm is dominant in a specific six-digit NAICS code with a particular size standard.

(B) SBA does not contemplate a finding of affiliation where a tribally-owned concern appears to have obtained an unfair competitive advantage in a local market, but remains competitive, but not dominant, on a national basis.

(3) *Ownership.* (i) For corporate entities, a Tribe must unconditionally own at least 51 percent of the voting stock and at least 51 percent of the aggregate of all classes of stock. For non-corporate entities, a Tribe must unconditionally own at least a 51 percent interest.

(ii) A Tribe may not own 51% or more of another firm which, either at the time of application or within the previous two years, has been operating in the 8(a) program under the same primary NAICS code as the applicant. A Tribe may, however, own a Participant or other applicant that conducts or will conduct secondary business in the 8(a) BD program under the NAICS code which is the primary NAICS code of the applicant concern. In addition, once an applicant is admitted to the 8(a) BD program, it may not receive an 8(a) sole source contract that is a follow-on contract to an 8(a) contract that was performed immediately previously by another Participant (or former Participant) owned by the same Tribe. For purposes of this paragraph, the same primary NAICS code means the six digit NAICS code having the same corresponding size standard.

(iii) The restrictions of §124.105(h) do not apply to tribes; they do, however, apply to non disadvantaged individuals or other business concerns that are partial owners of a tribally-owned concern.

(4) *Control and management.* (i) The management and daily business operations of a Tribally-owned concern must be controlled by the Tribe. The Tribally-owned concern may be controlled by the Tribe through one or more individuals who possess sufficient management experience of an extent and complexity needed to run the concern, or through management as follows:

(A) Management may be provided by committees, teams, or Boards of Directors which are controlled by one or more members of an economically disadvantaged tribe, or

(B) Management may be provided by non-Tribal members if the concern can demonstrate that the Tribe can hire and fire those individuals, that it will retain control of all management decisions common to boards of directors, including strategic planning, budget approval, and the employment and compensation of officers, and that a written management development plan exists which shows how Tribal members will develop managerial skills sufficient to manage the concern or similar Tribally-owned concerns in the future.

(ii) Members of the management team, business committee members, officers, and directors are precluded from engaging in any outside employment or other business interests which conflict with the management of the concern or prevent the concern from achieving the objectives set forth in its business development plan. This is not intended to preclude participation in tribal or other activities which do not interfere with such individual's responsibilities in the operation of the applicant concern.

(iii) The individuals responsible for the management and daily operations of a tribally-owned concern cannot manage more than two Program Participants at the same time.

(A) An individual's officer position, membership on the board of directors or position as a tribal leader does not necessarily imply that the individual is responsible for the management and daily operations of a given concern. SBA looks beyond these corporate formalities and examines the totality of the information submitted by the applicant to determine which individual(s) manage the actual day-to-day operations of the applicant concern.

(B) Officers, board members, and/or tribal leaders may control a holding company overseeing several tribally-owned or ANC-owned companies, provided they do not actually control the day-to-day management of more than two current 8(a) BD Program Participant firms.

(5) *Individual eligibility limitation.* SBA does not deem an individual involved in the management or daily business operations of a tribally-owned concern to have used his or her individual eligibility within the meaning of § 124.108(b).

(6) *Potential for success.* A Tribally-owned applicant concern must possess reasonable prospects for success in competing in the private sector if admitted to the 8(a) BD program. A Tribally-owned applicant may establish potential for success by demonstrating that:

(i) It has been in business for at least two years, as evidenced by income tax returns (individual or consolidated) for each of the two previous tax years showing operating revenues in the primary industry in which the applicant is seeking 8(a) BD certification; or

(ii) The individual(s) who will manage and control the daily business operations of the firm have substantial technical and management experience, the applicant has a record of successful performance on contracts from governmental or nongovernmental sources in its primary industry category, and the applicant has adequate capital to sustain its operations and carry out its business plan as a Participant; or

(iii) The Tribe has made a firm written commitment to support the operations of the applicant concern and it has the financial ability to do so.

(7) *Other eligibility criteria.* (i) As with other 8(a) applicants, a tribally-owned applicant concern shall not be denied admission into the 8(a) program due solely to a determination that specific contract opportunities are unavailable to assist the development of the concern unless:

(A) The Government has not previously procured and is unlikely to procure the types of products or services offered by the concern; or

(B) The purchase of such products or services by the Federal Government will not be in quantities sufficient to support the developmental needs of the applicant and other program participants providing the same or similar items or services.

(ii) Except for the tribe itself, the concern's officers, directors, and all shareholders owning an interest of 20% or more must demonstrate good character. *See* § 124.108(a).

[63 FR 35739, June 30, 1998, as amended at 74 FR 45753, Sept. 4, 2009; 76 FR 8255, Feb. 11, 2011; 81 FR 48580, July 25, 2016]

§ 124.110 Do Native Hawaiian Organizations have any special rules for applying to the 8(a) BD program?

(a) Concerns owned by economically disadvantaged Native Hawaiian Organizations, as defined in § 124.3, are eligible for participation in the 8(a) program and other federal programs requiring SBA to determine social and economic disadvantage as a condition of eligibility. Such concerns must meet all eligibility criteria set forth in §§ 124.101 through 124.108 and § 124.112 to the extent that they are not inconsistent with this section.

(b) A concern owned by a Native Hawaiian Organization must qualify as a small business concern as defined in part 121 of this title. The size standard corresponding to the primary industry classification of the applicant concern applies for determining size. SBA will determine the concern's size independently, without regard to its affiliation with the Native Hawaiian Organization or any other business enterprise owned by the Native Hawaiian Organization, unless the Administrator determines that one or more such concerns owned by the Native Hawaiian Organization have obtained, or are likely to obtain, a substantial unfair competitive advantage within an industry category. In determining whether an NHO-owned concern has obtained, or is likely to obtain, a substantial unfair competitive advantage within an industry category, SBA will examine the firm's participation in the relevant six digit NAICS code nationally.

(1) SBA will consider the firm's percentage share of the national market and other relevant factors to determine whether the firm is dominant in a specific six-digit NAICS code with a particular size standard.

(2) SBA does not contemplate a finding of affiliation where an NHO-owned concern appears to have obtained an unfair competitive advantage in a local market, but remains competitive, but not dominant, on a national basis.

(c) An NHO must establish that it is economically disadvantaged and that its business activities will principally benefit Native Hawaiians. Once an NHO establishes that it is economically disadvantaged in connection with the application of one NHO-owned firm, it need not reestablish such status in order to have other businesses that it owns certified for 8(a) BD program participation, unless specifically requested to do so by the AA/BD. If a different NHO identifies that it will serve and benefit the same Native Hawaiian community as an NHO that has already established its economic disadvantage status, that NHO need not establish its economic disadvantage status in connection with an 8(a) BD application of a business concern that it owns, unless specifically requested to do so by the AA/BD.

(1) In order to establish that an NHO is economically disadvantaged, it must demonstrate that it will principally benefit economically disadvantaged Native Hawaiians. To do this, the NHO must provide data showing the economic condition of the Native Hawaiian community that it intends to serve, including:

(i) The number of Native Hawaiians in the community that the NHO intends to serve;

(ii) The present Native Hawaiian unemployment rate of those individuals;

(iii) The per capita income of those Native Hawaiians, excluding judgment awards;

(iv) The percentage of those Native Hawaiians below the poverty level; and

(v) The access to capital of those Native Hawaiians.

(2) An NHO should describe any activities that it has done to benefit Native Hawaiians at the time its NHO-owned firm applies to the 8(a) BD program. In addition, the NHO must include statements in its bylaws or operating agreements identifying the benefits Native Hawaiians will receive from the NHO. The NHO must have a detailed plan that shows how revenue earned by the NHO will principally benefit Native Hawaiians. As part of an annual review conducted for an NHO-owned Participant, SBA will review how the NHO is fulfilling its obligation to principally benefit Native Hawaiians.

(d) An NHO must control the applicant or Participant firm. To establish that it is controlled by an NHO, an applicant or Participant must demonstrate that the NHO controls its board of directors, managing members, managers or managing partners.

(1) The NHO need not possess the technical expertise necessary to run the NHO-owned applicant or Participant firm. The NHO must have managerial experience of the extent and complexity needed to run the concern.

Management experience need not be related to the same or similar industry as the primary industry classification of the applicant or Participant.

(2) An individual responsible for the day-to-day management of an NHO-owned firm need not establish personal social and economic disadvantage.

(e) A Native Hawaiian Organization cannot own 51% or more of another firm which, either at the time of application or within the previous two years, has been operating in the 8(a) program under the same primary NAICS code as the applicant. A Native Hawaiian Organization may, however, own a Participant or an applicant that conducts or will conduct secondary business in the 8(a) BD program under the same NAICS code that a current Participant owned by the Native Hawaiian Organization operates in the 8(a) BD program as its primary NAICS code. In addition, once an applicant is admitted to the 8(a) BD program, it may not receive an 8(a) sole source contract that is a follow-on contract to an 8(a) contract that was performed immediately previously by another Participant (or former Participant) owned by the same Native Hawaiian Organization. For purposes of this paragraph, the same primary NAICS code means the six digit NAICS code having the same corresponding size standard.

(f) SBA does not deem an individual involved in the management or daily business operations of a Participant owned by a Native Hawaiian Organization to have used his or her individual eligibility within the meaning of §124.108(b).

(g) An NHO-owned firm's eligibility for 8(a) BD participation is separate and distinct from the individual eligibility of the NHO's members, directors, or managers. The eligibility of an NHO-owned concern is not affected by the former 8(a) BD participation of one or more of the NHO's individual members.

(h) An applicant concern owned by a NHO must possess reasonable prospects for success in competing in the private sector if admitted to the 8(a) BD program. An applicant concern owned by a NHO may establish potential for success by demonstrating that:

(1) It has been in business for at least two years, as evidenced by income tax returns (individual or consolidated) for each of the two previous tax years showing operating revenues in the primary industry in with the applicant is seeking 8(a) BD certification; or

(2) The individual(s) who will manage and control the daily business operations of the firm have substantial technical and management experience, the applicant has a record of successful performance on contracts from governmental or nongovernmental sources in its primary industry category, and the applicant has adequate capital to sustain its operations and carry out its business plan as a Participant; or

(3) The NHO has made a firm written commitment to support the operations of the applicant concern and it has the financial ability to do so.

[63 FR 35739, June 30, 1998, as amended at 76 FR 8256, Feb. 11, 2011; 77 FR 28237, May 14, 2012; 81 FR 48580, July 25, 2016; 81 FR 71983, Oct. 19, 2016]

§124.111 Do Community Development Corporations (CDCs) have any special rules for applying to the 8(a) BD program?

(a) Concerns owned at least 51 percent by CDCs (or a wholly owned business entity of a CDC) are eligible for participation in the 8(a) BD program and other federal programs requiring SBA to determine social and economic disadvantage as a condition of eligibility. These concerns must meet all eligibility criteria set forth in §124.101 through §124.108 and §124.112 to the extent that they are not inconsistent with this section.

(b) A concern that is at least 51 percent owned by a CDC (or a wholly owned business entity of a CDC) is considered to be controlled by such CDC and eligible for participation in the 8(a) BD program, provided it meets all eligibility criteria set forth or referred to in this section and its management and daily business operations are conducted by one or more individuals determined to have managerial experience of an extent and complexity needed to run the concern.

(c) A concern that is at least 51 percent owned by a CDC (or a wholly owned business entity of a CDC) must qualify as a small business concern as defined in part 121 of this title. The size standard corresponding to the primary industry classification of the applicant concern applies for determining size. SBA will determine the concern's size independently, without regard to its affiliation with the CDC or any other business enterprise owned by the CDC, unless the Administrator determines that one or more such concerns owned by the CDC have obtained, or are likely to obtain, a substantial unfair competitive advantage within an industry category. In determining whether a CDC-owned concern has obtained, or is likely to obtain, a substantial unfair competitive advantage within an industry category, SBA will examine the firm's participation in the relevant six digit NAICS code nationally.

(1) SBA will consider the firm's percentage share of the national market and other relevant factors to determine whether the firm is dominant in a specific six-digit NAICS code with a particular size standard.

(2) SBA does not contemplate a finding of affiliation where a CDC-owned concern appears to have obtained an unfair competitive advantage in a local market, but remains competitive, but not dominant, on a national basis.

(d) A CDC cannot own 51% or more of another firm which, either at the time of application or within the previous two years, has been operating in the 8(a) program under the same primary NAICS code as the applicant. A CDC may, however, own a Participant or an applicant that conducts or will conduct secondary business in the 8(a) BD program under the same NAICS code that a current Participant owned by the CDC operates in the 8(a) BD program as its primary SIC code. In addition, once an applicant is admitted to the 8(a) BD program, it may not receive an 8(a) sole source contract that is a follow-on contract to an 8(a) contract that was performed immediately previously by another Participant (or former Participant) owned by the same CDC. For purposes of this paragraph, the same primary NAICS code means the six digit NAICS code having the same corresponding size standard.

(e) SBA does not deem an individual involved in the management or daily business operations of a CDC-owned concern to have used his or her individual eligibility within the meaning of § 124.108(b).

(f) An applicant concern owned by a CDC must possess reasonable prospects for success in competing in the private sector if admitted to the 8(a) BD program. An applicant concern owned by a CDC may establish potential for success by demonstrating that:

(1) It has been in business for at least two years, as evidenced by income tax returns (individual or consolidated) for each of the two previous tax years showing operating revenues in the primary industry in with the applicant is seeking 8(a) BD certification; or

(2) The individual(s) who will manage and control the daily business operations of the firm have substantial technical and management experience, the applicant has a record of successful performance on contracts from governmental or nongovernmental sources in its primary industry category, and the applicant has adequate capital to sustain its operations and carry out its business plan as a Participant; or

(3) The CDC has made a firm written commitment to support the operations of the applicant concern and it has the financial ability to do so.

(g) A CDC-owned applicant and all of its principals must have good character as set forth in § 124.108(a).

[63 FR 35739, June 30, 1998, as amended at 76 FR 8257, Feb. 11, 2011; 77 FR 28237, May 14, 2012; 81 FR 48581, July 25, 2016]

§ 124.112 What criteria must a business meet to remain eligible to participate in the 8(a) BD program?

(a) *Standards.* In order for a concern (except those owned by Indian tribes, ANCs, Native Hawaiian Organizations or CDCs) to remain eligible for 8(a) BD program participation, it must continue to meet all eligibility criteria contained in § 124.101 through § 124.108. For concerns owned by Indian tribes, ANCs, Native Hawaiian Organizations or CDCs to remain eligible, they must meet the criteria set forth in this § 124.112 to the extent that they are not inconsistent with § 124.109, § 124.110 and § 124.111, respectively. The concern must inform SBA in writing of any changes in circumstances which would adversely affect its program eligibility, especially economic disadvantage and ownership and control. Any concern that fails to meet the eligibility requirements after being admitted to the program will be subject to termination or early graduation under §§ 124.302 through 124.304, as appropriate.

(b) *Submissions supporting continued eligibility.* As part of an annual review, each Participant must annually submit to the servicing district office the following:

(1) A certification that it meets the 8(a) BD program eligibility requirements as set forth in § 124.101 through § 124.108 and paragraph (a) of this section;

(2) A certification that there have been no changed circumstances which could adversely affect the Participant's program eligibility. If the Participant is unable to provide such certification, the Participant must inform SBA of any changes and provide relevant supporting documentation.

(3) Personal financial information for each disadvantaged owner;

(4) A record from each individual claiming disadvantaged status regarding the transfer of assets for less than fair market value to any immediate family member, or to a trust any beneficiary of which is an immediate family member, within two years of the date of the annual review. The record must provide the name of the recipient(s) and family relationship, and the difference between the fair market value of the asset transferred and the value received by the disadvantaged individual.

(5) A record of all payments, compensation, and distributions (including loans, advances, salaries and dividends) made by the Participant to each of its owners, officers or directors, or to any person or entity affiliated with such individuals;

(6) If it is an approved protégé, a narrative report detailing the contracts it has had with its mentor and benefits it has received from the mentor/protégé relationship. See § 124.520(b)(4) for additional annual requirements;

(7) A listing of any fees paid to agents or representatives to assist the Participant in obtaining or seeking to obtain a Federal contract;

(8) A report for each 8(a) contract performed during the year explaining how the performance of work requirements are being met for the contract, including any 8(a) contracts performed as a joint venture; and

(9) Such other information as SBA may deem necessary. For other required annual submissions, *see* §§ 124.601 through 124.603.

(c) *Eligibility reviews.* (1) Upon receipt of specific and credible information alleging that a Participant no longer meets the eligibility requirements for continued program eligibility, SBA will review the concern's eligibility for continued participation in the program.

(2) Sufficient reasons for SBA to conclude that a socially disadvantaged individual is no longer economically disadvantaged include, but are not limited to, excessive withdrawals of funds or other assets withdrawn from the concern by its owners, or substantial personal assets, income or net worth of any disadvantaged owner. SBA may also consider access by the Participant firm to a significant new source of capital or loans since the financial condition of the Participant is considered in evaluating the disadvantaged individual's economic status.

(d) *Excessive withdrawals.* (1) The term withdrawal includes, but is not limited to, the following: Cash dividends; distributions in excess of amounts needed to pay S Corporation, LLC or partnership taxes; cash and property withdrawals; payments to immediate family members not employed by the Participant; bonuses to officers; and investments on behalf of an owner. Although officers' salaries are generally not considered withdrawals for purposes of this paragraph, SBA will count those salaries as withdrawals where SBA believes that a firm is attempting to circumvent the excessive withdrawal limitations through the payment of officers' salaries. SBA will look at the totality of the circumstances in determining whether to include any specific amount as a withdrawal under this paragraph.

(2) If SBA determines that funds or assets have been excessively withdrawn from the Participant for the personal

benefit of one or more owners or managers, or any person or entity affiliated with such owners or managers, and such withdrawal was detrimental to the achievement of the targets, objectives, and goals contained in the Participant's business plan, SBA may:

(i) Initiate termination proceedings under §§ 124.303 and 124.304 where the withdrawals detrimentally affect the achievement of the Participant's targets, objectives and goals set forth in its business plan, or its overall business development;

(ii) Initiate early graduation proceedings under §§ 124.302 and 124.303 where the withdrawals do not adversely affect the Participant's business development; or

(iii) Require an appropriate reinvestment of funds or other assets, as well as any other actions SBA deems necessary to counteract the detrimental effects of the withdrawals, as a condition of the Participant maintaining program eligibility.

(3) Withdrawals are excessive if in the aggregate during any fiscal year of the Participant they exceed (i) $250,000 for firms with sales up to $1,000,000; (ii) $300,000 for firms with sales between $1,000,000 and $2,000,000; and (iii) $400,000 for firms with sales exceeding $2,000,000.

(4) The fact that a concern's net worth has increased despite withdrawals that are deemed excessive will not preclude SBA from determining that such withdrawals were detrimental to the attainment of the concern's business objectives or to its overall business development.

(5) The excessive withdrawal analysis does not apply to Participants owned by Tribes, ANCs, NHOs, or CDCs where a withdrawal is made for the benefit of the Tribe, ANC, NHO, CDC or the native or shareholder community. It does, however, apply to withdrawals from a firm owned by a Tribe, ANC, NHO, or CDC that do not benefit the relevant entity or community. Thus, if funds or assets are withdrawn from an entity-owned Participant for the benefit of a non-disadvantaged manager or owner that exceed the withdrawal thresholds, SBA may find that withdrawal to be excessive. For example, a $1,000,000 payout to a non-disadvantaged manager would be deemed an excessive withdrawal.

(e) *Change in primary industry classification.* (1) A Participant may request that the primary industry classification contained in its business plan be changed by filing such a request with its servicing SBA district office. SBA will grant such a request where the Participant can demonstrate that the majority of its total revenues during a three-year period have evolved from one NAICS code to another.

(2) SBA may change the primary industry classification contained in a Participant's business plan where the greatest portion of the Participant's total revenues during the Participant's last three completed fiscal years has evolved from one NAICS code to another. As part of its annual review, SBA will consider whether the primary NAICS code contained in a Participant's business plan continues to be appropriate.

(i) Where SBA believes that the primary industry classification contained in a Participant's business plan does not match the Participant's actual revenues over the Participant's most recently completed three fiscal years, SBA may notify the Participant of its intent to change the Participant's primary industry classification and afford the Participant the opportunity to respond.

(ii) A Participant may challenge SBA's intent to change its primary industry classification by demonstrating why it believes the primary industry classification contained in its business plan continues to be appropriate, despite an increase in revenues in a secondary NAICS code beyond those received in its designated primary industry classification. The Participant should identify: All non-federal work that it has performed in its primary NAICS code; any efforts it has made and any plans it has to make to receive contracts to obtain contracts in its primary NAICS code; all contracts that it was awarded that it believes could have been classified under its primary NAICS code, but which a contracting officer assigned another reasonable NAICS code; and any other information that it believes has a bearing on why its primary NAICS code should not be changed despite performing more work in another NAICS code.

(iii) As long as the Participant provides a reasonable explanation as to why the identified primary NAICS code continues to be its primary NAICS code, SBA will not change the Participant's primary NAICS code.

(iv) Where an SBA change in the primary NAICS code of an entity-owned firm results in the entity having two Participants with the same primary NAICS code, the second, newer Participant will not be able to receive any 8(a) contracts in the six-digit NAICS code that is the primary NAICS code of the first, older Participant for a period of time equal to two years after the first Participant leaves the 8(a) BD program.

(f) *Graduation determination.* As part of the final annual review performed by SBA prior to the expiration of a Participant's nine-year program term, SBA will determine if the Participant has met the targets, objectives and goals set forth in its business plan and, thus, whether the Participant will be considered to have graduated from the 8(a) BD program at the expiration of its program term. A firm that has not met the targets, objectives and goals set forth in its business plan at the end of its nine-year term in the 8(a) BD program will not be considered to have graduated from the 8(a) BD program, but rather to have merely completed its program term.

[63 FR 35739, June 30, 1998, as amended at 76 FR 8257, Feb. 11, 2011; 77 FR 28237, May 14, 2012; 81 FR 48581, July 25, 2016; 81 FR 71983, Oct. 19, 2016]

APPLYING TO THE 8(a) BD PROGRAM

§ 124.201 May any business submit an application?

Any concern or any individual on behalf of a business has the right to apply for 8(a) BD program participation whether or not there is an appearance of eligibility.

§ 124.202 How must an application be filed?

An application for 8(a) BD program admission must be filed in an electronic format. An electronic application can be found by going to the 8(a) BD page of SBA's Web site (*http://www.sba.gov*). The SBA district office will provide an applicant with information regarding the 8(a) BD program.

[81 FR 48581, July 25, 2016]

§ 124.203 What must a concern submit to apply to the 8(a) BD program?

Each 8(a) BD applicant concern must submit those forms and attachments required by SBA when applying for admission to the 8(a) BD program. These forms and attachments may include, but not be limited to, financial statements, copies of signed Federal personal and business tax returns, individual and business bank statements, personal history statements, and any additional documents SBA deems necessary to determine eligibility. In all cases, the applicant must provide a signature from each individual claiming social and economic disadvantage status. The electronic signing protocol will ensure the Agency is able to specifically identify the individual making the representation. The individual(s) upon whom eligibility is based take responsibility for the accuracy of all information submitted on behalf of the applicant.

[81 FR 48581, July 25, 2016]

§ 124.204 How does SBA process applications for 8(a) BD program admission?

(a) The AA/BD is authorized to approve or decline applications for admission to the 8(a) BD program. The DPCE will receive, review and evaluate all 8(a) BD applications. SBA will advise each program applicant within 15 days after the receipt of an application whether the application is complete and suitable for evaluation and, if not, what additional information or clarification is required to complete the application. SBA will process an application for 8(a) BD program participation within 90 days of receipt of a complete application package by the DPCE. Incomplete packages will not be processed.

(b) SBA, in its sole discretion, may request clarification of information contained in the application at any time in the application process. SBA will take into account any clarifications made by an applicant in response to a request for such by SBA.

(c) The burden of proof to demonstrate eligibility is on the applicant concern. If a concern does not provide requested information within the allotted time provided by SBA, or if it submits incomplete information, SBA may presume that disclosure of the missing information would adversely affect the firm or would demonstrate lack of eligibility in the area to which the information relates.

(d) An applicant must be eligible as of the date the AA/BD issues a decision. The decision will be based on the facts set forth in the application, any information received in response to SBA's request for clarification made pursuant to paragraph (b) of this section, and any changed circumstances since the date of application.

(e) Changed circumstances for an applicant concern occurring subsequent to its application and which adversely affect eligibility will be considered and may constitute grounds for decline. The applicant must inform SBA of any changed circumstances that could adversely affect its eligibility for the program (particularly economic disadvantage and ownership and control) during its application review. Failure to inform SBA of any such changed circumstances constitutes good cause for which SBA may terminate the Participant if non-compliance is discovered after admittance.

(f) The decision of the AA/BD to approve or deny an application will be in writing. A decision to deny admission will state the specific reasons for denial, and will inform the applicant of any appeal rights.

(g) If the AA/BD approves the application, the date of the approval letter is the date of program certification for purposes of determining the concern's program term.

[63 FR 35739, June 30, 1998, as amended at 74 FR 45753, Sept. 4, 2009; 76 FR 8258, Feb. 11, 2011]

§ 124.205 Can an applicant ask SBA to reconsider SBA's initial decision to decline its application?

(a) An applicant may request the AA/BD to reconsider his or her initial decline decision by filing a request for reconsideration with SBA. The applicant may submit a revised electronic application or submit its request for reconsideration to the SBA DPCE unit that originally processed its application by personal delivery, first class mail, express mail, facsimile transmission followed by first class mail, or commercial delivery service. The applicant must submit its request for reconsideration within 45 days of its receipt of written notice that its application was declined. If the date of actual receipt of such written notice cannot be determined, SBA will presume receipt to have occurred ten calendar days after the date the notice was sent to the applicant. The applicant must provide any additional information and documentation pertinent to overcoming the reason(s) for the initial decline, whether or not available at the time of initial application, including information and documentation regarding changed circumstances.

(b) The AA/BD will issue a written decision within 45 days of SBA's receipt of the applicant's request. The AA/BD may either approve the application, deny it on the same grounds as the original decision, or deny it on other grounds. If denied, the AA/BD will explain why the applicant is not eligible for admission to the 8(a) BD program and give specific reasons for the decline.

(c) If the AA/BD declines the application solely on issues not raised in the initial decline, the applicant can ask for reconsideration as if it were an initial decline.

[63 FR 35739, June 30, 1998, as amended at 74 FR 45753, Sept. 4, 2009; 76 FR 8258, Feb. 11, 2011]

§ 124.206 What appeal rights are available to an applicant that has been denied admission?

(a) An applicant may appeal a denial of program admission to SBA's Office of Hearings and Appeals (OHA), if it is based solely on a negative finding of social disadvantage, economic disadvantage, ownership, control, or any combination of these four criteria. A denial decision that is based at least in part on the failure to meet any other eligibility criterion is not appealable and is the final decision of SBA.

(b) The applicant may appeal an initial decision of the AA/BD without requesting reconsideration, or may appeal the decision of the AA/BD on reconsideration.

(c) The applicant may initiate an appeal by filing a petition in accordance with part 134 of this chapter with OHA within 45 days after the applicant receives the Agency decision.

(d) If an appeal is filed with OHA, the written decision of the Administrative Law Judge is the final Agency decision. If an appealable decision is not appealed, the decision of the AA/BD is the final Agency decision.

[63 FR 35739, June 30, 1998, as amended at 67 FR 47246, July 18, 2002; 74 FR 45753, Sept. 4, 2009]

§ 124.207 Can an applicant reapply for admission to the 8(a) BD program?

A concern which has been declined for 8(a) BD program admission may submit a new application for admission to the program 12 months after the date of the final Agency decision to decline.

EXITING THE 8(a) BD PROGRAM

§ 124.301 What are the ways a business may leave the 8(a) BD program?

A concern participating in the 8(a) BD program may leave the program by any of the following means:

(a) Expiration of the program term established pursuant to § 124.2;

(b) Voluntary withdrawal or voluntary early graduation;

(c) Graduation pursuant to § 124.302;

(d) Early graduation pursuant to the provisions of §§ 124.302 and 124.304; or

(e) Termination pursuant to the provisions of §§ 124.303 and 124.304.

[76 FR 8258, Feb. 11, 2011]

§ 124.302 What is graduation and what is early graduation?

(a) *General.* SBA may graduate a firm from the 8(a) BD program at the expiration of its program term (graduation) or prior to the expiration of its program term (early graduation) where SBA determines that:

(1) The concern has successfully completed the 8(a) BD program by substantially achieving the targets, objectives, and goals set forth in its business plan, and has demonstrated the ability to compete in the marketplace without assistance under the 8(a) BD program; or

(2) One or more of the disadvantaged owners upon whom the Participant's eligibility is based are no longer economically disadvantaged.

(b) *Criteria for determining whether a Participant has met its goals and objectives.* In determining whether a Participant has substantially achieved the targets, objectives and goals of its business plan and in assessing the overall competitive strength and viability of a Participant, SBA considers the totality of circumstances, including the following factors:

(1) Degree of sustained profitability;

(2) Sales trends, including improved ratio of non-8(a) sales to 8(a) sales since program entry;

(3) Business net worth, financial ratios, working capital, capitalization, and access to credit and capital;

(4) Current ability to obtain bonding;

(5) A comparison of the Participant's business and financial profiles with profiles of non-8(a) BD businesses having the same primary four-digit SIC code as the Participant;

(6) Strength of management experience, capability, and expertise; and

(7) Ability to operate successfully without 8(a) contracts.

(c) *Exceeding the size standard corresponding to the primary NAICS code.* SBA may graduate a Participant prior to the expiration of its program term where the firm exceeds the size standard corresponding to its primary NAICS code, as adjusted during the program, for three successive program years unless the firm is able to demonstrate that it has taken steps to change its industry focus to another NAICS code that is contained in the goals, targets and objectives of its business plan.

(d) *Excessive withdrawals.* SBA may graduate a Participant prior to the expiration of its program term where excessive funds or other assets have been withdrawn from the Participant (see § 124.112(d)(3)), causing SBA to determine that the Participant has demonstrated the ability to compete in the marketplace without assistance under the 8(a) BD program.

[63 FR 35739, 35772, June 30, 1998, as amended at 76 FR 8258, Feb. 11, 2011]

§ 124.303 What is termination?

(a) SBA may terminate the participation of a concern in the 8(a) BD program prior to the expiration of the concern's Program Term for good cause. Examples of good cause include, but are not limited to, the following:

(1) Submission of false information in the concern's 8(a) BD application, regardless of whether correct information would have caused the concern to be denied admission to the program, and regardless of whether correct information was given to SBA in accompanying documents or by other means.

(2) Failure by the concern to maintain its eligibility for program participation, including failure by an individual owner or manager to continue to meet the requirements for economic disadvantage set forth in § 124.104 where such status is needed for eligibility.

(3) Failure by the concern for any reason, including the death of an individual upon whom eligibility was based, to maintain ownership, full-time day-to-day management, and control by disadvantaged individuals.

(4) Failure by the concern to obtain prior written approval from SBA for any changes in ownership or business structure, management or control pursuant to §§ 124.105 and 124.106.

(5) Failure by the concern to disclose to SBA the extent to which non-disadvantaged persons or firms participate in the management of the Participant business concern.

(6) Failure by the concern or one or more of the concern's principals to maintain good character.

(7) A pattern of failure to make required submissions or responses to SBA in a timely manner, including a failure to provide required financial statements, requested tax returns, reports, updated business plans, information requested by SBA's Office of Inspector General, or other requested information or data within 30 days of the date of request.

(8) Cessation of business operations by the concern.

(9) Failure by the concern to pursue competitive and commercial business in accordance with its business plan, or failure in other ways to make reasonable efforts to develop and achieve competitive viability.

(10) A pattern of inadequate performance by the concern of awarded section 8(a) contracts.

(11) Failure by the concern to pay or repay significant financial obligations owed to the Federal Government.

(12) Failure by the concern to obtain and keep current any and all required permits, licenses, and charters, including suspension or revocation of any professional license required to operate the business.

(13) Excessive withdrawals that are detrimental to the achievement of the targets, objectives, and goals contained in the Participant's business plan, including transfers of funds or other business assets from the concern for the personal benefit of any of its owners or managers, or any person or entity affiliated with the owners or managers (*see* § 124.112(d)).

(14) Unauthorized use of SBA direct or guaranteed loan proceeds or violation of an SBA loan agreement.

(15) Submission by or on behalf of a Participant of false information to SBA, including false certification of compliance with non-8(a) business activity targets under § 124.507 or failure to report changes that adversely affect the program eligibility of an applicant or program participant under § 124.204 and § 124.112, where responsible officials of the 8(a) BD Participant knew or should have known the submission to be false.

(16) Debarment, suspension, voluntary exclusion, or ineligibility of the concern or its principals pursuant to 2 CFR parts 180 and 2700 or FAR subpart 9.4 (48 CFR part 9, subpart 9.4). * * *

(17) Conduct by the concern, or any of its principals, indicating a lack of business integrity. Such conduct may be demonstrated by information related to a criminal indictment or guilty plea, a criminal conviction, or a judgment or settlement in a civil case.

(18) Willful failure by the Participant business concern to comply with applicable labor standards and obligations.

(19) Material breach of any terms and conditions of the 8(a) BD Program Participation Agreement.

(20) Willful violation by a concern, or any of its principals, of any SBA regulation pertaining to material issues.

(b) The examples of good cause listed in paragraph (a) of this section are intended to be illustrative only. Other grounds for terminating a Participant from the 8(a) BD program for cause may exist and may be used by SBA.

[63 FR 35739, June 30, 1998, as amended at 76 FR 8258, Feb. 11, 2011]

§ 124.304 What are the procedures for early graduation and termination?

(a) *General.* The same procedures apply to both early graduation and termination of Participants from the 8(a) BD program.

(b) *Letter of Intent to Terminate or Graduate Early.* When SBA believes that a Participant should be terminated or graduated prior to the expiration of its program term, SBA will notify the concern in writing. The Letter of Intent to Terminate or Graduate Early will set forth the specific facts and reasons for SBA's findings, and will notify the concern that it has 30 days from the date it receives the letter to submit a written response to SBA explaining why the proposed ground(s) should not justify termination or early graduation.

(c) *Recommendation and decision.* Following the 30-day response period, the Assistant Administrator for DPCE (AA/DPCE) or designee will consider the proposed early graduation or termination and any information submitted in response by the concern. Upon determining that early graduation or termination is not warranted, the AA/DPCE or designee will notify the Participant in writing. If early graduation or termination appears warranted, the AA/DPCE will make such a recommendation to the AA/BD, who will then make a decision whether to early graduate or terminate the concern. SBA will act in a timely manner in processing early graduation and termination actions.

(d) *Notice requirements.* Upon deciding that early graduation or termination is warranted, the AA/BD will issue a Notice of Early Graduation or Termination. The Notice will set forth the specific facts and reasons for the decision, and will advise the concern that it may appeal the decision in accordance with the provisions of part 134 of this title.

(e) *Appeal to OHA.* Procedures governing appeals of early graduation or termination to SBA's OHA are set forth in part 134. If a Participant does not appeal a Notification of Early Graduation or Termination within 45 days after the Participant receives the Notification, the decision of the AA/BD is the final agency decision effective on the date the appeal right expired.

(f) *Effect or early graduation or termination.* (1) After the effective date of early graduation or termination, a Participant is no longer eligible to receive any 8(a) BD program assistance. However, such concern is obligated to complete previously awarded 8(a) contracts, including any priced options which may be exercised.

(2) When SBA early graduates or terminates a firm from the 8(a) BD program, the firm will generally not qualify as an SDB for future procurement actions. If the firm believes that it does qualify as an SDB and seeks to certify itself as an SDB, as part of its SDB certification the firm must identify:

(i) That it has been early graduated or terminated;

(ii) The statutory or regulatory authority that qualifies the firm for SDB status; and

(iii) Where applicable, the circumstances that have changed since the early graduation or termination or that do not prevent it from qualifying as an SDB.

(3) Where a concern certifies that it qualifies as an SDB pursuant to paragraph (f)(2) of the section, the procuring activity contracting officer may protest the SDB status of the firm to SBA pursuant to § 124.1010 where questions regarding the firm's SDB status remain.

[63 FR 35739, June 30, 1998, as amended at 67 FR 47246, July 18, 2002; 74 FR 45753, Sept. 4, 2009; 76 FR 8258, Feb. 11, 2011]

§ 124.305 What is suspension and how is a Participant suspended from the 8(a) BD program?

(a) Except as set forth in paragraph (h) of this section, at any time after SBA issues a Letter of Intent to Terminate an 8(a) Participant pursuant to § 124.304, the AA/BD may suspend 8(a) contract support and all other forms of 8(a) BD program assistance to that Participant until the issue of the Participant's termination from the program is finally determined. The AA/BD may suspend a Participant when he or she determines that suspension is needed to protect the interests of the Federal Government, such as where information showing a clear lack of program eligibility or conduct indicating a lack of business integrity exists, including where the concern or one of its principals submitted false statements to the Federal Government. SBA will suspend a Participant where SBA determines that the Participant submitted false information in its 8(a) BD application.

(b) SBA will issue a Notice of Suspension to the Participant's last known address by certified mail, return receipt requested. Suspension is effective as of the date of the issuance of the Notice. The Notice will provide the following information:

(1) The basis for the suspension;

(2) A statement that the suspension will continue pending the completion of further investigation, a final program termination determination, or some other specified period of time;

(3) A statement that awards of competitive and non-competitive 8(a) contracts, including those which have been "self-marketed" by a Participant, will not be made during the pendency of the suspension unless it is determined by the head of the relevant procuring agency or an authorized representative to be in the best interest of the Government to do so, and SBA adopts that determination;

(4) A statement that the concern is obligated to complete previously awarded section 8(a) contracts;

(5) A statement that the suspension is effective nationally throughout SBA;

(6) A statement that a request for a hearing on the suspension will be considered by an Administrative Law Judge at OHA, and granted or denied as a matter of discretion.

(7) A statement that the firm's participation in the program is suspended effective on the date the Notice is served, and that the program term will resume only if the suspension is lifted or the firm is not terminated.

(c) The Participant may appeal a Notice of Suspension by filing a petition in accordance with part 134 of this chapter with OHA within 45 days after the concern receives the Notice of Suspension pursuant to paragraph (b) of this section. It is contemplated that in most cases a hearing on the issue of the suspension will be afforded if the Participant requests one, but authority to grant a hearing is within the discretion of the Administrative Law Judge in OHA. A suspension remains in effect pending the result of its appeal.

(d) SBA has the burden of showing that adequate evidence exists that protection of the Federal Government's interest requires suspension before OHA or the AA/BD makes a final determination regarding the termination action.

(1) The term "adequate evidence" means information contained in the record before the AA/BD at the time of his or her suspension decision that is sufficient to support the reasonable belief that the Government's interests need to be protected.

(2) SBA need not demonstrate that an act or omission actually occurred in order for OHA to uphold a suspension. SBA's burden in a suspension proceeding is limited to demonstrating that it had a reasonable belief that a particular act or omission occurred, and that that act or omission requires suspension to protect the interests of the Government.

(3) Unless the Administrative Law Judge consolidates the suspension and termination proceedings, OHA's review is limited to determining whether the Government's interests need to be protected, and will not consider the merits of the termination action.

(e) If there is a timely appeal, the decision of the Administrative Law Judge is the final SBA decision. If there is not a timely appeal, the decision of the AA/BD is the final Agency decision.

(f) Upon the request of SBA, OHA may consolidate suspension and termination proceedings when the issues presented are identical.

(g) Any program suspension which occurs under this section is effective until such time as SBA lifts the suspension or the Participant's participation in the program is fully terminated. If the concern is ultimately not terminated from the 8(a) BD program, the suspension will be lifted and the length of the suspension will be added to the concern's program term.

(h)(1) SBA will suspend a Participant from receiving further 8(a) BD program benefits when termination proceedings have not been commenced pursuant to § 124.304 where:

(i) A Participant requests a change of ownership and/or control and SBA discovers that a change of ownership or control has in fact occurred prior to SBA's approval; or

(ii) A disadvantaged individual who is involved in the ownership and/or control of the Participant is called to active military duty by the United States, his or her participation in the firm's management and daily business operations is critical to the firm's continued eligibility, and the Participant elects not to designate a non-disadvantaged individual to control the concern during the call-up period pursuant to § 124.106(h); or

(iii) A Participant has a principal place of business located in a federally declared disaster area and elects to suspend its participation in the 8(a) BD program for a period of up to one year from the date of the disaster declaration to allow the firm to recover from the disaster and take full advantage of the program. A Participant that elects to be suspended may request that the suspension be lifted prior to the end date of the original request; or

(iv) Federal appropriations for one or more federal departments or agencies have lapsed, SBA has previously accepted an offer for a sole source 8(a) award on behalf of the Participant, award is pending, and the Participant elects to suspend its participation in the 8(a) BD program during the lapse in federal appropriations.

(2) A suspension initiated under paragraph (h) of this section will be commenced by the issuance of a notice similar to that required for termination-related suspensions under paragraph (b) of this section, except that a suspension issued under paragraph (h) is not appealable.

(3) Where a Participant is suspended pursuant to paragraph (h)(1)(i) of this section and SBA approves the change of ownership and/or control, the length of the suspension will be added to the firm's program term only where the change in ownership or control results from the death or incapacity of a disadvantaged individual or where the firm requested prior approval and waited at least 60 days for SBA approval before making the change.

(4) Where a Participant is suspended pursuant to paragraph (h)(1)(ii) of this section, the Participant must notify SBA when the disadvantaged individual returns to control the firm so that SBA can immediately lift the suspension. When the suspension is lifted, the length of the suspension will be added to the concern's program term.

(5) Where a Participant is suspended pursuant to (h)(1)(iv) of this section, the Participant must notify SBA when the lapse in appropriation ends so that SBA can immediately lift the suspension. When the suspension is lifted, the length of the suspension will be added to the concern's program term.

(6) *Effect of suspension.* Once a suspension is issued pursuant to this section, a Participant cannot receive any additional 8(a) BD program assistance, including new 8(a) contract awards, for as long as the Participant is suspended. This includes any procurement requirements that the firm has self-marketed and those that have been accepted into the 8(a) BD program on behalf of the suspended concern. However, the suspended Participant must complete any previously awarded 8(a) contracts.

(i) SBA does not recognize the concept of de facto suspension. Adding time to the end of a Participant's program term equal to the length of a suspension will occur only where a concern's program participation has been formally suspended in accordance with the procedures set forth in this section.

(j) A suspension from 8(a) BD participation under this section has no effect on a concern's eligibility for non-8(a)

Federal Government contracts. However, a debarment or suspension under the Federal Acquisition Regulation (48 CFR, chapter 1) will disqualify a concern from receiving all Federal Government contracts, including 8(a) contracts.

[63 FR 35739, June 30, 1998, as amended at 67 FR 47246, July 18, 2002; 74 FR 45753, Sept. 4, 2009; 76 FR 8259, Feb. 11, 2011; 81 FR 48582, July 25, 2016]

BUSINESS DEVELOPMENT

§ 124.401 Which SBA field office services a Participant?

The SBA district office which serves the geographical territory where a Participant's principal place of business is located normally will service the concern during its participation in the 8(a) BD program.

§ 124.402 How does a Participant develop a business plan?

(a) *General.* In order to assist the SBA servicing office in determining the business development needs of its portfolio Participants, each Participant must develop a comprehensive business plan setting forth its business targets, objectives, and goals.

(b) *Submission of initial business plan.* Each Participant must submit a business plan to its SBA servicing office as soon as possible after program admission. The Participant will not be eligible for 8(a) BD program benefits, including 8(a) contracts, until SBA approves its business plan.

(c) *Contents of business plan.* The business plan must contain at least the following:

(1) A detailed description of any products currently being produced and any services currently being performed by the concern, as well as any future plans to enter into one or more new markets;

(2) The applicant's designation of its primary industry classification, as defined in § 124.3;

(3) An analysis of market potential, competitive environment, and the concern's prospects for profitable operations during and after its participation in the 8(a) BD program;

(4) An analysis of the concern's strengths and weaknesses, with particular attention on ways to correct any financial, managerial, technical, or work force conditions which could impede the concern from receiving and performing non-8(a) contracts;

(5) Specific targets, objectives, and goals for the business development of the concern during the next two years;

(6) Estimates of both 8(a) and non-8(a) contract awards that will be needed to meet its targets, objectives and goals; and

(7) Such other information as SBA may require.

§ 124.403 How is a business plan updated and modified?

(a) *Annual review.* Each Participant must annually review its business plan with its assigned Business Opportunity Specialist (BOS), and modify the plan as appropriate. The Participant must submit a modified plan and updated information to its BOS within thirty (30) days after the close of each program year. It also must submit a capability statement describing its current contract performance capabilities as part of its updated business plan.

(b) *Contract forecast.* As part of the annual review of its business plan, each Participant must annually forecast in writing its needs for contract awards for the next program year. The forecast must include:

(1) The aggregate dollar value of 8(a) contracts to be sought, broken down by sole source and competitive opportunities where possible;

(2) The aggregate dollar value of non-8(a) contracts to be sought;

(3) The types of contract opportunities to be sought, identified by product or service; and

(4) Such other information as SBA may request to aid in providing effective business development assistance to the Participant.

(c) *Transition management strategy.* Beginning in the first year of the transitional stage of program participation, each Participant must annually submit a transition management strategy to be incorporated into its business plan. The transition management strategy must describe:

(1) How the Participant intends to meet the applicable non-8(a) business

activity target imposed by § 124.507 during the transitional stage of participation; and

(2) The specific steps the Participant intends to take to continue its business growth and promote profitable business operations after the expiration of its program term.

[63 FR 35739, 35772, June 30, 1998, as amended at 76 FR 8259, Feb. 11, 2011]

§ 124.404 What business development assistance is available to Participants during the two stages of participation in the 8(a) BD program?

(a) *General.* Participation in the 8(a) BD program is divided into two stages, a developmental stage and a transitional stage. The developmental stage will last four years, and the transitional stage will last five years, unless the concern has exited the program by one of the means set forth in § 124.301 prior to the expiration of its program term.

(b) *Developmental stage of program participation.* A Participant, if otherwise eligible, may receive the following assistance during the developmental stage of program participation:

(1) Sole source and competitive 8(a) contract support;

(2) Financial assistance pursuant to § 120.375 of this title;

(3) The transfer of technology or surplus property owned by the United States pursuant to § 124.405; and

(4) Training to aid in developing business principles and strategies to enhance their ability to compete successfully for both 8(a) and non-8(a) contracts.

(c) *Transitional stage of program participation.* A Participant, if otherwise eligible, may receive the following assistance during the transitional stage of program participation:

(1) The same assistance as that provided to Participants in the developmental stage;

(2) Assistance from procuring agencies (in cooperation with SBA) in forming joint ventures, leader-follower arrangements, and teaming agreements between the concern and other Participants or other business concerns with respect to contracting opportunities outside the 8(a) BD program for research, development, or full scale engineering or production of major systems (these arrangements must comply with all relevant statutes and regulations, including applicable size standard requirements); and

(3) Training and technical assistance in transitional business planning.

§ 124.405 How does a Participant obtain Federal Government surplus property?

(a) *General.* (1) Pursuant to 15 U.S.C. 636(j)(13)(F), eligible Participants may receive surplus Federal Government property from State Agencies for Surplus Property (SASPs). The procedures set forth in 41 CFR Part 101–44 and this section will be used to transfer surplus property to eligible Participants.

(2) The property which may be transferred to SASPs for further transfer to eligible Participants includes all personal property which has been determined to be "donable" as defined in 41 CFR 101–44.001–3.

(b) *Eligibility to receive Federal surplus property.* To be eligible to receive Federal surplus property, on the date of transfer a concern must:

(1) Be in the 8(a) BD program;

(2) Be in compliance with all program requirements, including any reporting requirements;

(3) Not be debarred, suspended, or declared ineligible under part 9, subpart 9.4 of the Federal Acquisition Regulations, Title 48 of the Code of Federal Regulations;

(4) Not be under a pending 8(a) BD program suspension, termination or early graduation proceeding; and

(5) Be engaged or expect to be engaged in business activities making the item useful to it.

(c) *Use of acquired surplus property.* (1) Eligible Participants may acquire surplus Federal property from any SASP located in any state, provided the concern represents and agrees in writing:

(i) As to what the intended use of the surplus property is to be and that this use is consistent with the objectives of the concern's 8(a) business plan;

(ii) That it will use the property to be acquired in the normal conduct of its business activities or be liable for the fair rental value from the date of its receipt;

(iii) That it will not sell or transfer the property to be acquired to any party other than the Federal Government during its term of participation in the 8(a) program and for one year after it leaves the program;

(iv) That, at its own expense, it will return the property to a SASP or transfer it to another Participant if directed to do so by SBA because it has not used the property as intended within one year of receipt;

(v) That, should it breach its agreement not to sell or transfer the property, it will be liable to the Government for the established fair market value or the sale price, whichever is greater, of the property sold or transferred; and

(vi) That it will give SBA access to inspect the property and all records pertaining to it.

(2) A firm receiving surplus property pursuant to this section assumes all liability associated with or stemming from the use of the property.

(3) If the property is not placed in use for the purposes for which it was intended within one year of its receipt, SBA may direct the concern to deliver the property to another Participant or to the SASP from which it was acquired.

(4) Failure to comply with any of the commitments made under paragraph (c)(1) of this section constitutes a basis for termination from the 8(a) program.

(d) *Procedures for acquiring Federal Government surplus property.* (1) Participants may participate in the surplus property distribution program administered by the SASPs to the same extent, but with no special priority over, other authorized transferees. *See* 41 CFR subpart 101–44.2.

(2) Each Participant seeking to acquire Federal Government surplus property from a SASP must:

(i) Certify in writing to the SASP that it is eligible to receive the property pursuant to paragraph (b) of this section;

(ii) Make the written representations and agreement required by paragraph (c)(1) of this section; and

(iii) Identify to the SASP its servicing SBA field office.

(3) Upon receipt of the required certification, representations, agreement, and information set forth in paragraph (d)(2) of this section, the SASP must contact the appropriate SBA field office and obtain SBA's verification that the concern seeking to acquire the surplus property is eligible, and that the identified use of the property is consistent with the concern's business activities. SASPs may not release property to a Participant without this verification.

(4) The SASP and the Participant must agree on and record the fair market value of the surplus property at the time of the transfer to the Participant. The SASP must provide to SBA a written record, including the agreed upon fair market value, of each transaction to a Participant when any property has been transferred.

(e) *Costs.* Participants acquiring surplus property from a SASP must pay a service fee to the SASP which is equal to the SASP's direct costs of locating, inspecting, and transporting the surplus property. If a Participant elects to incur the responsibility and the expense for transporting the acquired property, the concern may do so and no transportation costs will be charged by the SASP. In addition, the SASP may charge a reasonable fee to cover its costs of administering the program. In no instance will any SASP charge a Participant more for any service than their established fees charged to other transferees.

(f) *Title.* The title to surplus property acquired from a SASP will pass to the Participant when the Participant executes the applicable SASP distribution documents and takes possession of the property.

(g) *Compliance.* (1) SBA will periodically review whether Participants that have received surplus property have used and maintained the property as agreed. This review may include site visits to visually inspect the property to ensure that it is being used in a manner consistent with the terms of its transfer.

(2) Participants must provide SBA with access to all relevant records upon request.

(3) Where SBA receives credible information that transferred surplus property may have been disposed of or otherwise used in a manner that is not

consistent with the terms of the transfer, SBA may investigate such claim to determine its validity.

(4) SBA may take any action to correct any noncompliance involving the use of transferred property still in possession of the Participant or to enforce any terms, conditions, reservations, or restrictions imposed on the property by the distribution document. Actions to enforce compliance, or which may be taken as a result of noncompliance, include the following:

(i) Requiring that the property be placed in proper use within a specified time;

(ii) Requiring that the property be transferred to another Participant having a need and use for the property, returned to the SASP serving the area where the property is located for distribution to another eligible transferee or to another SASP, or transferred through GSA to another Federal agency;

(iii) Recovery of the fair rental value of the property from the date of its receipt by the Participant; and

(iv) Initiation of proceedings to terminate the Participant from the 8(a) BD program.

(5) Where SBA finds that a recipient has sold or otherwise disposed of the acquired surplus property in violation of the agreement covering sale and disposal, the Participant is liable for the agreed upon fair market value of the property at the time of the transfer, or the sale price, whichever is greater. However, a Participant need not repay any amount where it can demonstrate to SBA's satisfaction that the property is no longer useful for the purpose for which it was transferred and receives SBA's prior written consent to transfer the property. For example, if a piece of equipment breaks down beyond repair, it may be disposed of without being subject to the repayment provision, so long as the concern receives SBA's prior consent.

(6) Any funds received by SBA in enforcement of this section will be remitted promptly to the Treasury of the United States as miscellaneous receipts.

CONTRACTUAL ASSISTANCE

§ 124.501 What general provisions apply to the award of 8(a) contracts?

(a) Pursuant to section 8(a) of the Small Business Act, SBA is authorized to enter into all types of contracts with other Federal agencies regardless of the place of performance, including contracts to furnish equipment, supplies, services, leased real property, or materials to them or to perform construction work for them, and to contract the performance of these contracts to qualified Participants. This includes set-asides, partial set-asides and reserves of Multiple Award Contracts and set-asides of orders issued against Multiple Award Contracts. Where practicable, simplified acquisition procedures should be used for 8(a) contracts at or below the simplified acquisition threshold. Where appropriate, SBA will delegate the contract execution function to procuring activities. In order to receive and retain a delegation of SBA's contract execution and review functions, a procuring activity must report all 8(a) contract awards, modifications, and options to SBA.

(b) 8(a) contracts may either be sole source awards or awards won through competition with other Participants. In addition, for multiple award contracts not set aside for the 8(a) BD program, a procuring agency may set aside specific orders to be competed only among eligible 8(a) Participants, regardless of the place of performance. Such an order may be awarded as an 8(a) award where the order was offered to and accepted by SBA as an 8(a) award and the order specifies that the performance of work and/or non-manufacturer rule requirements apply as appropriate.

(c) Admission into the 8(a) BD program does not guarantee that a Participant will receive 8(a) contracts.

(d) A requirement for possible award may be identified by SBA, a particular Participant or the procuring activity itself. SBA will submit the capability statements provided to SBA annually under § 124.403 to appropriate procuring activities for the purpose of matching requirements with Participants.

(e) Participants should market their capabilities to appropriate procuring activities to increase their prospects of receiving sole source 8(a) contracts.

(f) An 8(a) participant that identifies a requirement that appears suitable for award through the 8(a) BD program may request SBA to contact the procuring activity to request that the requirement be offered to the 8(a) BD program.

(g) A concern must be a current Participant in the 8(a) BD program at the time of award, except as provided in §124.507(d).

(h) A Participant must certify that it qualifies as a small business under the size standard corresponding to the NAICS code assigned to each 8(a) contract. 8(a) BD program personnel will verify size prior to award of an 8(a) contract. If the Participant is not verified as small, it may request a formal size determination from the appropriate General Contracting Area Office under part 121 of this title.

(i) Any person or entity that misrepresents its status as a "small business concern owned and controlled by socially and economically disadvantaged individuals" in order to obtain any 8(a) contracting opportunity will be subject to possible criminal, civil and administrative penalties, including those imposed by section 16(d) of the Small Business Act, 15 U.S.C. 645(d).

[63 FR 35739, June 30, 1998, as amended at 76 FR 8259, Feb. 11, 2011; 78 FR 61132, Oct. 2, 2013; 81 FR 48582, July 25, 2016]

§ 124.502 How does an agency offer a procurement to SBA for award through the 8(a) BD program?

(a) A procuring activity contracting officer indicates his or her formal intent to award a procurement requirement as an 8(a) contract by submitting a written offering letter to SBA. The procuring activity may transmit the offering letter to SBA by electronic mail, if available, or by facsimile transmission, as well as by mail or commercial delivery service.

(b) Contracting officers must submit offering letters to the following locations:

(1) For competitive 8(a) requirements and those sole source requirements for which no specific Participant is nominated (i.e., open requirements) other than construction requirements, to the SBA district office serving the geographical area in which the procuring activity is located;

(2) For competitive and open construction requirements, to the SBA district office serving the geographical area in which the work is to be performed or, in the case of such contracts to be performed overseas, to the Office of 8(a) BD located in SBA Headquarters;

(3) For sole source requirements offered on behalf of a specific Participant, to the SBA district office servicing that concern.

(c) An offering letter must contain the following information:

(1) A description of the work to be performed;

(2) The estimated period of performance;

(3) The NAICS code that applies to the principal nature of the acquisition;

(4) The anticipated dollar value of the requirement, including options, if any;

(5) Any special restrictions or geographical limitations on the requirement;

(6) The location of the work to be performed for construction procurements;

(7) Any special capabilities or disciplines needed for contract performance;

(8) The type of contract to be awarded, such as firm fixed price, cost reimbursement, or time and materials;

(9) The acquisition history, if any, of the requirement, including specifically whether the requirement is a follow-on requirement, and whether any portion of the contract was previously performed by a small business outside of the 8(a) BD program;

(10) The names and addresses of any small business contractors which have performed on this requirement during the previous 24 months;

(11) A statement that prior to the offering no solicitation for the specific acquisition has been issued as a small business set-aside, or as a small disadvantaged business set-aside if applicable, and that no other public communication (such as a notice in the Commerce Business Daily) has been made

showing the procuring activity's clear intent to use any of these means of procurement;

(12) Identification of any specific Participant that the procuring activity contracting officer nominates for award of a sole source 8(a) contract, if appropriate, including a brief justification for the nomination, such as one of the following:

(i) The Participant, through its own efforts, marketed the requirement and caused it to be reserved for the 8(a) BD program; or

(ii) The acquisition is a follow-on or renewal contract and the nominated concern is the incumbent;

(13) Bonding requirements, if applicable;

(14) Identification of all Participants which have expressed an interest in being considered for the acquisition;

(15) Identification of all SBA field offices which have requested that the requirement be awarded through the 8(a) BD program;

(16) A request, if appropriate, that a requirement whose estimated contract value is under the applicable competitive threshold be awarded as an 8(a) competitive contract;

(17) A statement that the necessary justification and approval under the Federal Acquisition Regulation has occurred where a requirement whose estimated contract value exceeds $22,000,000 is offered to SBA as a sole source requirement on behalf of a specific Participant; and

(18) Any other information that the procuring activity deems relevant or which SBA requests.

[63 FR 35739, June 30, 1998, as amended at 81 FR 48582, July 25, 2016]

§ 124.503 How does SBA accept a procurement for award through the 8(a) BD program?

(a) *Acceptance of the requirement.* Upon receipt of the procuring activity's offer of a procurement requirement, SBA will determine whether it will accept the requirement for the 8(a) BD program. SBA's decision whether to accept the requirement will be sent to the procuring activity in writing within 10 working days of receipt of the written offering letter if the contract is valued at more than the simplified acquisition threshold, and within two days of receipt of the offering letter if the contract is valued at or below the simplified acquisition threshold, unless SBA requests, and the procuring activity grants, an extension. SBA is not required to accept any particular procurement offered to the 8(a) BD program.

(1) Where SBA decides to accept an offering of a sole source 8(a) procurement, SBA will accept the offer both on behalf of the 8(a) BD program and in support of a specific Participant. As part of its acceptance of a sole source requirement, SBA will determine the eligibility of the Participant identified in the offering letter, using the same analysis set forth in § 124.507(b)(2). Where a procuring agency offers a sole source 8(a) procurement on behalf of a joint venture, SBA will conduct an eligibility review of the lead 8(a) party to the joint venture as part of its acceptance, and will approve the joint venture prior to award pursuant to § 124.513(e).

(2) Where SBA decides to accept an offering of a competitive 8(a) procurement, SBA will accept the offer on behalf of the 8(a) BD program. For a competitive 8(a) procurement, SBA will determine the eligibility of the apparent successful offeror pursuant to § 124.507(b).

(3) Where SBA has delegated its contract execution functions to a procuring activity, the procuring activity may assume that SBA accepts its offer for the 8(a) program if the procuring activity does not receive a reply to its offer within five days.

(4) In the case of procurement requirements valued at or below the Simplified Acquisition Procedures threshold:

(i) Where a procuring activity makes an offer to the 8(a) program on behalf of a specific Program Participant and does not receive a reply to its offer within two days, the procuring activity may assume the offer is accepted and proceed with award of an 8(a) contract;

(ii) Where SBA has delegated its 8(a) contract execution functions to an agency, SBA may authorize the procuring activity to award an 8(a) contract without requiring an offer and acceptance of the requirement for the

8(a) program. In such a case, the procuring activity must notify SBA of all 8(a) awards made under this authority.

(5) Where SBA does not respond to an offering letter within the normal 10-day time period, the procuring activity may seek SBA's acceptance through the AA/BD. The procuring activity may assume that SBA accepts its offer for the 8(a) program if it does not receive a reply from the AA/BD within 5 days of his or her receipt of the procuring activity request.

(b) *Verification of NAICS code.* As part of the acceptance process, SBA will verify the appropriateness of the NAICS code designation assigned to the requirement by the procuring activity contracting officer.

(1) SBA will accept the NAICS code assigned to the requirement by the procuring activity contracting officer as long as it is reasonable, even though other NAICS codes may also be reasonable.

(2) If SBA and the procuring activity are unable to agree as to the proper NAICS code designation for the requirement, SBA may either refuse to accept the requirement for the 8(a) BD program, appeal the contracting officer's determination to the head of the agency pursuant to §124.505, or appeal the NAICS code designation to OHA under part 134 of this title.

(c) *Sole source award where procuring activity nominates a specific Participant.* SBA will determine whether an appropriate match exists where the procuring activity identifies a particular Participant for a sole source award.

(1) Once SBA determines that a procurement is suitable to be accepted as an 8(a) sole source contract, SBA will normally accept it on behalf of the Participant recommended by the procuring activity, provided that:

(i) The procurement is consistent with the Participant's business plan;

(ii) The Participant complies with its applicable non-8(a) business activity target imposed by §124.509(d);

(iii) The Participant is small for the size standard corresponding to the NAICS code assigned to the requirement by the procuring activity contracting officer; and

(iv) The Participant has submitted required financial statements to SBA.

(2) If an appropriate match exists, SBA will advise the procuring activity whether SBA will participate in contract negotiations or whether SBA will authorize the procuring activity to negotiate directly with the identified Participant. Where SBA has delegated its contract execution functions to a procuring activity, SBA will also identify that delegation in its acceptance letter.

(3) If an appropriate match does not exist, SBA will notify the Participant and the procuring activity, and may then nominate an alternate Participant.

(d) *Open requirements.* When a procuring activity does not nominate a particular concern for performance of a sole source 8(a) contract (open requirement), the following additional procedures will apply:

(1) If the procurement is a construction requirement, SBA will examine the portfolio of Participants that have a bona fide place of business within the geographical boundaries served by the SBA district office where the work is to be performed to select a qualified Participant. If none is found to be qualified or a match for a concern in that district is determined to be impossible or inappropriate, SBA may nominate a Participant with a bona fide place of business within the geographical boundaries served by another district office within the same state, or may nominate a Participant having a bona fide place of business out of state but within a reasonable proximity to the work site. SBA's decision will ensure that the nominated Participant is close enough to the work site to keep costs of performance reasonable.

(2) If the procurement is not a construction requirement, SBA may select any eligible, responsible Participant nationally to perform the contract.

(3) In cases in which SBA selects a Participant for possible award from among two or more eligible and qualified Participants, the selection will be based upon relevant factors, including business development needs, compliance with competitive business mix requirements (if applicable), financial condition, management ability, technical capability, and whether award

will promote the equitable distribution of 8(a) contracts.

(e) *Formal technical evaluations.* Except for requirements for architectural and engineering services, SBA will not authorize formal technical evaluations for sole source 8(a) requirements. A procuring activity:

(1) Must request that a procurement be a competitive 8(a) award if it requires formal technical evaluations of more than one Participant for a requirement below the applicable competitive threshold amount; and

(2) May conduct informal assessments of several Participants' capabilities to perform a specific requirement, so long as the statement of work for the requirement is not released to any of the Participants being assessed.

(f) *Repetitive acquisitions.* A procuring activity contracting officer must submit a new offering letter to SBA where he or she intends to award a follow-on or repetitive contract as an 8(a) award. This enables SBA to determine:

(1) Whether the requirement should be a competitive 8(a) award;

(2) A nominated firm's eligibility, whether or not it is the same firm that performed the previous contract;

(3) The affect that contract award would have on the equitable distribution of 8(a) contracts; and

(4) Whether the requirement should continue under the 8(a) BD program.

(g) *Basic Ordering Agreements (BOAs).* A Basic Ordering Agreement (BOA) is not a contract under the FAR. See 48 CFR 16.703(a). Each order to be issued under the BOA is an individual contract. As such, the procuring activity must offer, and SBA must accept, each task order under a BOA in addition to offering and accepting the BOA itself.

(1) SBA will not accept for award on a sole source basis any task order under a BOA that would cause the total dollar amount of task orders issued to exceed the applicable competitive threshold amount set forth in §124.506(a).

(2) Where a procuring activity believes that task orders to be issued under a proposed BOA will exceed the applicable competitive threshold amount set forth in §124.506(a), the procuring activity must offer the requirement to the program to be competed among eligible Participants.

(3) Once a concern's program term expires, the concern otherwise exits the 8(a) BD program, or becomes other than small for the NAICS code assigned under the BOA, new orders will not be accepted for the concern.

(4) A procuring agency may offer, and SBA may accept, an order issued under a BOA to be awarded through the 8(a) BD program where the BOA itself was not accepted for the 8(a) BD program, but rather was awarded on an unrestricted basis.

(h) *Task or Delivery Order Contracts, including Multiple Award Contracts*—(1) *Contracts set-aside for exclusive competition among 8(a) Participants.* (i) A task or delivery order contract, Multiple Award Contract, or order issued against a Multiple Award Contract that is set-aside exclusively for 8(a) Program Participants, partially set-aside for 8(a) Program Participants or reserved solely for 8(a) Program Participants must follow the established 8(a) competitive procedures. This includes an offering to and acceptance into the 8(a) program, SBA eligibility verification of the apparent successful offerors prior to contract award, compliance with the performance of work requirements set forth in §124.510, and compliance with the nonmanufacturer rule (*see* §121.406(b)), if applicable.

(ii) An agency is not required to offer or receive acceptance of individual orders into the 8(a) BD program if the task or delivery order contract or Multiple Award Contract was set-aside exclusively for 8(a) Program Participants, partially set-aside for 8(a) Program Participants or reserved solely for 8(a) Program Participants, and the individual order is to be competed among all 8(a) contract holders.

(iii) A concern awarded a task or delivery order contract or Multiple Award Contract that was set-aside exclusively for 8(a) Program Participants, partially set-aside for 8(a) Program Participants or reserved solely for 8(a) Program Participants may generally continue to receive new orders even if it has grown to be other than small or has exited the 8(a) BD program, and agencies may continue to take credit toward their prime contracting goals for orders awarded to 8(a) Participants. However, agencies may not take SDB or small business credit for an order where the concern has been asked by the procuring agency to recertify its size, 8(a) or SDB status and is unable to do so (*see* § 121.404(g)), or where ownership or control of the concern has changed and SBA has granted a waiver to allow performance to continue (*see* § 124.515).

(iv) An agency may issue a sole source award against a Multiple Award Contract that has been set-aside exclusively for 8(a) Program Participants, partially set-aside for 8(a) Program Participants or reserved solely for 8(a) Program Participants if the required dollar thresholds for sole source awards are met. Where an agency seeks to award an order on a sole source basis (i.e., to one particular 8(a) contract holder without competition among all 8(a) contract holders), the agency must offer and SBA must accept the order into the 8(a) program on behalf of the identified 8(a) contract holder.

(2) *Allowing orders issued to 8(a) Participants under Multiple Award Contracts that were not set-aside for exclusive competition among eligible 8(a) Participants to be considered 8(a) awards.* In order for an order issued to an 8(a) Participant and placed against a Multiple Award Contract to be considered an 8(a) award, where the Multiple Award contract was not initially set-aside, partially set-aside or reserved for exclusive competition among 8(a) Participants, the following conditions must be met:

(i) The order must be offered to and accepted into the 8(a) BD program;

(ii) The order must be competed exclusively among 8(a) concerns;

(iii) The order must require the concern comply with applicable limitations on subcontracting provisions (*see* § 125.6) and the nonmanufacturer rule, if applicable, (*see* § 121.406(b)) in the performance of the individual order; and

(iv) SBA must verify that a concern is an eligible 8(a) concern prior to award of the order in accordance with § 124.507.

(3) *Reserves.* A procuring activity must offer and SBA must accept a requirement that is reserved for 8(a) Participants (*i.e.*, an acquisition where the contracting officer states an intention to make one or more awards to only 8(a) Participants under full and open competition). However, a contracting officer does not have to offer the requirement to SBA where the acquisition has been reserved for small businesses, even if the contracting officer states an intention to make one or more awards to several types of small business including 8(a) Participants since any such award to 8(a) Participants would not be considered an 8(a) contract award.

(i) Requirements where SBA has delegated contract execution authority. Except as provided in paragraph (a)(4)(i) of this section, where SBA has delegated its 8(a) contract execution authority to the procuring activity, the procuring activity must still offer and SBA must still accept all requirements intended to be awarded as 8(a) contracts.

(j) *Contracting Among Small Business Programs*—(1) *Acquisitions Valued At or Below the Simplified Acquisition Threshold.* The contracting officer shall set aside any acquisition with an anticipated dollar value exceeding the Micro-purchase Threshold but not exceeding the Simplified Acquisition Threshold (defined in the FAR at 48 CFR 2.101) for small business concerns when there is a reasonable expectation that offers will be obtained from at least two small business concerns that are competitive in terms of quality and delivery and award will be made at fair market prices. This requirement does not preclude a contracting officer from making an award to a small business under the 8(a) BD, HUBZone, SDVO SBC or WOSB Programs.

(2) *Acquisitions Valued Above the Simplified Acquisition Threshold.* (i) The contracting officer shall set aside any acquisition with an anticipated dollar value exceeding the Simplified Acquisition Threshold (defined in the FAR at 48 CFR 2.101) for small business concerns when there is a reasonable expectation that offers will be obtained from at least two small business concerns that are competitive in terms of quality and delivery and award will be made at fair market prices. However, after conducting market research, the

contracting officer shall first consider a set-aside or sole source award (if the sole source award is permitted by statute or regulation) under the 8(a) BD, HUBZone, SDVO SBC or WOSB programs before setting aside the requirement as a small business set-aside. There is no order of precedence among the 8(a) BD, HUBZone, SDVO SBC or WOSB programs. The contracting officer must document the contract file with the rationale used to support the specific set-aside, including the type and extent of market research conducted. In addition, the contracting officer must document the contract file showing that the apparent successful offeror's System for Award Management (SAM) (or any successor system) certifications and associated representations were reviewed.

(ii) SBA believes that Progress in fulfilling the various small business goals, as well as other factors such as the results of market research, programmatic needs specific to the procuring agency, anticipated award price, and the acquisition history, will be considered in making a decision as to which program to use for the acquisition.

[63 FR 35739, June 30, 1998, as amended at 70 FR 51248, Aug. 30, 2005; 71 FR 66444, Nov. 15, 2006; 74 FR 45753, Sept. 4, 2009; 75 FR 62280, Oct. 7, 2010; 76 FR 8259, Feb. 11, 2011; 77 FR 1860, Jan. 12, 2012; 78 FR 61133, Oct. 2, 2013; 81 FR 48582, July 25, 2016]

§ 124.504 What circumstances limit SBA's ability to accept a procurement for award as an 8(a) contract?

SBA will not accept a procurement for award as an 8(a) contract if the circumstances identified in paragraphs (a) through (d) of this section exist.

(a) *Prior intent to award as a small business set-aside, or use the HUBZone, Service Disabled Veteran-Owned Small Business, or Women-Owned Small Business programs.* The procuring activity issued a solicitation for or otherwise expressed publicly a clear intent to award the contract as a small business set-aside, or to use the HUBZone, Service Disabled Veteran-Owned Small Business, or Women-Owned Small Business programs prior to offering the requirement to SBA for award as an 8(a) contract. However, the AA/BD may permit the acceptance of the requirement under extraordinary circumstances.

(b) *Competition prior to offer and acceptance.* The procuring activity competed a requirement among Participants prior to offering the requirement to SBA and receiving SBA's formal acceptance of the requirement.

(1) Any competition conducted without first obtaining SBA's formal acceptance of the procurement for the 8(a) BD program will not be considered an 8(a) competitive requirement.

(2) SBA may accept the requirement for the 8(a) BD program as a competitive 8(a) requirement, but only if the procuring activity agrees to resolicit the requirement using appropriate competitive 8(a) procedures.

(c) *Adverse impact.* SBA has made a written determination that acceptance of the procurement for 8(a) award would have an adverse impact on an individual small business, a group of small businesses located in a specific geographical location, or other small business programs. The adverse impact concept is designed to protect small business concerns which are performing Government contracts awarded outside the 8(a) BD program, and does not apply to follow-on or renewal 8(a) acquisitions. SBA will not consider adverse impact with respect to any requirement offered to the 8(a) program under Simplified Acquisition Procedures.

(1) In determining whether the acceptance of a requirement would have an adverse impact on an individual small business, SBA will consider all relevant factors.

(i) In connection with a specific small business, SBA presumes adverse impact to exist where:

(A) The small business concern has performed the specific requirement for at least 24 months;

(B) The small business is performing the requirement at the time it is offered to the 8(a) BD program, or its performance of the requirement ended within 30 days of the procuring activity's offer of the requirement to the 8(a) BD program; and

(C) The dollar value of the requirement that the small business is or was performing is 25 percent or more of its most recent annual gross sales (including those of its affiliates). For a multi-year requirement, the dollar value of the last 12 months of the requirement will be used to determine whether a small business would be adversely affected by SBA's acceptance.

(ii) Except as provided in paragraph (c)(2) of this section, adverse impact does not apply to "new" requirements. A new requirement is one which has not been previously procured by the relevant procuring activity.

(A) Where a requirement is new, no small business could have previously performed the requirement and, thus, SBA's acceptance of the requirement for the 8(a) BD program will not adversely impact any small business.

(B) Procurements for construction services (*e.g.*, the building of a specific structure) are generally deemed to be new requirements. However, recurring indefinite delivery or indefinite quantity task or delivery order construction services are not considered new (*e.g.*, a recurring procurement requiring all construction work at base X).

(C) The expansion or modification of an existing requirement will be considered a new requirement where the magnitude of change is significant enough to cause a price adjustment of at least 25 percent (adjusted for inflation) or to require significant additional or different types of capabilities or work.

(D) SBA need not perform an impact determination where a new requirement is offered to the 8(a) BD program.

(2) In determining whether the acceptance of a requirement would have an adverse impact on a group of small businesses, SBA will consider the effects of combining or consolidating various requirements being performed by two or more small business concerns into a single contract which would be considered a "new" requirement as compared to any of the previous smaller requirements. SBA may find adverse impact to exist if one of the existing small business contractors meets the presumption set forth in paragraph (c)(1)(i) of this section.

(3) In determining whether the acceptance of a requirement would have an adverse impact on other small business programs, SBA will consider all relevant factors, including but not limited to, the number and value of contracts in the subject industry in the 8(a) BD program as compared with other small business programs.

(d) *Release for non-8(a) competition.* (1) Except as set forth in (d)(4) of this section, where a procurement is awarded as an 8(a) contract, its follow-on or renewable acquisition must remain in the 8(a) BD program unless SBA agrees to release it for non-8(a) competition. If a procuring agency would like to fulfill a follow-on or renewable acquisition outside of the 8(a) BD program, it must make a written request to and receive the concurrence of the AA/BD to do so. In determining whether to release a requirement from the 8(a) BD program, SBA will consider:

(i) Whether the agency has achieved its SDB goal;

(ii) Where the agency is in achieving its HUBZone, SDVO, WOSB, or small business goal, as appropriate; and

(iii) Whether the requirement is critical to the business development of the 8(a) Participant that is currently performing it.

(2) SBA may decline to accept the offer of a follow-on or renewable 8(a) acquisition in order to give a concern previously awarded the contract that is leaving or has left the 8(a) BD program the opportunity to compete for the requirement outside of the 8(a) BD program.

(i) SBA will consider release under paragraph (2) only where:

(A) The procurement awarded through the 8(a) BD program is being or was performed by either a Participant whose program term will expire prior to contract completion, or by a former Participant whose program term expired within one year of the date of the offering letter;

(B) The concern requests in writing that SBA decline to accept the offer prior to SBA's acceptance of the requirement for award as an 8(a) contract; and

(C) The concern qualifies as a small business for the requirement now offered to the 8(a) BD program.

(ii) In considering release under paragraph (2), SBA will balance the importance of the requirement to the concern's business development needs against the business development needs of other Participants that are qualified to perform the requirement. This determination will include consideration of whether rejection of the requirement would seriously reduce the pool of similar types of contracts available for award as 8(a) contracts. SBA will also seek the views of the procuring agency.

(3) SBA will release a requirement under this paragraph only where the procuring activity agrees to procure the requirement as a small business, HUBZone, SDVO small business, or WOSB set-aside.

(4) The requirement that a follow-on procurement must be released from the 8(a) BD program in order for it to be fulfilled outside the 8(a) BD program does not apply to orders offered to and accepted for the 8(a) BD program pursuant to § 124.50(3)(h)(2).

[63 FR 35739, 35772, June 30, 1998, as amended at 74 FR 45753, Sept. 4, 2009; 76 FR 8259, Feb. 11, 2011; 78 FR 61133, Oct. 2, 2013; 81 FR 34260, May 31, 2016; 81 FR 48582, July 25, 2016]

§ 124.505 When will SBA appeal the terms or conditions of a particular 8(a) contract or a procuring activity decision not to use the 8(a) BD program?

(a) *What SBA may appeal.* The Administrator of SBA may appeal the following matters to the head of the procuring agency:

(1) A contracting officer's decision not to make a particular procurement available for award as an 8(a) contract;

(2) A contracting officer's decision to reject a specific Participant for award of an 8(a) contract after SBA's acceptance of the requirement for the 8(a) BD program; and

(3) The terms and conditions of a proposed 8(a) contract, including the procuring activity's NAICS code designation and estimate of the fair market price.

(b) *Procedures for appeal.* (1) SBA must notify the contracting officer of the SBA Administrator's intent to appeal an adverse decision within 5 working days of SBA's receipt of the decision.

(2) Upon receipt of the notice of intent to appeal, the procuring activity must suspend further action regarding the procurement until the head of the procuring agency issues a written decision on the appeal, unless the head of the procuring agency makes a written determination that urgent and compelling circumstances which significantly affect interests of the United States will not permit waiting for a consideration of the appeal.

(3) The SBA Administrator must send a written appeal of the adverse decision to the head of the procuring agency within 15 working days of SBA's notification of intent to appeal or the appeal may be considered withdrawn.

(4) By statute (15 U.S.C. 637(a)(1)(A)), the procuring agency head must specify in writing the reasons for a denial of an appeal brought by the Administrator under this section.

§ 124.506 At what dollar threshold must an 8(a) procurement be competed among eligible Participants?

(a) *Competitive thresholds.* (1) The Federal Acquisition Regulatory Council (FAR Council) has the responsibility of adjusting each acquisition-related dollar threshold on October 1, of each year that is evenly divisible by five. Acquisition-related dollar thresholds are defined as dollar thresholds that are specified in law as a factor in defining the scope of the applicability of a policy, procedure, requirement, or restriction provided in that law to the procurement of property or services by an executive agency as determined by the FAR Council. 41 U.S.C. 431a(c). Part 124, Subpart A, 8(a) Business Development, contains acquisition-related dollar thresholds subject to inflationary adjustments. The FAR Council shall publish a notice of the adjusted dollar thresholds in the FEDERAL REGISTER. The adjusted dollar thresholds shall take effect on the date of publication.

(2) A procurement offered and accepted for the 8(a) BD program must be competed among eligible Participants if:

(i) There is a reasonable expectation that at least two eligible Participants will submit offers at a fair market price;

(ii) The anticipated award price of the contract, including options, will exceed $7,000,000 for contracts assigned manufacturing NAICS codes and $4,000,000 for all other contracts; and

(iii) The requirement has not been accepted by SBA for award as a sole source 8(a) procurement on behalf of a tribally-owned or ANC-owned concern.

(3) For all types of contracts, the applicable competitive threshold amounts will be applied to the procuring activity estimate of the total value of the contract, including all options.

Example to paragraph (a)(3). If the anticipated award price for a professional services requirement is determined to be $3.8 million and it is accepted as a sole source 8(a) requirement on that basis, a sole source award will be valid even if the contract price arrived at after negotiation is $4.2 million.

(4) Where the estimate of the total value of a proposed 8(a) contract is less than the applicable competitive threshold amount and the requirement is accepted as a sole source requirement on that basis, award may be made even though the contract price arrived at through negotiations exceeds the competitive threshold, provided that the contract price is not more than ten percent greater than the competitive threshold amount.

(5) A proposed 8(a) requirement with an estimated value exceeding the applicable competitive threshold amount may not be divided into several separate procurement actions for lesser amounts in order to use 8(a) sole source procedures to award to a single contractor.

(b) *Exemption from competitive thresholds for Participants owned by Indian Tribes, ANCs and NHOs.* (1) A Participant concern owned and controlled by an Indian Tribe or an ANC may be awarded a sole source 8(a) contract where the anticipated value of the procurement exceeds the applicable competitive threshold if SBA has not accepted the requirement into the 8(a) BD program as a competitive procurement.

(2) A Participant concern owned and controlled by an NHO may be awarded a sole source Department of Defense (DoD) 8(a) contract where the anticipated value of the procurement exceeds the applicable competitive threshold if SBA has not accepted the requirement into the 8(a) BD program as a competitive procurement.

(3) There is no requirement that a procurement must be competed whenever possible before it can be accepted on a sole source basis for a Tribally-owned or ANC-owned concern, or a concern owned by an NHO for DoD contracts, but a procurement may not be removed from competition to award it to a Tribally-owned, ANC-owned or NHO-owned concern on a sole source basis.

(4) A joint venture between one or more eligible Tribally-owned, ANC-owned or NHO-owned Participants and one or more non-8(a) business concerns may be awarded sole source 8(a) contracts above the competitive threshold amount, provided that it meets the requirements of § 124.513.

(5) An agency may not award an 8(a) sole source contract for an amount exceeding $22,000,000 unless the contracting officer justifies the use of a sole source contract in writing and has obtained the necessary approval under the Federal Acquisition Regulation.

(c) *Competition below thresholds.* The AA/BD, on a nondelegable basis, may approve a request from a procuring activity to compete a requirement that is below the applicable competitive threshold amount among eligible Participants.

(1) This authority will be used primarily when technical competitions are appropriate or when a large number of potential awardees exist.

(2) The AA/BD may consider whether the procuring activity has made and will continue to make available a significant number of its contracts to the 8(a) BD program on a noncompetitive basis.

(3) The AA/BD may deny a request if the procuring activity previously offered the requirement to the 8(a) BD program on a noncompetitive basis and the request is made following the inability of the procuring activity and the potential sole source awardee to reach an agreement on price or some other material term or condition.

(d) *Sole source above thresholds.* Where a contract opportunity exceeds the applicable threshold amount and there is not a reasonable expectation that at least two eligible 8(a) Participants will submit offers at a fair price, the AA/BD may accept the requirement for a sole source 8(a) award if he or she determines that an eligible Participant in the 8(a) portfolio is capable of performing the requirement at a fair price.

[63 FR 35739, June 30, 1998, as amended at 74 FR 45753, Sept. 4, 2009; 74 FR 46887, Sept. 14, 2009; 76 FR 8260, Feb. 11, 2011; 78 FR 61133, Oct. 2, 2013; 81 FR 48582, July 25, 2016]

§ 124.507 What procedures apply to competitive 8(a) procurements?

(a) *FAR procedures.* Procuring activities will conduct competitions among and evaluate offers received from Participants in accordance with the Federal Acquisition Regulation (48 CFR, chapter 1).

(b) *Eligibility determination by SBA.* In either a negotiated or sealed bid competitive 8(a) acquisition, the procuring activity will request that the SBA district office servicing the apparent successful offeror determine that firm's eligibility for award.

(1) Within 5 working days after receipt of a procuring activity's request for an eligibility determination, SBA will determine whether the firm identified by the procuring activity is eligible for award.

(2) Eligibility is based on 8(a) BD program criteria, including whether the Participant is:

(i) A small business under the NAICS code assigned to the requirement;

(ii) In compliance with any applicable competitive business mix target established or remedial measure imposed by § 124.509 that does not include the denial of future 8(a) contracts;

(iii) In compliance with the continued eligibility reporting requirements set forth in § 124.112(b);

(iv) In the developmental stage of program participation if the solicitation restricts offerors to the developmental stage of participation; and

(v) A concern with a bona fide place of business in the applicable geographic area if the procurement is for construction.

(3) Where the apparent successful offeror is a joint venture and SBA has not approved the joint venture prior to receiving notification of the apparent successful offeror, review of the joint venture will be part of the eligibility determination conducted under this paragraph (b). If SBA cannot approve the joint venture within 5 days of receiving a procuring activity's request for an eligibility determination, and the procuring activity does not grant additional time for review, SBA will be unable to verify the eligibility of the joint venture for award.

(4) If SBA determines that the apparent successful offeror is ineligible, SBA will notify the procuring activity. The procuring activity will then send to SBA the identity of the next highest evaluated firm for an eligibility determination. The process is repeated until SBA determines that an identified offeror is eligible for award.

(5) Except to the extent set forth in paragraph (d) of this section, SBA determines whether a Participant is eligible for a specific 8(a) competitive requirement as of the date that the Participant submitted its initial offer which includes price.

(6) If the procuring activity contracting officer believes that the apparent successful offeror is not responsible to perform the contract, he or she must refer the concern to SBA for a possible Certificate of Competency in accord with § 125.5 of this title.

(c) *Restricted competition*—(1) *Competition within stages of program participation.* SBA may accept a competitive 8(a) requirement that is limited to Participants in the developmental stage of program participation, or may accept a requirement to be competed among firms both in the developmental and transitional stages of program participation.

(2) *Construction competitions.* Based on its knowledge of the 8(a) BD portfolio, SBA will determine whether a competitive 8(a) construction requirement should be competed among only those Participants having a bona fide place of business within the geographical boundaries of one or more SBA district offices, within a state, or within the state and nearby areas. Only those Participants with bona fide places of business within the appropriate geographical boundaries are eligible to submit offers.

(i) A Participant may have bona fide places of business in more than one location.

(ii) In order for a Participant to establish a bona fide place of business in a particular geographic location, the SBA district office serving the geographic area of that location must determine if that location in fact qualifies as a bona fide place of business under SBA's requirements.

(A) A Participant must submit a request for a bona fide business determination to the SBA district office servicing it.

(B) The servicing district office will forward the request to the SBA district office serving the geographic area of the particular location for processing.

(iii) The effective date of a bona fide place of business is the date that the evidence (paperwork) shows that the business in fact regularly maintained its business at the new geographic location.

(iv) In order for a Participant to be eligible to submit an offer for a 8(a) procurement limited to a specific geographic area, it must receive from SBA a determination that it has a bona fide place of business within that area prior to submitting its offer for the procurement.

(3) *Competition for all non-construction requirements.* Except for construction requirements, all eligible Participants regardless of location may submit offers in response to competitive 8(a) solicitations. The only geographic restrictions pertaining to 8(a) competitive requirements, other than those for construction requirements, are any imposed by the solicitations themselves.

(d) *Award to firms whose program terms have expired.* A concern that has completed its term of participation in the 8(a) BD program may be awarded a competitive 8(a) contract if it was a Participant eligible for award of the contract on the initial date specified for receipt of offers contained in the contract solicitation, and if it continues to meet all other applicable eligibility criteria.

(1) Amendments to the solicitation extending the date for submissions of offers will be disregarded.

Example to paragraph (d)(1). The program term for 8(a) Participant X is scheduled to expire on December 19. A solicitation for a competitive 8(a) procurement specifies that initial offers are due on December 15. The procuring activity amends the solicitation to extend the date for the receipt of offers to January 5. X submits its offer on January 5 and is selected as the apparent successful offeror. X is eligible for award because it was an eligible 8(a) Participant on the initial date set forth in the solicitation for the receipt of offers.

(2) For a negotiated procurement, a Participant may submit revised offers, including a best and final offer, and be awarded a competitive 8(a) contract if it was eligible as of the initial date specified for the receipt of offers in the solicitation, even though its program term may expire after that date.

[63 FR 35739, June 30, 1998, as amended at 76 FR 8260, Feb. 11, 2011; 81 FR 48582, July 25, 2016]

§ 124.508 How is an 8(a) contract executed?

(a) An 8(a) contract can be awarded in the following ways:

(1) As a tripartite agreement in which the procuring activity, SBA and the Participant all sign the appropriate contract documents. There may be separate prime and subcontract documents (i.e., a prime contract between the procuring activity and SBA and a subcontract between SBA and the selected 8(a) concern) or a combined contract document representing both the prime and subcontract relationships; or

(2) Where SBA has delegated contract execution authority to the procuring activity, directly by the procuring activity through a contract between the procuring activity and the Participant.

(b) Where SBA receives a contract for signature valued at or below the simplified acquisition threshold, it will sign the contract and return it to the procuring activity within three (3) days of receipt.

(c) In order to be eligible to receive a sole source 8(a) contract, a firm must be a current Participant on the date of award. (*See* § 124.507(d) for competitive 8(a) awards.)

§ 124.509 What are non-8(a) business activity targets?

(a) *General.* (1) To ensure that Participants do not develop an unreasonable reliance on 8(a) awards, and to ease their transition into the competitive marketplace after graduating from the 8(a) BD program, Participants must make maximum efforts to obtain business outside the 8(a) BD program. Work performed by an 8(a) Participant for any Federal department or agency other than through an 8(a) contract, including work performed on orders under the General Services Administration Multiple Award Schedule program, and work performed as a subcontractor, including work performed as a subcontractor to another 8(a) Participant on an 8(a) contract, qualifies as work performed outside the 8(a) BD program.

(2) During both the developmental and transitional stages of the 8(a) BD program, a Participant must make substantial and sustained efforts, including following a reasonable marketing strategy, to attain the targeted dollar levels of non-8(a) revenue established in its business plan. It must attempt to use the 8(a) BD program as a resource to strengthen the firm for economic viability when program benefits are no longer available.

(b) *Required non-8(a) business activity targets during transitional stage*—(1) *General.* During the transitional stage of the 8(a) BD program, a Participant must achieve certain targets of non-8(a) contract revenue (i.e., revenue from other than sole source or competitive 8(a) contracts). These targets are called non-8(a) business activity targets and are expressed as a percentage of total revenue. The targets call for an increase in non-8(a) revenue over time.

(2) *Non-8(a) business activity targets.* During their transitional stage of program participation, Participants must meet the following non-8(a) business activity targets each year:

Participant's year in the transitional stage	Non-8(a) business activity targets (required minimum non-8(a) revenue as a percentage of total revenue)
1	15
2	25
3	35
4	45
5	55

(3) *Compliance with non-8(a) business activity targets.* SBA will measure the Participant's compliance with the applicable non-8(a) business activity target at the end of each program year in the transitional stage based on the Participant's latest fiscal year-end total revenue. Thus, at the end of the first year in the transitional stage of program participation, SBA will compare the Participant's non-8(a) revenue to its total revenue during that first year. If appropriate, SBA will require remedial measures during the subsequent program year. Thus, for example, non-compliance with the required non-8(a) business activity target in year one of the transitional stage would cause SBA to initiate remedial measures under paragraph (d) of this section for year two in the transitional stage.

(4) *Certification of compliance.* A Participant must certify as part of its offer that it complies with the applicable non-8(a) business activity target or with the measures imposed by SBA under paragraph (d) of this section before it can receive any 8(a) contract during the transitional stage of the 8(a) BD program.

(c) *Reporting and verification of business activity.* (1) Once admitted to the 8(a) BD program, a Participant must provide to SBA as part of its annual review:

(i) Annual financial statements with a breakdown of 8(a) and non-8(a) revenue in accord with § 124.602; and

(ii) An annual report within 30 days from the end of the program year of all non-8(a) contracts, options, and modifications affecting price executed during the program year.

(2) At the end of each year of participation in the transitional stage, the BOS assigned to work with the Participant will review the Participant's total revenues to determine whether the non-8(a) revenues have met the applicable target. In determining compliance, SBA will compare all 8(a) revenues received during the year, including those from options and modifications, to all non-8(a) revenues received during the year.

(d) *Consequences of not meeting competitive business mix targets.* (1) Except as set forth in paragraph (e) of this section, beginning at the end of the first year in the transitional stage (the fifth year of participation in the 8(a) BD program), any firm that does not meet its applicable competitive business mix target for the just completed program year will be ineligible for sole source 8(a) contracts in the current program year, unless and until the Participant corrects the situation as described in paragraph (d)(2) of this section.

(2) If SBA determines that an 8(a) Participant has failed to meet its applicable competitive business mix target during any program year in the transitional stage of program participation, SBA may increase its monitoring of the Participant's contracting activity during the ensuing program year. SBA will also notify the Participant in writing that the Participant will not be eligible for further 8(a) sole source contract awards until it has demonstrated to SBA that it has complied with its non-8(a) business activity requirements as described in paragraphs (d)(2)(i) and (d)(2)(ii) of this section. In order for a Participant to come into compliance with the non-8(a) business activity target and be eligible for further 8(a) sole source contracts, it may:

(i) Wait until the end of the current program year and demonstrate to SBA as part of the normal annual review process that it has met the revised non-8(a) business activity target; or

(ii) At its option, submit information regarding its non-8(a) revenue to SBA quarterly throughout the current program year in an attempt to come into compliance before the end of the current program year. If the Participant satisfies the requirements of paragraphs (d)(2)(ii)(A) or (d)(2)(ii)(B) of this section, SBA will reinstate the Participant's ability to get sole source 8(a) contracts prior to its annual review.

(A) To qualify for reinstatement during the first six months of the current program year (i.e., at either the first or second quarterly review), the Participant must demonstrate that it has received non-8(a) revenue and new non-8(a) contract awards that are equal to or greater than the dollar amount by which it failed to meet its non-8(a) business activity target for the just completed program year. For this purpose, SBA will not count options on existing non-8(a) contracts in determining whether a Participant has received new non-8(a) contract awards.

(B) To qualify for reinstatement during the last six months of the current program year (i.e., at either the nine-month or one year review), the Participant must demonstrate that it has achieved its non-8(a) business activity target as of that point in the current program year.

Example 1 to paragraph (d)(2). Firm A had $10 million in total revenue during year 2 in the transitional stage (year 6 in the program), but failed to meet the minimum non-8(a) business activity target of 25 percent. It had 8(a) revenues of $8.5 million and non-8(a) revenues of $1.5 million (15 percent). Based on total revenues of $10 million, Firm A should have had at least $2.5 million in non-8(a) revenues. Thus, Firm A missed its target by $1 million (its target ($2.5 million) minus its actual non-8(a) revenues ($1.5 million)). Because Firm A did not achieve its non-8(a) business activity target, it cannot receive 8(a) sole source awards until correcting that situation. The firm may wait until the next annual review to establish that it has met the revised target, or it can choose to report contract awards and other non-8(a) revenue to SBA quarterly. Firm A elects to submit information to SBA quarterly in year 3 of the transitional stage (year 7 in the program). In order to be eligible for sole source 8(a) contracts after either its 3 month or 6 month review, Firm A must show that it has received non-8(a) revenue and/or been awarded new non-8(a) contracts totaling $1 million (the amount by which it missed its target in year 2 of the transitional stage).

Example 2 to paragraph (d)(2). Firm B had $10 million in total revenue during year 2 in the transitional stage (year 6 in the program), of which $8.5 million were 8(a) revenues and $1.5 million were non-8(a) revenues. At its first two quarterly reviews during year 3 of the transitional stage (year 7 in the program), Firm B could not demonstrate that it had received at least $1 million in non-8(a) revenue and new non-8(a) awards. In order to be eligible for sole source 8(a) contracts after its 9 month or 1 year review, Firm B must show that at least 35% (the non-8(a) business activity target for year 3 in the transitional stage) of all revenues received during year 3 in the transitional stage as of that point are from non-8(a) sources.

(3) In determining whether a Participant has achieved its required non-8(a) business activity target at the end of any program year in the transitional stage, or whether a Participant that failed to meet the target for the previous program year has achieved the required level of non-8(a) business at

its nine-month review, SBA will measure 8(a) support by adding the base year value of all 8(a) contracts awarded during the applicable program year to the value of all options and modifications executed during that year.

(4) As a condition of eligibility for new 8(a) contracts, SBA may also impose other requirements on a Participant that fails to achieve the non-8(a) business activity targets. These include requiring the Participant to obtain management assistance, technical assistance, and/or counseling, and/or attend seminars relating to management assistance, business development, financing, marketing, accounting, or proposal preparation.

(5) SBA may initiate proceedings to terminate a Participant from the 8(a) BD program where the firm makes no good faith efforts to obtain non-8(a) revenues.

(e) *Waiver of sole source prohibition.* (1) The AA/BD, or his or her designee, may waive the requirement prohibiting a Participant from receiving further sole source 8(a) contracts when a Participant does not meet its non-8(a) business activity target where a denial of a sole source contract would cause severe economic hardship on the Participant so that the Participant's survival may be jeopardized, or where extenuating circumstances beyond the Participant's control caused the Participant not to meet its non-8(a) business activity target. A firm receiving a waiver will be able to self market its capabilities and receive one or more sole source 8(a) contracts during the next program year. At its next annual review, SBA will reevaluate the firm's circumstances and determine whether the waiver should be extended an additional program year. The decision to grant or deny a request for a waiver is at SBA's discretion, and no appeal may be taken with respect to that decision.

(2) The SBA Administrator on a non-delegable basis may waive the requirement prohibiting a Participant from receiving further sole source 8(a) contracts when the Participant does not meet its non-8(a) business activity target where the head of a procuring activity represents to the SBA Administrator that award of a sole source 8(a) contract to the Participant is needed to achieve significant interests of the Government.

[63 FR 35739, June 30, 1998, as amended at 74 FR 45754, Sept. 4, 2009; 76 FR 8261, Feb. 11, 2011]

§ 124.510 What limitations on subcontracting apply to an 8(a) contract?

(a) To assist the business development of Participants in the 8(a) BD program, there are limitations on the percentage of an 8(a) contract award amount that may be spent on subcontractors. The prime contractor recipient of an 8(a) contract must comply with the limitations on subcontracting at § 125.6 of this chapter.

(b) Indefinite delivery and indefinite quantity contracts. In order to ensure that the required limitations on subcontracting requirements on an indefinite delivery or indefinite quantity 8(a) award are met by the Participant, the Participant cannot subcontract more than the required percentage to subcontractors that are not similarly situated entities for each performance period of the contract (*i.e.*, during the base term and then during each option period thereafter). However, the contracting officer, in his or her discretion, may require the Participant to meet the applicable limitation on subcontracting or comply with the nonmanufacturer rule for each order.

(1) This includes Multiple Award Contracts that were set-aside or partially set-aside for 8(a) BD Participants.

(2) For orders that are set aside for eligible 8(a) Participants under full and open contracts or reserves, the Participant must meet the applicable limitation on subcontracting requirement and comply with the nonmanufacturer rule, if applicable, for each order.

[81 FR 34260, May 31, 2016]

§ 124.511 How is fair market price determined for an 8(a) contract?

(a) The procuring activity determines what constitutes a "fair market price" for an 8(a) contract.

(1) The procuring activity must derive the estimate of a current fair market price for a new requirement, or a requirement that does not have a satisfactory procurement history, from a price or cost analysis. This analysis

may take into account prevailing market conditions, commercial prices for similar products or services, or data obtained from any other agency. The analysis must also consider any cost or pricing data that is timely submitted by SBA.

(2) The procuring activity must base the estimate of a current fair market price for a requirement that has a satisfactory procurement history on recent award prices adjusted to ensure comparability. Adjustments will take into account differences in quantities, performance, times, plans, specifications, transportation costs, packaging and packing costs, labor and material costs, overhead costs, and any other additional costs which may be appropriate.

(b) Upon the request of SBA, a procuring activity will provide to SBA a written statement detailing the method it has used to estimate the current fair market price for the 8(a) requirement. This statement must be submitted within 10 working days of SBA's request. The procuring activity must identify the information, studies, analyses, and other data it used in making its estimate.

(c) The procuring activity's estimate of fair market price and any supporting data may not be disclosed by SBA to any Participant or potential contractor.

(d) The concern selected to perform an 8(a) contract may request SBA to protest the procuring activity's estimate of current fair market price to the Secretary of the Department or head of the agency in accordance with § 124.505.

§ 124.512 Delegation of contract administration to procuring agencies.

(a) SBA may delegate, by the use of special clauses in the 8(a) contract documents or by a separate agreement with the procuring activity, all responsibilities for administering an 8(a) contract to the procuring activity except the approval of novation agreements under 48 CFR 42.302(a)(25). Tracking compliance with the performance of work requirements set forth in § 124.510 is included within the functions performed by the procuring activity as part of contract administration.

(b) This delegation of contract administration authorizes a contracting officer to execute any priced option or in scope modification without SBA's concurrence. The contracting officer must, however, submit copies to the SBA servicing district office of all modifications and options exercised within 15 business days of their occurrence, or by another date agreed upon by SBA.

(c) SBA may conduct periodic compliance on-site agency reviews of the files of all contracts awarded pursuant to Section 8(a) authority.

[63 FR 35739, June 30, 1998, as amended at 76 FR 8261, Feb. 11, 2011]

§ 124.513 Under what circumstances can a joint venture be awarded an 8(a) contract?

(a) *General.* (1) If approved by SBA, a Participant may enter into a joint venture agreement with one or more other small business concerns, whether or not 8(a) Participants, for the purpose of performing one or more specific 8(a) contracts.

(2) A joint venture agreement is permissible only where an 8(a) concern lacks the necessary capacity to perform the contract on its own, and the agreement is fair and equitable and will be of substantial benefit to the 8(a) concern. However, where SBA concludes that an 8(a) concern brings very little to the joint venture relationship in terms of resources and expertise other than its 8(a) status, SBA will not approve the joint venture arrangement.

(b) *Size of concerns to an 8(a) joint venture.* (1) A joint venture of at least one 8(a) Participant and one or more other business concerns may submit an offer as a small business for a competitive 8(a) procurement, or be awarded a sole source 8(a) procurement, so long as each concern is small under the size standard corresponding to the NAICS code assigned to the procurement.

(2) Notwithstanding the provisions of paragraph (b)(1) of this section, a joint venture between a protégé firm and its approved mentor (*see* § 124.520) will be deemed small provided the protégé qualifies as small for the size standard corresponding to the NAICS code assigned to the contract and has not

reached the dollar limits set forth in § 124.519.

(3) SBA approval of a joint venture agreement pursuant to paragraph (e) of this section does not equate to a formal size determination. As such, despite SBA's approval of a joint venture, the size status of a joint venture that is the apparent successful offeror for a competitive 8(a) contract may be protested pursuant to § 121.1001(a)(2) of this chapter. *See* § 124.517(b).

(c) *Contents of joint venture agreement.* Every joint venture agreement to perform an 8(a) contract, including those between mentors and protégés authorized by § 124.520, must contain a provision:

(1) Setting forth the purpose of the joint venture;

(2) Designating an 8(a) Participant as the managing venturer of the joint venture and an employee of an 8(a) Participant as the project manager responsible for performance of the contract. The individual identified as the project manager of the joint venture need not be an employee of the 8(a) Participant at the time the joint venture submits an offer, but, if he or she is not, there must be a signed letter of intent that the individual commits to be employed by the 8(a) Participant if the joint venture is the successful offeror. The individual identified as the project manager cannot be employed by the mentor and become an employee of the 8(a) Participant for purposes of performance under the joint venture;

(3) Stating that with respect to a separate legal entity joint venture the 8(a) Participant(s) must own at least 51% of the joint venture entity;

(4) Stating that the 8(a) Participant(s) must receive profits from the joint venture commensurate with the work performed by the 8(a) Participant(s);

(5) Providing for the establishment and administration of a special bank account in the name of the joint venture. This account must require the signature of all parties to the joint venture or designees for withdrawal purposes. All payments due the joint venture for performance on an 8(a) contract will be deposited in the special account; all expenses incurred under the contract will be paid from the account as well;

(6) Itemizing all major equipment, facilities, and other resources to be furnished by each party to the joint venture, with a detailed schedule of cost or value of each, where practical. If a contract is indefinite in nature, such as an indefinite quantity contract or a multiple award contract where the level of effort or scope of work is not known, the joint venture must provide a general description of the anticipated major equipment, facilities, and other resources to be furnished by each party to the joint venture, without a detailed schedule of cost or value of each, or in the alternative, specify how the parties to the joint venture will furnish such resources to the joint venture once a definite scope of work is made publicly available;

(7) Specifying the responsibilities of the parties with regard to negotiation of the contract, source of labor, and contract performance, including ways that the parties to the joint venture will ensure that the joint venture and the 8(a) partner(s) to the joint venture will meet the performance of work requirements set forth in paragraph (d) of this section, where practical. If a contract is indefinite in nature, such as an indefinite quantity contract or a multiple award contract where the level of effort or scope of work is not known, the joint venture must provide a general description of the anticipated responsibilities of the parties with regard to negotiation of the contract, source of labor, and contract performance, not including the ways that the parties to the joint venture will ensure that the joint venture and the 8(a) partner(s) to the joint venture will meet the performance of work requirements set forth in paragraph (d) of this section, or in the alternative, specify how the parties to the joint venture will define such responsibilities once a definite scope of work is made publicly available;

(8) Obligating all parties to the joint venture to ensure performance of the 8(a) contract and to complete performance despite the withdrawal of any member;

(9) Designating that accounting and other administrative records relating

to the joint venture be kept in the office of the 8(a) Participant managing venturer, unless approval to keep them elsewhere is granted by the District Director or his/her designee upon written request;

(10) Requiring the final original records be retained by the 8(a) Participant managing venturer upon completion of the 8(a) contract performed by the joint venture;

(11) Stating that quarterly financial statements showing cumulative contract receipts and expenditures (including salaries of the joint venture's principals) must be submitted to SBA not later than 45 days after each operating quarter of the joint venture; and

(12) Stating that a project-end profit and loss statement, including a statement of final profit distribution, must be submitted to SBA no later than 90 days after completion of the contract.

(d) *Performance of work.* (1) For any 8(a) contract, including those between a protégé and a mentor authorized by §124.520, the joint venture must perform the applicable percentage of work required by §124.510 of this chapter.

(2) The 8(a) partner(s) to the joint venture must perform at least 40% of the work performed by the joint venture.

(i) The work performed by the 8(a) partner(s) to a joint venture must be more than administrative or ministerial functions so that the 8(a) partners gain substantive experience.

(ii) The amount of work done by the partners will be aggregated and the work done by the 8(a) partner(s) must be at least 40% of the total done by all partners. In determining the amount of work done by a non-8(a) partner, all work done by the non-8(a) partner and any of its affiliates at any subcontracting tier will be counted.

(e) *Prior approval by SBA.* (1) SBA must approve a joint venture agreement prior to the award of an 8(a) contract on behalf of the joint venture. A Participant may submit a joint venture agreement to SBA for approval at any time, whether or not in connection with a specific 8(a) procurement.

(2) Where a joint venture has been established and approved by SBA for one 8(a) contract, a second or third 8(a) contract may be awarded to that joint venture provided an addendum to the joint venture agreement, setting forth the performance requirements on that second or third contract, is provided to and approved by SBA prior to contract award.

(i) After approving the structure of the joint venture in connection with the first contract, SBA will review only the addendums relating to performance of work on successive contracts.

(ii) SBA must approve the addendums prior to the award of any successive 8(a) contract to the joint venture.

(iii) If a second or third contract to be awarded a joint venture is not an 8(a) contract, the Participant would not have to submit an addendum setting forth contract performance for the non-8(a) contract(s) to SBA for approval.

(3) Where a joint venture has been established and approved by SBA without a corresponding specific 8(a) contract award (including where a joint venture is established in connection with a blanket purchase agreement (BPA), basic agreement (BA), or basic ordering agreement (BOA)), the Participant must submit an addendum to the joint venture agreement, setting forth the performance requirements, to SBA for approval for each of the three 8(a) contracts authorized to be awarded to the joint venture. In the case of a BPA, BA or BOA, each order issued under the agreement would count as a separate contract award, and SBA would need to approve the addendum for each order prior to award of the order to the joint venture.

(f) *Past performance and experience.* When evaluating the past performance and experience of an entity submitting an offer for an 8(a) contract as a joint venture approved by SBA pursuant to this section, a procuring activity must consider work done individually by each partner to the joint venture as well as any work done by the joint venture itself previously.

(g) *Contract execution.* Where SBA has approved a joint venture, the procuring activity will execute an 8(a) contract in the name of the joint venture entity or the 8(a) Participant, but in either case will identify the award as one to an 8(a) joint venture or an 8(a) mentor-protégé joint venture, as appropriate.

(h) *Amendments to joint venture agreement.* All amendments to the joint venture agreement must be approved by SBA.

(i) *Inspection of records.* The joint venture partners must allow SBA's authorized representatives, including representatives authorized by the SBA Inspector General, during normal business hours, access to its files to inspect and copy all records and documents relating to the joint venture.

(j) *Certification of compliance.* Prior to the performance of any 8(a) contract by a joint venture, the 8(a) BD Participant to the joint venture must submit a written certification to the contracting officer and SBA, signed by an authorized official of each partner to the joint venture, stating as follows:

(i) The parties have entered into a joint venture agreement that fully complies with paragraph (c) of this section;

(ii) The parties will perform the contract in compliance with the joint venture agreement and with the performance of work requirements set forth in paragraph (d) of this section.

(iii) The parties have obtained SBA's approval of the joint venture agreement and any addendum to that agreement and that there have been no modifications to the agreement that SBA has not approved.

(k) *Performance of work reports.* An 8(a) Participant to a joint venture must describe how it is meeting or has met the applicable performance of work requirements for each 8(a) contract it performs as a joint venture.

(1) As part of its annual review, the 8(a) Participant(s) to the joint venture must explain for each 8(a) contract performed during the year how the performance of work requirements are being met for the contract.

(2) At the completion of every 8(a) contract awarded to a joint venture, the 8(a) Participant(s) to the joint venture must submit a report to the local SBA district office explaining how the performance of work requirements were met for the contract.

(l) *Basis for suspension or debarment.* The Government may consider the following as a ground for suspension or debarment as a willful violation of a regulatory provision or requirement applicable to a public agreement or transaction:

(1) Failure to enter a joint venture agreement that complies with paragraph (c) of this section;

(2) Failure to perform a contract in accordance with the joint venture agreement or performance of work requirements in paragraph (d) of this section; or

(3) Failure to submit the certification required by paragraph (e) of this section or comply with paragraph (i) of this section.

[63 FR 35739, June 30, 1998, as amended at 69 FR 29208, May 21, 2004; 76 FR 8261, Feb. 11, 2011; 77 FR 28238, May 14, 2012; 81 FR 34261, May 31, 2016; 81 FR 48582, July 25, 2016; 81 FR 71983, Oct. 19, 2016]

§ 124.514 Exercise of 8(a) options and modifications.

(a) *Unpriced options.* The exercise of an unpriced option is considered to be a new contracting action.

(1) If a concern has graduated or been terminated from the 8(a) BD program or is no longer small under the size standard corresponding to the NAICS code for the requirement, negotiations to price the option cannot be entered into and the option cannot be exercised.

(2) If the concern is still a Participant and otherwise eligible for the requirement on a sole source basis, the procuring activity contracting officer may negotiate price and exercise the option provided the option, considered a new contracting action, meets all regulatory requirements, including the procuring activity's offering and SBA's acceptance of the requirement for the 8(a) BD program.

(3) If the estimated fair market price of the option exceeds the applicable threshold amount set forth in § 124.506, the requirement must be competed as a new contract among eligible Participants.

(b) *Priced options.* The procuring activity contracting officer may exercise a priced option to an 8(a) contract whether the concern that received the award has graduated or been terminated from the 8(a) BD program or is no longer eligible if to do so is in the best interests of the Government.

(c) *Modifications beyond the scope.* A modification beyond the scope of the initial 8(a) contract award is considered to be a new contracting action. It will be treated the same as an unpriced option as described in paragraph (a) of this section.

(d) *Modifications within the scope.* The procuring activity contracting officer may exercise a modification within the scope of the initial 8(a) contract whether the concern that received the award has graduated or been terminated from the 8(a) BD program or is no longer eligible if to do so is in the best interests of the Government.

§ 124.515 Can a Participant change its ownership or control and continue to perform an 8(a) contract, and can it transfer performance to another firm?

(a) An 8(a) contract (or 8(a) order where the underlying contract is not an 8(a) contract) must be performed by the Participant that initially received it unless a waiver is granted under paragraph (b) of this section.

(1) An 8(a) contract or order, whether in the base or an option year, must be terminated for the convenience of the Government if:

(i) One or more of the individuals upon whom eligibility for the 8(a) BD program was based relinquishes or enters into any agreement to relinquish ownership or control of the Participant such that the Participant would no longer be controlled or at least 51% owned by disadvantaged individuals; or

(ii) The contract is transferred or novated for any reason to another firm.

(2) The procuring activity may not assess repurchase costs or other damages against the Participant due solely to the provisions of this section.

(b) The SBA Administrator may waive the requirements of paragraph (a)(1) of this section if requested to do so by the 8(a) contractor when:

(1) It is necessary for the owners of the concern to surrender partial control of such concern on a temporary basis in order to obtain equity financing;

(2) Ownership and control of the concern that is performing the 8(a) contract will pass to another Participant, but only if the acquiring firm would otherwise be eligible to receive the award directly as an 8(a) contract;

(3) Any individual upon whom eligibility was based is no longer able to exercise control of the concern due to physical or mental incapacity or death;

(4) The head of the procuring agency, or an official with delegated authority from the agency head, certifies that termination of the contract would severely impair attainment of the agency's program objectives or missions; or

(5) It is necessary for the disadvantaged owners of the initial 8(a) awardee to relinquish ownership of a majority of the voting stock of the concern in order to raise equity capital, but only if—

(i) The concern has graduated from the 8(a) BD program;

(ii) The disadvantaged owners will maintain ownership of the largest single outstanding block of voting stock (including stock held by affiliated parties); and

(iii) The disadvantaged owners will maintain control of the daily business operations of the concern.

(c) The 8(a) contractor must request a waiver in writing prior to the change of ownership and control except in the case of death or incapacity. A request for waiver due to incapacity or death must be submitted within 60 days after such occurrence. The Participant seeking to change ownership or control must specify the grounds upon which it requests a waiver, and must demonstrate that the proposed transaction would meet such grounds.

(d) SBA determines the eligibility of an acquiring Participant under paragraph (b)(2) of this section by referring to the items identified in § 124.507(b)(2) and deciding whether at the time of the request for waiver (and prior to the transaction) the acquiring Participant is a responsible and eligible concern with respect to each contract for which a waiver is sought. As part of the waiver request, the acquiring firm must certify that it is a small business for the size standard corresponding to the NAICS code assigned to each contract for which a waiver is sought.

(e) Anyone other than a procuring agency head who submits a certification regarding the impairment of the agency's objectives under paragraph (b)(4) of this section, must also certify delegated authority to make the certification.

(f) In processing a request for a waiver under paragraph (b)(2) of this section, SBA will treat a transfer of all a Participant's operating assets to another Participant the same as the transfer of an ownership interest, provided the Participant that transfers its assets to another eligible Participant:

(1) Voluntarily graduates from the 8(a) BD program; and

(2) Ceases its business operations, or presents a plan to SBA for its orderly dissolution.

(g) A concern performing an 8(a) contract must notify SBA in writing immediately upon entering into an agreement or agreement in principle (either oral or written) to transfer all or part of its stock or other ownership interest or assets to any other party. Such an agreement could include an oral agreement to enter into a transaction to transfer interests in the future.

(h) The Administrator has discretion to decline a request for waiver even though legal authority exists to grant the waiver.

(i) The 8(a) contractor may appeal SBA's denial of a waiver request by filing a petition with OHA pursuant to part 134 of this chapter within 45 days after the contractor receives the Administrator's decision.

[63 FR 35739, June 30, 1998, as amended at 67 FR 47246, July 18, 2002; 81 FR 48584, July 25, 2016]

§ 124.516 Who decides contract disputes arising between a Participant and a procuring activity after the award of an 8(a) contract?

For purposes of the Disputes Clause of a specific 8(a) contract, the contracting officer is that of the procuring activity. A dispute arising between an 8(a) contractor and the procuring activity contracting officer will be decided by the procuring activity, and appeals may be taken by the 8(a) contractor without SBA involvement.

§ 124.517 Can the eligibility or size of a Participant for award of an 8(a) contract be questioned?

(a) The eligibility of a Participant for a sole source or competitive 8(a) requirement may not be challenged by another Participant or any other party, either to SBA or any administrative forum as part of a bid or other contract protest.

(b) The size status of the apparent successful offeror for a competitive 8(a) procurement may be protested pursuant to § 121.1001(a)(2) of this chapter. The size status of a nominated Participant for a sole source 8(a) procurement may not be protested by another Participant or any other party.

(c) A Participant cannot appeal SBA's determination not to award it a specific 8(a) contract because the concern lacks an element of responsibility or is ineligible for the contract, other than the right set forth in § 124.501(h) to request a formal size determination where SBA cannot verify it to be small.

(d)(1) The NAICS code assigned to a sole source 8(a) requirement may not be challenged by another Participant or any other party either to SBA or any administrative forum as part of a bid or contract protest. Only the AA/BD may appeal a NAICS code designation with respect to a sole source 8(a) requirement.

(2) In connection with a competitive 8(a) procurement, any interested party who has been adversely affected by a NAICS code designation may appeal the designation to SBA's OHA pursuant to § 121.1103 of this title.

(e) Anyone with information questioning the eligibility of a Participant to continue participation in the 8(a) BD program or for purposes of a specific 8(a) contract may submit such information to SBA under § 124.112(c).

[63 FR 35739, June 30, 1998, as amended at 74 FR 45754, Sept. 4, 2009]

§ 124.518 How can an 8(a) contract be terminated before performance is completed?

(a) *Termination for default.* A decision to terminate a specific 8(a) contract for default can be made by the procuring activity contracting officer after consulting with SBA. The contracting officer must advise SBA of any intent to terminate an 8(a) contract for default in writing before doing so. SBA may provide to the Participant any program benefits reasonably available in order to assist it in avoiding termination for default. SBA will advise the contracting officer of this effort. Any procuring activity contracting officer who believes grounds for termination continue to exist may terminate the 8(a) contract for default, in accordance with the Federal Acquisition Regulations (48 CFR chapter 1). SBA will have no liability for termination costs or reprocurement costs.

(b) *Termination for convenience.* After consulting with SBA, the procuring activity contracting officer may terminate an 8(a) contract for convenience when it is in the best interests of the Government to do so. A termination for convenience is appropriate if any disadvantaged owner of the Participant performing the contract relinquishes ownership or control of such concern, or enters into any agreement to relinquish such ownership or control, unless a waiver is granted pursuant to § 124.515.

(c) *Substitution of one 8(a) contractor for another.* Where a procuring activity contracting officer demonstrates to SBA that an 8(a) contract will otherwise be terminated for default, SBA may authorize another Participant to complete performance and, in conjunction with the procuring activity, permit novation of the contract without invoking the termination for convenience or waiver provisions of § 124.515.

§ 124.519 Are there any dollar limits on the amount of 8(a) contracts that a Participant may receive?

(a) A Participant (other than one owned by an Indian Tribe, ANC or NHO) may not receive sole source 8(a) contract awards where it has received a combined total of competitive and sole source 8(a) contracts in excess of the dollar amount set forth in this section during its participation in the 8(a) BD program.

(1) For a firm having a receipts-based primary NAICS code at time of program entry, the limit above which it can no longer receive sole source 8(a) contracts is five times the size standard corresponding to its primary NAICS code which is determined as of the date of SBA's acceptance of the requirement for the 8(a) BD program or $100,000,000, whichever is less.

(2) For a firm having an employee-based primary NAICS code at time of program entry, the limit above which it can no longer receive sole source 8(a) contracts is $100,000,000.

(3) SBA will not consider 8(a) contracts awarded under $100,000 in determining whether a Participant has reached the limit identified in paragraphs (a)(1) and (a)(2) of this section.

(b) Once the limit is reached, a firm may not receive any more 8(a) sole source contracts, but may remain eligible for competitive 8(a) awards.

(c) SBA includes the dollar value of 8(a) options and modifications in determining whether a Participant has reached the limit identified in paragraph (a) of this section. If an option is not exercised or the contract value is reduced by modification, SBA will deduct those values.

(d) A Participant's eligibility for a sole source award in terms of whether it has exceeded the dollar limit for 8(a) contracts is measured as of the date that the requirement is accepted for the 8(a) program without taking into account whether the value of that award will cause the limit to be exceeded.

(e) The AA/BD may waive the requirement prohibiting a Participant from receiving sole source 8(a) contracts in excess of the dollar amount set forth in this section where the head of a procuring activity represents that award of a sole source 8(a) contract to the Participant is needed to achieve significant interests of the Government.

[63 FR 35739, June 30, 1998, as amended at 76 FR 8262, Feb. 11, 2011; 77 FR 28238, May 14, 2012]

§ 124.520 What are the rules governing SBA's Mentor/Protégé program?

(a) *General.* The mentor/protégé program is designed to encourage approved mentors to provide various forms of business development assistance to protégé firms. This assistance may include technical and/or management assistance; financial assistance in the form of equity investments and/or loans; subcontracts (either from the mentor to the protégé or from the protégé to the mentor); trade education; and/or assistance in performing prime contracts with the Government through joint venture arrangements. Mentors are encouraged to provide assistance relating to the performance of non-8(a) contracts so that protégé firms may more fully develop their capabilities. The purpose of the mentor/protégé relationship is to enhance the capabilities of the protégé, assist the protégé with meeting the goals established in its SBA-approved business plan, and to improve its ability to successfully compete for contracts.

(b) *Mentors.* Any concern that demonstrates a commitment and the ability to assist developing 8(a) Participants may act as a mentor and receive benefits as set forth in this section. This includes businesses that have graduated from the 8(a) BD program, firms that are in the transitional stage of program participation, other small businesses, and large businesses.

(1) In order to qualify as a mentor, a concern must demonstrate that it:

(i) Is capable of carrying out its responsibilities to assist the protégé firm under the proposed mentor-protégé agreement;

(ii) Possesses good character;

(iii) Does not appear on the federal list of debarred or suspended contractors; and

(iv) Can impart value to a protégé firm due to lessons learned and practical experience gained because of the 8(a) BD program, or through its knowledge of general business operations and government contracting.

(2) Generally a mentor will have no more than one protégé at a time. However, the AA/BD may authorize a concern to mentor more than one protégé at a time where it can demonstrate that the additional mentor/protégé relationship will not adversely affect the development of either protégé firm (*e.g.*, the second firm may not be a competitor of the first firm). Under no circumstances will a mentor be permitted to have more than three protégés at one time in the aggregate under the mentor-protégé programs authorized by §§ 124.520 and 125.9 of this chapter.

(3) In order to demonstrate that it is capable of carrying out its responsibilities to assist the protégé firm under the proposed mentor-protégé agreement, a firm seeking to be a mentor may submit to the SBA copies of the federal tax returns it submitted to the IRS, or audited financial statements, including any notes, or in the case of publicly traded concerns, the filings required by the Securities and Exchange Commission (SEC), for the past three years.

(4) Once approved, a mentor must annually certify that it continues to possess good character and a favorable financial position.

(c) *Protégés.* (1) In order to initially qualify as a protégé firm, a concern must:

(i) Qualify as small for the size standard corresponding to its primary NAICS code or identify that it is seeking business development assistance with respect to a secondary NAICS code and qualify as small for the size standard corresponding to that NAICS code; and

(ii) Demonstrate how the business development assistance to be received through its proposed mentor-protégé relationship would advance the goals and objectives set forth in its business plan.

(2) Only firms that are in good standing in the 8(a) BD program (e.g., firms that do not have termination or suspension proceedings against them, and are up to date with all reporting requirements) may qualify as a protégé.

(3) A protégé firm may generally have only one mentor at a time. The AA/BD may approve a second mentor for a particular protégé firm where the second relationship will not compete or otherwise conflict with the business development assistance set forth in the first mentor/protégé relationship and either:

(i) The second relationship pertains to a, secondary NAICS code; or

(ii) The protégé firm is seeking to acquire a specific expertise that the first mentor does not possess.

(4) The AA/BD may authorize a Participant to be both a protégé and a mentor at the same time where the Participant can demonstrate that the second relationship will not compete or

otherwise conflict with the first mentor-protégé relationship.

(d) *Benefits.* (1) A mentor and protégé may joint venture as a small business for any government prime contract or subcontract, including procurements with a dollar value less than half the size standard corresponding to the assigned NAICS code and 8(a) sole source contracts, provided the protégé qualifies as small for the procurement and, for purposes of 8(a) sole source requirements, the protégé has not reached the dollar limit set forth in § 124.519.

(i) SBA must approve the mentor/protégé agreement before the two firms may submit an offer as a joint venture on a particular government prime contract or subcontract in order for the joint venture to receive the exclusion from affiliation.

(ii) In order to receive the exclusion from affiliation for both 8(a) and non-8(a) procurements, the joint venture must meet the requirements set forth in § 124.513(c).

(iii) Once a protégé firm graduates or otherwise leaves the 8(a) BD program or grows to be other than small for its primary NAICS code, it will not be eligible for any further 8(a) contracting benefits from its 8(a) BD mentor-protégé relationship. Leaving the 8(a) BD program, growing to be other than small for its primary NAICS code, or terminating the mentor-protégé relationship while a protégé is still in the program, does not, however, generally affect contracts previously awarded to a joint venture between the protégé and its mentor. A protégé firm that graduates or otherwise leaves the 8(a) BD program but continues to qualify as a small business may transfer its 8(a) mentor-protégé relationship to a small business mentor-protégé relationship. In order to effectuate such a transfer, a firm must notify SBA of its intent to transfer its 8(a) mentor-protégé relationship to a small business mentor-protégé relationship. The transfer will occur without any application or approval process.

(A) A joint venture between a protégé firm that continues to qualify as small and its mentor may certify its status as small for any Government contract or subcontract so long as the protégé (and/or the joint venture) has not been determined to be other than small for the size standard corresponding to the procurement at issue (or any higher size standard).

(B) Where the protégé firm no longer qualifies as small, the receipts and/or employees of the protégé and mentor would generally be aggregated in determining the size of any joint venture between the mentor and protégé after that date.

(C) Except for contracts with durations of more than five years (including options), a contract awarded to a joint venture between a protégé and a mentor as a small business continues to qualify as an award to small business for the life of that contract and the joint venture remains obligated to continue performance on that contract.

(D) For contracts with durations of more than five years (including options), where size re-certification is required no more than 120 days prior to the end of the fifth year of the contract and no more than 120 days prior to exercising any option thereafter, once the protégé firm no longer qualifies as small for its primary NAICS code, the joint venture must aggregate the receipts/employees of the partners to the joint venture in determining whether it continues to qualify as and can recertify itself to be a small business under the size standard corresponding to the NAICS code assigned to that contract. The rules set forth in § 121.404(g)(3) of this chapter apply in such circumstances.

(2) Notwithstanding the requirements set forth in §§ 124.105(g) and (h), in order to raise capital for the protégé firm, the mentor may own an equity interest of up to 40% in the protégé firm.

(3) Notwithstanding the mentor/protégé relationship, a protégé firm may qualify for other assistance as a small business, including SBA financial assistance.

(4) No determination of affiliation or control may be found between a protégé firm and its mentor based on the mentor/protégé agreement or any assistance provided pursuant to the agreement.

(5) Where appropriate, procuring activities may provide incentives in the contract evaluation process to a firm

that will provide significant subcontracting work to its SBA-approved protégé firm.

(e) *Written agreement.* (1) The mentor and protégé firms must enter a written agreement setting forth an assessment of the protégé's needs and providing a detailed description and timeline for the delivery of the assistance the mentor commits to provide to address those needs (*e.g.*, management and/or technical assistance, loans and/or equity investments, cooperation on joint venture projects, or subcontracts under prime contracts being performed by the mentor). The mentor/protégé agreement must:

(i) Address how the assistance to be provided through the agreement will help the protégé firm meet the goals established in its SBA-approved business plan;

(ii) Establish a single point of contact in the mentor concern who is responsible for managing and implementing the mentor/protégé agreement; and

(iii) Provide that the mentor will provide such assistance to the protégé firm for at least one year.

(2) A firm seeking SBA's approval to be a protégé must identify any other mentor-protégé relationship it has through another federal agency or SBA and provide a copy of each such mentor-protégé agreement to SBA.

(i) The 8(a) BD mentor-protégé agreement must identify how the assistance to be provided by the proposed mentor is different from assistance provided to the protégé through another mentor-protégé relationship, either with the same or a different mentor.

(ii) A firm seeking SBA's approval to be a protégé may terminate a mentor-protégé relationship it has through another agency and use any not yet provided assistance identified in the other mentor-protégé agreement as part of the assistance that will be provided through the 8(a) BD mentor-protégé relationship. Any assistance that has already been provided through another mentor-protégé relationship cannot be identified as assistance that will be provided through the 8(a) BD mentor-protégé relationship.

(3) The written agreement must be approved by the AA/BD. The agreement will not be approved if SBA determines that the assistance to be provided is not sufficient to promote any real developmental gains to the protégé, or if SBA determines that the agreement is merely a vehicle to enable the mentor to receive 8(a) contracts.

(4) The agreement must provide that either the protégé or the mentor may terminate the agreement with 30 days advance notice to the other party to the mentor/protégé relationship and to SBA.

(5) SBA will review the mentor-protégé relationship annually during the protégé firm's annual review to determine whether to approve its continuation for another year. Unless rescinded in writing at that time, the mentor-protégé relationship will automatically renew without additional written notice of continuation or extension to the protégé firm. The term of a mentor-protégé agreement may not exceed three years, but may be extended for a second three years. A protégé may have two three-year mentor-protégé agreements with different mentors, and each may be extended an additional three years provided the protégé has received the agreed-upon business development assistance and will continue to receive additional assistance through the extended mentor-protégé agreement.

(6) SBA must approve all changes to a mentor/protégé agreement in advance.

(7) If control of the mentor changes (through a stock sale or otherwise), the previously approved mentor-protégé relationship may continue provided that, after the change in control, the mentor expresses in writing to SBA that it acknowledges the mentor-protégé agreement and certifies that it will continue to abide by its terms.

(8) SBA may terminate the mentor-protégé agreement at any time if it determines that the protégé is not adequately benefiting from the relationship or that the parties are not complying with any term or condition of the mentor protégé agreement. In the event SBA terminates the relationship, the mentor-protégé joint venture is obligated to complete any previously awarded contracts unless the procuring agency issues a stop work order.

(f) *Decision to decline mentor/protégé relationship.* (1) Where SBA declines to approve a specific mentor/protégé agreement, the protégé may request the AA/BD to reconsider the Agency's initial decline decision by filing a request for reconsideration with its servicing SBA district office within 45 calendar days of receiving notice that its mentor/protégé agreement was declined. The protégé may revise the proposed mentor/protégé agreement and provide any additional information and documentation pertinent to overcoming the reason(s) for the initial decline to its servicing district office.

(2) The AA/BD will issue a written decision within 45 calendar days of receipt of the protégé's request. The AA/BD may approve the mentor/protégé agreement, deny it on the same grounds as the original decision, or deny it on other grounds. If denied, the AA/BD will explain why the mentor/protégé agreement does not meet the requirements of § 124.520 and give specific reasons for the decline.

(3) If the AA/BD declines the mentor/protégé agreement solely on issues not raised in the initial decline, the protégé can ask for reconsideration as if it were an initial decline.

(4) If SBA's final decision is to decline a specific mentor/protégé agreement, the 8(a) firm seeking to be a protégé cannot attempt to enter another mentor/protégé relationship with the same mentor for a period of 60 calendar days from the date of the final decision. The 8(a) firm may, however, submit another proposed mentor/protégé agreement with a different proposed mentor at any time after the SBA's final decline decision.

(g) *Evaluating the mentor/protégé relationship.* (1) In its annual business plan update required by § 124.403(a,) the protégé must report to SBA for the protégé's preceding program year:

(i) All technical and/or management assistance provided by the mentor to the protégé;

(ii) All loans to and/or equity investments made by the mentor in the protégé;

(iii) All subcontracts awarded to the protégé by the mentor, and the value of each subcontract;

(iv) All federal contracts awarded to the mentor/protégé relationship as a joint venture (designating each as an 8(a), small business set aside, or unrestricted procurement), the value of each contract, and the percentage of the contract performed and the percentage of revenue accruing to each party to the joint venture; and

(v) A narrative describing the success such assistance has had in addressing the developmental needs of the protégé and addressing any problems encountered.

(2) The protégé must report the mentoring services it receives by category and hours.

(3) The protégé must annually certify to SBA whether there has been any change in the terms of the agreement.

(4) SBA will review the protégé's report on the mentor/protégé relationship as part of its annual review of the firm's business plan pursuant to § 124.403. SBA may decide not to approve continuation of the agreement if it finds that the mentor has not provided the assistance set forth in the mentor/protégé agreement or that the assistance has not resulted in any material benefits or developmental gains to the protégé.

(h) *Consequences of not providing assistance set forth in the mentor/protégé agreement.* (1) Where SBA determines that a mentor has not provided to the protégé firm the business development assistance set forth in its mentor/protégé agreement, SBA will notify the mentor of such determination and afford the mentor an opportunity to respond. The mentor must respond within 30 days of the notification, explaining why it has not provided the agreed upon assistance and setting forth a definitive plan as to when it will provide such assistance. If the mentor fails to respond, does not supply adequate reasons for its failure to provide the agreed upon assistance, or does not set forth a definite plan to provide the assistance:

(i) SBA will terminate its mentor/protégé agreement;

(ii) The firm will be ineligible to again act as a mentor for a period of two years from the date SBA terminates the mentor/protégé agreement; and

(iii) SBA may recommend to the relevant procuring agency to issue a stop work order for each Federal contract for which the mentor and protégé are performing as a small business joint venture pursuant to paragraph (d)(1) of this section in order to encourage the mentor to comply with its mentor/protégé agreement. Where a protégé firm is able to independently complete performance of any such contract, SBA may also authorize a substitution of the protégé firm for the joint venture.

(2) SBA may consider a mentor's failure to comply with the terms and conditions of an SBA-approved mentor/protégé agreement as a basis for debarment on the grounds, including but not limited to, that the mentor has not complied with the terms of a public agreement under 2 CFR 180.800(b).

(i) *Results of mentor-protégé relationship.* (1) In order to assess the results of a mentor-protégé relationship upon its completion, the protégé must report to SBA whether it believed the mentor-protégé relationship was beneficial and describe any lasting benefits to the protégé.

(2) Where a protégé does not report the results of a mentor-protégé relationship upon its completion, SBA will not approve a second mentor-protégé relationship either under this section or under § 125.9 of this chapter.

[63 FR 35739, June 30, 1998, as amended at 69 FR 29208, May 21, 2004; 74 FR 45754, Sept. 4, 2009; 76 FR 8262, Feb. 11, 2011; 77 FR 28238, May 14, 2012; 81 FR 48584, July 25, 2016]

§ 124.521 What are the requirements for representing 8(a) status, and what are the penalties for misrepresentation?

(a) *Presumption of Loss Based on the Total Amount Expended.* In every contract, subcontract, cooperative agreement, cooperative research and development agreement, or grant which is set aside, reserved, or otherwise classified as intended for award to 8(a) Participants, there shall be a presumption of loss to the United States based on the total amount expended on the contract, subcontract, cooperative agreement, cooperative research and development agreement, or grant whenever it is established that a business concern other than an 8(a) Participant willfully sought and received the award by misrepresentation.

(b) *Deemed Certifications.* The following actions shall be deemed affirmative, willful and intentional certifications of 8(a) status:

(1) Submission of a bid or proposal for an 8(a) sole source or competitive contract.

(2) Registration on any Federal electronic database for the purpose of being considered for award of a Federal grant, contract, subcontract, cooperative agreement, or cooperative research and development agreement, as a small disadvantaged business (SDB).

(c) *Signature Requirement.* Each offer for an 8(a) contract shall contain a certification concerning the 8(a) status of a business concern seeking the contract. An authorized official must sign the certification on the same page containing the 8(a) status claimed by the concern.

(d) *Limitation of Liability.* Paragraphs (a)–(c) of this section may be determined not to apply in the case of unintentional errors, technical malfunctions, and other similar situations that demonstrate that a misrepresentation of 8(a) status was not affirmative, intentional, willful or actionable under the False Claims Act, 31 U.S.C. 3729, et seq. A prime contractor acting in good faith should not be held liable for misrepresentations made by its subcontractors regarding the subcontractors' 8(a) status. Relevant factors to consider in making this determination may include the firm's internal management procedures governing representation or certification as an eligible 8(a) Participant, the clarity or ambiguity of the representation or certification requirement, and the efforts made to correct an incorrect or invalid representation or certification in a timely manner. An individual or firm may not be held liable where government personnel have erroneously identified a concern as an eligible 8(a) Participant without any representation or certification having been made by the concern and where such identification is made without the knowledge of the individual or firm.

[78 FR 38818, June 28, 2013]

MISCELLANEOUS REPORTING REQUIREMENTS

§ 124.601 What reports does SBA require concerning parties who assist Participants in obtaining federal contracts?

(a) Each Participant must submit semi-annually a written report to its assigned BOS that includes a listing of any agents, representatives, attorneys, accountants, consultants and other parties (other than employees) receiving fees, commissions, or compensation of any kind to assist such Participant in obtaining or seeking to obtain a Federal contract. The listing must indicate the amount of compensation paid and a description of the activities performed for such compensation.

(b) Failure to submit the report is good cause for the initiation of a termination proceeding pursuant to §§ 124.303 and 124.304.

[63 FR 35739, June 30, 1998, as amended at 76 FR 8264, Feb. 11, 2011]

§ 124.602 What kind of annual financial statement must a Participant submit to SBA?

(a) Except as set forth in paragraph (a)(1) of this section, Participants with gross annual receipts of more than $10,000,000 must submit to SBA audited annual financial statements prepared by a licensed independent public accountant within 120 days after the close of the concern's fiscal year.

(1) Participants with gross annual receipts of more than $10,000,000 which are owned by a Tribe, ANC, NHO, or CDC may elect to submit unaudited financial statements within 120 days after the close of the concern's fiscal year, provided the following additional documents are submitted simultaneously:

(i) Audited annual financial statements for the parent company owner of the Participant, prepared by a licensed independent public accountant, for the equivalent fiscal year;

(ii) Certification from the Participant's Chief Executive Officer and Chief Financial Officer (or comparable positions) that each individual has read the unaudited financial statements, affirms that the statements do not contain any material misstatements, and certifying that the statements fairly represent the Participant's financial condition and result of operations.

(2) In the first year that a Participant's gross receipts exceed $10,000,000, a Participant may provide an audited balance sheet, with the income and cash flow statements receiving the level of service required for the previous year (review or none, depending on sales the year before the audit is required).

(3) The servicing SBA District Director may waive the requirement for audited financial statements for good cause shown by the Participant.

(4) Circumstances where waivers of audited financial statements may be granted include, but are not limited to, the following:

(i) The concern has an unexpected increase in sales towards the end of its fiscal year that creates an unforeseen requirement for audited statements;

(ii) The concern unexpectedly experiences severe financial difficulties which would make the cost of audited financial statements a particular burden; and

(iii) The concern has been a Participant less than 12 months.

(b)(1) Participants with gross annual receipts between $2,000,000 and $10,000,000 must submit to SBA reviewed annual financial statements prepared by a licensed independent public accountant within 90 days after the close of the concern's fiscal year.

(2) The servicing SBA District Director may waive the requirement for reviewed financial statements for good cause shown by the Participant.

(c) Participants with gross annual receipts of less than $2,000,000 must submit to SBA an annual statement prepared in-house or a compilation statement prepared by a licensed independent public accountant, verified as to accuracy by an authorized officer, partner, limited liability member, or sole proprietor of the Participant, including signature and date, within 90 days after the close of the concern's fiscal year.

(d) Any audited or reviewed financial statements submitted to SBA pursuant to paragraphs (a) or (b) of this section must be prepared in accordance with

Generally Accepted Accounting Principles.

(e) While financial statements need not be submitted until 90 or 120 days after the close of a Participant's fiscal year, depending on the receipts of the concern, a Participant seeking to be awarded an 8(a) contract between the close of its fiscal year and such 90 or 120-day time period must submit a final sales report signed by the CEO or President to SBA in order for SBA to determine the concern's eligibility for the 8(a) contract. This report must show a breakdown of 8(a) and non-8(a) sales.

(f) Notwithstanding the amount of a Participant's gross annual receipts, SBA may require audited or reviewed statements whenever they are needed to obtain more complete information as to a concern's assets, liabilities, income or expenses, such as when the concern's capacity to perform a specific 8(a) contract must be determined, or when they are needed to determine continued program eligibility.

(g) Participants owned by Tribes, ANCs, NHOs and CDCs may submit consolidated financial statements prepared by the parent entity that include schedules for each 8(a) Participant instead of separate audited financial statements for each individual 8(a) Participant. If one Participant must submit an audited financial statement, then the consolidated statement and the schedules for each 8(a) Participant must be audited.

[63 FR 35739, June 30, 1998, as amended at 76 FR 8264, Feb. 11, 2011]

§ 124.603 What reports regarding the continued business operations of former Participants does SBA require?

Former Participants must provide such information as SBA may request concerning the former Participant's continued business operations, contracts, and financial condition for a period of three years following the date on which the concern graduates or is terminated from the program. Failure to provide such information when requested will constitute a violation of the regulations set forth in this part, and may result in the nonexercise of options on or termination of contracts awarded through the 8(a) BD program, debarment, or other legal recourse.

§ 124.604 Report of benefits for firms owned by Tribes, ANCs, NHOs and CDCs.

As part of its annual financial statement submission (*see* § 124.602), each Participant owned by a Tribe, ANC, NHO or CDC must submit to SBA information showing how the Tribe, ANC, NHO or CDC has provided benefits to the Tribal or native members and/or the Tribal, native or other community due to the Tribe's/ANC's/NHO's/CDC's participation in the 8(a) BD program through one or more firms. This data includes information relating to funding cultural programs, employment assistance, jobs, scholarships, internships, subsistence activities, and other services provided by the Tribe, ANC, NHO or CDC to the affected community.

[76 FR 8264, Feb. 11, 2011, as amended at 81 FR 48585, July 25, 2016]

Management and Technical Assistance Program

§ 124.701 What is the purpose of the 7(j) management and technical assistance program?

Section 7(j)(1) of the Small Business Act, 15 U.S.C. 636(j)(1), authorizes SBA to enter into grants, cooperative agreements, or contracts with public or private organizations to pay all or part of the cost of technical or management assistance for individuals or concerns eligible for assistance under sections 7(a)(11), 7(j)(10), or 8(a) of the Small Business Act.

§ 124.702 What types of assistance are available through the 7(j) program?

Through its private sector service providers, SBA may provide a wide variety of management and technical assistance to eligible individuals or concerns to meet their specific needs, including:

(a) Counseling and training in the areas of financing, management, accounting, bookkeeping, marketing, and operation of small business concerns; and

(b) The identification and development of new business opportunities.

§ 124.703 Who is eligible to receive 7(j) assistance?

The following businesses are eligible to receive assistance from SBA through its service providers:

(a) Businesses which qualify as small under part 121 of this title, and which are located in urban or rural areas with a high proportion of unemployed or low-income individuals, or which are owned by such low-income individuals; and

(b) Businesses eligible to receive 8(a) contracts.

§ 124.704 What additional management and technical assistance is reserved exclusively for concerns eligible to receive 8(a) contracts?

In addition to the management and technical assistance available under § 124.702, Section 7(j)(10) of the Small Business Act authorizes SBA to provide additional management and technical assistance through its service providers exclusively to small business concerns eligible to receive 8(a) contracts, including:

(a) Assistance to develop comprehensive business plans with specific business targets, objectives, and goals;

(b) Other nonfinancial services necessary for a Participant's growth and development, including loan packaging; and

(c) Assistance in obtaining equity and debt financing.

Subpart B—Eligibility, Certification, and Protests Relating to Federal Small Disadvantaged Business Programs

SOURCE: 63 FR 35772, June 30, 1998, unless otherwise noted.

§ 124.1001 General applicability.

(a) This subpart defines a Small Disadvantaged Business (SDB). It also establishes procedures by which SBA determines whether a particular concern qualifies as an SDB in response to a protest challenging the concern's status as disadvantaged. Unless specifically stated otherwise, the phrase "socially and economically disadvantaged individuals" in this subpart includes, Indian tribes, ANCs, CDCs, and NHOs.

(b) In order for a concern to represent that it is an SDB in order to receive a benefit as a prime contractor on a Federal Government procurement, it must:

(1) Be a current Participant, as defined in § 124.3 of this part, in SBA's 8(a) BD as described in § 124.1 of this part, program;

(2) Have been certified by SBA as an SDB within three years of the date it seeks to certify as an SDB;

(3) Have received certification from the procuring agency that it qualifies as an SDB; or

(4) Have submitted an application for SDB certification to the procuring agency and must not have received a negative determination regarding that application.

(c) A firm may represent that it qualifies as an SDB for any Federal subcontracting program if it believes in good faith that it is owned and controlled by one or more socially and economically disadvantaged individuals.

[73 FR 57494, Oct. 3, 2008]

§ 124.1002 What is a Small Disadvantaged Business (SDB)?

(a) *Reliance on 8(a) criteria.* In determining whether a firm qualifies as an SDB, the criteria of social and economic disadvantage and other eligibility requirements established in subpart A of this part apply, including the requirements of ownership and control and disadvantaged status, unless otherwise provided in this subpart. Qualified Private Certifiers must use the 8(a) criteria applicable to ownership and control in determining whether a particular firm is actually owned and controlled by one or more individuals claiming disadvantaged status.

(b) *SDB eligibility criteria.* A small disadvantaged business (SDB) is a concern:

(1) Which qualifies as small under part 121 of this title for the size standard corresponding to the applicable four digit North American Industry Classification System (NAICS) code.

(i) For purposes of SDB certification, the applicable NAICS code is that which relates to the primary business activity of the concern;

(ii) For purposes related to a specific Federal Government contract, the applicable NAICS code is that assigned by the contracting officer to the procurement at issue;

(2) Which is at least 51 percent unconditionally owned by one or more socially and economically disadvantaged individuals as set forth in § 124.105. For the requirements relating to tribes and ANCs, NHOs, or CDCs, *see* §§ 124.109, 124.110, and 124.111, respectively.

(3) Except for tribes, ANCs, NHOs, and CDCs, whose management and daily business operations are controlled by one or more socially and economically disadvantaged individuals. For the requirements relating to tribes and ANCs, NHOs, or CDCs, *see* §§ 124.109, 124.110, and 124.111, respectively.

(c) *Disadvantaged status.* In assessing the personal financial condition of an individual claiming economic disadvantage, his or her net worth must be less than $750,000 after taking into account the exclusions set forth in § 124.104(c)(2).

(d) *Additional eligibility criteria.* (1) Except for Tribes, ANCs, CDCs, and NHOs, each individual claiming disadvantaged status must be a citizen of the United States.

(2) The other eligibility requirements set forth in § 124.108 for 8(a) BD program participation do not apply to SDB eligibility.

(e) *Potential for success not required.* The potential for success requirement set forth in § 124.107 does not apply as an eligibility requirement for an SDB.

(f) *Joint ventures.* Joint ventures are permitted for SDB procurement mechanisms (such as price evaluation adjustments, evaluation factors or subfactors, monetary subcontracting incentives, or SDB set-asides), provided that the requirements set forth in this paragraph are met.

(1) The disadvantaged participant(s) to the joint venture must have:

(i) Received an SDB certification from SBA; or

(ii) Submitted an application for SDB certification to SBA or a Private Certifier, and must not have received a negative determination regarding that application.

(2) For purposes of this paragraph, the term joint venture means two or more concerns forming an association to engage in and carry out a single, specific business venture for joint profit. Two or more concerns that form an ongoing relationship to conduct business would not be considered "joint venturers" within the meaning of this paragraph, and would also not be eligible to be certified as an SDB. The entity created by such a relationship would not be owned and controlled by one or more socially and economically disadvantaged individuals. Each contract for which a joint venture submits an offer will be evaluated on a case by case basis.

(3) Except as set forth in 13 CFR 121.103(h)(3), a concern that is owned and controlled by one or more socially and economically disadvantaged individuals entering into a joint venture agreement with one or more other business concerns is considered to be affiliated with such other concern(s) for size purposes. If the exception does not apply, the combined annual receipts or employees of the concerns entering into the joint venture must meet the applicable size standard corresponding to the NAICS code designated for the contract.

(4) An SDB must be the managing venturer of the joint venture, and an employee of the managing venturer must be the project manager responsible for performance of the contract.

(5) The joint venture must perform any applicable percentage of work required of SDB offerors, and the SDB joint venturer(s) must perform a significant portion of the contract.

(g) *Ownership restrictions for non-disadvantaged individuals.* The ownership restrictions set forth in § 124.105 (g) and (h) for non-disadvantaged individuals and concerns do not apply for purposes of determining SDB eligibility.

(h) *Full-time requirement for SDB purposes.* An SDB is considered to be managed on a full-time basis by a disadvantaged individual if such individual works for the concern during all of the hours the concern operates. For example, if a concern operates 20 hours per week and the disadvantaged manager works for the firm during those twenty hours, that individual will be considered as working full time for the firm.

[63 FR 35772, June 30, 1998, as amended at 69 FR 29208, May 21, 2004; 76 FR 8264, Feb. 11, 2011; 81 FR 48585, July 25, 2016]

§ 124.1003 How does a firm become certified as an SDB?

(a) All firms that are current Participants in SBA's 8(a) BD program are automatically deemed to be certified SDBs.

(b) Any firm seeking to be certified as an SDB in order to represent that it qualifies and is eligible to obtain a benefit on a federal prime contract as an SDB may apply to the procuring agency for such certification.

(c) A procuring agency may accept a certification from another entity (*e.g.*, a private certifying entity, or a state or local government) that a firm qualifies as an SDB if the agency deems it appropriate.

[73 FR 57494, Oct. 3, 2008]

§ 124.1004 What is a misrepresentation of SDB status?

(a) Any person or entity that misrepresents a firm's status as a "small business concern owned and controlled by socially and economically disadvantaged individuals" ("SDB status") in order to obtain an 8(d) or SDB contracting opportunity or preference will be subject to the penalties imposed by section 16(d) of the Small Business Act, 15 U.S.C. 645(d), as well as any other penalty authorized by law.

(b)(1) A representation of SDB status on a federal prime contract will be deemed a misrepresentation of SDB status if the firm does not meet the requirements of § 124.1001(b).

(2) A representation of SDB status on a subcontract to a federal prime contract will be deemed a misrepresentation of SDB status if the firm does not have a good faith belief that it is owned and controlled by one or more socially and economically disadvantaged individuals. Any certification by a firm that SBA found not to qualify as an SDB in connection with an SDB protest or otherwise will be deemed a misrepresentation of SDB status if the firm has not overcome the reason(s) for the negative determination.

(3) Any representation of SDB status by a firm that SBA has found not to qualify as an SDB in connection with a protest or SBA-initiated SDB determination will be deemed a misrepresentation of SDB status if the firm has not overcome the reason(s) set forth in SBA's written decision.

[73 FR 57494, Oct. 3, 2008]

§ 124.1005 How long does an SDB certification last?

(a) A firm that is certified to be an SDB will generally be certified for a period of three years from the date of the certification.

(b) A firm's SDB certification will extend beyond three years where SBA finds the firm to be an SDB:

(1) In connection with a protest challenging the firm's SDB status (*see* § 124.1013(h)(2));

(2) In connection with an SBA-initiated SDB determination (*see* § 124.1006); or

(3) As part of an 8(a) BD annual review.

(c) A firm that completes its nine-year program term in the 8(a) BD program will continue to be deemed a certified SDB firm for a period of three years from the date of its last 8(a) annual review.

[73 FR 57494, Oct. 3, 2008]

§ 124.1006 Can SBA initiate a review of the SDB status of a firm claiming to be an SDB?

SBA may initiate an SDB determination on any firm that has been certified to be an SDB by a procuring agency or that has represented itself to be an SDB on a subcontract to a federal prime contract whenever it receives credible information calling into question the SDB status of the firm. Upon its completion of an SDB determination, SBA will issue a written decision regarding the SDB status of the questioned firm. If SBA finds that the firm continues to qualify as an SDB, the determination remains in effect for three years from the date of the decision.

[73 FR 57494, Oct. 3, 2008]

§ 124.1007 Who may protest the disadvantaged status of a concern?

(a) In connection with a requirement for which the apparent successful offeror has invoked an SDB evaluation adjustment or an SDB set-aside, the following entities may protest the disadvantaged status of the apparent successful offeror:

(1) Any other concern which submitted an offer for that requirement, unless the contracting officer has found the concern to be non-responsive or outside the competitive range, or SBA has previously found the protesting concern to be ineligible for the requirement at issue;

(2) The procuring activity contracting officer; or

(3) SBA.

(b) In connection with an 8(d) subcontract, or a requirement for which the apparent successful offeror received an evaluation adjustment for proposing one or more SDB subcontractors, the procuring activity contracting officer or SBA may protest the disadvantaged status of a proposed subcontractor. Other interested parties may submit information to the contracting officer or SBA in an effort to persuade the contracting officer or SBA to initiate a protest.

(c) An interested party seeking to protest both the disadvantaged status and size of an apparent successful SDB offeror must submit two separate protests, one as to disadvantaged status pursuant to this subpart, and one as to size pursuant to part 121 of this title. An interested party seeking to protest only size of an apparent successful SDB offeror must submit a size protest to the contracting officer pursuant to part 121.

[63 FR 35772, June 30, 1998. Redesignated at 73 FR 57495, Oct. 3, 2008]

§ 124.1008 When will SBA not decide an SDB protest?

(a) SBA will not decide a protest as to disadvantaged status of any concern other than the apparent successful offeror.

(b) SBA will not normally consider a post award protest. SBA may consider a post award protest in its discretion where it determines that a protest decision after award would have a practical effect (e.g., where the contracting officer agrees to terminate the contract if the protest is sustained).

(c) SBA will not decide an untimely protest (see § 124.1020(c)).

(d) SBA will not decide a non-specific protest or one that does not present credible evidence that the protested concern's circumstances have materially changed since SBA certified it as an SDB, or that the protested concern's SDB application contained false or misleading information (*see* § 124.1021).

(e) An interested party may appeal SBA's dismissal of a protest for lack of specificity, timeliness, or a basis upon which SBA will consider a protest to Associate Administrator for Government Contracting and Business Development (AA/GC&BD) pursuant to § 124.1024.

[63 FR 35772, June 30, 1998. Redesignated at 73 FR 57495, Oct. 3, 2008; 74 FR 45754, Sept. 4, 2009; 74 FR 51229, Oct. 6, 2009]

§ 124.1009 Who decides disadvantaged status protests?

In response to a protest challenging the disadvantaged status of a concern, the SBA's AA/BD, or designee, will determine whether the concern is disadvantaged.

[76 FR 8264, Feb. 11, 2011]

§ 124.1010 What procedures apply to disadvantaged status protests?

(a) *General.* The protest procedures described in this section are separate and distinct from those governing size protests and appeals. All protests relating to whether a concern is a "small" business for purposes of any Federal program, including SDB set-asides and SDB evaluation adjustments, must be filed and processed pursuant to part 121 of this title.

(b) *Filing.* (1) All protests challenging the disadvantaged status of a concern with respect to a particular Federal procurement requirement must be submitted in writing to the procuring activity contracting officer, except in cases where the contracting officer or SBA initiates a protest.

(2) Any contracting officer who initiates a protest must submit the protest in writing to SBA in accord with paragraph (c) of this section.

(3) In cases where SBA initiates a protest, the protest must be submitted in writing to the DC/SDBCE and notification provided in accord with § 124.1022(a).

(c) *Timeliness of protest*—(1) *SDB evaluation adjustment and set-aside protests*—(i) *General.* In order for a protest to be timely, it must be received by the contracting officer prior to the close of business on the fifth day, exclusive of Saturdays, Sundays and legal holidays, after the bid opening date for sealed bids, or after the receipt from the contracting officer of notification of the identity of the prospective awardee in negotiated acquisitions.

(ii) *Oral protests.* An oral protest relating to an SDB set-aside or SDB evaluation adjustment made to the contracting officer within the allotted 5-day period will be considered a timely protest only if the contracting officer receives a confirming letter postmarked, FAXed, or delivered no later than one calendar day after the date of such oral protest.

(iii) *Protests of contracting officers or SBA.* The time limitations in paragraph (c)(1)(i) of this section do not apply to contracting officers or SBA, and they may file protests before or after awards, except to the extent set forth in paragraph (c)(3) of this section.

(iv) *Untimely protests.* A protest received after the time limits set forth in this paragraph (c)(1) will be dismissed by SBA.

(2) *Section 8(d) protests.* In connection with an 8(d) subcontract, the contracting officer or SBA must submit a protest to the DC/SDBCE prior to the completion of performance by the intended 8(d) subcontractor.

(3) *Premature protests.* A protest in connection with any procurement which is submitted by any person, including the contracting officer, before bid opening or notification of intended award, whichever applies, will be considered premature, and will be returned to the protestor without action. A contracting officer that receives a premature protest must return it to the protestor without submitting it to the SBA.

(d) *Referral to SBA.* (1) Any contracting officer who receives a protest that is not premature must promptly forward it to the SBA's DC/SDBCE, 409 3rd Street, SW, Washington, DC 20416.

(2) A contracting officer's referral of a protest to SBA must contain the following:

(i) The written protest and any accompanying materials;

(ii) The date on which the protest was received by the contracting officer;

(iii) A copy of the protested concern's selfrepresentation as an SDB, and the date of such self-representation; and

(iv) The date of bid opening or the date on which notification of the apparent successful offeror was sent to all unsuccessful offerors, as applicable.

[63 FR 35772, June 30, 1998. Redesignated at 73 FR 57495, Oct. 3, 2008]

§ 124.1011 What format, degree of specificity, and basis does SBA require to consider an SDB protest?

(a) *Format.* An SDB protest need not be in any specific format in order for SBA to consider it.

(b) *Specificity.* A protest must be sufficiently specific to provide reasonable notice as to all grounds upon which the protested concern's disadvantaged status is challenged.

(1) SBA will dismiss a protest that merely asserts that the protested concern is not disadvantaged, without setting forth specific facts or allegations.

(2) The contracting officer must forward to SBA any non-premature protest received, notwithstanding whether he or she believes it is sufficiently specific or timely.

(c) *Basis.* SBA will consider a protest challenging whether the apparent successful offeror is owned and controlled by one or more socially and economically disadvantaged individuals, including whether one or more of the individuals claiming disadvantaged status is in fact socially or economically disadvantaged, only if the protest presents credible evidence that the firm's circumstances have materially changed since SBA certified it as an SDB, or that the firm's SDB application contained false or misleading information.

[63 FR 35772, June 30, 1998. Redesignated at 73 FR 57495, Oct. 3, 2008]

§ 124.1012 What will SBA do when it receives an SDB protest?

(a) Upon receipt of a protest challenging the disadvantaged status of a concern, the DC/SDBCE, or designee, will immediately notify the protestor and the contracting officer of the date the protest was received and whether it will be processed or dismissed for lack of timeliness or specificity.

(b) In cases where the protest is timely and sufficiently specific, the DC/SDBCE, or designee, will also immediately advise the protested concern of the protest and forward a copy of it to the protested concern.

(1) The DC/SDBCE, or designee, is authorized to ask the protested concern to provide any or all of the following information and documentation, completed so as to show the circumstances existing on the date of self-representation: SBA Form 1010A, "Statement of Personal Eligibility" for each individual claiming disadvantaged status; SBA Form 1010B, "Statement of Business Eligibility;" SBA Form 413, "Personal Financial Statement," for each individual claiming disadvantaged status; information as to whether the protested concern, or any of its owners, officers or directors, have applied for admission to or participated in the SBA's 8(a) BD program and if so, the name of the company which applied or participated and the date of the application or entry into the program; business tax returns for the last two completed fiscal years prior to the date of self-representation; personal tax returns for the last two years prior to the date of self-representation for all individuals claiming disadvantaged status, all officers, all directors and for any individual owning at least 10% of the business entity; annual business financial statements for the last two completed fiscal years prior to the date of self-representation; a current monthly or quarterly business financial statement no older than 90 days; articles of incorporation; corporate by-laws; partnership agreements; limited liability company articles of organization; and any other relevant information as to whether the protested concern is disadvantaged.

(2) SBA's disadvantaged status determination need not be limited to consideration only of the issues raised in the protest. SBA may consider other applicable criteria.

(3) Unless the protest presents specific credible information which calls into question the veracity of application or other documents previously submitted to SBA by a current Participant in SBA's 8(a) BD program, SBA will allow the Participant to submit, in lieu of the information specified in paragraph (b)(1) of this section, a sworn affidavit or declaration that circumstances concerning the ownership and control of the business and the disadvantaged status of its principals have not changed since its application or entry into the program or its most recent annual review, and a copy of its most recently completed annual review.

(i) If the ownership or control of the business or the disadvantaged status of any principals have changed, the protested concern must comply with paragraph (b)(1) of this section.

(ii) An affidavit or declaration may be allowed only if SBA admitted the protested concern to the 8(a) BD program, or conducted an annual review of the protested concern, during the 12month period preceding the date on which SBA receives the protest, and if proceedings to suspend, terminate or early graduate the concern from the 8(a) BD program are not pending.

(c) Within 10 working days of the date that notification of the protest was received from the DC/SDBCE or designee, the protested concern must submit to the DC/SDBCE or designee, by personal delivery, FAX, or mail, the information and documentation requested pursuant to paragraph (b)(1) of this section or the affidavit permitted by paragraph (b)(2) of this section. Materials submitted must be received by the close of business on the 10th working day.

(1) SBA will consider only materials submitted timely, and the late or nonsubmission of materials needed to make a disadvantaged status determination may result in sustaining the protest.

(2) The burden is on the protested concern to demonstrate its disadvantaged status, whether or not it is currently shown on the list of qualified SDBs.

(3) The protested concern must timely submit to SBA any information it deems relevant to a determination of its disadvantaged status.

[63 FR 35772, June 30, 1998. Redesignated at 73 FR 57495, Oct. 3, 2008]

§ 124.1013 How does SBA make disadvantaged status determinations in considering an SDB protest?

(a) *General.* The DC/SDBCE, or designee, will determine a protested concern's disadvantaged status within 15 working days after receipt of a protest.

(b) *Award of contract.* (1) The contracting officer may award a contract after receipt of a protest if the contracting officer determines in writing that an award must be made to protect the public interest. Notwithstanding such a determination, the provisions of paragraph (h) of this section apply to the procurement in question.

(2) If SBA does not issue its determination within 15 business days (or request an extension that is granted), the contracting officer may award the contract if he or she determines in writing that there is an immediate need to award the contract and that waiting until SBA makes its determination will be disadvantageous to the Government, Notwithstanding such a determination, the provisions of paragraph (h) of this section apply to the procurement in question.

(c) *Withdrawal of protest.* If a protest is withdrawn, SBA will not complete a new disadvantaged status determination, and a previous SDB certification will stand.

(d) *Basis for determination.* (1) Except with respect to a concern which is a current Participant in SBA's 8(a) BD program and is authorized under § 124.1013(b)(3) to submit an affidavit concerning its disadvantaged status, the disadvantaged status determination will be based on the protest record, including reasonable inferences therefrom, as supplied by the protested concern, SBA or others.

(2) SBA may in its discretion make a part of the protest record information already in its files, and information submitted by the protestor, the protested concern, the contracting officer, or other persons contacted for additional specific information.

(e) *Disadvantaged status.* In evaluating the social and economic disadvantage of individuals claiming disadvantaged status, SBA will consider the same information and factors set forth in §§ 124.103 and 124.104. As provided in § 124.1002(c), individuals claiming disadvantaged status must have a net worth that is less than $750,000, after taking into account the exclusions set forth in § 124.104(c)(2).

(f) *Disadvantaged status determination.* SBA will render a written determination including the basis for its findings and conclusions.

(g) *Notification of determination.* After making its disadvantaged status determination, the SBA will immediately notify the contracting officer, the protestor, and the protested concern of its determination. SBA will promptly provide by certified mail, return receipt requested, a copy of its written determination to the same entities, consistent with law.

(h) *Results of an SBA disadvantaged status determination.* A disadvantaged status determination becomes effective immediately.

(1) A contracting officer may award a contract to a protested concern after the DC/SDBCE has determined either that the protested concern is an eligible SDB or has dismissed all protests against it. If the AA/GCBD subsequently overturns the initial determination or dismissal, the contracting officer may apply the appeal decision to the procurement in question.

(2) A contracting officer shall not award a contract to a protested concern that the DC/SDBCE has determined is not an eligible SDB for the procurement in question.

(i) If a contracting officer receives such a determination after contract award, and no appeal has been filed, the contracting officer shall terminate the award.

(ii) If a timely appeal is filed after contract award, the contracting officer must consider whether performance can be suspended until an appellate decision is rendered.

(iii) If the AA/GCBD affirms the initial determination finding that the protested concern ineligible, the contracting officer shall either terminate the contract or not exercise the next option.

(3) The contracting officer must update the Federal Procurement Data System and other procurement reporting databases to reflect the final agency SDB decision (the decision of the

AA/SDBCE if no appeal is filed or the decision of the AA/GCBD).

(4) A concern found to be ineligible is precluded from applying for SDB certification for 12 months from the date of the final agency decision (whether by the DC/SDBCE, without an appeal, or by the AA/GCBD on appeal). A concern found to be ineligible is also precluded from representing itself as an SDB for a subcontract unless it overcomes the reasons for the protest (*e.g.*, it changes its ownership to satisfy the definition of an SDB set forth in § 124.1002).

[63 FR 35772, June 30, 1998. Redesignated at 73 FR 57495, Oct. 3, 2008, as amended at 74 FR 45754, Sept. 4, 2009; 76 FR 5684, Feb. 2, 2011]

§ 124.1014 Appeals of disadvantaged status determinations.

(a) *Who may appeal.* Appeals of protest determinations may be filed with the SBA's AA/GC&BD by the protested concern, the protestor, or the contracting officer.

(b) *Timeliness of appeal.* An appeal must be in writing and must be received by the AA/GC&BD no later than 5 working days after the date of receipt of the protest determination. SBA will dismiss any appeal received after the five-day time period.

(c) *Notice of appeal.* Notice of the appeal must be provided by the party bringing an appeal to the procuring activity contracting officer and either the protested concern or original protestor, as appropriate.

(d) *Grounds for appeal.* SBA will reexamine a protest determination only if there was a clear and significant error in the processing of the protest, or if the DC/SDBCE, or designee, failed to consider a significant material fact contained within the information supplied by the protestor or the protested concern. SBA will not consider protest determination appeals based on additional information or changed circumstances which were not disclosed at the time of the decision of the DC/SDBCE or designee, or which are based on disagreement with the findings and conclusions contained in the determination.

(e) *Contents of appeal.* No specific format is required for the appeal. However, the appeal must identify the protest determination which is appealed, and set forth a full and specific statement as to why the determination is erroneous under paragraph (c) of this section.

(f) The appeal will be decided by the AA/GC&BD, within 5 working days of its receipt, if practicable.

(g) The appeal decision will be based only on the information and documentation in the protest record as supplemented by the appeal. SBA will provide a copy of the decision to the contracting officer, the protestor, and the protested concern, consistent with law.

(h) The decision of the AA/GC&BD, is the final decision of the SBA, and cannot be further appealed to OHA.

[63 FR 35772, June 30, 1998. Redesignated at 73 FR 57495, Oct. 3, 2008, as amended at 76 FR 5684, Feb. 2, 2011]

§ 124.1015 What are the requirements for representing SDB status, and what are the penalties for misrepresentation?

(a) *Presumption of Loss Based on the Total Amount Expended.* In every contract, subcontract, cooperative agreement, cooperative research and development agreement, or grant which is set aside, reserved, or otherwise classified as intended for award to SDB concerns, there shall be a presumption of loss to the United States based on the total amount expended on the contract, subcontract, cooperative agreement, cooperative research and development agreement, or grant whenever it is established that a business concern other than a SDB willfully sought and received the award by misrepresentation.

(b) *Deemed Certifications.* The following actions shall be deemed affirmative, willful and intentional certifications of SDB status:

(1) Submission of a bid, proposal, application or offer for a Federal grant, contract, subcontract, cooperative agreement, or cooperative research and development agreement reserved, set aside, or otherwise classified as intended for award to SDBs.

(2) Submission of a bid, proposal, application or offer for a Federal grant, contract, subcontract, cooperative agreement or cooperative research and development agreement which in any

way encourages a Federal agency to classify the bid or proposal, if awarded, as an award to a SDB.

(3) Registration on any Federal electronic database for the purpose of being considered for award of a Federal grant, contract, subcontract, cooperative agreement, or cooperative research and development agreement, as a SDB.

(c) *Signature Requirement*. Each offer, proposal, bid, or application for a Federal contract, subcontract, or grant shall contain a certification concerning the SDB status of a business concern seeking the Federal contract, subcontract or grant. An authorized official must sign the certification on the same page containing the SDB status claimed by the concern.

(d) *Limitation of Liability*. Paragraphs (a) through (c) of this section may be determined not to apply in the case of unintentional errors, technical malfunctions, and other similar situations that demonstrate that a misrepresentation of SDB status was not affirmative, intentional, willful or actionable under the False Claims Act, 31 U.S.C. 3729, et seq. A prime contractor acting in good faith should not be held liable for misrepresentations made by its subcontractors regarding the subcontractors' SDB status. Relevant factors to consider in making this determination may include the firm's internal management procedures governing SDB status representation or certification, the clarity or ambiguity of the representation or certification requirement, and the efforts made to correct an incorrect or invalid representation or certification in a timely manner. An individual or firm may not be held liable where government personnel have erroneously identified a concern as a SDB without any representation or certification having been made by the concern and where such identification is made without the knowledge of the individual or firm.

(e) *Penalties for Misrepresentation*. (1) *Suspension or debarment*. The SBA suspension and debarment official or the agency suspension and debarment official may suspend or debar a person or concern for misrepresenting a firm's status as a SDB pursuant to the procedures set forth in 48 CFR subpart 9.4.

(2) *Civil Penalties*. Persons or concerns are subject to severe penalties under the False Claims Act, 31 U.S.C. 3729–3733, the Program Fraud Civil Remedies Act, 31 U.S.C. 3801–3812, and any other applicable laws or regulations, including 13 CFR part 142.

(3) *Criminal Penalties*. Persons or concerns are subject to severe criminal penalties for knowingly misrepresenting the SDB status of a concern in connection with procurement programs pursuant to section 16(d) of the Small Business Act, 15 U.S.C. 645(d), as amended, 18 U.S.C. 1001, 18 U.S.C. 287, and any other applicable laws. Persons or concerns are subject to criminal penalties for knowingly making false statements or misrepresentations to SBA for the purpose of influencing any actions of SBA pursuant to section 16(a) of the Small Business Act, 15 U.S.C. 645(a), as amended, including failure to correct "continuing representations" that are no longer true.

[78 FR 38818, June 28, 2013, as amended at 81 FR 31491, May 19, 2016]

§ 124.1016 What must a concern do in order to be identified as a SDB in any Federal procurement database?

(a) In order to be identified as a SDB in the System for Award Management (SAM) database (or any successor thereto), a concern must certify its SDB status in connection with specific eligibility requirements at least annually.

(b) If a firm identified as a SDB in SAM fails to certify its status within one year of a status certification, the firm will not be listed as a SDB in SAM, unless and until the firm recertifies its SDB status.

[78 FR 38819, June 28, 2013]

PART 125—GOVERNMENT CONTRACTING PROGRAMS

Sec.

Subpart A—Definitions for the Service-Disabled Veteran-Owned Small Business Concern Program

Subpart B—Eligibility Requirements for the SDVO SBC Program

Subpart C—Contracting with SDVO SBCs

Subpart D—Protests Concerning SDVO SBCs

Subpart E—Penalties and Retention of Records

AUTHORITY: 15 U.S.C. 632(p), (q), 634(b)(6), 637, 644, 657(f), 657q, and 657s; 38 U.S.C. 501 and 8127.

SOURCE: 61 FR 3312, Jan. 31, 1996, unless otherwise noted.

§ 125.1 What definitions are important to SBA's Government Contracting Programs?

Chief Acquisition Officer means the employee of a Federal agency designated as such pursuant to section 16(a) of the Office of Federal Procurement Policy Act (41 U.S.C. 414(a)).

Commercial off-the-shelf item has the same definition as set forth in 41 U.S.C. 101 (as renumbered) and Federal Acquisition Regulation (FAR) 2.101 (48 U.S.C. 2.101).

Consolidation of contract requirements, consolidated contract, or consolidated requirement means a solicitation for a single contract or a Multiple Award Contract to: (1) Satisfy two or more requirements of the Federal agency for goods or services that have been provided to or performed for the Federal agency under two or more separate contracts each of which was lower in cost than the total cost of the contract for which the offers are solicited, the total cost of which exceeds $2 million (including options); or (2) Satisfy requirements of the Federal agency for construction projects to be performed at two or more discrete sites.

Contract, unless otherwise noted, has the same definition as set forth in FAR

2.101 (48 U.S.C. 2.101) and includes orders issued against Multiple Award Contracts and orders competed under agreements where the execution of the order is the contract (*e.g.*, a Blanket Purchase Agreement (BPA), a Basic Agreement (BA), or a Basic Ordering Agreement (BOA)).

Contract bundling, bundled requirement, bundled contract, or bundling means the consolidation of two or more procurement requirements for goods or services previously provided or performed under separate smaller contracts into a solicitation of offers for a single contract or a Multiple Award Contract that is likely to be unsuitable for award to a small business concern (but may be suitable for award to a small business with a Small Business Teaming Arrangement) due to:

(1) The diversity, size, or specialized nature of the elements of the performance specified;

(2) The aggregate dollar value of the anticipated award;

(3) The geographical dispersion of the contract performance sites; or

(4) Any combination of the factors described in paragraphs (e)(1), (2), and (3) of this section.

Cost of materials means costs of the items purchased, handling and associated shipping costs for the purchased items (which includes raw materials), commercial off-the-shelf items (and similar common supply items or commercial items that require additional manufacturing, modification or integration to become end items), special tooling, special testing equipment, and construction equipment purchased for and required to perform on the contract. In the case of a supply contract, cost of materials includes the acquisition of services or products from outside sources following normal commercial practices within the industry.

General Services Administration (GSA) Schedule Contract means a Multiple Award Contract issued by GSA and includes the Federal Supply Schedules and other Multiple Award Schedules.

Multiple Award Contract means a contract that is:

(1) A Multiple Award Schedule contract issued by GSA (*e.g.*, GSA Schedule Contract) or agencies granted Multiple Award Schedule contract authority by GSA (*e.g.*, Department of Veterans Affairs) as described in FAR part 38 and subpart 8.4;

(2) A multiple award task-order or delivery-order contract issued in accordance with FAR subpart 16.5, including Governmentwide acquisition contracts; or

(3) Any other indefinite-delivery, indefinite-quantity contract entered into with two or more sources pursuant to the same solicitation.

Office of Small and Disadvantaged Business Utilization (OSDBU) or the Office of Small Business Programs (OSBP) means the office in each Federal agency having procurement powers that is responsible for ensuring that small businesses receive a fair proportion of Federal contracts in that agency. The office is managed by a Director, who is responsible and reports directly to the head of the agency or deputy to the agency (except that for DoD, the Director reports to the Secretary or the Secretary's designee).

Partial set-aside (or partially set-aside) means, for a Multiple Award Contract, a contracting vehicle that can be used when: market research indicates that a total set-aside is not appropriate; the procurement can be broken up into smaller discrete portions or discrete categories such as by Contract Line Items, Special Item Numbers, Sectors or Functional Areas or other equivalent; and two or more small business concerns, 8(a) BD Participants, HUBZone SBCs, SDVO SBCs, WOSBs or EDWOSBs are expected to submit an offer on the set-aside part or parts of the requirement at a fair market price.

Reserve means, for a Multiple Award Contract,

(1) An acquisition conducted using full and open competition where the contracting officer makes—

(i) Two or more contract awards to any one type of small business concern (*e.g.*, small business, 8(a), HUBZone, SDVO SBC, WOSB or EDWOSB) and competes any orders solely amongst the specified types of small business concerns if the "rule of two" or any alternative set-aside requirements provided in the small business program have been met;

(ii) Several awards to several different types of small businesses (*e.g.*, one to 8(a), one to HUBZone, one to SDVO SBC, one to WOSB or EDWOSB) and competes any orders solely amongst all of the small business concerns if the "rule of two" has been met; or

(iii) One contract award to any one type of small business concern (*e.g.*, small business, 8(a), HUBZone, SDVO SBC, WOSB or EDWOSB) and subsequently issues orders directly to that concern.

(2) An award on a bundled contract to one or more small businesses with a Small Business Teaming Arrangement.

"*Rule of Two*" refers to the requirements set forth in §§ 124.506, 125.2(f), 125.19(c), 126.607(c) and 127.503 of this chapter that there is a reasonable expectation that the contracting officer will obtain offers from at least two small businesses and award will be made at fair market price.

Senior Procurement Executive (SPE) means the employee of a Federal agency designated as such pursuant to section 16(c) of the Office of Federal Procurement Policy Act (41 U.S.C. 414(c)).

Separate contract means a contract or order (including those placed against a GSA Schedule Contract or an indefinite delivery, indefinite quantity contract) that has previously been performed by any business, including an other-than-small business or small business concern.

Separate smaller contract means a contract that has previously been performed by one or more small business concerns or was suitable for award to one or more small business concerns.

Similarly situated entity is a subcontractor that has the same small business program status as the prime contractor. This means that: For a HUBZone requirement, a subcontractor that is a qualified HUBZone small business concern; for a small business set-aside, partial set-aside, or reserve a subcontractor that is a small business concern; for a SDVO small business requirement, a subcontractor that is a self-certified SDVO SBC; for an 8(a) requirement, a subcontractor that is an 8(a) certified Program Participant; for a WOSB or EDWOSB contract, a subcontractor that has complied with the requirements of part 127. In addition to sharing the same small business program status as the prime contractor, a similarly situated entity must also be small for the NAICS code that the prime contractor assigned to the subcontract the subcontractor will perform.

Single contract means any contract or order (including those placed against a GSA Schedule Contract or an indefinite delivery, indefinite quantity contract) resulting in one or more awardee(s).

Subcontract or subcontracting means, except for purposes of § 125.3, that portion of the contract performed by a business concern, other than the business concern awarded the contract, under a second contract, purchase order, or agreement for any parts, supplies, components, or subassemblies which are not available commercial off-the-shelf items, and which are manufactured in accordance with drawings, specifications, or designs furnished by the contractor, or by the government as a portion of the solicitation. Raw castings, forgings, and moldings are considered as materials, not as subcontracting costs. Where the prime contractor has been directed by the Government as part of the contract to use any specific source for parts, supplies, or components subassemblies, the costs associated with those purchases will be considered as part of the cost of materials, not subcontracting costs.

Substantial bundling means any bundling that meets or exceeds the following dollar amounts (if the acquisition strategy contemplates Multiple Award Contracts or multiple award orders issued against a GSA Schedule Contract or a task or delivery order contract awarded by another agency, these thresholds apply to the cumulative estimated value of the Multiple Award Contracts or orders, including options):

(1) $8.0 million or more for the Department of Defense;

(2) $6.0 million or more for the National Aeronautics and Space Administration, the General Services Administration, and the Department of Energy; and

(3) $2.5 million or more for all other agencies.

[78 FR 61134, Oct. 2, 2013, as amended at 81 FR 34261, May 31, 2016]

§ 125.2 What are SBA's and the procuring agency's responsibilities when providing contracting assistance to small businesses?

(a) *General.* The objective of the SBA's contracting programs is to assist small business concerns, including 8(a) BD Participants, HUBZone small business concerns, Service Disabled Veteran-Owned Small Business Concerns, Women-Owned Small Businesses and Economically Disadvantaged Women-Owned Small Businesses, in obtaining a fair share of Federal Government prime contracts, subcontracts, orders, and property sales. Therefore, these regulations apply to all types of Federal Government contracts, including Multiple Award Contracts, and contracts for architectural and engineering services, research, development, test and evaluation. Small business concerns must receive any award (including orders, and orders placed against Multiple Award Contracts) or contract, part of any such award or contract, any contract for the sale of Government property, or any contract resulting from a reverse auction, regardless of the place of performance, which SBA and the procuring or disposal agency determine to be in the interest of:

(1) Maintaining or mobilizing the Nation's full productive capacity;

(2) War or national defense programs;

(3) Assuring that a fair proportion of the total purchases and contracts for property, services and construction for the Government in each industry category are placed with small business concerns; or

(4) Assuring that a fair proportion of the total sales of Government property is made to small business concerns.

(b) *SBA's responsibilities in the acquisition planning process*—(1) *SBA Procurement Center Representative (PCR) Responsibilities*—

(i) *PCR Review*—(A) SBA has PCRs who are generally located at Federal agencies and buying activities which have major contracting programs. At the SBA's discretion, PCRs will review all acquisitions that are not totally set aside for small businesses to determine whether a set-aside or sole source award to a small business under one of SBA's programs is appropriate and to identify alternative strategies to maximize the participation of small businesses in the procurement. PCRs also advocate for the maximum practicable utilization of small business concerns in Federal contracting, including by advocating against the consolidation or bundling of contract requirements, as defined in § 125.1, and reviewing any justification provided by the agency for consolidation or bundling. This review includes acquisitions that are Multiple Award Contracts where the agency has not set-aside all or part of the acquisition or reserved the acquisition for small businesses. It also includes acquisitions where the agency has not set-aside orders placed against Multiple Award Contracts for small business concerns.

(B) PCRs will work with the cognizant Small Business Specialist (SBS) and agency OSDBU or OSBP as early in the acquisition process as practicable to identify proposed solicitations that involve bundling, and with the agency acquisition officials to revise the acquisition strategies for such proposed solicitations, where appropriate, to increase the probability of participation by small businesses, including small business contract teams and Small Business Teaming Arrangements, as prime contractors.

(C) In conjunction with their duties to promote the set-aside of procurements for small business, PCRs may identify small businesses that are capable of performing particular requirements.

(D) PCRs will also ensure that any Federal agency decision made concerning the consolidation of contract requirements considers the use of small businesses and ways to provide small businesses with maximum opportunities to participate as prime contractors and subcontractors in the acquisition or sale of real property.

(E) PCRs will review whether, for bundled and consolidated contracts that are recompeted, the amount of savings and benefits was achieved under the prior bundling or consolidation of contract requirements, that such savings and benefits will continue to be realized if the contract remains bundled or consolidated, or such savings and benefits would be greater if the procurement requirements were divided into separate solicitations suitable for award to small business concerns.

(F) PCRs also advocate competitive procedures and recommend the breakout for competition of items and requirements which previously have not been competed when appropriate. They may appeal the failure by the buying activity to act favorably on a recommendation in accord with the appeal procedures in paragraph (b)(2) of this section. PCRs also review restrictions and obstacles to competition and make recommendations for improvement.

(ii) *PCR recommendations.* The PCR must recommend to the procuring activity alternative procurement methods that would increase small business prime contract participation if a PCR believes that a proposed procurement includes in its statement of work goods or services currently being performed by a small business and is in a quantity or estimated dollar value the magnitude of which renders small business prime contract participation unlikely; will render small business prime contract participation unlikely (*e.g.*, ensure geographical preferences are justified); or is for construction and seeks to package or consolidate discrete construction projects. If a PCR does not believe a bundled or consolidated requirement is necessary or justified the PCR shall advocate against the consolidation or bundling of such requirement and recommend to the procuring activity alternative procurement methods which would increase small business prime contract participation. Such alternatives may include:

(A) Breaking up the procurement into smaller discrete procurements, especially construction acquisitions that can be procured as separate projects;

(B) Breaking out one or more discrete components, for which a small business set-aside may be appropriate;

(C) Reserving one or more awards for small businesses when issuing Multiple Award Contracts;

(D) Using a partial set-aside;

(E) Stating in the solicitation for a Multiple Award Contract that the orders will be set-aside for small businesses; and

(F) Where the bundled or consolidated requirement is necessary and justified, the PCR will work with the procuring activity to tailor a strategy that preserves small business contract participation to the maximum extent practicable.

(iii) *PCR Recommendations for Small Business Teaming Arrangements and Subcontracting.* The PCR will work to ensure that small business participation is maximized both at the prime contract level such as through Small Business Teaming Arrangements and through subcontracting opportunities. This may include the subcontracting considerations in source selections set forth in §125.3(g), as well as the following:

(A) Reviewing an agency's oversight of its subcontracting program, including its overall and individual assessment of a contractor's compliance with its small business subcontracting plans. The PCR will furnish a copy of the information to the SBA Commercial Market Representative (CMR) servicing the contractor;

(B) Recommending that the solicitation and resultant contract specifically state the small business subcontracting goals that are expected of the contractor awardee;

(C) Recommending that the small business subcontracting goals be based on total contract dollars in addition to goals based on a percentage of total subcontracted dollars;

(D) Recommending that separate evaluation factors be established for evaluating the offerors' proposed approach to small business subcontracting participation in the subject procurement, the extent to which the offeror has met its small business subcontracting goals on previous contracts; and/or the extent to which the offeror actually paid small business subcontractors within the specified number of days;

(E) Recommending that a contracting officer include an evaluation factor in a solicitation which evaluates an offeror's commitment to pay small business subcontractors within a specified number of days after receipt of payment from the Government for goods and services previously rendered by the small business subcontractor.

The contracting officer will comparatively evaluate the proposed timelines. Such a commitment shall become a material part of the contract. The contracting officer must consider the contractor's compliance with the commitment in evaluating performance, including for purposes of contract continuation (such as exercising options);

(F) For bundled and consolidated requirements, recommending that a separate evaluation factor with significant weight be established for evaluating the offeror's proposed approach to small business utilization, the extent to which the offeror has met its small business subcontracting goals on previous contracts; and the extent to which the other than small business offeror actually paid small business subcontractors within the specified number of days;

(G) For bundled or consolidated requirements, recommending the solicitation state that the agency must evaluate offers from teams of small businesses the same as other offers, with due consideration to the capabilities and past performance of all proposed subcontractors. It may also include recommending that the agency reserve at least one award to a small business prime contractor with a Small Business Teaming Arrangement;

(H) For Multiple Award Contracts and multiple award requirements above the substantial bundling threshold, recommending or requiring that the solicitation state that the agency will solicit offers from small business concerns and small business concerns with Small Business Teaming Arrangements;

(I) For consolidated contracts, ensuring that agencies have provided small business concerns with appropriate opportunities to participate as prime contractors and subcontractors and making recommendations on such opportunities as appropriate; and

(J) Recommending paragraphs (B) through (I) above apply to an ordering agency placing an order against a Multiple Award Contract or Agreement.

(iv) PCRs will consult with the agency OSDBU regarding agency decisions to convert an activity performed by a small business concern to an activity performed by a Federal employee.

(v) PCRs may receive unsolicited proposals from small business concerns and will transmit those proposals to the agency personnel responsible for reviewing such proposals. The agency personnel shall provide the PCR with information regarding the disposition of such proposal.

(2) *Appeals of PCR recommendations.* In cases where there is disagreement between a PCR and the contracting officer over the suitability of a particular acquisition for a small business set-aside, partial set-aside or reserve, whether or not the acquisition is a bundled, substantially bundled or consolidated requirement, the PCR may initiate an appeal to the head of the contracting activity. If the head of the contracting activity agrees with the contracting officer, SBA may appeal the matter to the Secretary of the Department or head of the agency. The time limits for such appeals are set forth in FAR subpart 19.5 (48 CFR 19.5).

(c) *Procuring Agency Responsibilities*—(1) *Requirement to Foster Small Business Participation.* The Small Business Act requires each Federal agency to foster the participation of small business concerns as prime contractors and subcontractors in the contracting opportunities of the Government regardless of the place of performance of the contract. In addition, Federal agencies must ensure that all bundled and consolidated contracts contain the required analysis and justification and provide small business concerns with appropriate opportunities to participate as prime contractors and subcontractors. Agency acquisition planners must:

(i) Structure procurement requirements to facilitate competition by and among small business concerns, including small business concerns owned and controlled by service-disabled veterans, qualified HUBZone small business concerns, 8(a) BD small business concerns (including those owned by ANCs, Indian Tribes and NHOs), and small business concerns owned and controlled by women;

(ii) Avoid unnecessary and unjustified bundling of contracts or consolidation of contract requirements that inhibits or precludes small business participation in procurements as prime contractors;

(iii) Follow the limitations on use of consolidated contracts;

(iv) With respect to any work to be performed the amount of which would exceed the maximum amount of any contract for which a surety may be guaranteed against loss under 15 U.S.C. 694b, to the extent practicable, place contracts so as to allow more than one small business concern to perform such work;

(v) Provide SBA the necessary information relating to the acquisition under review at least 30 days prior to issuance of a solicitation. This includes providing PCRs (to the extent allowable pursuant to their security clearance) copies of all documents relating to the acquisition under review, including, but not limited to, the performance of work statement/statement of work, technical data, market research, hard copies or their electronic equivalents of Department of Defense (DoD) Form 2579 or equivalent, and other relevant information. The DoD Form 2579 or equivalent must be sent electronically to the PCR (or if a PCR is not assigned to the procuring activity, to the SBA Office of Government Contracting Area Office serving the area in which the buying activity is located);

(vi) Provide opportunities for the participation of small business concerns during acquisition planning processes and in acquisition plans; and

(vii) Invite the participation of the appropriate Director of Small and Disadvantaged Business Utilization in acquisition planning processes and provide that Director with access to acquisition plans.

(2) *Requirement for market research.* Each agency, as part of its acquisition planning, must conduct market research to determine the type and extent of foreseeable small business participation in the acquisition. In addition, each agency must conduct market research and any required analysis and justifications before proceeding with an acquisition strategy that could lead to a bundled, substantially bundled, or consolidated contract. The purpose of the market research and analysis is to determine whether the bundling or consolidation of the requirements is necessary and justified and all statutory requirements for such a strategy have been met. Agencies should be as broad as possible in their search for qualified small businesses, using key words as well as NAICS codes in their examination of the System for Award Management (SAM) and the Dynamic Small Business Search (DSBS), and must not place unnecessary and unjustified restrictions when conducting market research (*e.g.*, requiring that small businesses prove they can provide the best scientific and technological sources) when determining whether to set-aside, partially set-aside, reserve or sole source a requirement to small businesses. During the market research phase, the acquisition team must consult with the applicable PCR (or if a PCR is not assigned to the procuring activity, the SBA Office of Government Contracting Area Office serving the area in which the buying activity is located) and the activity's Small Business Specialist.

(3) *Proposed Acquisition Strategy.* A procuring activity must provide to the applicable PCR (or to the SBA Office of Government Contracting Area Office serving the area in which the buying activity is located if a PCR is not assigned to the procuring activity) at least 30 days prior to a solicitation's issuance:

(i) A copy of a proposed acquisition strategy (*e.g.*, DoD Form 2579, or equivalent) whenever a proposed acquisition strategy:

(A) Includes in its description goods or services the magnitude of the quantity or estimated dollar value of which would render small business prime contract participation unlikely;

(B) Seeks to package or consolidate discrete construction projects;

(C) Is a bundled or substantially bundled requirement; or

(D) Is a consolidation of contract requirements;

(ii) A written statement explaining why, if the proposed acquisition strategy involves a bundled or consolidated requirement, the procuring activity believes that the bundled or consolidated requirement is necessary and justified; the analysis required by paragraph (d)(2)(i) of this section; the acquisition plan; any bundling information required under paragraph (d)(3) of this section; and any other relevant information. The PCR and agency OSDBU or OSBP, as applicable, must then work together to develop alternative acquisition strategies identified in paragraph (b)(1) of this section to enhance small business participation;

(iii) All required clearances for the bundled, substantially bundled, or consolidated requirement; and

(iv) A written statement explaining why—if the description of the requirement includes goods or services currently being performed by a small business and the magnitude of the quantity or estimated dollar value of the proposed procurement would render small business prime contract participation unlikely, or if a proposed procurement for construction seeks to package or consolidate discrete construction projects—

(A) The proposed acquisition cannot be divided into reasonably small lots to permit offers on quantities less than the total requirement;

(B) Delivery schedules cannot be established on a basis that will encourage small business participation;

(C) The proposed acquisition cannot be offered so as to make small business participation likely; or

(D) Construction cannot be procured through separate discrete projects.

(4) *Procuring Agency Small Business Specialist (SBS) Responsibilities.*

(i) As early in the acquisition planning process as practicable—but no later than 30 days before the issuance of a solicitation, or prior to placing an order without a solicitation—the procuring activity must coordinate with the procuring activity's SBS when the acquisition strategy contemplates an acquisition meeting the dollar amounts set forth for substantial bundling. If the acquisition strategy contemplates Multiple Award Contracts or orders under the GSA Multiple Award Schedule Program or a task or delivery order contract awarded by another agency, these thresholds apply to the cumulative estimated value of the Multiple Award Contracts or orders, including options. The procuring activity is not required to coordinate with its SBS if the contract or order is entirely set-aside for small business concerns, or small businesses under one of SBA's small business programs, as authorized under the Small Business Act.

(ii) The SBS must notify the agency OSDBU or OSBP if the agency's acquisition strategy or plan includes bundled or consolidated requirements that the agency has not identified as bundled, or includes unnecessary or unjustified bundling of requirements. If the strategy involves substantial bundling, the SBS must assist in identifying alternative strategies that would reduce or minimize the scope of the bundling.

(iii) The SBS must coordinate with the procuring activity and PCR on all required determinations and findings for bundling and/or consolidation, and acquisition planning and strategy documentation.

(5) *OSDBU and OSBP Oversight Functions.* The Agency OSDBU or OSBP must:

(i) Conduct annual reviews to assess the:

(A) Extent to which small businesses are receiving their fair share of Federal procurements, including contract opportunities under programs administered under the Small Business Act;

(B) Adequacy of the bundling or consolidation documentation and justification; and

(C) Adequacy of actions taken to mitigate the effects of necessary and justified contract bundling or consolidation on small businesses (*e.g.*, review agency oversight of prime contractor subcontracting plan compliance under the subcontracting program);

(ii) Provide a copy of the assessment under paragraph (c)(5)(i) of this section to the agency head and SBA's Administrator;

(iii) Identify proposed solicitations that involve significant bundling of contract requirements, and work with the agency acquisition officials and the SBA to revise the procurement strategies for such proposed solicitations to increase the probability of participation by small businesses as prime contractors through Small Business Teaming Arrangements;

(iv) Facilitate small business participation as subcontractors and suppliers, if a solicitation for a substantially bundled contract is to be issued;

(v) Assist small business concerns to obtain payments, required late payment interest penalties, or information regarding payments due to such concerns from an executive agency or a contractor, in conformity with chapter 39 of Title 31 or any other protection for contractors or subcontractors (including suppliers) that is included in the FAR or any individual agency supplement to such Government-wide regulation;

(vi) Cooperate, and consult on a regular basis with the SBA with respect to carrying out these functions and duties;

(vii) Make recommendations to contracting officers as to whether a particular contract requirement should be awarded to any type of small business. The Contracting Officer must document any reason not to accept such recommendations and include the documentation in the appropriate contract file; and

(viii) Coordinate on any acquisition planning and strategy documentation, including bundling and consolidation determinations at the agency level.

(6) *Communication on Achieving Goals.* All Senior Procurement Executives, senior program managers, Directors of OSDBU or Directors of OSBP must communicate to their subordinates the importance of achieving small business goals and ensuring that a fair proportion of awards are made to small businesses.

(d) *Contract Consolidation and Bundling*—(1) *Limitation on the Use of Consolidated Contracts.* (i) An agency may not conduct an acquisition that is a consolidation of contract requirements unless the Senior Procurement Executive or Chief Acquisition Officer for the Federal agency, before carrying out the acquisition strategy:

(A) Conducts adequate market research;

(B) Identifies any alternative contracting approaches that would involve a lesser degree of consolidation of contract requirements;

(C) Makes a written determination, which is coordinated with the agency's OSDBU/OSBP, that the consolidation of contract requirements is necessary and justified;

(D) Identifies any negative impact by the acquisition strategy on contracting with small business concerns; and

(E) Ensures that steps will be taken to include small business concerns in the acquisition strategy.

(ii) A Senior Procurement Executive or Chief Acquisition Officer may determine that an acquisition strategy involving a consolidation of contract requirements is necessary and justified.

(A) A consolidation of contract requirements may be necessary and justified if the benefits of the acquisition strategy substantially exceed the benefits of each of the possible alternative contracting approaches identified under paragraph (d)(1)(i)(B).

(B) The benefits may include cost savings and/or price reduction, quality improvements that will save time or improve or enhance performance or efficiency, reduction in acquisition cycle times, better terms and conditions, and any other benefits that individually, in combination, or in the aggregate would lead to: benefits equivalent to 10 percent of the contract or order value (including options) where the contract or order value is $94 million or less; or benefits equivalent to 5 percent of the contract or order value (including options) or $9.4 million, whichever is greater, where the contract or order value exceeds $94 million.

(C) Savings in administrative or personnel costs alone do not constitute a sufficient justification for a consolidation of contract requirements in a procurement unless the expected total amount of the cost savings, as determined by the Senior Procurement Executive or Chief Acquisition Officer, is expected to be substantial in relation to the total cost of the procurement. To be substantial, such administrative or personnel cost savings must be at least 10 percent of the contract value (including options).

(iii) Each agency must ensure that any decision made concerning the consolidation of contract requirements considers the use of small businesses and ways to provide small businesses with opportunities to participate as prime contractors and subcontractors in the acquisition.

(iv) If the consolidated requirement is also considered a bundled requirement, then the contracting officer must instead follow the provisions regarding bundling set forth in paragraphs (d)(2) through (7) of this section.

(2) *Limitation on the Use of Contract Bundling.*

(i) When the procuring activity intends to proceed with an acquisition involving bundled or substantially bundled procurement requirements, it must document the acquisition strategy to include a determination that the bundling is necessary and justified, when compared to the benefits that could be derived from meeting the agency's requirements through separate smaller contracts.

(ii) A bundled requirement is necessary and justified if, as compared to the benefits that the procuring activity would derive from contracting to meet those requirements if not bundled, it would derive measurably substantial benefits. The procuring activity must quantify the identified benefits and explain how their impact would be measurably substantial. The benefits may include cost savings and/or price reduction, quality improvements that will save time or improve or enhance performance or efficiency, reduction in acquisition cycle times, better terms and conditions, and any other benefits that individually, in combination, or in the aggregate would lead to:

(A) Benefits equivalent to 10 percent of the contract or order value (including options), where the contract or order value is $94 million or less; or

(B) Benefits equivalent to 5 percent of the contract or order value (including options) or $9.4 million, whichever is greater, where the contract or order value exceeds $94 million.

(iii) Notwithstanding paragraph (d)(2)(ii) of this section, the Senior Procurement Executives or the Under Secretary of Defense for Acquisition and Technology (for other Defense Agencies) in the Department of Defense and the Deputy Secretary or equivalent in civilian agencies may, on a non-delegable basis, determine that a bundled requirement is necessary and justified when:

(A) There are benefits that do not meet the thresholds set forth in paragraph (d)(2)(ii) of this section but, in the aggregate, are critical to the agency's mission success; and

(B) The procurement strategy provides for maximum practicable participation by small business.

(iv) The reduction of administrative or personnel costs alone must not be a justification for bundling of contract requirements unless the administrative or personnel cost savings are expected to be substantial, in relation to the dollar value of the procurement to be bundled (including options). To be substantial, such administrative or personnel cost savings must be at least 10 percent of the contract value (including options).

(v) In assessing whether cost savings and/or a price reduction would be achieved through bundling, the procuring activity and SBA must compare the price that has been charged by small businesses for the work that they have performed and, where available, the price that could have been or could be charged by small businesses for the work not previously performed by small business.

(vi) The substantial benefit analysis set forth in paragraph (d)(2)(ii) of this section is still required where a requirement is subject to a Cost Comparison Analysis under OMB Circular A–76.

(3) *Limitations on the Use of Substantial Bundling.* Where a proposed procurement strategy involves a Substantial Bundling of contract requirements, the procuring agency must, in the documentation of that strategy, include a determination that the anticipated benefits of the proposed bundled contract justify its use, and must include, at a minimum:

(i) The analysis for bundled requirements set forth in paragraph (d)(2)(i) of this section;

(ii) An assessment of the specific impediments to participation by small business concerns as prime contractors that will result from the substantial bundling;

(iii) Actions designed to maximize small business participation as prime contractors, including provisions that encourage small business teaming for the substantially bundled requirement;

(iv) Actions designed to maximize small business participation as subcontractors (including suppliers) at any tier under the contract or contracts that may be awarded to meet the requirements; and

(v) The identification of the alternative strategies that would reduce or minimize the scope of the bundling, and the rationale for not choosing those alternatives (*i.e.*, consider the strategies under paragraph (b)(1)(ii) of this section).

(4) *Significant Subcontracting Opportunities in Justified Consolidated, Bundled and Substantially Bundled Requirements.*

(i) Where a justified consolidated, bundled, or substantially bundled requirement offers a significant opportunity for subcontracting, the procuring agency must designate the following factors as significant factors in evaluating offers:

(A) A factor that is based on the rate of participation provided under the subcontracting plan for small business in the performance of the contract; and

(B) For the evaluation of past performance of an offeror, a factor that is based on the extent to which the offeror attained applicable goals for small business participation in the performance of contracts.

(ii) Where the offeror for such a contract qualifies as a small business concern, the procuring agency must give to the offeror the highest score possible for the evaluation factors identified above.

(5) *Notification to Current Small Business Contractors of Intent to Bundle.* The procuring activity must notify each small business which is performing a contract that it intends to bundle that requirement with one or more other requirements at least 30 days prior to the issuance of the solicitation for the bundled or substantially bundled requirement. The procuring activity, at that time, should also provide to the small business the name, phone number and address of the applicable SBA PCR (or if a PCR is not assigned to the procuring activity, the SBA Office of Government Contracting Area Office serving the area in which the buying activity is located). This notification must be documented in the contract file.

(6) *Notification to Public of Rationale for Bundled Requirement.* The head of a Federal agency must publish on the agency's Web site a list and rationale for any bundled requirement for which the agency solicited offers or issued an award. The notification must be made within 30 days of the agency's data certification regarding the validity and verification of data entered in that Federal Procurement Data Base to the Office of Federal Procurement Policy. However, to foster transparency in Federal procurement, the agency is encouraged to provide such notification before issuance of the solicitation.

(7) *Notification to SBA of Recompeted Bundled or Consolidated Requirement.* For each bundled or consolidated contract that is to be recompeted (even if additional requirements have been added or deleted) the procuring agency must notify SBA's PCR as soon as possible but no later than 30 days prior to issuance of the solicitation of:

(i) The amount of savings and benefits achieved under the prior bundling or consolidation of contract requirements;

(ii) Whether such savings and benefits will continue to be realized if the contract remains bundled or consolidated; and

(iii) Whether such savings and benefits would be greater if the procurement requirements were divided into separate solicitations suitable for award to small business concerns.

(e) *Multiple Award Contract*—(1) *General.*

(i) The contracting officer must set-aside a Multiple Award Contract if the requirements for a set-aside are met. This includes set-asides for small businesses, 8(a) Participants, HUBZone SBCs, SDVO SBCs, WOSBs or EDWOSBs.

(ii) The contracting officer in his or her discretion may partially set-aside or reserve a Multiple Award Contract, or set aside, or preserve the right to set aside, orders against a Multiple Award Contract that was not itself set aside for small business. The ultimate decision of whether to use any of the above-mentioned tools in any given procurement action is a decision of the contracting agency.

(iii) The procuring agency contracting officer must document the contract file and explain why the procuring agency did not partially set-aside or reserve a Multiple Award Contract, or set-aside orders issued against a Multiple Award Contract, when these authorities could have been used.

(2) *Total Set-aside of Multiple Award Contracts.*

(i) The contracting officer must conduct market research to determine whether the "rule of two" can be met. If the "rule of two" can be met, the contracting officer must follow the procedures for a set-aside set forth in paragraph (f) of this section.

(ii) The contracting officer must assign a NAICS code to the solicitation for the Multiple Award Contract and each order pursuant to § 121.402(c) of this chapter. *See* § 121.404 for further determination on size status for the Multiple Award Contract and each order issued against that contract.

(iii) When drafting the solicitation for the contract, agencies should consider an "on-ramp" provision that permits the agency to refresh the awards by adding more small business contractors throughout the life of the contract. Agencies should also consider the need to "off-ramp" existing contractors that no longer qualify as small for the size standard corresponding to the NAICS code assigned to the contract (*e.g.*, termination for convenience).

(iv) A business must comply with the applicable limitations on subcontracting provisions (*see* § 125.6) and the nonmanufacturer rule (*see* § 121.406(b)), if applicable, during each performance period of the contract (e.g., the base term and each subsequent option period). However, the contracting officer, in his or her discretion, may require the contractor perform the applicable amount of work or comply with the nonmanufacturer rule for each order awarded under the contract.

(3) *Partial Set-asides of Multiple Award Contracts.*

(i) A contracting officer may partially set-aside a multiple award contract when: market research indicates that a total set-aside is not appropriate; the procurement can be broken up into smaller discrete portions or discrete categories such as by Contract Line Items, Special Item Numbers, Sectors or Functional Areas or other equivalent; and two or more small business concerns, 8(a) BD Participants, HUBZone SBCs, SDVO SBCs, WOSBs or EDWOSBs are expected to submit an offer on the set-aside part or parts of the requirement at a fair market price. A contracting officer has the discretion, but is not required, to set-aside the discrete portions or categories for different small businesses participating in SBA's small business programs (*e.g.*, CLIN 0001, 8(a) set-aside; CLIN 0002, HUBZone set-aside; CLIN 0003, SDVO SBC set-aside; CLIN 0004, WOSB set-aside; CLIN 0005 EDWOSB set-aside; CLIN 0006, small business set-aside). If the contracting officer decides to partially set-aside a Multiple Award Contract, the contracting officer must follow the procedures for a set-aside set forth in paragraph (f) of this section for the part or parts of the contract that have been set-aside.

(ii) The contracting officer must assign a NAICS code and corresponding size standard to the solicitation for the Multiple Award Contract and each order issued against the Multiple Award Contract pursuant to § 121.402(c) of this chapter. *See* § 121.404 for further determination on size status for the Multiple Award Contract and each order issued against that contract.

(iii) A contracting officer must state in the solicitation that the small business will not compete against other-than-small businesses for any order issued against that part or parts of the Multiple Award Contract that are set-aside.

(iv) A contracting officer must state in the solicitation that the small business will be permitted to compete against other-than-small businesses for an order issued against the portion of the Multiple Award Contract that has not been partially set-aside if the small business submits an offer for the non-set-aside portion. The business concern will not have to comply with the limitations on subcontracting (*see* § 125.6) and the nonmanufacturer rule for any order issued against the Multiple

Award Contract if the order is competed and awarded under the portion of the contract that is not set-aside.

(v) When drafting the solicitation for the contract, agencies should consider an "on ramp" provision that permits the agency to refresh these awards by adding more small business contractors to that portion of the contract that was set-aside throughout the life of the contract. Agencies should also consider the need to "off ramp" existing contractors that no longer qualify as small for the size standard corresponding to the NAICS code assigned to the contract (*e.g.*, termination for convenience).

(vi) The small business must submit one offer that addresses each part of the solicitation for which it wants to compete. A small business (or 8(a) Participant, HUBZone SBC, SDVO SBC or ED/WOSB) is not required to submit an offer on the part of the solicitation that is not set-aside. However, a small business may choose to submit an offer on the part or parts of the solicitation that have been set-aside and/or on the parts that have not been set-aside.

(vii) A small business must comply with the applicable limitations on subcontracting provisions (*see* § 125.6) and the nonmanufacturer rule (*see* § 121.406(b)), if applicable, during each performance period of the contract (e.g., during the base term and then during option period thereafter). However, the contracting officer, in his or her discretion, may require the contractor perform the applicable amount of work or comply with the nonmanufacturer rule for each order awarded under the contract.

(4) *Reserves of Multiple Award Contracts Awarded in Full and Open Competition.* (i) A contracting officer may reserve one or more awards for small business where:

(A) The market research and recent past experience evidence that—

(*1*) At least two small businesses, 8(a) BD Participants, HUBZone SBCs, SDVO SBCs, WOSBs or EDWOSBs could perform one part of the requirement, but the contracting officer was unable to divide the requirement into smaller discrete portions or discrete categories by utilizing individual Contract Line Items (CLINs), Special Item Numbers (SINs), Functional Areas (FAs), or other equivalent; or

(*2*) At least one small business, 8(a) BD Participant, HUBZone SBC, SDVO SBC, WOSB or EDWOSB can perform the entire requirement, but there is not a reasonable expectation of receiving at least two offers from small business concerns, 8(a) BD Participants, HUBZone SBCs, SDVO SBCs, WOSBs or EDWOSBs at a fair market price for all the work contemplated throughout the term of the contract; or

(B) The contracting officer makes:

(1) Two or more contract awards to any one type of small business concern (*e.g.*, small business, 8(a), HUBZone, SDVO SBC, WOSB or EDWOSB) and competes any orders solely amongst the specified types of small business concerns if the "rule of two" or any alternative set-aside requirements provided in the small business program have been met;

(2) Several awards to several different types of small businesses (*e.g.*, one to 8(a), one to HUBZone, one to SDVO SBC, one to WOSB or EDWOSB) and competes any orders solely amongst all of the small business concerns if the "rule of two" has been met; or

(3) One contract award to any one type of small business concern (*e.g.*, small business, 8(a), HUBZone, SDVO SBC, WOSB or EDWOSB) and subsequently issues orders directly to that concern.

(ii) If the contracting officer decides to reserve a multiple award contract established through full and open competition, the contracting officer must assign a NAICS code to the solicitation for the Multiple Award Contract and each order issued against the Multiple Award Contract pursuant to § 121.402(c) of this chapter. *See* § 121.404 for further determination on size status for the Multiple Award Contract and each order issued against that contract.

(iii) A contracting officer must state in the solicitation that if there are two or more contract awards to any one type of small business concern (*e.g.*, small business, 8(a), HUBZone, SDVO SBC, WOSB or EDWOSB), the agency may compete any orders solely amongst the specified types of small business concerns if the "rule of two" or an alternative set-aside requirement provided in the small business program have been met.

(iv) A contracting officer must state in the solicitation that if there are several awards to several different types of small businesses (*e.g.*, one to 8(a), one to HUBZone, one to SDVO SBC, one to WOSB or EDWOSB), the agency may compete any orders solely amongst all of the small business concerns if the "rule of two" has been met.

(v) A contracting officer must state in the solicitation that if there is only one contract award to any one type of small business concern (*e.g.*, small business, 8(a), HUBZone, SDVO SBC, WOSB or EDWOSB), the agency may issue orders directly to that concern for work that it can perform.

(vi) A contracting officers may, but is not required to, set forth targets in the contract showing the estimated dollar value or percentage of the total contract to be awarded to small businesses.

(vii) A small business offeror must submit one offer that addresses each part of the solicitation for which it wants to compete.

(viii) Small businesses are permitted to compete against other-than-small businesses for an order issued against the Multiple Award Contract if agency issued the small business a contract for those supplies or services.

(ix) A business must comply with the applicable limitations on subcontracting provisions (*see* § 125.6) and the nonmanufacturer rule (*see* § 121.406(b)), if applicable, for any order issued against the Multiple Award Contract if the order is set aside or awarded on a sole source basis. However, a business need not comply with the limitations on subcontracting provisions (*see* § 125.6) and the nonmanufacturer rule for any order issued against the Multiple Award Contract if the order is competed amongst small and other-than-small business concerns.

(5) *Reserve of Multiple Award Contracts that are Bundled.*

(i) If the contracting officer decides to reserve a multiple award contract established through full and open competition that is a bundled contract, the contracting officer must assign a NAICS code to the solicitation for the Multiple Award Contract and each order issued against the Multiple Award Contract pursuant to § 121.402(c) of this chapter. *See* § 121.404 for further determination on size status for the Multiple Award Contract and each order issued against that contract.

(ii) The Small Business Teaming Arrangement must comply with the applicable limitations on subcontracting provisions (*see* § 125.6) and the nonmanufacturer rule (*see* § 121.406(b)), if applicable, on all orders issued against the Multiple Award Contract, although the cooperative efforts of the team members will be considered in determining whether the subcontracting limitations requirement is met (*see* § 125.6(j)).

(iii) Team members of the Small Business Teaming Arrangement will not be affiliated for the specific solicitation or contract (*see* § 121.103(b)(8)).

(6) *Set-aside of orders against Full and Open Multiple Award Contracts.*

(i) Notwithstanding the fair opportunity requirements set forth in 10 U.S.C. 2304c and 41 U.S.C. 253j, the contracting officer has the authority to set-aside orders against Multiple Award Contracts that were competed on a full and open basis.

(ii) The contracting officer may state in the solicitation and resulting contract for the Multiple Award Contract that:

(A) Based on the results of market research, orders issued against the Multiple Award Contract will be set-aside for small businesses or any subcategory of small businesses whenever the "rule of two" or any alternative set-aside requirements provided in the small business program have been met; or

(B) The agency is preserving the right to consider set-asides using the "rule of two" or any alternative set-aside requirements provided in the small business program, on an order-by-order basis.

(iii) For the acquisition of orders valued at or below the simplified acquisition threshold (SAT), the contracting officer may set-aside the order for small businesses, 8(a) BD Participants, HUBZone SBCs, SDVO SBCs, WOSBs or EDWOSBs in accordance with the relevant program's regulations. For the acquisition of orders valued above the SAT, the contracting officer shall first consider whether there is a reasonable expectation that offers will be obtained from at least two 8(a) BD Participants, HUBZone SBCs, SDVO SBCs, WOSBs or EDWOSBs in accordance with the program's regulations, before setting aside the requirement as a small business set-aside. There is no order of precedence among the 8(a) BD, HUBZone, SDVO SBC or WOSB programs.

(iv) The contracting officer must assign a NAICS code to the solicitation for each order issued against the Multiple Award Contract pursuant to §121.402(c) of this chapter. *See* §121.404 for further determination on size status for each order issued against that contract.

(v) A business must comply with applicable limitations on subcontracting provisions (*see* §125.6) and the nonmanufacturer rule (*see* §121.406(b)), if applicable in the performance of each order that is set-aside against the contract.

(7) *Tiered evaluation of offers, or cascading.* An agency cannot create a tiered evaluation of offers or "cascade" unless it has specific statutory authority to do so. This is a procedure used in negotiated acquisitions when the contracting officer establishes a tiered or cascading order of precedence for evaluating offers that is specified in the solicitation, which states that if no award can be made at the first tier, it will evaluate offers at the next lower tier, until award can be made. For example, unless the agency has specific statutory authority to do so, an agency is not permitted to state an intention to award one contract to an 8(a) BD Participant and one to a HUBZone SBC, but only if no awards are made to 8(a) BD Participants.

(f) *Contracting Among Small Business Programs*—(1) *Acquisitions Valued At or Below the Simplified Acquisition Threshold.* The contracting officer shall set aside any acquisition with an anticipated dollar value exceeding the Micro-purchase Threshold but not exceeding the Simplified Acquisition Threshold (defined in the FAR at 48 CFR 2.101) for small business concerns when there is a reasonable expectation that offers will be obtained from at least two small business concerns that are competitive in terms of quality and delivery and award will be made at fair market prices. This requirement does not preclude a contracting officer from making an award to a small business under the 8(a) BD, HUBZone, SDVO SBC or WOSB Programs.

(2) *Acquisitions Valued Above the Simplified Acquisition Threshold.* (i) The contracting officer shall set aside any acquisition with an anticipated dollar value exceeding the Simplified Acquisition Threshold (defined in the FAR at 48 CFR 2.101) for small business concerns when there is a reasonable expectation that offers will be obtained from at least two small business concerns that are competitive in terms of quality and delivery and award will be made at fair market prices. However, after conducting market research, the contracting officer shall first consider a set-aside or sole source award (if the sole source award is permitted by statute or regulation) under the 8(a) BD, HUBZone, SDVO SBC or WOSB programs before setting aside the requirement as a small business set-aside. There is no order of precedence among the 8(a) BD, HUBZone, SDVO SBC or WOSB programs. The contracting officer must document the contract file with the rationale used to support the specific set-aside, including the type and extent of market research conducted. In addition, the contracting officer must document the contract file showing that the apparent successful offeror's certifications in the System for Award Management (SAM) (or successor system) and associated representations were reviewed.

(ii) SBA believes that Progress in fulfilling the various small business goals, as well as other factors such as the results of market research, programmatic needs specific to the procuring agency, anticipated award price, and the acquisition history, will be considered in making a decision as to which program to use for the acquisition.

[61 FR 3312, Jan. 31, 1996, as amended at 63 FR 31908, June 11, 1998; 64 FR 57370, Oct. 25, 1999; 65 FR 45833, July 26, 2000; 68 FR 60012, Oct. 20, 2003; 74 FR 46887, Sept. 14, 2009; 75 FR 62281, Oct. 7, 2010; 76 FR 63547, Oct. 12, 2011; 77 FR 1860, Jan. 12, 2012; 78 FR 61135, Oct. 2, 2013; 81 FR 34261, May 31, 2016; 81 FR 48585, July 25, 2016]

§ 125.3 What types of subcontracting assistance are available to small businesses?

(a) *General.* The purpose of the subcontracting assistance program is to provide the maximum practicable subcontracting opportunities for small business concerns, including small business concerns owned and controlled by veterans, small business concerns owned and controlled by service-disabled veterans, certified HUBZone small business concerns, certified small business concerns owned and controlled by socially and economically disadvantaged individuals, and small business concerns owned and controlled by women. The subcontracting assistance program implements section 8(d) of the Small Business Act, which includes the requirement that, unless otherwise exempt, other than small business concerns awarded contracts that offer subcontracting possibilities by the Federal Government in excess of $650,000, or in excess of $1,500,000 for construction of a public facility, must submit a subcontracting plan to the appropriate contracting agency. The Federal Acquisition Regulation sets forth the requirements for subcontracting plans in 48 CFR 19.7, and the clause at 48 CFR 52.219–9.

(1) Subcontract under this section means a legally binding agreement between a contractor that is already under contract to another party to perform work and a third party (other than one involving an employer-employee relationship), hereinafter referred to as the subcontractor, for the subcontractor to perform a part or all of the work that the contractor has undertaken.

(i) Subcontract award data reported by prime contractors and subcontractors shall be limited to awards made to their immediate next-tier subcontractors. Credit cannot be taken for awards made beyond the immediate next-tier, except as follows:

(A) The contractor or subcontractor has been designated to receive a small business or small disadvantaged business credit from an ANC or Indian Tribe; or

(B) Purchases from a corporation, company, or subdivision that is an affiliate of the prime contractor or subcontractor are not included in the subcontracting base. Subcontracts by first-tier affiliates shall be treated as subcontracts of the prime.

(C) Where the prime contractor has an individual subcontracting plan, the prime contractor shall establish two sets of small business subcontracting goals, one goal for the first tier and one goal for lower tier subcontracts awarded by other than small subcontractors with individual subcontracting plans. Under individual subcontracting plans the prime contractor shall receive credit for small business concerns performing as first tier subcontractors (first tier goal) and subcontractors at any tier pursuant to the subcontracting plans required under paragraph (c) of this section in an amount equal to the dollar value of work awarded to such small business concerns (lower tier goal). Other-than-small, lower tier subcontractors must have their own individual subcontracting plans if the subcontract is at or above the subcontracting plan threshold, and are required to make a good faith effort to meet their subcontracting plan goals. The prime contractor and any subcontractor with a subcontracting plan are responsible for reporting on subcontracting performance under their contracts or subcontracts at their first tier. The prime contractor's performance under its individual subcontracting plan will be calculated using its own reporting at the first tier for its first tier goal and its subcontractors' first tier reports under their plans for the lower tier subcontracting goals. The prime contractor's performance under the individual subcontracting plan must be evaluated based on its combined performance under the first tier and lower tier goal.

(D) Other-than-small prime contractors and subcontractors with subcontracting plans shall report on their subcontracting performance on the Summary Subcontracting report (SSR) at their first tier only.

(ii) Only subcontracts involving performance in the United States or its outlying areas should be included, with the exception of subcontracts under a contract awarded by the U.S. Department of State or any other agency that has statutory or regulatory authority to require subcontracting plans for subcontracts performed outside the United States and its outlying areas and subcontracts for foreign military sales unless waived in accordance with agency regulations.

(iii) The following should not be included in the subcontracting base: internally generated costs such as salaries and wages; employee insurance; other employee benefits; payments for petty cash; depreciation; interest; income taxes; property taxes; lease payments; bank fees; fines, claims, and dues; Original Equipment Manufacturer relationships during warranty periods (negotiated up front with product); utilities such as electricity, water, sewer, and other services purchased from a municipality or solely authorized by the municipality to provide those services in a particular geographical region; and philanthropic contributions. Utility companies may be eligible for additional exclusions unique to their industry, which may be approved by the contracting officer on a case-by-case basis. Exclusions from the subcontracting base include but are not limited to those listed above.

(2) Subcontracting goals required under paragraph (c) of this section must be established in terms of the total dollars subcontracted and as a percentage of total subcontract dollars. However, a contracting officer may establish additional goals as a percentage of total contract dollars.

(3) A prime contractor has a history of unjustified untimely or reduced payments to subcontractors if the prime contractor has reported itself to a contracting officer in accordance with paragraph (c)(5) of this section on three occasions within a 12 month period.

(b) *Responsibilities of prime contractors.* (1) Prime contractors (including small business prime contractors) selected to receive a Federal contract that exceeds the simplified acquisition threshold, that will not be performed entirely outside of any state, territory, or possession of the United States, the District of Columbia, or the Commonwealth of Puerto Rico, and that is not for services which are personal in nature, are responsible for ensuring that small business concerns have the maximum practicable opportunity to participate in the performance of the contract, including subcontracts for subsystems, assemblies, components, and related services for major systems, consistent with the efficient performance of the contract.

(2) A small business cannot be required to submit a formal subcontracting plan or be asked to submit a formal subcontracting plan, a small-business prime contractor is encouraged to provide maximum practicable opportunity to other small businesses to participate in the performance of the contract, consistent with the efficient performance of the contract.

(3) Efforts to provide the maximum practicable subcontracting opportunities for small business concern may include, as appropriate for the procurement, one or more of the following actions:

(i) Breaking out contract work items into economically feasible units, as appropriate, to facilitate small business participation;

(ii) Conducting market research to identify small business subcontractors and suppliers through all reasonable means, such as performing online searches via the System for Award Management (SAM) (or any successor system), posting Notices of Sources Sought and/or Requests for Proposal on SBA's SUB-Net, participating in Business Matchmaking events, and attending pre-bid conferences;

(iii) Soliciting small business concerns as early in the acquisition process as practicable to allow them sufficient time to submit a timely offer for the subcontract;

(iv) Providing interested small businesses with adequate and timely information about the plans, specifications, and requirements for performance of the prime contract to assist them in submitting a timely offer for the subcontract;

(v) Negotiating in good faith with interested small businesses;

(vi) Directing small businesses that need additional assistance to SBA;

(vii) Assisting interested small businesses in obtaining bonding, lines of credit, required insurance, necessary equipment, supplies, materials, or services;

(viii) Utilizing the available services of small business associations; local, state, and Federal small business assistance offices; and other organizations; and

(ix) Participating in a formal mentor-protégé program with one or more small-business protégés that results in developmental assistance to the protégés.

(c) *Additional responsibilities of other than small contractors.* (1) In addition to the responsibilities provided in paragraph (b) of this section, a prime contractor selected for award of a contract or contract modification that exceeds $700,000, or $1,500,000 in the case of construction of a public facility, is responsible for the following:

(i) Submitting and negotiating before award an acceptable subcontracting plan that reflects maximum practicable opportunities for small businesses in the performance of the contract as subcontractors or suppliers at all tiers of performance. A prime contractor may submit a commercial plan, described in paragraph (c)(2) of this section, instead of an individual subcontracting plan, when the product or service being furnished to the Government meets the definition of a commercial item under 48 CFR 2.101;

(ii) Making a good-faith effort to achieve the dollar and percentage goals and other elements in its subcontracting plan;

(iii) The contractor may not prohibit a subcontractor from discussing any material matter pertaining to payment or utilization with the contracting officer;

(iv) When developing an individual subcontracting plan (also called individual contract plan), the contractor must decide whether to include indirect costs in its subcontracting goals. If indirect costs are included in the goals, these costs must be included in the Individual Subcontract Report (ISR) in www.esrs.gov (eSRS) or Subcontract Reports for Individual Contracts (the paper SF–294, if authorized). If indirect costs are excluded from the goals, these costs must be excluded from the ISRs (or SF–294 if authorized); however, these costs must be included on a prorated basis in the Summary Subcontracting Report (SSR) in the eSRS system. A contractor authorized to use a commercial subcontracting plan must include all indirect costs in its SSR;

(v) The contractor must assign to each subcontract, and to each solicitation, if a solicitation is utilized, the NAICS code and corresponding size standard that best describes the principal purpose of the subcontract (see §121.410 of this chapter). A formal solicitation is not required for each subcontract, but the contractor must provide some form of written notice of the NAICS code and size standard assigned to potential offerors prior to acceptance and award of the subcontract. The prime contractor (or subcontractor) may rely on a subcontractor's electronic representations and certifications, if the solicitation for the subcontract contains a clause which provides that the subcontractor verifies by submission of the offer that the size or socioeconomic representations and certifications are current, accurate and complete as of the date of the offer for the subcontract. Electronic submission may include any method acceptable to the prime contractor (or subcontractor) including, but not limited to, size or socioeconomic representations and certifications made in SAM (or any successor system). A prime contractor (or subcontractor) may not require the use of SAM (or any successor system) for purposes of representing size or socioeconomic status in connection with a subcontract;

(vi) The contractor must submit timely and accurate ISRs and SSRs in eSRS (or any successor system), or if information for a particular procurement cannot be entered into eSRS (or any successor system), submit a timely

SF–294, Subcontracting Report for Individual Contract. When a report is rejected by the contracting officer, the contractor must make the necessary corrections and resubmit the report within 30 days of receiving the notice of rejection;

(vii) The contractor must cooperate in the reviews of subcontracting plan compliance, including providing requested information and supporting documentation reflecting actual achievements and good-faith efforts to meet the goals and other elements in the subcontracting plan;

(viii) The contractor must provide pre-award written notification to unsuccessful small business offerors on all subcontracts over the simplified acquisition threshold (as defined in the FAR at 48 CFR 2.101)'' in paragraphs (c)(1)(viii) and (ix) for which a small business concern received a preference. The written notification must include the name and location of the apparent successful offeror and if the successful offeror is a small business, veteran-owned small business, service-disabled veteran-owned small business, HUBZone small business, small disadvantaged business, or women-owned small business;

(ix) As a best practice, the contractor may provide the pre-award written notification cited in paragraph (c)(1)(viii) of this section to unsuccessful and small business offerors on subcontracts at or below the simplified acquisition threshold (as defined in the FAR at 48 CFR 2.101)'' in paragraphs (c)(1)(viii) and (ix) and should do so whenever practical; and

(x) Except when subcontracting for commercial items, the prime contractor must require all subcontractors (except small business concerns) who receive subcontracts in excess of $1,500,000 in the case of a subcontract for the construction of any public facility, or in excess of $700,000 in the case of all other subcontracts, and which offer further subcontracting possibilities, to adopt a subcontracting plan of their own consistent with this section, and must ensure at a minimum that all subcontractors required to maintain subcontracting plans pursuant to this paragraph will review and approve subcontracting plans submitted by their subcontractors; monitor their subcontractors' compliance with their approved subcontracting plans; ensure that subcontracting reports are submitted by their subcontractors when required; acknowledge receipt of their subcontractors' reports; compare the performance of their subcontractors to their subcontracting plans and goals; and discuss performance with their subcontractors when necessary to ensure their subcontractors make a good-faith effort to comply with their subcontracting plans; and

(xi) The prime contractor must provide a written statement of the types of records it will maintain to demonstrate procedures which have been adopted to ensure subcontractors at all tiers comply with the requirements and goals set forth in the subcontracting plan established in accordance with paragraph (c)(1)(x) of this section, including the establishment of source lists of small business concerns, small business concerns owned and controlled by veterans, small business concerns owned and controlled by service-disabled veterans, qualified HUBZone small business concerns, small business concerns owned and controlled by socially and economically disadvantaged individuals, and small business concerns owned and controlled by women; the efforts to identify and award subcontracts to such small business concerns; and size or socioeconomic certifications or representations received in connection with each subcontract.

(2) A commercial plan, also referred to as an annual plan or company-wide plan, is the preferred type of subcontracting plan for contractors furnishing commercial items. A commercial plan covers the offeror's fiscal year and applies to the entire production of commercial items sold by either the entire company or a portion thereof (e.g., division, plant, or product line). Once approved, the plan remains in effect during the contractor's fiscal year for all Federal government contracts in effect during that period. The contracting officer of the agency that originally approved the commercial plan will exercise the functions of the contracting officer on behalf of all agencies that award contracts covered by the plan.

(3) An offeror must represent to the contracting officer that it will make a good faith effort to acquire articles, equipment, supplies, services, or materials, or obtain the performance of construction work from the small business concerns that it used in preparing the bid or proposal, in the same scope, amount, and quality used in preparing and submitting the bid or proposal. Merely responding to a request for a quote does not constitute use in preparing a bid or offer. An offeror used a small business concern in preparing the bid or proposal if:

(i) The offeror references the small business concern as a subcontractor in the bid or proposal or associated small business subcontracting plan;

(ii) The offeror has a subcontract or agreement in principle to subcontract with the small business concern to perform a portion of the specific contract; or

(iii) The small business concern drafted any portion of the bid or proposal or the offeror used the small business concern's pricing or cost information or technical expertise in preparing the bid or proposal, where there is written evidence (including email) of an intent or understanding that the small business concern will be awarded a subcontract for the related work if the offeror is awarded the contract.

(4) If a prime contractor fails to acquire articles, equipment, supplies, services or materials or obtain the performance of construction work as described in (c)(3), the prime contractor must provide the contracting officer with a written explanation. This written explanation must be submitted to the contracting officer prior to the submission of the invoice for final payment and contract close-out.

(5) A prime contractor shall notify the contracting officer in writing if upon completion of the responsibilities of the small business subcontractor (i.e., the subcontractor is entitled to payment under the terms of the subcontract), the prime contractor pays a reduced price to a small business subcontractor for goods and services provided for the contract or the payment to a small business subcontractor is more than 90 days past due under the terms of the subcontract for goods and services provided for the contract and for which the Federal agency has paid the prime contractor. "Reduced price" means a price that is less than the price agreed upon in a written, binding contractual document. The prime contractor shall include the reason for the reduction in payment to or failure to pay a small business subcontractor in any written notice.

(6) If at the conclusion of a contract the prime contractor did not meet all of the small business subcontracting goals in the subcontracting plan, the prime contractor shall provide the contracting officer with a written explanation as to why it did not meet the goals of the plan so that the contracting officer can evaluate whether the prime contractor acted in good faith as set forth in paragraph (d)(3) of this section.

(7) The additional prime contractor responsibilities described in paragraph (c)(1) of this section do not apply if:

(i) The prime contractor is a small business concern;

(ii) The prime contract or contract modification is a personal services contract; or

(iii) The prime contract or contract modification will be performed entirely outside of any state, territory, or possession of the United States, the District of Columbia, or the Commonwealth of Puerto Rico.

(8) A prime contractor that identifies a small business by name as a subcontractor in a proposal, offer, bid or subcontracting plan must notify those subcontractors in writing prior to identifying the concern in the proposal, bid, offer or subcontracting plan.

(9) Anyone who has a reasonable basis to believe that a prime contractor or a subcontractor may have made a false statement to an employee or representative of the Federal Government, or to an employee or representative of the prime contractor, with respect to subcontracting plans must report the matter to the SBA Office of Inspector General. All other concerns as to whether a prime contractor or subcontractor has complied with SBA regulations or otherwise acted in bad faith may be reported to the Government Contracting Area Office where the firm is headquartered.

(d) *Contracting officer responsibilities.* The contracting officer (or administrative contracting officer if specifically delegated in writing to accomplish this task) is responsible for evaluating the prime contractor's compliance with its subcontracting plan, including:

(1) Ensuring that all contractors submit their subcontracting reports into the eSRS (or any successor system) or, if applicable, the SF-294, Subcontracting Report for Individual Contracts, within 30 days after the report ending date (e.g., by October 30th for the fiscal year ended September 30th).

(2) Reviewing all ISRs, and where applicable, SSRs, in eSRS (or any successor system) within 60 days of the report ending date (e.g., by November 30th for a report submitted for the fiscal year ended September 30th) and either accepting or rejecting the reports in accordance with the Federal Acquisition Regulation (FAR) provisions set forth in 48 CFR subpart 19.7, 52.219-9, and the eSRS instructions (www.esrs.gov). The authority to acknowledge or reject SSRs for commercial plans resides with the contracting officer who approved the commercial plan. If a report is rejected, the contracting officer must provide an explanation for the rejection to allow prime contractors the opportunity to respond specifically to perceived deficiencies.

(3) Evaluating whether the prime contractor made a good faith effort to comply with its small business subcontracting plan. Evidence that a large business prime contractor has made a good faith effort to comply with its subcontracting plan or other subcontracting responsibilities includes supporting documentation that:

(i) The contractor performed one or more of the actions described in paragraph (b) of this section, as appropriate for the procurement;

(ii) Although the contractor may have failed to achieve its goal in one socioeconomic category, it over-achieved its goal by an equal or greater amount in one or more of the other categories; or

(iii) The contractor fulfilled all of the requirements of its subcontracting plan.

(4) Evaluating the prime contractor's written explanation concerning the prime contractor's failure to use a small business concern in performance in the same scope, amount, and quality used in preparing and submitting the bid or proposal, and considering that information when rating the contractor for past performance purposes.

(5) Evaluating the prime contractor's written explanation concerning its payment of a reduced price to a small business subcontractor for goods and services upon completion of the responsibilities of the subcontractor or its payment to a subcontractor more than 90 days past due under the terms of the subcontract for goods and services provided for the contract and for which the Federal agency has paid the prime contractor, and considering that information when rating the contractor for past performance purposes.

(6) Evaluating whether the prime contractor has a history of unjustified untimely or reduced payments to subcontractors, and if so, recording the identity of the prime contractor in the Federal Awardee Performance and Integrity Information System (FAPIIS), or any successor database.

(7) In his or her discretion, requiring the prime contractor (other than a prime contractor with a commercial plan) to update its subcontracting plan when an option is exercised.

(8) Requiring the prime contractor (other than a contractor with a commercial plan) to submit a subcontracting plan if the value of a modification causes the value of the contract to exceed the subcontracting plan threshold and to the extent that subcontracting opportunities exist.

(9) In his or her discretion, requiring a subcontracting plan if a prime contractor's size status changes from small to other than small as a result of a size recertification.

(10) Where a subcontracting plan is amended in connection with an option, or added as a result of a recertification or modification, the changes to any existing plan are for prospective subcontracting opportunities and do not apply retroactively. However, since achievements must be reported on the ISR (or the SF-294, if applicable) on a cumulative basis from the inception of the

contract, the contractor's achievements prior to the modification or option will be factored into its overall achievement on the contract from inception.

(e) *CMR Responsibilities*. Commercial Market Representatives (CMRs) are SBA's subcontracting specialists. CMRs are responsible for:

(1) Facilitating the matching of large prime contractors with small business concerns;

(2) Counseling large prime contractors on their responsibilities to maximize subcontracting opportunities for small business concerns;

(3) Instructing large prime contractors on identifying small business concerns by means of SAM (or any successor system), SUB-Net, Business Matchmaking events, and other resources and tools;

(4) Counseling small business concerns on how to market themselves to large prime contractors;

(5) Maintaining a portfolio of large prime contractors and conducting Subcontracting Orientation and Assistance Reviews (SOARs). SOARs are conducted for the purpose of assisting prime contractors in understanding and complying with their small business subcontracting responsibilities, including developing subcontracting goals that reflect maximum practicable opportunity for small business; maintaining acceptable books and records; and periodically submitting reports to the Federal government; and

(6) Conducting periodic reviews, including compliance reviews in accordance with paragraph (f) of this section.

(f) *Compliance reviews*. (1) A prime contractor's performance under its subcontracting plan is evaluated by means of on-site compliance reviews and follow-up reviews, as a supplement to evaluations performed by the contracting agency, either on a contract-by-contract basis or, in the case of contractors having multiple contracts, on an aggregate basis. A compliance review is a surveillance review that determines a contractor's achievements in meeting the goals and other elements in its subcontracting plan for both open contracts and contracts completed during the previous twelve months. A follow-up review is done after a compliance review, generally within six to eight months, to determine if the contractor has implemented SBA's recommendations.

(2) All compliance reviews begin with a validation of the prime contractor's most recent ISR (or SF–294, if applicable) or SSR. A compliance review includes:

(i) An evaluation of whether the prime contractor assigned the proper NAICS code and corresponding size standard to a subcontract, and a review of whether small business subcontractors qualify for the size or socio-economic status claimed;

(ii) Validation of the prime contractor's methodology for completing its subcontracting reports; and

(iii) Consideration of whether the prime contractor is monitoring its other than small subcontractors with regard to their subcontracting plans, determining achievement of their proposed subcontracting goals, and reviewing their subcontractors' ISRs (or SF–294s, if applicable).

(3) Upon completion of the review and evaluation of a contractor's performance and efforts to achieve the requirements in its subcontracting plans, the contractor's performance will be assigned one of the following ratings: Outstanding, Highly Successful, Acceptable, Marginal, or Unsatisfactory. The factors listed in paragraph (c) of this section will be taken into consideration, where applicable, in determining the contractor's rating. However, a contractor may be found Unsatisfactory, regardless of other factors, if it cannot substantiate the claimed achievements under its subcontracting plan.

(4) Any contractor that receives a marginal or unsatisfactory rating must provide a written corrective action plan to SBA, or to both SBA and the agency that conducted the compliance review if the agency conducting the review has an agreement with SBA, within 30 days of its receipt of the official compliance report.

(5) Any contractor that fails to comply with paragraph (f)(4) of this section, or any contractor that fails to demonstrate a good-faith effort, as set forth in paragraph (d) of this section:

(i) May be considered for liquidated damages under the procedures in 48 CFR 19.705–7 and the clause at 52.219–16; and

(ii) Shall be in material breach of such contract or subcontract, and such failure to demonstrate good faith must be considered in any past performance evaluation of the contractor. This action shall be considered by the contracting officer upon receipt of a written recommendation to that effect from the CMR. The CMR's recommendation must include a copy of the compliance report and any other relevant correspondence or supporting documentation. Furthermore, if the CMR has a reasonable basis to believe that a contractor has made a false statement to an employee or representative of the Federal Government, or to an employee or representative of the prime contractor, the CMR must report the matter to the SBA Office of Inspector General. All other concerns as to whether a prime contractor or subcontractor has complied with SBA regulations or otherwise acted in bad faith may be reported to the Area Government Contracting Office where the firm is headquartered.

(6) Reviews and evaluations of contractors with commercial plans are identical to reviews and evaluations of other contractors, except that contractors with commercial subcontracting plans do not submit the SF–294, Subcontracting Report for Individual Contracts. Instead, goal achievement is determined by comparing the goals in the approved commercial subcontracting plan against the cumulative achievements on the SF–295, Summary Subcontract Report, for the same period. The same ratings criteria set forth in paragraph (f)(3) of this section apply to contractors with commercial plans.

(7) SBA is authorized to enter into agreements with other Federal agencies or entities to conduct compliance reviews and otherwise further the objectives of the subcontracting program. Copies of these agreements will be published on *http://www.sba.gov/GC*. SBA is the lead agency on all joint compliance reviews with other agencies.

(8) The head of the contracting agency shall ensure that:

(i) The agency collects and reports data on the extent to which contractors of the agency meet the goals and objectives set forth in subcontracting plans; and

(ii) The agency periodically reviews data collected and reported pursuant to paragraph (f)(8)(i) of this section for the purpose of ensuring that such contractors comply in good faith with the requirements of this section.

(g) *Subcontracting consideration in source selection.* (1) A contracting officer may include an evaluation factor in a solicitation which evaluates:

(i) An offeror's proposed approach to small business subcontracting participation in the subject procurement;

(ii) The extent to which the offeror has met its small business subcontracting plan goals on previous covered contracts; and/or

(iii) The extent to which the offeror timely paid its small business subcontractors under covered contracts.

(2) A contracting officer may include an evaluation factor in a solicitation which evaluates an offeror's commitment to pay small business subcontractors within a specific number of days after receipt of payment from the Government for goods and services previously rendered by the small business subcontractor.

(i) The contracting officer will comparatively evaluate the proposed timelines.

(ii) Such a commitment shall become a material part of the contract.

(iii) The contracting officer must consider the contractor's compliance with the commitment in evaluating performance, including for purposes of contract continuation (such as exercising options).

(3) A small business concern submitting an offer shall receive the maximum score, credit or rating under an evaluation factor described in paragraph (g) of this section without having to submit any information in connection with this factor.

(4) A contracting officer shall include a significant evaluation factor for the criteria described in paragraphs (g)(1)(i) and (g)(1)(ii) of this section in a bundled contract or order as defined in § 125.2.

(5) Paragraph (g) of this section may apply to solicitations for orders against multiple award contracts, (including a Federal Supply Schedule or Multiple Award Schedule contract, a Government-wide acquisition contract (GWAC), or a multi-agency contract (MAC)), blanket purchase agreements or basic ordering agreements.

(h) *Multiple award contracts.* (1) Except where a prime contractor has a commercial plan, the contracting officer shall require a subcontracting plan for each multiple award indefinite delivery, indefinite quantity contract (including Multiple Award Schedule), where the estimated value of the contract exceeds the subcontracting plan thresholds in paragraph (a) of this section and the contract has subcontracting opportunities.

(2) Contractors shall submit small business subcontracting reports for individual orders to the contracting agency on an annual basis.

(3) The agency funding the order shall receive credit towards its small business subcontracting goals. More than one agency may not receive credit towards its subcontracting goals for a particular subcontract.

(4) The agency funding the order may in its discretion establish small business subcontracting goals for individual orders, blanket purchase agreements or basic ordering agreements.

(i) *Subcontracting consideration in bundled and consolidated contracts.* (1) For bundled requirements, the agency must evaluate offers from teams of small businesses the same as other offers, with due consideration to the capabilities of all proposed subcontractors.

(2) For substantial bundling, the agency must design actions to maximize small business participation as subcontractors (including suppliers) at any tier under the contract or contracts that may be awarded to meet the requirements.

(3) For significant subcontracting opportunities in consolidated contracts, bundled requirements, and substantially bundled requirements, *see* § 125.2(d)(4).

[69 FR 75824, Dec. 20, 2004, as amended at 74 FR 46887, Sept. 14, 2009; 78 FR 42403, July 16, 2013; 78 FR 59798, Sept. 30, 2013; 78 FR 61142, Oct. 2, 2013; 81 FR 34262, May 31, 2016; 81 FR 94250, Dec. 23, 2016; 83 FR 12852, Mar. 26, 2018]

§ 125.4 What is the Government property sales assistance program?

(a) The purpose of SBA's Government property sales assistance program is to:

(1) Insure that small businesses obtain their fair share of all Federal real and personal property qualifying for sale or other competitive disposal action; and

(2) Assist small businesses in obtaining Federal property being processed for disposal, sale, or lease.

(b) SBA property sales assistance primarily consists of two activities:

(1) Obtaining small business set-asides when necessary to insure that a fair share of Government property sales are made to small businesses; and

(2) Providing advice and assistance to small businesses on all matters pertaining to sale or lease of Government property.

(c) The program is intended to cover the following categories of Government property:

(1) Sales of timber and related forest products;

(2) Sales of strategic material from national stockpiles;

(3) Sales of royalty oil by the Department of Interior's Minerals Management Service;

(4) Leases involving rights to minerals, petroleum, coal, and vegetation; and

(5) Sales of surplus real and personal property.

(d) SBA has established specific small business size standards and rules for the sale or lease of the different kinds of Government property. These provisions are contained in §§ 121.501 through 121.514 of this chapter.

§ 125.5 What is the Certificate of Competency Program?

(a) *General.* (1) The Certificate of Competency (COC) Program is authorized under section 8(b)(7) of the Small Business Act (15 U.S.C. 637(b)(7)). A

COC is a written instrument issued by SBA to a Government contracting officer, certifying that one or more named small business concerns possess the responsibility to perform a specific Government procurement (or sale) contract, including any contract deriving from a reverse auction. The COC Program is applicable to all Government procurement actions, including Multiple Award Contracts and orders placed against Multiple Award Contracts, where the contracting officer has used any issues of capacity or credit (responsibility) to determine suitability for an award. With respect to Multiple Award Contracts, contracting officers generally determine responsibility at the time of award of the contract. However, if a contracting officer makes a responsibility determination as set forth in paragraph (a)(2) of this section for an order issued against a Multiple Award Contract, the contracting officer must refer the matter to SBA for a COC. The COC procedures apply to all Federal procurements, regardless of the location of performance or the location of the procuring activity.

(2) A contracting officer must refer a small business concern to SBA for a possible COC, even if the next apparent successful offeror is also a small business, when the contracting officer:

(i) Denies an apparent successful small business offeror award of a contract or order on the basis of responsibility (including those bases set forth in paragraphs (a)(1)(ii) and (iii) of this section);

(ii) Refuses to consider a small business concern for award of a contract or order after evaluating the concern's offer on a non-comparative basis (e.g., a pass/fail, go/no go, or acceptable/unacceptable) under one or more responsibility type evaluation factors (such as experience of the company or key personnel or past performance); or

(iii) Refuses to consider a small business concern for award of a contract or order because it failed to meet a definitive responsibility criterion contained in the solicitation.

(3) A small business offeror referred to SBA as nonresponsible may apply to SBA for a COC. Where the applicant is a non-manufacturing offeror on a supply contract, the COC applies to the responsibility of the non-manufacturer, not to that of the manufacturer.

(b) *COC Eligibility.* (1) The offeror seeking a COC has the burden of proof to demonstrate its eligibility for COC review. (i) To be eligible for a COC, an offeror must qualify as a small business under the applicable size standard in accordance with part 121 of this chapter.

(ii) To be eligible for a COC, an offeror must qualify as a small business under the applicable size standard in accordance with part 121 of this chapter, and must have agreed to comply with the applicable limitations on subcontracting and the nonmanufacturer rule, where applicable.

(2) SBA will determine a concern ineligible for a COC if the concern, or any of its principals, appears in the "Parties Excluded From Federal Procurement Programs" section found in the U.S. General Services Administration Office of Acquisition Policy Publication: List of Parties Excluded From Federal Procurement or Nonprocurement Programs. If a principal is unable to presently control the applicant concern, and appears in the Procurement section of the list due to matters not directly related to the concern itself, responsibility will be determined in accordance with paragraph (f)(2) of this section.

(3) An eligibility determination will be made on a case-by-case basis, where a concern or any of its principals appears in the Nonprocurement Section of the publication referred to in paragraph (b)(2) of this section.

(c) *Referral of nonresponsibility determination to SBA.* (1) The contracting officer must refer the matter in writing to the SBA Government Contracting Area Office (Area Office) serving the area in which the headquarters of the offeror is located. The referral must include a copy of the following:

(i) Solicitation;

(ii) Offer submitted by the concern whose responsibility is at issue for the procurement (its Best and Final Offer for a negotiated procurement);

(iii) Abstract of Bids, where applicable, or the Contracting Officer's Price Negotiation Memorandum;

(iv) Preaward survey, where applicable;

(v) Contracting officer's written determination of nonresponsibility;

(vi) Technical data package (including drawings, specifications, and Statement of Work); and

(vii) Any other justification and documentation used to arrive at the nonresponsibility determination.

(2) Contract award must be withheld by the contracting officer for a period of 15 working days (or longer if agreed to by SBA and the contracting officer) following receipt by the appropriate Area Office of a referral which includes all required documentation.

(3) The COC referral must indicate that the offeror has been found responsive to the solicitation, and also identify the reasons for the nonresponsibility determination.

(d) *Application for COC.* (1) Upon receipt of the contracting officer's referral, the Area Office will inform the concern of the contracting officer's negative responsibility determination, and offer it the opportunity to apply to SBA for a COC by a specified date.

(2) The COC application must include all information and documentation requested by SBA and any additional information which the firm believes will demonstrate its ability to perform on the proposed contract. The application should be returned as soon as possible, but no later than the date specified by SBA.

(3) Upon receipt of a complete and acceptable application, SBA may elect to visit the applicant's facility to review its responsibility. SBA personnel may obtain clarification or confirmation of information provided by the applicant by directly contacting suppliers, financial institutions, and other third parties upon whom the applicant's responsibility depends.

(e) *Incomplete applications.* If an application for a COC is materially incomplete or is not submitted by the date specified by SBA, SBA will close the case without issuing a COC and will notify the contracting officer and the concern with a declination letter.

(f) *Reviewing an application.* (1) The COC review process is not limited to the areas of nonresponsibility cited by the contracting officer. SBA may, at its discretion, independently evaluate the COC applicant for all elements of responsibility, but it may presume responsibility exists as to elements other than those cited as deficient. SBA may deny a COC for reasons of nonresponsibility not originally cited by the contracting officer.

(2) A small business will be rebuttably presumed nonresponsible if any of the following circumstances are shown to exist:

(i) Within three years before the application for a COC, the concern, or any of its principals, has been convicted of an offense or offenses that would constitute grounds for debarment or suspension under FAR subpart 9.4 (48 CFR part 9, subpart 9.4), and the matter is still under the jurisdiction of a court (e.g., the principals of a concern are incarcerated, on probation or parole, or under a suspended sentence); or

(ii) Within three years before the application for a COC, the concern or any of its principals has had a civil judgment entered against it or them for any reason that would constitute grounds for debarment or suspension under FAR subpart 9.4 (48 CFR part, subpart 9.4).

(3) Where a contracting officer finds a concern to be non-responsible for reasons of financial capacity on an indefinite delivery or indefinite quantity task or delivery order contract, the Area Director will consider the firm's maximum financial capacity. If the Area Director issues a COC, it will be for a specific amount that is the limit of the firm's financial capacity for that contract. The contracting officer may subsequently determine to exceed the amount, but cannot deny the firm award of an order or contract on financial grounds if the firm has not reached the financial maximum the Area Director identified in the COC letter.

(g) *Decision by Area Director ("Director").* After reviewing the information submitted by the applicant and the information gathered by SBA, the Area Director will make a determination, either final or recommended as set forth in the following chart:

Contracting actions	SBA official or office with authority to make decision	Finality of decision; options for contracting agencies
$100,000 or less, or in accordance with Simplified Acquisition Threshold procedures.	Director may approve or deny	Final. The Director will notify both applicant and contracting agency in writing of the decision.
Between $100,000 and $25 million	(1) Director may deny (2) Director may approve, subject to right of appeal and other options.	(1) Final. (2) Contracting agency may proceed under paragraph (h) or paragraph (i) of this section.
Exceeding $25 million	(1) Director may deny (2) Director must refer to SBA Headquarters recommendation for approval.	(1) Final. (2) Contracting agency may proceed under paragraph (j) of this section.

(h) *Notification of intent to issue on a contract or order with a value between $100,000 and $25 million.* Where the Director determines that a COC is warranted, he or she will notify the contracting officer (or the procurement official with the authority to accept SBA's decision) of the intent to issue a COC, and of the reasons for that decision, prior to issuing the COC. At the time of notification, the contracting officer or the procurement official with the authority to accept SBA's decision has the following options:

(1) Accept the Director's decision to issue the COC and award the contract to the concern. The COC issuance letter will then be sent, including as an attachment a detailed rationale of the decision; or

(2) Ask the Director to suspend the case for one of the following purposes:

(i) To forward a detailed rationale for the decision to the contracting officer for review within a specified period of time;

(ii) To afford the contracting officer the opportunity to meet with the Area Office to review all documentation contained in the case file;

(iii) To submit any information which the contracting officer believes SBA has not considered (at which time, SBA will establish a new suspense date mutually agreeable to the contracting officer and SBA); or

(iv) To permit resolution of an appeal by the contracting agency to SBA Headquarters under paragraph (i) of this section.

(i) *Appeals of Area Director determinations.* For COC actions with a value exceeding $100,000, contracting agencies may appeal a Director's decision to issue a COC to SBA Headquarters by filing an appeal with the Area Office processing the COC application. The Area Office must honor the request to appeal if the contracting officer agrees to withhold award until the appeal process is concluded. Without such an agreement from the contracting officer, the Director must issue the COC. When such an agreement has been obtained, the Area Office will immediately forward the case file to SBA Headquarters.

(1) The intent of the appeal procedure is to allow the contracting agency the opportunity to submit to SBA Headquarters any documentation which the Area Office may not have considered.

(2) SBA Headquarters will furnish written notice to the Director, OSDBU or OSBP of the procuring agency, with a copy to the contracting officer, that the case file has been received and that an appeal decision may be requested by an authorized official. If the contracting agency decides to file an appeal, it must notify SBA Headquarters through its Director, OSDBU, within 10 working days (or a time period agreed upon by both agencies) of its receipt of the notice under paragraph (h) of this section. The appeal and any supporting documentation must be filed within 10 working days (or a different time period agreed to by both agencies) after SBA receives the request for a formal appeal.

(3) The SBA Director, Office of Government Contracting (D/GC) will make a final determination, in writing, to issue or to deny the COC.

(j) *Decision by SBA Headquarters where contract value exceeds $25 million.* (1) Prior to taking final action, SBA Headquarters will contact the contracting agency at the secretariat level or agency equivalent and afford it the following options:

(i) Ask SBA Headquarters to suspend the case so that the agency can meet with Headquarters personnel and review all documentation contained in the case file; or

(ii) Submit to SBA Headquarters for evaluation any information which the contracting agency believes has not been considered.

(2) After reviewing all available information, the AA/GC will make a final decision to either issue or deny the COC. If the AA/GC's decision is to deny the COC, the applicant and contracting agency will be informed in writing by the Area Office. If the decision is to issue the COC, a letter certifying the responsibility of the firm will be sent to the contracting agency by Headquarters and the applicant will be informed of such issuance by the Area Office. Except as set forth in paragraph (l) of this section, there can be no further appeal or reconsideration of the decision of the AA/GC.

(k) *Notification of denial of COC.* The notification to an unsuccessful applicant following either an Area Director or a Headquarters denial of a COC will briefly state all reasons for denial and inform the applicant that a meeting may be requested with appropriate SBA personnel to discuss the denial. Upon receipt of a request for such a meeting, the appropriate SBA personnel will confer with the applicant and explain the reasons for SBA's action. The meeting does not constitute an opportunity to rebut the merits of the SBA's decision to deny the COC, and is for the sole purpose of giving the applicant the opportunity to correct deficiencies so as to improve its ability to obtain future contracts either directly or, if necessary, through the issuance of a COC.

(l) *Reconsideration of COC after issuance.* (1) An approved COC may be reconsidered and possibly rescinded, at the sole discretion of SBA, where an award of the contract has not occurred, and one of the following circumstances exists:

(i) The COC applicant submitted false or omitted materially adverse information;

(ii) New materially adverse information has been received relating to the current responsibility of the applicant concern; or

(iii) The COC has been issued for more than 60 days (in which case SBA may investigate the business concern's current circumstances and the reason why the contract has not been issued).

(2) Where SBA reconsiders and reaffirms the COC the procedures under paragraph (h) of this section do not apply.

(m) *Effect of a COC.* By the terms of the Act, a COC is conclusive as to responsibility. Where SBA issues a COC on behalf of a small business with respect to a particular contract, contracting officers are required to award the contract without requiring the firm to meet any other requirement with respect to responsibility. Where SBA issues a COC with respect to a referral in paragraph (a)(2)(ii) or (a)(2)(iii) of this section, the contracting officer is not required to issue an award to that offeror if the contracting officer denies the contract for reasons unrelated to responsibility.

(n) *Effect of Denial of COC.* Denial of a COC by SBA does not preclude a contracting officer from awarding a contract to the referred firm, nor does it prevent the concern from making an offer on any other procurement.

(o) *Monitoring performance.* Once a COC has been issued and a contract awarded on that basis, SBA will monitor contractor performance.

[61 FR 3312, Jan. 31, 1996; 61 FR 7987, Mar. 1, 1996, as amended at 72 FR 50041, Aug. 30, 2007; 78 FR 61142, Oct. 2, 2013; 81 FR 34262, May 31, 2016; 81 FR 48585, July 25, 2016]

§ 125.6 What are the prime contractor's limitations on subcontracting?

(a) *General.* In order to be awarded a full or partial small business set-aside contract with a value greater than the simplified acquisition threshold (as defined in the FAR at 48 CFR 2.101)" in paragraph (a) introductory text; and an 8(a) contract, an SDVO SBC contract, a HUBZone contract, a WOSB or EDWOSB contract pursuant to part 127 of this chapter, a small business concern must agree that:

(1) In the case of a contract for services (except construction), it will not pay more than 50% of the amount paid by the government to it to firms that are not similarly situated. Any work that a similarly situated subcontractor

further subcontracts will count towards the 50% subcontract amount that cannot be exceeded.

(2)(i) In the case of a contract for supplies or products (other than from a nonmanufacturer of such supplies), it will not pay more than 50% of the amount paid by the government to it to firms that are not similarly situated. Any work that a similarly situated subcontractor further subcontracts will count towards the 50% subcontract amount that cannot be exceeded. Cost of materials are excluded and not considered to be subcontracted.

(ii) In the case of a contract for supplies from a nonmanufacturer, it will supply the product of a domestic small business manufacturer or processor, unless a waiver as described in §121.406(b)(5) of this chapter is granted.

(A) For a multiple item procurement where a waiver as described in §121.406(b)(5) of this chapter has not been granted for one or more items, more than 50% of the value of the products to be supplied by the nonmanufacturer must be the products of one or more domestic small business manufacturers or processors.

(B) For a multiple item procurement where a waiver as described in §121.406(b)(5) of this chapter is granted for one or more items, compliance with the limitation on subcontracting requirement will not consider the value of items subject to a waiver. As such, more than 50% of the value of the products to be supplied by the nonmanufacturer that are not subject to a waiver must be the products of one or more domestic small business manufacturers or processors.

(C) For a multiple item procurement, the same small business concern may act as both a manufacturer and a nonmanufacturer.

Example 1 to paragraph (a)(2). A contract calls for the supply of one item valued at $1,000,000. The market research shows that there are no small business manufacturers that produce this item, and the contracting officer seeks and is granted a contract specific waiver for this item. In this case, a small business nonmanufacturer may supply an item manufactured by a large business.

Example 2 to paragraph (a)(2). A contract is for $1,000,000 and calls for the acquisition of 10 items. Market research shows that nine of the items can be sourced from small business manufacturers and one item is subject to an SBA class waiver. The projected value of the item that is waived is $10,000. Therefore, at least 50% of the value of the items not subject to a waiver, or 50% of $990,000, must be supplied by one or more domestic small business manufacturers, and the prime small business nonmanufacturer may act as a manufacturer for one or more items.

Example 3 to paragraph (a)(2). A contract is for $1,000,000 and calls for the acquisition of 10 items. Market research shows that only four of these items are manufactured by small businesses. The value of the items manufactured by small business is estimated to be $400,000. The contracting officer seeks and is granted waivers on the other six items. Therefore, the value of the items granted waivers is excluded from the calculation and at least 50% of $400,000 would have to be spent by the prime contractor on items it manufactures itself, or on items manufactured by one or more other small business concerns.

Example 4 to paragraph (a)(2). A contract is for $1,000,000 and calls for the acquisition of 10 items. Market research shows that eight of the items can be sourced from small business manufacturers, and the estimated value of these items is $800,000. At least 50% of the value of the contract (*i.e.*, at least $500,000) will be spent on items manufactured by one or more small business concerns. As such, the contracting officer is not required to request contract specific waivers for the other two items valued at $200,000. In this case, the prime contractor can meet the requirement by sourcing some of the items from small businesses manufacturers and some from large businesses without a waiver and still satisfy the requirement.

(3) In the case of a contract for general construction, it will not pay more than 85% of the amount paid by the government to it to firms that are not similarly situated. Any work that a similarly situated subcontractor further subcontracts will count towards the 85% subcontract amount that cannot be exceeded. Cost of materials are excluded and not considered to be subcontracted.

(4) In the case of a contract for special trade contractors, no more than 75% of the amount paid by the government to the prime may be paid to firms that are not similarly situated. Any work that a similarly situated subcontractor further subcontracts will count towards the 75% subcontract amount

that cannot be exceeded. Cost of materials are excluded and not considered to be subcontracted.

(b) *Mixed contracts.* Where a contract combines services and supplies, the contracting officer shall select the appropriate NAICS code as prescribed in § 121.402(b) of this chapter. The contracting officer's selection of the applicable NAICS code is determinative as to which limitation on subcontracting and performance requirement applies. In no case shall the requirements of paragraph (a)(1) and (a)(2) of this section both apply to the same contract. The relevant limitation on subcontracting in paragraph (a)(1) or (a)(2) of this section shall apply only to that portion of the contract award amount.

Example 1 to paragraph (b). A procuring agency is acquiring both services and supplies through a small business set-aside. The total value of the requirement is $3,000,000, with the supply portion comprising $2,500,000, and the services portion comprising $500,000. The contracting officer appropriately assigns a manufacturing NAICS code to the requirement. The cost of material is $500,000. Thus, because the services portion of the contract and the cost of materials are excluded from consideration, the relevant amount for purposes of calculating the performance of work requirement is $2,000,000 and the prime and/or similarly situated entities must perform at least $1,000,000 and the prime contractor may not subcontract more than $1,000,000 to non-similarly situated entities.

Example 2 to paragraph (b). A procuring agency is acquiring both services and supplies through a small business set-aside. The total value of the requirement is $3,000,000, with the services portion comprising $2,500,000, and the supply portion comprising $500,000. The contracting officer appropriately assigns a services NAICS code to the requirement. Thus, because the supply portion of the contract is excluded from consideration, the relevant amount for purposes of calculating the performance of work requirement is $2,500,000 and the prime and/or similarly situated entities must perform at least $1,250,000 and the prime contractor may not subcontract more than $1,250,000 to non-similarly situated entities.

(c) *Subcontracts to similarly situated entities.* A small business concern prime contractor that receives a contract listed in paragraph (a) of this section and spends contract amounts on a subcontractor that is a similarly situated entity shall not consider those subcontracted amounts as subcontracted for purposes of determining whether the small business concern prime contractor has violated paragraph (a) of this section, to the extent the subcontractor performs the work with its own employees. Any work that the similarly situated subcontractor does not perform with its own employees shall be considered subcontracted SBA will also exclude a subcontract to a similarly situated entity from consideration under the ostensible subcontractor rule (§ 121.103(h)(4)).

Example 1 to paragraph (c): An SDVO SBC sole source contract is awarded in the total amount of $500,000 for hammers. The prime contractor is a manufacturer and subcontracts 51% of the total amount received, less the cost of materials ($100,000) or $204,000, to an SDVO SBC subcontractor that manufactures the hammers in the U.S. The prime contractor does not violate the limitation on subcontracting requirement because the amount subcontracted to a similarly situated entity (less the cost of materials) is excluded from the limitation on subcontracting calculation.

Example 2 to paragraph (c): A competitive 8(a) BD contract is awarded in the total amount of $10,000,000 for janitorial services. The prime contractor subcontracts $8,000,000 of the janitorial services to another 8(a) BD certified firm. The prime contractor does not violate the limitation on subcontracting for services because the amount subcontracted to a similarly situated entity is excluded from the limitation on subcontracting.

Example 3 to paragraph (c): A WOSB set-aside contract is awarded in the total amount of $1,000,000 for landscaping services. The prime contractor subcontracts $500,001 to an SDVO SBC subcontractor that is not also a WOSB under the WOSB program. The prime contractor is in violation of the limitation on subcontracting requirement because it has subcontracted more than 50% of the contract amount to an SDVO SBC subcontractor, which is not considered similarly situated to a WOSB prime contractor.

(d) *HUBZone procurement for commodities.* In the case of a HUBZone contract for the procurement of agricultural commodities, a HUBZone SBC may not purchase the commodity from a subcontractor if the subcontractor will supply the commodity in substantially the final form in which it is to be supplied to the Government.

(e) *Determining compliance with applicable limitation on subcontracting.* The period of time used to determine compliance for a total or partial set-aside contract will be the base term and then each subsequent option period. For an order set aside under a full and open contract or a full and open contract with reserve, the agency will use the period of performance for each order to determine compliance unless the order is competed among small and other-than-small businesses (in which case the subcontracting limitations will not apply).

(1) The contracting officer, in his or her discretion, may require the concern to comply with the applicable limitations on subcontracting and the nonmanufacturer rule for each order awarded under a total or partial set-aside contract.

(2) Compliance will be considered an element of responsibility and not a component of size eligibility.

(3) Work performed by an independent contractor shall be considered a subcontract, and may count toward meeting the applicable limitation on subcontracting where the independent contractor qualifies as a similarly situated entity.

(f) *Inapplicability of limitations on subcontracting.* The limitations on subcontracting do not apply to:

(1) Small business set-aside contracts with a value that is greater than the micro-purchase threshold but less than or equal to the simplified acquisition threshold (as both terms are defined in the FAR at 48 CFR 2.101); or

(2) Subcontracts (except where a prime is relying on a similarly situated entity to meet the applicable limitations on subcontracting).

(g) *Request to change applicable limitation on subcontracting.* SBA may use different percentages if the Administrator determines that such action is necessary to reflect conventional industry practices among small business concerns that are below the numerical size standard for businesses in that industry group. Representatives of a national trade or industry group or any interested SBC may request a change in subcontracting percentage requirements for the categories defined by six digit industry codes in the North American Industry Classification System (NAICS) pursuant to the following procedures:

(1) *Format of request.* Requests from representatives of a trade or industry group and interested SBCs should be in writing and sent or delivered to the Director, Office of Government Contracting, U.S. Small Business Administration, 409 3rd Street SW., Washington, DC 20416. The requester must demonstrate to SBA that a change in percentage is necessary to reflect conventional industry practices among small business concerns that are below the numerical size standard for businesses in that industry category, and must support its request with information including, but not limited to:

(i) Information relative to the economic conditions and structure of the entire national industry;

(ii) Market data, technical changes in the industry and industry trends;

(iii) Specific reasons and justifications for the change in the subcontracting percentage;

(iv) The effect such a change would have on the Federal procurement process; and

(v) Information demonstrating how the proposed change would promote the purposes of the small business, 8(a), SDVO, HUBZone, WOSB, or EDWOSB programs.

(2) *Notice to public.* Upon an adequate preliminary showing to SBA, SBA will publish in the FEDERAL REGISTER a notice of its receipt of a request that it considers a change in the subcontracting percentage requirements for a particular industry. The notice will identify the group making the request, and give the public an opportunity to submit information and arguments in both support and opposition.

(3) *Comments.* SBA will provide a period of not less than 30 days for public comment in response to the FEDERAL REGISTER notice.

(4) *Decision.* SBA will render its decision after the close of the comment period. If SBA decides against a change, SBA will publish notice of its decision in the FEDERAL REGISTER. Concurrent with the notice, SBA will advise the requester of its decision in writing. If SBA decides in favor of a change, SBA will propose an appropriate change to this part.

(h) *Penalties*. Whoever violates the requirements set forth in paragraph (a) of this section shall be subject to the penalties prescribed in 15 U.S.C. 645(d), except that the fine shall be treated as the greater of $500,000 or the dollar amount spent, in excess of permitted levels, by the entity on subcontractors. A party's failure to comply with the spirit and intent of a subcontract with a similarly situated entity may be considered a basis for debarment on the grounds, including but not limited to, that the parties have violated the terms of a Government contract or subcontract pursuant to FAR 9.406–2(b)(1)(i) (48 CFR 9.406–2(b)(1)(i)).

[81 FR 34262, May 31, 2016; 81 FR 67093, Sept. 30, 2016; 83 FR 12852, Mar. 26, 2018]

EDITORIAL NOTE: At 81 FR 48585, July 25, 2016, § 125.6 was amended; however, the amendment could not be incorporated due to inaccurate amendatory instruction.

§ 125.7 Acquisition-related dollar thresholds.

The Federal Acquisition Regulatory Council (FAR Council) has the responsibility of adjusting each acquisition-related dollar threshold on October 1, of each year that is evenly divisible by five. Acquisition-related dollar thresholds are defined as dollar thresholds that are specified in law as a factor in defining the scope of the applicability of a policy, procedure, requirement, or restriction provided in that law to the procurement of property or services by an executive agency as determined by the FAR Council. 41 U.S.C. 431a(c). Part 125, Government Contracting Programs, contains acquisition-related dollar thresholds subject to inflationary adjustments. The FAR Council shall publish a notice of the adjusted dollar thresholds in the FEDERAL REGISTER. The adjusted dollar thresholds shall take effect on the date of publication.

[74 FR 46887, Sept. 14, 2009]

§ 125.8 What requirements must a joint venture satisfy to submit an offer for a procurement or sale set aside or reserved for small business?

(a) *General*. A joint venture of two or more business concerns may submit an offer as a small business for a Federal procurement, subcontract or sale so long as each concern is small under the size standard corresponding to the NAICS code assigned to the contract, or qualify as small under one of the exceptions to affiliation set forth in § 121.103(h)(3) of this chapter.

(b) *Contents of joint venture agreement*. (1) A joint venture agreement between two or more entities that individually qualify as small need not be in any specific form or contain any specific conditions in order for the joint venture to qualify as a small business.

(2) Every joint venture agreement to perform a contract set aside or reserved for small business between a protégé small business and its SBA-approved mentor authorized by § 125.9 or § 124.520 of this chapter must contain a provision:

(i) Setting forth the purpose of the joint venture;

(ii) Designating a small business as the managing venturer of the joint venture, and an employee of the small business managing venturer as the project manager responsible for performance of the contract. The individual identified as the project manager of the joint venture need not be an employee of the small business at the time the joint venture submits an offer, but, if he or she is not, there must be a signed letter of intent that the individual commits to be employed by the small business if the joint venture is the successful offeror. The individual identified as the project manager cannot be employed by the mentor and become an employee of the small business for purposes of performance under the joint venture;

(iii) Stating that with respect to a separate legal entity joint venture, the small business must own at least 51% of the joint venture entity;

(iv) Stating that each participant must receive profits from the joint venture commensurate with the work performed by the concern;

(v) Providing for the establishment and administration of a special bank account in the name of the joint venture. This account must require the signature of all parties to the joint venture or designees for withdrawal purposes. All payments due the joint venture for performance on a contract set aside or reserved for small business will be deposited in the special account; all expenses incurred under the contract will be paid from the account as well;

(vi) Itemizing all major equipment, facilities, and other resources to be furnished by each party to the joint venture, with a detailed schedule of cost or value of each, where practical. If a contract is indefinite in nature, such as an indefinite quantity contract or a multiple award contract where the level of effort or scope of work is not known, the joint venture must provide a general description of the anticipated major equipment, facilities, and other resources to be furnished by each party to the joint venture, without a detailed schedule of cost or value of each, or in the alternative, specify how the parties to the joint venture will furnish such resources to the joint venture once a definite scope of work is made publicly available;

(vii) Specifying the responsibilities of the parties with regard to negotiation of the contract, source of labor, and contract performance, including ways that the parties to the joint venture will ensure that the joint venture and the small business partner(s) to the joint venture will meet the performance of work requirements set forth in paragraph (d) of this section, where practical. If a contract is indefinite in nature, such as an indefinite quantity contract or a multiple award contract where the level of effort or scope of work is not known, the joint venture must provide a general description of the anticipated responsibilities of the parties with regard to negotiation of the contract, source of labor, and contract performance, not including the ways that the parties to the joint venture will ensure that the joint venture and the small business partner(s) to the joint venture will meet the performance of work requirements set forth in paragraph (d) of this section, or in the alternative, specify how the parties to the joint venture will define such responsibilities once a definite scope of work is made publicly available;

(viii) Obligating all parties to the joint venture to ensure performance of a contract set aside or reserved for small business and to complete performance despite the withdrawal of any member;

(ix) Designating that accounting and other administrative records relating to the joint venture be kept in the office of the small business managing venturer, unless approval to keep them elsewhere is granted by the District Director or his/her designee upon written request;

(x) Requiring that the final original records be retained by the small business managing venturer upon completion of any contract set aside or reserved for small business that was performed by the joint venture;

(xi) Stating that quarterly financial statements showing cumulative contract receipts and expenditures (including salaries of the joint venture's principals) must be submitted to SBA not later than 45 days after each operating quarter of the joint venture; and

(xii) Stating that a project-end profit and loss statement, including a statement of final profit distribution, must be submitted to SBA no later than 90 days after completion of the contract.

(c) *Performance of work.* (1) For any contract set aside or reserved for small business that is to be performed by a joint venture between a small business protégé and its SBA-approved mentor authorized by § 125.9, the joint venture must perform the applicable percentage of work required by § 125.6, and the small business partner to the joint venture must perform at least 40% of the work performed by the joint venture.

(2) The work performed by the small business partner to a joint venture must be more than administrative or ministerial functions so that it gains substantive experience.

(3) The amount of work done by the partners will be aggregated and the work done by the small business protégé partner must be at least 40% of the total done by the partners. In determining the amount of work done by a mentor participating in a joint venture with a small business protégé, all work done by the mentor and any of its affiliates at any subcontracting tier will be counted.

(d) *Certification of compliance.* Prior to the performance of any contract set aside or reserved for small business by a joint venture between a protégé small business and a mentor authorized by § 125.9, the small business partner to the joint venture must submit a written certification to the contracting officer and SBA, signed by an authorized official of each partner to the joint venture, stating as follows:

(1) The parties have entered into a joint venture agreement that fully complies with paragraph (b) of this section;

(2) The parties will perform the contract in compliance with the joint venture agreement and with the performance of work requirements set forth in paragraph (c) of this section.

(e) *Past performance and experience.* When evaluating the past performance and experience of an entity submitting an offer for a contract set aside or reserved for small business as a joint venture established pursuant to this section, a procuring activity must consider work done individually by each partner to the joint venture as well as any work done by the joint venture itself previously.

(f) *Contract execution.* The procuring activity will execute a contract set aside or reserved for small business in the name of the joint venture entity or a small business partner to the joint venture, but in either case will identify the award as one to a small business joint venture or a small business mentor-protégé joint venture, as appropriate.

(g) *Inspection of records.* The joint venture partners must allow SBA's authorized representatives, including representatives authorized by the SBA Inspector General, during normal business hours, access to its files to inspect and copy all records and documents relating to the joint venture.

(h) *Performance of work reports.* In connection with any contract set aside or reserved for small business that is awarded to a joint venture between a protégé small business and a mentor authorized by § 125.9, the small business partner must describe how it is meeting or has met the applicable performance of work requirements for each contract set aside or reserved for small business that it performs as a joint venture.

(1) The small business partner to the joint venture must annually submit a report to the relevant contracting officer and to the SBA, signed by an authorized official of each partner to the joint venture, explaining how the performance of work requirements are being met for each contract set aside or reserved for small business that is performed during the year.

(2) At the completion of every contract set aside or reserved for small business that is awarded to a joint venture between a protégé small business and a mentor authorized by § 125.9, the small business partner to the joint venture must submit a report to the relevant contracting officer and to the SBA, signed by an authorized official of each partner to the joint venture, explaining how and certifying that the performance of work requirements were met for the contract, and further certifying that the contract was performed in accordance with the provisions of the joint venture agreement that are required under paragraph (b) of this section.

(i) *Basis for suspension or debarment.* For any joint venture between a protégé small business and a mentor authorized by § 125.9, the Government may consider the following as a ground for suspension or debarment as a willful violation of a regulatory provision or requirement applicable to a public agreement or transaction:

(1) Failure to enter a joint venture agreement that complies with paragraph (b) of this section;

(2) Failure to perform a contract in accordance with the joint venture agreement or performance of work requirements in paragraph (c) of this section; or

(3) Failure to submit the certification required by paragraph (d) of this section or comply with paragraph (g) of this section.

(j) *Compliance with performance of work requirements.* Any person with information concerning a joint venture's compliance with the performance of work requirements may report that information to SBA and/or the SBA Office of Inspector General.

[81 FR 48585, July 25, 2016, as amended at 81 FR 94941, Dec. 27, 2016]

§ 125.9 What are the rules governing SBA's small business mentor-protégé program?

(a) *General.* The small business mentor-protégé program is designed to enhance the capabilities of protégé firms by requiring approved mentors to provide business development assistance to protégé firms and to improve the protégé firms' ability to successfully compete for federal contracts. This assistance may include technical and/or management assistance; financial assistance in the form of equity investments and/or loans; subcontracts (either from the mentor to the protégé or from the protégé to the mentor); trade education; and/or assistance in performing prime contracts with the Government through joint venture arrangements. Mentors are encouraged to provide assistance relating to the performance of contracts set aside or reserved for small business so that protégé firms may more fully develop their capabilities.

(b) *Mentors.* Any concern that demonstrates a commitment and the ability to assist small business concerns may act as a mentor and receive benefits as set forth in this section. This includes other than small businesses.

(1) In order to qualify as a mentor, a concern must demonstrate that it:

(i) Is capable of carrying out its responsibilities to assist the protégé firm under the proposed mentor-protégé agreement;

(ii) Possesses good character;

(iii) Does not appear on the federal list of debarred or suspended contractors; and

(iv) Can impart value to a protégé firm due to lessons learned and practical experience gained or through its knowledge of general business operations and government contracting.

(2) In order to demonstrate that it is capable of carrying out its responsibilities to assist the protégé firm under the proposed mentor-protégé agreement, a firm seeking to be a mentor may submit to the SBA copies of the federal tax returns it submitted to the IRS, or audited financial statements, including any notes, or in the case of publicly traded concerns, the filings required by the Securities and Exchange Commission (SEC), for the past three years.

(3) Once approved, a mentor must annually certify that it continues to possess good character and a favorable financial position.

(4) Generally, a mentor will have no more than one protégé at a time. However, SBA may authorize a concern to mentor more than one protégé at a time where it can demonstrate that the additional mentor-protégé relationship will not adversely affect the development of either protégé firm (*e.g.*, the second firm may not be a competitor of the first firm). Under no circumstances will a mentor be permitted to have more than three protégés at one time in the aggregate under the mentor-protégé programs authorized by §§ 124.520 and 125.9 of this chapter.

(c) *Protégés.* (1) In order to initially qualify as a protégé firm, a concern must qualify as small for the size standard corresponding to its primary NAICS code or identify that it is seeking business development assistance with respect to a secondary NAICS code and qualify as small for the size standard corresponding to that NAICS code.

(i) A firm may self-certify that it qualifies as small for its primary or identified secondary NAICS code.

(ii) Where a firm is other than small for the size standard corresponding to its primary NAICS code and seeks to qualify as a small business protégé in a secondary NAICS code, the firm must demonstrate how the mentor-protégé relationship is a logical business progression for the firm and will further develop or expand current capabilities. SBA will not approve a mentor-protégé relationship in a secondary NAICS code in which the firm has no prior experience.

(2) A protégé firm may generally have only one mentor at a time. SBA may approve a second mentor for a particular protégé firm where the second relationship will not compete or otherwise conflict with the assistance set forth in the first mentor-protégé relationship and:

(i) The second relationship pertains to an unrelated NAICS code; or

(ii) The protégé firm is seeking to acquire a specific expertise that the first mentor does not possess.

(3) SBA may authorize a small business to be both a protégé and a mentor at the same time where the small business can demonstrate that the second relationship will not compete or otherwise conflict with the first mentor-protégé relationship.

(4) Where appropriate, SBA may examine the Service-Disabled Veteran-Owned Small Business status or Women-Owned Small Business status of a concern seeking to be a protégé that claims such status in any Federal procurement database.

(d) *Benefits.* (1) A protégé and mentor may joint venture as a small business for any government prime contract or subcontract, provided the protégé qualifies as small for the procurement. Such a joint venture may seek any type of small business contract (*i.e.*, small business set-aside, 8(a), HUBZone, SDVO, or WOSB) for which the protégé firm qualifies (*e.g.*, a protégé firm that qualifies as a WOSB could seek a WOSB set-aside as a joint venture with its SBA-approved mentor).

(i) SBA must approve the mentor-protégé agreement before the two firms may submit an offer as a joint venture on a particular government prime contract or subcontract in order for the joint venture to receive the exclusion from affiliation.

(ii) In order to receive the exclusion from affiliation, the joint venture must meet the requirements set forth in §125.8(b)(2), (c), and (d).

(iii) Once a protégé firm no longer qualifies as a small business for the size standard corresponding to its primary NAICS code, it will not be eligible for any further contracting benefits from its mentor-protégé relationship. However, a change in the protégé's size status does not generally affect contracts previously awarded to a joint venture between the protégé and its mentor.

(A) Except for contracts with durations of more than five years (including options), a contract awarded to a joint venture between a protégé and a mentor as a small business continues to qualify as an award to small business for the life of that contract and the joint venture remains obligated to continue performance on that contract.

(B) For contracts with durations of more than five years (including options), where size re-certification is required under §121.404(g)(3) of this chapter no more than 120 days prior to the end of the fifth year of the contract and no more than 120 days prior to exercising any option thereafter, once the protégé no longer qualifies as small for the size standard corresponding to its primary NAICS code, the joint venture must aggregate the receipts/employees of the partners to the joint venture in determining whether it continues to qualify as and can re-certify itself to be a small business under the size standard corresponding to the NAICS code assigned to that contract. The rules set forth in §121.404(g)(3) of this chapter apply in such circumstances.

(2) In order to raise capital, the protégé firm may agree to sell or otherwise convey to the mentor an equity interest of up to 40% in the protégé firm.

(3) Notwithstanding the mentor-protégé relationship, a protégé firm may qualify for other assistance as a small business, including SBA financial assistance.

(4) No determination of affiliation or control may be found between a protégé firm and its mentor based solely on the mentor-protégé agreement or any assistance provided pursuant to the agreement. However, affiliation may be found for other reasons set forth in §121.103 of this chapter.

(5) Where appropriate, procuring activities may provide incentives in the contract evaluation process to a firm that will provide significant subcontracting work to its SBA-approved protégé firm.

(e) *Written agreement.* (1) The mentor and protégé firms must enter a written agreement setting forth an assessment of the protégé's needs and providing a detailed description and timeline for the delivery of the assistance the mentor commits to provide to address those needs (*e.g.*, management and/or technical assistance, loans and/or equity investments, cooperation on joint venture projects, or subcontracts under prime contracts being performed by the mentor). The mentor-protégé agreement must:

(i) Address how the assistance to be provided through the agreement will help the protégé firm meet its goals as defined in its business plan;

(ii) Establish a single point of contact in the mentor concern who is responsible for managing and implementing the mentor-protégé agreement; and

(iii) Provide that the mentor will provide such assistance to the protégé firm for at least one year.

(2) A firm seeking SBA's approval to be a protégé must identify any other mentor-protégé relationship it has through another federal agency or SBA and provide a copy of each such mentor-protégé agreement to SBA.

(i) The small business mentor-protégé agreement must identify how the assistance to be provided by the proposed mentor is different from assistance provided to the protégé through another mentor-protégé relationship, either with the same or a different mentor.

(ii) A firm seeking SBA's approval to be a protégé may terminate a mentor-protégé relationship it has through another agency and use any not yet provided assistance identified in the other mentor-protégé agreement as part of the assistance that will be provided through the small business mentor-protégé relationship. Any assistance that has already been provided through another mentor-protégé relationship cannot be identified as assistance that will be provided through the small business mentor-protégé relationship.

(3) The written agreement must be approved by the Associate Administrator for Business Development (AA/BD) or his/her designee. The agreement will not be approved if SBA determines that the assistance to be provided is not sufficient to promote any real developmental gains to the protégé, or if SBA determines that the agreement is merely a vehicle to enable the mentor to receive small business contracts.

(4) The agreement must provide that either the protégé or the mentor may terminate the agreement with 30 days advance notice to the other party to the mentor-protégé relationship and to SBA.

(5) SBA will review the mentor-protégé relationship annually to determine whether to approve its continuation for another year. Unless rescinded in writing as a result of the review, the mentor-protégé relationship will automatically renew without additional written notice of continuation or extension to the protégé firm. The term of a mentor-protégé agreement may not exceed three years, but may be extended for a second three years. A protégé may have two three-year mentor-protégé agreements with different mentors, and each may be extended an additional three years provided the protégé has received the agreed-upon business development assistance and will continue to receive additional assistance through the extended mentor-protégé agreement.

(6) SBA must approve all changes to a mentor-protégé agreement in advance, and any changes made to the agreement must be provided in writing. If the parties to the mentor-protégé relationship change the mentor-protégé agreement without prior approval by SBA, SBA shall terminate the mentor-protégé relationship and may also propose suspension or debarment of one or both of the firms pursuant to paragraph (h) of this section where appropriate.

(7) If control of the mentor changes (through a stock sale or otherwise), the previously approved mentor-protégé relationship may continue provided that, after the change in control, the mentor expresses in writing to SBA that it acknowledges the mentor-protégéagreement and certifies that it will continue to abide by its terms.

(8) SBA may terminate the mentor-protégé agreement at any time if it determines that the protégé is not benefiting from the relationship or that the parties are not complying with any term or condition of the mentor protégé agreement. In the event SBA terminates the relationship, the mentor-protégé joint venture is obligated to complete any previously awarded contracts unless the procuring agency issues a stop work order.

(f) *Decision to decline mentor-protégé relationship.* (1) Where SBA declines to approve a specific mentor-protégé agreement, the protégé may request the AA/BD or designee to reconsider the Agency's initial decline decision by filing a request for reconsideration within 45 calendar days of receiving notice that its mentor-protégé agreement was declined. The protégé may revise the proposed mentor-protégé agreement and provide any additional information and documentation pertinent to overcoming the reason(s) for the initial decline.

(2) SBA will issue a written decision within 45 calendar days of receipt of the protégé's request. SBA may approve the mentor-protégé agreement, deny it on the same grounds as the original decision, or deny it on other grounds.

(3) If SBA declines the mentor-protégé agreement solely on issues not raised in the initial decline, the protégé can ask for reconsideration as if it were an initial decline.

(4) If SBA's final decision is to decline a specific mentor-protégé agreement, the small business concern seeking to be a protégé cannot attempt to enter into another mentor-protégé relationship with the same mentor for a period of 60 calendar days from the date of the final decision. The small business concern may, however, submit another proposed mentor-protégé agreement with a different proposed mentor at any time after the SBA's final decline decision.

(g) *Evaluating the mentor-protégé relationship.* (1) Within 30 days of the anniversary of SBA's approval of the mentor-protégé agreement, the protégé must report to SBA for the preceding year:

(i) All technical and/or management assistance provided by the mentor to the protégé;

(ii) All loans to and/or equity investments made by the mentor in the protégé;

(iii) All subcontracts awarded to the protégé by the mentor and all subcontracts awarded to the mentor by the protégé, and the value of each subcontract;

(iv) All federal contracts awarded to the mentor-protégé relationship as a joint venture (designating each as a small business set-aside, small business reserve, or unrestricted procurement), the value of each contract, and the percentage of the contract performed and the percentage of revenue accruing to each party to the joint venture; and

(v) A narrative describing the success such assistance has had in addressing the developmental needs of the protégé and addressing any problems encountered.

(2) The protégé must report the mentoring services it receives by category and hours.

(3) The protégé must annually certify to SBA whether there has been any change in the terms of the agreement.

(4) SBA will review the protégé's report on the mentor-protégé relationship, and may decide not to approve continuation of the agreement if it finds that the mentor has not provided the assistance set forth in the mentor-protégé agreement or that the assistance has not resulted in any material benefits or developmental gains to the protégé.

(h) *Consequences of not providing assistance set forth in the mentor-protégé agreement.* (1) Where SBA determines that a mentor has not provided to the protégé firm the business development assistance set forth in its mentor-protégé agreement, SBA will notify the mentor of such determination and afford the mentor an opportunity to respond. The mentor must respond within 30 days of the notification, explaining why it has not provided the agreed upon assistance and setting forth a definitive plan as to when it will provide such assistance. If the mentor fails to respond, does not supply adequate reasons for its failure to provide the agreed upon assistance, or does not set forth a definite plan to provide the assistance:

(i) SBA will terminate the mentor-protégé agreement;

(ii) The firm will be ineligible to again act as a mentor for a period of two years from the date SBA terminates the mentor-protégé agreement; and

(iii) SBA may recommend to the relevant procuring agency to issue a stop work order for each federal contract for which the mentor and protégé are performing as a small business joint venture in order to encourage the mentor to comply with its mentor-protégé agreement. Where a protégé firm is able to independently complete performance of any such contract, SBA may recommend to the procuring agency to authorize a substitution of the protégé firm for the joint venture.

(2) SBA may consider a mentor's failure to comply with the terms and conditions of an SBA-approved mentor-protégé agreement as a basis for debarment on the grounds, including but not limited to, that the mentor has not complied with the terms of a public agreement under 2 CFR 180.800(b).

(i) *Results of mentor-protégé relationship.* (1) In order to assess the results of a mentor-protégé relationship upon its completion, the protégé must report to SBA whether it believed the mentor-protégé relationship was beneficial and describe any lasting benefits to the protégé.

(2) Where a protégé does not report the results of a mentor-protégé relationship upon its completion, SBA will not approve a second mentor-protégé relationship either under this section or under § 124.520 of this chapter.

[81 FR 48585, July 25, 2016]

§ 125.10 Mentor-Protégé programs of other agencies.

(a) Except as provided in paragraph (c) of this section, a Federal department or agency may not carry out a mentor-protégé program for small business unless the head of the department or agency submits a plan to the SBA Administrator for the program and the SBA Administrator approves the plan. Before starting a new mentor protégé program, the head of a department or agency must submit a plan to the SBA Administrator. Within one year of the effective date of this section, the head of a department or agency must submit a plan to the SBA for any previously existing mentor-protégé program that the department or agency seeks to continue.

(b) The SBA Administrator will approve or disapprove a plan submitted under paragraph (a) of this section based on whether the proposed program:

(1) Will assist protégés to compete for Federal prime contracts and subcontracts; and

(2) Complies with the provisions set forth in §§ 125.9 and 124.520 of this chapter, as applicable.

(c) Paragraph (a) of this section does not apply to:

(1) Any mentor-protégé program of the Department of Defense;

(2) Any mentoring assistance provided under a Small Business Innovation Research Program or a Small Business Technology Transfer Program; and

(3) A mentor-protégé program operated by a Department or agency on January 2, 2013, for a period of one year after the effective date of this section.

(d) The head of each Federal department or agency carrying out an agency-specific mentor-protégé program must report annually to SBA:

(1) The participants (both protégé firms and their approved mentors) in its mentor-protégé program. This includes identifying the number of participants that are:

(i) Small business concerns;

(ii) Small business concerns owned and controlled by service-disabled veterans;

(iii) Small business concerns owned and controlled by socially and economically disadvantaged individuals;

(iv) Small business concerns owned and controlled by Indian tribes, Alaska Native Corporations, Native Hawaiian Organizations, and Community Development Corporations; and

(v) Small business concerns owned and controlled by women;

(2) The assistance provided to small businesses through the program; and

(3) The progress of protégé firms under the program to compete for Federal prime contracts and subcontracts.

[81 FR 48585, July 25, 2016]

Subpart A—Definitions for the Service-Disabled Veteran-Owned Small Business Concern Program

SOURCE: 69 FR 25267, May 5, 2004, unless otherwise noted.

§ 125.11 What definitions are important in the Service-Disabled Veteran-Owned (SDVO) Small Business Concern (SBC) Program?

Contracting officer has the meaning given such term in section 27(f)(5) of the Office of Federal Procurement Policy Act (41 U.S.C. 423(f)(5)).

Daily business operations include, but are not limited to, the marketing, production, sales, and administrative functions of the firm, as well as the supervision of the executive team, and the implementation of policies.

ESOP has the meaning given the term "employee stock ownership plan" in section 4975(e)(7) of the Internal Revenue Code of 1986 (26 U.S.C. 4975(e)(7)).

Extraordinary circumstances, for purposes of this part, are only the following:

(1) Adding a new equity stakeholder;

(2) Dissolution of the company;

(3) Sale of the company;

(4) The merger of the company; and

(5) Company declaring bankruptcy.

Negative control has the same meaning as that set forth in § 121.103(a)(3) of this chapter.

Participant means a veteran-owned small business concern that has verified status in the Vendor Information Pages database, available at *https://www.vip.vetbiz.gov/.*

Permanent caregiver, for purposes of this part, is the spouse, or an individual, 18 years of age or older, who is legally designated, in writing, to undertake responsibility for managing the well-being of the service-disabled veteran with a permanent and severe disability, as determined by Department of Veterans Affairs' Veterans Benefits Administration, to include housing, health and safety. A permanent caregiver may, but does not need to, reside in the same household as the service-disabled veteran with a permanent and severe disability. In the case of a service-disabled veteran with a permanent and severe disability lacking legal capacity, the permanent caregiver shall be a parent, guardian, or person having legal custody. There may be no more than one permanent caregiver per service-disabled veteran with a permanent and severe disability.

(1) A permanent caregiver may be appointed, in a number of ways, including:

(i) By a court of competent jurisdiction;

(ii) By the Department of Veterans Affairs, National Caregiver Support Program, as the Primary Family Caregiver of a Veteran participating in the Program of Comprehensive Assistance for Family Caregivers (this designation is subject to the Veteran and the caregiver meeting other specific criteria as established by law and the Secretary and may be revoked if the eligibility criteria do not continue to be met); or

(iii) By a legal designation.

(2) Any appointment of a permanent caregiver must in all cases be accompanied by a written determination from the Department of Veterans Affairs that the veteran has a permanent and total service-connected disability as set forth in 38 CFR 3.340 for purposes of receiving disability compensation or a disability pension. The appointment must also delineate why the permanent caregiver is given the appointment, must include the consent of the veteran to the appointment and how the appointment would contribute to managing the veteran's well-being.

Service-connected has the meaning given that term in 38 U.S.C. 101(16).

Service-disabled veteran is a veteran who possesses either a valid disability rating letter issued by the Department of Veterans Affairs, establishing a service-connected rating between 0 and 100 percent, or a valid disability determination from the Department of Defense or is registered in the Beneficiary Identification and Records Locator Subsystem maintained by Department of Veterans Affairs' Veterans Benefits Administration as a service-disabled veteran. Reservists or members of the National Guard disabled from a disease or injury incurred or aggravated in line of duty or while in training status also qualify.

Service-disabled veteran with a permanent and severe disability means a veteran with a service-connected disability that has been determined by the Department of Veterans Affairs, in writing, to have a permanent and total service-connected disability as set forth in 38 CFR 3.340 for purposes of receiving disability compensation or a disability pension.

Small business concern means a concern that, with its affiliates, meets the size standard corresponding to the NAICS code for its primary industry, pursuant to part 121 of this chapter.

Small business concern owned and controlled by service-disabled veterans (also known as a Service-Disabled Veteran-Owned SBC) means any of the following:

(1) A small business concern—

(i) Not less than 51 percent of which is owned by one or more service-disabled veterans or, in the case of any publicly owned business, not less than 51 percent of the stock (not including any stock owned by an ESOP) of which is owned by one or more service-disabled veterans; and

(ii) The management and daily business operations of which are controlled by one or more service-disabled veterans or, in the case of a veteran with permanent and severe disability, the spouse or permanent caregiver of such veteran;

(2) A small business concern—

(i) Not less than 51 percent of which is owned by one or more service-disabled veterans with a disability that is rated by the Secretary of Veterans Affairs as a permanent and total disability who are unable to manage the daily business operations of such concern; or

(ii) In the case of a publicly owned business, not less than 51 percent of the stock (not including any stock owned by an ESOP) of which is owned by one or more such veterans.

Surviving spouse has the meaning given the term in 38 U.S.C. 101(3).

Unconditional ownership means ownership that is not subject to conditions precedent, conditions subsequent, executory agreements, voting trusts, restrictions on or assignments of voting rights, or other arrangements causing or potentially causing ownership benefits to go to another (other than after death of incapacity). The pledge or encumbrance of stock or other ownership interest as collateral, including seller-financed transactions, does not affect the unconditional nature of ownership if the terms follow normal commercial practices and the owner retains control absent violations of the terms.

Veteran has the meaning given the term in 38 U.S.C. 101(2). A Reservist or member of the National Guard called to Federal active duty or disabled from a disease or injury incurred or aggravated in line of duty or while in training status also qualify as a veteran.

Veteran owned small business concern means a small business concern:

(1) Not less than 51 percent of which is owned by one or more veterans or, in the case of any publicly owned business, not less than 51 percent of the stock of which is owned by one or more veterans; and

(2) The management and daily business operations of which are controlled by one or more veterans. All of the provisions of subpart B of this part apply for purposes of determining ownership and control.

[83 FR 48912, Sept. 28, 2018]

Subpart B—Eligibility Requirements for the SDVO SBC Program

SOURCE: 69 FR 25267, May 5, 2004, unless otherwise noted.

§ 125.12 Who does SBA consider to own an SDVO SBC?

Generally, a concern must be at least 51% unconditionally and directly owned by one or more service-disabled veterans. More specifically:

(a) *Ownership must be direct.* Ownership by one or more service disabled veterans must be direct ownership. A concern owned principally by another business entity that is in turn owned and controlled by one or more service-disabled veterans does not meet this requirement. Ownership by a trust, such as a living trust, may be treated as the functional equivalent of ownership by service-disabled veterans where the trust is revocable, and service-disabled veterans are the grantors, trustees, and the current beneficiaries of the trust.

(b) *Ownership of a partnership.* In the case of a concern which is a partnership, at least 51% of aggregate voting interest must be unconditionally owned by one or more service-disabled veterans. The ownership must be reflected in the concern's partnership agreement.

(c) *Ownership of a limited liability company.* In the case of a concern which is a limited liability company, at least 51% of each class of member interest must be unconditionally owned by one or more service-disabled veterans.

(d) *Ownership of a corporation.* In the case of a concern which is a corporation, at least 51% of the aggregate of all stock outstanding and at least 51% of each class of voting stock outstanding must be unconditionally owned by one or more service-disabled veterans. In the case of a publicly owned business, not less than 51 percent of the stock (not including any stock owned by an ESOP) must be unconditionally owned by one or more veterans.

(e) *Stock options' effect on ownership.* In determining unconditional ownership, SBA will disregard any unexercised stock options or similar agreements held by service-disabled veterans. However, any unexercised stock options or similar agreements (including rights to convert non-voting stock or debentures into voting stock) held by non-service-disabled veterans sill be treated as exercised, except for any ownership interests which are held by investment companies licensed under the Small Business Investment Act of 1958.

(f) *Change of ownership.* A concern may change its ownership or business structure so long as one or more service-disabled veterans own and control it after the change.

(g) *Dividends and distributions.* One or more service-disabled veterans must be entitled to receive:

(1) At least 51 percent of the annual distribution of profits paid to the owners of a corporation, partnership, or limited liability company concern;

(2) 100 percent of the value of each share of stock owned by them in the event that the stock or member interest is sold; and

(3) At least 51 percent of the retained earnings of the concern and 100 percent of the unencumbered value of each share of stock or member interest owned in the event of dissolution of the corporation, partnership, or limited liability company.

(4) An eligible individual's ability to share in the profits of the concern must be commensurate with the extent of his/her ownership interest in that concern.

(h) *Community property.* Ownership will be determined without regard to community property laws.

(i) *Surviving spouse.* (1) A small business concern owned and controlled by one or more service-disabled veterans immediately prior to the death of a service-disabled veteran who was the owner of the concern, the death of whom causes the concern to be less than 51 percent owned by one or more service-disabled veterans, will continue to qualify as a small business concern owned and controlled by service-disabled veterans during the time period if:

(i) The surviving spouse of the deceased veteran acquires such veteran's ownership interest in such concern;

(ii) Such veteran had a service-connected disability (as defined in 38 U.S.C. 101(16)) rated as 100 percent disabling under the laws administered by the Secretary of Veterans Affairs or such veteran died as a result of a service-connected disability; and

(iii) For a participant, immediately prior to the death of such veteran, and during the period described in paragraph (i)(2) of this section, the small business concern is included in the database described in 38 U.S.C. 8127(f).

(2) The time period described in paragraph (i)(1)(iii) of this section is the time period beginning on the date of the veteran's death and ending on the earlier of—

(i) The date on which the surviving spouse remarries;

(ii) The date on which the surviving spouse relinquishes an ownership interest in the small business concern; or

(iii) The date that is 10 years after the date of the death of the veteran.

[69 FR 25267, May 5, 2004. Redesignated at 81 FR 48585, July 25, 2016. Amended at 83 FR 48913, Sept. 28, 2018]

§ 125.13 Who does SBA consider to control an SDVO SBC?

(a) *General.* To be an eligible SDVO SBC, the management and daily business operations of the concern must be controlled by one or more service-disabled veterans (or in the case of a veteran with permanent and severe disability, the spouse or permanent caregiver of such veteran). Control by one or more service-disabled veterans means that both the long-term decisions making and the day-to-day management and administration of the business operations must be conducted by one or more service-disabled veterans (or in the case of a veteran with permanent and severe disability, the spouse or permanent caregiver of such veteran).

(b) *Managerial position and experience.* A service-disabled veteran (or in the case of a service-disabled veteran with permanent and severe disability, the spouse or permanent caregiver of such veteran) must hold the highest officer position in the concern (usually President or Chief Executive Officer) and must have managerial experience of the extent and complexity needed to run the concern. The service-disabled veteran manager (or in the case of a veteran with permanent and severe disability, the spouse or permanent caregiver of such veteran) need not have the technical expertise or possess the required license to be found to control the concern if the service-disabled veteran can demonstrate that he or she has ultimate managerial and supervisory control over those who possess the required licenses or technical expertise.

(c) *Control over a partnership.* In the case of a partnership, one or more service-disabled veterans (or in the case of a veteran with permanent and severe disability, the spouse or permanent caregiver of such veteran) must serve as general partners, with control over all partnership decisions.

(d) *Control over a limited liability company.* In the case of a limited liability company, one or more service-disabled veterans (or in the case of a veteran with permanent or severe disability, the spouse or permanent caregiver of such veteran) must serve as managing members, with control over all decisions of the limited liability company.

(e) *Control over a corporation.* One or more service-disabled veterans (or in the case of a veteran with permanent and severe disability, the spouse or permanent caregiver of such veteran) must control the Board of Directors of the concern.

(1) SBA will deem service-disabled veteran individuals to control the Board of Directors where:

(i) A single service-disabled veteran individual owns 100% of all voting stock of an applicant or concern;

(ii) A single service-disabled veteran individual owns at least 51% of all voting stock of an applicant or concern, the individual is on the Board of Directors and no super majority voting requirements exist for shareholders to approve corporation actions. Where super majority voting requirements are provided for in the concern's articles of incorporation, its by-laws, or by state law, the service-disabled veteran individual must own at least the percent of the voting stock needed to overcome any such super majority voting requirements; or

(iii) More than one service-disabled veteran shareholder seeks to qualify the concern (*i.e.*, no one individual owns 51%), each such individual is on the Board of Directors, together they own at least 51% of all voting stock of the concern, no super majority voting requirements exist, and the service-disabled veteran shareholders can demonstrate that they have made enforceable arrangements to permit one of them to vote the stock of all as a block without a shareholder meeting. Where the concern has super majority voting requirements, the service-disabled veteran shareholders must own at least that percentage of voting stock needed to overcome any such super majority ownership requirements. In the case of super majority ownership requirements, the service-disabled veteran shareholders can demonstrate that they have made enforceable arrangements to permit one of them to vote the stock of all as a block without a shareholder meeting.

(2) Where an applicant or concern does not meet the requirements set forth in paragraph (e)(1) of this section,

the service-disabled veteran individual(s) upon whom eligibility is based must control the Board of Directors through actual numbers of voting directors or, where permitted by state law, through weighted voting (*e.g.*, in a concern having a two-person Board of Directors where one individual on the Board is service-disabled veteran and one is not, the service-disabled veteran vote must be weighted—worth more than one vote—in order for the concern to be eligible). Where a concern seeks to comply with this paragraph (e)(2):

(i) Provisions for the establishment of a quorum cannot permit non-service-disabled veteran Directors to control the Board of Directors, directly or indirectly; and

(ii) Any Executive Committee of Directors must be controlled by service-disabled veteran directors unless the Executive Committee can only make recommendations to and cannot independently exercise the authority of the Board of Directors.

(3) Non-voting, advisory, or honorary Directors may be appointed without affecting service-disabled veteran individuals' control of the Board of Directors.

(4) Arrangements regarding the structure and voting rights of the Board of Directors must comply with applicable state law.

(f) *Super majority requirements.* One or more service-disabled veterans must meet all super majority voting requirements. An applicant must inform the Department of Veterans Affairs, when applicable, of any super majority voting requirements provided for in its articles of incorporation, its by-laws, by state law, or otherwise. Similarly, after being verified, a participant must inform the Department of Veterans Affairs of changes regarding super majority voting requirements.

(g) *Licenses.* A firm must obtain and keep current any and all required permits, licenses, and charters, required to operate the business.

(h) *Unexercised rights.* A service-disabled veteran owner's unexercised right to cause a change in the control or management of the applicant concern does not in itself constitute control and management, regardless of how quickly or easily the right could be exercised.

(i) *Control by non-service-disabled veterans.* Non-service-disabled veteran individuals or entities may not control the firm. There is a rebuttable presumption that non-service-disabled veteran individuals or entities control or have the power to control a firm in any of the following circumstances, which are illustrative only and not inclusive:

(1) The non-service-disabled veteran individual or entity who is involved in the management or ownership of the firm is a current or former employer or a principal of a current or former employer of any service-disabled veteran individual upon whom the firm's eligibility is based. However, a firm may provide evidence to demonstrate that the relationship does not give the non-service-disabled veteran actual control over the concern and such relationship is in the best interests of the concern.

(2) One or more non-service-disabled veterans receive compensation from the firm in any form as directors, officers or employees, including dividends, that exceeds the compensation to be received by the highest-ranking officer (usually CEO or President). The highest ranking officer may elect to take a lower amount than the total compensation and distribution of profits that are received by a non-veteran only upon demonstrating that it helps the concern.

(3) In circumstances where the concern is co-located with another firm in the same or similar line of business, and that firm or an owner, director, officer, or manager, or a direct relative of an owner, director, officer, or manager of that firm owns an equity interest in the concern.

(4) In circumstances where the concern shares employees, resources, equipment, or any type of services, whether by oral or written agreement with another firm in the same or similar line of business, and that firm or an owner, director, officer, or manager, or a direct relative of an owner, director, officer, or manager of that firm owns an equity interest in the concern.

(5) A non-service-disabled veteran individual or entity, having an equity interest in the concern, provides critical financial or bonding support.

(6) In circumstances where a critical license is held by a non-service-disabled individual, or other entity, the non-service-disabled individual or entity may be found to control the firm. A critical license is considered any license that would normally be required of firms operating in the same field or industry, regardless of whether a specific license is required on a specific contract.

(7) Business relationships exist with non-service-disabled veteran individuals or entities which cause such dependence that the applicant or concern cannot exercise independent business judgment without great economic risk.

(j) *Critical financing.* A non-service-disabled veteran individual or entity may be found to control the concern through loan arrangements with the concern or the service-disabled veteran(s). Providing a loan or a loan guaranty on commercially reasonable terms does not, by itself, give a non-service-disabled veteran individual or entity the power to control a firm, but when taken into consideration with other factors may be used to find that a non-service-disabled firm or individual controls the concern.

(k) *Normal business hours.* There is a rebuttable presumption that a service-disabled veteran does not control the firm when the service-disabled veteran is not able to work for the firm during the normal working hours that businesses in that industry normally work. This may include, but is not limited to, other full-time or part-time employment, being a full-time or part-time student, or any other activity or obligation that prevents the service-disabled veteran from actively working for the firm during normal business operating hours.

(l) *Close proximity.* There is rebuttable presumption that a service-disabled veteran does not control the firm if that individual is not located within a reasonable commute to firm's headquarters and/or job-sites locations, regardless of the firm's industry. The service-disabled veteran's ability to answer emails, communicate by telephone, or to communicate at a distance by other technological means, while delegating the responsibility of managing the concern to others is not by itself a reasonable rebuttal.

(m) *Exception for "extraordinary circumstances."* SBA will not find that a lack of control exists where a service-disabled veteran does not have the unilateral power and authority to make decisions in "extraordinary circumstances." The only circumstances in which this exception applies are those articulated in the definition.

(n) *Exception for active duty.* Notwithstanding the provisions of this section requiring a service-disabled veteran to control the daily business operations and long-term strategic planning of a concern, where a service-disabled veteran individual upon whom eligibility is based is a reserve component member in the United States military who has been called to active duty, the concern may elect to designate in writing one or more individuals to control the concern on behalf of the service-disabled veteran during the period of active duty. The concern will not be considered ineligible based on the absence of the service-disabled veteran during the period of active duty. The concern must keep records evidencing the active duty and the written designation of control, and provide those documents to VA, and if requested to SBA.

[69 FR 25267, May 5, 2004. Redesignated at 81 FR 48585, July 25, 2016. Amended at 83 FR 48914, Sept. 28, 2018]

§ 125.14 What size standards apply to SDVO SBCs?

(a) At time of contract offer, an SDVO SBC must be small within the size standard corresponding to the NAICS code assigned to the contract.

(b) If the contracting officer is unable to verify that the SDVO SBC is small, the concern shall be referred to the responsible SBA Government Contracting Area Director for a formal size determination in accordance with part 121 of this chapter.

[69 FR 25267, May 5, 2004. Redesignated at 81 FR 48585, July 25, 2016]

§ 125.15 May an SDVO SBC have affiliates?

A concern may have affiliates provided that the aggregate size of the concern and all its affiliates is small as defined in part 121 of this chapter.

[69 FR 25267, May 5, 2004. Redesignated at 81 FR 48585, July 25, 2016]

§ 125.16 May 8(a) Program participants, HUBZone SBCs, Small and Disadvantaged Businesses, or Women-Owned Small Businesses qualify as SDVO SBCs?

Yes, 8(a) Program participants, HUBZone SBCs, Small and Disadvantaged Businesses, and Women-Owned SBCs, may also qualify as SDVO SBCs if they meet the requirements in this subject.

[70 FR 56814, Sept. 29, 2005. Redesignated at 81 FR 48585, July 25, 2016]

Subpart C—Contracting with SDVO SBCs

SOURCE: 69 FR 25268, May 5, 2004, unless otherwise noted.

§ 125.17 What are SDVO contracts?

SDVO contracts, including Multiple Award Contracts (*see* § 125.1), are those awarded to an SDVO SBC through any of the following procurement methods:

(a) Sole source awards to an SDVO SBC;

(b) Set-aside awards, including partial set-asides, based on competition restricted to SDVO SBCs;

(c) Awards based on a reserve for SDVO SBCs in a solicitation for a Multiple Award Contract (*see* § 125.1); or

(d) Orders set-aside for SDVO SBCs against a Multiple Award Contract, which had been awarded in full and open competition.

[78 FR 61143, Oct. 2, 2013. Redesignated at 81 FR 48585, July 25, 2016]

§ 125.18 What requirements must an SDVO SBC meet to submit an offer on a contract?

(a) *Representation of SDVO SBC status.* An SDVO SBC must submit the following representations with its initial offer (which includes price) on a specific contract:

(1) It is an SDVO SBC;

(2) It is small under the NAICS code assigned to the procurement;

(3) It will comply with the limitations on subcontracting requirements set forth in § 125.6;

(4) If applicable, it is an eligible joint venture; and

(5) If applicable, it is an eligible nonmanufacturer.

(b) *Joint ventures.* An SDVO SBC may enter into a joint venture agreement with one or more other SBCs or its SBA-approved mentor for the purpose of performing an SDVO contract.

(1) *Size of concerns to an SDVO SBC joint venture.* (i) A joint venture of at least one SDVO SBC and one or more other business concerns may submit an offer as a small business for a competitive SDVO SBC procurement or sale, or be awarded a sole source SDVO contract, so long as each concern is small under the size standard corresponding to the NAICS code assigned to the procurement or sale.

(ii) A joint venture between a protégé firm that qualifies as an SDVO SBC and its SBA-approved mentor (*see* §§ 125.9 and 124.520 of this chapter) will be deemed small provided the protégé qualifies as small for the size standard corresponding to the NAICS code assigned to the SDVO procurement or sale.

(2) *Contents of joint venture agreement.* Every joint venture agreement to perform an SDVO contract, including those between a protégé firm that qualifies as an SDVO SBC and its SBA-approved mentor authorized by § 124.520 or § 125.9 of this chapter, must contain a provision:

(i) Setting forth the purpose of the joint venture;

(ii) Designating an SDVO SBC as the managing venturer of the joint venture, and an employee of the SDVO SBC managing venturer as the project manager responsible for performance of the contract;

(iii) Stating that with respect to a separate legal entity joint venture, the SDVO SBC must own at least 51% of the joint venture entity;

(iv) Stating that the SDVO SBC(s) must receive profits from the joint venture commensurate with the work performed by the SDVO SBC;

(v) Providing for the establishment and administration of a special bank account in the name of the joint venture. This account must require the signature of all parties to the joint venture or designees for withdrawal purposes. All payments due the joint venture for performance on an SDVO contract will be deposited in the special account; all expenses incurred under the contract will be paid from the account as well;

(vi) Itemizing all major equipment, facilities, and other resources to be furnished by each party to the joint venture, with a detailed schedule of cost or value of each, where practical. If a contract is indefinite in nature, such as an indefinite quantity contract or a multiple award contract where the level of effort or scope of work is not known, the joint venture must provide a general description of the anticipated major equipment, facilities, and other resources to be furnished by each party to the joint venture, without a detailed schedule of cost or value of each, or in the alternative, specify how the parties to the joint venture will furnish such resources to the joint venture once a definite scope of work is made publicly available;

(vii) Specifying the responsibilities of the parties with regard to negotiation of the contract, source of labor, and contract performance, including ways that the parties to the joint venture will ensure that the joint venture and the SDVO small business partner(s) to the joint venture will meet the performance of work requirements set forth in paragraph (b)(3) of this section, where practical. If a contract is indefinite in nature, such as an indefinite quantity contract or a multiple award contract where the level of effort or scope of work is not known, the joint venture must provide a general description of the anticipated responsibilities of the parties with regard to negotiation of the contract, source of labor, and contract performance, not including the ways that the parties to the joint venture will ensure that the joint venture and the SDVO small business partner(s) to the joint venture will meet the performance of work requirements set forth in paragraph (d) of this section, or in the alternative, specify how the parties to the joint venture will define such responsibilities once a definite scope of work is made publicly available;

(viii) Obligating all parties to the joint venture to ensure performance of the SDVO contract and to complete performance despite the withdrawal of any member;

(ix) Designating that accounting and other administrative records relating to the joint venture be kept in the office of the SDVO SBC managing venturer, unless approval to keep them elsewhere is granted by the District Director or his/her designee upon written request;

(x) Requiring that the final original records be retained by the SDVO SBC managing venturer upon completion of the SDVO contract performed by the joint venture;

(xi) Stating that quarterly financial statements showing cumulative contract receipts and expenditures (including salaries of the joint venture's principals) must be submitted to SBA not later than 45 days after each operating quarter of the joint venture; and

(xii) Stating that a project-end profit and loss statement, including a statement of final profit distribution, must be submitted to SBA no later than 90 days after completion of the contract.

(3) *Performance of work.* (i) For any SDVO contract, including those between a protégé and a mentor authorized by § 125.9 or § 124.520 of this chapter, the joint venture must perform the applicable percentage of work required by § 125.6.

(ii) The SDVO SBC partner(s) to the joint venture must perform at least 40% of the work performed by the joint venture.

(A) The work performed by the SDVO SBC partner(s) to a joint venture must be more than administrative or ministerial functions so that they gain substantive experience.

(B) The amount of work done by the partners will be aggregated and the work done by the SDVO SBC partner(s) must be at least 40% of the total done by all partners. In determining the amount of work done by a non-SDVO SBC partner, all work done by the non-

SDVO SBC partner and any of its affiliates at any subcontracting tier will be counted.

(4) *Certification of Compliance.* Prior to the performance of any SDVO contract as a joint venture, the SDVO SBC partner to the joint venture must submit a written certification to the contracting officer and SBA, signed by an authorized official of each partner to the joint venture, stating as follows:

(i) The parties have entered into a joint venture agreement that fully complies with paragraph (b)(2) of this section;

(ii) The parties will perform the contract in compliance with the joint venture agreement and with the performance of work requirements set forth in paragraph (b)(3) of this section.

(5) *Past performance and experience.* When evaluating the past performance and experience of an entity submitting an offer for an SDVO contract as a joint venture established pursuant to this section, a procuring activity must consider work done individually by each partner to the joint venture as well as any work done by the joint venture itself previously.

(6) *Contract execution.* The procuring activity will execute an SDVO contract in the name of the joint venture entity or the SDVO SBC, but in either case will identify the award as one to an SDVO joint venture or an SDVO mentor-protégé joint venture, as appropriate.

(7) *Inspection of records.* The joint venture partners must allow SBA's authorized representatives, including representatives authorized by the SBA Inspector General, during normal business hours, access to its files to inspect and copy all records and documents relating to the joint venture.

(8) *Performance of work reports.* An SDVO SBC partner to a joint venture must describe how it is meeting or has met the applicable performance of work requirements for each SDVO contract it performs as a joint venture.

(i) The SDVO SBC partner to the joint venture must annually submit a report to the relevant contracting officer and to the SBA, signed by an authorized official of each partner to the joint venture, explaining how and certifying that the performance of work requirements are being met.

(ii) At the completion of every SDVO contract awarded to a joint venture, the SDVO SBC partner to the joint venture must submit a report to the relevant contracting officer and to the SBA, signed by an authorized official of each partner to the joint venture, explaining how and certifying that the performance of work requirements were met for the contract, and further certifying that the contract was performed in accordance with the provisions of the joint venture agreement that are required under paragraph (b)(2) of this section.

(9) *Basis for suspension or debarment.* The Government may consider the following as a ground for suspension or debarment as a willful violation of a regulatory provision or requirement applicable to a public agreement or transaction:

(i) Failure to enter a joint venture agreement that complies with paragraph (b)(2) of this section;

(ii) Failure to perform a contract in accordance with the joint venture agreement or performance of work requirements in paragraph (b)(3) of this section; or

(iii) Failure to submit the certification required by paragraph (b)(4) of this section or comply with paragraph (b)(7) of this section.

(10) Any person with information concerning a joint venture's compliance with the performance of work requirements may report that information to SBA and/or the SBA Office of Inspector General.

(c) *Non-manufacturers.* An SDVO SBC which is a non-manufacturer may submit an offer on an SDVO contract for supplies if it meets the requirements of the non-manufacturer rule set forth at §121.406(b)(1) of this chapter.

(d) *Multiple Award Contracts.* (1) *Total Set-Aside Contracts.* The SDVO SBC must comply with the applicable limitations on subcontracting provisions (*see* §125.6) and the nonmanufacturer rule (*see* §121.406(b)), if applicable, in the performance of a contract totally set-aside for SDVO SBCs. However, the contracting officer, in his or her discretion, may require the concern to perform the applicable amount of work or comply with the nonmanufacturer rule for each order awarded under the contract.

(2) *Partial Set-Aside Contracts.* For orders awarded under a partial set-aside contract, the SDVO SBC must comply with the applicable limitations on subcontracting provisions (*see* § 125.6) and the nonmanufacturer rule (*see* § 121.406(b)), if applicable, during each performance period of the contract—e.g., during the base term and then during each option period thereafter. For orders awarded under the non-set-aside portion, the SDVO SBC need not comply with any limitations on subcontracting or nonmanufacturer rule requirements. However, the contracting officer, in his or her discretion, may require the concern to perform the applicable amount of work or comply with the nonmanufacturer rule for each order awarded under the contract.

(3) *Orders.* The SDVO SBC must comply with the applicable limitations on subcontracting provisions (*see* § 125.6) and the nonmanufacturer rule (*see* § 121.406(b)), if applicable, in the performance of each individual order that has been set-aside for SDVO SBCs.

(4) *Reserves.* The SDVO SBC must comply with the applicable limitations on subcontracting provisions (*see* § 125.6) and the nonmanufacturer rule (*see* § 121.406(b)), if applicable, in the performance of an order that is set aside for SDVO SBCs. However, the SDVO SBC will not have to comply with the limitations on subcontracting provisions and the nonmanufacturer rule for any order issued against the Multiple Award Contract if the order is competed amongst SDVO SBCs and one or more other-than-small business concerns.

(e) *Recertification.* (1) A concern that represents itself and qualifies as an SDVO SBC at the time of initial offer (or other formal response to a solicitation), which includes price, including a Multiple Award Contract, is considered an SDVO SBC throughout the life of that contract. This means that if an SDVO SBC is qualified at the time of initial offer for a Multiple Award Contract, then it will be considered an SDVO SBC for each order issued against the contract, unless a contracting officer requests a new SDVO SBC certification in connection with a specific order. Where a concern later fails to qualify as an SDVO SBC, the procuring agency may exercise options and still count the award as an award to an SDVO SBC. However, the following exceptions apply to this paragraph (e)(1):

(i) Where an SDVO contract is novated to another business concern, the concern that will continue performance on the contract must certify its status as an SDVO SBC to the procuring agency, or inform the procuring agency that it does not qualify as an SDVO SBC, within 30 days of the novation approval. If the concern is not an SDVO SBC, the agency can no longer count the options or orders issued pursuant to the contract, from that point forward, towards its SDVO goals.

(ii) Where a concern that is performing an SDVO SBC contract acquires, is acquired by, or merges with another concern and contract novation is not required, the concern must, within 30 days of the transaction becoming final, recertify its SDVO SBC status to the procuring agency, or inform the procuring agency that it no longer qualifies as an SDVO SBC. If the contractor is not an SDVO SBC, the agency can no longer count the options or orders issued pursuant to the contract, from that point forward, towards its SDVO goals. The agency and the contractor must immediately revise all applicable Federal contract databases to reflect the new status.

(iii) Where there has been an SDVO SBC status protest on the solicitation or contract, *see* § 125.27(e) for the effect of the status determination on the contract award.

(2) For the purposes of contracts (including Multiple Award Contracts) with durations of more than five years (including options), a contracting officer must request that a business concern recertify its SDVO SBC status no more than 120 days prior to the end of the fifth year of the contract, and no more than 120 days prior to exercising any option.

(3) A business concern that did not certify itself as an SDVO SBC, either initially or prior to an option being exercised, may recertify itself as an

SDVO SBC for a subsequent option period if it meets the eligibility requirements at that time.

(4) Recertification does not change the terms and conditions of the contract. The limitations on subcontracting, nonmanufacturer and subcontracting plan requirements in effect at the time of contract award remain in effect throughout the life of the contract.

(5) Where the contracting officer explicitly requires concerns to recertify their status in response to a solicitation for an order, SBA will determine eligibility as of the date the concern submits its self-representation as part of its response to the solicitation for the order.

(6) A concern's status may be determined at the time of a response to a solicitation for an Agreement and each order issued pursuant to the Agreement.

[69 FR 25268, May 5, 2004, as amended at 70 FR 14527, Mar. 23, 2005; 78 FR 61143, Oct. 2, 2013; 81 FR 34264, May 31, 2016. Redesignated at 81 FR 48585, July 25, 2016, as amended at 81 FR 48590, July 25, 2016; 81 FR 94941, Dec. 27, 2016; 83 FR 12852, Mar. 26, 2018]

§ 125.19 Does SDVO SBC status guarantee receipt of a contract?

No, SDVO SBCs should market their capabilities to appropriate procuring agencies in order to increase their prospects of having a procurement set-aside for SDVO contract award.

[69 FR 25268, May 5, 2004. Redesignated at 81 FR 48585, July 25, 2016]

§ 125.20 Who decides if a contract opportunity for SDVO competition exists?

The contracting officer for the contracting activity decides if a contract opportunity for SDVO competition exists.

[69 FR 25268, May 5, 2004. Redesignated at 81 FR 48585, July 25, 2016]

§ 125.21 What requirements are not available for SDVO contracts?

A contracting activity may not make a requirement available for a SDVO contract if:

(a) The contracting activity otherwise would fulfill that requirement through award to Federal Prison Industries, Inc. under 18 U.S.C. 4124 or 4125, or to Javits-Wagner-O'Day Act participating non-profit agencies for the blind and severely disabled, under 41 U.S.C. 46 *et seq.*, as amended; or

(b) An 8(a) participant currently is performing that requirement or SBA has accepted that requirement for performance under the authority of the section 8(a) program, unless SBA has consented to release of the requirement from the section 8(a) program.

[69 FR 25268, May 5, 2004. Redesignated at 81 FR 48585, July 25, 2016]

§ 125.22 When may a contracting officer set-aside a procurement for SDVO SBCs?

(a) The contracting officer first must review a requirement to determine whether it is excluded from SDVO contracting pursuant to § 125.21.

(b) *Contracting Among Small Business Programs.* (1) *Acquisitions Valued At or Below the Simplified Acquisition Threshold.* The contracting officer shall set aside any acquisition with an anticipated dollar value exceeding the Micro-purchase Threshold but not exceeding the Simplified Acquisition Threshold (defined in the FAR at 48 CFR 2.101) for small business concerns, regardless of the place of performance, when there is a reasonable expectation that offers will be obtained from at least two small business concerns that are competitive in terms of quality and delivery and award will be made at fair market prices. This requirement does not preclude a contracting officer from making an award to a small business under the 8(a) BD, HUBZone, SDVO SBC or WOSB Programs.

(2) *Acquisitions Valued Above the Simplified Acquisition Threshold.* (i) The contracting officer shall set aside any acquisition with an anticipated dollar value exceeding the Simplified Acquisition Threshold (defined in the FAR at 48 CFR 2.101) for small business concerns, regardless of the place of performance, when there is a reasonable expectation that offers will be obtained from at least two small business concerns that are competitive in terms of quality and delivery and award will be made at fair market prices. However, after conducting market research, the contracting officer shall first consider

a set-aside or sole source award (if the sole source award is permitted by statute or regulation) under the 8(a) BD, HUBZone, SDVO SBC or WOSB programs before setting aside the requirement as a small business set-aside. There is no order of precedence among the 8(a) BD, HUBZone, SDVO SBC or WOSB programs. The contracting officer must document the contract file with the rationale used to support the specific set-aside, including the type and extent of market research conducted. In addition, the contracting officer must document the contract file showing that the apparent successful offeror's certifications in System for Award Management (SAM) (or any successor system) and associated representations were reviewed.

(ii) SBA believes that Progress in fulfilling the various small business goals, as well as other factors such as the results of market research, programmatic needs specific to the procuring agency, anticipated award price, and the acquisition history, will be considered in making a decision as to which program to use for the acquisition.

(c) If the CO decides to set-aside the requirement for competition restricted to SDVO SBCs, the CO must:

(1) Have a reasonable expectation that at least two responsible SDVO SBCs will submit offers; and

(2) Determine that award can be made at fair market price.

[69 FR 25268, May 5, 2004, as amended at 75 FR 62281, Oct. 7, 2010; 77 FR 1860, Jan. 12, 2012; 78 FR 61144, Oct. 2, 2013. Redesignated at 81 FR 48585, July 25, 2016, as amended at 81 FR 48591, July 25, 2016; 83 FR 12852, Mar. 26, 2018]

§ 125.23 When may a contracting officer award sole source contracts to SDVO SBCs?

A contracting officer may award a sole source contract to an SDVO SBC only when the contracting officer determines that:

(a) None of the provisions of §§ 125.21 or 125.22 apply;

(b) The anticipated award price of the contract, including options, will not exceed:

(1) $6,500,000 for a contract assigned a manufacturing NAICS code, or

(2) $4,000,000 for all other contracts;

(c) A SDVO SBC is a responsible contractor able to perform the contract; and

(d) Contract award can be made at a fair and reasonable price.

[69 FR 25268, May 5, 2004, as amended at 74 FR 46887, Sept. 14, 2009; 81 FR 34265, May 31, 2016. Redesignated at 81 FR 48585, July 25, 2016; 83 FR 12852, Mar. 26, 2018]

§ 125.24 Are there SDVO contracting opportunities at or below the simplified acquisition threshold?

Yes, if the requirement is at or below the simplified acquisition threshold, the contracting officer may set-aside the requirement for consideration among SDVO SBCs using simplified acquisition procedures or may award a sole source contact to an SDVO SBC.

[69 FR 25268, May 5, 2004. Redesignated at 81 FR 48585, July 25, 2016]

§ 125.25 May SBA appeal a contracting officer's decision not to make a procurement available for award as an SDVO contract?

The Administrator may appeal a contracting officer's decision not to make a particular requirement available for award as an SDVO sole source or a SDVO set-aside contact at or above the simplified acquisition threshold.

[69 FR 25268, May 5, 2004. Redesignated at 81 FR 48585, July 25, 2016]

§ 125.26 What is the process for such an appeal?

(a) *Notice of appeal.* When the contacting officer rejects a recommendation by SBA's Procurement Center Representative to make a requirement available for award as an SDVO contract, he or she must notify the Procurement Center Representative as soon as practicable. If the Administrator intends to appeal the decision, SBA must notify the contracting officer no later than five business days after receiving notice of the contracting officer's decision.

(b) *Suspension of action.* Upon receipt of notice of SBA's intent to appeal, the contracting officer must suspend further action regarding the procurement until the Secretary of the department or head of the agency issues a written decision on the appeal, unless the Secretary of the department or head of the agency makes a written determination that urgent and compelling circumstances which significantly affect the interests of the United States compel award of the contract.

(c) *Deadline for appeal.* Within 15 business days of SBA's notification to the CO, SBA must file its formal appeal with the Secretary of the department or head of the agency, or the appeal will be deemed withdrawn.

(d) *Decision.* The Secretary of the department or head of the agency must specify in writing the reasons for a denial of an appeal brought under this section.

[69 FR 25268, May 5, 2004. Redesignated at 81 FR 48585, July 25, 2016]

Subpart D—Protests Concerning SDVO SBCs

SOURCE: 69 FR 25269, May 5, 2004, unless otherwise noted.

§ 125.27 Who may protest the status of an SDVO SBC?

(a) *For Sole Source Procurements.* SBA or the contracting officer may protest the proposed awardee's service-disabled veteran status.

(b) For all other procurements, including Multiple Award Contracts (*see* § 125.1), any interested party may protest the apparent successful offeror's SDVO SBC status.

[69 FR 25269, May 5, 2004, as amended at 78 FR 61144, Oct. 2, 2013. Redesignated at 81 FR 48585, July 25, 2016]

§ 125.28 How does one file a service disabled veteran-owned status protest?

(a) *General.* The protest procedures described in this part are separate from those governing size protests and appeals. All protests relating to whether an eligible SDVO SBC is a "small" business for purposes of any Federal program are subject to part 121 of this chapter and must be filed in accordance with that part. If a protester protests both the size of the SDVO SBC and whether the concern meets the SDVO SBC requirements set forth in § 125.15(a), SBA will process each protest concurrently, under the procedures set forth in part 121 of this chapter and this part. SBA does not review issues concerning the administration of an SDVO contract.

(b) *Format.* Protests must be in writing and must specify all the grounds upon which the protest is based. A protest merely asserting that the protested concern is not an eligible SDVO SBC, without setting forth specific facts or allegations is insufficient. *Example:* A protester submits a protest stating that the awardee's owner is not a service-disabled veteran. The protest does not state any basis for this assertion. The protest allegation is insufficient.

(c) *Filing.* An interested party, other than the contracting officer or SBA, must deliver their protests in person, by facsimile, by express delivery service, or by U.S. mail (postmarked within the applicable time period) to the contracting officer. The contracting officer or SBA must submit their written protest directly to the Director, Office of Government Contracting.

(d) *Timeliness.* (1) For negotiated acquisitions, an interested party must submit its protest by close of business on the fifth business day after notification by the contracting officer of the apparent successful offeror.

(2) For sealed bid acquisitions, an interested party must submit its protest by close of business on the fifth business day after bid opening.

(3) Any protest submitted after the time limits is untimely, unless it is from SBA or the CO.

(4) Any protest received prior to bid opening or notification of intended awardee, whichever applies, is premature.

(e) *Referral to SBA.* The contracting officer must forward to SBA any non-premature protest received, notwithstanding whether he or she believes it is sufficiently specific or timely. The contracting officer must send all protests, along with a referral letter, directly to the Director, Office of Government Contracting, U.S. Small Business Administration, 409 Third Street, SW., Washington, DC 20416 or by fax to (202) 205–6390, marked Attn: Service-Disabled Veteran Status Protest. The CO's referral letter must include information pertaining to the solicitation that may be necessary for SBA to determine timeliness and standing, including: the solicitation number; the name, address, telephone number and facsimile number of the CO; whether the contract was sole source or set-aside; whether the protester submitted an offer; whether the protested concern was the apparent successful offeror; when the protested concern submitted its offer (*i.e.*, made the self-representation that it was a SDVO SBC); whether the procurement was conducted using sealed bid or negotiated procedures; the bid opening date, if applicable; when the protest was submitted to the CO; when the protester received notification about the apparent successful offeror, if applicable; and whether a contract has been awarded.

[69 FR 25269, May 5, 2004, as amended at 70 FR 14527, Mar. 23, 2005; 72 FR 50041, Aug. 30, 2007. Redesignated at 81 FR 48585, July 25, 2016]

§ 125.29 What are the grounds for filing an SDVO SBC protest?

(a) *Status.* In cases where the protest is based on service-connected disability, permanent and severe disability, or veteran status, the Director, Office of Government Contracting will only consider a protest that presents specific allegations supporting the contention that the owner(s) cannot provide documentation from the VA, DoD, or the U.S. National Archives and Records Administration to show that they meet the definition of service-disabled veteran or service disabled veteran with a permanent and severe disability as set forth in § 125.8.

(b) *Ownership and control.* In cases where the protest is based on ownership and control, the Director, Office of Government Contracting will consider a protest only if the protester presents credible evidence that the concern is not 51% owned and controlled by one or more service-disabled veterans. In the case of a veteran with a permanent and severe disability, the protester must present credible evidence that the concern is not controlled by the veteran, spouse or permanent caregiver of such veteran.

[70 FR 14527, Mar. 23, 2005, as amended at 72 FR 50041, Aug. 30, 2007; 81 FR 34265, May 31, 2016. Redesignated at 81 FR 48585, July 25, 2016]

§ 125.30 How will SBA process an SDVO protest?

(a) *Notice of receipt of protest.* Upon receipt of the protest, SBA will notify the contracting officer and the protester of the date SBA received the protest and whether SBA will process the protest or dismiss it under paragraph (b) of this section.

(b) *Dismissal of protest.* If SBA determines that the protest is premature, untimely, nonspecific, or is based on non-protestable allegations, SBA will dismiss the protest and will send the contracting officer and the protester a notice of dismissal, citing the reason(s) for the dismissal. The dismissal notice must also advise the protester of his/her right to appeal the dismissal to SBA's Office of Hearings and Appeals (OHA) in accordance with part 134 of this chapter.

(c) *Notice to protested concern.* If SBA determines that the protest is timely, sufficiently specific and is based upon protestable allegations, SBA will:

(1) Notify the protested concern of the protest and of its right to submit information responding to the protest within ten business days from the date of the notice; and

(2) Forward a copy of the protest to the protested concern, with a copy to the contracting officer if one has not already been made available.

(d) *Time period for determination.* SBA will determine the SDVO SBC status of the protested concern within 15 business days after receipt of the protest, or within any extension of that time which the contracting officer may grant SBA. If SBA does not issue its determination within the 15-day period, the contracting officer may award the contract, unless the contracting officer has granted SBA an extension.

(e) *Award of contract.* (1) The contracting officer may award a contract after receipt of a protest if the contracting officer determines in writing that an award must be made to protect the public interest. Notwithstanding such a determination, the provisions of paragraph (g) of this section apply to the procurement in question.

(2) If SBA does not issue its determination within 15 business days (or request an extension that is granted), the contracting officer may award the contract if he or she determines in writing that there is an immediate need to award the contract and that waiting until SBA makes its determination will be disadvantageous to the Government. Notwithstanding such a determination, the provisions of paragraph (g) of this section apply to the procurement in question.

(f) *Notification of determination.* SBA will notify the contracting officer, the protester, and the protested concern in writing of its determination.

(g) *Effect of determination.* (1) A contracting officer may award a contract to a protested concern after the Director, Office of Government Contracting (D/GC) has determined either that the protested concern is an eligible SDVO or has dismissed all protests against it. If OHA subsequently overturns the D/GC's determination or dismissal, the contracting officer may apply the OHA decision to the procurement in question.

(2) A contracting officer shall not award a contract to a protested concern that the D/GC has determined is not an eligible SDVO for the procurement in question.

(i) If a contracting officer receives such a determination after contract award, and no OHA appeal has been filed, the contracting officer shall terminate the award.

(ii) If a timely OHA appeal is filed after award, the contracting officer must consider whether performance can be suspended until an appellate decision is rendered.

(iii) If OHA affirms the D/GC's determination finding the protested concern ineligible, the contracting officer shall either terminate the contract or not exercise the next option.

(3) The contracting officer must update the Federal Procurement Data System and other procurement reporting databases to reflect the final agency decision (the D/GC's decision if no appeal is filed or OHA's decision).

(4) A concern found to be ineligible may not submit an offer as an SDVO SBC on a future procurement unless it demonstrates to SBA's satisfaction that it has overcome the reasons for the protest (*e.g.*, it changes its ownership to satisfy the definition of an SDVO SBC set forth in § 125.8) and SBA issues a decision to this effect.

[70 FR 14528, Mar. 23, 2005, as amended at 76 FR 5684, Feb. 2, 2011. Redesignated at 81 FR 48585, July 25, 2016]

§ 125.31 What are the procedures for appealing an SDVO status protest?

The protested concern, the protester, or the contracting officer may file an appeal of an SDVO status protest determination with OHA in accordance with part 134 of this chapter.

[76 FR 5685, Feb. 2, 2011. Redesignated at 81 FR 48585, July 25, 2016]

Subpart E—Penalties and Retention of Records

SOURCE: 69 FR 25270, May 5, 2004, unless otherwise noted.

§ 125.32 What are the requirements for representing SDVO SBC status, and what are the penalties for misrepresentation?

(a) *Presumption of Loss Based on the Total Amount Expended.* In every contract, subcontract, cooperative agreement, cooperative research and development agreement, or grant which is set aside, reserved, or otherwise classified as intended for award to SDVO SBCs, there shall be a presumption of loss to the United States based on the total amount expended on the contract, subcontract, cooperative agreement, cooperative research and development agreement, or grant whenever it is established that a business concern other than a SDVO SBC willfully sought and received the award by misrepresentation.

(b) *Deemed Certifications.* The following actions shall be deemed affirmative, willful and intentional certifications of SDVO SBC status:

(1) Submission of a bid, proposal, application or offer for a Federal grant, contract, subcontract, cooperative agreement, or cooperative research and

development agreement reserved, set aside, or otherwise classified as intended for award to SDVO SBCs.

(2) Submission of a bid, proposal, application or offer for a Federal grant, contract, subcontract, cooperative agreement or cooperative research and development agreement which in any way encourages a Federal agency to classify the bid or proposal, if awarded, as an award to a SDVO SBC.

(3) Registration on any Federal electronic database for the purpose of being considered for award of a Federal grant, contract, subcontract, cooperative agreement, or cooperative research and development agreement, as a SDVO SBC.

(c) *Signature Requirement.* Each offer, proposal, bid, or application for a Federal contract, subcontract, or grant shall contain a certification concerning the SDVO SBC status of a business concern seeking the Federal contract, subcontract or grant. An authorized official must sign the certification on the same page containing the SDVO SBC status claimed by the concern.

(d) *Limitation of Liability.* Paragraphs (a) through (c) of this section may be determined not to apply in the case of unintentional errors, technical malfunctions, and other similar situations that demonstrate that a misrepresentation of SDVO SBC status was not affirmative, intentional, willful or actionable under the False Claims Act, 31 U.S.C. §§3729, et seq. A prime contractor acting in good faith should not be held liable for misrepresentations made by its subcontractors regarding the subcontractors' SDVO SBC status. Relevant factors to consider in making this determination may include the firm's internal management procedures governing SDVO SBC status representations or certifications, the clarity or ambiguity of the representation or certification requirement, and the efforts made to correct an incorrect or invalid representation or certification in a timely manner. An individual or firm may not be held liable where government personnel have erroneously identified a concern as a SDVO SBC without any representation or certification having been made by the concern and where such identification is made without the knowledge of the individual or firm.

(e) *Penalties for Misrepresentation.* (1) *Suspension or debarment.* The SBA suspension and debarment official or the agency suspension and debarment official may suspend or debar a person or concern for misrepresenting a firm's status as a SDVO SBC pursuant to the procedures set forth in 48 CFR subpart 9.4.

(2) *Civil Penalties.* Persons or concerns are subject to severe penalties under the False Claims Act, 31 U.S.C. 3729–3733, the Program Fraud Civil Remedies Act, 31 U.S.C. 3801–3812, and any other applicable laws or regulations, including 13 CFR part 142.

(3) *Criminal Penalties.* Persons or concerns are subject to severe criminal penalties for knowingly misrepresenting the SDVO SBC status of a concern in connection with procurement programs pursuant to section 16(d) of the Small Business Act, 15 U.S.C. 645(d), as amended, 18 U.S.C. 1001, 18 U.S.C. 287, and any other applicable laws. Persons or concerns are subject to criminal penalties for knowingly making false statements or misrepresentations to SBA for the purpose of influencing any actions of SBA pursuant to section 16(a) of the Small Business Act, 15 U.S.C. 645(a), as amended, including failure to correct "continuing representations" that are no longer true.

[78 FR 38819, June 28, 2013, as amended at 81 FR 31492, May 19, 2016. Redesignated at 81 FR 48585, July 25, 2016]

§ 125.33 What must a concern do in order to be identified as a SDVO SBC in any Federal procurement databases?

(a) In order to be identified as a SDVO SBC in the System for Award Management (SAM) database (or any successor thereto), a concern must certify its SDVO SBC status in connection with specific eligibility requirements at least annually.

(b) If a firm identified as a SDVO SBC in SAM fails to certify its status within one year of a status certification, the firm will not be listed as a SDVO SBC in SAM, unless and until the firm recertifies its SDVO SBC status.

[78 FR 38820, June 28, 2013. Redesignated at 81 FR 48585, July 25, 2016]

PART 126—HUBZONE PROGRAM

Subpart A—Provisions of General Applicability

Subpart B—Requirements to be a Qualified HUBZone SBC

Subpart C—Certification

Subpart D—Program Examinations

Subpart E—Maintaining HUBZone Status

Subpart F—Contractual Assistance

Subpart G—Contract Performance Requirements

Subpart H—Protests

Subpart I—Penalties

AUTHORITY: 15 U.S.C. 632(a), 632(j), 632(p), 644 and 657a.

SOURCE: 63 FR 31908, June 11, 1998, unless otherwise noted.

EDITORIAL NOTE: Nomenclature changes to part 126 appear at 72 FR 50041, Aug. 30, 2007.

Subpart A—Provisions of General Applicability

§ 126.100 What is the purpose of the HUBZone program?

The purpose of the HUBZone program is to provide federal contracting assistance for qualified SBCs located in historically underutilized business zones in an effort to increase employment opportunities, investment, and economic development in such areas.

§ 126.101 Which government departments or agencies are affected directly by the HUBZone program?

(a) The HUBZone Program applies to all federal departments or agencies that employ one or more contracting officers.

(b) The HUBZone program does not apply to contracts awarded by state and local governments. However, state and local governments may use the List of qualified HUBZone SBCs to identify qualified HUBZone SBCs for similar programs authorized under state or local law.

[63 FR 31908, June 11, 1998, as amended at 66 FR 4645, Jan. 18, 2001; 69 FR 29420, May 24, 2004]

§ 126.102 What is the effect of the HUBZone program on the section 8(d) subcontracting program?

The HUBZone Act of 1997 amended the section 8(d) subcontracting program to include qualified HUBZone SBCs in the formal subcontracting plans described in § 125.3 of this title.

§ 126.103 What definitions are important in the HUBZone program?

Administrator means the Administrator of the United States Small Business Administration (SBA).

AA/BD means SBA's Associate Administrator for Business Development.

AA/GC&BD means Associate Administrator, Office of Government Contracting & Business Development.

Agricultural commodity has the same meaning as in section 102 of the Agricultural Trade Act of 1978 (7 U.S.C. 5602).

Alaska Native Corporation (ANC) has the same meaning as the term "Native Corporation" in section 3 of the ANCSA, 43 U.S.C. 1602.

Alaska Native Village has the same meaning as the term "Native village" in section 3 of the ANCSA, 43 U.S.C. 1602.

ANCSA means the Alaska Native Claims Settlement Act, as amended.

Attempt to maintain means making substantive and documented efforts such as written offers of employment, published advertisements seeking employees, and attendance at job fairs.

Base closure area means:

(1) Lands within the external boundaries of a military installation that were closed through a privatization process under the authority of:

(i) The Defense Base Closure and Realignment Act of 1990 (part A of title XXIX of division B of Pub. L. 101–510; 10 U.S.C. 2687 note);

(ii) Title II of the Defense Authorization Amendments and Base Closure and Realignment Act (Pub. L. 100–526; 10 U.S.C. 2687 note);

(iii) 10 U.S.C. 2687; or

(iv) Any other provision of law authorizing or directing the Secretary of Defense or the Secretary of a military department to dispose of real property at the military installation for purposes relating to base closures of redevelopment, while retaining the authority to enter into a leaseback of all or a portion of the property for military use;

(2) The census tract or nonmetropolitan county (excluding any qualified census tract and any qualified nonmetropolitan county) in which the lands described in paragraph (1) of this definition are wholly contained;

(3) A census tract or nonmetropolitan county (excluding any qualified census tract and any qualified non-metropolitan county) the boundaries of which intersect the area described in paragraph (1) of this definition; and

(4) A census tract or nonmetropolitan county (excluding any qualified census tract and any qualified non-metropolitan county) the boundaries of which are contiguous to the area described in paragraph (2) or paragraph (3) of this definition.

Certify means the process by which SBA determines that a HUBZone SBC is qualified for the HUBZone program and entitled to be included in SBA's "List of Qualified HUBZone SBCs."

Citizen means a person born or naturalized in the United States. SBA does not consider holders of permanent visas and resident aliens to be citizens.

Community Development Corporation (CDC) means a corporation that has received financial assistance under Part 1 of Subchapter A of the Community Economic Development Act of 1981, 42 U.S.C. 9805–9808.

Concern means a firm which satisfies the requirements in §§ 121.105(a) and (b) of this title.

Contract opportunity means a situation in which a requirement for a procurement exists, none of the exclusions from § 126.605 applies, and any applicable conditions in § 126.607 are met.

Contracting Officer (CO) has the meaning given that term in 41 U.S.C. 423(f)(5), which defines a CO as a person who, by appointment in accordance with applicable regulations, has the authority to enter into a Federal agency procurement contract on behalf of the Government and to make determinations and findings with respect to such a contract.

County means the political subdivisions recognized as a county by a state or commonwealth or which is an equivalent political subdivision such as a parish, borough, independent city, or *municipio*, where such subdivisions are not subdivisions within counties.

County unemployment rate is the rate of unemployment for a county based on the most recent data available from the United States Department of Labor, Bureau of Labor Statistics. The appropriate data may be found in the DOL/BLS publication titled "Supplement 2, Unemployment in States and Local Areas." This publication is available for public inspection at the Department of Labor, Bureau of Labor Statistics, Division of Local Area Unemployment Statistics located at 2 Massachusetts Ave., NE, Room 4675, Washington DC 20212. A copy is also available at SBA, Office of D/HUB, 409 3rd Street, SW., Washington DC 20416.

DAA/GC&BD means SBA's Deputy Associate Administrator for Government Contracting and Business Development.

D/HUB means SBA's Director Office of HUBZone;

De-certify means the process by which SBA determines that a concern is no longer a qualified HUBZone SBC and removes that concern from its List.

Employee means all individuals employed on a full-time, part-time, or other basis, so long as that individual works a minimum of 40 hours per month. This includes employees obtained from a temporary employee agency, leasing concern, or through a union agreement or co-employed pursuant to a professional employer organization agreement. SBA will consider the totality of the circumstances, including criteria used by the IRS for Federal income tax purposes and those set forth in SBA's Size Policy Statement No. 1, in determining whether individuals are employees of a concern. Volunteers (*i.e.*, individuals who receive deferred compensation or no compensation, including no in-kind compensation, for work performed) are not considered employees. However, if an individual has an ownership interest in and works for the HUBZone SBC a minimum of 40 hours per month, that owner is considered an employee regardless of whether or not the individual receives compensation.

HUBZone means a historically underutilized business zone, which is an area located within one or more:

(1) Qualified census tracts;

(2) Qualified non-metropolitan counties;

(3) Lands within the external boundaries of an Indian reservation;

(4) Qualified base closure areas;

(5) Redesignated areas; or

(6) Qualified disaster areas.

HUBZone small business concern (HUBZone SBC) means an SBC that is:

(1) At least 51% owned and controlled by 1 or more persons, each of whom is a United States citizen;

(2) An ANC owned and controlled by Natives (as determined pursuant to section 29(e)(1) of the ANCSA, 43 U.S.C. 1626(e)(1));

(3) A direct or indirect subsidiary corporation, joint venture, or partnership of an ANC qualifying pursuant to section 29(e)(1) of the ANCSA, 43 U.S.C. 1626(e)(1)), if that subsidiary, joint venture, or partnership is owned and controlled by Natives (as determined pursuant to section 29(e)(2) of the ANCSA, 43 U.S.C. 1626(e)(2));

(4) Wholly owned by one or more Indian Tribal Governments, or by a corporation that is wholly owned by one or more Indian Tribal Governments;

(5) An SBC that is owned in part by one or more Indian Tribal Governments or in part by a corporation that is wholly owned by one or more Indian Tribal Governments, if all other owners are either United States citizens or SBCs;

(6) An SBC that is wholly owned by a CDC or owned in part by one or more CDCs, if all other owners are either United States citizens or SBCs;

(7) An SBC that is a small agricultural cooperative organized or incorporated in the United States, wholly owned by one or more small agricultural cooperatives organized or incorporated in the United States or owned in part by one or more small agricultural cooperatives organized or incorporated in the United States, provided that all other owners are small business concerns or United States citizens;

(8) Wholly owned by one or more Native Hawaiian Organizations, or by a corporation that is wholly owned by one or more Native Hawaiian Organizations; or

(9) Owned in part by one or more Native Hawaiian Organizations or by a corporation that is wholly owned by one or more Native Hawaiian Organizations, if all other owners are either United States citizens or small business concerns.

Indian reservation (1) Has the same meaning as the term "Indian country" in 18 U.S.C. 1151, except that such term does not include:

(i) Any lands that are located within a State in which a tribe did not exercise governmental jurisdiction as of December 21, 2000, unless that tribe is recognized after that date by either an Act of Congress or pursuant to regulations of the Secretary of the Interior for the administrative recognition that an Indian group exists as an Indian tribe (25 CFR part 83); and

(ii) Lands taken into trust or acquired by an Indian tribe after December 21, 2000 if such lands are not located within the external boundaries of an Indian reservation or former reservation or are not contiguous to the lands held in trust or restricted status as of December 21, 2000; and

(2) In the State of Oklahoma, means lands that:

(i) Are within the jurisdictional areas of an Oklahoma Indian tribe (as determined by the Secretary of the Interior); and

(ii) Are recognized by the Secretary of the Interior as of December 21, 2000, as eligible for trust land status under 25 CFR part 151.

Indian Tribal Government means the governing body of any Indian tribe, band, nation, pueblo, or other organized group or community which is recognized as eligible for the special programs and services provided by the United States to Indians because of their status as Indians.

Interested party means any concern that submits an offer for a specific HUBZone sole source or set-aside contract (including Multiple Award Contracts) or order, any concern that submitted an offer in full and open competition and its opportunity for award will be affected by a price evaluation preference given a qualified HUBZone SBC, any concern that submitted an offer in a full and open competition and its opportunity for award will be affected by a reserve of an award given to a qualified HUBZone SBC, the contracting activity's contracting officer, or SBA.

Lands within the external boundaries of an Indian reservation include all lands within the perimeter of an Indian reservation, whether tribally owned and governed or not. For example, land that is individually owned and located within the perimeter of an Indian reservation is "lands within the external boundaries of an Indian reservation." By contrast, an Indian-owned parcel of land that is located outside the perimeter of an Indian reservation is not "lands within the external boundaries of an Indian reservation."

List refers to the database of qualified HUBZone SBCs that SBA has certified.

Median household income has the meaning used by the Bureau of the Census, United States Department of Commerce, in its publication titled, "1990 Census of Population, Social and Economic Characteristics," Report Number CP–2, pages B–14 and B–17. This publication is available for inspection at any local Federal Depository Library. For the location of a Federal Depository library, call toll-free (888) 293–6498 or contact the Bureau of the Census, Income Statistics Branch, Housing and Economic Statistics Division, Washington D.C. 20233–8500.

Metropolitan statistical area means an area as defined in section 143(k)(2)(B) of the Internal Revenue Code of 1986, (Title 26 of the United States Code).

Native Hawaiian Organization (NHO) means any community service organization serving Native Hawaiians in the State of Hawaii which is a not-for-profit organziation chartered by the State of Hawaii, is controlled by Native Hawaiians, and whose business activities will principally benefit such Native Hawaiians.

Non-metropolitan has the meaning used by the Bureau of the Census, United States Department of Commerce, in its publication titled, "1990 Census of Population, Social and Economic Characteristics," Report Number CP–2, page A–9. This publication is available for inspection at any local Federal Depository Library. For the location of a Federal Depository Library, call toll-free (888) 293–6498 or contact the Bureau of the Census, Population Distribution Branch, Population Division, Washington D.C. 20233–8800.

Person means a natural person.

Principal office means the location where the greatest number of the concern's employees at any one location perform their work. However, for those concerns whose "primary industry" (see 13 CFR 121.107) is service or construction (see 13 CFR 121.201), the determination of principal office excludes the concern's employees who perform the majority of their work at job-site locations to fulfill specific contract obligations.

Qualified base closure area means:

(1) A base closure area that is treated as a HUBZone for a period of not less than 8 years, beginning on the date the military installation undergoes final closure and ending on the latter of the following:

(i) The date the Administrator makes a final determination as to whether or not to implement the applicable designations in accordance with the results of the decennial census conducted after the area was initially designated as a base closure area; or

(ii) The date 8 years after the base closure area was initially designated as a HUBZone.

(2) However, if a base closure area was treated as a HUBZone at any time after 2010, it shall be treated as a HUBZone until such time as the Administrator makes a final determination as to whether or not to implement the applicable designations in accordance with the results of the 2020 decennial census.

Qualified census tract has the meaning given that term in section 42(d)(5)(B)(ii) of the Internal Revenue Code of 1986. However, for any metropolitan statistical area in the Commonwealth of Puerto Rico, the term "qualified census tract" has the meaning given that term in section 42(d)(5)(B)(ii) of the Internal Revenue Code of 1986 as applied without regard to subclause (II) of such section, except that this clause shall apply only until December 22, 2027, or the date on which the Financial Oversight and Management Board for the Commonwealth of Puerto Rico created by the Puerto Rico Oversight, Management, and Economic Stability Act ceases to exist, whichever event occurs first.

Qualified disaster area means any census tract or nonmetropolitan county located in an area for which the President has declared a major disaster under section 401 of the Robert T. Stafford Disaster Relief and Emergency Assistance Act (42 U.S.C. 5170), or located in an area in which a catastrophic incident has occurred if such census tract or nonmetropolitan county ceased to be categorized as either a qualified census tract or qualified nonmetropolitan county, as applicable, during the period beginning 5 years before the date on which the President declared the major disaster or the catastrophic incident occurred and ending 2 years after such date. However, the following exceptions apply:

(1) In the case of a major disaster declared by the President, a census tract or nonmetropolitan county may be a qualified disaster area only during the 5-year period beginning on the date on which the President declared the major disaster for the area in which the census tract or nonmetropolitan county is located; and

(2) In the case of a catastrophic incident, a census tract or nonmetropolitan county may be a qualified disaster area only during the 10-year period beginning on the date on which the catastrophic incident occurred in the area in which the census tract or nonmetropolitan county is located.

Qualified HUBZone SBC means a HUBZone SBC that SBA certifies as qualified for federal contracting assistance under the HUBZone program.

Qualified non-metropolitan county means any county that was not located in a metropolitan statistical area at the time of the most recent census taken for purposes of selecting qualified census tracts under section 42(d)(5)(C)(ii) of the Internal Revenue Code of 1986, and in which:

(i) The median household income is less than 80% of the non-metropolitan State median household income, based on the most recent data available from the Bureau of the Census of the Department of Commerce; or

(ii) The unemployment rate is not less than 140 percent of the average unemployment rate for the United States or for the State in which such county is located, whichever is less, based on the most recent data available from the Secretary of Labor.

Redesignated area means any census tract or any non-metropolitan county that ceases to be a qualified HUBZone, except that such census tracts or non-metropolitan counties may be "redesignated areas" only until the later of:

(1) The date on which the Census Bureau publicly releases the first results from the 2010 decennial census; or

(2) Three years after the date on which the census tract or non-metropolitan county ceased to be so qualified. The date on which the census tract or non-metropolitan county ceases to be qualified is the date that the official government data, which affects the eligibility of the HUBZone, is released to the public.

Reside means to live in a primary residence at a place for at least 180 days, or as a currently registered voter, and with intent to live there indefinitely.

Small agricultural cooperative means an association (corporate or otherwise), comprised exclusively of other small agricultural cooperatives, small business concerns, or U.S. citizens, pursuant to the provisions of the Agricultural Marketing Act, 12 U.S.C. 1141j, whose size does not exceed the applicable size standard pursuant to part 121 of this chapter. In determining such size, an agricultural cooperative is treated as a "business concern" and its member shareholders are not considered affiliated with the cooperative by virtue of their membership in the cooperative.

Small business concern (SBC) means a concern that, with its affiliates, meets the size standard for its primary industry, pursuant to part 121 of this chapter.

Small disadvantaged business (SDB) means a concern that is small pursuant to part 121 of this chapter, is owned and controlled by one or more socially and economically disadvantaged individuals, tribes, ANCs, Native Hawaiian Organizations, or CDCs and has been certified pursuant to subpart A or B, part 124 of this chapter.

Statewide average unemployment rate is the rate based on the most recent data available from the Bureau of Labor Statistics, United States Department of Labor, Division of Local Area Unemployment Statistics, 2 Massachusetts Ave., NE., Room 4675, Washington, DC 20212. A copy is also available at SBA, Office of D/HUB, 409 3rd Street, SW., Washington DC 20416.

[63 FR 31908, June 11, 1998, as amended at 66 FR 4645, Jan. 18, 2001; 69 FR 29421, May 24, 2004; 70 FR 51248, Aug. 30, 2005; 72 FR 50041, Aug. 30, 2007; 74 FR 45754, Sept. 4, 2009; 74 FR 56702, Nov. 3, 2009; 78 FR 61144, Oct. 2, 2013; 81 FR 51313, Aug. 4, 2016; 82 FR 48904, Oct. 23, 2017]

Subpart B—Requirements to be a Qualified HUBZone SBC

§ 126.200 What requirements must a concern meet to receive SBA certification as a qualified HUBZone SBC?

(a) *Concerns owned by Indian Tribal Governments*—(1) *Ownership.* (i) The concern must be wholly owned by one or more Indian Tribal Governments;

(ii) The concern must be wholly owned by a corporation that is wholly owned by one or more Indian Tribal Governments;

(iii) The concern must be owned in part by one or more Indian Tribal Governments and all other owners are either United States citizens or SBCs; or

(iv) The concern must be owned in part by a corporation, which is wholly owned by one or more Indian Tribal Governments, and all other owners are either United States citizens or SBCs.

(2) *Size.* The concern, with its affiliates, must meet the size standard corresponding to its primary industry classification as defined in part 121 of this chapter.

(3) *Other Requirements.* The concern must either:

(i) Maintain a principal office located in a HUBZone and ensure that at least 35% of its employees reside in a HUBZone as provided in paragraph (b)(4) of this section; or

(ii) Certify that when performing a HUBZone contract, at least 35% of its employees engaged in performing that contract will reside within any Indian reservation governed by one or more of the Indian Tribal Government owners, or reside within any HUBZone adjoining such Indian reservation. A HUBZone and Indian reservation are adjoining when the two areas are next to and in contact with each other; and

(iii) The concern will "attempt to maintain" (see § 126.103) that applicable employment percentage stated above during the performance of any HUBZone contract it receives.

(b) *Concerns owned by U.S. citizens, ANCs or CDCs*—(1) *Ownership.* (i) The concern must be at least 51% owned and controlled by persons who are United States citizens;

Example: A concern that is a partnership owned 50% by an individual who is a United States citizen and 50% by someone who is not a United States citizen, is not an eligible concern because it is not at least 51% owned by United States citizens.

(ii) The concern must be an ANC owned and controlled by Natives (determined pursuant to section 29(e)(1) of the ANCSA); or a direct or indirect subsidiary corporation, joint venture, or partnership of an ANC qualifying pursuant to section 29(e)(1) of ANCSA, if that subsidiary, joint venture, or partnership is owned and controlled by Natives (determined pursuant to section 29(e)(2)) of the ANCSA);

(iii) The concern must be wholly owned by one or more NHOs, or by a corporation that is wholly owned by one or more NHOs, or owned in part by one or more NHOs, if all other owners are either United States citizens or small business concerns; or

(iv) The concern must be wholly owned by a CDC, or owned in part by one or more CDCs, if all other owners are either United States citizens or SBCs.

(2) *Size.* The concern, together with its affiliates, must qualify as a small business under the size standard corresponding to its primary industry classification as defined in part 121 of this chapter.

(3) *Principal office.* The concern's principal office must be located in a HUBZone.

(4) *Employees.* At least 35% of the concern's employees must reside in a HUBZone. When determining the percentage of employees that reside in a HUBZone, if the percentage results in a fraction, round up to the nearest whole number;

Example 1: A concern has 25 employees, 35% or 8.75 employees must reside in a HUBZone. Thus, 9 employees must reside in a HUBZone.

Example 2: A concern has 95 employees, 35% or 33.25 employees must reside in a HUBZone. Thus, 34 employees must reside in a HUBZone.

(5) *Contract Performance.* The concern must represent, as provided in the application, that it will "attempt to maintain" (*see* § 126.103) having 35% of its employees reside in a HUBZone during the performance of any HUBZone contract it receives.

(6) *Subcontracting.* The concern must represent, as provided in the application, that it will comply with the applicable limitations on subcontracting requirements in connection with any procurement that it receives as a qualified HUBZone SBC, as set forth in § 126.5 and § 126.700.

(c) *Concerns owned by small agricultural cooperatives*—(1) *Ownership.* (i) A small agricultural cooperative organized or incorporated in the United States;

(ii) A small business concern wholly owned by one or more small agricultural cooperatives organized or incorporated in the United States; or

(iii) A small business concern owned in part by one or more small agricultural cooperatives organized or incorporated in the United States, provided that all other owners are small business concerns or United States citizens.

(2) *Size.* The small agricultural cooperative must meet the size standard corresponding to its primary industry classification as defined in part 121 of this chapter. However, in determining such size, an agricultural cooperative is treated as a "business concern" and its member shareholders are not considered affiliated with the cooperative by virtue of their membership in the cooperative.

(3) *Principal office.* The cooperative's principal office must be located in a HUBZone.

(4) *Employees.* At least 35% of the cooperative's employees must reside in a HUBZone. When determining the percentage of employees that reside in a HUBZone, if the percentage results in a fraction, round up to the nearest whole number.

(5) *Contract Performance.* The concern must represent, as provided in the application, that it will "attempt to maintain" (see § 126.103) having 35% of its employees reside in a HUBZone during the performance of any HUBZone contract it receives.

[69 FR 29422, May 24, 2004, as amended at 70 FR 51249, Aug. 30, 2005; 81 FR 34265, May 31, 2016; 81 FR 51314, Aug. 4, 2016; 83 FR 12852, Mar. 26, 2018]

§ 126.201 Who does SBA consider to own a HUBZone SBC?

An owner of a SBC seeking HUBZone certification or a qualified HUBZone SBC is a person who owns any legal or equitable interest in such SBC. If an Employee Stock Ownership Plan owns all or part of the concern, SBA considers each stock trustee and plan member to be an owner. If a trust owns all or part of the concern, SBA considers each trustee and trust beneficiary to be an owner. In addition:

(a) *Corporations.* SBA considers any person who owns stock, whether voting or non-voting, to be an owner. SBA considers options to purchase stock and the right to convert debentures into voting stock to have been exercised.

Example: U.S. citizens own all of the stock of a corporation. A corporate officer, a non-U.S. citizen, owns no stock in the corporation but owns options to purchase stock in the corporation. SBA will consider the options exercised and the individual to be an owner. Therefore, if that corporate officer has options to purchase 50% or more of the corporate stock, pursuant to § 126.200, the corporation would not be eligible to be a qualified HUBZone SBC because it is not at least 51% owned and controlled by persons who are U.S. citizens.

(b) *Partnerships.* SBA considers all partners, whether general or limited, to be owners in a partnership.

(c) *Sole proprietorships.* The proprietor is the owner.

(d) *Limited liability companies.* SBA considers each member to be an owner of a limited liability company.

[69 FR 29422, May 24, 2004, as amended at 70 FR 51249, Aug. 30, 2005; 71 FR 69183, Nov. 30, 2006]

§ 126.202 Who does SBA consider to control a HUBZone SBC?

Control means both the day-to-day management and long-term decision-making authority for the HUBZone SBC. Many persons share control of a concern, including each of those occupying the following positions: officer, director, general partner, managing partner, managing member and manager. In addition, key employees who possess expertise or responsibilities related to the concern's primary economic activity may share significant control of the concern. SBA will consider the control potential of such key employees on a case by case basis.

[69 FR 29422, May 24, 2004]

§ 126.203 What size standards apply to HUBZone SBCs?

(a) *At time of application for certification.* A HUBZone SBC must meet SBA's size standards for its primary industry classification as defined in § 121.201 of this title. If SBA is unable to verify that a concern is small, SBA may deny the concern status as a qualified HUBZone SBC, or SBA may request a formal size determination from the responsible Government Contracting Area Director or designee.

(b) *At time of initial contract offer.* A HUBZone SBC must be small for the size standard corresponding to the NAICS code assigned to the contract.

[63 FR 31908, June 11, 1998, as amended at 69 FR 29422, May 24, 2004]

§ 126.204 May a qualified HUBZone SBC have affiliates?

A concern may have affiliates provided that the aggregate size of the concern and all of its affiliates is small as defined in part 121 of this title, except as otherwise provided for small agricultural cooperatives in § 126.103.

[70 FR 51249, Aug. 30, 2005]

§ 126.205 May participants in other SBA programs be certified as qualified HUBZone SBCs?

Participants in other SBA programs may be certified as qualified HUBZone SBCs if they meet all of the requirements set forth in this part. Participation in other SBA Programs is not a requirement for participation in the HUBZone Program.

[69 FR 29422, May 24, 2004]

§ 126.206 May non-manufacturers be certified as qualified HUBZone SBCs?

Non-manufacturers (referred to in the HUBZone Act of 1997 as "regular dealers") may be certified as qualified HUBZone SBCs if they meet all of the requirements set forth in § 126.200. For purposes of this part, a "non-manufacturer" is defined in § 121.406(b)(1)(i) and (ii) of this title.

[66 FR 4645, Jan. 18, 2001]

§ 126.207 May a qualified HUBZone SBC have offices or facilities in another HUBZone or outside a HUBZone?

A qualified HUBZone SBC may have offices or facilities in another HUBZone or even outside a HUBZone and still be a qualified HUBZone SBC. However, in order to be certified as a qualified HUBZone SBC and if required by § 126.200, the concern's principal office must be located in a HUBZone.

[69 FR 29423, May 24, 2004]

Subpart C—Certification

§ 126.300 How may a concern be certified as a qualified HUBZone SBC and what information will SBA consider?

A concern must apply to SBA for certification. SBA will consider the information provided by the concern in order to determine whether the concern qualifies. SBA, in its discretion, may rely solely upon the information submitted to establish eligibility, may request additional information, or may verify the information before making a determination. SBA may draw an adverse inference and deny the certification where a concern fails to cooperate with SBA or submit information requested by SBA. If SBA determines that the concern is a qualified HUBZone SBC, it will issue a certification to that effect and add the concern to the List.

[69 FR 29423, May 24, 2004]

§ 126.301 Is there any other way for a concern to obtain certification?

No. SBA certification is the only way to qualify for HUBZone program status.

§ 126.302 When may a concern apply for certification?

A concern may apply to SBA and submit the required information whenever it can represent that it meets the eligibility requirements, subject to § 126.309. All representations and supporting information contained in the application must be complete and accurate as of the date of submission. The application must be signed by an officer of the concern who is authorized to represent the concern.

§ 126.303 Where must a concern submit its application and certification?

A concern seeking certification as a HUBZone SBC must submit either an electronic application to SBA via *https://eweb1.sba.gov/hubzone/internet/* or a written application to the D/HUB, U.S. Small Business Administration, 409 3rd Street, SW., Washington, DC 20416. Certification pages must be validated electronically or signed by a person authorized to represent the concern.

[69 FR 29423, May 24, 2004]

§ 126.304 What must a concern submit to SBA?

(a) To be certified by SBA as a qualified HUBZone SBC, a concern must submit a completed application and represent to SBA that it meets the requirements set forth in § 126.200. After submitting the application, applicants must notify SBA of any material changes that could affect its eligibility. The concern must also submit any additional information required by SBA.

(b) Concerns applying for HUBZone status based on a location within the external boundaries of an Indian reservation must use SBA's maps (located at *https://eweb1.sba.gov/hubzone/internet/*) to verify that the location is within the external boundaries of an Indian reservation. If, however, SBA's maps indicate that the location is not within the external boundaries of an Indian reservation and the concern disagrees, then the concern must submit official documentation from the appropriate Bureau of Indian Affairs (BIA) Land Titles and Records Office with jurisdiction over the concern's area, confirming that it is located within the external boundaries of an Indian reservation. BIA lists the Land Titles and Records Offices and their jurisdiction in 25 CFR 150.4 and 150.5.

(c) Concerns applying for HUBZone status based on a location within a qualified base closure area must use SBA's List of Qualified Base Closure Areas (located at *http://www.sba.gov/hubzone*) to verify that the location is within a qualified base closure area. If a concern disagrees with the failure of SBA's List of Qualified Base Closure Areas to include a particular area as a qualified base closure area, then the concern must submit relevant documentation from the Department of Defense, Office of Economic Adjustment, or the military department responsible for closing that installation.

(d) If the concern was decertified for failure to notify SBA of a material change affecting its eligibility pursuant to § 126.501, it must include with its application for certification a full explanation of why it failed to notify SBA of the material change. If SBA is not satisfied with the explanation provided, SBA may decline to certify the concern.

[69 FR 29423, May 24, 2004, as amended at 70 FR 51249, Aug. 30, 2005]

§ 126.305 What format must the certification to SBA take?

A concern must submit the required information in either a written or electronic application form provided by SBA. An electronic application must be sufficiently authenticated for enforcement purposes.

§ 126.306 How will SBA process the certification?

(a) The D/HUB or designee is authorized to approve or decline applications for certification. SBA will receive and review all applications and request supporting documents. SBA must receive all required information, supporting documents, and completed HUBZone representation before it will begin processing a concern's application. SBA will not process incomplete packages. SBA will make its determination within ninety (90) calendar days after receipt of a complete package whenever practicable. The decision of the D/HUB or designee is the final agency decision.

(b) SBA may request additional information or clarification of information contained in an application or document submission at any time.

(c) The burden of proof to demonstrate eligibility is on the applicant concern. If a concern does not provide requested information within the allotted time provided by SBA, or if it submits incomplete information, SBA may presume that disclosure of the missing information would adversely affect the business concern or demonstrate a lack of eligibility in the area or areas to which the information relates.

(d) The applicant must be eligible as of the date it submitted its application and up until and at the time the D/HUB issues a decision. The decision will be based on the facts set forth in the application, any information received in response to SBA's request for clarification, and any changed circumstances since the date of application.

(e) Any changed circumstance occurring after an applicant has submitted an application will be considered and may constitute grounds for decline. After submitting the application and signed representation, an applicant must notify SBA of any changes that could affect its eligibility. The D/HUB may propose decertification for any HUBZone SBC that failed to inform SBA of any changed circumstances that affected its eligibility for the program during the processing of the application.

(f) If SBA approves the application, SBA will send a written notice to the concern and automatically enter it on the List described in § 126.307.

(g) A decision to deny eligibility must be in writing and state the specific reasons for denial.

[63 FR 31908, June 11, 1998, as amended at 69 FR 29423, May 24, 2004; 70 FR 58974, Oct. 11, 2005; 81 FR 48591, July 25, 2016]

§ 126.307 Where will SBA maintain the List of qualified HUBZone SBCs?

Qualified HUBZone SBCs are identified by running a search on the Dynamic Small Business Search at *http://dsbs.sba.gov/dsbs/search/dsp_dsbs.cfm*. In addition, requesters may obtain a copy of the List by writing to the D/HUB at U.S. Small Business Administration, 409 3rd Street SW., Washington, DC 20416 or at *hubzone@sba.gov*.

[78 FR 61144, Oct. 2, 2013]

§ 126.308 What happens if SBA inadvertently omits a qualified HUBZone SBC from the List?

A HUBZone SBC that has received SBA's notice of certification, but is not on the List within 10 business days thereafter, should immediately notify the D/HUB in writing at U.S. Small Business Administration, 409 Third Street, SW., Washington, DC 20416 or via e-mail at *hubzone@sba.gov*. The concern must appear on the List to be eligible for HUBZone contracts.

[69 FR 29423, May 24, 2004]

§ 126.309 May a declined or decertified concern seek certification at a later date?

A concern that SBA has declined or decertified may seek certification after ninety (90) calendar days from the date of decline or decertification if it believes that it has overcome all reasons for decline or decertification through changed circumstances and is currently eligible. A concern found to be ineligible during a HUBZone status protest is precluded from applying for HUBZone certification for ninety (90) calendar days from the date of the final agency decision (the D/HUB's decision if no appeal is filed or the decision of the AA/GCBD) pursuant to 13 CFR 126.803(d)(5).

[76 FR 43574, July 21, 2011]

Subpart D—Program Examinations

§ 126.400 Who will conduct program examinations?

SBA field staff or others designated by the D/HUB will conduct program examinations.

§ 126.401 What is a program examination and what will SBA examine?

(a) *General.* A program examination is an investigation by SBA officials, which verifies the accuracy of any certification made or information provided as part of the HUBZone application process or in connection with a HUBZone contract. Thus, examiners may verify that the concern currently meets the program's eligibility requirements, and that it met such requirements at the time of its application for certification, its most recent recertification, or its certification in connection with a HUBZone contract.

(b) *Scope of review.* Examiners may conduct the review, or parts of the review, at one or all of the concern's offices. SBA will determine the location of the examination. Examiners may review any information related to the concern's eligibility requirements including, but not limited to, documentation related to the location and ownership of the concern, the employee percentage requirements, and the concern's "attempt to maintain" (*see* § 126.103) this percentage. The concern must document each employee's residence address through employment records. The examiner also may review property tax, public utility or postal records, and other relevant documents. The concern must retain documentation demonstrating satisfaction of the employee residence and other qualifying requirements for 6 years from date of submission of the application and any recertifications issued to SBA.

[69 FR 29423, May 24, 2004]

§ 126.402 When may SBA conduct program examinations?

SBA may conduct a program examination at any time after the concern submits its application, during the processing of the application, and at any time while the concern is certified as a qualified HUBZone SBC.

[69 FR 29423, May 24, 2004]

§ 126.403 May SBA require additional information from a HUBZone SBC?

(a) At the discretion of the D/HUB, SBA has the right to require that a HUBZone SBC submit additional information as part of the certification process, or at any time thereafter. SBA may draw an adverse inference from the failure of a HUBZone SBC to cooperate with a program examination or provide requested information.

(b) In order to gauge the success of the program, SBA requires that a HUBZone SBC submit updated financial information and information relating to the number of its employees.

[69 FR 29424, May 24, 2004]

Subpart E—Maintaining HUBZone Status

§ 126.500 How does a qualified HUBZone SBC maintain HUBZone certification?

Any qualified HUBZone SBC seeking to remain on the List must recertify every three years to SBA that it remains a qualified HUBZone SBC (*See* § 126.501 for ongoing obligations). Concerns wishing to remain in the program without any interruption must recertify their continued eligibility to SBA within 30 calendar days after the third anniversary of their date of certification and each subsequent three-year period. Failure to do so will result in SBA initiating decertification proceedings. Once decertified, the concern then would have to submit a new application for certification pursuant to § 126.309. The recertification to SBA must be in writing and must represent that the circumstances relative to eligibility that existed on the date of certification showing on the List have not materially changed and that the concern meets any new eligibility requirements.

[69 FR 29424, May 24, 2004]

§ 126.501 What are a qualified HUBZone SBC's ongoing obligations to SBA?

A qualified HUBZone SBC must immediately notify SBA of any material change that could affect its eligibility. Material change includes, but is not limited to, a change in the ownership, business structure, or principal office of the concern, or a failure to meet the 35% HUBZone residency requirement (*See* § 126.200 for certain eligibility requirements). The notification must be in writing, and must be sent or delivered to the D/HUB to comply with this requirement. Failure of a qualified HUBZone SBC to notify SBA of such a material change may result in decertification and removal from the List pursuant to § 126.504. In addition, SBA may seek the imposition of penalties under § 126.900. If the concern later becomes eligible for the program, it must apply for certification pursuant to §§ 126.300 through 126.306.

[69 FR 29424, May 24, 2004]

§ 126.502 Is there a limit to the length of time a qualified HUBZone SBC may be on the List?

There is no limit to the length of time a qualified HUBZone SBC may remain on the List so long as it continues to follow the provisions of §§ 126.200, 126.500, and 126.501.

§ 126.503 What happens if SBA is unable to verify a qualified HUBZone SBC's eligibility or determines that the concern is no longer eligible for the program?

If SBA is unable to verify a qualified HUBZone SBC's eligibility or determines it is not eligible for the program, SBA may propose decertification of the concern.

(a) *Proposing Decertification.* Except as set forth in paragraph (c) of this section, the Deputy D/HUB or designee will first notify the qualified HUBZone SBC in writing that SBA is proposing to decertify it, the reasons for the proposed de-certification, and that the SBC must rebut each of the reasons SBA sets forth. The qualified HUBZone SBC will have 30 calendar days from the date that it receives SBA's notification to respond, in writing, to the D/HUB or designee.

(b) *SBA's Decision.* The D/HUB or designee will consider the reasons for proposed decertification and the qualified HUBZone SBC's response before making a written decision whether to decertify. The D/HUB may draw an adverse inference where a qualified HUBZone SBC fails to cooperate with SBA or provide the information requested. The D/HUB's decision is the final agency decision.

(c) *Decertifying Pursuant to a Protest.* SBA will decertify a qualified HUBZone SBC and remove its name from the List without first proposing it for decertification if the D/HUB upholds a protest pursuant to § 126.803 and the D/HUB's decision is not overturned pursuant to § 126.805.

[69 FR 29424, May 24, 2004, as amended at 70 FR 51250, Aug. 30, 2005]

§ 126.504 When is a concern removed from the List?

If SBA determines at any time that a HUBZone SBC is not qualified, SBA may de-certify the HUBZone SBC, remove the concern from the List, and seek imposition of penalties pursuant to § 126.900. An adverse finding in the resolution of a protest also may result in de-certification and removal from the List, and the imposition of penalties pursuant to § 126.900. Failure to notify SBA of a material change which could affect a concern's eligibility will result in immediate de-certification, removal from the List, and SBA may seek the imposition of penalties under § 126.900.

[63 FR 31908, June 11, 1998. Redesignated at 69 FR 29424, May 24, 2004]

Subpart F—Contractual Assistance

§ 126.600 What are HUBZone contracts?

HUBZone contracts are contracts awarded to a qualified HUBZone SBC, regardless of the place of performance, through any of the following procurement methods:

(a) Sole source awards to qualified HUBZone SBCs;

(b) Set-aside awards, including partial set-asides, based on competition restricted to qualified HUBZone SBCs;

(c) Awards to qualified HUBZone SBCs through full and open competition after a price evaluation preference is applied to an other than small business in favor of qualified HUBZone SBCs;

(d) Awards based on a reserve for HUBZone SBCs in a solicitation for a Multiple Award Contract (*see* § 125.1); or

(e) Orders set-aside for HUBZone SBCs against a Multiple Award Contract, which had been awarded in full and open competition.

[78 FR 61144, Oct. 2, 2013, as amended at 81 FR 48591, July 25, 2016]

§ 126.601 What additional requirements must a qualified HUBZone SBC meet to bid on a contract?

(a) The Federal Acquisition Regulatory Council (FAR Council) has the responsibility of adjusting each acquisition-related dollar threshold on October 1 of each year that is evenly divisible by five. Acquisition-related dollar thresholds are defined as dollar thresholds that are specified in law as a factor in defining the scope of the applicability of a policy, procedure, requirement, or restriction provided in that law to the procurement of property or services by an executive agency as determined by the FAR Council. 41 U.S.C. 431a(c). Part 126, Subpart F, Contract Assistance, contains acquisition-related dollar thresholds subject to inflationary adjustments. The FAR Council shall publish a notice of the adjusted dollar thresholds in the FEDERAL REGISTER. The adjusted dollar thresholds shall take effect on the date of publication.

(b) In order to submit an offer on a specific HUBZone contract, the qualified HUBZone SBC, together with its affiliates, must be small under the size standard corresponding to the NAICS code assigned to the contract.

(c) A firm must be a qualified HUBZone SBC both at the time of its initial offer and at the time of award in order to be eligible for a HUBZone contract.

(d) At the time a qualified HUBZone SBC submits its initial offer, and where applicable its final offer, on a specific HUBZone contract, it must certify to the CO that:

(1) It is a qualified HUBZone SBC that appears on SBA's List;

(2) There has been no material change in its circumstances since the date of certification shown on the List that could affect its HUBZone eligibility;

(3) It is small under the NAICS code assigned to the procurement; and

(4) If the qualified HUBZone SBC was certified pursuant to § 126.200(b), it must represent that it will "attempt to maintain" (*See* § 126.103) the required percentage of employees who are HUBZone residents during the performance of a HUBZone contract. If the qualified HUBZone SBC was certified pursuant to § 126.200(a), then it must represent that at least 35% of its employees engaged in performing the HUBZone contract reside within any Indian reservation governed by one or more of its Indian Tribal Government owners or reside within any HUBZone adjoining any such Indian reservation.

(e) If submitting an offer as a joint venture, each qualified HUBZone SBC must make the certifications in paragraph (c) of this section separately under its own name.

(f) A qualified HUBZone SBC may submit an offer on a HUBZone contract for supplies as a nonmanufacturer if it meets the requirements of the nonmanufacturer rule set forth at § 121.406 of this chapter.

(g) *Multiple Award Contracts*—(1) *Total Set-Aside Contracts.* The qualified HUBZone SBC must comply with the applicable limitations on subcontracting provisions (*see* § 126.700) and the nonmanufacturer rule (*see* § 126.601), if applicable, in the performance of a contract totally set-aside for HUBZone SBCs. However, the contracting officer, in his or her discretion, may require the concern to perform the applicable amount of work or comply with the nonmanufacturer rule for each order awarded under the contract.

(2) *Partial Set-Aside Contracts.* For orders awarded under a partial set-aside contract, the qualified HUBZone SBC must comply with the applicable limitations on subcontracting provisions (*see* § 126.700) and the nonmanufacturer rule (*see* § 126.601), if applicable, during each performance period of the contract—e.g., during the base term and then during each subsequent option thereafter. For orders awarded under the non-set-aside portion, the qualified HUBZone SBC need not comply with any limitations on subcontracting or nonmanufacturer rule requirements. However, the contracting officer, in his or her discretion, may require the concern to perform the applicable amount of work or comply with the nonmanufacturer rule for each order awarded under the contract.

(3) *Orders.* The qualified HUBZone SBC must comply with the applicable limitations on subcontracting provisions (*see* § 126.700) and the nonmanufacturer rule (*see* § 126.601), if applicable, in the performance of each individual order that has been set-aside for HUBZone SBCs.

(4) *Reserves.* The qualified HUBZone SBC must comply with the applicable limitations on subcontracting provisions (*see* § 126.700) and the nonmanufacturer rule (*see* § 126.601), if applicable, in the performance of an order that is set aside for HUBZone SBCs. However, the qualified HUBZone SBC will not have to comply with the limitations on subcontracting provisions and the nonmanufacturer rule for any order issued against the Multiple Award Contract if the order is competed amongst qualified HUBZone SBCs and one or more other-than-small business concerns.

(h) *Recertification.* (1) A concern that is a qualified HUBZone SBC at the time of initial offer and contract award, including a Multiple Award Contract, is considered a HUBZone SBC throughout the life of that contract. This means that if a HUBZone SBC is certified at the time of initial offer and contract award for a Multiple Award Contract, then it will be considered a HUBZone SBC for each order issued against the contract, unless a contracting officer requests a new HUBZone SBC certification in connection with a specific order. Where a concern is later decertified, the procuring agency may exercise options and still count the award as an award to a HUBZone SBC. However, the following exceptions apply to this paragraph (h)(1):

(i) Where a HUBZone contract (or a contract awarded through full and open competition based on the HUBZone price evaluation preference) is novated to another business concern, the concern that will continue performance on the contract must certify its status as a HUBZone SBC to the procuring agency, or inform the procuring agency that it does not qualify as a HUBZone SBC, within 30 days of the novation approval. If the concern cannot certify that it qualifies as a HUBZone SBC, the agency can no longer count the options or orders issued pursuant to the contract, from that point forward, towards its HUBZone goals.

(ii) Where a concern that is performing a HUBZone contract acquires, is acquired by, or merges with another concern and contract novation is not required, the concern must, within 30 days of the transaction becoming final, recertify its HUBZone SBC status to the procuring agency, or inform the procuring agency that it has been decertified or no longer qualifies as a HUBZone SBC. If the contractor is unable to recertify its status as a HUBZone SBC, the agency can no longer count the options or orders issued pursuant to the contract, from that point forward, towards its HUBZone goals. The agency must immediately revise all applicable Federal contract databases to reflect the new status.

(iii) Where there has been a HUBZone status protest on the solicitation or contract, *see* § 126.803(d) for the effect of the status determination on the contract award.

(2) For the purposes of contracts (including Multiple Award Contracts) with durations of more than five years (including options), a contracting officer must request that a business concern recertify its HUBZone SBC status

no more than 120 days prior to the end of the fifth year of the contract, and no more than 120 days prior to exercising any option.

(3) A business concern that did not certify itself as a HUBZone SBC, either initially or prior to an option being exercised, may recertify itself as a HUBZone SBC for a subsequent option period if it meets the eligibility requirements at that time.

(4) Recertification does not change the terms and conditions of the contract. The limitations on subcontracting, nonmanufacturer and subcontracting plan requirements in effect at the time of contract award remain in effect throughout the life of the contract.

(5) Where the contracting officer explicitly requires concerns to recertify their status in response to a solicitation for an order, SBA will determine eligibility as of the date the concern submits its self-representation as part of its response to the solicitation for the order and at the time of award.

(6) A concern's status may be determined at the time of submission of its initial response to a solicitation for and award of an Agreement and each order issued pursuant to the Agreement.

[69 FR 29424, May 24, 2004, as amended at 74 FR 46887, Sept. 14, 2009; 78 FR 61144, Oct. 2, 2013; 81 FR 34265, May 31, 2016; 83 FR 12852, Mar. 26, 2018]

§ 126.602 Must a qualified HUBZone SBC maintain the employee residency percentage during contract performance?

(a) Qualified HUBZone SBCs eligible for the program pursuant to § 126.200(b) must meet the HUBZone residency requirement at all times while certified in the program. However, the qualified HUBZone SBC may "attempt to maintain" (*see* § 126.103) the required percentage of employees who reside in a HUBZone during the performance of any HUBZone contract awarded to the concern on the basis of its HUBZone status, except as set forth in paragraph (d).

(b) For indefinite delivery, indefinite quantity contracts, including Multiple Award Contracts, the qualified HUBZone SBC must attempt to maintain the residency requirement during the performance of each order that is set-aside for HUBZone SBCs.

(c) A qualified HUBZone SBC eligible for the program pursuant to § 126.200(a) must have at least 35% of its employees engaged in performing a HUBZone contract residing within any Indian reservation governed by one or more of the concern's Indian Tribal Government owners, or residing within any HUBZone adjoining any such Indian reservation. To monitor compliance, SBA will conduct program examinations, pursuant to §§ 126.400 through 126.403, where appropriate.

(d) Every time a qualified HUBZone SBC submits an offer and is awarded a HUBZone contract, it must meet all of the HUBZone Program's eligibility requirements, including the employee residency requirement at the time it submits its initial offer and up until and including the time of award. This means that if a HUBZone SBC is performing on a HUBZone contract and submits an offer for another HUBZone contract, it can no longer attempt to maintain the HUBZone residency requirement; rather, it must meet the requirement at the time it submits its initial offer and up until and including the time of award.

[78 FR 61145, Oct. 2, 2013]

§ 126.603 Does HUBZone certification guarantee receipt of HUBZone contracts?

HUBZone certification does not guarantee that a qualified HUBZone SBC will receive HUBZone contracts. Qualified HUBZone SBCs should market their capabilities to appropriate contracting activities in order to increase the prospect that the contracting activity will adopt an acquisition strategy that includes HUBZone contract opportunities.

[69 FR 29425, May 24, 2004]

§ 126.604 Who decides if a contract opportunity for HUBZone set-aside competition exists?

The contracting officer for the contracting activity makes this decision.

§ 126.605 What requirements are not available for HUBZone contracts?

A contracting activity may not make a requirement available for a HUBZone contract if:

(a) The contracting activity otherwise would fulfill that requirement through award to Federal Prison Industries, Inc. under 18 U.S.C. 4124 or 4125, or to Javits-Wagner-O'Day Act participating non-profit agencies for the blind and severely disabled, under 41 U.S.C. 46 *et seq.*, as amended; or

(b) An 8(a) participant currently is performing the requirement through the 8(a)BD program or SBA has accepted the requirement for award through the 8(a)BD program, unless SBA has consented to release the requirement from the 8(a)BD program.

[63 FR 31908, June 11, 1998, as amended at 69 FR 29425, May 24, 2004]

§ 126.606 May a CO request that SBA release a requirement from the 8(a)BD program for award as a HUBZone contract?

A CO may request that SBA release an 8(a) requirement for award as a HUBZone contract. However, SBA will grant its consent only where neither the incumbent nor any other 8(a) participant can perform the requirement. The request must be made to the AA/BD, who will make a determination after consulting with the D/HUB.

[69 FR 29425, May 24, 2004, as amended at 74 FR 45754, Sept. 4, 2009]

§ 126.607 When must a contracting officer set aside a requirement for qualified HUBZone SBCs?

(a) The contracting officer first must review a requirement to determine whether it is excluded from HUBZone contracting pursuant to § 126.605.

(b) *Contracting Among Small Business Programs.* (1) *Acquisitions Valued At or Below the Simplified Acquisition Threshold.* The contracting officer shall set aside any acquisition with an anticipated dollar value exceeding the Micropurchase Threshold but not exceeding the Simplified Acquisition Threshold (defined in the FAR at 48 CFR 2.101) for small business concerns when there is a reasonable expectation that offers will be obtained from at least two small business concerns that are competitive in terms of quality and delivery and award will be made at fair market prices. This requirement does not preclude a contracting officer from making an award to a small business under the 8(a) BD, HUBZone, SDVO SBC or WOSB Programs.

(2) *Acquisitions Valued Above the Simplified Acquisition Threshold.* (i) The contracting officer shall set aside any acquisition with an anticipated dollar value exceeding the Simplified Acquisition Threshold (defined in the FAR at 48 CFR 2.101) for small business concerns when there is a reasonable expectation that offers will be obtained from at least two small business concerns that are competitive in terms of quality and delivery and award will be made at fair market prices. However, after conducting market research, the contracting officer shall first consider a set-aside or sole source award (if the sole source award is permitted by statute or regulation) under the 8(a) BD, HUBZone, SDVO SBC or WOSB programs before setting aside the requirement as a small business set-aside. There is no order of precedence among the 8(a) BD, HUBZone, SDVO SBC or WOSB programs. The contracting officer must document the contract file with the rationale used to support the specific set-aside, including the type and extent of market research conducted. In addition, the contracting officer must document the contract file showing that the apparent successful offeror's certifications in the System for Award Management (SAM) (or any successor system) and associated representations were reviewed.

(ii) SBA believes that Progress in fulfilling the various small business goals, as well as other factors such as the results of market research, programmatic needs specific to the procuring agency, anticipated award price, and the acquisition history, will be considered in making a decision as to which program to use for the acquisition.

(c) If the contracting officer decides to set aside the requirement for competition restricted to qualified HUBZone SBCs, the contracting officer must:

(1) Have a reasonable expectation after reviewing SBA's list of qualified

HUBZone SBCs that at least two responsible qualified HUBZone SBCs will submit offers; and

(2) Determine that award can be made at fair market price.

[63 FR 31908, June 11, 1998, as amended at 70 FR 51250, Aug. 30, 2005; 75 FR 62281, Oct. 7, 2010; 77 FR 1860, Jan. 12, 2012; 78 FR 61146, Oct. 2, 2013]

§ 126.608 Are there HUBZone contract opportunities at or below the simplified acquisition threshold or micropurchase threshold?

A CO may make a requirement available as a HUBZone set-aside if it is at or below the simplified acquisition threshold. In addition, a CO may award a requirement as a HUBZone contract to a qualified HUBZone SBC at or below the micropurchase threshold.

[69 FR 29425, May 24, 2004]

§ 126.609 [Reserved]

§ 126.610 May SBA appeal a contracting officer's decision not to make a procurement available for award as a HUBZone contract?

(a) The Administrator may appeal a CO's decision not to make a particular requirement available for award as a HUBZone contract to the Secretary of the department or head of the agency.

(b) An appeal is initiated by SBA's Procurement Center Representative to the CO, and may be in response to information supplied by the D/HUB, his or her designee, or other interested parties.

[69 FR 29425, May 24, 2004]

§ 126.611 What is the process for such an appeal?

(a) *Notice of appeal.* When the contracting officer rejects a recommendation by SBA's Procurement Center Representative to make a requirement available for award as a HUBZone contract, he or she must notify the Procurement Center Representative as soon as practicable. If the Administrator intends to appeal the decision, SBA must notify the contracting officer no later than five business days after receiving notice of the contracting officer's decision.

(b) *Suspension of action.* Upon receipt of notice of SBA's intent to appeal, the contracting officer must suspend further action regarding the procurement until the head of the contracting activity issues a written decision on the appeal, unless the head of the contracting activity makes a written determination that urgent and compelling circumstances which significantly affect the interests of the United States compel award of the contract.

(c) *Deadline for appeal.* Within 15 business days of SBA's notification to the CO, SBA must file its formal appeal with the Secretary of the department or head of the agency, or the appeal will be deemed withdrawn.

(d) *Decision.* The contracting activity must specify in writing the reasons for a denial of an appeal brought under this section.

[63 FR 31908, June 11, 1998, as amended at 69 FR 29425, May 24, 2004]

§ 126.612 When may a CO award sole source contracts to qualified HUBZone SBCs?

A contracting officer may award a sole source contract to a qualified HUBZone SBC only when the contracting officer determines that:

(a) None of the provisions of §§ 126.605 or 126.607 apply;

(b) The anticipated award price of the contract, including options, will not exceed:

(1) $7,000,000 for a contract assigned a manufacturing NAICS code, or

(2) $4,000,000 for all other contracts.

(c) Two or more qualified HUBZone SBCs are not likely to submit offers;

(d) A qualified HUBZone SBC is a responsible contractor able to perform the contract; and

(e) In the estimation of the CO, contract award can be made at a fair and reasonable price.

[63 FR 31908, June 11, 1998, as amended at 69 FR 29425, May 24, 2004; 74 FR 46887, Sept. 14, 2009; 83 FR 12852, Mar. 26, 2018]

§ 126.613 How does a price evaluation preference affect the bid of a qualified HUBZone SBC in full and open competition?

(a)(1) Where a CO will award a contract on the basis of full and open competition, the CO must deem the price offered by a qualified HUBZone SBC to be lower than the price offered by another offeror (other than another SBC) if the price offered by the qualified HUBZone SBC is not more than 10% higher than the price offered by the otherwise lowest, responsive, and responsible offeror. For a best value procurement, the CO must apply the 10% preference to the otherwise successful offer of a large business and then determine which offeror represents the best value to the Government, in accordance with the terms of the solicitation. This does not apply if the HUBZone SBC will receive the contract as part of a reserve for HUBZone SBCs.

(2) Where, after considering the price evaluation adjustment, the price offered by a qualified HUBZone SBC is equal to the price offered by a large business (or, in a best value procurement, the total evaluation points received by a qualified HUBZone SBC is equal to the total evaluation points received by a large business), award shall be made to the qualified HUBZone SBC.

Example 1: In a full and open competition, a qualified HUBZone SBC submits an offer of $98, a non-HUBZone SBC submits an offer of $95, and a large business submits an offer of $93. The lowest, responsive, responsible offeror would be the large business. However, the CO must apply the HUBZone price evaluation preference. In this example, the qualified HUBZone SBC's offer is not more than 10% higher than the large business' offer and, consequently, the qualified HUBZone SBC displaces the large business as the lowest, responsive, and responsible offeror.

Example 2: In a full and open competition, a qualified HUBZone SBC submits an offer of $103, a non-HUBZone SBC submits an offer of $100, and a large business submits an offer of $93. The lowest, responsive, responsible offeror would be from the large business. The CO must then apply the HUBZone price evaluation preference. In this example, the qualified HUBZone SBC's offer is more than 10% higher than the large business' offer and, consequently, the qualified HUBZone SBC does not displace the large business as the lowest, responsive, and responsible offeror. In addition, the non-HUBZone SBC's offer at $100 does not displace the large business' offer because a price evaluation preference is not applied to change an offer and benefit a non-HUBZone SBC.

Example 3: In a full and open competition, a qualified HUBZone SBC submits an offer of $98 and a non-HUBZone SBC submits an offer of $93. The CO would not apply the price evaluation preference in this procurement because the lowest, responsive, responsible offeror is a SBC.

Example 4: In a full and open competition, a qualified HUBZone SBC submits an offer of $98 and a large business submits an offer of $93. The contracting officer has stated in the solicitation that one contract will be reserved for a HUBZone SBC. The contracting officer would not apply the price evaluation preference when determining which HUBZone SBC would receive the contract reserved for HUBZone SBCs, but would apply the price evaluation preference when determining the awardees for the non-reserved portion.

(b)(1) For purchases by the Secretary of Agriculture of agricultural commodities, the price evaluation preferences shall be:

(i) 10%, for the portion of a contract to be awarded that is not greater than 25% of the total volume being procured for each commodity in a single invitation for bids (IFB);

(ii) 5%, for the portion of a contract to be awarded that is greater than 25%, but not greater than 40%, of the total volume being procured for each commodity in a single IFB; and

(iii) Zero, for the portion of a contract to be awarded that is greater than 40% of the total volume being procured for each commodity in a single IFB.

(2) The 10% and 5% price evaluation preferences for agricultural commodities apply to all offers from qualified HUBZone SBCs up to the 25% and 40% volume limits specified in paragraph (b)(1) of this section. As such, more than one qualified HUBZone SBC may receive a price evaluation preference for any given commodity in a single IFB.

Example: There is an IFB for 100,000 pounds of wheat. Bid 1 (from a large business) is $1/pound for 100,000 pounds of wheat. Bid 2 (from a HUBZone SBC) is $1.05/pound for 20,000 pounds of wheat. Bid 3 (from a HUBZone SBC) is $1.04/pound for 20,000 pounds. Bid 3 receives a 10% price evaluation adjustment for 20,000 pounds, since 20,000 is less than 25% of 100,000 pounds. With the 10% price evaluation adjustment, Bid 1 changes from $20,000 for the first 20,000 pounds to $22,000. Bid 3's price of $20,800 ($1.04 × 20,000) is now lower than any other bid for 20,000 pounds. Thus, Bid 3 will be accepted for the full 20,000 pounds. Bid 2 receives a 10% price evaluation adjustment for that amount of its bid when added to the volume in Bid 3 that does not exceed 25% of the total volume being procured. Since 25,000 pounds is 25% of the total volume of wheat under the IFB, and Bid 3 totaled 20,000 pounds, a 10% price evaluation adjustment will be applied to the first 5,000 pounds of Bid 2. With the price evaluation adjustment, the price for Bid 1, as measured against Bid 2, for 5,000 pounds changes from $5,000 to $5,500. Bid 2's price of $5,250 ($1.05 × 5,000) is lower than Bid 1 for 5,000 pounds. Bid 2 will then receive a 5% price evaluation adjustment for the remaining 15,000 pounds, since the total volume of Bids 3 and 2 receiving an adjustment does not exceed 40% of the total volume of wheat under the IFB (*i.e.*, 40,000 pounds). With the 5% price evaluation adjustment, Bid 1's price for the next 15,000 pounds changes from $15,000 to $15,750. Bid 2's price for that 15,000 pounds is also $15, 750 ($1.05 × 15,000). Because the evaluation price for Bid 2 is *not more than* 10% higher than the price offered by Bid 1, Bid 2's price is deemed to be lower than the price offered by Bid 1. Since the evaluation price for both the first 5,000 pounds (receiving a 10% price evaluation adjustment) and the remaining 15,000 pounds (receiving a 5% price evaluation adjustment) is less than Bid 1, Bid 2 will be accepted for the full 20,000 pounds.

(c) For purchases by the Secretary of Agriculture of agricultural commodities for export operations through international food aid programs administered by the Farm Service Agency, the price evaluation preference shall be 5% on the first portion of a contract to be awarded that is not greater than 20% of the total volume being procured for each commodity in a single IFB.

(d) A contract awarded to a qualified HUBZone SBC under a preference described in paragraph (b) of this section shall not be counted toward the fulfillment of any requirement partially set aside for competition restricted to SBCs.

[69 FR 29425, May 24, 2004, as amended at 70 FR 51250, Aug. 30, 2005; 78 FR 61146, Oct. 2, 2013]

§ 126.614 [Reserved]

§ 126.615 May a large business participate on a HUBZone contract?

Except as provided in § 126.618, a large business may not participate as a prime contractor on a HUBZone award, but may participate as a subcontractor to an otherwise qualified HUBZone SBC, subject to the contract performance requirements set forth in § 126.700.

[81 FR 48591, July 25, 2016, as amended at 81 FR 71983, Oct. 19, 2016]

§ 126.616 What requirements must a joint venture satisfy to submit an offer on a HUBZone contract?

(a) *General.* A qualified HUBZone SBC may enter into a joint venture agreement with one or more other SBCs, or with an approved mentor authorized by § 125.9 of this chapter (or, if also an 8(a) BD Participant, with an approved mentor authorized by § 124.520 of this chapter), for the purpose of submitting an offer for a HUBZone contract. The joint venture itself need not be certified as a qualified HUBZone SBC.

(b) *Size.* (1) A joint venture of at least one qualified HUBZone SBC and one or more other business concerns may submit an offer as a small business for a HUBZone procurement or sale so long as each concern is small under the size standard corresponding to the NAICS code assigned to the procurement or sale.

(2) A joint venture between a protégé firm and its SBA-approved mentor (*see* § 125.9 of this chapter) will be deemed small provided the protégé qualifies as small for the size standard corresponding to the NAICS code assigned to the HUBZone procurement or sale.

(c) *Contents of joint venture agreement.* Every joint venture agreement to perform a HUBZone contract, including those between a protégé firm that is a certified HUBZone SBC and its SBA-approved mentor authorized by § 124.520 or § 125.9 of this chapter, must contain a provision:

(1) Setting forth the purpose of the joint venture;

(2) Designating a HUBZone SBC as the managing venturer of the joint venture, and an employee of the HUBZone SBC managing venturer as the project manager responsible for performance of the contract. The individual identified as the project manager of the joint venture need not be an employee of the HUBZone SBC at the time the joint venture submits an offer, but, if he or she is not, there must be a signed letter of intent that the individual commits to be employed

by the HUBZone SBC if the joint venture is the successful offeror. The individual identified as the project manager cannot be employed by the mentor and become an employee of the HUBZone SBC for purposes of performance under the joint venture;

(3) Stating that with respect to a separate legal entity joint venture, the HUBZone SBC must own at least 51% of the joint venture entity;

(4) Stating that the HUBZone SBC(s) must receive profits from the joint venture commensurate with the work performed by the HUBZone SBC;

(5) Providing for the establishment and administration of a special bank account in the name of the joint venture. This account must require the signature of all parties to the joint venture or designees for withdrawal purposes. All payments due the joint venture for performance on a HUBZone contract will be deposited in the special account; all expenses incurred under the contract will be paid from the account as well;

(6) Itemizing all major equipment, facilities, and other resources to be furnished by each party to the joint venture, with a detailed schedule of cost or value of each, where practical. If a contract is indefinite in nature, such as an indefinite quantity contract or a multiple award contract where the level of effort or scope of work is not known, the joint venture must provide a general description of the anticipated major equipment, facilities, and other resources to be furnished by each party to the joint venture, without a detailed schedule of cost or value of each, or in the alternative, specify how the parties to the joint venture will furnish such resources to the joint venture once a definite scope of work is made publicly available;

(7) Specifying the responsibilities of the parties with regard to negotiation of the contract, source of labor, and contract performance, including ways that the parties to the joint venture will ensure that the joint venture and the HUBZone partner(s) to the joint venture will meet the performance of work requirements set forth in paragraph (d) of this section, where practical. If a contract is indefinite in nature, such as an indefinite quantity contract or a multiple award contract where the level of effort or scope of work is not known, the joint venture must provide a general description of the anticipated responsibilities of the parties with regard to negotiation of the contract, source of labor, and contract performance, not including the ways that the parties to the joint venture will ensure that the joint venture and the HUBZone partner(s) to the joint venture will meet the performance of work requirements set forth in paragraph (d) of this section, or in the alternative, specify how the parties to the joint venture will define such responsibilities once a definite scope of work is made publicly available;

(8) Obligating all parties to the joint venture to ensure performance of the HUBZone contract and to complete performance despite the withdrawal of any member;

(9) Designating that accounting and other administrative records relating to the joint venture be kept in the office of the HUBZone SBC managing venturer, unless approval to keep them elsewhere is granted by the District Director or his/her designee upon written request;

(10) Requiring that the final original records be retained by the HUBZone SBC managing venturer upon completion of the HUBZone contract performed by the joint venture;

(11) Stating that quarterly financial statements showing cumulative contract receipts and expenditures (including salaries of the joint venture's principals) must be submitted to SBA not later than 45 days after each operating quarter of the joint venture; and

(12) Stating that a project-end profit and loss statement, including a statement of final profit distribution, must be submitted to SBA no later than 90 days after completion of the contract.

(d) *Limitations on subcontracting.* (1) For any HUBZone contract to be performed by a joint venture between a qualified HUBZone SBC and another qualified HUBZone SBC, the aggregate of the qualified HUBZone SBCs to the joint venture, not each concern separately, must perform the applicable percentage of work required by § 125.6 of this chapter.

(2) For any HUBZone contract to be performed by a joint venture between a qualified HUBZone SBC and a small business concern or its SBA-approved mentor authorized by § 125.9 or § 124.520 of this chapter, the joint venture must perform the applicable percentage of work required by § 125.6 of this chapter, and the HUBZone SBC partner to the joint venture must perform at least 40% of the work performed by the joint venture.

(i) The work performed by the HUBZone SBC partner to a joint venture must be more than administrative or ministerial functions so that it gains substantive experience.

(ii) The amount of work done by the partners will be aggregated and the work done by the HUBZone SBC partner must be at least 40% of the total done by the partners. In determining the amount of work done by a mentor participating in a joint venture with a HUBZone qualified protégé, all work done by the mentor and any of its affiliates at any subcontracting tier will be counted.

(e) *Certification of compliance.* Prior to the performance of any HUBZone contract as a joint venture, the HUBZone SBC partner to the joint venture must submit a written certification to the contracting officer and SBA, signed by an authorized official of each partner to the joint venture, stating as follows:

(i) The parties have entered into a joint venture agreement that fully complies with paragraph (c) of this section;

(ii) The parties will perform the contract in compliance with the joint venture agreement and with the performance of work requirements set forth in paragraph (d) of this section.

(f) *Past performance and experience.* When evaluating the past performance and experience of an entity submitting an offer for a HUBZone contract as a joint venture established pursuant to this section, a procuring activity must consider work done individually by each partner to the joint venture as well as any work done by the joint venture itself previously.

(g) *Contract execution.* The procuring activity will execute a HUBZone contract in the name of the joint venture entity or the HUBZone SBC, but in either case will identify the award as one to a HUBZone joint venture or a HUBZone mentor-protégé joint venture, as appropriate.

(h) *Inspection of records.* The joint venture partners must allow SBA's authorized representatives, including representatives authorized by the SBA Inspector General, during normal business hours, access to its files to inspect and copy all records and documents relating to the joint venture.

(i) *Performance of work reports.* The HUBZone SBC partner to a joint venture must describe how it is meeting or has met the applicable performance of work requirements for each HUBZone contract it performs as a joint venture.

(1) The HUBZone SBC partner to the joint venture must annually submit a report to the relevant contracting officer and to the SBA, signed by an authorized official of each partner to the joint venture, explaining how the performance of work requirements are being met for each HUBZone contract performed during the year.

(2) At the completion of every HUBZone contract awarded to a joint venture, the HUBZone SBC partner to the joint venture must submit a report to the relevant contracting officer and to the SBA, signed by an authorized official of each partner to the joint venture, explaining how and certifying that the performance of work requirements were met for the contract, and further certifying that the contract was performed in accordance with the provisions of the joint venture agreement that are required under paragraph (c) of this section.

(j) *Basis for suspension or debarment.* The Government may consider the following as a ground for suspension or debarment as a willful violation of a regulatory provision or requirement applicable to a public agreement or transaction:

(1) Failure to enter a joint venture agreement that complies with paragraph (c) of this section;

(2) Failure to perform a contract in accordance with the joint venture agreement or performance of work requirements in paragraph (d) of this section; or

(3) Failure to submit the certification required by paragraph (e) of this

section or comply with paragraph (h) of this section.

(k) Any person with information concerning a joint venture's compliance with the performance of work requirements may report that information to SBA and/or the SBA Office of Inspector General.

[81 FR 48591, July 25, 2016, as amended at 81 FR 94942, Dec. 27, 2016; 83 FR 12852, Mar. 26, 2018]

§ 126.617 Who decides contract disputes arising between a qualified HUBZone SBC and a contracting activity after the award of a HUBZone contract?

For purposes of the Disputes Clause of a specific HUBZone contract, the contracting activity will decide disputes arising between a qualified HUBZone SBC and the contracting activity.

[69 FR 29426, May 24, 2004]

§ 126.618 How does a HUBZone SBC's participation in a Mentor-Protégé relationship affect its participation in the HUBZone Program?

(a) A qualified HUBZone SBC may enter into a mentor-protégé relationship under § 125.9 of this chapter (or, if also an 8(a) BD Participant, under § 124.520 of this chapter) or in connection with a mentor-protégé program of another agency, provided that such relationships do not conflict with the underlying HUBZone requirements.

(b) For purposes of determining whether an applicant to the HUBZone Program or a HUBZone SBC qualifies as small under part 121 of this chapter, SBA will not find affiliation between the applicant or qualified HUBZone SBC and the firm that is its mentor in an SBA-approved mentor-protégé relationship (including a mentor that is other than small) on the basis of the mentor-protégé agreement or the assistance provided to the protégé firm under the agreement. SBA will not consider the employees of the mentor in determining whether the applicant or qualified HUBZone SBC meets (or continues to meet) the 35% HUBZone residency requirement or the principal office requirement, or in determining the size of the applicant or qualified HUBZone SBC for any employee-based size standard.

(c) A qualified HUBZone SBC that is a prime contractor on a HUBZone contract may subcontract work to its mentor.

(1) The HUBZone SBC must meet the applicable performance of work requirements set forth in § 125.6(c) of this chapter.

(2) SBA may find affiliation between a prime HUBZone contractor and its mentor subcontractor where the mentor will perform primary and vital requirements of the contract. *See* § 121.103(h)(4) of this chapter.

[81 FR 48593, July 25, 2016]

Subpart G—Contract Performance Requirements

§ 126.700 What are the limitations on subcontracting requirements for HUBZone contracts?

A prime contractor receiving an award as a qualified HUBZone SBC must meet the limitations on subcontracting requirements set forth in § 125.6 of this chapter.

[81 FR 34265, May 31, 2016]

§ 126.701 Can these subcontracting percentages requirements change?

Yes. The Administrator may change the subcontracting percentage requirements if the Administrator determines that such action is necessary to reflect conventional industry practices.

§ 126.702 How can the subcontracting percentage requirements be changed?

SBA may change the required subcontracting percentage for a specific industry if the Administrator determines that such action is necessary to reflect conventional industry practices among SBCs that are below the numerical size standard for businesses in that industry group. The procedures for requesting changes in subcontracting percentages are set forth in § 125.6 of this chapter.

[69 FR 29427, May 24, 2004]

Subpart H—Protests

§ 126.800 Who may protest the status of a qualified HUBZone SBC?

(a) *For sole source procurements.* SBA or the contracting officer may protest the proposed awardee's qualified HUBZone SBC status.

(b) For all other procurements, including Multiple Award Contracts (*see* § 125.1), SBA, the contracting officer, or any other interested party may protest the apparent successful offeror's qualified HUBZone SBC status.

[63 FR 31908, June 11, 1998, as amended at 69 FR 29427, May 24, 2004; 78 FR 61146, Oct. 2, 2013]

§ 126.801 How does one file a HUBZone status protest?

(a) *General.* The protest procedures described in this part are separate from those governing size protests and appeals. All protests relating to whether a qualified HUBZone SBC is other than small for purposes of any Federal program are subject to part 121 of this chapter and must be filed in accordance with that part. If a protester protests both the size of the HUBZone SBC and whether the concern meets the HUBZone qualifying requirements set forth in § 126.200, SBA will process protests concurrently, under the procedures set forth in part 121 of this chapter and this part. SBA does not review issues concerning the administration of a HUBZone contract.

(b) *Format.* Protests must be in writing and state all specific grounds for the protest. A protest merely asserting that the protested concern is not a qualified HUBZone SBC, without setting forth specific facts or allegations, is insufficient.

(c) *Filing.* (1) An interested party other than a contracting officer or SBA must submit its written protest to the contracting officer.

(2) A contracting officer and SBA must submit their protest to the D/HUB.

(3) Protestors may deliver their protests in person, by facsimile, by express delivery service, or by U.S. mail (postmarked within the applicable time period).

(d) *Timeliness.* (1) For negotiated acquisitions, an interested party must submit its protest by close of business on the fifth business day after notification by the contracting officer of the apparent successful offeror.

(2) For sealed bid acquisitions:

(i) An interested party must submit its protest by close of business on the fifth business day after bid opening, or

(ii) If the price evaluation preference was not applied at the time of bid opening, by close of business on the fifth business day from the date of identification of the apparent successful offeror.

(3) Any protest submitted after the time limits is untimely, unless it is from SBA or the CO.

(4) Any protest received prior to bid opening or notification of intended award, whichever applies, is premature.

(e) *Referral to SBA.* The CO must forward to SBA any non-premature protest received, notwithstanding whether he or she believes it is sufficiently specific or timely. The CO must send the protests, along with a referral letter, to D/HUB, U.S. Small Business Administration, 409 3rd Street, SW, Washington, DC 20416. The CO's referral letter must include information pertaining to the solicitation that may be necessary for SBA to determine timeliness and standing, including: the solicitation number; the name, address, telephone number and facsimile number of the CO; the type of HUBZone contract at issue; if the procurement was conducted using full and open competition with a HUBZone price evaluation preference, and whether the protester's opportunity for award was affected by the preference; if the procurement was a HUBZone set-aside, whether the protester submitted an offer; whether the protested concern was the apparent successful offeror; whether the procurement was conducted using sealed bid or negotiated procedures; the bid opening date, if applicable; when the protest was submitted to the CO; and whether a contract has been awarded.

[63 FR 31908, June 11, 1998, as amended at 69 FR 29427, May 24, 2004]

§ 126.802 Who decides a HUBZone status protest?

The D/HUB or designee will determine whether the concern has qualified HUBZone status.

§ 126.803 How will SBA process a HUBZone status protest?

(a) *Notice of receipt of protest.* (1) SBA immediately will notify the contracting officer and the protestor of the date SBA receives a protest and whether SBA will process the protest or dismiss it in accordance with § 126.804.

(2) If SBA determines the protest is timely and sufficiently specific, SBA will notify the protested HUBZone SBC of the protest and the identity of the protestor. The protested HUBZone SBC may submit information responsive to the protest within 5 business days.

(b) *Time period for determination.* (1) SBA will determine the HUBZone status of the protested HUBZone SBC within 15 business days after receipt of a protest.

(2) The contracting officer may award a contract after receipt of a protest if the contracting officer determines in writing that an award must be made to protect the public interest. Notwithstanding such a determination, the provisions of paragraph (d) of this section apply to the procurement in question.

(3) If SBA does not issue its determination within 15 business days (or request an extension that is granted), the contracting officer may award the contract if he or she determines in writing that there is an immediate need to award the contract and that waiting until SBA makes its determination will be disadvantageous to the Government. Notwithstanding such a determination, the provisions of paragraph (d) of this section apply to the procurement in question.

(c) *Notice of determination.* SBA will notify the contracting officer, the protestor, and the protested concern of its determination.

(d)(1) *Effect of determination.* The determination is effective immediately and is final unless overturned on appeal by the AA/GC&BD, or designee, pursuant to § 126.805. If SBA upholds the protest, SBA will decertify the concern.

(2) A contracting officer may award a contract to a protested concern after the D/HUB has determined either that the protested concern is an eligible HUBZone or has dismissed all protests against it. If the AA/GCBD subsequently overturns the initial determination or dismissal, the contracting officer may apply the appeal decision to the procurement in question.

(3) A contracting officer shall not award a contract to a protested concern that the D/HUB has determined is not an eligible HUBZone for the procurement in question.

(i) If a contracting officer receives such a determination after contract award, and no appeal has been filed, the contracting officer shall terminate the award.

(ii) If a timely appeal is filed after contract award, the contracting officer must consider whether performance can be suspended until an appellate decision is rendered.

(iii) If the AA/GCBD affirms the initial determination finding the protested concern ineligible, the contracting officer shall either terminate the contract or not exercise the next option.

(4) The contracting officer must update the Federal Procurement Data System and other procurement reporting databases to reflect the final agency HUBZone decision (the D/HUB's decision if no appeal is filed or the decision of the AA/GCBD).

(5) A concern found to be ineligible is precluded from applying for HUBZone certification for ninety (90) calendar days from the date of the final agency decision (the D/HUB's decision if no appeal is filed or the decision of the AA/GCBD).

[63 FR 31908, June 11, 1998, as amended at 69 FR 29427, May 24, 2004; 74 FR 45754, Sept. 4, 2009; 76 FR 5685, Feb. 2, 2011; 76 FR 43574, July 21, 2011]

§ 126.804 Will SBA decide all HUBZone status protests?

SBA will decide all protests not dismissed as premature, untimely or nonspecific.

§ 126.805 What are the procedures for appeals of HUBZone status determinations?

(a) *Who may appeal.* The protested HUBZone SBC, the protestor, or the CO may file appeals of protest determinations with the AA/GC&BD, or designee.

(b) *Timeliness of appeal.* The AA/GC&BD, or designee must receive the appeal no later than five business days after the date of receipt of the protest determination. SBA will dismiss any appeal received after the five-day period.

(c) *Method of Submission.* The party appealing the decision may deliver its appeal in person, by facsimile, by express delivery service, or by U.S. mail (postmarked within the applicable time period).

(d) *Notice of appeal.* The party bringing an appeal must provide notice of the appeal to the contracting activity contracting officer and either the protested HUBZone SBC or original protestor, as appropriate.

(e) *Grounds for appeal.* (1) SBA will reexamine a protest determination only if there was a clear and significant error in the processing of the protest or if the D/HUB failed completely to consider a significant fact contained within the information supplied by the protestor or the protested HUBZone SBC.

(2) SBA will not consider additional information or changed circumstances that were not disclosed at the time of the D/HUB's decision or that are based on disagreement with the findings and conclusions contained in the determination.

(f) *Contents of appeal.* The appeal must be in writing. The appeal must identify the protest determination being appealed and set forth a full and specific statement as to why the decision is erroneous or what significant fact the D/HUB failed to consider.

(g) *Decision.* The AA/GC&BD, or designee will make a decision within five business days of receipt of the appeal, if practicable, and will base his or her decision only on the information and documentation in the protest record as supplemented by the appeal. SBA will provide a copy of the decision to the CO, the protestor, and the protested HUBZone SBC, consistent with law. The ADA/GC&BD's decision is the final agency decision.

[63 FR 31908, June 11, 1998, as amended at 69 FR 29427, May 24, 2004; 74 FR 45754, Sept. 4, 2009; 76 FR 5685, Feb. 2, 2011]

Subpart I—Penalties

§ 126.900 What are the requirements for representing HUBZone status, and what are the penalties for misrepresentation?

(a) *Presumption of Loss Based on the Total Amount Expended.* In every contract, subcontract, cooperative agreement, cooperative research and development agreement, or grant which is set aside, reserved, or otherwise classified as intended for award to HUBZone SBCs, there shall be a presumption of loss to the United States based on the total amount expended on the contract, subcontract, cooperative agreement, cooperative research and development agreement, or grant whenever it is established that a business concern other than a HUBZone SBC willfully sought and received the award by misrepresentation.

(b) *Deemed Certifications.* The following actions shall be deemed affirmative, willful and intentional certifications of HUBZone SBC status:

(1) Submission of a bid, proposal, application or offer for a Federal grant, contract, subcontract, cooperative agreement, or cooperative research and development agreement reserved, set aside, or otherwise classified as intended for award to HUBZone SBCs.

(2) Submission of a bid, proposal, application or offer for a Federal grant, contract, subcontract, cooperative agreement or cooperative research and development agreement which in any way encourages a Federal agency to classify the bid or proposal, if awarded, as an award to a HUBZone SBC.

(3) Registration on any Federal electronic database for the purpose of being considered for award of a Federal grant, contract, subcontract, cooperative agreement, or cooperative research and development agreement, as a HUBZone SBC.

(c) *Signature Requirement.* Each offer, proposal, bid, or application for a Federal contract, subcontract, or grant shall contain a certification concerning the HUBZone SBC status of a business concern seeking the Federal contract, subcontract or grant. An authorized official must sign the certification on the same page containing the

HUBZone status claimed by the concern.

(d) *Limitation of Liability*. Paragraphs (a)–(c) of this section may be determined not to apply in the case of unintentional errors, technical malfunctions, and other similar situations that demonstrate that a misrepresentation of HUBZone status was not affirmative, intentional, willful or actionable under the False Claims Act, 31 U.S.C. §§3729, et seq. A prime contractor acting in good faith should not be held liable for misrepresentations made by its subcontractors regarding the subcontractors' HUBZone status. Relevant factors to consider in making this determination may include the firm's internal management procedures governing HUBZone status representations or certifications, the clarity or ambiguity of the representation or certification requirement, and the efforts made to correct an incorrect or invalid representation or certification in a timely manner. An individual or firm may not be held liable where government personnel have erroneously identified a concern as a HUBZone SBC without any representation or certification having been made by the concern and where such identification is made without the knowledge of the individual or firm.

(e) *Penalties for Misrepresentation*. (1) *Suspension or debarment*. The SBA suspension and debarment official or the agency suspension and debarment official may suspend or debar a person or concern for misrepresenting a firm's status as a HUBZone SBC pursuant to the procedures set forth in 48 CFR subpart 9.4.

(2) *Civil Penalties*. Persons or concerns are subject to severe penalties under the False Claims Act, 31 U.S.C. 3729–3733, the Program Fraud Civil Remedies Act, 31 U.S.C. 3801–3812, and any other applicable laws or regulations, including 13 CFR part 142.

(3) *Criminal Penalties*. Persons or concerns are subject to severe criminal penalties for knowingly misrepresenting the HUBZone status of a concern in connection with procurement programs pursuant to section 16(d) of the Small Business Act, 15 U.S.C. 645(d), as amended, 18 U.S.C. 1001, 18 U.S.C. 287, and any other applicable laws. Persons or concerns are subject to criminal penalties for knowingly making false statements or misrepresentations to SBA for the purpose of influencing any actions of SBA pursuant to section 16(a) of the Small Business Act, 15 U.S.C. 645(a), as amended, including failure to correct "continuing representations" that are no longer true.

[78 FR 38820, June 28, 2013, as amended at 81 FR 31492, May 19, 2016]

PART 127—WOMEN-OWNED SMALL BUSINESS FEDERAL CONTRACT PROGRAM

Subpart A—General Provisions

Sec.

Subpart B—Eligibility Requirements To Qualify as an EDWOSB or WOSB

Subpart C—Certification of EDWOSB or WOSB Status

Subpart D—Eligibility Examinations

Subpart E—Federal Contract Assistance

Subpart F—Protests

Subpart G—Penalties

AUTHORITY: 15 U.S.C. 632, 634(b)(6), 637(m), 644 and 657r.

SOURCE: 75 FR 62282, Oct. 7, 2010, unless otherwise noted.

Subpart A—General Provisions

§ 127.100 What is the purpose of this part?

Section 8(m) of the Small Business Act authorizes certain procurement mechanisms to ensure that Women-Owned Small Businesses (WOSBs) have an equal opportunity to participate in Federal contracting. This part implements these mechanisms and ensures that the program created, referred to as the WOSB Program, is substantially related to this important Congressional goal in accordance with applicable law.

§ 127.101 What type of assistance is available under this part?

This part authorizes contracting officers to restrict competition or award sole source contracts or orders to eligible Economically Disadvantaged Women-Owned Small Businesses (EDWOSBs) for certain Federal contracts or orders in industries in which the Small Business Administration (SBA) determines that WOSBs are underrepresented in Federal procurement. It also authorizes contracting officers to restrict competition or award sole source contracts or orders to eligible WOSBs for certain Federal contracts or orders in industries in which SBA determines that WOSBs are substantially underrepresented in Federal procurement and has waived the economically disadvantaged requirement.

[80 FR 55021, Sept. 14, 2015]

§ 127.102 What are the definitions of the terms used in this part?

For purposes of this part:

8(a) Business Development (8(a) BD) concern means a concern that SBA has certified as an 8(a) BD program participant and whose term has not expired or otherwise left the 8(a) BD program early.

AA/GC&BD means SBA's Associate Administrator for Government Contracting and Business Development.

Citizen means a person born or naturalized in the United States. Resident aliens and holders of permanent visas are not considered to be citizens.

Concern means a firm that satisfies the requirements in § 121.105 of this chapter.

Contracting officer has the meaning given to that term in Section 27(f)(5) of the Office of Federal Procurement Policy Act (codified at 41 U.S.C. 423(f)(5)).

D/GC means SBA's Director for Government Contracting.

Economically Disadvantaged WOSB (EDWOSB) means a concern that is small pursuant to part 121 of this chapter and that is at least 51 percent owned and controlled by one or more women who are citizens and who are economically disadvantaged in accordance with §§ 127.200, 127.201, 127.202 and 127.203. An EDWOSB automatically qualifies as a WOSB.

EDWOSB requirement means a Federal requirement for services or supplies for which a contracting officer has restricted competition or awarded a sole source contract or order to eligible EDWOSBs, including Multiple Award Contracts, partial set-asides, reserves, sole source awards, and orders set aside for EDWOSBs issued against a Multiple Award Contract.

Immediate family member means father, mother, husband, wife, son, daughter, stepchild, brother, sister, grandfather, grandmother, grandson, granddaughter, father-in-law, mother-in-law, son-in-law, and daughter-in-law.

Interested party means any concern that submits an offer for a specific EDWOSB or WOSB requirement (including Multiple Award Contracts), any concern that submitted an offer in a full and open competition and its opportunity for award will be affected by a reserve of an award given a WOSB or EDWOSB, the contracting activity's contracting officer, or SBA.

Primary industry classification means the six-digit North American Industry Classification System (NAICS) code designation that best describes the primary business activity of the concern. The NAICS code designations are described in the NAICS manual available via the Internet at *http://www.census.gov/NAICS*. In determining the primary industry in which a concern is engaged, SBA will consider the factors set forth in § 121.107 of this chapter.

Same or similar line of business means business activities within the same four-digit "Industry Group" of the NAICS Manual as the primary industry classification of the WOSB or EDWOSB.

Substantial underrepresentation is determined by a study using a reliable and relevant methodology.

System for Award Management (SAM) (or any successor system) means a federal system that consolidates various federal procurement systems (*e.g.*, Central Contractor Registration (CCR), Federal Agency Registration (Fedreg), Online Representations and Certifications Application (ORCA), Excluded Parties List System (EPLS)) and the Catalog of Federal Domestic Assistance into one system.

Underrepresentation is determined by a study using a reliable and relevant methodology.

WOSB means a concern that is small pursuant to part 121 of this chapter, and that is at least 51 percent owned and controlled by one or more women who are citizens in accordance with §§ 127.200, 127.201 and 127.202.

WOSB Program Repository means a secure, Web-based application that collects, stores and disseminates documents to the contracting community and SBA, which verify the eligibility of a business concern for a contract to be awarded under a WOSB or EDWOSB requirement.

WOSB requirement means a Federal requirement for services or supplies for which a contracting officer has restricted competition or awarded a sole source contract or order to eligible WOSBs, including Multiple Award Contracts, partial set-asides, reserves, sole source awards, and orders set aside for WOSBs issued against a Multiple Award Contract.

[75 FR 62282, Oct. 7, 2010, as amended at 78 FR 61146, Oct. 2, 2013; 80 FR 55022, Sept. 14, 2015]

Subpart B—Eligibility Requirements To Qualify as an EDWOSB or WOSB

§ 127.200 What are the requirements a concern must meet to qualify as an EDWOSB or WOSB?

(a) *Qualification as an EDWOSB.* To qualify as an EDWOSB, a concern must be:

(1) A small business as defined in part 121 of this chapter for its primary industry classification; and

(2) Not less than 51 percent unconditionally and directly owned and controlled by one or more women who are United States citizens and are economically disadvantaged.

(b) *Qualification as a WOSB.* To qualify as a WOSB, a concern must be:

(1) A small business as defined in part 121 of this chapter; and

(2) Not less than 51 percent unconditionally and directly owned and controlled by one or more women who are United States citizens.

§ 127.201 What are the requirements for ownership of an EDWOSB and WOSB?

(a) *General.* To qualify as an EDWOSB one or more economically disadvantaged women must unconditionally and directly own at least 51 percent of the concern. To qualify as a WOSB, one or more women must unconditionally and directly own at least 51 percent of the concern. Ownership will be determined without regard to community property laws.

(b) *Requirement for unconditional ownership.* To be considered unconditional, the ownership must not be subject to any conditions, executory agreements, voting trusts, or other arrangements that cause or potentially cause ownership benefits to go to another. The pledge or encumbrance of stock or other ownership interest as collateral, including seller-financed transactions, does not affect the unconditional nature of ownership if the terms follow normal commercial practices and the owner retains control absent violations of the terms.

(c) *Requirement for direct ownership.* To be considered direct, the qualifying women must own 51 percent of the concern directly. The 51 percent ownership may not be through another business entity or a trust (including employee stock ownership plan) that is, in turn, owned and controlled by one or more women or economically disadvantaged women. However, ownership by a trust, such as a living trust, may be treated as the functional equivalent of ownership by a woman or economically disadvantaged woman where the trust is revocable, and the woman is the grantor, the trustee, and the sole current beneficiary of the trust.

(d) *Ownership of a partnership.* In the case of a concern that is a partnership, at least 51 percent of each class of partnership interest must be unconditionally owned by one or more women or in the case of an EDWOSB, economically disadvantaged women. The ownership must be reflected in the concern's partnership agreement. For purposes of this requirement, general and limited partnership interests are considered different classes of partnership interest.

(e) *Ownership of a limited liability company.* In the case of a concern that is a limited liability company, at least 51 percent of each class of member interest must be unconditionally owned by one or more women or in the case of an EDWOSB, economically disadvantaged women.

(f) *Ownership of a corporation.* In the case of a concern that is a corporation, at least 51 percent of each class of voting stock outstanding and 51 percent of the aggregate of all stock outstanding must be unconditionally owned by one or more women, or in the case of an EDWOSB, economically disadvantaged women. In determining unconditional ownership of the concern, any unexercised stock options or similar agreements held by a woman will be disregarded. However, any unexercised stock option or other agreement, including the right to convert non-voting stock or debentures into voting stock, held by any other individual or entity will be treated as having been exercised.

§ 127.202 What are the requirements for control of an EDWOSB or WOSB?

(a) *General.* To qualify as a WOSB, the management and daily business operations of the concern must be controlled by one or more women. To qualify as an EDWOSB, the management and daily business operations of the concern must be controlled by one or more women who are economically disadvantaged. Control by one or more women or economically disadvantaged women means that both the long-term decision making and the day-to-day management and administration of the business operations must be conducted by one or more women or economically disadvantaged women.

(b) *Managerial position and experience.* A woman, or in the case of an EDWOSB an economically disadvantaged woman, must hold the highest officer position in the concern and must have managerial experience of the extent and complexity needed to run the concern. The woman or economically disadvantaged woman manager need not have the technical expertise or possess the required license to be found to control the concern if she can demonstrate that she has ultimate managerial and supervisory control over those who possess the required licenses or technical expertise. However, if a man possesses the required license and has an equity interest in the concern, he may be found to control the concern.

(c) *Limitation on outside employment.* The woman or economically disadvantaged woman who holds the highest officer position of the concern must manage it on a full-time basis and devote full-time to the business concern during the normal working hours of business concerns in the same or similar line of business. The woman or economically disadvantaged woman who holds the highest officer position may not engage in outside employment that prevents her from devoting sufficient time and attention to the daily affairs of the concern to control its management and daily business operations.

(d) *Control over a partnership.* In the case of a partnership, one or more women, or in the case of an EDWOSB, economically disadvantaged women, must serve as general partners, with control over all partnership decisions.

(e) *Control over a limited liability company.* In the case of a limited liability company, one or more women, or in the case of an EDWOSB, economically disadvantaged women, must serve as management members, with control over all decisions of the limited liability company.

(f) *Control over a corporation.* One or more women, or in the case of an EDWOSB, economically disadvantaged women, must control the Board of Directors of the concern. Women or economically disadvantaged women are considered to control the Board of Directors when either:

(1) One or more women or economically disadvantaged women own at least 51 percent of all voting stock of the concern, are on the Board of Directors and have the percentage of voting stock necessary to overcome any super majority voting requirements; or

(2) Women or economically disadvantaged women comprise the majority of voting directors through actual numbers or, where permitted by state law, through weighted voting.

(g) *Involvement in the concern by other individuals or entities.* Men or other entities may be involved in the management of the concern and may be stockholders, partners or limited liability members of the concern. However, no males or other entity may exercise actual control or have the power to control the concern.

§ 127.203 What are the rules governing the requirement that economically disadvantaged women must own EDWOSBs?

(a) *General.* To qualify as an EDWOSB, the concern must be at least 51 percent owned by one or more women who are economically disadvantaged. A woman is economically disadvantaged if she can demonstrate that her ability to compete in the free enterprise system has been impaired due to diminished capital and credit opportunities as compared to others in the same or similar line of business. SBA does not take into consideration community property laws when determining economic disadvantage when the woman has no direct, individual or separate ownership interest in the property.

(b) *Limitation on personal net worth.* (1) In order to be considered economically disadvantaged, the woman's personal net worth must be less than $750,000, excluding her ownership interest in the concern and her equity interest in her primary personal residence.

(2) Income received from an EDWOSB that is an S corporation, LLC or partnership will be excluded from net worth where the EDWOSB provides documentary evidence demonstrating that the income was reinvested in the business concern or the distribution was solely for the purposes of paying taxes arising in the normal course of operations of the business concern. Losses from the S corporation, LLC or partnership, however, are losses to the EDWOSB only, not losses to the individual, and cannot be used to reduce an individual's net worth.

(3) Funds invested in an Individual Retirement Account (IRA) or other official retirement account that are unavailable until retirement age without a significant penalty will not be considered in determining a woman's net worth. In order to properly assess whether funds invested in a retirement account may be excluded from a woman's net worth, she must provide information about the terms and restrictions of the account to SBA and certify that the retirement account is legitimate.

(c) *Factors to be considered.* (1) *General.* The personal financial condition of the woman claiming economic disadvantage, including her personal income for the past three years (including bonuses, and the value of company stock given in lieu of cash), her personal net worth and the fair market value of all of her assets, whether encumbered or not, will be considered in determining whether she is economically disadvantaged.

(2) *Spouse's financial situation.* SBA may consider a spouse's financial situation in determining a woman's access to credit and capital. When married, an individual claiming economic disadvantage must submit separate financial information for her spouse, unless the individual and the spouse are legally separated. SBA will consider a spouse's financial situation in determining an individual's access to credit and capital where the spouse has a role in the business (e.g., an officer, employee or director) or has lent money to, provided credit or financial support to, or guaranteed a loan of the business. SBA may also consider the spouse's financial condition if the spouse's business is in the same or similar line of business as the EDWOSB or WOSB and the spouse's business and WOSB share similar names, Web sites, equipment or employees. In addition, all transfers to a spouse within two years of a certification will be attributed to a woman claiming economic disadvantage as set forth in paragraph (d) of this section.

(3) *Income.*

(i) When considering a woman's personal income, if the adjusted gross yearly income averaged over the three years preceding the certification exceeds $350,000, SBA will presume that she is not economically disadvantaged. The presumption may be rebutted by a showing that this income level was unusual and not likely to occur in the future, that losses commensurate with and directly related to the earnings were suffered, or by evidence that the income is not indicative of lack of economic disadvantage.

(ii) Income received by an EDWOSB that is an S corporation, LLC, or partnership will be excluded from an individual's income where the EDWOSB provides documentary evidence demonstrating that the income was reinvested in the EDWOSB or the distribution was solely for the purposes of paying taxes arising in the normal course of operations of the business concern. Losses from the S corporation, LLC or partnership, however, are losses to the EDWOSB only, not losses to the individual, and cannot be used to reduce a woman's personal income.

(4) *Fair market value of all assets.* A woman will generally not be considered economically disadvantaged if the fair market value of all her assets (including her primary residence and the value of the business concern) exceeds $6 million. The only assets excluded from this determination are funds excluded under paragraph (b)(3) of this section as being invested in a qualified

IRA account or other official retirement account.

(d) *Transfers within two years.* Assets that a woman claiming economic disadvantage transferred within two years of the date of the concern's certification will be attributed to the woman claiming economic disadvantage if the assets were transferred to an immediate family member, or to a trust that has as a beneficiary an immediate family member. The transferred assets within the two-year period will not be attributed to the woman if the transfer was:

(1) To or on behalf of an immediate family member for that individual's education, medical expenses, or some other form of essential support; or

(2) To an immediate family member in recognition of a special occasion, such as a birthday, graduation, anniversary, or retirement.

Subpart C—Certification of EDWOSB or WOSB Status

§ 127.300 How is a concern certified as an EDWOSB or WOSB?

(a) *General.* At the time a concern submits an offer on a specific contract (including a Multiple Award Contract) or order reserved for competition among EDWOSBs or WOSBs under this Part, it must be registered in the System for Award Management (SAM) (or any successor system), have a current representation posted on SAM (or any successor system) that it qualifies as an EDWOSB or WOSB, and have provided the required documents to the WOSB Program Repository, or if the repository is unavailable, be prepared to submit the documents to the contracting officer if selected as the apparent successful offeror.

(b) *Form of certification.* In conjunction with its required registration in the SAM (or any successor system), the concern must submit a copy of the Women-Owned Small Business Program Certification (WOSB or EDWOSB) to the WOSB Program Repository and representations to the electronic annual representations and certifications at *http://orca.bpn.gov*, that it is a qualified EDWOSB or WOSB. The Women-Owned Small Business Program Certification (WOSB or EDWOSB) and representation must state, subject to penalties for misrepresentation, that:

(1) The concern is an EDWOSB or WOSB or is certified as an EDWOSB or WOSB by a certifying entity approved by SBA, and there have been no changes in its circumstances affecting its eligibility since certification;

(2) The concern meets *each* of the applicable individual eligibility requirements described in subpart B of this part, including that:

(i) It is a small business concern under the size standard assigned to the particular procurement;

(ii) It is at least 51 percent owned and controlled by one or more women who are United States citizens, or it is at least 51 percent owned and controlled by one or more women who are United States citizens and are economically disadvantaged; and

(iii) Neither SBA, in connection with an examination or protest, nor an SBA-approved certifier has issued a decision currently in effect finding that it does not qualify as an EDWOSB or WOSB.

(c) *Documents provided to contracting officer.* All of the documents set forth in paragraphs (d) and (e) of this section must be provided to the contracting officer to verify eligibility at the time of initial offer. The documents will be provided via the WOSB Program Repository or, if the repository is unavailable, directly to the contracting officer. The documents must be retained for a minimum of six (6) years.

(d) *Third-Party Certification.* (1) Prior to certification in SAM (or any successor system), the WOSB or EDWOSB that has been certified as a WOSB or EDWOSB by a certifying entity approved by SBA, including those certifiers from which SBA will accept certifications from the U.S. Department of Transportation's (DOT) Disadvantaged Business Enterprise (DBE) Program, or by SBA as an 8(a) BD Participant, must provide a copy of the third-party Certification to the WOSB Program Repository. If the WOSB Program Repository is unavailable, then prior to the award of a WOSB or EDWOSB contract, the apparent successful offeror WOSB or EDWOSB that has been certified as a EDWOSB or WOSB by a certifying entity approved by SBA must provide a copy of the third-party Certification to the contracting officer verifying that it was a WOSB or EDWOSB at the time of initial offer.

(2) The EDWOSB or WOSB must also provide a copy of the joint venture agreement, if applicable.

(3) The EDWOSB or WOSB must also provide a signed copy of the Women-Owned Small Business Program Certification (WOSB or EDWOSB).

(4) The EDWOSB or WOSB must also provide any additional documents as requested by SBA in writing that are necessary to satisfy the WOSB Program requirements.

(5) Within thirty (30) days of the WOSB Program Repository becoming available, the WOSB or EDWOSB must provide the same documents to the repository.

(e) *Non-Third Party Certification.* A concern that has not been certified as a WOSB or EDWOSB by a third-party certifier approved by SBA or as a DBE or by SBA as an 8(a) BD Participant must also provide documents to the WOSB Program Repository. If the WOSB Program Repository is unavailable, then prior to award of a WOSB or EDWOSB contract, the apparent successful offeror must provide a copy of the documents to the contracting officer verifying that it was a WOSB or EDWOSB at the time of initial offer. Within thirty (30) days of the WOSB Program Repository becoming available, the WOSB or EDWOSB must provide the same documents to the WOSB Program Repository. These documents must be signed and include the following:

(1) Birth certificates, Naturalization papers, or unexpired passports for owners who are women;

(2) Copy of the joint venture agreement, if applicable;

(3) For limited liability companies:

(i) Articles of organization (also referred to as certificate of organization or articles of formation) and any amendments; and

(ii) Operating agreement, and any amendments;

(4) For corporations:

(i) Articles of incorporation and any amendments;

(ii) By-laws and any amendments;

(iii) All issued stock certificates, including the front and back copies, signed in accord with the by-laws;

(iv) Stock ledger; and

(v) Voting agreements, if any;

(5) For partnerships, the partnership agreement and any amendments;

(6) For sole proprietorships (and corporations, limited liability companies and partnerships if applicable), the assumed/fictitious name certificate(s);

(7) A signed copy of the Women-Owned Small Business Program Certification-WOSBs; and

(8) For EDWOSBs, in addition to the above:

(i) SBA Form 413, Personal Financial Statement, available to the public at *http://www.sba.gov/tools/Forms/index.html*, for each woman claiming economic disadvantage; and

(ii) A signed copy of the Women-Owned Small Business Program Certification–EDWOSBs.

(f) *Update of certification and documents.* (1) The concern must update its Women-Owned Small Business Program Certification (WOSB or EDWOSB) and EDWOSB and WOSB representations and self-certification in SAM (or any successor system) as necessary, but at least annually, to ensure they are kept current, accurate, and complete. The certification and representations are effective for a period of one year from the date of submission or update.

(2) The WOSB or EDWOSB must update the documents submitted to the contracting officer via the WOSB Program Repository as necessary to ensure they are kept current, accurate and complete. If the WOSB Program Repository is not available, the WOSB or EDWOSB must provide current, accurate and complete documents to the contracting officer for each contract award. Within thirty (30) days of the WOSB Program Repository becoming available, the WOSB or EDWOSB must provide the same documents to the WOSB Program Repository.

[75 FR 62282, Oct. 7, 2010, as amended at 78 FR 61146, Oct. 2, 2013]

§ 127.301 When may a contracting officer accept a concern's self-certification?

(a) *General.* (1) *Third-Party Certifications.* A contracting officer may accept a concern's self-certification in SAM (or any successor system) as accurate for a specific procurement reserved for award under this Part if the apparent successful offeror WOSB or EDWOSB provided the required documents, which are set forth in § 127.300(d), and there has been no protest or other credible information that calls into question the concern's eligibility as a EDWOSB or WOSB. An example of such credible evidence includes information that the concern was determined by SBA or an SBA-approved certifier not to qualify as an EDWOSB or WOSB.

(2) *Non-Third Party Certification.* A contracting officer may accept a concern's self-certification in SAM (or any successor system) if the apparent successful offeror WOSB or EDWOSB has provided the required documents, which are set forth in § 127.300(e), and there has been no protest or other credible information that calls into question the concern's eligibility as an EDWOSB or WOSB.

(b) *Referral to SBA.* When the contracting officer has information that calls into question the eligibility of a concern as an EDWOSB or WOSB or the concern fails to provide all of the required documents to verify its eligibility, the contracting officer shall refer the concern to SBA for verification of the concern's eligibility by filing an EDWOSB or WOSB status protest pursuant to subpart F of this part. If the apparent successful offeror WOSB or EDWOSB fails to submit any of the required documents, the contracting officer cannot award a WOSB or EDWOSB contract to that business concern.

[75 FR 62282, Oct. 7, 2010, as amended at 77 FR 1861, Jan. 12, 2012; 78 FR 61146, Oct. 2, 2013]

§ 127.302 What third-party certifications may a concern use as evidence of its status as a qualified EDWOSB or WOSB?

In order for a concern to use a certification by another entity as evidence of its status as a qualified EDWOSB or WOSB in support of its representations in SAM (or any successor system) pursuant to § 127.300(b), the concern must have a current, valid certification from:

(a) SBA as an 8(a) BD Program participant; or

(b) An entity designated as an SBA-approved certifier on SBA's Web site located at *http://www.sba.gov/GC.*

[75 FR 62282, Oct. 7, 2010, as amended at 78 FR 61147, Oct. 2, 2013]

§ 127.303 How will SBA select and identify approved certifiers?

(a) *General.* SBA may enter into written agreements to accept the EDWOSB or WOSB certification of a Federal agency, State government, or national certifying entity if SBA determines that the entity's certification process complies with SBA-approved certification standards and tracks the EDWOSB or WOSB eligibility requirements set forth in subpart B of this part. The written agreement will include a provision authorizing SBA to terminate the agreement if SBA subsequently determines that the entity's certification process does not comply with SBA-approved certification standards or is not based on the same EDWOSB or WOSB eligibility requirements as set forth in subpart B of this part.

(b) *Required certification standards.* In order for SBA to enter into an agreement to accept the EDWOSB or WOSB certification of a Federal agency, State government, or national certifying entity, the entity must establish the following:

(1) It will render fair and impartial EDWOSB or WOSB eligibility determinations.

(2) It will retain the documents submitted by the approved WOSB or EDWOSB for a period of six (6) years from the date of certification (initial and any recertification) and provide any such documents to SBA in response to a status protest or eligibility examination or agency investigation or audit.

(3) Its certification process will require applicant concerns to pre-register in SAM (or any successor system)and

submit sufficient information as determined by SBA to enable it to determine whether the concern qualifies as an EDWOSB or WOSB. This information must include documentation demonstrating whether the concern is:

(i) A small business concern under SBA's size standards for its primary industry classification;

(ii) At least 51 percent owned and controlled by one or more women who are United States citizens; and

(iii) In the case of a concern applying for EDWOSB certification, at least 51 percent owned and controlled by one or more women who are United States citizens and economically disadvantaged.

(4) It will not decline to accept a concern's application for EDWOSB or WOSB certification on the basis of race, color, national origin, religion, age, disability, sexual orientation, or marital or family status.

(c) *List of SBA-approved certifiers.* SBA will maintain a list of approved certifiers, including certifiers from which SBA will accept DOT DBE certifications, on SBA's Internet Web site at *http://www.sba.gov/GC.* Any interested person may also obtain a copy of the list from the local SBA district office or SBA Area Office for Government Contracting.

[75 FR 62282, Oct. 7, 2010, as amended at 78 FR 61147, Oct. 2, 2013]

§ 127.304 How does a concern obtain certification from an approved certifier?

A concern that seeks EDWOSB or WOSB certification from an SBA-approved certifier must submit its application directly to the approved certifier in accordance with the specific application procedures of the particular certifier. Any interested party may obtain such certification information and application by contacting the approved certifier at the address provided on SBA's list of approved certifiers.

§ 127.305 May a concern determined not to qualify as an EDWOSB or WOSB submit a self-certification for a particular EDWOSB or WOSB requirement?

A concern that SBA or an SBA-approved certifier determines does not qualify as an EDWOSB or WOSB may not represent itself to be an EDWOSB or WOSB, as applicable, unless SBA subsequently determines that it is an eligible EDWOSB or WOSB pursuant to the examination procedures under § 127.405, and there have been no material changes in its circumstances affecting its eligibility since SBA's eligibility determination. Any concern determined not to be a qualified EDWOSB or WOSB may request that SBA conduct an examination to determine its EDWOSB or WOSB eligibility at any time once it believes in good faith that it satisfies all of the eligibility requirements to qualify as an EDWOSB or WOSB.

Subpart D—Eligibility Examinations

§ 127.400 What is an eligibility examination?

(a) *Purpose of examination.* Eligibility examinations are investigations that verify the accuracy of any certification made or information provided as part of the certification process (including third-party certifications) or in connection with an EDWOSB or WOSB requirement. In addition, eligibility examinations may verify that a concern meets the EDWOSB or WOSB eligibility requirements at the time of the examination. SBA will, in its sole discretion, perform eligibility examinations at any time after a concern self-certifies in SAM (or any successor system) that it is an EDWOSB or WOSB. SBA may conduct the examination, or parts of the examination, at one or all of the concern's offices.

(b) *Determination on conduct of an examination.* SBA may consider protest allegations set forth in a protest in determining whether to conduct an examination of a concern pursuant to subpart D of this part, notwithstanding a dismissal or denial of a protest pursuant to § 127.604. SBA may also consider information provided to the D/GC by a third-party that questions the eligibility of a WOSB or EDWOSB that has certified its status in SAM in determining whether to conduct an eligibility examination.

[75 FR 62282, Oct. 7, 2010, as amended at 78 FR 61147, Oct. 2, 2013]

§ 127.401 What is the difference between an eligibility examination and an EDWOSB or WOSB status protest pursuant to subpart F of this part?

(a) *Eligibility examination.* An eligibility examination is the formal process through which SBA verifies and monitors the accuracy of any certification made or information provided as part of the certification process or in connection with an EDWOSB or WOSB requirement. If SBA is conducting an eligibility examination on a concern that has submitted an offer on a pending EDWOSB or WOSB procurement and SBA has credible information that the concern may not qualify as an EDWOSB or WOSB, then SBA may initiate a protest pursuant to § 127.600 to suspend award of the contract for fifteen (15) business days pending SBA's determination of the concern's eligibility.

(b) *EDWOSB or WOSB protests.* An EDWOSB or WOSB status protest provides a mechanism for challenging or verifying the EDWOSB or WOSB eligibility of a concern in connection with a specific EDWOSB or WOSB requirement. SBA will process EDWOSB or WOSB protests in accordance with the procedures and timeframe set forth in subpart F, and will determine the EDWOSB or WOSB eligibility of the protested concern as of the date the concern represented its EDWOSB or WOSB status as part of its initial offer including price. SBA's protest determination will apply to the specific procurement to which the protest relates and to future procurements.

[75 FR 62282, Oct. 7, 2010, as amended at 78 FR 61147, Oct. 2, 2013]

§ 127.402 How will SBA conduct an examination?

(a) *Notification.* No less than five (5) business days before commencing an examination, SBA will notify the concern in writing that it will conduct an examination to verify the status of the concern as an EDWOSB or WOSB. However, SBA reserves the right to conduct a site visit without prior notification to the concern.

(b) *Request for information.* SBA will request that the concern or contracting officer provide documentation and information related to the concern's EDWOSB or WOSB eligibility. These documents will include those submitted under § 127.300 and any other pertinent documents requested by SBA at the time of eligibility examination to verify eligibility, including but not limited to, documents submitted by a concern in connection with any WOSB or EDWOSB certification. SBA may also request copies of proposals or bids submitted in response to an EDWOSB or WOSB solicitation. In addition, EDWOSBs will be required to submit signed copies of SBA Form 413, Personal Financial Statement, the three most recent personal income tax returns (including all schedules and W–2 forms) for the women claiming economic disadvantage and their spouses, unless the individuals and their spouses are legally separated, and SBA Form 4506–T, Request for Tax Transcript Form, available to the public at *http://www.sba.gov/tools/Forms/index.html.* SBA may draw an adverse inference where a concern fails to cooperate in providing the requested information. The WOSB or EDWOSB must retain documentation demonstrating satisfaction of the eligibility requirements for six (6) years from date of self-certification.

§ 127.403 What happens if SBA verifies the concern's eligibility?

If SBA verifies that the concern satisfies the applicable EDWOSB or WOSB eligibility requirements, then the D/GC will send the concern a written decision to that effect and will allow the concern's EDWOSB or WOSB designation in SAM (or any successor system) to stand and the concern may continue to self-certify its EDWOSB or WOSB status.

[75 FR 62282, Oct. 7, 2010, as amended at 78 FR 61147, Oct. 2, 2013]

§ 127.404 What happens if SBA is unable to verify a concern's eligibility?

(a) *Notice of proposed determination of ineligibility.* If SBA is unable to verify that the concern qualifies as an EDWOSB or WOSB, then the D/GC will send the concern a written notice explaining the reasons SBA believes the concern did not qualify at the time of certification or does not qualify as an EDWOSB or WOSB. The notice will advise the concern that it has fifteen (15) calendar days from the date of the notice to respond.

(b) *SBA determination.* Following the fifteen (15) day response period, the D/GC or designee will consider the reasons of proposed ineligibility and any information the concern submitted in response, and will send the concern a written decision with its findings. The D/GC's decision is effective immediately and remains in full force and effect unless a new examination verifies the concern is an eligible EDWOSB or WOSB or the concern is certified by a third-party certifier.

(1) If SBA determines that the concern does not qualify as an EDWOSB or WOSB, then the D/GC will send the concern a written decision explaining the basis of ineligibility, and will require that the concern remove its EDWOSB or WOSB designation in SAM (or any successor system) within five (5) calendar days after the date of the decision.

(2) If the concern has already certified itself as a WOSB or EDWOSB on a pending procurement the concern must immediately inform the officials responsible for the procurement of the adverse determination.

(3) If SBA determines that the concern did not qualify as an EDWOSB or WOSB at the time it submitted its initial offer for an EDWOSB or WOSB requirement, the contracting officer may terminate the contract, not exercise any option, or not award further task or delivery orders.

(4) Whether or not a contracting officer decides to allow or not allow an ineligible concern to fully perform a contract under paragraph (b)(2) of this section, the contracting officer cannot count the award as one to an EDWOSB or WOSB and must update the Federal Procurement Data System–Next Generation (FPDS–NG) and other databases from the date of award accordingly.

(c) A concern that has been found to be ineligible may not represent itself as a WOSB or EDWOSB until it cures the reason for its ineligibility and SBA determines that the concern qualifies as a WOSB or EDWOSB. A concern that believes in good faith that it has cured the reason(s) for its ineligibility may request an examination under the procedures set forth in this section.

[75 FR 62282, Oct. 7, 2010, as amended at 78 FR 61147, Oct. 2, 2013]

§ 127.405 What is the process for requesting an eligibility examination?

(a) *General.* A concern may request that SBA conduct an examination to verify its eligibility as an EDWOSB or WOSB at any time after it is determined by SBA not to qualify as an EDWOSB or WOSB, if the concern believes in good faith that it satisfies all of the EDWOSB or WOSB eligibility requirements under subpart B of this part.

(b) *Format.* The request for an examination must be in writing and must specify the particular reasons the concern was determined not to qualify as an EDWOSB or WOSB.

(c) *Submission of request.* The concern must submit its request directly to the Director for Government Contracting, U.S. Small Business Administration, 409 Third Street, SW., Washington, DC 20416, or by fax to (202) 205–6390, marked "*Attn:* Request for Women-Owned Small Business Eligibility Examination."

(d) *Notice of receipt of request.* SBA will immediately notify the concern in writing once SBA receives its request for an examination. SBA will request that the concern provide documentation and information related to the concern's EDWOSB or WOSB eligibility and may draw an adverse inference if the concern fails to cooperate in providing the requested information.

(e) *Determination of eligibility.* The D/GC will send the concern a written decision finding that it either qualifies or does not qualify as an EDWOSB or WOSB.

(1) If the D/GC determines that the concern does not qualify as an EDWOSB or WOSB, the decision will explain the specific reasons for the adverse determination and advise the concern that it is prohibited from self-certifying as an EDWOSB or WOSB. If the concern self-certifies as an EDWOSB or WOSB notwithstanding SBA's adverse determination, the concern will be subject to the penalties under subpart G of this part.

(2) If the D/GC determines that the concern qualifies as an EDWOSB or WOSB, then the D/GC will send the concern a written decision to that effect and will advise the concern that it may self-certify as an EDWOSB or WOSB, as applicable.

(f) *Effect of decision.* The D/GC's decision is effective immediately and remains in full force and effect unless a new examination verifies the concern is an eligible EDWOSB or WOSB or the concern is certified by a third-party certifier. If the concern has already certified itself as a WOSB or EDWOSB on a pending procurement the concern must immediately inform the officials responsible for the procurement of the adverse determination.

(g) *Determinations of Ineligibility.* A concern that has been found to be ineligible shall not represent itself as a WOSB or EDWOSB until it cures the reason for its ineligibility and SBA determines that the concern qualifies as a WOSB or EDWOSB. A concern that believes in good faith that it has cured the reason(s) for its ineligibility may request an examination under the procedures set forth in this section.

Subpart E—Federal Contract Assistance

§ 127.500 In what industries is a contracting officer authorized to restrict competition or make a sole source award under this part?

A contracting officer may restrict competition or make a sole source award under this part only in those industries in which SBA has determined that WOSBs are underrepresented or substantially underrepresented in Federal procurement, as specified in § 127.501, regardless of the place of performance.

[80 FR 55022, Sept. 14, 2015, as amended at 81 FR 48593, July 25, 2016]

§ 127.501 How will SBA determine the industries that are eligible for EDWOSB or WOSB requirements?

(a) Based upon its analysis, SBA will designate by NAICS Industry Subsector Code those industries in which WOSBs are underrepresented and substantially underrepresented.

(b) In determining the extent of underrepresentation of WOSBs, SBA may request that the head of any Federal department or agency provide SBA, data or information necessary to analyze the extent of underrepresentation of WOSBs.

[75 FR 62282, Oct. 7, 2010, as amended at 80 FR 55022, Sept. 14, 2015]

§ 127.502 How will SBA identify and provide notice of the designated industries?

SBA will post on its Internet Web site at *http://www.sba.gov* a list of NAICS Industry Subsector industries it designates under § 127.501. The list of designated industries also may be obtained from the local SBA district office and may be posted on the General Services Administration Internet Web site.

§ 127.503 When is a contracting officer authorized to restrict competition or award a sole source contract or order under this part?

(a) *Competition restricted to EDWOSBs.* For requirements in industries designated by SBA as underrepresented pursuant to § 127.501, a contracting officer may restrict competition to EDWOSBs if the contracting officer has a reasonable expectation based on market research that:

(1) Two or more EDWOSBs will submit offers for the contract; and

(2) Contract award may be made at a fair and reasonable price.

(b) *Competition restricted to WOSBs.* For requirements in industries designated by SBA as substantially underrepresented pursuant to § 127.501, a contracting officer may restrict competition to WOSBs if the contracting officer has a reasonable expectation based on market research that:

(1) Two or more WOSBs will submit offers (this includes EDWOSBs, which are also WOSBs); and

(2) Contract award may be made at a fair and reasonable price.

(c) *Sole source awards to EDWOSBs.* For requirements in industries designated by SBA as underrepresented pursuant to § 127.501, a contracting officer may issue a sole source award to an EDWOSB when the contacting officer determines that:

(1) The EDWOSB is a responsible contractor with respect to performance of the requirement and the contracting officer does not have a reasonable expectation that 2 or more EDWOSBs will submit offers;

(2) The anticipated award price of the contract (including options) will not exceed $6,500,000 in the case of a contract assigned a North American Industry Classification System (NAICS) code for manufacturing, or $4,000,000 in the case of any other contract opportunity; and

(3) In the estimation of the contracting officer, the award can be made at a fair and reasonable price.

(d) *Sole source awards to WOSBs.* For requirements in industries designated by SBA as substantially underrepresented pursuant to § 127.501, a contracting officer may issue a sole source award to a WOSB when the contacting officer determines that:

(1) The WOSB is a responsible contractor with respect to performance of the requirement and the contracting officer does not have a reasonable expectation that 2 or more WOSBs will submit offers;

(2) The anticipated award price of the contract (including options) will not exceed $6,500,000 in the case of a contract assigned a NAICS code for manufacturing, or $4,000,000 in the case of any other contract opportunity; and

(3) In the estimation of the contracting officer, the award can be made at a fair and reasonable price.

(e) *8(a) BD requirements.* A contracting officer may not restrict competition to eligible EDWOSBs or WOSBs if an 8(a) BD Participant is currently performing the requirement under the 8(a) BD Program or SBA has accepted the requirement for performance under the authority of the 8(a) BD program, unless SBA consented to release the requirement from the 8(a) BD program.

(f) *Contracting Among Small Business Programs.* (1) *Acquisitions Valued At or Below the Simplified Acquisition Threshold.* The contracting officer shall set aside any acquisition with an anticipated dollar value exceeding the Micro-purchase Threshold but not exceeding the Simplified Acquisition Threshold (defined in the FAR at 48 CFR 2.101) for small business concerns when there is a reasonable expectation that offers will be obtained from at least two small business concerns that are competitive in terms of quality and delivery and award will be made at fair market prices. This requirement does not preclude a contracting officer from making an award to a small business under the 8(a) BD, HUBZone, SDVO SBC or WOSB Programs.

(2) *Acquisitions Valued Above the Simplified Acquisition Threshold.* (i) The contracting officer shall set aside any acquisition with an anticipated dollar value exceeding the Simplified Acquisition Threshold (defined in the FAR at 48 CFR 2.101) for small business concerns when there is a reasonable expectation that offers will be obtained from at least two small business concerns that are competitive in terms of quality and delivery and award will be made at fair market prices. However, after conducting market research, the contracting officer shall first consider a set-aside or sole source award (if the sole source award is permitted by statute or regulation) under the 8(a) BD, HUBZone, SDVO SBC or WOSB programs before setting aside the requirement as a small business set-aside. There is no order of precedence among the 8(a) BD, HUBZone, SDVO SBC or WOSB programs. The contracting officer must document the contract file with the rationale used to support the specific set-aside, including the type

and extent of market research conducted. In addition, the contracting officer must document the contract file showing that the apparent successful offeror's certifications in SAM (or any successor system) and associated representations were reviewed.

(ii) SBA believes that Progress in fulfilling the various small business goals, as well as other factors such as the results of market research, programmatic needs specific to the procuring agency, anticipated award price, and the acquisition history, will be considered in making a decision as to which program to use for the acquisition.

(g) *Contract file.* When restricting competition to WOSBs or EDWOSBs in accordance with § 127.503, the contracting officer must document the contract file accordingly, including the type and extent of market research and the fact that the NAICS code assigned to the contract is for an industry that SBA has designated as an underrepresented or, with respect to WOSBs, substantially underrepresented, industry. In addition, the contracting officer must document the contract file showing that the apparent successful offeror's documents and certifications in SAM (or any successor system) and associated representations were reviewed.

(h) *Recertification.* (1) A concern that represents itself and qualifies as a WOSB or EDWOSB at the time of initial offer (or other formal response to a solicitation), which includes price, including a Multiple Award Contract, is considered a WOSB or EDWOSB throughout the life of that contract. This means that if a WOSB/EDWOSB is qualified at the time of initial offer for a Multiple Award Contract, then it will be considered an WOSB/EDWOSB for each order issued against the contract, unless a contracting officer requests a new WOSB or EDWOSB certification in connection with a specific order. Where a concern later fails to qualify as a WOSB/EDWOSB, the procuring agency may exercise options and still count the award as an award to a WOSB/EDWOSB. However, the following exceptions apply to this paragraph (h)(1):

(i) Where a WOSB/EDWOSB contract is novated to another business concern, the concern that will continue performance on the contract must certify its status as a WOSB/EDWOSB to the procuring agency, or inform the procuring agency that it does not qualify as a WOSB/EDWOSB, within 30 days of the novation approval. If the concern cannot certify its status as a WOSB/EDWOSB, the agency may no longer be able to count the options or orders issued pursuant to the contract, from that point forward, towards its women-owned small business goals.

(ii) Where a concern that is performing a WOSB/EDWOSB contract acquires, is acquired by, or merges with another concern and contract novation is not required, the concern must, within 30 days of the transaction becoming final, recertify its WOSB/EDWOSB status to the procuring agency, or inform the procuring agency that it no longer qualifies as a WOSB/EDWOSB. If the concern is unable to recertify its status as a WOSB/EDWOSB, the agency may no longer be able to count the options or orders issued pursuant to the contract, from that point forward, towards its women-owned small business goals. The agency and the contractor must immediately revise all applicable Federal contract databases to reflect the new status if necessary.

(iii) Where there has been a WOSB or EDWOSB status protest on the solicitation or contract, *see* § 127.604(f) for the effect of the status determination on the contract award.

(2) For the purposes of contracts (including Multiple Award Contracts) with durations of more than five years (including options), a contracting officer must request that a business concern recertify its WOSB/EDWOSB status no more than 120 days prior to the end of the fifth year of the contract, and no more than 120 days prior to exercising any option.

(3) A business concern that did not certify itself as a WOSB/EDWOSB, either initially or prior to an option being exercised, may recertify itself as a WOSB/EDWOSB for a subsequent option period if it meets the eligibility requirements at that time.

(4) Recertification does not change the terms and conditions of the contract. The limitations on subcontracting, nonmanufacturer and subcontracting plan requirements in effect at the time of contract award remain in effect throughout the life of the contract.

(5) Where the contracting officer explicitly requires concerns to recertify their status in response to a solicitation for an order, SBA will determine eligibility as of the date the concern submits its self-representation as part of its response to the solicitation for the order.

(6) A concern's status may be determined at the time of a response to a solicitation for an Agreement and each order issued pursuant to the Agreement.

[75 FR 62282, Oct. 7, 2010, as amended at 77 FR 1861, Jan. 12, 2012; 78 FR 26506, May 7, 2013; 78 FR 61147, Oct. 2, 2013; 79 FR 31849, June 3, 2014; 80 FR 55022, Sept. 14, 2015; 83 FR 12852, Mar. 26, 2018]

§ 127.504 What additional requirements must a concern satisfy to submit an offer on an EDWOSB or WOSB requirement?

(a) In order for a concern to submit an offer on a specific EDWOSB or WOSB requirement, the concern must ensure that the appropriate representations and certifications in SAM (or any successor system) are accurate and complete at the time it submits its offer to the contracting officer, including, but not limited to, the fact that:

(1) It is small under the size standard corresponding to the NAICS code assigned to the contract;

(2) It is listed in SAM (or any successor system) as an EDWOSB or WOSB; and

(3) There has been no material change in any of its circumstances affecting its EDWOSB or WOSB eligibility.

(b) The concern must also meet the applicable limitations on subcontracting requirements as set forth in § 125.6 of this chapter.

[75 FR 62282, Oct. 7, 2010, as amended at 78 FR 61147, Oct. 2, 2013; 81 FR 34265, May 31, 2016]

§ 127.505 May a non-manufacturer submit an offer on an EDWOSB or WOSB requirement for supplies?

An EDWOSB or WOSB that is a non-manufacturer, as defined in § 121.406(b) of this chapter, may submit an offer on an EDWOSB or WOSB contract for supplies, if it meets the requirements under the non-manufacturer rule set forth in § 121.406(b) of this chapter.

§ 127.506 May a joint venture submit an offer on an EDWOSB or WOSB requirement?

A joint venture, including those between a protégé and a mentor under § 125.9 of this chapter (or, if also an 8(a) BD Participant, under § 124.520 of this chapter), may submit an offer on a WOSB Program contract if the joint venture meets all of the following requirements:

(a)(1) A joint venture of at least one WOSB or EDWOSB and one or more other business concerns may submit an offer as a small business for a WOSB Program procurement or sale so long as each concern is small under the size standard corresponding to the NAICS code assigned to the procurement or sale.

(2) A joint venture between a protégé firm and its SBA-approved mentor (*see* § 125.9 and § 124.520 of this chapter) will be deemed small provided the protégé qualifies as small for the size standard corresponding to the NAICS code assigned to the WOSB Program procurement or sale.

(b) The EDWOSB or WOSB participant of the joint venture must be designated in SAM (or any successor system)as an EDWOSB or WOSB;

(c) *Contents of joint venture agreement.* The parties to the joint venture must enter into a written joint venture agreement. The joint venture agreement must contain a provision:

(1) Setting forth the purpose of the joint venture.

(2) Designating a WOSB as the managing venturer of the joint venture, and an employee of the WOSB managing venturer as the project manager responsible for performance of the contract. The individual identified as the project manager of the joint venture need not be an employee of the WOSB at the time the joint venture submits

an offer, but, if he or she is not, there must be a signed letter of intent that the individual commits to be employed by the WOSB if the joint venture is the successful offeror. The individual identified as the project manager cannot be employed by the mentor and become an employee of the WOSB for purposes of performance under the joint venture;

(3) Stating that with respect to a separate legal entity joint venture, the WOSB must own at least 51% of the joint venture entity;

(4) Stating that the WOSB(s) must receive profits from the joint venture commensurate with the work performed by the WOSB;

(5) Providing for the establishment and administration of a special bank account in the name of the joint venture. This account must require the signature of all parties to the joint venture or designees for withdrawal purposes. All payments due the joint venture for performance on a WOSB Program contract will be deposited in the special account; all expenses incurred under the contract will be paid from the account as well;

(6) Itemizing all major equipment, facilities, and other resources to be furnished by each party to the joint venture, with a detailed schedule of cost or value of each, where practical. If a contract is indefinite in nature, such as an indefinite quantity contract or a multiple award contract where the level of effort or scope of work is not known, the joint venture must provide a general description of the anticipated major equipment, facilities, and other resources to be furnished by each party to the joint venture, without a detailed schedule of cost or value of each, or in the alternative, specify how the parties to the joint venture will furnish such resources to the joint venture once a definite scope of work is made publicly available;

(7) Specifying the responsibilities of the parties with regard to negotiation of the contract, source of labor, and contract performance, including ways that the parties to the joint venture will ensure that the joint venture and the WOSB Program participant(s) in the joint venture will meet the performance of work requirements set forth in paragraph (d) of this section, where practical. If a contract is indefinite in nature, such as an indefinite quantity contract or a multiple award contract where the level of effort or scope of work is not known, the joint venture must provide a general description of the anticipated responsibilities of the parties with regard to negotiation of the contract, source of labor, and contract performance, not including the ways that the parties to the joint venture will ensure that the joint venture and the WOSB Program participant(s) in the joint venture will meet the performance of work requirements set forth in paragraph (d) of this section, or in the alternative, specify how the parties to the joint venture will define such responsibilities once a definite scope of work is made publicly available;

(8) Obligating all parties to the joint venture to ensure performance of the WOSB contract and to complete performance despite the withdrawal of any member;

(9) Designating that accounting and other administrative records relating to the joint venture be kept in the office of the WOSB managing venturer, unless approval to keep them elsewhere is granted by the District Director or his/her designee upon written request;

(10) Requiring that the final original records be retained by the WOSB managing venturer upon completion of the WOSB Program contract performed by the joint venture;

(11) Stating that quarterly financial statements showing cumulative contract receipts and expenditures (including salaries of the joint venture's principals) must be submitted to SBA not later than 45 days after each operating quarter of the joint venture; and

(12) Stating that a project-end profit and loss statement, including a statement of final profit distribution, must be submitted to SBA no later than 90 days after completion of the contract.

(d) *Performance of work.* (1) For any WOSB Program contract, the joint venture (including one between a protégé and a mentor authorized by § 125.9 or § 124.520 of this chapter) must perform the applicable percentage of work required by § 125.6 of this chapter.

(2) The WOSB partner(s) to the joint venture must perform at least 40% of

the work performed by the joint venture.

(i) The work performed by the WOSB partner(s) to a joint venture must be more than administrative or ministerial functions so that they gain substantive experience.

(ii) The amount of work done by the partners will be aggregated and the work done by the WOSB partner(s) must be at least 40% of the total done by all partners. In determining the amount of work done by the non-WOSB partner, all work done by the non-WOSB partner and any of its affiliates at any subcontracting tier will be counted.

(e) *Certification of compliance.* Prior to the performance of any WOSB Program contract as a joint venture, the WOSB Program participant in the joint venture must submit a written certification to the contracting officer and SBA, signed by an authorized official of each partner to the joint venture, stating as follows:

(i) The parties have entered into a joint venture agreement that fully complies with paragraph (c) of this section;

(ii) The parties will perform the contract in compliance with the joint venture agreement and with the performance of work requirements set forth in paragraph (d) of this section.

(f) *Past performance and experience.* When evaluating the past performance and experience of an entity submitting an offer for a WOSB Program contract as a joint venture established pursuant to this section, a procuring activity must consider work done individually by each partner to the joint venture as well as any work done by the joint venture itself previously.

(g) *Contract execution.* The procuring activity will execute a WOSB Program contract in the name of the joint venture entity or the WOSB, but in either case will identify the award as one to a WOSB Program joint venture or a WOSB Program mentor-protégé joint venture, as appropriate.

(h) *Submission of joint venture agreement.* The WOSB Program participant must provide a copy of the joint venture agreement to the contracting officer.

(i) *Inspection of records.* The joint venture partners must allow SBA's authorized representatives, including representatives authorized by the SBA Inspector General, during normal business hours, access to its files to inspect and copy all records and documents relating to the joint venture.

(j) *Performance of work reports.* The WOSB Program participant in the joint venture must describe how it is meeting or has met the applicable performance of work requirements for each WOSB Program contract it performs as a joint venture.

(1) The WOSB partner to the joint venture must annually submit a report to the relevant contracting officer and to the SBA, signed by an authorized official of each partner to the joint venture, explaining how the performance of work requirements are being met for each WOSB Program contract performed during the year.

(2) At the completion of every WOSB Program contract awarded to a joint venture, the WOSB partner to the joint venture must submit a report to the relevant contracting officer and to the SBA, signed by an authorized official of each partner to the joint venture, explaining how and certifying that the performance of work requirements were met for the contract, and further certifying that the contract was performed in accordance with the provisions of the joint venture agreement that are required under paragraph (c) of this section.

(k) *Basis for suspension or debarment.* The Government may consider the following as a ground for suspension or debarment as a willful violation of a regulatory provision or requirement applicable to a public agreement or transaction:

(1) Failure to enter a joint venture agreement that complies with paragraph (c) of this section;

(2) Failure to perform a contract in accordance with the joint venture agreement or performance of work requirements in paragraph (d) of this section; or

(3) Failure to submit the certification required by paragraph (e) or comply with paragraph (i) of this section.

(l) Any person with information concerning a joint venture's compliance with the performance of work requirements may report that information to SBA and/or the SBA Office of Inspector General.

[75 FR 62282, Oct. 7, 2010, as amended at 78 FR 61147, Oct. 2, 2013; 81 FR 34265, May 31, 2016; 81 FR 48593, July 25, 2016; 81 FR 94942, Dec. 27, 2016]

§ 127.507 Are there EDWOSB and WOSB contracting opportunities at or below the simplified acquisition threshold?

If the requirement is valued at or below the simplified acquisition threshold, the contracting officer may set aside the requirement or award the requirement on a sole source basis as set forth in § 127.503.

[80 FR 55022, Sept. 14, 2015]

§ 127.508 May SBA appeal a contracting officer's decision not to make a requirement available for award as a WOSB Program contract?

The Administrator may appeal a contracting officer's decision not to make a particular requirement available for award under the WOSB Program.

§ 127.509 What is the process for such an appeal?

(a) *Notice of appeal.* When the contacting officer rejects a recommendation by SBA's Procurement Center Representative to make a requirement available for the WOSB Program, he or she must notify the Procurement Center Representative as soon as practicable. If the Administrator intends to appeal the decision, SBA must notify the contracting officer no later than five (5) business days after receiving notice of the contracting officer's decision.

(b) *Suspension of action.* Upon receipt of notice of SBA's intent to appeal, the contracting officer must suspend further action regarding the procurement until the Secretary of the department or head of the agency issues a written decision on the appeal, unless the Secretary of the department or head of the agency makes a written determination that urgent and compelling circumstances which significantly affect the interests of the United States compel award of the contract.

(c) *Deadline for appeal.* Within fifteen (15) business days of SBA's notification to the CO, SBA must file its formal appeal with the Secretary of the department or head of the agency, or the appeal will be deemed withdrawn.

(d) *Decision.* The Secretary of the department or head of the agency must specify in writing the reasons for a denial of an appeal brought under this section.

Subpart F—Protests

§ 127.600 Who may protest the status of a concern as an EDWOSB or WOSB?

(a) *For sole source procurements.* SBA or the contracting officer may protest the proposed awardee's EDWOSB or WOSB status.

(b) *For all other EDWOSB or WOSB requirements.* An interested party may protest the apparent successful offeror's EDWOSB or WOSB status.

[80 FR 55022, Sept. 14, 2015]

§ 127.601 May a protest challenging the size and status of a concern as an EDWOSB or WOSB be filed together?

An interested party seeking to protest both the size and the EDWOSB or WOSB status of an apparent successful offeror on an EDWOSB or WOSB requirement must file two separate protests, one size protest pursuant to part 121 of this chapter and one EDWOSB or WOSB status protest pursuant to this subpart. An interested party seeking to protest only the size of an apparent successful EDWOSB or WOSB offeror must file a size protest to the contracting officer pursuant to part 121 of this chapter.

§ 127.602 What are the grounds for filing an EDWOSB or WOSB status protest?

SBA will consider a protest challenging the status of a concern as an EDWOSB or WOSB if the protest presents sufficient credible evidence to show that the concern may not be owned and controlled by one or more women who are United States citizens and, if the protest is in connection with an EDWOSB contract, that the concern is not at least 51 percent owned and controlled by one or more women who are economically disadvantaged. In addition, SBA will consider a protest challenging the status of a concern as an EDWOSB or WOSB if the contracting officer has protested because the WOSB or EDWOSB apparent successful offeror has failed to provide all of the required documents, as set forth in § 127.300.

§ 127.603 What are the requirements for filing an EDWOSB or WOSB protest?

(a) *Format.* Protests must be in writing and must specify all the grounds upon which the protest is based. A protest merely asserting that the protested concern is not an eligible EDWOSB or WOSB, without setting forth specific facts or allegations, is insufficient.

(b) *Filing.* Protestors may deliver their written protests in person, by facsimile, by express delivery service, e-mail, or by U.S. mail (received by the applicable date) to the following:

(1) To the contracting officer, if the protestor is an offeror for the specific contract; or

(2) To the D/GC, if the protest is initiated by the contracting officer or SBA. IF SBA initiates a protest, the D/GC will notify the contracting officer of such protest.

(c) *Timeliness.* (1) For negotiated acquisitions, a protest from an interested party must be received by the contracting officer prior to the close of business on the fifth business day after notification by the contracting officer of the apparent successful offeror or notification of award.

(2) For sealed bid acquisitions, a protest from an interested party must be received by close of business on the fifth business day after bid opening.

(3) Any protest received after the time limit is untimely, unless it is from SBA or the contracting officer. A contracting officer or SBA may file an EDWOSB or WOSB protest at any time after bid opening or notification of intended awardee, whichever applies.

(4) Any protest received prior to bid opening or notification of intended awardee, whichever applies, is premature.

(5) A timely filed protest applies to the procurement in question even if filed after award.

(d) *Referral to SBA.* The contracting officer must forward to SBA any protest received, notwithstanding whether he or she believes it is premature, sufficiently specific, or timely. The contracting officer must send all protests, along with a referral letter and documents, directly to the Director for Government Contracting, U.S. Small Business Administration, 409 Third Street, SW., Washington, DC 20416, or by fax to (202) 205–6390, Attn: Women-Owned Small Business Status Protest. The contracting officer's referral letter must include information pertaining to the solicitation that may be necessary for SBA to determine timeliness and standing, including: the solicitation number; the name, address, telephone number and facsimile number of the contracting officer; whether the protestor submitted an offer; whether the protested concern was the apparent successful offeror; when the protested concern submitted its offer; whether the procurement was conducted using sealed bid or negotiated procedures; the bid opening date, if applicable; when the protest was submitted to the contracting officer; when the protestor received notification about the apparent successful offeror, if applicable; and whether a contract has been awarded. In addition, the contracting officer must send copies of any documents provided to the contracting officer pursuant to § 127.300 (if the repository is unavailable). The D/GC or designee will decide the merits of EDWOSB or WOSB status protests.

§ 127.604 How will SBA process an EDWOSB or WOSB status protest?

(a) *Notice of receipt of protest.* Upon receipt of the protest, SBA will notify the contracting officer and the protestor of the date SBA received the protest and whether SBA will process the protest or dismiss it under paragraph (b) of this section. The contracting officer may award the contract after receipt of a protest if the contracting officer determines in writing that an award must be made to protect the public interest. Notwithstanding such a determination, the provisions of paragraph (f) of this section apply to the procurement in question.

(b) *Dismissal of protest.* If SBA determines that the protest is premature, untimely, nonspecific, or is based on nonprotestable allegations, SBA will dismiss the protest and will send the contracting officer and the protestor a notice of dismissal, citing the reason(s) for the dismissal. Notwithstanding SBA's dismissal of the protest, SBA may, in its sole discretion, consider the protest allegations in determining whether to conduct an examination of the protested concern pursuant to subpart D of this part or submit a protest itself.

(c) *Notice to protested concern.* If SBA determines that the protest is timely, sufficiently specific and is based upon protestable allegations, SBA will:

(1) Notify the protested concern of the protest and request information and documents responding to the protest within five (5) business days from the date of the notice. These documents will include those that verify the eligibility of the concern, respond to the protest allegations, and copies of proposals or bids submitted in response to an EDWOSB or WOSB requirement. In addition, EDWOSBs will be required to submit signed copies of SBA Form 413, Personal Financial Statement, the three most recent personal income tax returns (including all schedules and W–2 forms) for the women claiming economic disadvantage and their spouses, unless the individuals and their spouses are legally separated, and SBA Form 4506–T, Request for Tax Transcript Form. SBA may draw an adverse inference where a concern fails to cooperate in providing the requested information and documents; and

(2) Forward a copy of the protest to the protested concern.

(d) *Time period for determination.* SBA will determine the EDWOSB or WOSB status of the protested concern within fifteen (15) business days after receipt of the protest, or within any extension of that time that the contracting officer may grant SBA. If SBA does not issue its determination within the fifteen (15) business day period (or within any extension of that time the contracting officer has granted), the contracting officer may award the contract if he or she determines in writing that there is an immediate need to award the contract and that waiting until SBA makes its determination will be disadvantageous to the Government. Notwithstanding such a determination, the provisions of paragraph (f) of this section apply to the procurement in question. The determination must be included in the contract file and a written copy sent to the D/GC.

(e) *Notification of determination.* SBA will notify the contracting officer, the protestor, and the protested concern in writing of its determination. If SBA sustains the protest, SBA will issue a decision explaining the basis of its determination and requiring that the concern remove its designation in SAM (or any successor system) as an EDWOSB or WOSB, as appropriate. Regardless of a decision not to sustain the protest, SBA may, in its sole discretion, consider the protest allegations in determining whether to conduct an examination of the protested concern pursuant to subpart D of this part.

(f) *Effect of determination.* SBA's determination is effective immediately and is final unless overturned by SBA's Office of Hearings and Appeals (OHA) on appeal pursuant to § 127.605.

(1) A contracting officer may award the contract to a protested concern after the D/GC either has determined that the protested concern is an eligible WOSB or EDWOSB or has dismissed all protests against it. If OHA subsequently overturns the D/GC's determination or dismissal, the contracting officer may apply the OHA decision to the procurement in question.

(2) A contracting officer shall not award the contract to a protested concern that the D/GC has determined is not an EDWOSB or WOSB for the procurement in question.

(i) If a contracting officer receives such a determination after contract award, and no OHA appeal has been filed, the contracting officer shall terminate the award.

(ii) If a timely OHA appeal has been filed after contract award, the contracting officer must consider whether performance can be suspended until an appellate decision is rendered.

(iii) If OHA affirms the D/GC's determination finding that the protested concern is ineligible, the contracting officer shall either terminate the contract, not exercise the next option or not award further task or delivery orders.

(3) The contracting officer must update the Federal Procurement Data System and other procurement reporting databases to reflect the final agency decision (the D/GC's decision if no appeal is filed or OHA's decision).

(4) A concern that has been found to be ineligible may not submit an offer as a WOSB or EDWOSB on another procurement until it cures the reason(s) for its ineligibility and SBA issues a decision to this effect. A concern that believes in good faith that it has cured the reason(s) for its ineligibility may request an examination under the procedures set forth in § 127.405.

[75 FR 62282, Oct. 7, 2010, as amended at 77 FR 1861, Jan. 12, 2012; 78 FR 61148, Oct. 2, 2013]

§ 127.605 What are the procedures for appealing an EDWOSB or WOSB status protest decision?

The protested concern, the protestor, or the contracting officer may file an appeal of a WOSB or EDWOSB status protest determination with SBA's Office of Hearings and Appeals (OHA) in accordance with part 134 of this chapter.

Subpart G—Penalties

§ 127.700 What are the requirements for representing EDWOSB or WOSB status, and what are the penalties for misrepresentation?

(a) *Presumption of Loss Based on the Total Amount Expended.* In every contract, subcontract, cooperative agreement, cooperative research and development agreement, or grant which is set aside, reserved, or otherwise classified as intended for award to EDWOSBs or WOSBs, there shall be a presumption of loss to the United States based on the total amount expended on the contract, subcontract, cooperative agreement, cooperative research and development agreement, or grant whenever it is established that a business concern other than a EDWOSB or WOSB willfully sought and received the award by misrepresentation.

(b) *Deemed Certifications.* The following actions shall be deemed affirmative, willful and intentional certifications of EDWOSB or WOSB status:

(1) Submission of a bid, proposal, application or offer for a Federal grant, contract, subcontract, cooperative agreement, or cooperative research and development agreement reserved, set aside, or otherwise classified as intended for award to EDWOSBs or WOSBs.

(2) Submission of a bid, proposal, application or offer for a Federal grant, contract, subcontract, cooperative agreement or cooperative research and development agreement which in any way encourages a Federal agency to classify the bid or proposal, if awarded, as an award to a EDWOSB or WOSB.

(3) Registration on any Federal electronic database for the purpose of being considered for award of a Federal grant, contract, subcontract, cooperative agreement, or cooperative research and development agreement, as an EDWOSB or WOSB.

(c) *Signature Requirement.* Each offer, proposal, bid, or application for a Federal contract, subcontract, or grant shall contain a certification concerning the EDWOSB or WOSB status of a business concern seeking the Federal contract, subcontract or grant. An authorized official must sign the certification on the same page containing the EDWOSB or WOSB status claimed by the concern.

(d) *Limitation of Liability.* Paragraphs (a)–(c) of this section may be determined not to apply in the case of unintentional errors, technical malfunctions, and other similar situations that demonstrate that a misrepresentation of EDWOSB or WOSB status was not affirmative, intentional, willful or actionable under the False Claims Act, 31 U.S.C. §§ 3729, et seq. A prime contractor acting in good faith should not be held liable for misrepresentations made by its subcontractors regarding the subcontractors' EDWOSB or WOSB status. Relevant factors to consider in making this determination may include the firm's internal management procedures governing EDWOSB or WOSB status representations or certifications, the clarity or ambiguity of the representation or certification requirement, and the efforts made to correct an incorrect or invalid representation or certification in a timely manner. An individual or firm may not be held liable where government personnel have erroneously identified a concern as an EDWOSB or WOSB without any representation or certification having been made by the concern and where such identification is made without the knowledge of the individual or firm.

(e) *Penalties for Misrepresentation.* (1) *Suspension or debarment.* The SBA suspension and debarment official or the agency suspension and debarment official may suspend or debar a person or concern for misrepresenting a firm's status as an EDWOSB or WOSB pursuant to the procedures set forth in 48 CFR subpart 9.4.

(2) *Civil Penalties.* Persons or concerns are subject to severe penalties under the False Claims Act, 31 U.S.C. 3729–3733, the Program Fraud Civil Remedies Act, 31 U.S.C. 3801–3812, and any other applicable laws or regulations, including 13 CFR part 142.

(3) *Criminal Penalties.* Persons or concerns are subject to severe criminal penalties for knowingly misrepresenting the EDWOSB or WOSB status of a concern in connection with procurement programs pursuant to section 16(d) of the Small Business Act, 15 U.S.C. 645(d), as amended, 18 U.S.C. 1001, 18 U.S.C. 287, and any other applicable laws. Persons or concerns are subject to criminal penalties for knowingly making false statements or misrepresentations to SBA for the purpose of influencing any actions of SBA pursuant to section 16(a) of the Small Business Act, 15 U.S.C. 645(a), as amended, including failure to correct "continuing representations" that are no longer true.

[78 FR 38820, June 28, 2013, as amended at 81 FR 31492, May 19, 2016]

§ 127.701 What must a concern do in order to be identified as an EDWOSB or WOSB in any Federal procurement databases?

(a) In order to be identified as an EDWOSB or WOSB in the System for Award Management (SAM) database (or any successor thereto), a concern must certify its EDWOSB or WOSB status in connection with specific eligibility requirements at least annually.

(b) If a firm identified as an EDWOSB or WOSB in SAM fails to certify its status within one year of a status certification, the firm will not be listed as an EDWOSB or WOSB in SAM, unless and until the firm recertifies its EDWOSB or WOSB status.

[78 FR 38821, June 28, 2013]

PART 130—SMALL BUSINESS DEVELOPMENT CENTERS

AUTHORITY: Sections 5(b)(6) and 21 of the Small Business Act, as amended, 15 U.S.C. 634(b)(6) and 648; Pub. L. 101–515, 101 Stat. 2101; Pub. L. 101–574, 104 Stat. 2814; Pub. L.

102–366, 106 Stat. 986; and Pub. L. 102–395, 106 Stat. 1828.

SOURCE: 60 FR 31056, June 13, 1995, unless otherwise noted.

§ 130.100 Introduction.

(a) *Objective.* The SBDC Program creates a broad-based system of assistance for the small business community by linking the resources of Federal, State and local governments with the resources of the educational community and the private sector. Although SBA is responsible for the general management and oversight of the SBDC Program, a partnership exists between SBA and the recipient organization for the delivery of assistance to the small business community.

(b) *Incorporation of amended references.* All references in these regulations to OMB Circulars, other SBA regulations, Standard Operating Procedures, and other sources of SBA policy guidance incorporate all ensuing changes or amendments to such sources.

§ 130.110 Definitions.

Applicant organization. An entity, described in § 130.200(a), which applies to establish and operate an SBDC network.

Application. The written submission by a new applicant organization or an existing recipient organization explaining its projected SBDC activities for the upcoming budget period and requesting SBA funding for use in its operations.

Area of Service. The State or territory, or portion of a State or territory (when there is more than one SBDC in a State or territory), or the District of Columbia, in which an applicant organization proposes to provide services or in which a recipient organization provides services.

Budget period. The 12-month period in which expenditure obligations are incurred by an SBDC network, coinciding with either the calendar year or the Federal fiscal year.

Cash Match. Non-Federal funds allocated specifically to the operation of the SBDC network equalling no less than fifty percent of the Federal funds. Cash Match includes direct costs committed by the applicant or recipient organization and sponsoring SBDC organizations, to the extent that such costs are committed as part of the verified, specific, line item direct costs prior to funding. Cash Match does not include indirect costs, overhead costs or in-kind contributions.

Cognizant Agency. The Federal agency, other than SBA, from which a recipient organization or sponsoring SBDC organization receives its largest grant or greatest amount of Federal funding, and from which it obtains an indirect cost rate for budgetary and funding purposes, applicable throughout the Federal government.

Cooperative Agreement. The written contract between SBA and a recipient organization, describing the conditions under which SBA awards Federal funds and recipient organizations provide services to the small business community.

Cosponsorship. A "Cosponsorship" as defined in and governed by § 8(b)(1)(A) of the Act and SBA's Standard Operating Procedures.

Counseling. Individual advice, guidance or instruction given to a small business person or entity.

Direct costs: "Direct costs" as defined in Office of Management and Budget (OMB) Circulars A–21, A–87 and A–122. Recipient organizations must allocate at least 80 percent of the Federal funds provided through the Cooperative Agreement to the direct costs of program delivery.

Dispute. Dispute means a program or financial disagreement which the recipient organization requests be handled with SBA in a formal manner.

Grants and Cooperative Agreement Appeals Committee. The SBA committee, appointed by the SBA Administrator, which resolves appeals arising from financial Disputes between a recipient organization and SBA.

Grants Management Specialist. An SBA employee designated by the AA/SBDCs who is responsible for the financial review, award, and administration of one or more SBDC Cooperative Agreements.

In-kind contributions. Property, facilities, services or other non-monetary contributions from non-federal sources. *See* OMB Circular A–87, A–102, or A–110, as appropriate.

Indirect costs. "Indirect costs" as defined in Office of Management and Budget (OMB) Circular A–21, A–87 or A–122.

Lead Center. The entity which administers and operates the SBDC network.

Lobbying. Lobbying as described in OMB Circulars A–21, A–87 and A–122, and Pub. L. 101–121, section 319.

Overmatched Amount. Non-Federal Contributions to SBDC project costs, including cash, in-kind contributions and indirect costs, in excess of the statutorily required amount.

Program Announcement. SBA's annual publication of requirements which an applicant or recipient organization must address in its initial or renewal application.

Program income. Income earned or received by the SBDC network from any SBDC supported activity as defined in Attachment D of OMB Circular A–110 and Attachment E of OMB Circular A–102.

Program manager. An SBA employee responsible for overseeing the operations of one or more SBDCs.

Project officer. An SBA employee who negotiates the annual Cooperative Agreement and monitors the ongoing operations of an SBDC.

Project period. The period of time, usually in twelve (12) month increments, during which the SBDC network operates, beginning on the day of award and continuing over a number of budget periods.

Recipient organization. The name given to an applicant organization after funding is approved and the applicant organization enters into a Cooperative Agreement. The recipient organization receives the Federal funds and is responsible for establishing the Lead Center.

Recognized Organization. The organization whose members include a majority of SBDCs and which is recognized as an SBDC representative by SBA in accordance with §21(a)(3)(A) of the Small Business Act, 15 U.S.C. 648(a)(3)(A).

SBDC Director. The full-time senior manager designated by each recipient organization and approved by SBA.

SBDC network. The Lead Center and SBDC service providers.

SBDC service providers. SBDC network participants, including the Lead Center, subcenters (at times referred to as regional centers), satellite locations, and any other entity authorized by the recipient organization to perform SBDC services.

Specialized Services. SBDC services other than Counseling and Training.

Sponsoring SBDC organizations. Organizations or entities which establish one or more SBDC service providers as part of the SBDC network under a contract or agreement with the recipient organization.

Training. The provision of advice, guidance and instruction to groups of prospective and existing small business persons and entities, whether by in-person group sessions or by such communication modes as teleconferences, videos, publications and electronic media.

§ 130.200 Eligible entities.

(a) *Recipient Organization.* The following entities are eligible to operate an SBDC network:

(1) A public or private institution of higher education;

(2) A land-grant college or university;

(3) A college or school of business, engineering, commerce or agriculture;

(4) A community or junior college;

(5) An entity formed by two or more of the above entities; or

(6) Any entity which was operating as a recipient organization as of December 31, 1990.

(b) *SBDC Service Providers.* SBDC service providers are not required to meet the eligibility requirements of a recipient organization.

§ 130.300 Small Business Development Centers (SBDCs). [Reserved]

§ 130.310 Area of service.

The AA/SBDC shall designate in writing the Area of Service of each recipient organization, consistent with the State plan. More than one recipient organization may be located in a State or Territory if the AA/SBDC determines it is necessary or beneficial to implement the Program effectively and to provide services to all interested small businesses.

§ 130.320 Location of lead centers and SBDC service providers.

(a) The recipient organization must locate its Lead Center and SBDC service providers so that services are readily accessible to small businesses in the Area of Service.

(b) The locations of the Lead Center and the SBDC service providers will be reviewed by SBA as part of the application review process for each budget period.

§ 130.330 Operating requirements.

(a) The Lead Center must be an independent entity within the recipient organization, having its own staff, including a full-time SBDC Director.

(b) A Lead Center must provide administrative services and coordination for the SBDC network, including program development, program management, financial management, reports management, promotion and public relations, program assessment and evaluation, and internal quality control.

(c) The Lead Center shall be open to the public throughout the year during the normal business hours of the recipient organization. Anticipated closures shall be included in the annual renewal application. Emergency closures shall be reported to the SBA Project Officer as soon as is feasible. Other SBDC service providers shall be open during the normal business hours of their sponsoring SBDC organizations.

(d) The Lead Center and other SBDC service providers must have a conflict of interest policy applicable to their SBDC consultants, employees, instructors and volunteers.

(e) The SBDC network shall comply with 13 CFR parts 112, 113 and 117, which require that no person shall be excluded on the grounds of age, color, handicap, marital status, national origin, race, religion or sex from participation in, be denied that benefits of, or otherwise be subjected to discrimination under, any program or activity for which the recipient organization received Federal financial assistance from SBA.

§ 130.340 SBDC services and restrictions on service.

(a) *Services.* The SBDC network must provide prospective and existing small business persons and entities with Counseling, Training and Specialized Services, concerning the formation, financing, management and operation of small business enterprises, reflecting local needs. The recipient organization shall primarily utilize institutions of higher education to provide services to the small business community. To the extent possible, SBDCs shall use other Federal, State, and local government programs that assist small business. Services periodically should be assessed and improved to keep pace with changing small business needs.

(b) *Access to Capital.* (1) SBDCs are encouraged to provide counseling services that increase a small business concern's access to capital, such as business plan development, financial statement preparation and analysis, and cash flow preparation and analysis.

(2) SBDCs should help prepare their clients to represent themselves to lending institutions. While SBDCs may attend meetings with lenders to assist clients in preparing financial packages, the SBDCs may not take a direct role in representing clients in loan negotiations.

(3) SBDCs should inform their clients that financial packaging assistance does not guarantee receipt of a loan.

(4) SBDCs may not make loans, service loans or make credit decisions regarding the award of loans.

(5) With respect to SBA guaranty programs, SBDCs may assist clients to formulate a business plan, prepare financial statements, complete forms which are part of a loan application, and accompany an applicant appearing before SBA. Unless authorized by the SBA Administrator with respect to a specific program, an SBDC may not advocate, recommend approval or otherwise attempt in any manner to influence SBA to provide financial assistance to any of its clients. An SBDC cannot collect fees for helping a client to prepare an application for SBA financial assistance.

(c) *Special emphasis initiatives.* From time to time, SBA may identify portions of the general population to be targeted for assistance by SBDCs. Support of SBA special emphasis initiatives will be negotiated each year as part of the application process and included in the Cooperative Agreement when appropriate.

§ 130.350 Specific program responsibilities.

(a) *Policy development.* SBA will establish Program policies and procedures to improve the delivery of services by SBDCs to the small business community, and to enhance compliance with applicable laws, regulations, OMB Circulars and Executive Orders. In doing so, SBA should consult, to the extent practicable, with the Recognized Organization.

(b) *Responsibilities of SBDC Directors.* The SBDC Director shall direct and monitor program activities and financial affairs of the SBDC network to deliver effective services to the small business community, comply with applicable laws, regulations, OMB Circulars and Executive Orders, and implement the Cooperative Agreement. The SBDC Director has authority to control expenditures under the Lead Center's budget. SBDC Directors may manage other programs in addition to the SBDC Program if the programs serve small businesses and do not duplicate the services provided by the SBDC network. However, SBDC Directors may not receive additional compensation for managing these programs. The SBDC Director shall serve as the principal contact point for all matters involving the SBDC network.

§ 130.360 SBDC advisory boards.

(a) *State/Regional Advisory Boards.* (1) The Lead Center must establish an advisory board to advise, counsel, and confer with the SBDC Director on matters pertaining to the operation of the SBDC network.

(2) The advisory board shall be referred to as a State SBDC Advisory Board in an Area of Service having only one recipient organization, and a Regional SBDC Advisory Board in an Area of Service having more than one recipient organization.

(3) These advisory boards must include small business owners and other representatives from the entire Area of Service.

(4) New Lead Centers must establish a State or Regional SBDC Advisory Board no later than the second budget period.

(5) A State or Regional SBDC Advisory Board member may also be a member of the National SBDC Advisory Board.

(6) The reasonable cost of travel of any Board member for official Board activities may be paid out of the SBDC's budgeted funds.

(b) *National SBDC Advisory Board.* (1) SBA shall establish a National SBDC Advisory Board consisting of nine members who are not Federal employees, appointed by the SBA Administrator. The Board shall elect a Chair. Three members of the Board shall be from universities or their affiliates and six shall be from small businesses or associations representing small businesses. Board members shall serve staggered three year terms, with three Board members appointed each year. The SBA Administrator may appoint successors to fill unexpired terms.

(2) The National SBDC Advisory Board shall advise and confer with SBA's AA/SBDCs on policy matters pertaining to the operation of the SBDC program. The Board shall meet with the AA/SBDCs at least semiannually.

§ 130.400 Application procedure. [Reserved]

§ 130.410 New applications.

(a) If SBA declines to renew an existing recipient organization or the recipient organization declines to reapply, SBA may accept applications from other organizations interested in becoming a recipient organization. An eligible entity may apply by submitting an application to the SBA District Office in the Area of Service in which the applicant proposes to provide services.

(b) An application for initial funding of a new SBDC network must include a letter by the Governor, or his or her designee, of the Area of Service in which the SBDC will operate, or other evidence, confirming that the applicant's designation as an SBDC would be consistent with the plan adopted by the State government and approved by SBA. No such requirement is imposed on subsequent applications from existing recipient organizations.

(c) The application must set forth the eligible entity or entities proposing to operate the SBDC network; a list of the Lead Center and other SBDC service providers by name, address and telephone number; the geographic areas to be serviced; the resources to be used; the services that will be provided; the method for delivering the services, including a description of how and to what extent academic, private and public resources will be used; a budget; a listing of the proposed members of the State or Regional Advisory Board and other relevant information set forth in the Program Announcement.

(d) SBA officials may request supplemental information or documentation to revise or complete an application.

(e) Upon written recommendation for approval by the SBA District Director, the proposal shall be submitted to the AA/SBDCs for review.

§ 130.420 Renewal applications.

(a) SBDCs shall comply with the requirements in the annual Program Announcement, including format and due dates, to receive consideration of their renewal applications. The SBA Project Officer, with the concurrence of the Program Manager, may grant an extension. The recipient organization shall submit the renewal application to the SBA office in the District in which the recipient organization is located. The annual Program Announcement will include a timetable for SBA review.

(b) After review by the SBA Project Officer and written recommendation for approval by the District Director, the Program Manager and Grants Management Specialist shall review the renewal application for conformity with the Program Announcement, OMB Circulars and all other statutory, financial and regulatory requirements. SBA officials may request supplemental information and documentation prior to issuing the Cooperative Agreement.

§ 130.430 Application decisions.

(a) The AA/SBDCs may approve, conditionally approve, or reject any application. In the event of a rejection, the AA/SBDCs shall communicate the reasons for rejection to the applicant and the appropriate SBA field office. If the approval is conditional, the conditions and applicable remedies shall be specified as special terms and conditions in the Cooperative Agreement. Upon approval or conditional approval, the Grants Management specialist may issue a Cooperative Agreement.

(b) In considering the application, significant factors shall include:

(1) The applicant's ability to contribute Matching Funds;

(2) For renewal Proposals, the quality of prior performance;

(3) The results of any examination conducted pursuant to § 130.810(b) of these regulations; and

(4) Any certification resulting from any certification program developed by the Recognized Organization.

(c) In the event of a conditional approval, SBA may conditionally fund a recipient organization for one or more specified periods of time up to a maximum of one budget period. If the recipient organization fails to resolve the specified matters to the AA/SBDCs' satisfaction within the allotted time period, SBA has the right to discontinue funding the SBDC, subject to the provisions of § 130.700.

§ 130.440 Maximum grant.

No recipient shall receive an SBDC grant exceeding the greater of the minimum statutory amount, or its pro rata share of all SBDC grants as determined by the statutory formula set forth in section 21(a)(4) of the Act.

§ 130.450 Matching funds.

(a) The recipient organization must provide total Matching Funds equal to the total amount of SBA funding. At least 50% of the Matching Funds must be Cash Match. The remaining 50% may be provided through any allowable combination of additional cash, in-kind contributions, or indirect costs.

(b) All sources of Matching Funds must be identified as specifically as possible in the budget proposal. Cash sources shall be identified by name and account. All applicants must submit a

Certification of Cash Match and Program Income executed by an authorized official of the recipient organization or any sponsoring SBDC organization providing Cash Match through a subcontract agreement. The account containing such cash must be under the direct management of the SBDC Director, or, if provided by a sponsoring SBDC organization, its subcenter Director. If a political entity is providing such cash and the funds have not been appropriated prior to issuance of the Cooperative Agreement, the recipient organization must certify that sufficient funds will be available from the political entity prior to the use of Federal dollars.

(c) The Grants Management Specialist is responsible for determining whether Matching Funds or Cash Match meet the requirements of the Act and appropriate OMB circulars.

(d) *Overmatched Amounts.* (1) SBDC are encouraged to furnish Overmatched Amounts.

(2) An Overmatched Amount can be applied to additional Matching Funds requirements necessitated by any supplemental funding increase received by the SBDC during the budget period, as long as the total Cash Match provided by the SBDC is 50% or more of the total SBA funds provided during the budget period.

(3) If used in the manner described in paragraph (d)(2) of this section, such Overmatched Amount is reclassified as committed Matching Funds.

(4) Allowable Overmatched Amounts which have not been used in the manner described in paragraph (d)(2) of this section may, with the approval of the AA/SBDCs, be used as a credit to offset any confirmed audit disallowances applicable only to the budget period in which the Overmatched Amount exists and the two previous budget periods. Such offsetting funds shall be considered Matching Funds.

(e) *Impermissible sources of Matching Funds.* Under no circumstances may the following be used as sources of the Matching Funds of the recipient organization:

(1) Uncompensated student labor;

(2) SCORE, ACE, or SBI volunteers;

(3) Program income or fees collected from small businesses receiving assistance;

(4) Funds or indirect or in-kind contributions from any other Federal source.

§ 130.460 Budget justification.

The SBDC Director, as a part of the renewal application, or the applicant organization's authorized representative in the case of a new SBDC application, shall prepare and submit to the SBA Project Officer the budget justification for the upcoming budget period. The budget shall be reviewed annually upon submission of a renewal application.

(a) *Direct costs.* Unless otherwise provided in applicable OMB circulars, at least eighty percent (80%) of SBA funding must be allocated to direct costs of Program delivery.

(b) *Indirect costs.* If the applicant organization waives all indirect costs to meet the Matching Funds requirement, one hundred percent (100%) of SBA funding must be allocated to program delivery. If some, but not all, indirect costs are waived to meet the Matching Funds requirement, the lesser of the following may be allocated as indirect costs of the Program and charged against the Federal contribution:

(1) Twenty percent (20%) of Federal contribution, or

(2) The amount remaining after the waived portion of indirect costs is subtracted from the total indirect costs.

(c) *Separate SBDC service provider budgets.* (1) The applicant organization shall include separate budgets for all subcontracted SBDC service providers in conformity with OMB requirements. Applicable direct cost categories and indirect cost base/rate agreements shall be included for the Lead Center and all SBDC service providers, using a rate equal to or less than the negotiated predetermined rate. If no such rate exists, the sponsoring SBDC organization or SBDC service provider shall negotiate a rate with its Cognizant Agency. In the event the sponsoring SBDC organization or SBDC service provider does not have a Cognizant Agency, the rate shall be negotiated with the SBA Project Officer in accordance with OMB guidelines (see OMB Circular A–21).

(2) The amount of cash, in-kind contributions and indirect costs for the Lead Center and all sub-contracted SBDC service providers shall be indicated in accordance with OMB requirements.

(d) *Cost principles.* Principles for determining allowable costs are contained in OMB Circulars A–21 (cost principles for grants, contracts, and other agreements with educational institutions), A–87 (cost principles for programs administered by State and local governments), and A–122 (cost principles for nonprofit organizations).

(e) *Costs associated with lobbying.* No portion of the Federal contribution received by an SBDC may be used for lobbying activities, either directly by the SBDC or indirectly through outside organizations, except those activities permitted by OMB. Restrictions on and reports of lobbying activities by the SBDC shall be in accordance with OMB requirements, Section 319 of Public Law No. 101–121, and the annual Program Announcement.

(f) *Salaries.* (1) If a recipient organization is an educational institution, the salaries of the SBDC Director and the subcenter Directors must approximate the average annualized salary of a full professor and an assistant professor, respectively, in the school or department in which the SBDC is located. If a recipient organization is not an educational institution, the salaries of the SBDC Director and the subcenter Directors must approximate the average salaries of parallel positions within the recipient organization. In both cases, the recipient organization should consider the Director's longevity in the Program, the number of subcenters and the individual's experience and background.

(2) Salaries for all other positions within the SBDC should be based upon level of responsibility, and be comparable to salaries for similar positions in the area served by the SBDC.

(3) Recruitment and salary increases for SBDC Directors, subcenter Directors and staff members should conform to the administrative policy of the recipient organization.

(g) *Travel.* All travel must be separately identified in the proposed budget as planned in-State, planned out-of-State, unplanned in-State or unplanned out-of-State. All proposed travel must use coach class, apply directly to specific work of the SBDC or be incurred in the normal course of Program administration, and conform to the written travel policies of the recipient organization or the sponsoring SBDC organization. (Per diem rates, including lodging, shall not exceed those authorized by the recipient organization.) Transportation costs must be justified in writing, including the estimated cost, number of persons traveling, and the benefit to be derived by the small business community from the proposed travel. A specific projected amount, based on the SBDC's past experience, where appropriate, must also be included in the budget for unplanned travel. A more detailed justification must be given for unplanned out-of-State travel. Any proposed unplanned out-of-State travel exceeding the approved budgeted amount for travel must be submitted to the Project Officer for approval on a case-by-case basis. Travel outside the United States must have prior approval by the AA/SBDCs on a case-by-case basis.

(h) *Dues.* Costs of memberships in business, technical, and professional organizations shall be allowable expenses. The use of Federal funds to pay dues for business, technical and professional organizations shall be permitted, provided that the payments are included in the budget proposal, are approved by the SBA and comply with § 130.460(e).

§ 130.470 Fees.

An SBDC may charge clients a reasonable fee to cover the costs of Training sponsored or cosponsored by the SBDC, costs of services provided by or obtained from third parties, or the costs of providing Specialized Services. Fees may not be imposed for Counseling.

§ 130.480 Program income.

(a) Program income for recipient organizations or SBDC service providers based in universities or nonprofit organizations shall be subject to OMB requirements (see OMB Circular A–110). Program income for recipient organizations or SBDC service providers based in State or local governments shall be subject to OMB requirements (see the provisions of §7.e and Attachment E of OMB Circular A–102) and 13 CFR 143.25.

(b) Program income, including any interest earned on Program income, must be used to expand the quantity or quality of services, resources or outreach provided by the SBDC network. It cannot be used to satisfy the requirements for Matching Funds. The Project Officer shall monitor the use of Program income. Any unused Program income will be carried over to a subsequent budget period.

(c) SBDCs must report in detail on standard SBA forms receipts and expenditures of program income, including any income received through cosponsored activities. A narrative description of how Program income was used to accomplish Program objectives shall be included.

§ 130.500 Funding.

The SBA funds Cooperative Agreements through its internal Letter of Credit Replacement System (LORS), using SBA standard forms to establish and modify letters of credit. SBDCs must use SBA standard forms to draw down funds required to meet their estimated or actual expenses and to submit quarterly cash transactions reports used by SBA to monitor the frequency of drawdowns and the cash-on-hand balance. Repeated drawdowns in excess of immediate cash needs may result in the cancellation of the letter of credit. If interest results from the deposit of any drawdowns in an interest-bearing account, SBDCs, other than State government sponsored SBDCs, must report and return such interest annually to SBA.

§ 130.600 Cooperative agreement. [Reserved]

§ 130.610 General terms.

Upon approval of the initial or renewal application, SBA will enter into a Cooperative Agreement with the recipient organization, setting forth the programmatic and fiscal responsibilities of the recipient organization and SBA, the scope of the project to be funded, and the budget of the program year covered by the Cooperative Agreement. Administrative requirements are contained in 13 CFR 143 and applicable OMB Circulars.

§ 130.620 Revisions and amendments to cooperative agreement.

(a) *Requests for revisions.* The recipient organization may request at any time one or more revisions to the Cooperative Agreement on an appropriate SBA form signed by the recipient organization's authorized representative (including a revised budget and budget narrative, if applicable). Revisions will normally relate to changes in scope, work or funding during the specified budget year.

(b) *Revisions which require amendment to Cooperative Agreement.* The Cooperative Agreement shall list the revisions which require Project Officer concurrence, review by the Program Manager and the Grants Management Specialist, approval of the AA/SBDCs and amendment of the Cooperative Agreement. No application for an amendment shall be effective until it is approved and incorporated into the Cooperative Agreement. Revisions which require amendments shall include:

(1) Any change in project scope or objectives;

(2) The addition or deletion of any subgrants or contracts;

(3) The addition of any new budget line items;

(4) Budget revisions and fund reallocations exceeding the limit established by applicable administrative regulations or OMB Circulars, either individually or in the aggregate (*see* paragraphs (c)(1) and (c)(2) of this section);

(5) Any proposed sole-source or one-bid contracts exceeding the limits established by applicable regulations or OMB Circulars; and

(6) The carryover from one budget period to the next budget period of unobligated, unexpended SBA funds allocable under the Cooperative Agreement to nonrecurring, nonseverable bona

fide needs of the SBDC network as provided in applicable OMB Circulars and the annual Program Announcement.

(c) *Revisions which do not require amendments to the Cooperative Agreement*—(1) *Budget revisions.* Any budget revision, except those which are covered by paragraph (b)(4) of this section. Budget revisions require approval of the SBA Project Officer and the AA/SBDCs as prescribed by applicable OMB Circulars or 13 CFR 143.30.

(2) *Reallocation of funds.* Reallocation of funds must be conducted in accordance with applicable OMB Circulars or 13 CFR 143.30. Additional guidance on this matter may be included in the annual Program Announcement.

§ 130.630 Dispute resolution procedures.

(a) *Financial Disputes.* (1) A recipient organization wishing to resolve a financial Dispute formally must submit a written statement describing the subject of the Dispute, together with any relevant documents or other evidence bearing on the Dispute, to the Grants Management Specialist, with copies to the Project Officer. The Grants Management Specialist shall respond in writing to the recipient organization within 30 calendar days of receipt of the descriptive statement.

(2) If the recipient organization receives an unfavorable decision from the Grants Management Specialist, it may file an appeal with the AA/SBDCs within 30 calendar days of issuance of the unfavorable decision. The AA/SBDCs shall respond in writing to the recipient organization within 15 calendar days of receipt of the appeal.

(3) If the recipient organization receives an unfavorable decision from the AA/SBDCs, it may make a final appeal to the SBA Grants and Cooperative Agreements Appeals Committee (the "Committee") within 30 calendar days of the date of issuance of the AA/SBDCs' written decision. Copies of the appeal shall also be sent to the Grants Management Specialist and the Project Officer.

(4) Appeals must be in writing. Formal briefs and other technical forms of pleading are not required. Requests for a hearing will not be granted unless there are material facts substantially in dispute. Appeals must contain at least the following:

(i) Name and address of the recipient organization;

(ii) The SBA field office;

(iii) The Cooperative Agreement;

(iv) A statement of the grounds for appeal, with reasons why the appeal should be sustained;

(v) The specific relief desired on appeal; and

(vi) If a hearing is requested, a statement of the material facts which are substantially in dispute.

(5) The AA/SBDCs or the Committee may request from the SBDC or the District Office additional information or documentation at any stage in the proceedings.

(6) If a request for a hearing is granted, the Committee will provide the recipient organization with written instructions, and will afford the parties an opportunity to present their positions to the Committee.

(7) The Committee will reach a decision on the merits of the appeal within 30 days of the hearing date.

(8) The Chairperson, with advice from the Office of General Counsel, shall prepare and transmit a written final decision to the recipient organization with copies to the Grants Management Specialist and the Project Officer.

(9) *Expedited Dispute appeal process.* By an affirmative vote constituting a majority of its total membership, the Committee may shorten response times to attain final resolution of a Dispute before the issuance date of a new Cooperative Agreement. At any time within 120 days of the end of the budget period, the recipient organization may submit a written request to use an expedited process. If a Dispute affects refunding, the Committee must meet to consider the matter prior to the end of the budget period, provided that the recipient organization has supplied the Committee with all requested documentation.

(b) *Programmatic (non-financial) Disputes.* (1) If a programmatic Dispute is not resolved at the SBA District Office level, the recipient organization may request its submission to the next SBA administrative level having authority to review such matter. The Project Officer shall refer the Dispute in writing, including comments of the SBDC Director, within 15 calendar days of receipt of the request.

(2) If the programmatic Dispute is not resolved at an intermediate SBA administrative level within 15 calendar days of receipt thereof, it shall be forwarded, in writing, to the AA/SBDCs for final resolution. All comments of the SBDC Director must be included in any package forwarded to the AA/SBDCs.

(3) The AA/SBDCs shall transmit a final, written decision to the recipient organization, the SBDC Director, the SBA Project Officer and other appropriate SBA field office personnel within 30 calendar days of receipt of such documentation, unless an extension of time is mutually agreed upon by the recipient organization and the AA/SBDCs.

§ 130.700 Suspension, termination and non-renewal.

(a) *General.* After SBA has entered into a Cooperative Agreement with a recipient organization, it shall not suspend, terminate or fail to renew the agreement unless SBA gives the recipient organization written notice setting forth the reasons and affording the recipient organization an opportunity for a hearing. Subject to this requirement and the provisions of § 130.700(c) regarding non-renewal procedures for nonperformance, the applicable general procedures for suspension and termination are contained in 13 CFR 143.43 and 143.44, and in OMB Circular A–110, Attachment L.

(b) *Causes.* Causes which may lead to suspension, termination, or failure to renew include non-performance, poor performance, unwillingness to implement changes to improve performance, or any of the following reasons:

(1) Disregard or material violation of these regulations;

(2) A willful or material failure to perform under the Cooperative Agreement or under these regulations;

(3) Conduct reflecting a lack of business integrity or honesty;

(4) A conflict of interest causing real or perceived detriment to a small business concern, a contractor, the SBDC or SBA;

(5) Improper use of Federal funds;

(6) Failure of a Lead Center or its subcenters to consent to audits or examination or to maintain required documents or records;

(7) Failure of the SBDC Director to work at the SBDC Lead Center on a full-time basis;

(8) Failure promptly to suspend or terminate the employment of an SBDC Director, subcenter Director or other key employee upon receipt of knowledge by the recipient organization and/or SBA that such individual is engaging in or has engaged in conduct resulting in a criminal conviction or civil judgment which would cause the public to question the SBDC's business integrity, taking into consideration such factors as the magnitude, repetitiveness, harm caused and remoteness in time of the activity or activities underlying the conviction or judgment.

(9) Violation of the SBDC's standards of conduct as specified in these rules and as established by the SBDC pursuant to these rules; or

(10) Any other cause not otherwise specified which materially and adversely affects the operation or integrity of an SBDC or the SBDC program.

(c) *Non-Renewal Procedure.* (1) Subject to § 130.700(a), when an SBA District Director believes there is sufficient evidence of SBDC nonperformance, poor performance or unwillingness to implement changes to improve performance, under the terms of the Cooperative Agreement or these regulations, the District Director shall notify the SBDC Director and any other appropriate official of the recipient organization of an intention not to approve its renewal application.

(2) Notice can be submitted at any time during the budget period, but normally should be sent no later than 3 months prior to the due date for renewal applications at the District Office.

(3) The notice shall specifically cite the reasons for the intention not to renew. It must allow the recipient organization 60 days within which to change its operations to correct the problems cited in the notice, and to report to the Project Officer, in writing, regarding the results of such changes.

(4) If the recipient organization is unwilling or unable to address the specific problem areas to the satisfaction of the SBA District Office within the 60-day period, the SBA Project Officer shall have ten (10) calendar days after expiration of the 60 days to submit to the AA/SBDCs a written description of the unresolved issues, a summary of the positions of the District Office on the issues, and any supportive documentation.

(5) The AA/SBDCs shall transmit a written, final decision to the recipient organization, the SBDC Director, the SBA Project Officer and other appropriate SBA field office personnel within 30 calendar days of receipt of such documentation, unless an extension of time is mutually agreed upon by the recipient organization and the AA/SBDCs.

(6) The AA/SBDCs shall consider written documentation of the issues to be resolved, including all relevant correspondence between the Project Officer, District Director and any other SBA personnel and the affected recipient organization. At a minimum, such documentation shall commence with the first written notice of issues invoking the non-renewal procedure. In addition, the AA/SBDCs also may communicate with the recipient organization and appropriate SBA personnel.

(7) If the AA/SBDCs determines that the evidence submitted establishes nonperformance, ineffective performance or an unwillingness to implement suggested changes to improve performance, the AA/SBDCs shall have full discretion to order non-renewal of the SBDC. The SBA District Office shall then pursue proposals from other organizations interested in applying for SBDC designation. The incumbent SBDC shall have until the end of the budget period or 120 days, whichever is longer, to conclude operations and to submit close-out documents to the SBA District Office. Close-out procedures shall conform with applicable OMB Circulars.

(d) *Effect of action on subcenter.* If competing applications are being accepted, a subcenter of the previously funded recipient organization may apply for designation as the recipient organization, so long as the subcenter was not involved in the conduct leading to non-renewal or termination of the former recipient organization.

§ 130.800 Oversight of the SBDC program.

SBA shall monitor and oversee the Cooperative Agreement and ongoing operations of the SBDC network to ensure the effective and efficient use of Federal funds for the benefit of the small business community.

§ 130.810 SBA review authority.

(a) *Site visits.* The AA/SBDCs, or a representative, on notice to the SBDC Director, is authorized to make programmatic and financial review visits to SBDC service providers to inspect records and client files, and to analyze and assess SBDC activities.

(b) *SBA examinations.* SBA examiners shall perform a biannual programmatic and financial examination of each SBDC.

(c) *Certification program.* SBA may provide financial support to the Recognized Organization to develop and implement an SBDC certification program.

(d) *Audits.* The examinations by SBA examiners shall not substitute for audits required of Federal grantees under the Single Audit Act of 1984 or applicable OMB guidelines (see Circulars A–110, A–128 and A–133), nor shall such internal review substitute for audits to be conducted by the SBA Office of Inspector General under authority of the Inspector General Act of 1978, as amended (see § 130.830(b)).

§ 130.820 Reports and recordkeeping.

(a) *Records.* The recipient organization shall maintain the records required for a Lead Center audit and SBA reports. Lead Centers and other SBDC service providers shall maintain detailed, complete and accurate client activity files, specifying counseling, training and other assistance provided.

(b) *Reports.* The recipient organization shall submit client service evaluations and performance and financial reports for SBA review to determine the quality of services provided by the SBDC, the completeness and accuracy of SBDC records, and actual SBDC network accomplishments compared to performance objectives.

(c) *Performance reports.* For recipient organizations in the Program for more than three years, interim reports shall be due 30 days after completion of six months of operation each year; for those recipient organizations in the Program three years or less, reports shall be due 30 days after completion of each of the first three quarters. The annual report shall include the second semiannual or the fourth quarter report and shall be due December 30 for fiscal year and March 30 for calendar year SBDCs. These reports shall reflect accurately the activities, accomplishments and deficiencies of the SBDC network.

(d) *Financial reports.* The recipient organization shall provide three quarterly and one annual financial report to the SBA Project Officer as set forth in the Program Announcement and the Cooperative Agreement, in compliance with OMB Circulars.

(e) *Availability of records.* As required by OMB (see Circular A–133), all SBDC service provider records shall be made available to SBA for review upon request.

§ 130.830 Audits and investigations.

(a) *Access to records.* Applicable OMB Circulars set forth the requirements concerning record access and retention.

(b) *Audits*—(1) *Pre-award audit.* Applicant organizations that propose to enter the Program for the first time may be subject to a pre-award audit conducted by or coordinated with the SBA Office of Inspector General. The purpose of a pre-award audit is to verify the adequacy of the accounting system, the suitability of posed costs and the nature and source of proposed Matching Funds.

(2) *Interim or final audits.* The recipient organization or SBA may conduct SBDC network audits. All audits will be conducted according to *Government Auditing Standards*, promulgated by the Comptroller General of the United States.

(i) The recipient organization will conduct its audits as a single audit of a recipient organization pursuant to OMB Circulars A–102, A–110, A–128, and A–133, as applicable.

(ii) The SBA Office of Inspector General or its agents will conduct, supervise, or coordinate SBA's audits, which may, at SBA's discretion, be audits of the SBDC network, even though single audits may have been performed. In such instances, SBA will conduct such audits in compliance with *Government Auditing Standards* and all applicable OMB Circulars.

(c) *Investigations.* SBA may conduct investigations as it deems necessary to determine whether any person or entity has engaged in acts or practices constituting a violation of the Act, any rule, regulation or order issued under that Act, or any other applicable Federal law.

PART 134—RULES OF PROCEDURE GOVERNING CASES BEFORE THE OFFICE OF HEARINGS AND APPEALS

Subpart A—General Rules

Subpart B—Rules of Practice

Subpart C—Rules of Practice for Appeals From Size Determinations and NAICS Code Designations

Subpart D—Rules of Practice for Appeals Under the 8(a) Program

Subpart E—Rules of Practice for Appeals From Service-Disabled Veteran Owned Small Business Concern Protests

Subpart F—Implementation of the Equal Access to Justice Act

Subpart G—Rules of Practice for Appeals From Women-Owned Small Business Concern (WOSB) and Economically Disadvantaged WOSB Concern (EDWOSB) Protests

Subpart H—Rules of Practice for Employee Disputes

Subpart I—Rules of Practice for Petitions for Reconsideration of Size Standards

Subpart J—Rules of Practice for Protests of Eligibility for Inclusion in the U.S. Department of Veterans Affairs (VA) Center for Verification and Evaluation (CVE) Database (CVE Protests)

Subpart K—Rules of Practice for Appeals of Denials and Cancellations of Verification for Inclusion in the U.S. Department of Veterans Affairs (VA) Center for Verification and Evaluation (CVE) Database (CVE Appeals)

AUTHORITY: 5 U.S.C. 504; 15 U.S.C. 632, 634(b)(6), 634(i), 637(a), 648(l), 656(i), and 687(c); 38 U.S.C. 8127(f); E.O. 12549, 51 FR 6370, 3 CFR, 1986 Comp., p. 189.

Subpart J issued under 38 U.S.C. 8127(f)(8)(B).

Subpart K issued under 38 U.S.C. 8127(f)(8)(A).

SOURCE: 61 FR 2683, Jan. 29, 1996, unless otherwise noted.

EDITORIAL NOTE: Nomenclature changes to part 134 appear at 72 FR 50042, Aug. 30, 2007.

Subpart A—General Rules

§ 134.101 Definitions.

As used in this part:

AA/OHA means the Assistant Administrator for OHA, who is also the Chief Hearing Officer.

Act means the Small Business Act, 15 U.S.C. 631 *et seq.*

Address means the primary home or business address of a person or entity, including the street location or postal box number, city or town, state, and postal zip code.

Administrative Judge means a Hearing Officer, as described at 15 U.S.C. 634(i), appointed by OHA to adjudicate cases.

Appeal petition has the same meaning as petition.

Area Office means a Government Contracting Area Office or a Disaster Area Office of the Small Business Administration.

Business day means any day other than a Saturday, Sunday, or a Federal holiday.

Day means a calendar day, unless a Judge specifies otherwise.

Hearing means the presentation and consideration of argument and evidence. A hearing need not include live testimony or argument.

Investment Act means the Small Business Investment Act of 1958, 15 U.S.C. 661 *et seq.*

Judge means the Administrative Judge or Administrative Law Judge who decides an appeal or petition brought before OHA, or the AA/OHA when he or she acts as an Administrative Judge.

NAICS code means North American Industry Classification System code.

OHA means the Office of Hearings and Appeals.

Party means the petitioner, appellant, respondent, or intervenor, and the contracting officer in a NAICS code appeal.

Person means an individual or any form of business entity.

Petition (or *appeal petition*) means a written complaint, a written appeal from an SBA determination, or a written request for the initiation of proceedings before OHA.

Petitioner means the person who initially files a petition before OHA.

Pleading means a petition, an order to show cause commencing a case, an appeal petition, an answer, a response, or any amendment or supplement to those documents.

Respondent means any person or governmental agency against which a case has been brought before OHA.

SBA means the Small Business Administration.

Size determination means a formal size determination made by an Area Office and includes decisions by Government Contracting Area Directors that determine whether two or more concerns are affiliated for purposes of SBA's financial assistance programs, or other programs for which an appropriate SBA official requested an affiliation determination.

Size Standard Petition means a petition for reconsideration of a revised, modified, or established size standard filed with OHA pursuant to 15 U.S.C. 632(a)(9) and subpart I of this part.

Step One and *Step Two* refer to the steps of the Employee Dispute Resolution Process, see § 134.801(a) for more information.

[61 FR 2683, Jan. 29, 1996, as amended at 67 FR 47246, July 18, 2002; 69 FR 29208, May 21, 2004; 75 FR 47438, Aug. 6, 2010; 82 FR 25506, June 2, 2017]

§ 134.102 Jurisdiction of OHA.

OHA has authority to conduct proceedings in the following cases:

(a) The revocation or suspension of Small Business Investment Company licenses, cease and desist orders, and the removal or suspension of directors and officers of licensees, under the Investment Act and part 107 of this chapter;

(b) Alleged violations of those civil rights laws which are effectuated by parts 112, 113, 117, and 136 of this chapter;

(c) The revocation of the privilege of a person to conduct business with SBA under the Act and part 103 of this chapter;

(d) [Reserved]

(e) The suspension or termination of surety bond program participants under 15 U.S.C. 694a *et seq.* and part 115 of this chapter;

(f) [Reserved]

(g) Allowance of fees and expenses under the Equal Access to Justice Act, 5 U.S.C. 504;

(h) Debarment from appearance before the SBA because of post-employment restrictions under 18 U.S.C. 207 and part 105 of this chapter;

(i) Collection of debts owed to SBA and the United States under the Debt

Collection Act of 1982, the Debt Collection Improvement Act of 1996, and part 140 of this chapter;

(j) Appeals from the following SBA 8(a) program determinations under the Act and part 124 of this chapter:

(1) Denial of program admission based solely on a negative finding as to social disadvantage, economic disadvantage, ownership or control; program termination; program graduation; or denial of a waiver of the requirement to perform to completion an 8(a) contract; and

(2) Program suspension;

(k) Appeals from size determinations and NAICS code designations under part 121 of this chapter;

(l) The imposition of civil penalties and assessments against persons who make false claims or statements to SBA under the Program Fraud Civil Remedies Act, 31 U.S.C. 3801–3812 and part 142 of this chapter;

(m)–(n) [Reserved]

(o) The suspension, termination, or non-renewal of cooperative agreements with Women's Business Centers and Small Business Development Centers under the Act and part 130 of this chapter;

(p) Certain matters involving debarments and suspensions under 2 CFR parts 180 and 2700;

(q) Appeals from the Service-Disabled Veteran-owned SBC Program ownership and control status under part 125 of this chapter;

(r) Appeals from SBA Employee Dispute Resolution Process cases (Employee Disputes) under Standard Operating Procedure (SOP) 37 71 (available at *http://www.sba.gov/tools/resourcelibrary/sops/index.html* or through OHA's Web site *http://www.sba.gov/oha*) and subpart H of this part;

(s) Appeals from Women-Owned Small Business or Economically-Disadvantaged Women-Owned Small Business protest determinations under part 127 of this chapter;

(t) Petitions for reconsideration of revised, modified, or established size standards pursuant to 15 U.S.C. 632(a)(9);

(u) Protests of eligibility for inclusion in the Department of Veterans Affairs Center for Verification and Evaluation (CVE) database; and

(v) Appeals of denials and cancellations of inclusion in the CVE database.

[61 FR 2683, Jan. 29, 1996, as amended at 66 FR 47074, Sept. 11, 2001; 67 FR 47246, July 18, 2002; 69 FR 25271, May 5, 2004; 69 FR 29208, May 21, 2004; 70 FR 17587, Apr. 7, 2005; 72 FR 39730, July 20, 2007; 73 FR 56954, Oct. 1, 2008; 75 FR 47438, Aug. 6, 2010; 75 FR 62292, Oct. 7, 2010; 82 FR 25506, June 2, 2017; 83 FR 13628, Mar. 30, 2018]

§ 134.103 [Reserved]

Subpart B—Rules of Practice

§ 134.201 Scope of the rules in this subpart.

(a) The rules of practice in this subpart apply to all OHA proceedings except:

(1) Where another subpart of this part, pertaining to a specific type of OHA proceeding, provides a different rule; or

(2) Where another part of this chapter, pertaining to a specific type of OHA proceeding (or SBA program allowing appeals to OHA), provides a different rule (see § 134.102).

(b) For specific types of OHA proceedings, the rules of practice are located as follows:

(1) For appeals from size determinations and NAICS code designations, in subpart C of this part (§ 134.301 *et seq.*);

(2) For 8(a) BD appeals, in subpart D of this part (§ 134.401 *et seq.*);

(3) For appeals from Service-Disabled Veteran-Owned Small Business Concern protest determinations, in subpart E of this part (§ 134.501 *et seq.*);

(4) For applications under the Equal Access to Justice Act, in subpart F of this part (§ 134.601 *et seq.*);

(5) For appeals from Women-Owned Small Business (WOSB) and Economically-Disadvantaged WOSB protest determinations, in subpart G of this part (§ 134.701 *et seq.*);

(6) For appeals relating to SBA employee disputes, in subpart H of this part (§ 134.801 *et seq.*);

(7) For Size Standard Petitions, in subpart I of this part (§§ 134.901 *through* 134.918);

(8) For protests of eligibility for inclusion in the Center for Verification

and Evaluation (CVE) database, in subpart J of this part;

(9) For appeals of denials and cancellations of inclusion in the CVE database, in subpart K of this part; and

(10) For proceedings under the Program Fraud Civil Remedies Act, in part 142 of this chapter.

(c) If a rule in this subpart conflicts with a rule pertaining to OHA in another subpart of this part or in another part of this chapter, the latter rule shall govern.

[75 FR 47438, Aug. 6, 2010, as amended at 82 FR 25506, June 2, 2017; 83 FR 13629, Mar. 30, 2018]

§ 134.202 Commencement of cases.

(a) A party other than the SBA may commence a case by filing an appeal petition.

(1) The filing deadline is contained in the SBA regulations governing the specific type of appeal.

(2) Where the SBA action or determination being appealed states a different time period (or deadline) for filing an appeal petition than does the applicable regulation, the longer time period (or later deadline) governs.

(b) The SBA may commence a case by issuing to the respondent an appropriate written order to show cause and filing the order to show cause with OHA.

(c) Cases concerning Small Business Investment Company license suspensions and revocations and cease and desist orders must be commenced with an order to show cause containing a statement of the matters of fact and law asserted by the SBA, the legal authority and jurisdiction under which a hearing is to be held, a statement that a hearing will be held, and the time and place for the hearing.

(d) *Calculation and modification of time periods and deadlines.* (1) *Calculation of a deadline when the time period is given in days.* (i) Do not count the day the time period begins, but do count the last day of the time period.

(ii) If the last day is Saturday, Sunday, or a Federal holiday, the time period ends on the next business day.

Example: On Monday, a Judge orders a party to file and serve a document within (or no later than) five days. The time period begins on Monday, so the first day to count is Tuesday. The second, third, and fourth days are Wednesday, Thursday, and Friday. The fifth day is Saturday, so the time period rolls over to the next business day, which is Monday. The deadline is Monday (or Tuesday if Monday is a Federal holiday).

(2) *Modification of a time period or deadline.* (i) A Judge may modify any time period or deadline, except:

(A) The time period governing commencement of a case (*i.e.*, when the appeal petition may be filed); and

(B) A time period established by statute.

(ii) A party may move for an extension of time pursuant to § 134.211.

[67 FR 47246, July 18, 2002, as amended at 70 FR 17587, Apr. 7, 2005; 75 FR 47439, Aug. 6, 2010]

§ 134.203 The appeal petition.

(a) A petition must contain the following:

(1) The basis of OHA's jurisdiction (see § 134.102);

(2) A copy of the SBA determination being appealed, if applicable, and the date the determination was received by the petitioner;

(3) A clear and concise statement of the factual basis of the case and applicable legal arguments;

(4) The relief being sought;

(5) The name, address, telephone number, facsimile number, e-mail address, and signature of the petitioner or its attorney; and

(6) A certificate of service (see § 134.204(d)).

(b) If the applicable subpart of this part 134 (or the program regulations) requires other documents or information with the appeal petition, these must also be included.

(c) A petition which does not contain all of the information required by paragraphs (a) and (b) of this section may be dismissed, with or without prejudice, at the Judge's own initiative, or upon motion of the respondent.

(d) *Format.* (1) An appeal petition should be on 8.5″ × 11″ paper with a clear type at least 12 point in size. Preferably, double-space the main text and use 1″ margins all around. Number each page. A separate cover letter is not needed. A table of contents is optional. Hard copies of documents sent by facsimile or electronic mail are not needed unless specifically requested.

(2) The maximum length of an appeal petition (not including attachments) is 20 pages, unless prior leave is sought by the petitioner and granted by the Judge. A table of authorities is required only for petitions citing more than twenty cases, regulations, or statutes.

(3) Clearly label any exhibits and attachments. Do not include documents already submitted to SBA in connection with the matter being appealed. SBA will submit these directly to OHA.

(e) *Motion for a more definite appeal petition.* A respondent, SBA, or a contracting officer (for NAICS appeals) may, not later than five days after receiving a petition, move for an order to the petitioner to provide a more definite appeal petition or otherwise comply with this section. A Judge may order a more definite appeal petition on his or her own initiative.

(1) A motion for a more definite appeal petition stays the respondent's time for filing an answer or response. The Judge will establish the time for filing and serving an answer or response.

(2) If the petitioner does not comply with the Judge's order to provide a more definite appeal petition or otherwise fails to comply with applicable regulations, the Judge may dismiss the petition with prejudice.

(f) *Notice and Order.* After an appeal petition is filed, OHA will issue a Notice and Order and serve it upon all known parties (or their attorneys). If a party does not receive a Notice and Order, it should contact OHA.

[67 FR 47247, July 18, 2002, as amended at 75 FR 47439, Aug. 6, 2010]

§ 134.204 Filing and service requirements.

All pleadings or other submissions must be filed with OHA and served on all other parties or their attorneys. Each submission requires a certificate of service.

(a) *Methods of filing and service.* E-mail, mail, delivery, and facsimile are all permitted unless a Judge orders otherwise.

(1) E-mail constitutes any system for sending and receiving messages electronically over a telecommunications network. The sender is responsible for ensuring that e-mail software and file formats are compatible with the recipient and for a successful, virus-free transmission.

(2) Mail includes any service provided by the U.S. Postal Service. Mail (except "Express Mail") is not recommended for time-sensitive filings.

(3) Delivery is personal delivery by a party, its employee, its attorney, or a commercial delivery service.

(4) Facsimile submissions should not exceed 30 pages. Contact OHA before faxing longer submissions. Follow-up originals or "hard copies" are not required unless OHA or another party specifically requests them.

(b) *Filing.* Filing is the receipt of pleadings and other submissions at OHA. Filers may call OHA to verify receipt. OHA's telephone number is (202) 401–8200.

(1) *OHA's address.* OHA accepts filings: by e-mail at *OHAFilings@sba.gov;* by mail or delivery at Office of Hearings and Appeals, U.S. Small Business Administration, 409 Third Street, SW., Washington, DC 20416; and by facsimile at (202) 205–7059.

(2) The date of filing is the date the submission is received at OHA. Any submission received at OHA after 5 p.m. eastern time is considered filed the next business day.

(3) *Exhibits.* An exhibit, whether an original or a copy, must be authenticated or identified to be what it purports to be. Parties are referred to 28 U.S.C. 1746.

(4) *Copies.* No extra copies of pleadings or other submissions need be filed. If a document is offered as an exhibit, a copy of the document will be accepted by the Judge unless—

(i) a genuine question is raised as to whether it is a true and accurate copy; or

(ii) it would be unfair, under the circumstances, to admit the copy instead of the original.

(c) *Service.* Service means sending a copy of a pleading or other submission filed with OHA to another party.

(1) Complete copies of all pleadings and other submissions filed with OHA must be served upon all other parties

or, if represented, their attorneys, at their record addresses.

(2) The date of service is as follows: for e-mail and facsimile, the date the copy is sent; for personal delivery, the date the copy is given to the party, its attorney, or the commercial delivery service (if one is used). For mail, date of service is postmark date; in absence of a legible postmark, there is a rebuttable presumption that the copy was mailed five days before the served party's receipt.

(3) *SBA address.* The correct office(s) of SBA must be served, as required by the applicable program regulations, by other subparts of part 134, or by the instructions on the SBA determination being appealed. If the SBA office for service is not specified elsewhere, serve: Office of General Counsel, U.S. Small Business Administration, 409 Third Street, SW., Washington, DC 20416.

(4) *Confidential information.* If a pleading or other submission contains proprietary or confidential information, that information may be redacted (deleted) from any copies served upon non-government parties. Counsel for those parties may access the redacted information only under the protective order procedure described in § 134.205.

(d) *Certificate of service.* A certificate of service shows how, when, and to whom service was made. Each submission to OHA must include a certificate of service. The certificate should state: "I certify that on [date], I served the foregoing [type of submission] by [e-mail, mail, Express Mail, personal delivery, commercial delivery service, facsimile] upon the following". List the name and address of each party served, and either the facsimile number or the e-mail address (if applicable). The individual serving the submission must sign the certificate and either print or type his or her name and title.

[75 FR 47439, Aug. 6, 2010]

§ 134.205 The appeal file, confidential information, and protective orders.

(a) *The appeal file.* The appeal file includes: all pleadings and other submissions; all admitted evidence; any recordings and transcripts of proceedings; the solicitation and amendments; in the case of an appeal of an SBA determination, the entire record on which that determination was based (*i.e.*, the administrative record, protest file, area office file); and any orders and decisions that have been issued.

(b) *Confidential business and financial information.* An appeal file usually contains confidential business and financial information pertaining to the party whose eligibility (as a small business, SDVO SBC, etc.) is at issue. A party may redact its own confidential business and financial information from the copies of its submissions it must serve on other non-government parties (usually protesters). A party served with redacted submissions must file and serve any objections to the redactions within two business days of its receipt of the submissions. The Judge then will rule on the objections and, if necessary, order the service of revised submissions.

(c) *Public access.* Except for confidential business and financial information, source selection sensitive information, income tax returns, and other exempt information, the appeal file is available to the public pursuant to the Freedom of Information Act (FOIA), 5 U.S.C. 552.

(d) *Party access.* A party in a pending appeal may examine and copy the party's own submissions as well as any information in the appeal file that is not exempt from disclosure under the FOIA. Party access to the appeal file in a pending appeal does not require a FOIA request or a protective order.

(e) *Counsel's access under a protective order.* On request, OHA will issue a protective order under which outside counsel for a non-government party in a pending appeal may be admitted, to examine and copy the appeal file (except for tax returns and privileged information). The protective order will set out the terms to which counsel must agree. The terms will restrict counsel's use of the protected information to the pending appeal and will prohibit any further disclosure. Violations of the terms of a protective order may result in sanctions to the party and referral of the attorney to bar disciplinary authorities. OHA's Web site contains detailed information on the protective order procedure.

(f) *Decisions.* OHA decisions are normally published without redactions on OHA's Web site. A decision may contain confidential business and financial information where that information is either decisionally-significant or otherwise necessary for a comprehensible decision. Where no protective order is in place, a party may request a redacted public decision by contacting OHA. Where a protective order is in place, the Judge will usually issue the unredacted decision under the protective order and then a redacted version for public release.

[75 FR 47440, Aug. 6, 2010]

§ 134.206 The answer or response.

(a)(1) Except in a case involving a petition appealing from an SBA determination, a respondent must file and serve an answer within 45 days after the filing of a petition or the service of an order to show cause, except that in debt collection cases, answers are due within 30 days.

(2) The answer must contain the following:

(i) An admission or denial of each of the factual allegations contained in the petition or order to show cause, or a statement that the respondent denies knowledge or information sufficient to determine the truth of a particular allegation;

(ii) Any affirmative defenses; and

(iii) The name, address, telephone number, facsimile number, and signature of the respondent or its attorney.

(3) Allegations in the petition or order to show cause that are not answered in accordance with paragraph (a)(2)(i) of this section will be deemed admitted unless injustice would occur.

(b) *Appeal of an SBA determination.* (1) *Notice and order.* Upon the filing of an appeal petition, OHA will issue a notice and order informing all known parties of the appeal petition and the deadline for filing and serving any responses to the appeal. The SBA response is due 45 days after the date the appeal petition is filed, unless a rule governing the particular type of appeal provides a different deadline.

(2) *SBA response.* If SBA is the respondent, SBA need not admit or deny the allegations in the petition, but must set forth the relevant facts and the legal arguments in support of SBA's determination.

(3) *Administrative record.* If SBA is to file and serve an authenticated copy of the administrative record (or protest file), the notice and order will provide further instructions.

(4) *Claim of privilege.* If SBA asserts a claim of privilege over any portion of the administrative record, SBA must serve the petitioner a redacted version, accompanied by a "Vaughn Index" describing each withheld item and justifying each claim of privilege. SBA also must file an unredacted copy for *in camera* inspection by the Judge. The Judge will afford the petitioner an opportunity to object to the administrative record and to challenge any claim of privilege asserted by SBA.

(c) If a petition or order to show cause is amended or if respondent is not properly served, the Judge will order the time to file an answer or response extended and will specify the date such answer or response is due. If respondent is not properly served with a petition appealing from an SBA determination, the Judge will issue an order directing that the petitioner serve respondent within a specified time and directing respondent to file and serve a response within 45 days after petitioner timely serves respondent in accordance with the order.

(d) If the respondent fails to timely file and serve an answer or response, that failure will constitute a default. Following such a default, the Judge may prohibit the respondent from participating further in the case. If SBA, as respondent to a petition appealing from an SBA determination, fails to timely file and serve its response or the administrative record (where required), the Judge will issue an order directing SBA to file and serve the administrative record by a specified date.

(e) *Reply.* A reply to a response is not permitted unless the Judge, upon motion or on his or her own initiative, orders a reply to be filed and served. A party moving for leave to reply should file and serve the proposed reply with its motion.

[67 FR 47247, July 18, 2002, as amended at 75 FR 47440, Aug. 6, 2010]

§ 134.207 Amendments and supplemental pleadings.

(a) *Amendments.* Upon motion (*see* § 134.211), and under terms needed to avoid prejudice to any non-moving party, the Judge may permit the filing and service of amendments to pleadings. However, an amendment will not be permitted if it would cause unreasonable delay in the determination of the matter. The proposed amendment must be filed and served with the motion. The Judge, on his or her own initiative, may order a party to file and serve an amendment to a pleading.

(b) *Supplemental pleadings.* Upon motion (*see* § 134.211), and under terms needed to avoid prejudice to any non-moving party, the Judge may permit the filing and service of a supplemental pleading setting forth relevant transactions or occurrences that have taken place since the filing of the original pleading. The proposed supplemental pleading must be filed and served with the motion. The Judge, on his or her own initiative, may order a party to file and serve a supplemental pleading.

(c) *8(a) appeals.* In 8(a) program appeals, amendments to pleadings and supplemental pleadings will be permitted by the Judge only upon a showing of good cause.

(d) *Answer or response.* In an order permitting the filing and service of an amended or supplemented petition or order to show cause, the Judge will establish the time for filing and serving an answer or response.

[61 FR 2683, Jan. 29, 1996, as amended at 67 FR 47248, July 18, 2002; 75 FR 47441, Aug. 6, 2010]

§ 134.208 Representation in cases before OHA.

(a) A party may represent itself, or be represented by an attorney. A partner may represent a partnership; a member may represent a limited liability company; and an officer may represent a corporation, trust, association, or other entity.

(b) An attorney for a party who did not appear on behalf of that party in the party's first filing with OHA must file and serve a written notice of appearance.

(c) An attorney seeking to withdraw from a case must file and serve a motion for the withdrawal of his or her appearance.

[67 FR 47248, July 18, 2002]

§ 134.209 Requirement of signature.

Every written submission to OHA, other than evidence, must be signed by the party filing that submission, or by the party's attorney. By signing the submission, a party or its attorney attests that the statements and allegations in that submission are true to the best of its knowledge, and that the submission is not being filed for the purpose of delay or harassment. False statements are subject to criminal penalties. Any misconduct is subject to sanctions (*see* § 134.219).

[61 FR 2683, Jan. 29, 1996, as amended at 75 FR 47441, Aug. 6, 2010]

§ 134.210 Intervention.

(a) *By SBA.* SBA may intervene as of right at any time in any case until 15 days after the close of record, or the issuance of a decision, whichever comes first.

(b) *By interested persons.* Any interested person may move to intervene at any time until the close of record by filing and serving a motion to intervene containing a statement of the moving party's interest in the case and the necessity for intervention to protect such interest. An interested person is any individual, business entity, or governmental agency that has a direct stake in the outcome of the appeal. The Judge may grant leave to intervene upon such terms as he or she deems appropriate.

[67 FR 47248, July 18, 2002]

§ 134.211 Motions.

(a) *Contents.* All motions must state the relief being requested, as well as the grounds and any authority for that relief. A motion must be filed, served, and accompanied by a certificate of service (*see* § 134.204).

(b) *Statement of whether motion is opposed.* Except when filing a motion to dismiss or a motion for summary decision, the moving party must make reasonable efforts before filing the motion to contact any non-moving party and determine whether it will oppose the motion and must state in the motion whether each non-moving party will oppose or not oppose the motion. If the moving party cannot determine whether a non-moving party will oppose the motion, the moving party must describe in the motion the efforts made to contact that non-moving party.

(c) *Response.* All non-moving parties must file and serve a response to the motion or be deemed to have consented to the relief sought. The response is due no later than 15 days after the motion is served, unless the Judge sets a different deadline. On motion, or on his or her own initiative, the Judge may permit a reply to a response and/or oral argument on the motion.

(d) *Service of orders.* OHA will serve upon all parties any written order issued in response to a motion.

(e) *Motion to dismiss.* A respondent may file a motion to dismiss any time before a decision is issued. If an answer or response to the appeal petition has not yet been filed, the motion to dismiss stays the respondent's time to answer or respond.

(f) *Motion for an extension of time.* Except for good cause shown, a motion for an extension of time must be filed at least two business days before the original deadline.

[61 FR 2683, Jan. 29, 1996, as amended at 63 FR 35766, June 30, 1998; 67 FR 47248, July 18, 2002; 75 FR 47441, Aug. 6, 2010]

§ 134.212 Summary judgment.

(a) *On motion by a party.* At any time before the close of record, a party may move for summary judgment as to all or any portion of the case, on the grounds that there is no genuine issue as to any material fact, and that the moving party is entitled to a decision in its favor as a matter of law.

(1) *Contents of motion.* The motion must include a statement of the material facts believed to be undisputed and the party's legal arguments. The motion may include supporting statements in accordance with 28 U.S.C. 1746. The motion must be filed, served, and accompanied by a certificate of service (*see* § 134.204).

(2) *Response.* No later than 15 days after the service of a motion for summary judgment, all non-moving parties must file and serve a response to the motion or be deemed to have consented to the motion for summary judgment.

(3) *Cross-motions.* In its response to a motion for summary judgment, a party may cross-move for summary judgment. The initial moving party must file and serve a response to any cross-motion for summary judgment within 15 days after the service of that cross-motion or be deemed to have consented to the cross-motion for summary judgment.

(4) *Stay.* If an answer or response to the appeal petition has not yet been filed, the motion for summary judgment stays the respondent's time to answer or respond. If the Judge denies the motion and an answer or response has not yet been filed, the respondent must file the answer or response within 15 days after the order deciding the motion unless otherwise ordered by the Judge.

(b) *On the Judge's own initiative.* The Judge may issue an order granting summary judgment as to all or any portion of the case in absence of a motion if there is no genuine issue to any material fact, and a party is entitled to a decision in its favor as a matter of law.

(c) *Appeal of an SBA determination.* If the SBA determination being appealed was based on multiple grounds, SBA may move for summary judgment on one or more of those grounds. If the Judge finds, as to any ground, that there is no genuine issue of material fact and that the SBA is entitled to a decision in its favor as a matter of law, the Judge will grant the motion for summary judgment and dismiss the rest of the appeal.

[75 FR 47441, Aug. 6, 2010]

§ 134.213 Discovery.

(a) *Motion.* A party may obtain discovery only upon motion, and for good cause shown.

(b) *Forms.* The forms of discovery which a Judge can order under paragraph (a) of this section include requests for admissions, requests for production of documents, interrogatories, and depositions.

(c) *Limitations.* Discovery may be limited in accordance with the terms of a protective order (see § 134.205). Further, privileged information and irrelevant issues or facts will not be subject to discovery.

(d) *Disputes.* If a dispute should arise between the parties over a particular discovery request, the party seeking discovery may file and serve a motion to compel discovery. Discovery may be opposed on the grounds of harassment, needless embarrassment, irrelevance, undue burden or expense, privilege, or confidentiality.

[61 FR 2683, Jan. 29, 1996, as amended at 63 FR 35766, June 30, 1998; 67 FR 47249, July 18, 2002; 75 FR 47441, Aug. 6, 2010]

§ 134.214 Subpoenas.

(a) *Availability.* At the request of a party, or upon his or her own initiative, a Judge may issue a subpoena requiring a witness to appear and testify, or to produce particular documents, at a specified time and place.

(b) *Requests.* A request for the issuance of a subpoena must be written, served upon all parties, and filed. The request must clearly identify the witness and any documents to be subpoenaed, and must set forth the relevance of the testimony or documents sought.

(c) *Service.* A subpoena may only be served by personal delivery. The individual making service shall prepare an affidavit stating the date, time, and place of the service. The party which obtained the subpoena must serve upon all other parties, and file with OHA, a copy of the subpoena and affidavit of service within 2 days after service is made.

(d) *Motion to quash.* A motion to limit or quash a subpoena must be filed and served within 10 days after service of the subpoena, or by the return date of the subpoena, whichever date comes first. Any response to the motion must be filed and served within 10 days after service of the motion, unless a shorter time is specified by the Judge. No oral argument will be heard on the motion unless the Judge directs otherwise.

[61 FR 2683, Jan. 29, 1996, as amended at 67 FR 47249, July 18, 2002; 75 FR 47441, Aug. 6, 2010]

EDITORIAL NOTE: At 75 FR 47441, Aug. 6, 2010, § 134.214 was amended; however, a portion of the amendment could not be incorporated due to inaccurate amendatory instruction.

§ 134.215 Interlocutory appeals.

(a) *General.* A motion for leave to take an interlocutory appeal from a Judge's ruling will not be entertained in those proceedings in which OHA issues final decisions. In all other cases, an interlocutory appeal will be permitted only if, upon motion by a party, or upon the Judge's own initiative, the Judge certifies that his or her ruling raises a question which is immediately appealable. Interlocutory appeals will be decided by the AA/OHA or a designee.

(b) *Motion for certification.* A party must file and serve a motion for certification no later than 20 days after issuance of the ruling to which the motion applies. A denial of the motion does not preclude objections to the ruling in any subsequent request for review of an initial decision.

(c) *Basis for certification.* The Judge will certify a ruling for interlocutory appeal only if he or she determines that:

(1) The ruling involves an important question of law or policy about which there is substantial ground for a difference of opinion; and

(2) An interlocutory appeal will materially expedite resolution of the case, or denial of an interlocutory appeal would cause undue hardship to a party.

(d) *Stay of proceedings.* A stay while an interlocutory appeal is pending will be at the discretion of the Judge.

[61 FR 2683, Jan. 29, 1996, as amended at 67 FR 47249, July 18, 2002]

§ 134.216 Alternative dispute resolution procedures.

(a) At any time during the pendency of a case, the parties may submit a joint motion requesting that the Judge permit the use of alternative dispute resolution procedures to assist in resolving the matter. If the motion is granted, the Judge will also stay the proceedings before OHA, in whole or in part, as he or she deems appropriate, pending the outcome of the alternative dispute resolution procedures.

(b) A Judge may offer alternative dispute resolution procedures to the parties at any time during the proceeding.

(c) The AA/OHA or a Judge may designate a Judge or attorney assigned to

OHA to serve as a neutral in alternative dispute resolution procedures. If OHA provides the neutral and the mediation fails to resolve all issues in the case, the OHA-provided neutral will not be involved in the adjudication.

[61 FR 2683, Jan. 29, 1996, as amended at 75 FR 47441, Aug. 6, 2010]

§ 134.217 Settlement.

At any time during the pendency of a case, the parties may submit a joint motion to dismiss the appeal if they have settled the case, and may file with such motion a copy of the settlement agreement. If the Judge has express authority, under statute, SBA regulation or SBA standard operating procedures, to review the contents of a settlement agreement for legality, the Judge may order the parties to file a copy of the settlement agreement. Otherwise, upon the filing of a joint motion to dismiss, the Judge will issue an order dismissing the case. Settlement negotiations, and rejected settlement agreements, are not admissible into evidence.

[61 FR 2683, Jan. 29, 1996, as amended at 67 FR 47249, July 18, 2002]

§ 134.218 Judges.

(a) *Assignment.* The AA/OHA will assign all cases subject to the Administrative Procedure Act, 5 U.S.C. 551 *et seq.*, to an Administrative Law Judge. The AA/OHA will assign all other cases before OHA to either an Administrative Law Judge or an Administrative Judge, or, if the AA/OHA is a duly licensed attorney, to himself or herself.

(b) *Authority.* Except as otherwise limited by this part, or by statute or other regulation, a Judge has the authority to take all appropriate action to ensure the efficient, prompt, and fair determination of a case, including, but not limited to, the authority to administer oaths and affirmations and to subpoena and examine witnesses.

(c) *Recusal.* Upon the motion of a party, or upon the Judge's own initiative, a Judge will promptly recuse himself or herself from further participation in a case whenever disqualification is appropriate due to conflict of interest, bias, or some other significant reason. A denial of a motion for recusal may be appealed within 5 days to the AA/OHA, or to the Administrative Law Judge if the AA/OHA is the Judge, but that appeal will not stay proceedings in the case.

[61 FR 2683, Jan. 29, 1996, as amended at 75 FR 47441, Aug. 6, 2010]

§ 134.219 Sanctions.

(a) A Judge may impose appropriate sanctions, except for fees, costs, or monetary penalties, which he or she deems necessary to serve the ends of justice, if a party or its attorney:

(1) Fails to comply with an order of the Judge;

(2) Fails to comply with the rules set forth in this part;

(3) Acts in bad faith or for purposes of delay or harassment;

(4) Submits false statements knowingly, recklessly, or with deliberate disregard for the truth; or

(5) Otherwise acts in an unethical or disruptive manner.

(b) Appropriate sanctions may include:

(1) Ordering a pleading or evidentiary filing to be struck from the record;

(2) Dismissing an appeal with prejudice;

(3) Suspending counsel from practice before OHA;

(4) Filing a complaint with the applicable State bar; and

(5) Taking any other action that is appropriate to further the administration of justice.

[75 FR 47441, Aug. 6, 2010]

§ 134.220 Prohibition against *ex parte* communications.

No person shall consult or communicate with a Judge concerning any fact, question of law, or SBA policy relevant to the merits of a case before that Judge except on prior notice to all parties, and with the opportunity for all parties to participate. In the event of such prohibited consultation or communication, the Judge will disclose the occurrence in accordance with 5 U.S.C. 557(d)(1), and may impose such sanctions as he or she deems appropriate.

§ 134.221 Prehearing conferences.

Prior to a hearing, the Judge, at his or her own initiative, or upon the motion of any party, may direct the parties or their attorneys to appear, by telephone or in person, in order to consider any matter which may assist in the efficient, prompt, and fair determination of the case. The conference may be recorded verbatim at the discretion of the Judge, and, if so, a party may purchase a transcript, at its own expense, from the recording service.

§ 134.222 Oral hearing.

(a) *Availability.* A party may obtain an oral hearing only if:

(1) It is required by regulation; or

(2) Following the motion of a party, or at his or her own initiative, the Judge orders an oral hearing upon concluding that there is a genuine dispute as to a material fact that cannot be resolved except by the taking of testimony and the confrontation of witnesses.

(b) *Place and time.* The place and time of oral hearings is within the discretion of the Judge, who shall give due regard to the necessity and convenience of the parties, their attorneys, and witnesses. The Judge may direct that an oral hearing be conducted by telephone.

(c) *Public access.* Unless otherwise ordered by the Judge, all oral hearings are public.

(d) *Payment of subpoenaed witnesses.* A party who obtains a witness's presence at an oral hearing by subpoena must pay to that witness the fees and mileage costs to which the witness would be entitled in Federal court.

(e) *Recording.* Oral hearings will be recorded verbatim. A transcript of a recording may be purchased by a party, at its own expense, from the recording service.

[61 FR 2683, Jan. 29, 1996, as amended at 63 FR 35766, June 30, 1998; 70 FR 17587, Apr. 7, 2005; 75 FR 47442, Aug. 6, 2010]

§ 134.223 Evidence.

(a) *Federal Rules of Evidence.* Unless contrary to a particular rule in this part, or an order of the Judge, the Federal Rules of Evidence will be used as a general guide in all cases before OHA.

(b) *Hearsay.* Hearsay evidence is admissible if it is deemed by the Judge to be relevant and reliable. Weight to be afforded hearsay evidence is at the discretion of the Judge.

[61 FR 2683, Jan. 29, 1996, as amended at 75 FR 47442, Aug. 6, 2010]

§ 134.224 [Reserved]

§ 134.225 The record.

(a) *Contents.* The record of a case before OHA will consist of all pleadings, motions, and other non-evidentiary submissions, all admitted evidence, all orders and decisions, and any transcripts of proceedings in the case.

(b) *Closure.* The Judge will set the date upon which the pre-decisional record of the case will be closed, and after which no additional evidence or argument will be accepted.

[61 FR 2683, Jan. 29, 1996, as amended at 75 FR 47442, Aug. 6, 2010]

§ 134.226 The decision.

(a) *Contents.* (1) Following close of record, the Judge will issue a decision containing findings of fact and conclusions of law, the reasons for such findings and conclusions, and any relief ordered. The record will constitute the exclusive basis for a decision.

(2) An OHA decision creates precedent, unless:

(i) Another regulation in this chapter applicable to a specific type of appeal provides that the OHA decision does not create precedent; or

(ii) the decision is designated as one not to be cited as precedent.

(3) A summary decision containing only cursory findings of fact and conclusions of law may be issued only if the Judge finds a full decision will not advance understanding of Federal statutes or applicable regulations, policies, or procedures and the underlying facts and law are of a routine and non-complex nature.

(b) *Time limits.* Decisions pertaining to the collection of debts owed to SBA and the United States under the Debt Collection Act of 1982, the Debt Collection Improvement Act of 1996, and Part 140 of this chapter must be made within 60 days after a petition is filed. Time limits for decisions in other types of cases, if any, are indicated either in the applicable program regulations or in other subparts of this part 134.

(c) *Service.* OHA will serve a copy of all written decisions on:

(1) Each party, or, if represented by counsel, on its counsel; and

(2) SBA's General Counsel, or his or her designee, if SBA is not a party.

[61 FR 2683, Jan. 29, 1996, as amended at 67 FR 47249, July 18, 2002; 70 FR 17587, Apr. 7, 2005; 75 FR 47442, Aug. 6, 2010]

§ 134.227 Finality of decisions.

(a) *Initial decisions.* Except as otherwise provided in paragraph (b) of this section, a decision by the Judge on the merits is an initial decision. However, unless a request for review is filed pursuant to § 134.228(a), or a request for reconsideration is filed pursuant to paragraph (c) of this section, an initial decision shall become the final decision of the SBA 30 days after its service.

(b) *Final decisions.* A decision by the Judge on the merits shall be a final decision in the following proceedings:

(1) Collection of debts owed to SBA and the United States under the Debt Collection Act of 1982, Debt Collection Improvement Act of 1996, and part 140 of this chapter;

(2) Appeals from SBA 8(a) program determinations under the Act and part 124 of this chapter;

(3) Appeals from size determinations and NAICS code designations under part 121 of this chapter;

(4) Size Standard Petitions; and

(5) In other proceedings as provided either in the applicable program regulations or in other subparts of this part 134.

(c) *Reconsideration.* Except as otherwise provided by statute, the applicable program regulations in this chapter, or this part 134, an initial or final decision of the Judge may be reconsidered. Any party in interest, including SBA where SBA did not appear as a party during the proceeding that led to the issuance of the Judge's decision, may request reconsideration by filing with the Judge and serving a petition for reconsideration within 20 days after service of the written decision, upon a clear showing of an error of fact or law material to the decision. The Judge also may reconsider a decision on his or her own initiative.

[67 FR 47249, July 18, 2002, as amended at 70 FR 17587, Apr. 7, 2005; 81 FR 48595, July 25, 2016; 82 FR 25507, June 2, 2017]

§ 134.228 Review of initial decisions.

(a) *Request for review.* Within 30 days after the service of an initial decision or a reconsidered initial decision of a Judge, any party, or SBA's Office of General Counsel, may file and serve a request for review by the Administrator. A request for review must set forth the filing party's specific objections to the initial decision, and any alleged support for those objections in the record, or in case law, statute, regulation, or SBA policy. A party must serve its request for review upon all other parties and upon SBA's Office of General Counsel.

(b) *Response.* Within 20 days after the service of a request for review, any party, or SBA's Office of General Counsel, may file and serve a response. A party must serve its response upon all other parties and upon SBA's Office of General Counsel.

(c) *Transfer of the record.* Upon receipt of all responses, or 30 days after the filing of a request for review, whichever is earlier, OHA will transfer the record of the case to the Administrator. The Administrator, or his or her designee, will then review the record.

(d) *Standard of review.* Upon review, the Administrator, or his or her designee, will sustain the initial decision unless it is based on an erroneous finding of fact or an erroneous interpretation or application of case law, statute, regulation, or SBA policy.

(e) *Order.* The Administrator, or his or her designee, will:

(1) Affirm, reverse, or modify the initial decision, which determination will become the final decision of the SBA upon issuance; or

(2) Remand the initial decision to the Judge for appropriate further proceedings.

[61 FR 2683, Jan. 29, 1996, as amended at 67 FR 47249, July 18, 2002]

§ 134.229 Termination of jurisdiction.

Except when the Judge reconsiders a decision or remands the case, the jurisdiction of OHA will terminate upon the issuance of a decision resolving all material issues of fact and law. If the Judge reconsiders a decision, OHA's jurisdiction terminates when the Judge issues the decision after reconsideration. If the Judge remands the case, the Judge may retain jurisdiction at his or her own discretion, and the remand order may include the terms and duration of the remand.

[67 FR 47249, July 18, 2002]

Subpart C—Rules of Practice for Appeals From Size Determinations and NAICS Code Designations

§ 134.301 Scope of the rules in this subpart C.

The rules of practice in this subpart C apply to all appeals to OHA from:

(a) Formal size determinations made by an SBA Government Contracting Area Office, under part 121 of this chapter, or by a Disaster Area Office, in connection with applications for disaster loans; and

(b) NAICS code designations, pursuant to part 121 of this chapter.

[61 FR 2683, Jan. 29, 1996, as amended at 67 FR 47249, July 18, 2002]

§ 134.302 Who may appeal.

Appeals from size determinations and NAICS code designations may be filed with OHA by the following, as applicable:

(a) Any person adversely affected by a size determination;

(b) Any person adversely affected by a NAICS code designation. However, with respect to a particular sole source 8(a) contract, only the Director, Office of Business Development may appeal a NAICS code designation;

(c) The Associate or Assistant Administrator for the SBA program involved, through SBA's Office of General Counsel; or

(d) The procuring agency contracting officer responsible for the procurement affected by a size determination.

[61 FR 2683, Jan. 29, 1996, as amended at 67 FR 47249, July 18, 2002; 74 FR 45754, Sept. 4, 2009; 75 FR 47442, Aug. 6, 2010]

§ 134.303 Advisory opinions.

The Office of Hearings and Appeals does not issue advisory opinions.

[67 FR 47249, July 18, 2002]

§ 134.304 Commencement of appeals from size determinations and NAICS code designations.

(a) Size appeals must be filed within 15 calendar days after receipt of the formal size determination.

(b) NAICS code appeals must be filed within 10 calendar days after issuance of the solicitation, or amendment to the solicitation affecting the NAICS code or size standard. However, SBA may file a NAICS code appeal at any time before offers or bids are due.

(c) An untimely appeal will be dismissed.

[76 FR 5685, Feb. 2, 2011]

§ 134.305 The appeal petition.

(a) *Form.* There is no required format for an appeal petition. However, it must include the following information:

(1) In a size appeal, a copy of the size determination being appealed;

(2) The solicitation or contract number, and the name, address, and telephone number of the contracting officer;

(3) A full and specific statement as to why the size determination or NAICS code designation is alleged to be in error, together with argument supporting such allegations; and

(4) The name, address, telephone number, facsimile number, and signature of the appellant or its attorney.

(b) *Service of size determination appeals.* The appellant must serve the appeal petition upon each of the following:

(1) The SBA official who issued the size determination;

(2) The contracting officer responsible for the procurement affected by a size determination;

(3) The business concern whose size status is at issue;

(4) All persons who filed protests; and

(5) SBA's Office of General Counsel, Associate General Counsel for Procurement Law, 409 Third Street, SW., Washington, DC 20416, facsimile (202) 205–6873, or e-mail at *OPLService@sba.gov.*

(c) *Service of NAICS appeals.* The appellant must serve:

(1) The contracting officer who made the NAICS code designation; and

(2) SBA's Office of General Counsel, Associate General Counsel for Procurement Law, 409 Third Street, SW., Washington, DC 20416, facsimile (202) 205–6873, or e-mail at *OPLService@sba.gov.*

(d) *Certificate of service.* The appellant must attach to the appeal petition a signed certificate of service meeting the requirements of § 134.204(d).

(e) *Dismissal.* An appeal petition which does not contain all of the information required in paragraph (a) of this section may be dismissed, with or without prejudice, by the Judge at his or her own initiative, or upon motion of a respondent.

[61 FR 2683, Jan. 29, 1996, as amended at 65 FR 57542, Sept. 25, 2000; 67 FR 47250, July 18, 2002; 69 FR 29208, May 21, 2004; 75 FR 47442, Aug. 6, 2010]

§ 134.306 Transmission of the case file and solicitation.

(a) Upon receipt of an appeal petition pertaining to a size determination, the Area Office which issued the size determination must immediately send to OHA the entire case file relating to that determination.

(b) Upon receipt of an appeal petition pertaining to a NAICS code designation, or a size determination made in connection with a particular procurement, the procuring agency contracting officer must immediately send to OHA an electronic link to or a paper copy of both the original solicitation relating to that procurement and all amendments.

[61 FR 2683, Jan. 29, 1996, as amended at 67 FR 47250, July 18, 2002; 75 FR 47442, Aug. 6, 2010]

§ 134.307 Service and filing requirements.

The provisions of § 134.204 apply to the service and filing of all pleadings and other submissions permitted under this subpart.

§ 134.308 Limitation on new evidence and adverse inference from non-submission in appeals from size determinations.

(a) Evidence not previously presented to the Area Office which issued the size determination being appealed will not be considered by a Judge unless:

(1) The Judge, on his or her own initiative, orders the submission of such evidence; or

(2) A motion is filed and served establishing good cause for the submission of such evidence. The offered new evidence must be filed and served with the motion.

(b) If the submission of evidence is ordered by a Judge, and the party in possession of that evidence does not submit it, the Judge may draw adverse inferences against that party.

[61 FR 2683, Jan. 29, 1996, as amended at 67 FR 47250, July 18, 2002]

§ 134.309 Response to an appeal petition.

(a) *Who may respond.* Any person served with an appeal petition, any intervenor, or any person with a general interest in an issue raised by the appeal may file and serve a response supporting or opposing the appeal. The response should present argument.

(b) *Time limits.* The Judge will issue a Notice and Order informing the parties of the filing of the appeal petition, establishing the close of record as 15 days after service of the Notice and Order, and informing the parties that OHA must receive any responses to the appeal petition no later than the close of record.

(c) *Service.* The respondent must serve its response upon the appellant and upon each of the persons identified in the certificate of service attached to the appeal petition pursuant to § 134.305.

(d) *Reply to a response.* No reply to a response will be permitted unless the Judge directs otherwise.

[61 FR 2683, Jan. 29, 1996, as amended at 67 FR 47250, July 18, 2002]

§ 134.310 Discovery.

Discovery will not be permitted in appeals from size determinations or NAICS code designations.

[61 FR 2683, Jan. 29, 1996, as amended at 67 FR 47250, July 18, 2002]

§ 134.311 Oral hearings.

Oral hearings will not be held in appeals from NAICS code designations, and will be held in appeals from size determinations only upon a finding by the Judge of extraordinary circumstances. If such an oral hearing is ordered, the proceeding shall be conducted in accordance with those rules of subpart B of this part as the Judge deems appropriate.

[61 FR 2683, Jan. 29, 1996, as amended at 67 FR 47250, July 18, 2002]

§ 134.312 Evidence.

To the extent the rules in this subpart permit the submission of evidence, the provisions of § 134.223 (a) and (b) apply.

§ 134.313 Applicability of subpart B provisions.

Except where inconsistent with this subpart C, the provisions of subpart B of this part apply to appeals from size determinations and NAICS code designations.

[67 FR 47250, July 18, 2002]

§ 134.314 Standard of review and burden of proof.

The standard of review is whether the size determination or NAICS code designation was based on clear error of fact or law. The appellant has the burden of proof, by a preponderance of the evidence, in both size and NAICS code appeals.

[61 FR 2683, Jan. 29, 1996, as amended at 67 FR 47250, July 18, 2002; 69 FR 29209, May 21, 2004]

§ 134.315 The record.

Where relevant, the provisions of § 134.225 apply. In an appeal under this subpart, the contents of the record also include the case file or solicitation submitted to OHA in accordance with § 134.306.

[61 FR 2683, Jan. 29, 1996, as amended at 75 FR 47442, Aug. 6, 2010]

§ 134.316 The decision.

(a) The Judge shall issue a size appeal decision, insofar as practicable, within 60 calendar days after close of the record.

(b) The Judge shall issue a NAICS code appeal decision as soon as practicable after close of the record.

(c) *Contents.* Following closure of the record, the Judge will issue a decision containing findings of fact and conclusions of law, reasons for such findings and conclusions, and any relief ordered. The Judge will not decide substantive issues raised for the first time on appeal, or which have been abandoned or become moot.

(d) *Finality.* The decision is the final decision of the SBA and becomes effective upon issuance. Where a size appeal is dismissed, the Area Office size determination remains in effect.

(e) *Service.* OHA will serve a copy of all written decisions on:

(1) Each party, or, if represented by counsel, on its counsel; and

(2) SBA's General Counsel, or his or her designee, if SBA is not a party.

(f) *Reconsideration.* The decision in a NAICS code appeal may not be reconsidered.

[61 FR 2683, Jan. 29, 1996, as amended at 67 FR 47250, July 18, 2002; 69 FR 29209, May 21, 2004; 76 FR 5685, Feb. 2, 2011]

§ 134.317 Return of the case file.

Upon issuance of the decision, OHA will return the case file to the transmitting Area Office. The remainder of the record will be retained by OHA.

[67 FR 47250, July 18, 2002]

§ 134.318 NAICS appeals.

(a) The regulations at §§ 121.402, 121.1102, and 121.1103 of this chapter also apply to NAICS code appeals.

(b) *Effect of OHA's decision.* If OHA grants the appeal (changes the NAICS code), and the contracting officer receives OHA's decision by the date offers are due, the contracting officer must amend the solicitation to reflect the new NAICS code. If the contracting officer receives OHA's decision after the date offers are due, OHA's decision will not apply to the pending procurement, but will apply to future solicitations for the same supplies or services.

(c) *Summary dismissal.* OHA may summarily dismiss a NAICS appeal either on the Judge's own initiative or on motion by a party. A summary dismissal may be with or without prejudice, and may be issued before the date set for close of record. Grounds for summary dismissal include: premature appeal, withdrawn appeal, settlement, cancellation of the procurement, and contract award.

[75 FR 47442, Aug. 6, 2010]

Subpart D—Rules of Practice for Appeals Under the 8(a) Program

SOURCE: 63 FR 35766, June 30, 1998, unless otherwise noted.

§ 134.401 Scope of the rules in this subpart D.

The rules of practice in this subpart D apply to all appeals to OHA from:

(a) Denials of 8(a) BD program admission based solely on a negative finding(s) of social disadvantage, economic disadvantage, ownership or control pursuant to § 124.206 of this title;

(b) Early graduation pursuant to §§ 124.302 and 124.304;

(c) Termination pursuant to §§ 124.303 and 124.304;

(d) Denials of requests to issue a waiver pursuant to § 124.515; and

(e) Suspensions pursuant to § 124.305(a).

§ 134.402 Appeal petition.

In addition to the requirements of § 134.203, an appeal petition must state, with specific reference to the determination and the record supporting such determination, the reasons why the determination is alleged to be arbitrary, capricious or contrary to law. This section does not apply to suspension appeals. For suspensions, see § 124.305 of this chapter.

[63 FR 35766, June 30, 1998, as amended at 67 FR 47250, July 18, 2002]

§ 134.403 Service of appeal petition.

Concurrent with its filing with OHA, the petitioner also must serve separate copies of the petition, including attachments, on two SBA officials.

(a) All 8(a) appeals must be served to: Director, Office of Business Development, U.S. Small Business Administration, 409 Third Street, SW., Washington, DC 20416, facsimile (202) 205–5206, or e-mail at *8aBD2@sba.gov*.

(b)(1) Appeals of early graduation or termination also must be served to: Associate General Counsel for Litigation, U.S. Small Business Administration, 409 Third Street, SW., Washington, DC 20416, facsimile (202) 205–7415, or e-mail at *OLITService@sba.gov*.

(2) Appeals of denial of program admission, suspension of program assistance, or denial of a request for waiver also must be served to: Associate General Counsel for Procurement Law, U.S. Small Business Administration, 409 Third Street, SW., Washington, DC 20416, facsimile (202) 205–6873, or e-mail at *OPLService@sba.gov*.

[75 FR 47442, Aug. 6, 2010]

§ 134.404 Deadline for filing appeal petition.

An 8(a) appeal petition must be filed within 45 calendar days after receipt of the SBA determination being appealed.

[75 FR 47442, Aug. 6, 2010]

§ 134.405 Jurisdiction.

(a) The Administrative Law Judge selected to preside over an appeal shall decline to accept jurisdiction over any matter if:

(1) The appeal does not, on its face, allege facts that, if proven to be true, would warrant reversal or modification of the determination, including appeals of denials of 8(a) BD program admission based in whole or in part on grounds other than a negative finding of social disadvantage, economic disadvantage, ownership or control;

(2) The appeal is untimely filed or is not otherwise filed in accordance with the requirements of this subpart or the

requirements in subparts A and B of this part; or

(3) The matter has been decided or is the subject of an adjudication before a court of competent jurisdiction over such matters.

(b) Once the Administrative Law Judge accepts jurisdiction over an appeal, subsequent initiation of an adjudication of the matter by a court of competent jurisdiction will not preclude the Administrative Law Judge from rendering a final decision on the matter.

(c) Jurisdiction of the Administrative Law Judge in a suspension case is limited to the issue of whether the protection of the Government's interest requires suspension pending resolution of the termination action, unless the Administrative Law Judge has consolidated the suspension appeal with the corresponding termination appeal.

[63 FR 35766, June 30, 1998; 75 FR 47443, Aug. 6, 2010]

§ 134.406 Review of the administrative record.

(a) Any proceeding conducted under § 134.401(a) through (d) shall be decided solely on a review of the written administrative record, except as provided in § 134.407 and in suspension appeals. For suspension appeals under § 134.401(e), see § 124.305(d) of this chapter.

(b) Except in suspension appeals, the Administrative Law Judge's review is limited to determining whether the Agency's determination is arbitrary, capricious, or contrary to law. As long as the Agency's determination is not arbitrary, capricious or contrary to law, the Administrative Law Judge must uphold it on appeal.

(1) The Administrative Law Judge must consider whether the decision was based on a consideration of the relevant factors and whether there has been a clear error of judgment.

(2) If the SBA's path of reasoning may reasonably be discerned, the Administrative Law Judge will uphold a decision of less than ideal clarity.

(c) *The administrative record.* (1) The administrative record must contain all documents that are relevant to the determination on appeal before the Administrative Law Judge and upon which the SBA decision-maker, and those SBA officials that recommended either for or against the decision, relied. The administrative record, however, need not contain all documents pertaining to the petitioner. For example, the administrative record in a termination proceeding need not include the Participant's entire business plan file, documents pertaining to specific 8(a) contracts, or the firm's application for participation in the 8(a) BD program if they are unrelated to the termination action. The SBA may claim privilege as to certain materials.

(2) The petitioner may object to the absence of a document, previously submitted to, or sent by, SBA, which the petitioner believes was erroneously omitted from the administrative record. The petitioner also may object to a claim of privilege made by the SBA. The petitioner's objections must be filed and served no later than 10 days of its receipt of the administrative record.

(3) In the absence of any objection by the petitioner or a finding by the Judge pursuant to paragraph (e) of this section that the record is insufficiently complete to decide whether the determination was arbitrary, capricious, or contrary to law, the administrative record submitted by SBA shall be deemed complete.

(d) Where the Agency files its response to the appeal petition after the date specified in § 134.206, the Administrative Law Judge may decline to consider the response and base his or her decision solely on a review of the administrative record.

(e) *Remand.* (1) The Administrative Law Judge may remand a case to the Director, Office of Business Development (or, in the case of a denial of a request for waiver under § 124.515 of this chapter, to the Administrator) for further consideration if he or she determines that, due to the absence in the written administrative record of the reasons upon which the determination was based, the administrative record is insufficiently complete to decide whether the determination is arbitrary, capricious, or contrary to law. In the event of such a remand, the Judge will not require the SBA to supplement the administrative record other than to supply the reason or reasons for the determination and any documents submitted to, or considered by, SBA in connection with any reconsideration permitted by regulation that occurs during the remand period. After such a remand, in the event the Judge finds that the reasons upon which the determination is based are absent from any supplemented record, the Judge will find the SBA determination to be arbitrary, capricious, or contrary to law.

(2) The Administrative Law Judge may also remand a case to the Director, Office of Business Development (or, in the case of a denial of a request for waiver under §124.515 of this chapter, to the Administrator) for further consideration where it is clearly apparent from the record that SBA made an erroneous factual finding (*e.g.*, SBA double counted an asset of an individual claiming disadvantaged status) or a mistake of law (*e.g.*, SBA applied the wrong regulatory provision in evaluating the case).

(3) The Administrative Law Judge may remand an eligibility, early graduation, or termination appeal to the Director, Office of Business Development, where the determination raises a new ground that was not in the initial SBA determination.

(4) A remand under this section will be for a reasonable period.

[63 FR 35766, June 30, 1998, as amended at 67 FR 47250, July 18, 2002; 74 FR 45754, Sept. 4, 2009; 75 FR 47443, Aug. 6, 2010; 81 FR 48595, July 25, 2016]

§ 134.407 Evidence beyond the record and discovery.

(a) Except in suspension appeals, the Administrative Law Judge may not admit evidence beyond the written administrative record nor permit any form of discovery unless he or she first determines that the petitioner, upon written submission, has made a substantial showing, based on credible evidence and not mere allegation, that the Agency determination in question may have resulted from bad faith or improper behavior.

(1) Prior to any such determination, the Administrative Law Judge must permit SBA to respond in writing to any allegations of bad faith or improper behavior.

(2) Upon a determination by the Administrative Law Judge that the petitioner has made such a substantial showing, the Administrative Law Judge may permit appropriate discovery, and accept relevant evidence beyond the written administrative record, which is specifically limited to the alleged bad faith or improper behavior.

(b) A determination by the Administrative Law Judge that the required showing set forth in paragraph (a) of this section has been made does not shift the burden of proof, which continues to rest with the petitioner.

[63 FR 35766, June 30, 1998, as amended at 67 FR 47251, July 18, 2002]

§ 134.408 Summary decision.

(a) *Generally.* In any appeal under this subpart D, either party may move or cross-move for summary decision, as provided in §134.212.

(b) *Summary decision based on fewer than all grounds.* If SBA has provided multiple grounds for the 8(a) determination being appealed, SBA may move for summary decision on one or more grounds.

(1) *Non-suspension cases.* Except in suspension appeals, if the Judge finds that there is no genuine issue of material fact as to whether SBA acted arbitrarily, capriciously, or contrary to law as to any such ground or grounds, and that the SBA is entitled to a decision in its favor as a matter of law, the Judge will grant the motion for summary decision and dismiss the appeal.

(2) *Suspension cases.* In suspension appeals, if the Judge finds that there is no genuine issue of material fact as to whether adequate evidence exists that protection of the Federal Government's interest requires suspension, as to any such ground or grounds for the proposed suspension, the SBA is entitled to a decision in its favor as a matter of law, and the Judge will grant the motion for summary decision and dismiss the appeal.

[67 FR 47251, July 18, 2002]

§ 134.409 Decision on appeal.

(a) A decision of the Administrative Law Judge under this subpart is the final agency decision, and is binding on the parties.

(b) The Administrative Law Judge shall issue a decision, insofar as practicable, within 90 days after an appeal petition is filed.

(c) The Administrative Law Judge may reconsider an appeal decision within 20 days of the decision if there is a clear showing of an error of fact or law material to the decision.

[63 FR 35766, June 30, 1998. Redesignated and amended at 67 FR 47251, July 18, 2002]

Subpart E—Rules of Practice for Appeals From Service-Disabled Veteran Owned Small Business Concern Protests

SOURCE: 70 FR 8927, Feb. 24, 2005, unless otherwise noted.

§ 134.501 What is the scope of the rules in this subpart E?

(a) The rules of practice in this subpart E apply to all appeals to OHA from formal protest determinations made by the Director, Office of Government Contracting (D/GC) in connection with a Service-Disabled Veteran-Owned Small Business Concern (SDVO SBC) protest relating to the status or ownership or control of the SDVO SBC, as set forth in § 125.29 of this chapter. This includes appeals from determinations by the D/GC that the protest was premature, untimely, nonspecific, or not based upon protestable allegations.

(b) Except where inconsistent with this subpart, the provisions of Subpart A and B of this part apply to appeals listed in paragraph (a) of this section.

(c) Appeals relating to formal size determinations and NAICS Code designations are governed by Subpart C of this part.

[70 FR 8927, Feb. 24, 2005, as amended at 81 FR 48595, July 25, 2016]

§ 134.502 Who may appeal?

Appeals from SDVO SBC protest determinations may be filed with OHA by the protested concern, the protester, or the contracting officer responsible for the procurement affected by the protest determination.

§ 134.503 When must a person file an appeal from an SDVO SBC protest determination?

Appeals from an SDVO SBC protest determination must be commenced by filing and serving an appeal petition within 10 business days after the appellant receives the SDVO SBC protest determination (*see* § 134.204 for filing and service requirements). An untimely appeal will be dismissed.

§ 134.504 [Reserved]

§ 134.505 What are the requirements for an appeal petition?

(a) *Format.* There is no required format for an appeal petition. However, it must include the following information:

(1) The solicitation or contract number, and the name, address, and telephone number of the contracting officer;

(2) A statement that the petition is appealing an SDVO SBC protest determination issued by the D/GC, a copy of the protest determination being appealed, and the date the petitioner received the SDVO SBC protest determination;

(3) A full and specific statement as to why the SDVO SBC protest determination is alleged to be based on a clear error of fact or law, together with an argument supporting such allegation; and

(4) The name, address, telephone number, facsimile number, e-mail address, and signature of the appellant or its attorney.

(b) *Service of appeal.* The appellant must serve the appeal petition upon each of the following:

(1) Director, Office of Government Contracting, U.S. Small Business Administration, 409 Third Street, SW., Washington, DC 20416, facsimile (202) 205–6390;

(2) The contracting officer responsible for the procurement affected by an SDVO SBC determination;

(3) The protested concern (the business concern whose SDVO SBC status is at issue) or the protester; and

(4) Associate General Counsel for Procurement Law, U.S. Small Business

Administration, 409 Third Street, SW., Washington, DC 20416, facsimile (202) 205–6873, or e-mail at *OPLService@sba.gov*.

(c) *Certificate of Service*. The appellant must attach to the appeal petition a signed certificate of service meeting the requirements of § 134.204(d).

[70 FR 8927, Feb. 24, 2005, as amended at 75 FR 47443, Aug. 6, 2010]

§ 134.506 What are the service and filing requirements?

The provisions of § 134.204 apply to the service and filing of all pleadings and other submissions permitted under this subpart unless otherwise indicated in this subpart.

§ 134.507 When does the D/GC transmit the protest file and to whom?

Upon receipt of an appeal petition, the D/GC will send to OHA a copy of the protest file relating to that determination. The D/GC will certify and authenticate that the protest file, to the best of his or her knowledge, is a true and correct copy of the protest file.

§ 134.508 What is the standard of review?

The standard of review for an appeal of a SDVO SBC protest determination is whether the D/GC's determination was based on clear error of fact or law. With respect to status determinations on whether the owner is a veteran, service-disabled veteran, or veteran with a permanent and severe disability, the Judge will not review the determinations made by the U.S. Department of Veteran's Affairs, U.S. Department of Defense, or such determinations identified by documents provided by the U.S. National Archives and Records Administration.

§ 134.509 When will a Judge dismiss an appeal?

(a) The Judge selected to preside over a protest appeal shall dismiss the appeal, if:

(1) The appeal does not, on its face, allege facts that if proven to be true, warrant reversal or modification of the determination;

(2) The appeal petition does not contain all of the information required in § 134.505;

(3) The appeal is untimely filed pursuant to § 134.503 or is not otherwise filed in accordance with the requirements of this subpart or the requirements in Subparts A and B of this part; or

(4) The matter has been decided or is the subject of an adjudication before a court of competent jurisdiction over such matters.

(b) Once Appellant files an appeal, subsequent initiation of litigation of the matter in a court of competent jurisdiction will not preclude the Judge from rendering a final decision on the matter.

§ 134.510 Who can file a response to an appeal petition and when must such a response be filed?

Although not required, any person served with an appeal petition may file and serve a response supporting or opposing the appeal if he or she wishes to do so. If a person decides to file a response, the response must be filed within 7 business days after service of the appeal petition. The response should present argument.

§ 134.511 Will the Judge permit discovery and oral hearings?

Discovery will not be permitted and oral hearings will not be held.

§ 134.512 What are the limitations on new evidence?

The Judge may not admit evidence beyond the written protest file nor permit any form of discovery. All appeals under this subpart will be decided solely on a review of the evidence in the written protest file, arguments made in the appeal petition and response(s) filed thereto.

§ 134.513 When is the record closed?

The record will close when the time to file a response to an appeal petition expires pursuant to 13 CFR 134.510.

§ 134.514 When must the Judge issue his or her decision?

The Judge shall issue a decision, insofar as practicable, within 15 business days after close of the record.

[70 FR 8927, Feb. 24, 2005, as amended at 76 FR 5685, Feb. 2, 2011]

§ 134.515 What are the effects of the Judge's decision?

(a) A decision of the Judge under this subpart is the final agency decision and is binding on the parties. For the effects of the decision on the contract or procurement at issue, please see § 125.31 of this chapter.

(b) The Judge may reconsider an appeal decision within twenty (20) calendar days after issuance of the written decision. Any party who has appeared in the proceeding, or SBA, may request reconsideration by filing with the Judge and serving a petition for reconsideration on all the parties to the appeal within twenty (20) calendar days after issuance of the written decision. The request for reconsideration must clearly show an error of fact or law material to the decision. The Judge may also reconsider a decision on his or her own initiative.

(c) The Judge may remand a proceeding to the D/GC for a new SDVO SBC determination if the latter fails to address issues of decisional significance sufficiently, does not address all the relevant evidence, or does not identify specifically the evidence upon which it relied. Once remanded, OHA no longer has jurisdiction over the matter, unless a new appeal is filed as a result of the new SDVO SBC determination.

[70 FR 8927, Feb. 24, 2005, as amended at 73 FR 56955, Oct. 1, 2008; 75 FR 62292, Oct. 7, 2010; 76 FR 5685, Feb. 2, 2011; 81 FR 48595, July 25, 2016]

Subpart F—Implementation of the Equal Access to Justice Act

SOURCE: 61 FR 2683, Jan. 29, 1996, unless otherwise noted. Redesignated at 63 FR 35766, June 30, 1998, and 70 FR 8927, Feb. 24, 2005.

§ 134.601 What is the purpose of this subpart?

The Equal Access to Justice Act, 5 U.S.C. 504, establishes procedures by which prevailing parties in certain administrative proceedings may apply for reimbursement of fees and other expenses. Eligible parties may receive awards when they prevail over SBA, unless SBA's position in the proceeding was "substantially justified" or, as provided in § 134.605(b), special circumstances make an award unjust. The rules of this subpart explain which OHA proceedings are covered, who may be eligible for an award of fees and expenses, and how to apply for such an award.

[61 FR 2683, Jan. 29, 1996. Redesignated at 63 FR 35766, June 30, 1998, and 70 FR 8927, Feb. 24, 2005, as amended at 75 FR 47443, Aug. 6, 2010]

§ 134.602 Under what circumstances may I apply for reimbursement?

You may apply for reimbursement under this subpart if you meet the eligibility requirements in § 134.606 and you prevail over SBA in a final decision in:

(a) The type of administrative proceeding which qualifies as an "adversary adjudication" under § 134.603; or

(b) An ancillary or subsidiary issue in that administrative proceeding that is sufficiently significant and discrete to merit treatment as a separate unit; or

(c) A matter which the agency orders to be determined as an "adversary adjudication" under 5 U.S.C. 554.

[61 FR 2683, Jan. 29, 1996. Redesignated at 63 FR 35766, June 30, 1998, and 70 FR 8927, Feb. 24, 2005, as amended at 75 FR 47443, Aug. 6, 2010]

§ 134.603 What is an adversary adjudication?

For purposes of this subpart, adversary adjudications are administrative proceedings before OHA which involve SBA as a party and which are required to be conducted by an Administrative Law Judge ("ALJ"). These adjudications ("administrative proceedings") include those proceedings listed in § 134.102 (a), (i), and (j)(1), but do not include other OHA proceedings such as those listed in § 134.102(k). In order for an administrative proceeding to qualify, SBA must have been represented by counsel or by another representative who enters an appearance and participates in the proceeding.

§ 134.604 What benefits may I claim?

You may seek reimbursement for certain reasonable fees and expenses incurred in prosecuting or defending a claim in an administrative proceeding.

§ 134.605 Under what circumstances are fees and expenses reimbursable?

(a) If you are a prevailing eligible party, you may receive an award for reasonable fees and expenses unless the position of the agency in the proceeding is found by the ALJ to be "substantially justified", or special circumstances exist which make an award unjust. The "position of the agency" includes not only the position taken by SBA in the administrative proceeding, but also the position which it took in the action which led to the administrative proceeding. No presumption arises that SBA's position was not substantially justified simply because it did not prevail in a proceeding. However, upon your assertion that the position of SBA was not substantially justified, SBA will be required to establish that its position was reasonable in fact and law.

(b) The ALJ may reduce or deny an award for reimbursement if you have unreasonably protracted the administrative proceeding or if other special circumstances would make the award unjust.

(c) Awards for fees and expenses incurred before the date on which an administrative proceeding was initiated are allowable only if you can demonstrate that they were reasonably incurred in preparation for the proceeding.

§ 134.606 Who is eligible for possible reimbursement?

(a) You are eligible for possible reimbursement if:

(1) You are an individual, owner of an unincorporated business, partnership, corporation, association, organization, or unit of local government; and

(2) You are a party, as defined in 5 U.S.C. 551(3); and

(3) You are the prevailing party; and

(4) You meet certain net worth and employee eligibility requirements set forth in § 134.607.

(b) You are not eligible for possible reimbursement if you participated in the administrative proceeding only on behalf of persons or entities that are ineligible.

[61 FR 2683, Jan. 29, 1996. Redesignated at 63 FR 35766, June 30, 1998, and 70 FR 8927, Feb. 24, 2005, as amended at 75 FR 47443, Aug. 6, 2010]

§ 134.607 How do I know which eligibility requirement applies to me?

Follow this chart to determine your eligibility. You should calculate your net worth and the number of your employees as of the date the administrative proceeding was initiated.

If your participation in the proceeding was:	Eligibility requirements:
(1) As an individual rather than a business owner.	(1) Personal net worth may not exceed 2 million dollars.
(2) As owner of an unincorporated business.	(2) Personal net worth may not exceed 7 million dollars, and No more than 500 employees.
(3) As a partnership, corporation, association, organization, or unit of local government.	(3) Business net worth may not exceed 7 million dollars, and No more than 500 employees.
(4) As a charitable or other tax-exempt organization described in 26 U.S.C. 501(c)(3) or a cooperative association as defined in 12 U.S.C. 1141j(a).	(4) No net worth limitations, and No more than 500 employees.

§ 134.608 What are the special rules for calculating net worth and number of employees?

(a) Your net worth must include the value of any assets disposed of for the purpose of meeting an eligibility standard, and must exclude any obligation incurred for that purpose. Transfers of assets, or obligations incurred, for less than reasonably equivalent value will be presumed to have been made for the purpose of meeting an eligibility standard.

(b) If you are an owner of an unincorporated business, or a partnership, corporation, association, organization, or unit of local government, your net worth must include the net worth of all of your affiliates. "Affiliates" are:

(1) Corporations or other business entities which directly or indirectly own or control a majority of the voting shares or other ownership interests in the applicant concern; and

(2) Corporations or other business entities in which the applicant concern directly or indirectly owns or controls a majority of the voting shares or other ownership interests.

(c) Your employees include all those persons regularly working for you at the time the administrative proceeding was initiated, whether or not they were at work on that date. Part-time employees must be included on a proportional basis. You must include the employees of all your affiliates in your total number of employees.

§ 134.609 What is the difference between a fee and an expense?

A fee is a charge to you for the professional services of attorneys, agents, or expert witnesses rendered in connection with your case. An expense is the cost to you of any study, analysis, engineering report, test, project, or similar matter prepared in connection with your case.

§ 134.610 Are there limitations on reimbursement for fees and expenses?

(a) Awards will be calculated on the basis of fees and expenses actually incurred. If services were provided by one or more of your employees, or were made available to you free, you may not seek an award for those services. If services were provided at a reduced rate, fees and expenses will be calculated at that reduced rate.

(b) In determining the reasonableness of the fees for attorneys, agents or expert witnesses, the ALJ will consider at least the following:

(1) That provider's customary fee for like services;

(2) The prevailing rate for similar services in the community in which that provider ordinarily performs services;

(3) The time actually spent in representing you; and

(4) The time reasonably spent in light of the difficulty and complexity of the issues.

(c) An award for the fees of an attorney or agent may not exceed $75 per hour, and an award for the fees of an expert witness may not exceed $25 per hour, regardless of the rate charged.

(d) An award for the reasonable cost of any study, analysis, engineering report, test, project or similar matter prepared on your behalf may not exceed the prevailing rate payable for similar services, and you may be reimbursed only if the study or other matter was necessary to the preparation of your case.

§ 134.611 What should I include in my application for an award?

(a) Your application must be in the form of a written petition which is served and filed in accordance with § 134.204. It must contain the following information:

(1) A statement that OHA has jurisdiction over the case pursuant to § 134.102(g);

(2) Identification of the administrative proceeding for which you are seeking an award;

(3) A statement that you have prevailed, and a list of each issue in which you claim the position of SBA was not substantially justified;

(4) Your status as an individual, owner of an unincorporated business, partnership, corporation, association, organization, or unit of local government;

(5) Your net worth and number of employees as of the date the administrative proceeding was initiated, or a statement that one or both of these eligibility requirements do not apply to you;

(6) The amount of fees and expenses you are seeking, along with the invoice or billing statement from each service provider;

(7) A description of any affiliates (as that term is defined in § 134.608), or a statement that no affiliates exist;

(8) A statement that the application and any attached statements and exhibits are true and complete to the best of your knowledge and that you understand a false statement on these documents is a felony punishable by fine and imprisonment under 18 U.S.C. 1001; and

(9)(i) Your name and address;

(ii) Your signature, or the signature of either a responsible official or your attorney; and

(iii) The address and telephone number of the person who signs the application.

(b) You should follow this chart to determine which further documents must be included with your application:

Party	Required documents
(1) Individual, owner of unincorporated business, partnership, corporation, association, organization, or unit of local government.	(1) Net worth exhibit.
(2) Organization qualified as tax-exempt under 26 U.S.C. 501(c)(3).	(2) Copy of a ruling by the Internal Revenue Service that you qualify as a 501(c)(3) organization or Statement that you were listed in the current edition of IRS Bulletin 78 as of the date the administrative proceeding was initiated.
(3) Tax-exempt religious organization not required to obtain a ruling from the Internal Revenue Service on its exempt status.	(3) Description of your organization and the basis for your belief you are exempt.
(4) Cooperative association as defined in 12 U.S.C. 1141j(a).	(4) Copy of your charter or articles of incorporation, and Copy of your bylaws.

[61 FR 2683, Jan. 29, 1996. Redesignated at 63 FR 35766, June 30, 1998, and 70 FR 8927, Feb. 24, 2005, as amended at 75 FR 47443, Aug. 6, 2010]

§ 134.612 What must a net worth exhibit contain?

(a) A net worth exhibit may be in any format, but it must contain:

(1) List of all assets and liabilities for you and each affiliate in detail sufficient to show your eligibility;

(2) Aggregate net worth for you and all affiliates; and

(3) Description of any transfers of assets from, or obligations incurred by, you or your affiliates within one year prior to the initiation of the administrative proceeding which reduced your net worth below the eligibility ceiling, or a statement that no such transfers occurred.

(b) The net worth exhibit must be filed with your application, but will not be part of the public record of the proceeding. Further, in accordance with the provisions of § 134.204(g), you need not serve your net worth exhibit on other parties.

§ 134.613 What documentation do I need for fees and expenses?

You must submit a separate itemized statement or invoice for the services of each provider for which you seek reimbursement. Each separate statement or invoice must contain:

(a) The hours worked in connection with the proceeding by each provider supplying a billable service;

(b) A description of the specific services performed by each provider;

(c) The rate at which fees were computed for each provider;

(d) The total charged by the provider on that statement or invoice; and

(e) The provider's verification that the statement or invoice is true to the best of his or her knowledge and that he or she understands that a false statement is punishable by fine and imprisonment under 18 U.S.C. 1001.

§ 134.614 What deadlines apply to my application for an award and where do I send it?

After you have prevailed in an administrative proceeding or in a discrete issue therein, you must serve, and file with OHA, your written application for an award, and its attachments, no later than 30 days after the decision in the administrative proceeding becomes final under § 134.227. The deadline for filing an application for an award may not be extended. If SBA or another party requests review of the decision in the underlying administrative proceeding, your request for an award for fees and expenses may still be filed, but it will not be considered by the ALJ until a final decision is rendered.

§ 134.615 How will proceedings relating to my application for fees and expenses be conducted?

Proceedings will be conducted in accordance with the provisions in subpart B of this part.

§ 134.616 How will I know if I receive an award?

The ALJ will issue an initial decision on the merits of your request for an award which will become final in 30 days unless a request for review is filed under § 134.228. The decision will include findings on your eligibility, on whether SBA's position was substantially justified, and on the reasonableness of the amount you requested. Where applicable, there will also be findings on whether you have unduly protracted the proceedings or whether other circumstances make an award unjust, and an explanation of the reason for the difference, if any, between the amount requested and the amount awarded. If you have sought an award against more than one federal agency, the decision will allocate responsibility for payment among the agencies with appropriate explanation.

§ 134.617 May I seek review of the ALJ's decision on my award?

You may request review of the ALJ's decision on your award by filing a request for review in accordance with § 134.228. You may seek judicial review of a final decision as provided in 5 U.S.C. 504(c)(2).

§ 134.618 How are awards paid?

If you are seeking payment of an award, you must submit a copy of the final decision, along with your certification that you are not seeking judicial review of either the decision in the adversary adjudication, or of the award, to the following address: Chief Financial Officer, Office of Financial Operations, SBA, P.O. Box 205, Denver, CO 80201–0205. SBA will pay you the amount awarded within 60 days of receipt of your request unless it is notified that you or another party has sought judicial review of the underlying decision or the award.

Subpart G—Rules of Practice for Appeals From Women-Owned Small Business Concern (WOSB) and Economically Disadvantaged WOSB Concern (EDWOSB) Protests

SOURCE: 75 FR 62292, Oct. 7, 2010, unless otherwise noted.

§ 134.701 What is the scope of the rules in this subpart G?

(a) The rules of practice in this subpart G apply to all appeals to OHA from formal protest determinations made by the Director for Government Contracting (D/GC) in connection with a Women-Owned Small Business Concern (WOSB) or Economically Disadvantaged WOSB Concern (EDWOSB) protest. Appeals under this subpart include issues related to whether the concern is owned and controlled by one or more women who are United States citizens and, if the appeal is in connection with an EDWOSB contract, that the concern is at least 51 percent owned and controlled by one or more women who are economically disadvantaged. This includes appeals from determinations by the D/GC that the protest was premature, untimely, nonspecific, or not based upon protestable allegations.

(b) Except where inconsistent with this subpart, the provisions of subparts A and B of this part apply to appeals listed in paragraph (a) of this section.

(c) Appeals relating to formal size determinations and NAICS Code designations are governed by subpart C of this part.

§ 134.702 Who may appeal?

Appeals from WOSB or EDWOSB protest determinations may be filed with OHA by the protested concern, the protestor, or the contracting officer responsible for the procurement affected by the protest determination.

§ 134.703 When must a person file an appeal from an WOSB or EDWOSB protest determination?

Appeals from a WOSB or EDWOSB protest determination must be commenced by filing and serving an appeal petition within ten (10) business days after the appellant receives the WOSB or EDWOSB protest determination (see § 134.204 for filing and service requirements). An untimely appeal must be dismissed.

§ 134.704 What are the effects of the appeal on the procurement at issue?

Appellate decisions apply to the procurement in question. If a timely OHA appeal has been filed after contract award, the contracting officer must consider whether performance can be suspended until an appellate decision is rendered. If OHA affirms the D/GC's determination finding that the protested concern is ineligible, the contracting officer shall either terminate the contract, not exercise the next option or not award further task or delivery orders. If OHA overturns the D/GC's dismissal or determination that the concern is an eligible EDWOSB or WOSB, the contracting officer may apply the OHA decision to the procurement in question.

§ 134.705 What are the requirements for an appeal petition?

(a) *Format.* There is no required format for an appeal petition. However, it must include the following information:

(1) The solicitation or contract number, and the name, address, and telephone number of the contracting officer;

(2) A statement that the petitioner is appealing a WOSB or EDWOSB protest determination issued by the D/GC and the date that the petitioner received it;

(3) A full and specific statement as to why the WOSB or EDWOSB protest determination is alleged to be based on a clear error of fact or law, together with an argument supporting such allegation; and

(4) The name, address, telephone number, facsimile number, and signature of the appellant or its attorney.

(b) *Service of appeal.* The appellant must serve the appeal petition upon each of the following:

(1) The D/GC at U.S. Small Business Administration, 409 3rd Street, SW., Washington, DC 20416, facsimile (202) 205–6390;

(2) The contracting officer responsible for the procurement affected by a WOSB or EDWOSB determination;

(3) The protested concern (the business concern whose WOSB or EDWOSB status is at issue) or the protester; and

(4) SBA's Office of General Counsel, Associate General Counsel for Procurement Law, U.S. Small Business Administration, 409 3rd Street, SW., Washington, DC 20416, facsimile number (202) 205–6873.

(c) *Certificate of Service.* The appellant must attach to the appeal petition a signed certificate of service meeting the requirements of § 134.204(d).

§ 134.706 What are the service and filing requirements?

The provisions of § 134.204 apply to the service and filing of all pleadings and other submissions permitted under this subpart unless otherwise indicated in this subpart.

§ 134.707 When does the D/GC transmit the protest file and to whom?

Upon receipt of an appeal petition, the D/GC will send to OHA a copy of the protest file relating to that determination. The D/GC will certify and authenticate that the protest file, to the best of his or her knowledge, is a true and correct copy of the protest file.

§ 134.708 What is the standard of review?

The standard of review for an appeal of a WOSB or EDWOSB protest determination is whether the D/GC's determination was based on clear error of fact or law.

§ 134.709 When will a Judge dismiss an appeal?

(a) The presiding Judge must dismiss the appeal if the appeal is untimely filed under § 134.703.

(b) The matter has been decided or is the subject of adjudication before a court of competent jurisdiction over such matters. However, once an appeal has been filed, initiation of litigation of the matter in a court of competent jurisdiction will not preclude the Judge from rendering a final decision on the matter.

§ 134.710 Who can file a response to an appeal petition and when must such a response be filed?

Although not required, any person served with an appeal petition may file and serve a response supporting or opposing the appeal if he or she wishes to do so. If a person decides to file a response, the response must be filed within seven (7) business days after service of the appeal petition. The response should present argument.

§ 134.711 Will the Judge permit discovery and oral hearings?

Discovery will not be permitted, and oral hearings will not be held.

§ 134.712 What are the limitations on new evidence?

The Judge may not admit evidence beyond the written protest file nor permit any form of discovery. All appeals under this subpart will be decided solely on a review of the evidence in the written protest file, arguments made in the appeal petition, and response(s) filed thereto.

§ 134.713 When is the record closed?

The record will close when the time to file a response to an appeal petition expires pursuant to § 134.710.

§ 134.714 When must the Judge issue his or her decision?

The Judge shall issue a decision, insofar as practicable, within fifteen (15) business days after close of the record.

§ 134.715 Can a Judge reconsider his decision?

(a) The Judge may reconsider an appeal decision within twenty (20) calendar days after issuance of the written decision. Any party who has appeared in the proceeding, or SBA, may request reconsideration by filing with the Judge and serving a petition for reconsideration on all the parties to the appeal within twenty (20) calendar days after service of the written decision. The request for reconsideration must clearly show an error of fact or law material to the decision. The Judge may also reconsider a decision on his or her own initiative.

(b) The Judge may remand a proceeding to the D/GC for a new WOSB or EDWOSB determination if the D/GC fails to address issues of decisional significance sufficiently, does not address all the relevant evidence, or does not identify specifically the evidence upon which it relied. Once remanded, OHA no longer has jurisdiction over the matter, unless a new appeal is filed as a result of the new WOSB or EDWOSB determination.

Subpart H—Rules of Practice for Employee Disputes

SOURCE: 75 FR 47443, Aug. 6, 2010, unless otherwise noted.

§ 134.801 Scope of rules.

(a) The rules of practice in this subpart H apply to the OHA appeal under the Employee Dispute Resolution Process (EDRP). Standard Operating Procedure (SOP) 37 71 sets out the EDRP. It is available at *http://www.sba.gov/tools/resourcelibrary/sops/index.html* or through OHA's Web site *http://www.sba.gov/oha*).

(b) The following rules, located in subparts A and B of this part, also apply to OHA appeals under the EDRP:

(1) Definitions (§ 134.101);

(2) Jurisdiction of OHA (§ 134.102(r) only);

(3) Scope of the rules in this subpart B (§ 134.201(a), (b)(6), and (c) only);

(4) Commencement of cases (§ 134.202(d) only, on deadlines and how to count days);

(5) Filing and service requirements (§ 134.204);

(6) Amendments and supplemental pleadings (§ 134.207);

(7) Requirement of signature (§ 134.209);

(8) Motions (§ 134.211);

(9) Summary decision (§ 134.212); and

(10) Sanctions (§ 134.219).

[75 FR 47443, Aug. 6, 2010, as amended at 82 FR 25507, June 2, 2017]

§ 134.802 [Reserved]

§ 134.803 Commencement of appeals from SBA Employee Dispute Resolution Process cases (Employee Disputes).

(a) An appeal from a Step Two decision must be commenced by filing an appeal petition within 15 calendar days from the date the Employee receives the Step Two decision.

(b) If the Step Two Official does not issue a decision within 15 calendar days of receiving the SBA Dispute Form from the Employee, the Employee must file his/her appeal petition at OHA no later than 15 calendar days from the date the Step Two decision was due.

(c) The rule for counting days is in § 134.202(d).

(d) OHA will dismiss an untimely appeal.

[75 FR 47443, Aug. 6, 2010, as amended at 82 FR 25507, June 2, 2017]

§ 134.804 The appeal petition.

(a) *Form.* There is no required format for an appeal petition. However, it must include the following:

(1) The completed SBA Dispute Form;

(2) A copy of the Step One and Step Two decisions, if any;

(3) Statement of why the Step Two decision (or Step One decision, if no Step Two decision was received), is alleged to be in error;

(4) Any other pertinent information the OHA Judge should consider;

(5) A request for mediation, if applicable; and

(6) If represented by an attorney, the attorney's contact information and signature.

(b) *Service of the appeal petition upon the SBA.* The Employee must serve copies of the entire appeal petition upon three SBA officials:

(1) The Step Two Official;

(2) Chief Human Capital Officer, U.S. Small Business Administration, 409 Third Street, SW., Washington, DC 20416; and

(3) Associate General Counsel for General Law, U.S. Small Business Administration, 409 Third Street, SW., Washington, DC 20416, e-mail: *OGLService@sba.gov*, except that an employee of the Office of Inspector General (OIG) must serve it upon the Counsel to the Inspector General, U.S. Small Business Administration, 409 Third Street, SW., Washington, DC 20416, e-mail: *ig.counseldiv@sba.gov*.

(c) The rules governing filing and service are in § 134.204.

(d) *Dismissal.* An appeal petition that does not meet all the requirements of this section may be dismissed by the Judge at his or her own initiative or upon motion of the SBA.

[75 FR 47443, Aug. 6, 2010, as amended at 82 FR 25507, June 2, 2017]

§ 134.805 After the appeal petition is filed.

(a) The AA/OHA will assign a Judge to adjudicate the case. If mediation is requested or offered, the AA/OHA will assign a different person to mediate the case.

(b) OHA will issue and serve upon the Employee and the SBA a notice and order informing the parties that an appeal has been filed, and setting the date for SBA's response and the close of record.

(c) The rules for amendments to pleadings and supplemental pleadings are in § 134.207.

(d) Unless otherwise instructed, OHA will serve all orders and the decision by email upon the Employee, or upon the attorney if represented by an attorney.

[75 FR 47443, Aug. 6, 2010, as amended at 82 FR 25507, June 2, 2017]

§ 134.806 Mediation.

Either the Employee or the SBA may request mediation, or OHA may offer mediation. OHA may designate a Judge or an OHA attorney to serve as a mediator. If the parties reach a settlement through mediation, they may file a joint motion to dismiss the appeal based on that settlement. If the parties do not reach a settlement, the mediation will conclude and the appeal will go to adjudication. An OHA-provided mediator will not be involved in a subsequent adjudication.

§ 134.807 SBA response.

(a) If the appeal goes to adjudication, SBA will file and serve the SBA's response to the appeal and any documentation, not already filed by the Employee, that SBA wishes OHA to consider.

(b) Unless the Judge orders a different date (either on his or her own initiative or on motion by a party), the SBA must file any response to the appeal petition no later than 15 calendar days from the conclusion of mediation or 15 calendar days from the filing of the appeal petition, whichever is later.

(c) The SBA's response is normally the last submission in an appeal, although the Judge may order or permit additional submissions. If a party wishes to file an additional submission, the party must file and serve a motion (see § 134.211) accompanied by the proposed submission.

[75 FR 47443, Aug. 6, 2010, as amended at 82 FR 25507, June 2, 2017]

§ 134.808 The decision.

(a) The Judge will decide the appeal within 45 calendar days (if practicable) from close of record. The decision will affirm, modify, remand, or reverse the Step One or Step Two decision.

(b) The standard of review and burden of proof will be determined by the specific issue presented.

(c) OHA's decision is an initial decision which becomes the final decision of the SBA 30 calendar days after issuance, unless a party files a request for review pursuant to § 134.809.

(d) OHA's decision is not precedential and it will not be published.

[75 FR 47443, Aug. 6, 2010, as amended at 82 FR 25507, June 2, 2017]

§ 134.809 Review of initial decision.

(a) If the Chief Human Capital Officer, General Counsel for SBA, or Counsel to the Inspector General (IG) believes OHA's decision is contrary to law, rule, regulation, or SBA policy, that official may file a Petition for Review (PFR) of the decision with the Deputy Administrator (or IG for disputes by OIG employees) for a final SBA Decision. Only the Chief Human Capital Officer, General Counsel, or Counsel to the IG may file a PFR of an OHA decision; the Employee may not.

(b) To file a PFR, the official must request a complete copy of the dispute file from the Assistant Administrator for OHA (AA/OHA) within five calendar days of receiving the decision. The AA/OHA will provide a copy of the dispute file to the official, the Employee, and the Employee's representative within five calendar days of the official's request. The official's PFR is due no later than 15 calendar days from the date the official receives the dispute file. The PFR must specify the objections to OHA's decision.

[82 FR 25507, June 2, 2017]

Subpart I—Rules of Practice for Petitions for Reconsideration of Size Standards

SOURCE: 82 FR 25507, June 2, 2017, unless otherwise noted.

§ 134.901 Scope of the rules in this subpart.

(a) The rules of practice in this subpart apply to Size Standard Petitions.

(b) Except where inconsistent with this subpart, the provisions of subparts A and B of this part apply to Size Standard Petitions listed in paragraph (a) of this section.

§ 134.902 Standing.

(a) A Size Standard Petition may be filed with OHA by any person that is adversely affected by the Administrator's decision to revise, modify, or establish a size standard.

(b) A business entity is not adversely affected unless it conducts business in the industry associated with the size standard that is being challenged and:

(1) The business entity qualified as a small business concern before the size standard was revised or modified; or

(2) The business entity qualifies as a small business under the size standard as revised or modified.

§ 134.903 Commencement of cases.

(a) A Size Standard Petition must be filed at OHA not later than 30 calendar days after the publication in the FEDERAL REGISTER of the final rule that revises, modifies, or establishes the challenged size standard. An untimely Size Standard Petition will be dismissed.

(b) A Size Standard Petition filed in response to a notice of proposed rulemaking is premature and will be dismissed.

(c) A Size Standard Petition challenging a size standard that has not been revised, modified, or established through publication in the FEDERAL REGISTER will be dismissed.

§ 134.904 Requirements for the Size Standard Petition.

(a) *Form*. There is no required form for a Size Standard Petition. However, it must include the following information:

(1) A copy of the final rule published in the FEDERAL REGISTER to revise, modify, or establish a size standard, or an electronic link to the final rule;

(2) A full and specific statement as to which size standard(s) in the final rule the Petitioner is challenging and why the process that was used to revise, modify, or establish each challenged size standard is alleged to be arbitrary, capricious, an abuse of discretion, or otherwise not in accordance with the law, together with argument supporting such allegation;

(3) A copy of any comments the Petitioner submitted in response to the proposed notice of rulemaking that pertained to the size standard(s) in question, or a statement that no such comments were submitted; and

(4) The name, mailing address, telephone number, facsimile number, email address, and signature of the Petitioner or its attorney.

(b) *Multiple size standards.* A Petitioner may challenge multiple size standards that were revised, modified, or established in the same final rule in a single Size Standard Petition, provided that the Petitioner demonstrates standing for each of the challenged size standards.

(c) *Format.* The formatting provisions of § 134.203(d) apply to Size Standard Petitions.

(d) *Service.* In addition to filing the Size Standard Petition at OHA, the Petitioner must serve a copy of the Size Standard Petition upon each of the following:

(1) SBA's Office of Size Standards, U.S. Small Business Administration, 409 3rd Street SW., Washington, DC 20416; facsimile number (202) 205–6390; or *sizestandards@sba.gov;* and

(2) SBA's Office of General Counsel, Associate General Counsel for Procurement Law, U.S. Small Business Administration, 409 3rd Street SW., Washington, DC 20416; facsimile number (202) 205–6873; or *OPLService@sba.gov.*

(e) *Certificate of service.* The Petitioner must attach to the Size Standard Petition a signed certificate of service meeting the requirements of § 134.204(d).

§ 134.905 Notice and order.

Upon receipt of a Size Standard Petition, OHA will assign the matter to a Judge in accordance with § 134.218. Unless it appears that the Size Standard Petition will be dismissed under § 134.910, the presiding Judge will issue a notice and order initiating the publication required by § 121.102(f) of this chapter; specifying a date for the Office of Size Standards to transmit to OHA a copy of the administrative record supporting the revision, modification, or establishment of the challenged size standard(s); and establishing a date for the close of record. Typically, the administrative record will be due seven calendar days after issuance of the notice and order, and the record will close 45 calendar days from the date of OHA's receipt of the Size Standard Petition.

§ 134.906 Intervention.

In accordance with § 134.210(b), interested persons with a direct stake in the outcome of the case may contact OHA to intervene in the proceeding and obtain a copy of the Size Standard Petition. In the event that the Size Standard Petition contains confidential information and the intervener is not a governmental entity, the Judge may require that the intervener's attorney be admitted to a protective order before obtaining a complete copy of the Size Standard Petition.

§ 134.907 Filing and service.

The provisions of § 134.204 apply to the filing and service of all pleadings and other submissions permitted under this subpart unless otherwise indicated in this subpart.

§ 134.908 The administrative record.

The Office of Size Standards will transmit to OHA a copy of the documentation and analysis supporting the revision, modification, or establishment of the challenged size standard by the date specified in the notice and order. The Chief, Office of Size Standards, will certify and authenticate that the administrative record, to the best of his or her knowledge, is complete and correct. The Petitioner and any interveners may, upon request, review the administrative record submitted to OHA. The administrative record will include the documentation and analysis supporting the revision, modification, or establishment of the challenged size standard.

§ 134.909 Standard of review.

The standard of review for deciding a Size Standard Petition is whether the process employed by the Administrator to revise, modify, or establish the size standard was arbitrary, capricious, an abuse of discretion, or otherwise not in accordance with the law. OHA will not adjudicate arguments that a different size standard should have been selected. The Petitioner bears the burden of proof.

§ 134.910 Dismissal.

The Judge must dismiss the Size Standard Petition if:

(a) The Size Standard Petition does not, on its face, allege specific facts that if proven to be true, warrant remand of the size standard;

(b) The Petitioner is not adversely affected by the final rule revising, modifying, or establishing a size standard;

(c) The Size Standard Petition is untimely or premature pursuant to § 134.903 or is not otherwise filed in accordance with the requirements in subparts A and B of this part; or

(d) The matter has been decided or is the subject of adjudication before a court of competent jurisdiction over such matters.

§ 134.911 Response to the Size Standard Petition.

Although not required, any intervener may file and serve a response supporting or opposing the Size Standard Petition at any time prior to the close of record. SBA may intervene as of right at any time in any case until 15 days after the close of record, or the issuance of a decision, whichever comes first. The response must present argument.

§ 134.912 Discovery and oral hearings.

Discovery will not be permitted. Oral hearings will not be held unless the Judge determines that the dispute cannot be resolved except by the taking of live testimony and the confrontation of witnesses.

§ 134.913 New evidence.

Disputes under this subpart ordinarily will be decided based on the pleadings and the administrative record. The Judge may admit additional evidence upon a motion establishing good cause.

§ 134.914 The decision.

The Judge will issue his or her decision within 45 calendar days after close of record, as practicable. The Judge's decision is final and will not be reconsidered.

§ 134.915 Remand.

If OHA grants a Size Standard Petition, OHA will remand the matter to the Office of Size Standards for further analysis. Once remanded, OHA no longer has jurisdiction over the matter unless a new Size Standard Petition is filed as a result of a new final rule published in the FEDERAL REGISTER.

§ 134.916 Effects of OHA's decision.

(a) If OHA grants a Size Standard Petition of a modified or revised size standard, SBA will take appropriate action to rescind that size standard and to restore the one that was in effect before the one challenged in the Size Standard Petition. The restored size standard will remain in effect until SBA issues a new size standard. The OHA decision does not affect the validity of a concern's size representation made under the challenged size standard prior to the effective date of the SBA action rescinding that challenged size standard. Such a concern remains eligible for award as a small business, and the procuring agency may count the award towards its small business goals. If the procuring agency amends the solicitation and requires new self-certifications, those self-certifications will be based on the size standard in effect on the day those self-certifications are made. If the size standard in question was newly established, the challenged size standard remains in effect while SBA conducts its further analysis on remand.

(b) If OHA denies a Size Standard Petition, the size standard remains as published in the Code of Federal Regulations.

§ 134.917 Equal Access to Justice Act.

A prevailing Petitioner is not entitled to recover attorney's fees. Size Standard Petitions are not proceedings that are required to be conducted by an Administrative Law Judge under § 134.603.

§ 134.918 Judicial review.

The publication of a final rule in the FEDERAL REGISTER is considered the final agency action for purposes of seeking judicial review.

Subpart J—Rules of Practice for Protests of Eligibility for Inclusion in the U.S. Department of Veterans Affairs (VA) Center for Verification and Evaluation (CVE) Database (CVE Protests)

SOURCE: 83 FR 13629, Mar. 30, 2018, unless otherwise noted.

§ 134.1001 Scope of rules.

(a) The rules of practice in this subpart apply to Department of Veterans Affairs' (VA) Center for Verification and Evaluation protests (CVE Protests).

(b) Except where inconsistent with this subpart, the provisions of subparts A and B of this part apply to protests listed in paragraph (a) of this section.

(c) The protest procedures described in this subpart are separate from those governing protests and appeals of a concern's size or status as a Service-Disabled Veteran-Owned Small Business Concern (SDVO SBC) for a non-Department of Veterans Affairs (non-VA) procurement. All protests relating to whether a veteran-owned concern is a "small" business for purposes of any Federal program are subject to part 121 of this chapter and must be filed in accordance with that part. If a protester protests both the size of the concern and the concern's eligibility for the CVE database, SBA will process each protest concurrently. SBA does not review issues concerning contract administration.

(d) Protests of a concern's eligibility for a non-VA procurement as a SDVO SBC are governed by 13 CFR part 125, subpart D.

(e) Appeals relating to determinations made by SBA's Director, Office of Government Contracting, regarding SDVO SBC status are governed by subpart E of this part.

(f) Appeals of denials and cancellations of verification for inclusion in the CVE database are governed by subpart K of this part.

§ 134.1002 Who may file a CVE Protest?

A CVE Protest may be filed by:

(a) The Secretary of the VA, or his/her designee; or

(b) In the case of a small business that is awarded a contract for a VA procurement, the contracting officer or an offeror.

§ 134.1003 Grounds for filing a CVE Protest.

(a) *Status.* In cases where the protest is based on service-connected disability, permanent and severe disability, or veteran status, the Judge will only consider a protest that presents specific allegations supporting the contention that the owner(s) cannot provide documentation from the VA, Department of Defense, or the U.S. National Archives and Records Administration to show that they meet the definition of veteran, service-disabled veteran, or service-disabled veteran with a permanent and severe disability.

(b) *Ownership and control.* In cases where the protest is based on ownership and control, the Judge will consider a protest only if the protester presents credible evidence that the concern is not 51% owned and controlled by one or more veterans or service-disabled veterans.

(c) *Date for determining eligibility.* (1) If the CVE Protest pertains to a procurement, the Judge will determine a protested concern's eligibility for inclusion in the CVE database as of the date of bid or initial offer, including price, and as of the date the CVE Protest was filed.

(2) If the CVE Protest does not pertain to a procurement, the Judge will

determine a protested concern's eligibility for inclusion in the CVE database as of the date the CVE Protest was filed.

§ 134.1004 Commencement of CVE Protests.

(a) *Timeliness.* (1) The Secretary of the VA, or his/her designee, may file a CVE Protest at any time.

(2) Where the CVE Protest is in connection with a VA procurement:

(i) An offeror must file a CVE Protest within five business days of notification of the apparent awardee's identity.

(ii) A contracting officer may file a CVE Protest at any time during the life of the VA contract.

(3) The rule for counting days is in § 134.202(d).

(4) An untimely protest will be dismissed.

(b) *Filing*—(1) *Private parties.* Interested parties, other than the contracting officer or Secretary of the VA or his/her designee, must deliver their CVE Protests in person, by email, by facsimile, by express delivery service, or by U.S. mail (postmarked within the applicable time period) to the contracting officer.

(2) *Referral to OHA.* The contracting officer must forward to OHA any non-premature CVE Protest received, notwithstanding whether he/she believes it is sufficiently specific or timely. The contracting officer must send all CVE Protests, along with a referral letter, directly to OHA, addressed to Office of Hearings and Appeals, U.S. Small Business Administration, 409 Third Street SW, Washington, DC 20416, by email at *OHAfilings@sba.gov*, or by facsimile to (202) 205–7059, marked Attn: CVE Protest. The referral letter must include information pertaining to the solicitation that may be necessary for OHA to determine timeliness and standing, including:

(i) The solicitation number;

(ii) The name, address, telephone number, email address, and facsimile number of the contracting officer;

(iii) Whether the contract was sole source or set-aside;

(iv) Whether the protester submitted an offer;

(v) Whether the protested concern was the apparent successful offeror;

(vi) Whether the procurement was conducted using sealed bid or negotiated procedures;

(vii) The bid opening date, if applicable;

(viii) When the protest was submitted to the contracting officer;

(ix) When the protester received notification about the apparent successful offeror, if applicable; and

(x) Whether a contract has been awarded.

(3) *Protests filed by Secretary of the VA.* The Secretary of VA or his/her designee must submit his/her CVE Protest directly to OHA in accordance with the procedures in § 134.204.

(4) *Protests filed by a contracting officer.* The contracting officer must submit his/her CVE Protest directly to OHA in accordance with the procedures in § 134.204. The protest should include in the referral letter the information set forth in paragraph (b)(2) of this section.

§ 134.1005 Contents of the CVE Protest.

(a) CVE Protests must be in writing. There is no required format for a CVE Protest, but it must include the following:

(1) The solicitation or contract number, if applicable;

(2) Specific allegations supported by credible evidence that the concern does not meet the eligibility requirements for inclusion in the CVE database, listed in § 134.1003;

(3) Any other pertinent information the Judge should consider; and

(4) The name, address, telephone number, and email address or facsimile number, if available, and signature of the protester or its attorney.

(b) If the protester intends to seek access to the CVE case file under § 134.205, the protester should include in its protest a request for a protective order. Unless good cause is shown, a protester must request a protective order within five days of filing the protest.

§ 134.1006 Service and filing requirements.

The provisions of § 134.204 apply to the service and filing of all pleadings and other submissions permitted under this subpart.

§ 134.1007 Processing a CVE Protest.

(a) *Notice and order.* If the Judge determines that the protest is timely, sufficiently specific, and based upon protestable allegations, the Judge will issue a notice and order, notifying the protester, the protested concern, the Director, CVE (D/CVE), VA Counsel, and, if applicable, the contracting officer of the date OHA received the protest, and order a due date for responses.

(b) *Dismissal of protest.* If the Judge determines that the protest is premature, untimely, nonspecific, or is based on non-protestable allegations, the Judge will dismiss the protest and will send the contracting officer, D/CVE, and the protester a notice of dismissal, citing the reason(s) for the dismissal. The dismissal is a final agency action.

(c) *Transmission of the case file.* Upon receipt of a notice and order, the D/CVE must deliver to OHA the entire case file relating to the protested concern's inclusion in the CVE database. The notice and order will establish the timetable for transmitting the case file to OHA. The D/CVE must certify and authenticate that the case file, to the best of his/her knowledge, is a true and correct copy of the case file.

(d) *Protective order.* A protester seeking access to the CVE case file must file a timely request for a protective order under § 134.205. Except for good cause shown, a protester must request a protective order within five days of filing the protest. Even after issuance of a protective order, OHA will not disclose income tax returns or privileged information.

(e) *Supplemental allegations.* If, after viewing documents in the CVE case file for the first time under a protective order, a protester wishes to supplement its protest with additional argument, the protester may do so. Any such supplement is due at OHA no later than 15 days from the date the protester receives or reviews the CVE case file.

(f) *Response*—(1) *Timing.* The protested concern, the D/CVE, the contracting officer, and any other interested party may respond to the protest and supplemental protest, if one is filed. The response is due no later than 15 days from the date the protest or supplemental protest was filed with OHA. The record closes the date the final response is due.

(2) *Service.* The respondent must serve its response upon the protester or its counsel and upon each of the persons identified in the certificate of service attached to the notice and order or, if a protective order is issued, in accordance with the terms of the protective order.

(3) *Reply to a response.* No reply to a response will be permitted unless the Judge directs otherwise.

(g) *Basis for decision.* The decision will be based primarily on the case file and information provided by the protester, the protested concern, and any other parties. However, the Judge may investigate issues beyond those raised in the protest and may use other information or make requests for additional information to the protester, the protested concern, or VA.

(h) *Award of contract.* The contracting officer may award a contract during the period between the date he/she receives a protest and the date the Judge issues a decision only if the contracting officer determines that an award must be made to protect the public interest and notifies the Judge in writing of any such determination. Notwithstanding such a determination, the provisions of paragraph (j) of this section shall apply to the procurement in question.

(i) *The decision.* OHA will serve a copy of the written decision on each party, or, if represented by counsel, on its counsel. The decision is considered the final agency action, and it becomes effective upon issuance.

(j) *Effect of decision.* (1) A contracting officer may award a contract to a protested concern after the Judge has determined either that the protested concern is eligible for inclusion in the CVE database or has dismissed all protests against it.

(2) A contracting officer shall not award a contract to a protested concern that the Judge has determined is not eligible for inclusion in the CVE database. If the contract has already been awarded, then the awarded contract shall be deemed void ab initio (invalid from the outset), and the contracting officer shall rescind the contract and award the contract to the next eligible concern in line for the award.

(3) The contracting officer must update the Federal Procurement Data System and other procurement reporting databases to reflect the Judge's decision.

(4) If the Judge finds the protested concern ineligible for inclusion in the CVE database, D/CVE must immediately remove the protested concern from the CVE database.

(5) A concern found to be ineligible may not submit an offer on a future VA procurement until the protested concern reapplies to the Vendor Information Pages Verification Program and has been reentered into the CVE database.

§ 134.1008 Discovery.

Discovery will not be permitted in CVE Protest proceedings.

§ 134.1009 Oral hearings.

Oral hearings will be held in CVE Protest proceedings only upon a finding by the Judge of extraordinary circumstances. If such an oral hearing is ordered, the proceeding shall be conducted in accordance with those rules of subpart B of this part as the Judge deems appropriate.

§ 134.1010 Standard of review and burden of proof.

The protested concern has the burden of proving its eligibility, by a preponderance of the evidence.

§ 134.1011 Weight of evidence.

The Judge will give greater weight to specific, signed, factual evidence than to general, unsupported allegations or opinions. In the case of refusal or failure to furnish requested information within a required time period, the Judge may assume that disclosure would be contrary to the interests of the party failing to make disclosure.

§ 134.1012 The record.

Where relevant, the provisions of § 134.225 apply. In a protest under this subpart, the contents of the record also include the case file or solicitation submitted to OHA in accordance with § 134.1007.

§ 134.1013 Request for reconsideration.

The decision on a CVE Protest may not be appealed. However:

(a) The Judge may reconsider a CVE Protest decision. Any party that has appeared in the proceeding, or the Secretary of VA or his/her designee, may request reconsideration by filing with OHA and serving a petition for reconsideration on all the parties to the CVE Protest within twenty (20) calendar days after service of the written decision. The request for reconsideration must clearly show an error of fact or law material to the decision. The Judge may also reconsider a decision on his or her own initiative.

(b) If the Judge reverses his or her initial decision on reconsideration, the contracting officer must follow § 134.1007(j) in applying the new decision's results.

Subpart K—Rules of Practice for Appeals of Denials and Cancellations of Verification for Inclusion in the U.S. Department of Veterans Affairs (VA) Center for Verification and Evaluation (CVE) Database (CVE Appeals)

SOURCE: 83 FR 13631, Mar. 30, 2018, unless otherwise noted.

§ 134.1101 Scope of rules.

(a) The rules of practice in this subpart apply to appeals of denials and cancellations of verification for inclusion in the U.S. Department of Veterans Affairs Center for Verification and Evaluation Database (CVE Appeals).

(b) Except where inconsistent with this subpart, the provisions of subparts A and B of this part apply to appeals listed in paragraph (a) of this section.

(c) Appeals relating to determinations made by SBA's Director, Office of Government Contracting regarding Service-Disabled Veteran-Owned Small Business Concern (SDVO SBC) status are governed by subpart E of this part.

(d) Protests of a concern's eligibility for inclusion in the VA CVE database are governed by subpart J of this part.

§ 134.1102 Who may file a CVE Appeal?

A concern that has been denied verification of its CVE status or has had its CVE status cancelled may appeal the denial or cancellation to OHA.

§ 134.1103 Grounds for filing a CVE Appeal.

Denials and cancellations of verification of CVE status may be appealed to OHA, so long as the denial or cancellation is not based on the failure to meet any veteran or service-disabled veteran eligibility criteria. Such denials and cancellations are final VA decisions and not subject to appeal to OHA.

§ 134.1104 Commencement of CVE Appeals.

(a) A concern whose application for CVE verification has been denied or whose CVE status has been cancelled must file its appeal within 10 business days of receipt of the denial or cancellation.

(b) The rule for counting days is in § 134.202(d).

(c) OHA will dismiss an untimely appeal.

§ 134.1105 The appeal petition.

(a) *Format.* CVE Appeals must be in writing. There is no required format for an appeal petition; however, it must include the following:

(1) A copy of the denial or cancellation and the date the appellant received it;

(2) A statement of why the cancellation or denial is in error;

(3) Any other pertinent information the Judge should consider; and

(4) The name, address, telephone number, and email address or facsimile number, if available, and signature of the appellant or its attorney.

(b) *Service.* The appellant must serve copies of the entire appeal petition upon the Director, Center for Verification and Evaluation (D/CVE) and VA Counsel at *CVEAppealsService@va.gov.*

(c) *Certificate of service.* The appellant must attach to the appeal petition a signed certificate of service meeting the requirements of § 134.204(d).

(d) *Dismissal.* An appeal petition that does not meet all the requirements of this section may be dismissed by the Judge at his/her own initiative or upon motion of a respondent.

§ 134.1106 Service and filing requirements.

The provisions of § 134.204 apply to the service and filing of all pleadings and other submissions permitted under this subpart.

§ 134.1107 Transmission of the case file.

Once a CVE Appeal is filed, the D/CVE must deliver to OHA the entire case file relating to the denial or cancellation. The Judge will issue a notice and order establishing the timetable for transmitting the case file to OHA. The D/CVE must certify and authenticate that the case file, to the best of his/her knowledge, is a true and correct copy of the case file.

§ 134.1108 Response to an appeal petition.

(a) *Who may respond.* The D/CVE or his/her designee or counsel for VA may respond to the CVE Appeal. The response should present arguments to the issues presented on appeal.

(b) *Time limits.* The notice and order will inform the parties of the filing of the appeal petition, establish the close of record as 15 days after service of the notice and order, and inform the parties that OHA must receive any responses to the appeal petition no later than the close of record.

(c) *Service.* The respondent must serve its response upon the appellant and upon each of the persons identified in the certificate of service attached to the appeal petition pursuant to § 134.1105.

(d) *Reply to a response.* No reply to a response will be permitted unless the Judge directs otherwise.

§ 134.1109 Discovery and oral hearings.

Discovery will not be permitted and oral hearings will not be held.

§ 134.1110 New evidence.

Except for good cause shown, evidence beyond the case file will not be admitted.

§ 134.1111 Standard of review and burden of proof.

The standard of review is whether the D/CVE denial or cancellation was based on clear error of fact or law. The appellant has the burden of proof, by a preponderance of the evidence.

§ 134.1112 The decision.

(a) *Timing.* The Judge shall decide a CVE Appeal, insofar as practicable, within 60 calendar days after close of the record.

(b) *Contents.* Following closure of the record, the Judge will issue a decision containing findings of fact and conclusions of law, reasons for such findings and conclusions, and any relief ordered.

(c) *Basis for decision.* Decisions under this subpart will be based primarily on the evidence in the CVE case file, arguments made on appeal, and any response(s) thereto. However, the Judge, in his/her sole discretion, may consider issues beyond those raised in the pleadings and the denial or cancellation letter.

(d) *Finality.* The decision is the final agency decision and becomes effective upon issuance. Where OHA dismisses an appeal of a D/CVE denial or cancellation, the D/CVE determination remains in effect.

(e) *Service.* OHA will serve a copy of all written decisions on each party, or, if represented by counsel, on its counsel.

(f) *Effect.* If the Judge grants the appeal and finds the appellant eligible for inclusion in the CVE database, the D/CVE must immediately reinstate or include the appellant, as the case may be, in the CVE database.

(g) *Reconsideration.* A decision of the Judge may be reconsidered. Any party that has appeared in the proceeding, or the Secretary of VA or his or her designee, may request reconsideration by filing with OHA and serving a petition for reconsideration on all parties to the CVE Appeal within twenty (20) calendar days after service of the written decision, upon a clear showing of an error of fact or law material to the decision. The Judge also may reconsider a decision on his or her own initiative.

PART 136—ENFORCEMENT OF NONDISCRIMINATION ON THE BASIS OF HANDICAP IN PROGRAMS OR ACTIVITIES CONDUCTED BY THE SMALL BUSINESS ADMINISTRATION

Sec.

AUTHORITY: 29 U.S.C. 794.

SOURCE: 53 FR 19760, May 31, 1988, unless otherwise noted.

§ 136.101 Purpose.

The purpose of this part is to effectuate section 119 of the Rehabilitation, Comprehensive Services, and Developmental Disabilities Amendments of 1978, which amended section 504 of the Rehabilitation Act of 1973 to prohibit discrimination on the basis of handicap in programs or activities conducted by Executive agencies or the United States Postal Service.

§ 136.102 Application.

This part applies to all programs or activities conducted by the Small Business Administration except for programs or activities conducted outside the United States that do not involve individuals with handicaps in the United States.

§ 136.103 Definitions.

For purposes of this part, the term—

Agency means the Small Business Administration.

Assistant Attorney General. Assistant Attorney General means the Assistant Attorney General, Civil Rights Division, United States Department of Justice.

Auxiliary aids means services or devices that enable persons with impaired sensory, manual, or speaking skills to have an equal opportunity to participate in, and enjoy the benefits of, programs or activities conducted by the Agency. For example, auxiliary aids useful for persons with impaired vision include readers, Brailled materials, audio recordings, and other similar services and devices. Auxiliary aids useful for persons with impaired hearing include telephone handset amplifiers, telephones compatible with hearing aids, telecommunication devices for deaf persons (TDD's), interpreters, notetakers, written materials, and other similar services and devices.

Complete complaint means a written statement that contains the complainant's name and address and describes the Agency's alleged discriminatory actions in sufficient detail to inform the Agency of the nature and date of the alleged violation of section 504. It shall be signed by the complainant or by someone authorized to do so on his or her behalf. Complaints filed on behalf of classes or third parties shall describe or identify (by name, if possible) the alleged victims of discrimination.

Facility means all or any portion of buildings, structures, equipment, roads, walks, parking lots, rolling stock or other conveyances, or other real or personal property.

Individual with handicaps means any person who has a physical or mental impairment that substantially limits one or more major life activities, has a record of such an impairment, or is regarded as having such an impairment. As used in this definition, the phrase:

(1) *Physical or mental impairment* includes—

(i) Any physiological disorder or condition, cosmetic disfigurement, or anatomical loss affecting one or more of the following body systems: Neurological; musculoskeletal; special sense organs; respiratory, including speech organs; cardiovascular; reproductive; digestive; genitourinary; hemic and lymphatic; skin; and endocrine; or

(ii) Any mental or psychological disorder, such as mental retardation, organic brain syndrome, emotional or mental illness, and specific learning disabilities. The term *physical or mental impairment* includes, but is not limited to, such diseases and conditions as orthopedic, visual, speech, and hearing impairments, cerebral palsy, epilepsy, muscular dystrophy, multiple sclerosis, cancer, heart disease, diabetes, mental retardation, emotional illness, and drug addiction and alcoholism.

(2) *Major life activities* includes functions such as caring for one's self, performing manual tasks, walking, seeing, hearing, speaking, breathing, learning, and working.

(3) *Has a record of such an impairment* means has a history of, or has been misclassified as having, a mental or physical impairment that substantially limits one or more major life activities.

(4) *Is regarded as having an impairment* means—

(i) Has a physical or mental impairment that does not substantially limit major life activities but is treated by the Agency as constituting such a limitation;

(ii) Has a physical or mental impairment that substantially limits major life activities only as a result of the attitudes of others toward such impairment; or

(iii) Has none of the impairments defined in paragraph (1) of this definition but is treated by the Agency as having such an impairment.

Qualified individual with handicaps means—

(1) With respect to any Agency program or activity under which a person is required to perform services or to achieve a level of accomplishment, an individual with handicaps who meets the essential eligibility requirements and who can achieve the purpose of the program or activity without modifications in the program or activity that

the Agency can demonstrate would result in a fundamental alteration in its nature;

(2) With respect to any other program or activity, an individual with handicaps who meets the essential eligibility requirements for participation in, or receipt of benefits from, that program or activity; and

(3) For purposes of employment, a person who qualifies under the definition contained at 29 CFR 1613.702(f), which is made applicable to this part by § 136.140.

Respondent means the organizational unit in which a complainant alleges that discrimination occurred.

Section 504 means section 504 of the Rehabilitation Act of 1973 ((Pub. L. 93–112, 87 Stat. 394) (29 U.S.C. 794)), as amended by the Rehabilitation Act Amendments of 1974 (Pub. L. 93–516, 88 Stat. 1617), and the Rehabilitation, Comprehensive Services, and Developmental Disabilities Amendments of 1978 (Pub. L. 95–602, 92 Stat. 2955) and the Rehabilitation Act Amendments of 1986 (Pub. L. 99–506, 100 Stat. 1810). As used in this part, section 504 applies only to programs or activities conducted by SBA and not to activities of recipients of assistance from SBA.

§§ 136.104–136.109 [Reserved]

§ 136.110 Self-evaluation.

(a) The Agency shall, by July 17, 1989, evaluate its current policies and practices, and the effects thereof, that do not or may not meet the requirements of this part, and, to the extent modification of any such policies and practices is required, the Agency shall proceed to make the necessary modifications.

(b) The Agency shall provide an opportunity to interested persons, including individuals with handicaps or organizations representing individuals with handicaps, to participate in the self-evaluation process by submitting comments (both oral and written).

(c) The Agency shall, for at least three years following the self-evaluation, maintain on file and make available for public inspection:

(1) A description of areas examined and any problems identified; and

(2) A description of any modifications made.

§ 136.111 Notice.

The Agency shall make available to employees, applicants, participants, beneficiaries, and other interested persons such information regarding the provisions of this part and its applicability to the programs or activities conducted by the Agency, and make such information available to them in such manner as the Administrator finds necessary to apprise such persons of the protections against discrimination assured them by section 504 and this part.

§§ 136.112–136.129 [Reserved]

§ 136.130 General prohibition against discrimination.

(a) No qualified individual with handicaps shall, on the basis of handicap, be excluded from participation in, be denied the benefits of, or otherwise be subjected to discrimination under any program or activity conducted by the Agency.

(b) The Agency, in providing any aid, benefit, or service, may not, directly or through contractual, licensing, or other arrangements, on the basis of handicap:

(1) Deny a qualified individual with handicaps the opportunity to participate in or benefit from the aid, benefit, or service;

(2) Afford a qualified individual with handicaps an opportunity to participate in or benefit from the aid, benefit, or service that is not equal to that afforded others;

(3) Provide a qualified individual with handicaps with an aid, benefit, or service that is not as effective in affording equal opportunity to obtain the same result, to gain the same benefit, or to reach the same level of achievement as that provided to others;

(4) Provide different or separate aid, benefits, or services to individuals with handicaps or to any class of individuals with handicaps than is provided to others unless such action is necessary to provide qualified individuals with handicaps with aid, benefits, or services that are as effective as those provided to others;

(5) Deny a qualified individual with handicaps the opportunity to participate as a member of planning, voluntary (such as SCORE or Ace) or advisory boards; or

(6) Otherwise limit a qualified individual with handicaps in the enjoyment of any right, privilege, advantage, or opportunity enjoyed by others receiving the aid, benefit, or service.

(c) The Agency shall permit a qualified individual with handicaps the opportunity to participate in any of the Agency's programs or activities, despite the existence of permissibly separate or different programs or activities especially designed to accommodate qualified individuals with handicaps.

(d) The Agency may not, directly or through contractual or other arrangements, utilize criteria or methods of administration the purpose of effect of which would—

(1) Subject qualified individuals with handicaps to discrimination on the basis of handicap; or

(2) Defeat or substantially impair accomplishment of the objectives of a program or activity with respect to individuals with handicaps.

(e) The Agency may not, in determining the site or location of a facility, make selections the purpose or effect of which would:

(1) Exclude individuals with handicaps from, deny them the benefits of, or otherwise subject them to discrimination under any program or activity conducted by the Agency; or

(2) Defeat or substantially impair the accomplishment of the objectives of a program or activity with respect to individuals with handicaps.

(f) The Agency, in the selection of procurement contactors, may not use criteria that subject qualified individuals with handicaps to discrimination on the basis of handicap.

(g) The Agency may not administer a licensing or certification program in a manner that subjects qualified individuals with handicaps to discrimination on the basis of handicap, nor may the Agency establish requirements for the programs or activities of licensees or certified entities that subject qualified individuals with handicaps to discrimination on the basis of handicap. However, the programs or activities of entities that are licensed or certified by the Agency are not, themselves, covered by this part.

(h) The exclusion of individuals without handicaps from the benefits of a program limited by Federal statute or Executive Order to individuals with handicaps or the exclusion of a specific class of individuals with handicaps from a program limited by Federal statute or Executive Order to a different class of individuals with handicaps is not prohibited by this part.

(i) The Agency shall administer programs and activities in the most integrated setting appropriate to the needs of qualified individuals with handicaps.

§§ 136.131–136.139 [Reserved]

§ 136.140 Employment.

(a) No qualified individual with handicaps shall, on the basis of handicap, be subjected to discrimination in employment under any program, or activity conducted by the Agency.

(b) The definitions, requirements and procedures of section 501 of the Rehabilitation Act of 1973 (29 U.S.C. 791) as established by the EEOC in 29 CFR part 1613, shall apply to employment in federally conducted programs or activities.

§§ 136.141–136.148 [Reserved]

§ 136.149 Program accessibility: Discrimination prohibited.

Except as otherwise provided in § 136.150, no qualified individual with handicaps shall, because the Agency's facilities are inaccessible to or unusable by individuals with handicaps, be denied the benefits of, be excluded from participation in, or otherwise be subjected to discrimination under any program or activity conducted by the Agency.

§ 136.150 Program accessibility: Existing facilities.

(a) *General.* The Agency shall operate each program or activity so that the program or activity, when viewed in its entirety, is readily accessible to and usable by individuals with handicaps. This paragraph does not—

(1) Necessarily require the Agency to make each of its existing facilities accessible to and usable by individuals with handicaps; or

(2) Require the Agency to take any action that it can demonstrate would result in a fundamental alteration in the nature of a program or activity or in undue financial and administrative burdens. In those circumstances where Agency personnel believe that the proposed action would fundamentally alter the program or activity or would result in undue financial and administrative burdens, the Agency has the burden of proving that compliance with § 136.150(a) would result in such alteration or burdens. The decision that compliance would result in such alteration or burdens must be made by the Administrator or Deputy Administrator after considering all Agency resources available for use in the funding and operation of the conducted program or activity and must be accompanied by a written statement of the reasons for reaching that conclusion. The Administrator or Deputy Administrator's decision shall be made within 30 days of the initial decision by Agency personnel that an action would result in such an alteration or burdens. If an action would result in such an alteration or such burdens, the Agency shall take any other action that would not result in such an alteration or such burdens but would, nevertheless, ensure that individuals with handicaps receive the benefits and services of the program or activity.

(b) *Methods.* The Agency may comply with the requirements of this section through such means as redesign of equipment, reassignment of services to accessible buildings, assignment of aids to beneficiaries, home visits, delivery of services at alternate accessible sites, alteration of existing facilities and construction of new facilities, use of accessible rolling stock, or any other methods that result in making its programs or activities readily accessible to and usable by individuals with handicaps. The Agency is not required to make structural changes in existing facilities where other methods are effective in achieving compliance with this section. The Agency, in making alterations to existing buildings, shall meet accessibility requirements to the extent compelled by the Architectural Barriers Act of 1968, as amended (42 U.S.C. 4151–4157), and any regulations implementing it. In choosing among available methods for meeting the requirements of this section, the Agency shall give priority to those methods that offer programs and activities to qualified individuals with handicaps in the most integrated setting appropriate.

(c) *Time period for compliance.* The Agency shall comply with the obligations established under this section by September 13, 1988, except that where structural changes in facilities are undertaken, such changes shall be made by July 15, 1991, but in any event as expeditiously as possible.

(d) *Transition plan.* In the event that structural changes to facilities will be undertaken to achieve program accessibility, the Agency shall develop, by January 16, 1989, a transition plan setting forth the steps necessary to complete such changes. The Agency shall provide an opportunity to interested persons, including individuals with handicaps or organizations representing individuals with handicaps, to participate in the development of the transition plan by submitting comments (both oral and written). A copy of the transition plan shall be made available for public inspection. The plan shall, at a minimum:

(1) Identify physical obstacles in the Agency's facilities that limit the accessibility of its programs or activities to individuals with handicaps;

(2) Describe in detail the methods that will be used to make the facilities accessible;

(3) Specify the schedule for taking the steps necessary to achieve compliance with this section and, if the time period of the transition plan is longer than one year, identify steps that will be taken during each year of the transition period; and

(4) Indicate the official responsible for implementation of the plan.

§ 136.151 Program accessibility: New construction and alterations.

Each building or part of a building that is constructed or altered by, on behalf if, or for the use of the Agency shall be designed, constructed, or altered so as to be readily accessible to and usable by individuals with handicaps. The definitions, requirements, and standards of the Architectural Barriers Act (42 U.S.C. 4151–4157), as established in 41 CFR 101–19.600—101–19.607, apply to buildings covered by this section.

§§ 136.152–136.159 [Reserved]

§ 136.160 Communications.

(a) The Agency shall take appropriate steps to ensure effective communication with applicants, participants, personnel of other Federal entities, and members of the public.

(1) The Agency shall furnish appropriate auxiliary aids where necessary to afford an individual with handicaps an equal opportunity to participate in, and enjoy the benefits of, a program or activity conducted by the Agency.

(i) In determining what type of auxiliary aid is necessary, the Agency shall give primary consideration to the requests of the individual with handicaps.

(ii) The Agency need not provide individually prescribed devices, readers for personal use or study, or other devices of a personal nature.

(2) Where the Agency communicates with applicants and beneficiaries by telephone, telecommunication devices for deaf persons (TDD's) or equally effective telecommunication systems shall be used.

(b) The Agency shall ensure that interested persons, including persons with impaired vision or hearing, can obtain information as to the existence and location of accessible services, activities, and facilities.

(c) The Agency shall provide a sign at each primary entrance to each of its inaccessible facilities, directing users to a location at which they can obtain information about accessible facilities. The international symbol for accessibility shall be used at each primary entrance of an accessible facility.

(d) This section does not require the Agency to take any action that it can demonstrate would result in a fundamental alteration in the nature of a program or activity or in undue financial and administrative burdens. In those circumstances where Agency personnel believe that the proposed action would fundamentally alter the program or activity or would result in undue financial and administrative burdens, the Agency has the burden of proving that compliance with § 136.160 would result in such alteration or burdens. The decision that compliance would result in such alteration or burdens must be made by the Administrator or Deputy Administrator after considering all Agency resources available for use in the funding and operation of the conducted program or activity and must be accompanied by a written statement of the reasons for reaching that conclusion. The Administrator or Deputy Administrator's decision shall be made within 30 days of the initial decision by Agency personnel that an action would result in such an alteration or burdens. If an action required to comply with this section would result in such as alteration or such burdens, the Agency shall take any other action that would not result in such an alteration or such burdens but would nevertheless ensure that, to the maximum extent possible, individuals with handicaps receive the benefits and services of the program or activity.

§§ 136.161–136.169 [Reserved]

§ 136.170 Compliance procedures.

(a) *Applicability.* Except as provided in paragraph (b) of this section, this section applies to all allegations of discrimination on the basis of handicap in programs or activities conducted by the Agency.

(b) *Employment complaints.* The Agency shall process complaints alleging violations of section 504 with respect to employment according to the procedures established by EEOC in 29 CFR part 1613 pursuant to section 501 of the Rehabilitation Act of 1973 (29 U.S.C. 791).

(c) *Filing a complaint*—(1) *Who may file.* Any person who believes that he or she has been subjected to discrimination prohibited by this part may file a complaint. An authorized representative of such person may file a complaint on his or her behalf. Any person who believes that any specific class of persons has been subjected to discrimination prohibited by this part and who is a member of that class, or the authorized representative of a member of that class, may file a complaint.

(2) *Confidentiality.* The Chief, Assistant Administrator, Office of Equal Employment Opportunity & Civil Rights Compliance (AA/EEOCCR), shall hold in confidence the identity of any person submitting a complaint, unless the person submits written authorization otherwise, except to the extent necessary to carry out the purposes of this part, including the conduct of any investigation, hearing, or proceeding under this part, or to cooperate with the Office of Inspector General in the performance of its responsibilities under the Inspector General Act of 1978, as amended.

(3) *When to file.* Complaints shall be filed within 180 days of the alleged act of discrimination, except when this deadline is extended by the AA/EEOCCR for good cause shown. For purposes of determining when a complaint is timely filed under this paragraph, a complaint mailed to the Agency shall be deemed filed on the date it is postmarked. Any other complaint shall be deemed filed on the date it is received by the Agency.

(4) *How to file.* Complaints may be delivered or mailed to the AA/EEOCCR Small Business Administration, 1441 L Street NW.—Room 501, Washington, DC 20416. Any other SBA official receiving a complaint under this part shall forward such complaint immediately to the AA/EEOCCR.

(d) *Notification to the Architectural and Transportation Barriers Compliance Board.* The agency shall promptly send to the Architectural and Transportation Barriers Compliance Board a copy of any complaint alleging that a building or facility that is subject to the Architectural Barriers Act of 1968, as amended, 42 U.S.C. 4151–4157 is not readily accessible to and usable by individuals with handicaps.

(e) *Acceptance of complaint.* (1) The AA/EEOCCR shall accept a complete complaint that is filed in accordance with paragraph (c) of this section and over which the Agency has jurisdiction. The AA/EEOCCR shall notify the complainant and the respondent of receipt and acceptance of the complaint.

(2) If the AA/EEOCCR receives a complaint that is not complete, he or she shall notify the complainant, within 30 days of receipt of the incomplete complaint, that additional information is needed. If the complainant fails to furnish the necessary information within 30 days of receipt of this notice, the AA/EEOCCR shall dismiss the complaint without prejudice.

(3) If the AA/EEOCCR receives a complaint over which the Agency does not have jurisdiction, he or she shall promptly notify the complainant and shall make reasonable efforts to refer the complaint to the appropriate Government entity.

(f) *Investigation/Conciliation.* (1) Within 180 days of the receipt of a complete complaint the AA/EEOCCR shall complete the investigation of the complaint and attempt informal resolution. If no informal resolution is achieved, the AA/EEOCCR shall issue a letter of findings.

(2) The AA/EEOCCR may require Agency employees to cooperate in the investigation and attempted resolution of complaints. Employees who are required to participate in any investigation under this section shall do so as part of their official duties and during regular duty hours.

(3) The AA/EEOCCR shall furnish the complainant and the respondent with a copy of the investigative report and provide the complainant and respondent with an opportunity for informal resolution of the complaint.

(4) If a complaint is resolved informally, the terms of the agreement shall be reduced to writing and made part of the complaint file, with a copy of the agreement provided to the complainant and respondent. The written agreement may include a finding on the issue of discrimination and shall describe any corrective action to which the complainant and respondent have agreed.

(g) *Letter of findings.* If an informal resolution of the complaint is not reached, the AA/EEOCCR shall, within 180 days of receipt of the complete complaint, notify the complainant, the respondent and the Director, Office of Equal Employment Opportunity and

Compliance (OEEOC), of the results of the investigation in a letter sent by certified mail, return receipt requested, and containing—

(1) Findings of fact and conclusions of law;

(2) A description of a remedy for each violation found;

(3) A notice of the right of the complainant and respondent to appeal to the Director, OEEOC; and

(4) A notice of the right of the complainant and respondent to request a hearing.

The letter of findings becomes the final Agency decision if neither party files an appeal within the time prescribed in paragraph (h)(1) of this section. The AA/EEOCCR shall certify that the letter of findings is the final Agency decision on the complaint at the expiration of that time.

(h) *Filing an appeal.* (1) Any notice of appeal to the AA/EEOCCR, with or without a request for hearing, shall be filed by the complainant or the respondent in writing with the AA/EEOCCR within 30 days of receipt from him or her of the letter required by paragraph (g) of this section. The notice shall be accompanied by a certificate of service attesting that the party has served a copy of his or her notice of appeal on all other parties to the proceeding. The AA/EEOCCR may extend this time limit for good cause shown pursuant to the procedure in paragraph (h)(3) of this section.

(2) If a timely notice of appeal without a request for hearing is filed, any other party may file a written request for hearing within the time limit specified in paragraph (h)(1) of this section or within 10 days of his or her receipt of such notice of appeal, whichever is later.

(3) A party may appeal to the AA/EEOCCR from a decision of the AA/EEOCCR that an appeal is untimely. This appeal shall be filed with the AA/EEOCCR within 15 days of receipt of the decision from the AA/EEOCCR.

(4) Any request for hearing will be construed as a request for an oral hearing. The complainant's failure to file a timely request for a hearing in accordance with this part shall constitute waiver of the right to a hearing, but shall not preclude his or her submitting written information and argument to the AA/EEOCCR in connection with his or her notice of appeal.

(i) *Acceptance of appeal.* The AA/EEOCCR shall accept and process any timely filed appeal.

(1) If a notice of appeal is filed but no party requests a hearing, the AA/EEOCCR shall promptly transmit the complaint file, the letter of findings and the notice of appeal to the AA/EEOCCR.

(2) If a notice of appeal if filed and a party makes a timely request for a hearing, the AA/EEOCCR will transmit the notice of appeal, the request for hearing and the investigative file to the Office of Hearings and Appeals which office will assign the case to an administrative judge who will conduct a hearing in accordance with the procedures contained in 13 CFR part 134.

(j) *Decision.* (1) Where no request for a hearing is made, the AA/EEOCCR shall make the final Agency decision based on the contents of the complaint file, the letter of findings, the notice of appeal, and any responses to the notice of appeal filed by other parties. The decision shall be made within 60 days of receipt of the appeal or any response to the notice of appeal, whichever is applicable. If the AA/EEOCCR, determines that he or she needs additional information from any party, he or she shall request the information and provide the other party or parties an opportunity to respond to that information. The AA/EEOCCR shall have 60 days from receipt of the additional information or responses to such additional information, whichever is later, to make the decision. The AA/EEOCCR shall transmit his or her decision in writing to the parties. The decision shall set forth the findings, remedial actions, and reasons for the decision.

(2) Where a request for a hearing has been made, the administrative judge shall issue an initial decision, in writing, based on the hearing record, composed of the proposed findings of fact, conclusions of law, and remedies, to the parties and to the AA/EEOCCR within 30 days after receipt of the hearing transcripts, or within 30 days after the conclusion of the hearing if no transcript is made. This time limit may be extended with the permission

of the AA/EEOCCR. The decision of the administrative judge shall be deemed to be the final decision of the Agency after 30 days, unless a party files a petition for review with the AA/EEOCCR, pursuant to 13 CFR 134.228(a) or the AA/EEOCCR issues an order stating his or her decision to review the initial decision, pursuant to 13 CFR 134.228(a). *See* 13 CFR 134.227(b).

(3) Where a petition for review is filed or a review is ordered by the AA/EEOCCR the AA/EEOCCR shall make the final decision of the Agency based on information in the complaint file, the letter of findings, the hearing record, the initial decision, the petition for review, and any responses to the petition or order. The decision shall be made within 60 days of receipt of the petition for review, the order, or any responses to such petition or order, whichever is later. If the AA/EEOCCR determines that he or she needs additional information from any party, he or she shall request the information and provide the other party or parties an opportunity to respond to that information. The AA/EEOCCR shall have 60 days from receipt of the additional information or responses to such additional information, whichever is later, to make the decision. The AA/EEOCCR shall transmit his or her decision by letter to the parties. The decision shall set forth the findings, recommended remedial actions, and reasons for the decision. The decision shall adopt, reject, or modify the initial decision of the administrative judge. If the decision is to reject or modify the initial decision, the decision letter shall set forth in detail the specific reasons for the rejection or modification.

(4) Any respondent required to take action under the terms of the decision of the Agency shall do so promptly. The AA/EEOCCR may require periodic compliance reports specifying:

(i) The manner in which compliance with the provisions of the decision has been achieved;

(ii) The reasons any action required by the final decision has not been taken; and

(iii) The steps being taken to ensure full compliance.

(k) The time limit cited in paragraph (f) of this section may be extended with the permission of the Assistant Attorney General.

(l) The Agency may delegate its authority for conducting complaint investigations to other Federal agencies, except that the authority for making the final determination may not be delegated to another agency.

[53 FR 19760, May 31, 1988, as amended at 61 FR 2691, Jan. 29, 1996; 72 FR 50042, Aug. 30, 2007]

PART 140—DEBT COLLECTION

AUTHORITY: 5 U.S.C. 5514; 15 U.S.C. 634(b)(6); 31 U.S.C. 3711, 3716, 3720, 3720A and 3720D.

SOURCE: 60 FR 62191, Dec. 5, 1995, unless otherwise noted.

Subpart A—Overview

§ 140.1 What does this part cover?

This part establishes procedures which SBA may use in the collection, through offset or administrative wage garnishment, of delinquent debts owed to the United States. SBA's failure to comply with any provision of the regulations in this part is not available to any debtor as a defense against collection of the debt through judicial process or otherwise.

[70 FR 17587, Apr. 7, 2005]

Subpart B—Offset

§ 140.2 What is a debt and how can the SBA collect it through offset?

(a) A debt means an amount owed to the United States from loans made or guaranteed by the United States, and from fees, leases, rents, royalties, services, sales of real or personal property, overpayments, fines, penalties, damages, interest, forfeitures, or any other source. You are a debtor if you owe an amount to the United States from any of these sources.

(b) SBA may collect past-due debts through offset by using any of three procedures: administrative offset, salary offset, or IRS tax refund offset. A past-due debt is one which has been reduced to judgment, has been accelerated, or has been due for at least 90 days.

(1) *Administrative offset.* SBA may withhold money it owes to the debtor in order to satisfy the debt. This procedure is an "administrative offset" and is authorized by 31 U.S.C. 3716.

(2) *Salary offset.* If the debtor is a federal employee (a civilian employee as defined by 5 U.S.C. 2105, an employee of the U.S. Postal Service or Postal Rate Commission, or a member of the Uniformed Services or Reserve of the Uniformed Services), SBA may deduct payments owed to SBA or another federal agency from the debtor's paycheck. This procedure is a "salary offset" and is authorized by 5 U.S.C. 5514.

(i) Any amount deducted from salary in any one pay period will not exceed 15 percent of a debtor's disposable pay, unless the debtor agrees in writing to a greater percentage.

(ii) SBA also may collect against travel advances, training expenses, disallowed payments, retirement benefits, or any other amount due the employee, including lump-sum payments.

(iii) If an employee has terminated employment after salary offset has been initiated, there are no limitations on the amount that can be withheld or offset.

(3) *IRS tax refund offset.* SBA may request that IRS reduce a debtor's tax refund by the amount of the debt, as authorized by 31 U.S.C. 3720A. Where available, administrative and salary offsets must be used before collection is attempted through income tax offset. SBA may refer a debt to the IRS for a tax refund offset and take additional action against the debtor to collect the debt at the same time or in sequence. When SBA makes simultaneous or sequential referrals (within six months of the initial notice), only one review pursuant to the rules in this part and the statutes authorizing them is required.

§ 140.3 What rights do you have when SBA tries to collect a debt from you through offset?

(a) SBA must write to you and tell you that it proposes to collect the debt by reducing your federal paycheck, withholding money the Government owes you, and/or reducing your tax refund.

(b) In its written notice to you, SBA must tell you the nature and amount of the debt; that SBA will begin procedures to collect the debt through reduction of your federal paycheck, administrative offset, or reduction of your tax refund; that you have an opportunity to inspect and copy Government records relating to the debt at your expense; and that, before collection begins, you have an opportunity to agree with SBA on a schedule for repayment of your debt.

(c) SBA also must tell you that unless you respond within 60 days from the date of the notice, it will disclose to consumer reporting agencies (also known as credit bureaus or credit agencies) that you are responsible for the debt and the specific information it intends to disclose in order to establish your identity. The amount, status, history of the debt, and agency program under which it arose also will be disclosed.

(d) If you respond to SBA within 60 days from the date of the notice, SBA will not disclose the information to consumer reporting agencies until it considers your response and determines that you owe a past-due, legally enforceable debt.

(e) Within 60 days of the notice you may present evidence that all or part of the debt is not past due or not legally enforceable.

(1) Where a salary offset or administrative offset is proposed, you will have the opportunity to present your evidence to SBA's Office of Hearings and Appeals ("OHA"). The rules in part 134 of this title govern the procedural rights to which you are entitled. In order to have a hearing before OHA,

you must request a hearing within 15 days of receipt of the written notice described in this section. An OHA judge will issue a decision within 60 days of the date you filed your petition/request for a review or hearing with OHA, unless you were granted additional time within which to file your request for review.

(2) Where an income tax refund offset is proposed, you will have the opportunity to request a review and present your evidence to the appropriate SBA Commercial Loan Servicing Center at the address provided in the notice.

(f) SBA must consider any evidence you present and must first decide that a debt is past due and legally enforceable. A debt is legally enforceable if there is any forum, including a State or Federal Court or administrative agency, in which SBA's claim would not be barred on the date of offset. Non-judgment debts are enforceable for ten years; judgment debts are enforceable beyond ten years. You will be notified of SBA's decision at least 30 days before any offset deduction is made. You also will be notified of the amount, frequency, proposed beginning date, and duration of the deductions, as well as any obligation to pay interest, penalties, and administrative costs.

(g) If there is any substantial change in the status or amount of your debt, SBA will promptly report that change to each consumer reporting agency it originally contacted.

(h) SBA will obtain satisfactory assurances from each consumer reporting agency that the consumer reporting agency has complied with all federal laws relating to provision of consumer credit information.

(i) If your debt is being repaid by reduction of your income tax refund and you make any additional payments to SBA, SBA will notify the IRS of these payments and your new balance within 10 business days of receiving your payment.

(j) When the debt of a federal employee is reduced to court judgment, the employee is not entitled to further review by SBA, but is only entitled to notice of a proposed salary offset resulting from the judgment. The amount deducted may not exceed 15% of disposable pay, except when the deduction of a greater amount is necessary to completely collect the debt within the employee's remaining period of employment.

(k) When another federal agency asks SBA to offset a debt for it, SBA will not initiate the requested offset until it has received from the creditor agency a written certification that the debtor owes a debt, its amount, and that the provisions of all applicable statutes and regulations have been complied with fully.

(l) SBA may make an offset prior to completion of the procedures described in this part, if:

(1) Failure to make an offset would substantially prejudice the government's ability to collect the debt; and

(2) The time before the payment would otherwise be made to you does not reasonably permit the completion of the procedures.

(3) Such prior offset then must be followed by the completion of the procedures described in this part.

(m) Where an IRS tax refund offset is sought, SBA must follow the Department of the Treasury's regulations governing offset of a past-due, legally enforceable debt against tax overpayment.

Subpart C—Administrative Wage Garnishment

§ 140.11 What type of debt is subject to administrative wage garnishment, and how can SBA administratively garnish your pay?

(a) *General.* SBA may order your employer to pay SBA a portion of your disposable pay to satisfy delinquent non-tax debt you owe to the United States. This process is called "administrative wage garnishment" and is authorized by 31 U.S.C. 3720D.

(b) *Scope.* (1) This section provides procedures for SBA to collect delinquent non-tax debts through administrative wage garnishment.

(2) This section applies despite any State law.

(3) Nothing in this section prevents SBA from settling for less than the full amount of a debt. See, for example, the Federal Claims Collection Standards (FCCS), 31 CFR parts 900–904.

(4) SBA's receipt of payments under this section does not prevent SBA from pursuing other debt collection remedies. SBA may pursue debt collection remedies separately or together with administrative wage garnishment.

(5) This section does not apply to the collection of delinquent non-tax debt owed to the United States from the wages of Federal employees. Federal pay is subject to the Federal salary offset procedures set forth in 5 U.S.C. 5514 and other laws, including subpart B of this part.

(6) Nothing in this section requires SBA to duplicate notices or administrative proceedings required by contract, other laws, or regulations.

(c) *Definitions.* In this section the following definitions apply:

Agency means the SBA or any entity, public or private, that pursues recovery of the debt on SBA's behalf.

Business day means Monday through Friday excluding Federal legal holidays.

Day means calendar day. For purposes of computation, the last day of the period will be included unless it is a Saturday, a Sunday, or a Federal legal holiday.

Debt or *claim* means any amount of money, funds or property that has been determined by an appropriate official of the Federal Government to be owed to the United States by an individual, including debt administered by a third party as an agent for the Federal Government. Debt also includes accrued interest, administrative costs incurred in collection efforts by SBA or a lender participating in an SBA loan program, and penalties imposed pursuant to law or contract.

Debtor or you means an individual who owes a delinquent non-tax debt to the United States.

Delinquent non-tax debt means any debt not related to an obligation under the Internal Revenue Code of 1986, as amended, that has not been paid by the date specified in SBA's initial written demand for payment, or applicable agreement, unless other satisfactory payment arrangements have been made. For purposes of this section, the terms "debt" and "claim" are synonymous and refer to delinquent non-tax debt.

Disposable pay means that part of the debtor's compensation (including, but not limited to, salary, bonuses, commissions, and vacation pay) from an employer remaining after the deduction of health insurance premiums and any amounts required by law to be withheld. For purposes of this section, "amounts required by law to be withheld" include amounts for deductions such as social security taxes and withholding taxes, but do not include any amount withheld pursuant to a court order.

Employer means a person or entity that employs the services of others and that pays their wages or salaries. The term employer includes, but is not limited to, State and local Governments, but does not include an agency of the Federal Government.

Evidence of service means information retained by the Agency indicating the nature of the document to which it pertains, the date of mailing of the document, and to whom the document is being sent. Evidence of service may be retained electronically so long as the manner of retention is sufficient for evidentiary purposes.

Garnishment means the process of withholding amounts from an employee's disposable pay and the paying of those amounts to a creditor in satisfaction of a withholding order.

Withholding order means any order for withholding or garnishment of pay issued by an agency, or judicial or administrative body. For purposes of this section, the terms "wage garnishment order" and "garnishment order" have the same meaning as "withholding order."

(d) *When may the Agency initiate administrative wage garnishment proceedings?* Whenever the Agency determines you owe a delinquent non-tax debt, the Agency may initiate administrative wage garnishment proceedings to withhold a portion of your wages to satisfy the debt.

(e) *Notice Requirements.* (1) The Agency will send a written notice by first-class mail to your last known address at least 30 days before initiating garnishment. This pre-garnishment notice will inform you of:

(i) The type and amount of the debt;

(ii) The Agency's intent to collect the debt by making deductions from your pay until the debt is paid in full;

(iii) An explanation of your rights, including those listed below, and the timeframe within which you may exercise your rights.

(2) You have the right to:

(i) Inspect and copy non-privileged SBA records related to the debt;

(ii) Enter into a written repayment agreement with SBA under terms agreeable to SBA; and

(iii) Have a hearing before an SBA hearing official in accordance with paragraph (f) of this section concerning the existence or the amount of the debt or the terms of the proposed repayment schedule under the garnishment order. However, you are not entitled to a hearing concerning the terms of the proposed repayment schedule if those terms have been established by written agreement under paragraph (e)(2)(ii) of this section.

(3) The Agency will retain evidence of service showing when the Agency mailed the pre-garnishment notice.

(f) *What type of hearing must SBA give me?*—(1) *Procedural rules.* Procedural rules for the conduct of administrative wage garnishment hearings are established in this section.

(2) *Request for hearing.* You will be provided with a hearing, if you request one in writing disputing either the existence or amount of the debt or the terms of the repayment schedule (except a repayment schedule you and SBA agreed to in writing).

(3) *Type of hearing or review.* (i) You will have the right to an oral hearing only if the Hearing Official determines that the issues in dispute cannot be resolved solely by review of the documentary evidence, for example, when the Hearing Official finds that the validity of the claim turns on the issue of credibility or veracity.

(ii) If the Hearing Official determines an oral hearing is needed, he or she will set the time and location. You may choose whether the oral hearing is conducted in person or by telephone. You must pay all travel expenses for yourself and your witnesses to attend an in-person hearing. SBA will pay telephone charges for telephone hearings.

(iii) If no oral hearing is needed, the Hearing Official will accord you a "paper hearing," that is, the Hearing Official will decide the issues in dispute based upon a review of the written record. The Hearing Official will set a reasonable deadline for the submission of evidence.

(4) *Effect of timely request for hearing.* Subject to paragraph (f)(13) of this section (failure to appear), if the Hearing Official determines your written request for a hearing was received by the Hearing Official by the 15th business day after the Agency mailed the pre-garnishment notice, the Agency will not issue a garnishment order before the Hearing Official renders a decision.

(5) *Untimely request for hearing.* If the Hearing Official determines your written request for a hearing was not received by the Hearing Official by the 15th business day after the Agency mailed the pre-garnishment notice, the Agency will provide a hearing to you. However, the Agency may proceed with the issuance of a garnishment order and acceptance of payments unless the Hearing Official determines that the delay in filing the request was caused by factors over which you had no control, or that information received justifies a delay or cancellation of the garnishment order.

(6) *Hearing official.* A hearing official may be any qualified individual designated in the pre-garnishment notice.

(7) *Procedure.* After you request a hearing, the Hearing Official will decide what type of hearing to hold and will notify you and the SBA of:

(i) The date and time of a telephonic hearing;

(ii) The date, time, and location of an in-person oral hearing; or

(iii) The deadline for the submission of evidence for a written hearing.

(8) *Burden of proof.* (i) The SBA will have the burden of going forward to prove the existence or amount of the debt.

(ii) Thereafter, if you dispute the existence or amount of the debt, you must establish by a preponderance of the evidence that no debt exists or that the amount of the debt is incorrect. In addition, you may present evidence that the terms of the repayment schedule are unlawful, would cause you a financial hardship, or that collection of the debt may not be pursued due to operation of law.

(9) *Record.* The Hearing Official must maintain a summary record of any hearing provided under this section. A hearing is not required to be a formal evidentiary-type hearing; however, witnesses who testify in oral hearings will do so under oath or affirmation.

(10) *Date of decision.* The Hearing Official must render a written decision within 60 days of the date on which your request for a hearing was received by OHA. If the Hearing Official's decision is not rendered within that time, and the Agency had previously issued a garnishment order, the Agency must suspend garnishment beginning on the 61st day. This suspension must continue until the Hearing Official renders a decision.

(11) *Content of decision.* The written decision shall include:

(i) A summary of the facts presented;

(ii) The Hearing Official's findings, analysis and conclusions; and

(iii) The terms of any repayment schedule, if applicable.

(12) *Final agency action.* The decision of the hearing official is the final agency decision for the purposes of judicial review under the Administrative Procedure Act (5 U.S.C. 701 *et seq.*).

(13) *Failure to appear.* In the absence of good cause shown, a debtor who fails to appear at an oral hearing will be deemed as not having timely filed a request for a hearing.

(g) *Garnishment order.* (1) Unless the Agency receives an adverse decision from the Hearing Official or information it believes justifies delaying or canceling garnishment, the Agency will send the garnishment order to your employer by first-class mail, within the following time frames:

(i) If you did not make a timely request for a pre-garnishment hearing, within 30 days following the 15th business day after the Agency mailed the pre-garnishment notice;

(ii) If you did make a timely request for a pre-garnishment hearing, within 30 days after the final agency decision to proceed with garnishment; or,

(iii) As soon as reasonably possible thereafter.

(2) The garnishment order will be in a form prescribed by the Secretary of the Treasury, and will contain the signature of, or the image of the signature of, SBA's Administrator or his/her delegatee. The garnishment order will contain only the information necessary for compliance, including your name, address, and social security number, the instructions for garnishing your pay, and the address for sending payments.

(3) The Agency will retain evidence of service showing when it mailed the garnishment order.

(h) *Certification by employer.* Along with the garnishment order, the Agency will send your employer a certification, in a form determined by the Secretary of the Treasury. Your employer must complete and return this certification to us within the time stated in the certification instructions. The certification will include information about your employment status and the amount of your disposable pay available for garnishment.

(i) *Amounts withheld.* (1) Your employer must deduct the garnishment amount from your disposable pay during each pay period.

(2) Except as shown in paragraphs (i)(3) and (i)(4) of this section, the amount of garnishment will be the lesser of:

(i) The amount stated on the garnishment order, not to exceed 15% of your disposable pay; or,

(ii) The amount in 15 U.S.C. 1673(a)(2) (Restriction on Garnishment). This is the amount by which your disposable pay exceeds an amount equivalent to thirty times the minimum wage. See 29 CFR 870.10.

(3) If your pay is subject to other garnishment orders, the following applies:

(i) Unless otherwise provided by Federal law, the Agency garnishment orders must be paid in the amounts in paragraph (i)(2) of this section, and will have priority over other garnishment orders issued later. However, withholding orders for family support have priority over the Agency garnishment orders.

(ii) If amounts are being withheld from your pay because of a garnishment order issued before the Agency's garnishment order, or because of a garnishment order for family support issued at any time, the earlier or family support order will have priority, and the amount withheld because of the Agency garnishment order will be the lesser of:

(A) The amount calculated under paragraph (i)(2) of this section, or

(B) An amount equal to 25% of your disposable pay minus the amount withheld under the garnishment order(s) with priority.

(iii) If you owe more than one delinquent non-tax debt, the Agency may issue multiple garnishment orders if the amount withheld from your pay does not exceed the amount in paragraph (i)(2) of this section.

(4) You may give written consent for the Agency to garnish from your pay an amount greater than that in paragraphs (i)(2) and (i)(3) of this section.

(5) Your employer must promptly pay to the Agency all amounts withheld under a withholding order.

(6) Your employer is not required to change normal pay cycles to comply with the garnishment order.

(7) No assignment or allotment of your earnings that you have requested may interfere with or prohibit execution of the Agency 's garnishment order. The one exception to this rule is that you may assign or allot earnings because of a family support judgment or order.

(8) The garnishment order will state a reasonable time period within which your employer must begin wage garnishment. Your employer must withhold the designated amount from your wages each pay period until the Agency notifies your employer to stop wage garnishment.

(j) *Exclusions from garnishment.* The Agency may not garnish your wages if the Agency knows you have been involuntarily unemployed at any time during the last 12 months. You are responsible for informing the Agency of the facts and circumstances of your unemployment.

(k) *Financial hardship.* (1) If your wages are subject to a garnishment order issued by the Agency, you may, at any time, request a review of the amount being withheld from your wages based on a material change in circumstances that causes you financial hardship, such as disability, divorce, or catastrophic illness. You may send your request to the Director of SBA's loan servicing center in Birmingham, Alabama.

(2) If you request review under paragraph (k)(1) of this section, you must specifically state why the current amount of garnishment causes you financial hardship and you must send documentation supporting your claim.

(3) If the Agency finds financial hardship, the Agency will decide how much and how long to reduce the amount garnished from your pay. The Agency will notify your employer of any reductions.

(l) *Ending garnishment.* (1) After the Agency has recovered the amount you owe, including interest, penalties, and administrative costs consistent with the FCCS, the Agency will send a notice to your employer to stop wage garnishment with a copy to you.

(2) The Agency will review your account to ensure that garnishment has stopped if you have paid your debt in full.

(m) *Prohibited actions.* No employer may fire, refuse to employ, or take disciplinary action against you because of a withholding order issued by the Agency.

(n) *Refunds.* (1) The Agency must promptly refund any amount collected by administrative wage garnishment if either—

(i) A Judge, after a hearing held under paragraph (f) of this section, determines you do not owe a debt to the United States; or

(ii) The Agency determines that your employer continued submitting to the Agency withheld wages after you had paid your debt in full.

(2) Refunds of amounts collected will not earn interest unless required by federal law or contract.

(o) *Right of action.* The Agency may sue your employer for any amount that the employer fails to withhold from wages owed and payable to you in accordance with paragraphs (g) and (i) of this section. However, the Agency may not file such a suit until the collection action involving you has ended unless earlier filing is necessary to avoid expiration of any applicable statute of limitations period. For purposes of this section, the collection action involving you ends when the Agency stops the collection action in accordance with the FCCS or other applicable standards. In any event, the collection action involving you will be deemed ended if the Agency has not received any payments from you to satisfy your debt, in whole or in part, for a period of one (1) year.

[70 FR 17587, Apr. 7, 2005, as amended at 73 FR 63628, Oct. 27, 2008]

PART 142—PROGRAM FRAUD CIVIL REMEDIES ACT REGULATIONS

OVERVIEW AND DEFINITIONS

Sec.

PROCEDURES LEADING TO ISSUANCE OF A COMPLAINT

PROCEDURES FOLLOWING SERVICE OF A COMPLAINT

HEARING PROVISIONS

DECISIONS AND APPEALS

AUTHORITY: 15 U.S.C. 634(b); 31 U.S.C. 3803(g)(2).

SOURCE: 61 FR 2691, Jan. 29, 1996, unless otherwise noted.

OVERVIEW AND DEFINITIONS

§ 142.1 Overview of regulations.

(a) *Statutory basis.* This part implements the Program Fraud Civil Remedies Act of 1986, 31 U.S.C. 3801–3812 ("the Act"). The Act provides SBA and other federal agencies with an administrative remedy to impose civil penalties and assessments against persons making false claims and statements. The Act also provides due process protections to all persons who are subject to administrative proceedings under this part.

(b) *Possible remedies for program fraud.* In addition to any other penalty which may be prescribed by law, a person who submits, or causes to be submitted, a false claim or a false statement to SBA is subject to a civil penalty of not more than $11,181 for each statement or claim, regardless of whether property, services, or money is actually delivered or paid by SBA. If SBA has made any payment, transferred property, or provided services in reliance on a false claim, the person submitting it is also subject to an assessment of not more than twice the amount of the false claim. This assessment is in lieu of damages sustained by SBA because of the false claim.

[61 FR 2691, Jan. 29, 1996, as amended at 81 FR 31492, May 19, 2016; 82 FR 9969, Feb. 9, 2017; 83 FR 7363, Feb. 21, 2018]

§ 142.2 What kind of conduct will result in program fraud enforcement?

(a) Any person who makes, or causes to be made, a false, fictitious, or fraudulent claim or written statement to SBA is subject to program fraud enforcement. A "person" means any individual, partnership, corporation, association, or other legal entity.

(b) If more than one person makes a false claim or statement, each person is liable for a civil penalty. If more than one person makes a false claim which has induced SBA to make payment, an assessment is imposed against each person. The liability of each such person to pay the assessment is joint and several, that is, each is responsible for the entire amount.

(c) No proof of specific intent to defraud is required to establish liability under this part.

§ 142.3 What is a claim?

(a) Claim means any request, demand, or submission:

(1) Made to SBA for property, services, or money;

(2) Made to a recipient of property, services, or money from SBA or to a party to a contract with SBA for property or services, or for the payment of money. This provision applies only when the claim is related to the property, services or money from SBA or to the contract with SBA; or

(3) Made to SBA which decreases an obligation to pay or account for property, services, or money.

(b) A claim can relate to grants, loans, insurance, or other benefits, and includes SBA guaranteed loans made by participating lenders. A claim is made when it is received by SBA, an agent, fiscal intermediary, or other entity acting for SBA, or when it is received by the recipient of property, services, or money, or the party to the contract.

(c) Each voucher, invoice, claim form, or individual request or demand for property, services, or money constitutes a separate claim.

§ 142.4 What is a statement?

A "statement" means any written representation, certification, affirmation, document, record, or accounting or bookkeeping entry made with respect to a claim or with respect to a contract, bid or proposal for a contract, grant, loan or other benefit from SBA. "From SBA" means that SBA provides some portion of the money or property in connection with the contract, bid, grant, loan, or benefit, or is potentially liable to another party for some portion of the money or property under such contract, bid, grant, loan, or benefit. A statement is made, presented, or submitted to SBA when it is received by SBA or an agent, fiscal intermediary, or other entity acting for SBA.

§ 142.5 What is a false claim or statement?

(a) A claim submitted to SBA is a "false" claim if the person making the claim, or causing the claim to be made, knows or has reason to know that the claim:

(1) Is false, fictitious or fraudulent;

(2) Includes or is supported by a written statement which asserts or contains a material fact which is false, fictitious, or fraudulent;

(3) Includes or is supported by a written statement which is false, fictitious or fraudulent because it omits a material fact that the person making the statement has a duty to include in the statement; or

(4) Is for payment for the provision of property or services which the person has not provided as claimed.

(b) A statement submitted to SBA is a false statement if the person making the statement, or causing the statement to be made, knows or has reason to know that the statement:

(1) Asserts a material fact which is false, fictitious, or fraudulent; or

(2) Is false, fictitious, or fraudulent because it omits a material fact that the person making the statement has a duty to include in the statement. In addition, the statement must contain or be accompanied by an express certification or affirmation of the truthfulness and accuracy of the contents of the statement.

§ 142.6 What does the phrase "know or have reason to know" mean?

A person knows or has reason to know (that a claim or statement is false) if the person:

(a) Has actual knowledge that the claim or statement is false, fictitious, or fraudulent; or

(b) Acts in deliberate ignorance of the truth or falsity of the claim or statement; or

(c) Acts in reckless disregard of the truth or falsity of the claim or statement.

Procedures Leading to Issuance of a Complaint

§ 142.7 Who investigates program fraud?

The Inspector General, or his designee, is responsible for investigating allegations that a false claim or statement has been made. In this regard, the Inspector General has authority under the Program Fraud Civil Remedies Act and the Inspector General Act of 1978 (5 U.S.C. App. 3), as amended, to issue administrative subpoenas for the production of records and documents. The methods for serving a subpoena are set forth in part 101 of this chapter.

§ 142.8 What happens if program fraud is suspected?

(a) If the investigating official concludes that an action under this part is warranted, the investigating official submits a report containing the findings and conclusions of the investigation to a reviewing official. The reviewing official is the General Counsel or his designee. If the reviewing official determines that the report provides adequate evidence that a person submitted a false claim or statement, the reviewing official transmits to the Attorney General written notice of an intention to refer the matter for adjudication, with a request for approval of such referral. This notice will include the reviewing official's statements concerning:

(1) The reasons for the referral;

(2) The claims or statements upon which liability would be based;

(3) The evidence that supports liability;

(4) An estimate of the amount of money or the value of property, services, or other benefits requested or demanded in the false claim or statement;

(5) Any exculpatory or mitigating circumstances that may relate to the claims or statements known by the reviewing official or the investigating official; and

(6) The likelihood of collecting the proposed penalties and assessments.

(b) If at any time, the Attorney General or designee requests in writing that this administrative process be stayed, the Administrator must stay the process immediately. The Administrator may order the process resumed only upon receipt of the written authorization of the Attorney General.

§ 142.9 When will SBA issue a complaint?

SBA will issue a complaint:

(a) If the Attorney General (or designee) approves the referral of the allegations for adjudication; and

(b) In a case of submission of false claims, if the amount of money or the value of property or services demanded or requested in a false claim, or a group of related claims submitted at the same time, does not exceed $150,000. A group of related claims submitted at the same time includes only those claims arising from the same transaction (such as a grant, loan, application, or contract) which are submitted together as part of a single request, demand, or submission.

§ 142.10 What is contained in a complaint?

(a) A complaint is a written statement giving notice to the person alleged to be liable under 31 U.S.C. 3802 of the specific allegations being referred for adjudication and of the person's right to request a hearing with respect to those allegations. The person alleged to have made false statements or to have submitted false claims to SBA is referred to as the "defendant."

(b) The reviewing official may join in a single complaint false claims or statements that are unrelated or were not submitted simultaneously, regardless of the amount of money or the value of property or services demanded or requested.

(c) The complaint will state that SBA seeks to impose civil penalties, assessments, or both, against each defendant and will include:

(1) The allegations of liability against each defendant, including the statutory basis for liability, identification of the claims or statements involved, and the reasons liability allegedly arises from such claims or statements;

(2) The maximum amount of penalties and assessments for which each defendant may be held liable;

(3) A statement that each defendant may request a hearing by filing an answer and may be represented by a representative;

(4) Instructions for filing such an answer;

(5) A warning that failure to file an answer within 30 days of service of the complaint will result in imposition of the maximum amount of penalties and assessments.

(d) The reviewing official must serve any complaint on the defendant and provide a copy to the Office of Hearings and Appeals (OHA). If a hearing is requested, an Administrative Law Judge (ALJ) from OHA will serve as the Presiding Officer.

§ 142.11 How will the complaint be served?

(a) The complaint must be served on individual defendants directly, a partnership through a general partner, and on corporations or on unincorporated associations through an executive officer or a director, except that service also may be made on any person authorized by appointment or by law to receive process for the defendant.

(b) The complaint may be served either by:

(1) Registered or certified mail (return receipt requested) addressed to the defendant at his or her residence, usual dwelling place, principal office or place of business; or by

(2) Personal delivery by anyone 18 years of age or older.

(c) The date of service is the date of personal delivery or, in the case of service by registered or certified mail, the date of postmark.

(d) Proof of service—

(1) When service is made by registered or certified mail, the return postal receipt will serve as proof of service.

(2) When service is made by personal delivery, an affidavit of the individual serving the complaint, or written acknowledgment of receipt by the defendant or a representative, will serve as proof of service.

(e) When served with the complaint, the defendant also should be served with a copy of this part 142 and 31 U.S.C. 3801–3812.

PROCEDURES FOLLOWING SERVICE OF A COMPLAINT

§ 142.12 How does a defendant respond to the complaint?

(a) A defendant may file an answer with the reviewing official and the Office of Hearings and Appeals within 30 days of service of the complaint. An answer will be considered a request for an oral hearing.

(b) In the answer, a defendant—

(1) Must admit or deny each of the allegations of liability contained in the complaint (a failure to deny an allegation is considered an admission);

(2) Must state any defense on which the defendant intends to rely;

(3) May state any reasons why he or she believes the penalties, assessments, or both should be less than the statutory maximum; and

(4) Must state the name, address, and telephone number of the person authorized by the defendant to act as defendant's representative, if any.

(c) If the defendant is unable to file an answer which meets the requirements set forth in paragraph (b) of this section, the defendant may file with the reviewing official a general answer denying liability, requesting a hearing, and requesting an extension of time in which to file a complete answer. A general answer must be filed within 30 days of service of the complaint.

(d) If the defendant initially files a general answer requesting an extension of time, the reviewing official must promptly file with the ALJ the complaint, the general answer, and the request for an extension of time.

(e) For good cause shown, the ALJ may grant the defendant up to 30 additional days within which to file an answer meeting the requirements of paragraph (b) of this section. Such answer must be filed with OHA and a copy must be served on the reviewing official.

§ 142.13 What happens if a defendant fails to file an answer?

(a) If a defendant does not file any answer within 30 days after service of the complaint, the reviewing official will refer the complaint to the ALJ.

(b) Once the complaint is referred, the ALJ will promptly serve on the defendant a notice that an initial decision will be issued.

(c) The ALJ will assume the facts alleged in the complaint to be true and, if such facts establish liability under the statute, the ALJ will issue an initial decision imposing the maximum amount of penalties and assessments allowed under the statute.

(d) Except as otherwise provided in this section, when a defendant fails to file a timely answer, the defendant waives any right to further review of the penalties and assessments imposed in the initial decision.

(e) The initial decision becomes final 30 days after it is issued.

(f) If, at any time before an initial decision becomes final, a defendant files a motion with the ALJ asking that the case be reopened and describing the extraordinary circumstances that prevented the defendant from filing an answer, the initial decision will be stayed until the ALJ makes a decision on the motion. The reviewing official may respond to the motion.

(g) If, in his motion to reopen, a defendant demonstrates extraordinary circumstances excusing his failure to file a timely answer, the ALJ will withdraw the initial decision, and grant the defendant an opportunity to answer the complaint.

(h) A decision by the ALJ to deny a defendant's motion to reopen a case is not subject to review or reconsideration.

§ 142.14 What happens once an answer is filed?

(a) When the reviewing official receives an answer, he must file concurrently, the complaint and the answer with the ALJ, along with a designation of an SBA representative.

(b) When the ALJ receives the complaint and the answer, the ALJ will promptly serve a notice of oral hearing upon the defendant and the representative for SBA, in the same manner as the complaint, service of which is described in § 142.11. The notice of oral hearing must be served within six years of the date on which the claim or statement is made.

(c) The notice must include:

(1) The tentative time, place and nature of the hearing;

(2) The legal authority and jurisdiction under which the hearing is to be held;

(3) The matters of fact and law to be asserted;

(4) A description of the procedures for the conduct of the hearing;

(5) The name, address, and telephone number of the defendant's representative and the representative for SBA; and

(6) Such other matters as the ALJ deems appropriate.

HEARING PROVISIONS

§ 142.15 What kind of hearing is contemplated?

The hearing is a formal proceeding conducted by the ALJ during which a defendant will have the opportunity to cross-examine witnesses, present testimony, and dispute liability.

§ 142.16 At the hearing, what rights do the parties have?

(a) The parties to the hearing shall be the defendant and SBA. Pursuant to 31 U.S.C. 3730(c)(5), a private plaintiff in an action under the False Claims Act may participate in the hearing to the extent authorized by the provisions of that Act.

(b) Each party has the right to:

(1) Be represented by a representative;

(2) Request a pre-hearing conference and participate in any conference held by the ALJ;

(3) Conduct discovery;

(4) Agree to stipulations of fact or law which will be made a part of the record;

(5) Present evidence relevant to the issues at the hearing;

(6) Present and cross-examine witnesses;

(7) Present arguments at the hearing as permitted by the ALJ; and

(8) Submit written briefs and proposed findings of fact and conclusions of law after the hearing, as permitted by the ALJ.

§ 142.17 What is the role of the ALJ?

An ALJ from OHA serves as the Presiding Officer at all hearings, with authority as set forth in § 134.218(b) of this chapter.

§ 142.18 Can the reviewing official or ALJ be disqualified?

(a) A reviewing official or an ALJ may disqualify himself or herself at any time.

(b) Upon motion of any party, the reviewing official or ALJ may be disqualified as follows:

(1) The motion must be supported by an affidavit containing specific facts establishing that personal bias or other reason for disqualification exists, including the time and circumstances of the discovery of such facts;

(2) The motion must be filed promptly after discovery of the grounds for disqualification, or the objection will be deemed waived; and

(3) The party, or representative of record, must certify in writing that the motion is made in good faith.

(c) Once a motion has been filed to disqualify the reviewing official, the ALJ will halt the proceedings until resolving the matter of disqualification. If the ALJ determines that the reviewing official is disqualified, the ALJ will dismiss the complaint without prejudice. If the ALJ disqualifies himself or herself, the case will be promptly reassigned to another ALJ.

§ 142.19 How are issues brought to the attention of the ALJ?

All applications to the ALJ for an order or ruling are made by motion, stating the relief sought, the authority relied upon, and the facts alleged. Procedures for filing motions under this section are governed by § 134.211 of this chapter.

§ 142.20 How are papers served?

Except for service of a complaint or a notice of hearing under §§ 142.11 and 142.14(b) respectively, service of papers must be made as prescribed by § 134.204 of this chapter.

§ 142.21 How will the hearing be conducted and who has the burden of proof?

(a) The ALJ conducts a hearing in order to determine whether a defendant is liable for a civil penalty, assessment, or both and, if so, the appropriate amount of the civil penalty and/or assessment. The hearing will be recorded and transcribed, and the transcript of testimony, exhibits admitted at the hearing, and all papers and requests filed in the proceeding constitute the record for a decision by the ALJ.

(b) SBA must prove a defendant's liability and any aggravating factors by a preponderance of the evidence.

(c) A defendant must prove any affirmative defenses and any mitigating factors by a preponderance of the evidence.

(d) The hearing will be open to the public unless otherwise ordered by the ALJ for good cause shown.

§ 142.22 How is evidence presented at the hearing?

(a) Witnesses at the hearing must testify orally under oath or affirmation unless otherwise ordered by the ALJ. At the discretion of the ALJ, testimony may be admitted in the form of a written statement or deposition, a copy of which must be provided to all other parties, along with the last known address of the witness, in a manner which allows sufficient time for other parties to subpoena the witness for cross-examination at the hearing.

(b) The ALJ determines the admissibility of evidence in accordance with § 134.223 (a) and (b) of this chapter.

§ 142.23 Are there limits on disclosure of documents or discovery?

(a) Upon written request to the reviewing official, the defendant may review all non-privileged, relevant and material documents, records and other material related to the allegations contained in the complaint. After paying SBA a reasonable fee for duplication, the defendant may obtain a copy of the records described.

(b) Upon written request to the reviewing official, the defendant may obtain a copy of all exculpatory information in the possession of the reviewing official or investigating official relating to the allegations in the complaint. If the document would otherwise be privileged, only the portion of the document containing exculpatory information must be disclosed. As used in this section, the term "information" does not include legal materials such as statutes or case law obtained through legal research.

(c) The notice sent to the Attorney General from the reviewing official is not discoverable under any circumstances.

(d) Other discovery is available only as ordered by the ALJ and includes only those methods of discovery allowed by § 134.213 of this chapter.

§ 142.24 Can witnesses be subpoenaed?

A party seeking the appearance and testimony of any individual or the production of documents or records at a hearing may request in writing that the ALJ issue a subpoena. Any such request must be filed with the ALJ not less than 15 days before the scheduled hearing date unless otherwise allowed by the ALJ for good cause. A subpoena shall be issued by the ALJ in the manner specified by § 134.214 of this chapter.

§ 142.25 Can a party or witness object to discovery?

Any party or prospective witness may file a motion to quash a subpoena or to limit discovery or the disclosure of evidence. Motions to limit discovery or to object to the disclosure of evidence are governed by § 134.213 of this chapter. Motions to limit or quash subpoenas are governed by § 134.214(d) of this chapter.

§ 142.26 Can a party informally discuss the case with the ALJ?

No. Such discussions are forbidden as *ex parte* communications with the ALJ as set forth in § 134.220 of this chapter. This does not prohibit a party from communicating with other employees of OHA to inquire about the status of a case or to ask routine questions concerning administrative functions and procedures.

§ 142.27 Are there sanctions for misconduct?

The ALJ may sanction a party or representative, as set forth in § 134.219 of this chapter.

§ 142.28 Where is the hearing held?

The ALJ will hold the hearing in any judicial district of the United States:

(a) In which the defendant resides or transacts business; or

(b) In which the claim or statement on which liability is based was made, presented or submitted to SBA; or

(c) As agreed upon by the defendant and the ALJ.

§ 142.29 Are witness lists exchanged before the hearing?

(a) At least 15 days before the hearing or at such other time as ordered by the ALJ, the parties must exchange witness lists and copies of proposed hearing exhibits, including copies of any written statements or transcripts of deposition testimony that the party intends to offer in lieu of live testimony.

(b) If a party objects, the ALJ will not admit into evidence the testimony of any witness whose name does not appear on the witness list or any exhibit not provided to an opposing party unless the ALJ finds good cause for the omission or concludes that there is no prejudice to the objecting party.

(c) Unless a party objects within the time set by the ALJ, documents exchanged in accordance with this section are deemed to be authentic for the purpose of admissibility at the hearing.

DECISIONS AND APPEALS

§ 142.30 How is the case decided?

(a) The ALJ will issue an initial decision based only on the record. It will contain findings of fact, conclusions of law, and the amount of any penalties and assessments imposed.

(b) The ALJ will serve the initial decision on all parties within 90 days after close of the hearing or expiration of any allowed time for submission of post-hearing briefs. If the ALJ fails to meet this deadline, he or she shall promptly notify the parties of the reason for the delay and set a new deadline.

(c) The findings of fact must include a finding on each of the following issues:

(1) Whether any one or more of the claims or statements identified in the complaint violate this part; and

(2) If the defendant is liable for penalties or assessments, the appropriate amount of any such penalties or assessments, considering any mitigating or aggravating factors.

(d) The initial decision will include a description of the right of a defendant found liable for a civil penalty or assessment to file a motion for reconsideration with the ALJ or a notice of appeal with the Administrator.

§ 142.31 Can a party request reconsideration of the initial decision?

(a) Any party may file a motion for reconsideration of the initial decision with the ALJ within 20 days of receipt of the initial decision. If the initial decision was served by mail, there is a rebuttable presumption that the initial decision was received by the party 5 days from the date of mailing.

(b) A motion for reconsideration must be accompanied by a supporting brief and must describe specifically each allegedly erroneous decision.

(c) Any response to a motion for reconsideration must be filed within 20 days of receipt of such motion.

(d) The ALJ will dispose of a motion for reconsideration by denying it or by issuing a revised initial decision.

(e) If the ALJ issues a revised initial decision upon motion of a party, that party may not file another motion for reconsideration.

§ 142.32 When does the initial decision of the ALJ become final?

(a) The initial decision of the ALJ becomes the final decision of SBA, and shall be binding on all parties 30 days after it is issued, unless any party timely files a motion for reconsideration or any defendant adjudged to have submitted a false claim or statement timely appeals to the SBA Administrator, as set forth in § 142.33.

(b) If the ALJ disposes of a motion for reconsideration by denying it or by issuing a revised initial decision, the ALJ's order on the motion for reconsideration becomes the final decision of SBA 30 days after the order is issued, unless a defendant adjudged to have submitted a false claim or statement timely appeals to the Administrator, within 30 days of the ALJ's order, as set forth in § 142.33.

§ 142.33 What are the procedures for appealing the ALJ decision?

(a) Any defendant who submits a timely answer and is found liable for a civil penalty or assessment in an initial decision may appeal the decision.

(b) The defendant may file a notice of appeal with the Administrator within 30 days following issuance of the initial decision, serving a copy of the notice of appeal on all parties and the ALJ. The Administrator may extend this deadline for up to thirty additional days if an extension request is filed within the initial 30 day period and shows good cause.

(c) The defendant's appeal will not be considered until all timely motions for reconsideration have been resolved.

(d) If a timely motion for reconsideration is denied, a notice of appeal may be filed within 30 days following such denial or issuance of a revised initial decision, whichever applies.

(e) A notice of appeal must be supported by a written brief specifying why the initial decision should be reversed or modified.

(f) SBA's representative may file a brief in opposition to the notice of appeal within 30 days of receiving the defendant's notice of appeal and supporting brief.

(g) If a defendant timely files a notice of appeal, and the time for filing motions for reconsideration has expired, the ALJ will forward the record of the proceeding to the Administrator.

§ 142.34 Are there any limitations on the right to appeal to the Administrator?

(a) A defendant has no right to appear personally, or through a representative, before the Administrator.

(b) There is no right to appeal any interlocutory ruling.

(c) The Administrator will not consider any objection or evidence that was not raised before the ALJ unless the defendant demonstrates that the failure to object was caused by extraordinary circumstances. If the appealing defendant demonstrates to the satisfaction of the Administrator that extraordinary circumstances prevented the presentation of evidence at the hearing, and that the additional evidence is material, the Administrator may remand the matter to the ALJ for consideration of the additional evidence.

§ 142.35 How does the Administrator dispose of an appeal?

(a) The Administrator may affirm, reduce, reverse, compromise, remand, or settle any penalty or assessment imposed by the ALJ in the initial decision or reconsideration decision.

(b) The Administrator will promptly serve each party to the appeal and the ALJ with a copy of his or her decision. This decision must contain a statement describing the right of any person, against whom a penalty or assessment has been made, to seek judicial review.

§ 142.36 Can I obtain judicial review?

If the initial decision is appealed, the decision of the Administrator is the final decision of SBA and is not subject to judicial review unless the defendant files a petition for judicial review within 60 days after the Administrator serves the defendant with a copy of the final decision.

§ 142.37 What judicial review is available?

31 U.S.C. 3805 authorizes judicial review by the appropriate United States District Court of any final SBA decision imposing penalties or assessments, and specifies the procedures for such review. To obtain judicial review, a defendant must file a petition in a timely fashion.

§ 142.38 Can the administrative complaint be settled voluntarily?

(a) Parties may make offers of compromise or settlement at any time. Any compromise or settlement must be in writing.

(b) The reviewing official has the exclusive authority to compromise or settle the case from the date on which the reviewing official is permitted to issue a complaint until the ALJ issues an initial decision.

(c) The Administrator has exclusive authority to compromise or settle the case from the date of the ALJ's initial decision until initiation of any judicial review or any action to collect the penalties and assessments.

(d) The Attorney General has exclusive authority to compromise or settle the case while any judicial review or any action to recover penalties and assessments is pending.

(e) The investigating official may recommend settlement terms to the reviewing official, the Administrator, or the Attorney General, as appropriate. The reviewing official may recommend settlement terms to the Administrator or the Attorney General, as appropriate.

§ 142.39 How are civil penalties and assessments collected?

31 U.S.C. 3806 and 3808(b) authorize the Attorney General to bring specific actions for collection of such civil penalties and assessments including administrative offset under 31 U.S.C. 3716. The penalties and assessments may not, however, be administratively offset against an overpayment of federal taxes (then or later owed) to the defendant by the United States.

§ 142.40 What if the investigation indicates criminal misconduct?

(a) Any investigating official may:

(1) Refer allegations of criminal misconduct directly to the Department of Justice for prosecution or for suit under the False Claims Act or other civil proceeding;

(2) Defer or postpone a report or referral to the reviewing official to avoid interference with a criminal investigation or prosecution; or

(3) Issue subpoenas under other statutory authority.

(b) Nothing in this part limits the requirement that SBA employees report suspected violations of criminal law to the SBA Office of Inspector General or to the Attorney General.

§ 142.41 How does SBA protect the rights of defendants?

These procedures separate the functions of the investigating official, reviewing official, and the ALJ, each of whom report to a separate organizational authority in accordance with 31 U.S.C. 3801. Except for purposes of settlement, or as a witness or a representative in public proceedings, no investigating official, reviewing official, or SBA employee or agent who helps investigate, prepare, or present a case may (in such case, or a factually related case) participate in the initial decision or the review of the initial decision by the Administrator. This separation of functions and organization is designed to assure the independence and impartiality of each government official during every stage of the proceeding. The representative for SBA may be employed in the offices of either the investigating official or the reviewing official.

PART 143 [RESERVED]

PART 146—NEW RESTRICTIONS ON LOBBYING

AUTHORITY: Section 319, Pub. L. 101–121 (31 U.S.C. 1352); 15 U.S.C. 634(b)(6).

CROSS REFERENCE: See also Office of Management and Budget notice published at 54 FR 52306, December 20, 1989.

SOURCE: 55 FR 6737. 6747, Feb. 26, 1990, unless otherwise noted.

Subpart A—General

§ 146.100 Conditions on use of funds.

(a) No appropriated funds may be expended by the recipient of a Federal contract, grant, loan, or cooperative agreement to pay any person for influencing or attempting to influence an officer or employee of any agency, a Member of Congress, an officer or employee of Congress, or an employee of a Member of Congress in connection with any of the following covered Federal actions: the awarding of any Federal contract, the making of any Federal grant, the making of any Federal loan, the entering into of any cooperative agreement, and the extension, continuation, renewal, amendment, or modification of any Federal contract, grant, loan, or cooperative agreement.

(b) Each person who requests or receives from an agency a Federal contract, grant, loan, or cooperative agreement shall file with that agency a certification, set forth in appendix A, that the person has not made, and will not make, any payment prohibited by paragraph (a) of this section.

(c) Each person who requests or receives from an agency a Federal contract, grant, loan, or a cooperative agreement shall file with that agency a disclosure form, set forth in appendix B, if such person has made or has agreed to make any payment using nonappropriated funds (to include profits from any covered Federal action), which would be prohibited under paragraph (a) of this section if paid for with appropriated funds.

(d) Each person who requests or receives from an agency a commitment providing for the United States to insure or guarantee a loan shall file with that agency a statement, set forth in appendix A, whether that person has made or has agreed to make any payment to influence or attempt to influence an officer or employee of any agency, a Member of Congress, an officer or employee of Congress, or an employee of a Member of Congress in connection with that loan insurance or guarantee.

(e) Each person who requests or receives from an agency a commitment providing for the United States to insure or guarantee a loan shall file with that agency a disclosure form, set forth in appendix B, if that person has made or has agreed to make any payment to influence or attempt to influence an officer or employee of any agency, a Member of Congress, an officer or employee of Congress, or an employee of a Member of Congress in connection with that loan insurance or guarantee.

§ 146.105 Definitions.

For purposes of this part:

(a) *Agency*, as defined in 5 U.S.C. 552(f), includes Federal executive departments and agencies as well as independent regulatory commissions and Government corporations, as defined in 31 U.S.C. 9101(1).

(b) *Covered Federal action* means any of the following Federal actions:

(1) The awarding of any Federal contract;

(2) The making of any Federal grant;

(3) The making of any Federal loan;

(4) The entering into of any cooperative agreement; and,

(5) The extension, continuation, renewal, amendment, or modification of any Federal contract, grant, loan, or cooperative agreement.

Covered Federal action does not include receiving from an agency a commitment providing for the United States to insure or guarantee a loan. Loan guarantees and loan insurance are addressed independently within this part.

(c) *Federal contract* means an acquisition contract awarded by an agency, including those subject to the Federal Acquisition Regulation (FAR), and any other acquisition contract for real or personal property or services not subject to the FAR.

(d) *Federal cooperative agreement* means a cooperative agreement entered into by an agency.

(e) *Federal grant* means an award of financial assistance in the form of money, or property in lieu of money, by the Federal Government or a direct appropriation made by law to any person. The term does not include technical assistance which provides services instead of money, or other assistance in the form of revenue sharing, loans, loan guarantees, loan insurance, interest subsidies, insurance, or direct United States cash assistance to an individual.

(f) *Federal loan* means a loan made by an agency. The term does not include loan guarantee or loan insurance.

(g) *Indian tribe* and *tribal organization* have the meaning provided in section 4 of the Indian Self-Determination and Education Assistance Act (25 U.S.C. 450B). Alaskan Natives are included under the definitions of Indian tribes in that Act.

(h) *Influencing or attempting to influence* means making, with the intent to influence, any communication to or appearance before an officer or employee or any agency, a Member of Congress, an officer or employee of Congress, or an employee of a Member of Congress in connection with any covered Federal action.

(i) *Loan guarantee* and *loan insurance* means an agency's guarantee or insurance of a loan made by a person.

(j) *Local government* means a unit of government in a State and, if chartered, established, or otherwise recognized by a State for the performance of a governmental duty, including a local public authority, a special district, an intrastate district, a council of governments, a sponsor group representative organization, and any other instrumentality of a local government.

(k) *Officer or employee of an agency* includes the following individuals who are employed by an agency:

(1) An individual who is appointed to a position in the Government under title 5, U.S. Code, including a position under a temporary appointment;

(2) A member of the uniformed services as defined in section 101(3), title 37, U.S. Code;

(3) A special Government employee as defined in section 202, title 18, U.S. Code; and,

(4) An individual who is a member of a Federal advisory committee, as defined by the Federal Advisory Committee Act, title 5, U.S. Code appendix 2.

(l) *Person* means an individual, corporation, company, association, authority, firm, partnership, society, State, and local government, regardless of whether such entity is operated for profit or not for profit. This term excludes an Indian tribe, tribal organization, or any other Indian organization with respect to expenditures specifically permitted by other Federal law.

(m) *Reasonable compensation* means, with respect to a regularly employed officer or employee of any person, compensation that is consistent with the normal compensation for such officer or employee for work that is not furnished to, not funded by, or not furnished in cooperation with the Federal Government.

(n) *Reasonable payment* means, with respect to professional and other technical services, a payment in an amount that is consistent with the amount normally paid for such services in the private sector.

(o) *Recipient* includes all contractors, subcontractors at any tier, and subgrantees at any tier of the recipient of funds received in connection with a Federal contract, grant, loan, or cooperative agreement. The term excludes an Indian tribe, tribal organization, or any other Indian organization with respect to expenditures specifically permitted by other Federal law.

(p) *Regularly employed* means, with respect to an officer or employee of a person requesting or receiving a Federal contract, grant, loan, or cooperative agreement or a commitment providing for the United States to insure or guarantee a loan, an officer or employee who is employed by such person for at least 130 working days within one year immediately preceding the date of the submission that initiates agency consideration of such person for receipt of such contract, grant, loan, cooperative agreement, loan insurance commitment, or loan guarantee commitment. An officer or employee who is employed by such person for less than 130 working days within one year immediately preceding the date of the submission that initiates agency consideration of such person shall be considered to be regularly employed as soon as he or she is employed by such person for 130 working days.

(q) *State* means a State of the United States, the District of Columbia, the Commonwealth of Puerto Rico, a territory or possession of the United States, an agency or instrumentality of a State, and a multi-State, regional, or interstate entity having governmental duties and powers.

§ 146.110 Certification and disclosure.

(a) Each person shall file a certification, and a disclosure form, if required, with each submission that initiates agency consideration of such person for:

(1) Award of a Federal contract, grant, or cooperative agreement exceeding $100,000; or

(2) An award of a Federal loan or a commitment providing for the United States to insure or guarantee a loan exceeding $150,000.

(b) Each person shall file a certification, and a disclosure form, if required, upon receipt by such person of:

(1) A Federal contract, grant, or cooperative agreement exceeding $100,000; or

(2) A Federal loan or a commitment providing for the United States to insure or guarantee a loan exceeding $150,000,

Unless such person previously filed a certification, and a disclosure form, if required, under paragraph (a) of this section.

(c) Each person shall file a disclosure form at the end of each calendar quarter in which there occurs any event that requires disclosure or that materially affects the accuracy of the information contained in any disclosure form previously filed by such person under paragraphs (a) or (b) of this section. An event that materially affects the accuracy of the information reported includes:

(1) A cumulative increase of $25,000 or more in the amount paid or expected to be paid for influencing or attempting to influence a covered Federal action; or

(2) A change in the person(s) or individual(s) influencing or attempting to influence a covered Federal action; or,

(3) A change in the officer(s), employee(s), or Member(s) contacted to influence or attempt to influence a covered Federal action.

(d) Any person who requests or receives from a person referred to in paragraphs (a) or (b) of this section:

(1) A subcontract exceeding $100,000 at any tier under a Federal contract;

(2) A subgrant, contract, or subcontract exceeding $100,000 at any tier under a Federal grant;

(3) A contract or subcontract exceeding $100,000 at any tier under a Federal loan exceeding $150,000; or,

(4) A contract or subcontract exceeding $100,000 at any tier under a Federal cooperative agreement,

Shall file a certification, and a disclosure form, if required, to the next tier above.

(e) All disclosure forms, but not certifications, shall be forwarded from tier to tier until received by the person referred to in paragraphs (a) or (b) of this section. That person shall forward all disclosure forms to the agency.

(f) Any certification or disclosure form filed under paragraph (e) of this section shall be treated as a material representation of fact upon which all receiving tiers shall rely. All liability arising from an erroneous representation shall be borne solely by the tier filing that representation and shall not be shared by any tier to which the erroneous representation is forwarded. Submitting an erroneous certification or disclosure constitutes a failure to file the required certification or disclosure, respectively. If a person fails to file a required certification or disclosure, the United States may pursue all available remedies, including those authorized by section 1352, title 31, U.S. Code.

(g) For awards and commitments in process prior to December 23, 1989, but not made before that date, certifications shall be required at award or commitment, covering activities occurring between December 23, 1989, and the date of award or commitment. However, for awards and commitments in process prior to the December 23, 1989 effective date of these provisions, but not made before December 23, 1989, disclosure forms shall not be required at time of award or commitment but shall be filed within 30 days.

(h) No reporting is required for an activity paid for with appropriated funds if that activity is allowable under either Subpart B or C.

Subpart B—Activities by Own Employees

§ 146.200 Agency and legislative liaison.

(a) The prohibition on the use of appropriated funds, in § 146.100 (a), does not apply in the case of a payment of reasonable compensation made to an officer or employee of a person requesting or receiving a Federal contract, grant, loan, or cooperative agreement if the payment is for agency and legislative liaison activities not directly related to a covered Federal action.

(b) For purposes of paragraph (a) of this section, providing any information specifically requested by an agency or Congress is allowable at any time.

(c) For purposes of paragraph (a) of this section, the following agency and legislative liaison activities are allowable at any time only where they are not related to a specific solicitation for any covered Federal action:

(1) Discussing with an agency (including individual demonstrations) the qualities and characteristics of the person's products or services, conditions or terms of sale, and service capabilities; and,

(2) Technical discussions and other activities regarding the application or adaptation of the person's products or services for an agency's use.

(d) For purposes of paragraph (a) of this section, the following agencies and legislative liaison activities are allowable only where they are prior to formal solicitation of any covered Federal action:

(1) Providing any information not specifically requested but necessary for an agency to make an informed decision about initiation of a covered Federal action;

(2) Technical discussions regarding the preparation of an unsolicited proposal prior to its official submission; and,

(3) Capability presentations by persons seeking awards from an agency pursuant to the provisions of the Small Business Act, as amended by Public Law 95–507 and other subsequent amendments.

(e) Only those activities expressly authorized by this section are allowable under this section.

§ 146.205 Professional and technical services.

(a) The prohibition on the use of appropriated funds, in § 146.100 (a), does not apply in the case of a payment of reasonable compensation made to an officer or employee of a person requesting or receiving a Federal contract, grant, loan, or cooperative agreement or an extension, continuation, renewal, amendment, or modification of a Federal contract, grant, loan, or cooperative agreement if payment is for professional or technical services rendered directly in the preparation, submission, or negotiation of any bid, proposal, or application for that Federal contract, grant, loan, or cooperative agreement or for meeting requirements imposed by or pursuant to law as a condition for receiving that Federal contract, grant, loan, or cooperative agreement.

(b) For purposes of paragraph (a) of this section, *professional and technical services* shall be limited to advice and analysis directly applying any professional or technical discipline. For example, drafting of a legal document accompanying a bid or proposal by a lawyer is allowable. Similarly, technical advice provided by an engineer on the performance or operational capability of a piece of equipment rendered directly in the negotiation of a contract is allowable. However, communications with the intent to influence made by a professional (such as a licensed lawyer) or a technical person (such as a licensed accountant) are not allowable under this section unless they provide advice and analysis directly applying their professional or technical expertise and unless the advice or analysis is rendered directly and solely in the preparation, submission or negotiation of a covered Federal action. Thus, for example, communications with the intent to influence made by a lawyer that do not provide legal advice or analysis directly and solely related to the legal aspects of his or her client's proposal, but generally advocate one proposal over another are not allowable under this section because the lawyer is not providing professional legal services. Similarly, communications with the intent to influence made by an engineer providing an engineering analysis prior to the preparation or submission of a bid or proposal are not allowable under this section since the engineer is providing technical services but not directly in the preparation, submission or negotiation of a covered Federal action.

(c) Requirements imposed by or pursuant to law as a condition for receiving a covered Federal award include those required by law or regulation, or reasonably expected to be required by law or regulation, and any other requirements in the actual award documents.

(d) Only those services expressly authorized by this section are allowable under this section.

§ 146.210 Reporting.

No reporting is required with respect to payments of reasonable compensation made to regularly employed officers or employees of a person.

Subpart C—Activities by Other Than Own Employees

§ 146.300 Professional and technical services.

(a) The prohibition on the use of appropriated funds, in § 146.100 (a), does not apply in the case of any reasonable payment to a person, other than an officer or employee of a person requesting or receiving a covered Federal action, if the payment is for professional or technical services rendered directly in the preparation, submission, or negotiation of any bid, proposal, or application for that Federal contract, grant, loan, or cooperative agreement or for meeting requirements imposed by or pursuant to law as a condition for receiving that Federal contract, grant, loan, or cooperative agreement.

(b) The reporting requirements in § 146.110 (a) and (b) regarding filing a disclosure form by each person, if required, shall not apply with respect to professional or technical services rendered directly in the preparation, submission, or negotiation of any commitment providing for the United States to insure or guarantee a loan.

(c) For purposes of paragraph (a) of this section, *professional and technical services* shall be limited to advice and analysis directly applying any professional or technical discipline. For example, drafting or a legal document accompanying a bid or proposal by a lawyer is allowable. Similarly, technical advice provided by an engineer on the performance or operational capability of a piece of equipment rendered directly in the negotiation of a contract is allowable. However, communications with the intent to influence made by a professional (such as a licensed lawyer) or a technical person (such as a licensed accountant) are not allowable under this section unless they provide advice and analysis directly applying their professional or technical expertise and unless the advice or analysis is rendered directly and solely in the preparation, submission or negotiation of a covered Federal action. Thus, for example, communications with the intent to influence made by a lawyer that do not provide legal advice or analysis directly and solely related to the legal aspects of his or her client's proposal, but generally advocate one proposal over another are not allowable under this section because the lawyer is not providing professional legal services. Similarly, communications with the intent to influence made by an engineer providing an engineering analysis prior to the preparation or submission of a bid or proposal are not allowable under this section since the engineer is providing technical services but not directly in the preparation, submission or negotiation of a covered Federal action.

(d) Requirements imposed by or pursuant to law as a condition for receiving a covered Federal award include those required by law or regulation, or reasonably expected to be required by law or regulation, and any other requirements in the actual award documents.

(e) Persons other than officers or employees of a person requesting or receiving a covered Federal action include consultants and trade associations.

(f) Only those services expressly authorized by this section are allowable under this section.

Subpart D—Penalties and Enforcement

§ 146.400 Penalties.

(a) Any person who makes an expenditure prohibited herein shall be subject to a civil penalty of not less than $19,639 and not more than $196,387 for each such expenditure.

(b) Any person who fails to file or amend the disclosure form (see appendix B) to be filed or amended if required herein, shall be subject to a civil penalty of not less than $19,639 and not more than $196,387 for each such failure.

(c) A filing or amended filing on or after the date on which an administrative action for the imposition of a civil penalty is commenced does not prevent the imposition of such civil penalty for a failure occurring before that date. An administrative action is commenced with respect to a failure when an investigating official determines in writing to commence an investigation of an allegation of such failure.

(d) In determining whether to impose a civil penalty, and the amount of any such penalty, by reason of a violation by any person, the agency shall consider the nature, circumstances, extent, and gravity of the violation, the effect on the ability of such person to continue in business, any prior violations by such person, the degree of culpability of such person, the ability of the person to pay the penalty, and such other matters as may be appropriate.

(e) First offenders under paragraphs (a) or (b) of this section shall be subject to a civil penalty of $19,639, absent aggravating circumstances. Second and subsequent offenses by persons shall be subject to an appropriate civil penalty between $19,639 and $196,387, as determined by the agency head or his or her designee.

(f) An imposition of a civil penalty under this section does not prevent the United States from seeking any other remedy that may apply to the same conduct that is the basis for the imposition of such civil penalty.

[55 FR 6737. 6747, Feb. 26, 1990, as amended at 81 FR 31492, May 19, 2016; 82 FR 9969, Feb. 9, 2017; 83 FR 7363, Feb. 21, 2018]

§ 146.405 Penalty procedures.

Agencies shall impose and collect civil penalties pursuant to the provisions of the Program Fraud and Civil Remedies Act, 31 U.S.C. sections 3803 (except subsection (c)), 3804, 3805, 3806, 3807, 3808, and 3812, insofar as these provisions are not inconsistent with the requirements herein.

§ 146.410 Enforcement.

The head of each agency shall take such actions as are necessary to ensure that the provisions herein are vigorously implemented and enforced in that agency.

Subpart E—Exemptions

§ 146.500 Secretary of Defense.

(a) The Secretary of Defense may exempt, on a case-by-case basis, a covered Federal action from the prohibition whenever the Secretary determines, in writing, that such an exemption is in the national interest. The Secretary shall transmit a copy of each such written exemption to Congress immediately after making such a determination.

(b) The Department of Defense may issue supplemental regulations to implement paragraph (a) of this section.

Subpart F—Agency Reports

§ 146.600 Semi-annual compilation.

(a) The head of each agency shall collect and compile the disclosure reports (see appendix B) and, on May 31 and November 30 of each year, submit to the Secretary of the Senate and the Clerk of the House of Representatives a report containing a compilation of the information contained in the disclosure reports received during the six-month period ending on March 31 or September 30, respectively, of that year.

(b) The report, including the compilation, shall be available for public inspection 30 days after receipt of the report by the Secretary and the Clerk.

(c) Information that involves intelligence matters shall be reported only to the Select Committee on Intelligence of the Senate, the Permanent Select Committee on Intelligence of the House of Representatives, and the Committees on Appropriations of the Senate and the House of Representatives in accordance with procedures agreed to by such committees. Such information shall not be available for public inspection.

(d) Information that is classified under Executive Order 12356 or any successor order shall be reported only to the Committee on Foreign Relations of the Senate and the Committee on Foreign Affairs of the House of Representatives or the Committees on Armed Services of the Senate and the House of Representatives (whichever such committees have jurisdiction of matters involving such information) and to the Committees on Appropriations of the Senate and the House of Representatives in accordance with procedures agreed to by such committees. Such information shall not be available for public inspection.

(e) The first semi-annual compilation shall be submitted on May 31, 1990, and shall contain a compilation of the disclosure reports received from December 23, 1989 to March 31, 1990.

(f) Major agencies, designated by the Office of Management and Budget (OMB), are required to provide machine-readable compilations to the Secretary of the Senate and the Clerk of the House of Representatives no later than with the compilations due on May 31, 1991. OMB shall provide detailed specifications in a memorandum to these agencies.

(g) Non-major agencies are requested to provide machine-readable compilations to the Secretary of the Senate and the Clerk of the House of Representatives.

(h) Agencies shall keep the originals of all disclosure reports in the official files of the agency.

§ 146.605 Inspector General report.

(a) The Inspector General, or other official as specified in paragraph (b) of this section, of each agency shall prepare and submit to Congress each year, commencing with submission of the President's Budget in 1991, an evaluation of the compliance of that agency with, and the effectiveness of, the requirements herein. The evaluation may include any recommended changes that may be necessary to strengthen or improve the requirements.

(b) In the case of an agency that does not have an Inspector General, the agency official comparable to an Inspector General shall prepare and submit the annual report, or, if there is no such comparable official, the head of the agency shall prepare and submit the annual report.

(c) The annual report shall be submitted at the same time the agency submits its annual budget justifications to Congress.

(d) The annual report shall include the following: All alleged violations relating to the agency's covered Federal actions during the year covered by the report, the actions taken by the head of the agency in the year covered by the report with respect to those alleged violations and alleged violations in previous years, and the amounts of civil penalties imposed by the agency in the year covered by the report.

Appendix A to Part 146—Certification Regarding Lobbying

Certification for Contracts, Grants, Loans, and Cooperative Agreements

The undersigned certifies, to the best of his or her knowledge and belief, that:

(1) No Federal appropriated funds have been paid or will be paid, by or on behalf of the undersigned, to any person for influencing or attempting to influence an officer or employee of an agency, a Member of Congress, an officer or employee of Congress, or an employee of a Member of Congress in connection with the awarding of any Federal contract, the making of any Federal grant, the making of any Federal loan, the entering into of any cooperative agreement, and the extension, continuation, renewal, amendment, or modification of any Federal contract, grant, loan, or cooperative agreement.

(2) If any funds other than Federal appropriated funds have been paid or will be paid to any person for influencing or attempting to influence an officer or employee of any agency, a Member of Congress, an officer or employee of Congress, or an employee of a Member of Congress in connection with this Federal contract, grant, loan, or cooperative agreement, the undersigned shall complete and submit Standard Form-LLL, "Disclosure Form to Report Lobbying," in accordance with its instructions.

(3) The undersigned shall require that the language of this certification be included in the award documents for all subawards at all tiers (including subcontracts, subgrants, and contracts under grants, loans, and cooperative agreements) and that all subrecipients shall certify and disclose accordingly.

This certification is a material representation of fact upon which reliance was placed when this transaction was made or entered into. Submission of this certification is a prerequisite for making or entering into this transaction imposed by section 1352, title 31, U.S. Code. Any person who fails to file the required certification shall be subject to a civil penalty of not less than $10,000 and not more than $100,000 for each such failure.

Statement for Loan Guarantees and Loan Insurance

The undersigned states, to the best of his or her knowledge and belief, that:

If any funds have been paid or will be paid to any person for influencing or attempting to influence an officer or employee of any agency, a Member of Congress, an officer or employee of Congress, or an employee of a Member of Congress in connection with this commitment providing for the United States to insure or guarantee a loan, the undersigned shall complete and submit Standard Form-LLL, "Disclosure Form to Report Lobbying," in accordance with its instructions.

Submission of this statement is a prerequisite for making or entering into this transaction imposed by section 1352, title 31, U.S. Code. Any person who fails to file the required statement shall be subject to a civil penalty of not less than $10,000 and not more than $100,000 for each such failure.

APPENDIX B TO PART 146—DISCLOSURE FORM TO REPORT LOBBYING

DISCLOSURE OF LOBBYING ACTIVITIES

Approved by OMB 0348-0046

Complete this form to disclose lobbying activities pursuant to 31 U.S.C. 1352
(See reverse for public burden disclosure.)

1. Type of Federal Action:
☐ a. contract
b. grant
c. cooperative agreement
d. loan
e. loan guarantee
f. loan insurance

2. Status of Federal Action:
☐ a. bid/offer/application
b. initial award
c. post-award

3. Report Type:
☐ a. initial filing
b. material change

For Material Change Only:
year _______ quarter _____
date of last report _________

4. Name and Address of Reporting Entity:
☐ Prime ☐ Subawardee
Tier _____ , *if known*:

Congressional District, *if known*:

5. If Reporting Entity in No. 4 is Subawardee, Enter Name and Address of Prime:

Congressional District, *if known*:

6. Federal Department/Agency:

7. Federal Program Name/Description:

CFDA Number, *if applicable*: _____________

8. Federal Action Number, *if known*:

9. Award Amount, *if known*:
$

10. a. Name and Address of Lobbying Entity *(if individual, last name, first name, MI)*:

b. Individuals Performing Services *(including address if different from No. 10a) (last name, first name, MI)*:

(attach Continuation Sheet(s) SF-LLL-A, if necessary)

11. Amount of Payment *(check all that apply)*:
$ _________________ ☐ actual ☐ planned

12. Form of Payment *(check all that apply)*:
☐ a. cash
☐ b. in-kind; specify: nature _________________
value _________________

13. Type of Payment *(check all that apply)*:
☐ a. retainer
☐ b. one-time fee
☐ c. commission
☐ d. contingent fee
☐ e. deferred
☐ f. other; specify: _________________

14. Brief Description of Services Performed or to be Performed and Date(s) of Service, including officer(s), employee(s), or Member(s) contacted, for Payment Indicated in Item 11:

(attach Continuation Sheet(s) SF-LLL-A, if necessary)

15. Continuation Sheet(s) SF-LLL-A attached: ☐ Yes ☐ No

16. Information requested through this form is authorized by title 31 U.S.C. section 1352. This disclosure of lobbying activities is a material representation of fact upon which reliance was placed by the tier above when this transaction was made or entered into. This disclosure is required pursuant to 31 U.S.C. 1352. This information will be reported to the Congress semi-annually and will be available for public inspection. Any person who fails to file the required disclosure shall be subject to a civil penalty of not less than $10,000 and not more than $100,000 for each such failure.

Signature: _________________
Print Name: _________________
Title: _________________
Telephone No.: _____________ **Date:** _____________

Federal Use Only:

Authorized for Local Reproduction
Standard Form - LLL

INSTRUCTIONS FOR COMPLETION OF SF-LLL, DISCLOSURE OF LOBBYING ACTIVITIES

This disclosure form shall be completed by the reporting entity, whether subawardee or prime Federal recipient, at the initiation or receipt of a covered Federal action, or a material change to a previous filing, pursuant to title 31 U.S.C. section 1352. The filing of a form is required for each payment or agreement to make payment to any lobbying entity for influencing or attempting to influence an officer or employee of any agency, a Member of Congress, an officer or employee of Congress, or an employee of a Member of Congress in connection with a covered Federal action. Use the SF-LLL-A Continuation Sheet for additional information if the space on the form is inadequate. Complete all items that apply for both the initial filing and material change report. Refer to the implementing guidance published by the Office of Management and Budget for additional information.

1. Identify the type of covered Federal action for which lobbying activity is and/or has been secured to influence the outcome of a covered Federal action.
2. Identify the status of the covered Federal action.
3. Identify the appropriate classification of this report. If this is a followup report caused by a material change to the information previously reported, enter the year and quarter in which the change occurred. Enter the date of the last previously submitted report by this reporting entity for this covered Federal action.
4. Enter the full name, address, city, state and zip code of the reporting entity. Include Congressional District, if known. Check the appropriate classification of the reporting entity that designates if it is, or expects to be, a prime or subaward recipient. Identify the tier of the subawardee, e.g., the first subawardee of the prime is the 1st tier. Subawards include but are not limited to subcontracts, subgrants and contract awards under grants.
5. If the organization filing the report in item 4 checks "Subawardee", then enter the full name, address, city, state and zip code of the prime Federal recipient. Include Congressional District, if known.
6. Enter the name of the Federal agency making the award or loan commitment. Include at least one organizational level below agency name, if known. For example, Department of Transportation, United States Coast Guard.
7. Enter the Federal program name or description for the covered Federal action (item 1). If known, enter the full Catalog of Federal Domestic Assistance (CFDA) number for grants, cooperative agreements, loans, and loan commitments.
8. Enter the most appropriate Federal identifying number available for the Federal action identified in item 1 (e.g., Request for Proposal (RFP) number; Invitation for Bid (IFB) number; grant announcement number; the contract, grant, or loan award number; the application/proposal control number assigned by the Federal agency). Include prefixes, e.g., "RFP-DE-90-001."
9. For a covered Federal action where there has been an award or loan commitment by the Federal agency, enter the Federal amount of the award/loan commitment for the prime entity identified in item 4 or 5.
10. (a) Enter the full name, address, city, state and zip code of the lobbying entity engaged by the reporting entity identified in item 4 to influence the covered Federal action.

    (b) Enter the full names of the individual(s) performing services, and include full address if different from 10 (a). Enter Last Name, First Name, and Middle Initial (MI).
11. Enter the amount of compensation paid or reasonably expected to be paid by the reporting entity (item 4) to the lobbying entity (item 10). Indicate whether the payment has been made (actual) or will be made (planned). Check all boxes that apply. If this is a material change report, enter the cumulative amount of payment made or planned to be made.
12. Check the appropriate box(es). Check all boxes that apply. If payment is made through an in-kind contribution, specify the nature and value of the in-kind payment.
13. Check the appropriate box(es). Check all boxes that apply. If other, specify nature.
14. Provide a specific and detailed description of the services that the lobbyist has performed, or will be expected to perform, and the date(s) of any services rendered. Include all preparatory and related activity, not just time spent in actual contact with Federal officials. Identify the Federal official(s) or employee(s) contacted or the officer(s), employee(s), or Member(s) of Congress that were contacted.
15. Check whether or not a SF-LLL-A Continuation Sheet(s) is attached.
16. The certifying official shall sign and date the form, print his/her name, title, and telephone number.

Public reporting burden for this collection of information is estimated to average 30 mintues per response, including time for reviewing instructions, searching existing data sources, gathering and maintaining the data needed, and completing and reviewing the collection of information. Send comments regarding the burden estimate or any other aspect of this collection of information, including suggestions for reducing this burden, to the Office of Management and Budget, Paperwork Reduction Project (0348-0046), Washington, D.C. 20503.

DISCLOSURE OF LOBBYING ACTIVITIES
CONTINUATION SHEET

Approved by OMB
0348-0046

Reporting Entity: ______________________ **Page** _____ **of** _____

Authorized for Local Reproduction
Standard Form - LLL-A

PART 147—GOVERNMENTWIDE REQUIREMENTS FOR DRUG-FREE WORKPLACE (NONPROCUREMENT)

AUTHORITY: 41 U.S.C. 701–707.

SOURCE: 68 FR 66557, 66572, Nov. 26, 2003, unless otherwise noted.

Subpart A—Purpose and Coverage

§ 147.100 What does this part do?

This part carries out the portion of the Drug-Free Workplace Act of 1988 (41 U.S.C. 701 *et seq.*, as amended) that applies to grants. It also applies the provisions of the Act to cooperative agreements and other financial assistance awards, as a matter of Federal Government policy.

§ 147.105 Does this part apply to me?

(a) Portions of this part apply to you if you are either—

(1) A recipient of an assistance award from the SBA; or

(2) A(n) SBA awarding official. (See definitions of award and recipient in §§ 147.605 and 147.660, respectively.)

(b) The following table shows the subparts that apply to you:

If you are . . .	see subparts . . .
(1) A recipient who is not an individual	A, B and E.
(2) A recipient who is an individual	A, C and E.
(3) A(n) SBA awarding official	A, D and E.

§ 147.110 Are any of my Federal assistance awards exempt from this part?

This part does not apply to any award that the SBA Administrator or designee determines that the application of this part would be inconsistent with the international obligations of the United States or the laws or regulations of a foreign government.

§ 147.115 Does this part affect the Federal contracts that I receive?

It will affect future contract awards indirectly if you are debarred or suspended for a violation of the requirements of this part, as described in § 147.510(c). However, this part does not apply directly to procurement contracts. The portion of the Drug-Free Workplace Act of 1988 that applies to Federal procurement contracts is carried out through the Federal Acquisition Regulation in chapter 1 of Title 48 of the Code of Federal Regulations (the drug-free workplace coverage currently is in 48 CFR part 23, subpart 23.5).

Subpart B—Requirements for Recipients Other Than Individuals

§ 147.200 What must I do to comply with this part?

There are two general requirements if you are a recipient other than an individual.

(a) First, you must make a good faith effort, on a continuing basis, to maintain a drug-free workplace. You must agree to do so as a condition for receiving any award covered by this part. The specific measures that you must take in this regard are described in more detail in subsequent sections of this subpart. Briefly, those measures are to—

(1) Publish a drug-free workplace statement and establish a drug-free awareness program for your employees (see §§ 147.205 through 147.220); and

(2) Take actions concerning employees who are convicted of violating drug statutes in the workplace (see § 147.225).

(b) Second, you must identify all known workplaces under your Federal awards (see § 147.230).

§ 147.205 What must I include in my drug-free workplace statement?

You must publish a statement that—

(a) Tells your employees that the unlawful manufacture, distribution, dispensing, possession, or use of a controlled substance is prohibited in your workplace;

(b) Specifies the actions that you will take against employees for violating that prohibition; and

(c) Lets each employee know that, as a condition of employment under any award, he or she:

(1) Will abide by the terms of the statement; and

(2) Must notify you in writing if he or she is convicted for a violation of a criminal drug statute occurring in the workplace and must do so no more than five calendar days after the conviction.

§ 147.210 To whom must I distribute my drug-free workplace statement?

You must require that a copy of the statement described in § 147.205 be given to each employee who will be engaged in the performance of any Federal award.

§ 147.215 What must I include in my drug-free awareness program?

You must establish an ongoing drug-free awareness program to inform employees about—

(a) The dangers of drug abuse in the workplace;

(b) Your policy of maintaining a drug-free workplace;

(c) Any available drug counseling, rehabilitation, and employee assistance programs; and

(d) The penalties that you may impose upon them for drug abuse violations occurring in the workplace.

§ 147.220 By when must I publish my drug-free workplace statement and establish my drug-free awareness program?

If you are a new recipient that does not already have a policy statement as described in § 147.205 and an ongoing awareness program as described in § 147.215, you must publish the statement and establish the program by the time given in the following table:

If . . .	then you . . .
(a) The performance period of the award is less than 30 days.	must have the policy statement and program in place as soon as possible, but before the date on which performance is expected to be completed.
(b) The performance period of the award is 30 days or more.	must have the policy statement and program in place within 30 days after award.

If . . .	then you . . .
(c) You believe there are extraordinary circumstances that will require more than 30 days for you to publish the policy statement and establish the awareness program.	may ask the SBA awarding official to give you more time to do so. The amount of additional time, if any, to be given is at the discretion of the awarding official.

§ 147.225 What actions must I take concerning employees who are convicted of drug violations in the workplace?

There are two actions you must take if an employee is convicted of a drug violation in the workplace:

(a) First, you must notify Federal agencies if an employee who is engaged in the performance of an award informs you about a conviction, as required by § 147.205(c)(2), or you otherwise learn of the conviction. Your notification to the Federal agencies must—

(1) Be in writing;

(2) Include the employee's position title;

(3) Include the identification number(s) of each affected award;

(4) Be sent within ten calendar days after you learn of the conviction; and

(5) Be sent to every Federal agency on whose award the convicted employee was working. It must be sent to every awarding official or his or her official designee, unless the Federal agency has specified a central point for the receipt of the notices.

(b) Second, within 30 calendar days of learning about an employee's conviction, you must either—

(1) Take appropriate personnel action against the employee, up to and including termination, consistent with the requirements of the Rehabilitation Act of 1973 (29 U.S.C. 794), as amended; or

(2) Require the employee to participate satisfactorily in a drug abuse assistance or rehabilitation program approved for these purposes by a Federal, State or local health, law enforcement, or other appropriate agency.

§ 147.230 How and when must I identify workplaces?

(a) You must identify all known workplaces under each SBA award. A failure to do so is a violation of your drug-free workplace requirements. You may identify the workplaces—

(1) To the SBA official that is making the award, either at the time of application or upon award; or

(2) In documents that you keep on file in your offices during the performance of the award, in which case you must make the information available for inspection upon request by SBA officials or their designated representatives.

(b) Your workplace identification for an award must include the actual address of buildings (or parts of buildings) or other sites where work under the award takes place. Categorical descriptions may be used (e.g., all vehicles of a mass transit authority or State highway department while in operation, State employees in each local unemployment office, performers in concert halls or radio studios).

(c) If you identified workplaces to the SBA awarding official at the time of application or award, as described in paragraph (a)(1) of this section, and any workplace that you identified changes during the performance of the award, you must inform the SBA awarding official.

Subpart C—Requirements for Recipients Who Are Individuals

§ 147.300 What must I do to comply with this part if I am an individual recipient?

As a condition of receiving a(n) SBA award, if you are an individual recipient, you must agree that—

(a) You will not engage in the unlawful manufacture, distribution, dispensing, possession, or use of a controlled substance in conducting any activity related to the award; and

(b) If you are convicted of a criminal drug offense resulting from a violation occurring during the conduct of any award activity, you will report the conviction:

(1) In writing.

(2) Within 10 calendar days of the conviction.

(3) To the SBA awarding official or other designee for each award that you currently have, unless § 147.301 or the award document designates a central point for the receipt of the notices. When notice is made to a central point,

it must include the identification number(s) of each affected award.

§ 147.301 [Reserved]

Subpart D—Responsibilities of SBA Awarding Officials

§ 147.400 What are my responsibilities as a(n) SBA awarding official?

As a(n) SBA awarding official, you must obtain each recipient's agreement, as a condition of the award, to comply with the requirements in—

(a) Subpart B of this part, if the recipient is not an individual; or

(b) Subpart C of this part, if the recipient is an individual.

Subpart E—Violations of this Part and Consequences

§ 147.500 How are violations of this part determined for recipients other than individuals?

A recipient other than an individual is in violation of the requirements of this part if the SBA Administrator or designee determines, in writing, that—

(a) The recipient has violated the requirements of subpart B of this part; or

(b) The number of convictions of the recipient's employees for violating criminal drug statutes in the workplace is large enough to indicate that the recipient has failed to make a good faith effort to provide a drug-free workplace.

§ 147.505 How are violations of this part determined for recipients who are individuals?

An individual recipient is in violation of the requirements of this part if the SBA Administrator or designee determines, in writing, that—

(a) The recipient has violated the requirements of subpart C of this part; or

(b) The recipient is convicted of a criminal drug offense resulting from a violation occurring during the conduct of any award activity.

§ 147.510 What actions will the Federal Government take against a recipient determined to have violated this part?

If a recipient is determined to have violated this part, as described in §147.500 or §147.505, the SBA may take one or more of the following actions—

(a) Suspension of payments under the award;

(b) Suspension or termination of the award; and

(c) Suspension or debarment of the recipient under 13 CFR Part 145, for a period not to exceed five years.

§ 147.515 Are there any exceptions to those actions?

The SBA Administrator may waive with respect to a particular award, in writing, a suspension of payments under an award, suspension or termination of an award, or suspension or debarment of a recipient if the SBA Administrator determines that such a waiver would be in the public interest. This exception authority cannot be delegated to any other official.

Subpart F—Definitions

§ 147.605 Award.

Award means an award of financial assistance by the SBA or other Federal agency directly to a recipient.

(a) The term award includes:

(1) A Federal grant or cooperative agreement, in the form of money or property in lieu of money.

(2) A block grant or a grant in an entitlement program, whether or not the grant is exempted from coverage under the Governmentwide rule 13 CFR Part 147 that implements OMB Circular A–102 (for availability, see 5 CFR 1310.3) and specifies uniform administrative requirements.

(b) The term award does not include:

(1) Technical assistance that provides services instead of money.

(2) Loans.

(3) Loan guarantees.

(4) Interest subsidies.

(5) Insurance.

(6) Direct appropriations.

(7) Veterans' benefits to individuals (*i.e.*, any benefit to veterans, their families, or survivors by virtue of the service of a veteran in the Armed Forces of the United States).

§ 147.610 Controlled substance.

Controlled substance means a controlled substance in schedules I through V of the Controlled Substances

Act (21 U.S.C. 812), and as further defined by regulation at 21 CFR 1308.11 through 1308.15.

§ 147.615 Conviction.

Conviction means a finding of guilt (including a plea of nolo contendere) or imposition of sentence, or both, by any judicial body charged with the responsibility to determine violations of the Federal or State criminal drug statutes.

§ 147.620 Cooperative agreement.

Cooperative agreement means an award of financial assistance that, consistent with 31 U.S.C. 6305, is used to enter into the same kind of relationship as a grant (see definition of grant in § 147.650), except that substantial involvement is expected between the Federal agency and the recipient when carrying out the activity contemplated by the award. The term does not include cooperative research and development agreements as defined in 15 U.S.C. 3710a.

§ 147.625 Criminal drug statute.

Criminal drug statute means a Federal or non-Federal criminal statute involving the manufacture, distribution, dispensing, use, or possession of any controlled substance.

§ 147.630 Debarment.

Debarment means an action taken by a Federal agency to prohibit a recipient from participating in Federal Government procurement contracts and covered nonprocurement transactions. A recipient so prohibited is debarred, in accordance with the Federal Acquisition Regulation for procurement contracts (48 CFR part 9, subpart 9.4) and the common rule, Government-wide Debarment and Suspension (Nonprocurement), that implements Executive Order 12549 and Executive Order 12689.

§ 147.635 Drug-free workplace.

Drug-free workplace means a site for the performance of work done in connection with a specific award at which employees of the recipient are prohibited from engaging in the unlawful manufacture, distribution, dispensing, possession, or use of a controlled substance.

§ 147.640 Employee.

(a) *Employee* means the employee of a recipient directly engaged in the performance of work under the award, including—

(1) All direct charge employees;

(2) All indirect charge employees, unless their impact or involvement in the performance of work under the award is insignificant to the performance of the award; and

(3) Temporary personnel and consultants who are directly engaged in the performance of work under the award and who are on the recipient's payroll.

(b) This definition does not include workers not on the payroll of the recipient (e.g., volunteers, even if used to meet a matching requirement; consultants or independent contractors not on the payroll; or employees of subrecipients or subcontractors in covered workplaces).

§ 147.645 Federal agency or agency.

Federal agency or agency means any United States executive department, military department, government corporation, government controlled corporation, any other establishment in the executive branch (including the Executive Office of the President), or any independent regulatory agency.

§ 147.650 Grant.

Grant means an award of financial assistance that, consistent with 31 U.S.C. 6304, is used to enter into a relationship—

(a) The principal purpose of which is to transfer a thing of value to the recipient to carry out a public purpose of support or stimulation authorized by a law of the United States, rather than to acquire property or services for the Federal Government's direct benefit or use; and

(b) In which substantial involvement is not expected between the Federal agency and the recipient when carrying out the activity contemplated by the award.

§ 147.655 Individual.

Individual means a natural person.

§ 147.660 Recipient.

Recipient means any individual, corporation, partnership, association, unit of government (except a Federal agency) or legal entity, however organized, that receives an award directly from a Federal agency.

§ 147.665 State.

State means any of the States of the United States, the District of Columbia, the Commonwealth of Puerto Rico, or any territory or possession of the United States.

§ 147.670 Suspension.

Suspension means an action taken by a Federal agency that immediately prohibits a recipient from participating in Federal Government procurement contracts and covered nonprocurement transactions for a temporary period, pending completion of an investigation and any judicial or administrative proceedings that may ensue. A recipient so prohibited is suspended, in accordance with the Federal Acquisition Regulation for procurement contracts (48 CFR part 9, subpart 9.4) and the common rule, Governmentwide Debarment and Suspension (Nonprocurement), that implements Executive Order 12549 and Executive Order 12689. Suspension of a recipient is a distinct and separate action from suspension of an award or suspension of payments under an award.

PARTS 148–199 [RESERVED]

CHAPTER III—ECONOMIC DEVELOPMENT ADMINISTRATION, DEPARTMENT OF COMMERCE

PART 300—GENERAL INFORMATION

AUTHORITY: 42 U.S.C. 3121; 42 U.S.C. 3122; 42 U.S.C. 3211; 15 U.S.C. 3701; Department of Commerce Organization Order 10–4.

SOURCE: 71 FR 56675, Sept. 27, 2006, unless otherwise noted.

§ 300.1 Introduction and mission.

EDA was created by Congress pursuant to the Public Works and Economic Development Act of 1965 to provide financial assistance to both rural and urban distressed communities. EDA's mission is to lead the Federal economic development agenda by promoting innovation and competitiveness, preparing American regions for growth and success in the worldwide economy. EDA will fulfill its mission by fostering entrepreneurship, innovation and productivity through Investments in infrastructure development, capacity building and business development in order to attract private capital investments and new and better jobs to Regions experiencing substantial and persistent economic distress. EDA works in partnership with distressed Regions to address problems associated with long-term economic distress as well as to assist those Regions experiencing sudden and severe economic dislocations, such as those resulting from natural disasters, conversions of military installations, changing trade patterns and the depletion of natural resources. EDA Investments generally take the form of Grants to or Cooperative Agreements with Eligible Recipients.

[79 FR 76123, Dec. 19, 2014]

§ 300.2 EDA Headquarters and regional offices.

(a) EDA's Headquarters Office is located at: U.S. Department of Commerce, Economic Development Administration, 1401 Constitution Avenue NW., Washington, DC 20230.

(b) EDA has regional offices throughout the United States and each regional office's contact information may be found on EDA's Internet Web site at *http://www.eda.gov* or in the applicable announcement of Federal Funding Opportunity issued by EDA. Please contact the appropriate regional office to learn about EDA Investment opportunities in your Region.

[79 FR 76123, Dec. 19, 2014]

§ 300.3 Definitions.

As used in this chapter, the following terms shall have the following meanings:

Assistant Secretary means the Assistant Secretary for Economic Development within the Department.

Comprehensive Economic Development Strategy or *CEDS* means a strategy that meets the requirements of § 303.7 of this chapter.

Cooperative Agreement means the financial assistance award of EDA funds to an Eligible Recipient where substantial involvement is expected between EDA and the Eligible Recipient in carrying out a purpose or activity authorized under PWEDA or another statute. *See* 31 U.S.C. 6305.

Co-Recipient means one of multiple Recipients awarded Investment Assistance under a single award. Unless otherwise provided in the terms and conditions of the Investment Assistance, each Co-Recipient is jointly and severally liable for fulfilling the terms of the Investment Assistance.

Department means the U.S. Department of Commerce.

District Organization means an organization meeting the requirements of § 304.2 of this chapter.

Economic Development District or *District* or *EDD* means any Region in the United States designated by EDA as an Economic Development District under § 304.1 of this chapter (or such regulation as was previously in effect before the effective date of this section) and also includes any economic development district designated as such under section 403 of PWEDA, as in effect on February 10, 1999.

EDA means the Economic Development Administration within the Department.

Eligible Applicant means an entity qualified to be an Eligible Recipient or its authorized representative.

Eligible Recipient means any of the following:

(1) City or other political subdivision of a State, including a special purpose unit of State or local government engaged in economic or infrastructure development activities, or a consortium of political subdivisions;

(2) State;

(3) Institution of higher education or a consortium of institutions of higher education;

(4) Public or private non-profit organization or association, including a community or faith-based non-profit organization, acting in cooperation with officials of a political subdivision of a State;

(5) District Organization;

(6) Indian Tribe or a consortium of Indian Tribes; or

(7) Private individual or for-profit organization, but only for Training, Research and Technical Assistance Investments pursuant to § 306.1(d)(3) of this chapter.

Federal Agency means a department, agency or instrumentality of the United States government.

Federal Funding Opportunity or *FFO* means an announcement EDA publishes during the fiscal year at *http://www.grants.gov* and on EDA's Internet Web site at *http://www.eda.gov* that provides the funding amounts, application and programmatic requirements, funding priorities, special circumstances, and other information concerning a specific competitive solicitation for EDA's economic development assistance programs. EDA also may periodically publish FFOs on specific programs or initiatives.

Federally Declared Disaster means a Presidentially Declared Disaster, a fisheries resource disaster pursuant to section 312(a) of the Magnuson-Stevens Fishery Conservation and Management Act, as amended (16 U.S.C. 1861a(a)), or other Federally declared disasters pursuant to applicable law.

Grant means the financial assistance award of EDA funds to an Eligible Recipient, under which the Eligible Recipient bears responsibility for carrying out a purpose or activity authorized under PWEDA or another statute. *See* 31 U.S.C. 6304.

Immediate Family means a person's spouse (or domestic partner or significant other), parents, grandparents, siblings, children and grandchildren, but does not include distant relatives, such as cousins, unless the distant relative lives in the same household as the person.

In-Kind Contribution(s) means non-cash contributions, which may include contributions of space, equipment, services and assumptions of debt that are fairly evaluated by EDA and that satisfy applicable Federal uniform administrative requirements and cost principles as set out in 2 CFR part 200.

Indian Tribe means an entity on the list of recognized tribes published pursuant to the Federally Recognized Indian Tribe List Act of 1994, as amended (Pub. L. 103–454) (25 U.S.C. 479a *et seq.*), and any Alaska Native Village or Regional Corporation (as defined in or established under the Alaska Native Claims Settlement Act (43 U.S.C. 1601 *et seq.*). This term includes the governing body of an Indian Tribe, nonprofit Indian corporation (restricted to Indians), Indian authority, or other non-profit Indian tribal organization or entity; provided that the Indian tribal organization or entity is wholly owned by, and established for the benefit of, the Indian Tribe or Alaska Native Village.

Interested Party means any officer, employee or member of the board of directors or other governing board of the Recipient, including any other parties that advise, approve, recommend or otherwise participate in the business decisions of the Recipient, such as agents, advisors, consultants, attorneys, accountants or shareholders. An Interested Party also includes the Interested Party's Immediate Family and other persons directly connected to the Interested Party by law or through a business arrangement.

Investment or *Investment Assistance* means a Grant or Cooperative Agreement entered into by EDA and a Recipient.

Investment Rate means, as set forth in § 301.4 of this chapter, the amount of the EDA Investment in a particular Project expressed as a percentage of the total Project cost.

Local Share or *Matching Share* means the non-EDA funds and any In-Kind Contributions that are approved by EDA and provided by a Recipient or third party as a condition of an Investment. The Matching Share may include funds from another Federal Agency only if authorized by statute that allows such use, which may be determined by EDA's reasonable interpretation of such authority.

Presidentially Declared Disaster means a major disaster or emergency declared under the Robert T. Stafford Disaster Relief and Emergency Assistance Act, as amended (42 U.S.C. 5121 *et seq.*).

Project means the proposed or authorized activity (or activities) the purpose of which fulfills EDA's mission and program requirements as set forth in PWEDA or Stevenson-Wydler and this chapter and which may be funded in whole or in part by EDA Investment Assistance.

PWEDA means the Public Works and Economic Development Act of 1965, as amended (42 U.S.C. 3121 *et seq.*).

Recipient means an entity receiving EDA Investment Assistance, including any EDA-approved successor to the entity.

Region or *Regional* means an economic unit of human, natural, technological, capital or other resources, defined geographically. Geographic areas comprising a Region need not be contiguous or defined by political boundaries, but should constitute a cohesive area capable of undertaking self-sustained economic development. For the limited purposes of determining economic distress levels and Investment Rates pursuant to part 301 of this chapter, a Region also may comprise a specific geographic area defined solely by its level of economic distress, as set forth in §§ 301.3(a)(2) and 301.3(a)(3) of this chapter.

Regional Commission means any of the following:

(1) The Appalachian Regional Commission established under chapter 143 of title 40, United States Code;

(2) The Delta Regional Authority established under subtitle F of the Consolidated Farm and Rural Development Act (7 U.S.C. 2009aa *et seq.*);

(3) The Denali Commission established under the Denali Commission Act of 1998 (42 U.S.C. 3121 note; 112 Stat. 2681–637 *et seq.*); or

(4) The Northern Great Plains Regional Authority established under subtitle G of the Consolidated Farm and Rural Development Act (7 U.S.C. 2009bb *et seq.*).

Regional Innovation Clusters or *RICs* means networks of similar, synergistic, or complementary entities that support a single industry sector and its various supply chains. In general, RICs:

(1) Are based on a geographic area that may cross municipal, county, and other jurisdictional boundaries;

(2) May include catalysts of innovation and drivers of Regional economic growth, such as universities, government research centers, and other research and development resources;

(3) Have active channels for business transactions and communication; and

(4) Depend upon specialized infrastructure, labor markets, and services that build on the unique competitive assets of a location, including talent, technology, services, and hard and soft infrastructure, to spur innovation, job creation, and business expansion.

Special Impact Area means a Region served by a Project for which the requirements of section 302 of PWEDA and § 303.7 of this chapter have, upon an application filed by an Eligible Recipient pursuant to section 214 of PWEDA and part 310 of this chapter, been waived in whole or in part by the Assistant Secretary.

Special Need means a circumstance or legal status arising from actual or threatened severe unemployment or economic adjustment problems resulting from severe short-term or long-term changes in economic conditions, including:

(1) Substantial outmigration or population loss;

(2) Underemployment; that is, employment of workers at less than full-time or at less skilled tasks than their training or abilities permit;

(3) Military base closures or realignments, defense contractor reductions-in-force, or U.S. Department of Energy defense-related funding reductions;

(4) Natural or other major disasters or emergencies;

(5) Extraordinary depletion of natural resources;

(6) Closing or restructuring of an industrial firm or loss of a major employer;

(7) Negative effects of changing trade patterns; or

(8) Other circumstances set forth in an FFO.

State means a State of the United States, the District of Columbia, the Commonwealth of Puerto Rico, the U.S. Virgin Islands, Guam, American Samoa, the Commonwealth of the Northern Mariana Islands, the Republic of the Marshall Islands, the Federated States of Micronesia, and the Republic of Palau.

Stevenson-Wydler, for purposes of EDA, means the Stevenson-Wydler Technology Innovation Act of 1980, as amended (15 U.S.C. 3701 *et seq.*).

Subrecipient means an Eligible Recipient that receives a redistribution of Investment Assistance in the form of a subgrant, under part 309 of this chapter, from another Eligible Recipient to carry out part of a Federal program.

Trade Act, for purposes of EDA, means title II, chapters 3, 4 and 5, of the Trade Act of 1974, as amended (19 U.S.C. 2341 *et seq.*).

United States means all of the States.

[71 FR 56675, Sept. 27, 2006, as amended at 73 FR 62865, Oct. 22, 2008; 79 FR 76123, Dec. 19, 2014; 82 FR 57052, Dec. 1, 2017]

PART 301—ELIGIBILITY, INVESTMENT RATE AND APPLICATION REQUIREMENTS

AUTHORITY: 42 U.S.C. 3121; 42 U.S.C. 3141–3147; 42 U.S.C. 3149; 42 U.S.C. 3161; 42 U.S.C. 3175; 42 U.S.C. 3192; 42 U.S.C. 3194; 42 U.S.C. 3211; 42 U.S.C. 3233; Department of Commerce Delegation Order 10–4.

SOURCE: 71 FR 56675, Sept. 27, 2006, unless otherwise noted.

Subpart A—General

§ 301.1 Overview of eligibility requirements.

In order to receive EDA Investment Assistance, the following requirements must be met:

(a) The applicant must be an Eligible Applicant as set forth in subpart B of this part;

(b) The Region in which the Project will be located must meet the economic distress criteria set forth in subpart C of this part;

(c) The sources of funding for the Project must fulfill the Investment Rate and Matching Share requirements set forth in subpart D of this part;

(d) The Eligible Applicant must satisfy the formal application requirements set forth in subpart E of this part;

(e) The Project must meet the general requirements set forth in part 302 (General Terms and Conditions for Investment Assistance) and the specific program requirements (as applicable) set forth in part 303 (Planning Investments and Comprehensive Economic Development Strategies), part 304 (Economic Development Districts), part 305 (Public Works and Economic Development Investments), part 306 (Training, Research and Technical Assistance Investments), or part 307 (Economic Adjustment Assistance Investments) of this chapter; and

(f) EDA must select the Eligible Applicant's proposed Project.

[71 FR 56675, Sept. 27, 2006, as amended at 79 FR 76124, Dec. 19, 2014]

Subpart B—Applicant Eligibility

§ 301.2 Applicant eligibility.

(a) An Eligible Applicant for EDA Investment Assistance is defined in § 300.3 of this chapter.

(b) An Eligible Applicant that is a non-profit organization must include in its application for Investment Assistance a resolution passed by (or a letter signed by) an authorized representative of a general purpose political subdivision of a State, acknowledging that it is acting in cooperation with officials of such political subdivision. EDA, at its sole discretion, may waive this cooperation requirement for certain Projects of a significant Regional or national scope under part 306 or 307 of this chapter. *See* §§ 306.3(b), 306.6(b), and 307.5(b) of this chapter.

[71 FR 56675, Sept. 27, 2006, as amended at 82 FR 57053, Dec. 1, 2017]

Subpart C—Economic Distress Criteria

§ 301.3 Economic distress levels.

(a) *Part 305 (Public Works and Economic Development Investments) and part 307 (Economic Adjustment Assistance Investments).* (1) Except as otherwise provided by this paragraph (a), for a Project to be eligible for Investment Assistance under parts 305 or 307 of this chapter, the Project must be located in a Region that, on the date EDA receives an application for Investment Assistance, is subject to one or more of the following economic distress criteria:

(i) An unemployment rate that is, for the most recent 24-month period for which data are available, at least one percentage point greater than the national average unemployment rate;

(ii) Per capita income that is, for the most recent period for which data are available, 80 percent or less of the national average per capita income; or

(iii) A Special Need, as determined by EDA.

(2) A Project located within an Economic Development District, which is located in a Region that does not meet the economic distress criteria described in paragraph (a)(1) of this section, also is eligible for Investment Assistance under parts 305 or 307 of this chapter if EDA determines that the Project will be of "substantial direct benefit" to a geographic area within the District that meets the criteria of paragraph (a)(1) of this section. For this purpose, a Project provides a "substantial direct benefit" if it provides significant employment opportunities for unemployed, underemployed or low-income residents of the geographic area within the District.

(3) A Project located in a geographic area of poverty or high unemployment that meets the requirements of paragraph (a)(1) of this section, but which is located in a Region that overall does not meet the requirements of paragraph (a)(1) of this section, is eligible for Investment Assistance under parts 305 or 307 of this chapter without regard to political or other subdivisions or boundaries.

(4) *Data requirements to demonstrate economic distress levels.* EDA will determine the economic distress levels pursuant to this subsection at the time EDA receives an application for Investment Assistance as follows:

(i) For economic distress levels based upon per capita income requirements, EDA will base its determination upon the most recent American Community Survey ("*ACS*") published by the U.S. Census Bureau. For economic distress levels based upon the unemployment rate, EDA will base its determination upon the most recent data published by the Bureau of Labor Statistics ("*BLS*"), within the U.S. Department of Labor. For eligibility based upon either per capita income requirements or the unemployment rate, when the ACS or BLS data, as applicable, are not the most recent Federal data available, EDA will base its decision upon the most recent Federal data from other sources (including data available from the Census Bureau and the Bureaus of Economic Analysis, Labor Statistics, Indian Affairs, or any other Federal source determined by EDA to be appropriate). If no Federal data are available, an Eligible Applicant must submit to EDA the most recent data available from the State. The required data must be for the Region where the Project will be located (paragraph (a)(1) of this section), the geographic area where substantial direct Project benefits will occur (paragraph (a)(2) of this section), or the geographic area of poverty or high unemployment (paragraph (a)(3) of this section), as applicable.

(ii) For economic distress based upon a Special Need, EDA will conduct the independent analysis it deems necessary under the facts and circumstances of a given case. Eligible Applicants are encouraged to submit reliable data substantiating their claim of a Special Need.

(b) *Part 303 (Planning Investments) and part 306 (Training, Research and Technical Assistance Investments).* There are no minimum economic distress level requirements for Investment Assistance awarded to Projects under parts 303 or 306 of this chapter.

(c) *Part 304 (Economic Development Districts).* For EDA to designate a Region as an Economic Development District under part 304 of this chapter, such Region must:

(1) Contain at least one geographic area that fulfills the economic distress criteria set forth in paragraph (a)(1) of this section and is identified in an approved CEDS; and

(2) Meet the Regional eligibility requirements set forth in § 304.1 of this chapter.

(d) EDA reserves the right to reject any documentation of Project eligibility that it determines is inaccurate or otherwise unreliable.

[71 FR 56675, Sept. 27, 2006, as amended at 73 FR 62865, Oct. 22, 2008; 79 FR 76124, Dec. 19, 2014]

Subpart D—Investment Rates and Matching Share Requirements

§ 301.4 Investment rates.

(a) *Minimum Investment Rate.* There is no minimum Investment Rate for a Project.

(b) *Maximum Investment Rate*—(1) *General rule.* Except as otherwise provided by this paragraph (b) or paragraph (c) of this section, the maximum EDA Investment Rate for all Projects shall be determined in accordance with Table 1 in paragraph (b)(1)(ii) of this section. The maximum EDA Investment Rate shall not exceed the sum of 50 percent, plus up to an additional 30 percent based on the relative needs of the Region in which the Project is located, as determined by EDA.

(i)(A) *Relative needs.* In determining the relative needs of the Region in which the Project is located, EDA will prioritize allocations of its Investment Assistance to ensure that the level of economic distress of a Region, rather than a preference for a specific geographic area or a specific type of economic distress, is the primary factor in allocating its Investment Assistance. In making this determination, EDA will take into consideration the following measures of economic distress:

(*1*) The severity of the unemployment rate and the duration of the unemployment in the Region;

(*2*) The per capita income levels and the extent of underemployment in the Region;

(*3*) The outmigration of population and the extent to which such outmigration is causing economic injury in the Region; and

(*4*) Such other factors as EDA deems relevant in determining the relative needs of the Region in which the Project is located.

(B) A Project is eligible for the maximum allowable Investment Rate as determined by EDA between the time EDA receives the application for Investment Assistance and the time that EDA awards Investment Assistance to the Project; however, the burden is on the Eligible Applicant to establish the relative needs of the Region in which the Project is located.

(ii) *Table 1.* Table 1 of this paragraph sets forth the maximum allowable Investment Rate for Projects located in Regions subject to certain levels of economic distress. In cases where Table 1 produces divergent results (*i.e.*, where Table 1 produces more than one maximum allowable Investment Rate based on the Region's levels of economic distress), the higher Investment Rate produced by Table 1 shall be the maximum allowable Investment Rate for the Project.

TABLE 1

Projects located in regions in which:	Maximum allowable investment rates (percentage)
(A) The 24-month unemployment rate is at least 225% of the national average; or	80
(B) The per capita income is not more than 50% of the national average	80
(C) The 24-month unemployment rate is at least 200% of the national average; or	70
(D) The per capita income is not more than 60% of the national average	70
(E) The 24-month unemployment rate is at least 175% of the national average; or	60
(F) The per capita income is not more than 65% of the national average	60
(G) The 24-month unemployment rate is at least one percentage point greater than the national average; or	50
(H) The per capita income is not more than 80% of the national average	50

(2) *Projects subject to a Special Need.* EDA shall determine the maximum allowable Investment Rate for Projects subject to a Special Need (as determined by EDA pursuant to §301.3(a)(1)(iii)) based on the actual or threatened overall economic situation of the Region in which the Project is located. However, unless the Project is eligible for a higher Investment Rate pursuant to paragraph (b)(5) of this section, the maximum allowable Investment Rate for any Project subject to a Special Need shall be 80 percent.

(3) *Projects under part 303.*

(i) The minimum Investment Rate for Projects under part 303 of this chapter shall be 50 percent.

(ii) Except as otherwise provided in paragraph (b)(3)(iii) of this section or in paragraph (b)(5) of this section, the maximum allowable Investment Rate for Projects under part 303 of this chapter shall be the maximum allowable Investment Rate set forth in Table 1 for the most economically distressed county or other equivalent political unit (*e.g.*, parish) within the Region. The maximum allowable Investment Rate shall not exceed 80 percent.

(iii) In compelling circumstances, the Assistant Secretary may waive the application of the first sentence in paragraph (b)(3)(ii) of this section.

(4) *Projects under part 306.* Except as otherwise provided in paragraph (b)(5) of this section, the maximum allowable Investment Rate for Projects under part 306 of this chapter shall generally be determined based on the relative needs (as determined under paragraph (b)(1) of this section) of the Region which the Project will serve. As specified in section 204(c)(3) of PWEDA, the Assistant Secretary has the discretion to establish a maximum Investment Rate of up to 100 percent where the Project:

(i) Merits, and is not otherwise feasible without, an increase to the Investment Rate; or

(ii) Will be of no or only incidental benefit to the Eligible Recipient.

(5) *Special Projects.* Table 2 of this paragraph sets forth the maximum allowable Investment Rate for certain special Projects as follows:

TABLE 2

Projects	Maximum allowable investment rates (percentage)
Projects that involve broad Regional planning and coordination with other entities outside the Eligible Applicant's political jurisdiction or area of authority, under special circumstances determined by EDA, and Projects that effectively leverage other Federal Agency resources	80
Projects of Indian Tribes	100
Projects for which EDA receives appropriations under section 703 of PWEDA (42 U.S.C. 3233) and Projects to address and implement post-disaster economic recovery efforts in Presidentially Declared Disaster areas in a timely manner	100
Projects of States or political subdivisions of States that the Assistant Secretary determines have exhausted their effective taxing and borrowing capacity, or Projects of non-profit organizations that the Assistant Secretary determines have exhausted their effective borrowing capacity	100
Projects under parts 305 or 307 that receive performance awards pursuant to §308.2 of this chapter	100
Projects located in a District that receive planning performance awards pursuant to §308.3 of this chapter	100

(c) Federal Funding Opportunity announcements may provide additional Investment Rate criteria and standards to ensure that the level of economic distress of a Region, rather than a preference for a geographic area or a specific type of economic distress, is the primary factor in allocating Investment Assistance.

[71 FR 56675, Sept. 27, 2006, as amended at 73 FR 62865, Oct. 22, 2008; 75 FR 4262, Jan. 27, 2010; 79 FR 76125, Dec. 19, 2014]

§ 301.5 Matching share requirements.

The required Matching Share of a Project's eligible costs may consist of cash or In-Kind Contributions. In addition, the Eligible Applicant must provide documentation to EDA demonstrating that the Matching Share is committed to the Project, will be available as needed and is not or will not be conditioned or encumbered in any way that would preclude its use consistent with the requirements of the Investment Assistance. EDA shall determine at its sole discretion whether the Matching Share documentation adequately addresses the requirements of this section.

[82 FR 57053, Dec. 1, 2017]

§ 301.6 Supplementary Investment Assistance.

(a) Pursuant to a request made by an Eligible Applicant, EDA Investment Assistance may supplement a grant awarded in another "designated Federal grant program," if the Eligible Applicant qualifies for financial assistance under such program, but is unable to provide the required non-Federal share because of the Eligible Applicant's economic situation. For purposes of this section, a "designated Federal grant program" means a Federal grant program that:

(1) Provides assistance in the construction or equipping of public works, public service or development facilities;

(2) Is designated by EDA as eligible for supplementary Investment Assistance under this section; and

(3) Assists Projects that are otherwise eligible for Investment Assistance and consistent with the Eligible Applicant's CEDS.

(b) For a Project that meets the economic distress criteria provided in § 301.3(a), the Investment Assistance, combined with funds from a designated Federal grant program, may be at the maximum allowable Investment Rate, even if the designated Federal grant program has a lower grant rate. If the designated Federal grant program has a grant rate higher than the maximum EDA Investment Rate, the EDA Investment and other Federal funds together may exceed the EDA Investment Rate, provided that the EDA share of total funding does not exceed the maximum allowable Investment Rate.

[71 FR 56675, Sept. 27, 2006, as amended at 79 FR 76126, Dec. 19, 2014]

Subpart E—Application Requirements; Evaluation Criteria

§ 301.7 Investment Assistance application.

(a) For all EDA Investment Assistance programs, including the Public Works, Economic Adjustment Assistance, Planning, Local Technical Assistance, Research and National Technical Assistance, and University Center programs, EDA will publish an FFO that specifies application submission requirements and evaluation procedures and criteria. Each FFO will be published on the EDA Web site and at *http://www.grants.gov.* All forms required for EDA Investment Assistance may be obtained electronically from *http://www.grants.gov* or from the appropriate regional office.

(b) PWEDA does not require nor does EDA provide an appeals process for denial of applications or EDA Investment Assistance.

[75 FR 4262, Jan. 27, 2010, as amended at 79 FR 76126, Dec. 19, 2014; 82 FR 57053, Dec. 1, 2017]

§ 301.8 Application evaluation criteria.

EDA will screen all applications for the feasibility of the budget presented and conformance with EDA's statutory and regulatory requirements. EDA will assess the economic development needs of the affected Region in which the proposed Project will be located (or will service), as well as the capability of the Eligible Applicant to implement the proposed Project. EDA will also review applications for conformance with program-specific evaluation criteria set out in the applicable FFO.

[82 FR 57053, Dec. 1, 2017]

§ 301.9 Application selection criteria.

(a) EDA will review completed application materials for compliance with the requirements set forth in PWEDA, this chapter, the applicable FFO, and other applicable Federal statutes and regulations. From those applications that meet EDA's technical and legal requirements, EDA will select applications based on the:

(1) Availability of funds;

(2) Competitiveness of the applications in accord with the criteria set forth in §301.8; and

(3) Funding priority considerations identified in the applicable FFO.

(b) EDA will endeavor to notify applicants as soon as practicable regarding whether their applications are selected for funding.

[79 FR 76127, Dec. 19, 2014]

§301.10 Formal application requirements.

Each formal application for EDA Investment Assistance must:

(a) Include evidence of applicant eligibility (as set forth in §301.2) and of economic distress (as set forth in §301.3);

(b) Identify the sources of funds, both eligible Federal and non-EDA, and In-Kind Contributions that will constitute the required Matching Share for the Project (*see* the Matching Share requirements under §301.5); and

(c) For Projects under parts 305 or 307 of this chapter, include a CEDS acceptable to EDA pursuant to part 303 of this chapter or otherwise incorporate by reference a current CEDS that EDA approves for the Project. The requirements stated in the preceding sentence shall not apply to:

(1) Strategy Grants, as defined in §307.3 of this chapter; and

(2) A Project located in a Region designated as a Special Impact Area pursuant to part 310 of this chapter.

(d) Projects that propose the construction of a business, technology, or other type of incubator or accelerator, must include a feasibility study demonstrating the need for the Project and an operational plan based on industry best practices demonstrating the Eligible Applicant's plan for ongoing successful operations. EDA will provide further guidance in the applicable FFO. EDA may require the Recipient to demonstrate that the feasibility study has been conducted by an impartial third party, as determined by EDA.

[75 FR 4263, Jan. 27, 2010, as amended at 79 FR 76127, Dec. 19, 2014]

§301.11 Infrastructure.

(a) EDA will fund both construction and non-construction infrastructure necessary to meet a Region's strategic economic development goals and needs, which in turn results in job creation. This includes infrastructure used to develop basic economic development assets as described in §§305.1 and 305.2 of this chapter (*e.g.*, roads, sewers, and water lines), as well as infrastructure that supports innovation and entrepreneurship. The following are examples of innovation and entrepreneurship-related infrastructure that support job creation:

(1) *Business Incubation*. Business incubation includes both physical facilities and business support services to advance the successful development of start-up companies by providing entrepreneurs with an array of targeted resources and services.

(2) *Business Acceleration*. Business acceleration includes both physical facilities and an array of business support services to help new and existing businesses develop new processes or products, get products and services to market more efficiently, expand market opportunities, or increase sales and exports.

(3) *Venture Development Organization*. A venture development organization ("*VDO*") works to ensure that Regional economies operate as smoothly and efficiently as possible in support of innovation-based entrepreneurship. A VDO may make strategic investments of time, talent, and other resources toward innovation, entrepreneurship, and technology to help nurture and grow promising companies and ideas, thereby promoting and taking advantage of the innovation assets of a Region and addressing the needs of the high-growth, innovation-oriented start-up companies in the Region.

(4) *Proof of Concept Center*. A proof of concept center serves as a hub of collaborative and entrepreneurial activity designed to accelerate the commercialization of innovations into the marketplace. Such centers support innovation-based, high growth entrepreneurship through a range of services, including technology and market evaluation, business planning and

mentorship, network development, and early stage access to capital.

(5) *Technology Transfer.* Technology transfer is the process of transferring scientific findings from one organization to another for the purpose of further development and commercialization. The process typically includes: Identifying new technologies; protecting technologies through patents and copyrights; and forming development and commercialization strategies, such as marketing and licensing, for existing private sector companies or creating start-up companies based on the technology.

(b) In general, successful Projects, including innovation and entrepreneurship-related infrastructure, require the engagement of a broad range of Regional stakeholders and resources. Therefore through appropriate FFOs and program requirements, EDA will seek to advance interagency coordination by funding Projects that demonstrate effective leveraging of other Federal Agency resources based on a Region's strategic economic development goals and needs. For all types of Projects, EDA assistance may not be used to provide direct venture capital to a for-profit entity because of the restrictions set out in section 217 of PWEDA (42 U.S.C. 3154c) and part 309 of this chapter. Nonetheless, EDA may consider an application more competitive if it includes measures to address the need to provide entrepreneurs with access to early stage capital outside of the proposed EDA Project budget. *See* § 301.8(b).

[79 FR 76127, Dec. 19, 2014, as amended at 82 FR 57053, Dec. 1, 2017]

PART 302—GENERAL TERMS AND CONDITIONS FOR INVESTMENT ASSISTANCE

Sec.

AUTHORITY: 19 U.S.C. 2341 *et seq.;* 42 U.S.C. 3150; 42 U.S.C. 3152; 42 U.S.C. 3153; 42 U.S.C. 3192; 42 U.S.C. 3193; 42 U.S.C. 3194; 42 U.S.C. 3211; 42 U.S.C. 3212; 42 U.S.C. 3216; 42 U.S.C. 3218; 42 U.S.C. 3220; 42 U.S.C. 5141; 15 U.S.C. 3701; Department of Commerce Delegation Order 10–4.

SOURCE: 71 FR 56675, Sept. 27, 2006, unless otherwise noted.

§ 302.1 Environment.

EDA will undertake environmental reviews of Projects in accordance with the requirements of the National Environmental Policy Act of 1969, as amended (Pub. L. 91–190; 42 U.S.C. 4321 *et seq.*, as implemented under 40 CFR chapter V) ("*NEPA*"), and all applicable Federal environmental statutes, regulations, and Executive Orders. These authorities include the implementing regulations of NEPA requiring EDA to provide public notice of the availability of Project-specific environmental documents, such as environmental impact statements, environmental assessments, findings of no significant impact, and records of decision, to the affected or interested public, as specified in 40 CFR 1506.6(b). Depending on the Project's location, environmental information concerning specific Projects may be obtained from the individual serving as the Environmental Officer in the appropriate EDA regional office listed in the applicable FFO.

[79 FR 76128, Dec. 19, 2014]

§ 302.2 Procedures in disaster areas.

When non-statutory EDA administrative or procedural conditions for Investment Assistance awards under PWEDA cannot be met by an Eligible Applicant as the result of a disaster, EDA may waive such conditions.

§ 302.3 Project servicing for loans, loan guaranties and Investment Assistance.

EDA will provide Project servicing to borrowers who received EDA loans or EDA-guaranteed loans and to lenders who received EDA loan guaranties under an EDA-administered program. Project servicing includes loans made under PWEDA prior to the effective date of the Economic Development Administration Reform Act of 1998, the Trade Act, and the Community Emergency Drought Relief Act of 1977 (Pub. L. 95–31; 42 U.S.C. 5184 note).

(a) EDA will continue to monitor such loans and loan guaranties in accordance with the applicable loans or loan guaranty program(s).

(b) Borrowers and lenders shall submit to EDA any requests for modifications of their loan or loan guaranty agreements with EDA, as applicable. EDA shall consider and respond to such modification requests in accordance with applicable laws and policies, including the budgetary constraints imposed by the Federal Credit Reform Act of 1990, as amended (2 U.S.C. 661c(e)).

(c) In the event that EDA determines it necessary or desirable to take actions to protect or further the interests of EDA in connection with loans, loan guaranties or evidence of purchased debt, EDA may:

(1) Assign or sell at public or private sale or otherwise dispose of for cash or credit, in its discretion and upon such terms and conditions as it shall determine to be reasonable, any evidence of debt, contract, claim, personal or real property, or security assigned to or held by it in connection with any EDA loans, EDA-guaranteed loans or Investment Assistance extended under PWEDA;

(2) Collect or compromise all obligations assigned to or held by it in connection with any EDA loans, EDA-guaranteed loans or Investment Assistance awarded under PWEDA until such time as such obligations may be referred to the Attorney General of the United States for suit or collection; and

(3) Take any and all other actions determined to be necessary or desirable in purchasing, servicing, compromising, modifying, liquidating, or otherwise administratively processing or disposing of loans or loan guaranties made or evidence of purchased debt in connection with any EDA loans, EDA-guaranteed loans or Investment Assistance awarded under PWEDA.

[71 FR 56675, Sept. 27, 2006, as amended at 79 FR 76128, Dec. 19, 2014]

§ 302.4 Public information.

The rules and procedures regarding public access to EDA's records pursuant to the Freedom of Information Act of 1967, as amended (5 U.S.C. 552), and the Privacy Act of 1974, as amended (5 U.S.C. 552a), are at 15 CFR part 4.

§ 302.5 Relocation assistance and land acquisition policies.

Recipients of EDA Investment Assistance or any other types of assistance under PWEDA, the Trade Act, and Stevenson-Wydler (States and political subdivisions of States and non-profit organizations, as applicable) are subject to the Uniform Relocation Assistance and Real Property Acquisition Policies Act of 1970, as amended (Pub. L. 91–646; 42 U.S.C. 4601 *et seq.*). *See* 15 CFR part 11 and 49 CFR part 24 for specific compliance requirements.

[82 FR 57053, Dec. 1, 2017]

§ 302.6 Additional requirements; Federal policies and procedures.

Recipients are subject to all Federal laws and to Federal, Department, and EDA policies, regulations, and procedures applicable to Federal financial assistance awards, including 2 CFR part 200, Uniform Administrative Requirements, Cost Principles, and Audit Requirements for Federal Awards.

[82 FR 57053, Dec. 1, 2017]

§ 302.7 Amendments and changes.

(a) Recipients shall submit requests for amendments to Investment awards in writing to EDA for approval and shall provide such information and documentation as EDA deems necessary to justify the request.

(b) Any changes to Projects made without EDA's approval are made at the Recipient's risk of non-payment of costs, suspension, termination or other applicable EDA action with respect to the Investment.

§ 302.8 Pre-approval Investment Assistance costs.

Project activities carried out before approval of Investment Assistance shall be carried out at the sole risk of the Eligible Applicant. Such activity is subject to the rejection of the application, the disallowance of costs, or other adverse consequences as a result of non-compliance with EDA or Federal requirements, including procurement requirements, civil rights requirements, Federal labor standards, or Federal environmental, historic preservation, and related requirements.

[79 FR 76128, Dec. 19, 2014]

§ 302.9 Inter-governmental review of projects.

(a) When an Eligible Applicant is not a State, Indian Tribe, or other general purpose governmental authority, the Eligible Applicant must afford the appropriate general purpose local governmental authority (the "*Authority*") in the Region a minimum of 15 days to review and comment on a proposed Project under EDA's Public Works and Economic Development program or a proposed construction Project or RLF Grant under EDA's Economic Adjustment Assistance program. Under these programs, the Eligible Applicant shall furnish the following with its application:

(1) If no comments are received from the Authority, a statement of efforts made to obtain such comments; or

(2) If comments are received from the Authority, a copy of the comments and a statement of any actions taken to address such comments.

(b) As required by 15 CFR part 13 and Executive Order 12372, "Intergovernmental Review of Federal Programs," as amended, if a State has adopted a process under Executive Order 12372 to review and coordinate proposed Federal financial assistance and direct Federal development (commonly referred to as the "single point of contact review process"), all Eligible Applicants also must give State and local governments a reasonable opportunity to review and comment on the proposed Project, including review and comment from area-wide planning organizations in metropolitan areas, as provided for in 15 CFR part 13.

[79 FR 76128, Dec. 19, 2014]

§ 302.10 Attorneys' and consultants' fees, employment of expediters, and post-employment restriction.

(a) *Employment of expediters.* Investment Assistance awarded under PWEDA shall not directly or indirectly reimburse any attorneys' or consultants' fees incurred in connection with obtaining Investment Assistance and contracts under PWEDA. Such Investment Assistance shall not be awarded to any Eligible Applicant, unless the owners, partners, or officers of the Eligible Applicant certify to EDA the names of any attorneys, agents, and other persons engaged by or on behalf of the Eligible Applicant for the purpose of expediting an application made to EDA in connection with obtaining Investment Assistance under PWEDA and the fees paid or to be paid to the person(s) for expediting the application.

(b) *Post-employment restriction.* (1) In general, any Eligible Applicant that is a non-profit organization, District Organization, or for-profit entity, for the two-year period beginning on the date on which the Investment Assistance under PWEDA is awarded to the Eligible Applicant, must refrain from employing, offering any office or employment to, or retaining for professional services any person who, on the date on which the Investment Assistance is awarded or within the one-year period ending on that date:

(i) Served as an officer, attorney, agent, or employee of the Department; and

(ii) Occupied a position or engaged in activities that the Assistant Secretary determines involved discretion with respect to the award of Investment Assistance under PWEDA.

(2) In addition to the types of Eligible Applicants noted in this paragraph (b),

EDA may require another Eligible Applicant to execute an agreement to abide by the above-described post-employment restriction on a case-by-case basis; for example, when an institution of higher education implements activities under or related to the Investment Assistance through a separate non-profit organization or association.

[79 FR 76128, Dec. 19, 2014]

§302.11 Economic development information clearinghouse.

Pursuant to section 502 of PWEDA, EDA maintains an economic development information clearinghouse on its Internet Web site at *http://www.eda.gov.*

[79 FR 76128, Dec. 19, 2014]

§302.12 Project administration, operation and maintenance.

EDA shall approve Investment Assistance awards only if, as determined in its sole discretion, the Project for which such Investment Assistance is awarded will be properly and efficiently administered, operated and maintained.

§302.13 Maintenance of standards.

All laborers and mechanics employed by contractors or subcontractors on Projects receiving Investment Assistance under PWEDA shall be paid wages at rates not less than those prevailing on similar construction in the locality, as determined by the U.S. Secretary of Labor in accordance with subchapter IV of chapter 31 of title 40, United States Code. EDA shall not extend any Investment Assistance under this chapter for a Project without first obtaining adequate assurance that these labor standards will be maintained upon the construction work. The U.S. Secretary of Labor shall have, with respect to the labor standards specified in this provision, the authority and functions set forth in Reorganization Plan No. 14 of 1950 (15 FR 3176 (May 25, 1950); 64 Stat. 1267) and section 3145 of title 40, United States Code.

§302.14 Records.

(a) *Records.* Recipients of Investment Assistance under PWEDA shall keep such records as EDA shall require, including records that fully disclose:

(1) The total cost of the Project;

(2) The amount and disposition by the Recipient of the Investment Assistance;

(3) The amount and nature of the portion of Project costs provided by other sources; and

(4) Such other information as EDA determines will facilitate an effective audit.

(b) *Access to records.* The Recipient shall permit the Assistant Secretary, the Inspector General of the Department, the Comptroller General of the United States or any of their respective agents or representatives access to its properties in order to examine all books, correspondence, and records, including without limitation computer programs and data processing software, to verify the Recipient's compliance with Investment Assistance requirements.

[73 FR 62865, Oct. 22, 2008]

§302.15 Acceptance of certifications made by Eligible Applicants.

EDA will accept an Eligible Applicant's certifications, accompanied by evidence satisfactory to EDA, that the Eligible Applicant meets the requirements for receiving Investment Assistance.

§302.16 Accountability.

(a) *General.* Each Recipient must submit reports to EDA at intervals and in the manner that EDA shall require, except that EDA shall not require any report to be submitted more than ten years after the date of closeout of the Investment Assistance.

(b) *Data on Project effectiveness.* Each report must contain a data-specific evaluation of the effectiveness of the Investment Assistance provided in fulfilling the Project's purpose (including alleviation of economic distress and meeting Project goals) and in meeting the objectives of PWEDA. Data used by a Recipient in preparing reports shall be accurate and verifiable as determined by EDA, and from independent sources (whenever possible). EDA will use this data and report to fulfill its performance measurement reporting requirements under the Government Performance and Results Act of 1993, as amended (Pub. L. 103–62) and to monitor internal, Investment, and Project performance through an internal performance measurement system.

(c) *Reporting Project service benefits.* To enable EDA to determine the economic development effect of a Project that provides service benefits, EDA may require the Recipient to submit a Project service map and information from which to determine whether services are provided to all segments of the Region being assisted.

(d) *Consequences for failure to undertake good faith efforts.* (1) The Recipient must undertake good faith efforts to fulfill the purpose of the Project as set out in the terms of the Investment Assistance and must report regularly on Project goals. In the event that EDA determines that the Recipient is failing to make good faith efforts to meet these goals, or otherwise is failing to meets its obligations under the Investment Assistance, EDA shall take necessary actions to protect EDA's interest in the Project, including the following:

(i) Discontinue disbursement of funds pending correction;

(ii) Suspend the Investment Assistance;

(iii) Terminate the Investment Assistance;

(iv) Require reimbursement of the EDA share of the Project; or

(v) Institute formal Government-wide debarment and suspension proceedings against the Recipient.

(2) Before making a determination under this subsection, EDA shall provide the Recipient with reasonable notice and opportunity to respond. A determination under this subsection is final and cannot be appealed.

[79 FR 76129, Dec. 19, 2014]

§ 302.17 Conflicts of interest.

(a) *General.* It is EDA's and the Department's policy to maintain the highest standards of conduct to prevent conflicts of interest in connection with the award of Investment Assistance or its use for reimbursement or payment of costs (*e.g.*, procurement of goods or services) by or to the Recipient. A conflict of interest generally exists when an Interested Party participates in a matter that has a direct and predictable effect on the Interested Party's personal or financial interests. A conflict also may exist where there is an appearance that an Interested Party's objectivity in performing his or her responsibilities under the Project is impaired. For example, an appearance of impairment of objectivity may result from an organizational conflict where, because of other activities or relationships with other persons or entities, an Interested Party is unable to render impartial assistance, services or advice to the Recipient, a participant in the Project or to the Federal government. Additionally, a conflict of interest may result from non-financial gain to an Interested Party, such as benefit to reputation or prestige in a professional field.

(b) *Prohibition on direct or indirect financial or personal benefits.* (1) An Interested Party shall not receive any direct or indirect financial or personal benefits in connection with the award of Investment Assistance or its use for payment or reimbursement of costs by or to the Recipient.

(2) An Interested Party also shall not, directly or indirectly, solicit or accept any gift, gratuity, favor, entertainment or other benefit having monetary value, for himself or herself or for another person or entity, from any person or organization which has obtained or seeks to obtain Investment Assistance from EDA.

(3) Costs incurred in violation of any conflicts of interest rules contained in this chapter or in violation of any assurances by the Recipient may be denied reimbursement.

(4) *See* § 315.15 of this chapter for special conflicts of interest rules for Trade Adjustment Assistance Investments.

(c) *Special rules for Revolving Loan Fund ("RLF") Grants.* In addition to the rules set forth in this section:

(1) An Interested Party of a Recipient of an RLF Grant shall not receive, directly or indirectly, any personal or financial benefits resulting from the disbursement of RLF loans;

(2) A Recipient of an RLF Grant shall not lend RLF funds to an Interested Party; and

(3) Former board members of a Recipient of an RLF Grant and members of his or her Immediate Family shall

not receive a loan from such RLF for a period of two years from the date that the board member last served on the RLF's board of directors.

[71 FR 56675, Sept. 27, 2006, as amended at 73 FR 62866, Oct. 22, 2008; 79 FR 76129, Dec. 19, 2014]

§ 302.18 Post-approval requirements.

A Recipient must comply with all financial, performance, progress report, and other requirements set forth in the terms and conditions of the Investment Assistance, including any special award conditions and applicable Federal cost principles (collectively, "*Post-Approval Requirements*"). A Recipient's failure to comply with Post-Approval Requirements may result in the disallowance of costs, termination of the Investment Assistance award, or other adverse consequences to the Recipient.

[79 FR 76129, Dec. 19, 2014]

§ 302.19 Indemnification.

To the maximum extent permitted by law, a Recipient shall indemnify and hold EDA harmless from any liability that EDA may incur due to the actions or omissions of the Recipient.

§ 302.20 Civil rights.

(a) Discrimination is prohibited by a Recipient or Other Party (as defined in paragraph (b) of this section) with respect to a Project receiving Investment Assistance under PWEDA or Stevenson-Wydler or by an entity receiving Adjustment Assistance (as defined in § 315.2 of this chapter) under the Trade Act or any other type of assistance under Stevenson-Wydler, in accordance with the following authorities:

(1) Section 601 of Title VI of the Civil Rights Act of 1964, as amended (42 U.S.C. 2000d *et seq.*) (proscribing discrimination on the basis of race, color, or national origin), and the Department's implementing regulations found at 15 CFR part 8;

(2) 42 U.S.C. 3123 (proscribing discrimination on the basis of sex in Investment Assistance provided under PWEDA), 42 U.S.C. 6709 (proscribing discrimination on the basis of sex under the Local Public Works Program), Title IX of the Education Amendments of 1972, as amended (20 U.S.C. 1681 *et seq.*) (proscribing discrimination on the basis of sex in any education program or activity receiving Federal financial assistance, whether or not such program or activity is offered or sponsored by an educational institution), and the Department's implementing regulations found at 15 CFR part 8a;

(3) Section 504 of the Rehabilitation Act of 1973, as amended (29 U.S.C. 794) (proscribing discrimination on the basis of disabilities), and the Department's implementing regulations found at 15 CFR part 8b;

(4) The Age Discrimination Act of 1975, as amended (42 U.S.C. 6101 *et seq.*) (proscribing discrimination on the basis of age), and the Department's implementing regulations found at 15 CFR part 20; and

(5) Other Federal statutes, regulations and Executive Orders, as applicable.

(b) *Definitions.* (1) For purposes of this section, an "*Other Party*" means an "other party subject to this part," as defined in 15 CFR 8.3(l), and includes an entity which (or which is intended to) creates and/or saves 15 or more permanent jobs as a result of Investment Assistance; provided that such entity also is either specifically named in the application as benefiting from the Project, or is or will be located in an EDA building, port, facility, or industrial, commercial or business park constructed or improved in whole or in part with Investment Assistance prior to EDA's final disbursement of award funds.

(2) Additional applicable definitions are provided in 15 CFR part 8.

(c) No Recipient or Other Party shall intimidate, threaten, coerce or discriminate against any person for the purpose of interfering with any right or privilege secured by 42 U.S.C. 3123 or 42 U.S.C. 6709, or because the person has made a complaint, testified, assisted or participated in any manner in an investigation, proceeding or hearing under this section.

(d) All Recipients of Investment Assistance under PWEDA and Stevenson-Wydler, all Other Parties, and all entities receiving Adjustment Assistance under the Trade Act or any other type of assistance under Stevenson-Wydler must submit to EDA written assurances that they will comply with applicable laws, EDA regulations, Department regulations, and such other requirements as may be applicable, prohibiting discrimination.

(e) Reporting and other procedural matters are set forth in 15 CFR parts 8, 8a, 8b, 8c and 20.

[71 FR 56675, Sept. 27, 2006, as amended at 75 FR 4263, Jan. 27, 2010; 79 FR 76129, Dec. 19, 2014; 82 FR 57053, Dec. 1, 2017]

PART 303—PLANNING INVESTMENTS AND COMPREHENSIVE ECONOMIC DEVELOPMENT STRATEGIES

Subpart A—General

Subpart B—Partnership Planning Assistance

Subpart C—State and Short-Term Planning Assistance

AUTHORITY: 42 U.S.C. 3143; 42 U.S.C. 3162; 42 U.S.C. 3174; 42 U.S.C. 3211; Department of Commerce Organization Order 10–4.

SOURCE: 71 FR 56675, Sept. 27, 2006, unless otherwise noted.

Subpart A—General

§ 303.1 Overview of EDA's Planning Program.

The purpose of EDA Planning Investments is to provide support to Planning Organizations for the development, implementation, revision, or replacement of Comprehensive Economic Development Strategies, and for related State plans and short-term Planning Investments designed to create and retain new and better jobs, particularly for the unemployed and underemployed in the nation's most economically distressed Regions. EDA's Planning Investments support partnerships with District Organizations, Indian Tribes, community development corporations, non-profit Regional planning organizations, and other Eligible Recipients. Planning activities supported by these Investments must be part of a continuous process involving the active participation of the private sector, public officials, non-profit organizations, educational institutions, and private citizens, and include:

(a) Analyzing local economies;

(b) Defining economic development goals;

(c) Determining Project opportunities; and

(d) Formulating and implementing an economic development program that includes systematic efforts to reduce unemployment and increase incomes.

[71 FR 56675, Sept. 27, 2006, as amended at 79 FR 76129, Dec. 19, 2014]

§ 303.2 Definitions.

In addition to the defined terms set forth in § 300.3 of this chapter, the following terms used in this part shall have the following meanings:

Planning Investment means the award of EDA Investment Assistance under section 203 of PWEDA and this part.

Planning Organization means a Recipient whose purpose is to develop and implement a CEDS for a specific EDA-approved Region under section 203 of PWEDA.

Strategy Committee means the committee or other entity identified by the Planning Organization as responsible for the development, implementation, revision or replacement of the CEDS for the Planning Organization.

§ 303.3 Application requirements and evaluation criteria.

(a) For Planning Investment awards, EDA uses the general application evaluation criteria set forth in § 301.8 of this chapter. In addition, applications for Planning Investments must include information about the following:

(1) The proposed scope of work for the development, implementation, revision or replacement of the CEDS, or

the relation of the CEDS to the proposed short-term planning activities or the State plan;

(2) Qualifications of the Eligible Applicant to implement the goals and objectives resulting from the CEDS, short-term planning activities or the State plan;

(3) The involvement of the Region's business leadership at each stage of the preparation of the CEDS, short-term planning activities or State plan;

(4) Extent of broad-based representation and involvement of the Region's civic, business, labor, minority and other interests in the Eligible Applicant's economic development activities; and

(5) Feasibility of the proposed scope of work to create and retain new and better jobs through implementation of the CEDS.

(b) In addition to the criteria set forth in paragraph (a) of this section, funded Recipients are evaluated on the basis of the extent of continuing economic distress within the Region, their past performance, and the overall effectiveness of their CEDS.

(c) For Planning Investment awards to a State, the Assistant Secretary also shall consider the extent to which the State will integrate and coordinate its CEDS with local and Economic Development District plans.

(d) The Investment Rates for Planning Investments will be determined in accordance with § 301.4 of this chapter.

[71 FR 56675, Sept. 27, 2006, as amended at 79 FR 76129, Dec. 19, 2014]

§ 303.4 Award requirements.

(a) Planning Investments shall be coordinated with and effectively leverage any other available Federal, State, or local planning assistance and private sector investments.

(b) Except in compelling circumstances as determined by the Assistant Secretary, EDA will not provide Planning Investments for multiple CEDS that address the needs of an identical or substantially similar Region.

(c) EDA will provide a Planning Investment for the period of time required to develop, revise or replace, and implement a CEDS, generally in 36-month renewable Investment project periods.

[71 FR 56675, Sept. 27, 2006, as amended at 73 FR 62866, Oct. 22, 2008; 79 FR 76130, Dec. 19, 2014]

§ 303.5 Eligible administrative expenses.

In accordance with applicable Federal cost principles, Planning Investments may be used to pay the direct and indirect costs incurred by a Planning Organization in the development, implementation, revision or replacement of a CEDS and for related short-term planning activities.

Subpart B—Partnership Planning Assistance

§ 303.6 Partnership Planning and the EDA-funded CEDS process.

(a) *Partnership Planning Overview.* Partnership Planning Investments support a nationwide network of Planning Organizations to provide comprehensive economic development planning services to distressed Regions. EDA makes Partnership Planning Investments to enable Planning Organizations to manage and coordinate the development and implementation of CEDS to address the unique needs of their respective Regions.

(b) *CEDS Process.* If EDA awards Investment Assistance to a Planning Organization to develop, revise, or replace a CEDS, the Planning Organization must follow the procedures set forth in this section:

(1) *CEDS Strategy Committee.* The Planning Organization must appoint a Strategy Committee. The Strategy Committee must represent the main economic interests of the Region, which may include Indian tribes, the private sector, State and other public officials, community leaders, private individuals, representatives of workforce development boards, institutions of higher education, minority and labor groups, and others who can contribute to and benefit from improved economic development in the relevant Region. In addition, the Strategy Committee must demonstrate the capacity to undertake a collaborative and effective planning process.

(2) *Public notice and comment.* The Planning Organization must develop and submit to EDA a CEDS that complies with the requirements of § 303.7. Before submission to EDA, the Planning Organization must provide the public and appropriate governments and interest groups in the relevant Region with adequate notice of and opportunity to comment on the CEDS. The comment period shall be at least 30 days and the Planning Organization shall make the CEDS readily available through appropriate means of distribution, electronically and otherwise, throughout the comment period. The Planning Organization also shall make the CEDS available in hardcopy upon request. EDA may require the Planning Organization to provide any comments received and demonstrate how the comments were resolved.

(3) *Reports and updates.* (i) After obtaining EDA approval of the CEDS, the Planning Organization must submit annually an updated CEDS performance report to EDA.

(ii) The Planning Organization must submit a new or revised CEDS to EDA at least every five years, unless EDA or the Planning Organization determines that a new or revised CEDS is required earlier due to changed circumstances. In connection with the submission of a new or revised CEDS, the Planning Organization shall use its best efforts to obtain renewed commitments from participating counties or other areas within the District to support the economic development activities of the District. Provided the Planning Organization can document a good faith effort to obtain renewed commitments, the inability to secure renewed commitments shall not disqualify a CEDS update.

(iii) Any updated CEDS performance report that results in a change of the requirements set forth in § 303.7(b)(1)(iii) of the EDA-accepted CEDS or any new or revised CEDS, must be available for review and comment by the public in accordance with paragraph (b)(2) of this section.

(4) *Inadequate CEDS.* If EDA determines that implementation of the CEDS is inadequate, it will notify the Planning Organization in writing and the Planning Organization shall submit to EDA a new or revised CEDS.

(5) *Regional Commission notification.* If any part of a Region is covered by one or more of the Regional Commissions as set forth in section 404 of PWEDA, the Planning Organization shall ensure that a copy of the CEDS is provided to the Regional Commission(s).

[79 FR 76130, Dec. 19, 2014, as amended at 82 FR 57054, Dec. 1, 2017]

§ 303.7 Requirements for Comprehensive Economic Development Strategies.

(a) *General.* CEDS are designed to bring together the public and private sectors in the creation of an economic roadmap to diversify and strengthen Regional economies. The CEDS should analyze the Regional economy and serve as a guide for establishing Regional goals and objectives, developing and implementing a Regional plan of action, and identifying investment priorities and funding sources. Public and private sector partnerships are critical to the implementation of the integral elements of a CEDS set forth in paragraph (b) of this section. As a performance-based plan, the CEDS will serve a critical role in a Region's efforts to defend against economic dislocations due to global trade, competition and other events resulting in the loss of jobs and private investment.

(b) *Strategy requirements.* (1) A CEDS must be the result of a continuing economic development planning process, developed with broad-based and diverse public and private sector participation. Consistent with section 302 of PWEDA, each CEDS must promote Regional resiliency and be unique and responsive to the relevant Region. Each CEDS must include:

(i) A summary of economic development conditions of the Region;

(ii) An in-depth analysis of economic and community development strengths, weaknesses, opportunities, and threats (commonly known as a "*SWOT*" analysis);

(iii) Strategies and an implementation plan to build upon the Region's strengths and opportunities and resolve the weaknesses and threats facing the Region, which should not be inconsistent with applicable State and local economic development or workforce development strategies; and

(iv) Performance measures used to evaluate the Planning Organization's successful development and implementation of the CEDS.

(2) EDA will publish and periodically update specific CEDS content guidelines.

(c) *Consideration of non-EDA funded CEDS.* (1) In determining the acceptability of a CEDS prepared independently of EDA Investment Assistance or oversight for Projects under parts 305 and 307 of this chapter, EDA may in its discretion determine that the CEDS is acceptable so long as it includes all of the elements listed in paragraph (b) of this section. In certain circumstances, EDA may accept a non-EDA funded CEDS that does not contain all the elements listed in paragraph (b) of this section. In doing so, EDA shall consider the circumstances surrounding the application for Investment Assistance, including emergencies or natural disasters and the fulfillment of the requirements of section 302 of PWEDA.

(2) If the CEDS for a Project under parts 305 and 307 of this chapter is developed under another federally-supported program, it must include acceptable performance measures similar to those set forth in paragraph (b) of this section and information on the state of the Regional economy. To the maximum extent practicable, the CEDS shall be consistent and coordinated with any existing economic development plan for the Region.

[71 FR 56675, Sept. 27, 2006, as amended at 79 FR 76130, Dec. 19, 2014; 82 FR 57054, Dec. 1, 2017]

Subpart C—State and Short-Term Planning Assistance

§ 303.8 Requirements for State plans.

(a) As a condition of a State receiving a Planning Investment:

(1) The State must have or develop a CEDS that meets the requirements of § 303.7;

(2) Any State plan developed with Planning Investment Assistance must, to the maximum extent practicable, be developed cooperatively by the State, political subdivisions of the State, and the Economic Development Districts located wholly or partially in the State; and

(3) The State must submit to EDA an annual report on any State plan receiving Planning Investment Assistance.

(b) Before awarding a Planning Investment to a State, EDA shall consider the extent to which the State will take into account local and District economic development plans.

§ 303.9 Requirements for short-term Planning Investments.

(a) In addition to providing support for CEDS and State plans, EDA also may provide Investment Assistance to support short-term planning activities. EDA may provide such Investment Assistance to:

(1) Develop the economic development planning capacity of States, cities and other Eligible Applicants experiencing economic distress;

(2) Assist in institutional capacity building; or

(3) Undertake innovative approaches to economic development.

(b) Eligible activities may include updating a portion of a CEDS, economic analysis, development of economic development policies and procedures, and development of economic development goals.

(c) Applicants for short-term Planning Investments must provide performance measures acceptable to EDA that can be used to evaluate the success of the program and provide EDA with progress reports during the term of the Planning Investment, as set forth in the Investment agreement.

[71 FR 56675, Sept. 27, 2006, as amended at 79 FR 76130, Dec. 19, 2014]

PART 304—ECONOMIC DEVELOPMENT DISTRICTS

AUTHORITY: 42 U.S.C. 3122; 42 U.S.C. 3171; 42 U.S.C. 3172; 42 U.S.C. 3196; Department of Commerce Organization Order 10–4.

SOURCE: 71 FR 56675, Sept. 27, 2006, unless otherwise noted.

§ 304.1 Designation of Economic Development Districts: Regional eligibility.

Upon the request of a District Organization (as defined in § 304.2), EDA may designate a Region as an Economic Development District if such Region:

(a) Contains at least one geographic area that is subject to the economic distress criteria set forth in § 301.3(a)(1) of this chapter and is identified in an approved CEDS;

(b) Is of sufficient size or population and contains sufficient resources to foster economic development on a scale involving more than a single geographic area subject to the economic distress criteria set forth in § 301.3(a)(1) of this chapter;

(c) Has an EDA-approved CEDS that:

(1) Meets the requirements under § 303.7 of this chapter;

(2) Contains a specific program for intra-District cooperation, self-help, and public investment; and

(3) Is approved by each affected State and by the Assistant Secretary;

(d) Obtains commitments from at least a majority of the counties or other areas within the proposed District, as determined by EDA, to support the economic development activities of the District; and

(e) Obtains the concurrence with the designation request from the State (or States) in which the proposed District will be wholly or partially located.

[71 FR 56675, Sept. 27, 2006, as amended at 79 FR 76131, Dec. 19, 2014]

§ 304.2 District Organizations: Formation, organizational requirements and operations.

(a) *General.* A "*District Organization*" is an entity that satisfies the formation and organizational requirements under paragraphs (b) and (c) of this section.

(b) *Formation.* A District Organization must be organized as one of the following:

(1) A public organization formed through an inter-governmental agreement providing for the joint exercise of local government powers; or

(2) A public organization established under State-enabling legislation for the creation of multi-jurisdictional area-wide planning organizations; or

(3) A non-profit organization incorporated under the applicable non-profit statutes of the State in which it is incorporated.

(c) *Organization and governance.* (1) Each District Organization must meet the requirements of this paragraph (c) concerning membership composition, the maintenance of adequate staff support to perform its economic development functions, and its authorities and responsibilities for carrying out economic development functions. The District Organization's board of directors (or other governing body) also must meet these requirements.

(2) The District Organization must demonstrate that its governing body is broadly representative of the principal economic interests of the Region, which may include the private sector, public officials, community leaders, representatives of workforce development boards, institutions of higher education, minority and labor groups, and private individuals. In addition, the governing body must demonstrate the capacity to implement the EDA-approved CEDS.

(3) The District Organization must be assisted by a professional staff drawn from qualified persons in economic development, planning, business development or related disciplines.

(4) The governing bodies of District Organizations must provide access for persons who are not members to make their views known concerning ongoing and proposed District activities in accordance with the following requirements:

(i) The District Organization must hold meetings open to the public at least twice a year and also shall publish the date and agenda of such meetings sufficiently in advance to allow the public a reasonable time to prepare in order to participate effectively.

(ii) The District Organization shall adopt a system of parliamentary procedures to assure that board members and others have access to an effective opportunity to participate in the affairs of the District.

(iii) The District Organization shall provide information sufficiently in advance of decisions to give the public adequate opportunity to review and react to proposals. District Organizations should communicate technical data and other material to the public so they may understand the impact of public programs, available options and alternative decisions.

(iv) The District Organization must make available to the public such audited statements, annual budgets and minutes of public meetings, as may be reasonably requested.

(v) The District Organization and its board of directors must comply with all Federal and State financial assistance reporting requirements and the conflicts of interest provisions set forth in §302.17 of this chapter.

(d) *Operations.* (1) The District Organization shall engage in the full range of economic development activities listed in its EDA-approved CEDS. These activities may include:

(i) Coordinating and implementing economic development activities in the District;

(ii) Carrying out economic development research, planning, implementation and advisory functions identified in the CEDS; and

(iii) Coordinating the development and implementation of the CEDS with other local, State, Federal and private organizations.

(2) The District Organization may at its option contract for services to accomplish the activities listed in paragraphs (d)(1)(i) through (iii) of this section.

[71 FR 56675, Sept. 27, 2006, as amended at 79 FR 76131, Dec. 19, 2014; 82 FR 57054, Dec. 1, 2017]

§304.3 District modification and termination.

(a) *Modification.* Upon the request of a District Organization and with the concurrence of the State or States affected (unless such concurrence is waived by the Assistant Secretary), EDA may modify the geographic boundaries of a District, if it determines that such modification will contribute to a more effective program for economic development.

(b) *Termination.* EDA may, upon 60 days prior written notice to the District Organization, member counties, and other areas determined by EDA and each affected State, terminate a Region's designation as an Economic Development District when:

(1) A District or District Organization no longer meets the requirements of §§304.1 or 304.2; or

(2) EDA determines that the District Organization fails to execute its CEDS according to the development, implementation and other performance measures set forth therein; or

(3) A District Organization has requested termination.

(c) Prior to terminating a District Organization under paragraph (b)(2) of this section, EDA will consult with the District Organization and consider all facts and circumstances regarding the District Organization's operations. EDA will not terminate a District's designation based on circumstances beyond the control of the District Organization (e.g., natural disaster, plant closure, overall economic downturn, sudden and severe economic dislocation, or other situation).

(d) EDA may further modify or terminate a Region's designation as a District according to the standards set forth in an FFO.

[71 FR 56675, Sept. 27, 2006, as amended at 79 FR 76131, Dec. 19, 2014]

§304.4 Performance evaluations.

(a) EDA shall evaluate the management standards, financial accountability and program performance of each District Organization within three years after the initial Investment award and at least once every three years thereafter, so long as the District Organization continues to receive Investment Assistance. EDA's evaluation shall assess:

(1) The continuing Regional eligibility of the District, as set forth in §304.1;

(2) The management of the District Organization, as set forth in §304.2; and

(3) The implementation of the CEDS, including the District Organization's performance and contribution towards the retention and creation of employment, as set forth in §303.7 of this chapter.

(b) For peer review, EDA shall ensure the participation of at least one other District Organization in the performance evaluation on a cost-reimbursement basis.

[71 FR 56675, Sept. 27, 2006, as amended at 79 FR 76131, Dec. 19, 2014]

PART 305—PUBLIC WORKS AND ECONOMIC DEVELOPMENT INVESTMENTS

Subpart A—General

Subpart B—Requirements for Approved Projects

AUTHORITY: 42 U.S.C. 3211; 42 U.S.C. 3141; Department of Commerce Organization Order 10–4.

SOURCE: 71 FR 56675, Sept. 27, 2006, unless otherwise noted.

Subpart A—General

§ 305.1 Purpose and scope.

Public Works and Economic Development Investments ("*Public Works Investments*") intend to help the nation's most distressed communities revitalize, expand, and upgrade their physical infrastructure (as defined in § 301.11 of this chapter) to attract new industry, encourage business expansion, diversify local economies, and generate or retain long-term private sector jobs and investments. The primary goal of these Investments is to create new or retain existing, long-term private sector job opportunities in communities experiencing significant economic distress as evidenced by chronic high unemployment, underemployment, low per capita income, outmigration, or a Special Need. These Investments also intend to assist communities in attracting private capital investment and new and better job opportunities and to promote the successful long-term economic recovery of a Region.

[79 FR 76131, Dec. 19, 2014]

§ 305.2 Award requirements.

(a) *Project scope.* Public Works Investments may fund the following activities:

(1) Acquisition or development of land and improvements for use in a public works, public service or other type of development facility; or

(2) Acquisition, design and engineering, construction, rehabilitation, alteration, expansion, or improvement of such a facility, including related machinery and equipment.

(b) *Requirements.* A Public Works Investment may be made if EDA determines that:

(1) The Project will, directly or indirectly:

(i) Improve the opportunities for the successful establishment or expansion of industrial or commercial plants or facilities in the Region where the Project is located;

(ii) Assist in the creation of additional long-term employment opportunities in the Region; or

(iii) Primarily benefit the long-term unemployed and members of low-income families in the Region;

(2) The Project will fulfill a pressing need of the Region, or a part of the Region, in which the Project is located; and

(3) The Region in which the Project is located has a CEDS and the Project is consistent with the CEDS.

(c) Not more than 15 percent of the annual appropriations made available to EDA to fund Public Works Investments may be made in any one State.

[71 FR 56675, Sept. 27, 2006, as amended at 79 FR 76131, Dec. 19, 2014]

§ 305.3 Application requirements.

(a) Each application for Public Works Investment Assistance must:

(1) Include evidence of eligibility, as provided in part 301 of this chapter;

(2) Include, or incorporate by reference, a CEDS (as provided in § 303.7 of this chapter);

(3) Demonstrate how the proposed Project meets the criteria of § 305.2; and

(4) Demonstrate how the proposed Project meets the application evaluation criteria set forth in § 301.8 of this chapter.

(b) The Investment Rate for Public Works Investments will be determined in accordance with § 301.4 of this chapter.

[71 FR 56675, Sept. 27, 2006, as amended at 75 FR 4264, Jan. 27, 2010]

§ 305.4 Projects for design and engineering work.

In the case of Public Works Investment Assistance awarded solely for design and engineering work, the following additional application requirements and terms shall apply:

(a) EDA may determine that a separate Investment for design and engineering is warranted due to the technical complexity or environmental sensitivity of the construction Project;

(b) The purpose of the Investment may be limited to the development and production of all documents required for the construction of the proposed construction Project in a format and in sufficient quantity to permit advertisement and award of a construction contract soon after securing construction financing for the Project;

(c) EDA will not disburse any portion of the Investment Assistance until it receives and certifies compliance with the Investment award of all design and engineering contracts; and

(d) EDA's funding of the Project for design and engineering work does not in any way commit EDA to fund construction of the Project.

Subpart B—Requirements for Approved Projects

§ 305.5 Project administration by District Organization.

(a) When a District Organization is not the Recipient or co-Recipient of Investment Assistance, the District Organization may administer the Project for the Recipient if EDA determines fulfillment of the following conditions:

(1) The Recipient has requested (either in the application or by separate written request) that the District Organization for the Region in which the Project is located administer the Project;

(2) The Recipient certifies and EDA finds that:

(i) Administration of the Project is beyond the capacity of the Recipient's current staff and would require hiring additional staff or contracting for such services;

(ii) No local organization or business exists that could administer the Project in a more efficient or cost-effective manner than the staff of the District Organization; and

(iii) The staff of the District Organization would administer the Project without sub-contracting the work; and

(3) The allowable costs for the administration of the Project by the District Organization's staff will not exceed the amount that would be allowable to the Recipient.

(b) EDA must approve the request either by approving the application in which the request is made or by separate specific written approval.

§ 305.6 Allowable methods of procurement for construction services.

(a) Recipients shall seek EDA's prior written approval to use alternate construction procurement methods to the traditional design/bid/build procedures (including lump sum or unit price-type construction contracts). These alternate methods may include design/build, construction management at risk, and force account. If an alternate method is used, the Recipient shall submit to EDA for approval a construction services procurement plan and the Recipient must use a design professional to oversee the process. The Recipient shall submit the plan to EDA prior to advertisement for bids and shall include the following, as applicable:

(1) Justification for the proposed method for procurement of construction services, including a brief analysis of the appropriateness and benefits of using the method to successfully execute the Project and the Recipient's experience in using the method;

(2) The scope of work with cost estimates and schedules;

(3) A copy of the proposed construction contract;

(4) The name and qualifications of the selected design professional; and

(5) Procedures to be used to ensure full and open competition, including the selection criteria.

(b) For all procurement methods, the Recipient must comply with the procedures and standards set forth in 2 CFR part 200.

[71 FR 56675, Sept. 27, 2006, as amended at 73 FR 62866, Oct. 22, 2008; 79 FR 76131, Dec. 19, 2014; 82 FR 57054, Dec. 1, 2017]

§ 305.7 Services performed by the Recipient's own forces.

In certain circumstances, the Recipient may wish to consider having a portion or all of the design, construction, inspection, legal services or other work and/or services in connection with the Project performed by personnel who are employed by the Recipient either full-time or part-time. EDA may approve the use of such "in-house forces" if:

(a) The services are routinely performed by the Recipient for all construction Projects performed by the Recipient (for example, inspection or legal); or

(b) The Recipient has a special skill required for the construction of the Project (for example, construction of unique Indian structures); or

(c) The Recipient has made all reasonable efforts to obtain a contractor but has failed to do so because of uncontrollable factors such as the remoteness of the Project site or an overabundance of construction work in the Region; or

(d) The Recipient demonstrates substantial cost savings.

§ 305.8 Recipient-furnished equipment and materials.

The Recipient may wish to incorporate into the Project equipment or materials that it will secure through its own efforts, subject to the following requirements:

(a) EDA must approve any use of Recipient-furnished equipment and materials. EDA may require that major equipment items be subject to a lien in favor of EDA and also may require a statement from the Recipient regarding expected useful life and salvage value of such equipment;

(b) EDA may require the Recipient to establish that the expense claimed for such equipment or materials is competitive with current local market costs; and

(c) Acquisition of Recipient-furnished equipment or materials under this section also is subject to the requirements of 2 CFR part 200.

[71 FR 56675, Sept. 27, 2006, as amended at 79 FR 76132, Dec. 19, 2014; 82 FR 57054, Dec. 1, 2017]

§ 305.9 Project phasing and Investment disbursement.

(a) EDA may authorize in advance the award of construction contracts in phases, provided the Recipient submits a request that includes each of the following:

(1) Valid reasons justifying why the Project must be phased;

(2) Description of the specific elements to be completed in each phase;

(3) Detailed construction cost estimates for each phase;

(4) Time schedules for completing all phases of the Project;

(5) Certification that the Recipient can and will fund any overrun(s); and

(6) Certification that the Recipient is capable of paying incurred costs prior to the first disbursement of EDA funds.

(b) EDA will begin disbursement of funds after receipt of evidence sufficient to EDA of compliance with all Investment award conditions. EDA may approve the disbursement of funds prior to the tender of all construction contracts if the Recipient can demonstrate to EDA's satisfaction that a severe financial hardship will result without such approval.

§ 305.10 Bid underrun and overrun.

(a) *Underrun.* If at the construction contract bid opening, the lowest responsive bid is less than the total Project cost, the Recipient shall notify EDA immediately to determine relevant procedures.

(b) *Overrun.* (1) In the case of an overrun at the construction contract bid opening, the Recipient may:

(i) If provided for in the bid documents, take deductive alternatives to eliminate certain Project elements in case of insufficient funds in the exact order shown on the invitation for bid until at least one of the responsive bids, less deductive alternative(s), results in a price within the budget for that item of work;

(ii) Reject all bids and re-advertise if there is a rational basis to expect that re-advertising will result in a lower bid; or

(iii) Augment the Matching Share by an amount sufficient to cover the excess cost. The Recipient must furnish a letter to EDA identifying the source of the additional funds and confirming that the Matching Share meets the requirements of § 301.5 of this chapter.

(2) If the Recipient demonstrates to EDA's satisfaction that the options listed in paragraph (b)(1) of this section are not feasible and the Project cannot be completed otherwise, the Recipient may submit a written request to EDA for additional funding in accordance with applicable EDA guidance. The award of additional Investment Assistance is at EDA's sole discretion and will be considered in accord with EDA's competitive process requirements. EDA's consideration of a request for additional Investment Assistance does not indicate approval.

[79 FR 76132, Dec. 19, 2014]

§ 305.11 Contract awards; early construction start.

EDA must determine that the award of all contracts necessary for design and construction of the Project facilities is in compliance with the terms and conditions of the Investment award in order for the costs to be eligible for EDA reimbursement. Pending this determination, the Recipient may issue a notice permitting construction under the contract to commence. If construction commences prior to EDA's determination, the Recipient proceeds at its own risk until EDA review and concurrence. The EDA regional office will advise the Recipient of the requirements necessary to obtain EDA's determination.

§ 305.12 Project sign.

The Recipient shall be responsible for the construction, erection and maintenance in good condition throughout the construction period of a sign or signs at a conspicuous place at the Project site indicating that the Federal government is participating in the Project. The EDA regional office will provide mandatory specifications for the signage.

§ 305.13 Contract change orders.

(a) If it becomes necessary to alter the construction contracts post-execution, the Recipient and contractor shall agree to a formal contract change order.

(b) All contract change orders must receive EDA review for compliance with the terms and conditions of the Investment award, even if the Recipient is to pay for all additional costs resulting from the change or the change order reduces the contract price.

(c) Work on the Project may continue pending EDA review of the contract change order, but all such work will be at the Recipient's risk until EDA completes its review.

§ 305.14 Occupancy prior to completion.

Occupancy of any part of the Project prior to final acceptance is entirely at the Recipient's risk and must follow the requirements of local and State law.

PART 306—TRAINING, RESEARCH AND TECHNICAL ASSISTANCE INVESTMENTS

Subpart A—Local and National Technical Assistance

AUTHORITY: 42 U.S.C. 3147; 42 U.S.C. 3196; 42 U.S.C. 3211; Department of Commerce Organization Order 10–4.

SOURCE: 71 FR 56675, Sept. 27, 2006, unless otherwise noted.

Subpart A—Local and National Technical Assistance

§ 306.1 Purpose and scope.

(a) Local and National Technical Assistance Investments may be awarded to:

(1) Determine the causes of excessive unemployment, underemployment, low per capita income, outmigration or other problems throughout the nation;

(2) Formulate and implement economic development tools, models, and innovative techniques that will alleviate or prevent conditions of excessive unemployment or underemployment;

(3) Formulate and implement economic development programs to increase local, regional and national capacity;

(4) Evaluate the effectiveness and economic impact of programs, projects and techniques to alleviate economic distress and promote economic development;

(5) Conduct project planning and feasibility studies;

(6) Provide management and operational assistance;

(7) Establish business outreach centers;

(8) Disseminate information about effective programs, projects and techniques that alleviate conditions of economic distress and promote economic development;

(9) Assess, market and establish business clusters and associations; or

(10) Perform other activities determined by EDA to be appropriate under the Local and National Technical Assistance program.

(b) Investment Assistance may not be used to start or expand a private business.

(c) EDA may identify specific training, research or technical assistance Projects it will fund, which will be subject to competition. Ordinarily, these Projects are specified in an FFO, which will provide the specific requirements, timelines and the appropriate points of contact and addresses.

(d) In providing Local and National Technical Assistance under this subpart, EDA, in addition to making Investments, may:

(1) Provide Local and National Technical Assistance through officers or employees of the Department;

(2) Pay funds made available to carry out this subpart to Federal Agencies; or

(3) Employ private individuals, partnerships, businesses, corporations, or appropriate institutions under contracts entered into for this purpose.

[71 FR 56675, Sept. 27, 2006, as amended at 79 FR 76132, Dec. 19, 2014]

§ 306.2 Award requirements.

EDA selects Projects for Local and National Technical Assistance Investments in accordance with the general evaluation and selection criteria set forth in part 301 of this chapter and the extent to which the Project:

(a) Strengthens the capacity of local, State or national organizations and institutions to undertake and promote effective economic development programs targeted to Regions of distress;

(b) Benefits distressed Regions;

(c) Demonstrates innovative approaches to stimulate economic development in distressed Regions;

(d) Is consistent with an EDA-approved CEDS, as applicable, for the Region in which the Project is located; and

(e) Meets the criteria outlined in the applicable FFO.

§ 306.3 Application requirements.

(a) EDA will provide Investment Assistance under this subpart for the period of time required to complete the Project's scope of work, generally not to exceed 12 to 18 months.

(b) For a Project of significant Regional or national scope, EDA may waive the requirement set forth in § 301.2(b) of this chapter that the nonprofit organization act in cooperation with officials of a political subdivision of a State.

(c) The Investment Rate for Investments under this subpart shall be determined in accordance with § 301.4(b)(4) of this chapter.

[71 FR 56675, Sept. 27, 2006, as amended at 79 FR 76132, Dec. 19, 2014]

Subpart B—University Center Economic Development Program

§ 306.4 Purpose and scope.

The University Center Economic Development Program is intended to help improve the economies of distressed Regions. Institutions of higher education have many assets, such as faculty, staff, libraries, laboratories, and computer systems that can address local economic problems and opportunities. With Investment Assistance, institutions of higher education establish and operate research centers (*"University Centers"*) that provide technical assistance to public and private sector organizations with the goal of enhancing local economic development.

[79 FR 76132, Dec. 19, 2014]

§ 306.5 Award requirements.

EDA provides Investment Assistance to University Center Projects in accordance with the general evaluation and selection criteria set forth in part 301 of this chapter, the competitive selection process outlined in the applicable FFO, and the extent to which the Project:

(a) Addresses the economic development needs, issues and opportunities of the Region and will benefit distressed areas in the Region;

(b) Provides service and value that are unique and will maximize coordination with other organizations in the Region;

(c) Has the commitment and support (both financial and non-financial) of the highest management levels of the sponsoring institution;

(d) Outlines activities consistent with the expertise of the proposed staff, academic programs and other resources available within the sponsoring institution; and

(e) Documents past experience of the sponsoring institution in operating technical assistance programs.

§ 306.6 Application requirements.

(a) EDA will provide Investment Assistance under this subpart for the period of time required to complete the Project's scope of work, as specifically outlined in the applicable FFO.

(b) For a Project of significant Regional or national scope, EDA may waive the requirement set forth in § 301.2(b) of this chapter that the nonprofit organization act in cooperation with officials of a political subdivision of a State.

(c) The Investment Rate for Investments under this subpart shall be determined in accordance with § 301.4(b)(4) of this chapter.

(d) At least 80 percent of EDA funding must be allocated to direct costs of program delivery.

[71 FR 56675, Sept. 27, 2006, as amended at 79 FR 76132, Dec. 19, 2014]

§ 306.7 Performance evaluations of University Centers.

(a) EDA will:

(1) Evaluate each University Center within three years after the initial Investment award and at least once every three years thereafter, so long as such University Center continues to receive Investment Assistance; and

(2) Assess the University Center's contribution to providing technical assistance, conducting applied research, meeting program performance objectives (as evidenced by retention and creation of employment opportunities) and disseminating Project results in accordance with the scope of work funded during the evaluation period.

(b) The performance evaluation will determine in part whether a University Center can compete to receive Investment Assistance under the University Center Economic Development Program for the following Investment Assistance cycle.

(c) For peer review, EDA shall ensure the participation of at least one other University Center in the performance evaluation on a cost-reimbursement basis.

[71 FR 56675, Sept. 27, 2006, as amended at 79 FR 76132, Dec. 19, 2014]

PART 307—ECONOMIC ADJUSTMENT ASSISTANCE INVESTMENTS

Subpart A—General

Sec.

Subpart B—Revolving Loan Fund Program

AUTHORITY: 42 U.S.C. 3211; 42 U.S.C. 3149; 42 U.S.C. 3161; 42 U.S.C. 3162; 42 U.S.C. 3233; Department of Commerce Organization Order 10–4.

SOURCE: 71 FR 56675, Sept. 27, 2006, unless otherwise noted.

Subpart A—General

§ 307.1 Purpose.

The purpose of Economic Adjustment Assistance Investments is to address the needs of communities experiencing adverse economic changes that may occur suddenly or over time, including those caused by:

(a) Military base closures or realignments, defense contractor reductions in force, or U.S. Department of Energy defense-related funding reductions;

(b) Federally Declared Disaster;

(c) International trade;

(d) Long-term economic deterioration;

(e) Loss of a major community employer; or

(f) Loss of manufacturing jobs.

[71 FR 56675, Sept. 27, 2006, as amended at 79 FR 76132, Dec. 19, 2014]

§ 307.2 Criteria for Economic Adjustment Assistance Investments.

(a) Economic Adjustment Assistance Investments are intended to enhance a distressed community's ability to compete economically by stimulating private investment in targeted economic sectors through use of tools that:

(1) Help develop and implement a CEDS;

(2) Expand the capacity of public officials and economic development organizations to work effectively with businesses;

(3) Assist in overcoming major obstacles identified in the CEDS;

(4) Enable communities to plan and coordinate the use of Federal resources and other resources available to support economic recovery, development of Regional economies, or recovery from natural or other disasters; or

(5) Encourage the development of innovative public and private approaches to economic restructuring and revitalization.

(b) Economic Adjustment Assistance Investments may be made when the Project funded by the Investment will help the Region meet a Special Need. The Region in which a Project is located must have a CEDS with which the Project is consistent (except that this requirement shall not apply to Strategy Grants described in § 307.3).

§ 307.3 Use of Economic Adjustment Assistance Investments.

Economic Adjustment Assistance Investments may be used to develop a CEDS to alleviate long-term economic deterioration or a sudden and severe economic dislocation (a *"Strategy Grant"*), or to fund a Project implementing such a CEDS (an *"Implementation Grant"*).

(a) Strategy Grants support developing, updating or refining a CEDS.

(b) Implementation Grants support the execution of activities identified in a CEDS. Specific activities may be funded as separate Investments or as multiple elements of a single Investment. Examples of Implementation Grant activities include:

(1) Infrastructure (as defined in § 301.11 of this chapter) improvements, such as site acquisition, site preparation, construction, rehabilitation and equipping of facilities;

(2) Provision of business or infrastructure financing through the capitalization of Recipient-administered Revolving Loan Funds (*"RLFs"*), which may include loans and interest rate buy-downs to facilitate business lending activities;

(3) Market or industry research and analysis;

(4) Technical assistance, including organizational development such as business networking, restructuring or improving the delivery of business services, or feasibility studies;

(5) Public services;

(6) Training; and

(7) Other activities justified by the CEDS that satisfy applicable statutory and regulatory requirements.

[71 FR 56675, Sept. 27, 2006, as amended at 79 FR 76132, Dec. 19, 2014]

§ 307.4 Award requirements.

(a) *General.* EDA will select Economic Adjustment Assistance Projects in accordance with part 301 of this chapter and the additional criteria provided in paragraphs (b), (c), and (d) of this section, as applicable. Funding priority considerations for Economic Adjustment Assistance, including RLF Grants, may be set forth in an FFO.

(b) *Strategy Grants.* EDA will review Strategy Grant applications to ensure that the proposed activities conform to the CEDS requirements set forth in § 303.7 of this chapter. Strategy Grants shall comply with the applicable provisions of part 303 of this chapter.

(c) *Implementation Grants.* (1) EDA will review Implementation Grant applications for the extent to which the:

(i) Applicable CEDS meets the requirements in § 303.7 of this chapter; and

(ii) Proposed Project is identified as a necessary element of or consistent with the applicable CEDS.

(2) Implementation Grants involving construction shall comply with the provisions of subpart B of part 305 of this chapter.

(3) Implementation Grants that do not involve construction shall comply with the applicable provisions of subpart A of part 306 of this chapter.

(d) *See* § 307.7 for RLF award requirements.

[71 FR 56675, Sept. 27, 2006, as amended at 75 FR 4264, Jan. 27, 2010; 79 FR 76132, Dec. 19, 2014]

§ 307.5 Application requirements.

(a) Each application for Economic Adjustment Assistance must:

(1) Include or incorporate by reference (if so approved by EDA) a CEDS, except that a CEDS is not required when applying for a Strategy Grant; and

(2) Explain how the proposed Project meets the criteria set forth in § 307.2.

(b) For a technical assistance Project of significant Regional or national scope under this subpart, EDA may waive the requirement set forth in § 301.2(b) of this chapter that the nonprofit organization act in cooperation with officials of a political subdivision of a State.

Subpart B—Revolving Loan Fund Program

§ 307.6 Revolving Loan Funds established for lending.

Economic Adjustment Assistance Grants to capitalize or recapitalize RLFs most commonly fund business lending, but also may fund public infrastructure or other authorized lending activities. The requirements in this subpart apply to EDA-funded RLFs. Special award conditions may contain appropriate modifications of these requirements.

[82 FR 57054, Dec. 1, 2017]

§ 307.7 Revolving Loan Fund award requirements.

(a) For Eligible Applicants seeking to capitalize or recapitalize an RLF, EDA will review applications for the following, as applicable:

(1) Need for a new or expanded public financing tool to:

(i) Enhance other business assistance programs and services targeting economic sectors and locations described in the CEDS; or

(ii) Provide appropriate support for post-disaster economic recovery efforts in Presidentially Declared Disaster areas;

(2) Types of financing activities anticipated; and

(3) Capacity of the RLF organization to manage lending activities, create networks between the business community and other financial providers, and implement the CEDS.

(b) RLF Grants shall comply with the requirements set forth in this part, as well as relevant provisions of parts 300 through 303, 305, and 314 of this chapter and in the following publications:

(1) EDA's RLF Standard Terms and Conditions; and

(2) The Compliance Supplement, which is appendix XI to 2 CFR part 200 and is available on the OMB Web site at *https://www.whitehouse.gov/omb/circulars_default.*

[79 FR 76133, Dec. 19, 2014, as amended at 82 FR 57055, Dec. 1, 2017]

§ 307.8 Definitions.

In addition to the defined terms set forth in § 300.3 of this chapter, the following terms used in this part shall have the following meanings:

Allowable Cash Percentage means the average percentage of the RLF Capital Base maintained as RLF Cash Available for Lending by RLF Recipients in each EDA regional office's portfolio of RLF Grants over the previous year.

Closed Loan means any loan for which all required documentation has been received, reviewed and executed by an RLF Recipient.

Disbursement Phase means the period of loan activity where Grant funds awarded have not been fully disbursed to the RLF Recipient.

Exempt Security means a Security that is not subject to certain SEC or Federal Reserve Board rules.

Prudent Lending Practices means generally accepted underwriting and lending practices for public loan programs, based on sound judgment to protect Federal and lender interests. Prudent Lending Practices include loan processing, documentation, loan approval, collections, servicing, administrative procedures, collateral protection and recovery actions. Prudent Lending Practices provide for compliance with local laws and filing requirements to perfect and maintain a security interest in RLF collateral.

Recapitalization Grants are Investments of additional Grant funds to increase the RLF Capital Base.

Reporting Period, for purposes of this subpart only, is based on the RLF Recipient's fiscal year end and is on an annual or semi-annual basis as determined by EDA.

Revolving Phase means that stage of the RLF's business lending activities that commences immediately after all Grant funds have been disbursed to the RLF Recipient.

Risk Analysis System refers to a set of measures defined by EDA to evaluate a Recipient's administration of its RLF Grant and that may include but is not limited to capital, assets, management, earnings, liquidity, strategic results, and financial controls.

RLF Capital Base means the total value of RLF Grant assets administered by the RLF Recipient. It is equal to the amount of Grant funds used to capitalize (and recapitalize, if applicable), the RLF, plus Local Share, plus RLF Income less any eligible and reasonable administrative expenses, plus Voluntarily Contributed Capital, less any loan losses and disallowances. Except as used to pay for eligible and reasonable administrative costs associated with the RLF's operations, the RLF Capital Base is maintained in two forms at all times: As RLF Cash Available for Lending and as outstanding loan principal.

RLF Cash Available for Lending means the portion of the RLF Capital Base that is held as cash and available to make loans. This excludes loans that have been committed or approved but have not yet been funded.

RLF Income means interest earned on outstanding loan principal and RLF accounts holding RLF funds, all fees and charges received by the RLF, and other income generated from RLF operations. An RLF Recipient may use RLF Income only to capitalize the RLF for financing activities and to cover eligible and reasonable costs necessary to administer the RLF, unless otherwise provided for in the Grant agreement or approved in writing by EDA. RLF Income excludes repayments of principal and any interest remitted to the U.S. Treasury pursuant to generally accepted accounting principles (GAAP) and § 307.20(h).

RLF Recipient means the Eligible Recipient that receives an RLF Grant to manage an RLF in accordance with an RLF Plan, Prudent Lending Practices, the terms and conditions of the RLF Grant, and all applicable policies, laws, and regulations.

RLF Third Party, for purposes of this subpart B only, means an Eligible Recipient or for-profit entity selected by EDA through a request for applications or Cooperative Agreement to facilitate or manage the intended liquidation of an RLF.

Sale means an EDA-approved sale by an RLF Recipient of its RLF loan portfolio (or a portion thereof) to a third party. A third party may participate in a subsequent Securitization offered in a secondary market transaction and collateralized by the underlying RLF loan portfolio (or a portion thereof).

SEC or the *Commission* means the U.S. Securities and Exchange Commission.

Securitization refers to the financing technique of securing an investment of new capital with a stream of income generated by aggregating similar instruments such as loans or mortgages into a new transferable Security.

Security means any investment instrument issued by a corporation, government or other organization which offers evidence of debt or equity.

Voluntary Contributed Capital means an RLF Recipient's voluntary infusion of additional non-EDA funds into the RLF Capital Base that is separate from and exceeds any Local Share that is required as a condition of the RLF Grant. Voluntary Contributed Capital is an irrevocable addition to the RLF Capital Base and must be administered in accordance with EDA regulations and policies.

[71 FR 56675, Sept. 27, 2006, as amended at 73 FR 62867, Oct. 22, 2008; 75 FR 4264, Jan. 27, 2010; 82 FR 57055, Dec. 1, 2017]

§ 307.9 Revolving Loan Fund Plan.

All RLF Recipients shall manage RLFs in accordance with an RLF plan (the "*RLF Plan*" or "*Plan*") as described in this section. The Plan shall be submitted in electronic format to EDA for approval, unless EDA approves a paper submission.

(a) *Format and content.* (1) Part I of the Plan titled "Revolving Loan Fund Strategy" shall summarize the Region's CEDS or EDA-approved economic development plan, if applicable, and business development objectives, and shall describe the RLF's financing strategy, policy and portfolio standards.

(2) Part II of the Plan titled "Operational Procedures" must serve as the RLF Recipient's internal operating manual and set out administrative procedures for operating the RLF consistent with "Prudent Lending Practices," as defined in § 307.8, the RLF Recipient's environmental review and compliance procedures as set out in § 307.10, and EDA's conflicts of interest rules set out in § 302.17 of this chapter.

(b) *Evaluation of RLF Plans.* EDA will use the following criteria in evaluating Plans:

(1) The Plan must be consistent with the CEDS or EDA-approved economic development plan, if applicable, for the Region.

(2) The Plan must identify the strategic purpose of the RLF and must describe the selection of the financing strategy and lending criteria, including:

(i) An analysis of the local capital market and the financing needs of the targeted businesses; and

(ii) Financing policies and portfolio standards that are consistent with EDA's policies and requirements; and

(3) The Plan must demonstrate an adequate understanding of commercial loan portfolio management procedures,

including loan processing, underwriting, closing, disbursements, collections, monitoring, and foreclosures. It also shall provide sufficient administrative procedures to prevent conflicts of interest and to ensure accountability, safeguarding of assets and compliance with Federal and local laws.

(c) *Revision and Modification of RLF Plans.* (1) An RLF Recipient must update its Plan as necessary in accordance with changing economic conditions in the Region; however, at a minimum, an RLF Recipient must submit an updated Plan to EDA every five years.

(2) An RLF Recipient must notify EDA of any change(s) to its Plan. Any material modification, such as a merger, consolidation, or change in the EDA-approved lending area under § 307.18, a change in critical management staff, or a change to the strategic purpose of the RLF, must be submitted to EDA for approval prior to any revision of the Plan. If EDA approves the modification, the RLF Recipient must submit an updated Plan to EDA in electronic format, unless EDA approves a paper submission.

[71 FR 56675, Sept. 27, 2006, as amended at 73 FR 62867, Oct. 22, 2008; 75 FR 4264, Jan. 27, 2010; 79 FR 76133, Dec. 19, 2014]

§ 307.10 Pre-loan requirements.

(a) RLF Recipients must adopt procedures to review the impacts of prospective loan proposals on the physical environment. The Plan must provide for compliance with applicable environmental laws and other regulations, including parts 302 and 314 of this chapter. The RLF Recipient also must adopt procedures to comply, and ensure that potential borrowers comply, with applicable environmental laws and regulations.

(b) RLF Recipients must ensure that prospective borrowers, consultants, or contractors are aware of and comply with the Federal statutory and regulatory requirements that apply to activities carried out with RLF loans. Accordingly, RLF loan agreements shall include applicable Federal requirements to ensure compliance and RLF Recipients must adopt procedures to diligently correct instances of noncompliance, including loan call stipulations.

(c) All RLF loan documents and procedures must protect and hold the Federal government harmless from and against all liabilities that the Federal government may incur as a result of providing an RLF Grant to assist directly or indirectly in site preparation or construction, as well as the direct or indirect renovation or repair of any facility or site. These protections apply to the extent that the Federal government may become potentially liable as a result of ground water, surface, soil or other natural or man-made conditions on the property caused by operations of the RLF Recipient or any of its borrowers, predecessors or successors.

[71 FR 56675, Sept. 27, 2006, as amended at 79 FR 76133, Dec. 19, 2014]

§ 307.11 Pre-disbursement requirements and disbursement of funds to Revolving Loan Funds.

(a) *Pre-disbursement requirements.* (1) Within 60 calendar days before the initial disbursement of EDA funds, the RLF Recipient must provide the following in a form acceptable to EDA:

(i) Certification from the RLF Recipient that the Recipient's accounting system is adequate to identify, safeguard, and account for the entire RLF Capital Base, outstanding RLF loans, and other RLF operations.

(ii) The RLF Recipient's certification that standard RLF loan documents reasonably necessary or advisable for lending are in place and a certification from the RLF Recipient's legal counsel that the loan documents are adequate and comply with the terms and conditions of the RLF Grant, RLF Plan, and applicable State and local law. The standard loan documents must include, at a minimum, the following:

(A) Loan application;

(B) Loan agreement;

(C) Board of directors' meeting minutes approving the RLF loan;

(D) Promissory note;

(E) Security agreement(s);

(F) Deed of trust or mortgage (as applicable);

(G) Agreement of prior lien holder (as applicable); and

(H) Evidence demonstrating that credit is not otherwise available on terms and conditions that permit the completion or successful operation of the activity to be financed.

(iii) Evidence of fidelity bond coverage for persons authorized to handle funds under the RLF Grant award in an amount sufficient to protect the interests of EDA and the RLF. At a minimum, the amount of coverage shall be the maximum loan amount allowed for in the EDA-approved RLF Plan.

(2) The RLF Recipient is required to maintain the adequacy of the RLF's accounting system and maintain and update standard RLF loan documents at all times during the duration of the RLF's operation. In addition, the RLF recipient must maintain sufficient fidelity bond coverage as described in this subsection for the duration of the RLF's operation. The RLF Recipient shall maintain records and documentation to demonstrate the requirements set out in this paragraph (a) are maintained for the duration of the RLF's operation. *See also* § 307.13(b)(3).

(b) *Timing of request for disbursements.* An RLF Recipient shall request disbursements of Grant funds only to close a loan or disburse RLF funds to a borrower. The RLF Recipient must disburse the RLF funds to a borrower within 30 days of receipt of the Grant funds. Any Grant funds not disbursed within the 30 day period shall be refunded to EDA pursuant to paragraph (e) of this section.

(c) *Amount of disbursement.* The amount of a disbursement of Grant funds shall be the amount required to meet the Federal share requirement of a new RLF loan. RLF Income held during the disbursement phase may be used to reimburse eligible administrative costs. RLF Income earned and principal repaid during the Disbursement Phase must be placed in the RLF Capital Base and may be used to reimburse eligible and reasonable administrative costs, provide the requirements of § 307.12(a) and (b) are met, and increase the RLF Capital Base. RLF Income earned and principal repaid during the Disbursement Phase is not required to be used for new RLF loans, unless otherwise specified in the terms and conditions of an RLF Grant.

(d) *Interest-bearing account.* All Grant funds disbursed by EDA to the RLF Recipient for loan obligations incurred but not yet disbursed to an eligible RLF borrower must be deposited and held in an interest-bearing account by the Recipient until an RLF loan is made to a borrower.

(e) *Delays.* If the RLF Recipient receives Grant funds and the RLF loan disbursement is subsequently delayed beyond 30 days, the RLF Recipient must notify the applicable grants officer and return such non-disbursed funds to EDA. Grant funds returned to EDA shall be available to the RLF Recipient for future draw-downs. When returning prematurely drawn Grant funds, the RLF Recipient must clearly identify on the face of the check or in the written notification to the applicable grants officer "EDA," the Grant award number, the words "Premature Draw," and a brief description of the reason for returning the Grant funds.

(f) *Local Share.* (1) Cash Local Share of the RLF may only be used for lending purposes. The cash Local Share must be used either in proportion to the Grant funds or at a faster rate than the Grant funds.

(2) When an RLF has a combination of In-Kind Contributions, which must be specifically authorized in the terms and conditions of the RLF Grant and may be used to provide technical assistance to borrowers or for eligible RLF administrative costs, and cash Local Share, the cash Local Share and the Grant funds will be disbursed proportionately as needed for lending activities, provided that the last 20 percent of the Grant funds may not be disbursed until all cash Local Share has been expended. The full amount of the cash Local Share shall remain for use in the RLF.

(g) *Loan closing and disbursement schedule.* (1) RLF loan activity must be sufficient to draw down Grant funds in accordance with the schedule prescribed in the award conditions for loan closings and disbursements to eligible RLF borrowers. The schedule usually requires that the RLF Recipient lend the entire amount of the RLF Grant within three years of the Grant award.

(2) If an RLF Recipient fails to meet the prescribed lending schedule, EDA may de-obligate the non-disbursed balance of the RLF Grant. EDA may allow exceptions where:

(i) Closed Loans approved prior to the schedule deadline will commence and complete disbursements within 45 days of the deadline;

(ii) Closed Loans have commenced (but not completed) disbursement obligations prior to the deadline; or

(iii) EDA has approved a time schedule extension pursuant to paragraph (h) of this section.

(h) *Time schedule extensions.* (1) RLF Recipients shall promptly inform EDA in writing of any condition that may adversely affect their ability to meet the prescribed schedule deadlines. RLF Recipients must submit a written request to EDA for continued use of Grant funds beyond a missed deadline for disbursement of RLF funds. RLF Recipients must provide good reason for the delay in their extension request by demonstrating that:

(i) The delay was unforeseen or beyond the control of the RLF Recipient;

(ii) The financial need for the RLF still exists;

(iii) The current and planned use and the anticipated benefits of the RLF will remain consistent with the current CEDS and the RLF Plan; and

(iv) The proposal of a revised time schedule is reasonable. An extension request must also provide an explanation as to why no further delays are anticipated.

(2) EDA is under no obligation to grant a time extension. In the event an extension is denied, EDA may de-obligate all or part of the unused Grant funds and terminate the Grant.

[71 FR 56675, Sept. 27, 2006, as amended at 75 FR 4264, Jan. 27, 2010; 79 FR 76133, Dec. 19, 2014; 82 FR 57055, Dec. 1, 2017]

§ 307.12 Revolving Loan Fund Income requirements during the Revolving Phase; payments on defaulted and written off Revolving Loan Fund loans; Voluntarily Contributed Capital.

(a) *Revolving Loan Fund Income requirements during the Revolving Phase.* During the Revolving Phase, RLF Income must be placed into the RLF Capital Base for the purpose of making loans or paying for eligible and reasonable administrative costs associated with the RLF's operations. RLF Income may fund administrative costs, provided:

(1) Such RLF Income is earned and the administrative costs are accrued in the same fiscal year of the RLF Recipient;

(2) RLF Income earned, but not used for administrative costs during the same fiscal year of the RLF Recipient is made available for lending activities;

(3) RLF Income shall not be withdrawn from the RLF Capital Base in a subsequent fiscal year for any purpose other than lending without the prior written consent of EDA; and

(4) An RLF Recipient shall not use funds in excess of RLF Income for administrative costs unless directed otherwise in writing by EDA. In accordance with EDA's RLF Risk Analysis System, RLF Recipients are expected to keep administrative costs to a minimum in order to maintain the RLF Capital Base. The percentage of RLF Income used for administrative expenses will be one of the measures used in EDA's RLF Risk Analysis System to evaluate RLF Recipients. *See also* § 307.16.

(b) *Compliance guidance.* When charging costs against RLF Income, RLF Recipients must comply with applicable Federal uniform administrative requirements, cost principles, and audit requirements as detailed in this paragraph (b) and in the terms and conditions of the RLF Grant.

(1) *For RLF Grants made on or after December 26, 2014.* For RLFs awarded on or after December 26, 2014 or for RLFs that have received one or more Recapitalization Grants on or after December 26, 2014, the RLF Recipient must comply with the administrative and cost principles in 2 CFR part 200 ("Uniform Administrative Requirements, Cost Principles, and Audit Requirements for Federal Awards").

(2) *For RLF Grants made before December 26, 2014.* For RLFs awarded before December 26, 2014, unless otherwise indicated in the terms of the Grant, the RLF Recipient must comply with the following cost principles:

(i) 2 CFR part 225 (OMB Circular A–87 for State, local, and Indian tribal governments),

(ii) 2 CFR part 230 (OMB Circular A–122 for non-profit organizations other than institutions of higher education, hospitals or organizations named in OMB Circular A–122 as not subject to such Circular), and

(iii) 2 CFR part 220 (OMB Circular A–21 for educational institutions).

(3) *For all RLF Grants.* For all RLF Grants, regardless of when they were awarded, the audit requirements set out as subpart F to 2 CFR part 200 apply to audits of the RLF Recipient's fiscal years beginning on or after December 26, 2014. In addition, the Compliance Supplement, which is appendix XI to 2 CFR part 200, applies as appropriate.

(c) *Priority of payments on defaulted and written off RLF loans.* When an RLF Recipient receives proceeds on a defaulted or written off RLF loan that is not subject to liquidation pursuant to § 307.21, such proceeds shall be applied in the following order of priority:

(1) *First,* towards any costs of collection;

(2) *Second,* towards outstanding penalties and fees;

(3) *Third,* towards any accrued interest to the extent due and payable; and

(4) *Fourth,* towards any outstanding principal balance.

(d) *Voluntarily Contributed Capital.* An RLF Recipient that wishes to inject additional capital into the RLF Capital Base to augment the amount of resources available to lend must submit a written request that specifies the source of the funds to be added. Once an RLF Recipient elects to commit Voluntarily Contributed Capital and upon approval by EDA, the Voluntarily Contributed Capital becomes an irrevocable part of the RLF Capital Base and may not be subsequently withdrawn or separated from the RLF.

[71 FR 56675, Sept. 27, 2006, as amended at 73 FR 62867, Oct. 22, 2008; 79 FR 76134, Dec. 19, 2014; 82 FR 57056, Dec. 1, 2017]

§ 307.13 Records and retention.

(a) *Closed Loan files and related documents.* The RLF Recipient shall maintain Closed Loan files and all related documents, books of account, computer data files and other records over the term of the Closed Loan and for a three-year period from the date of final disposition of such Closed Loan. The date of final disposition of a Closed Loan is the date:

(1) Principal, interest, fees, penalties and all other costs associated with the Closed Loan have been paid in full; or

(2) Final settlement or discharge and cessation of collection efforts of any unpaid amounts associated with the Closed Loan have occurred.

(b) *Administrative records.* RLF Recipients must at all times:

(1) Maintain adequate accounting records and source documentation to substantiate the amount and percent of RLF Income expended for eligible RLF administrative costs.

(2) Retain records of administrative expenses incurred for activities and equipment relating to the operation of the RLF for three years from the actual submission date of the report that covers the fiscal year in which such costs were claimed.

(3) Consistent with § 307.11(a), for the duration of RLF operations, maintain records to demonstrate:

(i) The adequacy of the RLF's accounting system to identify, safeguard, and account for the entire RLF Capital Base, outstanding RLF loans, and other RLF operations;

(ii) That standard RLF loan documents reasonably necessary or advisable for lending are in place; and

(iii) Evidence of fidelity bond coverage for persons authorized to handle funds under the Grant award in an amount sufficient to protect the interests of EDA and the RLF.

(4) Make available for inspection retained records, including those retained for longer than the required period. The record retention periods described in this section are minimum periods and such prescription does not limit any other record retention requirement of law or agreement. In no event will EDA question claimed administrative costs that are more than three years old, unless fraud is at issue.

[71 FR 56675, Sept. 27, 2006, as amended at 73 FR 62867, Oct. 22, 2008; 79 FR 76134, Dec. 19, 2014; 82 FR 57057, Dec. 1, 2017]

§ 307.14 Revolving Loan Fund report.

(a) *Frequency of reports.* All RLF Recipients, including those receiving Recapitalization Grants for existing RLFs, must complete and submit an RLF report, using Form ED–209, in a format and at a frequency as required by EDA.

(b) *Report contents.* RLF Recipients must certify as part of the RLF report to EDA that the RLF is operating in accordance with the applicable RLF Plan and that the information provided is complete and accurate.

[82 FR 57057, Dec. 1, 2017]

§ 307.15 Prudent management of Revolving Loan Funds.

(a) *Accounting principles.* (1) RLFs shall operate in accordance with generally accepted accounting principles ("GAAP") as in effect in the United States and the provisions outlined in the audit requirements set out as subpart F to 2 CFR part 200 and the Compliance Supplement, which is appendix XI to 2 CFR part 200, as applicable.

(2) In accordance with GAAP, a loan loss reserve may be recorded in the RLF Recipient's financial statements to show the adjusted current value of an RLF's loan portfolio, provided this loan loss reserve is non-funded and is represented by a non-cash entry. However, loan loss reserves shall not be used to reduce the value of the RLF in the Schedule of Expenditures of Federal Awards ("SEFA") required as part of the RLF Recipient's audit requirements under 2 CFR part 200.

(b) *Interest rates*—(1) *General rule.* An RLF Recipient may make loans to eligible borrowers at interest rates and under conditions determined by the RLF Recipient to be appropriate in achieving the goals of the RLF. The minimum interest rate an RLF Recipient may charge is four percentage points below the lesser of the current money center prime interest rate quoted in the *Wall Street Journal*, or the maximum interest rate allowed under State law. In no event shall the interest rate be less than the lower of four percent or 75 percent of the prime interest rate listed in the *Wall Street Journal.*

(2) *Exception.* Should the prime interest rate listed in the *Wall Street Journal* exceed 14 percent, the minimum RLF interest rate is not required to be raised above 10 percent if doing so compromises the ability of the RLF Recipient to implement its financing strategy.

(c) *RLF leveraging.* (1) RLF loans must leverage additional investment of at least two dollars for every one dollar of such RLF loans. This leveraging requirement applies to the RLF portfolio as a whole rather than to individual loans and is effective for the duration of the RLF's operation. To be classified as leveraged, additional investment must be made within 12 months of approval of an RLF loan, as part of the same business development project, and may include:

(i) Capital invested by the borrower or others;

(ii) Financing from private entities;

(iii) The non-guaranteed portions and 90 percent of the guaranteed portions of any Federal loan; or

(iv) Loans from other State and local lending programs.

(2) Private investments shall not include accrued equity in a borrower's assets.

(d) *RLF certification course.* EDA may establish a mandatory RLF certification program to enhance RLF Recipients' ability to administer RLF Grants in a prudent manner. If so required by EDA, the RLF Recipient must satisfactorily complete this program, and may consider the cost of attending the certification courses as an administrative cost, provided the requirements set forth in § 307.12 are satisfied.

[71 FR 56675, Sept. 27, 2006, as amended at 73 FR 62868, Oct. 22, 2008; 75 FR 4264, Jan. 27, 2010; 79 FR 76134, Dec. 19, 2014; 82 FR 57057, Dec. 1, 2017]

§ 307.16 Risk Analysis System.

(a) EDA shall evaluate and manage RLF recipients using a Risk Analysis System that will focus on such risk factors as: capital, assets, management, earnings, liquidity, strategic results, and financial controls. Risk analysis ratings of each RLF Recipient's RLF program shall be conducted at least annually and will be based on the most recently submitted Form ED–209 RLF report.

(b) An RLF Recipient generally will be allowed a reasonable period of time to achieve compliance with risk factors as defined by EDA. However, persistent noncompliance with these factors and their limits as identified through EDA's Risk Analysis System over multiple Reporting Periods may result in EDA taking appropriate remedies for noncompliance as detailed in § 307.21.

[82 FR 57057, Dec. 1, 2017]

§ 307.17 Requirements for Revolving Loan Fund Cash Available for Lending.

(a) *General.* RLF Cash Available for Lending shall be deposited and held in an interest-bearing account by the Recipient and used for the purpose of making RLF loans that are consistent with an RLF Plan or such other purposes approved by EDA. To ensure that RLF funds are used as intended, each loan agreement must clearly state the purpose of each loan.

(b) *Allowable Cash Percentage.* EDA shall notify each RLF recipient by January 1 of each year of the Allowable Cash Percentage that is applicable to lending during the Recipient's ensuing fiscal year. During the Revolving Phase, RLF Recipients must manage their repayment and lending schedules so that at all times they do not exceed the Allowable Cash Percentage.

(c) *Restrictions on use of RLF Cash Available for Lending.* RLF Cash Available for Lending shall not be used to:

(1) Acquire an equity position in a private business;

(2) Subsidize interest payments on an existing RLF loan;

(3) Provide a loan to a borrower for the purpose of meeting the requirements of equity contributions under another Federal Agency's loan programs;

(4) Enable borrowers to acquire an interest in a business either through the purchase of stock or through the acquisition of assets, unless sufficient justification is provided in the loan documentation. Sufficient justification may include acquiring a business to save it from imminent closure or to acquire a business to facilitate a significant expansion or increase in investment with a significant increase in jobs. The potential economic benefits must be clearly consistent with the strategic objectives of the RLF;

(5) Provide RLF loans to a borrower for the purpose of investing in interest-bearing accounts, certificates of deposit, or any investment unrelated to the RLF; or

(6) Refinance existing debt, unless:

(i) The RLF Recipient sufficiently demonstrates in the loan documentation a "sound economic justification" for the refinancing (*e.g.*, the refinancing will support additional capital investment intended to increase business activities). For this purpose, reducing the risk of loss to an existing lender(s) or lowering the cost of financing to a borrower shall not, without other indicia, constitute a sound economic justification; or

(ii) RLF Cash Available for Lending will finance the purchase of the rights of a prior lien holder during a foreclosure action which is necessary to preclude a significant loss on an RLF loan. RLF funds may be used for this purpose only if there is a high probability of receiving compensation from the sale of assets sufficient to cover an RLF's costs plus a reasonable portion of the outstanding RLF loan within a reasonable time frame approved by EDA following the date of refinancing.

(7) Serve as collateral to obtain credit or any other type of financing without EDA's prior written approval;

(8) Support operations or administration of the RLF Recipient; or

(9) Undertake any activity that would violate the requirements found in part 314 of this chapter, including § 314.3 ("Authorized Use of Property") and § 314.4 ("Unauthorized Use of Property").

[82 FR 57057, Dec. 1, 2017]

§ 307.18 Addition of lending areas; consolidation and merger of RLFs.

(a)(1) An RLF Recipient shall make loans only within its EDA-approved lending area, as set forth and defined in the RLF Grant and the RLF Plan. An RLF Recipient may add a lending area (an "*Additional Lending Area*") to its existing lending area to create a new lending area (the "*New Lending Area*") only with EDA's prior written approval and subject to the following provisions and conditions:

(i) The Additional Lending Area must meet the economic distress criteria for Economic Adjustment Assistance Investments under this part and in accordance with § 301.3(a) of this chapter;

(ii) Prior to EDA's disbursement of additional funds to the RLF Recipient (for example, through a recapitalization), EDA shall determine a new Investment Rate for the New Lending Area based on the criteria set forth in § 301.4 of this chapter;

(iii) The RLF Recipient must demonstrate that the Additional Lending Area is consistent with its CEDS, or modify its CEDS for any such Additional Lending Area, in accordance with § 307.9(b)(1);

(iv) The RLF Recipient shall modify its Plan to incorporate the Additional Lending Area and revise its lending strategy, as necessary;

(v) The RLF Recipient shall execute an amended financial assistance award, as necessary; and

(vi) The RLF Recipient fulfills any other conditions reasonably requested by EDA.

(2) Following EDA approval, the New Lending Area designation shall remain in place until EDA approves a subsequent request for a New Lending Area.

(b) *Consolidation and merger of RLFs*—(1) *Single RLF Recipient.* An RLF Recipient with more than one EDA-funded RLF Grant may consolidate two or more EDA-funded RLFs into one combined RLF with EDA's prior written approval and provided:

(i) It is up-to-date with all reports in accordance with § 307.14;

(ii) It demonstrates a rational basis for undertaking the consolidation (for example, the lending area(s) and borrower criteria identified in different RLF Plans are compatible, or will be compatible, for all RLFs to be consolidated);

(iii) It amends and consolidates its Plan to account for the consolidation of RLFs, including items such as the New Lending Area (including any Additional Lending Area(s)), its lending strategy and borrower criteria;

(iv) Prior to EDA's disbursement of additional funds to the RLF Recipient (for example, through a recapitalization), EDA shall determine a new Investment Rate for the New Lending Area based on the criteria set forth in § 301.4 of this chapter; and

(v) The RLF Recipient fulfills any other conditions reasonably requested by EDA.

(2) *Multiple RLF Recipients.* Two or more RLF Recipients may merge their EDA-funded RLFs into one surviving RLF with EDA's prior written approval and provided:

(i) The replacement RLF Recipient is up-to-date with all reports in accordance with § 307.14;

(ii) The surviving RLF Recipient amends and consolidates its Plan to account for the merger of RLFs, including items such as the New Lending Area (including any Additional Lending Area(s)), its lending strategy and borrower criteria;

(iii) Prior to EDA's disbursement of additional funds to the surviving RLF Recipient (for example, through a recapitalization), EDA shall determine a new Investment Rate for the New Lending Area based on the criteria set forth in § 301.4 of this chapter;

(iv) EDA must provide written approval of the merger agreement(s), modifications and revisions to the Plans and any other related amendments thereto;

(v) All applicable RLF Grant assets of the discharging RLF Recipient(s) transfer to the surviving RLF Recipient as of the merger's effective date; and

(vi) The surviving RLF Recipient becomes fully responsible for administration of the RLF Grant assets transferred and fulfills all surviving RLF Grant requirements and any other conditions reasonably requested by EDA.

[71 FR 56675, Sept. 27, 2006, as amended at 73 FR 62869, Oct. 22, 2008; 79 FR 76135, Dec. 19, 2014; 82 FR 57058, Dec. 1, 2017]

§ 307.19 RLF loan portfolio Sales and Securitizations.

EDA may take such actions as appropriate to enable an RLF Recipient to sell or securitize RLF loans, except that EDA may not issue a Federal guaranty covering any issued Security. With prior approval from EDA, an RLF Recipient may enter into a Sale or a

Securitization of all or a portion of its RLF loan portfolio, provided:

(a) An RLF Recipient must use all proceeds from any Sale or Securitization (net of reasonable transaction costs) to make additional RLF loans;

(b) No Security collateralized by RLF loans and other RLF property and offered in a secondary market transaction pursuant to a Securitization shall be treated as an Exempt Security for purposes of the Securities Act of 1933, as amended (15 U.S.C. 77a *et seq.*), or the Securities Exchange Act of 1934, as amended (15 U.S.C. 78a *et seq.*) (the "*Exchange Act*"), unless exempted by a rule or regulation issued by the Commission; and

(c) Except as provided in paragraph (b), no provision of this section supersedes or otherwise affects the application of the "securities laws" (as such term is defined in section 3(a)(47) of the Exchange Act) or the rules, regulations or orders issued by the Commission or a self-regulatory organization under the Commission.

[71 FR 56675, Sept. 27, 2006, as amended at 79 FR 76135, Dec. 19, 2014]

§307.20 Noncompliance.

EDA will take appropriate compliance actions as detailed in §307.21 for the RLF Recipient's failure to operate the RLF in accordance with the RLF Plan, the terms and conditions of the RLF Grant, or this subpart, including but not limited to:

(a) Failing to obtain prior EDA approval for material changes to the RLF Plan, including provisions for administering the RLF;

(b) Failing to submit an updated RLF Plan to EDA in accordance with §307.9(c);

(c) Failing to submit timely progress, financial, and audit reports in the format required by the RLF Grant and §307.14, including the Form ED–209 RLF report;

(d) Failing to manage the RLF Grant in accordance with Prudent Lending Practices, as defined in §307.8;

(e) Holding RLF Cash Available for Lending so that it is 50 percent or more of the RLF Capital Base for 24 months without an EDA-approved extension request based on other EDA risk analysis factors or other extenuating circumstances;

(f) Making an ineligible loan;

(g) Failing to disburse the EDA funds in accordance with the time schedule prescribed in the RLF Grant;

(h) Failing to sequester funds or remit the interest on EDA's portion of the sequestered funds to the U.S. Treasury, as directed by EDA;

(i) Failing to comply with the audit requirements set forth in subpart F to 2 CFR part 200 and the related Compliance Supplement, including reference to the correctly valued EDA RLF Federal expenditures in the SEFA, timely submission of audit reports to the Federal Audit Clearinghouse, and the inclusion of the RLF program as an appropriately audited program;

(j) Failing to implement timely resolutions to audit findings or questioned costs contained in the annual audit, as applicable;

(k) Failing to comply with an EDA-approved corrective action plan to remedy persistent noncompliance with RLF-related findings;

(l) Failing to comply with the conflicts of interest provisions set forth in §302.17; and

(m) Making unauthorized use of RLF Cash Available for Lending in violation of §307.18(c).

[82 FR 57058, Dec. 1, 2017]

§307.21 Remedies for noncompliance.

(a) *General.* If an RLF Recipient fails to operate the RLF in accordance with the RLF Plan, the terms and conditions of the RLF Grant, or this subpart, as detailed in §307.20, EDA may require one or more of the following actions, as appropriate in the circumstances:

(1) Increased reporting requirements;

(2) Implementation of a corrective action plan;

(3) A special audit;

(4) Sequestration of RLF funds;

(5) Repayment of ineligible loans or other costs to the RLF;

(6) Transfer or merger of the RLF in accordance with §307.18;

(7) Suspension of the RLF Grant; or

(8) Termination of the RLF Grant, in whole or in part.

(b) *Disallowance of a portion of an RLF Grant, liquidation.* If the RLF Recipient engages in certain problematic practices, EDA may disallow a corresponding proportion of the Grant or direct the RLF Recipient to transfer loans to an RLF Third Party for liquidation. Problematic practices for which EDA may disallow a portion of an RLF Grant and recover the pro-rata Federal Share (as defined in § 314.5 of this chapter) include the RLF Recipient:

(1) Holding RLF Cash Available for Lending so that it is 50 percent or more of the RLF Capital Base for 24 months without an EDA-approved extension request;

(2) Failing to disburse the EDA funds in accordance with the time schedule prescribed in the RLF Grant; or

(3) Determining that it does not wish to further invest in the RLF or cannot maintain operations at the degree originally contemplated upon receipt of the RLF Grant and requests that a portion of the RLF Grant be disallowed, and EDA agrees to the disallowance.

(c) *Termination or suspension*. To maintain effective control over and accountability of RLF Grant funds and assets, EDA shall determine the manner and timing of any suspension or termination action. EDA may require the RLF Recipient to repay the Federal Share in a lump-sum payment or enter into a Sale, or EDA may agree to enter into a repayment agreement with the RLF Recipient for repayment of the Federal Share.

(d) *Termination, liquidation upon termination*. When EDA approves the termination of an RLF Grant, EDA must make all efforts to recover the pro rata Federal Share (as defined in § 314.5 of this chapter). EDA may assign or transfer assets of the RLF to an RLF Third Party for liquidation. The following terms will govern any liquidation:

(1) EDA shall have sole discretion in choosing the RLF Third Party;

(2) The RLF Third Party may be an Eligible Applicant or a for-profit organization not otherwise eligible for Investment Assistance;

(3) EDA may enter into an agreement with the RLF Third Party to liquidate the assets of one or more RLFs or RLF Recipients;

(4) EDA may allow the RLF Third Party to retain a portion of the RLF assets, consistent with the agreement referenced in paragraph (d)(3) of this section, as reasonable compensation for services rendered in the liquidation; and

(5) EDA may require additional reasonable terms and conditions.

(e) *Distribution of proceeds*. The proceeds resulting from any liquidation upon termination shall be distributed in the following order of priority:

(1) *First*, for any third party liquidation costs;

(2) *Second*, for the payment of EDA's Federal Share; and

(3) *Third*, if any proceeds remain, to the RLF Recipient.

(f) *RLF Recipient's request to terminate*. EDA may approve a request from an RLF Recipient to terminate an RLF Grant. The RLF Recipient must compensate the Federal Government for the pro rata Federal Share of the RLF Capital Base.

(g) *Distribution of proceeds upon termination*. Upon termination, distribution of proceeds shall occur in accordance with § 307.21(e).

[82 FR 57058, Dec. 1, 2017]

§ 307.22 Variances.

EDA may approve variances to the requirements contained in this subpart, provided such variances:

(a) Are consistent with the goals of the Economic Adjustment Assistance program and with an RLF Plan;

(b) Are necessary and reasonable for the effective implementation of the RLF;

(c) Are economically and financially sound; and

(d) Do not conflict with any applicable legal requirements, including Federal, State and local law.

PART 308—PERFORMANCE INCENTIVES

Sec.

AUTHORITY: 42 U.S.C. 3151; 42 U.S.C. 3154a; 42 U.S.C. 3154b; Department of Commerce Delegation Order 10–4.

SOURCE: 71 FR 56675, Sept. 27, 2006, unless otherwise noted.

§ 308.1 Use of funds in Projects constructed under projected cost.

(a) If the Assistant Secretary determines before closeout of a construction Project funded under parts 305 or 307 of this chapter that the cost of the Project, based on the designs and specifications that were the basis of the Investment Assistance, has decreased because of a decrease in costs, EDA may in its discretion approve the use of the excess funds (or a portion of the excess funds) by the Recipient to:

(1) Increase the Investment Rate of the Project to the maximum percentage allowable under § 301.4 of this chapter for which the Project was eligible at the time of the Investment award; or

(2) Further improve the Project consistent with its purpose.

(b) EDA, in its sole discretion, may use any amount of excess funds remaining after application of paragraph (a) of this section for other eligible Investments.

(c) In the case of Projects involving funds transferred from other Federal Agencies, EDA will consult with the transferring Agency regarding the use of any excess funds.

§ 308.2 Performance awards.

(a) A Recipient of Investment Assistance under parts 305 or 307 of this chapter may receive a performance award in connection with an Investment made on or after the date of enactment of section 215 of PWEDA in an amount not to exceed 10 percent of the amount of the Investment award.

(b) To receive a performance award, a Recipient must demonstrate Project performance in one or more of the areas listed in this paragraph, weighted at the discretion of the Assistant Secretary:

(1) Meet or exceed the Recipient's projection of jobs created;

(2) Meet or exceed the Recipient's projection of private sector capital invested;

(3) Meet or exceed target dates for Project start and completion stated at the time of Investment approval;

(4) Fulfill the application evaluation criteria set forth in § 301.8 of this chapter; or

(5) Demonstrate other unique Project performance characteristics as determined by the Assistant Secretary.

(c) A Recipient may receive a performance award no later than three years following the Project's closeout.

(d) A performance award may fund up to 100 percent of the cost of an eligible Project or any other authorized activity under PWEDA. For the purpose of meeting the non-Federal share requirement of PWEDA or any other statute, the amount of a performance award shall be treated as non-Federal funds.

(e) The applicable FFO will set forth the requirements, qualifications, guidelines and procedures for performance awards to be made during the applicable fiscal year, with all performance awards being subject to the availability of funds.

[71 FR 56675, Sept. 27, 2006, as amended at 75 FR 4265, Jan. 27, 2010; 79 FR 76136, Dec. 19, 2014]

§ 308.3 Planning performance awards.

(a) A Recipient of Investment Assistance awarded on or after the date of enactment of section 216 of PWEDA for a Project located in an EDA-funded Economic Development District may, at the discretion of the Assistant Secretary, receive a planning performance award in an amount not to exceed five percent of the amount of the applicable Investment award if EDA determines before closeout of the Project that:

(1) The Recipient, through the Project, actively participated in the economic development activities of the District;

(2) The Project demonstrated exceptional fulfillment of one or more components of, and is otherwise in accordance with, the applicable CEDS, including any job creation or job retention requirements; and

(3) The Recipient demonstrated exceptional collaboration with Federal, State, and local economic development entities throughout the development of the Project.

(b) The Recipient shall use the planning performance award to increase, up to 100 percent, the Federal share of the cost of a Project under this chapter.

(c) The applicable FFO may set forth additional requirements, qualifications and guidelines for planning performance awards.

[71 FR 56675, Sept. 27, 2006, as amended at 73 FR 62869, Oct. 22, 2008; 79 FR 76136, Dec. 19, 2014]

PART 309—REDISTRIBUTIONS OF INVESTMENT ASSISTANCE

AUTHORITY: 42 U.S.C. 3154c; 42 U.S.C. 3211; Department of Commerce Delegation Order 10–4.

SOURCE: 71 FR 56675, Sept. 27, 2006, unless otherwise noted.

§ 309.1 Redistributions under parts 303, 305 and 306.

(a) *General.* Except as provided in paragraph (b) of this section, a Recipient of Investment Assistance under parts 303, 305 or 306 of this chapter may directly expend such Investment Assistance or, with prior EDA approval, may redistribute such Investment Assistance in the form of a subgrant to another Eligible Recipient, generally referred to as a Subrecipient, that qualifies for Investment Assistance under the same part of this chapter as the Recipient, to fund required components of the scope of work approved for the Project. All subgrants made pursuant to this section shall be subject to the same terms and conditions applicable to the Recipient under the original Investment Assistance award and must satisfy the requirements of PWEDA and of this chapter. EDA may require the Eligible Recipient under the original Investment award to agree to special award conditions and the Subrecipient to provide appropriate certifications to ensure the Subrecipient's compliance with legal requirements.

(b) *Exception.* A Recipient may not make a subgrant of Investment Assistance received under parts 303 or 305 of this chapter to a for-profit entity.

[71 FR 56675, Sept. 27, 2006, as amended at 82 FR 57059, Dec. 1, 2017]

§ 309.2 Redistributions under part 307.

(a) A Recipient of Investment Assistance under part 307 of this chapter may directly expend such Investment Assistance or, with prior EDA approval, may redistribute such Investment Assistance in the form of:

(1) A subgrant to another Eligible Recipient, generally referred to a Subrecipient, that qualifies for Investment Assistance under part 307 of this chapter; or

(2) Pursuant to part 307, subpart B, a loan or other appropriate assistance to non-profit and private for-profit entities.

(b) All redistributions of Investment Assistance made pursuant to this section shall be subject to the same terms and conditions applicable to the Recipient under the original Investment Assistance award and must satisfy the requirements of PWEDA and of this chapter. EDA may require the Eligible Recipient under the original Investment Award to agree to special award conditions and the Subrecipient to provide appropriate certifications to ensure the Subrecipient's compliance with legal requirements.

[71 FR 56675, Sept. 27, 2006, as amended at 82 FR 57059, Dec. 1, 2017]

PART 310—SPECIAL IMPACT AREAS

AUTHORITY: 42 U.S.C. 3154; Department of Commerce Organization Order 10–4.

SOURCE: 71 FR 56675, Sept. 27, 2006, unless otherwise noted.

§ 310.1 Special Impact Area.

Upon the application of an Eligible Applicant, and with respect to that Eligible Applicant's Project only, the Assistant Secretary may designate the Region which the Project will serve as a Special Impact Area if the Eligible Applicant demonstrates that its proposed Project will:

(a) Directly fulfill a pressing need; and

(b) Be useful in alleviating or preventing conditions of excessive unemployment or underemployment, or assist in providing useful employment opportunities for the unemployed or underemployed residents of the Region.

[73 FR 62869, Oct. 22, 2008, as amended at 79 FR 76136, Dec. 19, 2014]

§310.2 Pressing need; alleviation of unemployment or underemployment.

(a) The Assistant Secretary may find a pressing need to exist if the Region which the Project will serve:

(1) Has a unique or urgent circumstance that would necessitate waiver of the CEDS requirements of §303.7 of this chapter;

(2) Involves a Project undertaken by an Indian Tribe;

(3) Is rural and severely distressed;

(4) Is undergoing a transition in its economic base as a result of changing trade patterns (e.g., the Region is certified as eligible by the North American Development Bank Program or the Community Adjustment and Investment Program);

(5) Exhibits a substantial reliance on a natural resource for its economic well-being;

(6) Has been designated as a Federally Declared Disaster area; or

(7) Has a Special Need.

(b) For purposes of this part, excessive unemployment exists if the 24-month unemployment rate is at least 225 percent of the national average or the per capita income is not more than 50 percent of the national average. A Region demonstrates excessive underemployment if the employment of a substantial percentage of workers in the Region is less than full-time or at less skilled tasks than their training or abilities would otherwise permit. Eligible Applicants seeking a Special Impact Area designation under this criterion must present appropriate and compelling economic and demographic data.

(c) Eligible Applicants may demonstrate the provision of useful employment opportunities by quantifying and evidencing the Project's prospective:

(1) Creation of jobs;

(2) Commitment of financial investment by private entities; or

(3) Application of innovative technology that will lead to the creation of jobs or the commitment of financial investment by private entities.

[71 FR 56675, Sept. 27, 2006, as amended at 79 FR 76136, Dec. 19, 2014]

PART 311 [RESERVED]

PART 312—REGIONAL INNOVATION PROGRAM

Subpart A—General Provisions

Subpart B—Regional Innovation Strategies Program

Subpart C—Regional Innovation Research and Information Program [Reserved]

AUTHORITY: 15 U.S.C. 3701 *et seq.;* Department of Commerce Organization Order 10–4.

SOURCE: 82 FR 3134, Jan. 11, 2017, unless otherwise noted.

Subpart A—General Provisions

§312.1 Purpose and scope of the Regional Innovation Program.

The purpose of the Regional Innovation Program is to encourage and support the development of regional innovation strategies. The Regional Innovation Program includes two sub-programs. One is focused on the formation and development of regional innovation clusters and implemented through the Regional Innovation Strategies Program. 15 U.S.C. 3722(b). The second program is focused on best practices, metrics and the collection and dissemination of information related to regional innovation strategies, achieved through the Regional Innovation Research and Information Program. 15 U.S.C. 3722(c). The Secretary has delegated to the Economic Development Administration the authority to implement and administer the Regional Innovation Program.

§ 312.2 General definitions from Public Works and Economic Development Act regulations inapplicable to this part.

The definitions contained in § 300.3 of this chapter do not apply to this part.

§ 312.3 General definitions.

As used in this part, the following terms shall have the following meanings:

Act or *Stevenson-Wydler* means the Stevenson-Wydler Technology Innovation Act of 1980, as amended (15 U.S.C. 3701 *et seq.*).

Assistant Secretary means the Assistant Secretary of Commerce for Economic Development within the Department.

Department of Commerce, Department, or *DOC* means the U.S. Department of Commerce.

Economic Development Organization means an organization whose primary purpose is to support the economic development of a community or region.

EDA means the Economic Development Administration within the Department.

Eligible applicant means an entity qualified to be an eligible recipient or its authorized representative.

Eligible recipient means a recipient that meets the requirements of § 312.6.

Equipment is defined at 2 CFR 200.33.

Federal agency means any executive agency as defined in 5 U.S.C. 105, and the military departments as defined in 5 U.S.C. 102, as well as any agency of the legislative branch of the Federal Government.

Federal funding opportunity or *FFO* means an announcement that EDA publishes during the fiscal year on a Federal Government grants platform or on EDA's Internet Web site at *http://www.eda.gov, https://www.eda.gov/oie/*, or any successor Web site, that provides the funding amounts, application and programmatic requirements, funding priorities, special circumstances, and other information concerning a specific competitive solicitation under EDA's Regional Innovation Program.

Federal interest is defined at 2 CFR 200.41, in accordance with 2 CFR 200.316.

Federal laboratory means any laboratory, any federally funded research and development center, or any center established under section 7 or section 9 of the Act that is owned, leased, or otherwise used by a Federal agency and funded by the Federal Government, whether operated by the government or by a contractor.

Grant means the financial assistance award of EDA funds to an eligible recipient, under which the Eligible Recipient bears responsibility for meeting a purpose or carrying out an activity authorized under Stevenson-Wydler. *See* 31 U.S.C. 6304.

In-kind contribution(s) means noncash contributions, which may include contributions of space, Equipment, services, and assumptions of debt that are fairly evaluated by EDA and that satisfy applicable Federal Uniform Administrative Requirements and Cost Principles as set out in 2 CFR part 200.

Indian tribe means an entity on the list of recognized tribes published pursuant to the Federally Recognized Indian Tribe List Act of 1994, as amended (Pub. L. 103–454) (25 U.S.C. 479a *et seq.*), and any Alaska Native Village or Regional Corporation (as defined in or established under the Alaska Native Claims Settlement Act (43 U.S.C. 1601 *et seq.*)). This term includes the governing body of an Indian tribe, nonprofit Indian corporation (restricted to Indians), Indian authority, or other nonprofit Indian tribal organization or entity; provided that the Indian tribal organization or entity is wholly owned by, and established for the benefit of, the Indian tribe or Alaska Native village.

Investment or *Investment assistance* means a grant entered into by EDA and a recipient.

Investment rate means, as set forth in §312.8, the amount of the EDA investment in a particular project expressed as a percentage of the total project cost.

Matching share or *Local share* means the non-EDA funds and any in-kind contribution(s) that are approved by EDA and provided by a recipient or third party as a condition of an investment. The matching share may include funds from another Federal agency only if authorized by a statute that allows such use, which may be determined by EDA's reasonable interpretation of such authority.

Nonprofit organization is defined at 2 CFR 200.70.

Office of Innovation and Entrepreneurship or *OIE* means the office established by 15 U.S.C. 3720.

Project means the proposed or authorized activity (or activities), the purpose of which fulfills EDA's mission and program requirements as set forth in the Act and this part, and which may be funded in whole or in part by EDA investment assistance.

Public-private partnership means a relationship formalized by contractual agreement between a public agency and a private-sector entity that reasonably defines the terms of collaboration in the delivery and financing of a public project.

Real property means any land, whether raw or improved, and includes structures, fixtures, appurtenances, and other permanent improvements, excluding moveable machinery and equipment.

Recipient means an entity receiving EDA investment assistance, including any successor to the entity approved by EDA in writing. If investment assistance is awarded to more than one recipient under a single award, the recipients are referred to as "co-recipients" and, unless otherwise provided in the terms and conditions of the investment assistance, each co-recipient is jointly and severally liable for fulfilling the terms of the investment assistance.

Region or *Regional* means an economic unit of human, natural, technological, capital, or other resources, defined geographically. Geographic areas comprising a region need not be contiguous or defined by political boundaries, but should constitute a cohesive area capable of undertaking self-sustained economic development.

Regional innovation clusters or *RICs* means a geographically bounded network of similar, synergistic, or complementary entities that are engaged in or with a particular industry sector and its related sectors; have active channels for business transactions and communication; share specialized infrastructure, labor markets, and services; and leverage the region's unique competitive strengths to stimulate innovation and create jobs.

Regional Innovation Program means the program enacted by Stevenson-Wydler at 15 U.S.C. 3722.

Regional Innovation Research and Information Program or *RIRI Program* means the program authorized by 15 U.S.C. 3722(c).

Regional Innovation Strategies Program or *RIS Program* means the cluster grant program authorized by 15 U.S.C. 3722(b).

Science or research park means a property-based venture that has: Master-planned property and buildings designed primarily for private-public research and development activities, high technology and science-based companies, and research and development support services; a contractual or operational relationship with one or more science- or research-related institutions of higher education or governmental or nonprofit research laboratories; a primary mission to promote research and development through industry partnerships, assisting in the growth of new ventures and promoting innovation-driven economic development; a role in facilitating the transfer of technology and business skills between researchers and industry teams; and a role in promoting technology-led economic development for the community or region in which the park is located.

Secretary means the Secretary of Commerce.

State means a State of the United States, the District of Columbia, the Commonwealth of Puerto Rico, the U.S. Virgin Islands, Guam, American Samoa, the Commonwealth of the Northern Mariana Islands, or any other territory or possession of the United States.

United States means all of the States.

Subpart B—Regional Innovation Strategies Program

§ 312.4 Purpose and scope of the Regional Innovation Strategies Program.

Under the RIS Program, EDA makes grants on a competitive basis to eligible applicants to foster connected, innovation-centric economic regions that support commercialization and entrepreneurship. The grants are intended to build public and private capacity to invent and improve products and services and to bring those products and services to market through a process often referred to as technology commercialization, as demonstrated by methodologically sound metrics for output and outcome.

§ 312.5 Regional Innovation Strategies Program definitions.

In addition to the defined terms set forth in subpart A of this part, the following term applies specifically to the RIS Program:

Institution of higher education means:

(1) An educational institution in any State that—

(i) Admits as regular students only persons having a certificate of graduation from a school providing secondary education, or the recognized equivalent of such a certificate, or persons who meet the requirements of 20 U.S.C. 1091(d);

(ii) Is legally authorized within such State to provide a program of education beyond secondary education;

(iii) Provides an educational program for which the institution awards a bachelor's degree or provides not less than a 2-year program that is acceptable for full credit toward such a degree, or awards a degree that is acceptable for admission to a graduate or professional degree program, subject to review and approval by the Secretary of Education; and

(iv) Is accredited by a nationally recognized accrediting agency or association, or if not so accredited, is an institution that has been granted preaccreditation status by such an agency or association that has been recognized by the Secretary of Education for the granting of preaccreditation status, and the Secretary of Education has determined that there is satisfactory assurance that the institution will meet the accreditation standards of such an agency or association within a reasonable time.

(2) *Additional institutions included.* For purposes of this subpart, the term *Institution of higher education* also includes—

(i) Any school that provides not less than a 1-year program of training to prepare students for gainful employment in a recognized occupation and that meets the provisions of paragraphs (1)(i), (ii), and (iv) of this definition; and

(ii) An educational institution in any State that, in lieu of the requirement in paragraph (1)(i) of this definition, admits as regular students individuals—

(A) Who are beyond the age of compulsory school attendance in the State in which the institution is located; or

(B) Who will be dually or concurrently enrolled in the institution and a secondary school.

§ 312.6 Eligible recipients.

A recipient eligible for investment assistance includes:

(a) A State;

(b) An Indian tribe;

(c) A city or other political subdivision of a State;

(d) An entity that is a nonprofit organization and whose application for funding under the RIS Program is supported by a State or a political subdivision of a State;

(e) An entity that is an institution of higher education, a public-private partnership, a science or research park, a Federal laboratory, or an economic development organization or similar entity, and whose application for funding under the RIS Program is supported by a State or a political subdivision of a State; or

(f) A consortium of any of the entities described in paragraphs (a) through (e) of this section.

§312.7 Eligible project activities.

(a) Activities eligible for a RIS Program grant include:

(1) Feasibility studies;

(2) Planning activities;

(3) Technical assistance;

(4) Developing or strengthening communication and collaboration between and among participants of a regional innovation cluster;

(5) Attracting additional participants to a regional innovation cluster;

(6) Facilitating market development of products and services of a regional innovation cluster, including through demonstration, deployment, technology transfer, and commercialization activities;

(7) Developing relationships between a regional innovation cluster and entities or clusters in other regions;

(8) Interacting with the public and State and local governments to meet the goals of the regional innovation cluster;

(9) Purchase of equipment and equipment-related modifications or renovations of a facility, but only to the extent that such equipment and any related modifications or renovations are used to support another eligible activity as described in this section (the recipient may be required to secure and record the Federal interest in the equipment); and

(10) Any other activity determined appropriate by the Assistant Secretary and consistent with section 27(b) of Stevenson-Wydler.

(b) An ineligible activity includes, but is not limited to:

(1) Use of Federal funds or matching share for equity investments;

(2) Acquisition or improvement of real property;

(3) Construction except to the extent provided in paragraph (a)(9) of this section; and

(4) Lending programs, such as a direct loan program or capitalizing a revolving loan fund.

§312.8 Investment rates.

(a) *Minimum investment rate.* There is no minimum investment rate for a project.

(b) *Maximum investment rate.* The maximum investment rate for a project shall not exceed 50 percent.

§312.9 Matching share requirements.

The required matching share of a project's eligible costs may consist of cash or in-kind contribution(s) whose value can be readily determined, verified, and justified. Applicants must show at the time of application that the matching share is committed to the project, will be available as needed, and is not or will not be conditioned or encumbered in any way that would preclude its use consistent with the requirements of the investment assistance. EDA shall determine at its sole discretion whether the matching share documentation adequately addresses the requirements of this section.

§312.10 Application components.

In addition to the criteria set forth in the FFO, to be considered for a RIS Program grant, eligible applicants must provide the following information:

(a) A description of the regional innovation cluster supported by the proposed activity;

(b) The extent to which the regional innovation cluster is supported by the private sector, State and local units of government, and other relevant stakeholders;

(c) The methods that participants in the regional innovation cluster will use to encourage and solicit participation by all types of entities that might benefit from participation, including newly formed entities and rival existing participants;

(d) The extent to which the regional innovation cluster is likely to stimulate innovation and have a positive effect on regional economic growth and development;

(e) The capacity of participants in the regional innovation cluster to access, or contribute to, a well-trained workforce;

(f) The ability of participants in the regional innovation cluster to attract additional funds to support the cluster with non-Federal funds; and

(g) The likelihood that participants in the regional innovation cluster will be able to sustain activities after the grant expires.

§312.11 Application evaluation and selection criteria.

(a) EDA will evaluate and select complete applications in accordance with the evaluation criteria, funding priority considerations, availability of funding, competitiveness of the application, and requirements set forth in section 27(b) of Stevenson-Wydler, the FFO, and other applicable Federal statutes and regulations. All awards are subject to the availability of funds.

(b) EDA will endeavor to notify applicants as soon as practicable regarding whether their applications are selected for funding.

(c) Stevenson-Wydler does not require nor does EDA provide an appeal process for denial of applications for EDA investment assistance.

§312.12 General terms and conditions for investment assistance.

RIS Program grants are subject to all requirements contained in part 302 of this chapter, except §§302.2, 302.3, 302.9, 302.10, and 302.17.

Subpart C—Regional Innovation Research and Information Program [Reserved]

§§312.13–312.17 [Reserved]

PART 313 [Reserved]

PART 314—PROPERTY

AUTHORITY: 42 U.S.C. 3211; Department of Commerce Organization Order 10–4.

SOURCE: 71 FR 56675, Sept. 27, 2006, unless otherwise noted.

§314.1 Definitions.

In addition to the defined terms set forth in §300.3 of this chapter, the following terms shall have the following meanings:

Adequate Consideration means the fair market value at the time of sale or lease of any Property, as adjusted, in EDA's sole discretion, by any services, property exchanges, contractual commitments, acts of forbearance or other considerations that are in furtherance of the authorized purposes of the Investment Assistance, which are received by the Recipient or Owner in exchange for such Property.

Disposition or *Dispose* means the sale, lease, abandonment or other disposition of any Property and also includes the Unauthorized Use of such Property.

Estimated Useful Life, as used in this part, means the period of years that constitutes the expected useful lifespan of a Project, as determined by EDA, during which EDA anticipates obtaining the economic development benefits of its Investment.

Federal Interest has the definition ascribed to it in §314.2(a).

Federal Share has the definition ascribed to it in §314.5.

Owner means a fee owner, transferee, lessee or optionee of any Property. The term Owner also includes the holder of other interests in a Property where the interests are such that the holder effectively controls the use of such Property.

Personal Property means all tangible and intangible property other than Real Property, including the RLF Capital Base as defined at §307.8.

Project Property means all Property that is acquired or improved, in whole or in part, with Investment Assistance and is required, as determined by EDA, for the successful completion and operation of a Project and/or serves as the economic justification of a Project. As appropriate to specify the type of Property referenced, this part refers to Project Property as "Project Real Property" or "Project Personal Property".

Property means Real Property, Personal Property and mixed property.

Real Property means any land, whether raw or improved, and includes structures, fixtures, appurtenances and other permanent improvements, excluding moveable machinery and equipment. Real Property includes land that is served by the construction of Project infrastructure (such as roads, sewers and water lines) where the infrastructure contributes to the value of such land as a specific purpose of the Project.

Successor Recipient means an EDA-approved transferee of Property pursuant to §314.3(d). A Successor Recipient must be an Eligible Recipient of Investment Assistance.

Unauthorized Use means any use of Property acquired or improved in whole or in part for purposes not authorized by EDA Investment Assistance, PWEDA or this chapter, as set forth in §314.4.

[71 FR 56675, Sept. 27, 2006, as amended at 79 FR 76136, Dec. 19, 2014; 82 FR 57059, Dec. 1, 2017]

§314.2 Federal Interest.

(a) Subject to the obligations and conditions set forth in this part and in relevant provisions of 2 CFR part 200, Project Property vests upon acquisition in the Recipient (or, if approved by EDA, in a Co-recipient or Subrecipient). Project Property shall be held in trust by the Recipient for the benefit of the Project for the Estimated Useful Life of the Project, during which period EDA retains an undivided equitable reversionary interest in the Property (the "Federal Interest"). The Federal Interest ensures compliance with EDA Project requirements, including those related to the purpose, scope, and use of a Project. The Recipient typically must secure the Federal Interest through a recorded lien, statement, or other recordable instrument setting forth EDA's Property interest in a Project (*e.g.*, a mortgage, covenant, or other statement of EDA's Real Property interest in the case of a Project involving the acquisition, construction, or improvement of a building. See §314.8.).

(b) When the Federal Government is fully compensated for the Federal Share of Project Property, the Federal Interest is extinguished and the Federal Government has no further interest in the Property, except as provided in §314.10(e)(3) regarding nondiscrimination requirements.

[82 FR 57059, Dec. 1, 2017]

§314.3 Authorized use of Project Property.

(a) *General.* During the Estimated Useful Life of the Project, the Recipient or Owner must use any Project Property only for authorized Project purposes as set out in the terms of the Investment Assistance. Such Property must not be Disposed of or encumbered without EDA's prior written authorization.

(b) *Project Property that is no longer needed for Project purposes.* Where EDA and the Recipient determine during the Estimated Useful Life of the Project that Project Property is longer needed for the original purpose of the Investment Assistance, EDA, in its sole discretion, may approve the use of such Property in other Federal grant programs or in programs that have purposes consistent with those authorized by PWEDA and by this chapter.

(c) *Real Property for sale or lease.* Where EDA determines that the authorized purpose of the Investment Assistance is to develop Real Property to be leased or sold, such sale or lease is permitted provided it is for Adequate Consideration and the sale is consistent with the authorized purpose of the Investment Assistance and with all applicable Investment Assistance requirements, including nondiscrimination and environmental compliance.

(d) *Property transfers and Successor Recipients.* EDA, in its sole discretion, may approve the transfer of any Project Property from a Recipient to a Successor Recipient (or from one Successor Recipient to another Successor Recipient). The Recipient will remain responsible for complying with the rules of this part and the terms and conditions of the Investment Assistance for the period in which it is the Recipient. Thereafter, the Successor Recipient must comply with the rules of this part and with the same terms and conditions as were applicable to the Recipient (unless such terms and conditions are otherwise amended by EDA). The same rules apply to EDA-approved transfers of Property between Successor Recipients.

(e) *Replacement Personal Property.* When acquiring replacement Personal Property of equal or greater value than Personal Property originally acquired with Investment Assistance, the Recipient may, with EDA's approval, trade in such Personal Property originally acquired or sell the original Personal Property and use the proceeds for the acquisition of the replacement Personal Property, provided that the replacement Personal Property is for use in the Project. The replacement Personal Property is subject to the same requirements as the original Personal Property.

(f) *Replacement Real Property.* In extraordinary and compelling circumstances, the Assistant Secretary may approve the replacement of Real Property used in a Project.

(g) *Incidental use of Project Property.* With EDA's prior written approval, a Recipient may undertake an incidental use of Project Property that does not interfere with the scope of the Project or the economic purpose for which the Investment was made, provided that the Recipient is in compliance with applicable law and the terms and conditions of the Investment Assistance, and the incidental use of the Property will not violate the terms and conditions of the Investment Assistance or otherwise undermine the economic purpose for which the Investment was made or adversely affect the economic useful life of the Property. Eligible Applicants and Recipients should contact the appropriate regional office (whose contact information is available via the Internet at *http://www.eda.gov*) for guidelines on obtaining approval for incidental use of Property under this section.

[82 FR 57059, Dec. 1, 2017]

§ 314.4 Unauthorized Use of Project Property.

(a) *Compensation of Federal Share upon an Unauthorized Use of Project Property.* Except as provided in §§ 314.3 (regarding the authorized use of Property) or 314.10 (regarding the release of the Federal Interest in certain Property), or as otherwise authorized by EDA, the Federal Government must be compensated by the Recipient for the Federal Share whenever, during the Estimated Useful Life of the Project, any Project Property is Disposed of, encumbered, or no longer used for the purpose of the Project; provided that for equipment and supplies, the requirements of 2 CFR part 200, including any supplements, shall apply.

(b) *Additional Unauthorized Uses of Project Property.* Additionally, prior to the release of the Federal Interest, Project Real Property or tangible Project Personal Property may not be used:

(1) In violation of the nondiscrimination requirements of § 302.20 of this chapter or in violation of the terms and conditions of the Investment Assistance; or

(2) For any purpose prohibited by applicable law.

(c) *Recovery of the Federal Share.* Where the Disposition, encumbrance, or use of any Project Property violates paragraph (a) or (b) of this section, EDA may assert the Federal Interest in the Project Property to recover the Federal Share for the Federal Government and may take such actions as authorized by PWEDA and this chapter, including the actions provided in §§ 302.3, 302.16, and 307.21 of this chapter. EDA may pursue its rights under paragraph (a) of this section and this paragraph (c) to recover the Federal Share, plus costs and interest. When the Federal Government is fully compensated for the Federal Share, the Federal Interest is extinguished as provided in § 314.2(b), and EDA will have no further interest in the ownership, use, or Disposition of the Property, except for the nondiscrimination requirements set forth in § 314.10(d)(3).

[71 FR 56675, Sept. 27, 2006, as amended at 79 FR 76137, Dec. 19, 2014; 82 FR 57059, Dec. 1, 2017]

§ 314.5 Federal Share.

(a) For purposes of this part, "Federal Share" means that portion of the current fair market value of any Project Property attributable to EDA's participation in the Project. EDA may rely on a current certified appraisal of the Project Property prepared by an appraiser licensed in the State where the Project Property is located to determine the fair market value. In extraordinary circumstances and at

EDA's sole discretion, where EDA is unable to determine the current fair market value, EDA may use other methods of determining the value of Project Property, including the amount of the award of Investment Assistance or the amount paid by a transferee. The Federal Share shall be the current fair market value or other valuation as determined by EDA of the Property after deducting:

(1) Reasonable repair expenses, if any, incurred to put the Property into marketable condition; and

(2) Sales, commission and marketing costs.

(b) The Federal Share excludes that portion of the current fair market value of the Property attributable to acquisition or improvements before or after EDA's participation in the Project, which are not included in the total Project costs. For example, if the total Project costs are $100, consisting of $50 of Investment Assistance and $50 of Matching Share, the Federal Share is 50 percent. If the Property is disposed of when its current fair market is $250, the Federal Share is $125 (*i.e.*, 50 percent of $250). If $10 is spent to put the Property into salable condition, the Federal Share is $120 (*i.e.*, 50 percent of ($250–$10)).

[73 FR 62870, Oct. 22, 2008, as amended at 79 FR 76137, Dec. 19, 2014; 82 FR 57060, Dec. 1, 2017]

§ 314.6 Encumbrances.

(a) *General.* Except as provided in paragraph (b) of this section or as otherwise authorized by EDA, Project Property must not be used to secure a mortgage or deed of trust or in any way otherwise encumbered, except to secure a grant or loan made by a Federal Agency or State agency or other public body participating in the same Project, so long as the Recipient discloses such an encumbrance in writing as part of its application for Investment Assistance or as soon as practicable after learning of the encumbrance.

(b) *Exceptions.* Subject to EDA's approval, which will not be unreasonably withheld or unduly delayed, paragraph (a) of this section does not apply in the following circumstances:

(1) *Shared first lien position.* EDA, at its discretion, may approve an encumbrance on Project Property where a lien holder and EDA enter into an inter-creditor agreement pursuant to which EDA and the other lien holder share a first lien position on terms satisfactory to EDA.

(2) *Utility encumbrances.* Encumbrances arising solely from the requirements of a pre-existing water or sewer facility or other utility encumbrances, which by their terms extend to additional Property connected to such facilities.

(3) *Pre-existing encumbrances.* Encumbrances already in place and disclosed to EDA at the time EDA approves the Project where EDA, in its sole discretion, determines that:

(i) The requirements of § 314.7(b) are met;

(ii) Consistent with paragraphs (b)(4)(iv) and (b)(5)(iv) of this section, the terms and conditions of the encumbrance are satisfactory; and

(iii) Consistent with paragraphs (b)(4)(v) and (b)(5)(v) of this section, there is a reasonable expectation that the Recipient will not default on its obligations.

(4) *Encumbrances proposed proximate to Project approval.* Encumbrances required to secure debt, including time and maturity-limited debt, that finances the Project Property at the same proximate time that EDA approves the Project when all of the following are met:

(i) EDA, in its sole discretion, determines that there is good cause and legal authority to waive paragraph (a) of this section;

(ii) All proceeds secured by the encumbrance on the Property shall be available only to the Recipient and shall be used only for the Project for which the Investment Assistance applies, for related activities of which the Project is an essential part, or other activities that EDA determines are authorized under PWEDA;

(iii) A grantor or lender will not provide funds without the security of a lien on the Property;

(iv) The terms and conditions of the encumbrance are satisfactory to EDA; and

(v) There is a reasonable expectation, as determined by EDA, that the Recipient will not default on its obligations. In determining whether an expectation is reasonable for purposes of this paragraph, EDA shall take into account whether:

(A) A Recipient that is a non-profit organization is joined in the Project with a co-Recipient that is a public body and all co-Recipients are jointly and severally responsible;

(B) A Recipient that is a non-profit organization is financially strong and is an established organization with sufficient organizational life to demonstrate stability over time;

(C) The approximate value of the Project Property so that the total amount of all debt plus the Federal share of cost as reflected on the EDA Investment award, and any amendments as applicable, does not exceed the value of the Project Property as improved; and

(D) Such other factors as EDA deems appropriate.

(5) *Encumbrances proposed after Project approval.* Encumbrances proposed to be incurred after Project approval where all of the following are met:

(i) EDA, in its sole discretion, determines that there is good cause and legal authority to waive paragraph (a) of this section;

(ii) All proceeds secured by the encumbrance on the Property shall be available only to the Recipient and shall be used only for the Project for which the Investment Assistance applies, for related activities of which the Project is an essential part, or other activities that EDA determines are authorized under PWEDA;

(iii) A grantor or lender will not provide funds without the security of a lien on the Property;

(iv) The terms and conditions of the encumbrance are satisfactory to EDA; and

(v) There is a reasonable expectation, as determined by EDA, that the Recipient will not default on its obligations. In determining whether an expectation is reasonable for purposes of this paragraph, EDA shall take into account whether:

(A) A Recipient that is a non-profit organization is joined in the Project with a co-Recipient that is a public body and all co-Recipients are jointly and severally responsible;

(B) A Recipient that is a non-profit organization is financially strong and is an established organization with sufficient organizational life to demonstrate stability over time;

(C) The Recipient's equity in the Project Property based on the appraised value of the Project Property at the time the encumbrance is requested so that the total amount of all debt plus the Federal share of cost as reflected on the EDA Investment award, and any amendments as applicable, does not exceed the value of the Project Property as improved; and

(D) Such other factors as EDA deems appropriate.

(c) *Unauthorized encumbrances.* Encumbering Project Property, other than as permitted in this section, is an Unauthorized Use of the Property under § 314.4.

[71 FR 56675, Sept. 27, 2006, as amended at 73 FR 62870, Oct. 22, 2008; 79 FR 76137, Dec. 19, 2014; 82 FR 57060, Dec. 1, 2017]

§ 314.7 Title.

(a) *General title requirement.* Except in those limited circumstances identified in paragraph (c) of this section, at the time Investment Assistance is awarded, the Recipient must hold title to Project Real Property, which, as noted in § 314.1 in the definition of "Real Property" includes land that is served by the construction of Project infrastructure (such as roads, sewers, and water lines) and where the infrastructure contributes to the value of such land as a specific purpose of the Project. The Recipient must maintain title to Project Real Property at all times during the Estimated Useful Life of the Project, except in those limited circumstances as provided in paragraph (c) of this section. The Recipient also must furnish evidence, satisfactory in form and substance to EDA, that title to Project Real Property (other than property of the United States) is vested in the Recipient and that any easements, rights-of-way, State or local government permits, long-term leases, or other items required for the Project have been or will be obtained by the

Recipient within an acceptable time, as determined by EDA.

(b) *Disclosure of encumbrances.* (1) The Recipient must disclose to EDA all encumbrances, including the following:

(i) Liens;

(ii) Mortgages;

(iii) Reservations;

(iv) Reversionary interests; and

(v) Other restrictions on title or on the Recipient's interest in the Property.

(2) No encumbrance will be acceptable if, as determined by EDA, the encumbrance interferes with the construction, use, operation or maintenance of the Project during its Estimated Useful Life.

(c) *Exceptions.* The following are exceptions to the requirements of paragraph (a) of this section that the Recipient hold title to Project Real Property at the time Investment Assistance is awarded and at all times during the Estimated Useful Life of the Project.

(1) *Project Real Property acquisition.* Where the acquisition of Project Real Property is contemplated as part of an Investment Assistance award, EDA may determine that an agreement for the Recipient to purchase the Project Real Property will be acceptable for purposes of paragraph (a) of this section if:

(i) The Recipient provides EDA with reasonable assurances that it will obtain fee title to the Real Property prior to or concurrent with the initial disbursement of the Investment Assistance; and

(ii) EDA, in its sole discretion, determines that the terms and conditions of the purchase agreement adequately safeguard the Federal Government's interest in the Project Real Property.

(2) *Leasehold interests.* EDA may determine that a long-term leasehold interest for a period not less than the Estimated Useful Life of Project Real Property will be acceptable for purposes of paragraph (a) of this section if:

(i) Fee title to the Real Property is not otherwise obtainable; and

(ii) EDA, in its sole discretion, determines that the terms and conditions of the lease adequately safeguard the Federal government's interest in the Real Property and demonstrate the economic development and public benefits of the leasehold transaction.

(3) *Railroad right-of-way construction.* When a Project includes construction within a railroad's right-of-way or over a railroad crossing, EDA may find it acceptable for the work to be completed by the railroad and for the railroad to continue to own, operate, and maintain that portion of the Project, if required by the railroad; and provided that, the construction is a minor but essential component of the Project.

(4) *State or local government owned roadway or highway construction.* When the Project includes construction on a State or local government owned roadway or highway the owner of which is not the Recipient, EDA may allow the Project to be constructed in whole or in part in the right-of-way of such public roadway or highway, provided that:

(i) All EDA-funded construction is completed in accordance with EDA requirements;

(ii) The Recipient confirms in writing to EDA, satisfactory to EDA, that:

(A) The Recipient is committed during the Estimated Useful Life of the Project to operate, maintain and repair all improvements for the Project consistent with the Investment Assistance; and

(B) If at any time during the Estimated Useful Life of the Project any or all of the improvements in the Project within the State or local government owned roadway or highway are relocated for any reason pursuant to requirements of the owner of the public roadway or highway, the Recipient shall be responsible for accomplishing such relocation, including expending the Recipient's own funds as necessary, so that the Project continues as authorized by the Investment Assistance; and

(iii) The Recipient obtains all written authorizations (*i.e.*, State or county permit(s)) necessary for the Project to be constructed within the public roadway or highway, copies of which shall be submitted to EDA. Such authorizations shall contain no time limits that EDA determines substantially restrict the use of the public roadway or highway for the Project during the Estimated Useful Life of the Project.

(5) *Construction of Recipient-owned facilities to serve Recipient or privately owned Real Property*—(i) *General.* At EDA's discretion, when an authorized purpose of the Project is to construct Recipient-owned facilities to serve Recipient or privately owned Project Real Property, including industrial or commercial parks, so that the Recipient or Owner may sell or lease parcels of the Project Real Property to private parties, such ownership, sale, or lease, as applicable, is permitted so long as:

(A) In cases where an authorized purpose of the Project is to sell Project Real Property, the Recipient or Owner, as applicable, provides evidence sufficient to EDA that it holds title to the Project Real Property intended for sale or lease prior to the disbursement of any portion of the Investment Assistance and will retain title until the sale of the Property in accordance with paragraphs (c)(5)(i)(C) through (E) of this section;

(B) In cases where an authorized purpose of the Project is to lease Project Real Property, the Recipient or Owner, as applicable, provides evidence sufficient to EDA that it holds title to the Project Real Property intended for lease prior to the disbursement of any portion of the Investment Assistance and will retain title for the entire Estimated Useful Life of the Project;

(C) The Recipient provides adequate assurances that the Project and the development of land and improvements on the Recipient or privately owned Project Real Property to be served by or that provides the economic justification for the Project will be completed according to the terms of the Investment Assistance;

(D) The sale or lease of any portion of the Project or of Project Real Property served by the Project or that provides the economic justification for the Project during the Project's Estimated Useful Life must be for Adequate Consideration and the terms and conditions of the Investment Assistance and the purpose(s) of the Project must continue to be fulfilled after such sale or lease; and

(ii) *Additional conditions on sale or lease.* EDA also may condition the sale or lease on the satisfaction by the Recipient, Owner, purchaser, or lessee (as the case may be) of any additional requirements that EDA may impose, including EDA's pre-approval of the sale or lease.

(iii) *Agreement between Recipient and Owner.* In addition to paragraphs (c)(5)(i) and (ii) of this section, when an authorized purpose of the Project is to construct facilities to serve privately owned Real Property, the Recipient and the Owner must agree to use the Real Property improved or benefitted by the EDA Investment Assistance only for the authorized purposes of the Project and in a manner consistent with the terms and conditions of the EDA Investment Assistance for the Estimated Useful Life of the Project.

(iv) *Unauthorized Use and compensation of Federal Share.* EDA may deem that a violation of this paragraph (c)(5) by the Recipient, Owner, purchaser, or lessee (as the case may be) constitutes an Unauthorized Use of the Real Property and the Recipient must agree to compensate EDA for the Federal government's Federal Share of the Project in the case of such Unauthorized Use.

[71 FR 56675, Sept. 27, 2006, as amended at 73 FR 62870, Oct. 22, 2008; 79 FR 76137, Dec. 19, 2014; 82 FR 57061, Dec. 1, 2017]

§ 314.8 Recorded statement for Project Real Property.

(a) For all Projects involving the acquisition, construction, or improvement of a building, as determined by EDA, the Recipient shall execute a lien, covenant, or other statement of the Federal Interest in such Project Real Property. The statement shall specify the Estimated Useful Life of the Project and shall include, but not be limited to, the Disposition, encumbrance and Federal Share requirements. The statement shall be satisfactory in form and substance to EDA.

(b) The statement of the Federal Interest must be perfected and placed of record in the Real Property records of the jurisdiction in which the Project Real Property is located, all in accordance with applicable law.

(c) Facilities in which the EDA Investment is only a small part of a large project, as determined by EDA, may be exempted from the requirements of this section.

(d) In extraordinary circumstances and at EDA's sole discretion, EDA may choose to accept another instrument to protect the Federal Interest in Project Real Property, such as an escrow agreement or letter of credit, provided that EDA determines such instrument is adequate and a recorded statement in accord with paragraph (a) of this section is not reasonably available. The terms and provisions of the relevant instrument shall be satisfactory to EDA in EDA's sole judgment. The costs and fees for escrow services and letters of credit shall be paid by the Recipient.

[71 FR 56675, Sept. 27, 2006, as amended at 79 FR 76138, Dec. 19, 2014; 82 FR 57061, Dec. 1, 2017]

§314.9 Recorded statement for Project Personal Property.

For all Projects which EDA determines involve the acquisition or improvement of significant items of Personal Property, including ships, machinery, equipment, removable fixtures, or structural components of buildings, the Recipient shall provide notice of the Federal Interest in all Project Personal Property by executing a Uniform Commercial Code Financing Statement (Form UCC-1, as provided by State law) or other statement of the Federal Interest in the Project Personal Property, acceptable in form and substance to EDA, which statement must be perfected and placed of record in accordance with applicable law, with continuances re-filed as appropriate. Whether or not a statement is required by EDA to be recorded, the Recipient must hold title to all Project Personal Property, except as otherwise provided in this part.

[82 FR 57062, Dec. 1, 2017]

§314.10 Procedures for release of the Federal Interest.

(a) *General.* As provided in §314.2, the Federal Interest in Project Property extends for the duration of the Estimated Useful Life of the Project, which is determined by EDA at the time of Investment award. Upon request of the Recipient, EDA will release the Federal Interest in Project Property upon expiration of the Estimated Useful Life as established in the terms and conditions of the Investment Assistance and in accord with the requirements of this section and part. This section provides procedures to obtain a release of the Federal Interest in Project Property.

(b) *Release of the Federal Interest after the expiration of the Estimated Useful Life.* At the expiration of a Project's Estimated Useful Life and upon the written request of a recipient, the Assistant Secretary may release the Federal Interest in Project Property if EDA determines that the Recipient has made a good faith effort to fulfill all terms and conditions of the Investment Assistance. The determination provided for in this paragraph (b) shall be established at the time of Recipient's written request and shall be based, at least in part, on the facts and circumstances provided in writing by the Recipient. For a Project in which a Recorded Statement as provided for in §§314.8 and 314.9 has been recorded, EDA will provide for the release by executing an instrument in recordable form. The release will terminate the Investment as of the date of its execution and satisfy the Recorded Statement. See paragraph (e) of this section for limitations and covenants of use that are applicable to any release of the Federal Interest.

(c) *Release prior to the expiration of the Estimated Useful Life.* If the Recipient will no longer use the Project Property in accord with the requirements of the terms and conditions of the Investment within the time period of the Estimated Useful Life, EDA will determine if such use by the Recipient constitutes an Unauthorized Use of Property and require compensation for the Federal Interest as provided in §314.4 and this section. EDA may release the Federal Interest in connection with such Property only upon receipt of full payment in compensation of the Federal Interest and thereafter will have no further interest in the ownership, use, or Disposition of the Property, except for the nondiscrimination requirements set forth in paragraph (e)(3) of this section.

(d) *Release of the Federal Interest before the expiration of the Estimated Useful Life, but 20 years after the award of Investment Assistance.* In accord with section 601(d)(2) of PWEDA, upon the request of a Recipient and before the expiration of the Estimated Useful Life of a Project, but where 20 years have elapsed since the award of Investment Assistance, EDA may release any Real Property or tangible Personal Property interest held by EDA, if EDA determines:

(1) The Recipient has made a good faith effort to fulfill all terms and conditions of the award of Investment Assistance; and

(2) The economic development benefits as set out in the award of Investment Assistance have been achieved.

(3) See paragraph (e) of this section for limitations and covenants of use that are applicable to any release of the Federal Interest.

(e) *Limitations and Covenant of Use.* (1) EDA's release of the Federal Interest pursuant to this section is not automatic; it requires EDA's approval, which will not be withheld except for good cause or as otherwise required by law, as determined in EDA's sole discretion. As deemed appropriate, EDA may require the Recipient to take some action as a condition of the release.

(2) In determining whether to release the Federal Interest, EDA will review EDA's legal authority to release its interest, including the Recipient's performance under and conformance with the terms and conditions of the Investment Assistance; any use of Project Property in violation of § 314.3 or § 314.4; and other such factors as EDA deems appropriate. When requesting a release of the Federal Interest pursuant to this section, the Recipient will be required to disclose to EDA the intended future use of the Real Property or the tangible Personal Property for which the release is requested.

(i) A Recipient not intending to use the Real Property or tangible Personal Property for explicitly religious activities following EDA's release will be required to execute a covenant of use. A covenant of use with respect to Real Property shall be recorded in the jurisdiction where the Real Property is located in accordance with § 314.8. A covenant of use with respect to items of tangible Personal Property shall be perfected and recorded in accordance with applicable law, with continuances re-filed as appropriate. *See* § 314.9. A covenant of use shall (at a minimum) prohibit the use of the Real Property or the tangible Personal Property for explicitly religious activities in violation of applicable Federal law.

(ii) EDA may require a Recipient (or its successors in interest) that intends or foresees the use of Real Property or tangible Personal Property for explicitly religious activities following the release of the Federal Interest to compensate EDA for the Federal Share of such Property. If such compensation is made, no covenant with respect to explicitly religious activities will be required as a condition of the release. EDA recommends that any Recipient who intends or foresees the use of Real Property or tangible Personal Property (including by successors of the Recipient) for explicitly religious activities to contact EDA well in advance of requesting a release pursuant to this section.

(3) Notwithstanding any release of the Federal Interest under this section, including a release upon a Recipient's compensation for the Federal Share, a Recipient must ensure that Project Property is not used in violation of nondiscrimination requirements set forth in § 302.20 of this chapter. Accordingly, upon the release of the Federal Interest, the Recipient must execute a covenant of use that prohibits use of Real Property or tangible Personal Property for any purpose that would violate the nondiscrimination requirements set forth in § 302.20 of this chapter.

(i) With respect to Real Property, the Recipient must record a covenant under this subsection in the jurisdiction where the Real Property is located in accordance with § 314.8.

(ii) With respect to items of tangible Personal Property, the Recipient must perfect and record a covenant under this subsection in accordance with applicable law, with continuances re-filed as appropriate, in accordance with § 314.9.

[79 FR 76139, Dec. 19, 2014, as amended at 82 FR 57062, Dec. 1, 2017]

PART 315—TRADE ADJUSTMENT ASSISTANCE FOR FIRMS

Subpart A—General Provisions

Subpart B—Certification of Firms

Subpart C—Protective Provisions

Subpart D—Adjustment Proposals

Subpart E—Assistance to Industries

AUTHORITY: 19 U.S.C. 2341 *et seq.*, as amended by Division B, Title I, Subtitle I, Part II of Pub. L. 111–5; 42 U.S.C. 3211; Department of Commerce Organization Order 10–4.

SOURCE: 74 FR 41598, Aug. 18, 2009, unless otherwise noted.

Subpart A—General Provisions

§315.1 Purpose and scope.

The regulations in this part set forth the responsibilities of the Secretary of Commerce under chapter 3 of title II of the Trade Act concerning Trade Adjustment Assistance for Firms. The statutory authority and responsibilities of the Secretary of Commerce relating to Adjustment Assistance are delegated to EDA. EDA certifies Firms as eligible to apply for Adjustment Assistance, provides technical Adjustment Assistance to Firms and other recipients, and provides assistance to organizations representing trade injured industries.

§315.2 Definitions.

In addition to the defined terms set forth in §300.3 of this chapter, the following terms used in this part shall have the following meanings:

Adjustment Assistance means technical assistance provided to Firms or industries under chapter 3 of title II of the Trade Act.

Adjustment Proposal means a Certified Firm's plan for improving its economic situation.

Certified Firm means a Firm which has been determined by EDA to be eligible to apply for Adjustment Assistance.

Confidential Business Information means any information submitted to EDA or a TAAC by a Firm that concerns or relates to trade secrets for commercial or financial purposes, which is exempt from public disclosure under 5 U.S.C. 552(b)(4), 5 U.S.C. 552b(c)(4) and 15 CFR part 4.

Contributed Importantly, with respect to an Increase in Imports, refers to a cause which is important but not necessarily more important than any other cause. Imports will not be considered to have Contributed Importantly if other factors were so dominant, acting singly or in combination, that the worker separation or threat thereof or decline in sales or production would have been essentially the same, irrespective of the influence of imports.

Decreased Absolutely means a Firm's sales or production has declined by a minimum of five percent relative to its sales or production during the applicable prior time period,

(1) Independent of industry or market fluctuations; and

(2) Relative only to the previous performance of the Firm, unless EDA determines that these limitations in a given case would not be consistent with the purposes of the Trade Act.

Directly Competitive means imported articles or services that compete with and are substantially equivalent for commercial purposes (*i.e.*, are adapted for the same function or use and are essentially interchangeable) as the Firm's articles or services. Any Firm that engages in exploring or drilling for oil or natural gas, or otherwise produces oil or natural gas, shall be considered to be producing articles directly competitive with imports of oil and with imports of natural gas.

Firm means an individual proprietorship, partnership, joint venture, association, corporation (includes a development corporation), business trust, cooperative, trustee in bankruptcy or receiver under court decree, and includes fishing, agricultural or service sector entities and those which explore, drill or otherwise produce oil or natural gas. *See also* the definition of Service Sector Firm. Pursuant to section 261 of chapter 3 of title II of the Trade Act (19 U.S.C. 2351), a Firm, together with any predecessor or successor firm, or any affiliated firm controlled or substantially beneficially owned by substantially the same person, may be considered a single Firm where necessary to prevent unjustifiable benefits. For purposes of receiving benefits under this part, when a Firm owns or controls other Firms, the Firm and such other Firms may be considered a single Firm when they produce or supply like or Directly Competitive articles or services or are exerting essential economic control over one or more production facilities. Accordingly, such other Firms may include a(n):

(1) *Predecessor*—see the following definition for Successor;

(2) *Successor*—a newly established Firm (that has been in business less than two years) which has purchased substantially all of the assets of a previously operating company (or in some cases a whole distinct division) (such prior company, unit or division, a 'Predecessor') and is able to demonstrate that it continued the operations of the Predecessor which has operated as an autonomous unit, provided that there were no significant transactions between the Predecessor unit and any related parent, subsidiary, or affiliate that would have affected its past performance, and that separate records are available for the Predecessor's operations for at least two years before the petition is submitted. The Successor Firm must have continued virtually all of the Predecessor Firm's operations by producing the same type of products or services, in the same plant, utilizing most of the same machinery and equipment and most of its former workers, and the Predecessor Firm must no longer be in existence;

(3) *Affiliate*—a company (either foreign or domestic) controlled or substantially beneficially owned by substantially the same person or persons that own or control the Firm filing the petition; or

(4) *Subsidiary*—a company (either foreign or domestic) that is wholly owned or effectively controlled by another company.

Increase in Imports means an increase of imports of Directly Competitive or Like Articles or Services with articles produced or services supplied by such Firm. EDA may consider as evidence of an Increase in Imports a certification from the Firm's customers that account for a significant percentage of the Firm's decrease in sales or production that they have increased their purchase of imports of Directly Competitive or Like Articles or Services from a foreign country, either absolutely or relative to their acquisition of such Like Articles or Services from suppliers located in the United States.

Like Articles or Services means any articles or services, as applicable, which are substantially identical in their intrinsic characteristics.

Partial Separation means, with respect to any employment in a Firm, either:

(1) A reduction in an employee's work hours to 80 percent or less of the employee's average weekly hours during the year of such reductions as compared to the preceding year; or

(2) A reduction in the employee's weekly wage to 80 percent or less of his/her average weekly wage during the year of such reduction as compared to the preceding year.

Person means an individual, organization or group.

Record means any of the following:

(1) A petition for certification of eligibility to qualify for Adjustment Assistance;

(2) Any supporting information submitted by a petitioner;

(3) The report of an EDA investigation with respect to petition; and

(4) Any information developed during an investigation or in connection with any public hearing held on a petition.

Service Sector Firm means a Firm engaged in the business of supplying services. For purposes of receiving benefits under this part, when a Service Sector Firm owns or controls other Service Sector Firms, the Service Sector Firm and such other Service Sector Firms may be considered a single Service Sector Firm when they furnish like or Directly Competitive services or are exerting essential economic control over one or more servicing facilities. Such other Service Sector Firm may be a Predecessor, Successor, Affiliate or Subsidiary, each as defined in the definition of Firm.

Significant Number or Proportion of Workers means five percent of a Firm's work force or 50 workers, whichever is less, unless EDA determines that these limitations in a given case would not be consistent with the purposes of the Trade Act. An individual farmer or fisherman is considered a Significant Number or Proportion of Workers.

Substantial Interest means a direct material economic interest in the certification or non-certification of the petitioner.

TAAC means a Trade Adjustment Assistance Center, as more fully described in §315.5.

Threat of Total or Partial Separation means, with respect to any group of workers, one or more events or circumstances clearly demonstrating that a Total or Partial Separation is imminent.

Total Separation means, with respect to any employment in a Firm, the laying off or termination of employment of an employee for lack of work.

§315.3 Confidential Business Information.

EDA will follow the procedures set forth in 15 CFR 4.9 for the submission of Confidential Business Information. Submitters should clearly mark and designate as confidential any Confidential Business Information.

§315.4 Eligible applicants.

(a) The following entities may apply for assistance to operate a TAAC:

(1) Universities or affiliated organizations;

(2) States or local governments; or

(3) Non-profit organizations.

(b) For purposes of §315.17 and to the extent funds are appropriated to implement section 265 of the Trade Act, organizations assisting or representing industries in which a substantial number of Firms or workers have been certified as eligible to apply for Adjustment Assistance under sections 223 and 251 of the Trade Act, include:

(1) Existing agencies;

(2) Private individuals;

(3) Firms;

(4) Universities;

(5) Institutions;

(6) Associations;

(7) Unions; or

(8) Other non-profit industry organizations.

§315.5 TAAC scope, selection, evaluation and awards.

(a) *TAAC purpose and scope.* (1) TAACs are available to assist Firms in obtaining Adjustment Assistance in all 50 U.S. States, the District of Columbia and the Commonwealth of Puerto Rico. TAACs provide Adjustment Assistance in accordance with this part either through their own staffs or by arrangements with outside consultants. Information concerning TAACs serving particular areas may be obtained from the TAAC Web site at *http://www.taacenters.org* or from EDA at *http://www.eda.gov.*

(2) Prior to submitting a petition for Adjustment Assistance to EDA, a Firm should determine the extent to which a TAAC can provide the required Adjustment Assistance. EDA will provide Adjustment Assistance through TAACs whenever EDA determines that such assistance can be provided most effectively in this manner. Requests for Adjustment Assistance will normally be made through TAACs.

(3) A TAAC generally provides Adjustment Assistance by providing assistance to a:

(i) Firm in preparing its petition for eligibility certification; and

(ii) Certified Firm in diagnosing its strengths and weaknesses, and developing and implementing an Adjustment Proposal.

(b) *TAAC selection.* (1) EDA invites currently funded TAACs to submit either new or amended applications, provided they have performed in a satisfactory manner and complied with previous or current conditions in their Cooperative Agreements with EDA and contingent upon availability of funds. Such TAACs shall submit an application on a form approved by OMB, as well as a proposed budget, narrative scope of work, and such other information as requested by EDA. Acceptance of an application or amended application for a Cooperative Agreement does not ensure funding by EDA.

(2) EDA may invite new applications through a Federal Funding Opportunity (‘*FFO*’) announcement. An application will require a narrative scope of work, proposed budget and such other information as requested by EDA. Acceptance of an application does not ensure funding by EDA.

(c) *TAAC evaluation.* (1) EDA generally evaluates currently funded TAACs based on:

(i) Performance under Cooperative Agreements with EDA and compliance with the terms and conditions of such Cooperative Agreements;

(ii) Proposed scope of work, budget and application or amended application; and

(iii) Availability of funds.

(2) EDA generally evaluates new TAACs based on:

(i) Competence in administering business assistance programs;

(ii) Background and experience of staff;

(iii) Proposed scope of work, budget and application; and

(iv) Availability of funds.

(d) *TAAC award requirements.* (1) EDA generally funds a TAAC for a three-year project period consisting of three separate funding periods of 12 months each.

(2) There are no matching share requirements for Adjustment Assistance provided by the TAACs to Firms for certification or for administrative expenses of the TAACs.

§ 315.6 Firm eligibility for Adjustment Assistance.

(a) Firms participate in the Trade Adjustment Assistance for Firms program in accordance with the following:

(1) Firms apply for certification through a TAAC by completing a petition for certification. The TAAC will assist Firms in completing such petitions (at no cost to the Firms);

(2) Firms certified in accordance with the procedures described in §§ 315.7 and 315.8 must prepare an Adjustment Proposal for Adjustment Assistance from the TAAC (‘Adjustment Proposal’) and submit it to EDA for approval; and

(3) EDA determines whether the Adjustment Assistance requested in the Adjustment Proposal is eligible based upon the evaluation criteria set forth in subpart D of this part. A Certified Firm may submit a request to the TAAC for Adjustment Assistance to implement an approved Adjustment Proposal.

(b) For certification, EDA evaluates Firms' petitions strictly on the basis of fulfillment of the requirements set forth in § 315.7.

(c) (1) Certified Firms generally receive Adjustment Assistance over a two-year period.

(2) The matching share requirements are as follows:

(i) Each Certified Firm must pay at least 25 percent of the cost of preparing its Adjustment Proposal. Each Certified Firm requesting $30,000 or less in total Adjustment Assistance in its approved Adjustment Proposal must pay at least 25 percent of the cost of that Adjustment Assistance. Each Certified Firm requesting more than $30,000 in total Adjustment Assistance in its approved Adjustment Proposal must pay at least 50 percent of the cost of that Adjustment Assistance.

(ii) Organizations representing trade-injured industries must pay at least 50 percent of the total cash cost of the Adjustment Assistance, in addition to appropriate in-kind contributions.

Subpart B—Certification of Firms

§ 315.7 Certification requirements.

(a) *General.* EDA may certify a Firm as eligible to apply for Adjustment Assistance under section 251(c) of the

Trade Act if it determines that the petition for certification meets one of the minimum certification thresholds set forth in paragraph (b) of this section. In order to be certified, a Firm must meet the criteria listed under any one of the 5 circumstances described in paragraph (b) of this section.

(b) *Minimum certification thresholds.* (1) *Twelve-month decline.* Based upon a comparison of the most recent 12-month period for which data are available and the immediately preceding twelve-month period:

(i) A Significant Number or Proportion of Workers in the Firm has undergone Total or Partial Separation or a Threat of Total or Partial Separation;

(ii) Either sales or production, or both, of the Firm has Decreased Absolutely; or sales or production, or both, of any article or service that accounted for not less than 25 percent of the total production or sales of the Firm during the 12-month period preceding the most recent 12-month period for which data are available have Decreased Absolutely; and

(iii) An Increase in Imports has Contributed Importantly to the applicable Total or Partial Separation or Threat of Total or Partial Separation, and to the applicable decline in sales or production or supply of services.

(2) *Twelve-month versus twenty-four month decline.* Based upon a comparison of the most recent 12-month period for which data are available and the immediately preceding 24-month period:

(i) A Significant Number or Proportion of Workers in the Firm has undergone Total or Partial Separation or a Threat of Total or Partial Separation;

(ii) Either average annual sales or production, or both, of the Firm has Decreased Absolutely; or average annual sales or production, or both, of any article or service that accounted for not less than 25 percent of the total production or sales of the Firm during the 24-month period preceding the most recent 12-month period for which data are available have Decreased Absolutely; and

(iii) An Increase in Imports has Contributed Importantly to the applicable Total or Partial Separation or Threat of Total or Partial Separation, and to the applicable decline in sales or production or supply of services.

(3) *Twelve-month versus thirty-six month decline.* Based upon a comparison of the most recent 12-month period for which data are available and the immediately preceding 36-month period:

(i) A Significant Number or Proportion of Workers in the Firm has undergone Total or Partial Separation or a Threat of Total or Partial Separation;

(ii) Either average annual sales or production, or both, of the Firm has Decreased Absolutely; or average annual sales or production, or both, of any article or service that accounted for not less than 25 percent of the total production or sales of the Firm during the 36-month period preceding the most recent 12-month period for which data are available have Decreased Absolutely; and

(iii) An Increase in Imports has Contributed Importantly to the applicable Total or Partial Separation or Threat of Total or Partial Separation, and to the applicable decline in sales or production or supply of services.

(4) *Interim sales or production decline.* Based upon an interim sales or production decline:

(i) Sales or production has Decreased Absolutely for, at minimum, the most recent six-month period during the most recent 12-month period for which data are available as compared to the same six-month period during the immediately preceding 12-month period;

(ii) During the same base and comparative period of time as sales or production has Decreased Absolutely, a Significant Number or Proportion of Workers in such Firm has undergone Total or Partial Separation or a Threat of Total or Partial Separation; and

(iii) During the same base and comparative period of time as sales or production has Decreased Absolutely, an Increase in Imports has Contributed Importantly to the applicable Total or Partial Separation or Threat of Total or Partial Separation, and to the applicable decline in sales or production or supply of services.

(5) *Interim employment decline.* Based upon an interim employment decline:

(i) A Significant Number or Proportion of Workers in such Firm has undergone Total or Partial Separation or a Threat of Total or Partial Separation during, at a minimum, the most recent six-month period during the most recent 12-month period for which data are available as compared to the same six-month period during the immediately preceding 12-month period; and

(ii) Either sales or production of the Firm has Decreased Absolutely during the 12-month period preceding the most recent 12-month period for which data are available; and

(iii) An Increase in Imports has Contributed Importantly to the applicable Total or Partial Separation or Threat of Total or Partial Separation, and to the applicable decline in sales or production or supply of services.

[74 FR 41598, Aug. 18, 2009, as amended at 75 FR 4265, Jan. 27, 2010]

§ 315.8 Processing petitions for certification.

(a) Firms shall consult with a TAAC for guidance and assistance in the preparation of their petitions for certification.

(b) A Firm seeking certification shall complete a *Petition by a Firm for Certification of Eligibility to Apply for Trade Adjustment Assistance* (Form ED–840P or any successor form) with the following information about such Firm:

(1) Identification and description of the Firm, including legal form of organization, economic history, major ownership interests, officers, directors, management, parent company, Subsidiaries or Affiliates, and production and sales facilities;

(2) Description of goods or services supplied or sold;

(3) Description of imported Directly Competitive or Like Articles or Services with those produced or supplied;

(4) Data on its sales, production and employment for the applicable 24-month, 36-month, or 48-month period, as required under § 315.7(b);

(5) One copy of a complete auditor's certified financial report for the entire period covering the petition, or if not available, one copy of the complete profit and loss statements, balance sheets and supporting statements prepared by the Firm's accountants for the entire period covered by the petition; publicly-owned corporations should submit copies of the most recent Form 10–K annual reports (or Form 10–Q quarterly reports, as appropriate) filed with the U.S. Securities and Exchange Commission for the entire period covered by the petition;

(6) Information concerning its major customers and their purchases (or its bids, if there are no major customers); and

(7) Such other information as EDA considers material.

(c) EDA shall determine whether the petition has been properly prepared and can be accepted. Promptly thereafter, EDA shall notify the petitioner that the petition has been accepted or advise the TAAC that the petition has not been accepted, but may be resubmitted at any time without prejudice when the specified deficiencies have been corrected. Any resubmission will be treated as a new petition.

(d) EDA will publish a notice of acceptance of a petition in the FEDERAL REGISTER.

(e) EDA will initiate an investigation to determine whether the petitioner meets the requirements set forth in section 251(c) of the Trade Act and § 315.7.

(f) A petitioner may withdraw a petition for certification if EDA receives a request for withdrawal before it makes a certification determination or denial. A Firm may submit a new petition at any time thereafter in accordance with the requirements of this section and § 315.7.

(g) Following acceptance of a petition, EDA will:

(1) Make a determination based on the Record as soon as possible after the petitioning Firm or TAAC has submitted all material. In no event may the determination period exceed 40 days from the date on which EDA accepted the petition; and

(2) Either certify the petitioner as eligible to apply for Adjustment Assistance or deny the petition. In either event, EDA shall promptly give written notice of action to the petitioner. Any written notice to the petitioner of a denial of a petition shall specify the reason(s) for the denial. A petitioner shall not be entitled to resubmit a petition within one year from the date of denial, provided, EDA may waive the one-year limitation for good cause.

§315.9 Hearings.

EDA will hold a public hearing on an accepted petition if the petitioner or any interested Person found by EDA to have a Substantial Interest in the proceedings submits a request for a hearing no later than 10 days after the date of publication of the notice of acceptance in the FEDERAL REGISTER, under the following procedures:

(a) The petitioner or any interested Person(s) shall have an opportunity to be present, to produce evidence and to be heard;

(b) A request for public hearing must be delivered by hand or by registered mail to EDA. A request by a Person other than the petitioner shall contain:

(1) The name, address and telephone number of the Person requesting the hearing; and

(2) A complete statement of the relationship of the Person requesting the hearing to the petitioner and the subject matter of the petition, and a statement of the nature of its interest in the proceedings.

(c) If EDA determines that the requesting party does not have a Substantial Interest in the proceedings, a written notice of denial shall be sent to the requesting party. The notice shall specify the reasons for the denial;

(d) EDA shall publish a notice of a public hearing in the FEDERAL REGISTER, containing the subject matter, name of petitioner, and date, time and place of the hearing; and

(e) EDA shall appoint a presiding officer for the hearing who shall respond to all procedural questions.

§315.10 Loss of certification benefits.

EDA may terminate a Firm's certification or refuse to extend Adjustment Assistance to a Firm for any of the following reasons:

(a) Failure to submit an acceptable Adjustment Proposal within two years after date of certification. While approval of an Adjustment Proposal may occur after the expiration of such two-year period, a Firm must submit an acceptable Adjustment Proposal before such expiration;

(b) Failure to submit documentation necessary to start implementation or modify its request for Adjustment Assistance consistent with its Adjustment Proposal within six months after approval of the Adjustment Proposal, where two years have elapsed since the date of certification. If the Firm anticipates needing a longer period to submit documentation, it should indicate the longer period in its Adjustment Proposal. If the Firm is unable to submit its documentation within the allowed time, it should notify EDA in writing of the reasons for the delay and submit a new schedule. EDA has the discretion to accept or refuse a new schedule;

(c) EDA has denied the Firm's request for Adjustment Assistance, the time period allowed for the submission of any documentation in support of such request has expired, and two years have elapsed since the date of certification; or

(d) Failure to diligently pursue an approved Adjustment Proposal where five years have elapsed since the date of certification.

§315.11 Appeals, final determinations and termination of certification.

(a) Any petitioner may appeal in writing to EDA from a denial of certification, provided that EDA receives the appeal by personal delivery or by registered mail within 60 days from the date of notice of denial under §315.8(g). The appeal must state the grounds on which the appeal is based, including a concise statement of the supporting facts and applicable law. The decision of EDA on the appeal shall be the final determination within the Department. In the absence of an appeal by the petitioner under this paragraph, the determination under §315.8(g) shall be final.

(b) A Firm, its representative or any other interested domestic party aggrieved by a final determination under paragraph (a) of this section may, within 60 days after notice of such determination, begin a civil action in the United States Court of International Trade for review of such determination, in accordance with section 284 of the Trade Act.

(c) Whenever EDA determines that a Certified Firm no longer requires Adjustment Assistance or for other good cause, EDA will terminate the certification and promptly publish notice of such termination in the FEDERAL REGISTER. The termination will take effect on the date specified in the published notice.

(d) EDA shall immediately notify the petitioner and shall state the reasons for any termination.

Subpart C—Protective Provisions

§ 315.12 Recordkeeping.

Each TAAC shall keep records that fully disclose the amount and disposition of Trade Adjustment Assistance for Firms program funds so as to facilitate an effective audit.

§ 315.13 Audit and examination.

EDA and the Comptroller General of the United States shall have access for the purpose of audit and examination to any books, documents, papers, and records of a Firm, TAAC or other recipient of Adjustment Assistance pertaining to the award of Adjustment Assistance.

§ 315.14 Certifications.

EDA will provide no Adjustment Assistance to any Firm unless the owners, partners, members, directors or officers thereof certify to EDA:

(a) The names of any attorneys, agents, and other Persons engaged by or on behalf of the Firm for the purpose of expediting applications for such Adjustment Assistance; and

(b) The fees paid or to be paid to any such Person.

§ 315.15 Conflicts of interest.

EDA will provide no Adjustment Assistance to any Firm under this part unless the owners, partners, or officers execute an agreement binding them and the Firm for a period of two years after such Adjustment Assistance is provided, to refrain from employing, tendering any office or employment to, or retaining for professional services any Person who, on the date such assistance or any part thereof was provided, or within one year prior thereto, shall have served as an officer, attorney, agent, or employee occupying a position or engaging in activities which involved discretion with respect to the provision of such Adjustment Assistance.

Subpart D—Adjustment Proposals

§ 315.16 Adjustment proposal requirements.

EDA evaluates Adjustment Proposals based on the following:

(a) EDA must receive the Adjustment Proposal within two years after the date of the certification of the Firm;

(b) The Adjustment Proposal must include a description of any Adjustment Assistance requested to implement such proposal, including financial and other supporting documentation as EDA determines is necessary, based upon either:

(1) An analysis of the Firm's problems, strengths and weaknesses and an assessment of its prospects for recovery; or

(2) If EDA so determines, other available information;

(c) The Adjustment Proposal must:

(1) Be reasonably calculated to contribute materially to the economic adjustment of the Firm (*i.e.*, that such proposal will constructively assist the Firm to establish a competitive position in the same or a different industry);

(2) Give adequate consideration to the interests of a sufficient number of separated workers of the Firm, by providing, for example, that the Firm will:

(i) Give a rehiring preference to such workers;

(ii) Make efforts to find new work for a number of such workers; and

(iii) Assist such workers in obtaining benefits under available programs; and

(3) Demonstrate that the Firm will make all reasonable efforts to use its own resources for its recovery, though under certain circumstances, resources of related Firms or major stockholders will also be considered; and

(d) The Adjustment Assistance identified in the Adjustment Proposal must consist of specialized consulting services designed to assist the Firm in becoming more competitive in the global marketplace. For this purpose, Adjustment Assistance generally consists of knowledge-based services such as market penetration studies, customized business improvements, and designs for new products. Adjustment Assistance does not include expenditures for capital improvements or for the purchase of business machinery or supplies.

Subpart E—Assistance to Industries

§315.17 Assistance to firms in import-impacted industries.

(a) Whenever the International Trade Commission makes an affirmative finding under section 202(B) of the Trade Act that increased imports are a substantial cause of serious injury or threat thereof with respect to an industry, EDA shall provide to the Firms in such industry assistance in the preparation and processing of petitions and applications for benefits under programs which may facilitate the orderly adjustment to import competition of such Firms.

(b) EDA may provide Adjustment Assistance, on such terms and conditions as EDA deems appropriate, for the establishment of industry-wide programs for new product development, new process development, export development or other uses consistent with the purposes of the Trade Act and this part.

(c) Expenditures for Adjustment Assistance under this section may be up to $10,000,000 annually per industry, subject to availability of funds, and shall be made under such terms and conditions as EDA deems appropriate.

PARTS 316–399 [RESERVED]

CHAPTER IV—EMERGENCY STEEL GUARANTEE LOAN BOARD

PART 400—EMERGENCY STEEL GUARANTEE LOAN PROGRAM

Subpart A—General

Subpart B—Board Procedures

Subpart C—Steel Guarantee Loans

AUTHORITY: Pub. L. 106–51, 113 Stat. 252 (15 U.S.C. 1841 note); Pub. L. 106–102, 113 Stat. 1338.

SOURCE: 64 FR 57933, Oct. 27, 1999, unless otherwise noted.

Subpart A—General

§ 400.1 Purpose.

This part is issued by the Emergency Steel Guarantee Loan Board pursuant to section 552 of title 5 of the United States Code and the Emergency Steel Loan Guarantee Act of 1999, Chapter 1 of Public Law 106–51, 113 Stat. 252, as amended by section 734 of Public Law 106–102, 113 Stat. 1338, the Gramm-Leach-Bliley Financial Modernization Act (1999).

[65 FR 70293, Nov. 22, 2000]

§ 400.2 Definitions.

(a) *Act* means the Emergency Steel Loan Guarantee Act of 1999, Chapter 1 of Public Law 106–51 (113 Stat. 252), as amended.

(b) *Administer, administering and administration*, mean the Lender's actions in making, disbursing, servicing (including, but not limited to care, preservation and maintenance of collateral), collecting and liquidating a loan and security.

(c) *Agent* means that Lender authorized to take such actions, exercise such powers, and perform such duties on behalf and in representation of all Lenders party to a Guarantee of a single loan, as is required by, or necessarily incidental to, the terms and conditions of the Guarantee.

(d) *Applicant* means the private banking or investment institution applying for a loan guarantee under this part.

(e) *Board* means the Emergency Steel Guarantee Loan Board.

(f) *Borrower* means a Qualified Steel Company which could receive a loan guaranteed by the Board under this Program.

(g) *Guarantee* means the written agreement between the Board and one or more Lenders, and approved by the Borrower, pursuant to which the Board guarantees repayment of a specified percentage of the principal of the loan, including the Special Terms and Conditions, the General Terms and Conditions, and all exhibits thereto.

(h) *Guaranteed Portion* means the portion of the principal of a loan that is subject to the Guarantee.

(i) *Lender* means a private banking or investment institution, eligible under § 400.201, that is a party to a Guarantee issued by the Board. With respect to a Guarantee of a single loan to which more than one Lender is a party, the term Lender means Agent.

(j) *Loan Documents* mean the loan agreement and all other instruments, and all documentation between the Lender and the Borrower evidencing the making, disbursing, securing, collecting, or otherwise administering of the loan. It includes any agreement and other documents relating to a Supplemental Guarantee. Loan Documents may not be modified without the prior written approval of the Board.

(k) *Program* means the Emergency Steel Guarantee Loan Program established by the Act.

(l) *Security* means all property, real or personal, required by the provisions of the Guarantee or by the Loan Documents to secure repayment of any indebtedness of the Borrower under the Loan Documents or Guarantee. It does not include a Supplemental Guarantee.

(m) *Qualified Steel Company* means a company that is incorporated under the laws of any State; is engaged in the production and manufacture of a product defined by the American Iron and Steel Institute as a basic steel mill product, including ingots, slab and billets, plates, flat-rolled steel, sections and structural products, bars, rail type products, pipe and tube, and wire rod; and has experienced layoffs, production losses, or financial losses since January 1, 1998. An iron ore company incorporated under the law of any state is considered a Qualified Steel Company for purposes of the Program.

(n) *Supplemental Guarantee* means a guarantee provided by one or more third parties, public or private, of part of the Unguaranteed Portion of a guaranteed loan.

(o) *Unguaranteed Portion* means the portion of the principal of a loan that is not covered by the Guarantee.

[64 FR 57933, Oct. 27, 1999, as amended at 65 FR 24104, Apr. 25, 2000; 66 FR 53079, Oct. 19, 2001]

Subpart B—Board Procedures

§ 400.100 Purpose and scope.

This subpart describes the Board's authorities and organizational structure, the means and rules by which the Board takes actions, and procedures for public access to Board records.

§ 400.101 Composition of the Board.

The Board consists of the Chairman of the Board of Governors of the Federal Reserve System, who acts as Chairman of the Board, the Chairman of the Securities and Exchange Commission, and the Secretary of Commerce.

§ 400.102 Authority of the Board.

Pursuant to the provisions of the Act, the Board is authorized to guarantee loans provided to Qualified Steel Companies by private banking and investment institutions in accordance with the procedures, rules, and regulations established by the Board, to make the determinations authorized by the Act, and to take such other actions as necessary to carry out its functions in accordance with the Act.

§ 400.103 Offices.

The principal offices of the Board are in the U.S. Department of Commerce, Washington, DC 20230.

[72 FR 63976, Nov. 14, 2007]

§ 400.104 Meetings and actions of the Board.

(a) *Place and frequency.* The Board meets, on the call of the Chairman, in order to consider matters requiring action by the Board. Time and place for any such meeting shall be determined by the members of the Board.

(b) *Quorum and voting.* Two voting members of the Board constitute a quorum for the transaction of business. All decisions and determinations of the Board shall be made by a majority vote of the voting members. All votes on determinations of the Board required by the Act shall be recorded in the minutes. A Board member may request that any vote be recorded according to individual Board members.

(c) *Agenda of meetings.* To the extent practicable, an agenda for each meeting shall be distributed to members of the Board at least two days in advance of the date of the meeting, together with copies of materials relevant to the agenda items.

(d) *Minutes.* The Secretary of the Board shall keep minutes of each Board meeting and of action taken without a meeting, a draft of which is to be distributed to each member of the Board as soon as practicable after each meeting or action. To the extent practicable, the minutes of a Board meeting shall be corrected and approved at the next meeting of the Board.

(e) *Use of conference call communications equipment.* Any member may participate in a meeting of the Board through the use of conference call, telephone or similar communications equipment, by means of which all persons participating in the meeting can simultaneously speak to and hear each other. Any member so participating in a meeting shall be deemed present for all purposes. Actions taken by the Board at meetings conducted through the use of such equipment, including the votes of each member, shall be recorded in the usual manner in the minutes of the meetings of the Board.

(f) *Actions between meetings.* When, in the judgment of the Chairman, circumstances occur making it desirable for the Board to consider action when it is not feasible to call a meeting, the relevant information and recommendations for action may be transmitted to the members by the Secretary of the Board and the voting members may communicate their votes to the Chairman in writing (including an action signed in counterpart by each Board member), electronically, or orally (including telephone communication). Any action taken under this paragraph has the same effect as an action taken at a meeting. Any such action shall be recorded in the minutes.

(g) *Delegations of authority.* The Board may delegate authority, subject to such terms and conditions as the Board deems appropriate, to the Executive Director, the General Counsel, or the Secretary of the Board, to take certain actions not required by the Act to be taken by the Board. All delegations shall be made pursuant to resolutions of the Board and recorded in writing, whether in the minutes of a meeting or otherwise. Any action taken pursuant to delegated authority has the effect of an action taken by the Board.

§400.105 Staff.

(a) *Executive Director.* The Executive Director of the Board advises and assists the Board in carrying out its responsibilities under the Act, provides general direction with respect to the administration of the Board's actions, directs the activities of the staff, and performs such other duties as the Board may require.

(b) *General Counsel.* The General Counsel of the Board provides legal advice relating to the responsibilities of the Board and performs such other duties as the Board may require.

(c) *Secretary of the Board.* The Secretary of the Board sends notice of all meetings, prepares minutes of all meetings, maintains a complete record of all votes and actions taken by the Board, has custody of all records of the Board and performs such other duties as the Board may require.

(d) An individual may hold more than one staff position.

[64 FR 57933, Oct. 27, 1999, as amended at 65 FR 70293, Nov. 22, 2000]

§400.106 *Ex parte* communications.

Oral or written communication, not on the public record, between any member of the Board and any party or parties interested in any matter pending before the Board concerning the substance of that matter is prohibited.

[66 FR 53079, Oct. 19, 2001]

§400.107 Freedom of Information Act.

(a) *Definitions.* All terms used in this section which are defined in 5 U.S.C. 551 or 5 U.S.C. 552 shall have the same meaning in this section. In addition the following definitions apply to this section:

(1) *FOIA*, as used in this section, means the "Freedom of Information Act," as amended, 5 U.S.C. 552.

(2) *Commercial use request* means a request from or on behalf of one who seeks information for a use or purpose that furthers the commercial, trade, or profit interests of the requester or the person on whose behalf the request is made.

(3) *Direct costs* mean those expenditures that the Board actually incurs in searching for, reviewing, and duplicating documents in response to a request made under paragraph (c) of this section. Direct costs include, for example, the labor costs of the employee performing the work (the basic rate of pay for the employee, plus 16 percent of that rate to cover benefits). Not included in direct costs are overhead expenses such as the costs of space and heating or lighting of the facility in which the records are kept.

(4) *Duplication* means the process of making a copy of a document in response to a request for disclosure of

records or for inspection of original records that contain exempt material or that otherwise cannot be inspected directly. Among others, such copies may take the form of paper, microfilm, audiovisual materials, or machine-readable documentation (e.g., magnetic tape or disk).

(5) *Educational institution* means a preschool, a public or private elementary or secondary school, or an institution of undergraduate higher education, graduate higher education, professional education, or an institution of vocational education that operates a program of scholarly research.

(6) *Noncommercial scientific institution* refers to an institution that is not operated on a "commercial" basis (as that term is used in this section) and which is operated solely for the purpose of conducting scientific research, the results of which are not intended to promote any particular product or industry.

(7) *News* means information about current events or that would be of current interest to the public. Examples of news media entities include, but are not limited to, television or radio stations broadcasting to the public at large, and publishers of newspapers and other periodicals (but only in those instances when they can qualify as disseminators of "news") who make their products available for purchase or subscription by the general public. "Freelance" journalists may be regarded as working for a news organization if they can demonstrate a solid basis for expecting publication through that organization, even though not actually employed by it.

(8) *Representative of the news media* means any person actively gathering news for an entity that is organized and operated to publish or broadcast news to the general public.

(9) *Review* means the process of examining documents, located in response to a request for access, to determine whether any portion of a document is exempt information. It includes doing all that is necessary to excise the documents and otherwise to prepare them for release. Review does not include time spent resolving general legal or policy issues regarding the application of exemptions.

(10) *Search* means the process of looking for material that is responsive to a request, including page-by-page or line-by-line identification within documents. Searches may be done manually or by computer.

(b) *Records available for public inspection and copying*—(1) *Types of records made available.* The information in this section is furnished for the guidance of the public and in compliance with the requirements of the Freedom of Information FOIA, as amended (5 U.S.C. 552)(FOIA). This section sets forth the procedures the Board follows to make publicly available the materials specified in 5 U.S.C. 552(a)(2). These materials shall be made available for inspection and copying at the Board's Freedom of Information Office pursuant to 5 U.S.C. 552(a)(2). Information routinely provided to the public as part of a regular Board activity (for example, press releases) may be provided to the public without following this section.

(2) *Reading room procedures.* Information available under this section is available for inspection and copying, from 9:00 a.m. to 5:00 p.m. weekdays, at the Freedom of Information Office of the Board, Steel Guarantee Loan Board, U.S. Department of Commerce, Washington, DC 20230.

(3) *Electronic records.* Information available under this section that was created on or after November 1, 1996, shall also be available on the Board's website found at *http://elb.osec.doc.gov* and at *http://elb.commerce.gov.*

(c) *Records available to the public on request*—(1) *Types of records made available.* All records of the Board that are not available under paragraph (b) of this section shall be made available upon request, pursuant to the procedures in this section and the exceptions set forth in the FOIA. The Board's policy is to make discretionary disclosures of records or information exempt from disclosure under the FOIA whenever disclosure would not foreseeably harm an interest protected by a FOIA exemption, but this policy does not create any right enforceable in court.

(2) *Procedures for requesting records.* A request for records shall reasonably describe the records in a way that enables the Board's staff to identify and

produce the records with reasonable effort and without unduly burdening or significantly interfering with any of the Board's operations. The request shall be submitted in writing to the Secretary of the Board, Steel Guarantee Loan Board, U.S. Department of Commerce, Washington, DC 20230; or sent by facsimile to the Secretary of the Board. The request shall be clearly marked *FREEDOM OF INFORMATION ACT REQUEST*.

(3) *Contents of request*. The request shall contain the following information:

(i) The name and address of the requester, and the telephone number at which the requester can be reached during normal business hours;

(ii) Whether the requested information is intended for commercial use, or whether the requester represents an educational or noncommercial scientific institution, or news media;

(iii) A statement agreeing to pay the applicable fees, or a statement identifying any fee limitation desired, or a request for a waiver or reduction of fees that satisfies paragraph (f) of this section.

(d) *Processing requests*—(1) *Priority of responses*. The date of receipt for any request, including one that is addressed incorrectly or that is referred to the Board by another agency, is the date the Secretary of the Board actually receives the request. The Secretary of the Board shall normally process requests in the order they are received. However, in the Secretary of the Board's discretion, the Board may use two or more processing tracks by distinguishing between simple and more complex requests based on the number of pages involved, or some other measure of the amount of work and/or time needed to process the request, and whether the request qualifies for expedited processing as described in paragraph (d)(2), of this section. When using multitrack processing, the Secretary of the Board may provide requesters in the slower track(s) with an opportunity to limit the scope of their requests in order to qualify for faster processing. The Secretary of the Board shall contact the requester by telephone or by letter, whichever is most efficient in each case.

(2) *Expedited processing*. (i) A person may request expedited access to records by submitting a statement, certified to be true and correct to the best of that person's knowledge and belief, that demonstrates a compelling need for the records, as defined in 5 U.S.C. 552(a)(6)(E)(v).

(ii) The Secretary of the Board shall notify a requester of the determination whether to grant or deny a request for expedited processing within ten working days of receipt of the request. If the Secretary of the Board grants the request for expedited processing, the Board shall process the request for access to information as soon as practicable. If the Secretary of the Board denies a request for expedited processing, the requester may file an appeal pursuant to the procedures set forth in paragraph (e) of this section, and the Board shall respond to the appeal within twenty days after the appeal was received by the Board.

(3) *Time limits*. The time for response to requests shall be 20 working days, except:

(i) In the case of expedited treatment under paragraph (d)(2) of this section;

(ii) Where the running of such time is suspended for payment of fees pursuant to paragraph (f)(2)(ii) of this section;

(iii) Where the estimated charge is less than $250, and the requester does not guarantee payment pursuant to paragraph (f)(2)(i) of this section; or

(iv) In unusual circumstances, as defined in 5 U.S.C. 552(a)(6)(B)(iii), the time limit may be extended for a period of time not to exceed 10 working days as provided by written notice to the requester, setting forth the reasons for the extension and the date on which a determination is expected to be dispatched; or such alternative time period as mutually agreed to by the Secretary of the Board and the requester when the Secretary of the Board notifies the requester that the request cannot be processed in the specified time limit.

(4) *Response to request*. In response to a request that satisfies paragraph (c) of this section, an appropriate search shall be conducted of records in the custody and control of the Board on the date of receipt of the request, and

a review made of any responsive information located. The Secretary of the Board shall notify the requester of:

(i) The Secretary of the Board's determination of the request and the reasons therefor;

(ii) The information withheld, and the basis for withholding; and

(iii) The right to appeal any denial or partial denial, pursuant to paragraph (e) of this section.

(5) *Referral to another agency.* To the extent a request covers documents that were created by, obtained from, classified by, or is in the primary interest of another agency, the Secretary of the Board may refer the request to that agency for a direct response by that agency and inform the requester promptly of the referral. The Secretary of the Board shall consult with another Federal agency before responding to a requester if the Board receives a request for a record in which:

(i) Another Federal agency subject to the FOIA has a significant interest, but not the primary interest; or

(ii) Another Federal agency not subject to the FOIA has the primary interest or a significant interest. Ordinarily, the agency that originated a record will be presumed to have the primary interest in it.

(6) *Providing responsive records.* (i) A copy of records or portions of records responsive to the request shall be sent to the requester by regular U.S. mail to the address indicated in the request, unless the requester elects to take delivery of the documents at the Board's Freedom of Information Office or makes other acceptable arrangements, or the Secretary of the Board deems it appropriate to send the documents by another means. The Secretary of the Board shall provide a copy of the record in any form or format requested if the record is readily reproducible in that form or format, but the Secretary of the Board need not provide more than one copy of any record to a requester.

(ii) The Secretary of the Board shall provide any reasonably segregable portion of a record that is responsive to the request after deleting those portions that are exempt under the FOIA or this section.

(iii) Except where disclosure is expressly prohibited by statute, regulation, or order, the Secretary of the Board may authorize the release of records that are exempt from mandatory disclosure whenever the Board or designated Board members determine that there would be no foreseeable harm in such disclosure.

(iv) The Board is not required in response to the request to create records or otherwise to prepare new records.

(7) *Prohibition against disclosure.* Except as provided in this part, no officer, employee, or agent of the Board shall disclose or permit the disclosure of any unpublished information of the Board to any person (other than Board officers, employees, or agents properly entitled to such information for the performance of official duties), unless required by law.

(e) *Appeals.* (1) Any person denied access to Board records requested under paragraph (c) of this section, denied expedited processing under paragraph (d) of this section, or denied a waiver of fees under paragraph (f) of this section may file a written appeal within 30 calendar days after the date of such denial with the Board. The written appeal shall prominently display the phrase *FREEDOM OF INFORMATION ACT APPEAL* on the first page, and shall be addressed to the General Counsel of the Board, Steel Guarantee Loan Board, U.S. Department of Commerce, Washington, DC 20230; or sent by facsimile to the General Counsel of the Board. The appeal shall include a copy of the original request, the initial denial, if any, and a statement of the reasons why the requested records should be made available and why the initial denial was in error.

(2) The General Counsel of the Board shall make a determination regarding any appeal within 20 working days of actual receipt of the appeal, and the determination letter shall notify the appealing party of the right to seek judicial review in event of denial.

(f) *Fee schedules; waiver of fees*—

(1) *Fee schedule.* The fees applicable to a request for records pursuant to paragraph (c) of this section are set forth in the uniform fee schedule at the end of this paragraph (f).

(i) *Search*. (A) Search fees shall be charged for all requests—other than requests made by educational institutions, noncommercial scientific institutions, or representatives of the news media—subject to the limitations of paragraph (f)(1)(iv) of this section. The Secretary of the Board shall charge for time spent searching even if no responsive record is located or if the Secretary of the Board withholds the record(s) located as entirely exempt from disclosure.

Search fees shall be the direct costs of conducting the search by the involved employees.

(B) For computer searches of records, requesters will be charged the direct costs of conducting the search, although certain requesters (as provided in paragraph (f)(3) of this section will be charged no search fee and certain other requesters (as provided in paragraph (f)(3)) are entitled to the cost equivalent of two hours of manual search time without charge. These direct costs include the costs, attributable to the search, of operating a central processing unit and operator/programmer salary.

(ii) *Duplication*. Duplication fees will be charged to all requesters, subject to the limitations of paragraph (f)(1)(iv) of this section. For a paper photocopy of a record (no more than one copy of which need be supplied), the fee shall be 15 cents per page. For copies produced by computer, such as tapes or printouts, the Secretary of the Board shall charge the direct costs, including operator time, of producing the copy. For other forms of duplication, the Secretary of the Board will charge the direct costs of that duplication.

(iii) *Review*. Review fees shall be charged to requesters who make a commercial use request. Review fees shall be charged only for the initial record review—the review done when the Secretary of the Board determines whether an exemption applies to a particular record at the initial request level. No charge will be made for review at the administrative appeal level for an exemption already applied. However, records withheld under an exemption that is subsequently determined not to apply may be reviewed again to determine whether any other exemption not previously considered applies, and the costs of that review are chargeable. Review fees shall be the direct costs of conducting the review by the involved employees.

(iv) *Limitations on charging fees*. (A) No search fee will be charged for requests by educational institutions, noncommercial scientific institutions, or representatives of the news media.

(B) No search fee or review fee will be charged for a quarter-hour period unless more than half of that period is required for search or review.

(C) Whenever a total fee calculated under this paragraph is $25 or less for any request, no fee will be charged.

(D) For requesters other than those seeking records for a commercial use, no fee will be charged unless the cost of search in excess of two hours plus the cost of duplication in excess of 100 pages totals more than $25.

(2) *Payment procedures*. All persons requesting records pursuant to paragraph (c) of this section shall pay the applicable fees before the Secretary of the Board sends copies of the requested records, unless a fee waiver has been granted pursuant to paragraph (f)(6) of this section. Requesters must pay fees by check or money order made payable to the Treasury of the United States.

(i) *Advance notification of fees*. If the estimated charges are likely to exceed $25, the Secretary of the Board shall notify the requester of the estimated amount, unless the requester has indicated a willingness to pay fees as high as those anticipated. Upon receipt of such notice, the requester may confer with the Secretary of the Board to reformulate the request to lower the costs. The processing of the request shall be suspended until the requester provides the Secretary of the Board with a written guarantee that payment will be made upon completion of the processing.

(ii) *Advance payment*. The Secretary of the Board shall require advance payment of any fee estimated to exceed $250. The Secretary of the Board shall also require full payment in advance where a requester has previously failed to pay a fee in a timely fashion. If an advance payment of an estimated fee exceeds the actual total fee by $1 or more, the difference shall be refunded to the requester. The time period for responding to requests under paragraph (d)(4) of this section, and the processing of the request shall be suspended until the Secretary of the Board receives the required payment.

(iii) *Late charges.* The Secretary of the Board may assess interest charges when fee payment is not made within 30 days of the date on which the billing was sent. Assessment of such interest will commence on the 31st day following the day on which the billing was sent. Interest is at the rate prescribed in 31 U.S.C. 3717.

(3) *Categories of uses.* The fees assessed depend upon the fee category. In determining which category is appropriate, the Secretary of the Board shall look to the identity of the requester and the intended use set forth in the request for records. Where a requester's description of the use is insufficient to make a determination, the Secretary of the Board may seek additional clarification before categorizing the request.

(i) *Commercial use requester.* The fees for search, duplication, and review apply when records are requested for commercial use.

(ii) *Educational, non-commercial scientific institutions, or representatives of the news media requesters.* The fees for duplication apply when records are not sought for commercial use, and the requester is a representative of the news media or an educational or non-commercial scientific institution, whose purpose is scholarly or scientific research. The first 100 pages of duplication, however, will be provided free.

(iii) *All other requesters.* For all other requests, the fees for search and duplication apply. The first two hours of search time and the first 100 pages of duplication, however, will be provided free.

(4) *Nonproductive search.* Fees for search may be charged even if no responsive documents are found. Fees for search and review may be charged even if the request is denied.

(5) *Aggregated requests.* A requester may not file multiple requests at the same time, solely in order to avoid payment of fees. If the Secretary of the Board reasonably believes that a requester is separating a request into a series of requests for the purpose of evading the assessment of fees or that several requesters appear to be acting together to submit multiple requests solely in order to avoid payment of fees, the Secretary of the Board may aggregate such requests and charge accordingly. It is considered reasonable for the Secretary of the Board to presume that multiple requests by one requester on the same topic made within a 30-day period have been made to avoid fees.

(6) *Waiver or reduction of fees.* A request for a waiver or reduction of the fees, and the justification for the waiver, shall be included with the request for records to which it pertains. If a waiver is requested and the requester has not indicated in writing an agreement to pay the applicable fees if the waiver request is denied, the time for response to the request for documents, as set forth in under paragraph (d)(4) of this section, shall not begin until a determination has been made on the request for a waiver or reduction of fees.

(i) *Standards for determining waiver or reduction.* The Secretary of the Board may grant a waiver or reduction of fees where it is determined both that disclosure of the information is in the public interest because it is likely to contribute significantly to public understanding of the operation or activities of the government, and that the disclosure of information is not primarily in the commercial interest of the requester. In making this determination, the following factors shall be considered:

(A) Whether the subject of the records concerns the operations or activities of the government;

(B) Whether disclosure of the information is likely to contribute significantly to public understanding of government operations or activities;

(C) Whether the requester has the intention and ability to disseminate the information to the public;

(D) Whether the information is already in the public domain;

(E) Whether the requester has a commercial interest that would be furthered by the disclosure; and, if so,

(F) Whether the magnitude of the identified commercial interest of the requester is sufficiently large, in comparison with the public interest in disclosure, that disclosure is primarily in the commercial interest of the requester.

(ii) *Contents of request for waiver.* A request for a waiver or reduction of fees shall include a clear statement of how the request satisfies the criteria set forth in paragraph (f)(6)(i) of this section.

(iii) *Burden of proof.* The burden shall be on the requester to present evidence or information in support of a request for a waiver or reduction of fees.

(iv) *Determination by Secretary of the Board.* The Secretary of the Board shall make a determination on the request for a waiver or reduction of fees and shall notify the requester accordingly. A denial may be appealed to the Board in accordance with paragraph (e) of this section.

(7) *Uniform fee schedule.*

Service	Rate
(i) Manual search	Actual salary rate of employee involved, plus 16 percent of salary rate.
(ii) Computerized search	Actual direct cost, including operator time.
(iii) Duplication of records:	
(A) Paper copy reproduction.	$.15 per page
(B) Other reproduction (e.g., computer disk or printout, microfilm, microfiche, or microform).	Actual direct cost, including operator time.
(iv) Review of records (includes preparation for release, *i.e.* excising).	Actual salary rate of employee conducting review, plus 16 percent of salary rate.

(g) *Reuest for confidential treatment of business information*—(1) *Submission of request.* Any submitter of information to the Board who desires confidential treatment of business information pursuant to 5 U.S.C. 552(b)(4) shall file a request for confidential treatment with the Board at the time the information is submitted or a reasonable time after submission.

(2) *Form of request.* Each request for confidential treatment of business information shall state in reasonable detail the facts supporting the commercial or financial nature of the business information and the legal justification under which the business information should be protected. Conclusory statements that release of the information would cause competitive harm generally will not be considered sufficient to justify confidential treatment.

(3) *Designation and separation of confidential material.* All information considered confidential by a submitter shall be clearly designated "*PROPRIETARY*" or "*BUSINESS CONFIDENTIAL*" in the submission and separated from information for which confidential treatment is not requested. Failure to segregate confidential commercial or financial information from other material may result in release of the nonsegregated material to the public without notice to the submitter.

(h) *Request for access to confidential commercial or financial information*—(1) *Request for confidential commercial or financial information.* A request by a submitter for confidential treatment of any business information shall be considered in connection with a request for access to that information.

(2) *Notice to the submitter.* (i) The Secretary of the Board shall notify a submitter who requested confidential treatment of information pursuant to 5 U.S.C. 552(b)(4), of the request for access.

(ii) Absent a request for confidential treatment, the Secretary of the Board may notify a submitter of a request for access to submitter's business information if the Secretary of the Board reasonably believes that disclosure of the information may cause substantial competitive harm to the submitter.

(iii) The notice given to the submitter by mail, return receipt requested, shall be given as soon as practicable after receipt of the request for access, and shall describe the request and provide the submitter seven working days from the date of notice, to submit written objections to disclosure of the information. Such statement shall specify all grounds for withholding any of the information and shall demonstrate why the information which is considered to be commercial or financial information, and that the information is a trade secret, is privileged or confidential, or that its disclosure is likely to cause substantial competitive harm to the submitter. If the submitter fails to respond to the notice within the time specified, the submitter will be considered to have no objection to the release of the information. Information a submitter provides under this paragraph may itself be subject to disclosure under the FOIA.

(3) *Exceptions to notice to submitter.* Notice to the submitter need not be given if:

(i) The Secretary of the Board determines that the request for access should be denied;

(ii) The requested information lawfully has been made available to the public;

(iii) Disclosure of the information is required by law (other than 5 U.S.C. 552); or

(iv) The submitter's claim of confidentiality under 5 U.S.C. 552(b)(4) appears obviously frivolous or has already been denied by the Secretary of the Board, except that in this last instance the Secretary of the Board shall give the submitter written notice of the determination to disclose the information at least seven working days prior to disclosure.

(4) *Notice to requester.* At the same time the Secretary of the Board notifies the submitter, the Secretary of the Board also shall notify the requester that the request is subject to the provisions of this section.

(5) *Determination by Secretary of the Board.* The Secretary of the Board's determination whether or not to disclose any information for which confidential treatment has been requested pursuant to this section shall be communicated to the submitter and the requester immediately. If the Secretary of the Board determines to disclose the business information over the objection of a submitter, the Secretary of the Board shall give the submitter written notice via mail, return receipt requested, or similar means, which shall include:

(i) A statement of reason(s) why the submitter's objections to disclosure were not sustained;

(ii) A description of the business information to be disclosed; and

(iii) A statement that the component intends to disclose the information seven working days from the date the submitter receives the notice.

(6) *Notice of lawsuit.* The Secretary of the Board shall promptly notify any submitter of information covered by this section of the filing of any suit against the Board to compel disclosure of such information, and shall promptly notify a requester of any suit filed against the Board to enjoin the disclosure of requested documents.

[64 FR 57933, Oct. 27, 1999, as amended at 65 FR 70293, Nov. 22, 2000]

§ 400.108 Restrictions on lobbying.

(a) No funds received through a loan guaranteed under this Program may be expended by the recipient of a Federal contract, grant, loan, loan Guarantee, or cooperative agreement to pay any person for influencing or attempting to influence an officer or employee of any agency, a Member of Congress, an officer or employee of Congress, or an employee of a Member of Congress in connection with any of the following covered Federal actions: the awarding of any Federal contract, the making of any Federal grant, the making of any Federal loan or loan Guarantee, the entering into of any cooperative agreement, and the extension, continuation, renewal, amendment, or modification of any Federal contract, grant, loan, loan Guarantee, or cooperative agreement.

(b) Each person who requests or receives from an agency a commitment providing for the United States to insure or guarantee a loan shall file with that agency a statement, set forth in the application form, whether that person has made or has agreed to make any payment to influence or attempt to influence an officer or employee of any agency, a Member of Congress, an officer or employee of Congress, or an employee of a Member of Congress in connection with that loan insurance or Guarantee.

(c) Each person who requests or receives from an agency a commitment providing for the United States to insure or guarantee a loan shall file with that agency a Standard Form-LLL if that person has made or has agreed to make any payment to influence or attempt to influence an officer or employee of any agency, a Member of Congress, an officer or employee of Congress, or an employee of a Member of Congress in connection with that loan insurance or Guarantee.

(d) Each person shall file a certification, contained in the application form, and a disclosure form (Standard Form-LLL), if required, with each submission that initiates agency consideration of such person for:

(1) Award of a Federal contract, grant, or cooperative agreement exceeding $100,000; or

(2) An award of a Federal loan or a commitment providing for the United States to insure or guarantee a loan exceeding $150,000.

(e) Each person shall file a certification, and a disclosure form, if required, upon receipt by such person of:

(1) A Federal contract, grant, or cooperative agreement exceeding $100,000; or

(2) A Federal loan or a commitment providing for the United States to insure or Guarantee a loan exceeding $150,000, unless such person previously filed a certification, and a disclosure form, if required, under paragraph (c) of this section.

(f) Each person shall file a disclosure form at the end of each calendar quarter in which there occurs any event that requires disclosure or that materially affects the accuracy of the information contained in any disclosure form previously filed by such person under paragraphs (d) or (e) of this section. An event that materially affects the accuracy of the information reported includes:

(1) A cumulative increase of $25,000 or more in the amount paid or expected to be paid for influencing or attempting to influence a covered Federal action; or

(2) A change in the person(s) or individual(s) influencing or attempting to influence a covered Federal action; or

(3) A change in the officer(s), employee(s), or Member(s) contacted to influence or attempt to influence a covered Federal action.

§400.109 Government-wide debarment and suspension (nonprocurement).

(a) Executive Order (E.O.) 12549 provides that, to the extent permitted by law, Executive departments and agencies shall participate in a governmentwide system for nonprocurement debarment and suspension. A person who is debarred or suspended shall be excluded from Federal financial and nonfinancial assistance and benefits under Federal programs and activities. Debarment or suspension of a participant in a program by one agency shall have governmentwide effect. The Board shall review the List of Debarred entities prior to making final loan Guarantee decisions. Suspension or debarment may be a basis for denying a loan Guarantee.

(b) This section applies to all persons who have participated, are currently participating or may reasonably be expected to participate in transactions under Federal nonprocurement programs. For purposes of this section such transactions will be referred to as "covered transactions".

(1) *Covered transaction.* For purposes of this section, a covered transaction is a primary covered transaction or a lower tier covered transaction. Covered transactions at any tier need not involve the transfer of Federal funds.

(i) Primary covered transaction. Except as noted in paragraph (b)(2) of this section, a primary covered transaction is any nonprocurement transaction between an agency and a person, regardless of type, including: grants, cooperative agreements, scholarships, fellowships, contracts of assistance, loans, loan Guarantees, subsidies, insurance, payments for specified use, donation agreements and any other nonprocurement transactions between a Federal agency and a person.

(ii) Lower tier covered transaction. A lower tier covered transaction is:

(A) Any transaction between a participant and a person other than a procurement contract for goods or services, regardless of type, under a primary covered transaction;

(B) Any procurement contract for goods or services between a participant and a person, regardless of type, expected to equal or exceed the Federal procurement small purchase threshold fixed at 10 U.S.C. 2304(g) and 41 U.S.C. 253(g) (currently $100,000) under a primary covered transaction;

(C) Any procurement contract for goods or services between a participant and a person under a covered transaction, regardless of amount, under which that person will have a critical influence on or substantive control over that covered transaction. Such persons may include loan officers or chief executive officers acting as principal investigators and providers of federally-required audit services.

(2) *Exceptions.* The following transactions are not covered:

(i) Statutory entitlements or mandatory awards (but not subtier awards thereunder which are not themselves mandatory), including deposited funds insured by the Federal Government;

(ii) Direct awards to foreign governments or public international organizations, or transactions with foreign governments or foreign governmental entities, public international organizations, foreign government owned (in whole or in part) or controlled entities, entities consisting wholly or partially of foreign governments or foreign governmental entities;

(iii) Benefits to an individual as a personal entitlement without regard to the individual's present responsibility (but benefits received in an individual's business capacity are not excepted);

(iv) Federal employment;

(v) Transactions pursuant to national or agency-recognized emergencies or disasters;

(vi) Incidental benefits derived from ordinary governmental operations; and

(vii) Other transactions where the application of this section would be prohibited by law.

(3) *Board covered transactions.* This section applies to the Board's loan Guarantees, subcontracts and transactions at any tier that are charges as direct or indirect costs, regardless of type.

(c) *Primary covered transactions.* Except to the extent prohibited by law, persons who are debarred or suspended shall be excluded from primary covered transactions as either participants or principals throughout the Executive Branch of the Federal Government for the period of their debarment, suspension, or the period they are proposed for debarment under 48 CFR part 9, subpart 9.4. Accordingly, no agency shall enter into primary covered transactions with such excluded persons during such period, except as permitted pursuant to paragraph (l) of this section.

(d) *Lower tier covered transactions.* Except to the extent prohibited by law, persons who have been proposed for debarment under 48 CFR part 9, subpart 9.4, debarred or suspended shall be excluded from participating as either participants or principals in all lower tier covered transactions (see paragraph (b)(1)(ii) of this section for the period of their exclusion.

(e) *Exceptions.* Debarment or suspension does not affect a person's eligibility for—

(1) Statutory entitlements or mandatory awards (but not subtier awards thereunder which are not themselves mandatory), including deposited funds insured by the Federal Government;

(2) Direct awards to foreign governments or public international organizations, or transactions with foreign governments or foreign governmental entities, public international organizations, foreign government owned (in whole or in part) or controlled entities, and entities consisting wholly or partially of foreign governments or foreign governmental entities;

(3) Benefits to an individual as a personal entitlement without regard to the individual's present responsibility (but benefits received in an individual's business capacity are not excepted);

(4) Federal employment;

(5) Transactions pursuant to national or agency-recognized emergencies or disasters;

(6) Incidental benefits derived from ordinary governmental operations; and

(7) Other transactions where the application of this section would be prohibited by law.

(f) Persons who are ineligible are excluded in accordance with the applicable statutory, executive order, or regulatory authority.

(g) Persons who accept voluntary exclusions are excluded in accordance with the terms of their settlements. The Board shall, and participants may, contact the original action agency to ascertain the extent of the exclusion.

(h) The Board may grant an exception permitting a debarred, suspended, or voluntarily excluded person, or a person proposed for debarment under 48 CFR part 9, subpart 9.4, to participate in a particular covered transaction upon a written determination by the agency head or an authorized designee stating the reason(s) for deviating from the Presidential policy established by

Executive Order 12549. However, in accordance with the President's stated intention in the Executive Order, exceptions shall be granted only infrequently. Exceptions shall be reported in accordance with the Executive Order.

(i) Notwithstanding the debarment, suspension, proposed debarment under 48 CFR part 9, subpart 9.4, determination of ineligibility, or voluntary exclusion of any person by an agency, agencies and participants may continue covered transactions in existence at the time the person was debarred, suspended, proposed for debarment under 48 CFR part 9, subpart 9.4, declared ineligible, or voluntarily excluded. A decision as to the type of termination action, if any, to be taken should be made only after thorough review to ensure the propriety of the proposed action.

(j) Agencies and participants shall not renew or extend covered transactions (other than no-cost time extensions) with any person who is debarred, suspended, proposed for debarment under 48 CFR part 9, subpart 9.4, ineligible or voluntary excluded, except as provided in paragraph (h) of this section.

(k) Except as permitted under paragraphs (h) or (i) of this section, a participant shall not knowingly do business under a covered transaction with a person who is—

(1) Debarred or suspended;

(2) Proposed for debarment under 48 CFR part 9, subpart 9.4; or

(3) Ineligible for or voluntarily excluded from the covered transaction.

(l) Violation of the restriction under paragraph (k) of this section may result in disallowance of costs, annulment or termination of award, issuance of a stop work order, debarment or suspension, or other remedies as appropriate.

(m) A participant may rely upon the certification of a prospective participant in a lower tier covered transaction that it and its principals are not debarred, suspended, proposed for debarment under 48 CFR part 9, subpart 9.4, ineligible, or voluntarily excluded from the covered transaction, unless it knows that the certification is erroneous. An agency has the burden of proof that a participant did knowingly do business with a person that filed an erroneous certification.

§ 400.110 Amendments.

The Board's rules in this chapter may be adopted or amended, or new rules may be adopted, only by majority vote of the Board.

[65 FR 70293, Nov. 22, 2000]

Subpart C—Steel Guarantee Loans

§ 400.200 Eligible Borrower.

(a) An eligible Borrower must be a Qualified Steel Company that can demonstrate:

(1) Credit is not otherwise available to it under reasonable terms or conditions sufficient to meet its financing needs, as reflected in the financial and business plans of the company;

(2) The prospective earning power of that company, together with the character and value of the security pledged, furnish reasonable assurance of repayment of the loan to be guaranteed in accordance with its terms;

(3) The company has agreed to permit audits by the General Accounting Office and an independent auditor acceptable to the Board prior to the issuance of the guarantee and while any such guaranteed loan is outstanding;

(4) It has experienced layoffs, production losses, or financial losses between January 1, 1998, and the date of application for the Guarantee, demonstrated as a comparison between employment, production, or net income existing on January 1, 1998 and on the date of application; and

(5) In the case of a purchaser of substantial assets of a Qualified Steel Company; the Qualified Steel Company is unable to re-organize itself.

(b) For purposes of this section, a company will be considered a purchaser of substantial assets of a Qualified Steel Company if the company's identifiable assets purchased from a Qualified Steel Company are 50 percent or more of the consolidated assets of that Qualified Steel Company and its subsidiaries.

(c) The Lender must provide with its application a letter from at least one lending institution other than the Lender to which the Borrower has applied for financial assistance dated within six months of submission of the application, indicating that the Borrower was denied for substantially the same loan it is now applying for, and the reasons the Borrower was unable to obtain the financing for which it applied. In addition, the Lender applying for a guarantee under this Program must certify that it would not make the loan without the Board's guarantee.

[64 FR 57933, Oct. 27, 1999, as amended at 65 FR 70293, Nov. 22, 2000]

§ 400.201 Eligible Lender.

(a) A lender eligible to apply to the Board for a Guarantee of a loan must be:

(1) A banking institution, such as a commercial bank or trust company, subject to regulation by the Federal banking agencies enumerated in 12 U.S.C. 1813; or

(2) An investment institution, such as an investment bank, commercial finance company, or insurance company, that is currently engaged in commercial lending in the normal course of its business.

(b)(1) If more than one banking or investment institution is applying to the Board for a Guarantee of a single loan, each one of the banking or investment institutions on the application must meet the requirements to be an eligible lender set forth in paragraph (a) of this section.

(2) An application for a Guarantee of a single loan submitted by a group of banking or investment institutions, as described in paragraph (b)(1) of this section, must identify one of the banking or investment institutions applying for such loan to act as agent for all. This agent is responsible for administering the loan and shall have those duties and responsibilities required of an agent, as set forth in the Guarantee.

(3) Each Lender, irrespective of any indemnities or other agreements between the Lenders and the Agent, shall be bound by all actions, and/or failures to act, of the Agent. The Board shall be entitled to rely upon such actions and/or failures to act of the Agent as binding the Lenders.

(c) Status as a Lender under paragraph (a) of this section does not assure that the Board will issue the Guarantee sought, or otherwise preclude the Board from declining to issue a Guarantee. In addition to evaluating an application pursuant to § 400.207, in making a determination to issue a Guarantee to a Lender, the Board will assess:

(1) The Agent Lender's level of regulatory capital, in the case of banking institutions, or net worth, in the case of investment institutions;

(2) Whether the Agent Lender possesses the ability to administer the loan, as required by § 400.211(b), including its experience with loans to steel companies;

(3) The scope, volume and duration of the Agent Lender's activity in administering loans;

(4) The performance of the Agent Lender's loan portfolio, including its current delinquency rate;

(5) The Agent Lender's loss rate as a percentage of loan amounts for its current fiscal year; and

(6) Any other matter the Board deems material to its assessment of the Agent Lender.

(d) A proposed loan for the purpose, in whole or in part, of refinancing existing credit provided by the Agent will not be approved unless the Board is satisfied that the Agent retains at least a substantially equivalent level of risk as a result of the refinancing.

[64 FR 57933, Oct. 27, 1999, as amended at 65 FR 24104, Apr. 25, 2000; 66 FR 53079, Oct. 19, 2001]

§ 400.202 Loan amount.

(a) The aggregate amount of loan principal guaranteed under this Program to a single Qualified Steel Company may not exceed $ 250 million.

(b) Of the aggregate amount of loans authorized to be guaranteed and outstanding at any one time, not more than $30 million shall be loans to iron ore companies.

§ 400.203 Guarantee percentage.

A guarantee issued by the Board may not exceed 85 percent of the amount of the principal of a loan to a Qualified Steel Company. Subject to the provisions of this part, one or more third parties, public or private, may guarantee repayment of part of the Unguaranteed Portion of a loan guaranteed by the Board.

[66 FR 53080, Oct. 19, 2001]

§400.204 Loan terms.

(a) All loans guaranteed under the Program shall be due and payable in full no later than December 31, 2005.

(b) Loans guaranteed under the Program must bear a rate of interest determined by the Board to be reasonable. The reasonableness of an interest rate will be determined with respect to current average yields on outstanding obligations of the United States with remaining periods of maturity comparable to the term of the loan sought to be guaranteed. The Board may reject an application to guarantee a loan if it determines the interest rate of such loan to be unreasonable.

(c)(1) The performance of all of the Borrower's obligations under the Loan Documents shall be secured by, and shall have the priority in, such Security as provided for within the terms and conditions of the Guarantee.

(2) Without limiting the Lender's or Borrower's obligations under paragraph (c) of this section, at a minimum, the loan shall be secured by:

(i) A fully perfected and enforceable security interest and/or lien, with first priority over conflicting security interests or other liens in all property acquired, improved or derived from the loan funds;

(ii) A fully perfected and enforceable security interest and/or lien in any other property of the Borrower's pledged to secure the loan, including accessions, replacements, proceeds, or property given by a third party as Security for the loan.

(3) The entire loan will be secured by the same Security with equal lien priority for the Guaranteed Portion and the Unguaranteed Portion of the loan. The Unguaranteed Portion of the loan will neither be paid first nor given any preference over the Guaranteed Portion. A Supplemental Guarantor shall not have a security interest, direct or indirect, in any asset of the Borrower or any affiliate thereof other than the Security.

(4) An Applicant's compliance with paragraph (c)(2) of this section does not assure a finding of reasonable assurance of repayment, or assure the Board's Guarantee of the loan.

(d) An eligible Lender may assess and collect from the Borrower such other fees and costs associated with the application and origination of the loan as are reasonable and customary, taking into consideration the amount and complexity of the credit. The Board may take such other fees and costs into consideration when determining whether to offer a Guarantee to the Lender.

[64 FR 57933, Oct. 27, 1999, as amended at 64 FR 72020, Dec. 23, 1999; 65 FR 70293, Nov. 22, 2000; 66 FR 53080, Oct. 19, 2001]

§400.205 Application process.

(a) *Application process.* An original application and three copies must be received by the Board no later than 5 p.m. EST, August 31, 2001 in the Board's offices at 1099—14th Street, NW, Suite 2600 East, Washington, DC 20005. Applications which have been provided to a delivery service with "delivery guaranteed" before 5 p.m. on August 31, 2001 will be accepted for review if the Applicant can document that the application was provided to the delivery service with delivery to the address listed in this section guaranteed prior to the closing date and time. A postmark is not sufficient to meet this deadline as the application must be received by the required date and time. Applications will not be accepted via facsimile machine transmission or electronic mail.

(b) Applications shall contain the following:

(1) A completed Form "Application for Steel Guarantee Loan";

(2) The information required for the completion of Form "Environmental Assessment and Compliance Findings for Related Environmental Laws" and attachments, as required by §400.206(a)(2)(i)(D);

(3) All Loan Documents that will be signed by the Lender and the Borrower, if the application is approved, including all terms and conditions of, and Security or additional Security to assure the Borrower's performance under, the loan;

(4) Certification by the chairman of the board and the chief executive officer of the Borrower acknowledging that the Borrower is aware that the Lender is applying to the Board for a Guarantee of a loan under the Program, as described in the Loan Documents; and agreeing to permit audits by the General Accounting Office, its designee, and an independent auditor acceptable to the Board prior to the issuance of the Guarantee and annually thereafter while such guarantee is outstanding;

(5) The Lender's full written underwriting analysis of the loan to be guaranteed by the Board;

(6) A certification by the Lender that the Lender meets each of the requirements of the Program as set forth in the Act and the Board's rules in this part;

(7) A description of all Security for the loan, including, as applicable, current appraisal of real and personal property, copies of any appropriate environmental site assessments, and current personal and corporate financial statements of any guarantors for the same period as required for the Borrower. Appraisals of real property shall be prepared by State licensed or certified appraisers, and be consistent with the "Uniform Standards of Professional Appraisal Practice," promulgated by the Appraisal Standards Board of the Appraisal Foundation. Financial statements of guarantors shall be prepared by independent Certified Public Accountants;

(8) Consolidated financial statements of the Borrower for the previous three years that have been audited by an independent certified public accountant, including any associated notes, as well as any interim financial statements and associated notes for the current fiscal year;

(9) A five year history and five year projection for revenue, cash flow, average realized prices and average realized production costs. If the loan funds are to be used to purchase substantial assets of an existing firm, a pro forma balance sheet at startup, and five years projected year end balance sheets and income statement at start-up;

(10) Documentation that credit is not otherwise available to the borrower under reasonable terms or conditions sufficient to meet its financial needs, as reflected in the financial or business plan of that company. The Lender must provide with its application those items required by § 400.200(c);

(11) Documentation sufficient to demonstrate that the Lender is eligible under § 400.201(a) and to allow the Board to make a determination to issue a Guarantee to such Lender as set forth in § 400.201(c); and

(12) A description of any Supplemental Guarantee(s) that will apply to the Unguaranteed Portion of the loan.

(c) No Guarantee will be made if either the Borrower or Lender has an outstanding, delinquent Federal debt until:

(1) The delinquent account has been paid in full;

(2) A negotiated repayment schedule is established and at least one payment has been received; or

(3) Other arrangements, satisfactory to the agency responsible for collecting the debt, are made.

[64 FR 57933, Oct. 27, 1999, as amended at 64 FR 72021, Dec. 23, 1999; 65 FR 24104, Apr. 25, 2000; 65 FR 70293, Nov. 22, 2000; 66 FR 53080, Oct. 19, 2001]

§ 400.206 Environmental requirements.

(a)(1) *In general.* Environmental assessments of the Board's actions will be conducted in accordance with applicable statutes, regulations, and Executive Orders. Therefore, each application for a Guarantee under the Program must be accompanied by information necessary for the Board to meet the requirements of applicable law.

(2) *Actions requiring compliance with NEPA.* (i) The types of actions classified as "major Federal actions" subject to NEPA procedures are discussed generally in 40 CFR parts 1500 through 1508.

(ii) With respect to this Program, these actions typically include:

(A) Any project, permanent or temporary, that will involve construction and/or installations;

(B) Any project, permanent or temporary, that will involve ground disturbing activities; and

(C) Any project supporting renovation, other than interior remodeling.

(3) *Environmental information required from the Lender.* (i) Environmental data or documentation concerning the use of the proceeds of any loan guaranteed under this Program must be provided by the Lender to the Board to assist the Board in meeting its legal responsibilities. The Lender may obtain this information from the Borrower. (ii) Such information includes:

(A) Documentation for an environmental threshold review from qualified data sources, such as a Federal, State or local agency with expertise and experience in environmental protection, or other sources, qualified to provide reliable environmental information;

(B) Any previously prepared environmental reports or data relevant to the loan at issue;

(C) Any environmental review prepared by Federal, State, or local agencies relevant to the loan at issue;

(D) The information required for the completion of Form XYZ, "Environmental Assessment and Compliance Findings for Related Environmental Laws;" and

(E) Any other information that can be used by the Board to ensure compliance with environmental laws.

(ii) All information supplied by the Lender is subject to verification by the Board.

(b) The regulations of the Council on Environmental Quality implementing NEPA require the Board to provide public notice of the availability of project specific environmental documents such as environmental impact statements, environmental assessments, findings of no significant impact, records of decision etc., to the affected public. See 40 CFR 1506.6(b). Environmental information concerning specific projects can be obtained from the Board by contacting: Executive Director, Emergency Steel Guarantee Loan Board, U.S. Department of Commerce, Washington, DC 20230.

(c) *National Environmental Policy Act*—(1) *Purpose.* The purpose of this paragraph (c) is to adopt procedures for compliance with the National Environmental Policy Act, 42 U.S.C. 4321 *et seq.*, by the Board. This paragraph supplements regulations at 40 CFR Chapter V.

(2) *Definitions.* For purposes of this section, the following definitions apply: *Categorical exclusion* means a category of actions which do not individually or cumulatively have a significant effect on the human environment and for which neither an environmental assessment nor an environmental impact statement is required.

Environmental assessment means a document that briefly discusses the environmental consequences of a proposed action and alternatives prepared for the purposes set forth in 40 CFR 1508.9.

EIS means an environmental impact statement prepared pursuant to section 102(2)(C) of NEPA.

FONSI means a finding of no significant impact on the quality of the human environment after the completion of an environmental assessment.

NEPA means the National Environmental Policy Act, 42 U.S.C. 4321, *et seq.*

Working capital loan means money used by an ongoing business concern to fund its existing operations.

(3) *Delegations to Executive Director.* (i) All incoming correspondence from Council on Environmental Quality (CEQ) and other agencies concerning matters related to NEPA, including draft and final EIS, shall be brought to the attention of the Executive Director. The Executive Director will prepare or, at his or her discretion, coordinate replies to such correspondence.

(ii) With respect to actions of the Board, the Executive Director will:

(A) Ensure preparation of all necessary environmental assessments and EISs;

(B) Maintain a list of actions for which environmental assessments are being prepared;

(C) Revise this list at regular intervals, and send the revisions to the Environmental Protection Agency;

(D) Make the list available for public inspection;

(E) Maintain a list of EISs; and

(F) Maintain a file of draft and final EISs.

(4) *Categorical exclusions.* (1) This paragraph describes various classes of Board actions that normally do not have a significant impact on the

human environment and are categorically excluded. The word "normally" is stressed; there may be individual cases in which specific factors require contrary action.

(ii) Subject to the limitations in paragraph (c)(4)(iii) of this section, the actions described in this paragraph have been determined not to have a significant impact on the quality of the human environment. They are categorically excluded from the need to prepare an environmental assessment or an EIS under NEPA.

(A) Guarantees of working capital loans; and

(B) Guarantees of loans for the refinancing of outstanding indebtedness of the Borrower, regardless of the purpose for which the original indebtedness was incurred.

(iii) Actions listed in paragraph (c)(4)(ii) of this section that otherwise are categorically excluded from NEPA review are not necessarily excluded from review if they would be located within, or in other cases, potentially affect:

(A) A floodplain;

(B) A wetland;

(C) Important farmlands, or prime forestlands or rangelands;

(D) A listed species or critical habitat for an endangered species;

(E) A property that is listed on or may be eligible for listing on the National Register of Historic Places;

(F) An area within an approved State Coastal Zone Management Program;

(G) A coastal barrier or a portion of a barrier within the Coastal Barrier Resources System;

(H) A river or portion of a river included in, or designated for, potential addition to the Wild and Scenic Rivers System;

(I) A sole source aquifer recharge area;

(J) A State water quality standard (including designated and/or existing beneficial uses and anti-degradation requirements); or

(K) The release or disposal of regulated substances above the levels set forth in a permit or license issued by an appropriate regulatory authority.

(5) *Responsibilities and procedures for preparation of an environmental assessment.* (i) the Executive Director will request that the Lender and Borrower provide information concerning all potentially significant environmental impacts of the Borrower's proposed project pursuant to 13 CFR 400.206. The Executive Director, consulting at his discretion with CEQ, will review the information provided by the Lender and Borrower. Though no specific format for an environmental assessment is prescribed, it shall be a separate document, suitable for public review and should include the following in conformance with 40 CFR 1508.9:

(A) *Description of the environment.* The existing environmental conditions relevant to the Board's analysis determining the environmental impacts of the proposed project, should be described. The no action alternative also should be discussed;

(B) *Documentation.* Citations to information used to describe the existing environment and to assess environmental impacts should be clearly referenced and documented. These sources should include, as appropriate, but not be limited to, local, tribal, regional, State, and Federal agencies, as well as, public and private organizations and institutions;

(C) *Evaluating environmental consequences of proposed actions.* A brief discussion should be included of the need for the proposal, of alternatives as required by 42 U.S.C. 4332(2)(E) and their environmental impacts. The discussion of the environmental impacts should include measures to mitigate adverse impacts and any irreversible or irretrievable commitments of resources to the proposed project.

(ii) The Executive Director, in preparing an environmental assessment, may:

(A) Tier upon the information contained in a previous EIS, as described in 40 CFR 1502.20;

(B) Incorporate by reference reasonably available material, as described in 40 CFR 1502.21; and/or

(C) Adopt a previously completed EIS reasonably related to the project for which the proceeds of the loan sought to be guaranteed under the Program will be used, as described in 40 CFR 1506.3.

(iii) Because of the statute's admonition to the Board to make its decisions as soon as possible after receiving applications, the Board will not:

(A) Publish notice of intent to prepare an environmental assessment, as describe in 40 CFR 1501.7;

(B) Conduct scoping, as described in 40 CFR 1501.7; and

(C) Seek comments on the environmental assessment, as described in 40 CFR 1503.1.

(iv) If, on the basis of an environmental assessment, it is determined that an EIS is not required, a FONSI, as described in 40 CFR 1508.13 will be prepared. The FONSI will include the environmental assessment or a summary of it and be available to the public from the Board. The Executive Director shall maintain a record of these decisions, making them available to interested parties upon request. Requests should be directed to the Executive Director, Emergency Steel Guarantee Loan Program, 1099—14th Street, NW, Suite 2600 East, Washington, DC 20005. Prior to a final loan guarantee decision, a copy of the NEPA documentation shall be sent to the Board for consideration.

(6) *Responsibilities and procedures for preparation of an environmental impact statement.* (i) If after an environmental assessment has been completed, it is determined that an EIS is necessary, it and other related documentation will be prepared by the Executive Director in accordance with section 102(2)(c) of NEPA, this section, and 40 CFR parts 1500 through 1508. The Executive Director may seek additional information from the applicant in preparing the EIS. Once the document is prepared, it shall be submitted to the Board. If the Board considers a document unsatisfactory, it shall be returned to the Executive Director for revision or supplementation prior to a loan guarantee decision; otherwise the Board will transmit the document to the Environmental Protection Agency.

(ii)(A) The following procedures, as discussed in 40 CFR parts 1500 through 1508, will be followed in preparing an EIS:

(*1*) The format and contents of the draft and final EIS shall be as discussed in 40 CFR 1502.

(*2*) The requirements of 40 CFR 1506.9 for filing of documents with the Environmental Protection Agency shall be followed.

(*3*) The Executive Director, consulting at his discretion with CEQ, shall examine carefully the basis on which supportive studies have been conducted to assure that such studies are objective and comprehensive in scope and in depth.

(*4*) NEPA requires that the decision making "utilize a systematic, interdisciplinary approach that will ensure the integrated use of the natural and social sciences and the environmental design arts." 42 U.S.C. 4332(A). If such disciplines are not present on the Board staff, appropriate use should be made of personnel of Federal, State, and local agencies, universities, nonprofit organizations, or private industry.

(B) Until the Board issues a record of decision as provided in 40 CFR 1502.2 no action concerning the proposal shall be taken which would:

(*1*) Have an adverse environmental impact; or

(*2*) Limit the choice of reasonable alternatives.

(*3*) 40 CFR 1506.10 places certain limitations on the timing of Board decisions on taking "major Federal actions." A loan guarantee shall not be made before the times set forth in 40 CFR 1506.10.

(iii) A public record of decision stating what the decision was; identifying alternatives that were considered, including the environmentally preferable one(s); discussing any national considerations that entered into the decision; and summarizing a monitoring and enforcement program if applicable for mitigating the environmental effects of a proposal; will be prepared. This record of decision will be prepared at the time the decision is made.

[64 FR 57933, Oct. 27, 1999, as amended at 64 FR 72021, Dec. 23, 1999; 65 FR 70294, Nov. 22, 2000]

§ 400.207 Application evaluation.

(a) *Eligibility screening.* Applications will be reviewed to determine whether the Lender and Borrower are eligible, the information required under § 400.205(b) is complete, and the proposed loan complies with applicable statutes and regulations. The Board can at any time reject an application that does not meet these requirements.

(b) *Evaluation criteria.* Applications that are determined to be eligible pursuant to paragraph (a) of this section shall be subject to a substantive review by the Board based upon the following evaluation factors, in order of importance:

(1) The ability of the Borrower to repay the loan by the date specified in the Loan Document, which shall be no later than December 31, 2005. Evaluation of this factor will consider the prospective earning power of the Borrower. An essential and necessary element of the Board's evaluation of whether this criterion is satisfied is whether the applicant has committed to undertake significant efforts to eliminate or reduce economically unviable capacity;

(2) The adequacy of the proposed provisions to protect the Government, including sufficiency of Security, the priority of the lien position in the Security, and the percentage of Guarantee requested; and

(3) Adequacy of the underwriting analysis performed by the Lender in preparing the application and the ability of the Lender to administer the loan in full compliance with the requisite standard of care set forth in § 400.211(b).

(c) *Decisions by the Board.* Upon completion of the evaluation of an application and as soon as possible after its receipt, the Board will approve or deny an eligible application that is timely received under this Program. The Board shall notify the Applicants and the Borrower in writing of the approval or denial of an application as soon as possible. Approvals for loan Guarantees shall be conditioned upon compliance with § 400.208.

[64 FR 57933, Oct. 27, 1999, as amended at 65 FR 70294, Nov. 22, 2000; 66 FR 53080, Oct. 19, 2001]

§ 400.208 Issuance of the Guarantee.

(a) The Board's decisions to approve any application for, and extend an offer of, guarantee under § 400.207 is conditioned upon:

(1) The Lender and Borrower obtaining any required regulatory or judicial approvals;

(2) The Lender and Borrower being legally authorized to enter into the loan under the terms and conditions submitted to the Board in the application;

(3) The Board's receipt of the Loan Documents and any related instruments, in form and substance satisfactory to the Board, and the Guarantee, all properly executed by the Lender, Borrower, and any other required party other than the Board; and

(4) No material adverse change in the Borrower's ability to repay the loan between the date of the Board's approval and the date the Guarantee is to be issued.

(b) The Board may withdraw its approval of an application and rescind its offer of Guarantee if the Board determines that the Lender or the Borrower cannot, or is unwilling to, provide adequate documentation and proof of compliance with paragraph (a) of this section within the time provided for in the offer.

(c) Only after receipt of all the documentation, required by this section, will the Board sign and deliver the Guarantee.

(d) A Borrower receiving a loan guaranteed by the Board under this Program shall pay a one-time guarantee fee of 0.5 percent of the amount of the principal of the loan. This fee must be paid no later than one year from the issuance of the Guarantee.

[64 FR 57933, Oct. 27, 1999, as amended at 65 FR 70294, Nov. 22, 2000; 66 FR 53080, Oct. 19, 2001]

§ 400.209 Funding for the Program.

The Act provides funding for the costs incurred by the Government as a result of granting Guarantees under the Program. While pursuing the goals of the Act, it is the intent of the Board to minimize the cost of the Program to the Government. The Board will estimate the risk posed by the guaranteed loans to the funds appropriated for the costs of the Guarantees under the Program and operate the Program accordingly.

§ 400.210 Assignment or transfer of loans.

(a) Neither the Loan Documents nor the Guarantee of the Board may be modified, in whole or in part, without the prior written approval of the Board.

(b) Upon notice to the Board and a certification by the assignor that the assignee is an Eligible Lender, and subject to the provisions of paragraphs (c) and (d) of this section and other provisions of this part, a Lender may assign or transfer its interest in the loan including the Loan documents and the Guarantee to a party that qualifies as an Eligible Lender pursuant to §400.201. Any other assignment or transfer will require the prior written approval of the Board.

(c) The provisions of paragraph (b) of this section shall not apply to transfers which occur by operation of law.

(d) The Agent must hold and may not assign or transfer an interest in a loan guaranteed under the Program equal to at least the lesser of $25 million or fifteen percent of the aggregate amount of the loan. In addition, the Agent must hold and may not assign or transfer an interest the Unguaranteed Portion of the loan equal to at least the minimum amount of the loan required to be held by the Agent under the preceding sentence multiplied by the percentage of the loan represented by the Unguaranteed Portion. A non-Agent Lender must hold and may not assign or transfer an interest in the Unguaranteed Portion of the loan representing no less than five percent of such Lender's total interest in the loan; provided, that a non-Agent Lender may transfer its interest in the Unguaranteed Portion after payment of the Guaranteed Portion has been made under the Guarantee.

[66 FR 53080, Oct. 19, 2001]

§400.211 Lender responsibilities.

The Lender shall have such obligations and duties to the Board as are set forth in the Guarantee.

[65 FR 70294, Nov. 22, 2000]

§400.212 Guarantee.

The Board shall adopt a form of Guarantee to be used by the Board under the Program, and shall publish the Guarantee on its website. Modifications to the provisions of the form of Guarantee must be approved and adopted by the Board.

[65 FR 70294, Nov. 22, 2000]

§400.213 Termination of obligations.

The Board shall have such rights to terminate the Guarantee as are set forth in the Guarantee.

[65 FR 70294, Nov. 22, 2000]

§400.214 Participations in guaranteed loans.

(a) Subject to paragraphs (b), (c) and (d) of this section, a Lender may distribute the risk of a portion of a loan guaranteed under the Program by sale of participations therein if:

(1) Neither the loan note nor the Guarantee is assigned, conveyed, sold, or transferred in whole or in part;

(2) The Lender remains solely responsible for the administration of the loan; and

(3) The Board's ability to assert any and all defenses available to it under the Guarantee and the law is not adversely affected.

(b) The following categories of entities may purchase participations in loans guaranteed under the Program:

(1) Eligible Lenders;

(2) Private investment funds and insurance companies that do not usually invest in commercial loans;

(3) Steel company suppliers or customers, who are interested in participating as a means of commencing or solidifying the supplier or customer relationship with the borrower; or

(4) Any other entity approved by the Board on a case-by-case basis.

(c) The Agent may not grant participations in that portion of its interest in a loan that may not be assigned or transferred under §400.210(d). A Lender, other than the Agent, may not grant participations in that portion of its interest in a loan that may not be assigned or transferred under §400.210(d).

(d) At least 5 percent of any participation interest in a loan must be unguaranteed.

[65 FR 70294, Nov. 22, 2000]

§400.215 Supplemental Guarantees.

The Board will allow the structure of a guaranteed loan to include one or more Supplemental Guarantees that cover the Unguaranteed Portion of the loan; provided that:

(a) There shall be no Supplemental Guarantee with respect to the Unguaranteed Portion required to be held by the Agent pursuant to § 400.210(c);

(b) The Loan Documents relating to any Supplemental Guarantee shall be acceptable in form and substance to the Board; and

(c) In approving the issuance of a Guarantee, the Board may impose any conditions with respect to Supplemental Guarantee(s) relating to the loan that it considers appropriate.

[66 FR 53080, Oct. 19, 2001]

PARTS 401–499 [RESERVED]

CHAPTER V—EMERGENCY OIL AND GAS GUARANTEED LOAN BOARD

PART 500—EMERGENCY OIL AND GAS GUARANTEED LOAN PROGRAM

AUTHORITY: Pub. L. 106–51, 113 Stat. 255 (15 U.S.C. 1841 note).

SOURCE: 64 FR 57947, Oct. 27, 1999, unless otherwise noted.

Subpart A—General

§ 500.1 Purpose.

This part is issued by the Emergency Oil and Gas Guaranteed Loan Board pursuant to section 552 of title 5 of the United States Code and the Emergency Oil and Gas Guaranteed Loan Act, Chapter 2 of Public Law 106–51. This part contains rules for making and servicing loans to qualified oil and gas guaranteed by the Board.

§ 500.2 Definitions.

(a) *Act* means the Emergency Oil and Gas Guaranteed Loan Program Act, Chapter 2 of Public Law 106–51.

(b) *Administer, administering and administration*, mean the Lender's actions in making, disbursing, servicing (including, but not limited to care, preservation and maintenance of collateral), collecting and liquidating a loan and security.

(c) *Agent* means that Lender authorized to take such actions, exercise such powers, and perform such duties on behalf and in representation of all Lenders party to a Guarantee of a single loan, as is required by, or necessarily incidental to, the terms and conditions of the Guarantee.

(d) *Applicant* means the private banking or investment institution applying for a loan guarantee under this part.

(e) *Board* means the Emergency Oil and Gas Guaranteed Loan Board.

(f) *Borrower* means a Qualified Oil and Gas Company which could receive a loan guaranteed by the Board under this Program.

(g) *Guarantee* means the written agreement between the Board and one or more Lenders, and approved by the Borrower, pursuant to which the Board guarantees repayment of a specified percentage of the principal of the loan, including the Special Terms and Conditions, the General Terms and Conditions, and all exhibits thereto.

(h) *Lender* means a private banking or investment institution, eligible under § 500.201, that is a party to a Guarantee issued by the Board. With respect to a Guarantee of a single loan to which more than one Lender is a party, the term Lender means Agent.

(i) *Loan Documents* mean the loan agreement and all other instruments, and all documentation between the Lender and the Borrower evidencing the making, disbursing, securing, collecting, or otherwise administering of the loan.

(j) *Program* means the Emergency Oil and Gas Guaranteed Loan Program established by the Act.

(k) *Security* means all property, real or personal, required by the provisions of the Guarantee or by the Loan Documents to secure repayment of any indebtedness of the Borrower under the Loan Documents or Guarantee.

(l) *Qualified Oil and Gas Company* means any company that: (A) is (i) an independent oil and gas company (within the meaning of section 57(a)(2)(B)(i) of the Internal Revenue Code of 1986) or; (ii) a small business concern under section 3 of the Small Business Act, 15 U.S.C. 632, (or a company based in Alaska, including an Alaska Native Corporation created pursuant to the Alaska Native Claims Settlement Act, 43 U.S.C. 1601 *et seq.*) that is an oil field service company whose main business is providing tools, products, personnel, and technical solutions on a contractual basis to exploration and production operators that drill, complete wells, and produce, transport, refine, and sell hydrocarbons and their byproducts as the main commercial business of the concern or company; and (B) has experienced layoffs, production losses, or financial losses since January 1997.

[64 FR 57947, Oct. 27, 1999, as amended at 65 FR 24106, Apr. 25, 2000]

Subpart B—Board Procedures

§ 500.100 Purpose and scope.

This subpart describes the Board's authorities and organizational structure, the means and rules by which the Board takes actions, and procedures for public access to Board records.

§ 500.101 Composition of the Board.

The Board consists of the Chairman of the Board of Governors of the Federal Reserve System, who acts as Chairman of the Board, the Chairman of the Securities and Exchange Commission, and the Secretary of Commerce.

§ 500.102 Authority of the Board.

Pursuant to the provisions of the Act, the Board is authorized to guarantee loans provided to Qualified Oil and Gas companies by private banking and investment institutions in accordance with the procedures, rules, and regulations established by the Board, to make the determinations authorized by the Act, and to take such other actions as necessary to carry out its functions in accordance with the Act.

§ 500.103 Offices.

The principal offices of the Board are in the U.S. Department of Commerce, Washington, D.C. 20230.

§ 500.104 Meetings and actions of the Board.

(a) *Place and frequency.* The Board meets, on the call of the Chairman, in order to consider matters requiring action by the Board. Time and place for any such meeting shall be determined by the members of the Board.

(b) *Quorum and voting.* Two voting members of the Board constitute a quorum for the transaction of business. All decisions and determinations of the Board shall be made by a majority vote of the voting members. All votes on determinations of the Board required by the Act shall be recorded in the minutes. A Board member may request that any vote be recorded according to individual Board members.

(c) *Agenda of meetings.* To the extent practicable, an agenda for each meeting shall be distributed to members of the Board at least two days in advance of the date of the meeting, together with copies of materials relevant to the agenda items.

(d) *Minutes.* The Secretary of the Board shall keep minutes of each Board meeting and of action taken without a meeting, a draft of which is to be distributed to each member of the Board as soon as practicable after each meeting or action. To the extent practicable, the minutes of a Board meeting shall be corrected and approved at the next meeting of the Board.

(e) *Use of conference call communications equipment.* Any member may participate in a meeting of the Board through the use of conference call, telephone or similar communications equipment, by means of which all persons participating in the meeting can simultaneously speak to and hear each other. Any member so participating in a meeting shall be deemed present for all purposes. Actions taken by the Board at meetings conducted through the use of such equipment, including the votes of each member, shall be recorded in the usual manner in the minutes of the meetings of the Board.

(f) *Actions between meetings.* When, in the judgment of the Chairman, circumstances occur making it desirable for the Board to consider action when it is not feasible to call a meeting, the relevant information and recommendations for action may be transmitted to the members by the Secretary of the Board and the voting members may communicate their votes to the Chairman in writing (including an action signed in counterpart by each Board member), electronically, or orally (including telephone communication). Any action taken under this paragraph has the same effect as an action taken at a meeting. Any such action shall be recorded in the minutes.

(g) *Delegations of authority.* The Board may delegate authority, subject to such terms and conditions as the Board deems appropriate, to the Executive Director, the General Counsel, or the Secretary of the Board, to take certain actions not required by the Act to be taken by the Board. All delegations shall be made pursuant to resolutions of the Board and recorded in writing, whether in the minutes of a meeting or otherwise. Any action taken pursuant to delegated authority has the effect of an action taken by the Board.

§ 500.105 Staff.

(a) *Executive Director.* The Executive Director of the Board advises and assists the Board in carrying out its responsibilities under the Act, provides general direction with respect to the administration of the Board's actions, directs the activities of the staff, and performs such other duties as the Board may require.

(b) *General Counsel.* The General Counsel of the Board provides legal advice relating to the responsibilities of the Board and performs such other duties as the Board may require.

(c) *Secretary of the Board.* The Secretary of the Board sends notice of all meetings, prepares minutes of all meetings, maintains a complete record of all votes and actions taken by the Board, has custody of all records of the Board and performs such other duties as the Board may require.

§ 500.106 *Ex parte* communications.

Oral or written communication, not on the public record, between the Board, or any member of the Board, and any party or parties interested in any matter pending before the Board concerning the substance of that matter is prohibited. This section also applies to the Board's staff and employees of the constituent agencies who are or reasonably may be expected to be involved in the decisional process of the matter pending before the Board.

§ 500.107 Freedom of Information Act.

(a) *Definitions.* All terms used in this section which are defined in 5 U.S.C. 551 or 5 U.S.C. 552 shall have the same meaning in this section. In addition the following definitions apply to this section:

(1) *FOIA,* as used in this section, means the "Freedom of Information Act," as amended, 5 U.S.C. 552.

(2) *Commercial use request* means a request from or on behalf of one who seeks information for a use or purpose that furthers the commercial, trade, or profit interests of the requester or the person on whose behalf the request is made.

(3) *Direct costs* mean those expenditures that the Board actually incurs in searching for, reviewing, and duplicating documents in response to a request made under paragraph (c) of this section. Direct costs include, for example, the labor costs of the employee performing the work (the basic rate of pay for the employee, plus 16 percent of that rate to cover benefits). Not included in direct costs are overhead expenses such as the costs of space and heating or lighting of the facility in which the records are kept.

(4) *Duplication* means the process of making a copy of a document in response to a request for disclosure of records or for inspection of original records that contain exempt material or that otherwise cannot be inspected directly. Among others, such copies may take the form of paper, microfilm, audiovisual materials, or machine-readable documentation (e.g., magnetic tape or disk).

(5) *Educational institution* means a preschool, a public or private elementary or secondary school, or an institution of undergraduate higher education, graduate higher education, professional education, or an institution of vocational education that operates a program of scholarly research.

(6) *Noncommercial scientific institution* refers to an institution that is not operated on a "commercial" basis (as that term is used in this section) and which is operated solely for the purpose of conducting scientific research, the results of which are not intended to promote any particular product or industry.

(7) *News* means information about current events or that would be of current interest to the public. Examples of news media entities include, but are not limited to, television or radio stations broadcasting to the public at large, and publishers of newspapers and other periodicals (but only in those instances when they can qualify as disseminators of "news") who make their products available for purchase or subscription by the general public. "Freelance" journalists may be regarded as working for a news organization if they can demonstrate a solid basis for expecting publication through that organization, even though not actually employed by it.

(8) *Representative of the news media* means any person actively gathering news for an entity that is organized and operated to publish or broadcast news to the general public.

(9) *Review* means the process of examining documents, located in response to a request for access, to determine whether any portion of a document is exempt information. It includes doing all that is necessary to excise the documents and otherwise to prepare them for release. Review does not include time spent resolving general legal or policy issues regarding the application of exemptions.

(10) *Search* means the process of looking for material that is responsive to a request, including page-by-page or line-by-line identification within documents. Searches may be done manually or by computer.

(b) *Records available for public inspection and copying*—(1) *Types of records made available.* The information in this section is furnished for the guidance of the public and in compliance with the requirements of the Freedom of Information Act, as amended (5 U.S.C. 552) (FOIA). This section sets forth the procedures the Board follows to make publicly available the materials specified in 5 U.S.C. 552(a)(2). These materials shall be made available for inspection and copying at the Board's Freedom of Information Office pursuant to 5 U.S.C. 552(a)(2). Information routinely provided to the public as part of a regular Board activity (for example, press releases) may be provided to the public without following this section.

(2) *Reading room procedures.* Information available under this section is available for inspection and copying, from 9:00 a.m. to 5:00 p.m. weekdays, at the Freedom of Information Office of the Board, Oil and Gas Guarantee Loan Board, U.S. Department of Commerce, Washington, D.C. 20230.

(3) *Electronic records.* Information available under this section that was created on or after November 1, 1996, shall also be available on the Board's website, found at *www.doc.gov.*

(c) *Records available to the public on request*—(1) *Types of records made available.* All records of the Board that are not available under paragraph (b) of this section shall be made available upon request, pursuant to the procedures in this section and the exceptions set forth in the FOIA. The Board's policy is to make discretionary disclosures of records or information exempt from disclosure under the FOIA whenever disclosure would not foreseeably harm an interest protected by a FOIA exemption, but this policy does not create any right enforceable in court.

(2) *Procedures for requesting records.* A request for records shall reasonably describe the records in a way that enables the Board's staff to identify and produce the records with reasonable effort and without unduly burdening or significantly interfering with any of the Board's operations. The request shall be submitted in writing to the Secretary of the Board, Oil and Gas Guarantee Loan Board, U.S. Department of Commerce, Washington, D.C. 20230; or sent by facsimile to the Secretary of the Board. The request shall

be clearly marked *FREEDOM OF INFORMATION ACT REQUEST*.

(3) *Contents of request*. The request shall contain the following information:

(i) The name and address of the requester, and the telephone number at which the requester can be reached during normal business hours;

(ii) Whether the requested information is intended for commercial use, or whether the requester represents an educational or noncommercial scientific institution, or news media;

(iii) A statement agreeing to pay the applicable fees, or a statement identifying any fee limitation desired, or a request for a waiver or reduction of fees that satisfies paragraph (f) of this section.

(d) *Processing requests*—(1) *Priority of responses*. The date of receipt for any request, including one that is addressed incorrectly or that is referred to the Board by another agency, is the date the Secretary of the Board actually receives the request. The Secretary of the Board shall normally process requests in the order they are received. However, in the Secretary of the Board's discretion, the Board may use two or more processing tracks by distinguishing between simple and more complex requests based on the number of pages involved, or some other measure of the amount of work and/or time needed to process the request, and whether the request qualifies for expedited processing as described in paragraph (d)(2) of this section. When using multitrack processing, the Secretary of the Board may provide requesters in the slower track(s) with an opportunity to limit the scope of their requests in order to qualify for faster processing. The Secretary of the Board shall contact the requester by telephone or by letter, whichever is most efficient in each case.

(2) *Expedited processing*. (i) A person may request expedited access to records by submitting a statement, certified to be true and correct to the best of that person's knowledge and belief, that demonstrates a compelling need for the records, as defined in 5 U.S.C. 552(a)(6)(E)(v).

(ii) The Secretary of the Board shall notify a requester of the determination whether to grant or deny a request for expedited processing within ten working days of receipt of the request. If the Secretary of the Board grants the request for expedited processing, the Board shall process the request for access to information as soon as practicable. If the Secretary of the Board denies a request for expedited processing, the requester may file an appeal pursuant to the procedures set forth in paragraph (e) of this section, and the Board shall respond to the appeal within twenty days after the appeal was received by the Board.

(3) *Time limits*. The time for response to requests shall be 20 working days, except:

(i) In the case of expedited treatment under paragraph (d)(2) of this section;

(ii) Where the running of such time is suspended for payment of fees pursuant to paragraph (f)(2)(ii) of this section;

(iii) Where the estimated charge is less than $250, and the requester does not guarantee payment pursuant to paragraph (f)(2)(i) of this section; or

(iv) In unusual circumstances, as defined in 5 U.S.C. 552(a)(6)(B)(iii), the time limit may be extended for a period of time not to exceed 10 working days as provided by written notice to the requester, setting forth the reasons for the extension and the date on which a determination is expected to be dispatched; or such alternative time period as mutually agreed to by the Secretary of the Board and the requester when the Secretary of the Board notifies the requester that the request cannot be processed in the specified time limit.

(4) *Response to request*. In response to a request that satisfies paragraph (c) of this paragraph, an appropriate search shall be conducted of records in the custody and control of the Board on the date of receipt of the request, and a review made of any responsive information located. The Secretary of the Board shall notify the requester of:

(i) The Secretary of the Board's determination of the request and the reasons therefor;

(ii) The information withheld, and the basis for withholding; and

(iii) The right to appeal any denial or partial denial, pursuant to paragraph (e) of this section.

(5) *Referral to another agency.* To the extent a request covers documents that were created by, obtained from, classified by, or is in the primary interest of another agency, the Secretary of the Board may refer the request to that agency for a direct response by that agency and inform the requester promptly of the referral. The Secretary of the Board shall consult with another Federal agency before responding to a requester if the Board receives a request for a record in which:

(i) Another Federal agency subject to the FOIA has a significant interest, but not the primary interest; or

(ii) Another Federal agency not subject to the FOIA has the primary interest or a significant interest. Ordinarily, the agency that originated a record will be presumed to have the primary interest in it.

(6) *Providing responsive records.* (i) A copy of records or portions of records responsive to the request shall be sent to the requester by regular U.S. mail to the address indicated in the request, unless the requester elects to take delivery of the documents at the Board's Freedom of Information Office or makes other acceptable arrangements, or the Secretary of the Board deems it appropriate to send the documents by another means. The Secretary of the Board shall provide a copy of the record in any form or format requested if the record is readily reproducible in that form or format, but the Secretary of the Board need not provide more than one copy of any record to a requester.

(ii) The Secretary of the Board shall provide any reasonably segregable portion of a record that is responsive to the request after deleting those portions that are exempt under the FOIA or this section.

(iii) Except where disclosure is expressly prohibited by statute, regulation, or order, the Secretary of the Board may authorize the release of records that are exempt from mandatory disclosure whenever the Board or designated Board members determine that there would be no foreseeable harm in such disclosure.

(iv) The Board is not required in response to the request to create records or otherwise to prepare new records.

(7) *Prohibition against disclosure.* Except as provided in this part, no officer, employee, or agent of the Board shall disclose or permit the disclosure of any unpublished information of the Board to any person (other than Board officers, employees, or agents properly entitled to such information for the performance of official duties), unless required by law.

(e) *Appeals.* (1) Any person denied access to Board records requested under paragraph (c) of this section, denied expedited processing under paragraph (d) of this section, or denied a waiver of fees under paragraph (f) of this section may file a written appeal within 30 calendar days after the date of such denial with the Board. The written appeal shall prominently display the phrase *FREEDOM OF INFORMATION ACT APPEAL* on the first page, and shall be addressed to the General Counsel of the Board, Oil and Gas Guaranteed Loan Board, U.S. Department of Commerce, Washington, D.C. 20230; or sent by facsimile to the General Counsel of the Board. The appeal shall include a copy of the original request, the initial denial, if any, and a statement of the reasons why the requested records should be made available and why the initial denial was in error.

(2) The General Counsel of the Board shall make a determination regarding any appeal within 20 working days of actual receipt of the appeal, and the determination letter shall notify the appealing party of the right to seek judicial review in event of denial.

(f) *Fee schedules; waiver of fees*—(1) *Fee schedule.* The fees applicable to a request for records pursuant to paragraph (c) of this section are set forth in the uniform fee schedule at the end of this paragraph (b).

(i) *Search.* (A) Search fees shall be charged for all requests—other than requests made by educational institutions, noncommercial scientific institutions, or representatives of the news media—subject to the limitations of paragraph (f)(1)(iv) of this section. The Secretary of the Board shall charge for time spent searching even if no responsive record is located or if the Secretary of the Board withholds the record(s) located as entirely exempt from disclosure. Search fees shall be the direct costs of conducting the search by the involved employees.

(B) For computer searches of records, requesters will be charged the direct costs of conducting the search, although certain requesters (as provided in paragraph (f)(3) of this section) will be charged no search fee and certain other requesters (as provided in paragraph (f)(3)) are entitled to the cost equivalent of two hours of manual search time without charge. These direct costs include the costs, attributable to the search, of operating a central processing unit and operator/programmer salary.

(ii) *Duplication*. Duplication fees will be charged to all requesters, subject to the limitations of paragraph (f)(1)(iv) of this section. For a paper photocopy of a record (no more than one copy of which need be supplied), the fee shall be 15 cents per page. For copies produced by computer, such as tapes or printouts, the Secretary of the Board shall charge the direct costs, including operator time, of producing the copy. For other forms of duplication, the Secretary of the Board will charge the direct costs of that duplication.

(iii) *Review*. Review fees shall be charged to requesters who make a commercial use request. Review fees shall be charged only for the initial record review—the review done when the Secretary of the Board determines whether an exemption applies to a particular record at the initial request level. No charge will be made for review at the administrative appeal level for an exemption already applied. However, records withheld under an exemption that is subsequently determined not to apply may be reviewed again to determine whether any other exemption not previously considered applies, and the costs of that review are chargeable. Review fees shall be the direct costs of conducting the review by the involved employees.

(iv) *Limitations on charging fees*. (A) No search fee will be charged for requests by educational institutions, noncommercial scientific institutions, or representatives of the news media.

(B) No search fee or review fee will be charged for a quarter-hour period unless more than half of that period is required for search or review.

(C) Whenever a total fee calculated under this paragraph is $25 or less for any request, no fee will be charged.

(D) For requesters other than those seeking records for a commercial use, no fee will be charged unless the cost of search in excess of two hours plus the cost of duplication in excess of 100 pages totals more than $25.

(2) *Payment procedures*. All persons requesting records pursuant to paragraph (c) of this section shall pay the applicable fees before the Secretary of the Board sends copies of the requested records, unless a fee waiver has been granted pursuant to paragraph (f)(6) of this section. Requesters must pay fees by check or money order made payable to the Treasury of the United States.

(i) *Advance notification of fees*. If the estimated charges are likely to exceed $25, the Secretary of the Board shall notify the requester of the estimated amount, unless the requester has indicated a willingness to pay fees as high as those anticipated. Upon receipt of such notice, the requester may confer with the Secretary of the Board to reformulate the request to lower the costs. The processing of the request shall be suspended until the requester provides the Secretary of the Board with a written guarantee that payment will be made upon completion of the processing.

(ii) *Advance payment*. The Secretary of the Board shall require advance payment of any fee estimated to exceed $250. The Secretary of the Board shall also require full payment in advance where a requester has previously failed to pay a fee in a timely fashion. If an advance payment of an estimated fee exceeds the actual total fee by $1 or more, the difference shall be refunded to the requester. The time period for responding to requests under paragraph (d)(4) of this section, and the processing of the request shall be suspended until the Secretary of the Board receives the required payment.

(iii) *Late charges*. The Secretary of the Board may assess interest charges when fee payment is not made within 30 days of the date on which the billing was sent. Assessment of such interest will commence on the 31st day following the day on which the billing was sent. Interest is at the rate prescribed in 31 U.S.C. 3717.

(3) *Categories of uses.* The fees assessed depend upon the fee category. In determining which category is appropriate, the Secretary of the Board shall look to the identity of the requester and the intended use set forth in the request for records. Where a requester's description of the use is insufficient to make a determination, the Secretary of the Board may seek additional clarification before categorizing the request.

(i) *Commercial use requester.* The fees for search, duplication, and review apply when records are requested for commercial use.

(ii) *Educational, non-commercial scientific institutions, or representatives of the news media requesters.* The fees for duplication apply when records are not sought for commercial use, and the requester is a representative of the news media or an educational or non-commercial scientific institution, whose purpose is scholarly or scientific research. The first 100 pages of duplication, however, will be provided free.

(iii) *All other requesters.* For all other requests, the fees for search and duplication apply. The first two hours of search time and the first 100 pages of duplication, however, will be provided free.

(4) *Nonproductive search.* Fees for search may be charged even if no responsive documents are found. Fees for search and review may be charged even if the request is denied.

(5) *Aggregated requests.* A requester may not file multiple requests at the same time, solely in order to avoid payment of fees. If the Secretary of the Board reasonably believes that a requester is separating a request into a series of requests for the purpose of evading the assessment of fees or that several requesters appear to be acting together to submit multiple requests solely in order to avoid payment of fees, the Secretary of the Board may aggregate such requests and charge accordingly. It is considered reasonable for the Secretary of the Board to presume that multiple requests by one requester on the same topic made within a 30-day period have been made to avoid fees.

(6) *Waiver or reduction of fees.* A request for a waiver or reduction of the fees, and the justification for the waiver, shall be included with the request for records to which it pertains. If a waiver is requested and the requester has not indicated in writing an agreement to pay the applicable fees if the waiver request is denied, the time for response to the request for documents, as set forth in paragraph (4)(d) of this section, shall not begin until a determination has been made on the request for a waiver or reduction of fees.

(i) *Standards for determining waiver or reduction.* The Secretary of the Board may grant a waiver or reduction of fees where it is determined both that disclosure of the information is in the public interest because it is likely to contribute significantly to public understanding of the operation or activities of the government, and that the disclosure of information is not primarily in the commercial interest of the requester. In making this determination, the following factors shall be considered:

(A) Whether the subject of the records concerns the operations or activities of the government;

(B) Whether disclosure of the information is likely to contribute significantly to public understanding of government operations or activities;

(C) Whether the requester has the intention and ability to disseminate the information to the public;

(D) Whether the information is already in the public domain;

(E) Whether the requester has a commercial interest that would be furthered by the disclosure; and, if so,

(F) Whether the magnitude of the identified commercial interest of the requester is sufficiently large, in comparison with the public interest in disclosure, that disclosure is primarily in the commercial interest of the requester.

(ii) *Contents of request for waiver.* A request for a waiver or reduction of fees shall include a clear statement of how the request satisfies the criteria set forth in paragraph (f)(6)(i) of this section.

(iii) *Burden of proof.* The burden shall be on the requester to present evidence or information in support of a request for a waiver or reduction of fees.

(iv) *Determination by Secretary of the Board.* The Secretary of the Board shall make a determination on the request for a waiver or reduction of fees and shall notify the requester accordingly. A denial may be appealed to the Board in accordance with paragraph (e) of this section.

(7) *Uniform fee schedule.*

Service	Rate
(i) Manual search	Actual salary rate of employee involved, plus 16 percent of salary rate.
(ii) Computerized search	Actual direct cost, including operator time.
(iii) Duplication of records:	
(A) Paper copy reproduction	$.15 per page.
(B) Other reproduction (e.g., computer disk or printout, microfilm, microfiche, or microform).	Actual direct cost, including operator time.
(iv) Review of records (includes preparation for release, *i.e.* excising).	Actual salary rate of employee conducting review, plus 16 percent of salary rate.

(g) *Request for confidential treatment of business information*—(1) *Submission of request.* Any submitter of information to the Board who desires confidential treatment of business information pursuant to 5 U.S.C. 552(b)(4) shall file a request for confidential treatment with the Board at the time the information is submitted or a reasonable time after submission.

(2) *Form of request.* Each request for confidential treatment of business information shall state in reasonable detail the facts supporting the commercial or financial nature of the business information and the legal justification under which the business information should be protected. Conclusory statements that release of the information would cause competitive harm generally will not be considered sufficient to justify confidential treatment.

(3) *Designation and separation of confidential material.* All information considered confidential by a submitter shall be clearly designated "*PROPRIETARY*" or "*BUSINESS CONFIDENTIAL*" in the submission and separated from information for which confidential treatment is not requested. Failure to segregate confidential commercial or financial information from other material may result in release of the nonsegregated material to the public without notice to the submitter.

(h) *Request for access to confidential commercial or financial information*—(1) *Request for confidential commercial or financial information.* A request by a submitter for confidential treatment of any business information shall be considered in connection with a request for access to that information.

(2) *Notice to the submitter.* (i) The Secretary of the Board shall notify a submitter who requested confidential treatment of information pursuant to 5 U.S.C. 552(b)(4), of the request for access.

(ii) Absent a request for confidential treatment, the Secretary of the Board may notify a submitter of a request for access to submitter's business information if the Secretary of the Board reasonably believes that disclosure of the information may cause substantial competitive harm to the submitter.

(iii) The notice given to the submitter by mail, return receipt requested, shall be given as soon as practicable after receipt of the request for access, and shall describe the request and provide the submitter seven working days from the date of notice, to submit written objections to disclosure of the information. Such statement shall specify all grounds for withholding any of the information and shall demonstrate why the information which is considered to be commercial or financial information, and that the information is a trade secret, is privileged or confidential, or that its disclosure is likely to cause substantial competitive harm to the submitter. If the submitter fails to respond to the notice within the time specified, the submitter will be considered to have no objection to the release of the information. Information a submitter provides under this paragraph may itself be subject to disclosure under the FOIA.

(3) *Exceptions to notice to submitter.* Notice to the submitter need not be given if:

(i) The Secretary of the Board determines that the request for access should be denied;

(ii) The requested information lawfully has been made available to the public;

(iii) Disclosure of the information is required by law (other than 5 U.S.C. 552); or

(iv) The submitter's claim of confidentiality under 5 U.S.C. 552(b)(4) appears obviously frivolous or has already been denied by the Secretary of the Board, except that in this last instance the Secretary of the Board shall give the submitter written notice of the determination to disclose the information at least seven working days prior to disclosure.

(4) *Notice to requester.* At the same time the Secretary of the Board notifies the submitter, the Secretary of the Board also shall notify the requester that the request is subject to the provisions of this section.

(5) *Determination by Secretary of the Board.* The Secretary of the Board's determination whether or not to disclose any information for which confidential treatment has been requested pursuant to this section shall be communicated to the submitter and the requester immediately. If the Secretary of the Board determines to disclose the business information over the objection of a submitter, the Secretary of the Board shall give the submitter written notice via mail, return receipt requested, or similar means, which shall include:

(i) A statement of reason(s) why the submitter's objections to disclosure were not sustained;

(ii) A description of the business information to be disclosed; and

(iii) A statement that the component intends to disclose the information seven working days from the date the submitter receives the notice.

(6) *Notice of lawsuit.* The Secretary of the Board shall promptly notify any submitter of information covered by this section of the filing of any suit against the Board to compel disclosure of such information, and shall promptly notify a requester of any suit filed against the Board to enjoin the disclosure of requested documents.

§ 500.108 Restrictions on lobbying.

(a) No funds received through a loan guaranteed under this Program may be expended by the recipient of a Federal contract, grant, loan, loan Guarantee, or cooperative agreement to pay any person for influencing or attempting to influence an officer or employee of any agency, a Member of Congress, an officer or employee of Congress, or an employee of a Member of Congress in connection with any of the following covered Federal actions: the awarding of any Federal contract, the making of any Federal grant, the making of any Federal loan or loan Guarantee, the entering into of any cooperative agreement, and the extension, continuation, renewal, amendment, or modification of any Federal contract, grant, loan, loan Guarantee, or cooperative agreement.

(b) Each person who requests or receives from an agency a commitment providing for the United States to insure or guarantee a loan shall file with that agency a statement, set forth in the application form, whether that person has made or has agreed to make any payment to influence or attempt to influence an officer or employee of any agency, a Member of Congress, an officer or employee of Congress, or an employee of a Member of Congress in connection with that loan insurance or Guarantee.

(c) Each person who requests or receives from an agency a commitment providing for the United States to insure or guarantee a loan shall file with that agency a Standard Form-LLL if that person has made or has agreed to make any payment to influence or attempt to influence an officer or employee of any agency, a Member of Congress, an officer or employee of Congress, or an employee of a Member of Congress in connection with that loan insurance or Guarantee.

(d) Each person shall file a certification, contained in the application form, and a disclosure form (Standard Form-LLL), if required, with each submission that initiates agency consideration of such person for:

(1) Award of a Federal contract, grant, or cooperative agreement exceeding $100,000; or

(2) An award of a Federal loan or a commitment providing for the United States to insure or guarantee a loan exceeding $150,000.

(e) Each person shall file a certification, and a disclosure form, if required, upon receipt by such person of:

(1) A Federal contract, grant, or cooperative agreement exceeding $100,000; or

(2) A Federal loan or a commitment providing for the United States to insure or Guarantee a loan exceeding $150,000, unless such person previously filed a certification, and a disclosure form, if required, under paragraph (c) of this section.

(f) Each person shall file a disclosure form at the end of each calendar quarter in which there occurs any event that requires disclosure or that materially affects the accuracy of the information contained in any disclosure form previously filed by such person under paragraphs (d) or (e) of this section. An event that materially affects the accuracy of the information reported includes:

(1) A cumulative increase of $25,000 or more in the amount paid or expected to be paid for influencing or attempting to influence a covered Federal action; or

(2) A change in the person(s) or individual(s) influencing or attempting to influence a covered Federal action; or

(3) A change in the officer(s), employee(s), or Member(s) contacted to influence or attempt to influence a covered Federal action.

§ 500.109 Government-wide debarment and suspension (nonprocurement).

(a) Executive Order (E.O.) 12549 provides that, to the extent permitted by law, Executive departments and agencies shall participate in a governmentwide system for nonprocurement debarment and suspension. A person who is debarred or suspended shall be excluded from Federal financial and nonfinancial assistance and benefits under Federal programs and activities. Debarment or suspension of a participant in a program by one agency shall have governmentwide effect. The Board shall review the List of Debarred entities prior to making final loan Guarantee decisions. Suspension or debarment may be a basis for denying a loan Guarantee.

(b) This section applies to all persons who have participated, are currently participating or may reasonably be expected to participate in transactions under Federal nonprocurement programs. For purposes of this section such transactions will be referred to as "covered transactions".

(1) *Covered transaction.* For purposes of this section, a covered transaction is a primary covered transaction or a lower tier covered transaction. Covered transactions at any tier need not involve the transfer of Federal funds.

(i) Primary covered transaction. Except as noted in paragraph (b)(2) of this section, a primary covered transaction is any nonprocurement transaction between an agency and a person, regardless of type, including: grants, cooperative agreements, scholarships, fellowships, contracts of assistance, loans, loan Guarantees, subsidies, insurance, payments for specified use, donation agreements and any other nonprocurement transactions between a Federal agency and a person.

(ii) Lower tier covered transaction. A lower tier covered transaction is:

(A) Any transaction between a participant and a person other than a procurement contract for goods or services, regardless of type, under a primary covered transaction;

(B) Any procurement contract for goods or services between a participant and a person, regardless of type, expected to equal or exceed the Federal procurement small purchase threshold fixed at 10 U.S.C. 2304(g) and 41 U.S.C. 253(g) (currently $100,000) under a primary covered transaction;

(C) Any procurement contract for goods or services between a participant and a person under a covered transaction, regardless of amount, under which that person will have a critical influence on or substantive control over that covered transaction. Such persons may include loan officers or chief executive officers acting as principal investigators and providers of federally-required audit services.

(2) *Exceptions.* The following transactions are not covered:

(i) Statutory entitlements or mandatory awards (but not subtier awards thereunder which are not themselves mandatory), including deposited funds insured by the Federal Government;

(ii) Direct awards to foreign governments or public international organizations, or transactions with foreign governments or foreign governmental entities, public international organizations, foreign government owned (in whole or in part) or controlled entities, entities consisting wholly or partially of foreign governments or foreign governmental entities;

(iii) Benefits to an individual as a personal entitlement without regard to the individual's present responsibility (but benefits received in an individual's business capacity are not excepted);

(iv) Federal employment;

(v) Transactions pursuant to national or agency-recognized emergencies or disasters;

(vi) Incidental benefits derived from ordinary governmental operations; and

(vii) Other transactions where the application of this section would be prohibited by law.

(3) *Board covered transactions.* This section applies to the Board's loan Guarantees, subcontracts and transactions at any tier that are charges as direct or indirect costs, regardless of type.

(c) *Primary covered transactions.* Except to the extent prohibited by law, persons who are debarred or suspended shall be excluded from primary covered transactions as either participants or principals throughout the Executive Branch of the Federal Government for the period of their debarment, suspension, or the period they are proposed for debarment under 48 CFR part 9, subpart 9.4. Accordingly, no agency shall enter into primary covered transactions with such excluded persons during such period, except as permitted pursuant to paragraph (l) of this section.

(d) *Lower tier covered transactions.* Except to the extent prohibited by law, persons who have been proposed for debarment under 48 CFR part 9, subpart 9.4, debarred or suspended shall be excluded from participating as either participants or principals in all lower tier covered transactions (see paragraph (b)(1)(ii) of this section) for the period of their exclusion.

(e) *Exceptions.* Debarment or suspension does not affect a person's eligibility for—

(1) Statutory entitlements or mandatory awards (but not subtier awards thereunder which are not themselves mandatory), including deposited funds insured by the Federal Government;

(2) Direct awards to foreign governments or public international organizations, or transactions with foreign governments or foreign governmental entities, public international organizations, foreign government owned (in whole or in part) or controlled entities, and entities consisting wholly or partially of foreign governments or foreign governmental entities;

(3) Benefits to an individual as a personal entitlement without regard to the individual's present responsibility (but benefits received in an individual's business capacity are not excepted);

(4) Federal employment;

(5) Transactions pursuant to national or agency-recognized emergencies or disasters;

(6) Incidental benefits derived from ordinary governmental operations; and

(7) Other transactions where the application of this section would be prohibited by law.

(f) Persons who are ineligible are excluded in accordance with the applicable statutory, executive order, or regulatory authority.

(g) Persons who accept voluntary exclusions are excluded in accordance with the terms of their settlements. The Board shall, and participants may, contact the original action agency to ascertain the extent of the exclusion.

(h) The Board may grant an exception permitting a debarred, suspended, or voluntarily excluded person, or a person proposed for debarment under 48 CFR part 9, subpart 9.4, to participate in a particular covered transaction upon a written determination by the agency head or an authorized designee stating the reason(s) for deviating from the Presidential policy established by Executive Order 12549. However, in accordance with the President's stated intention in the Executive Order, exceptions shall be granted only infrequently. Exceptions shall be reported in accordance with the Executive Order.

(i) Notwithstanding the debarment, suspension, proposed debarment under

48 CFR part 9, subpart 9.4, determination of ineligibility, or voluntary exclusion of any person by an agency, agencies and participants may continue covered transactions in existence at the time the person was debarred, suspended, proposed for debarment under 48 CFR part 9, subpart 9.4, declared ineligible, or voluntarily excluded. A decision as to the type of termination action, if any, to be taken should be made only after thorough review to ensure the propriety of the proposed action.

(j) Agencies and participants shall not renew or extend covered transactions (other than no-cost time extensions) with any person who is debarred, suspended, proposed for debarment under 48 CFR part 9, subpart 9.4, ineligible or voluntary excluded, except as provided in paragraph (h) of this section.

(k) Except as permitted paragraphs (h) or (i) of this section, a participant shall not knowingly do business under a covered transaction with a person who is—

(1) Debarred or suspended;

(2) Proposed for debarment under 48 CFR part 9, subpart 9.4; or

(3) Ineligible for or voluntarily excluded from the covered transaction.

(l) Violation of the restriction under paragraph (k) of this section may result in disallowance of costs, annulment or termination of award, issuance of a stop work order, debarment or suspension, or other remedies as appropriate.

(m) A participant may rely upon the certification of a prospective participant in a lower tier covered transaction that it and its principals are not debarred, suspended, proposed for debarment under 48 CFR part 9, subpart 9.4, ineligible, or voluntarily excluded from the covered transaction, unless it knows that the certification is erroneous. An agency has the burden of proof that a participant did knowingly do business with a person that filed an erroneous certification.

§500.110 Amendments.

The Board's rules in this chapter may be adopted or amended, or new rules may be adopted, only by majority vote of the Board. Authority to adopt or amend these rules may not be delegated.

Subpart C—Oil and Gas Guaranteed Loans

§500.200 Eligible Borrower.

(a) An eligible Borrower must be a Qualified Oil and Gas Company that can demonstrate:

(1) Credit is not otherwise available to it under reasonable terms or conditions sufficient to meet its financing needs, as reflected in the financial and business plans of the company;

(2) The prospective earning power of that company, together with the character and value of the security pledged, furnish reasonable assurance of repayment of the loan to be guaranteed in accordance with its terms;

(3) The company has agreed to permit audits by the General Accounting Office and an independent auditor acceptable to the Board prior to the issuance of the guarantee and while any such guaranteed loan is outstanding; and

(4) It has experienced layoffs, production losses, or financial losses between January 1, 1997, and the date of application for the Guarantee, demonstrated as a comparison between employment, production, or net income existing on January 1, 1997 and on the date of application.

(b) The Lender must provide with its application a letter from at least one lending institution other than the Lender to which the Borrower has applied for financial assistance, since January 1, 1997, indicating that the Borrower was denied for substantially the same loan they are now applying for, and the reasons the Borrower was unable to obtain the financing for which it applied. In addition, the Lender applying for a guarantee under this Program must certify that it would not make the loan without the Board's guarantee.

§500.201 Eligible Lender.

(a) A lender eligible to apply to the Board for a Guarantee of a loan must be:

(1) A banking institution, such as a commercial bank or trust company, subject to regulation by the Federal

banking agencies enumerated in 12 U.S.C. § 1813; or

(2) An investment institution, such as an investment bank, commercial finance company, or insurance company, that is currently engaged in commercial lending in the normal course of its business.

(b)(1) If more than one banking or investment institution is applying to the Board for a Guarantee of a single loan, each one of the banking or investment institutions on the application must meet the requirements to be an eligible lender set forth in paragraph (a) of this section.

(2) An application for a Guarantee of a single loan submitted by a group of banking or investment institutions, as described in paragraph (b)(1) of this section, must identify one of the banking or investment institutions applying for such loan to act as agent for all. This agent is responsible for administering the loan and shall have those duties and responsibilities required of an agent, as set forth in the Guarantee.

(3) Each Lender, irrespective of any indemnities or other agreements between the Lenders and the Agent, shall be bound by all actions, and/or failures to act, of the Agent. The Board shall be entitled to rely upon such actions and/or failures to act of the Agent as binding the Lenders.

(c) Status as a Lender under paragraph (a) of this section does not assure that the Board will issue the Guarantee sought, or otherwise preclude the Board from declining to issue a Guarantee. In addition to evaluating an application pursuant to § 500.207, in making a determination to issue a Guarantee to a Lender, the Board will assess:

(1) The Lender's level of regulatory capital, in the case of banking institutions, or net worth, in the case of investment institutions;

(2) Whether the Lender possesses the ability to administer the loan, as required by § 500.211(b), including its experience with loans to oil and gas companies;

(3) The scope, volume and duration of the Lender's activity in administering loans;

(4) The performance of the Lender's loan portfolio, including its current delinquency rate;

(5) The Lender's loss rate as a percentage of loan amounts for its current fiscal year; and

(6) Any other matter the Board deems material to its assessment of the Lender.

(d) In the case of the refinancing of an existing credit, the applicant must be a different lender than the holder of the existing credit.

[64 FR 57947, Oct. 27, 1999, as amended at 65 FR 24107, Apr. 25, 2000]

§ 500.202 Loan amount.

The aggregate amount of loan principal guaranteed under this Program to a single Qualified Oil and Gas Company may not exceed $10 million.

§ 500.203 Guarantee percentage.

A guarantee issued by the Board may not exceed 85 percent of the amount of the principal of a loan to a Qualified Oil and Gas Company.

§ 500.204 Loan terms.

(a) All loans guaranteed under the Program shall be due and payable in full no later than December 31, 2010.

(b) Loans guaranteed under the Program must bear a rate of interest determined by the Board to be reasonable. The reasonableness of an interest rate will be determined with respect to current average yields on outstanding obligations of the United States with remaining periods of maturity comparable to the term of the loan sought to be guaranteed. The Board may reject an application to guarantee a loan if it determines the interest rate of such loan to be unreasonable.

(c)(1) The performance of all of the Borrower's obligations under the Loan Documents shall be secured by, and shall have the priority in, such Security as provided for within the terms and conditions of the Guarantee.

(2) Without limiting the Lender's or Borrower's obligations under paragraph (c) of this section, at a minimum, the loan shall be secured by:

(i) A fully perfected and enforceable security interest and or lien, with first priority over conflicting security interests or other liens in all property acquired, improved, or derived from the loan funds; and

(ii) A fully perfected and enforceable security interest and or lien in any other property of the Borrower's pledged to secure the loan, including accessions, replacements, proceeds, or property given by a third party as Security for the loan, the priority of which shall be, at a minimum, equal in status with the existing highest voluntarily granted or acquired interest or lien;

(3) The entire loan will be secured by the same Security with equal lien priority for the guaranteed and the unguaranteed portions of the loan. The unguaranteed portion of the loan will neither be paid first nor given any preference over the guaranteed portion.

(4) An Applicant's compliance with paragraph (c)(2) of this section does not assure a finding of reasonable assurance of repayment, or assure the Board's Guarantee of the loan.

(d) An eligible Lender may assess and collect from the Borrower such other fees and costs associated with the application and origination of the loan as are reasonable and customary, taking into consideration the amount and complexity of the credit. The Board may take such other fees and costs into consideration when determining whether to offer a Guarantee to the Lender.

[64 FR 57947, Oct. 27, 1999, as amended at 64 FR 72024, Dec. 23, 1999]

§ 500.205 Application process.

(a) *Application process.* An original application and three copies must be received by the Board no later than 5 P.M. EST, February 28, 2000, in the U.S. Department of Commerce, 1401 Constitution Avenue, NW., room H–2500, Washington, DC 20230. Applications which have been provided to a delivery service on or before February 27, 2000, with "delivery guaranteed" before 5 P.M. on February 28, 2000, will be acceptabled for review if the Applicant can document that the application was provided to the delivery service with delivery to the address listed in this section guaranteed prior to the closing date and time. A postmark of February 27, 2000, is not sufficient to meet this deadline as the application must be received by the required date and time. Applications will not be accepted via facsimile machine transmission or electronic mail.

(b) Applications shall contain the following:

(1) A completed Form, "Application for Oil and Gas Guarantee Loan";

(2) The information required for the completion of Form "Environmental Assessment and Compliance Findings for Related Environmental Laws" and attachments, as required by § 500.206(a)(2)(i)(D), unless the project is categorically excluded under § 500.206(b);

(3) All Loan Documents that will be signed by the Lender and the Borrower, if the application is approved, including all terms and conditions of, and Security or additional Security to assure the Borrower's performance under, the loan;

(4) Certification by the chairman of the board and the chief executive officer of the Borrower acknowledging that the Borrower is aware that the Lender is applying to the Board for a Guarantee of a loan under the Program, as described in the Loan Documents, and agreeing to permit audits by the General Accounting Office, its designee, an independent auditor acceptable to the Board prior to the issuance of the Guarantee and annually thereafter while such guarantee is outstanding;

(5) The Lender's full written underwriting analysis of the loan to be guaranteed by the Board;

(6) A certification that the Lender has followed the same loan underwriting analysis with the loan to be guaranteed as it would follow for a loan not guaranteed by the Government; and a certification by the Lender, that the loan, Lender, and Borrower meet each of the requirements of the Program as set forth in the Act and the Board's rules in this part;

(7) A description of all Security for the loan, including, as applicable, current appraisal of real and personal property, copies of any appropriate environmental site assessments, and current personal and corporate financial statements of any guarantors for the

same periods as required for the Borrower. Appraisals of real property shall be prepared by State licensed or certified appraisers, and be consistent with the "Uniform Standards of Professional Appraisal Practice," promulgated by the Appraisal Standards Board of the Appraisal Foundation. Financial statements of guarantors shall be prepared by independent Certified Public Accountants;

(8)(i) An independent oil and gas company, as defined in section 201(c)(3)(A)(i) of the Act, is required to submit:

(A) For loans less than $5 million, three years of financial statements reviewed by a certified public accountant following generally accepted accounting principles, as well as any interim financial statements; or

(B) For loans of $5 million or greater, three years of financial statements must be submitted. The most recent year's statement must be audited by an independent certified public accountant. Statements from the prior two years must be reviewed by a certified public accountant following generally accepted accounting principles. In addition, any interim financial statements and associated notes must be submitted as well.

(ii) A service company, as defined in section 201(c)(3)(A)(ii) of the Act, is required to submit consolidated financial statements of the Borrower for the previous three years that have been audited by an independent certified public accountant, including any associated notes, as well as any interim financial statements and associated notes.

(9) A five year history and five year projection for revenue, cash flow, average realized prices and average realized production costs. If the loan funds are to be used to purchase substantial assets of an existing firm, a pro forma balance sheet at startup, and five years projected year end balance sheets and income statement at start-up;

(10) Documentation that credit is not otherwise available to the borrower under reasonable terms or conditions sufficient to meet its financial needs, as reflected in the financial or business plan of that company. The Lender must provide with its application those items required by § 500.200(b);

(11) Documentation sufficient to demonstrate that the Lender is eligible under § 500.201(a) and to allow the Board to make a determination to issue a Guarantee to such Lender as set forth in § 500.201(c).

(12) A report as to the Borrower's designation of the nature and value of project reserves from an independent petroleum engineer acceptable to the Board.

(c) No Guarantee will be made if either the Borrower or Lender has an outstanding, delinquent Federal debt until:

(1) The delinquent account has been paid in full;

(2) A negotiated repayment schedule is established and at least one payment has been received; or

(3) Other arrangements, satisfactory to the agency responsible for collecting the debt, are made.

[64 FR 57947, Oct. 27, 1999, as amended at 64 FR 72024, Dec. 23, 1999; 65 FR 6889, Feb. 11, 2000; 65 FR 24107, Apr. 25, 2000]

§ 500.206 Environmental requirements.

(a)(1) *In General.* Environmental assessments of the Board's actions will be conducted in accordance with applicable statutes, regulations, and Executive Orders. Therefore, each application for a Guarantee under the Program must be accompanied by information necessary for the Board to meet the requirements of applicable law.

(2) *Actions requiring compliance with NEPA.* (i) The types of actions classified as "major Federal actions" subject to NEPA procedures are discussed generally in 40 CFR parts 1500 through 1508.

(ii) With respect to this Program, these actions typically include:

(A) Any project, permanent or temporary, that will involve construction and/or installations;

(B) Any project, permanent or temporary, that will involve ground disturbing activities; and

(C) Any project supporting renovation, other than interior remodeling.

(3) *Environmental information required from the Lender.* (i) Environmental data or documentation concerning the use of the proceeds of any loan guaranteed

under this Program must be provided by the Lender to the Board to assist the Board in meeting its legal responsibilities. The Lender may obtain this information from the Borrower. Such information includes:

(A) Documentation for an environmental threshold review from qualified data sources, such as a Federal, State or local agency with expertise and experience in environmental protection, or other sources, qualified to provide reliable environmental information;

(B) Any previously prepared environmental reports or data relevant to the loan at issue;

(C) Any environmental review prepared by Federal, State, or local agencies relevant to the loan at issue;

(D) The information required for the completion of Form XYZ, "Environmental Assessment and Compliance Findings for Related Environmental Laws;" and

(E) Any other information that can be used by the Board to ensure compliance with environmental laws.

(ii) All information supplied by the Lender is subject to verification by the Board.

(b) The regulations of the Council on Environmental Quality implementing NEPA require the Board to provide public notice of the availability of project specific environmental documents such as environmental impact statements, environmental assessments, findings of no significant impact, records of decision etc., to the affected public. See 40 CFR 1506.6(b). Environmental information concerning specific projects can be obtained from the Board by contacting: Executive Director, Emergency Oil and Gas Guaranteed Loan Board, U.S. Department of Commerce, Washington, DC 20230.

(c) *National Environmental Policy Act*—(1) *Purpose.* The purpose of this paragraph (c) is to adopt procedures for compliance with the National Environmental Policy Act, 42 U.S.C. 4321 *et seq.*, by the Board. This paragraph supplements regulations at 40 CFR Chapter V.

(2) *Definitions.* For purposes of this section, the following definitions apply:

Categorical exclusion means a category of actions which do not individually or cumulatively have a significant effect on the human environment and for which neither an environmental assessment nor an environmental impact statement is required.

Environmental assessment means a document that briefly discusses the environmental consequences of a proposed action and alternatives prepared for the purposes set forth in 40 CFR 1508.9.

EIS means an environmental impact statement prepared pursuant to section 102(2)(C) of NEPA.

FONSI means a finding of no significant impact on the quality of the human environment after the completion of an environmental assessment.

NEPA means the National Environmental Policy Act, 42 U.S.C. 4321, *et seq.*

Working Capital Loan means money used by an ongoing business concern to fund its existing operations.

(3) *Delegations to Executive Director.* (i) All incoming correspondence from Council on Environmental Quality (CEQ) and other agencies concerning matters related to NEPA, including draft and final EIS, shall be brought to the attention of the Executive Director. The Executive Director will prepare or, at his or her discretion, coordinate replies to such correspondence.

(ii) With respect to actions of the Board, the Executive Director will:

(A) Ensure preparation of all necessary environmental assessments and EISs;

(B) Maintain a list of actions for which environmental assessments are being prepared;

(C) Revise this list at regular intervals, and send the revisions to the Environmental Protection Agency;

(D) Make the list available for public inspection;

(E) Maintain a list of EISs; and

(F) Maintain a file of draft and final EISs.

(4) *Categorical exclusions.* (i) This paragraph describes various classes of Board actions that normally do not have a significant impact on the human environment and are categorically excluded. The word "normally" is stressed; there may be individual cases in which specific factors require contrary action.

(ii) Subject to the limitations in paragraph (c)(4)(iii) of this section, the actions described in this paragraph have been determined not to have a significant impact on the quality of the human environment. They are categorically excluded from the need to prepare an environmental assessment or an EIS under NEPA.

(A) Guarantees of working capital loans; and

(B) Guarantees of loans for the refinancing of outstanding indebtedness of the Borrower, regardless of the purpose for which the original indebtedness was incurred.

(iii) Actions listed in paragraph (c)(4)(ii) of this section that otherwise are categorically excluded from NEPA review are not necessarily excluded from review if they would be located within, or in other cases, potentially affect:

(A) A floodplain;

(B) A wetland;

(C) Important farmlands, or prime forestlands or rangelands;

(D) A listed species or critical habitat for an endangered species;

(E) A property that is listed on or may be eligible for listing on the National Register of Historic Places;

(F) An area within an approved State Coastal Zone Management Program;

(G) A coastal barrier or a portion of a barrier within the Coastal Barrier Resources System;

(H) A river or portion of a river included in, or designated for, potential addition to the Wild and Scenic Rivers System;

(I) A sole source aquifer recharge area;

(J) A State water quality standard (including designated and/or existing beneficial uses and anti-degradation requirements); or

(K) The release or disposal of regulated substances above the levels set forth in a permit or license issued by an appropriate regulatory authority.

(5) *Responsibilities and procedures for preparation of an environmental assessment.* (i) The Executive Director will request that the Lender and Borrower provide information concerning all potentially significant environmental impacts of the Borrower's proposed project pursuant to 13 CFR 500.206. The Executive Director, consulting at his discretion with CEQ, will review the information provided by the Lender and Borrower. Though no specific format for an environmental assessment is prescribed, it shall be a separate document and should include the following in conformance with 40 CFR 1508.9:

(A) *Description of the environment.* The existing environmental conditions relevant to the Board's analysis determining the environmental impacts of the proposed project, should be described. The no action alternative also should be discussed;

(B) *Documentation.* Citations to information used to describe the existing environment and to assess environmental impacts should be clearly referenced and documented. Such references should include, as appropriate, but not be limited to, local, tribal, regional, State, and Federal agencies, as well as, public and private organizations and institutions;

(C) *Evaluating environmental consequences of proposed actions.* A brief discussion should be included of the need for the proposal, of alternatives as required by 42 U.S.C. 4332(2)(E) and their environmental impacts. The discussion of the environmental impacts should include measures to mitigate adverse impacts and any irreversible or irretrievable commitments of resources to the proposed project.

(ii) The Executive Director, in preparing an environmental assessment, may:

(A) Tier upon the information contained in a previous EIS, as described in 40 CFR 1502.20;

(B) Incorporate by reference reasonably available material, as described in 40 CFR 1502.21; and/or

(C) Adopt a previously completed EIS reasonably related to the project for which the proceeds of the loan sought to be guaranteed under the Program will be used, as described in 40 CFR 1506.3.

(iii) Because of the statute's admonition to the Board to make its decisions as soon as possible after receiving applications, the Board will not:

(A) Publish notice of intent to prepare an environmental assessment, as described in 40 CFR 1501.7;

(B) Conduct scoping, as described in 40 CFR 1501.7; and

(C) Seek comments on the environmental assessment, as described in 40 CFR 1503.1.

(iv) If, on the basis of an environmental assessment, it is determined that an EIS is not required, a FONSI, as described in 40 CFR 1508.13 will be prepared. The FONSI will include the environmental assessment or a summary of it and be available to the public from the Board. The Executive Director shall maintain a record of these decisions, making them available to interested parties upon request. Requests should be directed to the Executive Director Emergency Oil and Gas Guarantee Loan Program, 14th Street and Constitution Avenue, NW., Washington DC 20230. Prior to a final loan guarantee decision, a copy of the NEPA documentation shall be sent to their Board for consideration.

(6) *Responsibilities and procedures for preparation of an environmental impact statement.* (i) If after an environmental assessment has been completed, it is determined that an EIS is necessary, it and other related documentation will be prepared by the Executive Director in accordance with section 102(*2*)(c) of NEPA, this section, and 40 CFR parts 1500 through 1508. The Executive Director may seek additional information from the applicant in preparing the EIS. Once the document is prepared, it shall be submitted to the Board. If the Board considers a document unsatisfactory, it shall be returned to the Executive Director for revision or supplementation prior to a loan guarantee decision; otherwise the Board will transmit the document to the Environmental Protection Agency.

(ii)(A) The following procedures, as discussed in 40 CFR parts 1500 through 1508, will be followed in preparing an EIS:

(*1*) The format and contents of the draft and final EIS shall be as discussed in 40 CFR 1502.

(*2*) The requirements of 40 CFR 1506.9 for filing of documents with the Environmental Protection Agency shall be followed.

(*3*) The Executive Director, consulting at his discretion with CEQ, shall examine carefully the basis on which supportive studies have been conducted to assure that such studies are objective and comprehensive in scope and depth.

(*4*) NEPA requires that the decision making "utilize a systematic, interdisciplinary approach that will ensure the integrated use of the natural and social sciences and the environmental design arts." 42 U.S.C. 4332(A). If such disciplines are not present on the Board staff, appropriate use should be made of personnel of Federal, State, and local agencies, universities, non-profit organizations, or private industry.

(B) Until the Board issues a record of decision as provided in 40 CFR 1502.2 no action concerning the proposal shall be taken which would:

(*1*) Have an adverse environmental impact; or

(*2*) Limit the choice of reasonable alternatives.

(*3*) 40 CFR 1506.10 places certain limitations on the timing of Board decisions on taking "major Federal actions." A loan guarantee shall not be make before the times set forth in 40 CFR 1506.10.

(iii) A public record of decision stating what the decision was; identifying alternatives that were considered, including the environmentally preferable one(s); discussing any national considerations that entered into the decision; and summarizing a monitoring and enforcement program if applicable for mitigating the environmental effects of a proposal; will be prepared. This record of decision will be prepared at the time the decision is made.

[64 FR 57947, Oct. 27, 1999, as amended at 64 FR 72024, Dec. 23, 1999]

§500.207 Application evaluation.

(a) *Eligibility screening.* Applications will be reviewed to determine whether the Lender and Borrower are eligible, the information required under §500.205(b) is complete, and the proposed loan complies with applicable statutes and regulations. The Board can at any time reject an application that does not meet these requirements.

(b) *Evaluation criteria.* Applications that are determined to be eligible pursuant to paragraph (a) of this section shall be subject to a substantive review, on a competitive basis, by the Board based upon the following evaluation factors, in order of importance:

(1) The ability of the Borrower to repay the loan by the date specified in the Loan Document, which shall be no later than December 31, 2010;

(2) The adequacy of the proposed provisions to protect the Government, including sufficiency of Security, the priority of the lien position in the Security, and the percentage of Guarantee requested; and

(3) Adequacy of the underwriting analysis performed by the Lender in preparing the application and the ability of the Lender to administer the loan in full compliance with the requisite standard of care set forth in § 500.211(b).

(c) *Decisions by the Board.* Upon completion of the evaluation of the application and as soon as possible after the due date, the Board will approve or deny all eligible applications timely received under this Program. The Board shall notify all Applicants in writing of the approval or denial of the Guarantee applications as soon as possible. Approvals for loan Guarantees shall be conditioned upon compliance with § 500.208.

§ 500.208 Issuance of the Guarantee.

(a) The Board's decisions to approve any application for, and extend an offer of, guarantee under § 500.207 is conditioned upon:

(1) The Lender and Borrower obtaining any required regulatory or judicial approvals;

(2) The Lender and Borrower being legally authorized to enter into the loan under the terms and conditions submitted to the Board in the application;

(3) The Board's receipt of the Loan Documents, Guarantee, and any related instruments, properly executed by the Lender, Borrower, and any other required party other than the Board; and

(4) No material adverse change in the Borrower's ability to repay the loan between the date of the Board's approval and the date the Guarantee is to be issued.

(b) The Board may withdraw its approval of an application and rescind its offer of Guarantee if the Board determines that the Lender or the Borrower cannot, or is unwilling to, provide adequate documentation and proof of compliance with paragraph (a) of this section within the time provided for in the offer.

(c) Only after receipt of all the documentation, required by this section, will the Board sign and deliver the Guarantee.

(d) A Borrower receiving a loan guaranteed by the Board under this Program shall pay a one-time guarantee fee of 0.5 percent of the amount of the principal of the loan. This fee must be paid no later than one year from the issuance of the Guarantee.

§ 500.209 Funding for the Program.

The Act provides funding for the costs incurred by the Government as a result of granting Guarantees under the Program. While pursuing the goals of the Act, it is the intent of the Board to minimize the cost of the Program to the Government. The Board will estimate the risk posed by the guaranteed loans to the funds appropriated for the costs of the Guarantees under the Program and operate the Program accordingly.

§ 500.210 Assignment or transfer of loans.

(a) Neither the Loan Documents nor the Guarantee of the Board, or any interest therein, may be modified, assigned, conveyed, sold or otherwise transferred by the Lender, in whole or in part, without the prior written approval of the Board.

(b) Under no circumstances will the Board permit an assignment or transfer of less than 100 percent of a Lender's interest in the Loan Documents and Guarantee, nor will it permit an assignment or transfer to be made to a party which the Board determines not to be an Eligible Lender pursuant to § 500.201.

(c) The proscription under paragraph (a) of this section shall not apply to:

(1) Transfers which occur by operation of law, unless a primary purpose of the transaction leading to such a transfer was to assign, convey or sell the loan note or Guarantee without the

necessity of securing the Board's prior written approval; or

(2) An action or agreement by the Lender which has the effect of distributing the risks of the credit among other Lenders if:

(i) Neither the loan note nor the Guarantee is assigned, conveyed, sold, or transferred in whole or in part;

(ii) Both the unguaranteed and guaranteed portions of the loan are treated in the same manner;

(iii) The Lender remains solely responsible for the administration of the loan; and

(iv) The Board's ability to assert any and all defenses available to it under the Guarantee and the law is not adversely affected; or

(3) Transfer by a non-Agent Lender of the non-guaranteed portion of the loan after payment under the Guarantee has been made.

[64 FR 57947, Oct. 27, 1999, as amended at 65 FR 24107, Apr. 25, 2000]

§ 500.211 Lender responsibilities.

(a) *General.* Lender shall comply with all provisions of the Guarantee.

(b) *Standard of care.* The Lender shall exercise due care and diligence in administering the loan as would be exercised by a reasonable and prudent banking institution when administering a secured loan of such banking institution's own funds without a Federal guaranty. Such standard shall also apply to any and all approvals, determinations, permissions, acceptances, requirements, or opinion made, given, imposed or reached by Lender.

(c) *Representation to the Board.* In addition to any other representations required by the Guarantee, the Applicant shall represent to the Board that it has the ability to, and will, administer the loan, as well as to exercise the Applicant's rights and pursue its remedies, including conducting any liquidation of the Security or additional Security in full compliance with the standard of care, without the need for any advice, opinion, determination, recommendation, approval, disapproval, assistance (financial or other) or participation by the Board, except where the Board's consent is expressly required by the Guarantee, or where the Board, in its sole discretion and pursuant to the Guarantee, elects to provide same.

(d) *Covenants.* With respect to any loan guaranteed by the Board pursuant to the Act and this part, the Lender shall require the Loan Documents to contain such affirmative and negative covenants by the Borrower as are required by the terms and conditions of the Guarantee, such as the prohibition on the payment of dividends.

(e) *Monitoring.* In accordance with the Guarantee the Lender shall monitor Borrower's performance under the Loan Documents to detect any noncompliance by the Borrower with any provision thereof.

(f) *Reporting.* With respect to any loan guaranteed by the Board pursuant to the Act and this part the Lender shall provide the Board with the following information, in accordance with the Guarantee:

(1) Financial statements for the borrower, as provided in the Guarantee;

(2) Projected balance sheet, income statement, and cash flows for the Borrower for each year remaining on the term of the loan; and

(3) A completed signed copy of Form "Quarterly Compliance Statement" that includes information on the recent performance of the loan, within 15 days of the end of each calendar quarter.

(g) *Notices.* All written notices, requests, or demands made to the Board shall be mailed to the Board at the U.S. Department of Commerce, H2500, Washington, DC 20230, except as otherwise specified by the Guarantee or as directed by the Board. Lender shall notify the Board in writing without delay of:

(1) Deterioration in the internal risk rating of a loan guaranteed under this Program within 5 business days of such action by the Lender;

(2) The occurrence of each event of default under the Loan Documents or Guarantee promptly, but not later than 5 business days, of the Lender's learning of such occurrence; and

(3) Any other notification requirements as provided by law, or by the

terms of the Guarantee or Loan Documents.

[64 FR 57947, Oct. 27, 1999, as amended at 65 FR 24107, Apr. 25, 2000; 65 FR 51522, Aug. 24, 2000]

§ 500.212 Liquidation.

(a) The Board may take, or direct to be taken, any action in liquidating the Security which the Board determines to be necessary or proper, consistent with Federal law and regulations.

(b) Pursuant to the Guarantee, upon written demand by the Lender and whether or not the Board has made any payment under the Guarantee, the Board, at the Board's sole option shall have the right to require that the Lender, solely or jointly with the Board, conduct to completion the liquidation of any or all of the Security. The Board may choose to conduct the liquidation itself.

§ 500.213 Termination of obligations.

(a) The Board, in its discretion, shall be entitled to terminate all, or a portion, of the Board's obligations under the Guarantee, without further cause, in the event that:

(1) The Guarantee fee required by § 500.208(d) shall not have been paid;

(2) A Lender shall have released or covenanted not to sue the Borrower or any other guarantor, or agreed to the modification of any obligation of any party to any agreement related to the loan, without the prior written consent of the Board;

(3) A Lender has released the Board from its liability and obligations under the Guarantee;

(4) A Lender shall have made any incorrect or incomplete representation to the Board in any material respect in connection with the Application, the Guarantee or the Loan Documents;

(5) A Lender fails to make a demand for payment within 30 days of payment default; or

(6) A Lender fails to comply with any material provision of the Loan Documents or the Guarantee.

(b) Upon receipt of a written demand for payment made pursuant to the Guarantee, the Board shall be entitled to seek such certifications from the Lender, undertake such audits or investigations, or take such other action as is provided for by law or the Guarantee so as to determine whether the Lender has complied with all of the Lender's obligations under the Guarantee.

[64 FR 57947, Oct. 27, 1999, as amended at 65 FR 24107, Apr. 25, 2000]

§ 500.214 OMB control number. [Reserved]

PARTS 501–599 [RESERVED]

FINDING AIDS

A list of CFR titles, subtitles, chapters, subchapters and parts and an alphabetical list of agencies publishing in the CFR are included in the CFR Index and Finding Aids volume to the Code of Federal Regulations which is published separately and revised annually.

Table of CFR Titles and Chapters

(Revised as of January 1, 2019)

Title 1—General Provisions

Title 2—Grants and Agreements

Title 2—Grants and Agreements—Continued

Chap.	
XXVII	Small Business Administration (Parts 2700—2799)
XXVIII	Department of Justice (Parts 2800—2899)
XXIX	Department of Labor (Parts 2900—2999)
XXX	Department of Homeland Security (Parts 3000—3099)
XXXI	Institute of Museum and Library Services (Parts 3100—3199)
XXXII	National Endowment for the Arts (Parts 3200—3299)
XXXIII	National Endowment for the Humanities (Parts 3300—3399)
XXXIV	Department of Education (Parts 3400—3499)
XXXV	Export-Import Bank of the United States (Parts 3500—3599)
XXXVI	Office of National Drug Control Policy, Executive Office of the President (Parts 3600—3699)
XXXVII	Peace Corps (Parts 3700—3799)
LVIII	Election Assistance Commission (Parts 5800—5899)
LIX	Gulf Coast Ecosystem Restoration Council (Parts 5900—5999)

Title 3—The President

I	Executive Office of the President (Parts 100—199)

Title 4—Accounts

I	Government Accountability Office (Parts 1—199)

Title 5—Administrative Personnel

I	Office of Personnel Management (Parts 1—1199)
II	Merit Systems Protection Board (Parts 1200—1299)
III	Office of Management and Budget (Parts 1300—1399)
IV	Office of Personnel Management and Office of the Director of National Intelligence (Parts 1400—1499)
V	The International Organizations Employees Loyalty Board (Parts 1500—1599)
VI	Federal Retirement Thrift Investment Board (Parts 1600—1699)
VIII	Office of Special Counsel (Parts 1800—1899)
IX	Appalachian Regional Commission (Parts 1900—1999)
XI	Armed Forces Retirement Home (Parts 2100—2199)
XIV	Federal Labor Relations Authority, General Counsel of the Federal Labor Relations Authority and Federal Service Impasses Panel (Parts 2400—2499)
XVI	Office of Government Ethics (Parts 2600—2699)
XXI	Department of the Treasury (Parts 3100—3199)
XXII	Federal Deposit Insurance Corporation (Parts 3200—3299)
XXIII	Department of Energy (Parts 3300—3399)
XXIV	Federal Energy Regulatory Commission (Parts 3400—3499)
XXV	Department of the Interior (Parts 3500—3599)
XXVI	Department of Defense (Parts 3600—3699)

Chap.	
XXVIII	Department of Justice (Parts 3800—3899)
XXIX	Federal Communications Commission (Parts 3900—3999)
XXX	Farm Credit System Insurance Corporation (Parts 4000—4099)
XXXI	Farm Credit Administration (Parts 4100—4199)
XXXIII	Overseas Private Investment Corporation (Parts 4300—4399)
XXXIV	Securities and Exchange Commission (Parts 4400—4499)
XXXV	Office of Personnel Management (Parts 4500—4599)
XXXVI	Department of Homeland Security (Parts 4600—4699)
XXXVII	Federal Election Commission (Parts 4700—4799)
XL	Interstate Commerce Commission (Parts 5000—5099)
XLI	Commodity Futures Trading Commission (Parts 5100—5199)
XLII	Department of Labor (Parts 5200—5299)
XLIII	National Science Foundation (Parts 5300—5399)
XLV	Department of Health and Human Services (Parts 5500—5599)
XLVI	Postal Rate Commission (Parts 5600—5699)
XLVII	Federal Trade Commission (Parts 5700—5799)
XLVIII	Nuclear Regulatory Commission (Parts 5800—5899)
XLIX	Federal Labor Relations Authority (Parts 5900—5999)
L	Department of Transportation (Parts 6000—6099)
LII	Export-Import Bank of the United States (Parts 6200—6299)
LIII	Department of Education (Parts 6300—6399)
LIV	Environmental Protection Agency (Parts 6400—6499)
LV	National Endowment for the Arts (Parts 6500—6599)
LVI	National Endowment for the Humanities (Parts 6600—6699)
LVII	General Services Administration (Parts 6700—6799)
LVIII	Board of Governors of the Federal Reserve System (Parts 6800—6899)
LIX	National Aeronautics and Space Administration (Parts 6900—6999)
LX	United States Postal Service (Parts 7000—7099)
LXI	National Labor Relations Board (Parts 7100—7199)
LXII	Equal Employment Opportunity Commission (Parts 7200—7299)
LXIII	Inter-American Foundation (Parts 7300—7399)
LXIV	Merit Systems Protection Board (Parts 7400—7499)
LXV	Department of Housing and Urban Development (Parts 7500—7599)
LXVI	National Archives and Records Administration (Parts 7600—7699)
LXVII	Institute of Museum and Library Services (Parts 7700—7799)
LXVIII	Commission on Civil Rights (Parts 7800—7899)
LXIX	Tennessee Valley Authority (Parts 7900—7999)
LXX	Court Services and Offender Supervision Agency for the District of Columbia (Parts 8000—8099)
LXXI	Consumer Product Safety Commission (Parts 8100—8199)
LXXIII	Department of Agriculture (Parts 8300—8399)

Title 5—Administrative Personnel—Continued

Chap.	
LXXIV	Federal Mine Safety and Health Review Commission (Parts 8400—8499)
LXXVI	Federal Retirement Thrift Investment Board (Parts 8600—8699)
LXXVII	Office of Management and Budget (Parts 8700—8799)
LXXX	Federal Housing Finance Agency (Parts 9000—9099)
LXXXIII	Special Inspector General for Afghanistan Reconstruction (Parts 9300—9399)
LXXXIV	Bureau of Consumer Financial Protection (Parts 9400—9499)
LXXXVI	National Credit Union Administration (Parts 9600—9699)
XCVII	Department of Homeland Security Human Resources Management System (Department of Homeland Security—Office of Personnel Management) (Parts 9700—9799)
XCVIII	Council of the Inspectors General on Integrity and Efficiency (Parts 9800—9899)
XCIX	Military Compensation and Retirement Modernization Commission (Parts 9900—9999)
C	National Council on Disability (Parts 10000—10049)
CI	National Mediation Board (Part 10101)

Title 6—Domestic Security

I	Department of Homeland Security, Office of the Secretary (Parts 1—199)
X	Privacy and Civil Liberties Oversight Board (Parts 1000—1099)

Title 7—Agriculture

	SUBTITLE A—OFFICE OF THE SECRETARY OF AGRICULTURE (PARTS 0—26)
	SUBTITLE B—REGULATIONS OF THE DEPARTMENT OF AGRICULTURE
I	Agricultural Marketing Service (Standards, Inspections, Marketing Practices), Department of Agriculture (Parts 27—209)
II	Food and Nutrition Service, Department of Agriculture (Parts 210—299)
III	Animal and Plant Health Inspection Service, Department of Agriculture (Parts 300—399)
IV	Federal Crop Insurance Corporation, Department of Agriculture (Parts 400—499)
V	Agricultural Research Service, Department of Agriculture (Parts 500—599)
VI	Natural Resources Conservation Service, Department of Agriculture (Parts 600—699)
VII	Farm Service Agency, Department of Agriculture (Parts 700—799)
VIII	Grain Inspection, Packers and Stockyards Administration (Federal Grain Inspection Service), Department of Agriculture (Parts 800—899)

Title 7—Agriculture—Continued

Chap.	
IX	Agricultural Marketing Service (Marketing Agreements and Orders; Fruits, Vegetables, Nuts), Department of Agriculture (Parts 900—999)
X	Agricultural Marketing Service (Marketing Agreements and Orders; Milk), Department of Agriculture (Parts 1000—1199)
XI	Agricultural Marketing Service (Marketing Agreements and Orders; Miscellaneous Commodities), Department of Agriculture (Parts 1200—1299)
XIV	Commodity Credit Corporation, Department of Agriculture (Parts 1400—1499)
XV	Foreign Agricultural Service, Department of Agriculture (Parts 1500—1599)
XVI	Rural Telephone Bank, Department of Agriculture (Parts 1600—1699)
XVII	Rural Utilities Service, Department of Agriculture (Parts 1700—1799)
XVIII	Rural Housing Service, Rural Business-Cooperative Service, Rural Utilities Service, and Farm Service Agency, Department of Agriculture (Parts 1800—2099)
XX	Local Television Loan Guarantee Board (Parts 2200—2299)
XXV	Office of Advocacy and Outreach, Department of Agriculture (Parts 2500—2599)
XXVI	Office of Inspector General, Department of Agriculture (Parts 2600—2699)
XXVII	Office of Information Resources Management, Department of Agriculture (Parts 2700—2799)
XXVIII	Office of Operations, Department of Agriculture (Parts 2800—2899)
XXIX	Office of Energy Policy and New Uses, Department of Agriculture (Parts 2900—2999)
XXX	Office of the Chief Financial Officer, Department of Agriculture (Parts 3000—3099)
XXXI	Office of Environmental Quality, Department of Agriculture (Parts 3100—3199)
XXXII	Office of Procurement and Property Management, Department of Agriculture (Parts 3200—3299)
XXXIII	Office of Transportation, Department of Agriculture (Parts 3300—3399)
XXXIV	National Institute of Food and Agriculture (Parts 3400—3499)
XXXV	Rural Housing Service, Department of Agriculture (Parts 3500—3599)
XXXVI	National Agricultural Statistics Service, Department of Agriculture (Parts 3600—3699)
XXXVII	Economic Research Service, Department of Agriculture (Parts 3700—3799)
XXXVIII	World Agricultural Outlook Board, Department of Agriculture (Parts 3800—3899)
XLI	[Reserved]
XLII	Rural Business-Cooperative Service and Rural Utilities Service, Department of Agriculture (Parts 4200—4299)

Title 8—Aliens and Nationality

Chap.

I Department of Homeland Security (Immigration and Naturalization) (Parts 1—499)

V Executive Office for Immigration Review, Department of Justice (Parts 1000—1399)

Title 9—Animals and Animal Products

I Animal and Plant Health Inspection Service, Department of Agriculture (Parts 1—199)

II Grain Inspection, Packers and Stockyards Administration (Packers and Stockyards Programs), Department of Agriculture (Parts 200—299)

III Food Safety and Inspection Service, Department of Agriculture (Parts 300—599)

Title 10—Energy

I Nuclear Regulatory Commission (Parts 0—199)

II Department of Energy (Parts 200—699)

III Department of Energy (Parts 700—999)

X Department of Energy (General Provisions) (Parts 1000—1099)

XIII Nuclear Waste Technical Review Board (Parts 1300—1399)

XVII Defense Nuclear Facilities Safety Board (Parts 1700—1799)

XVIII Northeast Interstate Low-Level Radioactive Waste Commission (Parts 1800—1899)

Title 11—Federal Elections

I Federal Election Commission (Parts 1—9099)

II Election Assistance Commission (Parts 9400—9499)

Title 12—Banks and Banking

I Comptroller of the Currency, Department of the Treasury (Parts 1—199)

II Federal Reserve System (Parts 200—299)

III Federal Deposit Insurance Corporation (Parts 300—399)

IV Export-Import Bank of the United States (Parts 400—499)

V (Parts 500—599) [Reserved]

VI Farm Credit Administration (Parts 600—699)

VII National Credit Union Administration (Parts 700—799)

VIII Federal Financing Bank (Parts 800—899)

IX Federal Housing Finance Board (Parts 900—999)

X Bureau of Consumer Financial Protection (Parts 1000—1099)

XI Federal Financial Institutions Examination Council (Parts 1100—1199)

XII Federal Housing Finance Agency (Parts 1200—1299)

XIII Financial Stability Oversight Council (Parts 1300—1399)

Title 12—Banks and Banking—Continued

Chap.

XIV Farm Credit System Insurance Corporation (Parts 1400—1499)

XV Department of the Treasury (Parts 1500—1599)

XVI Office of Financial Research (Parts 1600—1699)

XVII Office of Federal Housing Enterprise Oversight, Department of Housing and Urban Development (Parts 1700—1799)

XVIII Community Development Financial Institutions Fund, Department of the Treasury (Parts 1800—1899)

Title 13—Business Credit and Assistance

I Small Business Administration (Parts 1—199)

III Economic Development Administration, Department of Commerce (Parts 300—399)

IV Emergency Steel Guarantee Loan Board (Parts 400—499)

V Emergency Oil and Gas Guaranteed Loan Board (Parts 500—599)

Title 14—Aeronautics and Space

I Federal Aviation Administration, Department of Transportation (Parts 1—199)

II Office of the Secretary, Department of Transportation (Aviation Proceedings) (Parts 200—399)

III Commercial Space Transportation, Federal Aviation Administration, Department of Transportation (Parts 400—1199)

V National Aeronautics and Space Administration (Parts 1200—1299)

VI Air Transportation System Stabilization (Parts 1300—1399)

Title 15—Commerce and Foreign Trade

SUBTITLE A—OFFICE OF THE SECRETARY OF COMMERCE (PARTS 0—29)

SUBTITLE B—REGULATIONS RELATING TO COMMERCE AND FOREIGN TRADE

I Bureau of the Census, Department of Commerce (Parts 30—199)

II National Institute of Standards and Technology, Department of Commerce (Parts 200—299)

III International Trade Administration, Department of Commerce (Parts 300—399)

IV Foreign-Trade Zones Board, Department of Commerce (Parts 400—499)

VII Bureau of Industry and Security, Department of Commerce (Parts 700—799)

VIII Bureau of Economic Analysis, Department of Commerce (Parts 800—899)

IX National Oceanic and Atmospheric Administration, Department of Commerce (Parts 900—999)

XI National Technical Information Service, Department of Commerce (Parts 1100—1199)

Title 15—Commerce and Foreign Trade—Continued

Chap.

XIII East-West Foreign Trade Board (Parts 1300—1399)

XIV Minority Business Development Agency (Parts 1400—1499)

SUBTITLE C—REGULATIONS RELATING TO FOREIGN TRADE AGREEMENTS

XX Office of the United States Trade Representative (Parts 2000—2099)

SUBTITLE D—REGULATIONS RELATING TO TELECOMMUNICATIONS AND INFORMATION

XXIII National Telecommunications and Information Administration, Department of Commerce (Parts 2300—2399) [Reserved]

Title 16—Commercial Practices

I Federal Trade Commission (Parts 0—999)

II Consumer Product Safety Commission (Parts 1000—1799)

Title 17—Commodity and Securities Exchanges

I Commodity Futures Trading Commission (Parts 1—199)

II Securities and Exchange Commission (Parts 200—399)

IV Department of the Treasury (Parts 400—499)

Title 18—Conservation of Power and Water Resources

I Federal Energy Regulatory Commission, Department of Energy (Parts 1—399)

III Delaware River Basin Commission (Parts 400—499)

VI Water Resources Council (Parts 700—799)

VIII Susquehanna River Basin Commission (Parts 800—899)

XIII Tennessee Valley Authority (Parts 1300—1399)

Title 19—Customs Duties

I U.S. Customs and Border Protection, Department of Homeland Security; Department of the Treasury (Parts 0—199)

II United States International Trade Commission (Parts 200—299)

III International Trade Administration, Department of Commerce (Parts 300—399)

IV U.S. Immigration and Customs Enforcement, Department of Homeland Security (Parts 400—599) [Reserved]

Title 20—Employees' Benefits

I Office of Workers' Compensation Programs, Department of Labor (Parts 1—199)

II Railroad Retirement Board (Parts 200—399)

III Social Security Administration (Parts 400—499)

Title 20—Employees' Benefits—Continued

Chap.

IV Employees' Compensation Appeals Board, Department of Labor (Parts 500—599)

V Employment and Training Administration, Department of Labor (Parts 600—699)

VI Office of Workers' Compensation Programs, Department of Labor (Parts 700—799)

VII Benefits Review Board, Department of Labor (Parts 800—899)

VIII Joint Board for the Enrollment of Actuaries (Parts 900—999)

IX Office of the Assistant Secretary for Veterans' Employment and Training Service, Department of Labor (Parts 1000—1099)

Title 21—Food and Drugs

I Food and Drug Administration, Department of Health and Human Services (Parts 1—1299)

II Drug Enforcement Administration, Department of Justice (Parts 1300—1399)

III Office of National Drug Control Policy (Parts 1400—1499)

Title 22—Foreign Relations

I Department of State (Parts 1—199)

II Agency for International Development (Parts 200—299)

III Peace Corps (Parts 300—399)

IV International Joint Commission, United States and Canada (Parts 400—499)

V Broadcasting Board of Governors (Parts 500—599)

VII Overseas Private Investment Corporation (Parts 700—799)

IX Foreign Service Grievance Board (Parts 900—999)

X Inter-American Foundation (Parts 1000—1099)

XI International Boundary and Water Commission, United States and Mexico, United States Section (Parts 1100—1199)

XII United States International Development Cooperation Agency (Parts 1200—1299)

XIII Millennium Challenge Corporation (Parts 1300—1399)

XIV Foreign Service Labor Relations Board; Federal Labor Relations Authority; General Counsel of the Federal Labor Relations Authority; and the Foreign Service Impasse Disputes Panel (Parts 1400—1499)

XV African Development Foundation (Parts 1500—1599)

XVI Japan-United States Friendship Commission (Parts 1600—1699)

XVII United States Institute of Peace (Parts 1700—1799)

Title 23—Highways

I Federal Highway Administration, Department of Transportation (Parts 1—999)

Title 23—Highways—Continued

Chap.

II National Highway Traffic Safety Administration and Federal Highway Administration, Department of Transportation (Parts 1200—1299)

III National Highway Traffic Safety Administration, Department of Transportation (Parts 1300—1399)

Title 24—Housing and Urban Development

SUBTITLE A—OFFICE OF THE SECRETARY, DEPARTMENT OF HOUSING AND URBAN DEVELOPMENT (PARTS 0—99)

SUBTITLE B—REGULATIONS RELATING TO HOUSING AND URBAN DEVELOPMENT

I Office of Assistant Secretary for Equal Opportunity, Department of Housing and Urban Development (Parts 100—199)

II Office of Assistant Secretary for Housing-Federal Housing Commissioner, Department of Housing and Urban Development (Parts 200—299)

III Government National Mortgage Association, Department of Housing and Urban Development (Parts 300—399)

IV Office of Housing and Office of Multifamily Housing Assistance Restructuring, Department of Housing and Urban Development (Parts 400—499)

V Office of Assistant Secretary for Community Planning and Development, Department of Housing and Urban Development (Parts 500—599)

VI Office of Assistant Secretary for Community Planning and Development, Department of Housing and Urban Development (Parts 600—699) [Reserved]

VII Office of the Secretary, Department of Housing and Urban Development (Housing Assistance Programs and Public and Indian Housing Programs) (Parts 700—799)

VIII Office of the Assistant Secretary for Housing—Federal Housing Commissioner, Department of Housing and Urban Development (Section 8 Housing Assistance Programs, Section 202 Direct Loan Program, Section 202 Supportive Housing for the Elderly Program and Section 811 Supportive Housing for Persons With Disabilities Program) (Parts 800—899)

IX Office of Assistant Secretary for Public and Indian Housing, Department of Housing and Urban Development (Parts 900—1699)

XII Office of Inspector General, Department of Housing and Urban Development (Parts 2000—2099)

XV Emergency Mortgage Insurance and Loan Programs, Department of Housing and Urban Development (Parts 2700—2799) [Reserved]

XX Office of Assistant Secretary for Housing—Federal Housing Commissioner, Department of Housing and Urban Development (Parts 3200—3899)

XXIV Board of Directors of the HOPE for Homeowners Program (Parts 4000—4099) [Reserved]

XXV Neighborhood Reinvestment Corporation (Parts 4100—4199)

Title 25—Indians

Chap.

I Bureau of Indian Affairs, Department of the Interior (Parts 1—299)

II Indian Arts and Crafts Board, Department of the Interior (Parts 300—399)

III National Indian Gaming Commission, Department of the Interior (Parts 500—599)

IV Office of Navajo and Hopi Indian Relocation (Parts 700—899)

V Bureau of Indian Affairs, Department of the Interior, and Indian Health Service, Department of Health and Human Services (Part 900—999)

VI Office of the Assistant Secretary, Indian Affairs, Department of the Interior (Parts 1000—1199)

VII Office of the Special Trustee for American Indians, Department of the Interior (Parts 1200—1299)

Title 26—Internal Revenue

I Internal Revenue Service, Department of the Treasury (Parts 1—End)

Title 27—Alcohol, Tobacco Products and Firearms

I Alcohol and Tobacco Tax and Trade Bureau, Department of the Treasury (Parts 1—399)

II Bureau of Alcohol, Tobacco, Firearms, and Explosives, Department of Justice (Parts 400—699)

Title 28—Judicial Administration

I Department of Justice (Parts 0—299)

III Federal Prison Industries, Inc., Department of Justice (Parts 300—399)

V Bureau of Prisons, Department of Justice (Parts 500—599)

VI Offices of Independent Counsel, Department of Justice (Parts 600—699)

VII Office of Independent Counsel (Parts 700—799)

VIII Court Services and Offender Supervision Agency for the District of Columbia (Parts 800—899)

IX National Crime Prevention and Privacy Compact Council (Parts 900—999)

XI Department of Justice and Department of State (Parts 1100—1199)

Title 29—Labor

SUBTITLE A—OFFICE OF THE SECRETARY OF LABOR (PARTS 0—99)

SUBTITLE B—REGULATIONS RELATING TO LABOR

I National Labor Relations Board (Parts 100—199)

Title 29—Labor—Continued

Title 30—Mineral Resources

Title 31—Money and Finance: Treasury

Title 31—Money and Finance: Treasury—Continued

Chap.

VIII Office of Investment Security, Department of the Treasury (Parts 800—899)

IX Federal Claims Collection Standards (Department of the Treasury—Department of Justice) (Parts 900—999)

X Financial Crimes Enforcement Network, Department of the Treasury (Parts 1000—1099)

Title 32—National Defense

SUBTITLE A—DEPARTMENT OF DEFENSE

I Office of the Secretary of Defense (Parts 1—399)

V Department of the Army (Parts 400—699)

VI Department of the Navy (Parts 700—799)

VII Department of the Air Force (Parts 800—1099)

SUBTITLE B—OTHER REGULATIONS RELATING TO NATIONAL DEFENSE

XII Defense Logistics Agency (Parts 1200—1299)

XVI Selective Service System (Parts 1600—1699)

XVII Office of the Director of National Intelligence (Parts 1700—1799)

XVIII National Counterintelligence Center (Parts 1800—1899)

XIX Central Intelligence Agency (Parts 1900—1999)

XX Information Security Oversight Office, National Archives and Records Administration (Parts 2000—2099)

XXI National Security Council (Parts 2100—2199)

XXIV Office of Science and Technology Policy (Parts 2400—2499)

XXVII Office for Micronesian Status Negotiations (Parts 2700—2799)

XXVIII Office of the Vice President of the United States (Parts 2800—2899)

Title 33—Navigation and Navigable Waters

I Coast Guard, Department of Homeland Security (Parts 1—199)

II Corps of Engineers, Department of the Army, Department of Defense (Parts 200—399)

IV Saint Lawrence Seaway Development Corporation, Department of Transportation (Parts 400—499)

Title 34—Education

SUBTITLE A—OFFICE OF THE SECRETARY, DEPARTMENT OF EDUCATION (PARTS 1—99)

SUBTITLE B—REGULATIONS OF THE OFFICES OF THE DEPARTMENT OF EDUCATION

I Office for Civil Rights, Department of Education (Parts 100—199)

II Office of Elementary and Secondary Education, Department of Education (Parts 200—299)

III Office of Special Education and Rehabilitative Services, Department of Education (Parts 300—399)

Title 34—Education—Continued

Chap.	
IV	Office of Career, Technical and Adult Education, Department of Education (Parts 400—499)
V	Office of Bilingual Education and Minority Languages Affairs, Department of Education (Parts 500—599) [Reserved]
VI	Office of Postsecondary Education, Department of Education (Parts 600—699)
VII	Office of Educational Research and Improvement, Department of Education (Parts 700—799) [Reserved]
	SUBTITLE C—REGULATIONS RELATING TO EDUCATION
XI	(Parts 1100—1199) [Reserved]
XII	National Council on Disability (Parts 1200—1299)

Title 35 [Reserved]

Title 36—Parks, Forests, and Public Property

I	National Park Service, Department of the Interior (Parts 1—199)
II	Forest Service, Department of Agriculture (Parts 200—299)
III	Corps of Engineers, Department of the Army (Parts 300—399)
IV	American Battle Monuments Commission (Parts 400—499)
V	Smithsonian Institution (Parts 500—599)
VI	[Reserved]
VII	Library of Congress (Parts 700—799)
VIII	Advisory Council on Historic Preservation (Parts 800—899)
IX	Pennsylvania Avenue Development Corporation (Parts 900—999)
X	Presidio Trust (Parts 1000—1099)
XI	Architectural and Transportation Barriers Compliance Board (Parts 1100—1199)
XII	National Archives and Records Administration (Parts 1200—1299)
XV	Oklahoma City National Memorial Trust (Parts 1500—1599)
XVI	Morris K. Udall Scholarship and Excellence in National Environmental Policy Foundation (Parts 1600—1699)

Title 37—Patents, Trademarks, and Copyrights

I	United States Patent and Trademark Office, Department of Commerce (Parts 1—199)
II	U.S. Copyright Office, Library of Congress (Parts 200—299)
III	Copyright Royalty Board, Library of Congress (Parts 300—399)
IV	National Institute of Standards and Technology, Department of Commerce (Parts 400—599)

Title 38—Pensions, Bonuses, and Veterans' Relief

I	Department of Veterans Affairs (Parts 0—199)
II	Armed Forces Retirement Home (Parts 200—299)

Title 39—Postal Service

Title 40—Protection of Environment

Title 41—Public Contracts and Property Management

Title 42—Public Health

Title 43—Public Lands: Interior

Title 44—Emergency Management and Assistance

Title 45—Public Welfare

Title 45—Public Welfare—Continued

Chap.	
V	Foreign Claims Settlement Commission of the United States, Department of Justice (Parts 500—599)
VI	National Science Foundation (Parts 600—699)
VII	Commission on Civil Rights (Parts 700—799)
VIII	Office of Personnel Management (Parts 800—899)
IX	Denali Commission (Parts 900—999)
X	Office of Community Services, Administration for Children and Families, Department of Health and Human Services (Parts 1000—1099)
XI	National Foundation on the Arts and the Humanities (Parts 1100—1199)
XII	Corporation for National and Community Service (Parts 1200—1299)
XIII	Administration for Children and Families, Department of Health and Human Services (Parts 1300—1399)
XVI	Legal Services Corporation (Parts 1600—1699)
XVII	National Commission on Libraries and Information Science (Parts 1700—1799)
XVIII	Harry S. Truman Scholarship Foundation (Parts 1800—1899)
XXI	Commission of Fine Arts (Parts 2100—2199)
XXIII	Arctic Research Commission (Parts 2300—2399)
XXIV	James Madison Memorial Fellowship Foundation (Parts 2400—2499)
XXV	Corporation for National and Community Service (Parts 2500—2599)

Title 46—Shipping

I	Coast Guard, Department of Homeland Security (Parts 1—199)
II	Maritime Administration, Department of Transportation (Parts 200—399)
III	Coast Guard (Great Lakes Pilotage), Department of Homeland Security (Parts 400—499)
IV	Federal Maritime Commission (Parts 500—599)

Title 47—Telecommunication

I	Federal Communications Commission (Parts 0—199)
II	Office of Science and Technology Policy and National Security Council (Parts 200—299)
III	National Telecommunications and Information Administration, Department of Commerce (Parts 300—399)
IV	National Telecommunications and Information Administration, Department of Commerce, and National Highway Traffic Safety Administration, Department of Transportation (Parts 400—499)
V	The First Responder Network Authority (Parts 500—599)

Title 48—Federal Acquisition Regulations System

Chap.	
1	Federal Acquisition Regulation (Parts 1—99)
2	Defense Acquisition Regulations System, Department of Defense (Parts 200—299)
3	Department of Health and Human Services (Parts 300—399)
4	Department of Agriculture (Parts 400—499)
5	General Services Administration (Parts 500—599)
6	Department of State (Parts 600—699)
7	Agency for International Development (Parts 700—799)
8	Department of Veterans Affairs (Parts 800—899)
9	Department of Energy (Parts 900—999)
10	Department of the Treasury (Parts 1000—1099)
12	Department of Transportation (Parts 1200—1299)
13	Department of Commerce (Parts 1300—1399)
14	Department of the Interior (Parts 1400—1499)
15	Environmental Protection Agency (Parts 1500—1599)
16	Office of Personnel Management, Federal Employees Health Benefits Acquisition Regulation (Parts 1600—1699)
17	Office of Personnel Management (Parts 1700—1799)
18	National Aeronautics and Space Administration (Parts 1800—1899)
19	Broadcasting Board of Governors (Parts 1900—1999)
20	Nuclear Regulatory Commission (Parts 2000—2099)
21	Office of Personnel Management, Federal Employees Group Life Insurance Federal Acquisition Regulation (Parts 2100—2199)
23	Social Security Administration (Parts 2300—2399)
24	Department of Housing and Urban Development (Parts 2400—2499)
25	National Science Foundation (Parts 2500—2599)
28	Department of Justice (Parts 2800—2899)
29	Department of Labor (Parts 2900—2999)
30	Department of Homeland Security, Homeland Security Acquisition Regulation (HSAR) (Parts 3000—3099)
34	Department of Education Acquisition Regulation (Parts 3400—3499)
51	Department of the Army Acquisition Regulations (Parts 5100—5199)
52	Department of the Navy Acquisition Regulations (Parts 5200—5299)
53	Department of the Air Force Federal Acquisition Regulation Supplement (Parts 5300—5399) [Reserved]
54	Defense Logistics Agency, Department of Defense (Parts 5400—5499)
57	African Development Foundation (Parts 5700—5799)
61	Civilian Board of Contract Appeals, General Services Administration (Parts 6100—6199)
99	Cost Accounting Standards Board, Office of Federal Procurement Policy, Office of Management and Budget (Parts 9900—9999)

Title 49—Transportation

Chap.

SUBTITLE A—OFFICE OF THE SECRETARY OF TRANSPORTATION (PARTS 1—99)

SUBTITLE B—OTHER REGULATIONS RELATING TO TRANSPORTATION

I Pipeline and Hazardous Materials Safety Administration, Department of Transportation (Parts 100—199)

II Federal Railroad Administration, Department of Transportation (Parts 200—299)

III Federal Motor Carrier Safety Administration, Department of Transportation (Parts 300—399)

IV Coast Guard, Department of Homeland Security (Parts 400—499)

V National Highway Traffic Safety Administration, Department of Transportation (Parts 500—599)

VI Federal Transit Administration, Department of Transportation (Parts 600—699)

VII National Railroad Passenger Corporation (AMTRAK) (Parts 700—799)

VIII National Transportation Safety Board (Parts 800—999)

X Surface Transportation Board (Parts 1000—1399)

XI Research and Innovative Technology Administration, Department of Transportation (Parts 1400—1499) [Reserved]

XII Transportation Security Administration, Department of Homeland Security (Parts 1500—1699)

Title 50—Wildlife and Fisheries

I United States Fish and Wildlife Service, Department of the Interior (Parts 1—199)

II National Marine Fisheries Service, National Oceanic and Atmospheric Administration, Department of Commerce (Parts 200—299)

III International Fishing and Related Activities (Parts 300—399)

IV Joint Regulations (United States Fish and Wildlife Service, Department of the Interior and National Marine Fisheries Service, National Oceanic and Atmospheric Administration, Department of Commerce); Endangered Species Committee Regulations (Parts 400—499)

V Marine Mammal Commission (Parts 500—599)

VI Fishery Conservation and Management, National Oceanic and Atmospheric Administration, Department of Commerce (Parts 600—699)

Alphabetical List of Agencies Appearing in the CFR

(Revised as of January 1, 2019)

Agency	CFR Title, Subtitle or Chapter
Administrative Conference of the United States	1, III
Advisory Council on Historic Preservation	36, VIII
Advocacy and Outreach, Office of	7, XXV
Afghanistan Reconstruction, Special Inspector General for	5, LXXXIII
African Development Foundation	22, XV
Federal Acquisition Regulation	48, 57
Agency for International Development	2, VII; 22, II
Federal Acquisition Regulation	48, 7
Agricultural Marketing Service	7, I, IX, X, XI
Agricultural Research Service	7, V
Agriculture, Department of	2, IV; 5, LXXIII
Advocacy and Outreach, Office of	7, XXV
Agricultural Marketing Service	7, I, IX, X, XI
Agricultural Research Service	7, V
Animal and Plant Health Inspection Service	7, III; 9, I
Chief Financial Officer, Office of	7, XXX
Commodity Credit Corporation	7, XIV
Economic Research Service	7, XXXVII
Energy Policy and New Uses, Office of	2, IX; 7, XXIX
Environmental Quality, Office of	7, XXXI
Farm Service Agency	7, VII, XVIII
Federal Acquisition Regulation	48, 4
Federal Crop Insurance Corporation	7, IV
Food and Nutrition Service	7, II
Food Safety and Inspection Service	9, III
Foreign Agricultural Service	7, XV
Forest Service	36, II
Grain Inspection, Packers and Stockyards Administration	7, VIII; 9, II
Information Resources Management, Office of	7, XXVII
Inspector General, Office of	7, XXVI
National Agricultural Library	7, XLI
National Agricultural Statistics Service	7, XXXVI
National Institute of Food and Agriculture	7, XXXIV
Natural Resources Conservation Service	7, VI
Operations, Office of	7, XXVIII
Procurement and Property Management, Office of	7, XXXII
Rural Business-Cooperative Service	7, XVIII, XLII
Rural Development Administration	7, XLII
Rural Housing Service	7, XVIII, XXXV
Rural Telephone Bank	7, XVI
Rural Utilities Service	7, XVII, XVIII, XLII
Secretary of Agriculture, Office of	7, Subtitle A
Transportation, Office of	7, XXXIII
World Agricultural Outlook Board	7, XXXVIII
Air Force, Department of	32, VII
Federal Acquisition Regulation Supplement	48, 53
Air Transportation Stabilization Board	14, VI
Alcohol and Tobacco Tax and Trade Bureau	27, I
Alcohol, Tobacco, Firearms, and Explosives, Bureau of	27, II
AMTRAK	49, VII
American Battle Monuments Commission	36, IV
American Indians, Office of the Special Trustee	25, VII
Animal and Plant Health Inspection Service	7, III; 9, I

Agency	CFR Title, Subtitle or Chapter
Appalachian Regional Commission	5, IX
Architectural and Transportation Barriers Compliance Board	36, XI
Arctic Research Commission	45, XXIII
Armed Forces Retirement Home	5, XI
Army, Department of	32, V
Engineers, Corps of	33, II; 36, III
Federal Acquisition Regulation	48, 51
Bilingual Education and Minority Languages Affairs, Office of	34, V
Blind or Severely Disabled, Committee for Purchase from People Who Are	41, 51
Broadcasting Board of Governors	22, V
Federal Acquisition Regulation	48, 19
Career, Technical, and Adult Education, Office of	34, IV
Census Bureau	15, I
Centers for Medicare & Medicaid Services	42, IV
Central Intelligence Agency	32, XIX
Chemical Safety and Hazardous Investigation Board	40, VI
Chief Financial Officer, Office of	7, XXX
Child Support Enforcement, Office of	45, III
Children and Families, Administration for	45, II, III, IV, X, XIII
Civil Rights, Commission on	5, LXVIII; 45, VII
Civil Rights, Office for	34, I
Council of the Inspectors General on Integrity and Efficiency	5, XCVIII
Court Services and Offender Supervision Agency for the District of Columbia	5, LXX
Coast Guard	33, I; 46, I; 49, IV
Coast Guard (Great Lakes Pilotage)	46, III
Commerce, Department of	2, XIII; 44, IV; 50, VI
Census Bureau	15, I
Economic Analysis, Bureau of	15, VIII
Economic Development Administration	13, III
Emergency Management and Assistance	44, IV
Federal Acquisition Regulation	48, 13
Foreign-Trade Zones Board	15, IV
Industry and Security, Bureau of	15, VII
International Trade Administration	15, III; 19, III
National Institute of Standards and Technology	15, II; 37, IV
National Marine Fisheries Service	50, II, IV
National Oceanic and Atmospheric Administration	15, IX; 50, II, III, IV, VI
National Technical Information Service	15, XI
National Telecommunications and Information Administration	15, XXIII; 47, III, IV
National Weather Service	15, IX
Patent and Trademark Office, United States	37, I
Secretary of Commerce, Office of	15, Subtitle A
Commercial Space Transportation	14, III
Commodity Credit Corporation	7, XIV
Commodity Futures Trading Commission	5, XLI; 17, I
Community Planning and Development, Office of Assistant Secretary for	24, V, VI
Community Services, Office of	45, X
Comptroller of the Currency	12, I
Construction Industry Collective Bargaining Commission	29, IX
Consumer Financial Protection Bureau	5, LXXXIV; 12, X
Consumer Product Safety Commission	5, LXXI; 16, II
Copyright Royalty Board	37, III
Corporation for National and Community Service	2, XXII; 45, XII, XXV
Cost Accounting Standards Board	48, 99
Council on Environmental Quality	40, V
Court Services and Offender Supervision Agency for the District of Columbia	5, LXX; 28, VIII
Customs and Border Protection	19, I
Defense Contract Audit Agency	32, I
Defense, Department of	2, XI; 5, XXVI; 32, Subtitle A; 40, VII
Advanced Research Projects Agency	32, I
Air Force Department	32, VII

Agency	CFR Title, Subtitle or Chapter
Army Department	32, V; 33, II; 36, III; 48, 51
Defense Acquisition Regulations System	48, 2
Defense Intelligence Agency	32, I
Defense Logistics Agency	32, I, XII; 48, 54
Engineers, Corps of	33, II; 36, III
National Imagery and Mapping Agency	32, I
Navy Department	32, VI; 48, 52
Secretary of Defense, Office of	2, XI; 32, I
Defense Contract Audit Agency	32, I
Defense Intelligence Agency	32, I
Defense Logistics Agency	32, XII; 48, 54
Defense Nuclear Facilities Safety Board	10, XVII
Delaware River Basin Commission	18, III
Denali Commission	45, IX
Disability, National Council on	5, C; 34, XII
District of Columbia, Court Services and Offender Supervision Agency for the	5, LXX; 28, VIII
Drug Enforcement Administration	21, II
East-West Foreign Trade Board	15, XIII
Economic Analysis, Bureau of	15, VIII
Economic Development Administration	13, III
Economic Research Service	7, XXXVII
Education, Department of	2, XXXIV; 5, LIII
Bilingual Education and Minority Languages Affairs, Office of	34, V
Career, Technical, and Adult Education, Office of	34, IV
Civil Rights, Office for	34, I
Educational Research and Improvement, Office of	34, VII
Elementary and Secondary Education, Office of	34, II
Federal Acquisition Regulation	48, 34
Postsecondary Education, Office of	34, VI
Secretary of Education, Office of	34, Subtitle A
Special Education and Rehabilitative Services, Office of	34, III
Educational Research and Improvement, Office of	34, VII
Election Assistance Commission	2, LVIII; 11, II
Elementary and Secondary Education, Office of	34, II
Emergency Oil and Gas Guaranteed Loan Board	13, V
Emergency Steel Guarantee Loan Board	13, IV
Employee Benefits Security Administration	29, XXV
Employees' Compensation Appeals Board	20, IV
Employees Loyalty Board	5, V
Employment and Training Administration	20, V
Employment Policy, National Commission for	1, IV
Employment Standards Administration	20, VI
Endangered Species Committee	50, IV
Energy, Department of	2, IX; 5, XXIII; 10, II, III, X
Federal Acquisition Regulation	48, 9
Federal Energy Regulatory Commission	5, XXIV; 18, I
Property Management Regulations	41, 109
Energy, Office of	7, XXIX
Engineers, Corps of	33, II; 36, III
Engraving and Printing, Bureau of	31, VI
Environmental Protection Agency	2, XV; 5, LIV; 40, I, IV, VII
Federal Acquisition Regulation	48, 15
Property Management Regulations	41, 115
Environmental Quality, Office of	7, XXXI
Equal Employment Opportunity Commission	5, LXII; 29, XIV
Equal Opportunity, Office of Assistant Secretary for	24, I
Executive Office of the President	3, I
Environmental Quality, Council on	40, V
Management and Budget, Office of	2, Subtitle A; 5, III, LXXVII; 14, VI; 48, 99
National Drug Control Policy, Office of	2, XXXVI; 21, III
National Security Council	32, XXI; 47, 2

Agency	CFR Title, Subtitle or Chapter
Presidential Documents	3
Science and Technology Policy, Office of	32, XXIV; 47, II
Trade Representative, Office of the United States	15, XX
Export-Import Bank of the United States	2, XXXV; 5, LII; 12, IV
Family Assistance, Office of	45, II
Farm Credit Administration	5, XXXI; 12, VI
Farm Credit System Insurance Corporation	5, XXX; 12, XIV
Farm Service Agency	7, VII, XVIII
Federal Acquisition Regulation	48, 1
Federal Aviation Administration	14, I
Commercial Space Transportation	14, III
Federal Claims Collection Standards	31, IX
Federal Communications Commission	5, XXIX; 47, I
Federal Contract Compliance Programs, Office of	41, 60
Federal Crop Insurance Corporation	7, IV
Federal Deposit Insurance Corporation	5, XXII; 12, III
Federal Election Commission	5, XXXVII; 11, I
Federal Emergency Management Agency	44, I
Federal Employees Group Life Insurance Federal Acquisition Regulation	48, 21
Federal Employees Health Benefits Acquisition Regulation	48, 16
Federal Energy Regulatory Commission	5, XXIV; 18, I
Federal Financial Institutions Examination Council	12, XI
Federal Financing Bank	12, VIII
Federal Highway Administration	23, I, II
Federal Home Loan Mortgage Corporation	1, IV
Federal Housing Enterprise Oversight Office	12, XVII
Federal Housing Finance Agency	5, LXXX; 12, XII
Federal Housing Finance Board	12, IX
Federal Labor Relations Authority	5, XIV, XLIX; 22, XIV
Federal Law Enforcement Training Center	31, VII
Federal Management Regulation	41, 102
Federal Maritime Commission	46, IV
Federal Mediation and Conciliation Service	29, XII
Federal Mine Safety and Health Review Commission	5, LXXIV; 29, XXVII
Federal Motor Carrier Safety Administration	49, III
Federal Prison Industries, Inc.	28, III
Federal Procurement Policy Office	48, 99
Federal Property Management Regulations	41, 101
Federal Railroad Administration	49, II
Federal Register, Administrative Committee of	1, I
Federal Register, Office of	1, II
Federal Reserve System	12, II
Board of Governors	5, LVIII
Federal Retirement Thrift Investment Board	5, VI, LXXVI
Federal Service Impasses Panel	5, XIV
Federal Trade Commission	5, XLVII; 16, I
Federal Transit Administration	49, VI
Federal Travel Regulation System	41, Subtitle F
Financial Crimes Enforcement Network	31, X
Financial Research Office	12, XVI
Financial Stability Oversight Council	12, XIII
Fine Arts, Commission of	45, XXI
Fiscal Service	31, II
Fish and Wildlife Service, United States	50, I, IV
Food and Drug Administration	21, I
Food and Nutrition Service	7, II
Food Safety and Inspection Service	9, III
Foreign Agricultural Service	7, XV
Foreign Assets Control, Office of	31, V
Foreign Claims Settlement Commission of the United States	45, V
Foreign Service Grievance Board	22, IX
Foreign Service Impasse Disputes Panel	22, XIV
Foreign Service Labor Relations Board	22, XIV
Foreign-Trade Zones Board	15, IV
Forest Service	36, II
General Services Administration	5, LVII; 41, 105

Agency	CFR Title, Subtitle or Chapter
Contract Appeals, Board of	48, 61
Federal Acquisition Regulation	48, 5
Federal Management Regulation	41, 102
Federal Property Management Regulations	41, 101
Federal Travel Regulation System	41, Subtitle F
General	41, 300
Payment From a Non-Federal Source for Travel Expenses	41, 304
Payment of Expenses Connected With the Death of Certain Employees	41, 303
Relocation Allowances	41, 302
Temporary Duty (TDY) Travel Allowances	41, 301
Geological Survey	30, IV
Government Accountability Office	4, I
Government Ethics, Office of	5, XVI
Government National Mortgage Association	24, III
Grain Inspection, Packers and Stockyards Administration	7, VIII; 9, II
Gulf Coast Ecosystem Restoration Council	2, LIX; 40, VIII
Harry S. Truman Scholarship Foundation	45, XVIII
Health and Human Services, Department of	2, III; 5, XLV; 45, Subtitle A
Centers for Medicare & Medicaid Services	42, IV
Child Support Enforcement, Office of	45, III
Children and Families, Administration for	45, II, III, IV, X, XIII
Community Services, Office of	45, X
Family Assistance, Office of	45, II
Federal Acquisition Regulation	48, 3
Food and Drug Administration	21, I
Indian Health Service	25, V
Inspector General (Health Care), Office of	42, V
Public Health Service	42, I
Refugee Resettlement, Office of	45, IV
Homeland Security, Department of	2, XXX; 5, XXXVI; 6, I; 8, I
Coast Guard	33, I; 46, I; 49, IV
Coast Guard (Great Lakes Pilotage)	46, III
Customs and Border Protection	19, I
Federal Emergency Management Agency	44, I
Human Resources Management and Labor Relations Systems	5, XCVII
Immigration and Customs Enforcement Bureau	19, IV
Transportation Security Administration	49, XII
HOPE for Homeowners Program, Board of Directors of	24, XXIV
Housing and Urban Development, Department of	2, XXIV; 5, LXV; 24, Subtitle B
Community Planning and Development, Office of Assistant Secretary for	24, V, VI
Equal Opportunity, Office of Assistant Secretary for	24, I
Federal Acquisition Regulation	48, 24
Federal Housing Enterprise Oversight, Office of	12, XVII
Government National Mortgage Association	24, III
Housing—Federal Housing Commissioner, Office of Assistant Secretary for	24, II, VIII, X, XX
Housing, Office of, and Multifamily Housing Assistance Restructuring, Office of	24, IV
Inspector General, Office of	24, XII
Public and Indian Housing, Office of Assistant Secretary for	24, IX
Secretary, Office of	24, Subtitle A, VII
Housing—Federal Housing Commissioner, Office of Assistant Secretary for	24, II, VIII, X, XX
Housing, Office of, and Multifamily Housing Assistance Restructuring, Office of	24, IV
Immigration and Customs Enforcement Bureau	19, IV
Immigration Review, Executive Office for	8, V
Independent Counsel, Office of	28, VII
Independent Counsel, Offices of	28, VI
Indian Affairs, Bureau of	25, I, V
Indian Affairs, Office of the Assistant Secretary	25, VI

Agency	CFR Title, Subtitle or Chapter
Indian Arts and Crafts Board	25, II
Indian Health Service	25, V
Industry and Security, Bureau of	15, VII
Information Resources Management, Office of	7, XXVII
Information Security Oversight Office, National Archives and Records Administration	32, XX
Inspector General	
Agriculture Department	7, XXVI
Health and Human Services Department	42, V
Housing and Urban Development Department	24, XII, XV
Institute of Peace, United States	22, XVII
Inter-American Foundation	5, LXIII; 22, X
Interior, Department of	2, XIV
American Indians, Office of the Special Trustee	25, VII
Endangered Species Committee	50, IV
Federal Acquisition Regulation	48, 14
Federal Property Management Regulations System	41, 114
Fish and Wildlife Service, United States	50, I, IV
Geological Survey	30, IV
Indian Affairs, Bureau of	25, I, V
Indian Affairs, Office of the Assistant Secretary	25, VI
Indian Arts and Crafts Board	25, II
Land Management, Bureau of	43, II
National Indian Gaming Commission	25, III
National Park Service	36, I
Natural Resource Revenue, Office of	30, XII
Ocean Energy Management, Bureau of	30, V
Reclamation, Bureau of	43, I
Safety and Enforcement Bureau, Bureau of	30, II
Secretary of the Interior, Office of	2, XIV; 43, Subtitle A
Surface Mining Reclamation and Enforcement, Office of	30, VII
Internal Revenue Service	26, I
International Boundary and Water Commission, United States and Mexico, United States Section	22, XI
International Development, United States Agency for	22, II
Federal Acquisition Regulation	48, 7
International Development Cooperation Agency, United States	22, XII
International Joint Commission, United States and Canada	22, IV
International Organizations Employees Loyalty Board	5, V
International Trade Administration	15, III; 19, III
International Trade Commission, United States	19, II
Interstate Commerce Commission	5, XL
Investment Security, Office of	31, VIII
James Madison Memorial Fellowship Foundation	45, XXIV
Japan–United States Friendship Commission	22, XVI
Joint Board for the Enrollment of Actuaries	20, VIII
Justice, Department of	2, XXVIII; 5, XXVIII; 28, I, XI; 40, IV
Alcohol, Tobacco, Firearms, and Explosives, Bureau of	27, II
Drug Enforcement Administration	21, II
Federal Acquisition Regulation	48, 28
Federal Claims Collection Standards	31, IX
Federal Prison Industries, Inc.	28, III
Foreign Claims Settlement Commission of the United States	45, V
Immigration Review, Executive Office for	8, V
Independent Counsel, Offices of	28, VI
Prisons, Bureau of	28, V
Property Management Regulations	41, 128
Labor, Department of	2, XXIX; 5, XLII
Employee Benefits Security Administration	29, XXV
Employees' Compensation Appeals Board	20, IV
Employment and Training Administration	20, V
Employment Standards Administration	20, VI
Federal Acquisition Regulation	48, 29
Federal Contract Compliance Programs, Office of	41, 60

Agency	CFR Title, Subtitle or Chapter
National Security Council and Office of Science and Technology Policy	47, II
National Technical Information Service	15, XI
National Telecommunications and Information Administration	15, XXIII; 47, III, IV, V
National Transportation Safety Board	49, VIII
Natural Resources Conservation Service	7, VI
Natural Resource Revenue, Office of	30, XII
Navajo and Hopi Indian Relocation, Office of	25, IV
Navy, Department of	32, VI
Federal Acquisition Regulation	48, 52
Neighborhood Reinvestment Corporation	24, XXV
Northeast Interstate Low-Level Radioactive Waste Commission	10, XVIII
Nuclear Regulatory Commission	2, XX; 5, XLVIII; 10, I
Federal Acquisition Regulation	48, 20
Occupational Safety and Health Administration	29, XVII
Occupational Safety and Health Review Commission	29, XX
Ocean Energy Management, Bureau of	30, V
Oklahoma City National Memorial Trust	36, XV
Operations Office	7, XXVIII
Overseas Private Investment Corporation	5, XXXIII; 22, VII
Patent and Trademark Office, United States	37, I
Payment From a Non-Federal Source for Travel Expenses	41, 304
Payment of Expenses Connected With the Death of Certain Employees	41, 303
Peace Corps	2, XXXVII; 22, III
Pennsylvania Avenue Development Corporation	36, IX
Pension Benefit Guaranty Corporation	29, XL
Personnel Management, Office of	5, I, XXXV; 5, IV; 45, VIII
Human Resources Management and Labor Relations Systems, Department of Homeland Security	5, XCVII
Federal Acquisition Regulation	48, 17
Federal Employees Group Life Insurance Federal Acquisition Regulation	48, 21
Federal Employees Health Benefits Acquisition Regulation	48, 16
Pipeline and Hazardous Materials Safety Administration	49, I
Postal Regulatory Commission	5, XLVI; 39, III
Postal Service, United States	5, LX; 39, I
Postsecondary Education, Office of	34, VI
President's Commission on White House Fellowships	1, IV
Presidential Documents	3
Presidio Trust	36, X
Prisons, Bureau of	28, V
Privacy and Civil Liberties Oversight Board	6, X
Procurement and Property Management, Office of	7, XXXII
Public Contracts, Department of Labor	41, 50
Public and Indian Housing, Office of Assistant Secretary for	24, IX
Public Health Service	42, I
Railroad Retirement Board	20, II
Reclamation, Bureau of	43, I
Refugee Resettlement, Office of	45, IV
Relocation Allowances	41, 302
Research and Innovative Technology Administration	49, XI
Rural Business-Cooperative Service	7, XVIII, XLII
Rural Development Administration	7, XLII
Rural Housing Service	7, XVIII, XXXV
Rural Telephone Bank	7, XVI
Rural Utilities Service	7, XVII, XVIII, XLII
Safety and Environmental Enforcement, Bureau of	30, II
Saint Lawrence Seaway Development Corporation	33, IV
Science and Technology Policy, Office of	32, XXIV
Science and Technology Policy, Office of, and National Security Council	47, II
Secret Service	31, IV
Securities and Exchange Commission	5, XXXIV; 17, II

Agency	CFR Title, Subtitle or Chapter
Selective Service System	32, XVI
Small Business Administration	2, XXVII; 13, I
Smithsonian Institution	36, V
Social Security Administration	2, XXIII; 20, III; 48, 23
Soldiers' and Airmen's Home, United States	5, XI
Special Counsel, Office of	5, VIII
Special Education and Rehabilitative Services, Office of	34, III
State, Department of	2, VI; 22, I; 28, XI
Federal Acquisition Regulation	48, 6
Surface Mining Reclamation and Enforcement, Office of	30, VII
Surface Transportation Board	49, X
Susquehanna River Basin Commission	18, VIII
Tennessee Valley Authority	5, LXIX; 18, XIII
Trade Representative, United States, Office of	15, XX
Transportation, Department of	2, XII; 5, L
Commercial Space Transportation	14, III
Emergency Management and Assistance	44, IV
Federal Acquisition Regulation	48, 12
Federal Aviation Administration	14, I
Federal Highway Administration	23, I, II
Federal Motor Carrier Safety Administration	49, III
Federal Railroad Administration	49, II
Federal Transit Administration	49, VI
Maritime Administration	46, II
National Highway Traffic Safety Administration	23, II, III; 47, IV; 49, V
Pipeline and Hazardous Materials Safety Administration	49, I
Saint Lawrence Seaway Development Corporation	33, IV
Secretary of Transportation, Office of	14, II; 49, Subtitle A
Transportation Statistics Bureau	49, XI
Transportation, Office of	7, XXXIII
Transportation Security Administration	49, XII
Transportation Statistics Bureau	49, XI
Travel Allowances, Temporary Duty (TDY)	41, 301
Treasury, Department of the	2, X;5, XXI; 12, XV; 17, IV; 31, IX
Alcohol and Tobacco Tax and Trade Bureau	27, I
Community Development Financial Institutions Fund	12, XVIII
Comptroller of the Currency	12, I
Customs and Border Protection	19, I
Engraving and Printing, Bureau of	31, VI
Federal Acquisition Regulation	48, 10
Federal Claims Collection Standards	31, IX
Federal Law Enforcement Training Center	31, VII
Financial Crimes Enforcement Network	31, X
Fiscal Service	31, II
Foreign Assets Control, Office of	31, V
Internal Revenue Service	26, I
Investment Security, Office of	31, VIII
Monetary Offices	31, I
Secret Service	31, IV
Secretary of the Treasury, Office of	31, Subtitle A
Truman, Harry S. Scholarship Foundation	45, XVIII
United States and Canada, International Joint Commission	22, IV
United States and Mexico, International Boundary and Water Commission, United States Section	22, XI
U.S. Copyright Office	37, II
Utah Reclamation Mitigation and Conservation Commission	43, III
Veterans Affairs, Department of	2, VIII; 38, I
Federal Acquisition Regulation	48, 8
Veterans' Employment and Training Service, Office of the Assistant Secretary for	41, 61; 20, IX
Vice President of the United States, Office of	32, XXVIII
Wage and Hour Division	29, V
Water Resources Council	18, VI
Workers' Compensation Programs, Office of	20, I, VII
World Agricultural Outlook Board	7, XXXVIII

List of CFR Sections Affected

All changes in this volume of the Code of Federal Regulations (CFR) that were made by documents published in the FEDERAL REGISTER since January 1, 2014 are enumerated in the following list. Entries indicate the nature of the changes effected. Page numbers refer to FEDERAL REGISTER pages. The user should consult the entries for chapters, parts and subparts as well as sections for revisions.

For changes to this volume of the CFR prior to this listing, consult the annual edition of the monthly List of CFR Sections Affected (LSA). The LSA is available at *www.govinfo.gov*. For changes to this volume of the CFR prior to 2001, see the "List of CFR Sections Affected, 1949–1963, 1964–1972, 1973–1985, and 1986–2000" published in 11 separate volumes. The "List of CFR Sections Affected 1986–2000" is available at *www.govinfo.gov*.

2014

13 CFR

79 FR Page

Chapter I

Policy statement 1303, 1309
107.50 Amended 62823
107.600 (c)(4) revised 62823
107.720 (b)(2), (c)(1) and (2) introductory text revised 62823
107.1120 (e) and (f) revised 62824
107.1150 Introductory text and (d)(2) amended; (d) introductory text, (1)(iii), (iv), (e)(1), (2)(iii) and (iv) revised 62824
115 Authority citation revised 2086
115.10 Amended 2086
115.12 (e)(3) and new (e)(4)(iii) removed; (e)(4) and (5) redesignated as (e)(3) and (4); (b), new (e)(4) introductory text revised; new (e)(3) and new (e)(4)(iii) amended; (e)(4)(iv) redesignated as (e)(4)(iii) 2086
115.13 (a)(5) amended 2087
115.17 (b)(2) amended 2087
115.19 Introductory text, (c)(1), (d) and (e)(2) amended 2087
115.30 (d)(2)(ii)(C) and (D) amended 2087
115.31 (d) amended 2087
115.32 (d)(1) amended 2087
115.35 (c)(1) and (4) amended 2087
115.36 (a)(3) amended 2087
115.67 (a) amended 2087

13 CFR—Continued

79 FR Page

Chapter I—Continued

115.69 Revised 2087
115.70 (a) amended 2087
120.102 Removed 15649
120.816 Redesignated from 120.820 15649
120.818 Added 15649
120.820 Redesignated as 120.816; new 120.820 added 15649
120.822 Removed 15649
120.823 Revised; eff. 4-21-15 15649
120.830 (a) revised 15651
120.835 (c) revised 15651
120.852 Removed 15651
120.882 (a) revised 15651
120.920 (b) revised 15651
120.925 Removed 15651
121.201 Table amended; interim 33655
Table corrected; interim 71296
121.301 (c)(2) introductory text and (d) revised; interim 33669
121.302 (c) revised; interim 33669
121.411 (d) through (h) correctly redesignated as (e) through (i) 29661
121.502 (a)(2) revised; interim 33669
121.512 (b) revised; interim 33669
123.6 Amended; interim 22862

13 CFR—Continued

79 FR Page

13 CFR—Continued

79 FR Page

13 CFR—Continued

79 FR Page

Chapter III—Continued

307.13 (a) introductory text, (b)(2) and (3) revised; eff. 1-20-15 76134
307.14 (c) revised; eff. 1-20-15 76134
307.15 (b)(1), (c)(1), (2), (d)(1) introductory text and (iii) revised; eff. 1-20-15 76134
307.16 (a)(1), (2)(i), (c)(1), (2)(i), (d)(1) introductory text and (i) revised; eff. 1-20-15 76134
307.17 (b)(6)(ii) and (c) revised; eff. 1-20-15 76135
307.18 Heading, (a)(1), (b) heading, (1) introductory text, (ii), (iii) and (2) introductory text revised; eff. 1-20-15 76135
307.19 (b) removed; (c) and (d) redesignated as new (b) and (c); new (c) revised; eff. 1-20-15 76135
307.20 (a) introductory text, (1), (2) and (c)(3) revised; eff. 1-20-15 76135
307.21 (a)(1) introductory text and (viii) revised; eff. 1-20-15 76135
308.2 (a), (b) introductory text, (c) and (d) revised; eff. 1-20-15 76136
308.3 (a) introductory text, (2), (3) and (b) revised; eff. 1-20-15 76136
310.1 Introductory text revised; eff. 1-20-15 76136
310.2 (a)(6), (b) and (c) introductory text revised; eff. 1-20-15 76136
314.1—314.6 (Subpart A) Subpart A heading removed; eff. 1-20-15 76136
314.1 Amended; eff. 1-20-15 76136
314.3 (a), (b) and (c) revised; eff. 1-20-15 76136
314.4 (c) revised; eff. 1-20-15 76137
314.5 (b) revised; eff. 1-20-15 76137
314.6 (b) revised; eff. 1-20-15 76137
314.7—314.8 (Subpart B) Subpart B heading removed; eff. 1-20-15 76137
314.7 (a), (b)(1) introductory text, (c)(1) introductory text, (2) introductory text, (3), (4) introductory text and (5) revised; (b) heading added; (c)(6) removed; eff. 1-20-15 76137
314.8 Heading revised; (d) added; eff. 1-20-15 76138
314.9 (Subpart C) Subpart C heading removed; eff. 1-20-15 76138
314.9 Revised; eff. 1-20-15 76138

13 CFR—Continued

79 FR Page

Chapter III—Continued

314.10 (Subpart D) Subpart D heading removed; eff. 1-20-15 76139
314.10 Revised; eff. 1-20-15 76139

2015

13 CFR

80 FR Page

Chapter I

105.401 (b)(3) amended; CFR correction 78967
120.701 (b) removed; (c) through (i) redesignated as new (b) through (h); new (c) revised 34046
120.707 (a) revised 34046
120.709 Amended 34046
120.710 (a) revised 34046
120.712 (c) removed; (d) and (e) redesignated as new (c) and (d); new (c) revised 34047
120.716 Added 34047
120.802 Amended; CFR correction 78967
120.1425 (d)(2) revised 34047
121.108 Heading revised; (e)(4) added 7536
121.109 Redesignated as 121.110; new 121.109 added 7536
121.110 Redesignated from 121.109 7536
121.1001 (b)(9) revised; (b)(10) redesignated as (b)(11); new (b)(10) added 7536
127.101 Revised 55021
127.102 Amended 55022
127.500 Revised 55022
127.501 Amended 55022
127.503 Heading, (a) heading and (b) heading revised; (c) through (f) redesignated as (e) through (h); new (c) and (d) added 55022
127.507 Revised 55022
127.600 Revised 55022
136.170 (h)(1), (j)(1) and (2) amended; CFR correction 78967
140.11 (i)(3)(ii) amended; CFR correction 78967

2016

13 CFR

81 FR Page

Chapter I

107 Authority citation revised 31491, 95424
107.50 Amended; eff. 1-27-17 95424

13 CFR—Continued

81 FR Page

Chapter I—Continued

107.210 (a) introductory text revised; eff. 1-27-17....................95424
107.503 (a) amended; eff. 1-27-17......95424
107.610 (g) added; eff. 1-27-17..........95424
107.630 (d) removed; (e) redesignated as new (d); eff. 1-27-17........95424
107.665 Added; interim..................31491
107.670 (b) amended; interim.........31491
107.720 (b)(2) and (3) revised; (b)(4) added; eff. 1-27-17......................95424
107.1100 (b) amended; (c) removed; eff. 1-27-17................................95424
107.1150 (b) amended; eff. 1-27-17...95424
109.20 Amended..............................41428
115.10 Amended..............................41428
115.11 Amended..............................23565
115.13 (a)(7) added..........................23565
115.14 Heading, (a)(4) and (b) revised; (c) added.........................23565
115.16 (e)(1) and (f)(1) revised.........23566
115.18 (a)(2) revised.......................23566
115.36 Heading revised; (a) designation and heading, (b) and (c) removed; (1), (2) and (3) redesignated as new (a), (b) and (c)..23566
115.60 (a)(1) amended; (a)(5) removed; (a)(6) redesignated as new (a)(5).................................23566
120 Authority citation revised......33125
120.151 Amended...........................41428
120.465 (b) amended; interim.........31491
120.882 (g) introductory text, (3), (10) and (13) revised; (g)(15)(vii) amended; interim.....................33125
121 Policy statement...................32635
121.103 (b)(9), (h)(3)(i) and (4) revised; (f)(1) and (2) added; (h) introductory text amended..........34258
(a)(8) added................................41428
(b)(2)(ii), (6) and (h)(3)(ii) revised; (h) introductory text amended 48578
(h) introductory text correctly revised.....................................71982
121.104 (a) introductory text revised...34258
121.108 (e)(2) revised; interim........31491
121.201 Table amended.....3947, 4466, 4486
Regulation at 79 FR 33655 confirmed......................................3956
Footnote 20 added........................34259
Table Footnote 5 correctly amended..................................93583

13 CFR—Continued

81 FR Page

Chapter I—Continued

121.301 Regulation at 79 FR 33669 confirmed..................................3956
Heading revised; (f) added............41428
121.302 Regulation at 79 FR 33669 confirmed..................................3956
121.402 (d) amended.......................34259
121.404 (f) revised; (g)(2)(i) amended; (g)(2)(ii)(D) added...............34259
(g)(2)(ii)(A) revised......................48578
Regulation at 78 FR 61131 withdrawn in part..................67093, 67901
121.406 (b)(3), (4) introductory text and (5) introductory text revised..............................4469, 4486
Heading, (a) introductory text, (b)(7) and (d) revised; (b)(4) amended; (e) redesignated as (f); new (e) added.......................34259
(b)(5) introductory text amended 48579
121.408 (a) revised..........................34259
121.409 Amended...........................34259
121.411 (i)(2) revised; interim.........31491
(b) amended; eff. 1-23-17...............94250
121.502 Regulation at 79 FR 33669 confirmed..................................3956
121.512 Regulation at 79 FR 33669 confirmed..................................3956
121.702 (a)(2) revised......................34259
(a)(1)(i) amended..........................48579
(b)(1)(i) correctly amended..........71983
121.1001 (a)(1)(i) and (2)(i) revised; (b)(11) redesignated as (b)(12); new (b)(11) added......................34259
(b)(10), (11) and (12) redesignated as (b)(11), (12) and (13); new (b)(10) added.............................48579
121.1203 Revised............................34260
121.1204 (b)(1)(ii) and (iii) revised..34260
121.1206 Added.............................34260
123 Authority citation revised......67903
123.2 Amended.............................67903
123.3 (a)(1) revised........................67903
123.6 Regulation at 79 FR 22862 confirmed...............................63367
123.11 Regulation at 79 FR 22862 confirmed...............................63367
(a)(2) revised...............................67903
123.13 (a) amended........................67903
123.18 Existing text designated as (a); new (a) amended; (b) added..67903
123.20 Existing text designated as (a); (b) added............................67903
123.21 Amended............................67903

13 CFR—Continued

81 FR Page

Chapter I—Continued

123.105 (a) introductory text and (4) revised; (a)(3) amended; (a)(5) added 67903

124 Authority citation revised 34260

124.103 (c)(1) amended; (c)(2)(iii) redesignated as (c)(2)(iv); new (c)(2)(iii) and (3) through (6) added; (c)(2)(ii) and new (iv) introductory text revised 48579

124.104 (b)(1) revised 48580

124.105 (h)(2) introductory text revised 48580

124.106 Introductory text amended 48580

124.108 (a)(1) revised; (a)(4) amended 48580

124.109 (c)(2)(iv) and (4)(iii) added 48580

124.110 (b) introductory text amended; (c) introductory text, (1) and (d) revised; (g) redesignated as (h); (b)(1), (2) and new (g) added 48580

(g) correctly revised 71983

124.111 (c) amended; (c)(1) and (2) added 48581

124.112 (e) redesignated as (e)(1); (e)(2) added 48581

(b)(8) correctly amended; (b)(9) correctly removed; (b)(10) correctly redesignated as new (b)(9) 71983

124.202 Revised 48581

124.203 Revised 48581

124.305 (h)(1)(ii) amended; (h)(5) redesignated as (h)(6); (h)(1)(iii), (iv) and new (5) added 48582

124.501 (a) and (b) amended 48582

124.502 (c)(9) revised; (c)(16) amended; (c)(17) redesignated as (c)(18); new (c)(17) added 48582

124.503 (a)(1) and (2) amended; (g)(4) added 48582

124.504 (c)(1)(ii)(B) revised 34260

(d)(4) amended 48582

124.506 (a)(2)(ii) amended 48582

124.507 (b)(3), (4) and (5) redesignated as (b)(4), (5) and (6); new (b)(3) added 48582

124.510 Revised 34260

124.513 (b) revised 34261

13 CFR—Continued

81 FR Page

Chapter I—Continued

(f) through (i) redesignated as (g), (h), (i) and (k); (b)(3), (e)(2)(iii), (3), new (f), (j) and (l) added; (c)(2), (6), (7), (d), (e)(1), new (g) and new (i) revised 48582

(c)(4) correctly revised 71983

124.515 (a) introductory text revised; (a)(1) introductory text amended 48584

124.520 (e)(2) through (5) redesignated as (e)(3) through (6); (a), (b) introductory text and (2) amended; (b)(1)(i), (3), (c)(1), (4), (d)(1)(iii) and new (e)(5) revised; (c)(5) removed; (d)(5), new (e)(2), (7), (8) and (i) added 48584

124.604 Amended 48585

124.1002 (b)(4) removed 48585

124.1015 (e)(2) revised; interim 31491

125 Authority citation revised 34261, 48585

125.1 (f), (g), (h), (m) and (u) removed; paragraph designations removed; amended 34261

125.2 (b)(1)(i)(F), (iv), (v), (c)(1)(vi) and (vii) added; (b)(2) removed; (b)(3) redesignated as new (b)(2); (b)(1)(i)(A), (ii) introductory text, (iii)(C), new (2) revised; (c)(1)(iv) and (v) amended 34261

(a) introductory text amended 48585

125.3 (c)(8), (9) and (f)(8) added; (f)(1) amended; (f)(5) revised 34262

(a)(1) introductory text, (c) heading and (1)(v) revised; (a)(1)(i)(C), (D), (x) and (xi) added; (c)(1), (i), (viii) and (ix) amended; eff. 1-23-17 94250

125.5 (b)(1)(ii) revised; (b)(1)(iii), (iv) and (v) revised; (f)(3) added 34262

(a)(1) amended 48585

125.6 Revised 34262

(b) introductory text and (5) amended 48585

(a) introductory text correctly revised 67093

Regulation at 81 FR 48585 removed 71983

125.8 Redesignated as 125.11; added 48585

(b)(2)(iv) correctly revised 94941

13 CFR—Continued

81 FR Page

13 CFR—Continued

81 FR Page

13 CFR—Continued

81 FR Page

Chapter I—Continued

134.515 (a) amended 48595

142.1 (b) amended; interim 31492

143 Regulation at 79 FR 76081 confirmed 1115

146.400 (a), (b) and (e) amended; interim 31492

2017

13 CFR

82 FR Page

Chapter I

102 Authority citation revised; eff. 1-3-18 46371

102.1—102.11 (Subpart A) Revised; eff. 1-3-18 46371

107 Regulation at 81 FR 95424 eff. date delayed to 3-21-17 8499

Authority citation revised 9969

Regulation at 81 FR 95424 eff. date further delayed to 5-20-17 14428

Regulation at 81 FR 95424 eff. date further delayed to 8-18-17 20133

Regulation at 81 FR 95424 withdrawn 39335

107.50 Regulation at 81 FR 95424 eff. date delayed to 3-21-17 8499

Regulation at 81 FR 95424 eff. date further delayed to 5-20-17 14428

Regulation at 81 FR 95424 eff. date further delayed to 8-18-17 20133

Amended 39340

Regulation at 81 FR 95424 withdrawn 39335

Amended 52184

107.210 Regulation at 81 FR 95424 eff. date delayed to 3-21-17 8499

Regulation at 81 FR 95424 eff. date further delayed to 5-20-17 14428

Regulation at 81 FR 95424 eff. date further delayed to 8-18-17 20133

(a) introductory text revised 39340

Regulation at 81 FR 95424 withdrawn 39335

107.300 Revised 52184

107.410 (b) amended 52185

107.503 Regulation at 81 FR 95424 eff. date delayed to 3-21-17 8499

Regulation at 81 FR 95424 eff. date further delayed to 5-20-17 14428

13 CFR—Continued

82 FR Page

Chapter I—Continued

Regulation at 81 FR 95424 eff. date further delayed to 8-18-17 20133

(a) amended 39340

Regulation at 81 FR 95424 withdrawn 39335

107.610 Regulation at 81 FR 95424 eff. date delayed to 3-21-17 8499

Regulation at 81 FR 95424 eff. date further delayed to 5-20-17 14428

Regulation at 81 FR 95424 eff. date further delayed to 8-18-17 20133

(g) added 39340

Regulation at 81 FR 95424 withdrawn 39335

107.630 Regulation at 81 FR 95424 eff. date delayed to 3-21-17 8499

Regulation at 81 FR 95424 eff. date further delayed to 5-20-17 14428

Regulation at 81 FR 95424 eff. date further delayed to 8-18-17 20133

(d) removed; (e) redesignated as new (d) 39340

Regulation at 81 FR 95424 withdrawn 39335

107.665 Amended; interim 9969

107.692 (b) through (e) amended 52185

107.720 Regulation at 81 FR 95424 eff. date delayed to 3-21-17 8499

Regulation at 81 FR 95424 eff. date further delayed to 5-20-17 14428

Regulation at 81 FR 95424 eff. date further delayed to 8-18-17 20133

(b)(2) and (3) revised; (b)(4) added 39340

Regulation at 81 FR 95424 withdrawn 39335

107.1100 Regulation at 81 FR 95424 eff. date delayed to 3-21-17 8499

Regulation at 81 FR 95424 eff. date further delayed to 5-20-17 14428

Regulation at 81 FR 95425 eff. date further delayed to 8-18-17 20133

(b) amended; (c) removed 39341

Regulation at 81 FR 95425 withdrawn 39335

13 CFR—Continued

13 CFR—Continued

13 CFR—Continued

82 FR Page

Chapter I—Continued

134.809 Revised 25507
134.901—134.918 (Subpart I) Added 25507
142.1 (b) amended; interim 9969
146.400 (a), (b) and (e) amended; interim 9969

Chapter III

300 Authority citation revised; eff. 1-2-18 57052
300.3 Amended; eff. 1-2-18 57052
301.2 (b) revised; eff. 1-2-18 57053
301.5 Revised; eff. 1-2-18 57053
301.7 (a) revised; eff. 1-2-18 57053
301.8 Revised; eff. 1-2-18 57053
301.11 (a) introductory text revised; eff. 1-2-18 57053
302 Authority citation revised; eff. 1-2-18 57053
302.5 Revised; eff. 1-2-18 57053
302.6 Revised; eff. 1-2-18 57053
302.20 (a) introductory text, (2), and (d) revised; eff. 1-2-18 57053
303.6 (b)(1) and (3)(ii) revised; eff. 1-2-18 57054
303.7 (c)(1) revised; eff. 1-2-18 57054
304.2 (c)(2) revised; eff. 1-2-18 57054
305.6 (b) revised; eff. 1-2-18 57054
305.8 (c) revised; eff. 1-2-18 57054
307.6 Revised; eff. 1-2-18 57054
307.7 (b) introductory text and (2) revised; eff. 1-2-18 57055
307.8 Amended; eff. 1-2-18 57055
307.11 Heading, (a), (c), (d), and (f)(2) revised; (g) and (h) added; eff. 1-2-18 57055
307.12 Heading, (a), (b), (c) heading and introductory text revised; (d) added; eff. 1-2-18 57056
307.13 (b)(2) revised; (b)(3) redesignated as (b)(4); new (b)(3) added; eff. 1-2-18 57057
307.14 Revised; eff. 1-2-18 57057
307.15 (c), (d) and (e) redesignated as (b), (c) and (d); (a), (1) and new (c) heading revised; (b) removed; eff. 1-2-18 57057
307.16 Revised; eff. 1-2-18 57057
307.17 Revised; eff. 1-2-18 57057
307.18 (a)(1) introductory text, (2), (b)(1) introductory text, (1)(i) and (2)(i) revised; eff. 1-2-18 57058
307.20 Revised; eff. 1-2-18 57058
307.21 Revised; eff. 1-2-18 57058
309.1 (a) revised; eff. 1-2-18 57059
309.2 (a)(1) and (b) revised; eff. 1-2-18 57059

13 CFR—Continued

82 FR Page

Chapter III—Continued

312 Added 3134
Regulation at 82 FR 3134 eff. date delayed to 3-21-17 8809
313 Removed 48760
314.1 Amended; eff. 1-2-18 57059
314.2 Revised; eff. 1-2-18 57059
314.3 Revised; eff. 1-2-18 57059
314.4 Heading, (a), (b) introductory text and (c) revised; (b) heading added; eff. 1-2-18 57060
314.5 (a) introductory text revised; eff. 1-2-18 57060
314.6 (a), (b)(3), (4)(v)(B), (5)(v)(B) and (c) revised; eff. 1-2-18 57060
314.7 (a), (c) introductory text, (1) introductory text, (ii), (2) introductory text, (4) heading, introductory text, (ii)(B), (iii), (5)(i) and (iii) revised; eff. 1-2-18 57061
314.8 Heading, (a), (b), and (d) revised; eff. 1-2-18 57061
314.9 Revised; eff. 1-2-18 57062
314.10 Section heading, (a) through (d), (e)(2) and (3) introductory text revised; eff. 1-2-18 57062

2018

13 CFR

83 FR Page

Chapter I

107.665 Amended 7363
120 Authority citation revised 19920
120 Policy statement 19921, 34021, 55478
120.465 (b) amended 7363
120.882 (g)(5), (6)(ii), (10), and (15) amended; (g)(6)(i) and (12) revised 19920
121 Notification 24919
121.103 (h)(3)(ii) revised 12851
121.201 Table amended; CFR correction 40660
121.404 (g) introductory text amended 12851
121.406 (a) amended; (d) revised 12851
125 Authority citation revised 48912
125.3 (c)(1)(viii) and (ix) amended 12852
125.6 (a) introductory text amended; (f)(1) revised 12852
125.11 Revised 48912
125.12 Introductory text revised; (b) and (d) amended; (g), (h), and (i) added 48913

13 CFR—Continued

83 FR Page

13 CFR—Continued

83 FR Page

www.ingramcontent.com/pod-product-compliance
Lightning Source LLC
LaVergne TN
LVHW052202200926
848481LV00001B/13